A COMPARATIVE GRAMMAR OF THE DRAVIDIAN OR SOUTH-INDIAN FAMILY OF LANGUAGES

A
COMPARATIVE GRAMMAR
OF THE
DRAVIDIAN
OR
SOUTH-INDIAN FAMILY OF LANGUAGES

BY THE

REV. ROBERT CALDWELL, D.D., LL.D.,

HONORARY MEMBER OF THE ROYAL ASIATIC SOCIETY,
FELLOW OF THE UNIVERSITY OF MADRAS,
MISSIONARY OF THE SOCIETY FOR THE PROPAGATION OF THE GOSPEL AT EDEYENGOODY, TINNEVELLY, SOUTHERN INDIA

SECOND EDITION, REVISED AND ENLARGED

GYAN

Published by

GYAN

Gyan Publishing House
5, Ansari Road
Daryaganj, New Delhi-110002
Phone: 011-47034999, 9811692060
E-mail: books@gyanbooks.com

Distribution Network
gyanbooks.com
India, USA, Canada, UK, Australia, France

ISBN : 978-81-212-4510-4 (HB)
First Published, 1875

2nd Impression 2020

Printed at: Gyan Press, Delhi.

A Comparative Grammar of the Dravidian
or
South-Indian Family of Languages
Author: Robert Caldwell

A COMPARATIVE GRAMMAR

OF THE

DRAVIDIAN

OR

SOUTH-INDIAN FAMILY OF LANGUAGES.

BY THE

REV. ROBERT CALDWELL, D.D., LL.D.,

HONORARY MEMBER OF THE ROYAL ASIATIC SOCIETY,
FELLOW OF THE UNIVERSITY OF MADRAS,
MISSIONARY OF THE SOCIETY FOR THE PROPAGATION OF THE GOSPEL AT
EDEYENGOODY, TINNEVELLY, SOUTHERN INDIA.

Second Edition, Revised and Enlarged.

LONDON:
TRÜBNER & CO., LUDGATE HILL.
1875.

PREFACE.

It is now nearly nineteen years since the first edition of this book was published, and a second edition ought to have appeared long ere this. The first edition was soon exhausted, and the desirableness of bringing out a second edition was often suggested to me. But as the book was a first attempt in a new field of research and necessarily very imperfect, I could not bring myself to allow a second edition to appear without a thorough revision. It was evident, however, that the preparation of a thoroughly revised edition, with the addition of new matter wherever it seemed to be necessary, would entail upon me more labour than I was likely for a long time to be able to undertake. The duties devolving upon me in India left me very little leisure for extraneous work, and the exhaustion arising from long residence in a tropical climate left me very little surplus strength. For eleven years, in addition to my other duties, I took part in the Revision of the Tamil Bible, and after that great work had come to an end, it fell to my lot to take part for one year more in the Revision of the Tamil Book of Common Prayer. I suffered also for some time from a serious illness of such a nature that it seemed to render it improbable that I should ever be able to do any literary work again. Thus year after year elapsed, and year after year the idea of setting myself to so laborious a task as that of preparing a second edition of a book of this kind grew more and more distasteful to me. I began to hope that it had become no longer necessary to endeavour to rescue a half-forgotten book from oblivion. At this juncture it was considered desirable that I should return for a time to my native land for the benefit of my health; and at the same time I was surprised to receive a new and more urgent request that I should bring out a second edition of this book—for which I was informed that a demand still existed. Accordingly I felt that I had now no option left, and arrived reluctantly at the conclusion that as the first edition was brought out during the period of my first return to this country on furlough, so it had become necessary that the period of my second furlough should be devoted to the preparation and publication of a second edition.

The first edition—chiefly on account of the novelty of the undertaking—was received with a larger amount of favour than it appeared to me to deserve. I trust that this second edition, revised and enlarged, will be found more really deserving of favour. Though reluctant to commence the work, no sooner had I entered upon it than my old interest in it revived, and I laboured at it *con amore.* I have endeavoured to be accurate and thorough throughout, and to leave no difficulty unsolved, or at least uninvestigated; and yet, notwithstanding all my endeavours, I am conscious of many deficiencies, and feel sure that I must have fallen into many errors. Of the various expressions of approval the first edition received, the one which gratified me most, because I felt it to be best deserved, was that it was evident I had treated the Dravidian languages "lovingly." I trust it will be apparent that I have given no smaller amount of loving care and labour to the preparation of this second edition. The reader must be prepared, however, to find that many of the particulars on which I have laboured most "lovingly," though exceedingly interesting to persons who have made the Dravidian languages their special study, possess but little interest for persons whose special studies lie in the direction of some other family of languages, or who are interested, not in the study of any one language or family of languages in particular, but only in philological studies in general, or in discussions respecting the origin of language in general.

It is now more than thirty-seven years since I commenced the study of Tamil, and I had not proceeded far in the study before I came to the conclusion that much light might be thrown on Tamil by comparing it with Telugu, Canarese, and the other sister idioms. On proceeding to make the comparison I found that my supposition was verified by the result, and also, as it appeared to me, that Tamil imparted still more light than it received. I have become more and more firmly persuaded, as time has gone on, that it is not a theory, but a fact, that none of these languages can be thoroughly understood and appreciated without some study of the others, and hence that a Comparative Grammar of the Dravidian Languages may claim to be regarded not merely as something that is useful in its way, but as a necessity.

I trust it will be found that I have not left much undone that seemed to be necessary for the elucidation of Tamil; but I hope this branch of work will now be taken up by persons who have made Telugu, Canarese, Malayâḷam, or Tuḷu their special study, so that the whole range of the Dravidian languages and dialects may be fully elucidated. One desideratum at present seems to be a Comparative Vocabulary of the Dravidian Languages, distinguishing the roots found, say, in the four most distinctive languages—Tamil, Telugu, Canarese, and Malayâḷam—from those found only in three, only in two, or only in one. An excellent illustration of what may be done in this direction has been furnished by Dr Gundert, whose truly scientific "Dictionary of Malayâḷam" has given a fresh stimulus to Drâvidian philology. Another thing which has long appeared to me to be a desideratum is a more thorough examination of all the South Indian alphabets, ancient and modern, with a careful comparison of them, letter by letter, not only with the alphabets of Northern India, ancient and modern, but also, and especially, with the characters found in ancient inscriptions in Ceylon, Java, and other places in the further East. It has been announced that a work on this subject, by Dr Burnell, M.C.S., entitled "South-Indian Palæography," is about to be published in Madras, but I regret that a copy of it has not yet arrived.

It has been my chief object throughout this work to promote a more systematic and scientific study of the Dravidian languages themselves—for their own sake, irrespective of theories respecting their relationship to other languages—by means of a careful inter-comparison of their grammars. Whilst I have never ceased to regard this as my chief object, I have at the same time considered it desirable to notice, as opportunity occurred, such principles, forms, and roots as appeared to bear any affinity to those of any other language or family of languages, in the hope of contributing thereby to the solution of the question of their ultimate relationship. That question has never yet been scientifically solved, though one must hope that it will be solved some day. It has not yet got beyond the region of theories, more or less plausible. My own theory is that the Dravidian languages occupy a position of their own between the languages of the Indo-European family and those of the Turanian or Scythian group—not quite a midway position, but one considerably nearer the latter than the former. The particulars in which they seem to me to accord with the Indo-European languages are numerous and remarkable, and some of them, it will be seen, are of such a nature that it is impossible, I think, to suppose that they have been accidental; but the relationship to which they testify—in so far as they do testify to any real relationship—appears to me to be very indefinite, as well as very remote. On the other hand the particulars in which they seem to me to accord with most of the so-called Scythian languages are not only so numerous, but are so distinctive and of so essential a nature, that they appear to me to amount to what is called a family likeness, and therefore naturally to suggest the idea of a common descent. The evidence is cumulative. It seems impossible to suppose that all the various remarkable resemblances that will be pointed out, section after section, in this work can have arisen merely from similarity in mental development—of which there is no proof—or similarity in external circumstances and history—of which also there is no proof—much less without any common cause whatever, but merely from the chapter of accidents. The relationship seems to me to be not merely morphological, but—in some shape or another, and however it may be accounted for—genealogical. The genealogical method of investigation has produced remarkable results in the case of the Indo-European family of languages, and there seems no reason why it should be discarded in relation to any other family or group; but this method is applicable, as it appears to me, not merely to roots and forms, but also to principles, contrivances, and adaptations. I have called attention to the various resemblances I have noticed, whether apparently important or apparently insignificant—not under the supposition that any one of them, or all together, will suffice to settle the difficult question at issue, but as an aid to inquiry, for the purpose of helping to point out the line in which further research seems likely—or not likely—to be rewarded with success. An ulterior and still more difficult question will be found to be occasionally discussed. It is this: Does there not seem to be reason for regarding the Dravidian family languages, not only as a link of connection between the Indo-European and Scythian groups, but—in some particulars, especially in relation to the pronouns—as the best surviving representative of a period in the history of human speech older than the Indo-European stage, older than the Scythian, and older than the separation of the one from the other.

Whilst pointing out extra-Dravidian affinities wherever they appeared to exist, it has always been my endeavour, as far as possible, to explain Dravidian forms by means of the Dravidian languages themselves. In this particular I think it will be found that a fair amount of progress has been made in this edition in comparison with the first—for which I am largely indebted to the help of Dr Gundert's suggestions. A considerable number of forms which were left unexplained in the first edition have now, more or less conclusively, been shown to have had a Dravidian origin, and possibly this process will be found to be capable of being carried further still. The Dravidian languages having been cultivated from so early a period, and carried by successive stages of progress to so high a point of refinement, we should be prepared to expect that in supplying themselves from time to time with inflexional forms they had availed themselves of auxiliary words already in use, with only such modifications in sound or meaning as were necessary to adapt them to the new purposes to which they were applied. Accordingly it does not seem necessary or desirable to seek for the origin of Dravidian forms out of the range of the Dravidian languages themselves, except in the event of those languages failing to afford us a tolerably satisfactory explanation. Even in that event, it must be considered more probable that the evidence of a native Dravidian origin has been obliterated by lapse of time than that the Dravidians, when learning to inflect their words, borrowed for this purpose the inflexional forms of their neighbours. It is a different question whether some of the Dravidian forms and roots may not have formed a portion of the linguistic inheritance which appears to have descended to the earliest Dravidians from the fathers of the human race. I should be inclined, however, to seek for traces of that inheritance only in the narrow area of the simplest and most necessary, and therefore probably the most primitive, elements of speech.

In preparing the second edition of this book, as in preparing the first, I have endeavoured to give European scholars, whether resident in Europe or in India, such information respecting the Dravidian languages as might be likely to be interesting to them. I have thought more, however, of the requirements of the natives of the country, than of those of foreigners. It has been my earnest and constant desire to stimulate the natives of the districts in which the Dravidian languages are spoken to take an intelligent interest in the comparative study of their own languages; and I trust it will be found that this object has in some measure been helped forward. Educated Tamilians have studied Tamil—educated Telugus have studied Telugu—the educated classes in each language-district have studied the language and literature of that district—with an earnestness and assiduity which are highly creditable to them, and which have never been exceeded in the history of any of the languages of the world—except, perhaps, by the earnestness and assiduity with which Sanskrit has been studied by the Brâhmans. One result of this long-continued devotion to grammatical studies has been the development of much intellectual acuteness; another result has been the progressive refinement of the languages themselves; and these results have acted and reacted one upon another. Hence, it is impossible for any European who has acquired a competent knowledge of any of the Dravidian languages—say Tamil—to regard otherwise than with respect the intellectual capacity of a people amongst whom so wonderful an organ of thought has been developed. On the other hand, in consequence of the almost exclusive devotion of the native *literati* to grammatical studies they have fallen considerably behind the educated classes in Europe in grasp and comprehensiveness. What they have gained in acuteness, they have lost in breadth. They have never attempted to compare their own languages with others—not even with other languages of the same family. They have never grasped the idea that such a thing as a family of languages existed. Consequently the interest they took in the study of their languages was not an intelligent, discriminating interest, and proved much less fruitful in results than might fairly have been expected. Their philology, if it can be called by that name, has remained up to our own time as rudimentary and fragmentary as it was ages ago. Not having become comparative, it has not become scientific and progressive. The comparative method of study has done much, in every department of science, for Europe; might it not be expected to do much for India also? If the natives of Southern India began to take an interest in the comparative study of their own languages and in comparative philology in general, they would find it in a variety of ways much more useful to them than the study of the grammar of their own language alone ever has been. They would cease to content themselves with learning by rote versified enigmas and harmonious platitudes. They would begin to discern the real aims and objects of language, and realise the fact that language has a history of its own, throwing light upon all other history, and rendering ethnology and archæology possible. They would find that philology studied in this manner enlarged the mind instead of cramping it, extended its horizon, and provided it with a plentiful store of matters of wide human interest. And the consequence probably would be that a more critical, scholarly habit of mind, showing itself in a warmer desire for the discovery of truth, would begin to prevail. Another result—not perhaps so immediate, but probably in the end as certain—a result of priceless value—would be the development of a good, readable, respectable, useful, Dravidian literature—a literature written in a style free at once from pedantry and from vulgarisms, and in matter, tone, and tendency, as well as in style, worthy of so intelligent a people as the natives of Southern India undoubtedly are.

I trust the interest taken in their language, literature, and antiquities by foreigners will not be without its effect in kindling amongst the natives of Southern India a little wholesome, friendly rivalry. If a fair proportion of the educated native inhabitants of each district were only to apply themselves to the study of the philology and archæology of their district with anything like the same amount of zeal with which the philology and archæology of Europe are studied by educated Europeans, the result would probably be that many questions which are now regarded as insoluble would speedily be solved, and that pursuits now generally regarded as barren would be found full of fruit.

Native pandits have never been surpassed in patient labour or in an accurate knowledge of details. They require in addition that zeal for historic truth and that power of discrimination, as well as of generalisation, which have hitherto been supposed to be special characteristics of the European mind. Both these classes of qualities seem to me to be combined in a remarkable degree in the articles recently contributed by learned natives to the Bombay *Indian Antiquary* on subjects connected with the languages and literature of Northern India; and those articles appear to me to be valuable not only in themselves, but also as giving the world a specimen of the kind of results that might be expected if learned natives of Southern India entered, in the same critical, careful spirit, on the cultivation of the similar, though hitherto much-neglected, field of literary labour, which may be regarded as specially their own.

I was much gratified last year on finding that this Comparative Grammar of the Dravidian Languages had ceased to be the only Indian Comparative Grammar that had appeared. Mr Beames has followed up this line of philological research by the publication of the first volume of a Comparative Grammar of the Modern Aryan Languages of India—that is, the North-Indian Vernaculars. I regret that the second volume of that valuable work has not yet been published. A Comparative Grammar of the Kôlarian tongues, the third great Indian family, has probably not yet been contemplated; but I am inclined to think that it would be found to be productive of important and interesting results.

I have endeavoured to make the second edition of this work more easily available for reference, as well as more complete, than the former one, by providing the reader with a full table of contents and an index of proper names, together with paradigms of nouns, numerals, pronouns, verbs, &c. I have also given a list of the books and papers bearing, directly or indirectly, on Dravidian philology which have appeared since the first edition of this work, and which have been referred to or made use of in this edition.

I have much pleasure in acknowledging the valuable help I have received from many friends. Amongst them are the following :—Rev. J. Brigel; C. P. Brown, Esq.; A. C. Burnell, Esq., Ph.D.; Rev. J. Clay; T. W. Rhys Davids, Esq.; Rev. E. Diez; Prof. Eggeling; Sir Walter Elliot, K.C.S.I.; the late C. Gover, Esq.; Rev. F. Kittel; Rev. F. Metz; Prof. Max Müller; N. P. Narasimmiengar, Esq.; Rev. Dr Pope;

P. Le Page Renouf, Esq.; Dr Rost; Prof. Teza; Dr Ernest Trumpp. I have especially to thank Colonel Yule, C.B., for much interesting and valuable information on points connected with topography and history; and the Rev. Dr Gundert for the invaluable help he was so kind as to render me in connection with every department of this work. I beg to thank the Indian and Colonial Governments and the various officers entrusted with the management of the late Indian census for the information with which I have been favoured respecting the numbers of the people speaking the various Dravidian languages.

R. CALDWELL.

OFFICE OF THE SOCIETY FOR THE PROPAGATION
OF THE GOSPEL,
19 DELAHAY STREET, WESTMINSTER,
LONDON, 1875.

BOOKS AND PAPERS BEARING ON DRAVIDIAN COMPARATIVE PHILOLOGY, PUBLISHED SUBSEQUENTLY TO THE FIRST EDITION OF THIS WORK, AND QUOTED OR REFERRED TO IN THIS EDITION.

Arden.—Progressive Grammar of the Telugu Language. By the Rev. A. H. ARDEN, M.A. Masulipatam, and Trübners, London, 1872.

Baer.—Historische Fragen mit Hülfe der Naturwissenschaften Beantwortet. Von Dr CARL ERNST v. BAER. St Petersburgh, 1873.

Batsch.—Brief Grammar and Vocabulary of the Orâon Language. By Rev. F. BATSCH. Journal of the Bengal Asiatic Society, vol. xxxv. Calcutta.

Beames.—Comparative Grammar of the Modern Aryan Languages of India. By J. BEAMES, Esq., B.C.S. Trübners, London, 1872.

Beames.—On the Present Position of Old Hindî in Oriental Philology. By J. BEAMES, Esq., B.C.S. Indian Antiquary for January 1872. Bombay, and Trübners, London.

Beames.—Kîrtans; or Hymns from the Earliest Bengali Poets. By J. BEAMES, Esq., B.C.S. Indian Antiquary for November 1872. Bombay, and Trübners, London.

Bellew.—From the Indus to the Tigris (including a Grammar and Vocabulary of the Brahui Language). By Dr BELLEW. Trübners, London, 1873.

Bleek.—Comparative Grammar of the South African Languages. By W. H. J. BLEEK, Esq., Ph.D. Trübners, London, 1862.

Bleek.—On the Position of the Australian Languages. By W. H. J. BLEEK, Esq., Ph.D. Journal of the Anthropological Society. London, 1871.

Bower.—On the Tamil Language and Literature. By the Rev. H. BOWER, D.D. Calcutta Review, vol. xxv.

Bower.—Lecture on Auveyar, a Tamil female poet. By the Rev. H. BOWER, D.D. Madras.

Brigel.—Tulu Grammar. By the Rev. J. BRIGEL. Mangalore, 1872.

Buehler.—On the Origin of Sanskrit Linguals. By Dr GEORGE BUEHLER. Madras Journal of Literature, July 1864.

Burnell.—An interesting passage in Kamârila-Bhaṭṭa's Tantravârttika. By A. C. BURNELL, Esq., Ph.D., M.C.S. Indian Antiquary for October 1872.

Burnell.—The Oldest-known South Indian Alphabet. By A. C. BURNELL, Esq., Ph.D., M.C.S. Indian Antiquary for November 1872.

Burnell.—Specimen of South Indian Dialects: 1. Konkani; 2. Coorg (*Kodagu*); Mâppila Malayâlam. Mangalore, 1872. (In progress.)

Caldwell.—On the Substitution of the Roman for the Indian Characters. By the Rev. Dr CALDWELL. Madras Journal of Literature for 1858–9.

Campbell.—Ethnology of India. By Sir GEORGE CAMPBELL, K.C.S.I. Journal of the Bengal Asiatic Society, vol. xxxvi. 1866

Campbell.—Specimens of Languages of India. By Sir GEORGE CAMPBELL, K.C.S.I. Calcutta, 1874.

Chitty.—The Tamil Plutarch. By SIMON CASIE CHITTY, Esq., Jaffna. Ceylon, 1859.

Cole.—Coorg Grammar. By Major R. A. COLE. Bangalore, 1867.

Cunningham.—The Ancient Geography of India. By General ALEXANDER CUNNINGHAM. London, 1871.

Dalton.—Descriptive Ethnology of Bengal. By Colonel E. T. DALTON, C.S.I. Calcutta, 1872.

Davids.—Conquest of South India in the Twelfth Century, by Parâkrama Bâhu the Great, king of Ceylon. By T. W. RHYS DAVIDS, Esq. Journal of the Bengal Asiatic Society, 1872.

Dawson.—Brief Grammar and Vocabulary of the Gônd Language. By the Rev. J. DAWSON. Journal of the Bengal Asiatic Society, 1871.

Edkins.—China's Place in Philology. By the Rev. JOSEPH EDKINS, D.D. Peking, 1870.

Eggeling.—On the Chera and Chalukya Dynasties. A paper read at the International Congress of Orientalists by Dr EGGELING, Secretary of the Royal Asiatic Society, London, 1874.

Frye.—On the Uriya and Khond Population of Orissa. By Lieut. J. P. FRYE. Journal of the Royal Asiatic Society. London, 1872.

Gazetteer.—The Central Provinces' Gazetteer. Nagpur, second edition, 1870.

Gover.—The Folk-Songs of Southern India. By C. E. GOVER, Esq. Madras, 1871.

Graeter.—Coorg Songs, with Outlines of Coorg Grammar. By Rev. A. GRAETER. Mangalore, 1870.

Graul.—Outlines of Tamil Grammar. By the Rev. C. GRAUL, D.D. Leipzig, 1856.

Graul.—Der Kural des Tiruvalluvar. By the Rev. C. GRAUL, D.D. Leipzig, 1856.

Graul.—Reise nach Ostindien. By the Rev. C. GRAUL, D.D. Three vols. Leipzig, 1856.

Growse.—On the Non-Aryan Element in Hindî Speech. By F. S. GROWSE, Esq., M.A., B.C.S. Indian Antiquary for April 1872.

Gundert.—Malayâlam Grammar. By the Rev. H. GUNDERT, Ph.D. Second edition. Mangalore, 1868.

Gundert.—Malayâlam Dictionary. By the Rev. H. GUNDERT, Ph.D. Mangalore, 1872.

Gundert.—On the Dravidian Elements in Sanskrit. By the Rev. H. GUNDERT, Ph.D. Journal of the German Oriental Society for 1869.

Hislop.—Papers relating to the Aboriginal Tribes of the Central Provinces, left in MS. by the late Rev. S. HISLOP. Edited, with Notes, by Sir RICHARD TEMPLE. Nagpur, 1866.

Hodgson.—Essays on the Languages, Literature, and Religion of Nepal, Tibet, and adjacent Countries. By BRIAN HODGSON, Esq., late British Resident, Nepal.

Hodson.—Canarese Grammar. By Rev. T. HODSON. Second edition. Bangalore, 1864.

Hunfalvy.—On the Study of the Turanian Languages. A paper read at the International Congress of Orientalists, London, 1874, by Professor HUNFALVY.

Hunter.—Comparative Dictionary of the Non-Aryan Languages of India and High Asia. By W. W. HUNTER, LL.D., B.C.S. Trübners, London, 1868.

Kennet.—Notes on Early-printed Tamil Books. By the Rev. C.E. KENNET. Indian Antiquary for June 1873.

Kittel.—On the Dravidian Element in Sanskrit Dictionaries. By the Rev. F. KITTEL. Indian Antiquary for August 1872.

Kittel.—Notes concerning the Numerals of the Ancient Dravidians. By the Rev. F. KITTEL. Indian Antiquary for January 1873.

Kittel.—Keśirâjâ's Jewel Mirror of Grammar (*Śabda maṇi darpaṇa*), a Grammar of Ancient Canarese. By the Rev. F. KITTEL. Mangalore, 1872.

Kittel.—Article on Old Canarese Literature, by the Rev. F. KITTEL, in Indian Antiquary for January 1875.

Koelle.—Grammar of the Bornu or Kanuri Language. By the Rev. S. W. KOELLE, London.

Marshall.—A Phrenologist among the Tudas. By Lieut.-Col. MARSHALL. Trübners, London, 1873.

Metz.—The Tribes inhabiting the Neilgherry Hills. By the Rev. F. METZ. Second edition. Mangalore, 1864.

Muir.—Original Sanskrit Texts. By J. MUIR, Esq., D.C.L., LL.D., late B.C.S. Second edition, five vols. Trübners, London, 1868.

Mueller.—Reise der Fregatte Novara, Linguistischer Theil. By Professor FRIEDRICH MUELLER. Vienna, 1868.

Mueller.—Lectures on the Science of Language. By Professor MAX MUELLER. Two vols. London, 1864.

Murdoch.—Classified Catalogue of Tamil-printed Books, with introductory notices. By J. MURDOCH, Esq., LL.D. Madras, 1865.

Nelson.—The Madura Country. A Manual compiled by order of the Madras Government. By J. H. NELSON, Esq., M.A., M.C.S. Madras, 1868.

Phillips.—Tumuli in the Salem District. By the Rev. MAURICE PHILLIPS. Indian Antiquary, 1873.

Pope.—A Larger Grammar of the Tamil Language in both dialects, with the Nannûl and other native authorities. By the Rev. G. U. POPE, D.D. Second edition. Madras, 1859.

Pope.—Tamil Handbook. By the Rev. G. U. POPE, D.D. Second edition. Madras, 1859.

Pope.—One Alphabet for all India. By the Rev. G. U. POPE, D.D. Madras, 1859.

Pope.—The Sermon on the Mount, in English, Tamil, Malayâlam, Canarese, and Telugu, in the Roman character. By the Rev. G. U. POPE, D.D. Madras, 1860.

Pope.—Outlines of the Grammar of the Tuda Language. By the Rev. G. U. POPE, D.D., included in Colonel Marshall's "Phrenologist among the Tudas." Trübners, London, 1873.

Priaulx.—India and Rome. Indian Travels of Apollonius of Tyana, and the Indian Embassies to Rome. By P. de B. PRIAULX, Esq., Quarrich. London, 1873.

Prinsep.—Essays on Indian Antiquities. By the late J. T. PRINSEP, Esq., B.C.S. Edited with Notes by EDWARD THOMAS, Esq., F.R.S., late B.C.S. Two vols. London, 1858.

Sanderson.—Canarese Dictionary, by the Rev. W. REEVES. Revised and enlarged by the Rev. D. SANDERSON. Bangalore, 1858.

Sayce.—Principles of Comparative Philology. By A. H. SAYCE. London, Trübner & Co., 1874.

Quatrefages.—Etude sur les Todas. Par M. DE QUATREFAGES DE BRÉAU. Journal des Savants, December 1873—January 1874. Paris.

Târanâtha's History of the Propagation of Buddhism in India; Tibetan and German. St Petersburgh, 1870.

Tennent.—Ceylon. By Sir EMERSON TENNENT. Two vols. London, 1860.

Tickell.—Brief Grammar and Vocabulary of the Ho, a Kolarian Language. By Colonel TICKELL. Journal of the Bengal Asiatic Society, vol. xxxv.

Travancore.—Inscriptions in Tinnevelly and South Travancore. By His Highness RÂMA VARMÂ, First Prince of Travancore. Indian Antiquary for December 1873.

Trumpp.—Grammar of the Sindhî Language. By Dr ERNEST TRUMPP. Trübners, London, 1872.

Yule.—Marco Polo, newly translated and edited with Notes, by Lieut.-Col. H. YULE, C.B. Two vols. London, 1871.

Yule.—Cathay and the Way Thither. By Lieut.-Col. H. YULE, C.B. Hakluyt Society, London, 1866.

Yule.—Map of Ancient India, with accompanying Memoir, in Dr WM. SMITH'S Atlas of Ancient Classical Geography. London, 1875.

Weber.—Indian Pronunciation of Greek, and Greek Pronunciation of Hindû Words. By Dr A. WEBER. Translated by E. REHATSEK, Esq. Indian Antiquary for May 1873.

Williams.—Application of the Roman Alphabet to the Languages of India. By Professor MONIER WILLIAMS. London, 1859.

Winslow.—Tamil Dictionary. Completed and edited by the Rev. M. WINSLOW, D.D. Madras, 1862.

CONTENTS.

2

COMPARATIVE GRAMMAR.

PART II.

PAGE

PART IV.

3

PAGE

PART VI.

PART VII.

INTRODUCTION.

DRAVIDIAN COMPARATIVE GRAMMAR.

INTRODUCTION.

It is the object of the following work to examine and compare the grammatical principles and forms of the various Dravidian languages, in the hope of contributing to a more thorough knowledge of their primitive structure and distinctive character. In pursuing this object, it will be the writer's endeavour to point out everything which appears likely to throw any light on the question of the relation which this family of languages bears to the principal families or groups into which the languages of Europe and Asia have been divided.

Whilst the grammatical structure of each Dravidian language and dialect will be investigated and illustrated in a greater or less degree, in proportion to its importance and to the writer's acquaintance with it, it will be his special and constant aim to throw light upon the structure of Tamil—a language which he has for more than thirty-seven years studied and used in the prosecution of his missionary labours, and which is probably the earliest cultivated, and most highly developed, of the Dravidian languages—in many respects the representative language of the family.

The idioms which are included in this word under the general term 'Dravidian,' constitute the vernacular speech of the great majority of the inhabitants of Southern India. With the exception of Orissa, and those districts of Western India and the Dekhan in which Gujarâtî and Marâṭhî are spoken, the whole of the peninsular portion of India, from the Vindhya mountains and the river Nerbudda (Narmadâ) to Cape Comorin (Kumârî), is peopled, and from the earliest period appears to have been peopled, by different branches of one and the same race, speaking different dialects of one and the same language—the language to which the term 'Dravidian' is here applied; and scattered offshoots from the same stem may be traced still farther north, as far as the Râjmahâl hills in Bengal, and even as far as the mountain fastnesses of Belûchistân.

Gujarâtî, Marâṭhî (with its offshoot, Koṅkaṇî), and Oriya, the language of Oḍra-dêśa, or Orissa, idioms which are derived from the decomposition of Sanskrit, form the vernacular speech of the Hindû population in the peninsular portion of India within their respective limits: besides which, and besides the Dravidian languages, various idioms which cannot be termed indigenous or vernacular are spoken or occasionally used by particular classes resident in Peninsular India.

Sanskrit, though it is improbable that it ever was the vernacular language of any district of country, whether in the north or in the south, is in every southern district read, and to some extent understood, by the Brâhmans—the descendants of those Brahmanical colonists of early times to whom the Dravidians appear to have been indebted for the higher arts of life and a considerable portion of their literary culture. Such of the Brâhmans as not only retain the name, but also discharge the functions of the priesthood, and devote themselves to professional studies, are generally able to converse in Sanskrit, though the vernacular language of the district in which they reside is that which they use in their families, and with which they are most familiar. They are styled, with reference to the language of their adopted district, Drâviḍa Brâhmans, Ândhra Brâhmans, Karṇâṭaka Brâhmans, &c.; and the Brâhmans of the several language-districts have virtually become distinct castes; but they are all undoubtedly descended from one and the same stock, and Sanskrit, though now regarded only as an accomplishment or as a professional acquirement, is properly the literary dialect of their ancestral tongue.

Hindûstânî is the distinctive language of the Muhammedan portion of the population in the Dekhan—most of which consists of the descendants of those warlike Paṭâns, or Afghâns, and other Muhammedans from Northern India by whom most of the peninsula was overrun some centuries ago. It may almost be regarded as the vernacular language in some parts of the Hyderabad country; but generally throughout Southern India the middle and lower classes of the Muhammedans make as much use of the language of the district in which they reside as of their ancestral tongue, if not more. Hindûstânî was never the ancestral language of the class of southern Muhammedans generally called by the English 'Lubbies,' but by natives on the eastern coast S'ônagas (Yavanas), and by those on the western coast Mâppiḷḷas. These are descendants of Arab merchants and their native converts, and speak Tamil or Malayâḷam.

Hebrew is used by the small colony of Jews resident in Cochin and the neighbourhood, in the same manner and for the same purposes as Sanskrit is used by the Brâhmans. Gujarâtî and Marâṭhî are spoken by the Gujarâtî bankers and the Pârsî shopkeepers who reside in the principal towns in the peninsula. The mixed race of 'country-born' Portuguese are rapidly forgetting (except in the territory of Goa itself) the corrupt Portuguese which their fathers and mothers were accustomed to speak, and learning English instead; whilst French still retains its place as the language of the French employés and their descendants in the settlements of Pondicherry (Puduchchêri), Carrical (Kâreikkâl), and Mahé (Mayyuṛi), which still belong to France.

Throughout the British territories in India, English is not only the language of the governing race, and of its 'East-Indian,' Eurasian, or 'Indo-British' offshoot, but is also used to a considerable and rapidly increasing extent by the natives of the country in the administration of justice and in commerce; and in the Presidency of Madras and the principal towns it has already won its way to the position which was formerly occupied by Sanskrit as the vehicle of all higher learning. Neither English, however, nor any other foreign tongue, appears to have the slightest chance of becoming the vernacular speech of any portion of the inhabitants of Southern India. The indigenous Dravidian languages, which have maintained their ground for more than two thousand years against Sanskrit, the language of a numerous, powerful, and venerated sacerdotal race, may be expected successfully to resist the encroachments of every other tongue.*

---

* I admit with Sir Erskine Perry (see his paper in the *Journal of the Royal Asiatic Society*), that English, the language of the governing race, ought to be employed as the language of public business in every part of British India; and I am certain that this end could be attained in a very short time by simply requiring every candidate for Government employment, from the highest to the lowest, to pass an examination in English. The natives would everywhere adapt themselves to this arrangement, not only without reluctance, but with alacrity and pleasure; and English schools and other facilities for the acquisition of English would multiply apace, as soon as it was found that the new rule could not be evaded.

[I leave the above paragraph unaltered, as a memento of the time when it was written (1855), though it would scarcely be necessary now to make any such recommendation, in so far, at least, as the Presidency of Madras is concerned. In 1861 a General Test Examination was instituted for the examination in general knowledge, including a knowledge of English, of all candidates for employment in the public service, in situations to which salaries of Rs. 25 per mensem and upwards were attached. In 1867 the rule was made applicable to salaries of Rs. 20 per mensem and upwards. This arrangement has been productive of much advantage both to the public service and to the community, even in the rural

Use of the Common Term 'Dravidian.'

I have designated the languages now to be subjected to comparison by a common term, because of the essential and distinctive grammatical characteristics which they all possess in common, and in virtue of which, joined to the possession in common of a large number of roots of primary importance, they justly claim to be considered as springing from a common origin, and as forming a distinct family of tongues.

This family was at one time styled by European writers 'Tamulian' or 'Tamulic;' but though Tamil is probably the oldest and most highly cultivated member of the family, and that which contains the largest proportion of the family inheritance of forms and roots; yet as it is, after all, but one dialect out of several, and does not claim to be the original speech out of which the other dialects have been derived; as it is also desirable to reserve the terms 'Tamil' and 'Tamilian' (or as they used sometimes to be erroneously written 'Tamul' and 'Tamulian') to denote the Tamil language itself and the people by whom it is spoken, I have preferred to designate this entire family by a term which is capable of a wider application.

One of the earliest terms used in Sanskrit to designate the family seems to have been that of *Ândhra-Drâviḍa-bhâshâ*, 'the Telugu-Tamil language,'* or rather, perhaps, 'the language of the Telugu and

---

districts, and I doubt not that the Government will ere long give the rule a still wider range of application.]

I do not think, however, that English is likely ever to become the vernacular language of any class of the Hindûs, or even that it is likely to be used to any considerable extent as a *lingua franca* beyond the circle of Government employés and the *alumni* of the universities. Before we can reasonably anticipate the employment of English as a conventional language, like Latin in the middle ages, or French in the more modern period in Europe, or like Hindûstani in the greater part of India since the period of Muhammedan supremacy, the number of the English resident in India should bear a much larger proportion to the mass of the inhabitants. That proportion is at present infinitesimally small—*e.g.*, the population of the two collectorates, or provinces, in Southern India with which I am best acquainted—Tinnevelly and Madura—amounts to very nearly four millions: the number of Englishmen (and Americans) resident in those two provinces is under a hundred and fifty! and that number includes the judges and magistrates who administer justice in those provinces, the officers of a single regiment of sepoys, a few planters and merchants, and the missionaries belonging to three missionary societies! Including women and children, the number is considerably under two hundred, with which handful of English people we have to contrast four millions of Hindûs!

* See an interesting article in the *Indian Antiquary* for October 1872, by Dr Burnell, M.C.S. "Kumârila says, 'It is now considered :—(as regards) words which are not known to the inhabitants of Âryâvarta (not Sanskrit), if they have

Tamil countries.' This term is used by Kumârila-bhaṭṭa, a controversial Brâhman writer of eminence, who is supposed to have lived at the end of the seventh century A.D.; and, though vague, it is not badly chosen, Telugu and Tamil being the dialects spoken by the largest number of people in Southern India. Canarese was probably supposed to be included in Telugu, and Malayâḷam in Tamil; and yet both dialects, together with any sub-dialects that might be included in them, were evidently regarded as forming but one *bhâshâ*.

The word I have chosen is 'Dravidian,' from Drâviḍa, the adjectival form of Draviḍa. This term, it is true, has sometimes been used, and is still sometimes used, in almost as restricted a sense as that of Tamil itself, so that though on the whole it is the best term I can find, I admit that it is not perfectly free from ambiguity. It is a term, however, which has already been used more or less distinctively by Sanskrit philologists, as a generic appellation for the South Indian peoples and their languages, and it is the only single term they seem ever to have used in this manner. I have, therefore, no doubt of the propriety of adopting it.

Manu says (x. 43, 44): "The following tribes of Kshatriyas have gradually sunk into the state of Vṛishalas (outcasts), from the extinction of sacred rites and from having no communication with Brâhmans, viz.—Pauṇḍrakas, Oḍras, *Draviḍas*, Kâmbojas, Yavanas, S'akas,

---

a meaning known to the *Mlechcha* (the aboriginal tribes?), is that to be accepted or not?' He suggests (but only to reject the notion) that by applications of affixes, &c., it may be possible to convert them into Sanskrit words. . . . Of the examples he gives, the first word *chôr* is the Tamil *chôr-u*, and means, as Kumârila states, boiled rice; *naḍer*, way, is the Tamil *naḍai*. So *pâmp*, snake, is perfectly correct. (The text has *pâp*, but the MSS. have *pâmp*. In Tamil it is written *pâmpu*, though pronounced *pâmbu*.) *âḷ*=person, and *vair*=*vayiru*, the belly, are common Tamil words, and their meanings are correctly given. It must, however, be remarked that the consonantal terminations of *chôr*, *pâmp*, and *vair*, have now assumed a vowel ending, which is written *u*, but is pronounced in a vague and indeterminate manner." Dr Burnell remarks, "Kumârila's evident acquaintance with this South Indian dialect (Tamil) is worth notice, as he is said to have been a native of the south." (Târanâtha, "History of Indian Buddhism.") The words Kumârila cites are mostly Tamil, not Telugu or Canarese. *naḍe* is Telugu as well as Tamil, but *chôr-u* and *vayir-u* are not in Telugu. The former is not in Canarese, and the latter appears under the shape of *basir-u*. *pâmbu*, Tamil, is *pâvu* in Canarese, and *pâmu* in Telugu. *âḷ*, in Canarese and Tamil, means a person; *âl-u*, in Telugu, a woman. Kumârila, however, calls *âḷ*, *strî-pratyayam*, a feminine affix (in grammar). The affix of the third person feminine singular in Tamil, Malayâlam, and Old Canarese is *âḷ*. Telugu occasionally uses *âl-u* in a similar manner, but generally it uses the neut. sing. affix for the fem. sing. Kumârila cites the lengthened form *âḷ* instead of *aḷ*, apparently because it is in that shape that the affix appears in verbs—*e.g.*, *pôn-âḷ*, she went.

Pâradas, Pahlavas, Chînas, Kirâtas, Daradas, and Khaśas." Of the tribes here mentioned the only tribe belonging to Southern India is that of the Draviḍas. This name, therefore, appears to have been supposed to denote the whole of the South Indian tribes. If any of those tribes were not intended to be included, it would probably be the Andhras, the Telugus of the interior, who had already been mentioned by name in the Aitareya Brâhmaṇa, and classed with Puṇḍras, Sabaras, and Pulindas, as degraded descendants of Viśvâmitra. The same statement is made in the Mahâ-bhârata; and in the two lists of degraded Kshatriyas therein given, the Draviḍas are the only South Indian tribe mentioned. It must be concluded, therefore, that the term is generically used, seeing that the more specific names of Pâṇḍyas, Chôlas, &c., had become well known in Northern India by that time. Doubtless it is in the same sense that Satyavrata, the Indian Noah, is called in the Bhâgavata Purâṇa 'the lord of Draviḍa' (Muir's "Sanskrit Texts," vol. i.)

The more distinctively philological writers of a later period used the term Drâviḍa in what appears to be substantially the same sense as that in which I propose that it should be used. The principal Prâkrits—that is, colloquial dialects—of ancient India were the Mahârâshtrî, the Saurasenî, and the Mâgadhî. Amongst minor or less known Prâkrit dialects the Drâviḍî, or language of the Draviḍas, was included. A Sanskrit philologist quoted by Muir (vol. ii. 46) speaks of the language of Drâviḍa as a *vibhâshâ*, or minor Prâkrit; and another (p. 50) speaks of 'the language proper to Draviḍas' (in which persons of that race should be represented as speaking in dramas) as the Drâviḍî. It is evident that we have here to understand not the Tamil alone, or any other South Indian language alone, but the Dravidian languages generally, supposed in a vague manner by North Indian writers to constitute only one tongue. This language of the Draviḍas was evidently included in what was called the Paiśâchî Prâkrit, a name which appears to have been applied promiscuously to a great number of provincial dialects, including dialects so widely differing from one another as 'the language of the Pâṇḍyas' (Tamil), and 'that of the Bhoṭas' (Tibetan). The only property these languages can have possessed in common must have been the contempt in which they were held by Brâhman philologists, in virtue of which it must have been that they were styled also Paiśâchî, the language of *piśâchas*, or demons. The more accurate term Drâviḍî has continued to be used occasionally by northern scholars up to our own time. As late as 1854, the learned Hindû philologist Bâbu Râjêndra Lâl Mitra (quoted by Muir, vol. ii. 127), speaks of the 'Drâviḍî' as one of the recognised Prâkrits, equally with the Saurasenî, and as being, like it, the parent of some of the present vernaculars of India. It thus appears that the word 'Drâviḍa,' from which the term 'Dravidian' has been formed, though sometimes used in a restricted sense, as equivalent to Tamil, is better fitted, notwithstanding, for use as a generic term; inasmuch as it not only has the advantage of being more remote from ordinary usage, and somewhat more vague, but has also the further and special advantage of having already been occasionally used by native philologists in a generic sense. By the adoption of this term 'Dravidian,' the word 'Tamiḷian' has been left free to signify that which is distinctively Tamil.

When the Bâbu referred to some of the present vernaculars as having originated in the so-called Drâviḍî-Prâkrit, the dialects to which he referred were doubtless those which have sometimes been styled by the North Indian Pandits 'the five Drâviras.' The colloquial languages of modern India are divided by the Pandits into two classes, each containing five dialects. These are denominated respectively 'the five Gauras' and 'the five Drâviras.' By the Gauḍa or Gâura languages are meant the 'bhâshâs,' or popular dialects of Northern India, at the head of which stands the Bangâlî, the Gâura proper. At present Bangâlî, Oriya, Hindî, with its daughter Hindûstânî, Panjâbî, Sindhî, Gujarâtî, and Marâṭhî are the languages which may be regarded as forming the 'Gaurian' class; to which I would add Cashmirian, Mârwârî, Assamese, and the court language of Nepâl, thus reckoning in this class eleven idioms instead of five. The five Drâviḍas or Drâviras, according to the Pandits, are 'the Telinga, the Karṇâṭaka, the Marâṭhî, the Gurjara, and the Drâvira,' or Tamil proper. The S'abda-kalpa-druma (Calcutta) gives the list thus: Drâviḍa, Karṇâṭa, Gujarâta, Mahârâshta, and Telinga. The Marâṭhî and Gujarâtî are erroneously included in this enumeration. It is true that the Mahârâshtra or Marâṭhî contains a small admixture of Dravidian roots and idioms, as might be expected from its local proximity to the Telugu and the Canarese; and both it and the Gurjara, or Gujarâtî, possess certain features of resemblance to the languages of the South, which are possibly derived from the same or a similar source; but, notwithstanding the existence of a few analogies of this nature, those two languages differ from the Dravidian family so widely and radically, and are so closely allied to the northern group, that there cannot be any hesitation in transferring them to that class. The three languages that remain in the classification of Dravidian tongues contained in the northern lists, viz., the Karṇâṭaka or Canarese, the Telinga or Telugu, and the Drâviḍa proper or Tamil, are not only members, but are certainly the principal members, of the Southern or Dravidian family. It will be observed that Malayâḷam and Tuḷu are not contained in the Sanskrit enumeration. The first was probably considered to be a dialect of Tamil, and was included in the denomination of the Drâviḍa proper; the second was probably unknown, or was erroneously considered a dialect of Canarese. The uncultivated dialects—the Tuda, Kôta, Gôṇḍ, and Khond—appear to have been unknown to the Pandits; and even had they been known, probably would not have been deemed worthy of notice.

No term belonging to the Dravidian languages themselves has ever been used to designate all the members of this family, nor are the native Tamil or Telugu grammarians, though deeply skilled in the grammar of their own tongues, sufficiently acquainted with *comparative* grammar to have arrived at the conclusion that all these idioms have a common origin and require to be designated by a common term. Some European scholars, who have confined their attention to the study of some one Dravidian idiom exclusively, have fallen into the same misapprehension of supposing these languages independent one of another. The Sanskrit Pandits seem to have had a clearer perception of grammatical affinities and differences than the Dravidian grammarians; and, though their generalisation was not perfectly correct, it has furnished us with the only common terms India possesses for denoting the northern and southern families of the Indian languages respectively.

It is not clear whether Varâha-mihira (A.D. 404) regarded the term 'Draviḍa' as generic or specific. [See Kern's translation of the Bṛihat-saṃhitâ, *Journal of the Royal Asiatic Society.*] He places the Draviḍas in the south-west, but mentions also an 'eastern half of the Draviḍas.' The western half may have been on the Malabar coast. Parâśara placed the Draviḍas in the east. This name seems to have been less firmly attached to a particular people than the more purely local and dynastic names of Chôla, Pâṇḍya, &c. Varâha-mihira mentions 'the Pâṇḍya king,' 'the king of Kalinga,' &c., but mentions 'the Draviḍa kings' in the plural. The local names he mentions are: Pâṇḍya, Chôla, Kêrala, Karṇâṭaka, Kalinga, Andhra. He mentions Kônchî (Kânchî), Kôllagiri (Quilon? North Malabar?), Lankâ, the rivers Kâvêrî and Tâmraparṇî, and the conch and pearl fisheries (in the Gulf of Manaar). In the Mahâ-bhârata the Draviḍas are distinguished not only from the Kalingas, &c., but even from the Chôlas. This is also the case in the Vishṇu Purâṇa. In this sense the term must have been intended to denote the Pâṇḍyas alone.

Enumeration of Dravidian Languages.

The idioms which I designate as 'Dravidian' are twelve in number, exclusive of the Brahuî. They are as follows:—

1. Cultivated Dialects.

1. Tamil.	4. Canarese.
2. Malayâḷam.	5. Tuḷu.
3. Telugu.	6. Kuḍagu or Coorg.

2. Uncultivated Dialects.

1. Tuda.	4. Khond or Ku.
2. Kôta.	5. Orâon.
3. Gônḍ.	6. Râjmahâl.

I. Tamil.—This language being probably the earliest cultivated of all the Dravidian idioms, the most copious, and that which contains the largest portion and the richest variety of indubitably ancient forms, it is deservedly placed at the head of the list. It includes two dialects, the classical and the colloquial, or the ancient and the modern, called respectively the 'S'en-Damiṛ' and the 'Koḍun-Damiṛ,' which differ one from the other so widely that they might almost be regarded as different languages. The Tamil language is spoken throughout the vast plain of the Carnatic, or country below the Ghauts, from Pulicat to Cape Comorin, and from the Ghauts, or central mountain range of Southern India, to the Bay of Bengal. It is also spoken in the southern part of the Travancore country on the western side of the Ghauts, from Cape Comorin to the neighbourhood of Trivandrum; and in the northern and north-western parts of Ceylon, where Tamilians commenced to form settlements prior even to the Christian era, and from whence they have gradually thrust out the Singhalese. All throughout Ceylon the *coolies* in the coffee plantations are Tamilians; the majority of the money-making classes even in Colombo are Tamilians; and it seems not unlikely that ere long the Tamilians will have excluded the Singhalese from almost every profitable employment in their own island. The majority of the domestic servants of Europeans and of the camp-followers in every part of the presidency of Madras being Tamil people, Tamil is the prevailing language in all the military cantonments in Southern India, whatever be the vernacular language of the district. Hence, at Cannanore in the Malayâḷam country, at Bangalore in the Canarese country, at Bellary in the Telugu country, and at Secunderabad, where Hindûstânî may be considered as the vernacular, the language which most frequently meets the ear in the bazaars is Tamil.

The majority of the Klings (Kalingas), or Hindûs, who are found in Pegu, Penang, Singapore, and other places in the further east, are Tamilians: a large proportion of the coolies who have emigrated in such numbers to the Mauritius and to the West Indian colonies are Tamilians; in short, wherever money is to be made, wherever a more apathetic or a more aristocratic people is waiting to be pushed aside, thither swarm the Tamilians, the Greeks or Scotch of the east, the least superstitious and the most enterprising and persevering race of Hindûs. Including Tamilians resident in military stations and distant colonies, and the Tamilian inhabitants of South Travancore, and Northern Ceylon, and excluding not only Muhammedans, &c., but also people of Telugu origin who are resident in the Tamil country, and who form probably ten per cent. of the whole population, the people who speak the Tamil language may be estimated at about fourteen and a half millions.

Madras, the chief city in the Tamil country, is also the chief city in the South Indian Presidency. The name by which it is known amongst natives everywhere is, not Madras, but Chennappa-paṭṭaṇam, abbreviated into Chenna-paṭṭaṇam, a name which it derived from Chennappa Nâyakkar, father-in-law of the Nâyakkar of Chinglepat, a petty local chieftain, a feudatory of the Chandragiri Râjâ, from whom the English obtained possession of a little fort on the coast which they converted into a fortified factory. The origin of the name by which it appears always to have been called by Europeans—Madras (officially Madraspatam)—has never been made out with certainty. Perhaps the most probable derivation is from the Telugu *maduru* (Tamil *madil*), the surrounding wall of a fort, a rampart. There is a ṇeighbouring town, Sadras, originally a Dutch settlement, the name of which closely resembles Madras. Sadras is an European corruption from Sadurei, which is an abbreviation of Sadurangam (= Sans. Chaturanga), the four constituent arms of an army. I have not been able to discover any authority for the statement sometimes made that Madras is derived from Mandrâj-paṭṭaṇam.

The proper spelling of the name Tamil is Tamiṛ, but through the change of *ṛ* into *ḷ* it is often pronounced Tamiḷ; and is often (though erroneously) written Tamul by Europeans. Tamul is the mode of writing the name which appears to have been introduced by the French; but the name given to the language by the Portuguese, and by which it was generally known amongst the earlier Europeans, was neither Tamul nor Tamil, but 'the Malabar'—a name founded on a misapprehension.

The Portuguese arrived first on the western coast of India, and naturally called the language they found spoken on that coast by the name by which the coast itself had long been called by their Arab predecessors—viz., Malabar. Sailing from Malabar on voyages of exploration, they made their acquaintance with various places on the eastern or Coromandel coast and also on the coast of Ceylon, and finding the language spoken by the fishing and sea-faring classes on the eastern coast similar to that spoken on the western, they came to the conclusion that it was identical with it, and called it in consequence by the same name—viz., Malabar, a name which has survived to our own day amongst the poorer classes of Europeans and Eurasians. The better educated members of those classes have long learned to call the language of the Malabar coast by its proper name Malayâḷam, and the language of the eastern coast Tamil. Though the early Portuguese did not distinguish Malayâḷam from Tamil (just as the Sanskrit pandits failed to do), they noticed that it was distinct from Telugu, the language spoken by the 'Badages,' as they called them, the *Vaḍugas*, Tam., or *Baḍagas*, Can., *i.e.* the northmen, the Telugu followers of the Nâyakkas of Madura, who were then spreading themselves over the Tamil country, and even making irruptions into South Travancore. A circumstance which naturally confirmed the Portuguese in their notion of the identity of the people and language of the Coromandel coast with those of Malabar was, that when they arrived at Cael, in Tinnevelly, on the Coromandel coast (properly Kâyal, see a note in Colonel Yule's "Marco Polo," vol. ii.), they found the king of Quilon (one of the most important places on the Malabar coast) residing there. The prince referred to would now be called king of Travancore, and it is clear from inscriptions in my possession that the kingdom of Travancore sometimes included a portion of Tinnevelly.

The following was inserted as a note in the first edition of this work. "Professor Max Müller supposed Malabar to be a different language from Tamil: nor did he confound it, as would have been natural enough, with Malayâḷam, for he gave a distinct place to each of the Dravidian dialects which actually exist, including Malayâḷam, and thereto he added Malabar, on the authority, I presume, of some grammar of the last century, in which Tamil was called by that name." The above note was written in vain. Dr Hunter, in his "Comparative Dictionary of the non-Aryan Languages of India and High Asia," has given his readers a list of words which he designates as Malabar. He says, "In two instances separate lists represent either the same language or varieties so close as to seem scarcely deserving of separate places. The first is the Toḍuva and Toḍu, the second, the Malabar. But after weighing Mr Caldwell's statements in his 'Dravidian Grammar,' and the considerations which Dr Rost kindly urged in correspondence, I thought it better to give Malabar a distinct place, as the vocabulary which passes under that name was collected at a period sufficiently remote to allow of dialectic changes between it and the language as now spoken. In this view, it is proper to add, Professor Max Müller coincided." I do not know which was the vocabulary referred to, and therefore cannot tell the date of its compilation. Its date, however, is of very little consequence, seeing that no dialectic changes whatever have taken place in Tamil since the arrival of Europeans in India. Every word contained in Dr Hunter's Malabar list is modern, colloquial Tamil of the most ordinary type. The alternative words are mostly Sanskrit, from which it may be concluded that the compiler of the vocabulary, or the person who made selections from it for Dr Hunter, did not take care to confine himself to genuine Dravidian words.*

Colebrooke, though writing in Northern India, was aware of the identity of Malabar with Tamil. He says ("Essay on the Sanskrit and Prâkrit Languages"), "The language of the province is the Tâmel, to which Europeans have given the name of Malabar." The identity, however, of the two languages was known at a much earlier date to persons who had the opportunity of acquiring local knowledge. In the very first book ever printed in Tamil characters—at Ambalakkâḍu, on the Malabar coast, in 1577 or 9—the language of the book is styled 'Malavar or Tamul.' The writer apparently regarded Tamil as the more correct word. See "Sounds: Alphabet."

The Sanskrit name corresponding to Tamil is Drâviḍa, a word which denotes both the country inhabited by the people called Draviḍas and the language spoken by them; and I have come to the conclusion that the words *Tamiṛ* and *Draviḍa*, though they seem to differ a good deal, are identical in origin. Supposing them to be one and the same word, it will be found much easier to derive *Tamiṛ* from *Draviḍa* than *Draviḍa* from *Tamiṛ*. It might naturally seem improbable at the outset that a Dravidian people residing in the extreme south should call themselves and be called by their neighbours, not by a Dravidian,

* I notice two errors. One is '*one*' for 'there,' which I cannot explain. It must have crept in from some other list. The other is the word for 'mosquito,' which can be made out clearly enough. It is the Tamil word for 'moustache.' It is not so surprising after all that Malabar should have acquired a place of its own in Indian philology side by side with Tamil, seeing that Malabar and Tamil, whatever they mean, are evidently different names. It is more surprising that Toḍu and Toḍuva should have been honoured with separate lists, seeing that it might have been concluded that they were only, like Tuḷu and Tuḷuva, different modes of writing one and the same name.

but by a Sanskrit name; but it is certain that Pâṇḍya, the name of the southernmost portion of the Dravidians, is Sanskrit, and a similar peculiarity meets us with regard to almost all the names of the South Indian peoples—Chôlas, Kêralas, Andhras, Kalingas, &c.—which, so far as is known at present, are Sanskrit, not Dravidian. The name Karṇâṭaka alone appears to have a Dravidian origin. If the other names were originally Dravidian, as this seems to have been, and as it might naturally be supposed they all must have been, their original shape and root-meaning have disappeared. What adds to the difficulty is, that though these words have a place in Sanskrit dictionaries and are accepted as Sanskrit by the Dravidian people, Sanskrit fails as completely as the Dravidian languages to furnish us with a clue to their original meaning. When we have traced them back to Sanskrit we are obliged to leave them there. The name Andhra appears, as has already been mentioned, in one of the Brâhmaṇas, but, like most of the Vedic proper names, it is incapable of explanation. May it not be, indeed, that those proper names belonged originally to some old North Indian vernacular—some præ-Aryan, though not necessarily non-Aryan—speech, which had disappeared before the literary history of Sanskrit commenced. If this were the case, it would be in vain to expect the derivation of such words as Draviḍa to be cleared up now. The compound *dr* is quite un-Dravidian. It would be *tira* in Tamil; but even if we suppose some such word as Tiraviḍa or Tiramiḍa to have been converted into Draviḍa by the Sanskrit-speaking people, we get no nearer to an explanation of the original meaning of the word.

The oldest form of Draviḍa—or, at least, the form which appears to have been most widely in use—appears to have been Dramiḍa; and this is the first step towards identifying the two words, Draviḍa and Tamiṛ. Both forms of the word are known in Tamil, but Dramiḍa (written Tiramiḍa) is preferred by the classics, and is placed first in ancient Tamil vocabularies. In Varâha-mihira's Bṛihat-sa*m*hitâ, according to Dr Kern, some manuscripts give Dramiḍa, instead of Draviḍa. Through the change of *ḍ* into *l*, the Draviḍas are called Dramilas in Târanâtha's Tibetan "History of the Propagation of Buddhism in India" (A.D. 1573), and Dr Gundert informs me that this is the form in which the word occurs again and again in the old Malayâḷam versions of the Purâṇas. In the Pâli of the Mahâwanso the form used is Damilo, the derivative of which is Dâmilo; and as initial *d* becomes *t* by rule in Tamil, we now reach the ordinary Tamil mode of writing the word, Tamiṛ or Tamil. Each of the changes that have taken place is in accordance with a recognised Dravidian law of sound.

Initial *dr* is always softened in the Prâkrits into *d*—*e.g.*, *drôha* becomes *dôhô*. In the same manner *śr* becomes *ś*, an example of which we have in the word S'ramaṇa, a Buddhist or Jaina ascetic, which in Tamil has become Samaṇa (in Pâli, Sammana; in the Greek of Clemens Alexandrinus the plural is Σαμαναιοί and Σεμνοί). The change of *v* into *m* or of *m* into *v*, even in Sanskrit itself, is seen in such words as *dhmâṅksha*, Sans. a crow, instead of *dhvâṅksha*, and especially in the affixes *mat* and *vat*, *man* and *van*, *min* and *vin*. Perhaps the most considerable change is from *ḍ* in Dravida to *ṛ* in Tamiṛ; but this also is quite in accordance with usage, as will appear in the chapter on "Sounds." Compare *nâḍi*, Sans. a measure, with the Tam.-Mal. *nâṛi* or *nâḻi*. A good illustration of this change is furnished by the name of one of the nations included under the general name of Tamil—viz., that of the Cholas. This name in the Sanskrit of one of Aśoka's inscriptions is Chôḍa, in ordinary Sanskrit Chôla, in Tamil S'ôra, in Telugu Chôḷa. In Telugu inscriptions it is often Chôḍa as in Aśoka's. The change of *d* to *t* in the beginning of a word is unavoidable in Tamil, but we have a reminiscence perhaps of the original sound in the name given to the language by the first Danish missionaries—viz., Lingua Damulica.

In the Indian segment of the very interesting set of Roman maps, called, from the name of the discoverer, the Peutinger Tables—(this segment at least seems to me anterior to Ptolemy's Geography)—we find a considerable portion of the country covered by two names—Andre Indi and Damirice. We can scarcely err in identifying these names with the Telugu and Tamil countries—the languages of which were called, as we have seen, by Kumârila-bhaṭṭa, some centuries later, the languages of the Ândhras and Drâviḍas. If so, the earliest appearance of the name Tamil in any foreign document, will be found also to be most perfectly in accordance with the native Tamil mode of spelling the name. Damirice evidently means Damir-ice. Compare the Αριάκη of Ptolemy and the Âryaka of Varâha-mihira. In another place in the same map a district is called Scytia Dymirice; and it appears to have been this word which, by a mistake of Δ for Λ, Ptolemy wrote Λυμιρίκη. The *D* retains its place, however, in the Cosmography of the anonymous geographer of Ravenna, who repeatedly mentions Dimirica as one of the three divisons of India, and the one farthest to the east. He shows also that the Tamil country must have been meant by the name, by mentioning Modura as one of the cities it contained. There can be little doubt that the name Tamil may also be identified with the Tchi-mo-lo of Hwen Thsang, a word which may also be read Dimala or even Dimara.

It is remarkable that native Tamil scholars, though generally willing enough to trace every word to a Sanskrit origin, have failed to see in Tamiṛ—or Tamiṛa, as it is also sometimes written—a *tadbhava* of Draviḍa or Dramiḍa, and have invented for the name of their language (like their neighbours the Telugu people—though perhaps with less reason), the meaning of 'sweetness or fragrance'—a meaning of the word Tamiṛ which has nothing to support or commend it, but its agreement with the estimate formed by the Tamilians of the euphoniousness of their native tongue. I accept their estimate of their language as in the main correct, but cannot accept their derivation of the word.

A discussion respecting the origin of the word Tamil would not be complete without some reference to the names of the three great subdivisions into which the Tamil people were divided in ancient times—Chêras, Chôlas, and Pâṇḍyas. The arrangement of the names is climatic, and denotes that the Pâṇḍyas were supposed in those times to have the pre-eminence—a supposition which appears to be in accordance with the facts of the case.

PAṆḌYA.—The Singhalese traditions preserved in the Mahâwamso represent Vijaya, the first sovereign of Ceylon, as marrying a daughter of the Pâṇḍya king, in consequence of which his son was called Pâṇḍuvaṁśadeva. Arjuna also, one of the five Pâṇḍava brothers, is related in the Mahâ-bhârata to have married a daughter of the king of the Pâṇḍyas in the course of his many wanderings. There is no certainty in these traditions; but it is certain that about the time of Pliny and the Periplus a portion of the Malabar coast was ruled over by the Pâṇḍyas, a proof that their power had considerably extended itself from its original seats; and I regard it as nearly certain that the Indian king who sent an embassy to Augustus was not Porus, but Pandion—*i.e.*, the king of the Pâṇḍyas, called in Tamil Pâṇḍiyan.*

* The statement generally made by the Greek and Latin historians who refer to this embassy is that it was sent by the Indi, without further explanation as to who those Indians were. Strabo says the embassy was from king Pandion, "or according to others" (whose opinion apparently he did not endorse) "from king Porus." One of those "others" was Nicolaus Damascenus, quoted by Strabo himself, who says he saw the ambassadors. The name Porus was already well known in Europe, through the historians of Alexander's career, and it was natural that Greeks should fall into the mistake of supposing every Indian king a successor of Porus, whereas the name Pandion was one which up to that time had never been heard of in Europe, and therefore was one which could not have been invented. This Indian embassy has a place in the Chronicon of Eusebius (320 A.D.), but neither in the ordinary (defective) Greek text of the Chronicon, nor in the Armenian version is the name of the king from whom it proceeded mentioned. The name appears, however, in the Chronographia of George the Syncellus (800 A.D.), whose work has been used to restore or complete the Greek text of the

If this be admitted, it is an interesting proof of the advanced social position occupied by the Pâṇḍyas—(probably in consequence of the foreign trade they carried on in connection with their settlements on the Malabar coast)—that after the termination of the political relations that subsisted between the successors of Alexander and the princes of Northern India, the Pâṇḍyas were the only Indian princes who perceived the advantages of an European alliance.

The Sanskrit Pâṇḍya is written in Tamil Pâṇḍiya, but the more completely Tamilised form Pâṇḍi is still more commonly used all over Southern India. I derive *Pâṇḍi*, not from the Tamil and Malayâḷam *paṇḍu*, ancient, though that is a very tempting derivation, but—as native scholars always derive the word—from the Sanskrit Pâṇḍu, the name of the father of the Pâṇḍava brothers. This very form Pâṇḍya, in the sense of a descendant of Pâṇḍu, is mentioned, as I am informed by Professor Max Müller, by Kâtyâyana, the immediate successor of Pâṇini. The second and most celebrated capital of the Pâṇḍyas—(the first was Kolkei on the Tâmraparṇi)—was Madurei, in English Madura, which is the Tamil mode of writing Mathurâ (the Muttra of our maps, and the Μέθορα of the Greeks) the name of the city which remained in the possession of the Pâṇḍavas at the conclusion of the great war. The Madura of the Pâṇḍyas is appropriately called in the Harivamśa, 'the Southern Mathurâ.' There is another (Maturâ) in Ceylon, and a fourth (Madûra) in the Eastern Archipelago.. The Singhalese annalists in the Mahâwanso call the king of the Pâṇḍyas sometimes Pâṇḍyava, sometimes Pâṇḍu; and this shows that there cannot be any doubt of the connection of the name of the Pâṇḍyas with that of the heroes of the great war, though the origin and nature of that connection cannot now be ascertained. Pâṇḍya must at first have been the name of the ruling family only. Its extension to the people followed the course which dynastic names have often taken in other parts of the world. Megasthenes speaks of a country in India which was called Πανδαίη, after the name of the only daughter of the Indian Hercules—that is, of Krishṇa. I have no doubt that the country referred to was that of the Pâṇḍyas. A writer who had heard of the Andaræ and Calingæ could not but have heard of the Pâṇḍyas also. He partly, it is true, misapprehended the legends related to him; but he was right in deriving the name of the Pâṇḍya country from the name of its rulers, and in connecting their name—in some fashion, however erroneously—with mythological heroes and heroines. The myth really

Chronicon, and who says, under the head of the 185th Olympiad, "Pandion, king of the Indians, sends an embassy to Augustus, requesting to become his friend and ally."

current at that time—if we may suppose the substance of the Mahâbhârata in its present shape then in existence—was that Arjuna, one of the Pâṇḍava brothers and Krishṇa's chief friend, had in the course of his wanderings in the south married a daughter of the king of the Pâṇḍyas. Everything related by Megasthenes respecting this country, especially the statement that it was there that pearls were procured, serves to identify it with the Pâṇḍya country. Pliny, apparently following another passage of Megasthenes, enumerates amongst the Indian nations a nation called Pandæ. It is not clear where he supposed their country was situated, but we cannot doubt that the Pâṇḍyas of Madura, wherever he thought they were located, were the people referred to. His statement that the Pandæ alone amongst Indian nations were ruled by women, though not correct (so far as is now known), if supposed to relate to the Pâṇḍyas of Madura, may be regarded as sufficiently applicable to the peculiar social usages of the Malabar coast, where almost every inheritance still runs in the female line, and where, in Pliny's own times at least, if not also in those of Megasthenes, the Pâṇḍyas of Madura had colonies. Pliny expressly mentions that a portion of the western coast was then under the rule of king Pandion, "far away from his mediterranean emporium of Modura;" yet he remarks also that this name, with others in the same neighbourhood, was new to him. He evidently had no idea that the subjects of king Pandion were identical with the Pandæ he himself had already referred to.

Chôla, the name of the Tamil people placed second in the list, is a word of unknown origin. It appears as Choḍa in one of Aśoka's inscriptions, and also in the Telugu inscriptions of the Châlukya dynasty. In modern Telugu this word appears as Chôḷa, in Tamil as Chôṛa or Sôṛa. We have here doubtless the Σῶραι, &c., of Ptolemy. It is difficult to identify the country called Choliya by Hwen Thsang with the country inhabited by the Chôlas, but it seems probable that the names are identical; and we know that the Northern Circars were ruled by an offshoot of the Chôlas in the eleventh century. The original seat of the Chôlas seems to have been the extensive, fertile valley of the Kâvêrî, including the Tanjore and Trichinopoly districts; but subsequently they ruled over the whole of the Tamil country north of the Kâvêrî. Their capital city in the earliest period was *Urieyûr* (literally the 'city of habitation'), called also *Kôṛi*, which appears to have been nearly identical with the modern Trichinopoly (*Tiriśirâppaḷḷi*). In the eleventh century the Chôlas reached the zenith of their power, and ruled—as is ascertained by inscriptions—over the whole Tamil country, including not only the country north of the Kâvêrî, but also the country of the Pâṇḍyas, South Travancore, the northern districts in Ceylon, and a portion of the Telugu country.

CHÊRA, the name of the third Tamilian people, is a word which presents itself to us in many shapes, as will be seen when we proceed to consider the Malayâḷam language. The language of the Chôlas never differed from that of the Pâṇḍyas; and originally the language of the Chêras also differed but little from that of the other two portions of the Tamil people, as appears from the Syrian and Jewish inscriptions of the eighth century. By whatever local or dynastic names they may have called themselves, they all—whether Chêras, Chôlas, or Pâṇḍyas—continued to be called Draviḍas, and the language they spoke in common was everywhere called by the one name of Drâviḍa or Tamil.

This idea of the original identity of the Chêras, or people of Kêrala, with the Chôlas and Pâṇḍyas, is quite in accordance with native traditions. According to Tamil tradition, *Chêran*, *Chôṛan*, and *Pâṇḍiyan* were three royal brothers, who at first lived and ruled in common at Kolkci, on the Tâmraparṇî, a river in Tinnevelly renowned in ancient song, on the banks of which the earliest civilisation in Southern India appears to have been built up. Eventually a separation took place: Pâṇḍiyan remained at home; Chêran and Chôran went forth to seek their fortunes, and founded kingdoms of their own to the north and west. We have a similar representation, perhaps merely an echo of the Tamil tradition, in the Hari-va*m*śa and several Purâṇas (see Muir's "Sanskrit Texts," vols. i. and ii.), in which Pâṇḍya, Kêrala, *Kôla*, and Chôla are represented as the four sons of Âkrîḍa, or of Dushyanta, the adopted son of Turvasu, a prince of the lunar line of the Kshatriyas. Who the *Kôlas* of this list were is not clear. The term is supposed by some to have been intended to denote the Canarese people, Karṇâṭa being given in this connection instead of Kôla by several Purâṇas. The Canarese people, however, are never called Kôlas either by themselves or by their Dravidian neighbours; and it seems most probable that the Kôls or Kolarians were referred to, perhaps under the impression (if so, an erroneous one, except in so far as the Orâons and Mâlers are concerned) that they also were Dravidians.

The Tamil language is called *Aravam* by the Mussulmans of the Dekhan, the Telugus, and the Canarese. What is the derivation of this term Aravam? Its origin appears to me very uncertain. Dr Gundert suggested that as Tamil literature excelled other literatures in ethics, it might have been perhaps from this circumstance that Tamilians were called Aravas. *Aravas* on this supposition would signify moralists, for *aram* in Tamil means virtue ; it might mean perhaps even Buddhists, for *Aravan*, Tam. 'the virtuous one,' is a name of Buddha. It would not be a valid objection to this derivation that the *r* of the Telugu and Canarese word *Aravam* is the ordinary liquid or semi-vowel, whilst the *r* of the Tamil *aram* is the hard rough **r**, for the hard **r** of Tamil generally changes into *r* in Telugu and Canarese; and this very word *aram*, Tam. virtue, is *aravu* in Canarese. Another theory derives the term from *arivu*, the Tamil word for knowledge, the Tamil people being supposed to be distinguished amongst the people of the south for their intelligence. Another derivation is from *Aruvâ*, the name of an unknown district somewhere in the Tamil country, which was reckoned one of the twelve districts in which, according to the Tamil grammarians, bad Tamil was spoken. A formidable, if not a fatal, objection to these derivations is, that they have all a Tamil origin, whereas *Aravam* is absolutely unknown in Tamil itself as a name either of the people or of their language. It is by the Telugus, Canarese, and Dekhanis that the name is used, and its derivation must, therefore, be sought out of the Tamil country. The opinion of the best Telugu pandits I have consulted is that *Arava* is a Sanskrit, not a Dravidian, word. It is to be divided as *a–rava*, destitute of sound ; and this name has been given, they suppose, to Tamil by the northern neighbours of the Tamilians on account of its being destitute of aspirates. Being the only language in India totally without aspirates, it was despised by outsiders for what was regarded as a defect, and was called in consequence *Arava*, which may be rendered 'unsonorous.' It was not likely, if this were the origin of the word, that the Tamil people would apply it to their own tongue. *Aravam-u* having come to be used in Telugu as the name of the language, the Telugu people went in time a step further, and called the people who spoke the language *Arava-lu*, Aravas. The Telugu word *Aravam-u*, 'the Tamil language,' is not to be confounded with the Tamil word *aravam*, sound. It is a curious circumstance that the latter word means sound, whilst the former means being without sound. The initial *a* of the Tamil word is not, as it might readily be supposed to be, the Sanskrit *a* privative, but is one of the devices employed in Tamil to render it possible for Tamil organs to pronounce an initial *r*. (Comp. *araśan*, king, from Sanskrit *râjâ*.) It may also be noticed that whilst the Sanskrit word *rava* means a loud sound, a noise, the Tamil form of the same word, *aravam*, means a very slight noise.

Mr Narasimmiengar, of the Mysore Commission, was so kind as to consult for me the best native Canarese scholars as to what they considered the origin of the term *Aravam̀*. They rejected the theory of the Telugu pandits, according to which it was derived from the Sanskrit *a-rava*, and stated that they considered it derived from the Canarese word *arȃvu*, 'half,' or 'deficient' (Can. root *are*, Tel. *ara*), a term by which they supposed the Tamil language had been designated by their forefathers, on account of what appeared to them its deficiencies. I am sorry to say the discussion of this point does not appear to me as yet to have produced any very satisfactory result. It is noteworthy, perhaps, that the people who are represented by Ptolemy as occupying, according to Colonel Yule, the portion of the Coromandel coast near Nellore, are called by him the Arvarni.

Whence has arisen the name *Tigaḷar* or *Tiguḷar*, ordinarily applied to the Tamilians by the Canarese? The Canarese, like the Telugus, call the Tamil people *Aravas* and Draviḍas, but the name *Tigaḷar* is given to the Tamilians by the Canarese alone. Mr Kittel informs me that in the oldest Canarese MSS. in which he has found this word it is written Tiguḷar, and that he has little doubt its original form was Tiguṛar. This word appears at present in Canarese in the form of *tegaḷa*, and means blame, abuse. As applied to the Tamilians it would mean the opprobrious people, which it is difficult to suppose would ever become current as the denomination of an entire race. No words resembling this have the meaning of blame or abuse in Tamil or Malayâḷam. In both languages *tigaṛ* means splendour; *tegiḷ*, *tegaḷ*, fulness. These meanings would doubtless be too complimentary for a name given to any people by foreigners, and yet the meaning deducible from the Canarese itself seems too uncivil. The Canarese pandits, consulted by Mr Narasimmiengar, derived the name from *tigadu* or *tigaru*, and explained it as meaning rude. This explanation accords substantially with Mr Kittel's. Mr Narasimmiengar adds, "The word Tigaḷaru has almost ceased to be one of reproach, and there are large communities, some of them Brâhmans, called by this name."

II. MALAYÂLAM.—This language claims to be placed next to Tamil in the list of Dravidian tongues, on account of the peculiarly close relationship to Tamil in which it stands. Malayâḷam is spoken along the Malabar coast, on the western side of the Ghauts, or Malaya range of mountains, from the vicinity of Chandragiri, near Mangalore, where it supersedes Canarese and Tuḷu, to Trivandrum (Tiruvanantapuram), where it begins to be superseded by Tamil. The people by whom this language is spoken in the native states of Travancore (Tiruvidâṅkôḍu or Tiravâṅkôḍu) and Cochin (Kochchi), and in the British Indian districts of Malabar and Canara, may be estimated at 3,750,000. All along the Malabar coast

Tamil intertwines itself with Malayâḷam. Though that coast was for many ages more frequented by foreigners than any other part of India; though Phœnicians, Greeks, Jews, Syrian or Persian Christians, and Arabs, traded in succession to the various ports along the coast; and though permanent settlements were formed by the last three classes; yet the Malayâḷam people continue to be of all Dravidians the most exclusive and superstitious, and shrink most sensitively from contact with foreigners. Hence the lines and centres of communication have been occupied, and a considerable portion of the commerce and public business of the Malabar States has been monopolised, especially in Travancore, by the less scrupulous and more adroit Tamilians.

Malayâḷam is also called *Malayâṛma,* another form of which is *Malayâyma;* but both words are substantially the same. The first part of each word is not the Sanskrit *Malaya,* 'a range of mountains' (probably identical with the Western and Southern Ghauts), but the Dravidian *mala,* 'a mountain,' from which doubtless the Sanskrit *malaya* itself was derived. The second part of the word, *âḷam* or *âṛma,* is an abstract neuter noun, between *mala* and which *y* is inserted by rule to prevent hiatus. *âḷam* is plainly a verbal derivative from the root *âḷ,* 'to possess,' 'to use,' 'to rule' (not to be confounded with *âṛam,* 'depth,' from the root *âṛ,* 'to be deep'). It bears the same relation to *âṛma,* originally *âḷma* (Tam. *âṇmei,* euphonised from *âḷmei*), that *tanam* (Mal.-Tam. 'quality') does to *tanma,* Mal. (Tam. *tanmei*); that is, it is more commonly used, but is reckoned less elegant. *âṛma* is softened from *âḷma,* as in Tam. *veḷḷâḷan,* a cultivator, is sometimes softened into *veḷḷâṛan.* More frequently *ṛ* changes to *ḷ,* but the change of *ḷ* to *ṛ* is also known. This *ṛ* is further softened in Malayâḷam to *y,* in consequence of which *Malayâṛma* becomes *Malayâyma.* In colloquial Tamil this softening process is sometimes carried so far that the *ḷ* disappears altogether and leaves no trace behind. Thus, *veḷḷâṇmei,* Tam. cultivation, becomes in Malayâḷam *veḷḷâyma,* but in colloquial Tamil *veḷḷâmei; naṭṭâṇmei,* Tam. the headship of a village, from *nâḍu* and *âṇmei,* becomes in Malayâlam *nâṭṭâyma,* but in colloquial Tamil *nâṭṭâmei.* *nâṭṭâṇma* is also found in Malayâḷam; and this supplies us with a clear proof of the descent of *âyma,* through *âṇma,* from *âḷma.* Perhaps the best rendering of the term Malayâḷam or Malayâṛma is the 'mountain region.' If we had a word in English for a mountain district ending in 'ship' like 'township,' it would come still nearer. When used as an abstract term in compounds *aṇmei* means use or possession—*e.g.,* *villâṇmei,* the use of the bow, from *vil,* bow. The appellative noun connected with this word *âṇmei* is *âḷan* or *âḷi,* each of which forms is in ordinary use both in Tamil and Malayâḷam—*e.g.*, *villâḷan* = *villâḷi*, Tam.-Mal. a bowman. The appellative noun corresponding to *Malayâḷam* or *Malayârma* is *Malayâḷi*, a man of Malayâḷam, a mountaineer.

The Malayâḷam *language* is not distinguished from Tamil by Sanskrit writers, the term Drâviḍa, as used by them, including both tongues; but the Malayâḷam *country* has a name of its own in Sanskrit, with special names for the various districts included in it, from Gokarṇam to Cape Comorin. The general name of this entire region in Sanskrit is Kêrala, a term which appears in the Kapur Di Giri version of Aśoka's edict, in the third century B.C., in which the king of this country is called *Kêralamputra*. *Kêralam* is found in all the Dravidian dialects in one shape or another. In Tamil, through the softening of *k* into *ś*, *c*, or *ch*, this word sometimes becomes *Sêralam*, more commonly still *Sêram*. Where the initial *k* is retained unchanged, it is followed by the Dravidian *ḷ*—*e.g.*, *Kêraḷam*—and this is the case also in Telugu and Canarese. In Malayâḷam we find *Keraḷam*, *Chêralam*, and *Chêram*, as in Tamil, and also *Kêram*. A man of *Kêraḷam* is called sometimes *Kêḷan* or *Kêḷu*, and though this is evidently a contraction of *Keraḷan*, it must be one of great antiquity, for we find it in Pliny's name of the king of the country, Celobotras, a form of the word which is thus seen to be as accurate as Ptolemy's Κηροβόθρος.

The Kerala of the ancients seems to have divided itself into two portions, one of which, the district lying along the sea coast, has always retained the Sanskritic name of Kêrala, whilst it also called itself by the Tamil name of Chera; the other, an inland district, including Coimbatore, Salem, and a portion of Mysore, seems to have dropped the name of Kerala altogether, and called itself exclusively either Chera or Kongu. It is to the latter district that the papers of Professor Dowson and Dr Eggeling on the Chera dynasty refer. Though, however, the districts and dynasties differed, I have no doubt that the *names* Kerala and Chera were originally one and the same, and it is certain that they are always regarded as synonymous in native Tamil and Malayâḷam lists of synonyms. In the various lists of the boundaries of Chera given by Tamil writers, the Malabar coast from Calicut southward—that is, the whole of southern Kerala—is invariably included. Probably Kêra was the earliest form of the word, Kêrala a Sanskritic derivative. The word *Koṅgu*, one of the names of the Chera country, means, like Kuḍagu (Coorg), crooked, curved, and is evidently a name derived from the configuration of the country. The meaning of *Kêram* is not so certain. One meaning of this word in Malayâḷam is 'a cocoa-nut palm.' This would furnish us with a very natural origin for the name of the country; but unfortunately it seems to be only a secondary meaning, the name of the country itself being probably the origin of this name of its most characteristic tree. No word allied to Malayâḷam, the native name of the language and the name most commonly used now for the country, seems to have been known to the earlier Greeks. A portion of the name appears for the first time in the "Christian Topography" of Cosmas Indicopleustes, about 545 A.D., who, writing especially about Ceylon, mentions amongst the adjacent countries, "Μαλί, whence the pepper comes." This form of the word is evidently identical with the Tamil *malei*, a hill, the hill country, a word which would be in common use then, as now, amongst the Tamil settlers in Ceylon. The distinctively Malayâḷam form of the same word is *mala*.

Malayâḷam being, as I conceive, a very ancient offshoot of Tamil, differing from it chiefly at present by its disuse of the personal terminations of the verbs and the larger amount of Sanskrit derivatives it has availed itself of, it might perhaps be regarded rather as a dialect of Tamil, than as a distinct member of the Dravidian family. Though its separation from Tamil must have taken place at a very early period, yet it seems to have participated, as time went on, in the progressive cultivation and refinement of Tamil,—possibly through the political influence the Tamilians acquired on the western coast in early times, an illustration of which we have seen in the fact that the author of the "Periplus" represents Nelkynda, one of the most important emporia on the western coast, as belonging to the Pâṇḍya king of Madura, the principal potentate in the Tamil country. The oldest Malayâḷam poetry, as I learn from Dr Gundert, imitated Tamil rather than Sanskrit. It eschewed all letters not included in the thirty-two adopted by Tamil, and the character employed was a character often used in inscriptions in the Tamil country, particularly in the south, and differing very widely from the Malayâḷam character now in use. The "Râma Charita," probably the oldest poem in the language, though not, after all, of any very great antiquity, was composed before the introduction of the Sanskrit alphabet, and exhibits substantially the same phase of the language as the Jewish and Syrian S'âsanas. Bearing this in mind, it is remarkable that the Brahmanisation of the language and literature should now have become so complete. This process appears to have been carried on systematically only during the last two or three centuries, yet one of the most marked characteristics of the Malayâḷam language, as we now find it, is the quantity of Sanskrit it contains. The proportion of Sanskrit words adopted by the Dravidian languages is least in Tamil, greatest in Malayâḷam; and the modern Malayâḷam character seems to have been derived in the main from the Grantha, the character in which Sanskrit is written in the Tamil country. In consequence of these things, the difference between Malayâḷam and Tamil, though originally slight, has progressively increased, so that the claim of Malayâḷam, as it now stands, to be considered, not as a mere dialect of Tamil, but as a sister language, cannot be called in question. Originally, it is true, I consider it to have been not a sister of Tamil, but a daughter. It may best be described as a much-altered offshoot.

The descent of Malayâḷam from Tamil may be illustrated by the word it uses to denote east. This is *kiṛakku*, meaning beneath, downwards, a word which corresponds to that which is used to denote west, viz., *mêlku*, above, upwards; both of which words necessarily originated, not in the western coast, but in the Tamil country, or the country on the eastern side of the Ghauts, where a lofty range of mountains rises everywhere to the westward, and where, consequently, to go westward is to go upwards, whilst to the eastward the country slopes downwards to the sea. The configuration of the Malayâḷam country, as of the whole of the western coast, is directly the reverse of this, the mountain range being to the eastward, and the sea to the westward. Notwithstanding this, the Malayâḷam word for east is identical with the Tamil word! To what can this coincidence point but the original identity of Malayâḷam with Tamil? The people by whom Malayâḷam is spoken must originally have been a colony of Tamilians. They must have entered the Malayâḷam country by the Paulghaut or Coimbatore gap, and from thence spread themselves along the coast, northward to the Chandragiri river, southward to the Neyyâṟu river near Trivandrum, at each of which points their further progress seems to have been stopped by settlements of colonists of a kindred race, who had already reached the western coast by different routes. Dr Gundert (Introduction to "Malayâḷam Dictionary"), whilst admitting Tamil and Malayâḷam to be very nearly related, appears to be unwilling to consider Malayâḷam as an offshoot of Tamil. He argues (in a private communication) that the words used in Malayâḷam for east and west cannot safely be regarded as proving the immigration of the Malayâḷam people from the east, and that if the analogous progress of the Aryans to the south be considered, it will appear probable that the Dravidians, like the Aryans, formed settlements on the western coast first, and afterwards made their acquaintance with the eastern. It is true, as he observes, that *paḍiññâṟu*, properly *paḍiññâyiṟu*, meaning the setting sun, is more commonly used in Malayâḷam for west than *mêlku*, but *paḍuññâyiṟu* is also a Tamil word, and Dr Gundert admits that both *mêlku* and *kiṛakku* must have originated in the Tamil country. The argument from the analogy of the Aryan immigration appears to prove too much. It would require us to regard the whole Tamil people as immigrants from the western coast, and the Tamil language as an offshoot from Malayâḷam, the geographical and philological difficulties in the way of both which suppositions appear to me to be insuperable.

Origin of the terms 'Coromandel' and 'Malabar.'—Before passing on to the rest of the Dravidian languages, it may be desirable to inquire into the origin of the names 'Coromandel' coast and 'Malabar' coast, by which the eastern and western coasts of the southern portion of the Indian peninsula, in which the Tamil and Malayâḷam languages are spoken, are usually designated.

1. *Coromandel.*—The best derivation of Coromandel is from the Tamil *Chôṛamaṇḍalam*, the Chôla country, from *Chôṛa*, the Tamil form of the name which is best known in its Sanskrit form of Chola, and *maṇḍalam* (a Sanskrit *tadbhava*), 'a district of country.' Undoubtedly Fra Paulino à St Bartolomæo was wrong in supposing Chôḷa-maṇḍalam to have meant 'the millet country.' The first word, Chôṛam though often pronounced like Chôḷam ('maize,' not 'millet'), is always written in Tamil Chôṛam, and the compound Chôṛa-maṇḍalam, 'the country of the Chôṛas, like Pâṇḍya-maṇḍalam, 'the country of the Pâṇḍyas,' has been in common use for ages. The first Portuguese, as I learn from Dr Gundert, always called by the name of Choramandala the fifth province of the Râyar's empire (the empire of the so-called Râyulu or Telugu kings of Vijayanagara), which they represented as extending from the frontiers of Quilon (that is, from near Cape Comorin) to Orissa. The Portuguese evidently adopted this name as the equivalent of Ma'bar, the name by which the greater part of the Coromandel coast had up to that time been generally called by the Muhammedans and those Europeans who derived their information from them. (See Ibn Batuta and Marco Polo.) This name Ma'bar, literally a ford or passage, was used originally to denote the coast of Madura, from which there was an easy passage by Râma's bridge to Ceylon. The application of the name was then indefinitely extended northwards. The change from Choramandala to Coromandel is one which would easily be made. The middle point appears to be Choromandel, the mode in which the name was written by the early Dutch.

In the first edition of this work, whilst assigning this origin to the term Coromandel coast, I suggested also that it was difficult to see how the first mariners could have become acquainted with this somewhat high-flown classical word. It seemed to me desirable, therefore, to seek for some more trite and easy derivation of the word Coromandel—some derivative that would suit the circumstances of mariners and factors; and this, I said, I think we find in *Karu-maṇal* (literally, black sand), the name of a small village on the eastern coast, near Pulicat (the first settlement of the Dutch), which is invariably pronounced and written Coromandel by the Europeans who are resident in Madras, some of whom annually take refuge in *Karumaṇal* or Coromandel during the hot land winds. Coromandel is often the first point which is sighted by ships from Europe bound to Madras; and the objects on which my own eyes first rested on approaching the coast, in January 1838, were the cocoanut trees of Coromandel and the distant Nagari hills. I fear, however, this easy derivation must be given up, and the more ancient one, which carries us back to the first arrival of the Portuguese in India, retained. I learn also from Mr C. P. Brown, that in a map of the Jaghire of Madras in "Kitchin's Atlas" (about 1790), the name of the village in question is written, not Coromandel, but *Karri mannel*, so that the application of the name Coromandel to this village by the English must be of recent date. One of the names given to the eastern coast in Telugu is *Kharamaṇḍalam*, from *khara*, Sans. hot; but this name has never been used so widely along the coast as to render it likely that it was the origin of the name Coromandel. Besides, this name was never used, as Chôṛamaṇḍalam was, as a political designation.

I am indebted to Colonel Yule, the learned editor of Marco Polo, for additional information regarding the use of the term Coromandel by the early Portuguese. He says—"It certainly was a name in use when the Portuguese arrived in India. This appears from its use in the short narrative of Hieronimo de Sto Stefano, dated in 1499, which is published at the end of Major's 'India' in the fifteenth century. After mentioning Ceylon he says, 'departing thence after twelve days we reached another place called Coromandel.' The city of Choromandel appears in 'Vaithema's Travels' (published in 1510); and in Barbosa, the most complete of the early Portuguese accounts, we have the country of Charamandel (in the Portuguese edition), Coromandel (in Ramusio's Italian), Cholmendel and Cholmender in a Spanish MS. translated by Lord Stanley of Alderley in the Hakluyt series. I believe both Spanish and Portuguese pronounce the *ch* as we do, so I should think it probable that the Italian Co was written Ço. This Cholmendel is remarkable, as the MS. is supposed to date about 1510, too early for theories about Chola-mandala. I had given up the hope of finding proof of the use of this name by the Muhammedans, but on turning to Rowlandson's translation of the 'Tohfat al Majâhidîn, or History of the Muhammedans in Malabar,' I have found (p. 153) that the Franks had built fortresses 'at Mielapoor and Nagapatam, and other seaports of Solmondul,' and the name occurs again in the next page." Colonel Yule, in mentioning this in the *Bombay Antiquary* for August 1874, adds—"The occurrence of this name in this form and in a Muhammedan writer upsets a variety of theories as to the origin of the name."

The Coromandel coast is evidently the Παραλία Σωρατῶν (or Σωριγῶν) of Ptolemy, and also the district τῆς ἰδίως λεγουμένης Παραλίας Τωριγγῶν (or Σωριγγῶν), in which the mouth of the Χαβῆρος, the Kâvêrî, was situated. These seem remarkable anticipations of the name by which the coast was known in later times.

2. *Malabar.*—The origin of the name Malabar has hitherto been enveloped in greater obscurity than that of the corresponding name Coromandel. The first part of the name (Mala) is evidently the Malayâḷam word for mountain, as in the name Malayâḷam itself, and we can scarcely err in concluding it to have been a perpetuation of the Malĕ of the later Greeks. I learn from Colonel Yule that in the relations of the Arabian navigators the name Malĕ held its place, nearly as Cosmos has it, without any such suffix as *bâr*, down to the eleventh or twelfth century. In 851 A.D. it occurs, he says, as Malai or Kulam-Malai, in 1150 as Malî and also Maliah. It is interesting to find the name of Quilon (Kulam, properly Kollam) as early as 851 associated with the name of the coast, in the compound term Kulam-Malai; but Colonel Yule has found Quilon mentioned by name prior even to 660,* which tends to show, as he observes, that the Quilon era (the first year of which corresponds to A.D. 824–5) did not in reality take its origin, as has been supposed, from the foundation of the city.

The first appearance of the affix *bâr* is in 1150, and from the time of its appearance, the word to which it is affixed—the first part of the compound—is frequently found to change. Colonel Yule gives the following Arabian forms,—Malîbâr, Manîbâr, Mulîbâr, Mûnîbâr, Mâlîbâr; and the following as the forms used by early European travellers, &c.—Minibar, Milibar, Melibar (Marco Polo), Minubar, Melibaria. From the time of the arrival of the Portuguese in India it seems always to have been called Malabar, as by ourselves, and in this form of the word *Mala*, mountain, is correctly given. It has been more difficult to ascertain the origin and meaning of the affix *bâr*. Lassen explained it as identical with the Sanskrit *vâra*, in the sense of 'a region;' Malaya-vâra = Malabar = the region of Malaya, the Western Ghauts.

* A letter in Assemani's Bibliotheca, from the Patriarch Jesajabus (died A.D. 660) to Simon, Metropolitan of Persia, blames his neglect of duty, saying that in consequence, not only is India, "which extends from the coast of the kingdom of Persia to COLON, a distance of 1200 parasangs, deprived of a regular ministry, but Persia itself is lying in darkness."—Colonel Yule.

The difficulty in the way of accepting this is that Malaya-vâra is a factitious word, not really found in Sanskrit, and never actually used by the people of the Malabar coast. The same difficulty stands in the way of Mala-vâram, Tam.-Mal. the foot of the mountains, and Malap-pâḍu, the mountain district. These derivations might be regarded at first sight as admissible; but they are Indian vernacular words, and if the name Malabar had been derived from them, we should expect to find them in use in India itself, whereas there is no trace of either of them having ever actually been used by any Indian people.

Dr Gundert suggested to me the possibility of the derivation of *bâr* from the Arabic *barr*, continent, as he considered it probable that the name of Malabar had first been brought into use by the Arabian navigators. Colonel Yule arrived independently at a similar conclusion. He preferred, however, the Persian *bâr* to the Arabic *barr*, and has given illustrations of the use of this Persian affix by the Arabs which appear to me to carry conviction. He says (in one of the private communications with which he has favoured me), "This affix *bâr* seems to have been much used by navigators. We have Zanzi-*bâr* (the country of the blacks), Kala-bâr (see the "Arabic Relations," by Reinaud, I., 17, where it is explained that "the word *bâr* signifies either a coast or a kingdom"); and even according to Johnson's "Persian Arabic Dictionary," Hindû-bâr. Burton says (*Journal of the Royal Geographical Society*, vol. xxix. p. 30) that at Zanzibar, in distinguishing the mainland from the island, they call the former Barr-el-Moli, or 'continent.' And in a note he adds, "The word Moli, commonly used in the corrupt Arabic of Zanzibar, will vainly be sought in the dictionaries. Query, if this word Moli for continent may not have shaped some of the forms of the name of Malabar that we have above. I suppose *bâr* itself is rather Persian than Arabic, and may be radically the same affix that we have in so many Indian names of countries, Marwar, Rajwar, &c." This Persian derivation seems to me so satisfactory that it may safely be accepted. *bâr*, country, may have been added to *Male* to distinguish the mainland from the adjacent islands, the Maldives and the Laccadives. The Mal*dives* may have been the *dives* or islands of Malĕ, whilst Mala*bâr* was the continent or mainland of Malĕ. Colonel Yule informs me that Pyrard de la Val and Moresby agree in calling the principal island Male; the first vowel of this name may be either long or short. In Singhalese the islands are called the *Mâl*dives, but in Tamil they are called *Mâl*dives; and this Tamil *mâl* differs considerably from Mala, the name of the Malabar coast, whilst it agrees perfectly with the name given to the islands by Ibn Batuta, who calls them Dhibatal-mahâl, from the name of the 'atoll' where the sultan of the islands lived—viz., Al-mahâl. Mahâl is always corrupted into *mâl* in Tamil.

The Persian *bâr*, one of the meanings of which is 'a country,' is regarded by Vuller (" Lexicon Pers.-Lat.") as identical in origin with the Sanskrit *vâra*, a noun of multitude. It does not follow, however, that it is identical with the affix *vâr* which we find in so many Indian names of countries, as Mârwâr, Dhârwâr, Kattywâr, &c. The apparent resemblance between this *wâr* and the Persian *bâr* and especially the Sanskrit *vâra* disappears on investigation. This *wâr* is written *vâḍ;* and Dr Trumpp assures me that its lineal descent from the Sanskrit *vâṭa* (*vâṭa, vâḍ, vâṛ*) is capable of proof. *vâṭa*, Sans. means not only 'an enclosure,' but also 'a district'—*e.g.*, *Prâchya-vâṭa*, the eastern district. Dr Eggeling informs me that he has found Dhârwâr written Dhârâ-varsha in an inscription of the seventh century. According to Dr Trumpp, however, the *wâr* of the modern Dharwar must have had a different origin, as *varsha* becomes in the Prâkrit, not *vâr*, but *varisô* or *varakhî*.

III. Telugu.—In respect of antiquity of culture and glossarial copiousness, Telugu is generally considered as ranking next to Tamil in the list of Dravidian idioms, whilst in point of euphonic sweetness it justly claims to occupy the first place. This language was sometimes called by the Europeans of the last generation the 'Gentoo,' from the Portuguese word for heathens or 'gentiles,' a term which was used at first to denote all Hindûs or 'natives,' but which came in time to mean the Telugus alone. The use of the term Gentoo for Telugu, like that of Malabar for Tamil, has now nearly disappeared. Telugu is spoken all along the eastern coast of the Peninsula, from the neighbourhood of Pulicat, where it supersedes Tamil, to Chicacole, where it begins to yield to the Oriya, and inland it prevails as far as the eastern boundary of the Marâṭha country and Mysore, including within its range the 'Ceded districts' and Karnûl, a considerable part of the territories of the Nizam, or the Hyderabad country, and a portion of the Nâgpûr country and Gôṇḍvana. The district thus described was called Telingânâ by the Muhammedans. The Telugu people, though not at present the most enterprising or migratory, are undoubtedly the most numerous branch of the Dravidian race. Including the Nâyuḍus (Tam. Nâyakkas = Sans. Nâyakas), Reḍḍis, and other Telugu tribes settled in the Tamil country, who are chiefly the descendants of those soldiers of fortune by whom the Pâṇḍya and Chôla kingdoms were subverted, and who number not much less than a million of souls; and including also the Telugu settlers in Mysore, and the indigenous Telugu inhabitants of the native states, the people who speak the Telugu language may be estimated as amounting to at least fifteen million and a half. The chief, if not the only, element of doubt in this calculation relates to the proportion of Telugu speaking people in the Nizam's territory.

Though the Telugu people cannot at present be described as the most migratory portion of the Dravidians, there was a time, when they appear to have exhibited this quality more conspicuously than any other branch of the race. Most of the Klings, or Hindûs, found in the eastern archipelago in our times, are, it is true, Tamilians; but the Tamilians, in trading and forming settlements in the East, have entered on a field formerly occupied by the Telugus, and not only so, but have actually inherited the name by which their Telugu predecessors were known. 'Kling' stood for 'Kalinga,' and Kalinga meant the seaboard of the Telugu country. The Hindûs, who in the early centuries of the Christian era formed settlements, built temples, and exercised dominion in Sumatra and Java, appear to have been Telugus, not Tamilians; and whilst the Tamil country was overrun by the Telugus in the sixteenth and seventeenth centuries, no corresponding settlement of Tamilians in the Telugu country to any considerable extent seems to have followed the establishment in that country (or at least in the portion of it specially called Kalinga) of a dynasty of Chôla kings in the eleventh or twelfth centuries.

Telugu is called Ândhra by Sanskrit writers—that is, the language of the Andhras, one of the two nations into which the Telugu people seems from the earliest times to have been divided. The other nation was the Kalingas. The Andhras seem to have been better known than the Kalingas to the early Aryans. They are mentioned as early as in the "Aitareya Brâhmaṇa of the Rig-veda," though represented therein as an uncivilised race; and in Puranic times a dynasty of Andhra kings is represented to have reigned in Northern India. The Andaræ are represented by Pliny (after Megasthenes) as a powerful people, and the Andre Indi have a place in the "Peutinger Tables" (north of the Ganges!) amongst the few Indian nations of which the author of those tables had heard. The first reference to their language I find made by any foreigner is in the memoirs of Hwen Thsang, the Chinese pilgrim, about the middle of the seventh century A.D., who states that the language of the Ândhras differed from that of Central India, whilst the forms of the written characters were for the most part the same. It is clear from this that Telugu culture had already made considerable progress, especially amongst the Ândhra branch of the nation. Hence it naturally happened that the name of the Ândhras, instead of that of the Kalingas, who inhabited the more remote seaboard, and were perhaps less cultured, was given by Sanskrit writers to the language which both branches of the nation spoke in common. It occupies the first place—not Kalinga or Trilinga—in the compound term, Ândhra-Drâviḍa-bhâshâ, by which Kumârila-bhaṭṭa, shortly after Hwen Thsang's date, designated what he appears to have supposed to be the one language spoken by the Dravidians.

Telugu is the name by which the language is called by the Telugu people themselves other; forms of which name are Teluṅgu, Teliṅga, Tailiṅga, Tenugu, and Tenuṅgu. The name has been corrupted still further in various directions by Muhammedans and other foreigners. One of the above-mentioned forms, Tenugu or Tenuṅgu, is sometimes represented by Telugu pandits as the original form of the word, and the meaning they attribute to it is sweetness. This derivation seems to have been an afterthought, suggested by the resemblance of the word to *têne*, honey; but there is more reason for it—both on account of the resemblance between the two words, and also on account of the exceedingly *melli*-fluous character of the Telugu language, than for the corresponding afterthought of the Tamil pandits, respecting the meaning of the word Tamiṛ.

The favourite derivation of Telugu pandits for Telugu or Teluṅgu, the ordinary name of their language, is from Trilinga, 'the language of the three lingas;' that is, as they represent, of the country of which three celebrated linga temples constituted the boundaries. This derivation was accepted by Mr A. D. Campbell, but is rejected by Mr C. P. Brown, who affirms it to be an invention of modern poets, and regards the name Telugu as devoid of any known root. Probably so much of the theory as is built on the connection of the name with certain temples may be unceremoniously discarded; but the derivation of the name itself from *trilinga* (without committing ourselves to the determination of the sense in which the word *linga* is used) may perhaps be found to be deserving of a better fate. If the derivation of Telugu from Trilinga be an invention, it must be admitted to have at least the merit of being an ingenious invention; for though it is quite true, as Mr Brown observes, that Trilinga, as a name of a country, is not found in any of the lists of Indian countries contained in the Purâṇas, yet the existence of such a name seems capable of being established by reliable evidence derived from other sources. Târanâtha, the Tibetan author already referred to, who derived his information, not from modern Telugu poets or pandits, but from Indian Buddhistical narratives (which, having been written before Buddhism disappeared from India, must have been of considerable antiquity), repeatedly designates the Telugu country Trilinga, and describes Kalinga as a portion of Trilinga, and Kalingapura as its capital. The name of Trilinga had reached Ptolemy himself at a time anterior probably to the date of the Purâṇas. It is true his Τρίγλυπτον (Τρίγλυφον?) τό καὶ Τρίλιγγον βασίλειον is placed by him to the east of the Ganges; but the names of places mentioned by Ptolemy seem generally much more reliable than the positions he assigns to them; and it is conceivable that the mariners or merchants from whom he derived his information spoke of the place in question merely as beyond the Ganges, without being certain whether it was east or south. We have seen that in like manner the "Peutinger Tables" place the Andre Indi—about whose identity with the Telugu people there can be no doubt—beyond the Ganges. The foreign name Trilingam must have been the name by which the place was called by the natives of the place, whilst Triglypton or Triglyphon must have been a translation of the name which had come into use amongst the Greeks. Hence the antiquity of Trilinga, as the name of a state, or of the capital city of a state, situated somewhere in India in Ptolemy's time, must be admitted to be established. The word *linga* forms the second portion of the name of several Indian nations mentioned by Pliny (after Megasthenes), as the Bolingæ, and the Maccocalingæ, a various reading of which is Maccolingæ.

Another name mentioned by Pliny, Modogalingam, involves some difficulty. He says—"Insula in Gange est magnæ magnitudinis gentem continens unam, Modogalingam nomine." Mr A. D. Campbell, in the Introduction to his "Telugu Grammar," represented the *modoga* of this name as the ancient Telugu word for three, and hence argued that Modogalingam was identical with Trilingam. If this identification were admitted, not only would the antiquity of Trilingam be firmly established, but also the opinion of the pandits that the original name of their language was Trilinga, and that this Trilinga became gradually Telinga, Telungu, Telugu, and Tenugu, would be confirmed. The Telugu word for 'three,' however, is not *modoga*, but *mûḍu*. *mûḍugu* might be used; but it is a poetical form, the use of which would be pedantic. Mr C. P. Brown prefers to write the name of the nation referred to by Pliny (after a MS. in Sillig's edition) "modo Galingam," and considers this Galingam equivalent to Calingam. The change of *c* (*k*) into *g* in such a connection would be quite in accordance with Telugu laws of sound, provided *modo*, as well as Calingam, were a Telugu word; and if it were Telugu it would more naturally represent *mûḍu*, three, than anything else. On this supposition, modo-Galingam would mean, not indeed 'the three lingas,' but 'the three Kalingas;' and it is remarkable that the corresponding expression Tri-kalinga has been found in actual use in India. General Cunningham, in his "Ancient Geography of India," mentions an inscription in which a line of kings assumed the title of 'lords of Tri-kalinga.' Dr Kern also, in his translation of Varâha-mihira's "Brihat-sa*m*hitâ," mentions that the name Tri-kalinga is found in one of the Purânas; and the same name has recently been found in an inscription on a copperplate, referred to in the proceedings of the Bengal Asiatic Society for 1872, p. 171. General Cunningham thinks it probable that there is a reference to these three Kalingas in the circumstance that Pliny mentions the Macco-Calingæ and the Gangarides-Calingæ as separate nations from the Calingæ; and that the Mahâ-bhârata mentions the Kalingas three times, and each time in connection with different neighbours. The circumstance that Modogalingam is represented as an 'island in the Ganges' presents no insuperable obstacle to its identification with Tri-kalinga or Telingâna. The term island has often been used very vaguely. Târanâtha calls the Tamil country an island; and Kalinga was supposed to be a Gangetic country by Sanskrit writers themselves, who generally agreed in representing it as the last of the districts visited by the Ganges. It is also to be remembered that the Godâvarî is often supposed by natives to be somehow identical with the Ganges. General Cunningham thinks Telinga derived, not from Trilinga, but from Tri-kalinga, but this derivation of the word needs to be historically confirmed. Kalinga and *linga* may probably in some way be connected, but the nature and history of the connection have not as yet been made out.

One of the names by which the Telugu language is known in the Tamil country is *Vaḍugu*, and a Telugu man, especially if a member of the Nâyakka caste, is called a *Vaḍugan*. The root of this is *vaḍa*, north, the Telugu country lying to the north of the Tamil. This word explains the name 'Badages,' by which certain marauding hordes were designated by the early Portuguese, and in the letters of St Francis Xavier. Mr C. P. Brown informs me that the early French missionaries in the Guntur country wrote a vocabulary "de la langue Talenga, dite vulgairement le Badega."

IV.—Canarese.—The next place is occupied by Canarese, properly the Kannaḍa, or Karṇâṭaka, which is spoken throughout the plateau of Mysore, in the southern Mahratta country, and in some of the western districts of the Nizam's territory, as far north as Beder. It is spoken also (together with Malayâḷam, Tuḷu, and Koṇkaṇi, but more extensively than any of them) in the district of Canara, properly Kannaḍiyam, on the Malabar coast, a district which was subjected for centuries to the rule of Canarese princes, and hence acquired the name by which it is at present known. The speech of the Badagas ('people from the north'), commonly called by the English Burghers, the most numerous class of people inhabiting the Neilgherry hills, is undoubtedly an ancient Canarese dialect. The Canarese, properly so called, includes, like the Tamil, two dialects—classical, commonly called Ancient Canarese, and the colloquial or modern; of which the former differs from the latter, not—as classical Telugu and Malayâḷam differ from the colloquial dialects of those languages—by containing a larger infusion of Sanskrit derivatives, but by the use of different inflexional terminations. The *dialect* called Ancient Canarese is not to be confounded with the *character* denoted by that name, which is found in many ancient inscriptions in the Maratha country, as well as in Mysore. The language of all really ancient inscriptions in the Haḷa Kannaḍa, or Ancient Canarese character, is Sanskrit, not Canarese.

The people that speak the Canarese language may be estimated at nine millions and a quarter; but, in the case of both Canarese and Telugu, the absence of a trustworthy census of the inhabitants of the Nizam's territory, requires such estimates to be considered as mere approximations. In that territory four languages—Canarese, Marâṭhi, Telugu, and Hindûstânî—are spoken by different classes in different districts; but it is difficult to ascertain the proportionate prevalence of each with any degree of certainty.

The term Karṇâṭa or Karṇâṭaka is said to have been a generic term, including both the Telugu and Canarese peoples and their languages, though it is admitted that it usually denoted the latter alone, and though it is to the latter that the abbreviated form Kannaḍam has been appropriated. *Karṇâṭaka* (that which belongs to *Karṇâṭa*) is regarded as a Sanskrit word by native pandits, but I agree with Dr Gundert in preferring to derive it from the Dravidian words *kar*, black, *nâḍ-u* (the adjectival form of which in Telugu is *nâṭ-i*), country—that is, the black country—a term very suitable to designate the "black, cotton soil," as it is called, of the plateau of the Southern Dekhan. The use of the term is of considerable antiquity, as we find it in Varâhamihira at the beginning of the fifth century A.D. Târanâtha also mentions Karṇâṭa. The word Karṇâṭa or Karṇâṭaka, though at first a generic term, became in process of time the appellation of the Canarese people and of their language alone, to the entire exclusion of the Telugu. Karṇâṭaka has now got into the hands of foreigners, who have given it a new and entirely erroneous application. When the Muhammedans arrived in Southern India, they found that part of it with which they first became acquainted—the country above the

Ghauts, including Mysore and part of Telingâna—called the Karṇâṭaka country. In course of time, by a misapplication of terms, they applied the same name, the Karṇâṭak, or Carnatic, to designate the country below the Ghauts, as well as that which was above. The English have carried the misapplication a step further, and restricted the name to the country below the Ghauts, which never had any right to it whatever. Hence the Mysore country, which is properly the Carnatic, is no longer called by that name by the English; and what is now geographically termed 'the Carnatic' is exclusively the country below the Ghauts, on the Coromandel coast, including the whole of the Tamil country, and the district of Nellore only in the Telugu country. The word Karṇâṭaka was further corrupted by the Canarese people themselves into Kannaḍa or Kannara, from which the language is styled by the English 'Canarese.'

V. TUḶU.—Next in the list of cultivated Dravidian languages stands Tuḷu or Tuḷuva. The claim of this peculiar and very interesting language to be ranked amongst the cultivated members of the family may perhaps be regarded as open to question, seeing that it is destitute of a literature in the proper sense of the term, and never had a character of its own. The Canarese character having been used by the Basle missionaries in the Tuḷu books printed by them at Mangalore—the only books ever printed in Tuḷu—that character has now become inseparably associated with the language. Notwithstanding its want of a literature, Tuḷu is one of the most highly developed languages of the Dravidian family. It looks as if it had been cultivated for its own sake, and it is well worthy of careful study. This language is spoken in a very limited district and by a very small number of people. The Chandragiri and Kalyânapuri rivers, in the district of Canara, are regarded as its ancient boundaries, and it does not appear ever to have extended much beyond them. The number of the Tuḷu-speaking people has been found not to exceed 300,000, and their country is broken in upon to such a degree by other languages that Tuḷu might be expected soon to disappear. All Tuḷu Christians are taught Canarese as well as Tuḷu. Tuḷu, however, shows, it is said, no signs of disappearing, and the people have the reputation of being the most conservative portion of the Dravidian race. The name Tuḷu means, according to Mr Brigel, mild, meek, humble, and is to be regarded therefore as properly denoting the people, not their language.

Tuḷu was supposed by Mr Ellis to be merely a dialect of Malayâḷam; but although Malayâḷam characters were and still are, ordinarily employed by Tuḷu Brâhmans in writing Sanskrit, in consequence of the prevalence of Malayâḷam in the vicinity, the supposition that Tuḷu was a dialect of Malayâḷam can no longer be entertained. The publication of Mr Brigel's "Tuḷu Grammar" has thrown much new light on this peculiarly interesting language. It differs far more widely from Malayâḷam than Malayâḷam does from Tamil. It differs widely, but not so widely, from Canarese; still less so from Coorg. The dialect from which it differs most widely is Tamil. There is a tradition mentioned by Mr Ellis, in his treatise on Mirasi right, to the effect that the ancient Kurumbars or nomadic shepherds, in the neighbourhood of Madras, were expelled and their lands given to Veḷḷâḷas from Tuḷuva; and this tradition is confirmed by the fact that certain Veḷḷâḷa families in that neighbourhood call themselves, and are called by others, Tuḷuva Veḷḷâḷas. Probably, however, the number of Tuḷuva immigrants was not very considerable, for there is no trace of any infusion of the peculiarities of Tuḷu into the colloquial Tamil of Madras, which, if it differs in any degree from the Tamil spoken in the rest of the Tamil country, differs, not in a Tuḷu, but in a Telugu direction.

VI. KUḌAGU OR COORG.—Last in the list of cultivated Dravidian languages is the language of Coorg; but though I have thought it best to give this language a place amongst the cultivated members of the family, the propriety of doing so seems to me still more doubtful than that of placing Tuḷu in this list. Coorg is a small but interesting district, formerly an independent principality, beautifully situated amongst the ridges of the Western Ghauts, between Mysore on the east and North Malabar and South Canara on the west. The native spelling of Coorg is usually *Koḍagu*, properly *Kuḍagu*, from *kuḍa*, west, a meaning of the word which is usual in Ancient Tamil. In the first edition of this work this language had not assigned to it a place of its own, but was included under the head of Canarese. It had been generally considered rather as an uncultivated dialect of Canarese, modified by Tuḷu, than as a distinct language. I mentioned then, however, that Dr Mögling, a German missionary, who had resided for some time amongst the Coorgs, was of opinion that their language was more closely allied to Tamil and Malayâḷam than to Canarese. It is not quite clear to me yet to which of the Dravidian dialects it is most closely allied. On the whole, however, it seems safest to regard it as standing about midway between Old Canarese and Tuḷu. Like Tuḷu it has the reputation of puzzling strangers by the peculiarities of its pronunciation. A grammar of the Coorg language has been published by Major Cole, Superintendent of Coorg, and some specimens of Coorg songs, with an epitome of the grammar by the

Rev. B. Gräter of Mangalore. "Like the similar dialects spoken by the tribes of the Nîlagiris, there can be no doubt that this language has preserved its form comparatively free from change owing to the retired position of the people who speak it. That the inhabitants of Coorg early settled on the Western Ghauts is shown by the primitive Dravidian custom of polyandria which they still follow. They are as yet far from being Brahmanised, and they have no literature in the proper sense of the word." Burnell's "Specimens of South Indian Dialects," No. 3.

The six languages which follow differ from those that have been mentioned in that they are entirely uncultivated, destitute of written characters, and comparatively little known.

VII. Tuda.—Toda, properly Tuda, is the language of the Tudas or Tudavars, a primitive and peculiarly interesting tribe inhabiting the Neilgherry (Nîlagiri) hills. It is now regarded as certain that the Tudas were not the original inhabitants of those hills, though it is still far from certain who the original inhabitants were. Their numbers could not at any time have exceeded a few thousands, and at present, probably through opium-eating and polyandria, and through the prevalence amongst them at a former period of female infanticide, they do not, it has been ascertained, number more than about 700 souls. I have to thank the Rev. F. Metz, the veteran missionary among the Neilgherry tribes, for much information respecting the Tudas and their language; and an interesting book has lately been written by Colonel Marshall, entitled "A Phrenologist among the Todas," in which everything that is known of this people is fully described. The same book contains a valuable epitome of the grammar of their language by the Rev. Dr Pope. Dr Pope connects the name of the Todas with the Tamil word *toṛa*, a herd; but the *d* of Tuda is not the lingual *d*, but the dental, which has no relationship to *ṛ* or *ḷ*. The derivation of the name may be regarded as at present unknown. See Appendix.

VIII. Kôta.—The language of the Kôtas, a small tribe of helot craftsmen inhabiting the Neilgherry hills, and numbering about eleven hundred souls. This language may be considered as a very old and very rude dialect of the Canarese, which was carried thither by a persecuted low-caste tribe at some very remote period. Besides the languages of the Todas and Kôtas, two other languages are vernacular on the Neilgherry hills—viz., the dialect spoken by the Burghers or Baḍagars (the northern people), an ancient but organised dialect of the Canarese; and the rude Tamil spoken by the Iruḷars ('people of the darkness') and Kuruburs (Can. *Kurubaru*, Tam. *Kurumbar*, shepherds), who are occasionally stumbled upon by adventurous sportsmen in the denser, deeper jungles, and the smoke of whose fires may occasionally be seen rising from the lower gorges of the hills. See Appendix.

IX. Gôṇḍ.—The language of the indigenous inhabitants of the extensive hilly and jungly tracts in Central India, formerly called Gôndwana. "In most old maps of India the territorial name Gôndwana is printed across the greater portion of the territory now known as the Central Provinces. Gôndwana extended from the Vindhya mountains to the Godâvarî, and embraced the Sâtpurâ range. Of the districts now under the Lieutenant-Governor of Bengal, it included Korea, Sirgûja, and Udaipûr; but Gônd colonies are found as far east as the Katak Tributary Mahâls, where they blend with the Kandhs and the Sauras, or Savaras, and they extend to Khandesh and Mâlwâ in the west, where they touch the Bhîls. A considerable proportion of the population of this tract (the core of India) are Gônds, and they are by far the most numerous of the aboriginal people still found there."—Colonel Dalton's "Ethnology of Bengal."

According to the recent census the various tribes included under the general name of Gôṇḍs number 1,634,578 souls. The Mâriâs are regarded as the purest, and are certainly the wildest, tribe of Gôṇḍs. They sometimes call themselves Kôhitûr, a name which is evidently identical with Kôîtôr, the name by which four out of the twelve tribes of Gôṇḍs call themselves. It has been asserted indeed that all the Gôṇḍs, when speaking of themselves in their own language, prefer to call themselves Kôîtôrs. This word is a plural appellative regularly formed from Kôî. Much valuable information concerning the Gôṇḍs is contained in Colonel Dalton's "Ethnology of Bengal;" in the papers left in MS. by the late Rev. S. Hislop, edited by Sir R. Temple; and in the *Gazetteer of the Central Provinces*. A grammar and vocabulary of the Gôṇḍ language were published by the Rev. J. G. Driberg, at Bishop's College, Calcutta, in 1849. A translation of the Gospels of St Matthew and St Mark into Gôṇḍ by the Rev. J. Dawson, published at Allahabad in 1872—73, furnishes us with a still more valuable contribution to the knowledge of the language. Mr Dawson has also recently published a brief grammar and vocabulary of the language in the *Journal of the Bengal Asiatic Society*. See Appendix.

X. Khond; more properly Ku. This is the language of the people who have hitherto been commonly called Khonds. By their neighbours in Orissa their name is said to be pronounced Kandhs; but by themselves they are called, it is said, Kus. They are a primitive race supposed to be allied to the Gôṇḍs, and inhabit the eastern parts of Gôndwana, Gûmsur, and the hilly ranges of Orissa, which constitute the Tributary Mahâls. Colonel Dalton says they are not found further north than the 22nd degree of latitude, and that they extend south as far as Bastar, whence their position as the aboriginal people is taken up by the Savaras or Sauras. They acquired a bad notoriety for a long time, through their horrid practice of stealing the children of their neighbours of the plains, and offering them up in sacrifice—a practice now entirely suppressed. The meaning of the name of this people is involved in obscurity. Some consider Khond a kindred word with Gôṇḍ, and derive both names from the Tamil word *kundru*, a hill, literally a small hill, the Telugu form of which is *koṇḍa*. This would be a very natural derivation for the name of a hill people; but, unfortunately, their nearest neighbours, the Telugus, call them, not Koṇḍs or Gôṇḍs, but Gônds, also Kôds; and as they call themselves *Kus*, according to Mr Latchmajî, the author of the grammar of their language, the existence of any connection between their name and *kundru* or *koṇḍa*, a hill, seems very doubtful. The term Ku is evidently allied to Kôî, the name by which the Gôṇḍs call themselves, and which they are fond of lengthening into Kôîtôr. The Khonds, according to the late census, number nearly 270,000 souls. See Appendix.

XI. The Mâler, commonly called the Râjmahâl, the language of the Pahârias, or hill people, who seem to have been the original inhabitants of the Râjmahâl hills in Bengal. The brief vocabulary of the language of this tribe contained in the "Asiatic Researches," vol. v., and the somewhat fuller lists of words belonging to the same language contained in Mr Hodgson's and Sir George Campbell's collections and in Colonel Dalton's "Ethnology of Bengal," lead to the supposition that the Râjmahâl idiom is in its basis Dravidian. This language is not to be confounded with the speech of the Santâls, a branch of the extensive Kôl family inhabiting at present the skirts of the Râjmahâl hills (but said to be mostly emigrants from the Hazârîbâgh district), who belong to a stock totally different from that of the Mâlers. Unfortunately very little is known of the grammatical structure of this language. The numbers of the people by whom it is spoken have been ascertained to amount to 41,000. See Appendix.

XII. Orâon.—The Orâons of Chûtiâ Nâgpûr and the neighbouring districts are estimated to amount to 263,000. A higher estimate has been made by Colonel Dalton, who has given a very full and interesting account of this tribe in his "Ethnology of Bengal." They have preserved, like the Mâlers, the rudiments of a language substantially Dravidian, as appears from the lists of words collected by Mr Hodgson and Colonel Dalton, and especially from an epitome of the grammar of their language prepared by the Rev. F. Batsch.

Their traditions are said to connect them with the Konkan, from which it is supposed they derive the name Khurũk, by which they invariably call themselves. They assert that for many generations they were settled on the Rohtâs and adjoining hills in the Patna district, and that when driven out from thence, one party emigrated to the Râjmahâl hills, the other went south-eastward till they arrived in the highlands of Chûtiâ Nâgpûr. This tradition of the original identity of the Mâlers and the Orâons is borne out by the evident affinity of their languages, and, as Colonel Dalton mentions, by the similarity of their customs. According to their traditions, the Orâons arrived in Chûtiâ Nâgpûr later than the Mûndas and other Kôlarians.

Tuda, Kôta, Gôṇḍ, and Ku, though rude and uncultivated, are undoubtedly to be regarded as essentially Dravidian dialects, equally with the Tamil, the Canarese, and the Telugu. I feel some hesitation in placing in the same category the Râjmahâl and the Orâon, seeing that they appear to contain so large an admixture of roots and forms belonging to some other family of tongues, probably the Kôlarian. I venture, however, to classify them as in the main Dravidian, because the Dravidian roots they contain are roots of primary importance, including the pronouns and the first four numerals, from which it may fairly be inferred that these dialects belonged originally to the Dravidian family. The Orâon was considered by Mr Hodgson as a connecting link between the Kôl dialects and the Mâler; the Mâler as a connecting link between the Kôl and the distinctively Tamilian families. The Mâler seems to me, on the whole, less distinctively Dravidian than the Orâon, perhaps because the Mâlers, or hill men of Râjmahâl, are locally more remote than the Orâons from the present seats of the Dravidian race. Sir George Campbell's lists of words belonging to the Mâler and Orâon dialects appear to contain a larger proportion of words that can be recognised as distinctively Dravidian than any previous lists. See Appendix.

The existence of a distinctively Dravidian element in two at least of these aboriginal dialects of the Central Provinces and Bengal being established, the Dravidian race can now be traced as far north as the confines of Bengal, if not also to the banks of the Ganges; and the supposition that this race was diffused at an early period through the greater part of India is thereby confirmed.

Colonel Dalton carries the Dravidian element still further than I have ventured to do. He says ("Ethnology of Bengal," p. 243), "The Dravidian element enters more largely into the composition of the population of Bengal than is generally supposed. I believe that a large majority of the tribes described as Hinduised aborigines might with propriety have been included in this group. The people called Bhûiyas, diffused through most of the Bengal districts, and massed in the jungle and tributary estates of Chûtiâ Nâgpûr and Orissa, certainly belong to it; and if I am right in my conjecture regarding the Kocch nation, they are of the same stock. I roughly estimate the Bhûiyas at two and a half millions, and the Kocch at a million and a half, so that we have in these two peoples about one-tenth of the Bengal population, who in all probability should be classed as Dravidian." I hesitate for the present to endorse this supposition, in the absence of lingual affinities of any kind and of physical characteristics—if there are any such even amongst the Dravidians themselves—that can be regarded as distinctively Dravidian.

Leaving these doubtful races out of account, I here exhibit the numbers, as far as can be ascertained by the census of 1871, of the various peoples and tribes by whom distinctively Dravidian languages are spoken. I have added together the census results obtained in each of the Indian Presidencies, and have also included the Dravidian inhabitants of Ceylon, and the Dravidian immigrants in Burma, the eastern archipelago, Mauritius, Demerara, &c. The only serious doubt I have is with regard to the numbers of the Telugu people, and this doubt is owing to the difficulty I have met with in endeavouring to estimate the proportion of the Telugu-speaking people inhabiting the Nizam's territory. I have estimated them at three millions. If the number should turn out to be higher or lower than this, a corresponding change will have to be made in the accompanying list.

The numbers of the several races by whom the languages and dialects mentioned above are spoken, appear to be as follows —

1. Tamil, ...	14,500,000
2. Telugu, ...	15,500,000
3. Canarese, ...	9,250,000
4. Malayâḷam, . . .	3,750,000
5. Tuḷu, ...	300,000
6. Kuḍagu or Coorg, . . .	150,000
Carry forward, ...	43,450,000

Brought forward, . .	43,450,000
7. Tuda, ...	752
8. Kôta, ...	1,112
9. Gôṇḍ, ...	1,634,578
10. Khond or Ku, . . .	269,501
11. Râjmahâl, ...	41,089
12. Orâon, ...	263,000
	45,660,032

According to this estimate the Dravidian-speaking peoples amount to nearly forty-six millions of souls.

In this enumeration of the Dravidian languages I have not included the idioms of the Ramûsis, the Lambâḍis, and various other wandering, predatory, or forest tribes. The Lambâḍis, the gipsies of the Peninsula, speak a dialect of Hindûstânî; the Ramûsis a *patois* of Telugu; the tribes inhabiting the hills and forests, corrupted dialects of the languages of the contiguous plains. None of these dialects is found to differ essentially from the speech of the more cultivated classes residing in the same neighbourhood. The Male-araśas, 'hill-kings' (in Malayâḷam, Mala-arayas), the hill tribe inhabiting the Southern Ghauts, speak corrupt Malayâḷam in the northern part of the range, where Malayâḷam is the prevailing language, and corrupt Tamil, with a tinge of Malayâḷam, in the southern, in the vicinity of Tamil-speaking districts.

In the above list of the Dravidian languages I have not included the Hô, the Mûnda, or any of the rest of the languages of the Kôls, the Savaras, and other rude tribes of Central India and of Bengal, called 'Kôlarian' by Sir George Campbell, and included by Mr Hodgson under the general term Tamulian. These languages might naturally be supposed to be allied to Gôṇḍ or Ku, to Orâon or Râjmahâl, and consequently to be of Dravidian origin; but though a few Dravidian words may perhaps be detected in some of them, their grammatical structure shows that they belong to a totally different family of languages. Without the evidence of similarity in grammatical structure, the discovery of a small number of similar words seems to prove only local proximity, or the existence of mutual intercourse at an earlier or later period, not the original relationship either of races or of languages.

I leave also out of account the languages of the north-eastern frontier of India, which are spoken by the Bôdos, Dhimâls, and other tribes inhabiting the mountains and forests between Kumaon and Assam. These were styled Tamulian by Mr Hodgson, on the supposition that all the aborigines of India, as distinguished from the Aryans, or Sanskrit-speaking race and its offshoots, belonged to one and the same stock; and that of this aboriginal race, the Tamilians of Southern India were to be considered the best representatives. But as the relationship of those north-eastern idioms to the languages of the Dravidian family, is unsupported by the evidence either of similarity in grammatical structure or of a similar vocabulary, and is founded only on such general grammatical analogies as are common to the whole range of the Scythian group of languages, it seems to me almost as improper to designate those dialects Tamilian or Dravidian, as it would be to designate them Turkish or Tungusian. Possibly they may form a link of connection between the Indo-Chinese or Tibetan family of tongues, and the Kôlarian; but even this is at present little better than an assumption. Professor Max Müller proposed to call all the non-Aryan languages of India, including the Sub-Himâlayan, the Kôl, and the Tamilian families, Nishâda-languages, the ancient aborigines being often termed Nishâdas in the Purâṇas. Philologically, I think, the use of this common term is to be deprecated, inasmuch as the Dravidian languages differ so widely from the others, that they possess very few features in common. For the present, I have no doubt that the safest common appellation is the negative one, non-Aryan, or non-Sanskritic.

Brahuî, the language of the mountaineers in the khanship of Kelat in Beluchistan, contains not only some Dravidian words, but a considerable infusion of distinctively Dravidian forms and idioms; in consequence of which this language has a better claim to be regarded as Dravidian or Tamilian than any of the languages of the Nepâl and Bhûtân frontier, which had been styled 'Tamulian' by Mr Hodgson. I have not included, however, the Brahuî in the list of Dravidian languages which are to be subjected to systematic comparison (though I shall give some account of it in the Appendix, and shall refer to it occasionally for illustration), because the Dravidian element contained in it bears but a small proportion to the rest of its component elements.

It is true that the great majority of the words in the Brahuî language seem altogether unconnected with Dravidian roots; but it will be evident from the analogies in structure, as well as in the vocabulary, which will be exhibited in the Appendix, that this language contains many grammatical forms essentially and distinctly Dravidian, together with a small proportion of important Dravidian words. The Brahuîs state that their forefathers came from Haleb (Aleppo); but even if this tradition could be regarded as a credible one, it would apply to the secondary or conquering race, apparently of Indo-European origin, not to their Dravidian predecessors. The previous existence of the latter race seems to have been forgotten, and the only evidence that they ever existed is that which is furnished by the Dravidian element which has been discovered in the language of their conquerors.

The Brahuî enables us to trace the Dravidian race beyond the Indus to the southern confines of Central Asia. The Brahuî language, considered as a whole, seems to be derived from the same source as the Panjâbî and Sindhî, but it evidently contains a Dravidian element; and the discovery of this Dravidian element in a language spoken beyond the Indus tends to show that the Dravidians, like the Aryans, the Græco-Scythians, and the Turco-Mongolians, must have entered India by the north-western route.. See Appendix.

The Dravidian Idioms not merely Provincial Dialects of the same Language.

Though I have described the twelve vernacular idioms mentioned in the foregoing list as dialects or varieties of one and the same original Dravidian language, it would be erroneous to consider them as dialects in the popular sense of the term—viz., as provincial peculiarities or varieties of speech. Of all those idioms no two are so nearly related to each other that persons who speak them can be mutually understood. The most nearly related are Tamil and Malayâḷam; and yet it is only the simplest and most direct sentences in the one language that are intelligible to those who speak only the other. Involved sentences in either language, abounding in verbal and nominal inflexions, or containing conditions and reasons, will be found by those who speak only the other language, to be unintelligible. Tamil, Malayâḷam, Telugu, and Canarese, have each a distinct and independent literary culture; and each of the three former—Tamil, Malayâḷam, and Telugu—has a system of written characters peculiar to itself. The modern Canarese *character* has been borrowed from that of the Telugu, and differs but slightly from it; but the Canarese *language* differs even more widely from Telugu than it does from Tamil; and the Ancient Canarese character is exceedingly unlike the character of the Telugu.

Of the six cultivated Dravidian dialects mentioned above—Tamil, Telugu, Canarese, Malayâḷam, Tuḷu, Kuḍuga—the farthest removed from each other are Tamil and Telugu. The great majority of the roots in both languages are, it is true, identical; but they are often so disguised in composition by peculiarities of inflexion and dialectic changes, that not one entire sentence in the one language is intelligible to those who are acquainted only with the other. The various Dravidian idioms, though sprung from a common origin, are therefore to be considered not as mere provincial dialects of the same speech, but as distinct though affiliated languages. They are as distinct one from the other as Spanish from Italian, Hebrew from Aramaic, Sindhî from Bengâlî. If the cultivated Dravidian idioms differ so materially from each other, it will naturally be supposed that the uncultivated idioms—Tuda, Kôta, Gôṇḍ, Khond, and the Orâon—must differ still more widely both from one another and from the cultivated languages. This supposition is in accordance with facts. So many and great are the differences and peculiarities observable amongst these rude dialects, that it has seemed to me to be necessary to prove, not that they differ, but that they belong, notwithstanding their differences, to the same stock as the more cultivated tongues, and that they have an equal right to be termed Dravidian.

Evidence that Tuda, Kôta, Gôṇḍ, Khond, and Orâon, are Dravidian tongues, and also evidence of the existence of a Dravidian element in Brahuî, has been transferred from the Introduction, in which it was included in the first edition, to the Appendix.

The Dravidian Languages independent of Sanskrit.

It was supposed by the Sanskrit Pandits (by whom everything with which they were acquainted was referred to a Brâhmanical origin), and too hastily taken for granted by the earlier European scholars, that the Dravidian languages, though differing in many particulars from the North Indian idioms, were equally with them derived from the Sanskrit. They could not but see that each of the Dravidian languages to which their attention had been drawn contained a certain proportion of Sanskrit words, some of which were quite unchanged, though some were so much altered as to be recognised with difficulty; and though they observed clearly enough that each language contained also many non-Sanskrit words and forms, they did not observe that those words and forms constituted the bulk of the language, or that it was in them that the living spirit of the language resided. Consequently they contented themselves with ascribing the non-Sanskrit portion of these languages to an admixture of a foreign element of unknown origin. According to this view there was no essential difference between the 'Drâviras' and the 'Gauras;' for the Bengâlî and other languages of the Gaurian group appear to contain also a small proportion of non-Sanskritic words and forms, whilst in the main they are corruptions of Sanskrit. This representation fell far short of the real state of the case, and the supposition of the derivation of the Dravidian languages from Sanskrit, though entertained in the past generation by a Colebrooke, a Carey, and a Wilkins, is now known to be entirely destitute of foundation. The orientalists referred to, though deeply learned in Sanskrit, and well acquainted with the idioms of Northern India, were unacquainted, or but very slightly acquainted, with the Dravidian languages. No person who has any acquaintance with the principles of comparative philology, and who has carefully studied the grammars and vocabularies of the Dravidian languages, and compared them with those of Sanskrit, can suppose the grammatical structure and inflexional forms of those languages and the greater number of their more important roots capable of being derived from Sanskrit by any process of development or corruption whatsoever.

The hypothesis of the existence of a remote original affinity between the Dravidian languages and Sanskrit, or rather between those languages and the Indo-European family of tongues, inclusive of Sanskrit, of such a nature as to allow us to give the Dravidian languages a place in the Indo-European group, is altogether different from the notion of the direct derivation of those languages from Sanskrit. The hypothesis of a remote original affinity is favoured by some interesting analogies both in the grammar and in the vocabulary, which will be noticed in their place. Some of those analogies are best accounted for by the supposition of the retention by the Dravidian family, as by Finnish and Turkish, of a certain number of roots and forms belonging to the præ-Aryan period, the period which preceded the final separation of the Indo-European group of tongues from the Scythian. I think I shall also be able to prove, with respect to one portion at least of the analogies referred to, that instead of the Dravidian languages having borrowed them from Sanskrit, or both having derived them from a common source, Sanskrit has not disdained to borrow them from its Dravidian neighbours. Whatever probabilities may be in favour of the hypothesis now mentioned, the older supposition of the direct derivation of the Dravidian languages from Sanskrit, in the same manner as Hindî, Bengâlî, and the other Gaurian dialects are directly derived from it, was certainly erroneous. (1.) It overlooked the circumstance that the non-Sanskritic portion of the Dravidian languages was very greatly in excess of the Sanskrit. (2.) It overlooked the still more material circumstance that the pronouns and numerals of the Dravidian languages, their verbal and nominal inflexions, and the syntactic arrangement of their words—everything, in short, which constitutes the living spirit of a language—were originally and radically different from Sanskrit. (3.) The orientalists who held the opinion of the derivation of the Dravidian languages from Sanskrit, relied mainly on the circumstance that all dictionaries of Dravidian languages contained a large number of Sanskrit words scarcely at all altered, and a still larger number which, though much altered, were evidently Sanskrit derivatives. They were not, however, aware that such words are never regarded by native scholars as of Dravidian origin, but are known and acknowledged to be derived from Sanskrit, and that they are arranged in classes, according to the degree in which they have been corrupted, or with reference to the medium through which they have been derived. They were also unaware that true Dravidian words, which form the great majority of the words in the southern vocabularies, are placed by native grammarians in a different class from the above-mentioned derivatives from Sanskrit, and honoured with the epithets 'national words' and 'pure words.' The Telugu grammarians, according to Mr A. D. Campbell, specify even the time when Sanskrit derivatives were first introduced into Telugu; by which we are doubtless to understand the time when the Brhâmans established themselves in the Telugu country. They say, "The adherents of king Ândhra-râya, who then resided on the banks of the Godâvarî, spoke Sanskrit derivatives, many of which words in course of time became corrupted. The other class of words consisting of nouns, verbals, and verbs, which were created by the god Brahmâ before the time of this king, are called 'pure (Telugu) words.' The date of the reign of this Ândhra-râya, or king of the Andhras or Ândhras, who is now worshipped at Chicacole as a deity, is unknown. Mr C. P. Brown says, "The name Ândhra Râya occurs in none of the inscriptions recorded in my 'Cyclic Tables.' Nor have I found it in any poem. It was perhaps a title assumed by some râjâ of whom nothing is recorded." An Andha-bhṛitya dynasty of kings commenced to reign in Magadha, according to Wilson (Vishṇu Purâṇa) in 18 B.C. Possibly, however, the Telugu king Ândhra-râya was merely a creation of the poets.

In general no difficulty is felt in distinguishing Sanskrit derivatives from the ancient Dravidian roots. There are a few cases only in which it may be doubtful whether particular words are Sanskrit or Dravidian —*e.g.*, *nîr*, water, and *mîn*, fish, are claimed as component parts of both languages, though I believe that both are of Dravidian origin.

COMPARATIVE LIST OF SIXTY WORDS OF PRIMARY IMPORTANCE (NOT INCLUDING PRONOUNS AND NUMERALS) IN SANSKRIT AND TAMIL.

	SANSKRIT.	TAMIL.		SANSKRIT.	TAMIL.
father,	*pitṛi,*	*appa(n).*	dog,	*śvan,*	*nây.*
mother,	*mâtṛi,*	*âyi.*	cat,	*viḍâla,*	*pûnei.*
son,	*sûnu,*	*maga(n).*	tiger,	*vyâghra,*	*kaḍu-vây.*
daughter,	*duhitṛi,*	*maga(ḷ).*	deer,	*mṛiga,*	*mân.*
head,	*śiras,*	*talei.*	monkey,	*kapi,*	*kurang-u.*
eye,	*akshi,*	*kaṇ.*	bear,	*śriksha,*	*karaḍi.*
ear,	*karṇa,*	*śevi.*	hog,	*śûkara,*	*pandri.*
mouth,	*mukha,*	*vây.*	snake,	*sarpa,*	*pâmbu.*
tooth,	*danta,*	*pal.*	bird,	*vayas,*	*paṟavei.*
hair,	*kêśa,*	*mayir.*	black,	*kâla,*	*kar-u.*
hand,	{ *hasta,* *kara,*† }	*kei.*	white,	*śukla,*	*veḷ.*
			red,	*rakta,*	*śe.*
foot,	*pad,*	*kâl.*	great,	*mahat,*	*per-u.*
sun,	*sûrya,*	*ñâyiṟ-u.*	small,	*alpa,*	*śiṟ-u.*
moon,	*chandra,*	*tiṅgaḷ.*	sweet,	*madhura,*	*in.*
sky,	*div,*	*vân.*	sour,	*amla,*	*puḷi.*
day,	*divasa,*	*nâḷ.*	salt,	*lavaṇa,*	*uppu.*
night,	*nak,*	*iravu.*	eat,	*bhaksh,*	*tin.*
fire,	*agni,*	*tî.*	drink,	*pâ,*	*kuḍi.*
water,	*ap, nîra,**	*nîr.*	come,	*ê,*	*vâ.*
fish,	{ *matsya,* *mîna,** }	*mîn.*	go,	*gam,*	*pô.*
			stand,	*sthâ,*	*nil.*
hill,	*parvata,*	*malei.*	sit,	*âs,*	*ir-u.*
tree,	*druma,*	*maram.*	walk,	*char,*	*êg-u.*
stone,	*aśman,*	*kal.*	run,	*dru,*	*ôḍ-u.*
house,	*veśman,*	*il.*	sleep,	*svap,*	*uṟang-u.*
village,	*grâma,*	*ûr.*	hear,	*śru,*	*kêḷ.*
elephant,	*hastin,*	*ânei.*	tell,	*vad,*	*śol.*
horse,	*aśva,*	*kudirei.*	laugh,	*has,*	*nagei.*
cow,	*gô,*	*â.*	weep,	*rud,*	*aṛ-u.*
buffalo,	*mahisha,*	*erumei.*	kill,	*han,*	*kol.*

(4.) The Orientalists who supposed the Dravidian languages to be derived from Sanskrit were not aware of the existence of uncultivated languages of the Dravidian family, in which Sanskrit words are not at all, or but very rarely, employed; and they were also not aware that

* See Glossarial Affinities, I. † See Glossarial Affinities, II.

some of the Dravidian languages which make use of Sanskrit derivatives, are able to dispense with those derivatives altogether, such derivatives being considered rather as luxuries or articles of finery than as necessaries. It is true it would now be difficult for Telugu to dispense with its Sanskrit: more so for Canarese; and most of all for Malayâḷam:—those languages having borrowed from Sanskrit so largely, and being so habituated to look up to it for help, that it would be scarcely possible for them now to assert their independence. Tamil, however, the most highly cultivated *ab intra* of all Dravidian idioms, can dispense with its Sanskrit altogether, if need be, and not only stand alone but flourish without its aid.

The ancient or classical dialect of the Tamil languages, called Shen-Tamil (S'en-Damiṛ) or correct Tamil, in which nearly all the literature has been written, contains exceedingly little Sanskrit; and differs from the colloquial dialect, or the language of prose, chiefly in the sedulous and jealous care with which it has rejected the use of Sanskrit derivatives and characters, and restricted itself to pure Ancient Dravidian sounds, forms, and roots. So completely has this jealousy of Sanskrit pervaded the minds of the educated classes amongst the Tamilians, that a Tamil poetical composition is regarded as in accordance with good taste and worthy of being called classical, not in proportion to the amount of Sanskrit it contains, as would be the case in some other dialects, but in proportion to its freedom from Sanskrit! The speech of the very lowest classes of the people in the retired country districts accords to a considerable extent with the classical dialect in dispensing with Sanskrit derivatives. In every country it is in the poetry and in the speech of the peasantry that the ancient condition of the language is best studied. It is in studied Tamil prose compositions, and in the ordinary speech of the Brâhmans and the more learned Tamilians, that the largest infusion of Sanskrit is contained; and the words that have been borrowed from Sanskrit are chiefly those which express abstract ideas of philosophy, science, and religion, together with the technical terms of the more elegant arts. Even in prose compositions on religious subjects, in which a larger amount of Sanskrit is employed than in any other department of literature, the proportion of Sanskrit which has found its way into Tamil is not greater than the amount of Latin contained in corresponding compositions in English. Let us, for example, compare the amount of Sanskrit contained in the Tamil translation of the Ten Commandments with the amount of Latin which is contained in the English version of the same formula, and which has found its way into it, either directly from ecclesiastical Latin, or indirectly, through the medium of Norman-French. Of forty-three nouns and adjectives in the English version twenty-nine are Anglo-Saxon, fourteen Latin : of fifty-three nouns and adjectives in Tamil (the difference in idiom causes this difference in the number) thirty-two are Dravidian, twenty-one Sanskrit. Of twenty verbs in English, thirteen are Anglo-Saxon, seven Latin : of thirty-four verbs in Tamil, twenty-seven are Dravidian, and only seven Sanskrit. Of the five numerals which are found in English, either in their cardinal or their ordinal shape, all are Anglo-Saxon : of the six numerals found in Tamil, five are Dravidian, one ('thousand') is Sanskrit. Putting all these numbers together for the purpose of ascertaining the percentage, I find that in the department of nouns, numerals, and verbs, the amount of the foreign element is in both instances the same—viz., as nearly as possible forty-five per cent. In both instances, also, all the pronouns, prepositions, adverbs, and conjunctions, and all the inflexional forms and connecting particles, are the property of the native tongue.

Archbishop Trench's expressions respecting the character of the contributions which our mother-English has received from Anglo-Saxon and from Latin respectively, are exactly applicable to the relation and proportion which the native Dravidian element bears to the Sanskrit contained in Tamil. "All its joints, its whole articulation, its sinews and its ligaments, the great body of articles, pronouns, conjunctions, prepositions, numerals, auxiliary verbs, all smaller words which serve to knit together, and bind the larger into sentences, these, not to speak of the grammatical structure of the language, are exclusively Anglo-Saxon (Dravidian). The Latin (Sanskrit) may contribute its tale of bricks, yea, of goodly and polished hewn stones, to the spiritual building, but the mortar, with all that holds and binds these together, and constitutes them into a house, is Anglo-Saxon (Dravidian) throughout."

Though the proportion of Sanskrit which we find to be contained in the Tamil version of the Ten Commandments happens to correspond so exactly to the proportion of Latin contained in the English version, it would be an error to conclude that the Tamil language is as deeply indebted to Sanskrit as English is to Latin. Tamil can readily dispense with the greater part or the whole of its Sanskrit, and by dispensing with it rises to a purer and more refined style; whereas English cannot abandon its Latin without abandoning perspicuity. Anglo-Saxon has no synonyms of its own for many of the words it has borrowed from Latin; so that if it were obliged to dispense with them, it would, in most cases, be under the necessity of using a very awkward periphrasis instead of a single word. Tamil, on the other hand, is peculiarly rich in synonyms; and generally it is not through any real necessity, but from choice and the fashion of the age, that it makes use of Sanskrit. If the Ten Commandments were expressed in the speech of the lower classes of the Tamil people, the proportion of Sanskrit would be very greatly diminished; and if we wished to raise the style of the translation to a refined and classical pitch, Sanskrit would almost entirely disappear. Of the entire number of words contained in this formula there is only one which could not be expressed with faultless propriety and poetic elegance in equivalents of pure Dravidian origin. That word is 'image!' Both word and thing are foreign to primitive Tamil usages and habits of thought, and were introduced into the Tamil country by the Brâhmans, with the Purânic system of religion and the worship of idols. (Through the predominant influence of the religion of the Brâhmans, the majority of the words expressive of religious ideas in actual use in modern Tamil are of Sanskrit origin, and though there are equivalent Dravidian words which are equally appropriate, and in some instances more so, such words have gradually become obsolete, and are now confined to the poetical dialect;) so that the use of them in prose compositions would sound affected and pedantic. This is the real and only reason why Sanskrit derivatives are so generally used in Tamil religious compositions.

In the other Dravidian languages, whatever be the nature of the composition or subject-matter treated of, the amount of Sanskrit employed is considerably larger than in Tamil; and the use of it has acquired more of the character of a necessity. This is in consequence of the literature of those languages having chiefly been cultivated by Brâhmans. Even in Telugu the principal grammatical writers and the most celebrated poets have been Brâhmans. There is only one work of note in that language which was not composed by a member of the sacred caste; and indeed the Telugu S'ûdras, who constitute *par excellence* the Telugu people, seem almost entirely to have abandoned to the Brâhmans the culture of their own language, with every other branch of literature and science. (In Tamil, on the contrary, few Brâhmans have written anything worthy of preservation. The language has been cultivated and developed with immense zeal and success by native Tamilians; and the highest rank in Tamil literature which has been reached by a Brâhman is that of a commentator. The commentary of Parimêlaṛagar on the Kuraḷ of Tiruvaḷḷuvar (supposed to have been a Pariar (Pareiya, see Appendix), yet the acknowledged and deified prince of Tamil authors) is the most classical production written in Tamil by a Brâhman.)

Professor Wilson observes that the spoken languages of the South were cultivated in imitation of Sanskrit, and but partially aspired to an independent literature; that the principal compositions in Tamil,

Telugu, Canarese, and Malayâḷam, are translations or paraphrases from Sanskrit works, and that they largely borrow the phraseology of their originals. This representation is not perfectly correct, in so far as Tamil is concerned; for the compositions that are universally admitted to be the finest in the language, viz., the Kuraḷ and the Chintâmaṇi, are perfectly independent of Sanskrit, and original in design as well as in execution; and though it is true that Tamil writers have imitated—I cannot say translated—the Râmâyaṇa, the Mahâ-bhârata, and similar works, they boast that the Tamil Râmâyaṇa of their own Kambar is greatly superior to the Sanskrit original of Vâlmîki.

(5.) Of all evidences of identity or diversity of languages the most conclusive are those which are furnished by a comparison of their grammatical structure; and by such a comparison the independence of the Dravidian languages of Sanskrit will satisfactorily and conclusively be established. By the same comparison (at the risk of anticipating a question which will be discussed more fully in the body of the work), the propriety of placing these languages, if not in the Scythian group, yet in a position nearer that group than the Indo-European, will be indicated.

The most prominent and essential differences in point of grammatical structure between the Dravidian languages and Sanskrit, are as follows:—

(i.) In the Dravidian languages all nouns denoting inanimate substances and irrational beings are of the neuter gender. The distinction of male and female appears only in the pronouns of the third person; in the adjectives (properly appellative nouns) which denote rational beings, and are formed by suffixing the pronominal terminations; and in the third person of the verb, which, being formed by suffixing the same pronominal terminations, has three forms in the singular and two in the plural, to distinguish the several genders, in accordance with the pronouns of the third person. In all other cases where it is required to mark the distinction of gender, separate words signifying 'male' and 'female' are prefixed; but, even in such cases, though the object denoted be the male or female of an animal, the noun which denotes it does not cease to be considered neuter, and neuter forms of the pronoun and verb are required to be conjoined with it. This rule presents a marked contrast to the rules respecting gender which we find in the vivid and highly imaginative Sanskrit, and in the other Indo-European languages, but it accords with the usage of the languages of the Scythian group.

(ii.) Dravidian nouns are inflected, not by means of case-terminations, but by means of suffixed post-positions and separable particles.

The only difference between the declension of the plural and that of the singular, is that the inflexional signs are annexed in the singular to the base, in the plural to the sign of plurality, exactly as in the Scythian languages. After the pluralising particle has been added to the base, all nouns, irrespective of number and gender, are declined in the same manner as in the singular.

(iii). Dravidian neuter nouns are rarely pluralised; neuter plurals are still more rare in the inflexions of the verb.

(iv.) The Dravidian dative *ku*, *ki*, or *ge*, bears no analogy to any dative case-termination which is found in Sanskrit or in any of the Indo-European languages; but it corresponds to the dative of the Oriental Turkish, to that of the language of the Scythian tablets of Behistun, and to that of several of the languages of the Finnish family.

(v.) In those connections in which prepositions are used in the Indo-European languages, the Dravidian languages, with those of the Scythian group, use post-positions instead,—which post-positions do not constitute a separate part of speech, but are simply nouns of relation or quality, adopted as auxiliaries. All adverbs are either nouns or the gerunds or infinitives of verbs, and invariably precede the verbs they qualify.

(vi.) In Sanskrit and the Indo-European tongues, adjectives are declined like substantives, and agree with the substantives to which they are conjoined in gender, number, and case. In the Dravidian languages, as in the Scythian, adjectives are incapable of declension. When used separately as abstract nouns of quality, which is the original and natural character of Dravidian adjectives, they are subject to all the affections of substantives; but when they are used adjectivally—*i.e.*, to qualify other substantives—they do not admit any inflexional change, but are simply prefixed to the nouns which they qualify.

(vii.) It is also a characteristic of these languages, as of the Mongolian, the Manchu, and several other Scythian languages, in contradistinction to the languages of the Indo-European family, that, wherever it is practicable, they use as adjectives the relative participles of verbs, in preference to nouns of quality, or adjectives properly so called; and that in consequence of this tendency, when nouns of quality are used, the formative termination of the relative participle is generally suffixed to them, through which suffix they partake of the character both of nouns and of verbs.

(viii.) The existence of two pronouns of the first person plural, one of which includes, the other excludes, the party addressed, is a peculiarity of the Dravidian dialects, as of many of the Scythian languages;

but is unknown to Sanskrit and the languages of the Indo-European family. The only thing at all resembling it in these languages is their use of the dual.

(ix.) The Dravidian languages have no passive voice. The passive is expressed by auxiliary verbs signifying 'to suffer,' &c.

(x.) The Dravidian languages like the Scythian, but unlike the Indo-European, prefer the use of continuative participles to conjunctions.

(xi.) The existence of a negative as well as an affirmative voice in the verbal system of these languages, constitutes another essential point of difference between them and Sanskrit: it equally constitutes a point of agreement between them and the Scythian tongues.

(xii.) It is a marked peculiarity of these languages, as of the Mongolian and the Manchu, and in a modified degree of many other Scythian languages, that they make use of relative participles instead of relative pronouns. There is no trace of the existence of a relative pronoun in any Dravidian language except the Gônd alone, which seems to have lost its relative participle, and uses instead the relative pronoun of the Hindî. The place of such pronouns is supplied in the Dravidian languages, as in the Scythian tongues mentioned above, by relative participles, which are formed from the present, preterite, and future participles of the verb by the addition of a formative suffix; which suffix is in general identical with the sign of the possessive case. Thus, 'the person who came,' is in Tamil *vand-a âḷ*, literally 'the who-came person;' *vand-u*, the preterite *verbal* participle signifying 'having come,' being converted into a *relative* participle, equivalent to 'the-who-came,' by the addition of the old possessive and adjectival suffix *a*.

(xiii.) The situation of the governing word is characteristic of each of these families of languages. In the Indo-European family it usually precedes the word governed: in the Dravidian and in all the Scythian languages, it is invariably placed after it; in consequence of which the nominative always occupies the first place in the sentence, and the one finite verb the last. The adjective precedes the substantive: the adverb precedes the verb: the substantive which is governed by a verb, together with every word that depends upon it or qualifies it, precedes the verb by which it is governed: the relative participle precedes the noun on which it depends: the negative branch of a sentence precedes the affirmative: the noun in the genitive case precedes that which governs it: the *pre*-position changes places with the noun and becomes a *post*-position in virtue of its governing a case: and finally the sentence is concluded by the one, all-governing, finite verb. In each of these important and highly characteristic peculiarities of syntax, the Dravidian languages and the Scythian are thoroughly agreed.*

Many other differences in grammatical structure, and many differences also in regard to the system of sounds, will be pointed out hereafter, in the course of the analysis; but in the important particulars which are mentioned above, the Dravidian languages evidently differ so considerably from the languages of the Indo-European family, and in particular from Sanskrit (notwithstanding the predominance for so many ages of the social and religious influence of the Sanskrit-speaking race), that it can scarcely be doubted that they belong to a totally different family of tongues. They are neither derived from Sanskrit, nor are capable of being affiliated to it: and it cannot have escaped the notice of the student, that in every one of those particulars in which the grammatical structure of the Dravidian languages differs from Sanskrit, it agrees with the structure of the Scythian languages, or the languages of Central and Northern Asia.

In some particulars—as might be expected from the contact into which the Sanskrit-speaking race was brought with the aboriginal races of India—Sanskrit appears to differ less widely than the other Indo-European tongues from the languages of the Scythian group. One of these particulars—the appearance in Sanskrit of consonants of the cerebral series—will be discussed further on in connection with the Dravidian system of sounds. Mr Edkins, in his "China's Place in Philology," has opened up a new line of inquiry in regard to the existence of Turanian influences in the grammatical structure of Sanskrit. He regards the inflexion of nouns by means of case-endings alone, without prepositions in addition, as the adoption by Sanskrit of a

* The only exceptions to the rule respecting the position of the governing word in the Dravidian languages are found in poetical compositions, in which, occasionally, for the sake of effect, the order of words required by rule is transposed.

I cannot forbear quoting here a sentence from "Aston's Grammar of the Japanese Written Languages" (London, 1872), a language which claims relationship not to the Chinese, but to the Scythian, or, as they are called in that work, the Altaic, family of tongues. It might have been supposed that the writer intended to describe the structure of the Dravidian languages. "As is the case in all languages of the Altaic family, every word in Japanese which serves to define another word invariably precedes it. Thus the adjective precedes the noun, the adverb the verb, the genitive the word which governs it, the objective case the verb, and the word governed by a preposition the preposition. The nominative case stands at the beginning of a sentence, and the verb at the end.

"Nouns have, properly speaking, no declension. Number and case are rarely expressed; but when they are, they are indicated by means of certain particles placed after the words which themselves suffer no change. Instead of a passive voice, verbs have derivative verbs with a conjugation resembling that of active verbs. Mood and tense are indicated by suffixes."

Turanian rule. He thinks also the position of the words in a Sanskrit prose sentence is Turanian rather than Aryan. It is an invariable law of the distinctively Turanian tongues that related sentences precede those to which they are related. It is another invariable law that the finite verb is placed at the end of the sentence. In both these particulars Mr Edkins thinks that Sanskrit has yielded to Turanian influences. This certainly seems to be the case with regard to the vernaculars which have been developed out of the old colloquial Sanskrit; but in so far as the Sanskrit of literature is concerned, the Turanian rule is far from being universally followed. Mr Edkins himself gives an illustration from a Sanskrit prose story (p. 315), which shows that a relative clause sometimes succeeds, instead of preceding, the indicative clause, and that the position of the finite verb is not always at the end of the sentence. Perhaps all that can be said with certainty is that in Sanskrit prose and in prosaic verse related sentences generally precede, and the finite verb generally comes last. Up to this point, therefore, it may perhaps fairly be held that Turanian influences have made themselves felt even in Sanskrit. We are safer, however, in dealing with facts than with causes; for on this theory it might be necessary to hold that Latin syntax is more 'Turanian' than Greek, and German more 'Turanian' than English.

Is there a Dravidian Element in the Vernacular Languages of Northern India?

The hypothesis of the direct derivation of the Dravidian tongues from Sanskrit, with the admixture of a proportion of words and forms from an unknown source, having been found untenable, some Oriental scholars adopted an opposite hypothesis, and attributed to the influence of the Dravidian languages that corruption of Sanskrit out of which the vernaculars of Northern India have arisen. It was supposed by the Rev. Dr Stevenson, of Bombay,* Mr Hodgson, of Nepâl,† and some other Orientalists, (1) that the North-Indian vernaculars had been derived from Sanskrit, not so much by the natural process of corruption and disintegration, as through the overmastering, remoulding power of the non-Sanskritic element contained in them; and (2) that this non-Sanskritic element was identical with the Dravidian speech, which they supposed to have been the speech of the ancient Nishâdas, and other aborigines of India.

* *Journal of the Asiatic Society of Bombay.*

† *Journal of the Asiatic Society of Bengal;* also "Aborigines of India," Calcutta, 1849.

The first part of this hypothesis appears to rest upon a better foundation than the second; but even the first part appears to me to be too strongly expressed, and to require considerable modification; for in some important particulars the corruption of Sanskrit into Hindî, Bengâlî, &c., has been shown to have arisen from that natural process of change which we see exemplified in Europe, in the corruption of Latin into Italian and Spanish. Nevertheless, on comparing the grammatical structure and essential character of Sanskrit with those of the vernaculars of Northern India, I feel persuaded—though here I am off my own ground, and must express myself with diffidence—that the direction in which those vernaculars have been differentiated from Sanskrit has to a considerable extent been non-Aryan, and that this must have been owing, in what way soever it may have been brought about, to the operation of non-Aryan influences.

The modifications which the grammar of the North Indian languages have received, being generally of one and the same character, and in one and the same direction, it may be concluded that there must have been a common modifying cause; and as the non-Sanskritic portion of those languages, which Professor Wilson styles "a portion of a primitive, unpolished, and scanty speech, the relics of a period prior to civilisation," has been calculated to amount to one-tenth of the whole, and in Marâṭhî to a fifth, it seems reasonable to infer that it was, in part at least, from that extraneous element that the modifying influences proceeded.

It is admitted that before the arrival of the Aryans, or Sanskrit-speaking colony of Brâhmans, Kshatriyas, and Vaiśyas, the greater part of Northern India was peopled by rude aboriginal tribes, called by Sanskrit writers Dasyus, Nishâdas, Mlêchchas, &c.; and it is the received opinion that those aboriginal tribes were of Scythian, or at least of non-Aryan, origin. On the irruption of the Aryans, it would naturally happen that the copious and expressive Sanskrit of the conquering race would almost overwhelm the vocabulary of the rude Scythian tongues spoken by the aboriginal tribes. Nevertheless, as the grammatical structure of the Scythian tongues possesses peculiar stability and persistency, and as the præ-Aryan tribes, who were probably more numerous than the Aryans, were not annihilated, but only reduced to a dependent position, and eventually, in most instances, incorporated in the Aryan community, it would seem almost necessarily to follow that they would modify, whilst they adopted, the language of their conquerors, and that this modification would consist, partly in the addition of new words, and partly also in the introduction of a new spirit and tendency.

This hypothesis seems to have the merit of according better than any other with existing phenomena. Seeing that the northern vernaculars possess, with the words of the Sanskrit, a grammatical structure which in the main appears to be Scythian, it seems more correct to represent those languages as having a Scythian basis, with a large and almost overwhelming Sanskrit addition, than as having a Sanskrit basis, with a small admixture of a Scythian element. The existence of a 'Tartarean or Chaldee,' that is, of a Scythian, element in the colloquial dialects of Northern India was first asserted by Sir W. Jones ("Asiatic Researches," vol. i.), and till of late has been generally admitted. It has recently been called in question in the *Indian Antiquary* (April 1872), in a paper by Mr Growse, B.C.S. His observations are confined to Hindî, and deal, not with its grammatical principles, but with the vocabulary only; but they prove the necessity of more extended research before the existence of any considerable amount of non-Sanskritic elements in that dialect can be regarded as certain.

The second part of the hypothesis of Dr Stevenson, viz., the identity of the non-Sanskritic element contained in those languages—supposing the existence of such an element established—with the languages of the Dravidian family, rests on a different foundation, and appears to me to be less defensible. According to the supposition in question, the Scythian or Dravidian element is substantially one and the same in all the vernacular languages of India, whether northern or southern, but is smallest in amount in those districts of Northern India which were first conquered by the Aryans; greater in the remoter districts of the Dekhan, Telingana, and Mysore; and greatest of all in the Tamil country, at the southern extremity of the peninsula, to which the aggressions of the Brâhmanical race had scarcely extended in the age of Manu and the Râmâyaṇa.

This hypothesis certainly appears at first sight to accord with the current of events in the ancient history of India; but whatever relationship, in point of blood and race, may originally have subsisted between the northern aborigines and the southern,—whatever *ethnological* evidences of their identity may be supposed to exist,—when we view the question *philologically*, and with reference to the evidence furnished by their languages alone, the hypothesis of their identity does not appear to me to have been established. It may be true that various analogies in point of grammatical structure appear to connect the non-Sanskritic element contained in the North-Indian idioms with the Scythian tongues. This connection, however (if it really exists), amounts only to a general relationship to the entire group of Scythian languages; and scarcely any special relationship to the Dravidian languages, *in contra-distinction* to those of the Turkish, the Finnish, or any other Scythian family, has yet been shown to exist. Indeed I conceive that the non-Aryan substratum of the North-Indian idioms presents as large a number of points of agreement with the Oriental Turkish, or with that Scythian tongue or family of tongues by which the New Persian has been modified, as with any of the Dravidian languages.

The principal particulars in which the grammar of the North-Indian idioms accords with that of the Dravidian languages are as follows:—(1), the inflexion of nouns by means of separate post-fixed particles added to the oblique form of the noun; (2), the inflexion of the plural by annexing to the unvarying sign of plurality the same suffixes of case as those by which the singular is inflected; (3), the use in several of the northern idioms of two pronouns of the first person plural, the one including, the other excluding, the party addressed; (4), the use of post-positions, instead of prepositions; (5), the formation of verbal tenses by means of participles; (6), the situation of the relative sentence before the indicative; (7), the situation of the governing word after the word governed. In the particulars above-mentioned, the grammar of the North-Indian idioms undoubtedly resembles that of the Dravidian family: but the argument founded upon this general agreement is to a considerable extent neutralised by the circumstance that those idioms accord in the same particulars, and to the same extent, with several other families of the Scythian group. None of those particulars in which the Dravidian languages differ from the Turkish or the Mongolian (and there are many such points of difference) has as yet been discovered, so far as I am aware, in the North-Indian idioms. For instance, those idioms contain no trace of the relative participle which is used in all the Dravidian tongues, except the Gônḍ, instead of a relative pronoun; they are destitute of the regularly inflected negative verb of the Dravidian languages; and they contain not one of the Dravidian pronouns or numerals—not even those which we find in the Medo-Scythic tablets of Behistun, and which still survive even in the languages of the Ostiaks, the Chinese, and the Lapps. If the non-Sanskritic element contained in the northern vernaculars had been Dravidian, we might also expect to find in their vocabularies a few primary Dravidian roots—such as the words for 'head,' 'foot,' 'eye,' 'ear,' &c.; but I have not been able to discover any reliable analogy in words belonging to this class. The only resemblances which have been pointed out are those which Dr Stevenson traced in a few words remote from ordinary use, and on which, in the absence of analogy in primary roots, and especially in grammatical structure, it is impossible to place any dependence.* The wideness of the difference between the Dravidian vocabulary and that of the languages of Northern India with respect to primary roots, together with the essential agreement of all the Dravidian vocabularies one with another, will appear from the following comparative view of the pronouns of the first and second persons singular. It sometimes happens that where one form of the pronoun is used in the nominative, another survives in the oblique cases, and a third in the verbal inflexions; it also sometimes happens that the ancient form of the pronoun differs from the modern. Where such is the case I have given all extant forms a place in the list, for the purpose of facilitating comparison.

Pronoun of the First Person Singular.

Gaurian Idioms.

(Sanskrit primary form, *aham*; secondary forms, *ma*, *mi*, *m*; Turkish primary form, *man*.)

Hindî,	*main.*
Bengâlî,	*mûi.*
Marâṭhî,	*mî.*
Gujarâtî,	*hun.*
Sindhi,	*man.*

Dravidian Idioms.

Tamil,	*nân, yân, ên, en.*
Canarese,	*ân, yân, nâ, nânu, en, êne.*
Tuḷu,	*yân, yen, e.*
Malayâḷam,	*ñân, ên, en, ena, eni, ini.*
Telugu,	*nênu, nê, ênu, ê, nâ, nu, ni.*
Tuda,	*ân, en, eni, ini.*
Kôta,	*âne, en, e.*
Gôṇḍ,	*annâ, nâ, ân, na.*
Ku,	*ânu, nâ, in, e.*
Râjmahâl,	*en.*
Orâon,	*enan.*

Pronoun of the Second Person Singular.

Gaurian Idioms.

(Sanskrit primary forms, *tvam*, *tav*, *te*: secondary form, *si*, *s*; Turkish primary form, *sen*.)

Hindî,	*tu, tun, te.*
Bengâlî,	*tûi, to.*
Marâṭhî,	*tûn, tu, to.*
Gujarâtî,	*tûn, ta.*
Sindhi,	*tun, to.*

Dravidian Idioms.

Tamil,	*nî, nin, nun, ei, i, ây, ôy.*
Canarese,	*nîn, nînu, nî, nin, ay, e, îye, î, i.*
Tuḷu,	*î, nin, ni.*
Malayâḷam,	*nî, nin.*
Telugu,	*nîvu, îvu, nî, nin, vu, vi.*
Tuda,	*nî, nin, i.*
Kôta,	*nî, nin, i.*
Gôṇḍ,	*imma, ni, î.*
Ku,	*înu, nî, i.*
Orâon.	*nîen.*
Râjmahâl,	*nin.*
Brahuî,	*nî, nâ.*
Scythic of the Behistun tablets,	*nî.*

---

* In many instances Dr Stevenson's lexical analogies are illusory, and disappear altogether on a little investigation. Thus, he supposes the North Indian *peḍ*, 'the belly, the womb,' to be allied to the first word in the Tamil compound *peṭṭa piḷḷei*, own child. That word should have been written *pettra* in English, to accord with the pronunciation of the Tamil word: the Tamil spelling of it,

From the striking dissimilarity existing between the Gaurian pronouns and the Dravidian, it is obvious that, whatever may have been the nature and origin of the influences by which the Gaurian languages were modified, those influences do not appear to have been distinctively Dravidian. In the pronouns of almost all the North-Indian languages we may notice the Scythic termination—the obscure *n*, which forms the final of most of the pronouns. We cannot fail also to notice the entire disappearance of the nominative of the Sanskrit pronoun of the first person singular, and the substitution for it of the Turkish-like *main* or *man*; but in no connection, in no number or case, in no compound or verbal inflexion, do we see any trace of the peculiar personal pronouns of the Dravidian family. Possibly further research may disclose the existence in the northern vernaculars of distinctively Dravidian forms and roots; but their existence does not appear to me as yet to be proved; for most of Dr Stevenson's analogies take too wide a range, and where they are supposed to be distinctively Dravidian they disappear on examination. I conclude, therefore, that the non-Sanskritic portion of the northern languages cannot safely be placed in the same category with the southern, except perhaps in the sense of both being Scythian rather than Aryan.

Thus far I had written in the first edition of this work. Since then the subject has been much discussed, especially in Muir's "Sanskrit Texts," vol. ii., and in Beames's "Comparative Grammar of the Modern Aryan Languages of India." The general result appears to be that it remains as certain as ever—it could scarcely become more certain—that few, if any, traces of *distinctively* Dravidian elements are discernible in the North-Indian vernaculars. On the one hand, Dr Gundert argues strongly—not indeed for the existence of Dravidian elements in those vernaculars, as distinguished from their existence in Sanskrit—but for the existence of such elements in Sanskrit itself. See his remarks on this subject (from the *Journal of the German Oriental Society for* 1869), in the section on Glossarial Affinities. On the other hand, Mr Growse* thus concludes a discussion of the question of the existence of traces of a non-Aryan element in the northern vernaculars—"The foregoing considerations demonstrate the soundness of the proposition laid down in the outset, viz., that the proportion of words in the Hindî vocabu-

---

however, is *peṟṟa*. It is the preterite relative participle of *peṟ-u*, 'to obtain,' signifying 'that was obtained.' *Peṟ-u*, 'to obtain,' has no connection with any word which signifies 'the womb,' and its derivative noun *pêṟ-u*, means 'a thing obtained, a birth, a favour.' The relationships of this root will be inquired into in the Glossarial Affinities.

* In an article "On the Non-Aryan Element in Hindi Speech," by F. S. Growse, Esq., M.A., B.C.S., in the *Indian Antiquary* for April 1872.

lary not connected with Sanskrit forms is exceedingly inconsiderable; such fact appearing—first, from the silence of the early grammarians as to the existence of any such non-Sanskritic element; secondly, from the discovery that many of the words hastily set down as barbarous are in reality traceable to a classic source; and, thirdly, from the unconscious adherence of the modern vernacular to the same laws of formation as influenced it in an admittedly Sanskritic stage of development."

The following more extended remarks in confirmation of the same view of the subject are from Mr Beames's "Comparative Grammar" (Introduction, pp. 9–10,* § 3):—"Next comes the class of words described as neither Sanskritic nor Aryan, but *x*. It is known that on entering India the Aryans found that country occupied by races of a different family from their own. With these races they waged a long and chequered warfare, gradually pushing on after each fresh victory, till at the end of many centuries they obtained possession of the greater part of the territories they now enjoy. Through these long ages, periods of peace alternated with those of war, and the contest between the two races may have been as often friendly as hostile. The Aryans exercised a powerful influence upon their opponents, and we cannot doubt but that they themselves were also, but in a less degree, subject to some influence from them. There are consequently to be found even in Sanskrit some words which have a very non-Aryan look, and the number of such words is much greater still in the modern languages, and there exists, therefore, a temptation to attribute to non-Aryan sources any words whose origin it is difficult to trace from Aryan beginnings.

"It may be as well here to point out certain simple and almost obvious limitations to the application of the theory that the Aryans borrowed from their alien predecessors. Verbal resemblance is, unless supported by other arguments, the most unsafe of all grounds on which to base an induction in philology. Too many writers, in other respects meritorious, seem to proceed on Fluellen's process, 'There is a river in Macedon, and there is also moreover a river in Monmouth, and there is salmon in both.' A certain Tamil word contains a *P*, so does a certain Sanskrit word, and *ergo*, the latter is derived from the former! Now, I would urge, that, in the first place, the Aryans were superior morally as well as physically to the aborigines, and probably therefore imparted to them more than they received from them. Moreover, the Aryans were in possession of a copious language before they came into India;

---

* "A Comparative Grammar of the Modern Non-Aryan Languages of India," &c., by John Beames, Esq., B.C.S. London, 1872.

they would therefore not be likely to borrow words of an ordinary, usual description, such as names for their clothing, weapons, and utensils, or for their cattle and tools, or for the parts of their bodies, or for the various relations in which they stood to each other. The words they would be likely to borrow would be names for the new plants, animals, and natural objects which they had not seen in their former abodes, and even this necessity would be reduced by the tendency inherent in all races to invent descriptive names for new objects. A third limitation is afforded by geographical considerations. Which were the tribes that the Aryans mixed with, either as friends or foes? Could the bulk of them have come into frequent and close contact with the Dravidians; and if so, when and how? These are questions which it is almost impossible to answer in the present state of our knowledge, but they are too important to be altogether set aside; and it may be therefore pointed out, merely as a contribution to the subject, that the tribes driven out of the valley of the Ganges by the Aryans were almost certainly Kols to the south, and semi-Tibetans to the north. It is fair to look with suspicion on an etymology which takes us from Sanskrit to Tamil, without exhibiting a connecting series of links through the intervening Kol tribes. If the above limitations are rigidly applied, they will narrow very much the area within which non-Aryan forms are possible in Sanskrit and its descendants, and will force us to have recourse to a far more extensive and careful research within the domain of Sanskrit itself than has hitherto been made, with a view to finding in that language the origin of modern words."

I coincide generally in the above remarks, especially in so far as they bear on the question of the influence of the Dravidian languages, properly so called, on the North-Indian or Aryan vernaculars. That influence, as I have always held, must have been but slight. It is a different question whether the influences by which the Aryan vernaculars have been moulded into their present shape may not have been in some degree Scythian or at least non-Aryan. Dravidian, Scythian, and non-Aryan are not convertible terms. Mr Beames himself says, in his chapter on "Vowel Changes," p. 128, "I am not in a position to point out how far, or in what direction, Aryan vocalism has been influenced by these alien races (on the northern and eastern frontier, in Central India, and on the south); but that some sort of influence has been at work is almost beyond a doubt." In treating of 'the breaking down of *a* and *â* into *e*' in the northern vernaculars, he says, "this seems to be one of those points where non-Aryan influences have been at work."—(P. 140.) In treating also of the cerebral *ḷ*, he says, "This curious heavy *ḷ* is very widely employed in the Dravidian group of languages, where it interchanges freely with *r* and *ḍ*, and it is also found in the Kôle family in Central India. The Marathas and Oriyas are perhaps of all the Aryan tribes those which have been for the longest time in contact with Koles and Dravidians, and it is not surprising, therefore, to find the cerebral *ḷ* more freely used by them than by others."—P. 245.

Dr Ernest Trumpp, in his "Grammar of the Sindhî Language," maintains that the northern vernaculars exhibit decided traces of non-Aryan influences. He thinks we shall be able "to trace out a certain residuum of vocables, which we must allot to an old aboriginal language, of which neither name nor extent is now known to us, but which in all probability was of the Tâtâr stock of languages, and spread throughout the length and breadth of India before the irruption of the Aryan race." In confirmation of this view he adduces the preference of cerebral consonants to dentals. "Nearly three-fourths," he thinks, "of the Sindhî words which commence with a cerebral are taken from some aboriginal non-Aryan idiom which in recent times has been termed Scythian, but which he would prefer to call Tâtâr." "And this," he proceeds to say, "seems to be very strong proof that the cerebrals have been borrowed from some idiom anterior to the introduction of the Aryan languages." In noticing the aversion of the Prâkrit to aspirates, he remarks that "this aversion seems to point to a Tâtâr underground current in the mouth of the common people, the Dravidian languages of the south being destitute of aspirates." He attributes also to Dravidian influences the pronunciation of *ch* and *j* in certain connections as *ts* and *dz*, by Marâṭhi as by Telugu.

To what Group of Languages are the Dravidian Idioms to be affiliated?

From the commencement of my Tamil studies I felt much interested in the problem of the ulterior relationship of the Dravidian family of languages; and before I was aware of the opinion which Professor Rask of Copenhagen was the first to express, I arrived by a somewhat similar process at a similar conclusion—viz., that the Dravidian languages are to be affiliated not so much to the Indo-European as to the Scythian group of tongues. I described the conclusion I arrived at as similar to Rask's, not the same, because I did not think it safe to place the Dravidian idioms unconditionally in the Scythian group, but preferred considering them more closely allied to the Scythian than to the Indo-European. In using the word 'Scythian,' I use it in the wide, general sense in which it was used by Rask, who first employed it to designate that group of tongues which comprises the Finnish, the Turkish, the Mongolian, and the Tungusian families. All these languages are formed on one and the same grammatical system, and in accordance with the same general laws. They all express grammatical relation by the simple agglutination of auxiliary words or particles; whilst in the Semitic languages grammatical relation is expressed by variations in the internal vowels of the roots, and in the Chinese and other isolative, monosyllabic languages, by the position of words in the sentence alone. The Indo-European languages appear to have been equally with the Scythian agglutinative in origin; but they have come to require to be formed into a class by themselves, through their allowing their agglutinated auxiliary words to sink into the position of mere signs of inflexion. The Scythian languages have been termed by some, the Tâtar family of tongues, by others the Finnish, the Altaïc, the Mongolian, or the Turanian; but as these terms have often been appropriated to designate one or two families, to the exclusion of the rest, they seem too narrow to be safely employed as common designations of the entire group. The term 'Scythian' having already been used by the classical writers in a vague, undefined sense, to denote generally the barbarous tribes of unknown origin that inhabited the northern parts of Asia and Europe, it seemed to me to be the most appropriate and convenient word which was available.

Professor Rask, who was the first to suggest that the Dravidian languages were probably Scythian, did little more than suggest this relationship. The evidence of it was left both by him and by the majority of succeeding writers in a very defective state. General statements of the Scythian relationship of the Dravidian languages, with a few grammatical illustrations, occupy a place in Prichard's "Researches," and have been repeated in several more recent works. Prichard himself wished to see the problem, not merely stated, but solved; but I believe it can never be definitely solved without previously ascertaining, by a careful intercomparison of dialects, what were the most ancient grammatical forms and the most essential characteristics of the Dravidian languages and of the various families of languages included in the Scythian group respectively. It was not till after I had commenced to carry the first edition of this work through the press that I became acquainted with Professor Max Müller's treatise "On the Present State of our Knowledge of the Turanian Languages," included in Bunsen's "Outlines of the Philosophy of Universal History." Notwithstanding the great excellence of that treatise, I did not find my own work forestalled by the Professor's. His was a general survey of the whole field. It was my object to endeavour to cultivate more thoroughly one portion of the field, or at least to prepare it for thorough cultivation. Whilst the principal features of the Dravidian tongues are strongly marked, and whilst their grammatical principles and syntactic arrangement are of too peculiar a nature to be easily mistaken, there is much in the phonic system of these languages, in their dialectic interchanges and displacements, and in their declensional and conjugational forms, which cannot be understood without special study.

In the course of the grammatical analysis and comparison of the Dravidian languages on which we are about to enter, I hope to help forward the solution of the problem of their ulterior relationship. It is a problem which has often up to a certain point been ingeniously elucidated, but which has never yet been thoroughly investigated. I am very far from regarding anything contained in the following work as a thorough investigation of this problem. The chief object I have in view is to contribute to a better knowledge of the Dravidian languages themselves. However interesting the question of affiliation may be, I regard that question as quite subsidiary to the object of the work in hand. Besides, I believe it will be found necessary for the satisfactory solution of the question, that the intercomparison of the various languages and families of languages of which the Scythian group is composed, should be carried much further than it has been carried as yet. An excellent beginning has been made in Boller's treatises : "Die Finnischen Sprachen" and "Die Conjugation in den Finnischen Sprachen," Schott's treatise "Über das Finnish-Tatarische Sprachengeschlecht," and Castrén's "De Affixis Personalibus Linguarum Altaicarum ;" in addition to which we have now Professor Hunfalvy's paper "On the Study of the Turanian Languages," in which he carefully compares the Hungarian, Vogul, Ostiak, and Finnish, and proves that the vocabularies of those four languages are of a common origin, and that their grammars are closely related. Till, however, the comparative study of the whole of these languages has been carried still further, one term of the comparison will always be liable to be misapprehended. My knowledge of the Scythian languages is only at second hand, and I am fully conscious of the truth of Böhtlingk's dictum, that "It is dangerous to write on languages of which we do not possess the most accurate knowledge." I trust, therefore, it will be remembered that if I advocate any particular theory on this question of affiliation, I do so with considerable diffidence.

Professors Pott and Friedrich Müller, followed by an increasing number of philologists, are unwilling to admit that the various languages of the so-called Scythian or Turanian class or group have had a common origin. They admit them to be morphologically or physiologically related, but do not concede to them any genealogical relationship. Dr Black also (*Journal of the Anthropological Society*, 1871) thinks it "not impossible that some or all of the Turanian languages exhibit only certain stages of development in one particular direction, taken either by members of different families, or by different branches of the same family." On the whole, however, the resemblances apparent amongst these languages, both in structure and vocabulary, as pointed out by Castrén and the other writers referred to, seem to me too numerous and essential to admit of any other conclusion than that of their original oneness. "These languages," appear to me, to use Professor Max Müller's words, to "share elements in common which they must have borrowed from the same source, and their formal coincidences, though of a different character from those of the Aryan and Semitic families, are such that it would be impossible to ascribe them to mere accident" ("Lecture I," 301). "The only coincidences we are likely to find," he says, "in agglutinative languages long separated, are such as refer to 'the radical materials of language, or to those parts of speech which it is most difficult to reproduce—pronouns, numerals, and prepositions. It is astonishing rather that any words of a conventional meaning should have been discovered as the common property of the Turanian languages than that most of their words and forms should be peculiar to each.'"

The various particulars which I adduced in the preceding section to prove that the Dravidian languages are essentially different from, and independent of, Sanskrit (each of which will be considered more fully under its own appropriate head) may also be regarded as contributing to show, both that the various languages of the Scythian group have sprung from a common origin, and also that the Dravidian languages—if not actually to be included in the Scythian group—stand to that group in some sort of relationship. In some important particulars the Dravidian languages have undoubtedly approximated to the Indo-European, especially in this, that instead of continuing to be purely agglutinative they have become partly inflexional. Several of the words of relation used as auxiliaries in declension and conjugation have ceased to be capable of being used as independent words. Still, it would be unnecessary on this account alone to disconnect these languages wholly from the Scythian group, for those auxiliary words, though they have now in some instances shrunk into the condition of fossilised relics, are always separable from the roots to which they are appended. They have never so far coalesced with the roots—as such words have generally done in the

Indo-European languages—as to form with the roots only one integral word, in which it is almost impossible to determine which is the root and which is the modificatory element. It is also to be remembered that the Turkish, Finnish, Hungarian, and Japanese languages, though in many particulars distinctively Turanian, have become still more inflexional than the Dravidian. Mr Edkins, in his "China's Place in Philology," has warmly supported both the positions I have advocated—viz., the original unity of all the Scythian languages and the affiliation of the Dravidian languages on the whole to the Scythian group. A considerable number of the minute coincidences on which he relies will probably disappear on further investigation; but the more this branch of philology is studied the more I think it will be evident that the main lines of his argument—especially with regard to the resemblances between the Dravidian languages and the Mongolian—are correct. I cannot say that I think the resemblances of the Dravidian languages to the Chinese very numerous. Mr Edkins holds the original unity, not only of the Scythian languages, but of all the languages of Europe and Asia, and argues that "what are called families of languages are only dialects of an earlier speech." This general principle seems to me to be in accordance, on the whole, with such facts as are known to us respecting the history of human speech, but it will probably be a considerable time before it is scientifically established. I may add that, to my own mind, the light which is thrown on the structure of the Dravidian languages by the study of the languages of the Scythian group has always seemed a strong confirmation of the theory of the existence in them of a Scythian element. The relative participle is one of the most distinguishing features of the Dravidian verb; but I never clearly understood the principle of the formation of that participle, till I saw how it was formed in the Mongolian and Manchu; and no person, however reluctant to see a Scythian element in the Dravidian languages, has ever, so far as I am aware, objected to the explanation of the origin of the relative participle given in the first edition of this work, or suggested another. (See "The Relative Participle," in Part V., on "The Verb.")

A remarkable confirmation, on the whole, of the Scythian theory has been furnished by the translation of the Behistun tablets. The inscriptions discovered at Behistun or Baghistân, in western Media, record the political autobiography of Darius Hystaspes in the Old Persian, in the Babylonian, and also in the language of the Scythians of the Medo-Persian empire; and the translation of the Scythian portion of those inscriptions has thrown a new light on the connection of the Dravidian languages with the Scythian group. The language of the second series of tablets was shown in Mr Norris's paper (in the *Journal of the Royal Asiatic Society*, vol. xv.) to be distinctively Scythian. Professor Oppert holds that the people by whom this language was spoken were Medians, but agrees with Mr Norris in considering the language Scythian—that is, Turanian. We are now enabled, therefore, to compare the Dravidian idioms with a fully developed language of the Scythian family, as spoken in the fifth century, B.C. : and whilst the language of the tablets has been shown to belong generally to the Scythian group, it has been found to bear a special relationship to a particular family included in that group—the Ugro-Finnish—a family which the Dravidian dialects have long appeared to me to resemble. The principal points of resemblance between the Dravidian dialects and the language of the tablets are as follows :—

(1.) The language of the tablets appears to accord with the Dravidian tongues in the use of consonants of the cerebral class, *ṭ*, *ḍ*, and *ṇ*. These sounds exist also in Sanskrit, but I have long suspected that Sanskrit borrowed them from the indigenous Dravidian languages (*vide* the section on "Sounds"); and I find that Mr Norris has expressed the same opinion.

(2.) The language of the tablets agrees with Tamil in regarding the same consonant as a surd in the beginning of a word, and as a sonant in the middle, and in pronouncing the same consonant as a sonant when single, and as a surd when doubled. (See in the section on "Sounds" illustrations of the Tamil rule.)

(3.) The genitive case of the language of the tablets is formed by suffixing the syllables *na*, *nina*, or *inna*. The analogous forms of the Dravidian languages are *nî* in the Telugu, *na* or *a* in Gôṇḍ or Brahui, and *in* in Tamil.

(4.) The dative of the tablets is *ikki* or *ikka*. There are analogies to this both in the Tâtar-Turkish and in the Ugrian families; but the form which is most perfectly in accordance with it is that of the Dravidian dative suffix *ku*, *ki*, *ka*, &c., preceded as the suffix generally is in Tamil and Malayâḷam, by an euphonic *u* or *i*, and a consequent doubling of the *k*. Compare *nin-ikka*, to thee, in the language of the tablets, with the corresponding *nin-a-ge*, in Canarese, and especially the Malayâḷam *nin-a-kku*.

(5.) The pronouns of the language of the tablets form their accusative by suffixing *un*, *in*, or *n*. Compare the Telugu accusative inflexion *nu* or *ni*, and the Canarese *am*, *ann-u*, &c.

(6.) The only numeral written in letters in the Scythian tablets is *kir*, one, with which appears to be connected the numeral adjective, or indefinite article, *ra*, or *irra*. In Telugu, 'one' is *oka*, and in Tamil *or*. The Ku numeral adjective 'one' is *ra*, corresponding to the Tamil *oru*, but more closely to the *ra* or *irra* of the tablets.

In the language of the tablets all ordinal numbers end in *im*, in Tamil in *âm*, in Samoïede in *im*.

(7.) The pronoun of the second person is exactly the same in the language of the inscriptions as in the Dravidian languages. In all it is *nî;* the oblique form, which is also the accusative, is *nin*. Unfortunately the plural of this pronoun is not contained in the tablets—the singular having been used instead of the plural in addressing inferiors.

(8.) The language of the tablets, like the Dravidian languages, makes use of a relative participle. A relative pronoun is used in addition to the relative participle; but Mr Norris supposes the use of this pronoun to be owing to the imitation of the Persian original. The particular particle which is used in the tablets in forming the relative participle differs from that which is generally used in the Dravidian languages; but the position and force of this particle, and the manner in which the participle formed by it is employed, are in perfect harmony with Dravidian usage. Perhaps the use of this relative participle is the most remarkable and distinctive characteristic of the grammar of every unaltered dialect of the Scythian family.

(9.) The negative imperative, or prohibitive, particle of the tablets is *inni*, in Gôṇḍ *minni*.

The conjugational system of the language of the tablets accords with that of the Hungarian, the Mordvin, and other languages of the Ugrian family, but differs considerably from the Dravidian languages, which form their tenses in a simpler manner, by the addition of particles of time to the root, and which form the persons of their verbs by the addition of the ordinary pronominal terminations to the particles of time. Notwithstanding this discrepancy in the inflexions of the verbs, the resemblances shown to subsist between the language of the tablets and the Dravidian idioms, most of which are in particulars of primary importance, seem to establish the existence of a radical, though very remote, connection. From the discovery of these analogies, we are led to conclude that the Dravidian race, though resident in India from a period long prior to the commencement of history, originated in the central tracts of Asia—the seed-plot of nations; and that from thence, after parting company with the Aryans and the Ugro-Turanians, and leaving a colony in Belûchistân, they entered India by way of the Indus.

Whilst I regard the grammatical structure and prevailing characteristics of the Dravidian idioms as in the main Scythian, I claim for them also, and have always claimed, as will be seen further on, the possession of certain remarkable affinities to the Indo-European family. In so far as they may be regarded as Scythian, they are allied not to the Turkish family, or to the Ugrian, or to the Mongolian, or to the Tungusian (each of which families differs materially from the others, notwithstanding generic points of resemblance), but to the group or class in which all these families are comprised. The Scythian family to which, on the whole, the Dravidian languages may be regarded as most nearly allied, is the Finnish or Ugrian, with some special affinities, as it appears, to the Ostiak branch of that family; and this supposition, which I had been led to entertain from the comparison of grammars and vocabularies alone, derives some confirmation from the fact brought to light by the Behistun tablets, that the ancient Scythic race, by which the greater part of Central Asia was peopled prior to the irruption of the Medo-Persians, belonged not to the Turkish, or to the Mongolian, but to the Ugrian stock. If we can venture to take for granted, at present, the conclusiveness of the evidence on which this hypothesis rests, the result at which we arrive is one of the most remarkable that the study of comparative philology has yet realised. How remarkable that distinct affinities to the speech of the Dravidians of inter-tropical India should be discoverable in the language of the Finns of Northern Europe, and of the Ostiaks and other Ugrians of Siberia; and, consequently, that the præ-Aryan inhabitants of the Dekhan should appear, from the evidence furnished by their language alone, in the silence of history, in the absence of all ordinary probabilities, to be allied to the tribes that appear to have overspread Europe before the arrival of the Teutons and the Hellenes, and even before the arrival of the Celts!* What a confirmation of the statement that "God hath made of *one* blood all nations of men, to dwell upon the face of the whole earth!"

In weighing the reasons which may be adduced for affiliating the Dravidian languages in the main to the Scythian group, it should be borne in mind that whilst the generic characteristics of the Scythian languages are very strongly marked and incapable of being mistaken, in a vast variety of minor particulars, and especially in their vocabularies, the languages comprised in this family differ from one another more widely than the various idioms of the Indo-European family mutually differ. Thus, whilst in nearly all the Indo-European languages the numerals are not only similar, but the same—(the Sanskrit

* Professor Hunfalvy does not admit that the Finno-Ugrian race arrived in Europe before the Celts, Teutons, and Slavonians. I adhere, however, to the ordinary belief prevailing amongst ethnologists, which appears to me in the main well-grounded. The late arrival of the Magyars in Hungary is of course admitted.

word for *one* being the only real exception to the rule of general identity)—not only do the numerals of every Scythian family differ so widely from those of every other as to present few or no points of resemblance, but even the numerals of any two languages of the same family are found to differ very widely. So great, indeed, is the diversity existing amongst the Scythian tongues, that, whilst the Indo-European idioms form but one family, the Scythian tongues form not so much a family as a group of families—a group held together not by the bond of identity in details, but only by the bond of certain general characteristics which they all possess in common. The Indo-European languages may be regarded as forming but a single genus, of which each language—(Sanskrit, Zend, Old Persian, Greek, Latin, Gothic, Lithuanian, Slavonic, Celtic)—forms a species; whilst the languages of the Scythian group, more prolific in differences, comprise at least five or six authenticated genera, each of which includes as many species as are contained in the solitary Indo-European genus, besides twenty or thirty isolated languages, which have up to this time resisted every effort to classify them.

This remarkable difference between the Indo-European languages and those of the Scythian stock seems to have arisen partly from the higher mental gifts and higher capacity for civilisation, with which the Indo-European tribes appear to have been endowed from the beginning, and still more from the earlier literary culture of their languages, and the better preservation, in consequence, of their forms and roots. It seems also to have arisen in part from their more settled habits, in comparison with the wandering, nomadic life led by most of the Scythian tribes. But, from whatever cause this difference may have arisen, it is obvious that in weighing evidences of relationship this circumstance must be taken into account; and that so minute an agreement of long-separated sister dialects of the Scythian stock is not to be expected as in parallel cases amongst the Indo-European dialects. Professor Max Müller, in his "Lectures on the Science of Language," adduces many instances of the rapidity and extent of the divergence which takes place between uncultivated dialects of the same language. Bishop Patteson also says, "In most cases the languages of two neighbouring islands may show their common derivation in their structure (the safest proof of all, I imagine), but nearly all the words will be different."—("Letter from Bishop Patteson to Professor Max Müller." Appendix to Life.)

The relationship of the Dravidian languages to the languages of the Scythian group,—whether the relation of lineal descent, or the relation of sisterhood, or the wider relationship for which I plead,—has not been universally admitted by students of Dravidian philology. From the brief remarks bearing on this question contained in Dr Pope's various publications, it is evident that that eminent Dravidian scholar considers the Dravidian languages in the main Indo-European. In the introduction to his "Tamil Hand-Book" (Madras, 1859), he says: "The more deeply they (the South Indian languages) are studied, the more close will their affinity to Sanskrit be seen to be, and the more evident it will appear that they possess a primitive and very near relationship to the languages of the Indo-European group. Yet they are certainly not mere Prakrits, or corruptions of Sanskrit. I have always supposed that their place was among the members of the last mentioned family, and that they were probably *disjecta membra* of a language coeval with Sanskrit, and having the same origin with it. They certainly contain many traces of a close connection with the Greek, the Gothic, the Persian, and the other languages of the same family, in points even where Sanskrit presents no parallel." In the introduction to his "Sermon on the Mount," in four Dravidian languages, with comparative vocabulary and inflexional tables (Madras, 1860), he says: "The writer would direct the attention of philologists to the deep-seated, radical affinities between these languages and the Celtic and Teutonic languages. Had leisure and space permitted, he was prepared to have exhibited in detail these analogies. In a next edition, or in some future work, he yet cherishes the hope of doing so. The subject of the affiliation of these languages is one which requires that further elucidation which nothing but a complete comparative lexicon could afford." The last reference he makes to the subject is in a prefatory notice to his "Outlines of the Grammar of the Tuda Language" (Bangalore, 1872), in which he says: "While agreeing in the main with Dr Caldwell, I yet think that the remarkable analogies between the Celtic and the Dravidian languages merit a more thorough investigation." I trust Dr Pope will ere long have time to favour philologers with the thorough investigation which this question undoubtedly merits. I may remark here, however, that in everything he says respecting the existence of 'analogies,' and 'affinities,' and 'traces of a close connection' between the Dravidian languages and various members of the Indo-European family, I not only perfectly coincide with him, but pointed out many of those particulars of agreement or resemblance myself (yet without deducing from them precisely the same conclusion) in every section of the first edition of this work. The theory I advocate, indeed, takes account of both sets of relationships—the Scythian and the Indo-European—though it regards the former as, on the whole, closer and more essential. With regard to Celtic affinities in particular, it is to be remembered that of all the members of the Indo-European family the Celtic is that which appears to have most in common with the Scythian group, and especially with the languages of the Finnish family—languages which may possibly have been widely spoken in Europe previously to the arrival of the Celts. It will be necessary, therefore, in each case to inquire whether the Celtic affinity may not also be a Scythian affinity.

I refer the reader to Appendix II. for some remarks on the philological portion of Mr Gover's "Folk-Songs of Southern India;" and also for a fuller explanation of the real nature of the theory respecting the relationship of the Dravidian languages to the languages of the Scythian group advocated in the first edition of this work.

At the very outset of my own inquiries, I thought I observed in the Dravidian languages the Indo-European analogies to which I have referred; and, rejecting affinities which are unreal and which disappear on investigation (such as the connection of the Tamil numerals *ondru* or *onnu*, one; *anju*, five; *eṭṭu*, eight; with *un-us*, *panch-an*, and *ashṭ-an*,—a connection which looks very plausible, but appears to me to be illusory (see section on "Numerals"),—I think it highly probable that a small number of the grammatical forms of the Dravidian languages and a more considerable number of their roots, are to be regarded as of cognate origin with corresponding forms and roots in the Indo-European languages. Notwithstanding the existence of a few analogies of this character, the most essential features of the grammar of the Dravidian idioms seem to me to be undoubtedly Scythian, and therefore I think the propriety of placing those idioms in the Scythian group is indicated. Though many Hebrew roots have been shown to be allied to Sanskrit, yet the Hebrew language does not cease to be regarded as Semitic rather than Indo-European; so, notwithstanding many interesting analogies with Sanskrit, Greek, Gothic, Celtic, and Persian, which may be discovered on a careful examination of the Dravidian tongues, and which will be pointed out in their order in each of the succeeding sections, the essential characteristics of those tongues are such as seem to me to require us to regard them as in the main Scythian. Dr Gustave Schlegel, in his "Sinico-Aryaca" (Batavia, 1872), a treatise on Chinese and Aryan affinities, endeavours to establish the existence of an ultimate relationship between the Chinese roots and those of the Aryan languages. Supposing this point established, it would not follow that Chinese is an Aryan tongue. It would only follow that it had succeeded in preserving certain exceedingly primitive forms of speech which had also been preserved in the languages of the Aryan family. Not Chinese only, but Sanskrit and Hebrew, are now known to have been originally monosyllabic; and the monosyllabic character of most Dravidian roots, if not of all, will appear in every section of this work. Dr Bleek (in a paper in the *Journal of the Anthropological Society* for 1871) has thrown out the idea that the Aryan family of languages may possibly have been exposed at an early period to Dravidian influences. He says: "The Aryan are distinguished from the other sex-denoting languages by the possession of a neuter gender. The Dravidian languages possess a neuter gender, which has as wide a range as in English, the most logically arranged of the Aryan languages. The distinctive marks of the neuter gender, in the Dravidian languages, even agree with those of our own languages to so great an extent that it does not appear probable that these two circles of languages (which are the only ones known to possess this threefold gender—*i.e.*, masculine, feminine, and neuter) should have developed the neuter gender quite independently of each other. The Dravidian languages have not as yet been proved to belong to our own sex-denoting family of languages; and although it is not impossible that they may be shown ultimately to be a member of this family, yet it may also be that at the time of the formation of the Aryan languages a Dravidian influence was exerted upon them, to which this, among other similarities, is due." The Dravidian languages had a neuter pronoun of the third person at the earliest period to which their forms can be traced; but I suspect it was at a later period of their history that gender made its appearance in the verb. When the Dravidians entered India their verb must, I think, have been without personal terminations, and therefore without gender. It will be seen hereafter that gender is more fully and systematically developed in the verb of the Dravidian literary dialects than in any other language in the world. This could not have been owing to the influence of Sanskrit, but must have been *ab intra.*

In stating that the Dravidian languages contain certain roots and forms allied to Sanskrit, and to the Indo-European languages generally, it is necessary to preclude misapprehension. During the long period of the residence of the Dravidian and Aryan races in the same country, the Dravidian vocabularies have borrowed largely from Sanskrit. It is necessary therefore to remind the reader that the analogies to which I refer are not founded on the existence in the Dravidian tongues of Sanskrit derivatives, but are such as are discoverable in the original structure and primitive vocabulary of those languages. Whilst the Dravidian languages have confessedly borrowed much from their more wealthy neighbours, Sanskrit, in some instances, has not disdained to borrow from the Dravidian: but in general there is no difficulty in distinguishing what the one language has borrowed from the other; and the statement I have now made relates not to derivatives, or words which may be supposed to be derivatives, but to radical, deep-seated analogies which it is difficult to explain on any supposition but that of a partial or distant relationship. In most instances the words and forms in which analogies are discoverable are allied not to Sanskrit alone, but to the entire Indo-European family: in not a few instances analogies are discoverable in Greek and Latin, which are not found in Sanskrit; and in many of those instances in which Sanskrit appears to exhibit the closest analogy, it is not the euphonised, systematised Sanskrit (Sa*m*skṛita) of written compositions, but the crude, original Sanskrit, which is discoverable by analysis and comparison,—the Vor-Sanskrit of W. von Humboldt.

I subjoin here a few illustrations of what I mean by primitive, underived Indo-Europeanisms discoverable in the Dravidian languages.

(1.) The use of *n*, as in Greek, to prevent *hiatus*.

(2.) The existence of gender in the pronouns of the third person and in verbs, and in particular the existence of a neuter gender.

(3.) The use of *d* or *t* as the sign of the neuter singular of demonstrative pronouns or pronouns of the third person.

(4.) The existence of a neuter plural, as in Latin, in short *a*.

(5.) The formation of the remote demonstrative from a base in *a*, the proximate from a base in *i*.

(6.) The formation of most preterites, as in Persian, by the addition of *d*.

(7.) The formation of some preterites by the reduplication of a portion of the root.

(8.) The formation of a considerable number of verbal nouns by lengthening the vowel of the verbal root. See also "Glossarial Affinities."

The illustrations given above form only a small portion of the analogous forms which will be adduced in the grammatical analysis and in the glossarial affinities: they will, however, suffice to render it probable that Indo-European analogies are really discoverable in the Dravidian languages. They also serve to illustrate the statement, that, though Sanskrit has long been the nearest neighbour of the Dravidian tongues, there are not a few Dravidian roots which seem more nearly allied to the western Indo-European idioms than to the Sanskritic or eastern. If therefore the Dravidian languages may be classified, as I am still inclined to classify them, as essentially and in the main Scythian, I must add that I consider them as of all Scythian tongues those which present the most numerous, ancient, and interesting analogies to the Indo-European languages. The position which this family occupies, if not mid-way between the two groups, seems to me to lie on that side of the Scythian group on which the Indo-European appears to have been severed from it, and on which the most distinct traces of the original identity of the families still remain. If this view be correct (as I think it will be shown to be), the Indo-Europeanisms discoverable in the Dravidian languages carry us back to a period beyond all history, beyond all mythology, not only prior to the separation of the western branches of the Indo-European race from the eastern, but prior also to the separation of the yet undivided Indo-European race from that portion of the common stock which was afterwards styled Scythian.

It is a curious circumstance that in the vocabulary of the Dravidian languages, especially in that of Tamil, a few Semitic analogies may also be discovered. In some instances the analogous roots are found in the Indo-European family, as well as in Hebrew, though the Hebrew form of the root is more closely analogous. For example, though we find in Latin *ave-o*, to desire, and in Sanskrit *av*, of which 'to desire' is a subordinate meaning; yet the corresponding Tamil words *avâ*, desire, and *âval* (signifying also desire, a verbal noun from a lost verb *âv-u*, to desire) seems still more directly allied to the Hebrew *âvah*, to desire, and the verbal noun *avvâh*, desire. In addition, however, to such general analogies as pervade several families of tongues, including the Dravidian, there are a few roots discoverable, I think, both in the Dravidian languages and in Hebrew, to which I am not aware of the existence of any resemblance in any language of the Indo-European family. Illustrations of these special analogies will be found under the head of "Glossarial Affinities: Semitic."

The Semitic analogies observable in Tamil are neither so numerous nor so important as the Indo-European, nor do they carry with them such convincing evidence; but taking them in connection with that more numerous and important class of analogous roots which are found in the Indo-European languages, as well as in Hebrew, but of which the Hebrew form is more closely allied to the Dravidian (see the "Glossarial Affinities"), these analogies, such as they are, constitute an additional element of interest in the problem of the origin and præ-historic connections of the Dravidian race. I do not adduce these analogies for the purpose of endeavouring to prove the existence of any relationship between the Dravidian language and Hebrew. Aware of the danger of proving nothing by attempting to prove too much, I content myself with merely stating those analogies, without attempting to deduce any inference from them. The Indo-European analogies are so intimately connected with the individuality and vital essence of the Dravidian languages, that it seems difficult to suppose them to be merely the result of early association, however intimate. It is only on the supposition of the existence of a remote or partial relationship that they appear to be capable of being fully explained. In the case of the Semitic analogies, however, the supposition of a relationship between the two families of tongues does not appear to be necessary. The analogies that appear to exist may be only accidental, or they can be accounted for on the hypothesis—a very easy and natural one—that the primitive Dravidians were at some early period before their arrival in India associated with a people speaking a Semitic language.

It seems proper here to notice the remarkable general resemblance which exists between the Dravidian pronouns and those of the aboriginal tribes of southern and western Australia. In whatever way it may be explained, the existence of a general resemblance seems to be unquestionable; but it has not hitherto been observed that the Australian pronouns of the first person are more nearly allied to the Tibetan than to the Dravidian. This will appear from the following comparative view of the pronoun of the first person singular.

	DRAVIDIAN.	AUSTRALIAN.	TIBETAN.	CHINESE.
I,	*nân, yân, nâ, en,*	*nga, ngaii, ngatsa, nganya,*	*nga, nge, nged,*	*ngo.*

Whilst the base of this pronoun seems to be closely allied to the corresponding pronoun in Tibetan, and in the Indo-Chinese family generally, the manner in which it is pluralised in the Australian dialects bears a marked resemblance to the Dravidian, and especially to Telugu. Telugu forms its plurals by suffixing *lu* to the singular; the Australian dialects by a similar addition of *lu, li, dlu, dli,* &c. In this particular some of the dialects of the north-eastern frontier of India exhibit also an agreement with Telugu—*e.g.,* compare Dhimal *nâ,* thou, with *nyel,* you. In the Australian dialects I find the following plurals and duals of the pronoun of the first person—we, or we two, *ngalu, ngadlu, ngadli, ngalata,* &c. Compare this with the manner in which the Telugu forms its plural—*e.g., vâṅḍ'u,* he, *vâṅḍlu,* they; and even with the Tamil 'plural exclusive' of the pronoun of the first person—*e.g., nân,* I, *nâṅgaḷ,* we.

The resemblance between the Australian pronouns of the second person, both singular and plural, and those of the Dravidian languages is more distinct and special, and is apparent, not only in the suffixes, but in the pronominal base itself. The normal forms of these pronouns in the Dravidian languages are—singular, *nîn,* plural, *nîm.* The personality resides in the crude root *nî*, thou, which is the same in both numbers, with the addition of a singular formative *n* (*nîn*, thou), and a pluralising formative *m* (*nî-m*, thous, or you). In some cases the pluralising particle *m* has been displaced, and *r*, which I regard as properly the sign of the epicene plural of the third person, has been substituted for it—*e.g.*, *nîr*, you (in Telugu *mîr-u*.) This abnormal form *nîr* is most used as a nominative, the older and more regular *nîm* retains its place in the compounds. Whilst *i* is the vowel which is almost invariably found in the singular of the pronoun of the second person, it is found that in the plural *i* often gives place to *u*, as in the classical Tamil *numa*, your, and the Brahui *num*, you. It is to be noticed also that the modern Canarese has softened *nîm* into *nîvu* or *nîwu*, in the nominative. It is singular, in whatever way it may be accounted for, that in each of the particulars now mentioned the Australian dialects resemble the Dravidian. See the following comparative view. Under the Australian head I class the dual together with the plural, as being substantially the same.

	DRAVIDIAN.	AUSTRALIAN.
thou,	*nîn, nin,*	*ninna, nginne, ngintoa, ningte.*
you,	*nîm, nim, nîr, num, nîvu,*	*nimedoo, nura, niwa, ngurle.*

Compare also the accusative of the first person singular in Tamil, *ennei*, me, with the Australian accusative *emmo.*

The grammatical structure of the Australian dialects exhibits a general agreement with the languages of the Scythian group. In the use of postpositions instead of prepositions; in the use of two forms of the first person plural, one inclusive of the party addressed, the other exclusive; in the formation of inceptive, causative, and reflective verbs by the addition of certain particles to the root; and, generally, in the agglutinative structure of words and in the position of words in a sentence, the dialects of Australia resemble the Dravidian—as also the Turkish, the Mongolian, and other Scythian languages; and in the same particulars, with one or two exceptions, they differ essentially from the dialects which are called Polynesian. The vocabularies of the Australian dialects which have been compiled do not appear to furnish additional confirmation to the resemblances pointed out above; but it is difficult to suppose these resemblances to be unreal or merely accidental, and it is obvious that the Australian dialects demand (and probably will reward) further examination.*

* See a paper "On the position of the Australian languages," by W. H. J. Bleek, Esq., Ph.D., read at a meeting of the Anthropological Society. London, 1871.

It is singular also, and still more difficult to be accounted for, that some resemblances may be traced between the Dravidian languages and the Bornu, or rather the Kanuri, one of the languages spoken in the Bornu country, in Central Africa. Most of the resemblances are, it is true, of a general nature—*e.g.*, the Kanuri is agglutinative in structure, it uses postpositions instead of prepositions, it adds to nouns and sentences syllables expressive of doubt, interrogation, and emphasis, in a peculiarly Dravidian manner, and its verb has a negative voice. It has an objective verb, as well as a subjective, like the Hungarian. The most distinctive resemblance to the Dravidian languages I notice is in the pronoun of the second person, which is *nī*, as in each of the Dravidian dialects. Even this, however, as has been shown, is common to the Dravidian with Brahui, Chinese, the language of the second Behistun tablets, and the Australian dialects. The Kanuri language differs so remarkably from the rest of the African tongues, that it is very desirable that its relationship should be fully investigated. See Koelle's "Grammar of Bornu."

Which Language or Dialect best represents the Primitive Condition of the Dravidian Tongues?

Before entering upon the grammatical comparison of the Dravidian dialects, it seems desirable to ascertain where we should look for their earliest characteristics. Some persons have been of opinion that what is called Shen-Tamil (*Śen-Damiṛ*), or the classical dialect of the Tamil language, is to be regarded as the best representative of the primitive Dravidian speech. Without underestimating the great value of the Shen-Tamil, I am convinced that no one dialect can be implicitly accepted as a mirror of Dravidian antiquity. A comparison of all the dialects that exist will be found our best and safest guide to a knowledge of the primitive speech from which the various existing dialects have diverged; and not only the Shen-Tamil, but every existing dialect, even the rudest, will be found to contribute its quota of help towards this end. The Tamil pronouns of the first and second person cannot be understood without a knowledge of Ancient or Classical Canarese; and the Khônd or Ku, one of the rudest dialects, the grammar of which was reduced to writing only a few years ago, is the only dialect which throws light on the masculine and feminine terminations of the Dravidian pronouns of the third person. Still it is unquestionable that the largest amount of assistance towards ascertaining the primitive condition of the Dravidian languages will be afforded by Tamil, and in particular by Shen-Tamil; and this naturally follows from the circumstance that of all the Dravidian idioms Tamil appears to have been the earliest cultivated.

(1.) *Literary, classical dialects of the Dravidian Languages: To what extent may they be regarded as representing the primitive condition of those Languages?*

It is a remarkable peculiarity of the Indian languages that, as soon as they begin to be cultivated, the literary style evinces a tendency to become a literary dialect distinct from the dialect of common life, with a grammar and vocabulary of its own. This is equally characteristic of the speech of the Aryans of the north and of that of the Dravidians of the south. The relation in which Sanskrit stands to the Prâkrits and the modern vernaculars is not identical with the relation in which the *dead* languages of Europe stand to the *living* languages descended from them. The so-called dead languages of Europe were at one time living tongues, spoken nearly as they were written, as, *e.g.*, the speeches of Demosthenes and Cicero testify. When we call those languages dead, we merely mean to describe them as the speech of the dead past, not that of the living present. Sanskrit cannot properly be called a dead language in this sense. Probably it was never the actual, every-day speech of any portion of the Aryans of India at any period of their history, however remote. Its name *Samskṛita*, the elaborated or developed speech, illustrates its origin. It was the language not of any race or district, but of a class—the class of bards and priests, the literary men of the first ages; or rather it was the language of literature; and as literary culture made progress, the language of literature became ever more copious, euphonious, and refined. If life means growth, and if growth means change, Sanskrit must be regarded as having for a long period been, not a dead, but a living tongue; though it must be admitted that it changed slowly, like everything else in India—more slowly, doubtless, than the colloquial dialects. The Sanskrit of the Purâṇas differed from the Sanskrit of the Vedas; and in the Vedas themselves the style of the later hymns differed from that of the earlier. The earliest Sanskrit extant is evidently the result of a process of refinement, originating in the literary activity of a still earlier period, of which no records survive. A composition is not necessarily ancient because written in Sanskrit; for all through the ages, down to very recent times, all the *literati* of Northern and Western India, with the exception of the Buddhists, together with a considerable proportion of the *literati* of the South, have been accustomed to regard Sanskrit as the most orthodox vehicle for the expression of every variety of orthodox thought.

"The great reformer Buddha, in the sixth century before Christ, adopted the popular speech as the vehicle of his teachings; his successors were infected with an unbounded *cacoethes scribendi*, and have left behind a literature of enormous extent. Here again, however, the fatal mistake common to all Indian writers was committed. No sooner had Prâkrit become the language of the Buddhists' scriptures, than it was at once regarded as sacred, and carefully preserved from change or development. It took with regard to the popular speech the same position that Sanskrit had taken in the earlier centuries. This seems to be the fate of all Indian languages: when once committed to writing they assume a literary type, and have a tendency to draw away from the vulgar living tongue of the people. In the present day we see the same process going on in Bengal. Few Bengâlî writers, save those whose minds have been to some extent moulded on English models of thought and feeling, are content to write as they speak. They must have something more elaborate and refined when they take pen in hand, and fill their pages with pompous and artificial Sanskrit words, which they readily admit are not 'understanded of the people.'"

This state of things is not peculiar to Northern India. We find precisely the same tendencies, with the same results, in the South. Each of the four cultivated Dravidian languages has split up into two dialects more or less distinct—a literary, classical dialect; and a popular, colloquial dialect. Classical Canarese is usually called 'Old Canarese;' but it may more properly be regarded neither as new nor as old, but simply as the language of Canarese literature, seeing that it is the language in which literary compositions seem always to have been written, at least from the twelfth century, when Kêśava's grammar was composed, down to the present day. 'Old Malayâḷam' seems to have a better title than Old Canarese to be called 'old,' inasmuch as it contains a considerable number of obsolete forms. Moreover, whilst modern Malayâḷam literature is intensely Sanskritic, the older literature was pervaded with the characteristics of the older or classical Tamil. The language of Telugu poetry differs considerably from that of everyday life, but it is not regarded as a different dialect, or designated by any special name. It is regarded by native Telugu scholars as differing from ordinary Telugu only in being purer and more elevated. The most appropriate name for any of the literary dialects, as it appears to me, is that by which the higher dialect of Tamil is designated. It is called Shen-Tamil (*Śen-Damiṛ*)—that is, classical or correct Tamil, literally 'straight Tamil,' by which name it is meant to be distinguished not merely from the colloquial Tamil of the masses, but still more from certain rude local dialects, said to be twelve in number, mentioned by the grammarians by name, and included under the generic designation of *Koḍun-Damir*—that is literally, 'crooked Tamil.' The name ordinarily given by Europeans to the literary dialect of Tamil is 'High Tamil;' and this appears to me to be a more accurate term, on the whole, than that ordinarily given to the literary dialect of Canarese; for though there is a sense in which each of these literary dialects may be described as 'old,' their most essential characteristic is the extraordinary amount of polish and refinement they have received. Classical Tamil bears nearly the same relation to the actual speech of the people that Sanskrit (that is, classical Indo-Aryan) did to the ancient Prâkrits, and now does to the modern Gaurian vernaculars. Even at the time the oldest extant High Tamil compositions were written, there was probably almost as wide a difference between the language of the vulgar and that affected by the *literati* as there is at present. It is inconceivable that so elaborately refined and euphonised a style of language as that of the classical poems and grammars, can ever have been the actual every-day speech of any class of the people. It contains, it is true, many ancient forms; but forms that had come to be regarded as vulgar by the time that literary culture had commenced (no matter how great their antiquity), seem to have been systematically rejected. The speech of the masses may therefore contain forms and words as old as, or even older than, the corresponding forms and words of the literature; and yet there is an important difference between the two to be borne in mind. No argument in favour of the antiquity of a word or form can be founded merely on the fact of its existence in the colloquial dialect; whereas the existence of a word or form in the classical dialect, especially in the grammars and vocabularies of that dialect, proves at least that it was in existence when that dialect was fixed, which certainly cannot have been less than a thousand years ago. There is an additional presumption in favour of its antiquity in the circumstance that all poets, even the earliest, have been accustomed to regard expressions that were considered more or less archaic in their own time, as peculiarly suitable to poetical compositions.

(2). *High antiquity of the literary cultivation of Tamil.*

The relatively high antiquity of the literary cultivation of Tamil being a matter of interest considered in itself, irrespective of its bearings on the question of Drâvidian comparative grammar, I shall here adduce a few of the evidences on which this conclusion rests.

1. Classical Tamil, which not only contains all the refinements which the Tamil has received, but also exhibits to some extent the primitive condition of the language, differs more from the colloquial Tamil than the classical dialect of any other Dravidian idiom differs from its ordinary dialect. It differs from colloquial Tamil so considerably that it might almost be considered as a distinct language: for not only is classical Tamil poetry as unintelligible to the unlearned Tamilian as the Æneid of Virgil to a modern Italian peasant, but even prose compositions written in the classical dialect might be read for hours in the hearing of a person acquainted only with the colloquial idiom, without his understanding a single sentence. Notwithstanding this, classical Tamil contains less Sanskrit, not more, than the colloquial dialect. It affects purism and national independence; and its refinements are all *ab intra*. As the words and forms of classical Tamil cannot have been invented all at once by the poets, but must have come into use slowly and gradually, the degree in which colloquial Tamil has diverged from the poetical dialect, notwithstanding the slowness with which language, like everything else, changes in the East, seems to me a proof of the high antiquity of the literary cultivation of Tamil.

2. Another evidence consists in the extraordinary copiousness of the Tamil vocabulary, and the number and variety of the grammatical forms of Shen-Tamil. The Shen-Tamil grammar is a crowded museum of obsolete forms, cast-off inflexions, and curious anomalies. Many of these will be pointed out from time to time in the body of this work. I may here refer especially to the extreme and almost naked simplicity of some of the conjugational forms of the oldest Tamil, particularly to the existence of an uninflected form of the verb, and of another form in which only the first rudimentary traces of inflection are seen. These particulars, as will be shown in the Part "on the Verb," seem to me to point to the arrest of the development of the Tamil verb at a very early period by the invention of writing, as in the still more remarkable instance of Chinese. The extraordinary copiousness of the Tamil vocabulary is shown by the fact that a school lexicon of the Tamil language, published by the American missionaries at Jaffna, contains no less than 58,500 words; notwithstanding which, it would be necessary to add several thousands of technical terms, besides provincialisms, and thousands upon thousands of authorised compounds, in order to render the list complete. Nothing strikes a Tamil scholar more, on examining the dictionaries of the other Dravidian dialects, than the paucity of their lists of synonyms in comparison with those of Tamil. The Tamil vocabulary contains not only those words which may be

regarded as appropriate to the language, inasmuch as they are used by Tamil alone, but also those which may be considered as the property of Telugu, Canarese, &c. Thus, the word used for 'house' in ordinary Tamil is *vîḍu;* but the vocabulary contains also, and occasionally uses, the word appropriate to Telugu, *il* (Tel. *illu*), and the distinctive Canarese word, *manei* (Can. *mana*); besides another synonym, *kuḍi*, which it has in common with Sanskrit and the whole of the Finnish languages. The grammar and vocabulary of Tamil are thus to a considerable extent the common repository of Dravidian forms and roots. We may conclude, therefore, that the literary cultivation of Tamil dates from a period prior to that of the other idioms, and not long subsequent to the final breaking up of the language of the ancient Dravidians into dialects.

3. Another evidence of the antiquity and purity of Tamil consists in the agreement of the ancient Canarese, the ancient Malayâḷam, the Tuḷu, and also the Tuḍa, Gôṇḍ, and Ku, with Tamil, in many of the particulars in which modern Canarese and modern Telugu differ from it.

4. The fact that in many instances the forms of Telugu roots and inflexions have evidently been softened down from the forms of Tamil, is a strong confirmation of the higher antiquity of the Tamilian forms. Instances of this will be given in the section on the phonetic system of these languages. It will suffice now to adduce, as an illustration of what is meant, the transposition of vowels in the Telugu demonstrative pronouns. The true Dravidian demonstrative bases are *a*, remote, and *i*, proximate; to which are suffixed the formatives of the genders, with *v* euphonic, to prevent *hiatus*. The Tamil demonstratives are *avan*, ille, and *ivan*, hic. The Telugu masculine formative answering to the Tamil *an*, is *ḍu*, *uḍu*, or *aḍu;* and hence the demonstratives in Telugu, answering to the Tamil *avan*, *ivan*, might be expected to be *avaḍu* and *ivaḍu*, instead of which we find *vâḍu*, ille, and *vîḍu*, hic. Here the demonstrative bases *a* and *i* have shifted from their natural position at the beginning of the word to the middle, whilst by coalescing with the vowel of the formative, or as a compensation for its loss, their quantity has been increased. The altered, abnormal form of the Telugu is evidently the later one; but as even the high dialect of the Telugu contains no other form, the period when the Telugu grammar was rendered permanent by written rules and the aid of written compositions, must have been subsequent to the origin of the corruption in question, and therefore subsequent to the literary cultivation of Tamil.

5. Another evidence of antiquity consists in the great corruption of many of the Sanskrit *tadbhavas* or derivatives found in Tamil.

The Sanskrit contained in Tamil may be divided into three portions of different dates.

(1.) The most recent portion was introduced by the three religious schools which divide amongst them the allegiance of the mass of the Tamil people. These are the school of the S'aiva-Siddhânta, or that of the philosophy of the Âgamas, the most popular system amongst the Tamil S'ûdras, the school of S'aṅkara Âchârya, the apostle of Advaita, and the chief rival of both, the school of S'rî Vaishṇava, founded by Râmânuja Âchârya. The period of the greatest activity and influence of those sects seems to have extended from about the eleventh century, A.D., to the sixteenth; * and the Sanskrit derivatives introduced by the adherents of these systems (with the exception of a few points wherein change was unavoidable) are pure, unchanged Sanskrit.

(2.) The school of writers, partly preceding the above and partly contemporaneous with them, by which the largest portion of the Sanskrit derivatives found in Tamil were introduced, was that of the Jainas, which flourished from about the ninth or tenth century, A.D., to the thirteenth. The period of the predominance of the Jainas (a predominance in intellect and learning—rarely a predominance in political power) was the Augustan age of Tamil literature, the period when the Madura College, a celebrated literary association, appears to have flourished, and when the Kuraḷ, the Chintâmaṇi, and the classical vocabularies and grammars were written. The Sanskrit derivatives found in the writings of this period are very considerably altered, so as to accord with Tamil euphonic rules. Thus *lôka*, Sans. the world, is changed into *ulagu; râjâ*, a king, into *araśu*.

Nearly the whole of the Sanskrit derivatives found in Telugu, Canarese, and Malayâḷam belong to the periods now mentioned, or at least they accord on the whole with the derivatives found in the Tamil

* It appears probable that it was during this period that the great temples of the Carnatic were erected. Those temples, the most stupendous works of the kind in the East, seem to have owed their existence to the enthusiasm and zeal of the adherents of the Śaiva-Siddhânta system. I have not yet been able to ascertain the exact date when any of the more celebrated temples was *erected;* but from inscriptions in my possession recording donations and endowments made to them, I am able to state that the greater number of the Śaiva temples were in existence in the twelfth century, many in the eleventh. I have not ascertained the existence of any Vaishṇava temple in the South before the twelfth century.

of those two periods, especially the former or more recent. They are divided, according to the degree of permutation or corruption to which they have been subjected, into the two classes of *tat-sama*, the same with it—*i.e.*, words which are identical with Sanskrit—and *tad-bhava*, of the same nature with it = derived from it—*i.e.*, words which are derived from a Sanskrit origin, but have been more or less corrupted or changed by local influences. The former class, or *tatsama* words, are scarcely at all altered, and generally look like words which have been used only by Brâhmans, or which had been introduced into the vernaculars at a period when the Sanskrit alphabetical and phonetic systems had become naturalised, through the predominance of the later forms of Hindûism. Sanskrit derivatives of the second class which have been altered more considerably, or *tadbhava* words, do not appear to have been borrowed direct from Sanskrit, but are represented by Telugu and Canarese grammarians themselves as words that have been borrowed from the Prâkrits, or colloquial dialects of the Sanskrit, spoken in ancient times in the contiguous Gaura provinces.

(3.) In addition to the Sanskrit *tatsama* and *tadbhava* derivatives of the two periods now mentioned—the modern Vedantic, Saiva, and Vaishnava periods, and the Jaina period—Tamil contains many derivatives belonging to the very earliest period of the literary culture of the language—derivatives which are probably of an earlier date than the introduction of Sanskrit into the other dialects. The derivatives of this class were not borrowed from the northern Prâkrits (though much more corrupted than even the derivatives borrowed from those Prâkrits by Canarese and Telugu), but appear to have been derived from oral intercourse with the first Brâhmanical priests, scholars, and astrologers, and probably remained unwritten for a considerable time. The Sanskrit of this period is not only greatly more corrupted than that of the period of the Jainas, but its corruptions are of a different character. The Jainas altered the Sanskrit which they borrowed in order to bring it into accordance with Tamil euphonic rules; whereas in the Sanskrit of the period now under consideration—the earliest period—the changes that have been introduced seem to be in utter defiance of rule. The following are instances of derivatives of this class :

(*a.*) The Sans. *śrî*, sacred, was altered into *tiru*, whilst a more recent alteration of the Sanskrit word is into *sirî*, *sirî*, and *sî*.

(*b.*) The Sans. *karman*, a work, is in the Tamil of the more modern periods altered into *karumam* and *kanmam;* but in the older Tamil it was corrupted into *kam*.

(*c.*) Several of the names of the Tamil months supply us with illustrations of early corruptions of Sanskrit. The Tamil months, though now solar-siderial, are named from the old lunar asterisms, the names of which asterisms, and still more the names of the months borrowed from them, are greatly corrupted. *E.g.*, the asterism *pûrva-âshâḍam*, is changed into *pûrâḍam* : *ashâḍam*, also, is changed into *âḍam*, from which is formed *âḍi*, the Tamil name of the month July—August. The name of the asterism *aśvinî* has been corrupted into *eippaśi*, which is the Tamil name of the month October—November. The change of *pûrva bhadra-pada*, the Sanskrit name of one of the asterisms, into *puraṭṭâśi* is still more extraordinary. *Pûrva-bhadra-pada* was first changed into *pûraṭṭâdi*, the name of the corresponding asterism in Tamil; and this, again, by the shortening of the first syllable and the change of *di* into *si*, became *puraṭṭâśi*, the Tamil month September —October. The corresponding names of the asterisms and months in Telugu, Canarese, &c., are pure, unchanged Sanskrit; and hence the greater antiquity of the introduction of those words into Tamil, or at least the greater antiquity of their use in Tamil written compositions, may safely be concluded.

6. The higher antiquity of the literary cultivation of Tamil may also be inferred from Tamil inscriptions. In Karṇâṭaka and Telingâna, every inscription of an early date and the majority even of modern inscriptions are written in Sanskrit. Even when the characters employed are those of the ancient Canarese or Telugu (characters which have been arranged to express the peculiar sounds of Sanskrit), Sanskrit is the language in which the inscription is found to be written, if it is one of any antiquity. In the Tamil country, on the contrary, *all* inscriptions belonging to an early period are written in Tamil; and I have not met with, or heard of, a single Sanskrit inscription in the Tamil country which appears to be older than the fourteenth century A.D., though I have obtained fac-similes of all the inscriptions I could hear of in South Tinnevelly and South Travancore—integral portions of the ancient Pâṇḍyan kingdom. The number of inscriptions I have obtained is about a hundred and fifty. They were found on the walls and floors of temples, and on rocks and pillars. The latest are written in Grantha, or the character in which Sanskrit is written by the Drâviḍa Brâhmans; those of an earlier age either in an old form of the existing Tamil character,* or in a still older character, which appears to

* I have long hoped at some period to make public the items of information contained in those inscriptions, not one of which is included in the inscriptions belonging to the Mackenzie collection of MSS. I may, however, mention here the following results I have arrived at:—1. The generally fictitious character of

have been common to the Tamil and the ancient Malayâḷam countries, and is the character in which the ancient *śâsanas* or documentary tablets in the possession of the Jews at Cochin and of the Syrian Christians in Travancore are written. This character is still used with some variations by the Muhammedan colonists in North Malayâḷam. It presents some points of resemblance to the modern Telugu-Canarese character, and also to the character in which some undeciphered inscriptions in Ceylon and the Eastern Islands are written.* The language of all the more ancient of these inscriptions is Tamil, and the style in which they are written is that of the classical dialect, without any of those double plurals (*e.g.*, *nîṅgal*, yous, instead of *nîr*, you), and other unauthorised novelties by which modern Tamil is disfigured; but it is free also from the affected brevity and involutions of the poetical style. As no inscription of any antiquity in Telingâna or Karṇâṭaka is found to be written in the Canarese or the Telugu *language*, whatever be the *character* employed, the priority of Tamil literary culture, as well as its national independence to a considerable extent, may fairly be concluded.

I may here remark that the Cochin and Travancore *śâsanas* or tablets which are referred to above, and which have been translated by Dr Gundert, prove amongst other things the substantial identity of ancient Malayâḷam with ancient Tamil. The date of these documents is probably not later than the ninth century A.D., nor earlier than the seventh; † for the technical terms of solar-siderial chronology (derived from the Sûrya-Siddhânta of Ârya-bhaṭṭa) which are employed in these

---

the long lists of kings of Madura, each with a high-sounding Sanskrit name, which are contained in the local *Purâṇas* and other legends, and which have been published by Professor Wilson in his "Historical Sketch of the Pandiyan Kingdom," and by Mr Taylor in his "Oriental Historical MSS." 2. The veracity and accuracy of most of the references to the Pâṇḍya and Chôla dynasties contained in the Mahâ-wanso and other historical records and compilations of the Singhalese Buddhists. 3. The fact, or proof of the fact, of the subjection of the whole of the Pâṇḍya country, including South Travancore, to the Chôlas in the eleventh and twelfth centuries. 4. The probable identification of Sundara Pâṇḍya, by whom the Jainas (sometimes erroneously termed Buddhists) were finally expelled from Madura, and whom Professor Wilson has placed in the eighth or ninth century A.D., with the 'Sender Bandi,' who is said by Marco Polo to have been reigning in the southern part of the peninsula during his visit to India in the end of the thirteenth century. The same Sundara Pâṇḍya is placed by native Hindû authorities some thousands of years before the Christian era. See "Relative Antiquity of Dravidian Literature."

* *Journal of the Madras Literary Society*, vol. xiii.

† I here allow the language of the first edition to stand, my conjecture having been found to be very near the mark. See Section on Dravidian Alphabets.

inscriptions were not introduced till the seventh century. The *śâsanas* were written at a time when the Kêrala dynasty was still predominant on the Malabar coast;* but though words and forms which are peculiar to Malayâḷam may be detected in them, the general style of the language in which they are written is Tamil, the inflexions of the nouns and verbs are Tamil, and the idiom is mostly Tamil; and we are therefore led to infer that at that period Tamil was the language at least of the court and of the educated classes in the Malayâḷam country, and that what is now called Malayâḷam, if it then existed at all, was probably nothing more than a patois current amongst the inhabitants of the hills and jungles in the interior. The fact that the *śâsanas* which were given by the ancient Malayâḷam kings to the Jews and Syrian Christians are in the Tamil language, instead of what is now called Malayâḷam, cannot be accounted for by the supposition of the subjection at that time of any part of the Malayâḷam country to the ancient kings of Madura; for the kings in question were Kêrala, not Pâṇḍya kings, with Kêrala names, titles, and insignia; and it is evident from the Greek geographers themselves, from whom alone we know anything of an ancient Pâṇḍya conquest, that it was only a few isolated places, on or near the Malabar coast, that were really under the rule of the Pâṇḍyas. The only part of the Malayâḷam country which at that period could have belonged *bonâ fide* to the Pâṇḍyas, was the southern part of the country of the Aïi or Paralia, *i.e.*, South Travancore, a district which has always been inhabited chiefly by Pâṇḍis, and where to the present day the language of the entire people is Tamil, not Malayâḷam.

From the various particulars mentioned above, it appears clear that the Tamil language was of all the Dravidian idioms the earliest cultivated; it also appears highly probable that in the endeavour to ascer-

---

* One of them is dated "in the thirty-sixth year of King Ravi Varmâ, *opposite the second year*." By this vexed expression, "opposite the second year," Mr Whish supposed that a reference was made to the "second cycle of a thousand years from the building of Quilon," a calculation according to which the present year, 1875, would be the fiftieth of the third cycle; but the same expression is exceedingly common in ancient Tamil inscriptions (*e.g.*, I have found "the seventh year of King Kulaśêkhara *opposite* the fifteenth year"); and it denotes, I conceive, the year of "the cycle of sixty" (which seems to have been at one time the prevailing calculation all over India), to which the year of the king's reign stands "opposite," or answers. Dr Burnell supposes the one year to be that of the king's age, and the other year that of his reign, to which it corresponds; but this supposition would hardly suit those cases where both numbers are under ten. I admit, however, that the year of the cycle of sixty, in all the authentic instances I am acquainted with, cited, not by its number, but by its name.

tain the characteristics of the primitive Dravidian speech, from which the various existing dialects have divaricated, most assistance will be furnished by Tamil. The amount and value of this assistance will appear in almost every portion of the grammatical comparison on which we are about to enter. It must, however, be borne in mind, as has already been intimated, that neither Tamil nor any other single dialect, ancient or modern, can be *implicitly* adopted as a faithful representative of the primitive Dravidian tongue. A careful comparison of the peculiarities of all the dialects will carry us up still further, probably up to the period of their mutual divergence, a period long anterior to that of grammars and vocabularies; and it is upon the result of such a comparison that most dependence is to be placed.

EARLIEST EXTANT WRITTEN RELICS OF THE DRAVIDIAN LANGUAGES.

The Dravidian words which are contained in the Râmâyaṇa, the Mahâ-bhârata, and other Sanskrit poems of undoubted antiquity, are so few that they throw no light whatever upon the ancient condition of the Dravidian languages prior to the ninth or tenth centuries A.D., the earliest date to which any extant Tamil compositions can safely be attributed.

The oldest Dravidian word found in any written record in the world appears to be the word for 'peacock' in the Hebrew text of the Books of Kings and Chronicles, in the list of the articles of merchandise brought from Tarshish or Ophir in Solomon's ships, about 1000 B.C. This word is *tuki* in Kings, *tûki* in Chronicles. The ordinary name at present for the peacock on the Malabar coast and in Tamil is *mayil* (Sans. *mayûra*); it is also sometimes called *śiki* (Sans. *śikhi*), a name given to it on account of its crest; but the ancient, poetical, purely Tamil-Malayâḷam name of the peacock is *tôkei*, the bird with the (splendid) tail. *Śikhi = avis cristata; tôkei = avis caudata.* The verbal root of the word *tôkei* is *tok'* or *tôk'*, *tuk* or *tûk'*, to hang; hence 'a scarf,' 'a skirt border,' is called *tôkkei.* The vowel of the root librates between *u* and *o:* half the derivatives have the one vowel, half the other. Hence there is no reason to suppose the Phœnicians in error when they represented *tuk* as the radical part of the word. That the vowel is short in Kings and long in Chronicles is also quite in accordance with the fact that in Tamil-Malayâḷam the vowel is sometimes short, sometimes long.

Though *tôkei*, as a verbal noun, is a derivative from *tôk'* or *tûk'*, yet the ultimate root appears to have been *to* or *tu.* Judging from analogy, the final *k'* or *ku* must have been a formative. A primary root with this addition becomes a verbal noun, and in the next stage of the language this verbal noun becomes in its turn a new, secondary verbal root. It is interesting to be able to trace the use of this Tamil-Malayâḷam formative *k'* or *ku* so early as the time of the Phœnician trade with India. Max Müller, speaking of this etymology (Lect. p. 209), remarks: "If this etymology be right, it would be an important confirmation of the antiquity of the Tamulic languages spoken in India before the advent of the Aryan tribes." I have no doubt that this etymology is right, and that the inference deduced from it is well founded. It may here be added that from the Dravidian *tôkei*, pronounced *tôgei*, would naturally be derived the Arabic *tawas*, the Greek ταῶς, and ultimately the Latin *pâvo* and our own *pea*-fowl. Minayeff has discovered in the Buddhistical writings a reference to voyages made by ancient Indian merchants to Babylon (called 'Baverû' = Old Cuneiform Persian 'Babiru'), in the second of which voyages they took thither the first *peacock* for sale. (See paper by Professor Weber in the *Indian Antiquary* for May 1873).

Of the names of the other articles of merchandise mentioned in Kings and Chronicles, *kôf*, an ape, has generally been identified with the Sanskrit *kapi*; and the Greek κῆπος, and even the English *ape*, have been supposed to have the same origin. It seems more probable, however, that the word has been derived from the old Egyptian *kâf*, an ape, a word which Mr Le Page Renouf informs me is in very common use in Egyptian inscriptions, and which he says is to all appearance as ancient as the language itself. The origin of the word used for 'ivory' (*shen habbim*, the tooth of the *habb*) still seems to me somewhat doubtful. On the whole, the most probable derivation seems to be from the old Egyptian *ab*, ivory. *Algum* may perhaps be the Sanskrit *valguka*, sandal wood, another meaning of which is 'beautiful,' a word which seems to be identical with, or derived from, the Tamil-Malayâḷam *aṛagu* or *aḷagu*, beauty. If so, *algum* will be more correct than *almug*. The fragrant wood called 'aloes' in Proverbs vii. 17, &c., was the Aquilaria Agallocha, the Hebrew word for which, *ahalim* or *ahaloth*, is evidently derived rather from the Tamil-Malayâḷam form of the word, *aghil*, than from the Sanskrit *agaru*, though both are ultimately identical.

The Greek word ὄρυζα, rice, must be one of considerable antiquity. It dates from the period, whenever that was, when rice was first introduced from India into Europe; and it cannot be doubted that we have here the Tamil word *ariśi*, rice deprived of the husk, this being the condition in which rice was then, as now, bought up in India for exportation to Europe. The distinctively Malayâḷam form of the word, *ari*, seems a corruption.

The earliest Dravidian word in Greek of which we know the date is *κάρπιον*, Ctesias's name for cinnamon. Herodotus describes cinnamon "as the *κάρφεα* (dry sticks), which we, after the Phœnicians, call *κιννάμωμον*." Liddell and Scott say, *in loc.* *κάρφος*, plural *καρφεα*, "this word bears a curious resemblance to the Arabic words *kerfat*, *kirfah*." This resemblance, however, must, I think, be accidental, seeing that Herodotus considered 'cinnamon' alone as a foreign word, and that *καρφος* is naturally derived from *κάρφω*, to wither. The word mentioned by Ctesias seems, however, to have a real resemblance to the Arabic word, and also to a Dravidian one. Ctesias, the author of the earliest Greek treatise on India, describes an odorous oil produced from an Indian tree having flowers like the laurel, which the Greeks called *μυροζόδα*, but which in India was called *κάρπιον*. From Ctesias's description (making allowance for its exaggerations) it is evident that cinnamon oil was meant, and in this opinion Wahl agrees. Uranius, a writer quoted by Stephen of Byzantium, mentions *κέρπαθον* as one of the productions of the Abasêni, the Arabian Abyssinians, by which we are doubtless to understand not so much the products of their country as the articles in which they traded. From the connection in which it is found, *κέρπαθον* would appear to be cinnamon, and we can scarcely err in identifying with it *kerfat*, or, more properly, *kirfah*, one of the names which cinnamon has received in Arabic. Some Arabic scholars derive *kirfah* from *karafa*, 'decortavit;' but Mr Hassoun does not admit this derivation, and considers *kirfah* a foreign word. We are thus brought back to Ctesias's *κάρπιον*, or the Indian word which *κάρπιον* represented. As this is a word of which we know the antiquity, the supposition that the Greeks or Indians borrowed it from the Arabs is quite inadmissible. What then is the Indian word Ctesias referred to? Not, as has been supposed, *kurundhu*, the Singhalese name for cinnamon, derived from the Sanskrit *kuruṇṭa;* but the Tamil-Malayâḷam word *karuppu* or *kârppu*—*e.g.*, *karappa-(t)tailam*, Mal. oil of cinnamon. Other forms of this word are *karappu*, *karuva*, and *karuvâ*, the last of which is the most common form in modern Tamil. Rheede refers to this form of the word when he says that "in his time in Malabar oils in high medical estimation were made from both the root and the leaves of the *karua* or wild cinnamon of that coast."

There are two meanings of *karu* in Tamil-Malayâḷam, 'black' and 'pungent,' and the latter doubtless supplies us with the explanation of *karuppu*, 'cinnamon.' A word with a related meaning to this is *karukku*, 'a medicinal preparation.' This name may have been given to cinnamon from what has been described as 'the sweet *burning* taste' of the bark, and especially of the oil. Wild cinnamon grows freely in Malabar, in the very region in which Ctesias's name for it, and the name adopted by the Arabians, is still in use. The cinnamon now grown in Ceylon is, it is true, of a much finer quality, but it is doubtful whether the cultivation of it had been introduced into Ceylon at that early period, and even if it had, it should be remembered that Ctesias, who derived all his information about India from Persian and Babylonian merchants, seems to have known nothing of Ceylon. I have little doubt that the Sanskrit *karpûra*, 'camphor,' is substantially the same as the Tamil-Malayâḷam *karuppu* and Ctesias's κάρπιον, seeing that it does not seem to have any root in Sanskrit, and that camphor and cinnamon are nearly related. The camphor of commerce is from a cinnamon tree, the *camphora officinarum*. If the identity of Ctesias's word with the Tamil-Malayâḷam *karuppa* be admitted, it follows that we have here the earliest Dravidian word quoted by the Greeks, and that at that early time Tamil roots were sometimes converted into verbal nouns by the addition of the formative *pu*, as they are at present, just as we have seen in the Hebrew *tûki*, the alternative formative *ku* or *kei*, used, as at present, for the same purpose.

It is a remarkable circumstance that the largest stock of primitive Dravidian words contained in any written documents of ancient times —the earliest authentic extant traces of the existence of the Dravidian languages, as distinguished from Sanskrit — are those which are found in the notices of the Greek geographers Ptolemy and the author of the "Periplus Maris Erythræi;" including also the "Natural History" of Pliny. Many of the names of places and tribes recorded by those geographers, not long after the commencement of the Christian era, are identical, letter for letter, with the names now in use. Several of those names have become obsolete, or cannot now be identified; but the signification of the compound words of which they consist is generally apparent, and in several of them we can detect the operation of some interesting dialectic peculiarity or euphonic rule which is still characteristic of these languages. I subjoin a few examples of Dravidian words of this class recorded by the Greeks, beginning with the names of Dravidian peoples and princes.

(1.) ὁ Πανδίων—ἡ χώρα Πανδιόνων (Κανδιόνων is evidently an error)—the Pâṇḍya king and people. This name is, as we have seen, of Sanskrit origin, and Pandæ, the form which Pliny, after Megasthenes, gives in his list of Indian nations, comes very near the Sanskrit. The more recent local information of Pliny himself, as well as the notices of

Ptolemy and the Periplus, supply us with the Draviḍian form of the word. The Tamil sign of the masculine singular is *an*, and Tamil inserts *i* euphonically after *ṇḍ*, consequently Πανδίων, and still better, the plural form of the word Πανδιόνες faithfully represents the Tamil masculine singular Pâṇḍiyan. Ptolemy is quite correct in giving the same name to the people and their prince. The people were Pâṇḍyas, the prince *the* Pâṇḍya, or the Pâṇḍya-dêva. The form of the masculine singular in ancient Canarese, corresponding to the Tamil *an*, is *am;* in Telugu it is *uḍu*, so that Pâṇḍiyuḍu in Telugu answers to Pâṇḍiyan in Tamil. Consequently we learn, that as early as the Christian era, Tamil differed dialectically from the other Dravidian idioms, and in particular that its mode of forming the masculine singular was then the same as it is now. We also learn from the expression Μόδουρα βασίλειον Πανδιόνος that the Pâṇḍyas had transferred their capital from Kolkei on the Tâmraparṇî to Madura on the Veigei (or Vêghavatî) before the Christian era. Μόδουρα itself (in Pliny Modura) is the Sanskrit Mathurâ, pronounced in the Tamil manner. The corresponding city in Northern India, Muttra, is written by the Greeks Μέθορα.

(2.) ὁ Κηροβόθρος. The prince called by this name by Ptolemy is called ὁ Κηπροβότρος by the author of the Periplus. The insertion of π is clearly an error, but more likely to be an error of a copyist than that of the author, who himself had visited the territories of the prince in question. He is called Cælobothras in Pliny's text, but one of the MSS. gives it more correctly as Celobotras. The name in Sanskrit, and in full, is *Keralaputra*, but both *Kêra* and *Kêḷa* are Dravidian abbreviations of *Kêrala*. They are Malayâḷam, however, not Tamil abbreviations; and the district over which Keralaputra ruled is that in which the Malayâḷam language is now spoken.

(3.) Σῶραι νομάδες—'Αρκατου βασίλειον Σῶρα—"Ορθουρα βασίλειον Σώρναγος—Παραλία Σωρητῶν (or Σωριγῶν); also Παραλία Τωριγγῶν (which should evidently have been Σωρίγγῶν, seeing that it included the mouth of the river Χαβήρος). Without entering here on any minute topographical discussions with regard to details, it seems evident to me that the word Σῶρα, which we meet alone and in various combinations in these notices, represents the name of the northern portion of the Tamilian nation. This name is *Chôla* in Sanskrit, *Chôḷa* in Telugu; but in Tamil *Sôṛa* or *Chôṛa*. Ptolemy's accuracy, or rather perhaps that of his informants, with regard to the name of this people is remarkable; for in Tamil they appear not only as *Sôṛas*, but also as *Sôṛagas* and *Sôṛiyas*, and even as *Sôṛiṅgas*; their country also is called *Sôṛagam*. The *ṛ* of the Tamil word *Sôṛa* is a peculiar sound, not contained in Telugu, in which it is generally represented by *ḍ*, nor in Sanskrit and Pali, in which it is represented by *ḍ* or *ḷ*. The transliteration of this letter by the Greeks as ρ seems to show that then, as now, the use of this peculiar *ṛ* was a dialectic peculiarity of Tamil. The Indian equivalent of the name of the king Sornax has not survived (as those of ὁ Πανδίων and ὁ Κηροβόθρος have), and it is fruitless to guess what it may have been; but as we know from native poems that the name of the ancient capital of the Sôṛas was Ureiyûr (pronounced Oreiyûr), we may safely identify this name with Ptolemy's "Ορθουρα, the capital of the Παραλία Σωρητῶν.

(4.) 'Αρκατοῦ βασίλειον Σῶρα. "Αρκατος is here represented, not as a country, people, or city, but as the name of a prince. As General Cunningham has pointed out, Σῶρα is represented as the name of a city, where a king called "Αρκατος reigned. Though this was evidently Ptolemy's meaning, yet one is strongly tempted to suppose that here the names given by the natives of the country to his informants had got transposed. The name Σῶρα is identical with that of the people of the district, whom Ptolemy himself calls Σῶραι νομαδες, and "Αρκατος answers exceedingly well, in situation as well as in sound, to Arcot, the capital of the Carnatic in Muhammedan times. There is a distinct tradition that the inhabitants of that part of the Chôla or Sôṛa country which lies between Madras and the Ghauts, including Arcot as its centre, were Kurumbars or wandering shepherds—nomads—for several centuries after the Christian era. General Cunningham objects to this identification that Arcot is quite a modern name; but it must, as Colonel Yule has pointed out, be at least as old as 1340 A.D., for it is mentioned by Ibn Batuta. The name is properly *âr'-kâḍ'*, Tam. the six forests, and the Hindûs of the place regard it as an ancient city, though not mentioned by name in the Purāṇas, and point out the 'six forests' in which six of the *rishis* of the ancient period had their hermitages. If this identification be admitted, we have here another instance of the antiquity of the dialectic peculiarities of Tamil, for the oblique form of the word *kâḍ'* is *kâṭṭ'*, and the word ordinarily used in Telugu for forest is not *kâḍ'*, but *aḍavi* or *aṭavi*.

(5.) Κάρουρα βασίλειον Κηροβόθρου. Karûr is mentioned in Tamil traditions as the ancient capital of the Chêra, Kêra, or Kêrala kings, and is generally identified with Karûr, an important town in the Coimbatore district, originally included in the Chera kingdom. *Karûr* means the black town, and I consider it identical with *Kâṛagam* and *Kaḍâram*, names of places which I have frequently found in inscriptions in the Tamil country, and which are evidently the poetical equivalents of *Karûr*. The meaning of each of the names is the same. Ptolemy's word Κάρουρα represents the Tamil name of the place with perfect accuracy; *kar* means black, and *ûr* (sometimes pronounced *ûr-u*), a town. Neither of these words seems to have altered in the least in sound or signification for 1800 years.

(6.) *Modogalingam nomine*, Pliny. I have already, in p. 32, discussed the meaning of this name. I add here that if *modo* be regarded as a Telugu word, meaning three, we have here an interesting illustration of the antiquity of Dravidian dialectic peculiarities; for three is in Telugu *mûḍu*, in Tamil *mûndru*, in Canarese *mûru*, in Tuḷu *mûji.*

(7.) *Damirice*, and also *Scytia Dymirice*, Peutinger Tables; *Dimirica*, in the Ravenna Cosmography, see p. 14. The Dymir of Dymirice was supposed by Dr Burnell to represent the word Tamir, and if so, the Damir of Damirice will come still nearer thereto. The portion of the Malabar coast immediately to the north of Dymirice is called, by Ptolemy and the author of the "Periplus," Ἀριακη, and it seems probable that this was the district to which the name of Âryaka was given by Varâha-mihira several centuries afterwards (*Journal of the Royal Asiatic Society*, vol. v.) It appears probable, therefore, that the difference between the Aryans and the Dravidians can be traced in the names given by the Greeks to those portions of the Malabar coast which we know from other sources of information have always been inhabited by Aryans and Dravidians respectively.

(8.) I content myself with simply noting the following names of places on the Malabar coast. Μουζιρὶς appears to be the Muyiri of Muyiri-cotta; Τύνδις is Tuṇḍi; and the Kynda of Nelkynda (or as Ptolemy has it Μέλ-Κυνδα, *i.e.*, probably Western Kynda) seems to be Kannettri, the southern boundary of Kêrala proper. One MS. of Pliny writes the second part of this word not cyndon, but canidon. The first of these places was identified by Dr Gundert; for the remaining two we are indebted to Dr Burnell.

(9.) Cottonara, Pliny; Κοττοναρικῆ, Perip.; the district where the best pepper was produced. It is singular that this district was not mentioned by Ptolemy. Cottonara was evidently the name of the district; κοττονάρικον, the name of the pepper for which the district was famous. Dr Buchanan identifies Cottonara with Kaḍatta-nâḍu, the name of a district in the Calicut country celebrated for its pepper. Dr Burnell identifies it with Koḷatta-nâḍu, the district about Tellicherry, which he says is *the* pepper district. *kaḍatta*, in Malayâḷam, means transport, conveyance; *nâḍu*, Tam.-Mal., means a district.

(10.) Σάνγαρα. The author of the "Periplus" calls by this name the canoes formed out of single trees, in which pepper was brought from Cottonara to Barace. The Malayâḷam name of these boats is *changâḍam*, Tuḷu *jangâla*. Compare Sanskrit *samghâḍam*, a raft. I have never been able to explain κολανδιόφωντα, the name of the large vessels that sailed from the western coast to Ceylon and the Ganges.

(11.) Κοττιάρα. This is the name of a place in the country of the Ἄιοι of Ptolemy, in the Παραλία of the author of the "Periplus," identical in part with South Travancore. Apparently it is the Cottora of Pliny, and I have no doubt that it is the Cottara of the Peutinger Tables. It is not to be confounded with Cottonara, the place mentioned above. It is called by Ptolemy Κοττιάρα Μητρόπολις, and must have been a place of considerable importance. The town referred to is probably *Kôttâr-u*, or as it is ordinarily written by Europeans, Kotaur, the principal town in South Travancore, and now, as in the time of the Greeks, distinguished for its commerce. The name of the place is derived from *kôḍ-u*, Tam.-Mal. a fort, and *âr-u*, a river. It is a rule both in Tamil and in Malayâḷam that when a word like *kôḍ'* is the first member of a compound, the final *ḍ* must be doubled for the purpose of giving the word the force of an adjective: it is another rule that sonants when doubled become surds. Consequently the compound *kôḍ-u —âr-u* becomes by rule *Kôtt-âr-u*. If the identification of the place be correct, as it appears to me to be, we find here an interesting proof that in the time of the Greeks the same phonetic rules were in operation as now.

(12.) Κομάρια ἄκρον, Ptol.; Κομὰρ, Κομαρεὶ, Perip. Cape Comorin has derived its name from the Sanskrit *kumârî*, a virgin, one of the names of the goddess Durgâ, the presiding divinity of the place; but the shape this word has taken, especially in Κομὰρ, is distinctively Tamilian. In ordinary Tamil *kumârî* becomes *kumări;* and in the vulgar dialect of the people residing in the neighbourhood of the Cape, a virgin is neither *kumârî* nor *kumări*, but *kŭmăr*, pronounced *kŏmăr*. It is remarkable that this vulgar corruption of the Sanskrit is identical with the name given to the place by the author of the "Periplus." He says, "After this there is another place called Κομὰρ, where there is a βριάριον (probably Φρούριον, a fort; ἱερὸν is less likely), and a harbour, where also people come to bathe and purify themselves, . . . for it is related that a goddess was once accustomed to bathe there monthly." This monthly bathing in honour of the goddess Durgâ is still continued at Cape Comorin, but is not practised to the same extent as in ancient times. Kumârî formerly ranked as one of the five renowned sacred bathing places, a representation which accords with the statement of the author of the "Periplus." Through the continued encroachments of the sea, the harbour the Greek mariners found at Cape Comorin, and the fort (if that were meant) have completely disappeared; but a fresh-water well remains in the centre of a rock a little way out at sea. It is singular that Cape Comorin does not appear in any shape in the Peutinger Tables.

(13.) Παραλία. There are three Paralias mentioned by the Greeks, two by Ptolemy (the Paralia of the Soreti, and the Paralia properly so called, that of the Toringi), one by the author of the "Periplus." The Paralia mentioned by the latter corresponded to Ptolemy's country of the Ἄιοι and that of the Καρεοι, that is, to South Travancore and South Tinnevelly. It commenced at the Red Cliffs, south of Quilon, and included not only Cape Comorin, but also Κόλχοι, where the pearl fishing was carried on, and which belonged to King Pandion. Dr Burnell identifies Παραλία with Puraḷi, which he states is an old name for Travancore, but I am not quite able to adopt this view. It is true that, if the Greeks found any part of the Travancore coast called Puraḷi, they would naturally proceed to convert that name into a word of their own, bearing an intelligible and appropriate meaning; but, on the other hand, it is not clear that any part of the coast was ever called by that name. *Puraḷi* is stated by Dr Gundert ("Malayâḷam Dictionary" *in loc.*) to be the name of a fort belonging to the old kings of *Kôṭṭayagam* in the interior. Hence *Puraḷîśan*, lord of Puraḷi, was one of the titles of those kings. This title is now poetically applied to the kings of Travancore; but it seems probable that it was adopted by them at a comparatively late period, on their gaining possession of the territory to which the title belonged, in the same manner as they adopted the title of *Vanji-bhûpati*, lord of Vanji, a name of Karûr, the ancient Chera or Kerala capital. It is also to be remembered that the Paralia of the "Periplus" included not only the coast of South Travancore, but also the coast of Tinnevelly as far as Kolkei. It appears to me, therefore, that Παραλία is to be taken as a Greek word, though possibly it may have corresponded in meaning, if not in sound, to some native word meaning coast. This will appear probable from the next item.

(14.) οἱ Καρεοι. The Careï of Ptolemy inhabited the southern portion of Tinnevelly, between Cape Comorin and Kolkei; consequently their country constituted the eastern portion of the Paralia of the "Periplus." *Karei* is the Tamil word for coast or shore, from the verbal theme *karei*, to be melted down, to be washed away, and is obviously identical in meaning with the Greek Παραλία. Up to the present time several portions of the Tinnevelly coast (including that part where I have myself lived and laboured for more than thirty years) are called *Karei*, the coast, or *Karei-(ch)chuttru*, the coast circuit, and a caste of fishermen further north are called *Kareiyâr*, coast-people. There cannot be any doubt that the last portion of two names of places mentioned by Ptolemy represents the Tamil *karei*, coast, viz., Καλαικαρίας and Περιγκαρεῖ. If the latter word had been written Περυγκαρεῖ, it would have been perfectly accurate Tamil, letter for letter. The meaning is great shore; and *perum*, great, becomes *perung* before *k* by rule. *perum* itself, instead of *peru*, is a distinctively classical form.

(15.) ἡ Σωλήν. The Tâmraparṇî, the chief river in Tinnevelly, must be the river intended to be denoted by Ptolemy by this name, for it is the only river mentioned by him between Cape Comorin and the Kâvêrî, and it entered the sea south of Κόλχοι, the emporium of the pearl trade, which was certainly at the mouth of the Tâmraparṇî. It is difficult, however, to explain how it came to be called Σωλήν. This word means in Greek a shell-fish, a mussel; and it seems uncertain whether the Greeks called the river by this name, because the native name of it somewhat resembled this, or because of the fishing for chanks, as well as pearls, then as now, carried on at its mouth. The name by which the river seems always to have been called in India is Tâmraparṇî, a name which bears no resemblance whatever to Solen. In Tamil poetry it is often called the Porunei, which is merely a Tamilisation of the second portion of its Sanskrit name. *Tâmraparṇî*. Sans., would naturally mean the tree with red or copper leaves; applied to a river, it would seem to mean the river which resembles a red leaf. It is called by this name in the Mahâ-bhârata, though whether the passage in which it is mentioned is older than Ptolemy may be regarded as uncertain. The name Tâmra-parṇî being identical with the oldest name of Ceylon—Tâmbapaṇṇi in Pâli, Ταπρόβανη in Greek—it might have been supposed, if the river had been called by this name in the time of the Greeks, that they would have called it the Taprobane, the name by which they called Ceylon. Solen cannot have any connection with Sylaur, erroneously represented in Lassen as the name of the principal tributary of the Tâmraparṇî. This tributary is called the Chitra-nadî, commonly the Chittâr, which means in Tamil the small river, and it is physically impossible that it ever can have been, as Lassen conjectured, the principal stream, the mountain district it drains being very much smaller than that which the Tâmraparṇî drains.

(16.) Βηττιγώ. This, according to Ptolemy, was the name of the mountain range in which the Σωλήν—the Tâmraparṇî—took its rise, in addition to two rivers on the western coast, the Βάρις and Ψευδόστομος. The mountain range meant is evidently that of the Southern Ghauts—that is, the range of mountains stretching from the Coimbatore gap to Cape Comorin. The Tâmraparṇî rises in a beautiful conical mountain included in this range, visible from the mouth of the river, and visible also from Κόλχοι, the emporium frequented by the Greeks. When the Greeks asked where the river took its rise, they would naturally be directed to this conspicuous mountain, and on learning its name would naturally give the same name to the whole range. This mountain is commonly called by the English Agastier—that is, the *rishi* Agastya's hill—Agastya being supposed to have finally retired thither from the world after civilising the Dravidians; but the true Tamil name of the mountain is *Podigei,* pronounced *Pothigei* (the *Podiyam* of the poets) or *Peria* (the greater) *Podigei,* in contradistinction to a smaller mountain in the same neighbourhood. The root meaning of *podi* being 'to cover,' 'to conceal,' *podigei* may have meant 'a place of concealment;' but, whatever may have been its meaning, it seems to come as near the Greek Βηττιγώ as could be expected.

(17.) Κόλχοι ἐμπόριον. This place is mentioned both by Ptolemy and by the author of the "Periplus," both of whom agree in representing it as the headquarters of the pearl-fishery, and as belonging to King Pandion. It was the first place east of Cape Comorin frequented by the Greeks, and was situated to the north of the river Solen. It is one of the few places in India mentioned in the "Peutinger Tables," where it is called 'Colcis Indorum.' From the name of this place the Gulf of Manaar was called by the Greeks the Colchic Gulf. The Tamil name of the place is almost identical with the Greek. It is Kolkei; and though this is now euphonically pronounced *Korkei,* through the change of *l* before *k* into **r** by rule, yet it is still pronounced *Kolka* in Malayâḷam, and I have found it written *Kolkei* in an old Tamil inscription in the temple at Trichendoor. Doubtless it was so pronounced in the time of the Greeks, when euphonic refinements could not have advanced very far. Ko**r**kei is well known in Tamil traditions as the place where the germs of civil government made their first appearance amongst the Tamilians—the government set up in common by the three mythical-patriarchal brothers, *Śêran, Śôṛan,* and *Pâṇḍiyan.* Vîra-Râma, the poet-king, one of the later Pâṇḍyas, in a little poem called "Vettri-vêṟkei," styles himself *Korkei(y)âḷi*—that is, 'ruler of Korkei.' This place is now about three miles inland, but there are abundant traces of its having once stood on the coast, and I have found the tradition that it was once the seat of the pearl-fishery still surviving amongst its inhabitants. After the sea had retired from Κόλχοι, in consequence of the silt deposited by the river, a new emporium arose on the coast, which was much celebrated during the middle ages. This was Kâyal (meaning in Tamil 'the lagoon'), the Cael of Marco Polo. (See Colonel Yule's "Marco Polo," vol. ii.) Kâyal in turn became in time too far from the sea for the convenience of trade, and Tuticorin

(*Tûttrukuḍi*) was raised instead by the Portuguese from the position of a fishing village to that of the most important port on the southern Coromandel coast. The pearl-oyster has nearly disappeared now, I am sorry to say, from the coast, and the staple trade of Tuticorin has long been, not pearls, but cotton. The identification of Κόλχοι with Kolkei is one of much importance. Being perfectly certain, it helps forward other identifications. *Kol* in Tamil means 'to slay;' *kei*, is 'hand.' The meaning of *Kolkei*, therefore, is 'the hand of slaughter,' which is an old poetical term in Tamil for 'an army,' 'a camp,' the first instrument of government in a rude age. In so far as the two words included in this name are concerned, the Tamil language does not seem to have altered in the slightest from that day to this. The junction of the words has been euphonised, but the words themselves remain the same.

(18.) Κῶρυ. Ptolemy describes Κῶρυ as an island in the Argaric Gulf, or Palk's Straits. Elsewhere he describes it as a promontory, and correctly, for it was both—if it is to be identified, as I have no doubt it is, with Râmêśvaram, a long narrow island terminating in a long spit of land. The bay between Point Calymere and the island of Râmêśvaram is called 'Rama's bow,' and each end is called *Dhanu kôti*, 'the tip of the bow,' or simply *kôṭi* (in Tamil *kôḍi*), 'the tip,' 'end,' or 'corner.' The most celebrated of the two *kôḍis* was that at Râmêś-varam, and this word *kôḍi* would naturally take the form of *kôri* or *kôru*. The ease with which this change might take place is shown by the fact that it is this very word *kôṭi* which is meant when we speak of the high number called by the English a *crore*. It is remarkable that the Portuguese, without knowing anything about the Κῶρυ of the Greeks, called the same spit of land Cape Ramana*coru*.

(19.) Καλλιγικόν. According to Ptolemy, Κῶρυ, the Râmêśvaram spit of land, was also called Καλλιγικόν, but it seems probable that he was mistaken in this identification, and that we are to understand by Καλλιγικόν the promontory called Calingon by Pliny, by which it appears to me that Point Calymere was meant. The circumstance that there were two places called Κῶρυ—that is, two ends of the bow—one of which was at Point Calymere, seems to show how Ptolemy's informants may have come to speak of Κῶρυ as also called Καλλιγικόν. The Tamil name of Point Calymere is *Kaḷḷi-mêḍu*,—that is, 'the euphorbia eminence,'—and it seems probable that the Greek καλλι and the Tamil *kaḷḷi* are identical.

(20.) Κῶλις. In the various Greek and Roman geographers prior to the time of Ptolemy, the name Κῶλις occupies an important place. It appears first (in the shape of an appellative) in Strabo, who speaks of Ceylon as seven days' sail from the southernmost part of India, the inhabitants of which he calls Κωλίακοι; but it is probable that Strabo herein follows Onesicritus, a writer three centuries older, who represented Ceylon (Taprobane) as twenty days' sail from the same place. Pomponius Mela calls it Colis. Pliny, who reduces the number of days' sail from Ceylon to four, calls the place Coliacum, and describes it as the promontory of India which was nearest Ceylon, between which and it there was a shallow coral sea. Dionysius Periegetes, who brings Κῶλις into greater prominence than any other writer, transfers to it (by a poetical licence) the description of Aornis near the Indus, given by the writers of Alexander's period, and gives to Ceylon itself a name which seems to be derived from Κῶλις—viz., Κωλιας. In Ptolemy Κῶλις disappears, and Κῶρυ, a name previously unknown, comes up instead. I have no doubt that the words Κῶλις and Κῶρυ are identical, and that the places denoted by these names were one and the same—viz., the island-promontory of Râmêśvaram, the point of land from which there was always the nearest access from Southern India to Ceylon. The geographical knowledge of the present time might naturally wish to identify Κῶλις with Cape Comorin, as the southernmost point of India; but in the times preceding Ptolemy (*e.g.*, in the "Peutinger Tables") what we now call Cape Comorin was not known to be a cape; and the Cape Comorin of the period (that is, what was supposed to be the southernmost point of the Indian continent) was *Kôṭi*, or Râmêśvaram, the point from which the passage to Ceylon (Rama's or Adam's bridge, the Ma'bar of the Arabians) was most easily made. I do not consider Κῶλις a corruption of Κῶρυ. On the contrary, I regard both names as equally representing the same word. *Kôṭi*, 'the end of the bow,' 'the angle,'—that is, the angle or corner of the bay (the Argaric Gulf) lying between Point Calymere and the island of Râmêśvaram. Pomponius Mela regarded it as an 'angulus,' not of that bay merely, but of India, viewed as a whole. He supposed it to be the termination towards the east of the southern coast, which extended thus far in a straight line nearly due east and west from the Indus! Κῶλι-ς seems to me somewhat nearer the Indian original *Kôṭi* or *Kôḍi*, than Κῶρυ; and the change of the Sanskrit *ḍ* into the Tamilian *ṛ* or *ḷ*, we have already seen exemplified in the change of the *ḍ* of Draviḍ into the *ṛ* or *ḷ* of *Tamiṛ* or *Tamiḷ*.

(21.) *Malli, quorum Mons Maleus;* Pliny. This mountain seems to have been to the north of the country of the Calingas, and General Cunningham identifies it with Mahêndra Male in Ganjam. It is difficult to determine the situation of the places in India mentioned in Pliny; but it seems certain that, wherever the Mons Maleus may have been, its name embodied the well-known Dravidian word (which we see also in the Sanskrit *Malaya*) *malei*, 'a mountain.' The name of the people was probably derived from the same word, and signified, like the Tamil *maleiyar* and the Râjmahâl *Mâler* or *Maler*, 'mountaineers.'

(22.) It may be noticed that the rendering of the Sanskrit *Buddha* by Clemens Alexandrinus as Βούττα, and his rendering of the Sanskrit *śramaṇa* (Buddhistic ascetics) by Σεμνοί, accord better with the Tamil forms of these words (*Putta* and *Śamaṇa*) than with the Sanskrit originals.

(23.) It is remarkable how many names of places in Southern India mentioned by Ptolemy end in ουρ or ουρα, 'town.' There are twenty-three such places in all. The following are examples:—Σαλούρ, Κορέουρα, Ποδοπέρουρα, Παλούρα, 'Αρεμβούρ, Μαγούρ, Μαντιττούρ, Κορινδιούρ. In addition to these there is Καρούρα mentioned already. It is scarcely possible to doubt that Ποδοπέρουρα means *pudu-per-ûr*, 'new great-town;' or Παλουρα, *pâl-ûr*, 'milk-town.' Probably a letter or two in the rest may have been changed, so that we cannot be quite certain what they meant, except the places should be identified, which has not yet been done; but they *sound* wonderfully Tamil-like. The conjunctions of consonants (*nt*, *nd*, *mb*, *tt*) are exactly such as Tamil loves.

Some of the names of places mentioned by Ptolemy prove that the Brâhmans had by that time established themselves at various points in the Carnatic, and given names to some of the principal localities. Μόδουρα, Madura, is a Sanskrit word; so also is Πανδίων, the king's name. Χάβηρος, 'the yellow river,' the Kâvêrî, is claimed by Sanskrit, though possibly Dravidian. There is no doubt that Κομάρια, Cape Comorin, is Sanskrit; and probably Κῶρυ is Sanskrit also. Ptolemy says that Brâhmans (Βραχμάναι Μάγοι) dwelt in the country under the mountain Βηττιγώ, and as far as the country of the Βάτοι—εν οἷς πόλις ἥδε, Βράχμη. Can this Βράχμη be Brahmadêśam, an ancient town on the Tâmraparṇî, not far from the foot of the Podigei mountain, which I have found referred to in several ancient inscriptions?

At a later period than that of Ptolemy by several centuries, when the Indian trade had passed from the hands of the Greeks to those of the Persians, Cosmas Indico-pleustes, in his "Christian Topography," furnishes some interesting particulars respecting Ceylon and the Malabar coast, included in which he preserves for us a few Tamil words. I have already mentioned his name for the Malabar coast—Μαλὲ, the mountain region. He gives also the names of five places on the Malabar coast from which pepper was exported, three of which end in πάτανα, 'town,' a word which, though found in Sanskrit, is, I think, o Dravidian origin; and of these, one (Πουδοπάτανα) gives us the distinctively Tamil word *pudu*, new. There is still on the same coast a town called by this name, which, like many other '*Newtons*,' must be a town of considerable antiquity, seeing that it has long been regarded by native authorities as the northern boundary of Kêrala proper and of true Kêrala usages. This πουδο of Cosmas is slightly more correct than the ποδο of Ptolemy's ποδοπέρουρα. Colonel Yule (*Bombay Antiquary* for August 1874) identifies the place with the 'Bodfattan' of Ibn Batuta, and the 'Peudefitania' of Nicolo Conti.

Though the Greek geographers have not given us any information respecting the languages of India, beyond what little is furnished by the names of places contained in their works, the information derived from those lists is exceedingly interesting. The earliest extant traces of the Dravidian languages which possess reliable authority, are those with which we have been furnished by the ancient Greeks; and from an examination of the words which they have recorded, we seem to be justified in drawing the conclusion, not only that the Dravidian languages have remained almost unaltered for the last two thousand years, but probably also that the principal dialects that now prevail had a separate existence at the commencement of the Christian era, and prevailed at that period in the very same districts of country in which we now find them. The art of writing had probably been introduced, the grammar of the Dravidian languages had been fixed, and some progress made in the art of composition before the arrival of the Greek merchants;* and the extraordinary fixity with which those languages

* The arrival in India of those Grecian merchants appears to have been contemporaneous with the conquest of Egypt by the Romans. The earliest Roman coins found in India are those of the reign of Augustus. A large number of Roman imperial *aurei* were found some years ago on the Malabar coast; upwards of thirty types of which, commencing with the earlier coins of Augustus, and including many of Nero, were described by me in a paper published at Trivandrum in 1851 by the Rajah of Travancore, to whom the coins belonged.

It may be desirable to mention here the approximate dates of the Greek and Roman geographical writers referred to above.

B.C.—Herodotus 420; Ctesias 400; Onesicritus 325; Megasthenes 300.

A.D.—Strabo 20; Pomponius Mela 50; Pliny 77; Periplus Maris Erythræi 80; Dionysius Periegetes 86; Ptolemy 130; Arrian 150; Clemens Alexandrinus 200; Eusebius 320; Festus Avienus 380; Marcian 420; Cosmas Indicopleustes 535; Stephen of Byzantium 560; Ravennatis Anonymi Cosmographia, 7th century; Georgius Syncellus 800; Eustathius, the commentator on Dionysius Periegetes, 12th century; Uranius, a writer quoted by Stephen of Byzantium, date unknown. The date of the Peutinger Tables is unknown, but an examination of the Asian segment of those tables convinces me that the author could not have had any acquaintance with Ptolemy, and therefore probably lived at an earlier period.

appear to have been characterised ever since that period is in accordance with the history of all other Asiatic languages, from the date of the commencement of their literary cultivation.

If the Dravidian family of languages is allied, as I think it may be believed to be in the main, to the Scythian families, it may justly claim to be considered as one of the oldest congeners of the group. With the exception of the language of the Behistun tablets, no words belonging to any distinctively Scythian language can be traced up to the Christian era. Mr Norris says, "I know of nothing written in the Magyar language earlier than the fifteenth century, and of the other Ugrian languages we have nothing above fifty or sixty years old. The great Finnish heroic poem, the 'Kalevala,' may be of any age, but as it appears to have been brought down to us only by word of mouth, it has naturally varied, like all traditional poetry, with the varying forms of the language." The Uigurs or Oriental Turks acquired the art of writing from the Nestorian Christians, the Mongolians from the Uigurs; so that the literary cultivation of neither of those languages can be compared in point of antiquity with that of the Dravidian. Amongst the earliest records of the Scythian tongues that have been discovered, is a brief list of words recorded by the Chinese as peculiar to the old Turks of the Altaï; and of eight words contained in this list, all of which are found in the modern dialects of the Turkish, probably three, certainly two, are Dravidian. Those words as given by the Chinese are:—

	TURKISH OF THE ALTAÏ.	MODERN TURKISH.	TAMIL.
black,	*koro,*	*quarâ,*	*karu.*
old,	*kori,*	*gori,*	*kiṛa.*
chieftain,	*kân,*	*khân,*	*kôn,* or *kô.*

I am strongly inclined to consider the last Tamil word, *kôn* or *kô,* to be identical with the *kân, khân,* or *khâgan* of the Turko-Mongolian languages. The Ostiak, an Ugrian dialect, has *khon.* In the old Tamil inscriptions I have invariably found *kô* or *kôn* instead of the Sanskrit *râjâ:* but the word has become obsolete in modern Tamil, except in compounds, and in the honorific caste title *kôn,* assumed by shepherds. This conjunction of meanings (king and shepherd) is very interesting, and reminds one of the Homeric description of kings as ποιμένες λαῶν.

The Tamil literature now extant enables us to ascend, in studying the history of the language, only to the ninth or tenth century, A.D.: the Dravidian words handed down to us by the Greeks carry us up, as we have seen, to the Christian era. Beyond that period, the comparison of existing dialects is our only available guide to a knowledge of the primitive condition of the Dravidian language. The civilisation of the Tamil people, together with the literary cultivation of their language, may have commenced about the sixth or seventh century, B.C., but the separation of the primitive Dravidian speech into dialects must have taken place shortly after the arrival of the Dravidians in the districts they at present inhabit—an event of unknown, but certainly of very great antiquity. The Irish and the Welsh dialects of Celtic, the Old High and the Old Low dialects of Teutonic, and the Finnish and Magyar dialects of Ugrian, had probably become separate and distinct idioms before the tribes by which those dialects are spoken settled in their present habitations; but the various Dravidian dialects which are now spoken appear to have acquired a separate existence subsequently to the settlement of the Dravidians in the localities in which we now find them. Supposing their final settlement in their present abodes in Southern India to have taken place shortly after the Aryan irruption (though I think it probable that it took place before), every grammatical form and root which the various dialects possess in common, may be regarded as at least coeval with the century subsequent to the arrival of the Aryans. Every form and root which the Brahui possesses in common with the Dravidian tongues may be regarded as many centuries older still. The Brahui analogies enable us to ascend to a period anterior to the arrival in India of the Aryans (which cannot safely be placed later than 1600 B.C.); and they furnish us with the means of ascertaining, in some degree, the condition of the Dravidian languages before the Dravidians had finally abandoned their original abodes in the central tracts of Asia.

Political and Social Relation of the Primitive Dravidians to the Aryan and Præ-Aryan Inhabitants of Northern India.

The arrival of the Dravidians in India must have been anterior to the arrival of the Aryans, but there is some difficulty in determining whether the Dravidians were identical with the aborigines whom the Aryans found in possession of the northern provinces, and to whom the vernacular languages of Northern India are supposed to be indebted for the non-Sanskritic elements they contain, or whether they were a distinct and more ancient race. The question may be put thus:—Were the Dravidians identical with the Dasyus, by whom the progress of the Aryans was disputed, and who were finally subdued and incorporated with the Aryan race as their serfs and dependents? or were they a race unknown to the Aryans of the first age, which had already left, or been expelled from, Northern India, and migrated southwards towards the extremity of the peninsula before the Aryans arrived? This question of the relation of the Dravidians to the Aryanised aborigines of Northern India is confessedly involved in obscurity, and can be settled only by a more thorough investigation than any that has yet been made of the relation of the Dravidian languages to Sanskrit, the Prâkrits, and the northern vernaculars. We may, indeed, with tolerable safety regard the Dravidians as the earliest inhabitants of India, or at least as the earliest race that entered from the North-West; but it is not so easy to determine whether they were the people whom the Aryans found in possession and conquered, or whether they had already, before the arrival of the Aryans, moved on southwards out of the northern provinces, or been expelled from those provinces by the præ-historic irruption of another race. Some inquirers have held the identity of the Dravidians with the primitive S'ûdras; and something may be said in support of this hypothesis. I am not competent to pronounce a decided opinion on a point which lies so far beyond my own province, but the differences which appear to exist, and which I have already pointed out, between the Dravidian languages and the non-Sanskritic under-stratum of the northern vernaculars induce me to incline to the supposition that the Dravidian idioms belong to an older period of speech. If this supposition is correct, it seems to follow that the progenitors of the Scythian or non-Aryan portion of the S'ûdras and mixed classes now inhabiting the northern provinces must have made their way into India subsequently to the Dravidians, and also that the Dravidians must have retired before them from the greater part of Northern India, ere they were in their turn subdued by a new race of invaders. By whomsoever the Dravidians were expelled from Northern India—if they ever were really expelled—and through what causes soever they were induced to migrate southward, I feel persuaded that they were never expelled by the Aryans. Neither the subjugation of the Chôlas, Pâṇḍyas, and other Dravidians by the Aryans, nor the expulsion from Northern India by the Aryans of the races who afterwards became celebrated in the South, as Pâṇḍyas, Chôlas, Kêralas, Kalingas, Andhras, &c., is recognised by any Sanskrit authority, or any Dravidian tradition. Looking at the question from a purely Dravidian point of view, I feel convinced that the Dravidians never had any relations with the primitive Aryans but those of a peaceable and friendly character; and that if they were expelled from Northern India, and forced to take refuge in Gôṇḍvana and Daṇḍakâraṇya—the great Dravidian forest—prior to the dawn of their civilisation, the tribes that subdued and thrust them southwards must have been præ-Aryans.

Those præ-Aryan Scythians, by whom I have been supposing the

Dravidians to have been expelled from the northern provinces, are not to be confounded with the Kôls, Santâls, Bhîls, Dôms, and other aboriginal tribes of the North. Possibly these tribes had fled into the forests from the Dravidians prior to the præ-Aryan invasion, just as the British had taken refuge in Wales before the Norman conquest. It is also possible that the tribes referred to had never crossed the Indus at all, or occupied Northern India, but had entered it, like the Bhûtân tribes, by the North-East, and had passed from the jungles and swamps of lower Bengal to their present abodes—taking care always to keep on the outside of the boundary line of civilisation. At all events, we cannot suppose that it was through an irruption of those forest tribes that the Dravidians were driven southwards; nor does the non-Sanskritic element supposed to be contained in the northern vernaculars appear to accord distinctively with the peculiar structure of the Kôlarian languages. The tribes of Northern India whom the Aryans gradually incorporated in their community, as S'ûdras, whoever they were, must have been an organised and formidable race. They may have been identical with the 'Æthiopians from the East,' who, according to Herodotus, were brigaded with other Indians in the army of Xerxes, and who differed from other Æthiopians in being 'straight-haired.'

I admit that there is a difficulty in supposing that the Dravidians, who have proved themselves superior to the Aryanised S'ûdras of Northern India in mental power, independence, and patriotic feeling, should have been expelled from their original possessions by an irruption of the ancestors of those very S'ûdras. It is to be remembered, however, that the lapse of time may have effected a great change in the warlike, hungry, Scythian hordes that rushed down upon the first Dravidian settlements. It is also to be remembered that the dependent and almost servile position to which this secondary race of Scythians was early reduced by the Aryans, whilst the more distant Dravidians were enjoying freedom and independence, may have materially altered their original character. It is not therefore so improbable as it might at first sight appear, that after the Dravidians had been driven across the Vindhyas into the Dekhan by a newer race of Scythians, this new race, conquered in its turn by the Aryans and reduced to a dependent position, soon sank beneath the level of the tribes which it had expelled; whilst the Dravidians, retaining their independence in the southern forests into which they were driven, and submitting eventually to the Aryans, not as conquerors, but as colonists and instructors, gradually rose in the social scale, and formed communities and states in the extreme South, rivalling those of the Aryans in the North.*

* *Dekhan* is a corruption of the Sanskrit *dakshiṇa*, the south, literally, the

Mr Curzon (*Journal of the Royal Asiatic Society*, vol. xvi.) attempted to meet the difficulty I have stated by supposing that the Tamilians were never in possession of Âryâ-varta, or Northern India, at all; but that they were connected with the Malay race, and came to Southern India by sea, from the opposite coast of the Bay of Bengal, or from Ceylon. This theory seems, however, perfectly gratuitous; for it has been proved that the languages of the Gônḍs and Kus are Dravidian equally with Tamil itself; that the Orâon and the Râjmahâl are also substantially Dravidian; and that Brahui partakes so largely of the same character (not to speak of the language of the Scythic tablets of Behistun), as to establish a connection between the Dravidians and the ancient races west of the Indus. It has also been shown that in the time of Ptolemy, when every part of India had long ago been settled and civilised, the Dravidians were in quiet possession, not only of the south-eastern coast, but of the whole of the peninsula, up nearly to the mouths of the Ganges.

It is undeniable that immigrations from Ceylon to the southern districts of India have occasionally taken place. The Tîyars (properly *Tîvârs*, islanders) and the Îṛavars, Singhalese (from *Îṛam*, Ceylon, a word which appears to have been corrupted from the Sanskrit *Simhalam*, or rather from the Pali *Sihalam*, by the omission of the initial *s*), both of them Travancore castes, are certainly immigrants from Ceylon; but these and similar immigrants are not to be considered as Singhalese, in the proper sense of the term, but as offshoots from the Tamilian population of the northern part of the island. They were the partial reflux of the tide which peopled the northern and western parts of Ceylon with Tamilians. Bands of marauding Tamilians (*Sôlis, Pâṇḍis*, and other *Damilos—i.e.*, Chôlas, Pâṇḍyas, and other Tamilians) frequently invaded Ceylon, as we are informed by the Mahâ-wanso, both before and subsequently to the Christian era.

---

right (*dexter*), an appellation which took its rise from the circumstance that the Brâhman, in determining the position of objects, looked towards the East, which he called *pûrva*, the opposite region, when whatever lay to the southward was necessarily to the right. The South was to the primitive Dravidian what the East was to the Brâhman. He called it *ten*, of which the meaning in Tamil is 'opposite;' whilst the North was *vaḍa* (the north-wind *vâḍei*), which is probably connected with *vâḍ-u*, to wither—the north wind being regarded by Tamilians with as much dread as the south wind (mythologically the car of Kâma, the Indian Cupid) was associated with the idea of everything that was agreeable. Referring to the physical configuration of the Carnatic, the Dravidians called the East 'downward;' the West, the region of the Ghauts, 'upward.' The cocoa-nut, *tennei*, Tam. seems to mean 'the southern tree,' this tree having been brought, according to tradition, from Ceylon. Mr C. P. Brown derives *tenkâya*, cocoa-nut, from *tenki*, covert, shell, and *kâya* (Tam. *kây*), fruit.

On several occasions they acquired supreme power, and at length permanently occupied the northern provinces of the island. There is no direct affinity, however, between the Singhalese language—the language of the Singhalese, properly so-called, who appear to have been colonists from Magadha—and the language of the Tamilians; nor is there any reason for supposing that the natural course of migration (viz., from the mainland to the island) was ever inverted to such a degree as to justify the supposition that the whole mass of Dravidians entered India from Ceylon. Dr Gundert's suggestion, mentioned in p. 24, is better capable of being defended than Mr Curzon's, but is also, as it appears to me, encumbered with greater difficulties than the ordinary theory.

Original Use and Progressive Extension of the Term 'S'ûdra.'

The mass of the Dravidians are now so commonly designated S'ûdras, especially by Brâhmans and those Europeans who take their caste nomenclature from Brâhmans, and the Dravidians themselves are so generally content to be called by this name, that it cannot but be regarded as a remarkable circumstance that they were originally designated, without distinction or exception, as Kshatriyas, by the highest and most ancient authorities in such matters—viz., Manu and the Mahâ-bhârata. The references will be found in Muir's 'Sanskrit Texts,' vols. i., ii., in which will also be found extracts from various genealogical lists in which the Dravidians are represented to be the descendants of Kshatriya princes. It is true that they are represented also as having fallen from the rank of Kshatriyas into the condition of *vṛishalas*, 'outcasts or S'ûdras,' by the neglect of Brâhmanical rites; but this does not affect the statement made regarding what was supposed to have been their original condition. However remarkable this statement may be, in consequence of its contrariety to more modern ideas, its ethnological value must be admitted to be very small, seeing that not only are the S'akas, a Scythian race, and the Chinas, or Chinese, of all Mongolians the most Mongolian, described as originally Kshatriyas, equally with the Dravidians, but both they and the Dravidians are placed in the same category with the Yavanas or Greeks, of all Aryans the most normally Aryan. Perhaps the chief value of the statement consists in the proof it furnishes that the Dravidian inhabitants of the southern part of the peninsula were regarded from the earliest times as occupying a very different position from that attributed to the Nishâdas and other rude forest tribes (some of whom at least seem to have been equally Dravidians in origin) inhabiting the forests and hilly ranges in Central India, and occasionally disturbing the contemplations and interrupting the sacrifices of holy *rishis*. The latter are generally described as vile sinners, as ugly and uncouth as they were savage. Possibly also when we read of the râkhasas or giants so frequently met with by the *rishis* and epic heroes, we are to understand merely an irreconcilably hostile portion of those aboriginal tribes; whilst those of them that showed a friendly disposition, like Rama's allies, are half praised, half ridiculed, as intelligent monkeys—by an interesting anticipation of the Darwinian theory; according to which the monkey progenitors of the human race will have to be sought for in the tropics, probably in India. It is doubtful whether even the rude Dravidian and Kôlarian tribes of Central India ever deserved to be described in such terms; but the fact that the Pâṇḍyas, Chôlas, and other Dravidian races were represented at the same time as having been originally, not râkshasas or monkeys, but Kshatriyas, equally with the Solar and Lunar princes of Aryan India, proves conclusively that they at least were considered almost as civilised and as occupying almost as respectable a position as the orthodox Aryans themselves.

The term 'S'ûdra,' which is now the common appellation of the mass of the inhabitants of India, whether Gaurians or Dravidians, has been supposed to have been originally the name of a tribe dwelling near the Indus. Lassen recognises their name in that of the town Σύδρος on the lower Indus; and especially in that of the nations of the Σύδροι in Northern Arachosia. He supposes them to have been, with the Abhîras and Nishâdas, a black, long-haired race of aborigines, not originally a component part of the Aryan race, but brought under its influence by conquest; and that it was in consequence of the S'ûdras having been the first tribe that was reduced by the Aryans to a dependent condition, that the name 'S'ûdra' was afterwards, on the conquest of the aborigines in the interior part of the country, extended to all the servile classes. Whatever may have been the origin of the name 'S'ûdra,' it cannot be doubted that it was extended in course of time to all who occupied or were reduced to a dependent condition; whilst the name 'Dasyu' or 'Mlêchcha' continued to be the appellation of the unsubdued, non-Aryanised tribes.

Most writers on this subject seem to suppose that the whole of the S'ûdras, or primitive, servile classes of Northern India, to whom this name was progressively applied, belonged to a different race from their Aryan conquerors. Whilst I assent to every other part of the supposition, I am unable to assent to the universality of this. It seems to me to be probable that a considerable proportion of the servants, dependents, or followers of the Aryans belonged from the first to the Aryan race. As the Slavonian serfs are Slavonians, and the Magyar serfs Magyars, there is no improbability in the supposition that a large number of the Aryan serfs or S'ûdras (perhaps at the outset the majority) were Aryans; and I cannot on any other supposition account for the fact that so large a proportion of the component materials of the Prâkrits and northern vernaculars is Sanskrit.'

The supposition of the Aryan origin of a large number of the S'ûdras, seems also most in accordance with the very old mythological statement of the origin of the S'ûdras from Purusha's or Brahmâ's feet; for though the Brâhmans, Kshatriyas, and Vaiśyas, the twice-born classes, are represented as springing from more honourable parts of the body, yet the S'ûdras are represented to have sprung from the same divinity, though from an ignoble part; whereas the Nishâdas, or barbarian aborigines, are not represented to have sprung from Brahmâ at all, but formed what was called in later times a 'fifth class,' totally unconnected with the others. It appears probable from this mythological tradition that the S'ûdras were supposed in the first ages to differ from the 'twice-born' Aryans in rank only, not in blood. I regard as confirmatory of this view the statement of Manu that 'all who become outcasts are called Dasyus, whether they speak the language of the Mlêchchas or that of the Aryans:' for in the same manner, all who enjoyed the protection of the Aryans, as their dependents and servants, would naturally receive a common appellation, probably that of S'ûdras,—whether, as aborigines, they spoke 'the language of Mlêchchas,' (the non-Aryan vernacular,) or whether, as Aryans of an inferior rank in life, they spoke 'the language of Aryans,' (a colloquial dialect of Sanskrit). It is true that the three twice-born castes alone are called Aryans by the S'atapatha-Brâhmaṇa of the Rigveda: but as 'the four classes,' including the S'ûdras, but excluding the Dasyus and Nishâdas, are distinctly referred to in the Vedic hymns; as outcast Aryans are styled 'Dasyus' by Manu; and as the higher classes of the Tamilians monopolise the national name in this very manner, and pretend that the lower classes of their race are not Tamilians, I think that we may safely attribute the statement in question (in part, at least) to the pride of 'the twice-born.' Even the Vrâtyas, who are distinguished from the S'ûdras, and are regarded as an inferior class, did not differ from the Brâhmans in language, and must, therefore, have been Aryans.

The aboriginal non-Aryan inhabitants of India seem to have been subdued, and transformed from Dasyus and Mlêchchas into S'ûdras, by slow degrees. In the age of Manu, they retained their independence and the appellation of 'Mlêchchas' in Bengal, Orissa, and the Dekhan; but in the earlier period referred to in some of the historic legends of the Mahâ-bhârata, we find the Mlêchchas and Dasyus disputing the possession of Upper India itself with the Aryans. Sagara, the thirty-fifth king of the Solar dynasty, is related to have laboured in vain to subdue the heterodox aborigines residing on or near his frontier: and in the reign preceding his, in conjunction with certain tribes connected with the Lunar line, those aborigines had succeeded in overrunning his territories.*

The introduction of the Dravidians within the pale of Hindûism appears to have originated, not in conquest, but in the peaceable process of colonisation and progressive civilisation. There is no tradition extant of a warlike irruption of the Aryans into Southern India, or of the forcible subjugation of the Dravidians; though, if such an event ever took place, some remembrance of it would probably have survived. All existing traditions, and the names by which the Brâhmanical race is distinguished in Tamil — viz., *Eiyar*, fathers, instructors, and *Pârppâr*, overseers (probably the ἐπίσκοποι of Arrian)—tend to show that the Brâhmans acquired their ascendancy by their intelligence and their administrative skill.

* Sagara, finding himself unable to extirpate or enslave those heterodox tribes, entered into a compromise with them, by imposing upon them various distinguishing marks; by which, I think, we may understand their obstinate persistence in the use of the distinguishing marks to which they had been accustomed. One of those marks is worthy of notice in an inquiry into the relations of the early Dravidians. "The Pâradas," it is recorded, "wore their hair long in obedience to his commands." Professor Wilson observes, with reference to this statement (in his notes on the *Vishṇu Purâṇa*), "What Oriental people wore their hair long, except at the back of the head, is questionable; and the usage would be characteristic rather of the Teutonic and Gothic nations." The usage referred to is equally characteristic of the Dravidians. Up to the present day the custom of wearing the hair long, and twisted into a knot at the back of the head, is characteristic of all the more primitive castes in the southern provinces of the Tamil country, and of some of the castes that occupy a more respectable position in society. In ancient times this mode of wearing the hair was in use amongst all Dravidian soldiers; and sculptured representations prove that at a still earlier period it was the general Dravidian custom. The Kôtas of the Nilgherry Hills wear their hair in the same manner. The Tudas wear their hair long, but without confining it in a knot. Probably it was from the Dravidian settlers in Ceylon that the Singhalese adopted the same usage; for as early as the third century A.D., Agathemerus, a Greek geographer, describing Ceylon, says, "The natives cherish their hair as women among us, and twist it round their heads." There are pictures, Dr Gundert informs me, in the early Portuguese books of voyages, representing the Tîvâr and other Malayâḷam castes, in which they invariably appear with long hair. The wearing of the hair long appears to have been regarded by the early Dravidians as a distinctive sign of national independence: whilst the shaving of the hair of the head, with the exception of the *sikhâ* or *kuḍumi*, the lock at the back of the head, corresponding to the tail of the Chinese, seems to have been considered as a sign of Aryanisation, or submission to Aryan customs, and admission within the pale of Aryan protection.

The most adventurous immigrations from Northern India to the Dekhan were those of the offshoots of the Lunar dynasty, a dynasty which originated from the Solar, and whose chief city Ayôdhyâ, Oude, was the traditional starting point of most of their migrations. The Pâṇḍya kings of Madura were feigned to have sprung from the Lunar line. The title 'Pâṇḍya' is derived, as has already been mentioned, p. 16, from the name of the Pâṇḍavas of Northern India, the celebrated combatants in the great war of the Mahâ-bhârata, to whom every Cyclopean work of unknown antiquity is traditionally ascribed. This derivâtion of the *name* of Pâṇḍyas is doubtless correct; but there is very little reason to suppose that the kings of Madura, by whom this name was assumed, sprang from any of the royal dynasties of Northern India. The marriage of Arjuna to a daughter of the second king of the Pâṇḍyan dynasty, whilst on his travels in the South, according to the Mahâ-bhârata, falls far short of proving (what it is sometimes supposed to prove) that the Pâṇḍya kings were Kshatriyas. Besides, what are we to conclude from Arjuna's abandonment of his Pâṇḍyan bride shortly afterwards, according to the same story? The Aryan immigrants to the South appear to have been generally Brâhmanical priests and instructors, rather than Kshatriya soldiers; and the kings of the Pâṇḍyas, Chôlas, Kalingas, and other Dravidians, appear to have been simply Dravidian chieftains, whom their Brâhmanical preceptors and spiritual directors dignified with Aryan titles, and taught to imitate and emulate the grandeur and cultivated tastes of the Solar, Lunar, and Agni-kula races of kings.* In later times we may see the progress

* A similar opinion respecting the relation that subsisted between the Aryans and the early Dravidians was expressed by Professor Max Müller ("Report of British Association for 1847"). "Wholly different from the manner in which the Brâhmanical people overcame the north of India, was the way they adopted of taking possession of and settling in the country south of the Vindhya. They did not enter there in crushing masses with the destroying force of arms, but in the more peaceful way of extensive colonisation, under the protection and countenance of the powerful empires in the north. Though sometimes engaged in wars with their neighbouring tribes, these colonies generally have not taken an offensive but only a defensive part; and it appears that, after having introduced Brâhmanical institutions, laws, and religion, especially along the two coasts of the sea, they did not pretend to impose their language upon the much more numerous inhabitants of the Dekhan, but that they followed the wiser policy of adopting themselves the language of the aboriginal people, and of conveying through its medium their knowledge and instruction to the minds of uncivilised tribes. In this way they refined the rude language of the earlier inhabitants, and brought it to a perfection which rivals even the Sanskrit. By these mutual concessions, a much more favourable assimilation took place between the Aryan and aboriginal race; and the south of India became afterwards the last refuge of Brâhmanical science, when it was banished from the north by the intolerant Mahommedans.

of a similar process in Gôṇḍvana, where we find that Gôṇḍ chieftains have learned from their Brâhman preceptors, not only to style themselves Râjâhs, but even to assume the sacred thread of the 'twice-born' Kshatriyas. The gradual transformation of these semi-barbarous chieftains into Kshatriya princes (see Appendix: Dravidian physical type) shows how the Pâṇḍya and Chôla chieftains of the South may originally have been Dravidian Poligars (*Pâḷeiyakkâran*, the holder of a *pâḷeiyam*, a feudal estate), like those of Ramnad and Puducottah in later times, and may in process of time have risen in rank as in power, assuming as they did so the Kshatriya titles of Deva, Varmâ, &c., and finally, in some instances at least, succeeding in getting themselves recognised as Kshatriyas by the original Kshatriyas of the North.

Whilst it is evident that the entire mass of the Dravidians were regarded by Manu and the authors of the Mahâ-bhârata and the Purâṇas as Kshatriyas by birth, it is remarkable that the Brâhmans who settled amongst the Dravidians and formed them into castes, in imitation of the castes of the North, seem never at any time to have given the Dravidians—with the exception perhaps of the royal houses—a higher title than that of S'ûdra. They might have styled the agricultural classes Vaiśyas, and reserved the name of S'ûdra for the village servants and the unenslaved low castes; but acting apparently on the principle that none ought to be called either Kshatriyas or Vaiśyas but Aryans, and that the Dravidians were not Aryans, they seem always to have called them S'ûdras, however respectable their position.

In consequence of this the title S'ûdra conveys a higher meaning in Southern than in Northern India. The primitive S'ûdras of Northern India seem to have been slaves to the Aryans, or in a condition but little superior to that of slaves. They seem to have had no property of their own, and can scarcely be said to have had any civil rights. In Southern India, on the contrary, it was upon the middle and higher classes of the Dravidians that the title of 'S'ûdra' was conferred; and the classes that appeared to be analogous to the servile S'udras of Northern India, were not called 'S'ûdras, but 'Paḷḷas,' 'Pareiyas,' &c., names which they still retain. The application of the term 'S'ûdra' to the ancient Dravidian chieftains, soldiers, and cultivators does not prove that they had ever been reduced by the Brâhmans to a dependent position, or that they ever were slaves—as the northern S'ûdras appear

---

It is interesting and important to observe how the beneficial influence of a higher civilisation may be effectually exercised, without forcing the people to give up their own language and to adopt that of their foreign conquerors, a result by which, if successful, every vital principle of an independent and natural development is necessarily destroyed."

to have been—to any class of Aryans. The Brâhmans, who came in 'peaceably, and obtained the kingdom by flatteries,' may probably have persuaded the Dravidians that in calling them S'ûdras they were conferring upon them a title of honour. If so, their policy was perfectly successful; for the title of 'S'ûdra' has never been resented by the Dravidian castes; and hence, whilst in Northern India the S'ûdra is supposed to be a low-caste man, in Southern India he generally ranks next to the Brâhman. The term S'ûdra, however, is really, as we have seen, as inappropriate to any class of Dravidians as the term Kshatriya or Vaiśya. It is better to designate each Dravidian caste simply by its own name, as Veḷḷâḷas, Nâyakkas, &c., in accordance with the usage prevailing amongst the people themselves in each locality, without attempting to classify the various castes according to Manu's principles of classification, which in reality are quite inapplicable to them, if not, indeed, equally inapplicable to the castes now existing in the north.

Præ-Aryan Civilisation of the Dravidians.

Though the primitive Dravidians were probably unacquainted with the higher arts of life, they do not appear to have been by any means a barbarous and degraded people. Whatever may have been the condition of the forest tribes, it cannot be doubted that the Dravidians, properly so called, had acquired at least the elements of civilisation, prior to the arrival amongst them of the Brâhmans.

If we eliminate from the Tamil language the whole of its Sanskrit derivatives, the primitive Dravidian words that remain will furnish us with a faithful picture of the simple, yet far from savage, life of the non-Aryanised Dravidians. Mr Curzon holds that there is nothing in the shape of a record of the Tamil mind which can recall to us anything independent of an obvious Sanskrit origin; and that if the contrary supposition were tenable, we ought to find the remains of a literature embodying some record of a religion different from Hindûism. Traces of the existence amongst the non-Aryanised Dravidians, both ancient and modern, of a religion different from Hindûism, will be pointed out in the Appendix. At present I will merely adduce those records of the primitive Tamil mind, manners, and religion which the ancient vocabularies of the language, when freed from the admixture of Sanskrit, will be found to furnish.

From the evidence of the words in use amongst the early Tamilians, we learn the following items of information. They had 'kings,' who dwelt in 'strong houses,' and ruled over small 'districts of country.'

They had 'minstrels,' who recited 'songs' at 'festivals,' and they seem to have had alphabetical 'characters' written with a style on palmyra leaves. A bundle of those leaves was called 'a book;' they were without hereditary 'priests' and 'idols,' and appear to have had no idea of 'heaven' or 'hell,' of the 'soul' or 'sin;' but they acknowledged the existence of God, whom they styled *kô*, or king—a realistic title little known to orthodox Hindûism. They erected to his honour a 'temple,' which they called *Kô-il*, God's-house; but I cannot find any trace of the nature of the 'worship' which they offered to him. They had 'laws' and 'customs,' but no lawyers or judges. Marriage existed among them. They were acquainted with the ordinary metals, with the exception of 'tin,' 'lead,' and 'zinc;' with the planets which were ordinarily known to the ancients, with the exception of 'Mercury' and 'Saturn.' They had numerals up to a hundred,—some of them to a thousand; but were ignorant of the higher denominations, a 'lakh' and a 'crore.' They had 'medicines,' but no 'medical science,' and no 'doctors; 'hamlets' and 'towns,' but no 'cities;' 'canoes,' 'boats,' and even 'ships' (small 'decked' coasting vessels), but no foreign 'commerce;' no acquaintance with any people beyond sea, except in Ceylon, which was then, perhaps, accessible on foot at low water; and no word expressive of the geographical idea of 'island' or 'continent.' They were well acquainted with 'agriculture,' and delighted in 'war.' They were armed with 'bows' and 'arrows,' with 'spears' and 'swords.' All the ordinary or necessary arts of life, including 'spinning,' 'weaving,' and 'dyeing,' existed amongst them. They excelled in 'pottery,' as their places of sepulture show, but were unacquainted with the arts of the higher class. They had no acquaintance with 'sculpture' or 'architecture;' with 'astronomy,' or even 'astrology;' and were ignorant, not only of every branch of 'philosophy,' but even of 'grammar.' Their undeveloped intellectual condition is especially apparent in words relating to the operations of the mind. Their only words for the 'mind' were the 'diaphragm' (the φρῆν of the early Greeks), and 'the inner parts' or 'interior.' They had a word for 'thought,' but no word distinct from this for 'memory,' 'judgment,' or 'conscience;' and no word for 'will.' To express 'the will' they would have been obliged to describe it as 'that which in the inner parts says, I am going to do so and so.'

This brief illustration, from the primitive Tamil vocabulary, of the social condition of the Dravidians, prior to the arrival of the Brâhmans, will suffice to prove that the elements of civilisation already existed amongst them. They had not acquired much more than the elements; and in many things were centuries behind the Brâhmans whom they revered as instructors, and obeyed as overseers: but if they had been left altogether to themselves, it is open to dispute whether they would not now be in a better condition, at least in point of morals and intellectual freedom, than they are. The mental culture and the higher civilisation which they derived from the Brâhmans, have, I fear, been more than counterbalanced by the fossilising caste rules, the unpractical, pantheistic philosophy, and the cumbersome routine of inane ceremonies, which were introduced amongst them by the guides of their new social state.

Probable Date of Aryan Civilisation of the Dravidians.

It would appear from the unanimous voice of ancient legends that the earliest Dravidian civilisation was that of the Tamilians of the Pâṇḍya kingdom, and that the first place where they erected a city and established a state was Kolkei, on the Tâmraparṇî river (see p. 101), near the southern extremity of the peninsula. This civilisation was probably indigenous in its origin, but it seems to have been indebted for its rapid development at so early a period to the influence of a succession of small colonies of Aryans, chiefly Brâhmans, from Upper India, who were probably attracted to the South by the report of the fertility of the rich alluvial plains watered by the Kâvêrî, the Tâmraparṇî, and other peninsular rivers; or as the legends relate, by the fame of Râma's exploits, and the celebrity of the emblem of S'iva, which Râma discovered and worshipped at Ramisseram, or Râmêśvaram, a holy place on an island between the mainland and Ceylon. The leader of the first or most influential Brâhmanical colony is traditionally said to have been Agastya, a personage who is celebrated in Northern India as one of the authors of the Vedic hymns, then as the holiest of hermits, performing sacrifices and austerities in the remotest forests, and evermore penetrating farther and farther into the hitherto unknown South. In the South he is venerated as the earliest teacher of science and literature to the primitive Dravidian tribes. It is very doubtful whether Agastya (if there ever were such a person) was really the leader of the Brâhman immigration; more probably he is to be considered as its mythological embodiment. 'The Vindhya mountains,' it is said, 'prostrated themselves before Agastya;' by which I understand that they presented no obstacle to his resolute southward progress; for he is said to have penetrated as far south as the vicinity of Cape Comorin. He is called by way of eminence the *Tamiẓ muni*, or Tamilian sage, and is celebrated for the influence he acquired at the court of Kulaśêkhara, according to tradition the first Pâṇḍyan king, and for the numerous elementary treatises he composed for the enlightenment of his royal disciple; amongst which his arrangement of the grammatical principles of the language has naturally acquired most renown. He is mythologically represented as identical with the star Canopus, the brightest star in the extreme southern sky in India, and is worshipped near Cape Comorin as Agastêśvara. By the majority of orthodox Hindûs he is believed to be still alive, though invisible to ordinary eyes, and to reside somewhere on the fine conical mountain, commonly called 'Agasťya's hill,' from which the Porunei or Tâmraparṇî, the sacred river of Tinnevelly, takes its rise. (See p. 100.)

The age of Agastya and the date of the commencement of the Brâhmanical civilisation of the Tamilians cannot now be determined with certainty; but data exists for making an approximate estimate. It was certainly prior to the era of the Greek traders, for then the greater part of the country appears to have been already Brâhmanised, the principal places had received Sanskrit names, and the Pâṇḍya dynasty of kings had become known even in Europe. It seems as certainly subsequent to the era described in the Râmâyaṇa; for then the whole of the south of India seems to have been still inhabited by barbarians, who ate human flesh, consorted with demons, and disturbed the contemplations of hermits. The age of Agastya is apparently to be placed between those two eras. If we could be sure that the references to the civilised Chôlas, Draviḍas, &c., which are contained in the present text of the Mahâ-bhârata, formed originally part of that poem, the era of the commencement of Tamilian civilisation, and the date of the Agastyan colony from which it proceeded, might be brought within a still narrower compass, and placed between the age of the Râmâyaṇa and that of the Mahâ-bhârata. The genuineness of those references, and their age, if genuine, being as yet doubtful, and the era of Manu (in which there is an allusion to the Chinese, under the name of Chînas, which, like a similar allusion to the Chînas in the Mahâ-bhârata, looks very modern) being generally now placed lower than ever, it is hard to say where we are to look for trustworthy means of arriving at an approximate date. At first sight Ceylon seems to furnish us with the information required. The immigration into Ceylon of the colony of Aryans from Magadha, headed by Vijaya, is placed by the Mahâwanso about B.C. 550, or at least some time in the course of that century; and if this were regarded as certain, it might be argued that the Aryans must have become acquainted with, and formed establishments in, the Dekhan and the Coromandel coast, and must have taken some steps towards clearing and civilising the Daṇḍakâraṇya, or primitive forest of the peninsula, before they thought of founding a colony in

Ceylon. We have no documentary evidence, however, for any of these particulars earlier than the date of the composition of the Mahâwamso, which is placed between 459 and 477 A.D. Though the date of the arrival in Ceylon of the colony from Magadha is uncertain, it is quite certain that some such colony must have arrived in Ceylon several centuries before the Christian era. This appears from the evidence of language. Tâmraparṇî (in Pâli Tâmbapaṇṇi) was the name given by the Magadha colonists to the place where they landed in Ceylon (said to have been near Putlam), and afterwards to the whole island. This name, in the shape of Ταπροβάνη, became known to the Greeks as early as the time of Alexander the Great, and it is singular that this is also the name of the principal river in Tinnevelly on the opposite coast of India. (See p. 100.) This river Tâmraparṇî is mentioned by name in the Mahâ-bhârata as a river in which the gods had once bathed, and it is evident from this reference to it in the Mahâ-bhârata that it must have been known by that name from a very early period, and that there must have been some special reason for its celebrity. We are led, therefore, to infer that the Magadha colony which settled in Ceylon may previously have formed a settlement in Tinnevelly, at the mouth of the Tâmraparṇî river—perhaps at Kolkei, which appears, as we have already seen, to have been the earliest residence of the Pâṇḍya kings. Vijaya, the leader of the expedition into Ceylon, is related in the Mahâ-wanso to have married the daughter of the king of Pâṇḍi; and though it may be doubtful enough whether he really did so (for on the same authority we might believe that he married also the queen of the Singhalese demons); this at least is certain, that it was the persuasion of the earliest Singhalese writers, who were, on the whole, the most truthful and accurate of oriental annalists, that the Pâṇḍyan kingdom on the coast of India opposite to Ceylon (the first kingdom established on Aryan principles in the peninsula) existed prior to the establishment of the Magadha rule in the neighbouring island.

Dr Burnell, in an article in the *Indian Antiquary* for October 1872, attributes the introduction of Brâhmanical civilisation to a much later period. He thinks it not too much to infer that about 700 A.D. (the date of Kumârila-bhaṭṭa, who speaks of the language of the Telugu and Tamil people as a language of Mlechchas), Brâhmanical civilisation had but little penetrated the south of India. "Brâhmans had, no doubt, begun to find the South a promising field of labour, but there could have been very few settlers." . . . "I do not mean," he says, "to deny for a moment that a few Sanskrit names are found some centuries earlier in South India, such as are preserved to us by classical writers, but they occur only in the fertile deltas or important seaports of the South, and were probably introduced by Buddhist missionaries." A distinction may perhaps be drawn between the elementary Brâhmanical civilisation of the era of the introduction of which I have been treating and the development of Dravidian *literature*. There is no proof of Dravidian literature, such as we now have it, having originated much before Kumârila's time, 700 A.D., and its earliest cultivators appear to have been Jainas; but in so far as that species of civilisation which falls short of a national literature is concerned, the Dravidians may have been civilised, as I have supposed, and perhaps even to a certain degree Brâhmanised, some centuries before the Christian era. Doubtless the Jainas themselves used Sanskrit in Southern as in Northern India at the commencement of their work as teachers (probably for a century or two), before they set themselves to the task of developing amongst each of the Dravidian races a popular literature independent of the language of their rivals the Brâhmans. The early Sanskrit names of places in Southern India, with two exceptions, are neither Buddhistical nor Brâhmanical, but simply descriptive. One of those exceptions, however, *Kumârî*, Cape Comorin, is clearly Brâhmanical, not Buddhistical, as appears from the statement of the author of the "Periplus" himself; and the other, *Mathurâ*, Madura, is evidently a reminiscence of Mathurâ, the capital of the Yâdavas—and therefore of Brâhmanical origin.

It seems probable that Aryan merchants from the mouth of the Indus must have accompanied the Phœnicians and Solomon's servants in their voyages down the Malabar coast towards Ophir (wherever Ophir may have been), or at least have taken part in the trade. If Mr Edward Thomas's supposition (*Journal of the Royal Asiatic Society*, 1871) that the basis of the Lât character of Northern India was a previously existing Dravidian character, and Dr Burnell's (see "Dravidian Alphabets"), that the earliest character used in India was one which was borrowed by the Dravidians from traders who brought it from the Red Sea, and which was then borrowed by the Aryans from the Dravidians, be accepted, this early intercourse of the Dravidians with Phœnicians on the one hand, and with Aryans on the other, may account in some degree both for what they borrowed and for what they lent. Both those suppositions, however, await confirmation. It appears certain from notices contained in the Vedas that the Aryans of the age of Solomon practised foreign trade in ocean-going vessels, but it remains uncertain to what ports their ships sailed.

Relative Antiquity of Dravidian Literature.

Notwithstanding the antiquity of Dravidian civilisation, the antiquity of the oldest Dravidian literature extant is much inferior to that of Sanskrit. It can boast of a higher antiquity than that of any of the Aryan vernaculars of Northern India; but, except in this connection, and in comparison with the literature of the modern languages of Europe, it is questionable whether the word 'antiquity' is a suitable one to use respecting the literature of any of the Dravidian languages.

Age of Telugu Literature.—The earliest writer on Telugu grammar is said to have been a sage called Kaṇva, who lived at the court of Ândhra-râya, the king in whose reign Sanskrit is said to have been first introduced into the Telugu country, according to the tradition formerly mentioned. For this tradition there is probably a historical groundwork, the introduction of Sanskrit derivatives being necessarily contemporaneous with the immigration of the Brâhmans; and the statement that the first attempt to reduce the grammatical principles of the language to writing proceeded from a Brâhman residing at the court of a Telugu prince, is a very reasonable one. Kaṇva's work, if it ever existed, is now lost; and the oldest extant work on Telugu grammar (which is composed, like most Telugu grammars, in Sanskrit) was written by a Brâhman called Nannaya Bhaṭṭa, or Nannappa, who is also said to be the author of the greater part of the Telugu version of the Mahâ-bhârata, which is the oldest extant composition of any extent in Telugu. Nannappa lived in the reign of Vishnu Vardhana, a king of the Kalinga branch of the Châlukya family, who reigned at Rajamundry. The reign of this king is placed by Mr A. D. Campbell about the commencement of the Christian era; but Mr C. P. Brown, in his Cyclic tables, places it, on better authority, in the beginning of the twelfth century A.D. Appa-kavi, who ranks next to Nannaya Bhaṭṭa as a grammarian, wrote his commentaries not in Sanskrit, but in Telugu verse.

With the exception of a few works composed towards the end of the twelfth century, nearly all the Telugu works that are now extant appear to have been written in the fourteenth and subsequent centuries, after the establishment of the kingdom of Vijaya-nagara; and many of them were written in comparatively recent times. Though the Telugu literature which is now extant cannot boast of a high antiquity, the language must have been cultivated and polished, and many poems that are now lost must have been written in it long prior to the twelfth century—the date of Nannaya's translation of the Mahâ-bhârata: for as this translation is considered 'the great standard of Telugu poetry,' it cannot be supposed to have sprung into existence all at once, without the preparation of a previous literary culture. It must have been the crowning achievement of several centuries of earnest work.

There is a large collection of popular Telugu aphorisms on religious and moral subjects attributed to the poet Vêmana: more than two thousand go by his name, but a selection of about seven hundred has been translated by Mr C. P. Brown, who supposes Vemana may have lived in the sixteenth century. If, as I conceive, the strongly monotheistic, anti-Brâhmanical, anti-ceremonial tone with which most of the aphorisms are pervaded, is due, like the same tone in the poems of the Tamil 'Sittar' (which will be referred to presently), to the influence of Christian teaching, I should be inclined to place Vemana at least a century later, perhaps even as late as the beginning of the eighteenth century. In style his verses do not differ from the popular compositions of the present day.*

Age of Canarese Literature.—Much new light has been thrown on the antiquity of Canarese literature by the publication of the S'abdamaṇidarpaṇam ("Jewel-Mirror of Words"), the most ancient and esteemed grammar of classical Canarese, written by Kêśava or Kêśirâjâ, in the preface to which the editor, Mr Kittel, has carefully worked out an answer to various questions that naturally suggest themselves to the modern mind respecting the authorship of the book and its date. Kêśava was a Jaina, and the Jainas were the first to cultivate Canarese literature with zeal and success. Most of the poets he cites were Jainas, and if it be true that the earliest Jaina literature written in Northern India dates from the fourth century A.D., several additional centuries must be allowed for the appearance of an indigenous Jaina literature in so distant a region as the Canarese country. Kêśava cites eleven predecessors in the art of poetry by name, besides referring to others, and styles them frequently 'the poets of antiquity,' 'the ancients,' &c. He speaks of certain compositions as written in *Paḷa-Gannaḍam*, ancient Canarese, whilst he calls the language used by himself simply Canarese, though his language is regarded as ancient Canarese now. Already also the use of the peculiar vocalic *ṛ*, which is retained in Tamil and Malayâḷam, was beginning to be forgotten in Canarese, for he gives rules for its use, whilst he gives no rules for the use of the hard **r**, which disappeared from Canarese in still later times, though it is still retained in Tamil and Malayâḷam, and to a certain extent in Telugu. Both these letters are retained in the Baḍaga

* See Gover's "Folk-Songs of Southern India." Mr Gover was inclined to attribute to Vêmana a much higher antiquity.

dialect, an old Canarese patois spoken by the Badagas of the Neilgherry hills, a Canarese colony long separated from the parent stock. These circumstances tend to bring down Kêśava's date to at least 1000 A.D. It is brought down to about this date more conclusively by means of a reference made by a poet cited by Kêśava to 'the burning sword of Tailapa.' The dynasty of the Châlukyas, to which Tailapa belonged, reigned in Kalyâṇa from about 800 A.D. to 1189, when it was extinguished; and the Tailapa probably referred to (the warlike Tailapa II.) restored the dynasty in 973 A.D. Kêśava does not cite the Basava-Purâṇa, which is known to have been written in 1369 A.D., and therefore, probably, was anterior to it. He is mentioned by name as a famous author in a book written in 1637 A.D. The Hari-vamśa had been translated into Canarese before Kêśava wrote; but though the poets whose works he cites in illustration of his rules, were well acquainted with the incidents and characters of the Mahâ-bhârata and the Râmâyaṇa, these works do not appear to have been rendered into Canarese at that time. On the whole, therefore, but especially from the reference to Tailapa, Mr Kittel concludes that Kêśava lived about 1170 A.D., a period which, as will be seen, was one of great literary activity in the Tamil country also. It is a remarkable fact that at the time when Kêśava wrote, 'Sanskrit words in a fixed form, either as *tatsamas* or *tadbhavas*, apparently to the same amount as in our days, had already been appropriated by the Canarese people.' Kêśava's work is still the only true standard for all the niceties of the Canarese of the present day, the essential features of the language having remained wholly unchanged. In the *Indian Antiquary* for January 1875, Mr Kittel has followed up this account of Kêśava and his times by an article on old Canarese literature in general, under the four heads of Jaina, Lingâita, S'aiva, and Vaishnava.

Age of Malayâḷam Literature.—Interesting as the Malayâḷam language undoubtedly is, both in itself and on account of the light it throws on the point of development which had been reached by Tamil before Malayâḷam finally separated from it and set up for itself, it must be confessed that Malayâḷam literature can advance fewer claims to antiquity than the literature of any other cultivated member of the Dravidian family. The following is the substance of the information on this subject given us by Dr Gundert, our best authority as to Malayâḷam questions, in the preface to his Malayâḷam dictionary. If we except a few inscriptions in copper and stone, the history of Malayâḷam literature commences with the "Râma Charita," which is probably the oldest Malayâḷam poem still in existence. This poem was composed before the introduction of the Sanskrit alphabet now used in writing Malayâḷam, and is deserving of the particular attention of the scholar, as it exhibits the earliest phase of the language,—perhaps centuries before the arrival of the Portuguese. For several antiquated words this poem is the only authority. The bulk of the other great poems (the "Mâha-bhârata," the "Râmâyaṇa," and the versions of the Purâṇas) were composed within the last two or three centuries. Many Malayâḷam compositions of later date, especially such as are current among the Vedantists, evidently affect Tamil modes of expression.

Age of Tamil Literature.—Tamil literature is older than Telugu or Canarese, and considerably older than Malayâḷam, though the high antiquity which is ascribed to some portions of it by the Tamilian *literati* cannot be admitted.

The sage Agastya occupies in Tamil literature a place of still greater eminence and importance than that of Kaṇva in Telugu. Not only is the formation of the Tamil alphabet attributed to Agastya, and the first treatise upon Tamil grammar, together with the original settlement of the grammatical principles of the language; but he is also said to have taught the Tamilians the first principles of medicine, of chemistry or alchymy, of magic, of architecture, astronomy, and law; and about fifty treatises on these sciences, most of them apparently very modern, are attributed to his pen. Portions of the treatise on grammar attributed to him exist, but their authenticity is not generally admitted by well-informed Tamilians, who are peculiarly well versed in questions relating to grammar and grammatical works.

Though the literary cultivation of the Tamil language may have commenced, as the Tamilians believe, in the age of Agastya (premising, however, that it is undecided whether he was a real personage, or is only to be regarded as the mythological representative of a class or period), I feel quite certain that none of the works which are commonly ascribed to Agastya were written at so early an age. Probably there is not any one of them older than the tenth century A.D. Of the works attributed to him, those which advocate the system of the Siddhas (in Tamil *Śittar*), a mystical compound of monotheism, quietism, and alchemy, with a tinge of Christianity, must certainly have been written after the arrival of Europeans in India: and Agastya's name appears to have been used by the writers, as had been done by many successions of authors before, for the purpose of gaining the ear of the people for whose use the books were composed. We cannot doubt that the substance of the following stanza, which is contained in the *Ñâna nûṛu*, or 'Centum of Wisdom,' a small poem attributed to Agastya, has been borrowed from statements of Christianity, notwithstanding that Christianity is not directly named in it, or in any other work of this class :—

> "Worship thou the Light of the Universe; who is one;
> Who made the world in a moment, and placed good men in it;
> Who afterwards himself dawned upon the earth as a Guru;
> Who, without wife or family, as a hermit performed austerities;
> Who, appointing loving sages (siddhas) to succeed him,
> Departed again into heaven :—worship him."

It is a striking illustration of the uncritical structure of the ordinary Hindû mind, that this stanza is supposed, even by Tamil *literati*, to have been written by Agastya himself many thousands of years ago. Hindûs endeavour to give it an orthodox Hindû meaning, and native Christians regard it as a prophecy. Though there is not a single archaism in it; though it is written not only in the modern dialect, but in a colloquial idiom, abounding in solecisms, neither party entertains any doubt of its antiquity.

Next to the fabulous Agastya, though many centuries before the treatises ascribed to him, we may perhaps place the author of the Tol-kâppiyam (Tam. *tol*, ancient; Sans. *kâvya*, poem), or ancient book, a real person, though fabled to have been one of Agastya's disciples, who quarrelled with his master and set up for himself. The Tol-kâppiyam is generally admitted to be the oldest extant Tamil grammar, and has been supposed, though on somewhat slight evidence, to be the oldest Tamil composition now extant, with the exception of certain fragments to be referred to presently.

Though written by a S'aiva, its S'aivism is not that of the mystical schools of the Vêdânta or S'aiva-siddhânta; and in the chapters which are still in existence (for much of it is supposed to have been lost), native grammarians have noticed the existence of various grammatical forms which are considered, but I think without sufficient warrant, to be archaic. It is traditionally asserted that the author of this treatise, who is styled technically 'Tolkâppiyanâr,' the man of the ancient book, embodied in his work the substance of Agastya's grammatical elements. This tradition is on a par with that which ascribes so many anonymous works of modern times to Agastya himself: nevertheless, if any relics of poems of the first age of Tamil literature still survive, they are to be found amongst the poetical quotations which are contained in this and similar works, and in commentaries which have been written upon them. Some of those quotations are probably the very oldest specimens of the poetical style that are now extant. Whatever antiquity may be attributed to the Tolkâppiyam, it must have been preceded by many centuries of literary culture. It lays down rules for different kinds of poetical compositions, which must have been deduced from examples furnished by the best authors whose works were then in existence. A rule is simply an observed custom. Grammars, as well as poems, had preceded the Tolkâppiyam, for it continually cites rules which had been laid down by preceding grammarians. Hence the formula which so frequently recurs, *enmanâr pulavar*, 'the poets (*i.e.*, the grammarians) say.' [This form, *enmanâr* instead of *enbar*, is one of the supposed archaisms of this writer; but *enbar* appears to me more ancient as well as more regular.] In endeavouring to trace the commencement of Tamil literature, we are thus carried further and further back to an unknown period.

Even when we come down to the later period, if it were really later, of the Kural and the Chintâmaṇi, when Tamil literature is supposed to have reached the summit of its perfection, we find that the exact age even of those great compositions is unknown. We have not a single reliable date to guide us, and in the mist of conjecture a few centuries more or less seem to go for nothing. Tamil writers, like Hindû writers in general, hid their individuality in the shade of their writings. Even the names of most of them are unknown. They seem to have regarded individual celebrity, like individual existence, as worthless, and absorption into the Universal Spirit of the classical literature of their country as the highest good to which their compositions could aspire. Their readers followed in the same course, age after age. If the book was good, people admired it; but whether it was written by a man or by a divinity, or whether it wrote itself, as the Vedas were commonly supposed to have done, they neither knew nor cared. Still less did they care, of course, if the book were bad. The historical spirit, the antiquarian spirit, to a great degree even the critical spirit, are developments of modern times. If, therefore, I attempt to throw some light on the age of the principal Tamil works, I hope it may be borne in mind that, in my opinion, almost the only thing that is perfectly certain in relation to those works is, that they exist.

It will be convenient to arrange the principal extant works in cycles, which appear to follow one another, with more or less probability, in chronological order.

(1.) *The Jaina cycle.*—I might perhaps have called this instead *the cycle of the Madura Sangam or College*, seeing that two of the most renowned books of this period—the Nâlaḍiyâr and the Kural—are said to have received the imprimatur of the college; but in the accounts respecting the college and its proceedings that have been handed down to us the legendary element predominates to such a degree, and the books now extant ascribed to members of the college, or said to have been approved by them, are such commonplace productions in comparison with those two, that I prefer regarding the college as merely 'the shadow of a great name,' and describing the principal works of the period, not as those which emanated from the college, but as those of the Jaina cycle, from the internal evidence of the works themselves.

Leaving out of account the isolated stanzas already referred to, of high but unknown antiquity, which are quoted as examples in the grammatical and rhetorical works, the oldest Tamil works of any extent now extant are those which were written, or claim to have been written, by the Jainas, or which date from the era of the literary activity of the Jaina sect. The Jainas of the old Pâṇḍya country were animated by a national and anti-Brâhmanical feeling of peculiar strength; and it is chiefly to them that Tamil is indebted for its high culture and its comparative independence of Sanskrit.* The S'aiva and Vaishṇava writers of a later period, especially the S'aivas, imbibed much of the enthusiasm for Tamilic purity and literary independence by which the Jainas were distinguished; in consequence of which, though Tamil literature, as a whole, will not bear a comparison with Sanskrit literature, as a whole, it is the only vernacular literature in India which has not been contented with imitating Sanskrit, but has honourably attempted to emulate and outshine it. In one department at least, that of ethical apophthegms, it is generally maintained, and I think must be admitted, that Sanskrit has been outdone by Tamil. The Jaina period extended probably from the eighth or ninth century A.D., to the twelfth or thirteenth. In the reign of Sundara Pâṇḍya, called also Kûn or Kubja Pâṇḍya, the date of which will be considered further on, the adherents of the religious system of the Jainas are said to have been finally expelled from the Pâṇḍya country; consequently, all Tamil works which advocate or avow that system may be concluded to have been written before the middle of the thirteenth century A.D., and probably before the decadence of Jaina influence in the twelfth. An exception

* Dr Burnell, in the article already quoted, says—"All earlier civilisation in Southern India, so far as it is known, is connected with the Jainas. Hiwen Thsang, who visited the Telugu and Tamil countries in 639–40 A.D., mentions that the inhabitants were chiefly *Nirgranthas* (*i.e.*, Digambara Jainas). He mentions a few Buddhists, but has not a word about Brâhmans. The vague term by which the Tamil language is mentioned (by Kumârila), Ândhra-Drâviḍa-bhâshâ, is remarkable, as it indicates that a systematic study of the so-called Dravidian languages can hardly have begun in the eighth century. . . . There can be little doubt that Bhaṭṭa Kumârila regarded the South Indian (Dravidian) dialects as Mlechcha, or un-Brâhmanic, uncivilised languages. He does not say so expressly, but his words imply that he thought so."

must be made in behalf of the Chûḍâmaṇi Nighaṇṭu, a classical dictionary, by Maṇḍala-purusha, a Jaina writer of the sixteenth century, who enjoyed the protection of one of the kings of Vjaya-nagaram.

The Kuraḷ of Tiruvaḷḷuvar, a work which consists of 1330 distichs, or poetical aphorisms, on almost every subject connected with virtue, wealth, and pleasure (the three chief objects of human existence, according to Hindû writers—the three *purushârthas*), and which is regarded by all Tamilians (and perhaps justly) as the finest composition of which Tamil can boast, is generally regarded not only the best but the oldest Tamil poem of any extent which is now in existence. I think we should not be warranted in placing the date of the Kuraḷ later than the tenth century A.D.

The reasons which induce me to assign to it so high an antiquity are as follows :—

(1.) The Kuraḷ contains no trace of the distinctive doctrines of Sankara Âchârya. It teaches the old Ṣânkhya philosophy, but ignores Sankara's additions and developments, and would therefore appear to have been written before the school of Sankara had popularised itself in the South; though probably not before Sankara himself, who seems to have lived not later than the ninth century.

(2.) It contains no trace of the distinctive doctrines of the Âgama or S'aiva-siddhânta school—a school which, since about the eleventh century A.D., has exercised a more powerful influence on Tamil literature and the Tamil mind than any other. It exhibits no acquaintance even with the existence of this school.

(3.) There is no trace in the Kuraḷ of the mysticism of the modern Purânic system; of *Bhakti*, or exclusive, enthusiastic faith in any one deity of the Hindû Pantheon. The work appears to have been written before S'aivism and Vaishṇavism had been transformed from rival schools into rival sects; before the Purâṇas, as they now stand, had become the text-books of Hindû theology; and whilst the theosophy of the early Vedânta and the mythology of the Mahâ-bhârata comprised the entire creed of the majority of Hindûs.

(4.) The author of the Kuraḷ is claimed with nearly equal reason by S'aivas and Jainas. He is claimed also, but very feebly, by Vaishṇavas. On the whole, the arguments of the Jainas appear to me to preponderate, especially those which appeal to the Jaina titles by which God is described, and the Jaina *tone* that pervades the ethical part of the work:—*e.g.*, scrupulous abstinence from the destruction of life is frequently declared to be not only the chiefest excellence of the true ascetic, but also the highest virtue. Nevertheless, from the indistinctness and undeveloped character of the Jaina element contained in it, it seems probable that in Tiruvaḷḷuvar's age the Jainism of the Tamil country was rather an esoteric ethical school, than an independent objective system of religion, and was only in the process of development out of the older Hindûism. This would carry back the date of the Kuraḷ to the ninth or tenth century.

(5.) The Kuraḷ is referred to and quoted in grammars and prosodies which were probably written in the eleventh or twelfth century.

For these reasons, such as they are, we seem to be warranted in placing the Kuraḷ in the tenth century A.D., at least. It must be remembered, however, as in almost every similar inquiry pertaining to Indian literature, that the reasons for this conclusion possess only a very limited amount of probability, and are capable of being overruled by the first discovery of a reliable date or fact. There are reasons also for regarding it as possible that the Kuraḷ should be placed several centuries later. It is the concurrent voice of various traditions that Tiruvaḷḷuvar lived before the dissolution of the Madura College, and it is certain that the Kuraḷ is included in a poetical list of eighteen works which the college-board—(in this case tradition says it was literally *a board*)—sanctioned. Those traditions go on to state that the Kuraḷ was the very last work presented for the approval of the college, and that it was in consequence of the rejection of the Kuraḷ, in the first instance by the syndicate (on account of the low caste of its author), that the college ceased to exist. The board miraculously expanded itself to receive the Kuraḷ, and then miraculously contracted itself so as to thrust out all the existing members of the college, whereupon, unable to bear the disgrace, they are all said to have drowned themselves. If any weight could be attached to this tradition, it would bring down the date of the Kuraḷ considerably, for other traditions connect Nakkîrar (who is always represented as the president of the college) with the reign of Karikâla Chôla, who seems to have lived in the thirteenth century. Another tradition of a similar tendency is that which places Auveiyâr (Tiruvaḷḷuvar's sister) in the reign of Kulôtunga Chôla, who is known to have lived in the twelfth century. We must be cautious, however, of placing the Kuraḷ so late as Kulôtunga Chôla's reign, for it may be regarded as certain that it was in that reign that the Tamil Râmâyaṇa was completed and published; and Tamil scholars are of opinion that there is internal evidence in the Râmâyaṇa of its author's acquaintance with the Kuraḷ, especially in certain stanzas relating to the duties and qualifications of ambassadors.

It is a remarkable circumstance that the author of the Kural is represented to have been a Pareiya,—born, according to the legend, at

Meilâpûr, near Madras. Another legend represents him to have been the offspring of a Brâhman father by a Pareiya mother. His real name is unknown. The Vaḷḷuvas are the priestly division of the Pareiyas, and also soothsayers, and the author of the 'Kuraḷ' is known only as *Tiruvaḷḷuvar*, 'the sacred Vaḷḷuvan' or Pareiya priest. This is one of those traditions which are so repugnant to inveterate popular prejudice, that they appear too strange for fiction, and are probably founded on fact. It is a still more remarkable circumstance that certain poetical compositions of universal use and popularity in the Tamil country, and of considerable merit, are ascribed to a sister of Tiruvaḷḷuvar, a Pareiya woman! Auveyâr's real name, like that of her brother, is unknown,—*Auvei* or *Auveiyâr*, signifying 'a mother,' 'a venerable matron.'

The Jaina period produced another great ethical poem on "the three objects of existence," called the Nâlaḍiyâr. The style of the stanzas of which it is composed is more discursive and rhetorical than that of the Kuraḷ, and Dr Granl considers it on this account probably more ancient. There is a still stronger argument, I think, for its priority to the Kuraḷ. As it is admitted on every hand that the Kuraḷ excels all Tamil compositions of this kind, it seems improbable that a later writer of inferior power should have chosen the same subject and treated it according to the same rules. Kuraḷ means 'brief,' referring to the brevity of the verse employed: Nâḷaḍi means 'four feet,' referring probably to the four line stanza in which the poem is written. The name of the author is unknown, as well as his date. All that is known is that he was a Jaina, that he wrote in the Pâṇḍya country, which he frequently describes by well-chosen epithets, and that his work is included in the list of those said to have been sanctioned by the Madura College. Some native scholars are of opinion that the whole of the Nâlaḍi is not the composition of one author, but that on the contrary it appears by internal signs to be a collection of stanzas by different hands.

The Chintâmaṇi,* a brilliant, romantic epic, containing 15,000 lines, is the most celebrated Tamil poem written by an avowedly Jaina author. Partly from its Jaina origin, partly from the difficulty of its style, it is little known; but Beschi, who made the Chintâmaṇi the model on which he composed his Têmbâvaṇi, was probably right in asserting that the author "may with justice be called the prince of Tamil poets." The style is considered superior even to that of Kam-

---

* *Chintâmaṇi*, Sans. the gem which yields all one desires, a favourite title of books in all the Indian languages.

bar's Tamil Râmâyaṇa. The name of the author is unknown. It is the opinion of some native scholars that the Chintâmaṇi preceded the Kuraḷ. They think they can trace allusions in the Kuraḷ to matters contained in the Chintâmaṇi, also amplifications in the Kuraḷ of matters which the Chintâmaṇi expresses more briefly. These reasons are adduced still more confidently to prove the priority of the Kuraḷ to the Tamil Râmâyaṇa. It would be a remarkable circumstance if it were capable of being clearly proved that the Chintâmaṇi, which is without doubt the greatest epic poem in the Tamil language, is also the oldest Tamil composition of any extent now extant.

To this period also belongs the oldest classical dictionary of the Tamil language, called the Divâkaram (*divâ-kara*, the day-maker, the sun), a work ascribed to S'êndanâr, a writer who is said to have been a member of the Madura College. The other two classical Tamil dictionaries, the Pingalandei and the Chûḍâmaṇi Nighaṇṭu, were also the composition of Jainas. We have to place in this period, though probably near its close, the most celebrated and authoritative of Tamil grammars, the Nannûl of Pavaṇanti. This is regarded up to the present day as the standard grammar of the language, though its method, like that of all Indian grammars, is very perplexing. No Tamil grammar appears to have been written by a Jaina before the time of Pavaṇanti. The Jainas of the early period were great dictionary-makers, but they seem to have left the writing of grammars to S'aivas.

(2.) *The Tamil Râmâyaṇa Cycle.*—The Tamil version of the Râmâyaṇa is an imitation rather than a translation of Vâlmîki's celebrated poem. The Sanskrit original is sometimes rhetorical, sometimes simple, touching, and natural, sometimes prosaic and prolix. The Tamil imitation never condescends to be natural, much less prosaic, but is always elaborately rhetorical and ornate. It piles up epithet on epithet, simile on simile, till the thought is obscured and the narrative interrupted and almost forgotten. To the Tamil ear it seems the perfection of sweet harmonious rhythm, but to the severer European judgment its sweetness borders upon lusciousness, and its harmony too often suggests the idea of monotonous jingle. The difference between the Tamil and the Sanskrit Râmâyaṇa may be compared to the difference between Pope's Iliad and the Iliad of Homer; but this comparison, though a just one so far as it goes, gives only an imperfect idea at best of the difference between the two works. Notwithstanding its faults of style, from the point of view of a cultured taste, the Tamil Râmâyaṇa is undoubtedly a great poem, and in this department of composition the Chintâmaṇi alone can dispute with it for the palm of supremacy. The author, Kambar, is so called from the name of the district to which he belonged, Kamba-nâḍu, in the Tanjore country, a portion of the ancient Chôla-dêśa. "His fame as a poet having reached the ears of Râjendra Chôla, he was invited to his court, and honoured with the title of the king of poets. Several poets undertook to prepare a Tamil version of the Râmâyaṇa. When recited in the presence of Kulôtunga Chôla, who had succeeded to the throne, Kambar's version was preferred." * Several other works are attributed to him, of which the Êr-eṛubadu, seventy stanzas in praise of the plough, is best known.

So many great poets, authors of works held in high esteem to the present day, seem to have flourished in Kambar's time (in particular Pugaṛêndi, Oṭṭakkûttar, and Auveiyâr), that I have thought the literature of this period best described by the name of the Râmâyaṇa cycle, and it becomes in consequence a point of interest to endeavour to determine its date. Nothing has been definitely ascertained respecting the date of the first or Jaina cycle; but as Kambar's era synchronises with the reigns of the two most celebrated kings of the Chôla line, our prospect of being able to determine his date—the earliest date in Tamil literature which we are likely to be able at present to determine—seems more hopeful. If it were possible to accept the date which is supposed to be furnished by the Tamil Râmâyaṇa itself, our search would at once come to an end. In a stanza which is prefixed to the work, and which is commonly, but without any conclusive authority, attributed to the author himself, it is stated that it was finished in the year of the S'âlivâhana era corresponding to A.D. 886. This date used to be accepted as genuine, not only by natives, but by those few European scholars who had turned their attention to matters of this kind. If it were genuine, the Tamil version of the Râmâyaṇa might fairly claim to be the oldest Tamil composition now extant—a supposition to which the internal evidence of style is opposed; and the author to be regarded as the father of Tamil poetry. This date, though it is the only one with which I am acquainted in the whole range of Tamil literature, is, I fear, an unauthorised addition to Kambar's poem, prefixed to it by some admiring editor for the purpose of giving it a higher antiquity than it can justly claim. We must therefore fall back in this inquiry on the dates of the Chôla kings.

Kambar is connected with the reigns of Râjêndra Chôla and his successor Kulôtunga Chôla, not by any inscriptions or documents which leave no room for uncertainty, but only by traditions, legends,

---

* Murdoch's "Classified Catalogue of Tamil Printed Books; Notices of Tamil Authors," p. 87.

and stories; * but these are so numerous, and on the whole so consistent, and they are corroborated to such a degree by what appear to be undesigned coincidences, that I think their evidence, at least with regard to the point of contemporaneousness, may safely be accepted. I do not find it stated in any inscriptions that Kulôtunga was Râjêndra's *son*, but that he was his successor (whether his immediate successor or not) appears from an inscription I obtained at Kôṭṭâr, near Nagercoil, in the Tamil-speaking part of Travancore. This inscription is cut on the walls of a temple, and states that the temple in question was erected in Kôṭṭâr, called also 'the good town of the triple crowned Chôla,' by Kulôtunga S'ôṛa dêvar, 'to the great divinity Râjêndra S'ôṛêśvaram' (*i.e.*, to S'iva as worshipped by Râjêndra Chôla, or to Râjêndra Chôla himself considered as identified with S'iva after his death).† This inscription is dated in the thirty-first year of Kulôtunga S'ôṛa. [I have found several records of gifts made to this and other temples dedicated to Râjêndra Chôlêśvara in succeeding reigns, including one in the reign of Sundara Pâṇḍya. Only one of these inscriptions furnishes us with a date, and that unfortunately is a late one. It is a record in the same temple at Kôṭṭâr of a gift to the same Chôla king's divinity, and is dated in the S'aka year answering to A.D. 1370, in the fifth year of Parâkrama Pâṇḍi dêvar. Râjêndra himself is generally in inscriptions in the Pâṇḍya country called simply Râjêndra Chôla, but in one inscription I have found him called Râjêndra Chôla Pâṇḍiyan.]

What was Râjêndra's date? I have found two inscriptions at Cape Comorin, one in the fourth year of his reign, and another in the fifth, in each of which Râjêndra is related to have achieved a victory over Âhava Malla (a Jaina king of the Châlukya race) on the banks of the Tunga-bhadra. The date which I supposed to be contained in one of these inscriptions I found afterwards was unreliable; but an inscription found by Sir Walter Elliot (*Journal of the Royal Asiatic Society*) in the western Châlukya country, in which the same battle is mentioned (though the victory is claimed for the Châlukya king), places Âhava Malla, Râjêndra's contemporary, in the middle of the eleventh century. According to inscriptions obtained by Sir Walter Elliot in the Kalinga country or Northern Circars (at that time ruled over by the eastern branch of the Châlukya dynasty), which were

* These traditions have recently been collected in a book called the Vinôdarasa Manchari, by Vîrasvâmi Chettiâr, late head pandit of the Presidency College, Madras.

† Compare the Român title 'Divus Augustus,' that is, Augustus regarded as deified after his death.

utilised by Dr Eggeling in a paper read before the International Congress of Orientalists in 1874, Râjêndra Chôla commenced to reign in A.D. 1063, and ruled not only over the Chôla country, but over the Kalinga country, and, as my inscriptions prove, over the Pâṇḍya country also. The battle between him and Âhava Malla must, therefore, have taken place between 1063 and 1066. I have an inscription of Râjêndra Chôla's, belonging to the southern portion of the Pâṇḍya country, dated in the thirtieth year of his reign. This carries us down to A.D. 1093. When he died, and was succeeded by Kulôtunga Chôla, is at present uncertain, but Sir Walter Elliot places this event in A.D. 1112, after a reign of forty-nine years. I have an inscription dated in the forty-fourth year of Kulôtunga Chôla; but it is unnecessary to place the publication of Kambar's 'Râmâyaṇa' so late as this. Supposing that it was commenced in Râjêndra's reign, and finished in Kulôtunga's, as all traditions represent, its publication cannot have been much before A.D. 1100, and was probably not much after that date. Supposing that it was published as late as the twenty-fourth year of Kulôtunga's reign, this would be exactly 250 years after the date given in the stanza prefixed to the poem. It would, therefore, appear that the poem must have been antedated 250 years.

It seems certain that Kambar was posterior to Râmânuja, the celebrated founder of the S'rî Vaishṇava system. He refers to Râmânuja by name in a poem called the 'S'aḍagôpar Antâdi,' which is always attributed to him. It might be supposed doubtful whether this poem were really written by Kambar, but native scholars think there can be no doubt about its authorship, as Kambar's style, they say, was *sui generis*, and incapable of being imitated. As Râmânuja is placed by Professor Wilson, on what appears to be conclusive evidence, in the beginning of the twelfth century A.D.,* Kambar's date must be posterior to Râmânuja's. The supposition that he lived in the following century in the reigns of Râjêndra Chôla and Kulôtunga Chôla, will perfectly suit all the circumstances of the case.

The same traditions and stories which place the poets Pugaṛêndi and Oṭṭakkûttar, together with Kambar, in the reign of Kulôtunga Chôla, place also Auveiyâr, the reputed sister of Tiruvaḷḷuvar, in the same reign, and connect her by means of conversations and incidents with those three poets. I therefore place her tentatively in this cycle, though this will have the effect either of discrediting the tradition

* Brown, in his "Cyclic Tables," places King Vishnu Vardhana's conversion by Râmânuja in 1133 A.D.

which represents her as Tiruvaḷḷuvar's sister, or of bringing down the age of the Kurâḷ lower than the internal evidence of style and matter seems to warrant. This period, however, does not seem too late for Auveiyâr herself. The two sets of brief verses called the *Âtti-śûḍi* and the *Kondrei-vêndan*, each commencing with a consecutive letter of the Tamil alphabet, which are ascribed to Auveiyâr, appear to be of considerable antiquity: but the Advaita work which is called Auveiyâr's Kuraḷ must have been written subsequently to the arrival of the Muhammedans in Southern India; and the collection of moral epigrams (most of them possessed of real poetic merit) which is called the 'Mûdurei,' or 'proverbial wisdom,' appears to have been written after the arrival of Europeans, perhaps even after the arrival of the English. The proof of the modern origin of the 'Mûdurei' is contained in the following simile:—"As the turkey that had seen the forest peacock dance, fancied himself also to be a peacock, and spread his ugly wings and strutted, so is the poetry which is recited by a conceited dunce." As it is certain that the turkey is an American bird, which was brought to Europe from America, and introduced into India from Europe, there cannot be any doubt of the late origin of the 'Mûdurei,' *if this stanza was always an integral portion of it.* When I have mentioned this anachronism to native scholars, and have called their attention to the circumstance that the Tamil word for 'turkey' (like the words denoting 'tobacco,' 'potato,' &c.), is not an original root, but a descriptive compound—viz., *vân-kôṛi*, signifying 'the great fowl,' they have courageously maintained that the turkey was always found in India.

Another and more ingenious explanation has been advanced by Mr T. M. Scott of Madura, a warm admirer of Tamil poetry. In an edition of the 'Mûdurei' Mr Scott maintains that by *vân-kôṛi* we are to understand, not the turkey, but the pea-hen. Though this explanation is ingenious, I think it inadmissible, on grounds both of philology and of natural history. The pea-hen could not have been described as having 'ugly wings;' and if it had been the intention of the authoress to distinguish the hen from the cock, she would not have marred her purpose by styling the cock alone 'the pea-fowl,' and its hen 'the great fowl,' thereby necessarily suggesting the idea that what she called 'the great fowl' was a totally different bird. It would be safer to argue that the stanza in question was not originally contained in the collection—of which, however, no proof can be adduced.

(3.) *The S'aiva Revival Cycle.*—To this period belongs two large collections of hymns—an earlier and a later—in praise of S'iva and S'aiva temples, breathing an intensely religious spirit, and mostly advocating the S'aiva-siddhânta system of religious philosophy. The earlier collection, called *Tiru-vâśagam*, composed by *Mâṇikka-vâśagar* (Mâṇikya-vâchaka), one of the most enthusiastic propagators of Saivism, has a great reputation amongst the Tamil people up to the present day for its elevated tone and religious earnestness. The heretics that Mâṇikka-vâśagar chiefly confuted were Buddhists from Ceylon, according to the account of a great debate on the merits of the rival creeds related in the *Tiruvâdûr purâṇam;* we can scarcely err, therefore, in placing him earlier, perhaps at least a century earlier, than the other great apostle of S'aivism in the Tamil country, *Ñâna Sambandhar*, who flourished during the reign of Sundara-Pâṇḍya (the date of whose reign will be considered further on), and whose opponents were Jainas. Mâṇikka-vâśagar is not included amongst the sixty-three *Bhaktas* or S'aiva devotees, belonging to Ñâna Sambandhar's period, whose lives are recorded in the *Tiruttoṇḍar purâṇam*, and he is generally stated by Tamil writers to have lived at an earlier period. Some, it is true, place him later than the sixty-three, but, I think, with much less probability. A story contained in the Madurei Sthala purâṇam places Mâṇikka-vâśagar in the reign of Arimardana Pâṇḍya, whose minister he is represented to have been, and whose name stands tenth in the list of kings in that *purâṇa* before that of Sundara Pâṇḍya. I have no confidence in any name in that list before Sundara's, the name with which it ends; but we may conclude that the prince in question, or at least Mâṇikka-vâśagar, lived before Sundara.

The later and larger collection of Saiva hymns was composed chiefly by *Ñâna-Sambandhar*, a native of Sheally (*Śîgâṛi*), near Chellumbrum (*Chidambara*), a sacred S'aiva temple in the Chôla country, who together with his disciples (of whom the most eminent were *Sundarar* and *Appar*, who also were authors of numerous hymns) devoted themselves to uprooting Jainism and spreading Saivism throughout the Tamil country. The general title of these hymns is *Dêvâram* (*dêvârha*, Sans. worthy of God). *Sambandhar's* hymns, 384 in number, have been published in three volumes; *Sundarar's* and *Appar's* in one volume each. These three persons held the most distinguished place amongst 'the sixty-three devotees of Siva,' of each of whose life and labours, including a variety of romantic and miraculous exploits attributed to them, a memoir has been furnished in a popular book already referred to, the *Tiruttoṇḍar purâṇam* (the *purâṇa* of the holy disciples), commonly called the *Periya purâṇam*, or great *purâṇam*, composed by a poet called *Śêkkiṛâr*. Some of the incidents in *Sambandhar's* career, especially his reconversion of *Sundara Pâṇḍya*, king of Madura, from Jainism, and the impaling of eight thousand Jainas, who had been vanquished in discussion and outdone in miracles, are related also in the last portion of the *Tiruviḷeiyâḍal purâṇam*, the *Sthala purâṇa* of Madura. The date of the *Tiruttoṇḍar purâṇam* is unknown; but if it be true, as is related, that the *Tiruviḷeiyâḍal purâṇam* was translated from the Sanskrit original at the request of *Ati-vîra-râma Pâṇḍya*, the poet-king of Madura (as there seems no reason for doubting), it dates, as will be seen further on, from the sixteenth century A.D. Another of the sixty-three devotees, *Śeramân Perumâḷ*, who is said to have been a son of one of the S'êra or Kêraḷa kings, was also the author of some poems belonging to this cycle.

There seems no reason to doubt the propriety of placing the most famous poets and theologians of the Saiva revival in the time of Sundara Pâṇḍya, in whose reign they are invariably placed by native traditions, as well as by the books referred to; and as this reign is an important era, both for the history of Tamil literature and for the date of the almost final extinction of Jainism in the Tamil country by the S'aivas, it becomes as important to endeavour to ascertain the date of this king's reign as it was to fix that of Kulôtunga Chôla. In the first edition of this work, I stated that Sundara Pâṇḍya seemed to me to be identical with the Sender-bandi mentioned by Marco Polo, who visited Southern India in A.D. 1292. This identification, however, has not found much acceptance. Mr Nelson, in his "Madura Manual," after a long and elaborate discussion of the evidence before him, comes to the conclusion that Sundara lived in the latter half of the eleventh century, and therefore nearly two hundred years before Polo's Sender-bandi; and Colonel Yule, in private communications with which he has favoured me, states that he considers it clear from the statements of the Muhammedan historians, Wassaf and Rashiduddin, that there were two Sundars in Ma'bar about Polo's time, and that whilst he thinks Polo's Sender-bandi was identical with the earlier of the two, he is inclined to the opinion that this person was not a genuine king of Madura, but an adventurer, and therefore not the Sundara Pâṇḍya, the date of whose reign I am anxious to ascertain.

The question of the date of this Sundara Pâṇḍya, the last king of the old Pâṇḍya line, is beset with difficulties. Inscriptions belonging to his reign are very numerous. There are at least twenty in my own possession, but not one of them contains a date. If ever a dated inscription belonging to his reign should be discovered (which might readily happen if a thorough search were made, seeing that the district of country from which my inscriptions have been taken does not amount to more than a fifth part of the old Pâṇḍya country), all doubt would be at an end. It might be necessary in that event to abandon

Marco Polo's Sender-bandi altogether; but till then I feel reluctant to give him up. That the true Sundara Pâṇḍya, who impaled the Jainas, and with whose name the ancient list of Pâṇḍya kings breaks suddenly off, belongs rather to the end of the thirteenth century (Polo's era) than to the end of the eleventh, as Mr Nelson supposes, appears to me at present best to accord with the various items of evidence with which we have to deal. It is certain that Sundara lived after Râjêndra Chôla, for there is an inscription in my possession, as I have already mentioned, in which a gift is recorded to have been made in the thirty-second year of Sundara to the temple of Râjêndra S'ôṛêś-varam. This takes him out of the eleventh century altogether, A.D. 1112, according to Sir Walter Elliot's lists, being the last year of Râjêndra's reign. It is in the highest degree probable that Sundara was preceded also by Kulôtunga Chôla who, as we know from an inscription already referred to, ruled over the whole of the Pâṇḍya country, like Râjêndra himself, without a rival, shortly after Râjêndra's reign. It is certain that he was preceded by Vikrama Pâṇḍya, called also Vikrama Chôla-Pâṇḍi, who is related, in an inscription in my possession dated in Sundara's reign, to have previously made a gift to the temple on which the inscription is found, in conjunction with Vîra Chôla, both of whom appear to have reigned in the interval between Râjêndra Chôla and Sundara Pâṇḍya. I may add that his reign must have been subsequent (probably a considerable time subsequent) to the era of Râmânuja, who flourished in the beginning of the twelfth century A.D. In several of the inscriptions belonging to Sundara Pâṇḍya's reign in my possession, gifts to S'rî Vaishṇava establishments are recorded, and in one of these one of the witnesses to the gift is designated Râmânuja-dâsa, the servant or devotee of Râmânuja, a clear proof that Râmânuja was already deceased, and had already for a considerable time been regarded as a sacred personage. [The person referred to as Râmânuja in this connection could not have been Rama's younger brother, who is sometimes called by that name in the Râmâyaṇa.] This seems to me quite irreconcilable with the idea that Sundara reigned in the latter part of the eleventh century. Lastly, if we may consider it certain, as I think we may, that the same Sundara Pâṇḍya, called also Kubja Pâṇḍya, or in Tamil Kûn Pâṇḍiyan, was in some sense the last of the kings of the old Pâṇḍya line—(seeing that his name stands last in the list, that he is the last king mentioned in the Madura *Tiruviḷeiyâḍal purâṇam*, and that all traditions represent his reign as having been followed by a period of anarchy, during which several Muhammedan dynasties were established at Madura)—then it must be considered certain that his reign comes nearly down to the period of the two Sundaras mentioned by the Muhammedan historians, one of whom may have been the Sender-bandi of Marco Polo himself.

The statements of the Muhammedan historians respecting the first of their two Sundaras do not seem to me irreconcilable with the supposition of the identity of Polo's Sender with the Sundara Pâṇḍya of the inscriptions. If we leave out of account Wassaf's second Sundara, who flees to Delhi in 1310, we find him agreeing with Rashiduddin with respect to the Sundara who died in 1293, the man of four brothers, whom we may with very little hesitation identify with Marco Polo's Sender, who was reigning in 1292. Is it impossible also to identify this same Sundara with the Sundara of the inscriptions? I think not. It is clear from both the Muhammedan historians that at the close of the thirteenth century there reigned in Madura *a* Sundara Pâṇḍya who was Dewar—that is, as they interpreted the title, lord paramount—of Ma'bar = the Pâṇḍya-Chôla country. He was, it is true, one of four (or five) brothers 'who had acquired power in different directions,' yet still he alone was called Dewar, and said to have been possessed of immense wealth. Polo also, though he speaks of his brothers as 'kings,' yet speaks of Sender alone as 'a crowned king,' and gives him distinctively the title of Bandi; so that it is evident that in some respects he was regarded as supreme. There is no trace in Sundara's inscriptions of his brothers, or of his power being in any degree shared by them, or of the position he and they held being one that they had 'acquired,' instead of being one that they had inherited; but these are particulars which would not be likely to make their appearance in inscriptions; and there is nothing in the inscriptions or traditions inconsistent with the supposition that he had brothers who had acquired power together with himself. All that is necessary to stipulate for in order to bring the accounts into agreement, is that in some sense he alone should be Pâṇḍi Dêvar, or lord paramount, so that his name only should appear in the inscriptions, and in this, as it seems to me, no particular difficulty can be involved. Polo represents his Sender Bandi as ruling over Soli, which he describes as 'the best and noblest province of India.' Colonel Yule is quite right, I have no doubt, in identifying Soli with Tanjore—that is, with the Chôla country—but this, instead of being a difficulty in the way of identifying Sender Bandi with the Sundara Pâṇḍya of the inscriptions, is in reality an argument in favour of this identification; for whilst Sundara is called in some inscriptions simply Sundara Pâṇḍya, in a still larger number he is called Sundara Chôla-Pâṇḍya, and represented as having conquered the Chôla country and had himself consecrated there as Chôla king. It is clear, however, that Polo's Sender Bandi ruled not only over the Chôla country, but also over at least the coast district of Madura and Tinnevelly (the Pâṇḍya country), inasmuch as it is stated that it was in his territory that the pearl fishery was carried on. I find another point of agreement, not of diversity, in the traces we find in Sundara's court of Muhammedan influences. Rashiduddin represents his Sundara as succeeded by a Muhammedan, and Wassaf agrees with Rashid in giving him a Muhammedan minister. Now it is clear from an inscription in Nelson's "Madura Manual," recording the confirmation by Vîrappa Nâyakkar, in A.D. 1573, of a grant originally made by Kûn Pâṇḍi (*i.e.*, the Sundara Pâṇḍya of the inscriptions, called also Kûn Pâṇḍiyan) to a mosque in Madura, that Muhammedan influences had found a footing in the Pâṇḍyan country even in the time of the genuine Sundara Pâṇḍya; and we know that in those days Muhammedan power was extending so rapidly on every hand, that where it received an inch it would not be slow in taking an ell. It seems to follow, therefore, quite naturally that Sundara's name should stand last in the list of the ancient Pâṇḍyan line, and that tradition should represent the Madura country soon after as entirely in the hands of Muhammedans. This would be an extraordinary circumstance if Sundara (Kûn) Pâṇḍi lived in the latter part of the eleventh century, but not by any means extraordinary if he lived in the latter part of the thirteenth. I may add that, so far as can be ascertained from inscriptions, only one Sundara Pâṇḍya ever reigned. In whatever part of the Pâṇḍya country this name appears, the epithets by which he is described invariably show that the person referred to is one and the same. For instance, in the elaborate inscription at Madura, given by Mr Nelson, we find a curious play on the numerals up to six; and in an inscription obtained by me at Tirukôḷur, a place on the Tâmraparṇi river in Tinnevelly, I find the very same play on the numerals, though more briefly expressed. [Thus, "He who by means of ONE umbrella throws a cool shade over Two countries" (*i.e.*, the Pâṇḍya and Chôla countries), "who cultivates the THREE kinds of classical Tamil, who cherishes the FOUR Vedas, the FIVE species of sacrifice, and the SIX (orthodox S'aiva) sects." The Madura inscription goes on to EIGHT.] The Sundara Pâṇḍya of the inscriptions had a long reign. I have one inscription dated in the thirty-second year of his reign, that in which a gift is recorded to the temple of Râjêndra Chôleśvara. It was natural therefore, especially seeing that it synchronised with the S'aiva revival, that it should abound in inscriptions. Now, as there are no inscriptions in which there is any reference to any other prince of this name; as it is certain that we have inscriptions pertaining to earlier reigns, and certain also that we have dated inscriptions pertaining to subsequent reigns; and as the Sundara of the Muhammedans must be presumed to have had a long reign, seeing that he occupies so large a space in their description of the kingdom, ports, trade, &c., of Ma'bar, I do not see any valid reason (pending the discovery of a dated inscription) why we should hesitate to identify their Sundar, both with Polo's Sender and with the Sundara or Kûn Pâṇḍya of the inscriptions and the S'aiva revival. (See Appendix III.)

(4.) *The Vaishṇava Cycle.*—The poetical compositions of seven of the twelve Âṛvârs or Vaishṇava devotees, followers of Râmânuja, which are included in the *Nâlâyira (p)prabandham* or *Peria Prabandham* ('the Book of the Four Thousand Hymns' or 'the Great Book'), are still more numerous than those of Mânikya Vâchaḳar, Ñâna Sambandhar, and the other S'aiva devotees previously referred to, and are considered not inferior to them in religious fervour or poetical merit. As the Tiruvâśakam and collection of Dêvârams are regarded by the Saivas as "the Tamil Veda," so the same title is claimed by the Vaishṇavas for the *Nâlâyira (p)prabandham*, especially for those parts of it which are called *Peria tiru-moṛi*, 'the Great Sacred Word,' and *Tiru-vây-moṛi*, 'the Words of the Sacred Mouth.'

It is still more difficult to ascertain the date of these compositions with any degree of accuracy than that of the compositions of the S'aiva revival, not only in consequence of there being no chronological data in the poems themselves (a defect which they share with almost all Tamil, and indeed with almost all Hindû, poems), but also in consequence of there being no incidents on record connecting their authors with any of the Chôla or Pâṇḍya kings. Râmânuja's own date is fixed with tolerable accuracy to the beginning of the twelfth century, in consequence of the fame of his conversion of Peddata, the Jaina king of the Hoisala race, afterwards called Vishṇu Vardhana; and Ñâna Sambandhar's reconversion of Sundara Pâṇḍya from Jainism to S'aivism, furnishes us with the materials for approximately determining his age; but no such important conversion to the Vaishṇâva faith is attributed to any of the authors of the Nâlâyira (p)prabandham. We are, therefore, left very much in the dark as regards the age of the poems of this cycle, except with regard to one particular, viz., that they are all subsequent (probably several generations subsequent) to the era of Râmânuja, the great teacher whose system they advocate, and to whom they frequently refer by name. Probably we shall not greatly err if we attribute to the older of these compositions nearly the same date as Mâṇikya Vâchakaṛ's Tiruvâśagam; and place the latter, with the Dêvârams of Sambandhar, Sundarar, and Appar, somewhere about the era of Sundara Pâṇḍya's reign. This seems to have been a period of intense religious excitement all over Southern India, and the fame of the compositions of the prophet-poets of the one faith would naturally fire the genius of the not less highly gifted prophet-poets of the other. It is singular that there is no reference in one of these sets of poems to the other, but this does not prove that they were not contemporary; it only proves that they were widely sundered in feeling and aim. Our own Milton betrays no signs of having ever heard of Jeremy Taylor; our own Jeremy Taylor betrays no signs of having ever heard of Milton: yet both were contemporaries, and one the greatest poet, the other the greatest prose-writer, of his age. If there was so wide a separation between Puritans and Churchmen in the seventeenth century in England, we need not wonder that many centuries earlier the S'aiva and Vaishṇâva poets of the Tamil country, though probably contemporaries, or nearly so, believed that they had no ideas in common, and moved in the orbits of their several creeds far apart.

(5.) *The Cycle of the Literary Revival.*—After a long period (probably nearly two centuries) of literary inactivity, during which the name of not a single great writer can be mentioned, the Tamil mind again awoke. At the head of the poets of the new period stands *Ati-vîra-râma Pâṇḍya*, an elegant and prolific writer, without much original genius, whose chief aim seems to have been to reproduce the glory of the *Chintâmaṇi* and the other great classics of the earlier age. The most celebrated of the compositions attributed to him is the *Neiḍadam* (Naishada), a version of the story of Nala in eleven hundred Tamil stanzas, all of them exceedingly ornate, and many of them exceedingly voluptuous. Another celebrated composition attributed to him is the *Kâśi kâṇḍam*, which from its title might be supposed to be the *kâṇḍam*, or book, of that name which professes to form a portion of the Skanda purâṇa, but which in reality is an independent work. He is also said to have been the author of the admired Tamil versions of two of the Sanskrit Purâṇas, the Liṅga and the Kûrma. His best work from a moral point of view, and the only one in which he shows any real originality, is a little poem called the 'Vettri Vêrkei,' in the first line of which he mentions his own name—a great novelty in Tamil literature. We may attribute also to this period, I think, the Tamil version of the Mahâ-bhârata, mainly by Villi Puttûrâr, which, though not so celebrated as the Tamil Râmâyana of Kambar, is regarded as a very fine composition; together with a large number of translations from Sanskrit on all subjects, including most of the Purâṇas. Perhaps the most valuable, certainly the most thoughtful, compositions of this period, were the philosophical treatises in explanation of the Vedantic and

S'aiva Siddhantic doctrines, some of them translations from Sanskrit, and some imitations. In this class the Ñâna Vâśishṭham, the principal Tamil Vedantic poem; and the S'iva-ñâna-bôdham, with its commentary the S'iva-ñâṇa-siddhi, the most authoritative exposition in Tamil of the Âgama or S'aiva-Siddhantic system, may be regarded as worthy of special notice. Probably this was the period in which most of the medical treatises were composed; and also the erotic poems, which betoken a late period and a depraved taste. Most of the compositions included in the list of Tamil "Minor Poets," and some at least of those attributed to the members of the Madura College, appear to me to belong to this period—a period of translations and elegant extracts, of moral platitudes and pedantic conceits, rather than one of original thought.

Ati-Vîra-Râma Pâṇḍiyan has sometimes been regarded as a mythical person. His name never appears in any traditions respecting the political history of his country; and if really a reigning king, it is concluded that he could scarcely also have been a poet, but must most likely have been merely a patron of poets. It is difficult of course to ascertain whether he may not have received help from the poets of his court, especially in his long translations from the Sanskrit Purâṇas; but it is so rare a thing for a Hindû king to be also a celebrated poet, that it seems unlikely so many poems should have been attributed to him, especially poems evincing what natives regard as such exquisite taste, if he had not really been their author. However this may be, I find it to be certain that this personage really existed and reigned, and I find also a satisfactory reason why his name does not occur in the political history. 'Ati-Vîra-Râma' was not his real name, but his assumed literary name—his *nom de plume.* His real name, by which he was known as a reigning sovereign, was Vallabha Deva. I had many inscriptions in my possession pertaining to Vallabha Deva's reign, which were without date. At length I found a dated inscription, which turned out to be a peculiarly valuable one for Tamil literary history. This is an inscription in Sanskrit, in the Grantha character, found in the interior of the temple at Courtallum, Tinnevelly. It is in the fortieth year of Vallabha Deva, "*who is Ati-Vîra-Râma;*" and that this person with the double name is the very person we are in search of appears from this also that he is praised for his skill in *saṅgîta-sâhitya,* 'music and *belles lettres.*' This fortieth year of Vallabha Deva corresponds to the S'aka year 1527 (A.D. 1605). It thus appears that Ati-Vîra-Râma, the poet-king, came to the throne in A.D. 1565. A predecessor of his (apparently his immediate predecessor) was Vikrama Pâṇḍya (called also *Kâśi kaṇḍa*, he who visited Benares), the year of whose accession, according to an inscription in my possession, was A.D. 1543; and he again was preceded by Parâkrama Pâṇḍya, the year of whose accession, according to another inscription, was A.D. 1516. The power of these princes, however, could have been little better than nominal; for the lieutenants of the Râjâ of Vijayanagara, who came to Madura about the middle of that very century, at the unwise request, it is said, of the Pâṇḍya prince, to help him against the Chôlas, never returned to Vijayanagara, but founded a new local dynasty (the Nâyaks of Madura), who from that time forward relieved the Pâṇḍyan princes, first of the greater part, and then of the whole, of their power, and ruled the country in their own name, with scarcely any reference to Vijayanagara. I do not suppose that all or most of the works referred to as included in this cycle, were composed exactly within the limits of Ati-Vîra-Râma Pâṇḍiyan's reign. Doubtless some were earlier than his time, some later; but it was about his time that they were written. He appears to have been a great patron of literature, and his own name is the most distinguished amongst the writers of that time. It is related that it was at his request that the Madura Tiruviḷeiyâḍal Purâṇam was translated from Sanskrit; and doubtless this was not the only case of the kind that occurred.

(6.) *The Anti-Brahmanical Cycle.*—I refer here to the compositions of the so-called *S'ittar* school—a series of compositions which occupy a position of their own in Tamil literature as regards both matter and style, so that, whatever be their age, they cannot well be included in any other cycle. The Siddhas or 'sages' (in Tamil *S'ittar*) were a Tamil sect, the adherents of which retained S'iva as the name of God, but rejected everything in the S'aiva system which was inconsistent with pure theism. They cultivated alchymy (*rasâyana*) as sedulously as the Arabians, from whom they appear to have derived their knowledge of it. One of their number is said to have visited Arabia, and another refers to the Franks. Several of them refer to the Turukkas, the name by which the Indian Muhammedans are known in the South. The poems of the Siddha school are wholly modern and colloquial, with grammatical forms unknown to the ancients; but they make up by clearness and force for what they lack in classical refinement. The writers evidently believed what they wrote, and wished to produce an impression, especially on the common people. So far they are deserving of commendation; but it was a peculiarity of theirs of which we cannot approve, that most of them took to themselves without warrant the names of *Rishis* or of renowned teachers and poets. Thus one of them called himself Agastya, another Kapila, another S'aṅkara Âchârya, another Gautama, another Tiruvaḷḷuvar. What is surprising is that this audacity was perfectly successful. The writers are now almost universally supposed to have lived at an early period; and as the school has ceased to exist, this contributes to throw around their writings an air of antiquity. They are much quoted by native Christians, who generally fancy them to have been endowed with a prophetic spirit, and to have meant Christ by the Sat-Guru (true teacher) to whom they constantly refer. I have no doubt that they were more or less acquainted with Christianity, and that their prophecies were after the event, like those of the Sybils of ancient Europe. Who could doubt the allusions to Christianity in the following?—

> "God is one and the Veda is one;
> The disinterested, true Guru is one, and his initiatory rite one;
> When this is obtained his heaven is one;
> There is but one birth of men upon the earth,
> And only one way for all men to walk in:
> But as for those who hold four Vedas and six Shastras,
> And different customs for different people,
> And believe in a plurality of gods,
> Down they will go to the fire of hell!"

The author of this composition calls himself *Koṅkaṇar*, the name of one of the supposed disciples of Agastya. To me, however, he appears by the adoption of that name to identify himself with the neighbourhood of Goa (in the Koṅkaṇa country), the first place where Christian teachers from Europe formed a settlement. I quote the last stanza from a striking series of verses by a writer of this school on the identity of God and love—premising that the word used for God is S'ivam, the neuter of S'iva—

> "The ignorant think that God and love are different.
> None knows that God and love are the same.
> Did all men know that God and love are the same,
> They would dwell together in peace, considering love as God."

The writer calls himself *Tirumûla*, the name of another supposed disciple of Agastya. *Tirumûla* was the name also of one of 'the sixty-three' S'aiva devotees mentioned in the *Tiruttoṇḍar purâṇam;* but this must have been a different person, for no one can attribute the idea conveyed in the verse quoted above to any but a Christian source. Another of the writers of this school is called *Pattira-giriyâr* (from the name of the place to which he belonged). I quote one verse out of more than two hundred of his *Pulambals* or Lamentations, to illustrate the anti-Brahmanical feeling pervading the writings of this school.

"Oh! when will the time come that I shall burn the S'âstras, and prove the four Vedas to be a lie, and discover the mystery, and obtain salvation?"

Undoubtedly the most striking compositions emanating from members of this school are those contained in a book called *Śiva-vâkyam*, 'Words about God,' the author of which is known only as *Śiva-vâkyar*, from the name of his book. I quote the following specimens as illustrations both of his matter and style.

"As milk once drawn cannot again enter the udder, nor butter churned be recombined with milk;
As sound cannot return to a broken conch, nor the life be restored to the body it left;
As a decayed leaf and a fallen flower cannot be reunited to the parent tree;
So man once dead is subject to no future birth."

THE SHEPHERD OF THE WORLDS.

How many various flowers
Did I, in bye-gone hours,
Cull for the gods, and in their honour strew;
In vain how many a prayer
I breathed into the air,
And made, with many forms, obeisance due.

Beating my breast, aloud
How oft I called the crowd
To drag the village car; how oft I stray'd,
In manhood's prime, to lave
Sunwards the flowing wave,
And, circling Saiva fanes, my homage paid.

But they, the truly wise,
Who know and realise
Where dwells the SHEPHERD OF THE WORLDS,* will ne'er
To any visible shrine,
As if it were divine,
Deign to raise hands of worship or of prayer.

I quote the above poetical version of a remarkable stanza of S'iva-vâkyar's from "Specimens of Tamil Poetry," by my son, Mr R. C.

---

* Probably the poet by *Aṇḍar(k)kôn* meant only 'king of the gods,' but the words used suggest the more poetical meaning given above.

Caldwell, in the *Indian Antiquary* (Bombay) for April 1872. See also Mr Gover's "Dravidian Folk-songs."

The poems of the Sittar school should be attributed, I think, to the seventeenth century. Looking at their matter and style, we might suppose them to have been written during the last century; but the school from which these remarkable poems emanated has passed so entirely away without leaving a relic behind, that we seem to be obliged to place it a century earlier. Its nearest representative in the present day is the Brahma Samâj, some of the members of which advocate the semi-Christian theism of their school in excellent Tamil prose.

(7.) *The Modern Writers.*—I mean by these the writers of the eighteenth and nineteenth centuries, including perhaps a few who belonged to the close of the seventeenth. Books belonging to this period, though generally of little real value, appear to be exceedingly numerous —not perhaps because the number of books written was greater than in former times, but because many mediocre works which people would not care to preserve by copying have not yet had time to crumble of themselves into dust. Of the poems belonging to this period which have acquired a name, one of the earliest is the Tamil version of the Prabhu Linga Lîlâ, a translation from the Canarese, which is considered the finest composition in Tamil pertaining to the Vîra S'aiva or Jangama sect. Another is a small ethical treatise called the Nîti-neri-viḷakkam, a portion of which is much used in schools. These belong to the close of the seventeenth century, to which period also probably belong the poems of Paṭṭanattu Piḷḷei.

The post of honour, not only in the beginning of the eighteenth century, when they flourished, but throughout the entire modern period, is to be assigned to two contemporary poets, one a native, the other a foreigner. The former of these, Tâyumânavar ('he who became a mother also,' the name of the manifestation of S'iva worshipped at Trichinopoly), was a religious-minded S'aiva, in whose poems it is believed that a distinct tinge of Christianity can be traced. He appears to have had opportunities of becoming acquainted with Christianity; but however this may be, it is certain that his poems are characterised by much religious earnestness, as well as by much beauty of language. The other, whose poems occupy a still higher place in literature, was the celebrated Beschi, not a Tamilian, like every other Tamil poet, but an Italian, a missionary priest of the Jesuit order, who acquired such a mastery over Tamil, especially over its classical dialect, as no other European seems ever to have acquired over that or any other Indian language. His prose style in the colloquial dialect, though good, is not of preeminent excellence; but his poems in the classical dialect, especially his great poem, the Têmbâvaṇi, a long and highly wrought religious epic in the style of the Chintâmaṇi, are so excellent—from the point of view of Hindû ideas of excellence; that is, they are so elaborately correct, so highly ornamented, so invariably harmonious—that I have no doubt he may fairly claim to be placed by the votes of impartial native critics themselves in the very first rank of the Tamil poets of the second class; and when it is remembered that the first class comprises only three, or at the utmost four, works—the Kural, the Chintâmaṇi, the Râmâyaṇam, the Nâlâḍiyâr—it seems to me, the more I think of it, the more wonderful that a foreigner should have achieved so distinguished a position. Though the Têmbâvaṇi possesses great poetical merit and exhibits an astonishing command of the resources of the language, unfortunately it is tinged with the fault of too close an adherence to the manner and style of 'the ancients'—that is, of the Tamil classics —and is still more seriously marred by the error of endeavouring to Hindûise the facts and narratives of Scripture, and even the geography of Scripture, for the purpose of pleasing the Hindû taste. It is a remarkable illustration of the difference in the position occupied in India at present by poetry and prose respectively, that Beschi's poetry, however much admired, is now very little read, whilst his prose works, particularly his grammars and dictionaries of both the Tamil dialects, are in great demand.

The principal compositions of the latter part of the last century were dramas, hymns in praise of temples, and abbreviations of older works. In the present century an entirely new style of composition has appeared—viz., good colloquial prose, which, through the spread of European influences, seems likely to have a struggle for the mastery with poetry, in the Tamil literature of the future. The name of the father of this species of composition (in so far as Tamilians are concerned) deserves to be remembered. It was Tâṇḍava-râya Mudaliyâr, at one time a teacher in the College of Madras. To him we are indebted for the Tamil prose version of the Panchatantra, and, through the influence of his example, for versions of the Râmâyaṇa, the Mahâ-bhârata, &c., in the same style of flowing and elegant, yet perfectly intelligible, prose.

There has been a considerable amount of literary activity, according to Dr Gundert, in Malayâḷam during the period under consideration, the Kêrala Utpatti, or Origin of Kêrala, with some other works of importance, having been written, he supposes, during the last century, before Hyder's invasion.

The introduction of printing during the present century has given a powerful impulse, if not to the composition of new Tamil works, yet at least to the publication (and thereby to the preservation) of old ones. The following list of Tamil books printed in Madras up to 1865, compared with Bengâli books printed in Calcutta, is taken from Murdoch's "Classified Catalogue of Tamil Printed Books."

	Bengali.	Tamil.
Protestant Books and Tracts,	263	587
Roman Catholic Publications,	2	87
Muhammedan Books,	41	36
S'aiva do.	37	237
Vaishṇava do.	80	103
Vedantic do.	40	101
Braḥma Samâj do.	51	3
Jurisprudence,	49	19
Ethics,	59	48
Medicine,	24	43
Poetry and the Drama,	53	103
Tales,	53	42

Tamil works surpass Bengâli works in numbers, but it does not follow that they are of a higher character. Dr Murdoch asserts that they are not. He says, with regard to Madras publications, "Reprints of old books, or feeble modern imitations of them, constitute the great bulk of the issues of the native presses. There is far more intellectual activity in Bengal."

This is not the proper place for attempting to furnish the reader with an estimate of the intrinsic value of Dravidian poetry. I have only space to remark here that, whilst an elevated thought, a natural, expressive description, a pithy, sententious maxim, or a striking comparison, may sometimes be met with, unfortunately elegance of style has always been preferred to strength, euphony has been preferred to truthfulness, and poetic fire has been quenched in an ocean of conceits. Nothing can exceed the refined elegance and 'linked sweetness' of many Telugu and Tamil poems; but a lack of power and purpose, and a substitution of sound for sense, more or less characterise them all; and hence, whilst an anthology composed of well-selected extracts would please and surprise the English reader, every attempt to translate any Tamil or Telugu poem *in extenso* into English, has proved to be a failure.

It is deserving of notice that alliteration is of the essence of Dravidian poetry, as of the more modern Welsh; and that the Dravidians have as just a claim as the Welsh to the credit of the invention of rhyme. The rhyme of modern European poetry is supposed by some to have had a Welsh or Celtic origin; but Dravidian rhyme was invented by Dravidians. The chief peculiarity of Dravidian rhyme consists in its seat being, not at the end of the line, but at the beginning—a natural result of its origin in a love of alliteration. The rule in each Dravidian dialect is that the consonant which intervenes between the first two vowels in a line is the seat of *rhyme*. A single Tamil illustration must suffice:—

"sî*r*ei (t)têḍil,
ê*r*ei (t)têḍu."—AUVEIYÂR.

"If you seek for prosperity,
Seek for a plough."

The agreement of those two consonants constitutes the minimum of rhyme which is admissible; but often the entire first foot of one line rhymes with the same foot in the second; sometimes the second feet in each line also rhyme; and the rhyme is sometimes taken up again further on in the verse, according to fixed laws in each variety of metre.

The mental physiology of the Indo-European and Dravidian races respectively is illustrated by their literature. It is illustrated in a still greater degree by their languages, and even by the systems of sound which are characteristic of those languages. The languages of the Indo-European class are fond of combining clashing consonants, and welding them into one syllable by sheer force of enunciation; and it is certain that strength and directness of character and scorn of difficulties are characteristics not only of the Indo-European languages, but of the races by which those languages are spoken. On the other hand, the Dravidian family of languages prefers softening away difficulties to grappling with them: it aims at ease and softness of enunciation rather than impressiveness. Multiplying vowels, separating consonants, assimilating differences of sound, and lengthening out its words by successive agglutinations, it illustrates the mental characteristics of the races by which it is spoken, by the soft, sweet, garrulous effeminacy of its utterances.

Perhaps, however, the chief cause of the inferiority of Dravidian poetry, as a whole, to Indo-European poetry, as a whole, is to be found not so much in its preference of elegance to strength, as in its subjection to the authority of precedent and custom, which is at least as complete as anything we meet with in later Sanskrit.

Literature could never be expected to flourish, and where it had ceased to flourish could never be expected to revive, where the following distich (contained in the "Nan-nûl," or classical Tamil grammar) was accepted as a settled principle :—

> "On whatsoever subjects, in whatsoever expressions, with whatsoever arrangement,
> Classical writers have written, *so* to write is denoted *propriety of style*."

For the last two hundred years Dravidian literature appears to have made but little real progress. This is sometimes attributed by natives to the discouraging effect of foreign domination, but it seems far more largely owing to the natural tendency to decay and death which is inherent in a system of slavery to the authority of great names.

Now that native education has commenced to make real progress, and the advantages of European knowledge, European civilisation, and European Christianity are becoming known and felt by so many of the Hindûs themselves, it may be expected that the Dravidian mind will ere long shake itself free from its thraldom, and be stimulated to enter upon a new and brighter career. If the national mind and heart were stirred to so great a degree a thousand years ago by the diffusion of Jainism, and some centuries later by the dissemination of the S'aiva and Vaishṇava doctrines, it is reasonable to expect still more important results from the propagation of the grand and soul-stirring truths of Christianity, and from the contact of the minds of the youth with the ever-progressive literature and science of the Christian nations of the West.

It is a great and peculiar advantage of the English and vernacular education which so many Hindûs are now receiving from European missionaries and from Government teachers, that it is communicated to all who wish to receive it without distinction of caste. In former ages the education of the lower castes and classes was either prohibited or sedulously discouraged; but now the youth of the lower classes are being admitted to the same educational advantages as those enjoyed by the higher castes. The hitherto uncultivated minds of the lower and far most numerous classes of the Hindû community are now for the first time in history being brought within the range of humanising and elevating influences. A virgin soil is now for the first time being ploughed, turned up to the air and light, and sown with the seed of life; and in process of time we may reasonably expect to reap a rich crop of intellectual and moral results.

In the Appendix I have adduced the evidence formerly contained in the Introduction, proving that Tuda, Kôta, Gôṇḍ, and Ku are Dravidian tongues, and have also reprinted some remarks on the late Mr Gover's "Folk Songs of Southern India." I have added an excursus on Sundara Pâṇḍya, and I have endeavoured to answer the question, "Are the Pareiyas and the Tudas Dravidians?" and have subjoined some remarks "On the Dravidian physical type," and "On the religion of the ancient Dravidian tribes."

COMPARATIVE GRAMMAR.

NOTE ON TRANSLITERATION.

All foreign words, to whatever family of languages they may belong, are represented in this work in Roman characters, for the double purpose of preventing unnecessary expense and trouble, and of facilitating comparison.

Long vowels are invariably marked thus,—*á:* when no such accent is placed over a vowel, it is intended that it should be pronounced short. *E* and *o*, being invariably long in Sanskrit, are left unaccented in the transliteration of Sanskrit words in works treating of Sanskrit. The Dravidian languages having short *e* and *o*, as well as long, it is to be understood that they are to be pronounced short when unaccented.*

All vowels are pronounced in the Continental manner. *ei*, as will be explained, corresponds to the Sanskrit *ai.*

The "lingual" or "cerebral" consonants are denoted by a subscribed dot—*e.g.*, *ṭ*, *ḍ*, *ṇ:* the peculiar vocalic *r*, and the surd *l*, of the South Indian languages are denoted in a similar manner—*e.g.*, *ṛ*, *ḷ:* the obscure, inorganic nasal *n* or *m* is represented by *n* with a superscribed line—*e.g.*, *n̄:* the nasal of the guttural row of consonants, ordinarily represented by *ng*, is written *ṅ;* the nasal of the palatal row, ordinarily written *nj* or *ny*, is written *ñ;* and the hard rough *r* is represented by a heavier letter **r**.

The dental *d* in Tamil, and the corresponding *t* or *d* in Malayâlam, are pronounced in the middle of a word, or between two vowels, like the English *th* in than; and in Telugu, *j* and *ch*, when followed by certain vowels, are pronounced like *dz* and *ts:* but as these are merely peculiarities of *pronunciation*, and one consonant is not exchanged for another, no change has been made in the characters by which those sounds are represented.

I have found it very difficult to determine how the third consonant in Tamil, answering to the Sanskrit *ch*, should be represented. The difficulty is owing to the circumstance that its pronunciation, when doubled, differs considerably from its pronunciation when single. When single, its pronunciation closely resembles that of the Sanskrit

---

* Dr Burnell, in his "Specimens of South Indian Dialects," No. 1, Konkani (Mangalore, 1872), mentions that Professor H. H. Wilson, being accustomed to speak North Indian dialects only, used always to say *Tĕlugu*, instead of *Telugu*.

ś; when doubled, it is identical with that of the Sanskrit *chch.* I have thought it best, therefore, to represent it by these letters. This is the way in which I have dealt with the other Tamil letters, the pronunciation of which, when single, differs from their pronunciation when double ;—*e.g.*, *d*, which, when doubled, I have represented, as the pronunciation requires, as *tt;* and *ḍ*, which, when doubled, becomes in like manner *ṭṭ*.

There is a tendency in all the Dravidian languages to pronounce *e* as if it were *ye*, and *o* as if it were *wo.* In colloquial Tamil, this pronunciation, though often heard, is seldom represented in writing; but in modern Canarese and Telugu, *y* before *e*, and *v* or *w* before *o*, are often written as well as pronounced. In Canarese and Tuḷu grammars, it has become customary, in rendering words in the Roman character, to write *ye* for *e*, and *wo* for *o*, even where the native characters employed are *e* and *o* alone—*e.g.*, Can., *wondu*, one, and *yeradu*, two, instead of *ondu* and *eradu.* As this euphonic change seems to be a corruption, not a primitive dialectic peculiarity, and as it tends to hinder comparison with the other dialects, all such words will be written in this work without the *y* or *v*, and it will be left to the reader who is acquainted with the native usage to pronounce those words as usage requires. This usage prevails also, it seems, in Marâṭhi and Koṅkaṇi; and Dr Pope, in his "Outlines of the Grammar of the Tuda Language," points out the existence of traces of this usage even in English—*e.g.*, "ewe" is pronounced "yew" and "one" "won." This he attributes to Celtic influences. As regards the Dravidian languages, it does not seem necessary to suppose this peculiarity to be one of any great antiquity, seeing that the spelling of Dravidian words has always been phonetic; and hence *y* and *v* would have been written as well as pronounced, if this pronunciation had been prevalent at the time the languages were first committed to writing. The people in the neighbourhood of Madura, where the purest Tamil is supposed to be spoken, pride themselves on pronouncing initial *e* and *o* pure.*

* Europeans often notice the appearance of this peculiarity in the pronunciation of English by the people of South India. "Every" becomes "yevery," and "over" "wover." One of the best illustrations of this peculiarity I have heard was mentioned to me by some members of my family. As they were travelling along a road in Tinnevelly, they passed a finger-post at a cross road, on which the name of a place was inscribed in English. They did not catch the name as they passed, and therefore sent back a native girl to find it out for them. The girl knew very little English, and on her return said she could not make out the name, but could repeat the letters. "What were they?" Answer—"Yen, yeh, yell, yell, woe, woe, war!" These dreadful sounds represented the name "Nalloor."

DRAVIDIAN GRAMMAR.

PART I.

SOUNDS.

It will be my endeavour in this section to elucidate the laws of sound by which the Dravidian languages are characterised. Special notice will be taken of those regular interchanges of sound in the different dialects which enable us to identify words under the various shapes they assume, and to which it will frequently be necessary to allude in the subsequent sections of this work.

Dravidian Alphabets.—Before entering on the examination of the Dravidian sounds, it is desirable to make some preliminary observations on the alphabets of the Dravidian languages.

There are three different Dravidian alphabets at present in use, viz., the Tamil, the Malayâlam, and the Telugu-Canarese. I class the Telugu and the Canarese characters together, as constituting but one alphabet; for though there are differences between them, those differences are few and very unimportant. Tuḷu has ordinarily been written hitherto in the Malayâlam character, but Canarese characters are now used in the books printed at the German Mission Press at Mangalore. It is this character which is used in Brigel's Tuḷu Grammar. The Ku grammar of which I have made use is written in the characters of the Oriya—characters which are less appropriate than those of the Telugu would have been for expressing the Ku sounds. The other uncultivated dialects of this family have hitherto been content to have their sounds expressed in the Roman character.

The three Dravidian alphabets which have been mentioned above, viz., the Tamil, the Malayâlam, and the Telugu-Canarese, together with their older but now obsolete shapes, and the *Grantha*, or character in which Sanskrit is written in the Tamil country, have all been derived, it is supposed, from the early Deva-nâgarî, or rather from the still earlier characters contained in Aśoka's inscriptions—characters which have been altered and disguised by natural and local influences, and especially by the custom, universal in the Dekhan, of writing on the leaf of the palmyra palm with an iron stylus.

The following remarks of Mr Beames ("Comparative Grammar of the Modern Aryan Languages of India," Introduction, pp. 62–66) show clearly how these alterations have taken place :—"The Oriya characters, in their present form, present a marked similarity to those employed by the neighbouring non-Aryan nations, whose alphabets have been borrowed from the Sanskrit; I mean, the Telugu, Malayâlam, Tamil, Singhalese, and Burmese. The chief peculiarity in the type of all these alphabets consists in their spreading out the ancient Indian letters into the elaborate maze of circular and curving forms. This roundness is the prevailing mark of them all, though it is more remarkable in the Burmese than in any other; Burmese letters being entirely globular, and having hardly such a thing as a straight line among them. The straight, angular letters which Aśoka used are exhibited in the inscriptions found at Seoni on the Narmadâ (Nerbudda) in more than their pristine angularity, but adorned with a great number of additional lines and squares, which render them almost as complicated as the glagolitic alphabet of St Cyril. The next modification of these letters occurs in the inscriptions found at Amrâvatî on the Kistna, where the square boxes have been in many instances rounded off into semicircles. From this alphabet follow all the Dravidian and the Singhalese; probably also we may refer to this type the Burmese and even the Siamese, and the beautiful character in use in Java, which is evidently of Aryan origin, as its system of Pasangans, or separate forms for the second letter of a nexus, and Sandangans, or vowel and diacritical signs, sufficiently testify.

"Whether the Oriyas received the art of writing from Bengal or from Central India is a question still under dispute. . . . . Assuming that they got their alphabet from Central, rather than from Northern, India, the reason of its being so round and curling has now to be explained. In all probability, in the case of Oriya, as in that of the other languages which I have mentioned above, the cause is to be found in the material used for writing. The Oriyas and all the populations living on the coasts of the Bay of Bengal write on the Tâlpatra, or leaf of the fan-palm, or palmyra (*Borassus flabelliformis*). The leaf of this tree is like a gigantic fan, and is split up into strips about two inches in breadth or less, according to the size of the leaf, each strip being one naturally-formed fold of the fan. On these leaves, when dried and cut into proper lengths, they write with an iron style, or Lekhani, having a very fine sharp point. Now, it is evident that if the long, straight, horizontal mâtrâ, or top line of the Deva-nâgarî alphabet, were used, the style in forming it would split the leaf, because, being a palm, it has a longitudinal fibre, going from the stalk to the point. Moreover, the style being held in the right hand and the leaf in the left, the thumb of the left hand serves as a fulcrum on which the style moves, and thus naturally imparts a circular form to the letters. Perhaps the above explanation may not seem very convincing to European readers; but no one who has ever seen an Oriya working away with both hands at his Lekhani and Tâlpatra will question the accuracy of the assertion; and though the fact may not be of much value, I may add, that the native explanation of the origin of their alphabet agrees with this. . . . The Oriya letters, however, have departed less from the early type than those of their neighbours the Telingas. . . . Without going through the whole alphabet letter by letter, it may suffice to say in general terms, that the Oriya characters show signs of having arisen from a form of the Kuṭila character prevalent in Central India, and that its love of circular forms, common to it and the neighbouring nations, is due to the habit of writing on the Tâlpatra, Talipot, or palm-leaf, with an iron style."

It was supposed by Mr Ellis, and the supposition has gained currency, that before the immigration of the Brahmans into the Tamil country, the ancient Tamilians were acquainted with the art of writing; that the Brahmans recombined the Tamil characters which they found in use, adding a few which were necessary for the expression of sounds peculiar to Sanskrit; and that from this amalgamation, which they called *Grantha*, or the book (*grantha lipi*, or "the book character"), the existing Tamil characters have been derived. There can be little doubt of the derivation of the Tamil character in ordinary use from the Grantha; for some characters are identical with Grantha letters which are still in use, and others with more ancient forms of the Grantha; but the other part of the hypothesis, viz., the existence of a Præ-Sanskrit Tamil character, out of which the Grantha itself was developed, is more doubtful; and though it is true that there is a native Tamil word which signifies "a letter," and another which signifies "a book," yet there is no direct proof of the existence of Tamil characters older than the time of the arrival of the first Brahman immigrants. The character called *Haḷa Kannaḍa*, or old Canarese, and the various characters in which Tamil is found to be written in old inscriptions, seem to me to be founded on the basis of an alphabetical system which was originally intended for the use of Sanskrit.

Mr Edward Thomas, in an article on "Recent Pehlvi Decipherments," in the *Jour. R. A. S.* for 1871, has put forth a theory allied to, but not identical with, Mr Ellis's. He supposes the earliest characters in which Sanskrit or the Prakrits were expressed—that is, the characters used in Aśoka's edicts—to have had a Dravidian origin; that they were originally invented to meet the requirements of Turanian (Dravidian) dialects; and that the principal change effected when the "normal Dravidian alphabet" was converted into the "Prakrit or Lat alphabet," consisted in the system of means adopted for the expression of the aspirates. Mr Thomas considers that the Lat alphabet made a difference between short and long *e*, though the form used for the latter is made to do duty for *ai*. On the other hand, "the oldest known Dravidian alphabet," published by Dr Burnell, which is to be described presently, makes no difference between long *e* and short, which is one of the arguments that may be adduced in favour of the theory of the derivation of that alphabet from the Sanskritic alphabet of Aśoka.

The characters used in certain early Tamil inscriptions, such as the *śâsanas*, or royal grants, in the possession of the Jews of Cochin and the Syrian Christians on the Malabar coast, deserve special consideration. The inscriptions themselves were published and interpreted many years ago in the *Journal of the Madras Literary Society*. They are written in the Tamil language, though in an idiom which is slightly tinged with the peculiarities of Malayâlam. The alphabet of these inscriptions has been printed by Dr Burnell, of the Madras Civil Service, in the *Indian Antiquary* for August 1872 (Bombay). The characters have been taken from a facsimile of the copper *śâsanas* in the possession of the Jews and Syrians in Cochin, one of which has been ascertained, from the astronomical data contained in it, to be dated in A.D. 774. Dr Burnell says of these *śâsanas*, "Palæographically they are of the greatest value, for they are the oldest inscriptions in Southern India that have yet been discovered, and give the oldest form of the ancient Tamil alphabet. It appears to have fallen into disuse in the Tamil country about the tenth century, but was generally in use in Malabar up to the end of the seventeenth. It is still occasionally used for deeds in Malabar; but in a more modern form, and still more changed, it is the character used by the Mâpillas of North Malabar and the islands off the coast." I formed for myself an alphabet of these characters many years ago, and have found it used in inscriptions in Tinnevelly as late as the twelfth century, if not later; but an old variety of the existing Tamil character was also in use at the same time. The latter character seems to have been introduced into Tinnevelly and the extreme south of Travancore during the supremacy of the Chola kings. I am therefore inclined to call it the Chola character. Rajendra Chola's inscriptions (in the eleventh century A.D.) are in this character. I have found inscriptions of the time of Sundara Pândiya (called also Chola-Pândiya) in both characters; and though unable at present to determine with accuracy the date of Sundara's reign, I have no hesitation in placing it several generations later than that of Rajendra Chola. Dr Burnell considers the Tamil-Malayâlam character of the Jewish and Syrian inscriptions the origin of the character used in the Aśoka edicts, and thinks that "the only possible theory of the origin of the character of the Southern inscriptions is that it is an importation brought by traders from the Red Sea, and thence from Phœnicia, and is therefore of Egyptian origin eventually. In many respects the old Tamil alphabet resembles that of the Himyaritic inscriptions found in Yemen. In one respect it differs remarkably from that (the Himyaritic) alphabet, but agrees with the Ethiopic —in that the consonants are modified by the addition of the vowels." These suggestions are well worthy of further consideration; but for the present they seem to me to be hardly in accordance with the facts with which we are acquainted respecting the history of Indian culture. That the character of the Aśoka inscriptions (in the third century B.C.) was gradually modified into the Tamil-Malayâlam character (the earliest dated specimen of which belongs, as we have seen, to A.D. 774), in the lapse of centuries, and in the progress of literature from the original seats of the Aryans to the extreme south, may surely be regarded as more probable in itself than that the Aśoka character was nothing more than an adoption or imitation of the Tamil-Malayâlam character, even though we should grant that the latter may originally have presented some differences of form—of which, however, there is now no proof.

The fact that the "oldest known South Indian alphabet" makes no distinction between long and short *e*, or long and short *o*, but has only one character for each vowel, like the Sanskrit alphabets and the modern Malayâlam, whilst it has different characters for the long and short forms of the other vowels, *a*, *i*, *u*, tends to show that it was framed originally for the expression of Sanskrit sounds, not for those of the Dravidian languages. On the other hand, may it not be said that the fact that different characters are provided in Aśoka's alphabet for the expression of the dental and the lingual sounds respectively, points to the origination of that alphabet amongst a people in whose system of sounds that difference was of more essential importance than it is in Sanskrit? It will be seen, in the section on the Origin of the

Lingual or Cerebral Sounds, that whilst the difference in question seems to have been in Sanskrit the result of gradual development, it enters into the very essence of the means whereby the simplest and most necessary ideas are differentiated in Tamil and other Dravidian languages. On the whole, the question of the origination of the Indian written characters—that is, the question whether Aśoka's characters were derived from the Dravidian or the Dravidian from Aśoka's —does not yet appear to me to be conclusively settled. For the present, I am inclined, with Mr Beames, to prefer the latter solution.

Since the above was written, I have seen some of the inscriptions referred to by Dr Eggeling in his paper on the Chera Dynasty, read before the International Congress of Orientalists in London, 1874; and in these inscriptions, which are considerably older than the Syrian and Jewish ones (the oldest is dated in A.D. 247), I find that the characters used do not resemble those referred to by Dr Burnell, but agree substantially with those in which Sanskrit was written at that period in North India. The characters may best be described as an archaic form of the Haḷa Kannaḍa.

Much information on the subject of Indian characters is contained in Mr Edward Thomas's edition of "Prinsep's Essays on Indian Antiquities." The question of the origin of the South Indian characters is one which requires, and which would probably reward, further research. It is much to be wished that all the Southern alpbabets, ancient and modern, were compared with one another and with the characters used in Northern and Central India and Barma, and especially with those found in inscriptions in Ceylon. The characters which Jambulus professes to have found in use in Ceylon do not perfectly suit any characters which are known to have existed. The impression left on my mind is, that they were mainly "developed out of his inner consciousness."

The modern Telugu-Canarese differs considerably from the modern Tamiḷ, and departs more widely than the Tamil from the Deva-nâgarî type; but there is a marked resemblance between some of the Telugu-Canarese characters and the corresponding characters found in the *śâsanas* of Cochin. The modern Malayâlam character is manifestly derived from the Tamilian Grantha.

On the whole, there seems to be reason to conclude that all the alphabetical characters which are used or known in Southern India have a common origin, whether or no their origin is the same as that of the existing alphabets of Northern India, namely, the system of characters in which Sanskrit was first written. The greatness of the difference between the Southern and the modern Northern alphabets arises probably from the greater antiquity of the literary cultivation of the Southern vernaculars, as compared with the Northern. The Southern vernaculars appear to have begun to be cultivated in that early period when the "cave character" was used: the Northern vernaculars were not cultivated, and can scarcely be said to have existed, till after the "cave character" had become obsolete, and had been superseded by the later Deva-nâgarî. The Telugu and the Canarese alphabets have been arranged on the model of the Deva-nâgarî, or at least they correspond thereto in power and arrangement. The only difference is, that a short *e* and *o*, and a hard **r**, which is unknown to Sanskrit, are contained in those alphabets, together with a surd *ḷ*, which is not used in modern Sanskrit, but is found in the Sanskrit of the Vedas, as well as in the Dravidian languages. Old Canarese possesses also the vocalic *ṛ* of Tamil and Malayâlam. In other respects the characters of those alphabets are convertible equivalents of the Deva-nâgarî. The Malayâlam alphabet generally agrees with the Telugu and the modern Canarese: it differs from them in having the vocalic *ṛ* of the Tamil, in addition to the other characters mentioned above; and in having only one character for long and short *e*, and another for long and short *o*. The aspirated letters and sibilants which all those alphabets have borrowed from Sanskrit, are seldom used except in pronouncing and writing Sanskrit derivatives. Those letters are not really required for native Dravidian purposes; though, through the prevalence of Sanskrit influences, they have acquired a place in the pronunciation of a few words which are not derived from Sanskrit. The letters *ch* and *j* are pronounced in Telugu in certain situations *ts* and *dj*; but no additional characters are employed to represent those sounds.

The Tamil alphabet differs more widely than the Malayâlam or the Telugu-Canarese from the arrangement of the Deva-nâgarî. The grammar of the Tamil language having, to a considerable degree, been systematised and refined independently of Sanskrit influences, and Sanskrit modes of pronunciation being almost unknown to Tamilians, the phonetic system of Tamil demanded, and has secured for itself, a faithful expression in the Tamil alphabet. The materials of that alphabet appear to be wholly, or in the main, Sanskrit; but the use which is made of those materials is Tamilian.

The following are the principal peculiarities of the Tamil alphabet.

In common with the Telugu and Canarese alphabets, the Tamil alphabet possesses separate characters for long and short *e*, and for long and short *o*. Formerly it had but one character for the long and short sounds of these vowels; and it is believed that the marks by which the long are now distinguished from the short were first introduced by the celebrated missionary Beschi. The Tamil has no characters corresponding to the liquid semi-vowels *ṛi* and *ḷri*, which are classed amongst vowels by Sanskrit grammarians; and it has not adopted the *anusvâra*, or obscure nasal, of Sanskrit. Much use is made of nasals in Tamil; but those nasals are firm, decided sounds, not "echoes," and are classed amongst consonants by native grammarians. *m* is the natural sound of the Tamil nasal, and this sound is uniformly retained at the end of words and before labials. When followed by a guttural, *m* is changed into *ṅ*, the nasal of the guttural row of consonants; and it is changed in a similar manner into *ñ*, *ṇ*, or *n*, according as it is followed by a palatal, a cerebral, or a dental. The Tamil alphabet has nothing to correspond with the *half anusvâra* of the Telugu—a character and sound peculiar to that language. Nevertheless, the tendency to euphonise hard consonants by prefixing and combining nasals, from which the *half anusvâra* has arisen, is in full operation in Tamil.

Tamil makes no use whatever of aspirates, and has not borrowed any of the aspirated consonants of Sanskrit, nor even the isolated aspirate *h*. It professes to possess a letter, half vowel, half consonant, corresponding in some respects to the Sanskrit *visarga*, and called *âydam* (that which is subtle, minute). It is pronounced like a guttural *h*, but is only found in the poets, and is generally considered a pedantical invention of the grammarians.

In arranging the consonants, the Tamil alphabet follows the Deva-nâgarî in respect of the *vargas*, or rows, in which the Sanskrit consonants are classified and arranged. It adopts, however, only the first and the last consonant of each row, omitting altogether the intermediate letters. In the first or guttural row, the Tamil alphabet adopts *k*, and its corresponding nasal *ṅ*, omitting *kh*, *g*, and *gh*: in the second or palatal row, it adopts *ch*, and its corresponding nasal *ñ*, omitting *chh*, *j*, and *jh*: in the third or cerebral row, it adopts *ṭ*, and its nasal *ṇ*, omitting *ṭh*, *ḍ*, and *ḍh*: in the fourth or dental row, it adopts *t*, and its nasal *n*, omitting *th*, *d*, and *dh*: in the fifth or labial row, it adopts *p*, and its nasal *m*, omitting *ph*, *b*, and *bh*.

Thus the Tamil alphabet omits not only all the aspirated consonants of the Deva-nâgarî, but also all its soft or sonant letters. The *sounds* which are represented by the sonants of the Deva-nâgarî are as commonly used in Tamil as in Sanskrit; but in accordance with a peculiar law of sound (to be explained hereafter), which requires the same letter to be pronounced as a surd in one position, and as a sonant in another, Tamil uses one and the same *character* for representing both sounds; and the character which has been adopted for this purpose by the Tamil alphabet is that which corresponds to the first consonant—viz., the tenuis or surd in each of the Deva-nâgarî *vargas*.

In the *varga* of the semi-vowels, Tamil follows the Deva-nâgarî; but it subjoins to that *varga* a row of four letters which are not contained in the Deva-nâgarî. These letters are a deep liquid *r*, which will always be represented in this work as *ṛ*; a harsh, rough *r*, which will be represented as **r**; *ḷ*, a peculiar surd *l*, with a mixture of *r*; and *n*, a letter to which it is unnecessary to affix any distinctive mark, the difference between it and the *n* of the dental *varga* being one of form rather than of sound. This *n* is that which is invariably used as a final, and it is also much used, in combination with **r**, to represent the peculiar Tamil sound of *ndr*.

The Tamil alphabet is destitute of the Sanskrit sibilants *ś*, *sh*, and *s*. The second and third of these sibilants are occasionally used in pronouncing and writing Sanskrit derivatives; but these letters are never found in the ancient grammars of Tamil, or in the classics, nor have they a place in the Tamil alphabet: when used, they are borrowed from the Grantha, from which a few other letters also are occasionally borrowed to express Sanskrit sounds. The first of the three Sanskrit characters referred to above, namely, the *ś* of *Śiva*, is never used at all in pure Tamil: the Tamil palatal or semi-sibilant which corresponds to the Sanskrit *ch*, and which is pronounced as a soft *ś* or *sh* when single, and as *chch* or *ćć* when doubled, is the letter which is used instead.

The following comparative view of the Deva-nâgarî and the Tamil alphabets exhibits the relations which the one bears to the other.

Vowels.

Sanskrit	*a, â : i, î : u, û : ṛi, ṛî : lṛî : — ê : aî : — ô : aû : ñ : ah*
Tamil	*a, â : i, î : u, û : — — : — : e, ê : eî : o, ô : aû : — : — h*

Consonants.

Gutturals,	Sans.	*k,*	*kh*	:	*g,*	*gh*	:	*ṅ*
Ditto,	Tamil	*k,*	—	:	—	—	:	*ṅ*
Palatals,	Sans.	*ch,*	*chh*	:	*j,*	*jh*	:	*ñ*
Ditto,	Tamil	*ch,*	—	:	—	—	:	*ñ*
Linguals,	Sans.	*ṭ,*	*ṭh*	:	*ḍ,*	*ḍh*	:	*ṇ*
Ditto,	Tamil	*ṭ,*	—	:	—	—	:	*ṇ*
Dentals,	Sans.	*t,*	*th*	:	*d,*	*dh*	:	*n*
Ditto,	Tamil	*t,*	—	:	—	—	:	*n*
Labials,	Sans.	*p,*	*ph*	:	*b,*	*bh*	:	*m*
Ditto,	Tamil	*p,*	—	:	—	—	:	*m*

CONSONANTS—*continued.*

Semi-vowels,	Sans.	*y,*	*r,*	*l,*	*v*			
Ditto,	Tamil	*y,*	*r,*	*l,*	*v;*	*ṛ,*	*ḷ,*	**r**
Sibilants and aspirate,	Sans.	*ś,*	*sh,*	*s,*	*h*			
Ditto,	Tamil	—	—	—	—*			

* "Early Printing in India," a paper by Dr Burnell, M.C.S., in the *Bombay Antiquary* for March 1873.—"The art of printing was introduced into India by the Goa Jesuits about the middle of the sixteenth century, but they printed only in the Roman character at first. Father Estevaõ (*i.e.*, Stephens, an Englishman), about 1600, speaks of the Roman character as exclusively used for writing Konkanî, and the system of transcription which he used in his Konkanî Grammar (*Arte de lingoa Canarin*) and *Purann* is really worthy of admiration. It is based on the Portuguese pronunciation of the alphabet, but is accurate and complete, and has been used by the numerous Konkanî Roman Catholics of the west coast of India up to the present time. In the seventeenth century the Jesuits appear to have had two presses at Goa; in their College of St Paul at Goa, and in their house at Rachol. Few specimens of their work have been preserved, but there is ample evidence that they printed a considerable number of books, and some of large size. About the end of the seventeenth century, it became the practice at Goa to advance natives to high office in the Church, and from that time ruin and degradation began, and the labours of the early Jesuits disappeared. Literature was entirely neglected, and the productions of the early presses were probably used as waste paper by the monks, or left to certain destruction by remaining unused and uncared for on their bookshelves. There is, however, in the Cochin territory, a place quite as famous as Goa in the history of printing in India. Often mentioned by travellers in the seventeenth and eighteenth centuries, *Ambalacâtta* (*i.e.*, *Ambalakkâḍu*, or 'Churchwood') is not to be found on the maps, and recent inquirers have supposed that the site is forgotten, and that inquiry was useless. The late Major Carr appears to have arrived at this conclusion after visiting Goa in order to get information about it. The place, however, still remains, but as a small village with a scanty population of schismatic Nestorians; it is inland from Cranganore, and a few miles to the north of Angamali. The Jesuits appear to have built here a seminary and church dedicated to St Thomas soon after 1550, and in consequence of the results of the Synod of Udayompura, presided over by Alexius Menezes, Archbishop of Goa, in 1599, it became a place of great importance to the mission. Sanskrit, Tamil, Malayâlam, and Syriac were studied by the Portuguese Jesuits residing there with great success,[1] and several important works were printed, of which, however, we have only the names left us, as recorded by F. de Souza and others, and still later by Fr. Paulinus. The last tells us that 'Anno 1679 in oppido *Ambalacâtta* in lignum incisi alii characteres Tamulici per Ignatium *Aichamoni* indigenam Malabarensem, iisque in lucem prodiit opus inscriptum: *Vocabulario Tamuelco com a significaçao Portugueza composto pello P. Antem de Proença da Comp. de Jesu, Miss. de Maduré.*' The first Malabar-Tamil (? Malayâlam) types had been cut by a lay brother of the Jesuits, Joannes Gonsalves, at Cochin, in 1577. Ambalacâtta

1 The German Jesuit Hanxleden, who died at *Pâś'ûr* (in South Malabar) in 1732, possessed a comprehensive knowledge of Sanskrit literature.

DRAVIDIAN SYSTEM OF SOUNDS.—We now proceed to inquire into the sounds of the Dravidian letters, and the laws of sound or phonetic system of this family of languages; and in doing so, it will be found advantageous to adhere to the order and arrangement of the Deva-nâgarî alphabet. It is not my object to explain in detail the pronunciation of each letter, but such observations will be made on each vowel and consonant in succession as seem likely to throw light on the principles and distinctive character of the Dravidian system of sounds. Tamil grammarians designate vowels by a beautiful metaphor, as *uyir* or the *life* of a word; consonants as *mey*, or the *body;* and the junction of a vowel and consonant as *uyir mey*, or an *animated body*.

I. VOWELS.—(1.) *ă* and *â*. The sound of these vowels in the Dravidian languages corresponds to their sound in Sanskrit, as pronounced everywhere in India except in Bengal, where *ă* is pronounced as *ŏ*. In Tamil, *ă* is the heaviest of all the simple vowels, and therefore the most liable to change. It evinces a tendency to be weakened into *e*—(comp. Sanskrit *balan*, strength, with Tamil *belan;* Sanskrit *japa*, prayer, with Tamil *śebam*. See also the pronoun of the first person.) In the other dialects it maintains its place more firmly; but even in them it is ordinarily strengthened at the end of words by the addition of the euphonic syllable *vu*, consisting of the enunciative vowel *u*, and the *v* euphonically used to prevent hiatus. *Ă* has almost entirely disappeared from the end of nouns in Tamil, and has been succeeded by *u* or *ei*. Where final *a* changes into *ei* in Tamil, it generally changes into *e* in Canarese, or else it is propped up by the addition of *vu*. In Telugu, and especially in Malayâlam, this vowel is less subject to change. Neuter plurals of appellatives and pronouns, which originally ended in *a* in all the dialects, and which still end in *a* in Malayâlam, now end in most instances in *ei* in colloquial Tamil, in *i* in Telugu, and in *u* in Canarese. Thus, *ava*, those (things),

---

was destroyed by order of Tipu, when his army invaded Cochin and Travancore; a true barbarian and savage, he spared neither Christians nor Hindus, and to him attaches the infamy of destroying most of the ancient Sanskrit MSS. which time had spared in Southern India. Brahmans have yet stories current how in those times their ancestors had to flee to the forests with a few of their most precious books and possessions, leaving the remainder to the flames." I may add to the above Fr. Paulinus's statement, that the title of the book printed in 1577 was the "Doctrina Christiana," which was followed the next year by a book entitled the "Flos Sanctorum." After mentioning the Tamil Dictionary, printed in 1679, he adds, "From that period the Danish missionaries at Tranquebar have printed many works."

has become *avei* in Tamil, *avi* in Telugu, *avu* in Canarese: in Malayâlam alone it is still *ava*.

The long *â*, which is formed in Tamil by the coalescence of two short *a*'s, becomes poetically *ô*. *Viṇṇa-v-ar*, heavenly ones, becomes *viṇṇôr*. In old Canarese, even short *a* becomes sometimes *o*. The long final *â* of Sanskrit feminine abstracts becomes in Tamil *ei*—*e.g.*, *âśâ*, Sans., *desire*, Tam. *âśei; Chitrâ*, Sans., April—May, Tam., *Śittirei*. The same *â* becomes *e* in Canarese—*e.g.*, *Gangâ*, the Ganges, is in Canarese *Gange* or *Gange-yu*.

The diphthong into which final *a* and *â* are weakened in Tamil is represented more properly as *ei* than as *ai*. The origination of the Tamil *ei* from *a*, and the analogy of the Sanskrit diphthong *ai*, which is equivalent to *âĭ*, might lead us to regard the Tamil diphthong as *ai* rather than *ei*. It is curious, however, that though it originated from *a*, every trace of the sound of *a* has disappeared. It is represented in Grantha and Malayâlam by a double *e*, and in Telugu-Canarese by a character which is compounded of *e* and *i*: it accords in sound also very nearly with the sound of *ê* or *ey* in *Turkey*. It is also to be observed that the Tamil *ei* is the equivalent of the *e* of the Malayâlam accusative, and is the ordinary representative of the final *e* of Canarese substantives and verbal nouns. It is worthy of notice also that Kumârila-bhaṭṭa, in transliterating the Tamil *naḍei* into Sanskrit characters, writes it, not as *naḍai*, but as *naḍe*. He evidently considered the Dravidian *ei* nearer *e* than *ai*. I conclude, therefore, that this sound is best represented by the diphthong *ei*, which corresponds to the *εῖ* of the Greeks.

"The change from *a* to *e* is rare in bases, though more frequent in inflexions. Of this change among the modern languages Gujarati gives many instances. It must here be remarked that the spelling of most of these languages, owing to the want of a literary standard, is very irregular, and in the cases now about to be noticed, it is probable that the spelling has been made to conform to the pronunciation. If this had been done in Hindi and Panjabi, they too would to the eye seem to have changed the *a* into *e*. . . . . Instances also occur in which not only *a*, but even *â*, is thus modulated. This process, which is irregular and capricious, resembles our own English habit of turning *a* into *e*. . . . . The *e* in the modern Indian languages is never short, as in Prakrit, but is constantly long. . . . . The breaking down of *a* and *â* into *e* seems to be one of those points where non-Aryan influences have been at work. The Sanskrit admits of the modulation of *i* into *e* by the addition of an *a* sound, but it does not include within the range of its phonetic system the process of flattening *a* into *e* by the appendage of an *i* sound. This transition is foreign to the genius of the ancient language, in which *e* is always long. The Dravidian languages, however, possess a short *e* as one of their original simple vowel sounds, side by side with the *ê* corresponding to the Sanskrit *ê*. The Tamil further substitutes for the Sanskrit *ê*—*i.e.*, *â* + *i*—a sound of *ei*—*i.e.*, *e* + *i*. This short *e* of the Dravidians is often found in Canarese to replace the *a* and *â* of Sanskrit, and in Tamil *ei* corresponds thereto. . . . . It would be rash, in the present imperfect state of our knowledge on the obscure subject of the relations between the Dravidians and the early Aryans, to lay down any definite law on this point; but it is noteworthy that the Aryan tribes who came most closely into contact with Kols and Dravidians exhibit the greatest proclivity towards the use of these broken vowels."—*Beames*, pp. 137–141.

(2.) *i* and *î*. These vowels call for no remark.

(3.) *u* and *û*. In the Indo-European languages, and also in the Semitic, the vowels *û* and *û* are very decided, inflexible sounds, which admit of little or no interchange with other vowels, or euphonic softening. In the Dravidian languages, long *û* is sufficiently persistent; but short *u* is of all vowels the weakest and lightest, and is largely used, especially at the end of words, for euphonic purposes, or as a help to enunciation.

In grammatical written Telugu, every word without exception must end in a vowel; and if it has not naturally a vowel ending of its own, *u* is to be suffixed to the last consonant. This rule applies even to Sanskrit derivatives; and the neuter abstracts ending in *m*, which have been borrowed from Sanskrit, must end in *m-u* in Telugu. Though this *u* is always written, it is often dropped in pronunciation. In modern Canarese a similar rule holds, with this additional development, that *u* (or with the euphonic copula *v*, *vu*) is suffixed even to words that end in *a*—*e.g.*, compare the Tamil *sila*, few (things), and *pala*, many (things), with the corresponding Canarese *kela-vu* and *pala-vu*. The Tamil rule, with regard to the addition of *u* to words which end in a consonant, accords with the rule of the ancient Canarese. That rule is, that in words which end in any hard or surd consonant, viz., in *k*, *ch*, *ṭ*, *t*, or *p* (each of which is the leading consonant of a *varga*), or in the hard, rough **r**, which is peculiar to these languages, the hard consonant shall be followed by *u* (as *q* by *sh'vâ* in Hebrew), in consequence of its being impossible for Tamilian organs of speech to pronounce those letters without the help of a succeeding vowel. In most instances this enunciative *u* is not merely short, but so very short that its quantity is determined by grammarians to be equal only to a fourth of the quantity of a long vowel. In Malayâlam a short *a* sometimes replaces the short *u* of the Tamil. Dr Gundert considers this a peculiarity of the Malayâlam of Cochin and of the Syrian Christians. Foreigners, who are led more by the written sign than by the spoken sound, have often, he says, been led to regard this letter as *a*. The short *u* of Tamil is still further shortened in Northern Malayâlam, so that in the northern districts it is not written at all, but a small circle, or dot merely, over the letter is used to express the sound. This may be represented by our apostrophe—*e.g.*, *kiṛakk'* = *kiṛakk-u*. The same usage prevails still more extensively in Tulu, in which the pronunciation of this final *u* is still more like the Hebrew *sh'vâ*. After all vowels except *ô* and *û* it is hardly possible to catch the sound. In so far as it is enunciated at all, it resembles a very short German *ü*. The change of the Tamil *iladu* (there is not) into the Telugu *lêdu*, and many changes of the like nature, seem to be the result of a similar contraction of initial vowels.

It often happens (though it is not an invariable rule) that the final surd, to which enunciative *u* or *a* has been appended, is doubled, apparently for the purpose of furnishing a fulcrum for the support of the appended vowel. Thus, the Sanskrit *vâk*, speech, becomes in Tamil *vâk(k)-u*; *ap*, water, becomes *ap(p)-u*; and so in all similar cases. The rule is further extended in Tamil so as to apply to the final consonants of syllables, as well as to those of words. If a syllable, though in the middle of a word, terminates in one of the hard consonants above mentioned, and if the initial consonant of the succeeding syllable is one which cannot be assimilated to it, the final consonant is doubled, and *u* is affixed. Thus, *advaita*, Sans., induality, becomes in Tamil *attuveida*. The rule by which *d*, when thus doubled, becomes *t*, will be explained hereafter. In modern colloquial Tamil, *u* is suffixed to almost every final consonant,—to the semi-vowels and nasals, as well as the surds; and even in the ancient or classical Tamil it is sometimes suffixed to final *l*—*e.g.*, *śol(l)-u*, speak, instead of simply *śol*. The employment of *u* in the manner and for the purposes now mentioned is obviously quite foreign to Indo-European usages. It is not derived from Sanskrit, and is opposed to Sanskrit laws of sound. It will be termed the *enunciative u*, and will generally be separated off by a hyphen.

(4.) *e*, *ê*: *o*, *ô*. The Dravidian languages possess and largely employ the short sounds of the vowels *e* and *o* (epsilon and omicron), and most of them have different characters for those sounds, for the purpose of distinguishing them from the corresponding long vowels. Sanskrit is destitute of short *e* and *o*. The entire absence of those sounds from a language which attends so nicely as Sanskrit, to the minutest gradations of sound, cannot be the result of accident; and the importance of the place which they occupy in the Dravidian system of sounds, contributes to show that the Dravidian languages are independent of Sanskrit. In a few cases, in all the dialects, particularly in the instance of the demonstrative bases, as *a* and *i*, and the interrogative base *e*, the short vowel has sometimes been converted into a long one by becoming the seat of emphasis; but such cases are rare and exceptional, and in general the difference between short *e* and *o* and the corresponding long vowels is a difference which pertains not to euphony or the inflexional form, but to the bases or roots of words, and is essential to the difference in the signification—*e.g.*, in Tamil, *tĕḷ* means clear, and *têḷ* scorpion; *kăl*, stone, and *kâl*, foot.

"The first trace of the adoption of this short *e* by Aryan populations is found in Prakrit, and takes the form, not of a distinct sound, from the long Sanskrit *ê*, but of a shortening of that sound itself. Thus, words which in Sanskrit exhibit long *e*, followed by a single consonant, occur in Prakrit with *e* followed by a double consonant. As Prakrit is always very careful to preserve the quantity of Sanskrit words, it is apparent that the common people who spoke Prakrit, having come to regard *e* as a short sound, felt it necessary to double the following consonant, in order to preserve the quantity; the vowel, which in Sanskrit was long by nature, becoming thus long by position. . . . . These words were pronounced with a short *e*, as in English *get*, *bed;* and the barrenness of invention of the persons who reduced Prakrit to writing is shown by their omitting to provide a separate character for this new sound, as the Dravidians have done."—*Beames*, p. 141.

(5.) *ei.* It has already been mentioned that *ei*, unlike the Sanskrit diphthong *ai*, represents *e* and *i*, not *a* and *i*. The primitive Dravidian *a* changes into *e*, and this again into *ei*. Thus, the head is *tala* in Telugu and Malayâlam, *tale* in Canarese, and *tali* in Tamil. This Malayâlam *a* is not pure, but, according to Dr Gundert, is a modification of *ei*. Hence *e*, not *a*, appears in the dative. When *ei* is succeeded in Tamil by another *ei*, with only a single consonant between them, the first *ei*, though naturally long, is considered short by position, and is pronounced short accordingly—*e.g.*, *uḍeimei*, property, is regarded in prosody as *udĕimei*. In such cases, *ei* is seen to be equivalent to its original *ă* or *ĕ*.

(6.) *au.* This diphthong has a place in the Tamil alphabet; but it is not really a part of any of the Dravidian languages, and it has been placed in the alphabets solely in imitation of Sanskrit. It is used only in the pronunciation of Sanskrit derivatives; and when such derivatives are used in Tamil, they are more commonly pronounced without the aid of this diphthong. Ordinarily the diphthong is separated into its component elements; that is, the simple vowels *a* and *u*, from which it is derived, are pronounced separately, with the usual euphonic *v* of the Tamil between them to prevent hiatus.—*e.g.*, the Sanskrit noun *saukhyam*, health, is ordinarily pronounced and written in Tamil *savukkiyam*.

It is a peculiarity of the Tamil system of sounds, as distinguished from that of the other languages of the family, that the vowels *i*, *î*, *e*, *ê*, and *u*, acquire before certain consonants followed by *a* and its cognate *ei*, a compound, diphthongal sound, which is different from the sound which they have as simple vowels. Thus, *i* before *ṭ*, *ṇ*, *r*, *ṛ*, **r**, *l*, and *ḷ*, followed by *a* or *ei*, acquires something of the sound of *e*: *î*, before the same consonants, with the exception of the first *r* and the first *l*, and followed by *a* or *ei*, takes a sound resembling *ŭ*: *û* remains always unchanged; but *ŭ*, not only before the above-mentioned seven consonants, but before all single consonants, when it is not succeeded by *i*, *u*, or *e*, is pronounced nearly like *o*; and in Telugu, *o* is generally used in writing those words. *e*, before the consonants above mentioned, with the exception of the semi-vowels, loses its peculiarly slender sound, and is pronounced nearly as it would be if the succeeding consonant were doubled. *ê*, with the same exceptions, acquires a sound similar to *ô*. This change of *e* into *o* especially distinguishes Tuḷu. Thus, the Tamil *vêṇḍum*, must, is in Tuḷu *bôḍ*; *veḷḷi*, silver, is *boḷḷi*. These changes in the sounds of the Dravidian vowels under certain circumstances are not owing exclusively to the influence of the following consonants. They illustrate more especially the power of one Dravidian vowel to bring another vowel into harmony with itself. In all the changes now referred to, we see the power of the vowel *a* and its cognate *ei* penetrating into the preceding syllable. The circumstance most worthy of notice, in connection with these changes, is that each of the short vowels *i*, *u*, and *e*, retains its natural sound, if it is succeeded by another *i*, *u*, or *e*. Thus, *ura*, Tamil, infinitive, to have, to be, is pronounced *ora*, but the imperative *uru* is pronounced as it is written. This rule discloses a law of sound which is unlike anything that is discoverable in Sanskrit. So far as it goes, it corresponds to the Scythian law of harmonic sequences, which will be referred to hereafter.

The vowel *ă*, occurring in the last syllable of a word ending in *n*, *ṇ*, *r*, *ṛ*, *l*, or *ḷ*, acquires a slender sound resembling that of *e*—*e.g.*, *avar*, Tamil, they (honorifically, he), is pronounced *aver*. This change corresponds to the weakening of the sound of heavy vowels in the ultimate or penultimate syllables of words, which is sometimes observed in the Sanskrit family of tongues.

II. CONSONANTS.—Tamil grammarians divide all consonants into three classes—(1.) Surds, which they call *vallinam*, or the hard class, viz., *k*, *ch* or *ś*, *ṭ*, *t*, *p*, **r**; (2.) Nasals, which they call *mellinam*, or the soft class, viz., *ṅ*, *ñ*, *ṇ*, *n*, *m*, with final *n*; and (3.) Semi-vowels, which they call *iḍeiyinam*, or the medial class, viz., *y*, *r*, *l*, *v*, *ṛ*, *ḷ*.

In this enumeration, as I have already observed, the sonant equivalents of the surd consonants (viz., *g*, the sonant of *k*; *j*, the sonant of *ch* or *ś*; *ḍ*, the sonant of *ṭ*; *d*, the sonant of *t*; and *b*, the sonant of *p*) are omitted. In the Northern Dravidian dialects the difference between surds and sonants is generally expressed by the use of different characters for each sound, in imitation of the system of the Deva-nâgarî; but in Tamil and in Malayâlam, in accordance with the peculiar Dravidian law of the convertibility of surds and sonants, one set of consonants serves for both purposes, and the difference between them is expressed in the pronunciation alone.

It is desirable, before proceeding further, to inquire into this law, viz.:—

The Convertibility of Surds and Sonants.—We have seen that the Tamil alphabet adopts the first and last of each of the Deva-nâgarî *vargas*, or rows of consonants, viz., the unaspirated surd and the nasal of each *varga;* we have also seen that the Tamil has not separate characters for surds and sonants, but uses one and the same character —that which, properly speaking, represents the surd only—to express both. This rule does not apply merely to the written characters of the language, but is the expression of a law of sound which is inherent in the language itself.

There are distinct traces of the existence of this law in all the Dravidian dialects; but it is found most systematically and most fully developed in Tamil and Malayâlam. The law, as apparent in the Tamil-Malayâlam system of sounds, is as follows:—*k*, *ṭ*, *t*, *p*, the first unaspirated consonants of the first, third, fourth, and fifth *vargas*, are always pronounced as tenues or surds (*i.e.*, as *k*, *ṭ*, *t*, *p*) at the beginning of words, and whenever they are doubled. The same consonants are always pronounced as medials or sonants (*i.e.*, as *g*, *ḍ*, *d*, *b*) when single in the middle of words. A sonant cannot commence a word, neither is a surd admissible in the middle, except when doubled; and so imperative is this law, and so strictly is it adhered to, that when words are borrowed from languages in which a different principle prevails, as Sanskrit or English, the consonants of those words change from sonants to surds, or *vice versâ*, according to their position—*e.g.*, *danta*, Sans. a tooth, becomes in Tamil, *tandam; bhâgya*, Sans. happiness, becomes *pâkkiyam*. This rule applies also to the case of compounds. The first consonant of the second word, though it was a surd when it stood independent, is regarded as a sonant when it becomes a medial letter in a compounded word. This difference is marked in Telugu by a difference in the character which is employed—*e.g.*, *anna-dammulu* (for *anna-tammulu*), elder and younger brothers; *koṭṭa-baḍu* (for *koṭṭa-paḍu*), to be beaten; but in Tamil, and generally in Malayâlam, the difference appears in the pronunciation alone. This rule applies to all compounds in Telugu; but in Tamil, when the words stand in a case-relation to one another, or when the first is governed by the second, the initial surd of the second word is not softened, but doubled and hardened, in token of its activity—*e.g.*, instead of *koṭṭa-baḍu*, to be beaten, it prefers to say *koṭṭa-(p)paḍu*. In *dvandva* compounds Tamil agrees with Telugu.

A similar rule applies to the pronunciation of *ch* or *ć* (the Tamil *ś*), the first consonant of the second *varga*. When single, it is pronounced as a soft, weak sibilant, with a sound midway between *ś*, *sh*, and *ch*. This pronunciation is unchanged in the middle of words, and in all cases in which the letter is single; but when it is doubled, it is pronounced exactly like *chch* or *ćć*. The principle involved in this instance is the same as in the cases previously mentioned, but the operation of the rule is in some degree different. The difference consists in the pronunciation of this consonant in the beginning of a word, as well as in the middle, as a sonant—*i.e.*, as *ś*. By theory it should be pronounced as *ch* at the beginning of a word,—and it is worthy of notice that it always receives this pronunciation at the beginning of a word in vulgar colloquial Tamil: and in Malayâlam and Telugu it is written as well as pronounced *ch*. A somewhat similar rule prevails with respect to the rough **r** of the Tamil, which is pronounced as **r** when single, and like *ttr* when doubled.

The Tamilian rule which requires the same consonant to be pronounced as *k* in one position and as *g* in another—as *ṭ*, *t*, *p*, in one position, and as *ḍ*, *d*, *b*, in another—is not a mere dialectic peculiarity, the gradual result of circumstances, or a modern refinement invented by grammarians, but is essentially inherent in the language, and has been a characteristic principle of it from the beginning.

The Tamil characters were borrowed, I conceive, from the earlier Sanskrit, and the language of the Tamilians was committed to writing on or soon after the arrival of the first colony of Brahmans, probably several centuries before the Christian era. Yet even at that early period the Tamil alphabet was arranged in such a manner as to embody the peculiar Dravidian law of the convertibility of surds and sonants. The Tamil alphabet systematically passed by the sonants of the Sanskrit, and adopted the surds alone, considering one character as sufficient for the expression of both classes of sounds. This circumstance clearly proves that *ab initio* the Dravidian phonetic system, as represented in Tamil, its most ancient exponent, differed essentially from that of Sanskrit.

In none of the Indo-European languages do we find surds and sonants convertible; though Hebrew scholars will remember the existence in Hebrew of a rule which is somewhat similar to the Tamilian respecting *k*, *t*, *p*, and their equivalents. The Hebrew consonants composing the memorial words *begad kephath*, are pronounced in two different ways, according to their position. When any of those consonants begins a word, or in certain cases a syllable, it is to be pronounced hard—that is, as a surd or tenuis; and if it be an aspirated letter, it is then deprived of the aspirate which it naturally possesses. To denote this, such consonants have a point, called a *dagesh*, inscribed in them. When those consonants are found in any other position, they are pronounced as sonants, and two of them, *ph* and *th*, as aspirates. This rule resembles the Tamilian in some particulars; but the resemblance which will be found to exist between the Tamilian rule and the law of sounds which prevails in some of the languages of the Scythian family, amounts to identity. In the Finnish and Lappish there is a clearly marked distinction between surds and sonants: a sonant never commences a word or syllable in either tongue. But in the oldest specimen of any Scythian language which is extant—the Scythic version of the inscription at Behistun—Mr Norris ascertained (*Journal of the Royal Asiatic Society* for 1853) the existence of a law of convertibility of sonants and surds which is absolutely identical with the Tamilian. He ascertained that in that language, in the middle of a word, the same consonant was pronounced as a sonant when single and as a surd when doubled.

We now enter upon an examination of the Dravidian *consonants* in detail.

(1.) *The guttural varga: k, g, and their nasal ṅ* or *ng*. These consonants are pronounced in the Dravidian language precisely as in Sanskrit. *g*, the sonant of *k*, which is expressed by the same character in Tamil, is pronounced in Tamil-Malayâlam in a peculiarly soft manner. Its sound resembles that of an Irish *gh*, and is commonly used to express the *h* of other languages. Thus, the Sanskrit adjective *mahâ*, great, is written in Tamil *magâ*; but so soft is the *g*, that it may be considered as an equivalent to *h*, pronounced with less roughness than is usual with that aspirate.

(2.) *The palatal varga : ch* or *ś*, *j, and ñ.* It has been observed that the Tamil rejects the Sanskrit sibilants *ś*, *ṣh*, and *s*. The consonant which it adopts instead is *ch*, which is pronounced in Tamil in a manner somewhat similar to the soft aspirated *ś* of *Śiva*, or as a very soft *sh*, with as little sibilation or aspiration as possible. In fact, it may be regarded as a palatal, not as a sibilant; and when it is doubled, it takes precisely the sound of the Sanskrit palatal *ch* or *ć*, or its English equivalent in *which*. In Telugu, the sound of *ch* is that with which this consonant is pronounced, not only when doubled, but also when single; and a similar pronunciation prevails in the lowest colloquial dialect of the Tamil, in which *śey*, to do, is pronounced *chey*, as in Telugu. It is probably the ancient pronunciation of this letter which is retained by the lower classes. The very soft sound of it as *ś* is probably a refinement originating with the higher classes. When the Tamil alphabet was arranged, and *ś* was made the equivalent of *ch*, and even after the arrival of the Europeans in India, when the Portuguese wrote S'ôṛamandalam as Choramandel; and the missionary Ziegenbalg wrote Sûdṛa as Tshuddira, the harder palatal sound seems to have been the one in general use. This letter should perhaps be represented as *ch* in the Roman character, like the corresponding Telugu letter, but the sound of *ś* is the sound so generally heard at present, when the letter is single, that the use of *ch* or *ć* would be puzzling to the student of Tamil. I have, therefore, resolved to adhere to *ś* as in the former edition.

j, the second unaspirated consonant of this row, is not used in correct Tamil; but in Telugu it is both written and pronounced: in vulgar Tamil also *ch* is sometimes pronounced like *j*. The same sound of *j* is sometimes admitted in the use of those Sanskrit derivatives in which the letter *j* is found in Sanskrit; but ordinarily the Tamil sound of *ch* or *ś* is used instead.

ñ, the nasal of this row of consonants, is pronounced as in Sanskrit in all the Dravidian languages. *ñ*, *nj*, or *ñy*, as this letter is commonly transliterated in English, being a double letter, and liable to mislead, I think it better to represent this sound by *ñ*. The *n* of the lingual series will be represented as before by *ṇ*; the dental *n*, as before, by *n*, without any diacritical mark. We frequently find *ñ* (*nj*) used in Malayâlam, as an initial, where the Tamil uses *n*—*e.g.*, *ñân*, I, instead of the Tamil *nân*. Possibly both the Tamil *n* and the Malayâlam *ñ* are representatives of an ancient *y*, as will appear in the examination of the personal pronouns, *nân*, *ñân* = *yân*. Tamil *naṇḍu*, a crab, is *ñaṇḍu* in Malayâlam, and *yaṇḍri* in Canarese.

It is necessary here to notice the existence in Telugu of a peculiarly soft pronunciation of *ch* and *j*, with their aspirates, which is unknown in Sanskrit and the Northern vernaculars, and is found only in Telugu and in Marâṭhi. *Ch* is pronounced as *ts*, and *j* as *dz*, before all vowels except *i*, *î*, *e*, *ê*, and *ei*. Before these excepted vowels, the ordinary sounds of *ch* and *j* are retained. Whether the Telugu borrowed these sounds from the Marâṭhi, or the Marâṭhi from the Telugu, I can scarcely venture to express an opinion; but this is not the only particular in which those languages are found to agree. A sound represented as *zh* is much used in the Tuda dialect, especially in connection with *r* and *l*.

"Marâṭhi has two methods of pronouncing the palatals. In *tatsamas* and modern *tadbhavas*, and before the palatal vowels *i*, *î*, *ê*, and *aî*, *ch* and *j* are pronounced as in Sanskrit; but in early *tadbhavas*, *dêśajas*, and before the other vowels, *ch* sounds *ts*, and *j*, *dz*. This peculiarity is not shared by any of the cognate languages, while, on the other hand, the *ts* and *dz* sounds (so to speak, the unassimilated palatals) are characteristic of the lower state of development of the non-Aryan, Turanian, or what-you-call class of languages. Tibetan on the one side, and Telugu among the Dravidians on the other, retain them. Marâṭhi, from its juxtaposition to Telugu and other non-Aryan forms of speech, might naturally be expected to have undergone somewhat of their influence, and this pronunciation of the palatals is probably an instance in point. By the expression "unassimilated palatals" I mean that, whereas, in the Aryan palatals, the dental and sibilant of which they are composed have become so united into one sound that the elements can no longer be separately recognised, in the Turanian class the elements are still distinct."—*Beames*, p. 72. Dr Trumpp also attributes the pronunciation of *ch* and *j* in certain connections, as *ts* and *dz* in Marâṭhi, to Dravidian influences.

(3.) *The lingual or so-called cerebral varga: ṭ, ḍ, ṇ.* The pronunciation of the consonants of the cerebral *varga* in the Dravidian languages does not essentially differ from their pronunciation in Sanskrit. In expressing these consonants, with their aspirates, in Roman characters in this work, a dot will be placed under each, to distinguish them from the *t*, *d*, and *n*, of the dental row. Though *ṭ* is the surd consonant of the linguals, it is not pronounced at the beginning of any word in Tamil, like the other surds. Its sound is too hard and rough to admit of its use as an initial; and, therefore, in those few Sanskrit derivatives which commence with this letter, *ṭ* is preceded in Tamil by the vowel *i*, as a help to enunciation. When *ṭ* is thus preceded by a vowel, it is no longer an initial, and therefore no longer a surd; and hence it becomes *ḍ* by rule; so that the sound of *ṭ* is never heard in Tamil, except when *ḍ* is doubled. In the other Dravidian dialects, *ṭ* is sometimes pronounced singly, as in Sanskrit. Tamil differs from the other dialects in refusing to combine *ṭ* with *ṇ*, and changing it into *ḍ* when *ṇ* is combined with it. This peculiarity is founded upon a general Tamilian law of sound, which is that nasals will not combine with surds, but coalesce with sonants alone. In consequence of this peculiar law, such combinations as *ṇṭ*, *nt*, and *mp*, which are admissible in Telugu and Canarese, are inadmissible in Tamil, in which *ṇḍ*, *nd*, and *mb*, must be used instead. This rule applies also to *k* and *ch*, which, when combined with the nasals corresponding to them, become *g* and *j*. Thus, *maṇṭapa*, Sans. a porch, becomes in Tamil *maṇḍabam*; *anta*, Sans. end, becomes *andam*. Probably the difference between Tamil and the other Dravidian languages in this point arises from the circumstance that Tamil has remained so much freer than its sister idioms from Sanskrit influences. A similar rule respecting the conjunction of nasals with sonants alone is found in Finnish, and is possibly owing to that delicacy of ear which both Finns and Tamilians appear to possess.

I reserve to the close of this examination of the Dravidian consonants some observations on the circumstance that the consonants of the lingual or cerebral class are found in Sanskrit as well as in the languages of the Dravidian family.

(4.) *The dental varga: t, d, n.* The letters of the dental *varga* have generally the same sound in the Dravidian languages as in Sanskrit. The principal exception consists in the peculiarly soft pronunciation of *t* in Tamil and Malayâlam between two vowels: it is then pronounced, not as *d*, but with the sound of the soft English *th* in *that*. It is only when it is combined with a nasal (as in the word which was cited above, *andam*, end) that the sonant of *t* is pronounced in Tamil as *d*; the sound of *d* being, in such a conjunction, more natural and easy than that of *th*. As this peculiar sound of *th* is found only in Tamil and in Malayâlam, a daughter of Tamil, it is doubtful whether *th* is to be considered as the original sound of the sonant equivalent of *t*, or whether it is to be regarded as a corruption or further softening of *d*. On the whole, the latter supposition seems the more probable; and as the *th* of Tamil corresponds to the *d* of Telugu and of the other dialects in position and power, I shall always write it as *d*, even when quoting Tamil words, except where it is used as an initial, and is therefore a surd, when it will be written as *t*.

Another exception to the rule that the dental letters have the same pronunciation in the Dravidian languages as in Sanskrit consists in the pronunciation of the Sanskrit *t* in certain connections in Malayâlam as *l*—*e.g.*, *âltmâv'*, soul, for *âttmâv'* (Tam. *âttumâ*), from the Sans. *âtmâ; Kêraḷôlpatti*, for *Kêralôtpatti*, the title of the History of Malabar.

One of the sounds peculiar to the Tuda is the hard sound of *th*, as in the English word *thin*. This is the pronunciation to be given to the *th* in *atham*, he, she, it, they.

(5.) *The labial varga: p, b, m.* The pronunciation of *p*, and its sonant *b*, requires no remark. One of the peculiarities of Tuda is the existence in it of the sound of *f*—*e.g.*, *pûf*, an insect. In the other Dravidian dialects *f* is unknown, and *p* is used instead in words containing *f* borrowed from English. With regard to the use of *m* in combination, I have only to observe, that though it changes into *ṅ*, *ñ*, *ṇ* or *n*, when immediately succeeded by a guttural, a palatal, a lingual, or a dental, it is not to be confounded with the *anusvâra* of the Sanskrit alphabet. The true *anusvâra*—*i.e.*, the sound which *m* takes in Sanskrit before the semi-vowels, the sibilants, and the letter *h*—is unknown to the Dravidian languages. A character called by the name of *anusvâra*, but of a different power from the *anusvâra* of the Sanskrit, is in use in Telugu and Canarese; but it is used merely as the equivalent of the consonantal *m* in euphonic combinations, and even as a final. The Telugu has also a vocalic nasal, the half *anusvâra*, which, though it is used merely for euphony, bears a close resemblance to the true *anusvâra* of the Sanskrit. There is nothing in any of the Dravidian languages which corresponds to the use of the obscure nasal *anusvâra* as a final in Hindi and in the other Northern vernaculars.

The euphonic use of *m* or *n*, and its modifications, and its use to prevent *hiatus*, will be considered at the close of this section.

(6.) *The varga of the liquid consonants or semi-vowels: y, r, l, v: ṛ, ḷ, ṟ.* In classical Tamil neither *r* nor *l* can commence a word; each of them requires to be preceded by an euphonic auxiliary vowel; *r* by *i* or *a*, and *l* by *u*. This appears most distinctly in words borrowed from Sanskrit, as in these instances we are certain of the original form of the word. Thus *râjâ*, Sans., becomes in Tamil *irâśan* or *irâyan*, and also *araśan* or *arayan; rêvati*, Sans. the *nakshatra* of that name, becomes *iravati; rakta*, Sans. blood, becomes *irattam* or *arattam; rava*, Sans. sound, becomes *aravam*. The last word never becomes *iravam*. So also *lôka*, Sans. the world, becomes in Tamil *ulôgam*, and by a further change, through the preference of the Tamil for short vowels, *ulagam*, and still more elegantly *ulagu*. The same rule applies to the second set of semi-vowels, *ṛ*, *ḷ*, *ṟ*, which are the exclusive property of the Dravidian languages, and none of which can be pronounced without the help of preceding vowels.

Of these distinctively Dravidian semi-vowels, *ṟ* is used most largely by Tamil. It is used also in Malayâlam, and its use is one of the distinguishing features of old, as distinguished from modern, Canarese. Its sound resembles that of the English *r* (not the Irish or Scotch) after a long vowel, as in the word *farm;* but it is pronounced farther back in the mouth, and in a still more liquid manner. It is sometimes expressed in English books as *zh* or *rzh;* but this is merely a local pronunciation of the letter which is peculiar to the Northern districts of the Tamil country: it is at variance with its affinities and its interchanges, and is likely to mislead the learner. *ṟ* is the only Dravidian consonant which is pronounced differently in different districts. In the southern districts of the Tamil country, it is pronounced by the mass of the people exactly in the same manner as *ḷ*, which is the letter generally used instead of *ṟ* in modern Canarese. Between Tanjore and Pondicherry, it is softened into *rzh* or *zh;* and in Madras and the neighbourhood, this softening process has been carried to such a length, that in the speech of the vulgar, *ṟ* has become *y*, or a silent letter. Even in correct written Tamil *ṟ* sometimes disappears—*e.g.*, *poṟudu*, time, becomes *pôdu*. It sometimes changes into *y* in Malayâlam. Telugu, which commences to be spoken about two days' journey north of Madras, has lost this letter altogether. Generally it uses *ḍ* instead, as the Canarese uses *ḷ;* but sometimes it uses no substitute, after the manner of the vulgar Tamil of Madras. Looking at such Telugu words as *kinda*, below, answering to the Tamil *kîṟnda*, and *mingu*, to swallow, answering to the Tamil *viṟungu*, we cannot but suppose that Telugu had this letter originally, like Tamil, and that it lost it gradually through the operation of that softening process which, in the colloquial Tamil of Madras, converts *kîṟê*, below, to *kîê*. Though *ṟ* is generally changed into *ḷ* in Canarese, it appears to have become *r* in some words—*e.g.*, *ardu*, having wept, instead of *aṟadu*, Tamil. It is sometimes also assimilated—*e.g.*, *poṟudu*, Tamil, time, became *pottu* (*poṟudu*, *poṟdu*, *poddu*, *pottu*) in old Canarese, in modern Canarese *hottu*. The change of *ṟ* into *r* is common in Tuḷu.

ḷ is a peculiar heavy *l*, with a mixture of *ṟ*, which is found in all the Dravidian languages. It may be styled the cerebral *l;* and it is probably derived from the same source, whatever that source may be, from which the cerebral consonants *ṭ*, *ḍ*, and *ṇ*, have proceeded. A similar *ḷ* is found in Vedic Sanskrit, and an *ḷ* identical with it is common in several of the North Indian vernaculars.

"From the examples given in this and other sections, it must have struck the reader that a close connection, if not a certain degree of confusion, exists in some languages between *l* and *ḷ*. This latter letter is very common in Oriya, Bengali, and Gujarati; less in Panjabi; and is not found in the others. Its pronunciation defies description; sometimes it sounds like *ṛh*, again like *rz*, and again merely a harsh *l*. Its point of contact is high up in the palate, near *r*, and the tongue in uttering it is shaped as in uttering the simple *l*. It appears to be capriciously substituted by the vulgar, in those languages where it exists, for the common *l*, and in a considerable number of instances this substitution has become the rule. . . . . It will be noticed that this letter never occurs initially in any of the languages; and there appears to be no reason for doubting that the sound itself is of non-Aryan origin, notwithstanding the fact that the character is found in Vedic Sanskrit. We do not know how this character was pronounced in those days, beyond this—that it in some degree resembled *ḍ*. But the equivalent of *ḍ*, in the modern languages, is not ळ, but *lh*. Moreover, Panjabi has side by side with ळ a character, *ṛh*, which accurately corresponds to the Sanskrit *ḍ*."—*Beames*, p. 215.

The hard rough *r* of the Dravidian languages is not found in Sanskrit, and is not employed in pronouncing Sanskrit derivatives. It is found in Telugu poetry and elegant prose, and the grammarians insist upon using it; but in the modern dialect of the Telugu it is seldom used. In Canarese, the use of this letter is confined to the poets and the ancient dialect. It is evident that it was originally contained in all the dialects; though, possibly through the influence of the Sanskrit, it is now seldom used except in Tamil and Malayâlam, in which it holds as firm footing as ever. In some of the older Tamil alphabets I have found this letter appropriately expressed by a double *r*; and, to distinguish it from the softer letter, it will be represented in this work by a Clarendon **r**, emblematical of its greater strength.

In the use of this hard **r** in Tamil, there are two peculiarities which are worthy of notice.

(i.) **r**, when doubled, is pronounced as *ttr*, though written **rr**. The *t* of this compound sound differs both from the soft dental *t* of the fourth *varga*, and from the cerebral *ṭ*, and corresponds very nearly to the emphatic final *t* of our English interrogative *what?* This sound of *t* is not expressed in writing, but in pronunciation it is never omitted; and it is one of those peculiar Dravidian sounds which are not derived from Sanskrit, and are not found in it. The double *ttr* or *tt* of the Tamil (**rr**) is sometimes softened in Telugu to a single *ṭ*, and in Canarese still further into *t*—*e.g.*, *mâ***rr***u* (*mâttru*), Tam., of which one of the meanings is an answer, a word, is in Tel. *mâṭa*, in Can. *mâtu*. The *ṭ* is also sometimes doubled in Telugu—*e.g.*, Tam., *pa***rr***u* (*pattru*), a laying hold; Tel., *paṭṭu*; Can., both *paṭṭu* and *pattu* (*hattu*). Even in old Canarese a similar change often takes place.

(ii.) The letter *n* (not the dental *n*, but the final *n* of Tamil), a letter which is not found in Telugu, is often prefixed in Tamil to the rough **r** for the sake of euphony, when the compound *n***r** acquires the sound of *ndr*—a sound of which the Tamil, like the language of Madagascar, is exceedingly fond. In Tuḷu this sound is further softened to *ñj*—*e.g.*, *kan***r***u*, Tamil, a calf, is in Tuḷu, *kañji*. In another class of words, the *n* which is prefixed to **r** is radical, and should be followed by *d*, according to rule (*e.g.*, in the preterites of verbs whose root ends in *n*); but **r** is suffixed to *n* instead of *d*, in consequence of which the sound of *ndr* is substituted for that of *nd*.

I consider the **r** radical, and the *n* euphonically prefixed, in *mûn***r***u* (*mûndru*), Tam., three (for *mûru*, Can., the more ancient form of the word), and in *on***r***u* (*ondru*), Tam., one (for *oru*). The *n* I consider radical (or an euphonised form of the radical), and the **r** used euphonically instead of *d*, in the following examples:—*en***r***u* (*endru*), having spoken, instead of *endu*; *śen***r***u* (*śendru*), having gone, for *śendu* (which is instead of the less euphonic *śeldu*). In the speech of the vulgar in the Tamil country, and in Malayâlam, this compound *ndr* is further altered into *nn* or *ṇṇ*. In Telugu and Canarese *nd* seems always to be found instead of *ndr*. See Numerals I. and III.*

(7.) *The sibilants and the aspirate: ś, ṣh, s, h.* It has already been mentioned that Tamil is destitute of sibilants. The other Dravidian

* I quote here from Dr Gundert's communication. "Is *mûru* more ancient than *mûndru*? Canarese dislikes the nasals (except the half *anusvara*, which it likes to introduce—*e.g.*, *sainhya* instead of *sahya*, tolerable). *Kandru*, Tam. a calf; Can., *karu*. Which is the older? I suppose **r***u* in *mûndru*, three, and *ondru*, one, to be the formative *du*, *tu*, changed by its contact with final *n*. *mun*, *on*, appear to me the original forms, the one from the radical *mu*, to be before, to excel (whence *mun*, before, and probably Sans. *mukha*, the face; also Tam. *mûkk-u*, the nose, and the verb *mû*, to be old); the other, from the radical *o*, to be one. Many old nouns are formed with *n* (as *ēn*, Tam. what? This *n* changes into **r**, as in *pi***r**, from *pin*, after; also into *ṛ*—*e.g.*, *uḷar*, birth, the same as *uḷan* and *uḷavu*. *Oru*, one, appears to me therefore only the more liquid equivalent of the noun *on*. *Śen***r***u* or *śendru*, having gone, I should rather derive from *śel-ndu* than from *śeldu*, as the latter would have to become *śe***rr***u*, *śettru*." I place Dr Gundert's observations at the foot of the page, instead of incorporating them in the text as usual, because in this instance I am unable to adopt his view. A comparison of all the forms of the Dravidian numerals for "one" and "three" (see the chapter on Numerals) appears to me to confirm the supposition expressed in the text. The change of *śeldu* into *śendru* would be quite in accordance with many precedents found in old Tamil words—*e.g.*, *pandri*, a hog (literally, "a tusker"), from the radical *pal*, a tusk, with the usual formative *ti* or *di*. Compare also *nin***r***u* (*nindru*) for *nindu*, having stood, the euphonised form of *nildu*, from the root *nil*, to stand.

idioms freely use the sibilants and aspirates of Sanskrit in writing and pronouncing Sanskrit derivatives, and to some extent, through the prevalence of Sanskrit influences, in the pronunciation even of pure Dravidian words. In Tamil, the *ś* of S'iva, occurring in Sanskrit derivatives, is represented by the peculiar palatal which answers to the *ch* of the Sanskrit, and the sound of which, when single, closely resembles that of *ś*. The other sibilants, *ṣh* and *s*, are altogether excluded from pure classical Tamil. In later Tamil books, and in the speech and letters of the better-educated Tamilians of the present age, those sibilants are freely employed in writing and pronouncing words which have been borrowed from Sanskrit; and in such cases, the characters which are used to express them are taken from the Grantha. By the mass of the people, however, those letters are rarely pronounced aright; and in the remoter districts the vulgar substitute for them, in accordance with the genius of the language, those letters which the ancient grammars enjoin, and the use of which is exemplified in the Sanskrit derivatives employed in the Tamil classics. The substitutions are as follows:—*ṣh*, the lingual sibilant of the Sanskrit, is represented in general by the lingual *ḍ*; sometimes by the liquid *ṛ*; sometimes even by the dental *t* or *d*. *s*, the sharp sibilant of the Sanskrit, is sometimes represented by *t* or *d*; sometimes it is omitted altogether; sometimes it is changed into the Tamil *ch*, the equivalent of *ś*. When this sibilant stands at the beginning of a Sanskrit derivative, and when it is desired, in accordance with modern usage, to pronounce it with the unmodified Sanskrit sound, it is preceded (at least in pronunciation) by the vowel *i*, without which it cannot be enunciated, in that connection, by Tamil organs. Thus, *strî*, Sans. a woman, is always pronounced and generally written *istiri*.

Tamil and Malayâlam are destitute of the sound of *h*. I believe, indeed, that this sound was originally foreign to the Dravidian languages, and that it crept into Telugu and Canarese through the influence of Sanskrit. Tamil upholds its claim to a sterner independence, if not to a higher antiquity, than the other tongues, by not only refusing to use the letter *h*, but by refusing to pronounce or write the aspirated consonants included in the Sanskrit words which it borrows. Dr Trumpp ("Sindhi Grammar," p. xxvi.) mentions the aversion of the Prakrit to aspirates, and remarks, that "this aversion seems to point to a Tatar underground current in the mouth of the common people, the Dravidian languages of the South being destitute of aspirates." In modern Canarese *h* is regularly used as a substitute for *p*, as is sometimes the case in Marâṭhi; but ancient Canarese agrees in this particular with Tamil.

Origin of the Lingual or "Cerebral" Sounds.—In all the languages and dialects of India, whether they belong to the Aryan or to the Dravidian families, much use is made of a series of consonants—*ṭ*, *ḍ*, with their aspirates, and *ṇ*—which are called by Hindu grammarians "cerebrals" because they are pronounced far back in the mouth, with a hard, ringing sound. I have reserved to this place some observations on the existence of this peculiar class of sounds in two families of tongues which are so widely different from one another as the Dravidian and the Sanskrit.

It seems natural to suppose that one of those families must have borrowed the sounds in question from the other; but it remains to be determined which was the borrower, and which was the original proprietor. Hindi, Bengali, and the other vernaculars of Northern India have doubtless inherited the lingual consonants from Sanskrit, from the decomposition of which those languages have mainly arisen; but it is very difficult to suppose that they have been borrowed in this manner from Sanskrit by the Dravidian languages. On the contrary, I have long been persuaded that they were borrowed from the Dravidian languages by Sanskrit, after the arrival of the Sanskrit-speaking race in India. The reasons which lead me to adopt this view are these:—

(1.) The lingual consonants are essential component elements of a large number of primitive Dravidian roots, and are often necessary, especially in Tamil, for the discrimination of one root from another; whereas in most cases in Sanskrit, the use of cerebral consonants instead of dentals, and especially the use of the cerebral *ṇ*, instead of the dental *n*, is merely euphonic.

(2.) None of the lingual consonants has ever been discovered in any of the primitive languages which are related to Sanskrit. They are not found in Greek or Latin, in Gothic or Celtic, in Lithuanian, Slavonian, or modern Persian: they are not found in cuneiform Persian or Zend—those sister dialects, with which the Sanskrit finally shook hands on crossing the Indus and settling in Âryâ-varta. On the other hand, the Dravidian languages, which claim to have had an origin independent of Sanskrit, and which appear to have been spoken throughout India prior to the arrival of the Aryans, possess the lingual sounds in question, and, for aught that appears, were in possession of them always. They are found even in the Brahui. There is no trace of these sounds in the Aryan family of tongues west of the Indus; but no sooner does a member of that family cross the Indus, and obtain a lodgment in the ancient seats of the Dravidians and other allied tribes in India, than the lingual sounds make their appearance in their language. It is worthy of notice also, that the Prakrits, the earliest vernacular dialects of the Sanskrit, make a larger use of the linguals than Sanskrit itself.*

(3.) Those consonants which Tamil has borrowed from Sanskrit within the period of the existence of Dravidian literature have been greatly modified to accord with the Tamilian laws of sound and delicacy of ear. Thus Tamil omits the aspirates even of Sanskrit derivatives, and omits or changes all the sibilants. It systematically softens down all harsh sounds. Even the Sanskrit lingual-sibilant *ṣh* cannot be pronounced by Tamil organs. Hence it seems improbable that a series of harsh ringing sounds, like the cerebral *ṭ*, *ḍ*, and *ṇ*, should have been borrowed by Tamil from Sanskrit without change, and used in the pronunciation, not only of Sanskrit derivatives, but also of a large number of the most essential Dravidian roots.

(4.) Though Telugu has been more exposed to Sanskrit influences than Tamil, yet larger use is made of those sounds in Tamil than in Telugu—a circumstance which seems incompatible with the supposition of the derivation of those sounds from Sanskrit.

Putting all these considerations together, it appears to me probable that instead of the Dravidian languages having borrowed the lingual consonants from Sanskrit, Sanskrit has borrowed them from the Dravidian languages; and it will, I think, be shown in the "Glossarial Affinities," that Sanskrit has not disdained to borrow from the Dravidian languages words as well as sounds.

After the foregoing observations were written, I met with Mr Norris's paper on the language of the "Scythic tablets" of Behistun, and found a similar opinion expressed therein respecting the Dravidian origin of the Sanskrit cerebrals. Mr Norris says, "I will here express my conviction that the sounds called cerebral are peculiar to the Tartar or Finnish class of languages; that the really Indian languages are all of Tartar origin, or at least that their phonetic and grammatical affinities are Tartar; and that the writers of Sanskrit

* The Vedic Sanskrit possesses a peculiar *l*—resembling the lingual *ḷ* of the Dravidian languages—which has disappeared from the more modern Sanskrit. This *ḷ* is one of the most distinctive features of the Dravidian languages, especially of Canarese and Tamil, and its origin is probably the same as that of the other linguals. It is retained occasionally in Tamil and Telugu, and very frequently in Canarese and Malayâlam, in the rendering of Sanskrit words, though it has disappeared from those words in Sanskrit itself. It is retained also in Marâṭhi, Koṅkaṇi, and other neighbouring Aryan languages. The lingual *ḷ* of the Vedic Sanskrit is regarded, not as an independent consonant, but as a substitute for *ḍ*. It will be shown hereafter that *ḍ* often changes into *ḷ* in the Dravidian languages, and that *ḷ* in its turn sometimes changes into *ḍ*.

adopted the sound from their Indian neighbours, in the same way that the Scandinavians appear to have adopted a similar sound from their neighbours the Lapps, who are undoubtedly Tartars; the Icelanders, who retain the old Scandinavian language, pronouncing the words *falla* and *fullr* as though written *fadla* and *fudlr*.

"It is certainly the case that this peculiar articulation has not been noticed as cerebral, so far as I know, by the writers who have treated of those languages; but this may be accounted for from the fact that Tartars have had few, if any, native grammarians; that, generally speaking, their languages are unwritten, and that, where written, the alphabet, not having been adopted by themselves, but given to them by nations more civilised than themselves, the difference between the dentals and cerebrals was not striking enough to a foreigner to induce him to invent new characters to designate the sounds new to him. But the existence of a *t* or *d*, convertible into *l*, is well known to Finnish philologers. Castrén, a Finnlander, in his 'Ostiak Grammar,' uses distinct characters for the cerebral and dental *d* and *t*, though not giving them these denominations, and directs that the former should be pronounced somewhat aspirated, with the addition of *l*, as *dhl* or *dl*, and *thl* or *tl*; observing that similar sounds occur in the Lappish and Finnish tongues."

The theory of the origin of the lingual consonants advocated above has been found to be in accordance with Professor Benfey's views. In his "Complete Sanskrit Grammar," p. 73 (I quote Dr Muir's translation of the passage, "Sanskrit Texts," part ii. 460), the Professor says, "The mute cerebrals have probably been introduced from the phonetic system of the Indian aborigines into Sanskrit, in which, however, they have become firmly established."

On the other hand, Dr Bühler, Professor of Sanskrit in the Elphinstone College, Bombay, argues, in a very able paper in the *Madras Journal of Literature* for 1864 (pp. 116–136), that I have not established my position, and that it is more probable that the sounds in question have been developed by the Sanskrit independently of other tongues, and spontaneously. I regret that this valuable contribution to Indian philology has not, so far as I know, been reprinted in Europe. We are so far in agreement that Dr Bühler thinks I have "proved two things beyond all doubt—firstly, that the so-called 'cerebrals,' or, as they are now termed, linguals, of the Dravidian dialects are not derived from the Sanskrit; and, secondly, that they did not belong to the original sounds of the primitive Indo-European tongues."

He goes on to say, "Dr Caldwell's statements contain a little error in point of fact. He says, 'None of the linguals has ever been discovered in any of the primitive languages which are related to Sanskrit.' This is perfectly true in regard to *ṭ*, *ṭh*, *ḍh*, and *ṇ*, but the Sanskrit *ṛ*, *ṛi*, *ṛī*, and *sh*, are, according to the testimony of the grammarians and of the pronunciation of the modern Pandits, likewise lingual; the second and fourth of these sounds (*ṛi, sh*) are found in Zend exactly in the same words and forms as in Sanskrit; and the first (*r*) is common to all the Indo-European languages." I was aware that *sh* was a lingual sound, and also that it was contained in Zend as well as in Sanskrit; but the fact that this *sh* was unknown to the Dravidian languages, though in such common use in Sanskrit, was adduced by me (in paragraph 3) for the purpose of proving that the other linguals, which are in still more common use in the Dravidian dialects than in Sanskrit, could not have been borrowed from the Sanskrit by those dialects. My argument referred to the cerebrals or linguals of the third *varga* alone, viz., *ṭ, ḍ, ṇ;* and it is admitted by Dr Bühler that these sounds were not originally contained in any of the Indo-European languages, and that in Sanskrit itself, though their use is very ancient, they are an "innovation." I admit that *r, ṛi,* and *ṛî,* notwithstanding their vocalic softness, have a just claim to be ranked amongst linguals. The Indian *r,* whether in Sanskrit or in the vernaculars, I consider more decidedly lingual than the *r* of Europe. It is one of the most difficult letters to Europeans; and the Dravidian languages contain, besides the *r* they have in common with Sanskrit, two *r*'s of their own, more lingual and more difficult still. I did not enter into the consideration of the lingual characters of *r* in connection with my argument, because this consonant, whatever minute differences may be observed in its pronunciation in different countries, is the common property of all the organic languages of Europe and Asia, and also because, though the influence of a contiguous *r* is well known to have largely contributed to the development in Sanskrit of the lingual sounds *ṭ, ḍ, ṇ,* it is scarcely, if at all, possible to detect the operation of any such influence in the Dravidian languages, in which the lingual sounds seem to have occupied from the beginning an essential place of their own in the differentiation of roots.

The chief value of Dr Bühler's paper consists in the fulness and clearness with which he traces the progressive stages of the development in Sanskrit of the lingual sounds in question, especially through the phonetic influence of *r* and *ṣh.* He summarises his results thus:—"We have seen that the ancient linguals *r* and *sh* produced lingual mutes and nasals, either independently or assisted by the universal law of assimilation, and that also *ṛi* and *ṛî,* the two lingual vowels, the former of which at least belongs to the pre-Sanskritic period, brought about the same result. Hence the Hindû contracted a liking for these sounds, and changed not only *h,* which, on account of its changeable nature, easily lent itself to this proceeding, to *ḍh,* but also dentals to the corresponding linguals. Moreover, I have pointed out repeatedly how the predilection for linguals becomes stronger and stronger in course of time—how in the daughter-languages of Sanskrit, and in their daughters, laws which cause the production of linguals become more and more stringent."

He then states that the probability of the theory advocated by him would be considerably enhanced if it could be shown that languages, other than the Sanskrit, have independently developed sounds of the lingual class, and proceeds to argue that such sounds have actually been developed in modern times in various Teutonic and Slavonic dialects, especially in English, though they have not been distinguished as such in grammars. He quotes Professor H. H. Wilson as an English writer who has recognised the existence of linguals in his own language. Professor Wilson says ("Sanskrit Grammar," p. 3), "The Sanskrit consonants are generally pronounced as in English, and we have, it may be suspected, several of the sounds for which the Sanskrit alphabet has provided distinct signs, but of which signs are wanting with us. This seems to be the case with the *cerebrals*. We write but one *t* and one *d*, but their sounds differ in such words as *trumpet* and *tongue*, *drain* and *den*, in the first of which they are *cerebrals*, in the second dentals." There is no doubt, I think, that the sound of the English *t* and *d*, in such connections, is slightly lingual, and also this semi-lingual sound is developed through the influence of the contiguous *r*. The case would be stronger, however, I think, if *r* preceded the dental or nasal, instead of following it, and if the vowel preceding *r* were long, not short. Thus the sounds *t*, *d*, and *n*, in the English words *mart*, *yard*, and *barn*, seem to me to have more of the character of the Indian linguals than in *trumpet* and *drain*. Dr Bühler proceeds to observe that the proper persons to decide this question are the natives of India. He says, "Every Englishman who has learned either Mahrâṭhi, Guzerathi, Hindi, or Bengali, from a native teacher, will have observed that the S'âstrî or Munshî constantly corrects his pronunciation, not of the *linguals*, but of the *dentals*, and tells him that he (the pupil) always uses the former instead of the latter. The conclusion to be drawn from this fact is, that the Englishman is familiar with the first class of sounds only. Besides, the natives of India, in transliterating English words, constantly use their linguals to express the English so-called dentals. They write, for instance, ḍirektar, instead of *d*irector, *gavarnmenṭ*, instead of governme*nt*, &c."

There is undoubtedly a measure of truth in the supposition advocated above. The English *t*, *d*, and *n*, approach more nearly to the sound of the Indian linguals than to that of the dentals, especially when intensified by a contiguous *r*. The influence of *r* on a contiguous *d* in English is well known. Hence, in several grammars of the Indian vernaculars intended for the use of Englishmen, students are advised to begin learning the lingual sounds by fancying the *t*, *d*, or *n* of the vernacular preceded by *r*. It accords generally also with my experience that Englishmen have less difficulty in acquiring the lingual sounds than in learning the peculiarly soft, distinctively dental sounds of the Indian *t*, *d*, and *n*. Beyond this, however, I am unable to go. There is still a great gulf, I conceive, between the slightly lingualised English dentals and the true Indian linguals,—a gulf which many European students of the Indian languages are never able to pass as long as they live (though they themselves are generally the last people to suppose this to be the case). The difference between the two classes of sounds could not be better illustrated than by getting a native unacquainted with English to pronounce the two words referred to by Professor Bühler, which have become naturalised in the country, and especially the long list of similar words, with their native transliterations, given at the end of Dr Bühler's paper by the editor of the

Madras Literary Journal. Every person who has taught English to Indians knows how difficult it is to get them out of their lingual pronunciation of the English *t* and *d*.

Up to this point, all the lingual sounds referred to by Dr Bühler, whether in Sanskrit and the Indian vernaculars derived from it, or in the tongues of modern Europe, have been found to be, and have been admitted to be, merely phonetic developments. Does this appear to be the case also in the Dravidian languages? I do not find any appreciable difference between any one of these languages and the rest with regard to the use of *ṭ* or *ḍ*; but a considerable difference is apparent with regard to the use of *ṇ* and the peculiarly Dravidian linguals *ṛ*, **r**, and *ḷ*. Many words which have *ṇ* and *ḷ* in the other dialects have *n* and *l* in Telugu. Are we to explain this by supposing that Telugu remained unchanged, whereas in the other dialects, especially in Tamil and Malayâlam, a certain fondness for the lingual sounds (that is, for the more distinctive sounds, as compared with the less distinctive) developed itself more and more as time went on, as has been the case in Sanskrit and the North Indian vernaculars? I think not. On the contrary, the existence in several of the Dravidian languages of a tendency to soften down these distinctive sounds is capable of being proved by a comparison of the ancient dialects of those languages with the modern. Thus old Canarese had the deep, vocalic, lingual *ṛ* of the Tamil and Malayâlam, whilst the modern Canarese has lost it. This sound does not now exist in Telugu, and it cannot clearly be proved that it ever had it; but the analogy of all the other dialects leads us to conclude that it had it originally, and that it lost it in course of time, as we know that Canarese did. Even in Tamil, it seems merging, in most parts of the country, either into *ḷ* or *y*, and the true pronunciation is now seldom heard. Both in Canarese and in Telugu the use of the hard lingual **r**, of which Tamil and Malayâlam are so fond, has become almost entirely obsolete, though the use of this consonant by the poets testifies to its currency in olden times. In Tuḷu this **r** has altogether disappeared, its place being generally supplied by *j*. It seems probable, therefore, that in those instances in which Telugu has *n* and *l*, whilst the other dialects have *ṇ* and *ḷ*, Telugu represents, not the older, but the more modern, usage of the people. Even though it should be admitted that Tamil carried its predilection for lingual sounds beyond the first phase of the language into the period when its secondary themes, derivatives, and inflexional suffixes were formed, it would still have to be remembered—(and in this respect it would differ widely from the Sanskrit)—that the place those sounds held in the first phase of the language itself was certainly far from being merely phonetic. Large numbers of the oldest verbal roots in the language, representing the most primitive and necessary ideas, are differentiated from other roots solely by the difference between the two classes of consonants. The following Tamil instances will suffice :—

kudi,	to leap.	*en*,	to say.
kuḍi,	to drink.	*eṇ*,	to count.
pudei,	to hide.	*manei*,	a house.
puḍei,	to sift.	*maṇei*,	a stool.

kattu,	to make a noise.	*aru,*	to be scarce.
kaṭṭu,	to tie.	*a**r**u,*	to cut off.
kottu,	to dig.	*aṛu,*	to weep.
koṭṭu,	to drum.	*kol,*	to kill.
ari,	to gnaw.	*koḷ,*	to take.
*a**r**i,*	to know.	*tulei,*	to end.
aṛi,	to destroy.	*tuḷei,*	to bore.

When these instances of the use of the lingual consonants in Tamil, which is richest in linguals, and which may be accepted in this particular as the best representative of the Dravidian family, are compared with the uses to which the linguals are put in Sanskrit, as amply illustrated by Dr Bühler, it will be apparent at once that the position occupied by the linguals in the Dravidian dialects differs essentially from that occupied by them in Sanskrit and the dialects derived from it. They evidently pertain, not to the phonetic development or euphonic refinement of the Tamil, but to its system of roots, meanings, and laws of specialisation. They take us back to a point in the history of the language beyond which we cannot hope to be able to ascend. If Sanskrit were to be deprived of its linguals, there is hardly an idea or shade of thought it expresses now which it would not then be equally able to express; but if Tamil were deprived of its linguals, it would cease to be able to express some of the most rudimentary, necessary ideas, and would scarcely be worthy to be called a language.

The position occupied by the lingual consonants in Sanskrit and in the Dravidian languages respectively being now fully before us, we come back to the question at issue, How did these sounds first make their appearance in Sanskrit? The question, it appears to me, is mainly one of probabilities. Speaking generally, with a reservation of the slight modifications already admitted, these sounds are peculiar to India. We find them in both the varieties of highly-organised human speech, the Sanskritic and the Dravidian, which have existed in India side by side for three thousand years; and there is reason to believe that for an unknown period before that the Sanskrit-speaking race came into still closer contact with the Dravidians (or with some people speaking a language analogous in structure to that of the Dravidian tongues), not only after they arrived in India and occupied the seats of the Dravidians, but possibly even before they crossed the Indus, whilst on their way through the country of the Brahuis. Which, then, is the more probable supposition?—that these peculiarly Indian lingual sounds developed themselves spontaneously and quite independently in each of those varieties of speech, the Sanskritic and the Dravidian? or that they had a common origin, having developed themselves first in one family, and then spread from that to the other? The balance of probabilities seems to me in favour of the latter supposition; and if this supposition of a common origin be adopted, we seem then to be warranted in concluding that it was in the speech of the primitive Dravidians that these sounds originated, and that it was through Dravidian influences that a predilection for these sounds developed itself in the speech of the Indo-Aryan race. It is freely admitted by Dr Bühler that "the linguals of the Dravidian dialects are not derived from the Sanskrit." On the supposition, therefore, that they have a common origin, would it not follow that Sanskrit must have derived them from the Dravidian dialects?

Dr Bühler argues that "the possibility of the borrowing of sounds by one language from another has never yet been proved," and that "comparative philologists have admitted loan-theories too easily, without examining facts." "Regarding the borrowing of sounds," he says, "it may suffice for the present to remark, that it never has been shown to occur in the languages which were influenced by others in historical times, such as English, Spanish, and the other Romance languages, Persian, &c." "We find still stronger evidence," he says, "against the loan-theory in the well-known fact that nations which, like the Jews, the Parsees, the Slavonian tribes of Germany, the Irish, &c., have lost their mother-tongues, are, as nations, unable to adopt with the words and grammatical laws also the pronunciation of the foreign language." I am quite prepared to agree with Dr Bühler up to a certain point. I admit that many nations, possibly that most nations, even whilst adopting wholesale the words of other nations with whom they have been brought into close contact, are found to have retained their own pronunciation without acquiring the peculiarities of the pronunciation of those other nations. But admitting it to be a fact that ten nations have not borrowed sounds from other nations, it is unsafe to argue from this that the eleventh nation cannot have done so. It is merely a question of fact; and if we find it in any case to be a fact that this supposed impossibility has taken place, all we can do is to add this new fact to our existing stock of facts, and modify our theories accordingly. An interesting illustration of the necessity of leaving an opening for new facts may be discovered in a portion of Dr Bühler's own argument. "Let us consider," he says, "the case of the English. Though half of its words have been imported by the Norman race, though most of the old Saxon inflexions have perished in the struggle between the languages of the conqueror and the conquered, though in some instances even Norman affixes have entered the organism of the original language, the quietism of the Saxon organs of speech has opposed a passive and successful resistance to the introduction of foreign sounds. The English has received neither the clear French *a*, nor its *u*, nor its peculiar nasals. On the contrary, it has well preserved its broad, impure vowels and diphthongs, and it is now as difficult for an Englishman to pronounce the French *a* or *u*, as it was for his Saxon ancestors eight hundred years ago." This argument is well worked out. It proves conclusively that the English, whilst adopting much of the vocabulary of the Normans, did not adopt their pronunciation. But what shall we say about the Normans themselves? Not two hundred years had elapsed since the first settlement of the Northmen in France when they conquered England; and during that short time they had not only exchanged their own Norse for the French of the period, but had adopted those sounds—had acquired those peculiarities of pronunciation—which Dr Bühler treats as distinctively and inalienably French. The very sounds to which he refers—the clear French *a*, the *u*, and its peculiar nasals, and of which he says that it is as difficult for an Englishman to pronounce them now as for his Saxon ancestors eight hundred years ago—are sounds which the Northmen only a short time before their arrival in England had picked up from the race they conquered. What can be said of this, but that the imitativeness of the Normans is as much a fact in history, and as much entitled to throw whatever light it can on the possibilities of Indian philology, as the passiveness of the early English? May not this at least be inferred, that if the Normans had so much of the faculty of imitation as to be able to adopt the language of a race with which they came in contact, pronunciation and all, it requires no straining of the imagination to suppose the Sanskrit-speaking race imitative enough to adopt—not the language of the race that preceded them in India—not their pronunciation—but merely a certain peculiarity in their pronunciation of a few consonants with which they could not fail to be struck?

"The possibility of the borrowing of sounds by one nation from another" receives an illustration from the "click" of Southern Africa; and this illustration is all the more appropriate, seeing that the "click," somewhat like the lingual sounds of India, is not a new, independent, consonantal sound, but merely a peculiarity of pronunciation attaching to a certain class of consonants. Dr Bleek remarks, "The occurrence of clicks in the Kafir dialects decreases almost in proportion to their distance from the Hottentot border. Yet the most southern Tekeza dialects and the Se-suto have also (probably through Kafir influence) become to a slight extent possessed of this remarkable phonetic element."—*Bleek's Comparative Grammar*, p. 13. Bishop Callaway, in his preface to vol. i. part i. of his "Zulu Nursery Tales," Natal (and London, Trübner & Co.), says, "It is generally supposed that the sounds called clicks are a modern intrusion into the alliterative class of languages, arising from intercourse with the Hottentots." He adds, "The view that the clicks are not native to the alliterative languages is quite in accordance with the theory I have formed of their nature."

One of Dr Bühler's objections to the supposition of the lingual mode of pronouncing certain consonants by the Sanskrit-speaking race having been derived from the Dravidians is, that the words containing linguals which I had represented as borrowed from the Dravidian languages by the Sanskrit are not numerous enough to render this supposition admissible. The number of such words might easily be increased; but I do not attribute the adoption of lingual sounds by the Âryans to the influence of the words, whether few or many, borrowed by them from the Dravidians. It does not appear to me a necessary condition of the adoption of a peculiar pronunciation that "a great number of foreign words containing the particular letter should first be borrowed, and that the sound should thus become perfectly familiar to the people." In the case of the South African "click," each tribe retains its own words, whilst pronouncing them in the Hottentot fashion. But we need not go beyond the Sanskrit-speaking race itself for an illustration of the possibility of a peculiarity in pronunciation making its way, not by the introduction of new words, but by the modification of the pronunciation of words already in existence. Dr Bühler considers the lingual sounds of the Sanskrit an independent development, "a phonetic innovation which has outgrown in course of time its original and legitimate limits." He thinks it capable of proof that the dental sounds in Sanskrit are more ancient than the lingual, and that the predilection for lingual sounds went on gradually increasing. Supposing this granted, we are naturally led to inquire by what process the transformation of dentals to linguals became a characteristic of the language of the whole race? It must have arisen, according to his theory, not from the adoption of new words, but from a certain peculiarity in the pronunciation of old words passing, like a new fashion, from one person to another. One person must have made a beginning; that person's family must have imitated him; from one family the peculiarity must have spread to the other families of the *gôtra; gôtra* after *gôtra* must gradually have caught the infection; and then at last, when the usage became universal, the new literature of the race provided it with a lasting resting-place. It appears to me, therefore, that, on Dr Bühler's hypothesis, as well as on mine, the borrowing of sounds must have been carried on on a very extensive scale. My hypothesis merely serves to show how this process may have received its first impulse, and been accelerated in its course. Probably also the Indo-Aryans were not the only people in ancient or later times amongst whom borrowing prevailed. How could the whole of the members of any nation or race have acquired its stock of distinctive sounds and words—how could organised varieties of speech have taken possession of the large areas in which they are now found—had not the practice stigmatised as the "loan-theory" been in continual operation? Descent accounts for much; imitativeness, as it appears to me, for more.

After writing the above, I found a discussion of the same question by Mr Beames in §§ 59, 60, of his "Comparative Grammar of the Modern Aryan Languages of India." Mr Beames takes to some extent the same line as Dr Bühler, but he enters more fully into the investigation of the question of the relation of the cerebrals to the dentals. With much of what he says I fully agree.

"The connection between dentals and cerebrals rests on the principle, which I shall do my best to prove in this section, that these two classes of sounds are really the weaker and stronger branches respectively of one and the same group, which, as being produced by the instrumentality of the tongue, may be comprehended under the general name of linguals. From the nature of the case, it might be anticipated that Sanskrit, in its polished or classical stage, would incline to the use of the softer or dental branch, while, on the other hand, the popular speech, as represented by the Prakrits, would adhere to the harsher or cerebral forms. It will be seen in the sequel how far this anticipation is borne out by facts. . . . . The modern languages present at first sight an inextricable chaos and confusion. There are cases (α) where the Sanskrit has the dental, Prakrits and the moderns the cerebral; (β) where Sanskrit has dental, Prakrit cerebral, and the moderns dental; (γ) where Sanskrit and Prakrit have dental, the moderns cerebral; (δ) Sanskrit cerebral, Prakrit the same, but the moderns dental. There are also instances in which two words, apparently cognate, differ only in this letter—one having the cerebral, the other the dental. . . .

"There would seem to be some misapprehension as to the nature of the Aryan cerebrals, which are treated by European scholars as though they were a class of sounds unpronounceable by our organs, and only to be with difficulty learnt by persons who have heard them uttered by the natives of India. Inasmuch as they are only found in the Indian branch of the great Indo-Germanic family, it has been somewhat hastily concluded that they are foreign to that family; and as a set of sounds which, in name at least, is identical with them, is found in the Dravidian languages, it has been assumed that these sounds are of non-Aryan origin, and that they have sprung partly from a tendency to harshen the pronunciation of the dentals acquired by the Aryans from their non-Aryan neighbours since their arrival in India, and partly from a wholesale importation of non-Aryan words into Sanskrit and its modern descendants.

"Without absolutely denying the possibility that both of these theories may contain a certain amount of truth, I would bring forward some considerations to show that they are not either undoubtedly correct, or even necessary to account for the presence of these sounds.

"To go to the root of the matter, we may endeavour to get at a true perception of the real state of the question by analysing the sounds themselves. All consonants are produced by checking the outward flowing breath, through bringing into contact two of the organs of the mouth. Among these checks there is a regularly graduated series, produced by the contact of the tip of the tongue with the region extending from the centre of the palate to the edges of the upper teeth. This series may be called the lingual series. If the tongue-tip be applied to the highest point of this region—that is, to the centre of the hard or true palate—the sounds are harsh, and similar to the letter *r*. Contact a little lower down, or more towards the front, produces a sound less harsh, and so on; the more forward the contact the softer the sound, till at last, when we get to the edge of the teeth, the sound which results is extremely soft and smooth. The sounds of this series, as expressed by the Teutonic branch of the family, are among the harsher, though not absolutely the harshest, notes of the series. In expressing *t* and *d*, we Teutons touch with our tongues the gum or fleshy part of the palate just above the teeth. The Southern European races form the contact lower down, just where the osseous substance of the teeth issues from the gums, thus producing a softer sound than the Teutons. The Persians and Indians form it low down on the teeth, almost at their edge, thus producing the softest sound of all. This Indian sound, being the result of impact on the teeth, is a true dental. We Teutons have no dental sounds at all, and the Italians have only semi-dentals. The Indians have, however, in addition to their true dentals, another series produced by contact at a point a very little, if at all, higher than the Teutonic contact, so that they possess, so to speak, the highest and lowest notes of the scale, but not the intermediate ones.

"With the exception of the harsh Indian contact, the Teutonic is the highest in the scale, and the reason of this is probably that the race which uses it, living in a cold country, has preserved that nervous vigour which enables it to employ its organs of speech firmly and crisply. In the South of Europe the warmer climate has induced a certain amount of laxity, which has told on the articulation, and the point of contact has therefore fallen lower, to a position which requires less effort on the part of the speaker; while in the still hotter climate of Persia and India, greater relaxation has taken place, and the muscles of the tongue have become flaccid; the member itself is long and soft, and naturally seeks the lowest and easiest place of utterance. Thus it comes to pass that the words which the Teutons pronounce with *ṭ* and *ḍ* are pronounced by the Indians with *t* and *d*. While *daughter*, as pronounced by an Englishman, would be written by the Indians *ḍâṭar*, they themselves at an early period said *duhitâ*. If we could find out how the word was pronounced by the Aryans before they descended into the plains of India, we should probably have to write it *ḍuhaṭâ*, or rather, in those days the sounds represented by the letters *t* and *d* did not exist. . . . . The relaxation indicated by those letters must have taken place after the Aryans came into this country. Before that time, and probably for some centuries after it, their lingual contact was, we may fairly assume, as crisp and firm, and its place as high up in the palate, as that of their European brethren. In those days they knew of no distinction between *t* and *ṭ*, *d* and *ḍ*. They had, however, in their language words in which an *r* preceded or followed a dental, and in such combinations their lingual sounds assumed by degrees a harsher note, being produced by a contact nearer to the place of utterance of *r*, which is very high up in the palate. The people, though they gradually softened their place of contact, and brought it lower down in the mouth in the case of a single consonant, naturally retained a high contact when an *r* was in combination, and this habit must have become more and more marked as time went on. In proportion as the point of utterance of *t* and *d* sank lower in the mouth, the distance between it and the point of utterance of *r* got greater and greater, and the additional labour of moving the tongue from one point to the other increased, and to avoid this, the higher and harsher point of contact for *t* and *d* was retained. Then as the *r*, under the influence of other phonetic laws, began to be regularly omitted, nothing remained but the linguals at a high point of contact—that is, what we now call cerebrals. So that when at length the art of writing was introduced, the national pronunciation had by that time become so fixed that it was necessary to recognise the existence of two separate sets of lingual utterances, and to provide appropriate symbols for each. But when they were confronted by the task of assigning either cerebral or dental linguals to any individual word, the grammarians to whose lot it fell to reduce their already highly-developed language to writing, must have had a difficult problem to solve. It is perhaps not to be expected that we should be able at this distance of time to detect the principles on which they worked, or to ascertain what were the considerations which guided them in determining in each case whether to write a dental or a cerebral. It results, however, from the remarks just made, that what we now call the cerebrals are the real equivalents of the European *t* and *d*, and that it is not these, but the Indian dentals which are peculiar to those tongues. It is fair, therefore, to assume that the original form of such words as those which are given above as examples, is that which retains the cerebral, and that the dental form has grown out of the cerebral one by the process of weakening and softening which the Aryan organs of speech have undergone from the effects of climate. It would certainly be in full and complete harmony with the present theory that the Prakrits, regarded as the colloquial languages, should exhibit a more frequent use of the cerebral, while the Sanskrit, regarded as the language of literature, should prefer the softer dental; and, as has been stated above, it is actually asserted by several authors that this is the case. Unfortunately, however, an examination of such examples of Prakrit as are available by no means bears out this assertion, and the evidence of the modern languages, which is of almost conclusive importance in this respect, shows that both dental and cerebral are used with equal frequency, even in derivatives from a common root; and more than this, dentals are used in cases where the recorded Sanskrit word is written only with a cerebral.

"It must have struck every one who has resided in India that the native ear, though keen and subtle beyond belief in detecting minute differences of sound in native words, is very dull and blunt in catching foreign sounds. The ordinary peasant, who never mistakes *sát*, seven, for *sáṭ*, sixty, however softly or rapidly spoken, will often be quite unable to catch a single word of a sentence in his own language, however grammatically correct, and however distinctly uttered by an European, simply on account of some apparently trifling difference in pronunciation. Now we see something of this sort in the Prakrit of the plays. The slight differences or rudenesses of pronunciation among the lower classes were made much of by play-writers, and exaggerated almost grotesquely. This tendency probably led to the practice of writing every *n* in Prakrit as *ṇ*, and will also account for much of the irregularity in the employment of the cerebrals and dentals. Provincial peculiarities of pronunciation, such as exist in the present day in various parts of India, were seized upon and fixed, and words were spelt accordingly, without reference to their etymology.

"One of the most striking of these provincial peculiarities is the fondness of the Sindhi for cerebrals. This language has preserved the harsher point of contact, and has not allowed itself to be weak and soft. The sturdy Jats, wandering over their barren deserts, were engaged in a constant struggle with nature for the bare permission to exist, and there was therefore little risk of their becoming languid or effeminate in speech or in any other qualification.

"The further transition of the cerebrals and dentals into the semivowel *l* is a point attended with some obscurity. The process seems, like so many phonetic processes in the Indian languages, to work backwards and forwards, and to branch out into further collateral development, as into *ḷ* (ळ), *r*, and the like. *Ḷ* is a dental letter, and the change from *d* to *ḍ* and then to *l*, involving, as it does, a passage from a dental to a cerebral, and back again to the dental, can only be accounted for on the supposition advanced above, that originally there was no difference between the two classes of sounds, and that, subsequently to the rise and establishment of this difference, the popular ear has continued to recognise the close connection of the two, and to be a little uncertain when to use one, and when the other. . . . .

"I will now sum up what has been said about the cerebrals and dentals, and the two forms of *l*. The cerebrals are the harsher, the dentals the softer, forms of the lingual series. The former correspond very nearly to our English sounds, the latter are unlike any sound current in Europe, and have arisen from the debilitating effects of a hot climate. . . . . From all these circumstances we infer the original unity of all the lingual group, and its affinity to the European dentals."

Mr Beames has discussed the origin of the cerebral sounds, and the nature of the difference between them and the dentals so exhaustively, and I am so perfectly in agreement with him in much of what he says, that, though I have already given to the discussion of this subject too large a share of the space at my disposal, I have thought it best to reprint nearly all he has said *in extenso*, and allow it to speak for itself, contenting myself with making only a few remarks on that portion of his theory which runs counter to my own. I need not repeat anything I have said in my remarks on Dr Bühler's paper. Whilst I admit that the dentals of the European languages are only partially dentals, and that the dentals of the languages of India, being formed into a class by themselves separate from the cerebrals, are more perfectly worthy of being called by that name, I do not admit that the Indian cerebrals represent the original sounds of the letters of the lingual class better than the dentals.

In another passage (p. 264), Mr Beames speaks of the cerebrals as "regarded by the Pandits, who worked at a time when the usual lingual contact of their nation had passed down to a lower point of contact, as in some way derived from the dentals; an erroneous view, in which they have been followed by many European scholars." In this matter, as it appears to me, the Pandits have not fallen into error. Dentals were regarded as best representing the true pronunciation of old Aryan words, not only at the time when Pâṇini and the grammatical writers lived, but also at the time when Sanskrit compositions were first committed to writing. Cerebral sounds had by that time come to be sharply distinguished from dentals, and a separate set of characters had been invented for their expression; yet, on comparing the stock of words possessed in common by the Sanskrit and the other languages of the Indo-European group, it will be manifest that dentals were in almost every instance preferred. Cerebral sounds seem to have been treated as novelties, or at least as later developments, whereas dentals were regarded as a portion of the old Aryan inheritance. But this line of argument is capable of being carried much further back. Long before grammatical rules were formed—long before writing was introduced—at that early period when the Vedic hymns began to be composed, and sacrificial formulæ began to be handed down from priest to priest, the same distinction between dentals and cerebrals, and the same preference for dentals, evidently existed. I cannot do better than quote Mr Beames himself. He says (Introduction, p. 5), "Although Pâṇini lived in an age when the early Aryan dialects had already undergone much change from their pristine condition, yet among the Brahmans, for whom alone he laboured, there existed a traditional memory of the ancient, and then obsolete, form of many words. They would remember those archaic forms, because their religious and professional duties required them constantly to recite formulæ of great antiquity, and of such sacredness that every letter in them was supposed to be a divinity in itself, and which had consequently been handed down from primeval times absolutely unchanged."

Again, if Mr Beames's theory respecting the origin of the Sanskrit dentals and the antiquity of the cerebrals were perfectly tenable, it ought to be applicable also to the dentals and cerebrals of the Dravidian languages. It ought to be evident, or at least should appear probable, that the Dravidian dentals were a later class of sounds than the cerebrals, brought into existence by the heat of the climate. But there is no ground whatever for such a supposition, in so far as the Dravidian languages are concerned, for dentals as well as cerebrals show themselves, as I have already mentioned, in the oldest and most necessary roots in each dialect, and cerebrals are more largely used in Tamil, which is spoken in the extreme south of the peninsula, where the heat is greatest, than in Telugu, which is spoken where the heat is less intense. Moreover, the development of the cerebral sounds is not in any degree in the Dravidian languages, as in Sanskrit, owing to the influence of a contiguous *r*. It looks, indeed, as if it were to the heat of the Indian climate that the cerebral sounds—not the dentals—were owing. If it be admitted that the heat of the climate has an enervating effect on the organs of speech, as it certainly has on the organs of digestion, may it not be supposed that the introduction into the speech of the people of the harsh piquant sounds of the cerebral letters was owing to the same cause to which they were indebted for the introduction of hot, piquant curries into the list of their articles of food?

I quote here some observations of Mr Beames in confirmation of the line of argument taken by myself in my remarks on Dr Bühler's paper. "I am not in a position to point out how far or in what direction Aryan vocalism has been influenced by these alien races (Kols, Dravidians, &c.); but that some sort of influence has been at work is almost beyond a doubt. It may, however, be conjectured that the pronunciation has been affected more than the written language, because the latter is always by conscious and intentional efforts kept up to some known standard. To one who has spent some years in the Panjab or Hindustan, the ordinary pronunciation of the Bengalis and Oṛiyas certainly sounds uncouth and foreign, and as these two races are surrounded by and much mixed up with non-Aryans, it is probable that the contiguity of the latter will eventually be found to have had much to do with this peculiarity."—P. 128.

"This curious heavy *ḷ* is very widely employed in the Dravidian group of languages, where it interchanges freely with *r* and *d*, and it is also found in the Kol family of Central India. The Marathas and Oṛiyas are perhaps of all the Aryan tribes those which have been for the longest time in contact with Kols and Dravidians, and it is not surprising, therefore, to find the cerebral *l* more freely used by them than by the others. . . . . It is noticeable in many languages, that where a nation gets hold of, or invents, some peculiar sound, it straightway falls in love with it, and drags it into use at every turn, whether there be any etymological reason for it or no. We English, for instance, have dragged our favourite *th* into a number of words where it has no business to be; and similarly the Oṛiyas and Marathas bring in this beloved *ḷ* where *l* should be."—P. 445.

"Oṛiya and Maratha have long been spoken in tracts partly peopled by non-Aryans: in the case of the former, by Kols and Telingas; in that of the latter, by Gonds, Bhils, and Canarese. The Aryans of Gujarat also displaced non-Aryan tribes, and may from them have caught this trick of speech (the use of broken vowels and a short *e*), as may also the Bengalis from the numerous wild tribes on their frontiers."—P. 141. It will be seen that, whilst as regards the special question of the adoption of the cerebral sounds from the Dravidians by the Indo-Aryans, Mr Beames's opinion coincides, on the whole, with Dr Bühler's, as regards the general question of the possibility of peculiarities of pronunciation being borrowed by one people from another, with which it is very much mixed up, his opinion coincides with mine. I claim his vote also with regard to one of the cerebrals themselves—the cerebral *ḷ*.

Dr Trumpp, in his recently-published "Grammar of the Sindhi Language," advocates the view of this question I have taken. He thinks the North Indian vernaculars have been considerably influenced by the Dravidian, or at least non-Aryan, languages spoken by the Indian aborigines; and, in particular, attributes the cerebrals to this source. "The cerebrals," he says, "comprise the most non-Aryan elements of the language (the Sindhi)." He thinks "nearly three-fourths of the words which commence with a cerebral are taken from some aboriginal non-Aryan idiom, which in recent times has been termed Scythian, but which we should prefer to call Tâtâr." "This seems," he says, "to be very strong proof that the cerebrals have been borrowed from some idiom anterior to the introduction of the Aryan family of languages. The Sanskrit uses the cerebrals very sparingly, but in Prakrit, which is already considerably tinged with so-called 'provincial,' that is, with non-Aryan elements, they struggle hard to supplant the dentals."—P. 21. Hence the preference by natives of cerebrals to dentals in the transliteration of European words, of which so much use is made by Dr Bühler and Mr Beames, appears to be merely in accordance with the preference of cerebrals to dentals exhibited in the Prakrits, and which is found in full operation in the dialects which have sprung from the Prakrits. This preference simply proves, in Dr Trumpp's opinion, that the cerebrals are more familiar to the people of India than the dentals (p. 24). He attributes also to Dravidian influences the aversion of the Prakrit to aspirates, and the peculiar pronunciation certain letters (*ch* and *f*) have received in certain connections in Marâṭhi. Mr Edkins (in "China's Place in Philology") remarks that in the Malay alphabet a Dravidian influence may be suspected in the cerebral series of letters *ṭ*, *ḍ*, *ṇ*. The initial consonant in Malay is generally single, as in the Dravidian tongue.

The Dravidian *ḷ* (as will be seen under the next head) is interchangeable with the cerebral *ḍ*, through their middle point, the vocalic ṛ. All these letters indeed appear to have a cognate origin. They are so easily interchanged, that one is tempted to consider them all merely as varieties of one and the same sound.

Dialectic Interchange of Consonants.—Under this head I intend to consider, not the euphonic refinements which have been tabulated, and perhaps in part invented, by grammarians, but those natural, unintentional mutations and interchanges which are brought to view by a comparison of the various Dravidian dialects. These dialectic interchanges will be found to throw much light on the Dravidian laws of sound, whilst they enable us to identify many words and inflexional forms contained in the various dialects, which appear at first sight to be unconnected, but which are in reality the same.

Following, as before, as far as possible, the order of the Deva-nâgarî alphabet, I proceed to point out the dialectic changes to which each Dravidian consonant appears to be liable. I omit the aspirated consonants as not really Dravidian.

1. *The gutturals: k, g, ṅ.*

g being merely the sonant of *k*, in the changes now to be inquired into, *k* and *g* will be regarded as identical.

(i.) *k*, when used as a sonant—that is, as *g*—changes into *v*. Where we have *g* in Tamil, we sometimes find *v* in Telugu—*e.g.*, *âgu*, Tam. to become; *avu*, Tel. In *kâ*, the infinitive of this verb in Telugu, which corresponds to the Tamil *âga*, *k* (or *g*) reappears. It is in the middle of words, where it is a sonant, that this consonant evinces a tendency to be changed into *v*. This tendency constantly appears in the spoken language of the lower classes of the Tamil people in the Southern provinces; and has found a place even in the poets—*e.g.*, *nôva*, to be pained, instead of the more common *nôga*. *g* in the middle of a word is sometimes lost altogether, not merely softened into *v*—*e.g.*, *pagudi*, Tam. a share, has become *pâdi*, half; *śagaḍu*, a cart, *śâḍu*.

In Telugu, *v* is often not only pronounced, but written, instead of *g*—*e.g.*, *pagaḍamu*, coral, corrupted into *pavaḍamu*. Compare with this the change of the Sanskrit *laghu*, light, into the Latin *levis*. It will be seen that, *per contra*, *v* sometimes becomes *g* in Telugu. This change sometimes takes place in Malayâlam also—*e.g.*, *chuvanna*, red, is often *chuganna* (*śivanda*, Tam.)

(ii.) *k* changes into *ch* or *ś*. As the Tamil *ś* becomes *ch* when doubled, and is represented in the alphabet by the equivalent of the Deva-nâgarî *ch*, the change of *k* into *ch* is identical with that of *k* into *ś*. The former change appears in Telugu, the latter in Tamil.

Compare the change of the Greek and Latin *k* into the Sanskrit *ś*—*e.g.*, *δέκα* and *decem*, softened into *daśan*, ten.

Canarese generally retains *k*, the older pronunciation of this consonant; and where *k* is found in Canarese, we generally find *ch* in Telugu and *ś* in Tamil—*e.g.*, *kinna*, Can. small; *chinna*, Tel.; *śinna*, Tam.: *kivi*, Can. the ear; *chevi*, Tel.; *śevi*, Tam.: *gey*, Can. to do; *chêy*, Tel.; *śey*, Tam. Sometimes the older *k* is retained by Tamil as well as by Canarese, and the softening appears in Telugu only—*e.g.*, *keḍu*, Tam. and Can. to spoil; Tel. *cheḍu* or *cheṟu*. The word for *hand* is in Tamil *kei*, in Canarese *keiyi*, in Telugu *kei* (also *kêlu*); but there is another word in Telugu, *chê* (*cheyyi*), the hand, which is the ordinary instrumental affix (*cheta*), and this is evidently a softened form of *kei* or *kê*.

A similar change of *k* into *ch* appears in Sanskrit—*e.g.*, compare *vâch-as*, of speech, with the nominative *vâk*, speech.

(iii.) *kk* change systematically into *ch* or *chch*. This change may be regarded as the rule of the pronunciation of the lower classes of the Tamil people in the southern districts. Farther north, and in grammatical Tamil, it is rarely met with, but in the Telugu country the rule re-appears; and in a large class of words, especially in the formatives of verbs, the double *k* of the Tamil is replaced regularly by *ch* in Telugu. The following instances of this change are contained even in grammatical Tamil:—*kâychchu*, to boil, for the more regular *kâykku*, and *pâychchu*, to irrigate, for *pâykku*. A single illustration will suffice to illustrate the perfect conformity in this point between the vulgar pronunciation of Tamil in the extreme south and the regular grammatical use of *ch* for *kk* in Telugu. *Veikka*, Tam. to place (infinitive), is pronounced *veichcha* by the illiterate in the southern Tamil districts; and in grammatical Telugu the same word is both written and pronounced *veicha*.

(iv.) *k* appears sometimes to have changed into *t*. I cannot adduce a good instance of this change in the Dravidian languages; but I suspect that the *t* of some inflexional terminations in Gônd (*e.g.*, the nominative plural of the personal pronouns) has been derived from the Tamil *k*. Compare also *vâkili*, a doorway, Telugu, with the Malayâlam form of the same word, *vâtil* or *vâdil*. I am doubtful, however, whether this illustration can be depended upon, because the Tamil form of the same word is *vâśal*, classically *vâyil*, from *vây-il*, literally mouth-house. In other families of languages the interchange between *k* and *t* is not uncommon—*e.g.*, Doric *τῆνος*, he, instead of *ἐ-κεῖνος*.

2. *The palatals: ch* or *ś*, *j*, *ñj*.

I class the changes of *ch*, *ś*, and *j* together, those letters being in reality but one in the Dravidian languages. The only change to which this letter *ś* or *j* is liable, is that of being softened into *y*. In words borrowed by Tamil from Sanskrit, *y* is optionally used instead of *ś*, and very commonly instead of *j*. Thus *râjâ*, Sans. a king (in Tamil *râśâ*, and with the masculine formative, *râś-an*), becomes *rây-an*. In the southern provinces of the Tamil country this change of *ś* into *y* has become a characteristic of the pronunciation of the lower classes. In those provinces, in all words in which this letter occurs, whether Sanskrit or Tamil, the *ś* is changed into *y*—*e.g.*, they say *ariyi*, rice, instead of *ariśi*. In Malayâlam this becomes *ari*. Dr Gündert thinks the *d* of the Tuḷu *pudar*, name, derived from the *ś* of the corresponding Canarese *peśar*. If so, we have here a change of *ś* into *d*.

On comparing Canarese with Tamil, we often find *ś* where we should have expected *y*—*e.g.*, *heśar* (for *peśar*), Can. a name, instead of *peyar*, Tam. It seems unsafe, however, to assume that in these cases *y* was the original and *ś* the corruption. It may as well be that *ś* was the original and *y* the corruption. The Tamil *peyar* may therefore be a softened form of the Canarese *hesar* (Tuḷu, *pudar*), and what renders this more likely is that the Tamil *peyar* itself is still further softened into *pêr*. In high Tamil, as in Malayâlam, the softened form is often preferred by the poets as more elegant. It may possibly therefore be more ancient—*e.g.*, *peim*, green, is in both languages more poetical than *paśum*. All that is certain with regard to such cases is, that *y* and *ś* often change places. The existence, however, of a dialectic change from *ś* to *y*, as apparent especially in the southern districts, is clearly proved by the change Sanskrit derivatives have undergone.

3. *The linguals or cerebrals: ṭ, ḍ, ṇ.*

(i.) The lingual *ṭ*, when used as a sonant and pronounced as *ḍ*, is sometimes changed into the vocalic *ṛ* in Tamil—*e.g.*, *nâḍi*, Sans. a measure, is commonly written and pronounced in Tamil *nâṛi*; and this is colloquially pronounced *nâḷi* in the southern districts by a further change of *ṛ* into *ḷ*. In old Canarese this Sanskrit *ḍ* often becomes *ṛ*, as in Tamil. These letters are considered cognate, like *r* and **r**, *l* and *ḷ*. In Tuda, *ḍ* becomes *r*—*e.g.*, *nâḍ-u*, a district, becomes *nâr*. The counterpart of this change—viz., the change of *ṛ* into *ḍ*—is still more common in the Dravidian languages. (See *ṛ*.) In Telugu there are some instances of the change of *ḍ* into the hard, rough **r**—*e.g.*, *cheḍu*, to spoil (Tam. and Can. *keḍu*), should have for its transitive form *cheḍuchu*, answering to the Tamil *keḍukku*; whereas *che***r***uchu* is used instead.

(ii.) *ṇ*. This lingual nasal is frequently softened in Telugu into *n*, the nasal of the dental row. Tamil, perhaps the most authentic representative of the ancient speech of the Dravidians, makes much use of *ṇ*, as well as of the other cerebrals; and the colloquial Tamil goes beyond the grammatical Tamil in preferring *ṇ* to *n*. Telugu, on the other hand, whilst it uses the other cerebrals freely enough, often prefers *n* to *ṇ*. Thus it softens the Tamil (and old Dravidian) words *kaṇ*, eye, *viṇ*, heaven, *maṇ*, earth, into *kannu*, *vinnu*, and *mannu*. It softens even some Sanskrit words in a similar manner—*e.g.*, in addition to *guṇamu*, quality, a *tatsama* word, it uses also the *tadbhava*, *gonamu*. Malayâlam sometimes uses *ṇ* instead of *n*—*e.g.*, *niṇakku*, to thee, instead of, but also in addition to, *ninakku*. On the other hand, it sometimes softens *ṇ* into *n*, like Telugu—*e.g.*, *tuniyu*, daring, instead of the Tamil *tuṇivu*. So also *eṇbadu*, eighty, in Tamil, becomes *embadu* in Malayâlam. Tamil in general leaves *ṇ* unassimilated to succeeding consonants—thus, *peṇ*, Tam. a female, has become *peṇḍu*, without change; but this *ṇ* is hardened by assimilation into *ṭ* in *peṭṭei*, female. So *eṇṭu*, Can. eight, which must have been the original form of the word in Tamil (*eṇ*, eight, *ṭu*, properly *du*, the neuter formative), has become in Tamil *eṭṭu*. The *ṇ* has disappeared altogether in *peḍei*, for *peṭṭei*, Tam. female.

4. *The dentals: t, d, n.*

(i.) *t*, or its sonant equivalent *d*, changes into *r* in Tamil, especially between two vowels. In the interchange of the cerebral *ḍ* and *ṛ*, *ṛ* sometimes appears to have been the original sound, and *ḍ* the corruption; but in the change which is now referred to, it is *d* that appears to be the original sound, which is changed into *r*. This change may arise from the circumstance that the *r* into which *d* is altered is pronounced very like a dental, and bears a considerable resemblance to *d*. In the southern districts of the Tamil country, the change of *d* (when preceded and followed by a vowel) into *r* or **r** is exceedingly common in the pronunciation of the lower classes; but the same change has in some instances found its way into the written language—*e.g.*, *virei*, seed, or to sow, instead of the more correct *videi*. In Canarese *ad*, the inflexional increment, or basis of most of the oblique cases of certain singular nouns, changes in some instances into *ar*—*e.g.*, compare *id-ar-a*, of this, from *id-u*, this, with *mar-ad-a*, of a tree, from *mara*, a tree. In this instance the change from *d* to *r*, or some equivalent change, was obviously required by euphony: *id-ad-a* would have been intolerably monotonous, and *mar-ar-a* not less so. The *ar* of the Canarese *idara* is supposed by Dr Gundert to be the equivalent of the Tamil *an* in *idan*, of this. Even if this should be so, the change of *d* into *r* in Tamil, especially in the south, is indubitable. This change (of *d* into *r*) is not unknown to the

North Indian languages; and in that family it is often followed up by a further change of *r* into *l*. Some instances occur in Hindustani and Bengali—*e.g.*, *des*, ten, becomes *reh* in the compound numbers, as *bâ-reh*, twelve. An instance of the change of *r* into *l* is furnished by another compound numeral, sixteen, which is not *sô-reh*, but *sô-leh*. The Prakrit also changed *d* into *r*, as is seen in the instance of the word *raha*, ten, which has superseded *daha*, a softened form of the Sanskrit *daśa*, and which is used instead of *daha* at the end of compound numerals. It seems to me possible, but not very probable, that in these cases, and also in the use in Bengali and Marâṭhi of *l* instead of *d* or *t*, as a sign of the preterite and passive participles, we see an evidence of the ancient prevalence of Dravidian influences in Northern India. It may be noticed here that the Umbrian also regularly changed *d* into *r*—*e.g.*, *sedes* was written *seres*. As in Tamil, however, this change took place only when *d* came between two vowels.

(ii.) *t* or *d* sometimes changes in Malayâlam into *l*. This peculiarity is apparent chiefly in words borrowed from Sanskrit—*e.g.*, *paltmam*, a lotus, from Sans. *padma; Paltmanâbha*, also vulgarly *Palpanâba*, from *Padmanâbha*, the Travancore name of Vishnu, he who has a lotus navel; *tâlparyam*, from Sans. *tâtparya*, purpose. The Dravidian *taṟ*, pronounced *tat*, euphonised from *tan*, its own, the inflexion of *tân*, self, is also sometimes pronounced *tal*.

(iii.) *t* or *d* sometimes changes into *ś*.

This change appears in Tamil in the optional use of *ś* in the formatives of nouns, instead of *d*. Thus, *periśu*, large, or that which is large, is commonly used instead of *peridu*, the more correct form. The vulgar Tamil *vayaśu*, age, is derived, not directly from the Sanskrit *vayas*, as might be supposed, but from *vayadu*, the regular Tamil equivalent of *vayas*. In Telugu, also, *d* is frequently subject to this change. In Malayâlam *t* and *ś* interchange, especially in the speech of the vulgar. Dr Gundert mentions a curious instance of this interchange. The lower classes, he says, sometimes say *śeivatte têvikka*, to serve God, instead of *teivatte śêvikka*. We appear to have a remarkable instance of the softening of *d* into *ś*, of *ś* into *y*, and finally of the obliteration of the *y* itself, in the Dravidian word already mentioned, signifying a name. This in Tuḷu is *pudar*, in ancient Canarese *peśar*, in classical Tamil *peyar*, and finally in modern Tamil *pêr*. In Tuda *d* sometimes becomes *tsh* (or *ch*)—*e.g.*, *eid-u*, Can. five, becomes *ûtsh*.

(iv.) *nd* changes in Tamil into *ñj*. In this change *j* must be considered as identical with *ś*, being the sound which *ś* takes when preceded by a nasal; and it is always expressed by *ś* in Tamil. In this conjunction the dental *n* changes into *ñ*, which is the nasal of the palatal row. The change of *nd* into *ñj* especially takes place after the vowels *i* or *ei*. In general it is heard in the pronunciation of the lower classes only; but in a few instances it has found its way into grammatical compositions—*e.g.*, *eindu*, five, has changed into *eiñju*, and this again, I believe, into *añju*, a form which is found even in the Tamil classics. The change of *nd* into *ñj* is classical in Malayâlam. (See the numeral *five*.)

(v.) *tt* change into *chch* in Tamil after the vowels *i* and *ei*. The change to which I refer appears to be one of *dd* into *śś*, if the form of the Tamil letters is regarded; but it has already been explained that sonants become surds when doubled; and hence *dd* must be expressed as *tt*, and *śś* as *chch*, this being their pronunciation when in juxtaposition. The corruption of the double, soft dentals *tt* into the palatals *śś*, which are represented by *chch*, is peculiarly easy and natural. This *chch* which arises out of *tt*, though almost universally characteristic of the pronunciation of the mass of the Tamil people, as distinguished from the literati, is rarely found in grammatical compositions, except in the formatives of derivative nouns, especially after the semi-vowels *r* and *ṛ*—*e.g.*, *uṇar-chchi*, sensation, knowledge, instead of *uṇar-tti* which is more in accordance with analogy. In Malayâlam this change from *tt* to *ch* not only appears in the pronunciation of the vulgar, but is the rule of the language after the vowels *i* and *e*; and *ch* is written as well as pronounced—*e.g.*, compare *chirichcha*, that laughed, with the corresponding Tamil *śiritta*.

(vi.) *n* also changes, though still more rarely, into *m*—*e.g.*, *mîru*, you, in Telugu, appears to have been altered from *nîru*, the form which answers to the Tamil *nîr*, and which Telugu analogies would lead us to expect. (See the section on "The Pronoun.")

5. *The labials: p, b, m.*

(i.) *p* changes in Canarese into *h*. This remarkable rule applies to the initial *p* of nearly all words in modern Canarese, whether they are pure Dravidian words or Sanskrit derivatives—*e.g.*, *pattu*, Tam. ten (*padi*, Tel.) is in Canarese *hattu*. In like manner, *paṇa*, money, a Sanskrit derivative, is in modern Canarese *haṇa*. This change of *p* into *h* seems to have taken place in comparatively recent times; for in old Canarese, and in the dialect of the Badagas of the Nilgherries, *p* almost invariably maintains its ground. A change similar to this is occasionally apparent in the Marâṭhi, the neighbour of the Canarese on the north; the Sanskrit participle *bhûta-s*, one who has been, being altered in Marâṭhi to *hôtô*—*e.g.*, *hôtô-n*, I was. Compare also the

Prakrit *hô-mi*, I was, from *bhûta-smi*. A similar change of *p* into *h* appears in Armenian—*e.g.*, foot is in Armenian *het* (for *pet*), and father, *hayr* (for *payr*).

It is curious to notice the same change in the far East. What is *p* in Chinese became in Japanese first *f* then *h*.

(ii.) *b*, the sonant of *p*, sometimes changes into *m*—*e.g.*, *padi*, Tel. ten, becomes *midi* in *tom-midi*, nine, a compound which the analogy of both Tamil and Telugu would require to be *tom-badi*; *enbar*, they will say, is often in poetical Tamil *enmar*; *uṇ-bân*, Tam. being about to eat, the future verbal participle of *uṇ* in classical Tamil, becomes *uṇ-mân* in Malayâlam. *b* is also euphonically added to *m* in vulgar Tamil. I do not refer to such words as *pâmbu*, Tam. a snake, as compared with *pâmu*, Tel.; for in those instances the *m* itself is euphonic, and *bu* (in Can. *vu*) is the real formative; compare Can. *hâvu* (*pâvu*), a snake. Cases in which the *m* is radical and the *b* euphonic occur plentifully in colloquial Tamil—*e.g.*, *kôdumei*, wheat, commonly pronounced *kôdumbei*, from Sans. *gôdhûma*.

(iii.) *b* is often softened into *v* in Tamil. Most transitive verbs in Tamil form their future tense by means of *p* or *pp*; and in the corresponding intransitives we should expect to find the future formed by *b*, the sonant of *p*. Where the root ends in a nasal consonant, this *b* appears; but where it ends in a vowel, *b* is ordinarily changed into *v*. (See the section on "The Verb.") In some instances in the Tamil poets this *b* of the future is changed, not into *v*, but into *m*, according to the previous rule.

(iv.) *m* changes into *n*. This change is often apparent in the nominatives of neuter nouns in Tamil, the ordinary termination of many of which is *m*, but which optionally terminate in *n*—*e.g.*, *pala-n*, profit, a derivative from *phala*, Sans., is more commonly used than *pala-m*. In Telugu, *kola-nu*, a tank, answers to the Tamil *kuḷa-m*.

(v.) *m* changes into *v*. *mâman*, father-in-law, and *mâmi*, mother-in-law, in Tamil, are softened in Coorg into *mâvu* and *mâvi*; *nâm*, we, and *nîm*, you, in ancient Canarese, are softened in the modern colloquial dialect to *nâvu* and *nîvu*.

6. *The liquid consonants or semi-vowels: y, r, l, v, ṛ, ḷ, ṟ.*

(i.) *y* changes into *ñ* and *n*. In some cases, though it is certain that *y* and *n* interchange, it is uncertain which is the more ancient. Thus the Dravidian pronoun of the first person is *nân*, *ñân*, *yân*, *ân*; and it might be argued either that *yân* was derived from *nân*, through the middle point *ñân*, or that, through the same middle point, *nân* was derived from *yân*. On examining, however, words borrowed from Sanskrit, there can be no doubt that in some instances at least *y* was the original and *n* the corruption. Thus, *yuga*, Sans. a yoke, is in Tamil *nugam*, and *Yama*, the god of death, is sometimes *Yaman*, sometimes *Naman*. It is curious to trace the different forms this word assumes in Tamil. We find Yaman, Eman, Ñaman, and Naman. The European word "anchor" has become in Tamil *nangkuram* and *nangkûram*. The change of *y* into *n* in *yuga* and *Yama* is mentioned by Tamil grammarians themselves. We have probably an instance of the same tendency in the change of the formative of the Tamil relative participle *ya* (y + a) into *na*—*e.g.*, *śolliya*, that said, becomes *śollina*, and this *śonna*.

(ii.) *y* sometimes changes into *d* in Canarese and Tuḷu—*e.g.*, *dâva*, Can. who, which, what, alternates with *yâva; dâvadu*, what thing, with *yâvadu*. The latter word is *dâdavu* in Tuḷu.

(iii.) *y* changes into *ś*. It has been shown that *ch*, *ś*, and *j* are softened into *y* in Tamil. Notwithstanding this, and in direct opposition to it, we find in colloquial Tamil, especially in that of the southern districts, a tendency also to harden *y* into *ś*. Where *ś* ought to be, it is pronounced as *y*, and where *y* ought to be, it is pronounced as *ś*—*e.g.*, *paśi*, hunger, is mispronounced by the vulgar *payi*; whilst *vayaru*, the belly, is transformed into *vaśaru*. This change of *y* into *ś* is not confined to the south, though it is more frequently met with there. Even in Madras, *payangaḷ*, boys, is pronounced *paśangaḷ*, and *ayal*, near, is not only pronounced but written *aśal*. The change of *y* into *ś*, and again conversely of *ś* into *y*, might seem to be owing to some peculiar perversity, but doubtless there is a cause for the change in each case, and hence it is not always easy to determine which is the original and which the corruption. Where *y* is used euphonically to prevent hiatus, it does not change into *ś*.

"*y* is regularly changed to *j* in Hindi, Panjabi, Bengali, and Oriya; less frequently in Marâṭhi, Gujarathi, and Sindhi. In these three languages *y* retains its liquid sound of *y*. This change is by Vararuchi confined to initial *y*. The stress laid on an initial consonant being greater than that on one in the middle of a word, it is natural that *y* should be more often changed to *j* in the former position than in the latter."—*Beames*, p. 249.

(iv.) *r* changes to **r**. This, as might be expected, is a very common change. What is *r* in one dialect is often **r** in another, or *vice versa*. The following is an example of both sounds interchanging in one and the same dialect:—In Tamil there are two words for black, *karu* and *ka**r**u*. They are now independent, with meanings that somewhat divaricate, but there can be no doubt that they were originally identical.

(v.) *r* changes into *l*. *r* and *l* are found to be interchangeable in many families of languages. Dr Bleek, speaking of the Setshuana dialects, remarks, "One is justified in considering *r* in these dialects as a sort of floating letter, and rather intermediate between *l* and *r* than a decided *r* in sound." In the Dravidian family, this interchange of *r* and *l* is one of very common occurrence. Sometimes *l* is corrupted into *r;* but in a larger number of cases *r* appears to be the original, and *l* the corruption. In the case of the distinctively Dravidian *ṛ* and *ḷ*, the change is uniformly of the latter nature; and the change of the ordinary semi-vowel *r* into the corresponding *l*, though not uniform, is an exceedingly common one, and one which may be regarded as a characteristic of colloquial Tamil. It is common in Malayâlam also. It is especially at the beginning of words in Tamil that this change occurs, and it takes place as frequently in the case of derivatives from Sanskrit as in the case of Dravidian roots—*e.g.*, *rakṣhi*, to save (*raksh*, Sans.), is pronounced by the vulgar *lakṣhi* or *laṭchi*. In the middle of words *r* is less frequently changed into *l;* nevertheless where Tamil uses *r* we sometimes find *l* in Telugu—*e.g.*, *teri*, to appear, in Tamil, becomes *teli-yu* in Telugu. This is also the equivalent of the Tamil *teḷi*, clear; but I consider *teri* and *teḷi*, in Tamil, different forms of the same root. Similarly the *r* of Tamil sometimes becomes *l* in the middle of words in Malayâlam—*e.g.*, Tam. *pariśei*, a shield; Mal. *paliśa*.

Seeing that a tendency to change *r* into *l* still exists and operates in the Dravidian languages, especially in Tamil, it may be concluded that in these ancient roots which are the common property of several families of language, and in which an interchange appears to exist between *r* and *l*, *r* was the original and *l* the altered sound—*e.g.*, if the Dravidian *kar-u* or *kâr*, black, is connected, as it evidently is, with the Sanskrit *kâl-a*, black, it may be concluded that the Sanskrit form of the root is less ancient than the Dravidian; and this supposition seems to be confirmed by the existence of this root, *kar*, black, in many of the Scythian languages. Compare *kri*, the root of *krishna*, Sans. black.

The fact of the frequency of the interchange between *r* and *l* (irrespective of the question of priority) would lead us to suspect a remote connection between several sets of Dravidian roots which are now considered to be independent of each other—*e.g.*, compare *śir*, Tam. small, with *śil*, few; and *par* (probably another form of *per*), large, with *pal*, many. Another form of *śir*, small, is *śin*.

(vi.) *l* changes into *r*. Whilst the ordinary change is that of *r* into *l*, the change of *l* into *r* is occasionally met with, and forms one of the peculiarities of Tuḷu. Tuḷu generally changes the final *l* of the other Dravidian languages into *r*—*e.g.*, *vil*, Tam. a bow (*billu*, Can.) becomes in Tuḷu *bir*. In this instance it cannot be doubted that *l* was the original termination of the word, for we find the same root west of the Indus in the Brahui *billa*, a bow. A similar interchange between *l* and *r* takes place in Central Asia. The *l* of Manchu is *r* in Mongolian.

(vii.) *l* sometimes changes into **r**—*e.g.*, compare *nil*, Tam. to stand, with *ni**r**uttu*, to cause to stand.

In Zend and old Persian, *l* was unknown, and *r* was systematically used instead. In Telugu, *lu*, the pluralising suffix of nouns, is sometimes changed into *ru*. This change, however, of *l* into *r* is not systematic, as in Tuḷu, but exceptional. In Tamil, *l* is euphonically changed, not into *r*, but into **r** before all hard consonants—*e.g.*, *palpala*, various, becomes in written compositions *pa**r**pala*. This proves that a change of *l* into *r* is not contrary to Tamil laws of sound.

"*l* is constantly changed to *r* in Sindhi when non-initial. Instances are—Sans. *kâla*, black, Sind. *kârâ;* Sans. *sthala*, place, Sind. *tharu*. In the Prakrits the reverse is the case; in nearly all the dialects except the principal or Mahârâshtri, *r* is changed into *l*. This statement is made among others of the Magadhi dialect. In the modern Magadha country, that is, in Southern Bihar, however, the tendency is decidedly the other way; and throughout the Eastern Hindi area, from Oudh to the frontier of Bengal, the rustics constantly pronounce *r* where *l* is the correct sound. This I can testify from personal observation during many years' residence in these parts. Thus we ordinarily hear *kariâ* for *kâlâ*, black; and this peculiarity may be noticed occasionally in the speech of the lower orders in other parts of the Hindi area, as, for instance, in Marwari, *chârṇâ*, to wander, for *chalnâ*. In old Hindi poems many instances may be found, as *jangar* for *jangal*, forest, and the like. In fact, so great is the confusion between these two letters, that they may in some parts of India be said to be used indifferently, and the speakers appear to be unconscious that they are saying *r* instead of *l*. . . . .

"The semi-vowel *r* is a very persistent letter, and is never ejected or elided. In Prakrit it is changed into *l* (in certain words). There is very little tendency to change *r* into *l* in the Indians of the present day. The tendency, as I stated under *l*, is rather the other way, though writers on the Prakrits affirm that in all the minor dialects *r* is changed into *l*. As far as it concerns the real origin and root-form of words, the matter is one of little moment. If it be true that the cerebral sounds were not originally distinguished from the dentals, then it must follow that the semi-vowels of the respective groups were identical. If there was a time when ḍ was the same as *d*, there must also have been a time when *r* was not sounded differently from *l*; and just as in the present day we find that there exists confusion between ḍ and *d*, ṭ and *t*, so we are prepared to find that there is in the minds of the lower classes, in many provinces, a tendency to use *r* and *l* as the same sounds. It is of no import, then, whether we take *r* as the original and *l* as the corruption, or *vice versa*. We have no right to assume that the form found in classical Sanskrit is the true and original one; rather, in the present state of our knowledge, we should be disposed to be very sceptical upon this point."—*Beames*, pp. 247–250.

(viii.) *l* changes in the language of the Kus to ḍ. The change of ḍ into ḷ is common enough, but the regular change of *l* into ḍ is peculiar to this idiom—*e.g.*, *pâlu*, Tel. milk, is in Ku *pâḍu*; *illu*, house, is *iḍḍu*. Compare also the change of the Sanskrit *l* into ḍ in the North Indian vernaculars—*e.g.*, *tâli*, the intoxicating juice of the palmyra palm, is in those vernaculars *tâḍî*, whence the word used by the English, *toddy*. The Telugu name of the tree is *tâḍu*, equivalent to the Hindi *tâḍ* or *tâṛ*.

(ix.) The *r* and ṛ and the *l* and ḷ of the other dialects change in the dialect of the Tudas to *rsh*, *rzh*, and *lzsh*.

(x.) *v* is generally hardened in Canarese into *b* in the beginning of a word—*e.g.*, *vâṛ*, Tam. to flourish, becomes in Canarese *bâḷ*. Where *v* is not changed into *b*, viz., in the middle of words, Canarese generally softens it into *w*. The same softening is sometimes observed in the pronunciation of the lower classes of Tamilians. In Malayâlam the sound of *v* stands midway between the English *v* and *w*. This soft sound is common in colloquial Tamil also.

(xi.) The *v* euphonic of Tamil is sometimes changed into *g* in Telugu. Both *y* and *v* are used euphonically to prevent hiatus in Tamil; so in Telugu *g* is sometimes used not only instead of *v*, but also instead of *y*. Compare Tam. *aṟu-(v)-ar*, six persons, with the Tel. *âṟu-(g)-uru*. Compare also *gâru*, Tel. honorific singular (really plural) suffix, with *vâru*, he (they), its more correct form. This will perhaps explain the occasional use of *g* instead of *v* as the sign of the future tense in high Tamil—*e.g.*, *śeygên*, instead of *śeyvên*, I will do.

(xii.) *v* appears to change into *m* in Malayâlam. It has already been mentioned that *b* in Tamil sometimes becomes *m* in Malayâlam—*e.g.*, Tam. *uṇ-bân*, about to eat, is in Mal. *uṇ-mân*—but it is doubtful whether this might not rather be represented as a change of *v* into *m*—*e.g.*, where Tamil has *kân-bân*, about to see (the future verbal participle), Malayâlam uses optionally either *kâṇu-vân* or *kâṇ-mân;* so where Tamil says *vâṛvavan* (or *vâṛbavan*), he who flourishes, Malayâlam says either *vâṛvavan* or *vâṛumavan.* Here, in so far as Malayâlam itself is concerned, *b* disappears, and the interchange is between *v* and *m.* I have noticed, also, an interchange between *v* and *m* in the Finno-Ugrian languages; *m* in Finnish is *v* in Hungarian.

(xiii.) *ṛ* (the peculiar vocalic *ṛ* of Tamil) interchanges with five different consonants. Sometimes it becomes *ṇ*—*e.g.*, *miṛugu,* Tam. to sink, is changed in Telugu to *muṇugu;* and *kuṛi,* Tam. a hole, becomes in Canarese *kuṇi.* Ordinarily *ṛ* is changed in Telugu into *ḍ.* Neither Telugu nor modern Canarese possesses the Tamil *ṛ.* It is found, however, in old Canarese, of which it is a distinctive sign. In a very few instances Telugu uses *ṇ* or *ḷ* instead of *ṛ;* sometimes it omits the consonant altogether, without using a substitute, but in a large majority of instances it converts *ṛ* into *ḍ.* *ṛ* is ordinarily converted in Canarese into *ḷ,* and the same change characterises the pronunciation of the mass of the Tamil people in the southern districts of the country. In Malayâlam *ṛ* is sometimes converted into *ḷ,* but more frequently into *y.* Thus Malayâṛma (Malayâlam) is often written and pronounced Malayâyma. In Tuḷu, *ṛ* is generally changed into *r*—*e.g.*, Tam. *poṛudu,* time, Tuḷu, *pordu.* In Canarese this *r* is assimilated—*e.g.*, *hottu* (*pottu*) for the Tuḷu *pordu.* Compare also the Telugu *poddu.* We thus find *ṛ* interchanging with *ṇ*, *ḍ*, *ḷ*, *y*, and *r*, and lastly assimilating itself to the succeeding consonant.

This change of *ṛ* into *ḷ*, and the previous one of *ṛ* into *ḍ*, form the constituents of an important dialectic law. That law is, that the same consonant which is *ṛ* in Tamil is generally *ḍ* in Telugu, and always *ḷ* in modern Canarese. Thus a fowl is *kôṛ-i* in Tamil, *kôḍ-i* in Telugu, and *kôḷ-i* in Canarese. The numeral seven is *êṛ-u* in Tamil, *êḷ-u* in Telugu, and *êḷ-u* in Canarese. In the compound numeral *êḷnûru,* seven hundred, the Telugu *êḍ-u* is found to change, like the Canarese, into *êḷ-u.* The word signifying time which is included in the adverbial nouns then and now (literally that time and this time), is in Tamil *poṛu-du,* in Telugu *prodd-u* or *podd-u,* then *puḍ-u,* and in Malayâlam *pôḷ.* In the last instance, however, Malayâlam uses *ḷ* only when final. When followed by a vowel it is *ṛ*, as *ippôṛum, appôṛum,* now and then. It thus appears that *ḷ* and *ḍ* are as intimately allied as *ḍ* and *ṛ.* This is a point of some importance in the affiliation of languages, for an interchange of *d* and *l* is characteristic of the Ugrian family of languages, as well as of the Dravidian family and the North Indian vernaculars. The same word is written with *t* or *d* in Ostiak, and with *l* in Magyar and Finnish.

A corresponding interchange is ocasionally observed even in the Indo-European languages—*e.g.*, compare δακρυμα, a tear, with *lachryma.* Similar changes in several of the modern Romance dialects might also be adduced, but in those languages it is rarely met with, whereas it is a characteristic dialectic sign of several families of tongues belonging to the Scythian group.

(xiv.) **r** (the strong rough **r** of Tamil) is frequently changed in Tuḷu into *j*—*e.g.*, *mûṟu*, the original form of *mûndṟu*, Tam. three, becomes *mûji*; *âṟu*, Tam. six, becomes *âji*. It changes also in Tuḷu into *d*—*e.g.*, *nûdu*, one hundred, instead of *nûṟu*. It changes still more frequently into the soft *r*. The tendency of Tuḷu appears, therefore, to be to soften down this hard sound. This change of *r* into *j*, the equivalent of *ś*, is directly the converse of the change of *s* into *r*, which is so common in the Indo-European tongues.

(xv.) This strong **r** sometimes changes in Tamil into *n*—*e.g.*, *piṟ* in *piṟagu*, afterwards, is identical with *pin*, afterwards; *śiṟ-u*, little, is identical with *śinn-a*, little.

(xvi.) *ḷ* changes in Tuḷu into *ṇ*—*e.g.*, *kêṇ*, to hear, replaces the Tam.-Can. *kêḷ*. So also *koḷ*, to take, to buy, Tam.-Can., becomes in Tuḷu *koṇ*. In Telugu the latter word becomes *kon-u*. Even in Tamil the *ḷ* of *koḷ* is euphonised into *ṇ* in the gerund *koṇ-ḍu*.

(xvii.) *ḷ* sometimes changes in Malayâlam into *ṛ*, and this again into *y*. The name of the country and language is an instance of this. *âṛma* is for *âḷma* (euphonised in Tamil into *âṇmei*), from *âḷ*, to rule, to possess. It has already been shown that Malayâṛma becomes also Malayâyma.

Having now finished the consideration of the dialectic changes which pure Dravidian consonants undergo, it remains to point out the changes which take place in the Sanskrit sibilants, when words in which they occur are borrowed from Sanskrit by Tamil.

1. *ṣh*. The hard, lingual sibilant of Sanskrit is unknown to classical Tamil. Sometimes it is changed into *ś*, a change which ordinarily takes place at the present day in the pronunciation of the lower classes in the southern districts. *ṣh* is sometimes, though rarely, converted in Tamil into *ṛ*. Dr Gundert supplies me with some instances of this in old Malayâlam—*e.g.*, *kshaya*, Sans. loss, is in old Mal. written *kiṛayam*, and the name *Lakshmaṇan* in an old copy of the Ramayana is written *Ilaṛkkaṇan*. Here *ṛkk* stands for *ksh*. Sometimes *ṣh* is assimilated to a succeeding *ṇ*—*e.g.*, the name *Vishṇu* becomes sometimes, both in poetical Tamil and in Malayâlam, *Viṇṇu*.

This name appears also in poetical Tamil as *Viṇḍu*, a word which denotes the wind as well as Vishnu. Dr Gundert identifies the *viṇ* of *Viṇṇu*, Vishnu, with the Tam.-Mal. word *viṇ*, sky, a true Tamil word connected with the root *viḷ*, to be bright. The derivation of Vishnu from *viḷ* and *viṇ* looks very tempting, but I fear Sanskrit lexicographers will refuse to yield to the temptation. Most commonly *ṣh* is converted in Tamil into *ḍ*. This *ḍ* is sometimes softened down into the dental *d*. Thus, *manuṣhya*, Sans. man, becomes in classical Tamil *mâniḍa-n;* and this by a further change becomes *manida-n*. A very old example of the change of the Sanskrit *ṣh* into *ḍ*, in Tamil, can be adduced. The month *Âṣhâḍha*, Sans. July–August, has become in Tamil *Aḍi;* and this change dates probably from the earliest period of the cultivation of the Tamil language. In *Taiṣha*, January–February, the hard *ṣh*, instead of being changed, has been discarded altogether: the Tamil name of this month, as far back as the literature reaches, has been *Tei.*

2. *s.* The hissing sibilant of Sanskrit, answering to our English *s*, is ordinarily in Tamil converted into *d*, the sonant of *t*, which is pronounced as *th* in that—*e.g.*, *mâsam*, Sans. a month, becomes in classical Tamil *mâdam* (*mâtham*); and *manas*, the mind, becomes *manad-u* (*manath-u*). In this conversion of the Sanskrit *s* into *d* (or *th*) in Tamil, there is a change from the sibilant to the dental, which is exactly the reverse of that change from the dental to the semi-sibilant which has already been described.

"If asked to account for the connection between two sounds at first sight so widely opposed, I would refer to similar conditions in other languages, as, for instance, the substitution of τ for σ in Attic Greek, as μέλιττα, θάλαττα, for μέλισσα, θάλασσα. Among modern languages, the example of the Spanish may also be adduced, where *c* before the palatal vowels *e* and *i* is pronounced as *th*. From the same cause arises that defect in speaking called a lisp, which renders some Englishmen unable to pronounce sibilants or palatals otherwise than as half-obscure linguals. But whereas in England this is only an individual and personal peculiarity, in Spanish it becomes a law. The people of Madrid all lisp, not only in pronouncing *c* and *z*, but also in *s*. So also, to go to a different age and family of languages, the Chaldeans and Syrians lisp the Semitic *sh*, as in Heb. *shâlosh*, Chal. *telath*, Syriac *tloth*, three."—*Beames*, p. 216. Mr Beames goes on to explain physiologically the origin of this tendency to change *s* into *t*.

When *s* happens to be the first consonant of a Sanskrit derivative, it is sometimes omitted in Tamil altogether—*e.g.*, *sandhyâ*, evening, becomes *andi;* *sthânam*, a place, becomes *tânam*. More commonly in modern

Tamil an effort is made to pronounce this *s* with the help of the vowel *i*, which is prefixed to it in order to assist enunciation—*e.g.*, *istiri* (*strî*, Sans.), a woman. *ś*, the soft sibilant of Sanskrit, sometimes passes through similar changes. Generally it is represented by the corresponding *ś* or *ch* of the Dravidian languages, but sometimes it is converted, like the harder *s*, into *t*, as in the very ancient derivative *tiru*, sacred, for *Śrî*. Sometimes it is discarded altogether, especially when compounded with *r*. Thus, *Śrâvaṇa*, the month of August–September, is in Tamil *Avaṇi*. The Malayâlam *Ôṇam*, the ceremony of the month *Śrâvaṇa*, carries this change further still.

The Sanskrit sibilant never changes into *r* in Tamil. This change, though very common in languages of the Indo-European family, rarely, if ever, appears in the Dravidian. It may be conjectured, but cannot be proved to have taken place. The Tamil-Canarese root *ir*, to be, originally to sit (in Brahui *ar*), *may* be allied to the Indo-European substantive verb, best represented by the Sanskrit *as*.* The Tamil plural of rational beings *ar*, resembles the Sanskrit epicene nominative plural *as*; and perhaps, though more doubtfully still, the Tamil *iru*, iron, euphonised into *iru-mbu*, may be compared with the Sanskrit *ayas*, and the English word *iron* (which is allied to *ayas*, through the change of *s* into *r*), though I prefer connecting this word with the Tamil root *ir*, dark.

Euphonic Permutation of Consonants.—The permutation of consonants for euphonic reasons, though it throws less light on the laws of sound than dialectic interchange, includes a few points of considerable interest. Dravidian grammarians have bestowed more attention and care on euphonic permutation than on any other subject; and the permutations which the grammar of Tamil requires or allows are at least twice as numerous, and more than twice as perplexing to beginners, as those of Sanskrit. On examining the permutations of consonants prescribed in the classical grammars of Tamil, Telugu, and Canarese—the three principal languages of this family —it is evident that a considerable proportion of them are founded upon Sanskrit precedents. Another class in which Sanskrit rules of euphony have been, not imitated, but emulated and surpassed, may be regarded rather as prosodial than as grammatical changes. But

* This is affirmed, but I think too positively, by Mr Gover (*Cornhill Magazine* for November 1871, "Dravidian Folk-Songs"). "Tamil and Telugu (*qu.* Canarese?) possess at the present day the complete verb which has left such traces in our language as *are*, *art*, and *were*."

after these have been eliminated, a certain number of euphonic permutations remain, which are altogether peculiar to these languages, and which proceed from, and help to illustrate, their laws of sound. It will suffice to notice a few of those permutations; for the subject is too wide, and at the same time not of sufficient importance, to allow us to enter here on a minute investigation of it.

1. In *dvandva* compounds, *i.e.*, in nouns which are united together, not by copulative conjunctions, but by a common sign of plurality (in the use of which common sign the Dravidian languages resemble, and probably imitate, the Sanskrit), if the second member of the compound commences with the first or surd consonant of any of the five *vargas* (viz., *k*, *ch*, or *ś*, *ṭ*, *t*, *p*), the surd must be changed into the corresponding sonant or soft letter. In those Dravidian languages which have adhered to the alphabetical system of Sanskrit, as Telugu and Canarese, this conversion of the surd into the sonant is carried into effect and expressed by the employment of a different character. In Tamil, in which the same character is used to represent both surds and sonants, a different character is not employed, but the softening of the first consonant of the second word is always apparent in the pronunciation. This peculiar rule evidently proceeds from the Dravidian law that the same consonant which is a surd at the beginning of a word should be regarded as a sonant in the middle; for the first consonant of the second word, being placed in the middle of a compound, has become a medial by position. The existence of this rule in Telugu and Canarese, notwithstanding the Sanskrit influences to which they have been subjected, proves that the law of convertibility of surds and sonants is not confined to Tamil.

All the Dravidian dialects agree in softening the initial surd of the second member of *dvandva* compounds; but with respect to compounds in which the words stand to one another in a case-relation—*e.g.*, substantives of which the first is used adjectivally or to qualify the second, or an infinitive and its governing verb—Telugu pursues a different course from Tamil. The rule of Telugu is, that when words belong to the *druta* class, including all infinitives, are followed by any word commencing with a surd consonant, such consonant is to be converted (as in *dvandva* compounds) into its soft or sonant equivalent. The rule of Telugu on this point resembles that of the Lappish, and still more the rule of Welsh; and it has been observed that Welsh, possibly through the pre-historic influence of Finnish, is the most Scythic of all the Indo-European languages.

It is curious that in combinations of words which are similar to those referred to above, and uniformly after infinitives in *a*, Tamil, instead of softening, doubles and hardens the initial surd-sonant of the succeeding word. Tamil also invariably doubles, and consequently hardens, the initial surd of the second member of *tat-purusha* compounds, *i.e.*, compounds in which the words stand in a case-relation to each other. In such combinations, Canarese, though it is less careful of euphony than either Tamil or Telugu, requires that the initial surd of the second member of the compound should be softened: it requires, for instance, that *huli togalu*, a tiger's skin, shall be written and pronounced *huli dogalu*. Tamil, on the contrary, requires the initial surd in all such cases to be hardened and doubled—*e.g.*, the same compound in Tamil, viz., *puli tôl*, a tiger's skin, must be written and pronounced, not *puli dôl*, but *puli-(t)tôl*. This doubling and hardening of the initial is evidently meant to symbolise the transition of the signification of the first word to the second; and it will be seen that this expedient has been very frequently resorted to by Tamil.

When the first word is used not as a noun or adjective, but as a verb or relative participle, the initial surd of the second word becomes a sonant in Tamil also, as in Telugu—*e.g.*, compare *kây kombu*, a withering branch, with *kây-(k)kombu*, a branch with fruit.

2. The Tamil system of assimilating, or euphonically changing, concurrent consonants, is in many particulars almost identical with that of Sanskrit, and has probably been arranged in imitation of it. Nevertheless there are some exceptions which may be regarded as distinctively Dravidian, and which are founded upon Dravidian laws of sound—*e.g.*, the mutation of *l* into *n* in various unexpected combinations. Through this tendency to nasalisation, *pôl-da*, like, becomes *pôn-da*, or rather *pôn-dra; koḷ-ḍa*, taken, bought, becomes *koṇ-ḍa;* and the latter euphonic mutation has found its way in Telugu into the root itself, which is *kon-u*, to buy, instead of the older Tamil *koḷ*. Tuḷu also is *koṇ*. It does not appear to have been noticed even by Tamil grammarians, that *l*, in a few instances, has been converted into *n* before *k*. Thus *nân-ku*, pronounced *nân-gu*, four, is derived from *nâl-ku*, an older form of the word; and *Panguni*, the Tamil name of the month of March–April, has been altered from the Sanskrit *Phalguna*. In Telugu a corresponding tendency appears in the change of *l* into *ṇ* before *ṭ*—*e.g.*, *ilṭi*, of a house, is softened into *iṇṭi*. In all these cases *l* is undoubtedly the original; and these proofs of the priority of *l* to *n* corroborate the suspicion that the Latin *alius* is older than its Sanskrit equivalent *anyas*.

A rule of the Tuda, which seems to arise from considerations of euphony, may here be noticed. *th* and *sh* seem to be euphonically inserted between *l* and *k* and *r* and *k*—*e.g.*, *nilthken*, I stand, and *ershken*, I am, where we should have expected *nilken* and *erken*.

EUPHONIC NUNNATION OR NASALISATION.—Much use is made in the Dravidian languages, especially in Tamil and Telugu, of the nasals *ṅ*, *ñ*, *ṇ*, *n*, and *m* (to which some add *n̄* or *m*, the *half anusvâra* of the Telugu), for the purpose of euphonising the harder consonants of each *varga*. All the nasals referred to, with the exception of the *half anusvâra*, which is an inorganic sound, are regarded by native grammarians as modifications of the sound of *m*; the nature of each modification being determined by the manner in which *m* is affected by succeeding consonants. In Tamil, as in Sanskrit, all those modifications are expressed by the nasal consonants which constitute the final characters of each of the five *vargas*. In Telugu and Canarese one and the same character, which is called *anusvâra*, but which possesses a greater range of power than the *anusvâra* of Sanskrit, is used to represent the whole of the nasal modifications referred to. The pronunciation of this character, however, varies so as to accord with the succeeding consonant, as in Tamil.

The *nunnation*, or nasalisation, of the Dravidian languages is of three kinds.

1. The first kind of *nunnation* is used to a greater extent in Tamil than in any other dialect. It consists in the insertion of a nasal before the initial consonant of the formative suffix of many nouns and verbs. The formative syllable or suffix, the nature of which will be explained more particularly in the succeeding section, is added to the crude root of the verb or noun, and constitutes the inflexional theme, to which the signs of inflexion are annexed. The nasalised formative is used in Tamil in connection with the intransitive form of the verb and the isolated form of the noun. When the verb becomes transitive, and when the noun becomes adjectival, or is placed in a case-relation to some other noun, the nasal disappears, and the consonant to which it was prefixed—the initial consonant of the formative—is hardened and doubled. The nasal is modified in accordance with the nature of the initial consonant of the formative suffix: it becomes *ṅ* before *k* or *g*; *ñ* before *ś*, *ch*, or *j*; *ṇ* before *ṭ* or *ḍ*; *n* before *t* or *d*; and *m* before *p* or *b*. Telugu uses the *anusvâra* to express all these varieties of sound; and the half *anusvâra* in certain other cases.

(i.) Of the use of the first nasal *ṅ*, to emphasise and euphonise the formative suffix *k-u* or *g-u*, Tamil affords innumerable examples. One verb and noun will suffice—*e.g.*, *aḍa-ṅgu*, to refrain oneself, to keep in, is formed from the root *aḍa*, by the addition of the formative, intransitive suffix *gu*, which is euphonised into *ṅgu; kâ-ṅgei*, heat, is from *kâ* or *kây*, to burn (in Telugu *kâ-gu*); with the addition of the suffix *gei*, euphonised into *ṅgei*. The final *g* is nasalised, not only in the case of the addition of the formative, but sometimes also when it is radical—*e.g.*, from *pag-u*, to divide, we have *paṅg-u*, a portion. The tendency in Tamil to the nasalisation of this consonant may be illustrated by its treatment of a Sanskrit word. Sans. *śunaka* (from *śuna*), a dog, has become in Tamil (with the masculine termination *an*) *śunagan*, then *śuṇaṅgan*, then by a further change (*u* being pronounced like *o* before a consonant followed by *a*) *śôṇaṅgi*.

The insertion of the nasal before *k* or *g* probably accounts for the shape of the Tamil adverbs, or rather nouns of place, *aṅgu*, there, *iṅgu*, here, *eṅgu*, where. The demonstrative and interrogative bases *a*, *i*, and *e* are followed by *ku* or *gu*, the Tamil dative case sign, or rather sign of direction, whence *agu* (*k* becoming *g* before a vowel) is nasalised into *aṅgu*. Dr Gundert prefers to derive these nouns of place from the (supposititious) demonstrative nouns *am* and *im*, and the interrogative noun *em*, which last still survives in Tamil in the shape of *en; e.g.*, *en*, *ên*, what, why; and takes in Telugu the shape of *êmi*. By the addition of the directive *ku* to these nouns, *am*, &c., they would naturally become *aṅgu*, &c. I recognise distinct traces of these supposititious demonstrative nouns *am* or *an* and *im* or *in* in the formatives of nouns, in the inflexional increments, and in the case signs, as will be seen under each of those heads; probably also they are the bases of the poetical Tamil equivalents of *aṅgu*, &c., viz., *ambar*, there, *imbar*, here, *embar*, where. Still I feel doubtful whether in *aṅgu*, &c., we are to recognise those demonstrative nouns. If we compare *yâṅgu*, Tam. where, a poetical form of *eṅgu*, with *yâṇḍu*, another noun of place and time, which appears to me to be derived from *yâ*, one of the interrogative bases, and *ḍu*, the formative, nasalised into *ṇḍu*, as will be seen under the next head, it will appear probable that *yâṅgu* has been formed in this manner; and if *yâṅgu*, then also *âṅgu*, *îṅgu*, poetical, and *aṅgu*, *iṅgu*, and *eṅgu*, the common forms. Besides, if we compare these Tamil adverbial forms with the Gônd adverbs *aga*, there, *iga*, here, *inga*, now, *hike*, hither, *hoke*, thither; with the Canarese *âga*, *âgalu*, then, *îga*, now, *yâvâga*, when, *hâge*, in that manner, *hîge*, in this manner, alternating with their nasalised forms *hâṅge* and *hîṅge;* and with the Coorg *akka*, then, *ikka*, now, *ekka*, when—(remembering that demonstrative nouns of time and place are in these languages more or less equivalent—*e.g.*, in Tamil, *âṇḍu* means either there or then)—we shall conclude, I think, that the primitive form of the Tamil adverbial noun *aṅgu*, there, with its companions, was *agu*, and that *aṅgu* is only an instance of the fondness of the Tamil for nasalisation. (See "Demonstratives, their use as Adverbs.")

(ii.) Instances of the euphonic use of the nasal of the second *varga*, *ñ*, are more common in Telugu than in Tamil. Thus, *pañch-u*, Tel. to divide, is derived from *pag-u*, Tam. (changed into *pach-u*, and then nasalised into *pañch-u*), and is analogous to the Tamil noun *paṅg-u*, a portion, derived from the same verbal root. *reṭṭi-ñchu*, Tel. to double, is an example of the use of the euphonic nasal by verbs of the transitive class—a class in which that nasal is not used by any other dialect but Telugu.

(iii.) The cerebrals *ṭ* and *ḍ* are not used as formative suffixes of verbs, though some verbal roots end in those consonants; but they are not unfrequently used as formatives of neuter nouns—*e.g.*, *ira-ḍ-u*, the probable original of the Tamil numeral two, corresponding to the Canarese *era-ḍu*, has been euphonised to *ira-ṇḍ-u*. The Tamil adverbial nouns *â-ṇḍ-u*, there, *î-ṇḍ-u*, here, *yâ-ṇḍ-u*, where, are derived from *â* and *î*, the demonstrative bases, and *yâ*, the interrogative base, with the addition of the usual neuter formative *ḍ-u*, euphonised to *ṇḍu*. *Yâṇḍu*, where, when, is used also to signify a year; another form is *yâṇḍei*. In common Tamil the word for year is *âṇḍu*, but *yâṇḍu* is the form I have invariably found in inscriptions. *âṇḍu*, a year, the more recent word (or rather the obsolete form of this word *âṇḍei*), is the origin of the word *âṭṭei*, annual—*e.g.*, *âṭṭei-(k)-karmam*, Tam. and Mal. an annual ceremony. The omission of the nasal *ṇ* from the word *âṭṭei* shows that the nasal is a portion, not of the root, but of the formative, and that it is merely euphonic in origin. The adjectival shape of a noun, or that which appears in the inflexion, may be regarded, as a general rule, as its oldest shape. Compare *iraṭṭei*, Tam. double, from *iraṇḍu*, two, with the Canarese *eraḍu*, two. We see, therefore, that the original shape of the noun of place or time under consideration was not *âṇḍu*, but *âḍu*. What seems to place this beyond doubt is the fact that in Telugu the *ḍ* of these words is not nasalised in ordinary writing, and only slightly nasalised in pronunciation. They are *âḍa*, *îḍa*, *êḍa*, there, here, where; and the last word, *êḍa*, changed to *êḍu*, is used like the corresponding Tamil *yâṇḍu*, to signify a year. [It will be shown, under the head of the "Interrogative Pronouns," that the Tamil *yâ* takes also the weaker form of *e*, and in Telugu *ê*.] We see the same primitive, unnasalised form of these demonstrative nouns in the Tuḷu *aḍe*, thither, *iḍe*, hither, *oḍe*, whither. In Telugu a large number of masculine formatives in *ḍ-u* receive in pronunciation the obscure nasal *n̄*—*e.g.*, for *vâḍu-lu* or *vâḍ-lu*, they, *vân̄ḍ-lu* is commonly used. On comparing the Tamil *karaṇḍi*, a spoon, with *gariṭe*, the Telugu form of the same word, we find that sometimes the nasal is used by one dialect and rejected by another.

(iv.) We see an example of the euphonic use of *n*, the nasal of the dental *varga*, in the intransitive verb *tiru-nd-u*, Tam. to become correct, from *tiru*, the radical base, and *du*, the formative, euphonised into *ndu*: the transitive form of the same verb is *tiru-ttu*, to correct. An example of the nasalisation of a noun of this class is found in *maru-ndu*, Tam. a medicinal drug, medicine, which is derived from *maru*, fragrant, with the addition of the formative *du*, euphonised to *ndu*, comp. Tuḷu and ancient Canarese, *mardu*, modern Canarese, *maddu*. We find, I think, the same euphonic nasalisation in the Tamil demonstrative adjectives *anda*, that, *inda*, this, *enda*, which. These appear to have been formed from the neuter demonstrative pronouns *ad-u*, *id-u*, and the interrogative *e-du*, by the insertion of the euphonic nasal (as was probably done also in the case of *aṅgu*, &c., and *âṇḍu*, &c.), with the addition of *a*, the sign of the relative participle, so frequently used in the formation of adjectives (see "Adjectives"). *ad-u* would thus become *and-a* by an easy process. Dr Gundert derives these adjectives from *am*, *im*, &c., the demonstrative nouns referred to in the previous paragraph, and *da*, the formative of relative participles. This relative formative, however, is not *da*, but only *a*; and it would be necessary to put Dr Gundert's case thus. The demonstrative base *am* was developed into *andu*, by the addition of *du*, the neuter formative; and this *and-u*, by the addition of the relative participle sign *a*, became *and-a*. A confirmation of this view might be found in the Telugu *andu*, there, which is also the sign of the locative case, and *indu*, here, as compared with the Canarese *inda* (originally, as we know, *im*), the sign of the instrumental, but a locative case sign originally. This view is very plausible, but on the whole I prefer adhering to the view I have already taken, which accords with a still larger number of parallel instances of Tamil nasalisation. The Tuḷu demonstrative pronoun *indu* or *undu*, it (proximate), corroborates this view. It is simply a nasalised form of the Tam. and Can. *idu* (prox.), *udu* (intermediate). The Tamil *andru*, *indru*, &c., that day, this day, &c. (Can. *andu*, *indu*), may also be euphonisations of *adu* and *idu*, that and this; though this euphonisation would be more in accordance with rule if they were formed from demonstrative nouns in *al* and *il*, the existence of which we may surmise, but of which I can discover no distinct proof. Compare, however, the Canarese *alli*, *illi*, *elli*, there, here, where, which may either be derived from supposed demonstrative nouns, *al*, *il*, *el*, or from the demonstrative bases of those nouns, *a*, *i*, *e*, prefixed to *li*, an altered form of *il*, a house, which is used in Tamil, as *alli* is in Canarese, as a locative case sign. The Tamil *ittrei*, to-day, a secondary form of *indru*, to-day (also the corresponding *attrei*, that day, and *ettrei*, what day), would seem to indicate the origin of *indra*, &c., from a root *il* or *ir*, from which *ittrei*, &c., would naturally proceed like *ottrei*, single, from *or* or *or*. Compare *indru*, Tam. there is not, and *andru*, it is not, which are regularly derived from the negative bases *il* and *al*.

(v.) Many examples of the euphonic insertion of *m* before the suffix in *b* might be adduced, but the following will suffice : *tiru-mbu*, to turn (intransitively), of which the root is unquestionably *tiru*, as appears from the corresponding Telugu *tiru-gu* and Canarese *tiru-vu*. The Tamil form of the transitive of the same verb is *tiru-pp-u*, to turn. An example of a similar insertion of euphonic *m* before the formative *b* of a noun is seen in *eru-mbu*, Tam. an ant, when compared with the equivalent Canarese word *iru-ve*. The formatives *nd-u* and *mbu* are extremely common terminations of Tamil nouns ; and with few, if any exceptions, wherever those terminations appear, they will be found on examination to be euphonised suffixes to the root.

2. The second use to which the euphonic nasal is put is altogether peculiar to Tamil. It consists in the insertion of an euphonic *n* between the verbal theme and the *d*, which constitutes the sign of the preterite of a very large number of Tamil verbs. The same *d* ordinarily forms the preterite in ancient Canarese, and is not unknown to Telugu ; but in those languages the nasal *n* is not prefixed to it. The following are examples of this nasalisation of the sign of the preterite in Tamil : *vâṛ-nd-ên* (for *vâṛ-d-ên*), I flourished, from the root *vâṛ ;* in Canarese, *bâḷ :* compare old Canarese preterite, *bâḷ-d-en*. So also *viṛu-nd-u* (for *viṛu-d-u*), having fallen, from the root *viṛu* or *vîṛ ;* High Tamil, *vîṛ-d-u ;* Canarese equivalent, *bidd-u*. The corresponding Malayâlam *vîṉ-u*, is an example of the absorption of the dental in the nasal. In colloquial, or vulgar, Tamil this euphonic insertion of *n* is carried further than grammatical Tamil allows. Thus, *śey-d-a*, done, and *pey-d-a*, rained, are vulgarly pronounced *śey-ñj-a* and *pey-ñj-a*.

3. A third use of the euphonic nasal is the insertion, in Tamil, of *ṉ* or *n* before the final *ḍ* or *d* of some verbal roots. The same rule sometimes applies to roots and forms that terminate in the rough **r**, or even in the ordinary semi-vowel *r*. Thus, *kar-u*, Can. a calf, is *kan***r***-u* in Tamil (pronounced *kandr-u*) ; and *mûr-u*, Can. three, is in Tamil *mûn***r***-u* (pronounced *mûndr-u*). In the first and second classes of instances in which *nunnation* is used for purposes of euphony, the Dravidian languages pursue a course of their own, which is different

from the usages of the Scythian, as well as of the Syro-Arabian and Indo-European families of languages. In the Syro-Arabian languages, especially in Talmudic Hebrew, euphonic *n* is always a final, and is often emphatic as well as euphonic. In Turkish, *n* is used between the bases of words and their inflexions in a manner similar to its use in Sanskrit. In the North-Indian vernaculars an obscure nasal, *ñ*, is often used as a final. But none of these usages perfectly corresponds to the Dravidian nasalisation referred to under the first and second heads. In the third class of instances the Dravidian usage bears a close resemblance to the Indo-European. In the seventh class of Sanskrit verbal roots a nasal is inserted in the special tenses, so as to coalesce with a final dental—*e.g.*, *nid*, to revile, becomes *nindati*, he reviles. Compare also the root *uda*, water, with its derivative root *und*, to be wet. A similar nasalisation is found both in Latin and Greek. In Latin we find the unaltered root in the preterite, and a nasalised form in the present—*e.g.*, compare *scidi* with *scindo*, *cubui* with *cumbo*, *tetigi* with *tango*, *fregi* with *frango*. Compare also the Latin *centum* with the Greek ἑ-κατόν. In Greek, compare the roots μαθ and λαβ with the nasalised forms of those roots found in the present tense—*e.g.*, μανθ-άνω, to learn, and λαμβ-άνω, to take. The principle of euphonic nasalisation contained in these Sanskrit, Greek, and Latin examples, though not perfectly identical with the Dravidian usage, corresponds to it in a remarkable degree. The difference consists in this, that in the Indo-European languages the insertion of a nasal appears to be purely euphonic, whereas in Tamil it generally contributes to grammatical expression. The consonant to which *n* is prefixed by neuter verbs is not only deprived of the *n*, but also hardened and doubled, by transitives.

Prevention of Hiatus.—An examination of the means employed in the Dravidian languages to prevent hiatus between concurrent vowels, will bring to light some analogies with the Indo-European languages, especially with Greek.

In Sanskrit, and all other languages in which negation is effected by the use of "alpha privative," when this *a* is followed by a vowel, *n* is added to it to prevent hiatus, and *a* becomes *an*, *in*, or *un*. In the Latin and Germanic languages this *n*, which was used at first euphonically, has become an inseparable part of the privative particles *in* or *un*. In the greater number of the Indo-European languages this is almost the only conjuncture of vowels in which hiatus is prevented by the insertion of an euphonic *n*. In Sanskrit and Pâli, *n* is also used for the purpose of preventing hiatus between the final base-vowels of nouns or pronouns and their case terminations, in order that the vowels of the base may escape elision or corruption, and be preserved pure. In some instances (a probably older) *m* is used for this purpose instead of *n*. This usage is unknown in the cognate languages, with the exception of the use of *n* between the vowel of the base and the termination of the genitive plural in Zend and old high German. It is in Greek that the use of *n*, to prevent hiatus, has been most fully developed; for whilst in Sanskrit contiguous vowels are combined or changed, so that hiatus is unknown, in Greek, in which vowels are more persistent, *n* is used to prevent hiatus between contiguous vowels, and that not only when they belong to the same word, but also, and still more, when they belong to different words.

On turning our attention to the Dravidian languages, we may chance at first sight to observe nothing which resembles the system now mentioned. In Tamil and Canarese, and generally in the Dravidian languages, hiatus between contiguous vowels is prevented by the use of *v* or *y*. Vowels are rarely combined or changed in the Dravidian languages, as in Sanskrit, except in the case of compounds which have been borrowed directly from Sanskrit itself; nor are final vowels elided in these languages before words commencing with a vowel, with the exception of some short finals, which are considered as mere vocalisations. In Telugu and Canarese a few other unimportant vowels are occasionally elided. Ordinarily, however, for the sake of ease of pronunciation, and in order to the retention of the agglutinative structure which is natural to these languages, all vowels are preserved pure and pronounced separately; but as hiatus is dreaded with peculiar intensity, the awkwardness of concurrent vowels is avoided by the interposition of *v* or *y* between the final vowel of one word and the initial vowel of the succeeding one. The rule of Tamil, which in most particulars is the rule of Canarese also, is that *v* is used after the vowels *a*, *u*, and *o*, with their long vowels, and *au*, and that *y* is used after *i*, *e*, with their long vowels, and *ei*. Thus, in Tamil, *vara illei*, not come, is written and pronounced *vara-(v)-illei*, and *vaṛi-alla* (it is) not the way, becomes *vaṛi-(y)-alla*.

This use of *v* in one conjunction of vowels, and of *y* in another, is doubtless a result of the progressive refinement of the language. Originally, we may conclude that one consonant alone was used for this purpose, and this may possibly have been *v* changing into *m*, *n*, and *y*. In Malayâlam, as Dr Gundert observes, *y* has gradually encroached on the domain of *v*, pure *a* having become rare. Words like the Tamil *avan* $(a + (v) + n)$, he, remote; *ivan* $(i + (v) + n)$, he, proximate, changing in Telugu into *vâṅḍu* and *vîṅḍu*, prove sufficiently the great antiquity of *v*. They appear to me to prove that even in Telugu *y* is more recent than *v*. Possibly, also, the *n* of the Telugu is more recent than *m*. The only thing, however, perfectly certain, is that *m*, *n*, *v*, and *y* interchange in Telugu, Tuḷu, and Canarese, and *n*, *v*, and *y* in Tamil. Euphonic insertions between contiguous vowels are observed in the common conversation of Dravidians, as well as in written compositions; and they are found even in the barbarous dialects—*e.g.*, in the Ku, which was reduced to writing only a few years ago, *v* may optionally be used for euphony, as in Tamil. Thus, in Ku, one may say either *âălu*, she, or *â(v)ălu*. This insertion of *v* or *y* takes place, not only when a word terminating with a vowel is followed by a word beginning with another vowel, but also (as in Sanskrit) between the final vowels of substantives and the initial vowels of their case terminations—*e.g.*, *puḷi-(y)-il*, in the tamarind, *pilă-(v)-il*, in the jack. The use of *alpha privative* to produce negation being unknown to the Dravidian languages, there is nothing in any of them which corresponds to the use of *an*, *in*, or *un* privative, instead of *a*, in the Indo-European languages, before words beginning with a vowel.

The only analogy which may at first sight have appeared to exist between the Dravidian usage and the Greek, in respect of the prevention of hiatus, consists in the use of *v* or *y* by the Dravidian languages as an euphonic copula. When we enter more closely on the examination of the means by which hiatus is prevented, a real and remarkable analogy comes to light; for in many instances where Tamil uses *v*, Telugu and Tuḷu, like Greek, use *n*. By one of the two classes into which all words are arranged in Telugu for euphonic purposes, *y* is used to prevent hiatus when the succeeding word begins with a vowel; by the other, a very numerous class, *n* is used, precisely as in Greek. Thus, instead of *tinnagâ êgenu*, it went slowly, Telugu requires us to say *tinnagă-(n)-êgenu*. When *n* is used in Telugu to prevent hiatus, it is called *druta*, and words which admit of this euphonic appendage are called *druta prakrits*, words of the *druta* class. *Druta* means fleeting, and *the druta n* may be interpreted as *the n which often disappears*. The other class of words consists of those which use *y* instead of *n*, or prevent elision in the Sanskrit manner by *sandhi* or combination. Such words are called the *kala* class, and the rationale of their preferring *y* to *n* was first pointed out by Mr Brown. Whenever *n* (or its equivalent, *ni* or *nu*) could have a meaning of its own—*e.g.*, wherever it could be supposed to represent the copulative conjunction, or the case sign of the accusative or the locative, there its use is inadmissible, and either *y* or *sandhi* must be used instead.

Hence, there is no difference in principle between *n* and *y*, for the latter is used in certain cases instead of the former, merely for the purpose of preventing misapprehension; and it can scarcely be doubted that both letters were originally identical in origin and in use, like *v* and *y* in Tamil.

An euphonic peculiarity of Telugu may here be noticed. *ni* or *nu*, the equivalents of *n*, are used euphonically between the final vowel of any word belonging to the *druta* class (the class which uses *n* to prevent hiatus), and the hard, surd initial consonant of the succeeding word—which initial surd is at the same time converted into its corresponding sonant. They may also be optionally used before any initial consonant, provided always that the word terminating in a vowel to which they are affixed, belongs to the class referred to. It is deserving of notice, that in this conjunction *ni* or *nu* may be changed into that form of *m* (the Telugu *anusvâra*) which coalesces with the succeeding consonant. Occasionally, *m* is used in Telugu to prevent hiatus between two vowels where we should have expected to find *n*, or, in Tamil, *v*.

m may perhaps be regarded as the original form of the euphonic copula of Telugu, and *n* and *y* as a softening of the same. A distinct trace of the use, apparently a very ancient use, of *m* to prevent hiatus, instead of *n* or *v*, may be noticed in classical Canarese, in the accusative singular of certain nouns—*e.g.*, instead of *guru-v-am*, the accusative of *guru*, a teacher, *guru-m-am* may be used. On the other hand, in Tuḷu, an older *v* seems to have changed into *m*, and even into *mb*. Thus, *môḷ*, Tuḷu, she (prox.), stands for *imaḷ*, and that for *ivaḷ*: *mêr*, they (prox.), for *imar*, and that for *ivar*, whilst the sing. masc. of the same is *imbe*, for *ivan*. Compare the Tuḷu remote sing. masc., *âye*, he. The evidence of all the other dialects in favour of *v* being originally the euphonic vowel of the pronouns is so strong that the Tuḷu *m* must, I think, be regarded as a corruption. In colloquial Tamil *m* is used in some instances instead of *v*, where *v* alone is used, not only by the classics, but by scrupulously correct writers up to the present day—*e.g.*, *ennamô*, whatever it may be, instead of the more correct *ennavô*, from *enna*, what, and *ô*, the particle expressing doubt.

It may be noticed here, that where *n* is used in later Sanskrit to prevent hiatus between base vowels and case terminations, *y* is often used instead in the Sanskrit of the Vedas. I regard *m* as the original form of the euphonic copula of the Telugu, and *n* and *y* as a softening of the same.

It has been mentioned that *v* and *y* are the letters which are used in Tamil for preventing hiatus, where *n* and *y* are used by Telugu. On examining more closely the forms and inflexions of classical

Tamil, we shall find reason for advancing a step farther. In Tamil, also, *n* is used instead of *v* in a considerable number of instances, especially in the pronominal terminations of verbs in the classical dialect. Thus, the neuter plural demonstrative being *avei* (for *a-(v)-a* from *â-a*), we should expect to find the same *a-(v)-ei*, or the older *a-(v)-a*, in the third person plural neuter of verbs; but we find *a-(n)-a* instead—*i.e.*, we find the hiatus of *a-a* filled up with *n* instead of *v*—*e.g.*, *irukkindra(n)a*, they are (neuter), instead of *irukkindra(v)a*. So also, whilst in the separate demonstratives *avan*, he, and *avar*, they (epicene), the hiatus is filled up with *v*—*e.g.*, (*a-(v)-an*, *a-(v)-ar*), in the pronominal terminations of verbs in the classical dialect we find *a-(n)-an* often used instead of *a-(v)-an*, and *a-(n)-ar* instead of *a-(v)-ar*—*e.g.*, *irunda(n)an*, he was, instead of *irunda(v)an*, or its ordinary contraction *irundân*. We sometimes also find the same *n* in the neuter plural of appellative nouns and verbs in the classical dialect—*e.g.*, *poruḷa(n)a*, things that are real, realities, instead of *poruḷa(v)a*, or simply *poruḷa*. *varu-(n)-a* = *varubavei*, things that will come. We find the same use of *n* to prevent hiatus in the preterites and relative past participles of a large number of Tamil verbs—*e.g.*, *kâṭṭi(n)ên*, I showed; *kâṭṭi(n)a*, which showed; in which forms the *n* which comes between the preterite participle *kâṭṭi* and the terminations *ên* and *a*, is clearly used (as *v* in ordinary cases) to prevent hiatus. The euphonic character of this *n* (respecting which see the Section on "Verbs, Preterite Tense") is confirmed by the circumstance that *n* optionally changes in classical Tamil into *y*—*e.g.*, we may say *kâṭṭi(y)a*, that showed, instead of *kâṭṭi(n)a*. Another instance of the use of *n* in Tamil for the prevention of hiatus appears to be furnished by the numerals. The compound numerals between ten and twenty are formed by the combination of the word for ten with each numeral in rotation. The Tamil word for ten is *pattu*, but *padu* is used in the numerals above twenty, and *padi*, identical with the Telugu word for ten, is used in the numerals from eleven to eighteen inclusive. Between this *padi* and the units which follow, each of which, with the exception of *mûndru*, three, and *nâlu*, four, commences with a vowel, *n* is inserted for the prevention of hiatus where the modern Tamil would have used *v*. The euphonic character of this *n* appears to be established on comparing the Tamil and Canarese numerals with those of the Telugu, in most of which *h* is used instead of *n*—*e.g.*,

	TELUGU.	TAMIL AND CANARESE.
fifteen	*padi-(h)-ênu*	*padi-(n)-eindu* (Can. *eidu*)
sixteen	*padi-(h)-âru*	*padi-(n)-âru*
seventeen	*padi-(h)-êḍu*	*padi-(n)-êṛu* (Can. *êḷu*)

In the Tamil compound numeral, *padi-(n)-mûndru*, thirteen, we find the same *n* used as in the previous examples, though there is no hiatus to be prevented. Telugu has here *pada-mûḍu*, the Canarese *hadi-mûru;* and as Canarese uses *n*, like Tamil, in all the other compound numbers between eleven and eighteen inclusive, and dispenses with it here, I think it may be concluded that in the Tamil *padi(n)mundru*, the *n* has crept in through the influence of the numerals on each side of it, and in accordance with the euphonic tendencies of the language in general. Dr Gundert thinks *padin* hardly an example of *n* used for the prevention of hiatus. He prefers to regard the *in* of these numerals as the *in* of the oblique case, and considers *padin-mûndra* (in Malayâlam, *padim-mûṇu*) as decisive to this effect. He adduces also *ombadin-âyiram* (Tam. *onbadin*), nine thousand, and *eṇbadin kôḍi* (also capable of being used in Tamil), eighty crores. On the other hand, it may be replied that the *h* used by Telugu cannot be regarded as a sign of the oblique case, and that if it be admitted that it is used simply for the prevention of hiatus, this fact should be allowed to throw light on the use of *n* in the same words in the other languages. It would be quite natural, however, that *in*, the inflexional increment of the Tam.-Mal. oblique case, should be used instead of the merely euphonic *n*, where it appeared to fit in suitably. Identity of sound would recommend it for occasional use. In the Coorg dialect *n* appears in all the compounds after *padu*, the form of *pattu*, ten, used in construction—*e.g.*, *paḍunanje*, fifteen, *padunâru*, sixteen, *padunêḷu*, seventeen. Notwithstanding this, the inflexional increment of the Coorg does not contain *n*, but is either *ḍa* or *ra*. Similarly in Tuḷu, in which the possessive increment is *a*, *ta*, or *da*, and the locative *ḍ'* or *ṭ'*, *ḍu* or *ṭu*, *n* is inserted between *pad'*, ten, and the words for four, &c., in the compound numerals from fourteen to nineteen inclusive—*e.g.*, *pad'(n)ormba*, nineteen. The *n* thus inserted must surely be euphonic.

We have an indubitable instance of the use of *n*, even in common Tamil, to prevent hiatus, in appellative nouns ending in *ei*—*e.g.*, when an appellative noun is formed from *iḷei*, youth, or young, by annexing *an*, the sign of the masc. sing., the compound is not *iḷei-(y)-an*, but *iḷei-(ñ)-an*, or even *iḷei-(n)-an*. *ñ* is merely a more liquid form of *n*, and in Malayâlam regularly replaces *n* in the pronoun of the first person. Probably also *manâr*, the epicene plural of the future tense of the Tamil verb in some of the poets, is for *ma-ar*—*e.g.*, *enma-(n)-âr*, they will say, for *enmâr*, and that for *enbâr*, the more common form.

There is thus reason to suppose that originally Tamil agreed with Telugu in using a nasal instead of a semi-vowel to keep contiguous vowels separate. It may be objected that *n* evinces no tendency to change into *v*. I admit this; but if we suppose *m*, not *n*, to have been the nasal which was originally employed for this purpose, every difficulty will disappear; for *m* readily changes on the one hand to *v*, and on the other to *n*. Nor is it a merely gratuitous supposition that Telugu may have used *m* at a former period instead of *n*, for we have already noticed that *ni* or *nu*, the euphonic equivalents of *n*, are interchangeable in certain conjunctions with the *anusvâra* or assimilating *m*; that in two important instances (the copulative particle and the aorist formative) the *n* of Telugu replaces an older *m* of Tamil; that *m* is occasionally used instead of *n*, to prevent hiatus between contiguous vowels; and that in Sanskrit also, instead of the *n* which is ordinarily inserted between certain pronominal bases and their case terminations, an older *m* is sometimes employed. It may also be noticed that the *ni* or *nu*, which may be considered as the euphonic suffix of the accusative in Telugu, is replaced in old Canarese by *m*.

In Tuḷu, *n* is sometimes used to prevent hiatus. When the personal pronouns beginning with a vowel are suffixed to participles for the purpose of forming participial nouns, *n* is euphonically inserted where *v* would ordinarily be inserted in Tamil and Canarese—*e.g.*, *maḷpu-(n)-âye*, he who makes. Tamil agrees with Tuḷu in thus inserting *n* after past participles ending in *i*—*e.g.*, compare *paṇṇi-(n)-avan*, Tam. he who made, with *batti-(n)-âye*, Tuḷu, he who came. Sometimes this euphonic *n* is inserted in Tuḷu where *y* would be inserted in Tamil—*e.g.*, *dhore-(n)-âkulu*, Tuḷu, gentlemen, Tam. *durei-(y)-avargaḷ* (plural used honorifically for singular). In *amma-(n)-âkuḷu*, Tuḷu, mistresses, Tamil would run the vowels together. When the adverbial particle *aga* is added to the root of a verb, to denote the time at which an action takes place, *n* inserted between the concurrent vowels—*e.g.*, *maḷpu-(n)-aga*, when making. Compare with these particulars the uses of the *druta n* of Telugu. The emphatic particle *ê* becomes in Tuḷu not only *yê* or *vê*, according to the nature of the preceding vowel, as in Tamil, but also *nê*, after *a*, and sometimes after *e*—*e.g.*, *âye-(n)-ê*, he himself. *n* is inserted in like manner before *â* and *ô*, the interrogative particles, where *v* would be inserted in Tamil, as also before *ê* when used interrogatively.

The reader cannot fail to have observed that whilst the Dravidian languages accord to a certain extent with Sanskrit in the point which has now been discussed, they accord to a much larger extent with Greek, and in one particular (the prevention of hiatus between the contiguous vowels of *separate words*) with Greek alone. It is impossible to suppose that the Dravidian languages borrowed this usage from Sanskrit, seeing that it occupies a much less important place in Sanskrit than in the Dravidian languages, and has been much less fully developed.

It should be mentioned here that the letter *r* is in some instances used to prevent hiatus in each of the Dravidian idioms. In Tamil, *kâ*, the imperative singular of the verb to preserve, becomes in the plural, not *kâ-(v)-um*, but *kâ-(r)-um*. Canarese in certain cases inserts *r* or *ar* between the crude noun and the case terminations, instead of the more common *v*, *n*, or *d*—*e.g.*, *karid'-ar-a*, of that which is black. This *ar*, however, is probably only another form of *ad*. Telugu inserts *r* in a more distinctively euphonic manner, as, for instance, between certain nouns and *âlu*, the suffix by which the feminine gender is sometimes denoted—*e.g.*, *sundaru-(r)-âlu*, a handsome woman. Compare this with the Tamil *soundariya-(v)-aḷ*, in which the same separation is effected by the use of the more common euphonic *v*. *r* is inserted euphonically in Telugu in other connections also—*e.g.*, *poda-r-illu*, from *poda*, leaf, and *illu*, house = a bower.

The *d* which intervenes between the *i* of the preterite verbal participle and the suffixes of many Canarese verbs (*e.g.*, *mâḍi-(d)-a*, that did), though possibly in its origin a sign of the preterite, is now used simply as an euphonic insertion. This *d* becomes invariably *n* in Telugu and Tamil; and in Tamil it is sometimes softened further into *y*. *ṭ* is sometimes stated to be used in Telugu for a similar purpose—viz., to prevent hiatus between certain nouns of quality and the nouns which are qualified by them—*e.g.*, *karaku-ṭ-ammu*, a sharp arrow, but I have no doubt that this *ṭ* is identical with *ṭi*, and was originally an inflexional particle. *g* is in some instances used by Telugu to prevent hiatus, or at least as an euphonic formative, where Tamil would prefer to use *v*—*e.g.*, the rational plural noun of number, six persons, may either be *âru(g)ur-u* or *âru(v)ur-u*. *k* seems to be used for the same purpose in *padakoṇḍu* (*pada-k-oṇḍu*), eleven. *gâḍu*, he, for *vâḍu*, and *gâru*, they, for *vâru*, are instances of the use of *g* for *v* in Telugu.

Harmonic Sequence of Vowels.—In all the languages of the Scythian group (Finnish, Turkish, Mongolian, Manchu) a law has been observed which may be called "the law of harmonic sequence." The law is, that a given vowel occurring in one syllable of a word, or in the root, requires an analogous vowel, *i.e.* a vowel belonging to the same set (of which sets there are in Turkish four) in the following syllables of the same word, or in the particles appended to it, which, therefore, alter their vowels accordingly. This rule, of which some traces remain even in modern Persian, appears to pervade all the

Scythian languages, and has been regarded as a confirmation of the theory that all those languages have sprung from a common origin.

In Telugu a similar law of attraction, or harmonic sequence, is found to exist. Traces of it, indeed, appear in all the Dravidian languages, especially in Tuḷu, which in this particular comes nearest to Telugu; but it is in Telugu that it comes out most distinctly and regularly. The range of its operation in Telugu is restricted to two vowels *i* and *u;* but in principle it appears to be identical with the Scythian law, *u* being changed into *i*, and *i* into *u*, according to the nature of the preceding vowel. Thus the copulative particle is *ni* after *i, î, ei;* and *nu* after *u* and the other vowels. *ku*, the sign of the dative case, becomes in like manner *ki* after *i, î*, and *ei*. In the above-mentioned instances it is the vowels of the appended particles which are changed through the attraction of the vowels of the words to which they are suffixed; but in a large number of cases the suffixed particles retain their own vowels, and draw the vowels of the verb or noun to which they are suffixed, as also the vowels of any particles that may be added to them, into harmony with themselves. Thus, the Telugu pluralising termination or suffix being *lu*, the plural of *katti*, a knife, would naturally be *kattilu;* but the vowel of the suffix is too powerful for that of the base, and accordingly the plural becomes *kattulu*. So also, whilst the singular dative is *katti-ki*, the dative plural is, not *kattila-ki*, but *kattula-ku;* for *la*, the plural inflexion, has the same power as the pluralising particle *lu* to convert *katti* into *kattu*, besides being able to change *ki*, the dative post-position of the singular, into *ku*.

In the inflexion of verbs, the most influential particles in Telugu are those which are marks of time, and by suffixing which the tenses are formed. Through the attraction of those particles, not only the vowels of the pronominal fragments which are appended to them, but even the secondary vowels of the verbal root itself, are altered into harmony with the vowel of the particle of time. Thus, from *kalugu*, to be able, *du*, the aorist particle, and *nu*, the abbreviation of the pronoun *nênu*, I, is formed the aorist first person singular *kalugu-du-nu*, I am able. On the other hand, the past verbal participle of *kalugu*, is not *kalugi*, but *kaligi*, through the attraction of the final *i*, the characteristic of the tense; and the preterite of the first person singular, therefore, is not *kalugi-ti-nu*, but *kaligi-ti-ni*. Thus, the verbal root *kalu* becomes *kali; nu*, the abbreviation of *nênu*, becomes *ni;* and both have by these changes been brought into harmony with *ti*, an intermediate particle, which is probably an ancient sign of the preterite.

This remarkable law of the Telugu phonetic system evidently accords with the essential principles of the law of harmonic sequence by which the Scythian languages are characterised, and differs widely from the prevailing usage of the Indo-European languages. The change which is apparent in the pronominal terminations of the various tenses of the Telugu verb (*e.g.*, *nu* in the first person of the present tense, *ni* in the preterite), have been compared with the variation in Greek and Latin of the pronominal terminations of the verb according to the tense. But the change in Greek and Latin arises merely from euphonic corruption, whereas the Dravidian change takes place in accordance with a regular fixed phonic law, the operation of which is still apparent in every part of the grammar.

Though I have directed attention only to the examples of this law which are furnished by Telugu, in which it is most fully developed, traces of its existence could easily be pointed out in the other dialects. Thus, in the Canarese verbal inflexions, the final euphonic or enunciative vowel of the abbreviated personal pronouns is *u*, *e*, or *i*, according to the character of the preceding vowel—*e.g.*, *mâḍuttêv-e*, we do, *mâḍuttîr-i*, ye do, *mâḍidev-u*, we did. If in the means employed to prevent hiatus between contiguous vowels, the Dravidian languages appeared to have been influenced by Indo-European usages, still more decided traces of Scythian influences may be noticed in the phonetic law now mentioned.

Principles of Syllabation.—The chief peculiarity of Dravidian syllabation is its extreme simplicity and dislike of compound or concurrent consonants; and this peculiarity characterises Tamil, the earliest cultivated member of the family, in a more marked degree than any other Dravidian language. In Telugu, Canarese, and Malayâlam, the great majority of primitive Dravidian words—*i.e.*, words which have not been derived from Sanskrit, or altered through Sanskrit influences—and in Tamil all words without exception, including even Sanskrit derivatives, are divided into syllables on the following plan. Double or treble consonants at the beginning of syllables, like *str* in *strength*, are altogether inadmissible. At the beginning, not only of the first syllable of every word, but also of every succeeding syllable, only one consonant is allowed. If in the middle of a word of several syllables, one syllable ends with a consonant and the succeeding one commences with another consonant, the concurrent consonants must be euphonically assimilated, or else a vowel must be inserted between them. At the conclusion of a word, double and treble consonants, *ngth* in *strength*, are as inadmissible as at the beginning: and every word must terminate in Telugu, Tuḷu, and Canarese, in a vowel; in Tamil, either in a vowel or in a single semi-vowel, as *l* or *r*, or in a single nasal, as *n* or *m*. Malayâlam resembles Tamil in this, but evinces a more decided preference for vowel terminations. It is obvious that this plan of syllabation is extremely unlike that of Sanskrit.

The only double consonants which can stand together in the middle of a word in Tamil without an intervening vowel, are as follows. The various nasals, *ṅ*, *ñ*, *ṇ*, *n*, and *m*, may precede the sonant of the *varga* to which they belong; and hence *ṅ-g*, *ñ-ś*, or *ñ-ch*, *ṇ-ḍ*, *n-d*, *m-b*, may occur, also *ṅṅ*, *ññ*, *ṇṇ*, *nn*, *mm*, *ṇm*, and *nm*: the doubled surds, *kk*, *śś* or *chch*, *ṭṭ*, *tt*, *pp*, *ḷḷ*, **rr** (pronounced *ttr*; also *ṭk*, and *ṭp*; **r***k*, **r***ch*, and **r***p*; *yy*, *ll*, *vv*; and finally *n***r**, pronounced *ndr*. The only treble consonants which can coalesce in Tamil, under any circumstances, are the very soft, liquid ones, *ṛnd* and *ynd*. Tamilian laws of sound allow only the above-mentioned consonants to stand together in the middle of words without the intervention of a vowel. All other consonants must be assimilated—that is, the first must be made the same as the second, or else a vowel must be inserted between them to render each capable of being pronounced by Tamilian organs. In the other Dravidian dialects, through the influence of Sanskrit, nasals are combined, not with sonants only, but also with surds—*e.g.*, *pamp-u*, Tel. to send, *eṇṭ-u*, Can. eight. The repugnance of Tamil to this practice is so very decided, that it must be concluded to be non-Dravidian. Generally *i* is the vowel which is used for the purpose of separating unassimilable consonants, as appears from the manner in which Sanskrit derivatives are Tamilised. Sometimes *u* is employed instead of *i*. Thus the Sanskrit preposition *pra* is changed into *pira* in the compound derivatives which have been borrowed by Tamil; whilst *Krishna* becomes *Kiruṭṭina-n* (*ṭṭ* instead of *ṣh*), or even *Kiṭṭina-n*. Even such soft conjunctions of consonants as the Sanskrit *dya*, *dva*, *gya*, &c., are separated in Tamil into *diya*, *diva*, and *giya*. Another rule of Tamil syllabation is, that when the first consonant of an unassimilable double consonant is separated from the second and formed into a syllable by the intervention of a vowel, every such consonant (not being a semi-vowel) must be doubled before the vowel is suffixed. Thus, *tatva*, Sans. nature, becomes in Tamil *tat(t)uva*; *aprayôjana*, unprofitable, *ap(p)irayôśana*.

In consequence of these peculiarities of syllabation and the agglutinative structure of its inflexions, the Tamil language appears very verbose and lengthy when compared with Sanskrit and the languages of Europe. Nevertheless, each syllable being exceedingly simple, and the great majority of the syllables being short, rapidity of enunciation is made to compensate for the absence of contraction and compression.

Finnish, Hungarian, and other languages of the same stock, allow of only one consonant at the beginning of a syllable. When foreign words which begin with two consonants are pronounced by a Magyar, the consonants are separated by the insertion of a vowel—*e.g.*, *krâl* becomes *kirâly*. Where the first consonant is a sibilant, it is formed into a distinct syllable by a prefixed vowel—*e.g.*, *schola* becomes *iskôla*. How perfectly in accordance with Tamil this is, is known to every European resident in Southern India who has heard the natives speak of establishing, or sending their children to, an English *iskûl*. The same peculiarity has been discovered in the language of the Scythic tablets of Behistun. In rendering the word *Sparta* into Scythian, the translator is found to have written it with a preceding *i*—*e.g.*, *Isparta*, precisely as it would be written in the present day in Magyar or in Tamil.

Professor Max Müller, in his "Lectures on the Science of Language, Second Series," adduces many similar instances in other families of languages. "Many words in Latin begin with *sc*, *st*, *sp*. Some of these are found, in Latin inscriptions of the fourth century after Christ, spelt with an initial *i*—*e.g.*, *isperitus*. It seems that the Celtic nations were unable to pronounce an initial *s* before a consonant, or at least that they disliked it. Richards, as quoted by Pott, says, 'No British word begins with *s* when a consonant or *w* follows, without setting *y* before it; and when we borrow any words from another language which begin with an *s* and a consonant immediately following it, we prefix a *y* before such words, as from the Latin *schola*, *ysgol*; *spiritus*, *yspryd*.' The Spaniards in Peru, even when reading Latin, pronounce *estudium* for *studium*, *eschola* for *schola*. Hence the constant addition of the initial vowel in the Western, or chiefly Celtic, branch of the Roman family. French *espérer*, instead of Latin *sperare*; *stabilire*, became *establir*, lastly *établir*, to establish."—P. 195. "Words beginning with more than one consonant are most liable to phonetic corruption. It certainly requires an effort to pronounce distinctly two or three consonants at the beginning without intervening vowels, and we could easily understand that one of these consonants should be slurred over and allowed to drop. But if it is the tendency of language to facilitate pronunciation, we must not shirk the question how it came to pass that such troublesome forms were ever framed and sanctioned. Most of them owe their origin to contraction—that is to say, to an attempt to pronounce two syllables as one, and thus to save time and breath, though not without paying for it by an increased consonantal effort."—P. 187. "There are languages still in existence in which each syllable consists either of a vowel, or of a vowel preceded by one consonant only, and in which no syllable ever ends in a consonant. This is the case, for instance, in the Polynesian languages. A Hawaian finds it almost impossible to pronounce two consonants together. All syllables in Chinese are open or nasal. In South Africa, all the members of the great family of speech called by Dr Bleek the Bâ-ntu family, agree in general with regard to the simplicity of their syllables. In the other family of South African speech, the Hottentot, compound consonants are equally eschewed at the beginning of words. In Kafir we find *gold* pronounced *igolide*. If we look to the Finnish, and the whole Uralic class of the Northern Turanian languages, we meet with the same disinclination to admit double consonants at the beginning, or any consonants whatever at the end of words. No genuine Finnish word begins with a double consonant, for the assimilated and softened consonants, which are spelt as double letters, were originally simple sounds. The Esthonian, Lapp, Mordvinian, Ostiakian, and Hungarian, by dropping or weakening their final and unaccented vowels, have acquired a large number of words ending in simple and double consonants; but throughout the Uralic class, wherever we can trace the radical elements of language, we always find simple consonants and simple vowels."—P. 190.

The mode in which compound consonants are dealt with in Prakrit and the modern North Indian vernaculars, is investigated and explained by Mr Beames in chapter iv. of his "Comparative Grammar." The Prakrit rules for the assimilation of compound consonants bear a considerable resemblance, up to a certain point, to the Dravidian, especially in regard to the combination called by Mr Beames "the strong nexus" —that is, the combination, without a vowel, of the strong consonants only, such as *kt*, *tp*, &c., respecting which the rule of the Prakrits, as of Tamil, is that the first consonant should be assimilated to the next. Vararuchi expresses the Prakrit rule rather peculiarly by saying that the first consonant is elided, the second doubled. The corresponding Tamil rule applies only to the treatment of *tadbharas*, no such conjunction of consonants as *kt*, &c., being possible in words of purely Dravidian origin.

Minor Dialectic Peculiarities.

1. *Euphonic Displacement of Consonants.*

In the Dravidian languages, consonants are sometimes found to change places through haste or considerations of euphony, especially, but not exclusively, in the speech of the vulgar.

We have an example of this in the Tamil *taśei*, flesh, which by a displacement of consonants, and a consequent change of the surd into the sonant, has become *śadei : kudirei*, a horse, is in this manner often pronounced by the vulgar in the Tamil country *kuridei ;* and looking at the root-syllable of the Telugu word, *gur-ram*, it is hard to decide whether *kuridei* or *kudirei* is to be regarded as the true Dravidian original, though the apparent derivation of the word from *kudi*, Tam. to leap, inclines me to prefer *kudirei*. In many instances, through the operation of this displacement, we find one form of a word in Tamil, and another, considerably different, in Telugu or Canarese. Thus, *koppuḷ*, Tam. the navel, is in Telugu *pokkili*, in Malayâḷam *pokkuḷ* and *pokkiḷ ;* and *paḍar*, Tam. to spread as a creeper, is in Canarese *paraḍ-u*. In comparing words in the different dialects, it is always necessary to bear in mind the frequent recurrence of this displacement.

2. *Euphonic Displacement of Vowels.*

In Telugu we find many instances of a still more curious displacement of vowels. This displacement occurs most commonly in words which consist of three short syllables beginning with a vowel; and when it occurs, we find that the second vowel has disappeared, and that the first vowel has migrated from the beginning of the word to the second syllable, and at the same time been lengthened to compensate for the vowel that is lost. We have here to deal, therefore, with an euphonic amalgamation of vowels, as well as an euphonic displacement. I take as an example the Dravidian demonstrative pronouns, remote and proximate; and I select the plural, rather than the singular, to get rid of the disturbing element of a difference which exists in the formatives. In Tamil those pronouns are *avar*, they, remote; and *ivar*, they, proximate, corresponding to *illi* and *hi*. Canarese adds *u* to each word, so that they become *avaru* and *ivaru*. By analogy this is the form we should expect to find in Telugu also; but on examination, we find in Telugu *vâru* instead of *avaru*, and *vîru* instead of *ivaru*. The neuter demonstrative pronouns of Telugu being dissyllables, there is no displacement in their nominatives (*adi*, that, *idi*, this, corresponding closely to the Tamil *adu*, *idu*); but when they become trisyllables by the addition of the inflexional suffix *ni*, we find a displacement similar to that which has been described—*e.g.*, *adini*, it, or of it, becomes *dâni*, and *idini* becomes *dîni*. Many ordinary substantives undergo in Telugu a similar change—*e.g.*, *ural*, Tamil, a mortar, pronounced *oral*, should by analogy be *oralu* in Telugu; but instead of *oralu* we find *rôlu*. In each of the instances mentioned, the change seems to have been produced by the rejection of the second vowel, and the substitution for it of a lengthened form of the first. This unsettledness of the vowels, as Dr Gundert calls it, attaches chiefly to the enunciation of *l*, *r*, and other liquid consonants.

As soon as this peculiar law of the displacement of vowels is brought to light, a large number of Telugu words and forms, which at first sight appear to be widely different from Tamil and Canarese, are found to be the same or but slightly altered. Thus *kâdu*, Tel., it will not be, or it is not, is found to be the same as the Tamil *âgâdu; lêdu*, there is not, corresponds to the Tamil *illadu*, or *iladu;* and by an extension of a similar rule to monosyllables, we find *lô*, Tel. within, to be identical with *uḷ*, Tam.; *ôḷ*, old Canarese. A similar rule of displacement appears in Tuḷu, though in a less degree.

3. *Rejection of Radical Consonants.*

Telugu and Canarese evince a tendency to reject or soften away liquid consonants in the middle of words, even though such consonants should belong to the root, not to the formative. Thus, *neruppu*, Tam. fire, is softened into *nippu; elumbu*, a bone, into *emmu; uḍal* (pronounced *oḍal*), body, into *oḷḷu; poṛudu*, time, into *poddu; erudu*, an ox, into *eddu; marundu*, medicine, into *mandu*. For the last word Tuḷu has *mardu*, Can. *maddu* (ancient Can. *mardu*). For the Tam. *eṛupadu*, seventy, Can. has *eppattu;* for *eṛuppu*, Tam. to raise (root, Tam. *eṛu*, to rise, Can. *êlu*), Can. has *ebbisu*. For the Tam. *koṛuppu, koṛumei*, fat, Can. has *kobbe*, Tuḷu *komme*. So Tam. *erumei*, a buffalo, Tuḷu *erme*, Can. *emme*. Something similar to this process takes place, but not so systematically, in vulgar colloquial Tamil.

In a few instances, on the other hand, Telugu appears to have retained a radical letter which has disappeared in some connections from Tamil. For example, *ôḍu*, with, together with, is the suffix of the Tamil conjunctive case. On examining Telugu, we find that the corresponding suffix is *tôḍa*. It has already been shown that *ḍ* in Telugu corresponds to *ṛ* in Tamil; and consequently *tôḍa* would become in Tamil *tôṛa*. *tôṛa* (*tôṛa-mei*) is contained in Tamil, and means companionship—a meaning which appears also in many Telugu compounds; and thus by the help of Telugu we find that the Tamil *ôḍu* and *tôṛa* are closely allied, if not virtually identical; that the meaning of the suffix *ôḍu* accords with its use; and that there is also reason to conclude another pair of similar words to be allied, viz., *uḍan*, with, Can. *oḍane*, a suffix of the conjunctive case, in itself a noun signifying connection, and *toḍar*, a verbal root, to follow, to join on, written also *tuḍar*.

Dr Gundert is right in considering *ôḍu* a lengthened secondary form of *oḍu*, which is still used in Malayâlam poetry (and equally so in Tamil). Old Can. has *oḍa, oḍam*, modern Can. *oḍane;* Tuḷu *oṭṭugu*, with. Can. *oḍane* is of course the equivalent of the Tam. *uḍan*, together with. *oḍu*, therefore, he thinks, needs no explanation from

Tel. *tôḍu,* Tam. *tôṛa,* companionship, the root of which latter word is *toṛu* (found with this meaning in Tam. *toṛudi,* a crowd). *toḍar,* to follow, explains itself as a verbal noun of *toḍu,* to touch, to connect. These three roots he considers as altogether distinct from, and independent of, each other. It seems to me, however, on a comparison of the three roots, difficult to avoid the conclusion that they are substantially identical. The lengthening of the root vowel in secondary forms of roots is quite common in Tamil, and the close relationship of the radical meanings of the shorter forms, *oḍu, toḍu,* and *toṛu,* favours the supposition that they are only different forms of the same root. I cannot perceive any essential difference between the radical meanings of *oḍu* and *toḍu.* The formêr, as we see from its verbal noun *oṭṭu,* means to touch so as to adhere, the latter simply to touch. The slight variations apparent in form and meaning appear to me to be specialisations of a common root. See the section on the radiation of roots, through "Particles of Specialisation."

4. *Accent.*

It is generally stated that the Dravidian languages are destitute of accent, and that emphasis is conveyed by the addition of the *ê* emphatic alone. Though, however, the Dravidian languages are destitute of the Indo-Greek system of accents, the use of accent is not altogether unknown to them; and the position of the Dravidian accent, always an acute one, accords well with the agglutinative structure of Dravidian words. The accent is upon the first syllable of the word; that syllable alone, in most cases, constituting the base, prior to every addition of formatives and inflexional forms, and remaining always unchanged. The first syllable of every word may be regarded as the natural seat of accent; but if the word be compounded, a secondary accent distinguishes the first syllable of the second member of the compound.

As in other languages, so in the Dravidian, accent is carefully to be distinguished from quantity; and in enunciation an accented short vowel is more emphatic than an unaccented long one. Thus, in the intransitive Tamil verb *aḍangugiṛadu,* it is contained, the second syllable, *ang,* is long by position, yet the only accent is that which is upon the first syllable *aḍ,* which, though shorter than the second, is more emphatic. Another example is furnished by the compound verb *uḍeind'-irukkiadu,* it is broken; literally, having been broken it is. Though in this instance the second syllable of the first word of the compound is long, not only by position, but by nature, and the second syllable of the auxiliary word is long by position, yet the principal accent rests upon the first syllable of the first word, *uḍ,* the most emphatic portion of the compound, and the secondary accent rests upon *ir*, the first syllable and crude base of the auxiliary; hence it is pronounced *úḍeindírukhiradu*, every syllable except the two accented ones being enunciated lightly and with rapidity.

The general rule of the Dravidian languages, which fixes the accent in the first or root syllable, admits of one exception. In poetical Tamil one and the same form is used as the third person of the verb (in each tense, number, and gender) and as a participial noun—*e.g.*, *ôduvân* means either he will read, or one who reads—*i.e.*, a reader. Even in the colloquial dialect the third person neuter singular, especially in the future tense, is constantly used in both senses—*e.g.*, *ôduvadu*, means either it will read, or that which will read, or abstractly, yet more commonly still, a reading, or to read. The same form being thus used in a double sense, Tamil grammarians have determined that the difference in signification should be denoted by a difference in accent. Thus when *ôduvân* is a verb, meaning he will read, the accent is left in its natural place, on the root syllable—*e.g.*, *ốduvân*; but when it is an appellative or participial noun, meaning he who reads, the pronominal termination is to be pronounced more emphatically, that is, it becomes the seat of accent—*e.g.*, *ôduvấn*.

Dr Gundert (in an article in the *Journal of the German Oriental Society* for 1869) directs attention to a subject which I had not sufficiently discussed—viz., the changes which Sanskrit sounds undergo when Sanskrit words are Dravidianised. Old tadbhavas, he observes, are not to be regarded as mere corruptions. Most of the changes that have taken place when Sanskrit words have been adopted by the Dravidian dialects have been in accordance with rule, though some appear to be arbitrary. It would be easy, he says, to point out the laws in virtue of which, for instance, the Sans. *vrishabha*, an ox, has become *basava* in Can., Tel., and Tuḷu; in Tam. and Mal. *iḍaba* and *eḍava;* and also to show how the Sans. *parva*, a season, becomes in Tam. *paruva*, in Can. *habba;* and how *Brahma* has become in Tel. *Bomma*, and in Tam. *Pirama.* He contents himself, however, with pointing out some of the laws which appear in the formation of the oldest class of tadbhavas. One of these laws consists in the simple omission of non-Dravidian sounds, such as the sibilants. Thus, *sahasram*, Sans. for one thousand, becomes in Can. *savira*, in Tuḷu *sâra*, in Tam. *âyiram.* The latter has been formed, he thinks, thus—*sahasiram* = *a-a-iram* = *âyiram.* So, out of the Pali name for Ceylon, *Sîhalam*, the old Tamil formed *Îḷam.* The nakshatras *Mṛigaśîrsham* and *Śrâvaṇam*, have become in Mal. *Magayiram* and *Ôṇam.* *Śramana*, a Jaina ascetic, becomes in Tamil *Samaṇa-n*, and also *Amaṇa-n;* *Sîsam*, lead, becomes *îyam.*

Another rule, which shows itself especially in Canarese, is the shortening of the long vowels of Sanskrit. Thus, from Sans. *kumârî*, a young girl, comes Tamil *kumari* (whence *Comorin*), from *śrêshṭi*, a superior, comes *śeṭṭi* (chetty), the title of the merchant caste. A noticeable illustration is Sanskrit, *snêha*, oil, which in all the Dravidian dialects becomes *ney*. Another important rule consists in the separation of vowels. No old Dravidian word can commence with *l* or *r*. Hence *râjâ*, a king, becomes commonly *irâśâ*; *lôka*, *ulôgam*. The predilection for short vowels produces a further change in these words—*râjâ* becomes in Tamil *arasa-n* and *araya-n*; *lôka*, *ulagam*, and *ulagu*; Sans. *Rêvatî*, the nakshatra, becomes *Iravati*.

PART II.

ROOTS.

Before proceeding to examine and compare the grammatical forms of the Dravidian languages, it is desirable to examine the characteristics of Dravidian roots, and the nature of the changes which are effected in them by the addition of the grammatical forms. The manner in which various languages deal with their roots is strongly illustrative of their essential spirit and distinctive character; and it is chiefly with reference to their differences in this particular, that the languages of Europe and Asia admit of being arranged into classes.

Those classes are as follows:—(1.) The monosyllabic, uncompounded, or isolative languages, of which Chinese is the principal example, in which roots admit of no change or combination, and in which all grammatical relations are expressed either by auxiliary words or phrases, or by the position of words in a sentence. (2.) The Semitic or intro-mutative languages, in which grammatical relations are expressed by internal changes in the vowels of dissyllabic roots. (3.) The agglutinative languages, in which grammatical relations are expressed by affixes or suffixes added to the root or compounded with it. In the latter class I include both the Indo-European and the Scythian groups of tongues. They differ, indeed, greatly from one another in details, and that not only in their vocabularies but also in their grammatical forms; yet I include them both in one class, because they appear to agree, or to have originally agreed, in the principle of expressing grammatical relation by means of the agglutination of auxiliary words. The difference between them is rather in degree than in essence. Agreeing in original construction, they differ considerably in development. In the highly-cultivated languages of the Indo-European family, post-positional additions have gradually been melted down into inflexions, and sometimes even blended with the root; whilst in the less plastic languages of the Scythian group, the principle of agglutination has been more faithfully retained, and every portion and particle of every compound word has not only maintained its original position, but held fast its separate individuality. In this particular the Dravidian languages agree in general rather with the Scythian than the Indo-European; and hence in each dialect of the family there is, properly speaking, only one declension and one conjugation.

It is to be remembered that the three classes mentioned above, into which the languages of Europe and Asia have been divided, are not separated from one another by hard and fast lines of distinction. Their boundaries overlap one another. Probably all languages consisted at first of isolated monosyllables. The isolative languages have become partly agglutinative, and changes in the internal vowels of roots, which are specially characteristic of the Semitic languages, are not unknown in the agglutinative class, especially in the Indo-European family. Such internal changes may occasionally be observed even in the Dravidian languages.

I here proceed to point out the most notable peculiarities of the Dravidian root-system, and of the manner in which roots are affected by inflexional combinations.

Arrangement of Dravidian Roots into Classes.—Dravidian roots, considered by themselves, apart from formative additions of every kind, may be arranged into the three classes of—(1.) Verbal roots, capable in general of being used also as nouns, which constitute by far the most numerous class; (2.) Nouns which cannot be traced up to any extant verbs.

1. *Verbal Roots.*—The Dravidian languages differ from Sanskrit and Greek, and accord with the languages of the Scythian group, in generally using the crude root of the verb, without any addition, as the imperative of the second person singular. This is the general rule, and the few apparent exceptions that exist are to be regarded either as corruptions, or as euphonic or honorific forms of the imperative. In a few instances, both in Tamil and in Telugu, the second person singular of the imperative has cast off its final consonant, which is generally in such cases a soft guttural or a liquid; but in those instances the unchanged verbal theme is found in the less used second person plural, or in the infinitive.

A considerable proportion of Dravidian roots are used either as verbal themes or as nouns, without addition or alteration in either case; and the class in which they are to be placed depends solely on the connection. The use of any root as a noun may be, and in general is, derived from its use as a verb, which would appear to be the primary condition and use of most words belonging to this class;

but as such words, when used as nouns, are used without the addition of formatives or any other marks of derivation, they can scarcely be regarded as derivatives from verbs; but in respect of grammatical form, the verb and the noun must be considered either as twin sisters or as identical. The following will suffice as examples of this twofold condition or use of the same root:—*śol,* Tam. as a verb, means to speak; as a noun, a word; *tari,* Tam. as a verb, to lop, to chop off; as a noun, a stake, a loom; *muri,* Tam. as a verb, to break in two; as a noun, a fragment, a document written on a fragment of a palm-leaf, a bond. In these instances it is evident that the radical meaning of the word is unrestrained, and free to take either a verbal or a nominal direction. Moreover, as the Dravidian adjective is not separate from the noun, but is generally identical with it, each root may be said to be capable of a threefold use—viz., (1.) as a noun, (2.) as an adjective, and (3.) as a verb. Thus, in Tamil, *kaḍ-u,* if used as the nominative of a verb, or followed by case terminations, is a noun, and means harshness or pungency; if it is placed before another noun for the purpose of qualifying it, it becomes an adjective—*e.g., kaḍu-naḍei,* a sharp walk; *kaḍu-vây,* the tiger, literally harsh mouth; and when standing alone, or preceded by a pronoun of the second person, expressed or understood, it becomes a verb—*e.g., kaḍu,* be sharp. With the formative addition *gu,* the same root becomes *kaḍu-gu,* mustard, that which is pungent. Again, when the included vowel is lengthened, it becomes *kâḍu,* a forest, literally what is rough, harsh, or rugged.

It would appear that originally there was no difference in any instance between the verbal and the nominal form of the root in any Dravidian dialect. Gradually, however, as the dialects became more cultivated, and as logical distinctness was felt to be desirable, a separation commenced to take place. This separation was effected by modifying the theme by some formative addition, when it was desired to restrict it to one purpose alone, and prevent it from being used for others also. In many instances the theme is still used in poetry, in accordance with ancient usages, indifferently either as a verb or as a noun; but in prose more commonly as a noun only, or as a verb only.

2. *Nouns.*—In Sanskrit and the languages allied to it, all words, with the exception of a few pronouns and particles, are derived by native grammarians from verbal roots. In the Dravidian languages the number of nouns which are incapable of being traced up or resolved into verbs is more considerable. Still, such nouns bear but a small proportion to the entire number; and not a few which are generally considered to be underived roots are in reality verbal nouns or verbal derivatives.

Many Dravidian dissyllabic nouns have for their second syllable *al*, a particle which is a commonly used formative of verbal nouns in Tamil, and a sign of the infinitive in Canarese and Gônd. All nouns of this class may safely be concluded to have sprung from verbal roots. In most instances their themes are discoverable, though in a few no trace of the verb from which they have been derived is now apparent. I cannot doubt that the following Tamil words, generally regarded as primitives, are derived from roots which are still in use—viz., *viral*, a finger, from *viri*, to expand; *kaḍal*, the sea, from *kaḍa*, to pass beyond; *pagal*, day as distinguished from night, properly *mid*-day, from *pag-u*, to divide; *kuḍal*, a bowel, from *kuḍei*, to hollow out.

There are many words in the Dravidian, as in other languages, denoting primary objects which are identical with, or but slightly altered from, existing verbal roots, possessing a more generic signification. What is specially noticeable is the smallness of the change the roots have undergone in the Dravidian languages. One might suppose the name of the object to have been affixed to it only a few years ago. These languages present in consequence the appearance of fresh youth, yet doubtless the true inference is that they have remained substantially unchanged (possibly in consequence of the high cultivation they received) from a very early period. The change effected consists in general only in the addition to the root of a formative particle, or in the lengthening of the included vowel of the root. Either way the name of the object is simply a verbal noun with the signification of a noun of quality. The following illustrations are from Tamil:—*nilam*, the ground, from *nil*, to stand; *nâḍu*, the cultivated country, from *naḍu*, to plant; *kâḍu*, the forest, from *kaḍu*, to be rugged (compare also *kaḍam*, a rough way, a forest); *viṇ*, the sky, from *viḷ*, to be clear; *mîn*, a star, also a fish, from *min*, to glitter; *veḷḷi*, the planet Venus, also silver, from *veḷ*, white; *kudirei*, a horse, from *kudi*, to leap; *pandri* (*pal-ti*), a hog, from *pal*, a tusk; *âḍu*, a sheep, from *âḍu*, to frisk. (Dr Gundert carries this noun still further back, but with some risk of error, to *aḍu*, to fight or cook, the sheep being regarded as the fighting animal, or the animal that was cooked): *kaṇ*, the eye, identical with *kâṇ* (in the past tense *kaṇ*), to see; *mûkku*, the nose (Tel. *mukku*, Can. *mûgu*), from *mug-ar*, to smell; *nâkku*, the tongue, from *nakku*, to lick (compare the probably older *nâ*, the tongue, with *nây*, a dog, the animal that licks). Probably also *kei*, the hand, bears the same relation to *śey*, to do (Can. *gêyu*), that the Sanskrit *kara*, the hand, bears to *kar* (*kṛi*), to do. In Telugu, *chê*, the hand, is identical with *chê*, to do (*kei* also is used in Telugu). I may here remark that the names of animals in the Dravidian languages are not imitations of the sounds they make, but are predicative words, expressive of some one of their qualities.

Though the greater number of Dravidian nouns are undoubtedly to be regarded as verbal derivatives, a certain proportion remain which cannot now be traced to any ulterior source. In this class are to be included the personal pronouns; some of the particles of relation which answer to the case signs and prepositions of other languages; and a considerable number of common nouns, including some names of objects—*e.g.*, *kâl*, foot, *kal*, a stone, and most nouns of quality—*e.g.*, *kar*, black, *veḷ*, white, *se*, red, &c. A suspicion may be entertained that some of the apparently simple nouns belonging to this class are derived from verbal roots which have become obsolete. Thus, *mun*, before, a noun of relation, appears at first sight to be an underived radical, yet it is evident that it is connected with *mudal*, first; and this word, being a verbal noun in *dal*, is plainly derived from a verb in *mu*, now lost; so that, after all, *mun* itself appears to be a verbal derivative: *mêl*, above, may similarly be traced to a lost verb *mi*, apparent in the Telugu and Tamil *mîdu*, above; *mêl* is equivalent to *mi-y-al*: *kîṛ*, below, may be traced to *kiṛ* (found in *kiṛ-angu*, root).

A large majority of the Dravidian post-positions and adverbs, and of the particles employed in nominal and verbal inflexions are known to be verbs or nouns adapted to special uses. Every word belonging to the class of adverbs and prepositions in the Dravidian languages is either the infinitive or the participle of a verb, or the nominative, the genitive, or the locative of a noun; and even of the inflexional particles which are employed in the declension of nouns, and in conjugating verbs, nearly all are easily recognised to be derived from nouns or verbs. Thus, in Telugu, the signs of the instrumental ablative, *chê* and *chêta*, are the nominative and locative of the word hand. So also the Tamil locative of rest may be formed by the addition of any noun which signifies a place; and the locative of separation, a case denoting motion from a place, or rather the place from whence motion commences, is formed by the addition of *in* or of *il*, the ordinary sign of the locative of rest, which means 'here' or a house.

The same suffix added to the crude aoristic form of the verb, constitutes the subjunctive case in Tamil—*e.g.*, *var-il* or *var-in*, if (he, she, it, or they) come, literally, in (his or their) coming—that is, in the event of (his or their) coming.

Of the post-positions or suffixes which are used as signs of case, some distinctly retain their original meaning; in some, the original meaning shines more or less distinctly through the technical appropriation; but it is doubtful whether any trace whatever remains of the original meaning of *ku*, *ki*, or *ge*, the sign of the dative and particle of direction. The Dravidian dative has, therefore, assumed the character of a real grammatical case; and in this particular the Dravidian languages have been brought into harmony with the genius of the Indo-European grammar.

DRAVIDIAN ROOTS ORIGINALLY MONOSYLLABIC.—It may appear at first sight scarcely credible that the Dravidian roots were originally monosyllabic, when it is considered that the majority of the words in every Dravidian sentence are longer than those of (perhaps) any other language in Asia or Europe (*e.g.*, compare *irukkiṟadu*, Tamil, it is, with the Latin *est*), and are inferior in length only to the words of the polysynthetic languages of America.

The great length of Dravidian words arises partly from the separation of clashing consonants by the insertion of euphonic vowels, but chiefly from the successive agglutination of formative and inflexional particles and pronominal fragments. A considerable number of Dravidian verbal themes, prior to the addition of inflexional forms, are trisyllabic; but it will generally be found that the first two syllables have been expanded out of one by the euphonic insertion or addition of a vowel; whilst the last syllable of the apparent base is in reality a formative addition, which appears to have been the sign of a verbal noun in its origin, but which now serves to distinguish transitive verbs from intransitives. In some instances the first syllable of the verbal theme contains the root, whilst the second is a particle anciently added to it, and compounded with it for the purpose of expanding or restricting the signification. The syllables that are added to the inflexional base are those which denote case, tense, person, and number.

Hence, whatever be the length and complication of Dravidian words, they may invariably be traced up to monosyllabic roots, by a careful removal of successive accretions. Thus, when we analyse *perugugiṟadu*, Tam. it increases, we find that the final *adu* represents the pronoun it, *giṟ* is the sign of the present tense, and *perugu* is the base or verbal theme. Of this base, the final syllable *gu* is only a formative, restricting the verb to an intransitive or neuter signification; and by its removal we come to *peru*, the real root, which is used also as an adjective or noun of quality, signifying greatness or great. Nor is even this dissyllable *peru* the ultimate condition of the root; it is an euphonised form of *per*, which is found in the adjectives *per-iya* and *per-um*, great; and an euphonically lengthened but monosyllabic form of the same is *pêr*. Thus, by successive agglutinations, a word of six syllables has been found to grow out of one. In all these forms, and under every shape which the word can assume, the radical element remains unchanged, or is so slightly changed that it can readily be pointed out by the least experienced scholar. The root always stands out in distinct relief, unobscured, unabsorbed, though surrounded by a large family of auxiliary affixes. This distinctness and prominence of the radical element in every word is a characteristic feature of all the Scythian tongues (*e.g.*, of the Turkish and the Hungarian); whilst in the Semitic and Indo-European tongues the root is frequently so much altered that it can scarcely be recognised.

Dravidian roots, adds Dr Gundert, arrange themselves naturally in two classes, each originally monosyllabic; one class ending in a vowel generally long—*e.g.*, *â*, to become; *śâ*, to die; *pô*, to go; or ending in a consonant, in which case the vowel is short—*e.g.*, *aḍ'*, to approach; *aṇ'*, to be in contact; *nil*, to stand; *śel*, to go. (Additions to these monosyllabic roots are either formative particles, particles of specialisation, or helps to enunciation.)

It is desirable here to explain in detail the manner in which Dravidian roots, originally monosyllabic, have been lengthened by the insertion or addition of euphonic vowels, or by formative additions, or in both ways.

Euphonic Lengthening of Roots.*—Crude Dravidian roots are sometimes lengthened by the addition of an euphonic vowel to the base. This euphonic addition to the final consonant takes place in grammatical Telugu and Canarese in the case of all words ending in a consonant, whatever be the number of syllables they contain. Vowel additions to roots which contain two syllables and upwards, seem to be made solely for the purpose of helping the enunciation; but when the additions which have been made to some monosyllabic roots are examined, it will be found that they are intended not so much for vocalisation as for euphonisation.

When it is desired merely to help the enunciation of a final consonant, *u* is the vowel that is ordinarily employed for this purpose, and this *u* is uniformly elided when it is followed by another vowel; but *u* is not the only vowel which is added on to monosyllabic roots, though

* Dr Gundert considers the "euphonic lengthening of Dravidian roots" very doubtful. He prefers to consider the lengthened forms of the roots secondary verbal themes. On the other hand, the interchangeableness of the added vowels in the various dialects, as will presently be shown, seems to me to prove the correctness, on the whole, of the view I have taken. Some of the lengthened forms of Dravidian roots are undoubtedly to be regarded as secondary verbal themes. These will be considered further on.

perhaps it is most frequently met with; and in some of the instances under consideration, it becomes so intimately blended with the real base that it will not consent to be elided. Next to *u*, the vowel which is most commonly employed is *i*, then follows *a*, then *e* or *ei*, according to the dialect. Verbal roots borrowed from Sanskrit have generally *i* added to the final consonants in all the Dravidian languages, to which Telugu adds *nchu*, and Canarese *su*, formatives which will be noticed afterwards. Thus, *śap*, Sans. to curse, is in Tamil *śabi*, in Tel. *śapinchu*, in Can. *śabisu*. On comparing the various Dravidian idioms, it will be found that all these auxiliary or enunciative vowels are interchangeable. Thus, of Tamil verbs in *a*, *mara*, to forget, is in Canarese *mare;* of Tamil verbs in *i*, *kaḍi*, to bite, is in Telugu *karachu; geli*, to win, is in Canarese *gillu*. Of Tamil verbs in *ei*, *muḷei*, to sprout, is in Telugu *moluchu*. These final vowels being thus interchangeable equivalents, it appears to me evident that they are intended merely as helps to enunciation, that they are not essential parts of the themes to which they are suffixed, and that they do not add anything to their meaning.

Dr Gundert considers *u* to be the only enunciative or euphonic vowel. The other auxiliary vowels *a*, *i*, *ei*, &c., he considers the formative particles of secondary verbal themes. One Canarese dialect, he observes (the modern), prefers *e*—*e.g.*, *naḍe*, to walk, instead of the Tamil *naḍa;* the other (the ancient), *i*,—*e.g.*, *naḍi*. The radical form he considers to be *naḍ-u*, a root no longer used in Tamil in the sense of to walk, but meaning to plant. He suggests that *muḷei*, to sprout, may be from a lost *mûḷ*, to come forth, to protrude, whence *muḷ*, a thorn. This also he suggests may be a verbal noun, a derivative of *mu*, to be prominent, to be before. The verb *naḍa*, to walk, adduced by Dr Gundert, seems to me to prove that in this instance at least, and therefore probably in some other instances, the vowel added to the root is simply, as I have represented it to be, a help to enunciation. On comparing Tam.-Mal. *naḍa*, anc. Can. *naḍi*, mod. Can. *naḍe*, Tel. *naḍu*—all which forms convey exactly the same meaning—I feel obliged to conclude that the *a*, *i*, *e*, and *u* are interchangeable equivalents, and therefore merely euphonic. On the other hand, where a series of verbal roots followed by these vowels is met with in the vocabulary of one and the same dialect, and we find that each root so altered possesses a meaning of its own, I have no hesitation in classing the added vowels in question with Particles of Specialisation (which see). We may fairly conclude this to be the case with one of the verbs referred to by Dr Gundert—viz., *paḍu*. In this shape in Tamil it appears to mean primarily, to come in contact with, commonly, to lie down, to be caught, to suffer; *paḍi* is to settle down, to subside; *paḍei*, to lay down, to present food, &c. (*paḍei*, a layer in a building, an army). Compare also *paḍar*, to spread, *paḍal*, a slab, and *paḍagu*, a boat.

FORMATIVE ADDITIONS TO ROOTS.—Formative suffixes are appended to the crude bases of nouns as well as to those of verbs. They are added not only to verbal derivatives, but to nouns which appear to be primitive; but they are most frequently appended to verbs properly so called, of the inflexional bases of which they form the last syllable, generally the third. These particles seem originally to have been the formatives of verbal nouns, and the verbs to which they are suffixed seem originally to have had the force of secondary verbs; but whatever may have been the origin of these particles, they now serve to distinguish transitive verbs from intransitives, and the adjectival form of nouns from that which stands in an isolated position and is used as a nominative. In Tamil, in which these formatives are most largely used and most fully developed, the initial consonant of the formative is single when it marks the intransitive or neuter signification of the verb, or that form of the noun which governs verbs or is governed by them: when it marks the transitive or active voice of the verb, or the adjectival form of the noun—viz., that form of the noun which is assumed by the first of two nouns that stand in a case relation to one another—the initial consonant of the formative is doubled, and is at the same time changed from a sonant into a surd. The single consonant, which is characteristic of the intransitive formative, is often euphonised by prefixing a nasal, without, however, altering its signification or value. The Tamilian formatives are—(1.) *gu* or *ṅgu*, and its transitive *kku*, answering to the Telugu *chu* or *nchu*; (2.) *śu*, and its transitive *śśu* or *chchu*; (3.) *du* or *ndu*, and its transitive *ttu*, with its equivalent *ḍu* or *ṇḍu*, and its transitive *ṭṭu*; and (4.) *bu* or *mbu*, with its transitive *ppu*.

Though I call these particles *formatives*, they are not regarded in this light by native grammarians. They are generally suffixed even to the imperative, which is supposed by them to be the crude form of the verb; they form a portion of the inflexional base, to which all signs of gender, number, and case, and also of mood and tense, are appended; and hence it was natural that native grammarians should regard them as constituent elements of the root. I have no doubt, however, of the propriety of representing them as formatives, seeing that they contribute nothing to the signification of the root, and that it is only by means of a further change, *i.e.*, by being hardened and doubled, that they express a grammatical relation, viz., the difference between the transitive and the intransitive forms of verbs, and between adjectival and independent nouns.

In this particular, perhaps, more than in any other, the high grammatical cultivation of Tamil has developed a tendency to imitate the Indo-European tongues by retaining syllables of which it has lost the original distinctive meaning, and combining such syllables after a time with the radical element of the word, or using them for a new purpose.

I proceed to consider the various formatives more particularly, with examples of their use and force.

(1.) *ku*, pronounced *gu*, with its nasalised equivalent *ngu*, and its transitive *kku*. Tamil examples: *peru-gu*, intrans. to become increased, *peru-kku*, trans. to cause to increase; *aḍa-ngu*, to be contained, *aḍa-kku*, to contain. So also in the case of dissyllabic roots—*e.g.*, *â-gu*, to become, *â-kku*, to make; *nî-ngu*, to quit, *nî-kku*, to put away. There is a considerable number of nouns, chiefly trisyllabic, in which the same formative is employed. In this case, however, there is no difference between the isolated shape of the noun and the adjectival shape. Whatever particle is used, whether *gu*, *ngu*, or *kku*, it retains its position in all circumstances unchanged. Examples: *paḍa-gu*, a boat, *kiṛa-ngu*, a root, *karu-kku*, a sharp edge. From a comparison of the above examples, it is evident that *ng* is equivalent to *g*, and euphonised from it; and that *ng*, equally with *g*, becomes *kk* in a transitive connection. In a few instances, *kku*, the transitive formative, is altered in colloquial Tamil usage to *ch*, *chu*, according to a law of interchange already noticed—*e.g.*, *kâykku*, to boil (crude root *kây*, to be hot), is generally written and pronounced *kâychchu*. This altered form of the sign of the transitive, which is the exception in Tamil, is in Telugu the rule of the language, *kku* being regularly replaced in Telugu by *chu*.

In Telugu the intransitive formative *gu* is not euphonically altered into *ngu* as in Tamil; but an obscure nasal, the half *anusvâra*, often precedes the *gu*, and shows that in both languages the same tendency to nasalisation exists. It is remarkable, that whilst Tamil often nasalises the formative of the neuter, and never admits a nasal into the transitive formative, Telugu, in a large number of cases, nasalises the transitive, and generally leaves the neuter in its primitive, unnasalised condition. Thus in Telugu, whenever the base terminates in *i* (including a large number of Sanskrit derivatives), *chu* is converted into *nchu*; though neither in this nor in any case does the *kku* of the Tamil change into *ngku*. *E.g.*, from *raṭṭi*, double, Tamil forms *raṭṭi-kka* (infinitive), to double; whilst the Telugu form of the same is *reṭṭi-ncha*. *manni-ncha*, to forgive, in Telugu, corresponds in the same manner to the Tamil *manni-kka*. In some cases in Telugu the euphonic nasal is prefixed to *chu*, not after *i* only, but after other vowels besides. Thus, *perugu*, to increase, neut. is the same in Tamil and in Telugu, but instead of finding *peru-chu* to be the transitive or active (corresponding to the Tamil transitive *peru-kku*), we find *penchu*, corrupted from *per'-nchu*: so also instead of *pagu-kku*, Tam. to divide, we find in Telugu *panchu*, for *pag'-nchu*.

The identity of the Tamil *k* and the Telugu *ch* appears also from the circumstance that in many cases *vu* may optionally be used in Telugu instead of *chu*. This use of *vu* as the equivalent of *chu* points to a time when *gu* was the formative in ordinary use in Telugu as in Tamil; for *ch* has no tendency to be converted into *v*, *b*, or *p*, whilst *k* or *g* constantly evinces this tendency to change into *v*, not only in Telugu, but also in colloquial Tamil; and *v* is regularly interchangeable with *b* and its surd *p*. I conclude, therefore, that *gu* was the original shape of this formative in the Dravidian languages; and that its doubled, surd shape, *kku*, the formative of transitives, was softened in Telugu into *chu*, and in Canarese still further softened into *śu*.

(2.) *śu*, and its transitive *śśu*, pronounced *chchu*.—This formative is very rare in Tamil, and the examples which Telugu contains, though abundant, are not to the point, inasmuch as they are apparently altered from the older *ku* and *kku*, by the ordinary softening process by which *k* changes into *ś* or *ch*, and *kk* into *chch*. A Tamil example of this formative is seen in *aḍei-śu*, to take refuge, of which the transitive is *aḍei-chchu*, to enclose, to twine round.

(3.) *du* or *ndu*, with its transitive form *ttu*.—There appears to be no difference whatever between this formative and the other three, *gu*, *śu*, or *bu*, in meaning or grammatical relation; and as *gu* is euphonised in the intransitive to *ngu*, so is *du* to *ndu*; whilst in the transitive the doubled *d* (and its equivalent *nd*) changes by rule into *tt*. The euphonic change of *du* to *ndu* has so generally taken place, that *ndu* is invariably used instead of *du* in the formatives of verbs of this class; and it is only in the formatives of nouns that *du*, the more primitive form, is sometimes found to have survived. The formative *gu* remains unaltered in the adjectival form of nouns; but *du* changes into *ttu*, when used adjectivally, in the same manner as in the transitive voice of verbs. Tamil examples of this formative: *tiru-ndu*, to become correct, *tiru-ttu*, to correct; *maru-ndu*, medicine, adjectival form of the same, *maru-ttu*—*e.g.*, *maruttu-(p)pei*, a medicine bag. The primitive unnasalised *du* and its adjectival *ttu* are found in such words as *eru-du*, a bull, an ox, and *eru-ttu-(p)pûṭṭu*, the fastening of an ox's traces. Nearly all the verbs which take *du* or *ndu* as a formative are trisyllabic. Of the few dissyllabic verbs of this class in Tamil, the most interesting is *nîndu*, to swim, of which I am inclined to consider *nî* as the crude form. *Nîndu* is evidently an euphonised form of *nîdu* (*du* changed into *ndu*); for the verbal noun derived from it, *nîttal*, swimming, is without the nasal, and Telugu uses *îdu* for the verb itself, instead of *îndu*, Tuḷu *ñanda*, Can. *îsu*, *îju*. I have little doubt that the *du*, *ndu*, or *ju* of this word is simply a formative. It is open to question whether the initial *n* of the Tamil word is a corruption, owing to the fondness of the Tamil for nasal sounds, so that the original shape was *î* or *îdu*, or whether the Tel. and Can. word had the initial *n* originally, but lost it in course of time. Comparing the Tamil word with *nîr*, the word for water in all the Dravidian dialects, I am inclined to consider *nî* the primitive base, answering to the Greek *νέ-ω*, the Latin *no*, *nato*, and also to *nau*, Sans. a boat, of which Sanskrit does not appear to contain the root.

Derivative nouns formed from verbs which have formative suffixes, always prefer as their formative the transitive suffix, or that which doubles and hardens the initial consonant. Thus from *tiru-ndu*, Tam. to become correct, is formed *tiru-ttam*, correction; and from *tû-ngu*, to sleep, *tû-kkam*, sleep (comp. *tuyil*, sleep). In some instances the crude root of a verb is used as the intransitive, whilst the transitive is formed by the addition of *ttu* to the root. *E.g.*, *paḍu*, Tam. to lie down, *paḍu-ttu*, to lay; *tâṛ*, to be low, *tâṛ-ttu*, to lower; *nil* (Tel. *nilu*), to stand, *niṟu-ttu* (for *nilu-ttu*), to establish. In such cases Canarese uses *du* instead of the Tamil *ttu*—*e.g.*, *tâḻ-du*, to lower, instead of *tâṛ-ttu*. This transitive formative is sometimes represented as a causal; but it will be shown in the section on "The Verb" that *i* is the only real causal in the Dravidian languages. In all the cases now mentioned, where *ttu* is used as the formative of the transitive by Tamil, Telugu uses *chu* or *pu*.

I class under the head of this formative all those nouns in which the *cerebral* consonants *ḍ*, *ṇḍ*, and *ṭṭ*, are used in the same manner and for the same purpose as the dentals *d*, *nd*, and *tt*—*e.g.*, *kuru-ḍu*, blindness, adjectival form of the same, *kuru-ṭṭu*, blind; *ira-ṇḍu*, two, adjectival form, *ira-ṭṭu*, double. Telugu hardens, but does not double, the final *ḍ* of such nouns—*e.g.*, *ôḍ-u*, a leak, *ôṭi*, leaky. In some instances in Tamil the hard rough **r**, when used as a final, seems to be equivalent to *du*, or *ḍu*, and is doubled and pronounced with a *t*—*e.g.*, *kiṇa-ṟu*, a well, *kiṇa-ṟṟu* (pronounced *kiṇattru*), of a well.

(4.) *bu* or *mbu*, with its transitive *ppu*.—In Canarese, *bu*, the original form of this intransitive suffix, has been softened into *vu*, and in Tamil, *bu* has universally been euphonised into *mbu*. This Tamilian formative *mbu* is in some instances softened in Telugu nouns into *mu*. The *bu* or *mbu* of Tamil verbs is superseded by *vu* or *gu* in Telugu; and the forms answering to the Tamil transitive *ppu* are *pu* and *mpu*, rarely *ppu*. Example of the use of this formative by a verb: *nira-mbu*, Tam. to be full, *nira-ppu*, to fill; of which the crude base *nir* reappears in the related verbs *nir-a*, *nir-avu*, *nir-ei*, and *nir̤-ei*, to be full, to be level, &c. Telugu has *niṇdu* instead of *nirambu;* but the transitive *nimpu* answers very nearly to the Tamil *nirappu*. Example of a noun in *mbu* and *ppu: iru-mbu*, Tam. iron, adjectival form, *iru-ppu*, of iron—*e.g.*, *iruppu-(k)kôl*, an iron rod. In Telugu *irumbu* is softened into *inumu*, adjectival form *inupa*. Canarese still adheres to the original form of this suffix, generally softening *b* into *v*, but leaving it always unnasalised—*e.g.*, Canarese *hâvu*, a snake, properly *pâvu:* Tamil *pâmbu*, nasalised from *pâbu;* adjectival form *pâppu*—*e.g.*, *pâppu-(k)koḍi*, the serpent banner: Telugu, still further altered, *pâmu*. This example clearly illustrates the progressive euphonisation of the formative in question.

It has been mentioned that Telugu uses *pu* or *mpu* as a formative of transitive verbs where Tamil uses *ppu*. It should be added that even in those cases where Tamil uses the other formatives previously noticed, viz., *kku* and *ttu*, Telugu often prefers *pu*. Compare the following infinitives in Tamil and in Telugu—*e.g.*, *mêykka*, Tam. to feed cattle, *mêpa*, Tel.; *nirutta*, Tam. to establish, *nilupa*, Tel. Where *kku* in Tamil, and *pu* in Telugu, are preceded by *i*, this formative becomes in Telugu either *mpu* or *nchu*—*e.g.*, compare *oppuvi-kka*, Tamil, to deliver over, with the corresponding Telugu infinitive, *oppagi-mpa*, or *oppagi-ncha*.

It appears from the various particulars now mentioned, that transitive verbs and nouns used adjectivally must have been regarded by the primitive Tamilians as possessing some quality in common. The common feature possessed by each is doubtless the quality of transition; for it is evident that when nouns are used adjectivally there is a transition of the quality or act denoted by the adjectival noun to the noun substantive to which it is prefixed, which corresponds to the transition of the action denoted by the transitive verb to the accusative which it governs.

It is manifest that the various particles which are used as formatives do not essentially differ from one another either in signification, in the purpose for which they are used, in the manner in which they are affixed, or in the manner in which they are doubled and hardened. It seems to have been euphony only that determined which of the sonants *g*, *ś*, *ḍ*, *d*, or *b*, should be suffixed as a formative to any particular verb or noun. The only particular in which a grammatical principle appears to exist, is the doubling of the initial consonant of the formative, to denote or correspond with the putting forth of energy, which is inherent in the idea of active or transitive verbs, as distinguished from intransitives.

Whilst the use of these formatives appears to have originated mainly in considerations of euphony, Dr Gundert thinks that in some instances traces of a frequentative meaning may be discovered. He adduces *minungu*, to glitter, from *min*, to shine. This instance seems to carry weight. The other instances adduced by him, such as *veḷu-veḷukka*, are properly infinitives of iterative, mimetic verbs.

From the statements and examples given above, it may be concluded that wherever Dravidian verbs or nouns are found to terminate in any of the syllables referred to, there is reason to suspect that the first part of the word alone constitutes or contains the root. The final syllables *gu*, *ngu*, *kku*; *śu*, *chu*; *ḍu*, *ṇḍu*, *ṭṭu*; *du*, *ndu*, *ttu*; *bu*, *mbu*, *mpu*, *pu*, *ppu*; *mu*, *vu*, may as a general rule be rejected as formative additions. This rule will be found on examination to throw unexpected light on the derivation and relationship of many nouns which are commonly supposed to be primitive and independent, but which, when the syllables referred to above are rejected, are found to be derived from or allied to verbal roots which are still in use. I adduce, as examples, the following Tamil words:—*kombu*, a branch, a twig; *vêmbu*, the margosa-tree; *vambu*, abuse; *pâmbu*, a snake. As soon as the formative final, *mbu*, is rejected, the verbs from which these nouns are derived are brought to light. Thus, *ko-mbu*, a twig, is plainly derived from *ko-y*, to pluck off, to cut; *vê-mbu*, the margosa-tree, is from *vê-y*, to screen or shade (the shade of this tree being peculiarly prized); *va-mbu*, abuse, is from *vei*, properly *va-y* (corresponding to the Canarese *bayyu*), to revile; *pâ-mbu*, a snake, is from *pâ-y*, to spring. In these instances, the verbal base which is now in use ends in *y*, a merely euphonic addition, which does not belong to the root, and which disappears in the derivatives before the consonants which are added as formatives. The same principle applied to nouns ending in the other formative syllables will be found to yield similar results—*e.g.*, *marunda*, a medical drug, from *maru*, to be fragrant; and *kiṛangu*, a root, from *kiṛ*, to be beneath, the *i* of which, though long in the Tamil *kîṛ*, is short in the Telugu *kinda*, below.

Reduplication of the Final Consonant of the Root.—The principle of employing reduplication as a means of producing grammatical expression is recognised by the Dravidian languages as well as by those of the Indo-European family, though the mode in which the reduplication is effected and the objects in view are different. It is in Tamil that this reduplication is most distinctly apparent, and it should here be borne in mind, that when a Tamil consonant is doubled it is changed from a sonant into a surd. The final consonant of a Tamil root is doubled—(1.) for the purpose of changing a noun into an adjective, showing that it qualifies another noun, or of putting it in the genitive case—*e.g.*, from *mâḍu*, an ox, is formed *mâṭṭ-u(t)tôl*, ox-hide; (2.) for the purpose of converting an intransitive or neuter verb into a transitive—*e.g.*, from *ôḍ-u*, to run, is formed *ôṭṭu*, to drive; (3.) for the purpose of forming the preterite—*e.g.*, *tag-u*, to be fit, *takk-a*, that was fit; and (4.) for the purpose of forming derivative nouns from verbal themes—*e.g*, from *eṛud-u*, to write, is formed *eṛutt-u*, a letter. (See this subject further elucidated in the sections on "The Noun" and "The Verb.") It is remarkable that whilst the Indo-European tongues often mark the past tense by the reduplication of the *first* syllable, it is by the reduplication of the *last* letter that the Dravidian languages effect this purpose; and also, that whilst the Tibetan converts a *noun* into a *verb* by doubling the last consonant, this should be a Dravidian method of converting a *verb* into a *noun*. The rationale of the Dravidian reduplication seems to be, that it was felt to be a natural way to express the idea of *transition* both in the act and in the result. In Hebrew also the doubling of a consonant is intensitive or causative.

Up to this point it has been found that all Dravidian polysyllabic roots are traceable to a monosyllabic base, lengthened either by euphonic additions, or by the addition of formative particles. An important class of dissyllabic bases remains, of which the second syllable, whatever may have been its origin, is an inseparable particle of specialisation, into the nature and use of which we shall now inquire.

Particles of Specialisation.—The verbs and nouns belonging to the class of bases which are now under consideration, consist of a monosyllabic root or stem, containing the generic signification, and a second syllable, originally perhaps a formative addition, or perhaps the fragment of a lost root or lost postposition, by which the generic meaning of the stem is in some manner modified. The second syllable appears sometimes to expand and sometimes to restrict the signification, but in some instances, through the absence of synonyms, its force cannot now be ascertained. As this syllable is intended in some manner to specialise the meaning of the root, I call it "the particle of specialisation." It is certain in some cases, probable in many, that these particles of specialisation were originally formatives of verbal nouns. This will appear from a comparison of the verbs and nouns contained in the list of final particles which will be found near the end of this section.

The principle involved in the use of these particles of specialisation, and the manner in which it is carried into effect, correspond in a certain degree to a characteristic feature of the Semitic languages, which it appears to be desirable to notice here. As far back as the separate existence of the Semitic family of languages can be traced, every root is found to consist of two syllables, comprising generally three consonants. When Semitic biliteral roots are compared with their synonyms, or corresponding roots, in the Indo-European languages, and especially with those which are found in Sanskrit, a simpler and more primitive root-system has been brought to light. It has been ascertained in a considerable number of instances that whilst the first syllable of the Hebrew root corresponds with Sanskrit, the second syllable does not in any manner correspond to any Indo-European synonym. It is found also that the second syllable has not any essential connection with the first, and that a considerable number of families of roots exist in which the first syllable is the same in each case, whilst the second continually varies. It is therefore inferred that in such cases the first syllable alone (comprising two consonants, the initial and the final, together with the vowel used for enunciation) contains the radical base and generic signification, and that the second syllable, perhaps the fragment of an obsolete auxiliary verb, has been appended to the first and afterwards compounded with it, for the purpose of giving the generic signification a specific and definite direction. According to this view, which appears to be in the main correct, Hebrew roots are to be regarded, not singly and separately, as independent monads, but as arranged generically in clusters or groups, exhibiting general resemblances and special differences. The family likeness resides in the first syllable, the radical base; the individuality, or special peculiarity, in the second, the particle of specialisation.

It is true that in some instances the second syllable of Semitic roots meets with its counterpart in the Indo-European languages, as well as the first, or even instead of the first; but the peculiar rule or law now referred to is found to pervade so large a portion of the Hebrew roots, that it justly claims to be considered as a characteristic of the language. Thus, there is a family of Hebrew roots signifying generally to divide, to cleave, to separate, &c. The members of this family are *pâlâh*, *pâlaḥ*, *pâlag*, *pâlâ*, *pâlal;* and also (through the dialectic interchange of *l* with *r*) *pârash*, *pâras*, Chaldee *peras*. It cannot be doubted that in all these instances the first syllable *pâl* or *par*, or rather *p-r*, *p-l* (for the vowel belongs not to the root, but to the grammatical relation), expresses merely the general idea of division; whilst the second syllable (which is in some instances a reduplication of the final consonant of the biliteral) expresses, or is supposed to express, the particular mode in which the division or partition is effected. The first syllable, which is the same in all the members of this group of roots, is that which is to be compared with synonyms in other languages, whilst the second syllable is merely modal. In this instance we not only observe a distinct analogy between the Hebrew roots *p-r*, *p-l*, and the Greek *πόρ-ω*, the Latin *par-s*, *par-tis*, and the Sanskrit *phal*, to divide, but we also discover the existence of an analogy with the Dravidian languages. Compare with the Hebrew *p-r*, *p-l*, the Tamil *piri*, to divide, and *pâl*, a part; *piḷa* and *pôṛ*, to cleave; as also *pagir* and *pagu*, to portion out, to divide. See also the "Glossarial Affinities."

On turning our attention to the root-system of the Dravidian languages, we are struck with the resemblance which it bears to the Semitic root-system referred to above. We find in these languages groups of related roots, the first syllables of which are nearly or wholly identical, whilst their second syllables are different in each instance, and in consequence of this difference produce the required degree of diversity in the signification of each member of the group. We also find in these languages, as in Hebrew, that the generic particle or common base, and the added particle of specialisation, are so conjoined as to become one indivisible etymon. The specialising particle, which was probably a separable suffix, formative, or postposition at first, has become by degrees a component part of the word; and this word, so compounded, constitutes the base to which all formatives, properly so called, and all inflexional particles are appended.

This root-system exists in all the languages of the Dravidian family, but its nature and peculiarities are especially apparent in Tamil. Out of many such groups of related Tamil roots, I select as illustrations two groups which commence with the first letter of the alphabet.

1. Roots which radiate from the base syllable *aḍ*:—

aḍu to come near; also to cook, to kill, to unite, to belong to.

aḍangu } to be contained, to enclose.
aḍakku }

aḍi to drive in, commonly to beat. *aḍi*, as a noun, the basis of any thing, a footstep, a sole.

aḍei to attain, to get in, to roost; transitive, to enclose.
aḍeiśu to stuff in.
aḍar to be close together, to be crowded, to join battle.
aḍukku to place one thing upon another, to pile up. This verb and *aḍakku* are properly *aḍuk* and *aḍak*, but final *k* in Tamil is always vocalised by the help of *u*, and often doubled, as in this instance, before receiving the *u* and *a* of the root.
aṇḍu (Tel. *aṇṭu*), to approach. This verb seems to be identical with *aḍu*, the first in the list, and euphonised from it by the insertion of the nasal. Compare also the related verb *aṇ*.

It is obvious that all these roots are pervaded by a family resemblance. All contain the generic notion of nearness, expressed by the first or base syllable *aḍ;* whilst each, by means of the second syllable, or particle of specialisation, denotes some particular species of nearness.

2. Roots which radiate from the base syllable *aṇ* :—

aṇu, aṇugu to approach, to touch.
aṇi to put on, to wear.
aṇei to connect, to embrace; as a noun, a weir, a dam.
aṇavu to cleave to.
aṇṇu to resort to, to lean upon. (From this verb is derived *aṇṇal* or *aṇṇan*, an elder brother, one to lean upon, a derivation which has at least the merit of being poetical). The corresponding Telugu verb is *ânuta*.
aṇmu to be near.

The generic idea signified by the base syllable *aṇ* is evidently that of contact; and this group differs from the previous one as actual contact differs from contiguity or nearness. Probably *âṇi*, a nail, a fastening, is derived from the same verb, and it appears probable also that this is the origin of the Sanskrit *aṇi* or *âṇi*, the pin of an axle.

The illustrations given above prove, that the second syllables of the various verbs now adduced have not been added merely for purposes of euphony, but have been appended in order to expand, to restrict, or in some manner to modify and specialise the signification. It was shown in a previous part of this section, that the vowels *a, i, u, e,* and *ei* are sometimes added euphonically to monosyllabic roots. It is obvious, however, that this is not the only purpose for which those vowel additions are used; and it is of importance to know that when they are merely euphonic they are found to be interchangeable with other vowels, whereas when they are used as particles of specialisation they retain their individual character more firmly. Probably they had all a specialising signification at first, which they retain in some instances, but have lost in others.

The examples already given may suffice to illustrate the use of appended *vowels* as specialising particles. Syllables ending in consonants, especially in *l* and *r*, are also used very frequently for this purpose; and it seems desirable here to adduce examples of the use of particles of this class. As has already been observed in connection with "Formative Additions to Roots," all these syllables seem to have been originally formatives of verbal nouns, probably each of them with a specialising signification. Many of the verbal nouns so formed have then become secondary verbal themes. The following examples are mostly from Tamil, in which *l* and *r* may stand as finals. The other dialects add *u* to the final consonant of each of these particles. Tamil requires this euphonic addition of *u* only when a word ends in the hard, rough **r**, or in any consonant besides the nasals and semi-vowels.

Each word being considered either as a verb or as a noun according to circumstances, I give examples of nouns as well as of verbs. Some of the following words, though used as verbs, are more commonly used as nouns, and some, though used as nouns, are more commonly used as verbs. Some of the examples, again, are used either as nouns only or as verbs only:—

FINAL PARTICLES.	VERBS.	NOUNS.
ar	*vaḷar*, to grow.	*suḍar*, lustre.
ir	*tuḷir*, to sprout.	*ugir*, a finger nail.
ur		*nudur-u*, Tel. the forehead.
aṛ	*pugaṛ*, to praise.	*idaṛ*, a flower petal.
iṛ	*magiṛ*, to rejoice.	*aviṛ*, a grain of rice.
*a***r***-u*	*iḍa***r***-u*, to trip.	*kiṇa***r***-u*, a well.
*i***r***-u*		*ñâyi***r***-u*, the sun.
al	*suṛal*, to whirl.	*îral*, the liver.
il	*kuyil*, to utter a sound.	*veyil*, sunshine.
ul	*pagul-u*, Tel. to break.	
aḷ	*tuvaḷ*, to bend.	*tiṅgaḷ*, the moon.
iḷ		*madiḷ*, a fort wall.
uḷ	*uruḷ*, to roll.	*iruḷ*, darkness.

Of all the thirteen specialising particles ending in consonants of which examples have now been adduced, only one appears occasionally to be used as an equivalent for a vowel addition: *ar* alternates with *ei*—*e.g.*, *amar*, Tam. to rest, and *amei*, are apparently equivalent. The verb to grow, also, is in Tamil *vaḷar*, and in Canarese *baḷe*, which in Tamil would be *vaḷei*.

The original meaning of most of the particles used as formative suffixes or particles of specialisation, is now unknown, but there are two of which the meaning appears nearly certain; these are *il*, which survives as a substantive, meaning here or a house, the particle used as the most common case sign of the locative in Tamil-Malayâlam, and *uḷ*, which is still used both as a noun and as a verb; as a noun meaning within, and as a verb, to be. The force of these particles and their retention of the locative signification will appear in such instances as *vâyil*, a doorway, literally the mouth house (from *vây*, mouth); *veyil*, the heat of the sun, literally, that in which heat resides (from *vey*, to be hot). Dr Gundert suggests also *poruḷ*, wealth, which may come from *poru*, to unite; *aruḷ*, grace, from *aru*, to be scarce, precious; and *iruḷ*, darkness, from *ir*, to be dark, the root of *irâ*, night.

I here subjoin an example of another peculiar and interesting set of groups of roots found in the Dravidian languages, which are formed upon a plan differing considerably from that which has now been explained. The roots referred to are dissyllabic, but they contain only one consonant, which is preceded and followed by a vowel. This consonant appears to represent the ultimate or radical base, whilst the initial and final vowels alter in accordance with the particular shade of signification which it is desired to convey. When we compare *iḍu*, Tam. to press or crush, *oḍu*, to squeeze, to bring into a smaller compass, and *iḍi*, to bruise, to beat down, as also *aḍi*, to drive in, or *oḍi*, to break in two, and *uḍei* (pronounced *oḍei*), to break open; we cannot avoid the conclusion that the first four roots are closely related members of the same family or group; that the last two are in like manner mutually related; and that possibly the whole of them have an ulterior relationship, in virtue of their possessing in common the same nucleus or radical base, the central consonant *ḍ*, and the same generic signification.

The existence of clusters of roots, like these mentioned above, is not a peculiarity of the Dravidian languages alone. Max Müller (Lectures, ii. 313) observes, "We find in Sanskrit and in all the Aryan languages *clusters of roots*, expressive of one common idea, and differing from each other merely by one or two additional letters, either at the end or at the beginning." In illustration of this he says, "To go, would be expressed by *sar*, to creep by *sarp*; to shout by *nad*, to rejoice by *nand*; to join by *yu* or *yuj*, to glue together by *yauṭ*." In another place (i. 274) he says, "In the secondary roots we can generally observe that one of the consonants, in the Aryan languages generally the final, is liable to modification. The root retains its general meaning, which is slightly modified and determined by the changes of the final consonants." "These secondary roots," he says, "stand to the primaries in about the same relation as the triliteral Semitic roots to the more primitive biliteral." In the Dravidian languages the change under consideration is as often in the vowel of the root as in the consonant, and it is hard to say whether the initial vowel is not even more subject to modification than the final vowel.

Changes in Root Vowels.—As a general rule the vowels of Dravidian roots belong as essentially to the radical base as the consonants. They very rarely pertain, as in the Semitic languages, to the system of means by which grammatical relations are expressed, and they are still more rarely modified, as in the Indo-European languages, by the addition of inflexional forms, or in composition.

In the Semitic languages the radical base is destitute of vowels, and by itself unpronounceable. The insertion of vowels not only vocalises the consonants of the root, but constitutes it a grammatically inflected verb or noun, the signification of which varies with the variation of the interior vowels. In the Indo-European languages grammatical modifications are generally produced by additions to the root; and though in the earliest period of the history of those languages, the root, generally monosyllabic, is supposed to have remained unaltered by additions and combinations, yet the existence of that rigidity is scarcely capable of direct proof; for on examining the Sanskrit, Greek, Latin, and German, the most faithful representatives of the early condition of those languages, we find that the root-vowels of a large proportion of the words have been modified by the addition of the suffixes of case and tense; and in particular, that the reduplication of the root, by which the past tense appears usually to have been formed, is often found either to alter the quantity of the root-vowel, to change one vowel into another, or entirely to expunge it.

In the Scythian family of tongues, not only does the vowel belong essentially to the root, but in general it remains unalterable. It very rarely happens that the root-vowel sustains any change or modification on the addition to the root of the signs of gender, number, and case, or of person, tense, and mood; which, as a rule, are successively agglutinated to the root, not welded into combination with it. This rigidity or persistency is almost equally characteristic of the root-vowels of the Dravidian languages. In general, whatever be the length or weight of the additions made to a Dravidian root, and whether it stands alone or is combined with other words in a construct state, it is represented as fully and faithfully in the oblique cases as in the nominative, in the preterite and future as in the present tense or in the imperative. I proceed to point out some noticeable exceptions to this rule.

Exceptions.—Internal Changes in Roots.

1. One class of changes is purely euphonic. It has no relation to grammatical expression; but it seems desirable to mention it here in order to give a complete view of the subject. It is connected with one of the minor dialectic peculiarities referred to in the chapter on sounds, and consists in the occasional softening or rejection of the medial consonant of a dissyllabic root or verbal noun, together with the coalescence of the vowels that preceded and followed it. It has been shown that *g* has a tendency to be softened into *v* and then to disappear, and that *ś* sometimes changes in the same manner into *y*, when it sometimes becomes absorbed. When either of these consonants is a medial, it is apt to be thus softened down and rejected. Thus *dogal-u*, Can. skin, becomes in Tamil *tôl; peśar*, Can. a name, becomes in Tamil first *peyar*, and then *pêr*. So in Tamil, *togup-pu*, a collection, is softened into *tôp-pu*, which has the restricted meaning of a collection of trees, a tope. In like manner the medial *v* of the Tamil *avan*, he, disappears in the personal terminations of verbs, and the preceding and following vowels coalesce, when *avan* becomes *ân* or *ôn*. So also the length of the demonstrative roots, *a* remote, and *i* proximate, varies in different dialects, and even in different connections in the same dialect, through considerations of euphony.

2. The exceptions that follow in this and the following paragraphs are not euphonic merely, but real. They pertain to grammatical expression. In most of the Dravidian languages the quantity of the root-vowels of the pronouns of the first and second persons, both singular and plural, is short in the oblique cases. The nominatives of those pronouns are long—*e.g.*, *nân*, Tamil, I, *nâm*, we; *nî*, thou, *nîr*, you. But in Tamil, Canarese, Malayâlam, and Tuḷu, in all the oblique cases the vowels are shortened before receiving the suffixed inflexional particles. Thus, in Canarese, to me is not *nân-a-ge*, but *năn-a-ge;* to thee is not *nîn-a-ge*, but *nĭn-a-ge*. Telugu, Gônd, and Ku generally retain the quantity of the vowel of the nominative unaltered—*e.g.*, in Telugu we find *nî-ku*, to thee, as well as *nî*, thou; but in the accusative, *nin-u* or *ninn-u*, thee, the quantity is altered. It is open to us to regard the shorter form of the pronouns as the original, and the longer as the form that has been altered; and it will be seen, when the pronouns are under discussion, that this is the view I prefer. Singularly enough, this exception from the general rigidity of the root-vowels is a Scythian exception, as well as a Dravidian one. In the Scythian version of the Behistun tablets, whilst the nominative of the pronoun of the second person is *nî*, thou, as in the Dravidian languages, the possessive case is *uĭ*, thy, and the accusative *nin*, thee, corresponding in quantity to the Dravidian oblique cases—*e.g.*, Telugu *nin-u*, thee;

Tulu *nin-a*, thy, *nin-an'*, thee; High Tamil *nîn*, thy, and *nînnei*, thee.

3. Another class of exceptions consists of instances in which the quantity of a vowel is lengthened when a verbal root is formed, directly and without any extraneous addition, into a noun. The alteration which the root-vowel sustains is prior to any inflexional additions being made. If any formative particle is added to a verbal root to convert it into a noun, the quantity of the root-vowel remains unchanged. The lengthening of the root-vowel to which I refer takes place only in (some of) those cases in which the verbal base itself is used as a noun. Thus, the verb *keḍ-u*, to destroy or to become destroyed, may become a verbal noun by the addition of the formative *di*—*e.g.*, *keḍudi*, destruction, in which event the root-vowel remains unaltered; but the verbal base may also be used without addition as a verbal noun, in which case *keḍ-u* is lengthened into *kêḍ-u*.

The following Tamil examples of the lengthening of each of the five primary vowels will suffice to illustrate this usage:—

From *paḍ-u*, to suffer, is formed *pâḍ-u*, a suffering; from *min*, to shine, *mîn*, a star; from *śuḍ-u*, to burn, *śûḍ-u*, heat; from *per-u*, to obtain, *pêr-u*, a benefit obtained; and from *koḷ*, to receive, *kôḷ*, reception.

I am not aware of the existence of a similar rule in any of the Scythian languages, but it is well known in Sanskrit (*e.g.*, compare *vach*, to speak, with *vâch*, a word; *mar* (*mri*), to die, with *mâra*, death). Nevertheless, I can scarcely think it likely that it is from Sanskrit that the Dravidian languages have derived a usage which prevails among them to so great an extent, and which has every appearance of being an original feature of their own. If it is not to be regarded as an independently developed peculiarity, arising out of the same mental and lingual habitudes as those out of which the corresponding Sanskrit usage was developed, it is probably to be regarded as a relic of those pre-Sanskrit influences of which many traces seem to be discoverable in these languages. In one particular the Dravidian rule differs from the Sanskrit. In Sanskrit the root-vowel is often not only lengthened, but changed, according to certain rules, into another—*e.g.*, from *vid*, to know, comes *vêda*, knowledge, the Veda; whereas in the Dravidian languages the rule is that the root-vowel is simply lengthened—*e.g.*, from *viḍ-u*, Tam. to set free, comes *vîḍ-u*, emancipation, a house (meaning probably a tax-free tenement).

Dr Gundert derives *vêr*, Tam. a root, from *vir*, the radical part of *viri*, to expand (compare *viral*, a finger). If this derivation be accepted as correct, as I think it may, it will furnish an instance of the operation of the Sanskrit law in question. Another derivation which I regard as still more probable is that of *nêr*, Tam. straight, from *nira*, to be level. These very rare exceptions, however, do not nullify the rule.

I must here notice a class of verbal nouns formed after this manner which are much used adjectivally. All Dravidian adjectives, grammatically considered, are nouns, but some of them are used indiscriminately either as nouns or as adjectives; some exclusively as adjectives, some exclusively as nouns. The three adjectives *pêr*, large, *kâr*, black, and *âr*, precious, furnish good illustrations of the class of verbal nouns to which I refer. *pêr* and *âr* are used exclusively as adjectives, *kâr* both as an adjective and as a noun. As an adjective it means black, as a noun, blackness, a cloud, the rainy season, &c. The radical forms of these words are also in use. These are *per-u*, to be large, *kar-u*, to be black, and *ar-u*, to be precious. The final *u* is, as usual, merely enunciative; the roots are *per*, *kar*, and *ar*. When we find a Dravidian root in two shapes, one with a longer, the other with a shorter vowel, it may generally be assumed, and can often be proved, that the shorter form is the radical one. Where both forms are in use, as in the case of these three words, the longer form is considered more elegant, and is much used in combinations, especially before words beginning with a vowel. It is to the shorter and probably more ancient form that *mei*, the formative of abstract nouns, like our English nouns ending in *ness*, is suffixed—*e.g.*, *aru-mei*, preciousness. The same change in the internal vowel of the root is apparent in some of the numerals. The radical forms of the Tamil numerals one and two seem to be *or* and *ir*, and these are often lengthened, when the numeral is used not as a substantive but as an adjective, into *ôr* and *îr*. There are also two forms of the numerals three, six, and seven (*mu* and *mû*, *aru* and *âru*, *eṛu* and *êṛu*), but in these instances it is the shorter forms that are used adjectivally. These shorter forms cannot stand alone, they can be used only as adjectives, whereas the longer ones are used as numeral substantives. The formation of verbal nouns by means of the lengthening of the root-vowel throws as much light on the original meaning of some adjectives, or nouns of quality, as we have seen that it does (in the previous part of this section) in the case of certain nouns exclusively used as substantives. For instance, *pâṛ* (Tam.) desolate, is evidently a verbal noun from *paṛ-u*, to grow old. To grow mature or ripe is a secondary meaning, from which we have *paṛam*, a ripe fruit. Another form used adjectivally is *paṛa*, old. A verb of the secondary formation is *paṛagu*, to become used to anything.

When the final consonant of the crude root belongs to this class of hard letters, it cannot be enunciated by Dravidian organs, whether the preceding vowel be long or short, without the aid of a final euphonic *u*. Thus *paśu*, Tam. to be green, when lengthened becomes, not *pâś* (as *pêr*, *kâr*, &c.), but *pâśu*, green. A change sometimes takes place in the internal vowel of this word which has been supposed to accord with the Sanskrit change of a short vowel into a longer one of a different order, and of a naturally long vowel into a diphthong, on the change of a noun or verbal-root into an adjective. *paśum*, green (another form of *paśu*), is changed in certain conjunctions into *peim*—*e.g.*, *peim-pon* (Tam.) excellent, literally green, gold. This change, however, is merely euphonic. It has already been shown that *ś*, when medial, has a tendency to soften into *y*, and then to disappear, and when this takes place the preceding and following vowels coalesce. In consequence of this tendency, *paśum* naturally becomes *payum*, and this again, by a change which is almost imperceptible in pronunciation, *peim*. We have a parallel instance of this in the noun *kaśuppu* (Tam.), bitterness, which may optionally be written and pronounced *keippu;* *kaśuppu* changing first into *kayuppu* and then into *keippu*. It should also be observed that *peim* has not in the least superseded *paśum*. The one may be optionally used instead of the other, and this proves that both forms are grammatically equivalent. I should be prepared to admit that in these and similar instances *y* may possibly be older than *ś*. The process, on this supposition, would have to be reversed; *pei*, properly *payu*, would become *paśu*, but the result would be the same. The change in the internal vowel would still be owing merely to the euphonic substitution of one consonant for another.

I may here remark that forms like *paśum*, green, do not appear to me to be derived, as Beschi, following native grammarians, supposed, from *pasumei*, greenness, by the omission of the final *ei;* for *mei*, not *ei*, is the particle by which abstract nouns of quality are formed, and the initial *m* is the most essential portion of that particle. *Paśum* is evidently derived from *paś*, the crude verbal root, with the addition of *um*, the sign of the aoristic future, by means of which it becomes an aoristic relative participle, a class of participles which the Dravidian tongues delight to use as adjectives.

4. Another class of internal changes appears in those instances in which Tamil shortens the quantity of the root-vowel in the preterite tense of verbs. This shortening is observed in Canarese also, but the following illustrations are furnished by Tamil—*e.g.*, *vê*, to burn, has for its preterite participle, not *vêndu*, but *vendu;* *nô*, to be in pain, has for its preterite, not *nôndu*, but *nondu;* *kâṇ*, to see, becomes, not *kâṇḍu*, but *kaṇḍu*. Another instance is *śâ*, to die, which takes not

śâttu, but *śettu*. The Malayâlam and Canarese form of this participle, *śattu* or *chattu*, represents the root-vowel more accurately than the Tamil. In some instances Tamil retains in the preterite the long vowel of the root, whilst Canarese shortens it—*e.g.*, *î*, to give, has for its preterite in Tamil *îndu*, in Canarese *ittu*.

There are two verbs in Tamil, *vâ*, to come, and *tâ*, to give, which involve peculiarities of which it is difficult to give a satisfactory explanation. Each of them is regularly conjugated, except in the preterite and imperative, as if from roots in *var* and *tar* (*e.g.*, *varugirên*, I come, *tarugirên*, I give); each takes the root with the long vowel without *r* for its imperative singular, and inserts *r* between this form of the root and the personal termination in the imperative plural (*e.g.*, *vâ*, come, *tâ*, give; *vârum*, come ye, *târum*, give ye); and each forms its preterite by shortening the vowel without inserting *r*, as if from roots in *vâ* and *tâ*, after the manner described in the previous paragraph (*e.g.*, *vandên*, I came, *tandên*, I gave, like *nondên*, I felt pain, from the root *nô*). Dr Pope, in his "Tamil Handbook," p. 52, considers the *r* of these verbs euphonically inserted to prevent hiatus and the whole of the tenses built upon the roots in *vâ* and *tâ*. I should have no objection to this view if the *r* made its appearance in the plural imperative only, as in *kârum*, protect ye, from *kâ*, to protect, the only other instance I know of *r* being used for this purpose in Tamil, and one which I have already mentioned in the chapter on "Prevention of Hiatus." On the other hand, the appearance of the roots in *var* and *tar*, in every part of the verb, except the preterite and the singular imperative alone, and in all the verbal nouns without exception (*e.g.*, *varal*, *varattu*, *varuttu*, *varudal*, *varavu*, *varugei*, each of them meaning a coming), leads to the conclusion that *var* and *tar* (whatever be the origin of their difference from *vâ* and *tâ*) are treated in Tamil as verbal themes. If *r* were not a portion of the root, we should expect to find the present, future, infinitive, negative voice, verbal nouns, &c., formed from *vâ* and *tâ*, with the addition of *g* or *v* as a formative suffix, as we find to be the case with the parallel verbs *nô*, &c. Compare *nôga*, infinitive; *nôvu*, *nôdal*, &c., verbal nouns; *nôgâ*, negative. The Canarese roots are *bar* and *tar*. In Telugu the imperative singular is *vâ*, the plural *rammu*, and this seems to me to confirm the supposition that *r* is an essential part of the root. If the Telugu *r* represented only the supposed euphonic *r* of the Tamil, the root-consonant would be left without any representative at all. It appears to me improbable, moreover, because unsupported by usage, that the Tamil *v* has been changed into *r* in Telugu. It seems more in accordance with usage to recognise here a change similar to that which has converted the

Tamil *iladu*, there is not, into *lêdu* in Telugu, and *irâ*, night, into *rê*. See the chapter on "Euphonic Displacement of Vowels." Notwithstanding this, I am not disposed to regard the forms in *vâ* and *tâ* as having found their way into the conjugation of the verbs by mistake. It is evident that *vâ* and *tâ*, not *var* and *tar*, are the themes from which the preterites *vanden* and *tanden* have been formed, and which we find pure in the imperatives. We seem therefore driven to adopt Dr Gundert's suggestion, that *vâ* and *var*, and *tâ* and *tar*, are alternative roots—perhaps it would be preferable to say, different forms of the same root. This supposition need not be relinquished in consequence of its being regarded as probable that *tâ* is identical with the Indo-European root *dâ*, to give. The Dravidian *tar* may have sprung from a related form of the same root, of which possibly a trace may survive in the Greek δῶρον and the Hebrew *tan*. I may add that though the change in the length of the vowel in the preterite has a grammatical significance, its change of length in the imperative, from *râ*, Tel. singular, to *rammu*, honorific singular (plural), and from *vâ*, Tam. singular, to High Tam. *vammin*, plural, appears to be purely euphonic.

The changes in the internal vowels of Dravidian roots exhibited in the last three classes of instances mentioned in this section as exceptions to the ordinary stability of the Dravidian root-vowels, evidently accord, as far as they go, with usages prevalent in the Indo-European languages, inasmuch as one of the classes referred to furnishes us with instances of the lengthening of the root-vowel, when the verb is converted into a noun, whilst the other classes furnish us with examples of the shortening of the interior vowels of the root on receiving the addition of inflexional particles, to compensate for the additional weight thus imposed on the root-vowel, or for the purpose of distinguishing one tense from another. In regard, however, to changes in root-vowels, it would be erroneous to suppose the rule of the Scythian languages essentially and universally dissimilar to the Indo-European. In the Scythian languages, as in the Dravidian, stability in the root-vowels is the rule, change the exception. But exceptions exist (*e.g.*, compare *olen*, Finnish, I am, from the root *ol*, to be, with *lienen*, if I be; compare also Hungarian *leven*, from the same root, being, with *volt*, having been, and *lenni*, to be). In consequence of the existence of such exceptions as these, it is impossible to erect the difference between the two families of language, in this particular, into a hard and fast law of distinction. It would also be unsafe on this ground alone, to disconnect the Dravidian languages from the languages of the Scythian group and to connect them with the Indo-European.

PART III.

THE NOUN.

In this section it will be my endeavour to investigate the nature and affections of the Dravidian noun, with the view of ascertaining its method of expressing the relations of gender and number, and the principles on which that method proceeds, together with the characteristics and origin of its case system, or system of means for expressing the relationship of nouns with other parts of speech. It will be shown at the close of the section on "The Verb," how derivative nouns are formed from verbal roots; and the various classes of participial nouns will then also be investigated.

SECTION I.—GENDER AND NUMBER.

1. Gender.

When the Indo-European laws of gender are compared with those of the Scythian group of tongues, it will appear that in this point, as in many others, the Dravidian languages accord more closely with the Scythian than with the Indo-European family. In all the more primitive Indo-European languages, not only are words that denote rational beings and living creatures regarded as masculine or feminine, according to the sex of the objects referred to, but also inanimate objects and even abstract ideas have similar sexual distinctions attributed to them; so that many nouns which denote objects naturally destitute of gender, and which ought therefore to be regarded as neuters, are treated by the grammars of those languages as if the objects they denote were males and females, and are fitted not with neuter, but with masculine or feminine case terminations, and with pronouns of corresponding genders. This peculiar system is a proof of the highly imaginative and poetical character of the Indo-European mind, by which principles of resemblance were discerned in the midst of the greatest differences, and all things that exist were not only animated, but personified. It is from this personification that most of the ancient mythologies are supposed to have arisen. A similar remark applies to the Semitic languages also, in which the same or a similar usage respecting gender prevailed. In the progress of the corruption of the primitive Indo-European languages, a less imaginative but more natural usage gained ground. Nevertheless, in a majority of the modern colloquial dialects of this family, both in Europe and in India, the gender of nouns is still an important and difficult section of the grammar, and a standing impediment in the way of the idiomatic use of those languages by foreigners.

On the other hand, in the Manchu, Mongolian, Turkish, and Finnish families of tongues—the principal families of the Scythian group—a law or usage respecting the gender of nouns universally prevails, which is generically different from that of the Indo-European and the Semitic idioms. In those families, not only are all things which are destitute of reason and life denoted by neuter nouns, but no nouns whatever—not even nouns which denote human beings—are regarded as in themselves masculine or feminine. All nouns, as such, are neuter, or rather are destitute of gender. In those languages there is no mark of gender inherent in, or inseparably annexed to, the nominative of any noun (the crude root being generally the nominative); and in none of the oblique cases, or postpositions used as case terminations, is the idea of gender at all involved. The unimaginative Scythians reduced all things, whether rational or irrational, animate or inanimate, to the same dead level, and regarded them all as impersonal. They prefixed to common nouns, wherever they found it necessary, some word denoting sex, equivalent to male or female, he or she; but they invariably regarded such nouns as in themselves neuters, and generally they supplied them with neuter pronouns. The only exceptions to this rule in the Scythian languages consist in a few words, such as God, man, woman, husband, wife, which are so highly instinct with personality that of themselves, and without the addition of any word denoting sex, they necessarily convey the signification of masculine or feminine.

When our attention is turned to the Dravidian languages we find that, whilst their rules respecting gender differ widely from those of the Indo-European group, they are not quite identical with those of the Scythian. It seems probable, however, that the particulars in which the Dravidian rules respecting gender differ from those of the Scythian languages, and evince a tendency in the Indo-European direction, are not the result of direct Sanskritic influences, of which no trace is perceptible in this department of Dravidian grammar, but have arisen either from the progressive mental cultivation of the Dravidians themselves, or from an inheritance of pre-Sanskritic elements.

Dravidian nouns are divided into two classes, which Tamil grammarians denote by the technical terms of high-caste and casteless nouns, but which are called by Telugu grammarians *mahât*, majors, and *a-mahât*, minors. High-caste nouns, or majors, are those which denote "the celestial and infernal deities and human beings," or, briefly, all things endowed with reason; and in all the Dravidian dialects (with a peculiar exception which is found only in Telugu and Gônd) nouns of this class are treated in the singular as masculines or feminines respectively, and in the plural as epicenes, that is, without distinguishing between masculines and feminines, but distinguishing both from the neuter. The other class of nouns, called casteless, or minors, includes everything which is destitute of reason, whether animate or inanimate. This classification of nouns, though not so imaginative as that of the Indo-European and Semitic tongues, is decidedly more philosophical; for the difference between rational beings and beings or things which are destitute of reason is more momentous and essential than any difference that exists between the sexes. The new Persian, which uses one pluralising particle for nouns that denote animated beings, and another and different one for things that are destitute of life, is the only non-Dravidian language in which nouns are classified in a manner which is in any degree similar to the Dravidian system.* The peculiar Dravidian law of gender which has now been described would appear to be a result of progressive intellectual and grammatical cultivation; for the masculine, feminine, and epicene suffixes which form the terminations of Dravidian high-caste nouns, are properly fragments of pronouns or demonstratives of the third person, as are also most of the neuter formatives. It may, indeed, be stated as a general rule that all primitive Dravidian nouns are destitute of gender, and that every noun or pronoun in which the idea of gender is formally expressed, being a compound word, is necessarily of later origin than the uncompounded primitives. The technical term by which such nouns are denoted by Tamil grammarians is *pagu-padam*, divisible words, *i.e.*, compounds. Hence the poetical dialects, which retain many of the primitive landmarks, are fond of discarding the ordinary suffixes of gender or rationality, and treating all nouns as far as possible as abstract neuters. Thus, in poetical Tamil *Dêv-u*, God, a crude

* This is not the only particular in which the Dravidian idiom attributes greater importance than the Indo-European to reason and the mind. *We* make our bodies the seat of personality. When we are suffering from any bodily ailment, we say "*I* am ill;" whereas the Dravidians denote the mind—the conscious *self* or *âtman*—when they say *I*, and therefore prefer to say, more philosophically, "my body is ill."

noun destitute of gender, is reckoned more classical than *Dêv-an*, the corresponding masculine noun. This word is a Sanskrit derivative; but the same tendency to fall back upon the old Scythian rule appears in the case of many other words which are primitive Dravidian nouns —*e.g.*, *irei*, a king, a word which is destitute of gender, is more classical than *irei-(v)-an*, the commoner form, which possesses the masculine singular termination.

In the modern Tamil spoken by the educated classes, the words which denote sun and moon (*śûriy-an* and *śandir-an*, derived from the Sanskrit *sûrya* and *chandra*) are of the masculine gender, in accordance with Sanskrit usage and with the principles of the Brahmanical mythology; but in the old Tamil of the poets and the peasants, *ñâyiru*, the sun, also *poṛudu*, and *tiṅgal*, the moon, also *nilâ*, all pure Dravidian words, are neuter. All true Dravidian names of towns, rivers, &c., are in like manner destitute of every mark of personality or gender. In some few instances Malayâlam and Canarese retain the primitive laws of gender more faithfully than Tamil. Thus, in the Tamil word *peiyan*, a boy, we find the masculine singular termination *an;* whereas Malayâlam (with which agrees Canarese) uses the older word *peidal*, a word (properly a verbal noun) which is destitute of gender, to which it prefixes in a thoroughly Scythian manner words that signify respectively male and female, to form compounds signifying boy and girl—*e.g.*, *âṇ peidal*, a boy, *peṇ peidal*, a girl. The nature and origin of the terminations which are used to signify gender in the various Dravidian dialects will be inquired into under the head of "Number," with the consideration of which this subject is inseparably connected. Under this head I restrict myself to a statement of the general principles respecting gender which characterise the Dravidian languages.

A peculiarity of Telugu, which appears also in Gônd, should here be mentioned. Whilst those dialects agree with the other members of the Dravidian family in regarding masculines and feminines, and both combined, as constituting in the plural a common or epicene gender, they differ from the other dialects in this respect that they are wholly or virtually destitute of a feminine singular, and instead of the feminine singular use the singular of the neuter. This rule includes in its operation pronouns and verbs as well as substantives, and applies to goddesses and queens, as well as to ordinary women. The Telugu possesses, it is true, a few forms which are appropriate to the feminine singular, but they are rarely used, and that only in certain rare combinations and conjunctures. He and it are the only pronouns of the third person singular which are ordinarily made use of by fifteen millions of the Telugu people; and the colloquial dialect does not even possess any pronoun, equivalent to our pronoun she, which is capable of being applied to women of the lower as well as of the higher classes. Ordinarily every woman is spoken of in Telugu as a chattel or a thing, or as we are accustomed to speak of very young children (*e.g.*, *it* did so and so), apparently on the supposition either that women are destitute of reason, or that their reason, like that of infants, lies dormant. Whilst each woman taken singly is treated by Telugu grammar as a chattel or as a child, women taken collectively are regarded with as much respect as by the other Dravidian dialects. In the plural they are honoured with the same high-caste or rational suffixes and pronouns that are applied to men and gods.

Canarese and Malayâlam agree in this point with Tamil, and regard women, not in the plural only but also in the singular, as pertaining to the class of rationals: accordingly in those languages there is a feminine singular pronoun equivalent to she, which corresponds in the principle of its formation to the masculine he. With those languages agrees Ku, which, though the near neighbour of Telugu and Gônd, pursues in this respect a politer course than either. In the idioms of the Tudas and Kôtas, the rude aborigines of the Nilgherry hills, there is, properly speaking, only one pronoun of the third person, and that is without distinction of gender or number. *atham*, remote, *itham*, proximate, mean indiscriminately he, she, it, they. The pronouns *avan*, *avaḷ*, he, she, are also occasionally used, but Dr Pope thinks they have been recently introduced from the Tamil and Canarese. This usage reminds one of the employment in the old Hebrew of the same pronoun, *hû*, to signify both he and she, and still more of the use of the reflexive pronoun of the Latin *se*, for all genders and numbers. Compare *wuh*, Hindustani, he, she.

2. Number.

The Dravidian languages recognise only two numbers, the singular and the plural. The dual, properly so called, is unknown, and there is no trace extant of its use at any previous period. Several of the languages of this family contain two plurals of the pronoun of the first person, one of which includes the party addressed as well as the party of the speaker, and which may therefore be considered as a species of dual, whilst the other excludes the party addressed. As, however, this peculiarity is restricted to the personal pronouns, it will be examined in that connection. Under the head of "Number," we shall inquire into the Dravidian mode of forming the masculine, feminine, and neuter singular, and the epicene and neuter plural.

(1.) *Masculine Singular.*—It has already been intimated that the formatives by which the gender of nouns is occasionally expressed are identical with the terminations of the demonstrative pronouns. From a very early period of the history of these languages, particles or formatives of gender were suffixed to the demonstrative bases, by the addition of which suffixes demonstrative pronouns were formed. Those formatives of gender were not originally appended to or combined with *substantive* nouns; but their use was gradually extended as their utility was perceived, and nouns which included the idea of gender were made to express that idea by suffixing the gender terminations of the pronouns, whereby they became appellative nouns. The manner in which all these suffixes are added will be sufficiently illustrated by the instance of the masculine singular.

The masculine singular suffix of the Tamil is *an, ân,* or *ôn. An,* the shorter formative, is that which appears in the demonstrative pronoun *avan* (*a-*(*v*)*-an*), he; and by suffixing any of these formatives to an abstract or neuter noun, the noun ceases to be abstract and becomes a concrete masculine-singular appellative. Thus *mûpp-u,* age, by the addition of *an* becomes *mûpp-an,* an elder, literally age-he, or age-man; and from *Tamiṛ* comes *Tamiṛ-an,* a Tamilian, a Tamil-man. These and similar nouns are called generically "compound or divisible words" by Tamil grammarians. They are obviously compounded of a noun—generally a noun of quality or relation—and a suffix of gender, which appears also to have been a noun originally.

In the instances which have been adduced, the suffix of gender is annexed to the nominative or *casus rectus:* but in many cases it is annexed to the oblique case or inflexional base, viz., to that form of the noun to which the case signs are suffixed, and which, when used by itself, has the meaning of the genitive or locative. When the inflexion, or oblique case, is employed instead of the nominative in compounds of this nature, it generally conveys a possessive or locative signification—*e.g.*, *maleiy*in*an* (*malei-*(*y*)-in-*an*), a mountaineer, literally a man of or on the mountain; *paṭṭin*attan (*paṭṭin'*-att'*ân*), a citizen, literally a man of or in the city. Sometimes, however, the inflexional "in" is merely added euphonically—*e.g.*, there is no difference in meaning between *villan* (*vill-an*), a bowman, and *villinan* (*vill'*-in-*an*), which is considered a more elegant form. Words of this description are in some grammars called adjectives; but they are never regarded as such by any native grammarians: they cannot be simply prefixed for the purpose of qualifying other words, and it is evident from their construction that they are merely appellative nouns.

A subdivision of appellatives consists of words in which the suffixes of gender are annexed to adjectival forms—*e.g.*, *koḍiya-n*, a cruel man. I regard words of this class as participial nouns, and they will be investigated in the part on "The Verb," under the head of "Appellative Verbs;" but whatever be the nature of *koḍiya* (the first part of the compound), *koḍiya-n* is certainly not an adjective, for before it can be used adjectivally we must append to it the relative participle *âna*, that is—*e.g.*, *koḍiyan-âna*, that is a cruel man; and as the compound, cruel man, cannot be called an adjective in English, neither is *koḍiyan* an adjective in Tamil: it is properly an appellative noun. It may be said that the neuter plural of this word, viz., *koḍiya*, may be prefixed adjectivally to any substantive; but *koḍiya*, cruel things, the neuter plural of *koḍiyan*, is not really identical with the adjective *koḍiya*, cruel. It is totally distinct from it, though identical in appearance. The *a* of the former word is the neuter suffix of plurality; whereas the *a* of the latter is that of the possessive case and of the relative participle, as will be shown at the close of this part (see "Adjectival Formatives") and in the part on "Verbs."

Another species of Tamil appellative nouns is said by Beschi to be formed by annexing suffixes of gender to verbal roots—*e.g.*, *ôduvân*, a reader, from *ôdu*, to read; but this, I believe, is an error. Those words are to be regarded as participial nouns, and *ôduvân* is literally he who will read, *i.e.*, he who is accustomed to read. In the same manner, *ôdinan* is the participial noun of the preterite tense, and means he who read or is accustomed to read: *ôdugindravan*, the corresponding present participial noun, he who reads, belongs to the same class; and these forms are not to be confounded with appellative nouns properly so called. On the other hand, such words as *kâppan*, a protector, are true appellatives; but *kâppan* is not formed from the future tense of the verb (though *kâppân* means he will protect), but from *kâppu*, protection, a derivative noun, of which the final and formative *ppu* is from the same origin as the corresponding final of *mûppu*, old age. See the concluding section of the part on "The Verb."

The suffixes of gender which form the terminal portion of appellative nouns vary somewhat in form, but they are one and the same in origin, and their variations are merely euphonic. It is the vowel only that varies, never the consonant. When a neuter noun ends with a vowel which is essential to it, and is incapable of elision, and also when a noun happens to be a long monosyllable, *ân*, or in poetry *ôn*, is more commonly suffixed than *an*. In some cases *avan*, he, the full demonstrative pronoun, is suffixed instead of its termination only, and this mode is thought peculiarly elegant. Thus, from *vil* or *vill-u*, a bow, we may form *vill-an*, *vill-ân*, and *vill-ôn*, an archer, a bowman, and also *vill-avan*. Indeed, *ân* and *ôn* have evidently been formed, not from *an*, but from $a+v+n$, by the softening of the euphonic *v*, and the coalescence of the vowels. This corruption of *avan* into *ân* appears systematically in the third person masculine singular of the colloquial Tamil verb—*e.g.*, *pô-(n)-ân* (not *pô-(n)-avan*), he went.

The Canarese masculine singular suffix *anu* is identical with the Tamil *an*, the addition of *u* being merely a phonetic necessity of the modern dialect. In the older Canarese, the termination which was used was *am*, a particle which is to be regarded as the equivalent of *an*, *n* and *m* being interchangeable nasals. Malayâlam is in this particular perfectly identical with Tamil. The corresponding Telugu masculine singular formative is *ḍ-u*, *uḍ-u*, or *aḍ-u;* or rather *ṉḍ-u*, *uṉḍ-u*, or *aṉḍu*, the obscure *ṉ* being always pronounced, and being probably an essential part of the original form of the particle, and by suffixing the same formative to any substantive noun, it becomes a masculine singular—*e.g.*, *mag-aṉḍu*, a husband, a word which seems to be identical in origin with the Tamil *mag-an*, a son (the primitive and proper meaning of each word being a male). The masculine singular suffix of Telugu often takes the shape of *uṉḍ-u*, and in like manner the epicene plural suffix, which is in Tamil *ar-u*, is often *ur-u* in Telugu; but in these instances *a* changes into *u* through attraction.

As Tamil forms masculine appellatives by suffixing the demonstrative pronoun *avan*, so does Telugu sometimes suffix its full demonstrative pronoun *vâṉḍu* — *e.g.*, *chinna-vâṉḍu*, a boy (Tamil, *śinna-(v)-an*), literally he who is little. It is probable that the Telugu masculine singular suffix was originally *an* or *an-u*, as in Tamil-Canarese. *aṉḍu*, *uṉḍ-u*, or *ṉḍu*, is found only in the nominative in correct Telugu, and it is replaced in all the oblique cases by *ani* or *ni;* and that this *ni* is not merely an inflexional increment, but the representative of an old masculine singular suffix, appears on comparing it with *ri*, the corresponding oblique case suffix of the masculine-feminine plural, which is certainly formed from *ar-u*. When *vâniki*, to him, is compared with its plural *vâriki*, to them, it is evident that the former corresponds as closely to the Tamil *avanukku* as the latter to *avarukku;* and consequently that the *ni* of *vâniki* must be significant of the masculine singular. Probably the same termination survives in the demonstrative, *âyana*, he, a form which is more rarely used than *vâṉḍu*.

The Telugu *ṉḍ* being thus found to be identical with the Tam., Can., Mal. *ṉ*, and the old Can. *m*, the masculine suffixes *an*, *am*, and *aṉḍu* are also found to be identical. It is more difficult to determine the origin of this suffix *an*. *an* is sometimes used in Tam. and Mal. instead of *am* as a formative of neuter nouns, as will be shown hereafter in the section on the Nominative—*e.g.*, *palan* (Sans. *phala*), fruit, instead of *palam;* but I cannot see how this can be identical in origin with the suffix *an* which denotes the masculine, the Dravidian masculine being a distinctive one—that is, not merely a grammatical term, but a sign of sex. On looking around for an explanation of the origin of the masculine suffix, it appears to me that the Ku, though one of the most barbarous of the Dravidian dialects, throws more light than any other upon this point. It forms its demonstrative pronouns in a simple and truly primitive manner by prefixing *â*, the demonstrative base, to common nouns which signify *man* and *woman*. These nouns are *âñ-u*, a man, and *âl-u*, a woman; and *ââñ-u* (compare Tam. *a(v)an*), literally that man, is used to signify he, and *ââlu* (compare Tam. *a(v)aḷ*), that woman, to signify she. The Ku *âñ-u*, a man, seems certainly identical with the Tam. noun *âṇ*, a male, and probably also with *âḷ*, a man, a person. In the use to which this primitive root is put in the Ku word *â-âñ-u*, we may see, I think, the origin of *an*, the suffix of the masculine singular in most of the Dravidian dialects. The final *u*, of the Ku word *âñ-u*, being merely euphonic, the root appears to be *âñ* or *ân;* and as *ṇ* and *n* have been shown to be interchangeable, *ân* must be regarded as only another form of *âṇ*. *ṇ*, again, is not only often euphonised by suffixing *ḍu* (*e.g.*, *peṇ*, Tam. a female, colloquially and poetically *peṇḍ-u*), but it is also sometimes directly changed into *ḍ*, of which we have an instance in the classical Tamil *peḍ-ei*, a hen, a word which is derived by this process from, and is identical with *peṇ*, a female. Hence, the Telugu suffix *aṇḍ-u* might naturally be derived from an older form in *aṇ*, if it should appear that that form existed; and that it did exist, appears from the vulgar use to the present day of *ṇ* instead of *n* in some of the oblique cases (*e.g.*, *vâṇṇi*, him, instead of *vâni*), and from the *half anusvâra*, or obscure nasal, which precedes *ḍu* itself—*e.g.*, *vânḍu*, for *vâḍu*, he. A close connection appears thus to be established between the Tamil-Canarese *an* and the Telugu *aḍ-u*, through the middle point *aṇ*.

The only difficulty in the way of the perfect identification of the formative *an* with the Ku *añu*, a man, and with the Tamil *âṇ*, a male, lies in the length of the vowel of the latter words. Here again Ku comes to our assistance; for we find that the vowel was euphonically shortened in some instances in the very dialect in which the origin of the word itself was discovered. In Ku the *â* of *âñ-u* is long, both when it is used as an isolated word and in the demonstratives *ââñ-u*, he, and *ââl-u*, she; but when the demonstrative pronoun is appended to, and combined with, the relative participle of the verb, so as to form with it a participial noun, the *â* of *âñ-u* is shortened into *a*, and in this shortened form the connection of the Ku formative with the Tamil-Canarese is seen to be complete. Compare the Ku participial noun *gităñ-u*, he who did, with the corresponding Canarese *gêyidăn-u; gitâr-u*, Ku, they who did, with *gêyidar-u*, Can., and also *gital-u*, Ku, she who did, with *gêyidaḷ-u*, Can.

(2.) *Feminine Singular.*—Though Telugu and Gônd generally use the neuter singular to supply the place of the feminine singular, the other Dravidian dialects possess and constantly use a feminine singular formative which is quite distinct from that of the neuter. This formative is *aḷ* in Tamil, Malayâlam, and old Canarese, and by suffixing the sign of gender to the demonstrative base, the feminine singular demonstrative pronoun *avaḷ* (*a*(*v*)*aḷ*), she, is formed—a word which perfectly corresponds to *avan* (*a*(*v*)*an*), he. A numerous class of feminine singular appellative nouns is formed by suffixing the same particle to abstract or neuter nouns in their crude state—*e.g.*, compare *mag-aḷ*, Tam. a daughter, with *mag-an*, a son; *ill-âḷ*, housewife, a wife, and *ill-ân*, a husband, are formed from the addition of the pronouns *avaḷ* and *avan* (euphonised into *âḷ* and *ân*) to *il*, a home.

Telugu, in some connections, uses a feminine singular formative which appears to be identical with that of Tamil-Canarese. That formative is *âl-u*, which is used by Ku more largely than by Telugu; and its identity with Tamil-Canarese *aḷ*, will be found to furnish us with a clue to the origin and literal meaning of the latter. As *âñ-u*, in Ku, means a man, so *âl-u* means a woman: *ââl-u*, she, is literally that woman. The same word *âl-u*, means a woman, a wife, in poetical and vulgar Telugu also; and in Gônd there is a word which is apparently allied to it, *âr*, a woman. Even in Sanskrit we meet with *âli*, a woman's female friend. It is evident that *âl-u* would be shortened into *al* as easily as *âñ-u* into *an*, and the constant occurrence of a cerebral *ḷ* in Tamil and Canarese, where Telugu has the medial *l*, fully accounts for the change of the one semi-vowel into the other. The unchanged form of this suffix appears in Telugu in such words as *manama-*(*r*)*-âlu*, a granddaughter, compared with *manama-ṉḍu*, a grandson. The abbreviation of the vowel of the feminine suffix, which is characteristic of Tamil and Canarese, is exemplified in Telugu also, in the words *maradal-u*, a niece, and *kôḍal-u*, a daughter-in-law; in which words the feminine suffix *al-u*, is evidently identical both with Tamil-Canarese *aḷ* or *aḷ-u*, and also with *âl-u*, the older and more regular form of this suffix, which is capable of being used by itself as a noun. Probably the Telugu *âḍ-u*, adj. female, though now treated as a different word, is identical in origin with *âl-u*, through the very common interchange of *ḍ* and *ḷ*; an illustration of which we have in *kei-(y)-âḷu*, Tam. to use, which is converted in the colloquial dialect to *kei-(y)-âḍu*.* The feminine singular suffix *aḷ* appears in Tamil and Canarese in the terminations of verbs as well as in those of pronouns. Telugu, on the other hand, which uses the neuter demonstrative instead of the feminine singular, uses the final fragment of the same demonstrative as the termination of the feminine singular of its verb. It may be remarked that in some of the Caucasian dialects, *n* and *l* are used as masculine and feminine terminals, exactly as in Tamil—*e.g.*, in Avar, *emen*, is father, *evel*, is mother.

There is another mode of forming the feminine singular of appellative nouns, which is much used in all the Dravidian dialects, and which may be regarded as especially characteristic of Telugu. It consists in suffixing the Telugu neuter singular demonstrative, its termination, or a modification of it, to any abstract or neuter noun. The neuter singular demonstrative being used by Telugu instead of the feminine singular (it for she), this neuter suffix has naturally in Telugu supplied the place of a feminine suffix; and though in the other dialects the feminine pronouns are formed by means of feminine suffixes, not by those of the neuter, yet the less respectful Telugu usage has crept into the department of their appellative nouns. In Tamil, this neuter-feminine suffix is *atti* or *tti*. This will appear on comparing *veḷḷâḷ-atti*, a woman of the cultivator caste, with *veḷḷâḷ-an*, a man of the same caste; *oru-tti*, one woman, *una*, with *oru-(v)-an*, one man, *unus;* and *vaṇṇâ-tti*, a washerwoman, with *vaṇṇâ-n*, a washerman. *tt*, a portion of this suffix, is sometimes erroneously used in vulgar Tamil as a component element in the masculine appellative noun *oruttan*, one man, instead of the classical and correct *oruvan*. With this exception its use is exclusively feminine. The same suffix is *iti* or *ti* in Canarese—*e.g.*, *arasiti*, a queen (corresponding to the Tamil *râśâtti*), *okkalati*, a farmer's wife. The Telugu uses *adi* or *di*—*e.g.*, *kômaṭi-(y)-adi* or

---

* It is more doubtful whether the Tuḷu *âḷ*, Gônd-Telugu *âl-u*, a woman, is allied to the Tamil common noun *âḷ*, a person; and yet the existence of some alliance appears to me probable. *âḷ* appears to mean properly a subject person, a servant—male or female—a slave. It is derived from *âḷ* (Tel. *êl-u*), to rule, and this seems a natural enough origin for a word intended to signify a Hindu woman. The ordinary Tamil word which signifies a woman is *peṇ*, the literal signification of which is said to be desire, from the verbal root *peṇ*, to desire; but the word is generally restricted to mean, a young woman, a bride. Hence, taking into consideration the subject position of women in India, the word *âḷ*, one who is subject to rule, a person whose sole duty it is to obey, is as natural a derivation for a word signifying a woman, a female, as *peṇ;* and perhaps more likely to come into general use as a suffix of the feminine singular. Dr Gundert has no doubt of the identity of the Tamil *âḷ* and the Telugu *âlu:* their identity, however, is not admitted by Mr C. P. Brown.

komaṭi-di, a woman of the Komti caste; *mâla-di*, a Paria woman; *chinna-di*, a girl. It seems to me evident, not only that all these suffixes are identical, but that the Telugu form of the demonstrative neuter singular, viz., *adi*, it, which is used systematically by Telugu to signify she, is the root from whence they have all proceeded.

Another feminine singular suffix of appellatives occasionally used in the Dravidian languages may possibly have been derived from the imitation of Sanskrit. It consists in the addition of *i* to the crude or neuter noun; and it is only in quantity that this *i* differs from the long *ī*, which is so much used by Sanskrit as a feminine suffix. In the majority of cases it is only in connection with Sanskrit derivatives that this suffix is used; but it has also come to be appended to some pure Dravidian nouns—*e.g.*, *talei-(v)-i*, Tam. a lady (compare *talei-(v)-an*, a lord), from *talei*, a head; compare also the Gônd *perdgal*, a boy, with *perdgi*, a girl. This feminine suffix is not to be confounded with *i*, a suffix of agency, which is much used in the formation of nouns of agency and operation, and which is used by all genders indiscriminately. See "Verbal Derivatives," at the close of the part on "The Verb."

3. *Neuter Singular.*—There is but little which is worthy of remark in the singular forms of neuter Dravidian nouns. Every Dravidian noun is naturally neuter, or destitute of gender, and it becomes masculine or feminine solely in virtue of the addition of a masculine or feminine suffix. When abstract Sanskrit nouns are adopted by the Dravidians, the neuter nominative form of those nouns (generally ending in *am*) is preferred. Sanskrit masculines, with the exception of those which denote rational beings, are made to terminate in *am*, being treated as neuters; and there are also some neuter nouns of pure Dravidian origin which end in *am*, or take *am* as their formative. The Dravidian termination *am* is not to be regarded, however, as a sign of the neuter, or a neuter suffix, though such is often its character in Sanskrit. It is merely one of a numerous class of formatives, of which much use is made by the Dravidian dialect, and by the addition of which verbal roots are transformed into derivative nouns. Such formatives are to be regarded as forming a part of the noun itself, not of the inflexional additions. See "Verbal Derivatives," at the close of the section on "The Verb."

All animated beings destitute of reason are placed by Dravidian grammarians in the caste-less, or neuter class, and the nouns that denote such animals, both in the singular and in the plural, are uniformly regarded as neuter or destitute of gender, irrespective of the animal's sex. If it happen to be necessary to distinguish the sex of any animal that is included in this class, a separate word signifying male or female, he or she, is prefixed. Even in such cases, however, the pronoun with which the noun stands in agreement is neuter, and notwithstanding the specification of the animal's sex, the noun itself remains in the caste-less or neuter class. For this reason, suffixes expressive of the neuter gender, whether singular or plural, were not much required by Dravidian nouns. The only neuter singular suffix of the Dravidian languages, which is used in the same manner as the masculine *an* or *aḍu*, and the feminine *aḷ*, is that which constitutes the termination of the neuter singular of demonstrative pronouns and appellative nouns. This pronoun is in Tamil, Canarese, and Malayâlam, *adu*, that, *idu*, this; in Telugu *adi*, *idi*; in Gônd *ad*, *id*.

In the Tuḷu pronoun the *d* has dropped out. The pronoun 'that' is *avu*. Dr Gundert considers this simply a corruption, and he shows that the language had its neuter singular in *d* originally, like its sister languages, by adducing such words as *att'*, it is not, which was evidently *aldu*, originally, like the Tamil *allaud* (old Tam. *andru* = *aldu*), in which the suffix *du* or *d* is the formative of the neuter singular.

The same neuter demonstrative, or in some instances its termination only, is used in the conjugation of Dravidian verbs as the sign of the neuter singular of each tense, and in Telugu as the sign of the feminine singular also. The bases of the Dravidian demonstratives being *a* and *i* (*a* remote, *i* proximate), that part of each pronoun which is found to be annexed to those demonstrative vowels is evidently a suffix of number and gender; and as the final vowels of *ad-u*, *ad-i*, *id-u*, *id-i*, are merely euphonic, and have been added only for the purpose of helping the enunciation, it is evident that *d* alone constitutes the sign of the neuter singular. This view is confirmed by the circumstance that *d* never appears in the neuter plural of this demonstrative, but is replaced by *ei*, *u*, *i*, or short *a*, with a preceding euphonic *v* or *n*—*e.g.*, compare *adu* (*a-d-u*), Tam. that, with *ava* (*a-(v)-a*), Malayâlam, those. It will be shown afterwards that this final *a* is a sign of the neuter plural.

Appellative nouns which form their masculine singular in Tamil in *an*, and their feminine singular in *aḷ*, form their neuter singular by annexing *du*, with such euphonic changes as the previous consonant happens to require—*e.g.*, *nalla-du*, a good thing; *al-du*, euphonically *andru*, a thing that is not; *periya-du* or *peri-du*, great, a great thing. This neuter singular suffix *d* is largely used in all the dialects in the formation of verbal nouns—*e.g.*, *pôgira-du*, Tam. the act of going, *pôna-du*, the having gone, *pôva-du*, the being about to go. This form has been represented by some, but erroneously, as an infinitive: it is a concrete verbal or participial noun of the neuter gender, which has gradually come to be used as an abstract.

The affinities of the neuter singular suffix in *d* appears to be exclusively Indo-European, and they are found especially in the Indo-European pronouns and pronominals. We may observe this suffix in the Sanskrit *tat*, that; in *tyat*, that; in *adas*, a weakened form of *adat*, that; in *êtat*, this; and in the relative pronoun *yat*, who, which, what. We find it also in the Latin *illud*, *id*, &c. (compare the Latin *id* with the Tamil *id-u*, this); and in our English demonstrative neuter it (properly hit), the neuter of he, as also in what, the neuter of who. Compare also the Vedic it, an indeclinable pronoun, described as "a petrified neuter," which combines with the negative particle *na* to form *nêt*, if not, apparently in the same manner as in Telugu the aoristic neuter *lêdu*, there is not, is compounded of the negative *la* for *ila*, and the suffix *du*. Though the Dravidian languages appear in this point to be allied to the Sanskrit family, it would be unsafe to suppose that they borrowed this neuter singular suffix from Sanskrit. The analogy of the Dravidian neuter plural in *a*, which though Indo-European, is foreign to Sanskrit, and that of the remote and proximate demonstrative vowels *a* and *i*, which though known to the Indo-European family, are used more systematically and distinctively by the Dravidian languages than by any other class of tongues, would lead to the supposition that these particles were inherited by the Dravidian family, in common with Sanskrit, from a primitive pre-Sanskrit source.

The Plural: Principles of Pluralisation.—In the primitive Indo-European tongues, the plural is carefully distinguished from the singular; and with the exception of a few nouns of quantity which have the form of the singular, but a plural signification, the number of nouns is always denoted by their inflexional terminations. Nouns whose number is indefinite, like our modern English sheep, are unknown to the older dialects of this family. In the languages of the Scythian group a looser principle prevails, and number is generally left indefinite, so that it is the connection alone which determines whether a noun is singular or plural. Manchu restricts the use of its pluralising particle to words which denote animated beings: all other words are left destitute of signs of number. Even the Tartar, or Oriental Turkish, ordinarily pluralises the pronouns alone, and leaves the number of other nouns indeterminate. In Brahui also, the number of nouns is generally left undefined; and when it is desired to attach to any noun the idea of plurality, a word signifying many or several, is prefixed to it. Notwithstanding this rule, Brahui verbs are regularly pluralised; and the number of an indeterminate noun may often be ascertained from the number of the verb with which it agrees.

With respect to principles of pluralisation, most of the Dravidian tongues differ considerably from the Indo-European family, and accord on the whole with the languages of the Scythian stock. The number of Tamil nouns, especially of neuter nouns, is ordinarily indefinite; and it depends upon the connection whether any noun is to be regarded as singular or as plural. It is true that when more persons than one are referred to, the high-caste or rational pronouns that are used are almost invariably plural, and that even neuter nouns themselves are sometimes pluralised, especially in polished prose compositions; but the poets and the peasants, the most faithful guardians of antique forms of speech, rarely pluralise the neuter, and are fond of using the singular noun in an indefinite singular-plural sense, without specification of number, except in so far as it is expressed by the context. This rule is adhered to with especial strictness by Tamil, which in this, as in many other particulars, seems to exhibit most faithfully the primitive condition of the Dravidian languages. Thus in Tamil, *mâḍu*, ox, means either an ox or oxen, according to the connection; and even when a numeral which necessarily conveys the idea of plurality is prefixed, idiomatic speakers prefer to retain the singular or indefinite form of the noun. Hence they will rather say, *nâlu mâḍu mêygiṙadu*, literally four ox is feeding, than *nâlu mâḍugaḷ mêygindrana*, four oxen are feeding, which would sound stiff and pedantic. Telugu is an exception to this rule. In it neuter nouns are as regularly pluralised as masculines or feminines, and the verbs with which they agree are pluralised to correspond. In Tuda, on the other hand, the only words that appear to be ever pluralised are the pronouns and the verbs which have pronouns for their nominatives. In Coorg neuter nouns have no plural. We find a similar usage occasionally even in English, as Mr C. P. Brown points out, in the military phrases, a hundred *foot*, three hundred *horse*.

In Tamil, even when a neuter noun is pluralised by the addition of a pluralising particle, the verb is rarely pluralised to correspond; but the singular form of verb is still used for the plural—the number of the neuter singular being naturally indeterminate. This is almost invariably the practice in the speech of the lower classes; and the colloquial style of even the best educated classes exhibits a similar characteristic. Tamil contains, it is true, a plural form of the third person neuter of the verb; but the use of this neuter plural verb is ordinarily restricted to poetry, and even in poetry the singular number both of neuter nouns and of the verbs that correspond is much more commonly used than the plural. It should be remarked also, that the third person neuter of the Tamil future, or aorist, is altogether destitute of a plural. In this particular, therefore, the Tamil verb is more decidedly Scythian in character than the noun itself. Max Müller supposes that a Dravidian neuter plural noun, with its suffix of plurality, is felt to be a compound (like animal-mass for animals, or stone-heap for stones), and that it is on this account that it is followed by a verb in the singular. The explanation I have given seems to me preferable. The number of all Dravidian nouns, whether high-caste or caste-less, was originally indefinite: the singular, the primitive condition of every noun, was then the only number which was or could be recognised by verbal or nominal inflexions, and plurality was left to be inferred from the context. As civilisation made progress, the plural made its appearance, and effected a permanent settlement in the department of high-caste or masculine-feminine nouns and verbs; whilst the number of caste-less or neuter nouns, whether suffixes of plurality were used or not, still remained generally unrecognised by the verb in the Dravidian languages. Even where the form exists it is little used. It is curious, that in this point the Greek verb exhibits signs of Scythian influences, or of the influences of a culture lower than its own, viz., in the use of the singular verb for the neuter plural.

The Dravidian languages ordinarily express the idea of singularity or oneness, not by the addition of a singular suffix to nouns and pronouns, or by the absence of the pluralising particle (by which number is still left indeterminate), but by prefixing the numeral adjective one. Thus, *mâḍu*, Tam. ox, does not mean exclusively either an ox or oxen, but admits of either meaning according to circumstances; and if we wish distinctly to specify singularity, we must say *oru mâḍu*, one or a certain ox. Europeans in speaking the Dravidian dialects use this prefix of singularity too frequently, misled by their habitual use of an indefinite article in their own tongues. They also make too free a use, in Tamil, of the distinctively plural form of neuter nouns, when the objects to which they wish to refer are plural. Occasionally, when euphony or usage recommend it, this is done by Tamilians themselves, but as a general rule the neuter singular is used instead of the neuter plural, and that not in Tamil only, but also in almost all the languages of the Scythian group.

Another important particular in which the Indo-European languages differ from the Scythian is, that in the former the plural has a different set of case-terminations from the singular, by the use of which the idea of plurality is not separately expressed, but is compounded with that of case-relation; whilst in the latter family the plural uses the same set of case-terminations as the singular, and plurality is expressed by a sign of plurality common to all the cases, which is inserted between the singular, or crude form of the noun, and the case-terminations. I call it a sign of plurality, not a noun denoting plurality, for in many instances only a fraction of a word, perhaps only a single letter, remains. In the Indo-European languages, each inflexion includes the twofold idea of number and of case. Thus there is a genitive singular and a genitive plural, each of which is a complex idea; but there is no inflexion which can be called genitive, irrespective of number; and in many instances (this of the genitive being one) there is no apparent connection between the case-termination of the singular and that which is used in, and which constitutes, the plural.

In those few cases in which the sign of number and the sign of case seem to have been originally distinct, and to have coalesced into one, the sign of case seems to have preceded that of number—*e.g.*, the Gothic plural accusative *ns* is derived from *n* or *m*, the sign of the accusative singular, and *s*, the sign of plurality. When the Scythian family of languages is examined, it is found that each of their case-signs is fixed and unalterable. It expresses the idea of case and nothing more, and is the same in the plural as in the singular, with the exception of those few trivial changes which are required by euphony. The sign of plurality also is not only distinct from the case-sign, but is one and the same in all the cases. It is an unalterable postposition—a fixed quantity; and it is not post-fixed to the case-sign, much less compounded with it, as in the Indo-European languages, but is prefixed to it. It is attached directly to the root itself, and followed by the signs of the different cases.

In the Dravidian languages a similar simplicity and rigidity of structure characterises the use of the particles of plurality. They are added directly to the crude base of the noun (which is equivalent to the nominative singular), and are the same in each of the oblique cases as in the nominative. The signs of case are the same in the plural as in the singular, the only real difference being that in the singular they are suffixed to the crude noun itself, in the plural to the pluralising particle, after the addition of that particle to the crude noun. The only exception to this rule is in Tuḷu, in which *a*, the sign of the genitive, keeps its place in the singular, as in the other dialects, but is weakened to *e* in the plural.

In Hungarian, *hâz*, a house, is declined as follows:—

Singular.		Plural.	
Nom.	*hâz.*	Nom.	*hâzak.*
Gen.	*hâz-nak.*	Gen.	*hâz-ak-nak.*
Dat.	*hâz-nak.*	Dat.	*hâz-ak-nak.*
Acc.	*hâz-at.*	Acc.	*hâz-ak-at.*

In Tamil, *manei*, a house, is declined as follows:—

Singular.		Plural.	
Nom.	*manei.*	Nom.	*manei-gaḷ*
Acc.	*manei-(y)-ei.*	Acc.	*manei-gaḷ-ei.*
Instr.	*manei-(y)-âl.*	Instr.	*manei-gaḷ-âl.*
Conj.	*manei-(y)-ôḍu.*	Conj.	*manei-gaḷ-ôḍu.*
Dat.	*manei-kku.*	Dat.	*manei-gaḷ-(u)-kku.*
Ablat.	*manei-(y)-il-irundu.*	Ablat.	*manei-gaḷ-il-irundu.*
Gen.	*manei-(y)-inadu.*	Gen.	*manei-gaḷ-inadu.*
Locat.	*manei-(y)-iḍatt-il.*	Locat.	*manei-gaḷ-iḍatt-il.*
Voc.	*manei-(y)-ê.*	Voc.	*manei-gaḷ-ê.*

(See Paradigm of Nouns.)

We here see that the particular signs which are used to express plurality and as exponents of case, in Tamil and Hungarian respectively, are taken from the resources of each language; whilst the manner in which they are used in both languages is precisely the same.

The neuter of Dravidian nouns being identical with the crude base, when the pluralising particle is attached to a neuter noun, it is attached to it not as a substitute for any suffix of the singular, but directly and without any change: it is attached to it pure and simple. In the case of masculine and feminine nouns, including pronouns, a somewhat different method of pluralisation is necessary. The singular of the masculine and feminine is formed, as has already been pointed out, by the addition to the root of particles denoting a male or a female. Hence, to pluralise those nouns, it is necessary either to add a pluralising particle to the masculine and feminine suffixes, or to substitute for those suffixes an epicene pluralising particle. In all the Dravidian languages the primitive plan of pluralising these two classes of nouns seems to have been that of substituting for the masculine and feminine singular suffixes a suffix of plurality which applied in common to men and women, without distinction of sex. This is the mode which is still used in most of the dialects; but in Telugu it retains its place only in connection with pronouns and verbs, and has disappeared from substantives, which form their plural by means of a neuter suffix.

The classification of Dravidian nouns into rationals and irrationals has already been explained; it has also been shown that in the singular, the masculine of rational nouns is distinguished from the feminine. In the plural both those genders are combined; the high-caste particle of plurality, or plural of rational beings, is the same for both genders, and includes men and women, gods and goddesses, without distinction of sex. Irrational or neuter nouns have a particle of plurality different from this, and in general peculiar to themselves. Hence the Dravidian languages have one form of the plural which may be called epicene or masculine-feminine, and another which is ordinarily restricted to the neuter; and by means of these pluralising particles, gender and number are conjointly expressed in the plural by one and the same termination. The masculine-feminine plural expresses the idea of plurality conjointly with that of rationality; the neuter plural, the idea of plurality conjointly with that of irrationality.

Arrangements of this kind for giving combined expression to gender and number are very commonly observed in the Indo-European family; and even the plan of classing masculines and feminines together in the plural, without distinction of sex, is also very common. Thus, the Sanskrit plural in *as* is masculine-feminine; so is the Latin plural in *es*, and the Greek in *ες*. The chief difference with respect to this point between the Dravidian system and the Indo-European one lies in this, that in the Dravidian languages the masculine-feminine particle of plurality is carefully restricted to rational beings; whereas in the Indo-European languages irrational and even inanimate objects are often complimented with inflexional forms and pluralising particles which imply the existence, not only of vitality, but even of personality—that is, of self-conscious intelligence. A still closer analogy to the Dravidian system is that which is exhibited by the New Persian. That dialect possesses two pluralising particles, of which one, *ân*, is suffixed to nouns denoting living beings,* the other, *hâ*, to nouns denoting inanimate objects. The particles employed in Persian are different from those which are used in the Dravidian languages, but the prin-

---

* Bopp derives *ân*, the New Persian plural of animated beings, from the Sanskrit *ân*, the masculine plural accusative. I am inclined with Sir Henry Rawlinson to connect this particle with the Chaldaic and Cuthite plural *ân*, allied to *îm* and *în* (*e.g.*, *anân*, Chald. we); the New Persian being undoubtedly tinged with Chaldæo-Assyrian elements, through its connection with the Pehlvi. One is tempted to connect with this suffix our modern English plural suffix *en*, in breth*ren*. Bopp, however, holds that this *en* is an ancient formative suffix originally used by the singular as well as the plural. Compare mediæval Eng. *brethren* with Anglo-Saxon *brôdhra*. The Dutch use both *broeders*, the older form, and *broederin*, the more modern.

ciple is evidently analogous. The Persians specialise *life*, the Dravidians *reason;* and both of them class the sexes together indiscriminately in the plural.

In Telugu some confusion has been introduced between the epicene sign of plurality *ar-u*, and the neuter *lu*. The pronouns pluralise their masculines and feminines regularly by substituting *ar-u* for their masculine and feminine singular suffixes, whilst the substantives and some of the appellative nouns append *lu*, which is properly the neuter sign of plurality, instead of the more correct *ar-u*. Thus the Telugu demonstrative pronoun *vâr-u*, they (the plural of *vâṉḍu*, he), corresponding to the Canarese *avar-u*, exhibits the regular epicene plural; whilst *magaṉḍu*, a husband (in Tamil *magan*, a son), takes for its plural not *magaru*, but *magalu;* and some nouns of this class add *lu* to the masculine or feminine singular suffix—*e.g.*, *alluḍu*, a son-in-law, makes in the plural not *alluru*, nor even *alluḷu*, but *allundlu*, nasalised from *alluḍlu;* and instead of *vâru*, they, *vâṉḍlu* is colloquially used, a word which is formed on the same plan as the Low Tamil *avangaḷ*, they, instead of *avargaḷ*, or the higher and purer *avar*.

One of the few cases in which the irrational pluralising particle is used in the higher dialect of the Tamil instead of the rational epicene, is that of *makkaḷ* (*maggaḷ*), mankind, people. This is not really, however, an exception to the rule, for *makkaḷ* is regarded by Tamil grammarians as the plural of *maga* (from *mag-u*), and the primary meaning of this seems to be child, a naturally neuter noun. Another instance of this anomaly both in Tamil and Canarese, and one to which no exception can be taken, is that of the masculine noun *guru* (Sans.), a teacher. The plural of this word is in Tam. *gurukkaḷ*, in Can. *gurugaḷu*. Tuḷu also has *gurukuḷu*.

Tuḷu agrees with the other dialects in using *er* as its sign of plurality in personal nouns, but differs from most of them in using this form occasionally only, and using *gaḷ*, or the shape which *gaḷ* assumes in Tuḷu, as its ordinary plural of personal nouns, as well as of neuters. Thus, the plural pronouns of the third person in ordinary use in Tuḷu are *âkuḷu*, they (*rem.*), *môkuḷu*, they (*prox.*) It uses also *âr'* (Tam. *avar*) for the former, and *mêr'* (Tam. *ivar*) for the latter, but rather as honorific singulars than as plurals. It also uses *nîkuḷu* for you, instead of *îr'*, the latter having come to be used as an honorific singular.

The Ku rational plural is *ngâ*, which is properly an irrational one. The pronouns and participial nouns form their rational plural by the addition of *âru*, which is identical with the *ar* of the other dialects. Modern colloquial Tamil seems to have been influenced in some degree by the usage of Telugu, and has adopted the practice of adding the irrational plural to the rational one, thereby systematically forming a double plural *ar-gal*, instead of the old rational plural *ar*—*e.g.*, *avan*, he, and *avaḷ*, she, properly take *avar*, they, as their plural; but the plural preferred by modern Tamil is the double one *avargaḷ*. So also the plural of the second person is properly *nîr;* but the plural which is most commonly used is *nîṅ-gaḷ* (from *nîm*, an older form of *nîr*, and *gaḷ*), which is a double plural like *avar-gaḷ*. Two forms of the epicene plural being thus placed at the disposal of the Tamil people (the classical *nîr* and *avar*, and the colloquial *nîṅ-gaḷ* and *avar-gaḷ*), they have converted the former, in colloquial usage and in prose compositions, into an honorific singular, and the same practice is not unknown in Canarese. This usage, though universally prevalent now, was almost unknown to the poets. I have not observed in the poets, or in any of the old inscriptions in my possession, any instance of the use of the epicene plural as an honorific singular, except in connection with the names and titles of the divinities, whether those names and titles are applied to the gods themselves, or are conferred honorifically upon kings. Even in those cases, however, the corresponding pronoun follows the ordinary rule, and is very rarely honorific. In modern Telugu a double plural, similar to that of the Tamil, has gained a footing—*e.g.*, *vâra-lu* (for *vâr-u*), they, and *mîra-lu* (for *mîr-u*), you. In Malayâlam, *avar* is still constantly used for the ordinary epicene plural, and *avargaḷ* is used more commonly as an honorific singular. This use of *avargaḷ* is also common in Tamil, and the corresponding *gâru* equally so in Telugu. (Tam. *durei-avargaḷ* = Tel. *dora-gâru*, the gentleman, literally the gentlemen, his honour.) In Canarese, *avaru* is commonly used simply as a plural; *âtanu* is regarded as the honorific singular, though *avaru* also is sometimes used in this sense. *nîṅgaḷ* in Tamil and Malayâlam is both plural and honorific singular, like Can. *nîvu* and Tel. *mîru*.

Telugu, as has been observed, pluralises masculine and feminine substantive nouns by the addition, not of the rational, but of the neuter or irrational, sign of plurality. By a similar inversion of idiom, Gônd sometimes uses the rational plural to pluralise neuter nouns—*e.g.*, *kâwâlor*, crows. Such usages, however, are evidently exceptions to the general and more distinctively Dravidian rule, according to which the neuter pluralising particle is restricted to neuter nouns, and the epicene particle to rational or personal nouns, *i.e.*, masculines and feminines.

We shall now consider in detail the pluralising particles themselves.

1. *Epicene Pluralising Particle.*—This particle is virtually one and the same in all the dialects, and the different forms it has taken are owing merely to euphonic peculiarities. In Tamil nouns, pronouns,

and verbs, it assumes the forms of *ar*, *âr*, *ôr*; *ir*, *îr*: in Canarese and Telugu, *aru*, *aru*; *âre*, *êru*; *ri*, *ru*: in Tuḷu, *er*: in Ku, *âru*: in Gônd, *ôr*. The lengthened forms include the assimilated demonstrative vowel of the pronoun. The Brahui also forms the second person plural of its verb in *ere*, *ure*, &c., the third person in *ur* or *ar*. I regard *ar* (not simply *r*) as probably the primitive shape of this pluralising particle, from which the other forms have been derived by euphonic mutation. It is true that *nî*, thou, forms its plural in modern Tamil by simply adding *r*; but this does not prove that *r* alone was the primitive form of the epicene plural, for an older form of *nîr*, you, is *nî-(v)-ir* or *nî-(y)-ir*, from which *nîr* has evidently been derived. It might naturally be supposed that in this case *ir* is used instead of *ar*, through the attraction of the preceding long vowel *î*; but we also find *ir* used as a pluralising particle in *magaḷir*, High Tam. women, and also a longer form, *îr*, in *magaḷîr*; consequently *ir* has acquired a position of its own in the language, as well as *ar*. All that we can certainly conclude respecting the original shape of this particle is that the final *r*, which is plainly essential, was preceded by a vowel, and that that vowel was probably *a*. May we regard this *a* as identical with the demonstrative *a*? On this supposition, *ar* would be simply an older form of *a(v)ar*, and would mean those persons; *ir* would mean these persons. On the other hand, may we venture to identify *ir* and *îr* with the second numeral *ir* and *îr*, two? *nîr* would on this supposition have been originally a dual, meaning ye two. It is not impossible, indeed, that the plural may in all languages have been developed out of the dual. In Bornu, we, ye, they, mean literally we two, ye two, they two. The chief difficulty in the way of accepting this as the origin of the Tamil *ir* or *nîr*, you, is that the *ar* of *avar*, they, which is the form of the epicene plural most commonly used, would have to be regarded as a corruption and a mistake, which it does not appear to be. The Canarese rational plural suffix *andar*—*e.g.*, *avandar-u* (for *avar-u*), *illi*, and *ivandar-u* (for *ivar-u*), *hi* seems to be identical with the Tel. indefinite plural *andar-u*, *indar-u*, so many, the final *ar* of which is the ordinary suffix of the epicene plural. In old Canarese, *ir* is a plural vocative of epicenes.

Tamil and Malayâlam have another particle of plurality applicable to rational beings, viz., *mâr*, or in High Tamil *mar*, which has a considerable resemblance to *ar*, and is evidently allied to it. It is suffixed to the noun which it qualifies in a different manner from *ar*; for whilst *ar* is substituted for the masculine and feminine suffixes of the singular, not added to them, *mâr* is generally added to the singular suffix by idiomatic writers and speakers. Thus in Tamil, *purushan*

(Sans.) a man, a husband, when pluralised by suffixing *ar* becomes *purușhar;* but if *mâr* is used instead of *ar*, it is not substituted for *an*, the masculine singular suffix, but appended to it—*e.g.*, *purușhan-mâr*, not *purușha-mar*. *mâr*, it is true, is sometimes added to *ar*—*e.g.*, *purușhar-mâr;* but this is considered unidiomatical. *mâr* is also sometimes used as an isolated particle of plurality in a peculiarly Scythian manner—*e.g.*, *tây-tagappan-mâr*, Tam. mothers and fathers, parents; in which both mother and father are in the singular, and *mâr* is separately appended to pluralise both. Probably there was originally no difference in signification between *ar* and *mar* or *mâr*. In modern Tamil, *mâr* is suffixed to nouns signifying parents, priests, kings, &c., as a plural of honour, but it may be suffixed, if necessary, to any class of nouns denoting rational beings. In Malayâlam it is used with a wider range of application than in Tamil, and in cases in which an honorific meaning cannot be intended—*e.g.*, *kaḻḻan-mâr*, thieves. The antiquity of many of the forms of the Malayâlam grammar favours the supposition that in ancient Tamil, which was apparently identical with ancient Malayâlam, *mar* or *mâr* may generally have been used instead of *ar*, as the ordinary pluralising particle of high-caste nouns.

A few traces of the use of the particle *mâr*, as the ordinary sign of epicene plurality, survive in classical Tamil. *mar*, which is evidently equivalent to *mâr*, forms the epicene plural of a few nouns—*e.g.*, *eṇmar*, eight persons. As *ar* is older than *âr* (the latter being euphonised from *avar* by the coalescence of the vowels), so in like manner it may be concluded that *mar* is older than *mâr*. This *mar* again seems to have been derived from *var*, or to be an older form of it, *m* and *v* being sometimes found to change places. When the Tam. *nâlvar*, four persons, *eivar*, five persons, are compared with *eṇmar*, eight persons, it is evident that *mar* is equivalent to *var*, and probable that the use of *m* for *v* is an euphonic change. *nâlmar* would be impossible in classical Tamil; *eṇmar* is not only possible, but euphonic.

var is a very common formative of epicene appellative nouns in Tamil and Malayâlam, and often appears as *avar*, in which case we cannot but regard it as the pronominal *avar*, they, used as a plural formative—*e.g.*, *viṇṇavar*, Tam. the heavenly ones, from *viṇ*, heaven, with *avar* affixed. Compare this form with participial nouns like *śeyḍavar*, Tam. they who did, from *śeyd-(u)*, having done, and *avar*, they, and the identity in origin of the *avar* of *viṇṇavar* and that of *śeyḍavar* will be evident. This *avar*, again, seems to have been abbreviated into *var*, like the Telugu *avaru*, they, into *vâru*. The *v* of *eivar*, five persons, might be regarded as simply euphonic, as a soft consonant inserted to prevent hiatus, but this explanation is inadmissible in the case of *nâlvar*, four persons, there being no hiatus here to be provided against. This *var* being identical in use with *avar*, it may safely be concluded to be identical with it in origin; and if *var* is a pronominal form, an abbreviation of *avar*, may not *mar* be the same? The example of the lengthening of *ar* into *âr* (*i.e.*, the substitution of the plural pronoun itself in an euphonised form for the bare particle of plurality) would naturally lead to the lengthening of *var* into *vâr* (the origin of the *v* being by this time forgotten); and when once *mar* had established itself instead of *var*, this also would naturally be lengthened into *mâr*. Thus *tagappan-mâr* would come to be used instead of *tagappan-vâr*. This suffixing of the plural formative to the singular noun, which seems so irregular, may be compared with the mode in which the singular is still honorifically pluralised by the addition of the plural pronoun—*e.g.*, *tagappan-avargaḷ*, father, and especially with the still more common *tagappan-âr*, forms which, though used as singular, are grammatically plurals. *tagappan-mâr* is invariably used as a plural, but it seems not improbable that it is identical in origin with *tagappan-âr*.

In this explanation of *mâr* I have followed a suggestion of Dr Gundert; but I find myself unable to follow him also in supposing the Tamil verbal terminations *mar*, *mâr*, *manâr*, to be identical in origin with the pluralising particles *mar*, *mâr*, though I admit that at first sight it seems impossible to suppose them to be otherwise. These are poetical forms of the future tense only, which do not make their appearance in any other part of the verb, and the *m* they contain will be found, I think, on examination, to have a futuric, not a pronominal, signification. It appears to be identical with *b* or *v*, the sign of the future, and there appears no reason why *m* should not be used instead of *v* or *b* in this instance, as well as in others that have already been pointed out. The impersonal future of *en*, to say, in classical Tamil is *enba*. When the personal terminations of the third person plural are suffixed to the root, we find 'they will say' represented indifferently by *enbar*, or *enmar*, *enbâr*, *enmâr*, or *enmanâr*. The force of the future, according to Tamil grammarians, being conveyed by each of these forms in *m*, precisely as by each of the forms in *b*, I conclude that this future *m* must be regarded as independent of the *m* of the pluralising particle, and the resemblance between the two, however complete, to be after all accidental. Dr Gundert suggests that the final *âr* of *enmanâr*, preceded by *an*, may be explained by a comparison of it with *tagappan-âr*, a form already referred to, and here I am disposed to coincide with him.

We have now to inquire whether *ar*, *âr*, *mar*, and *mâr*, the Dravidian plurals of rationality, appear to sustain any relation to the plural terminations, or pluralising suffixes, of other languages. It might at first sight be supposed that the formation of the plural by the addition of *r* to the singular which characterises some of the Teutonic tongues, is analogous to the use of *r* or *ar* in the Dravidian languages. In the Icelandic the most common plural is that which terminates in *r*—sometimes the consonant *r* alone, sometimes the syllables *ar*, *ir*, *ur*—*e.g.*, *konungur*, kings. A relic of this plural may be traced in the vulgar English childer, for children. The same plural appears in the old Latin termination of the masculine plural in *or* which is found in the Eugubian tables—*e.g.*, *subator* for *subacti*, and *screhitor* for *scripti*. Compare also *mas*, the termination of the first person plural of verbs in Sanskrit, with *mar*, the corresponding termination in Irish, answering to the Doric *μες* and the ordinary Greek *μεν*. In these cases, however, the resemblance to the Dravidian plural *ar* is perhaps rather apparent than real; for the final *r* of these forms has been hardened from an older *s*, and the *s* of the Sanskrit nominative singular is hardened in some of the Teutonic tongues into *r*, equally with the *as* or *s* of the plural; whilst there is no evidence, on which we can rely, of the existence of a tendency in the Dravidian languages to harden *s* into *r*, and therefore no evidence for the supposition that the Dravidian epicene *ar* has been derived from, or is connected with, the Sanskrit masculine-feminine *as*. It should also be noted that the Irish *mar* is a compound of two forms, *ma*, the representative of the singular of the personal pronoun I, and *r*, the hardened equivalent of the plural suffix *s*; and that, therefore, it has no real resemblance to the Dravidian *mar*, which is entirely and exclusively a plural suffix of the third person.

There is more probability perhaps of the Dravidian plural suffixes being related to the pluralising particles of some of the Scythian languages. The Turkish plural suffix, which is inserted, as in the Dravidian languages, between the crude noun and each of the case-terminations, is *lar* or *ler*—*e.g.*, *ân-lar*, they. Dr Logan says, but on what authority does not appear, that *nar* is a plural suffix in Kôl. Mongolian nouns which end with a vowel are pluralised by the addition of *nar* or *ner*, a particle which is evidently related to, or identical with, the Turkish *lar* or *ler*: and the resemblance of this Mongol suffix *nar* to the Dravidian *mar*, both in the final *ar* and in the nasal prefix, is remarkable. It is well known that *m* evinces a tendency to be softened into *n* (witness the change of the Sanskrit *mama*, my, into *mana* in Zend); and in this manner it may perhaps be supposed that the Dravidian *mar* may be allied to the High Asian *nar*. The Tamil *iḷeiñar* (*iḷei-ñar*), young people, a plural appellative noun, formed from *iḷei*, youth, exhibits a form of pluralisation which at first sight seems very closely to resemble the Mongolian *nar*. Nay, *nar* is actually used in this very instance instead of *ñar* by some of the poets, and it is certain that *ñ* and *n* often change places. Unfortunately we find this *ñ* or *n* in the singular, as well as the plural; which proves it to be inserted merely for euphony in order to prevent hiatus, and therefore *ileiñar* must be re-divided, and represented not as *iḷei-ñar*, but as *iḷei-(ñ)-ar* or *iḷei-(n)-ar*, equivalent to *iḷei-(y)-ar*. The resemblance of the final syllable *nâr*, of the Tamil verb *enmanâr*, already commented on, to the Mongolian plural suffix *nar*, seems more reliable, and yet that also seems to disappear on further examination.

Turkish, besides its ordinary plural *lar* or *ler*, uses *z* as a plural suffix of the personal pronouns, as may be observed in *biz*, we, and *siz*, you; and the Turkish terminal *z* corresponds to the *r* of some other Scythian languages. Thus *yâz*, Turkish, summer, is in Magyar *yâr* or *ñâr* (compare the Tamil *ñâyiṟ-u*, the sun). It would almost appear, therefore, that the Turkish suffix of plurality has undergone a process of change and comminution similar to that of the Tamil, and that the Turkish *z* and the Tamil *r* are remotely connected, as the last remaining representatives or relics of *mar*, *nar*, and *lar*.

Though I call attention to these and similar Scythian correspondences, I wish it to be understood that I do so only in the hope that they will be inquired into more thoroughly, and the existence or otherwise of a real relationship between them and the Dravidian forms with which they correspond ascertained. I attribute much more weight to the resemblance between the Dravidian languages and those of the Scythian group in the use they make of these particles of plurality, and the manner in which they connect them with the case-sign than to any resemblance, however close, that can be traced between the particles themselves. We should look, I think, not so much at the linguistic materials used by the Scythian languages and the Dravidian respectively, as at the use they severally make of those materials.

2. *Pluralising Particles of the Neuter.*—There are two neuter pluralising particles used by the Dravidian languages:—

(1.) *The Neuter Plural Suffix gaḷ, with its Varieties.*—It has already been noticed that *gaḷ* is occasionally used in Tamil and Canarese as the plural suffix of rational nouns and pronouns; and that the corresponding Telugu *lu* is still more systematically used in this manner. Nevertheless, I have no doubt that it was originally and is essentially a suffix of the neuter plural. This suffix is in both dialects of the Tamil *gaḷ*—*e.g.*, *kei-gaḷ*, hands, with only such changes as are required by Tamilian rules of euphony. In accordance with one of those rules, when *g*, the initial consonant of *gaḷ*, is doubled, or preceded without an intermediate vowel by another consonant, *gaḷ* is regularly hardened into *kaḷ* or *kkaḷ*. Thus *kal-gaḷ*, stones, is changed by rule into *kar-kaḷ*. *gaḷ* is occasionally lengthened in Tamil poetry into *gâḷ*. In Malayâlam this particle is generally *gaḷ*, *kaḷ*, or *kkaḷ*, but sometimes the initial *k* coalesces with a preceding nasal and becomes *ṅ*—*e.g.*, *niṅ-ṅaḷ*, you, instead of *nim-kaḷ*, in Tamil *nîṅ-gaḷ*. In modern Canarese we have *gaḷ-u*, in ancient *gaḷ*, as in Tamil. The three southern idioms are in perfect agreement with respect to this particle, but when we advance further north we shall find its shape considerably modified.

In Telugu the corresponding neuter plural suffix is *lu*, of which the *l* answers, as is usual in Telugu, to the lingual *ḷ* of the other dialects: *l-u*, therefore, accords with the final syllable of the Canarese *gaḷ-u*. The only real difference between the Telugu and the Tamil-Canarese consists in the omission by the former of the initial consonant *k* or *g*. Traces, however, exist, in Telugu, of the use of a vowel before *lu*. Thus, in *gurrâlu*, horses, the long *â* is derived from the combination of the short final *a* of the inflexional base *gurra* and a vowel, evidently *a*, which must have preceded *lu*. We thus arrive at *al-u* as the primitive form of the Telugu plural; and it is obvious that *al-u* could easily have been softened from *gal-u*. Conjecture, however, is scarcely needed, for in some nouns ending in *n-u*, of which the Tamil equivalents end in *m*, the old Dravidian pluralising particle in *gaḷ* is exhibited in Telugu almost as distinctly as in Tamil. Thus, *kolan-u*, a tank (Tamil *kuḷam*), takes as its plural *kolan-kul-u*, a word cited in this form by Nannaya Bhaṭṭa (Tamil *kuḷaṅ-gaḷ*), and *gon-u*, the name of a species of tree, forms its plural in *gon-gul-u*. When *kul-u* and *gul-u* are compared with the Tamil-Canarese forms *kaḷ*, *gaḷ*, and *gaḷ-u*, it is obvious that they are not only equivalent but identical. An illustration of the manner in which the Telugu *lu* has been softened from *gal-u*, may be taken also from colloquial Tamil, in which *avar-gal*, they, is commonly pronounced *avâḷ*; *Pirâmaṇargaḷ*, Brahmans, *Pirâmaṇâḷ*. *k* or *g* is dropped or elided in a similar manner in many languages of the Scythian family. Tuḷu, though locally remote from Telugu, follows its example in many points, and amongst others in this. It often rejects the *k* or *g* of the plural, and uses merely *ḷu*, like Telugu. It uses the full form *kuḷu* more rarely.

The same form of the pluralising particle appears in the languages of some of the tribes of the north-eastern frontier—languages which possibly form a link of connection between the Dravidian and the Tibetan families. In the Miri or Abor-Miri dialect, *nô*, thou, forms its plural in *nôlü*, you; and in the Dhimâl, *nê*, thou, is pluralised into *nyêl*, you. The pronoun of the Mikir is pluralised by adding *li*—*e.g.*, *na-li*, you, whilst substantives have no plural form. In the Dhimâl, substantive nouns are pluralised by the addition of *galai*, which is possibly the origin of the pronominal plural *l*, though this particle or word, *galai*, is not compounded with, or agglutinated to, the noun, but placed after it separately. Though it is used as a separate word, it does not seem to retain any signification of its own independent of its use as a post-position. The resemblance of *galai* to the Tamil-Canarese *gaḷ* or *gaḷu*, is distinct and remarkable. The pluralising particle of the Naga also is *khala*.

It is not an uncommon occurrence to find one portion of a much-used prefix or suffix in one language or dialect of a family, and another portion of it in another member of the same family. Seeing, therefore, that the Telugu has adopted the latter portion of the particle *kaḷ*, *gaḷ*, or *gaḷu*, and omitted the initial *ka*, *ga*, or *k*, we may expect to find this *k* used as a pluralising particle in some other Dravidian dialect, and the final *ḷu* or *ḷ* omitted. Accordingly, in Gônd we find that the plural neuter is commonly formed by the addition of *k* alone—*e.g.*, *nai*, a dog, *naik*, dogs (compare Tamil *nâykaḷ*, pronounced *nâygaḷ*). The Seoni-Gônd forms its plural by adding *nk*—*e.g.*, *neli*, a field, *neḷnk*, fields. The Ku dialect uses *ngâ*, and also *skâ*, of all which forms *k* or *g* constitutes the basis.

k is sometimes found to interchange with *t*, especially in the languages of High Asia. This interchange appears also in the Gônd pluralising particle; for whilst *k* is the particle in general use, the pronouns of the first and second persons form their plurals, or double plurals, by the addition of *t* to the nominative—*e.g.*, *amat*, we, *imat*, you. The same interchange between *k* and *t* appears in Brahui. Though a separate word is usually employed by Brahui to denote plurality, a suffix in *k* is also sometimes used; but this *k* is found only in the nominative plural, and is replaced by *t* in the oblique cases.

When we turn to the grammatical forms of the Finnish family of languages, we find some tolerably distinct analogies to this Dravidian plural suffix. Compare with the Dravidian forms noticed above the Magyar plural in *k* or *ak*; the Lappish in *k*, *ch*, or *h*: also the *t* by which *k* is replaced in almost all the other dialects of the Finnish family; and observe the reappearance of the sound of *l* in the Ostiak plural suffix *tl*. In Ostiak, the dual suffix is *kan* or *gan*; in Samoïed-Ostiak, *ga* or *ka*; in Kamass, *gai*. Castren supposes these suffixes to be derived from the conjunctive particle *ka* or *ki*, also; but their resemblance to the Dravidian signs of plurality is worth noticing. Even Armenian forms its plural in *k*—*e.g.*, *tu*, thou, *tuk*, you; *siṛem*, I love; *siremk*, we love. In Turkish also, *k* is the sign of plurality in some forms of the first person plural of the verb—*e.g.*, *îlum*, I was, *îduk*, we were. *t*, on the other hand, is the sign of the plural in Mongolian, and in Calmuck is softened into *d*. Even in Zend, though a language of a different family, there is a neuter plural in *t*. Thus, for *imâni* (Sans.), these things, Zend has *imat*.

In those instances of the interchange of *t* and *k*, in which it can be ascertained with tolerable clearness which consonant was the one originally used and which was the corruption, *t* sometimes appears to be older than *k*. Thus, the Doric τῆνος is in better accordance with related words, and therefore probably older, than the Æolian κῆνος, the origin of ἐ-κεῖνος. The Semitic pronoun or pronominal fragment *ta*, thou (preserved in *attâ* and *antâ*), is also, I doubt not, a more accurate and older form than the equivalent or auxiliary suffix *kâ*. In several of the Polynesian dialects, *k* is found instead of an apparently earlier Sanskrit or pre-Sanskrit *t*. On the other hand, as Dr Gundert points out, *k* sometimes appears to be older than *t*, particularly in Greek —*e.g.*, compare Gr. τις with Sans. *kas*. If, in accordance with a portion of these precedents, where *k* and *t* are found to be interchanged, *t* is to be regarded as older than *k*, it would follow that *kaḷ*, the Dravidian plural suffix now under consideration, may originally have been *taḷ*. I cannot think that the Dravidian *gaḷ* has been derived, as Dr Stevenson supposed, from the Sanskrit *sakala* (in Tamil *sagala*), all. *kal*, the base of *sa-kala*, has been connected with ὅλ-ος; but *el*, the root signifying 'all,' which is found in all the Dravidian languages —Tel. *ella*; Tam.-Mal. *ellâ*, *ellâm*, *ellâvum* (the conjunction *um* intensifies the meaning)—if it were related to any Indo-European word at all, which is doubtful, would be connected, not with the Gr. ὅλ, Heb. *kol*, Sans. *sar-va*, &c., but with the Germanic *alla*, Eng. *all*.* The Dravidian *taḷa*, one of the meanings of which is a heap, a quantity, would suit very well; but even this derivation of *kaḷ* is destitute of evidence. The supposititious Dravidian *taḷ* may be compared with the Ostiak plural suffix *tl*; but in the absence of evidence it is useless to proceed with conjectural analogies.

The New Persian neuter plural, or plural of inanimate objects, which corresponds generally to the Dravidian neuter plural, is *hâ*, a form

* Dr Gundert is right, I think, in deriving this word from *el*, a boundary (Tam. *el-vei*, *el-gei*, *ellei*; Tel. *ella*); but I am unable to follow him in adding to *el* a negative *a*, so as to give *ellâ*, all, the idea of boundless. The Tamil *ellavar*, all (persons), compared with *ellavan*, the sun, from *el*, time, and several related words denoting measure, end, &c., lead me to the conclusion that the word *ellâ* or *ellâm*, all, is used affirmatively, in its natural sense, to signify whatever is included within the measure or limits of the thing referred to.

which Bopp derives with much probability from the Zend. It may here be mentioned, though I do not attach any importance to a resemblance which is certainly accidental, that the Tamil plural *gaḷ* sometimes resembles *ha* in the pronunciation of the peasantry—*e.g.*, *irukkiṟârgaḷ*, they are, is vulgarly pronounced *irukkiṟâha.*

(2.) *Neuter Plural Suffix in a.*—In addition to the neuter plural in *gaḷ*, with its varieties, we find in nearly all the Dravidian languages a neuter plural in short *a*, or traces of the use of it at some former period. *gaḷ*, though a neuter plural suffix, is occasionally used, especially in the modern dialects, as the plural suffix of rationals; but in those dialects in which *a* is used, its use is invariably restricted to neuters, and it seems therefore to be a more essentially neuter form than *gaḷ* itself.

We shall first examine the traces of the existence and use of this suffix which are contained in Tamil. *gaḷ* is invariably used in Tamil as the plural suffix of uncompounded neuter nouns; but *a* is preferred in the classical dialect for pluralising neuter compounds, that is, appellative nouns, or those which are compounded of a base and a suffix of gender, together with demonstrative pronouns, pronominal adjectives, and participial nouns. Even in the ordinary dialect, *a* is generally used as the suffix of the neuter plural in the conjugation of verbs.

The second line in one of the distichs of Tiruvaḷḷuvar's "Kuraḷ" contains two instances of the use of *a* as a neuter plural of appellative nouns—*e.g.*, *âgula nîra piṟa*, vain shows (are all) other (things). The first of these three words is used adjectivally; and in that case the final *a* is merely that which remains of the neuter termination *am*, after the regular rejection of *m*; but the next two words, *nîra* and *piṟa*, are undoubted instances of the use of *a* as a suffix of the neuter plural of appellatives. The much-used Tamil words *pala*, several, or many (things), and *śila*, some, or some (things), (from *pal* and *śil*), though commonly considered as adjectives, are in reality neuter plurals —*e.g.*, *piṇi pala*, diseases (are) many; *pala-(v)-in-pâl*, the neuter plural gender, literally the gender of the many (things). This is the case also in poetry in Malayâlam. The use of these words adjectivally, and with the signification, not of the collective, but of the distributive plural, has led some persons to overlook their origin and real meaning, but I have no doubt that they are plurals. So also *alla*, not, is properly a plural appellative. It is formed from the root *al*, not, by the addition of *a*, the plural suffix, and literally means things that are not, and the singular that corresponds to *alla* is *al-du*, not, euphonically *andru*, literally a thing that is not. In the higher dialect of Tamil, all nouns of quality and relation may be, and very frequently are, converted into appellatives and pluralised by the addition of *a*—*e.g.*, *ariya* (Kural), things that are difficult, *difficilia*. We have some instances in High Tamil of the use of *a* as the plural suffix even of substantive nouns—*e.g.*, *poruḷa*, substances, things that are real, realities (from the singular *poruḷ*, a thing, a substance); also *poruḷana* and *poruḷavei*,—with the addition of *ana* and *avei* (for *ava*), the plural neuters of the demonstrative pronouns.

The neuter plural of the third person of the Tamil verb, a form which is used occasionally in ordinary prose as well as in the classical dialect, ends in *ana*—*e.g.*, *irukkindrana*, they (neut.) are. *ana* is undoubtedly identical with *ava* (now *avei*), the neuter plural of the demonstrative pronoun, and is possibly an older form than *ava*. It is derived from the demonstrative base *a*, with the addition of *a*, the neuter plural suffix, and an euphonic consonant (*n* or *v*) to prevent hiatus—*e.g.*, *a*-(*n*)-*a* or *a*-(*v*)-*a*. Sometimes in classical Tamil this *a*, the sign of the neuter plural, is added directly to the temporal suffix of the verb, without the addition of the demonstrative base of the pronoun—*e.g.*, *mîṇḍa*, they (neut.) returned, instead of *mîṇḍana*. This final *a* is evidently a sign of the neuter plural, and of that alone.

Possibly we should also regard as a sign of the neuter plural the final *a* of the High Tamil possessive adjectives *ena*, my (things), *mea*; *nama*, our (things), *nostra*. The final *a* of *ena* would, on this supposition, be not only equivalent to the final *a* of the Latin *mea*, but really identical with it. These possessive adjectives are regarded by Tamil grammarians as genitives; and it will be shown hereafter that *a* is undoubtedly the most essential sign of the genitive in the Dravidian languages. The real nature of *ena* and *nama* will be discussed when the genitive case-terminations are inquired into. It should be stated, however, under this head, that Tamil grammarians admit that *ena* and *nama*, though, as they say, genitives, must be followed by nouns in the neuter plural—*e.g.*, *ena keigaḷ*, my hands; and this, so far as it goes, constitutes the principal argument in favour of regarding the final *a* of these words, not as a genitive, but as the ordinary neuter plural suffix of the high dialect.

In Malayâlam, the oldest daughter of Tamil, and a faithful preserver of many old forms, the neuter plurals of the demonstrative pronouns are *ava*, those (things), and *iva*, these (things). The existence, therefore, in Tamil and Malayâlam of a neuter plural in short *a*, answering to a neuter singular in *d*, is clearly established. In addition to *ava* and *iva*, *avattrugaḷ* and *ivattrugaḷ* are regularly used in Malayâlam, like the double plural *aveigaḷ*, *iveigaḷ*, in Tamil.

Canarese appears to have originally agreed with Tamil in all the particulars and instances mentioned above; but the neuter plural in *a* is now generally hidden in that dialect by the addition of euphonic *u*, or the addition of *avu*, they, neuter (corresponding to the Tamil *avei*) to the base. Thus *piṛa*, Tam. other (things), is in Canarese *heravu*. The neuter plural of the demonstrative pronoun is not *ava*, as it is in Malayâlam, and as it must have been in primitive Tamil, but *avu*. Though, however, the nominative is *avu*, all the oblique cases in the ancient Canarese reject the final *u* before receiving the case-suffixes, and must have been formed from the base of an older *ava*—*e.g.*, *avara* (*ava-ra*), of those things.

The Telugu plural neuters of the demonstratives are *avi*, those, *ivi*, these, answering to the singular neuters *adi* and *idi*. The oblique forms of the same demonstratives (or rather the bases of those oblique forms), to which the case-terminations are suffixed, are *vâ* remote, and *vî* proximate (*vâṭi*, *vîṭe*), which are evidently formed (by that process of displacement peculiar to Telugu) from the primitive bases *ava* and *iva*, like *vâru*, from *avaru*, and *vîru*, from *ivaru*. The neuter plural of the Telugu verb is formed by suffixing *avi* or *vi*.

Dr Gundert calls my attention here to the natural and easy transition from one vowel to another apparent on comparing the Malayâlam and old Tamil *ava* with the modern Tamil *avei*, and finally with the Telugu *avi*. So also Malayâlam and old Tamil *illa*, none, is *illei* in modern Tamil. Final *a* constantly lapses in the Dravidian languages into a weaker sound.

In Gônd the singular demonstratives are *ad* and *id*; the corresponding plurals *av* and *iv*. If Telugu and Gônd were the only extant dialects of the Dravidian family, we should naturally conclude that as *d* is the sign of the neuter singular, so *v* is the sign of the neuter plural. When the other extant dialects, however (Tamil, Malayâlam, and Canarese), are examined, we perceive that this *v* is not a sign of plurality, nor a sign of anything but of abhorrence of hiatus; and that it is merely an euphonic link between the preceding and succeeding vowels. Telugu and Gônd must therefore yield to the overpowering weight of evidence which is adducible in proof of this point from their sister dialects. Nor is there anything opposed to analogy in the supposition that Telugu has changed the *a*, which was the sign of the neuter plural of its pronouns and verbs, into *i*, and then, to represent the idea of plurality, adopted a consonant which was used originally merely to prevent hiatus. In the case of *avaru*, they, *illi*, converted into *vâru*, and *ivaru*, they, *hi*, converted into *vîru*, *v*, though only euphonic in its origin, has become an initial and apparently a radical;

and the old initial and essentially demonstrative vowels *a* and *i* have been thrust into a secondary place. The conversion, therefore, of *ava* into *vâ*, and of *iva* into *vî* (*vâṭi, vîṭi*), the oblique forms of the Telugu plural demonstratives, is directly in accordance with this analogy; and thus Telugu cannot be considered as opposed to the concurrent testimony of the other dialects, which is to the effect that *v* is merely euphonic, and that *a* is the sign of the neuter plural of the demonstrative pronouns.

I remarked it as a curious irregularity, that in Tuḷu *v* had become the sign of the neuter singular instead of *d*—*e.g.*, *avu*, it. Dr Gundert says that the *v* is not written. The word is written *au-u*, and he considers it merely a softened pronunciation of *adu*, so that there is no irregularity here after all. It is written *avu*, however, in Brigel's Grammar.

If short *a* be, as it has been shown to be, a sign of the neuter plural inherent in the Dravidian languages, and most used by the oldest dialects, we have now to inquire into the relationship which it apparently sustains to the neuter plural suffix of some of the Indo-European languages. I know of no plural in any of the Scythian tongues with which it can be compared; and we appear to be obliged to attribute to it, as well as to *d*, the suffix of the neuter singular, an origin which is allied to that of the corresponding Indo-European forms. In the use of *a* as a neuter plural suffix, it is evident that the Dravidian family has not imitated, or been influenced by, the Sanskrit, and that it was not through the medium of Sanskrit that Indo-European influences made their way into this department of the Dravidian languages; for the Dravidian neuter plural *a* differs widely from the Sanskrit neuter plural *âni*, and it is as certainly unconnected with the masculine-feminine plural *as* (softened in modern Sanskrit into *ah*). It is with the short *a*, which constitutes the neuter plural of Zend, Latin, and Gothic, that the Dravidian neuter plural *a* appears to be allied. Compare also the Old Persian neuter plural *â*.

It will be evident on recapitulating the various particulars that have been mentioned in this section, that grammatical gender has been more fully and systematically developed in the Dravidian languages than in perhaps any other language, or family of languages, in the world. Properly speaking, there is no such thing as gender in the Scythian languages. Gender appears in the Indo-European languages in the pronouns and pronominals, but not in the verb. In the Semitic languages the verb distinguishes between the masculine and feminine in the singular; but in the plural, as in the verb of the Indo-European languages, gender is ignored. In the Dravidian languages, on the other hand, not only is there a full equipment of sex-denoting pronouns, but there is the same development of gender in the verb also. We have verbal forms—without the necessity of using the separate pronouns as nominatives—for expressing *he is, she is, it is, they* (*persons*) *are, they* (*things*) *are*. This is a refinement of expressiveness in which the Dravidian languages appear to stand alone. Sanskrit is far less highly developed in this particular, so that if there were any borrowing, the Dravidian family must have been the lender, not the borrower. Probably, however, neither borrowed from the other, but both inherited elements of greater antiquity than either, which the Dravidian family has best preserved, and turned to best account. See Introduction and Appendix.

SECTION II.—FORMATION OF CASES.

Principles of Case-Formation.—The Indo-European and the Scythian families of tongues originally agreed in the principle of expressing the reciprocal relations of nouns by means of postpositions or auxiliary words. The difference between those families with respect to this point consists chiefly in the degree of faithfulness with which they have retained this principle.

In the Scythian tongues, postpositions, that is, appended auxiliary words, have generally held fast their individuality and separate existence. In the Indo-European tongues, on the contrary, the old postpositions or suffixes have been welded into combination with the roots to which they were appended, and converted into mere technical case-signs or inflexional terminations; whilst in the later corruptions to which those languages have been subjected, most of the case-terminations have been abandoned altogether, and prepositions, as in the Semitic tongues, have generally come to be employed instead of the older case-signs. It cannot reasonably be doubted that the case-terminations of the primitive dialects of the Indo-European family were originally postpositional words, which were added to the root to express relation, and at length blended into an inseparable union with it, through that love of composition by which every member of the family was characterised. In most instances the root and the original signification of those postpositions are now unknown, or they are ascertained with difficulty by means of analogy and comparison.

Both in Greek and in Latin we find some postpositions still used in a manner which illustrates the conversion of a portion of this class of words into case-endings—*e.g.*, in Latin *nobiscum*, and in Greek such words as ἀγρόθι, in the country; ἅλαδε, to the sea; and οὐρανόθεν, from heaven. The postpositional auxiliary words used in these instances are appended to their bases in a truly primitive manner. If there is any difference between them and the usage of the Scythian postpositions, it consists in this—that in most of the Scythian tongues θι, δε, θεν, would be written as separate words.

One of the Greek postpositions quoted above, δε, signifying direction to a place, has been supposed to be allied to *de*, the dative of the Manchu; and the Greek θεν has been conjectured to be allied to the Tartar ablative *din* or *den*. One may well be doubtful whether any such connection can be established; but in the manner in which the particles are appended to their bases a distinct analogy may be observed.

On turning our attention to the Dravidian languages, we find that the principle on which they have proceeded in the formation of cases is distinctively Scythian. All case-relations are expressed by means of postpositions, or postpositional suffixes. Most of the postpositions are, in reality, separate words; and in all the Dravidian dialects the postpositions retain traces of their original character as auxiliary nouns. Several case-signs, especially in the more cultivated dialects, have lost the faculty of separate existence, and can only be treated now as case-terminations; but there is no reason to doubt that they were all postpositional nouns originally. The dialect of the Tudas shows its want of literary cultivation in the paucity of its case-signs. There is no difference in it between the nominative, genitive, and accusative.

There is another point in which the Scythian principles of case-formation differ materially from the Indo-European. In the Indo-European family the case-endings of the plural differ from those of the singular. It is true, that on comparing the case-terminations of all the members of the family, some traces have been discovered of the existence of an original connection between the singular and the plural terminations of some of the cases; but in several instances—*e.g.*, in the instrumental case—no such connection between the singular and the plural has been brought to light by any amount of investigation; and it may be stated as a general rule that the languages of this family appear to have acted from the beginning upon the principle of expressing the case-relations of the singular by one set of forms, and the case-relations of the plural by another set. On the other hand, in all the languages of the Scythian group, the same case-signs are employed both in the singular and in the plural, without alteration, or with only such alterations as euphony is supposed to require. In the singular, the case-postpositions are appended directly to the nominative, which is identical with the base; in the plural they are appended, not to the nominative or base, but to the particle of pluralisation which has been suffixed to the base. In general, this is the only difference between the singular case-signs and those of the plural. The only exception of importance is, that in some of the Scythian tongues, especially in the languages of the Finnish family, the included vowel of the case-sign differs in the two numbers: it is generally *a* in the singular and *e* in the plural—a change which arises from the "law of harmonic sequences" by which those tongues are characterised, and which re-appears, but little modified, in Telugu and Tuḷu. It has already been remarked that in Tuḷu the *a* of the singular becomes *e* in the plural.

When the Dravidian languages are examined, it is found that they differ from those of the Indo-European family, and are, in general, in perfect accordance with the Scythian group, in their use of the same signs of case in the plural as in the singular. The only exceptions are the truly Scythian one apparent in Tuḷu, in the change in the case-sign vowel, mentioned above, from *a* in the singular to *e* in the plural, and the equally Scythian exception apparent in Telugu, in which the dative case-sign is either *ki* or *ku*, according to the nature of the vowel by which it is preceded or influenced; in consequence of which it is generally *ki* in the singular and *ku* in the plural. This identity of the singular and plural case-endings in the languages of the Scythian group, as well as in those of the Dravidian family, will be found greatly to facilitate the comparison of the case-signs of one language of either of those families with those of the other.

Number of Declensions.—There is only one declension, I conceive, properly so called, in the Dravidian languages, as in the Scythian family generally.

Those varieties of inflexional increments which have been called declensions by some scholars, both native and European, especially with reference to Canarese, Tuḷu, and Telugu, appear to me to constitute but one declension; for there is no difference between one so-called declension and another with respect to the signs of case. Those signs are precisely the same in all: the difference which exists relates solely to suffixes of gender, or to the euphonic and inflexional increments which are added to the bases before the addition of the case-signs.

On proceeding to analyse the case-formation of the Dravidian languages, we shall follow the order in which they have been arranged by Dravidian grammarians, which is the same as that of the Sanskrit. The imitation of Sanskrit in this particular was certainly an error; for whilst in Sanskrit there are eight cases only, the number of cases in Tamil, Telugu, &c., is almost indefinite. Every postposition annexed to a noun constitutes, properly speaking, a new case; and therefore the number of such cases depends upon the requirements of the speaker and the different shades of meaning he wishes to express. In particular, the "inflexion" or inflected form of the base, or oblique case, as it is sometimes called, which has sometimes a possessive, sometimes a locative, and sometimes an adjectival signification, ought to have had a place of its own. So also the social and conjunctive case. (See the Inflexion and the Instrumental Case.) Notwithstanding this, the usage of Dravidian grammarians has restricted the number of cases to eight; and though there are not a few disadvantages in this arrangement, it will conduce to perspicuity to adhere to the ordinary usage in the analysis on which we are about to enter. Tamil grammarians, in following the order of the Sanskrit cases, have also adopted or imitated the Sanskrit mode of denominating them—not by descriptive appellations, as dative or ablative, but by numbers. They have affixed a number to each case in the same order as in Sanskrit—*e.g.*, first case, second case, &c., to eighth case. Though a nominative, or first case, stands at the head of the Dravidian list of cases, the only cases, properly so called, which are used by these languages, are the oblique cases.

The Nominative—Absence of Nominative Case-Terminations.—In the Scythian languages in which nouns are inflected, as in the Dravidian, the nominative is not provided with a case-termination. With regard to Japanese, this is expressed by saying that the noun has no nominative. The Dravidian nominative singular is simply *peyar-ê*, the noun itself—the inflexional base of the noun—without addition or alteration; but it necessarily includes the formative, if there be one. The nominative plural differs from the nominative singular only by the addition to it of the pluralising particle. There are three apparent exceptions to this rule, or instances in which the nominative might appear to have terminations peculiar to itself, which it is desirable here to inquire into.

(1.) The neuter termination *am* might at first sight be supposed to be a nominative case-sign. In Sanskrit, *am* is the most common sign of the nominative neuter; and in Tamil also, all nouns ending in *am* (in Telugu *am-u*), whether Sanskrit derivatives or pure Dravidian words, are neuter abstracts. In Sanskrit the accusative of the neuter is identical with the nominative, but in the other cases *am* disappears. In Tamil, *am* is discarded by all the oblique cases of the singular without exception: every case retains it in the plural, but in the singular it is used by the nominative alone. This comprises the sum total of the reasons for regarding *am* as a termination of the nominative. On the other hand, though *am* disappears in Tamil from the oblique cases in the singular, it retains its place in every one of the cases in the plural. The particle of plurality is regularly suffixed to *am*, and the signs of case are then suffixed to the particle of plurality; which is a clear proof that, whatever *am* may be, it is not a mere termination or case-sign of the nominative. The Telugu regards *am* or *am-u* as part of the inflexional base, retains it in each case of *both* numbers alike, and suffixes to it in the singular the case-signs, in the plural the particle of plurality.

Ancient Canarese uses *am* in the nominative and accusative singular of nouns ending in *a*, and discards it in the plural. In that dialect a tree is *maram*, as in Tamil; but the plural nominative, trees, is not *maraṅgaḷ* (*maram-gaḷ*), but *maragaḷ*. Modern Canarese appears to make no use of *am* whatever, either in the singular or the plural, but it is evident that the final *vu* of many Canarese nouns is a softened form of *m*. Compare Tam. *maram*, a tree; Can. *maravu*.

Neuter nouns borrowed from Sanskrit by Tamil ordinarily retain (in the nominative alone, in the singular) the *am* of the Sanskrit nominative singular: this *am* is used in every one of the cases in the plural; so that even in Sanskrit derivatives *am* is regarded in Tamil, not as a case-sign, but as a portion of the inflexional base.

Whatever be the origin of the Tamil *am*, considered (as I think we must consider it) as a formative, not as a nominative case-sign, it does not appear to have been borrowed from Sanskrit, in which it is used for so different a purpose; and I believe it springs from a source altogether independent of Sanskrit. We find it added to many of the purest Dravidian roots, and by the addition of it many verbs of that class are converted into nouns. Thus *nil-am*, Tam. the ground, is from *nil*, to stand, *âḻ-am*, Tam. depth, is from *âḻ*, to be deep. See "Derivative Nouns," in the section on "The Verb." The best explanation of the origin of this *am* is probably that suggested by Dr Gundert, viz., that it is an obsolete demonstrative pronoun meaning 'it.' I am doubtful whether the Tamil demonstrative adjectives *anda*, that, *inda*, this, &c., and the demonstrative adverbs *angu*, there, &c., have originated in this supposed demonstrative pronoun *am*, because of the existence of equivalent forms (*âṇḍu*, *îṇḍu*, &c.), in which the nasal *m* or *n* is evidently an euphonic insertion; and also because the Tuḷu proximate demonstrative pronoun *indu* or *undu*, it, can clearly be identified with the unnasalised *idu* proximate, and *udu* intermediate, of Tamil and Canarese. (See section on "Euphonic Nomination.") In the case, however, of *am*, the suffix of so many Dravidian neuter nouns, the supposition that this was an ancient form of the demonstrative pronoun, regularly formed from the demonstrative root *a*, that, appears best to suit the use to which it is applied. It cannot indeed be regarded as a perfectly satisfactory explanation of the particle; for, given a supposed demonstrative *am*, formed from the demonstrative base *a*, it cannot fail to be asked, What, then, is the origin of the *m* of this supposititious *am?* Still, without being able to answer this question, we may readily suppose that a demonstrative *am*, it, was at one time current as an equivalent to *ad-u*. A parallel instance will then enable us to see how it came to be used as a suffix to nouns. In Tamil poetry *adu*, it, is frequently appended to neuter nouns as a sort of suffix of emphasis—*e.g.*, we may either say *pon*, gold, or *ponnadu* (*pon*, gold, *adu*, it). The only difference is that *adu* is separable from the word to which it is affixed, whereas wherever *am* was affixed, it seems to have adhered. The oblique cases of the Tamil reflexive pronouns, *tân*, *tâm*, are also suffixed to nouns in Tamil poetry instead of the oblique cases of those nouns themselves—*e.g.*, *marandanei(k)* (instead of *marattei*) *kaṇḍên*, I saw the tree (*accus*). The reflexive seems here to be used in a demonstrative sense. Though we do not now find a neuter demonstrative pronoun in *am* or *an* holding an independent position of its own in any of the Dravidian languages (as is the case with the neuter demonstrative *ad-u*), yet we may pretty safely conclude that such a form once existed. An evident trace of this ancient demonstrative *am* (or *an*, which would be quite equivalent to it) is found in the existence of the interrogative particles, or rather nouns, Tam. *en*, *ên*, Tel. *êmi*, what, why. If the interrogative *edu*, what, leads us necessarily to *adu*, that, may it not be regarded as almost equally certain that the interrogative *em* or *en*, what, points to a demonstrative *am* or *an*, that? Whatever be the origin of the neuter formative *am*, we must assign the same origin to the *an* which is sometimes substituted for it. Thus we may say in Tamil either *kaḍam* or *kaḍan*, debt; *uram* or *uran*, strength. When *adu* is appended to neuter nouns in Tamil as a separable formative, it can keep its place, if euphony is supposed to require it, in the oblique cases as well as in the nominative, and to it the case-signs may be affixed. This is also the case with the formative *an*, and herein it differs in use, if not in origin, from *am*. Thus *kaḍam* in Tamil loses *am* in the accusative, takes *attu* instead, and thus forms its accusative *kaḍattei;* whereas *kaḍan* retains *an*, and has *kaḍanei* for its accusative. In Malayâlam *an* sometimes alternates with *ar* as a formative of nouns—*e.g.*, *uḷan* or *uḷar*, being, equivalent to the more common *uḷava; uḷan-âgu*, to be born. I find a corroboration of this supposition of the original identity of *am* and *adu* in the use of *attu*, Tam., *ad*, Can., and *ti*, Tel., as inflexional increments or signs of the oblique cases of nouns, all these increments being, as it appears to me, only the different shapes which *adu* or *adi* takes in construction. In the inflexion of singular nouns in Tamil, *attu*, as in the example given above, is regularly used instead of the *am* of the nominative, from which we may conclude the identity of both *am* and *attu* (*adu*) in signification, and probably in origin, as different forms of the same demonstrative.

(2.) In Canarese the crude form of the personal pronouns is occasionally used instead of the nominative—*e.g.*, *nâ*, instead of *nânu*, I, and *tâ*, instead of *tânu*, self; and hence it might be supposed that the final *n* or *nu* of those pronouns constitutes a nominative termination. This supposition, however, is inadmissible; for in all the oblique cases, without exception, the final *n* or *nu* retains its place, and it is to it that the signs of case are added. Consequently it is evident that *n* is not a sign of the nominative, but a formative, which has been compounded with the inflexional base, or annexed to it, though it is capable of occasional separation from it.

(3.) In all the Dravidian languages, the quantity of the included vowels of the personal pronouns in some of the oblique cases (and in Tamil, Malayâlam, and Canarese in all the oblique cases) differs from the quantity of the same vowels in the nominative. In the nominative the vowel is invariably long, in the oblique cases generally short—*e.g.*, in Canarese we find *nânu*, I, *nanna*, my; *nînu*, thou, *ninna*, thy; *tânu*, self, *tanna*, of one's self. This is the only instance in these languages in which there is a difference between the nominative and the oblique cases of such a nature as almost to constitute the nominative a case by itself. In this instance, however, it is uncertain whether the nominative has been lengthened for the sake of emphasis, and we are to seek the true form of the root in the oblique cases, or whether the nominative is the true base, and the shortening of the quantity of the vowel in the oblique cases, prior to the addition of postpositions, has arisen from the euphonic tendencies of the language. Telugu shortens the root-vowel in the accusative only. In Tamil the shortened form, without any inflexional addition, is often used as a possessive—*e.g.*, *nin*, thy, from the obsolete *nîn*, thou—a usage which is in accordance with the ordinary Dravidian rule that the inflected form of every noun, or the basis of the oblique cases, is to be regarded as of itself a possessive or adjective. See "Roots: Internal Changes."

Before proceeding to consider the oblique case-signs *seriatim*, it is necessary to inquire into the changes which the base sustains prior to receiving the suffixes.

Inflexion or Inflexional Base of the Oblique Cases.—In a very large number of instances that form of the Dravidian noun which constitutes the crude base, and which is used as the nominative, constitutes also the inflexional base. The nominative of this class of nouns and the base of the oblique cases are identical; and the case-signs are added to the base or nominative without any link of connection, whether inflexional or euphonic, beyond the ordinary *v* or *y*, which is inserted to prevent hiatus between concurrent vowels. In a smaller number of instances (a number which constitutes, however, a very large minority), the base or nominative undergoes some alteration before receiving the addition of the terminations, or case-signs, of the oblique cases.

In the solitary instance of the personal pronouns, as pointed out under the preceding head, the nominative sustains a curtailment (viz., by the shortening of the quantity of the included vowel) on becoming the inflexional base, or base of the oblique cases: but in all other instances the alteration which the base sustains consists in an augmentation, which is sometimes optional and sometimes necessary; and it is to this augmented form (augmented by the addition of some inflexional increment) that the case-signs are attached. This Dravidian rule may be illustrated by Hebrew. In Hebrew the personal and other suffixes of substantives and verbal nouns are attached, not to the base or nominative, but to the construct state—*i.e.*, the state in which a noun stands when it is qualified by a subsequent noun. Just so in the Dravidian languages, in that large class of nouns in which the inflexional base of the noun, or its adjectival form, differs from the crude form or nominative, the signs of case are attached, not to the crude, natural form of the noun, but to the altered, inflected form—viz., to that form which a Dravidian noun assumes when it qualifies or is qualified by a subsequent noun, or when it stands to such noun in the relation of an adjective. This inflected form of the noun is frequently used by itself, without the addition of any case-termination, and when so used it has sometimes a locative, sometimes a possessive or adjectival force. Tamil grammarians hold that the inflexion is not a case-sign, though they cannot but admit that for almost every purpose for which the possessive or locative case-signs are used, the oblique case, or inflected form of the noun, may be used instead. They admit that it is used adjectivally: but it appears to me that its use as an adjectival formative is a secondary one, and that it was originally, like many other adjectival formatives in various languages, a sign of the possessive or locative. Its use eventually as the inflexional basis of all the cases is in perfect harmony with this view of its origin, and testifies to the existence of a period in the history of the language when each of the postpositions of case was known and felt to be a substantive, which required to be united to its base by a sign of localisation or relationship. At present, however, it is our object to seek out and arrange the various increments which are used for forming the inflexional base of the oblique cases, without reference to the other uses to which those increments are put.

(1.) *The inflexional increment 'in' with its dialectic varieties.*—The particle *in* constitutes the inflexion of certain classes of nouns in Tamil-Canarese; and the corresponding Telugu particles are *ni* and *na.* All these particles are, I believe, virtually one and the same. Tamil uses *in* in the singular and in the plural alike; and its original signification has been forgotten to such a degree that it is now often used merely as an euphonic link of connection between the base and its case-signs. For this reason its use both in Tamil and in Canarese is optional. In Telugu the corresponding particles are used only in the singular; and where they are used, their use is not euphonic merely, but is intended to constitute the *inflexion.* Ku, which in this respect is more nearly allied to Tamil than Telugu is, and more regular, uses *ni* as the inflexion of the plural as well as of the singular of all classes of nouns.

When *in* is used in Tamil as the inflexion of the neut. sing. demonstratives *adu,* that, *idu,* this, it is apt to be confounded with *an,* a termination which those pronouns often take, especially in the oblique cases, instead of *u.* Instead of *adu* and *idu,* we may say in Tamil *adan* and *idan.* In the nominative these forms are very rarely used; but the accusative, *adan-ei,* is more common, and the dative, *adarku* (*adan-ku*), still more so. *id-in-âl,* through this, *ad-in-âl,* through that, and cases similarly formed, must therefore be carefully distinguished from *idan-âl* and *adan-âl.* The *an* of the latter is a formative, which is probably of the same origin as the *am* of many neuter nouns (that *am* being often convertible into *an*); whereas *in* is an inflexional increment, and was probably a case-sign of the locative originally.

The use of *in* as an inflexional increment effects no alteration in the meaning of the case-sign which is suffixed to it. Where it is not followed by a case-sign, it is generally found to be used as a mode of expressing the genitive; but where a case-sign follows, it is merely euphonic, and its use is optional. Thus, we may say either *keiyâl* (*kei-(y)-âl*), with the hand, or *keiyin-âl* (*kei-(y)-in-âl*); either *kâlâl,* with the foot, or *kâlinâl* (*kâl-in-âl*). In the first of these instances (*kei-(y)-in-âl*), *y* is used to keep the initial vowel of *in* pure, in accordance with the ordinary rule of the language; from the use of which, in this instance, it is evident that *in,* though merely euphonic in its present application, was in its origin something more than a mere euphonic expletive.

in is not only attached as an inflexional increment to the crude base of Tamil nouns, but it is appended also to other inflexional increments, viz., to *attu*, and to the doubled final ḍ and **r** of certain classes of nouns. Thus, by the addition of *attu* to *mara-m*, a tree, we form *marattu*, the inflexional base of the oblique cases, by suffixing to which *âl*, the sign of the instrumental case, we form *marattâl*, by a tree; but we may also attach *in* to *attu*, forming *attin* (*att-in*), a doubled and euphonised increment—*e.g.*, *marattinâl* (*mara-attu-in-âl*). As *in* when standing alone, without the suffix of any case-sign, has acquired the force of the genitive, so also has the double increment, *attin*—*e.g.*, *marattin* signifies of a tree. In Tamil, *in* is the inflexion of all nouns except those which end in *am*, or in *ḍ-u* or **r**-*u*: in Canarese *in* is much more rarely used than in Tamil; but where it is used, its use is rather euphonic and optional than inflexional, and it cannot be used by itself to express the force of the genitive. As in Tamil *guruvil*, in a priest, and *guruvinil* are identical, so we may say in Canarese either *guruvalli* or *guruvinalli*. In Malayâlam the use of *in* before *il*, as in the last instance now adduced, is found, Dr Gundert says, only in pedantic poetry. Before the other inflexional increments it is common enough.

In Telugu the corresponding particles *ni* and *na* constitute the inflexion, or natural genitive of certain classes of nouns, and are also attached as inflexional increments to the base before suffixing the case-signs—*e.g.*, *dîniki* (*dî-ni-ki*), to it, *tammuniki* (*tammu-ni-ki*), to a younger brother, *guruva-na-ku*, to a spiritual teacher. These increments are attached only to the singular in Telugu. They constitute the singular inflexion—*i.e.*, the genitival or adjectival base of the noun; and though their use is now in many connections optional and merely euphonic, they doubtless contributed at the outset to grammatical expression; nor are they to be regarded as the inflexion of masculine nouns and pronouns alone, though they are chiefly used by them, for *dâniki*, to that, *dîniki*, to this, are neuters. The Telugu *ni*, and the Tamil-Canarese *in*, are doubtless identical in origin. The change in the position of the vowel is in accordance with the change of *il*, Tam. the negative particle, into *lê* in Telugu, and of *uḷ*, Tam. within, into *lô* in Telugu. It also corresponds to the change of the position of the vowel which is apparent when *in*, the Latin preposition, is compared with the corresponding Sanskrit preposition *ni*.

It will be seen that *in* is used not only as an inflexional increment, but as a genitive, an ablative, and a locative. We cannot be in error, therefore, I think, in regarding *in* in all these instances as one and the same particle, though in different connections it is used for different purposes, nor in concluding that originally it had only one meaning, and was used for only one purpose. A comparison of the various case-signs or increments appears to show that *in* was originally an equivalent form for *il*, and as *il* means 'here,' or a house (*e.g.*, *kô-v-il*, Tam. God's house, a temple), it seems evident that the first use of *il* in the inflexion of nouns must have been as a sign of the locative. It appears probable therefore that its equivalent *in* must also have had at first a locative signification. Dr Gundert says, "The oblique cases would all seem to be modified forms of the locative, as expressing something happening in or about the noun, whilst the nominative pronounces its totality." *in* being used in so many connections and in so general a way, in course of time it came to be regarded in some connections as merely an inflexional increment, that is, as an optional suffix to the base, and lastly, as little better than an euphonic expletive, which might be prefixed (its original meaning now having become obscured) to any case-sign, and even to *il*, its own earliest shape.

(2.) *The inflexional increments 'ad' and 'ar.'*—The particles *ad* and *ar* are extensively used by Canarese as inflexional increments. Their use exactly resembles that of *in* in the same language, though each is restricted to a particular class of words. *in* is used as an increment of the base in connection with nouns which end in *u*—*e.g.*, *guru*, a priest; and *ad* and *ar* are used in connection with neuter nouns and demonstratives, and with those alone. In the Canarese genitive case-endings, *ara*, *ada*, *ina*, and *a*, it will be seen that the real and only sign of the genitive is *a*, the final vowel of each; and therefore Dr Stevenson erred in comparing *ara* or *ra* (properly *ar-a* or *ad-a*) with the New Persian *râ*. *ad* and *ar* are prefixed to the signs of case, not by the genitive only, but by three cases besides—viz., by the accusative, the instrumental, and the locative. Thus we may say not only *idara* (*id-ar-a*), of this, and *marada* (*mar-a-da*), of a tree, but also *idaralli* (*id-ar-alli*), in this, and *maradinda* (*mar-ad-inda*), by a tree. Consequently *ad* and *ar*, whatever be their origin, do not appear to be signs of case, in so far as their use is concerned, but are used merely as increments of the base, or inflexional bonds of conjunction between the base and the case-signs, like *in*, *ni*, &c. Moreover, Canarese differs in its use of these increments from Telugu and Tamil in this, that it never suffixes them alone without the addition of the case-signs, and never gives them the signification of genitives or adjectival formatives.

ad and *ar* are evidently related. Are they also identical? Both are increments of the neuter alone; and where Canarese uses *ar*, Tuḷu uses *t*. *d* and *r* are known to change places dialectically, as in the southern provinces of the Tamil country, in which *adu*, it, is pronounced *aṟu;* and the Canarese increment *ad* is certainly, and *ar* probably, identical with that very word—viz., with the Tamil-Canarese demonstrative *adu* or *ad*, it. Dr Gundert thinks *ar* derived, not from *adu*, but from *an*, the equivalent of *aṟu*. I do not feel sure of this; but it is certain that *n* changes into ṟ before *k*—*e.g.*, *adaṟku*, Tam. to that—and that *n* and ṟ are sometimes found to change places —*e.g.*, comp. *piṟ-agu*, afterwards, with *pin*, afterwards.

Though Tamil has not regularly adopted the unchanged form of this demonstrative, *adu*, as an inflexional increment of the base in the declension of nouns, it makes use of it occasionally in a manner which perfectly illustrates the origin of the Canarese use of it. In classical Tamil, as I have already mentioned in discussing the origin of the increment *am*, the neuter demonstrative may optionally be added to any neuter noun in the singular, not for the purpose of altering the signification, but merely for the improvement of the euphony, and for the purpose of meeting the requirements of prosody. *adu* may thus be added even to the nominative—*e.g.*, we may not only write *pon*, gold, but also poetically *ponnadu*, gold, etymologically gold-that—*i.e.*, that (which is) gold. It is much more common, however, and more in accordance also with the Canarese usage, to use *ad-u* in the oblique cases; in which event it is inserted between the base and the case-sign, so as to become virtually (yet without losing its proper character) an inflexional increment—*e.g.*, instead of *ponnei*, the accusative of *pon*, gold, we may write *ponnadei* (*ponn-ad-ei*).

We may possibly connect with the Canarese *ar*, and therefore with *ad*, and ultimately with the neuter demonstrative itself, the euphonic consonant *r*, which is used in Telugu in certain instances to separate between a noun of quality used as an adjective and the feminine suffix *âlu*—*e.g.*, *sogasu-r-âlu*, a handsome woman. This would be quite in accordance with the peculiar Telugu usage of employing the neuter demonstrative singular in place of the feminine singular. I should prefer, however, to regard this *r* as used simply to prevent hiatus.

(3.) *The inflexional increment 'ṭi.'*—In Telugu *ṭi* or *ti* is the most common and characteristic inflexional increment of neuter singular nouns, and it is used in Telugu, like the corresponding *attu* in Tamil, not merely as an increment of the base, but as the inflexion, with the signification of the possessive case or of that of an adjective, as the context may require. Two instances of the use of this increment will suffice out of the very numerous class of neuter nouns which form their singular inflexion by the addition of *ṭi* or *ti* (or rather by the combination of that particle with their last syllable)—*e.g.*, *vâkili*, a doorway, inflexion *vâkiṭi; nuduru*, the forehead, inflexion *muduṭi*. In these instances of the use of *ṭi* or *ti*, the inflexional increment appears to be substituted for the last syllable; but it is certainly to be considered as an addition to the word—as a particle appended to it; and the blending of the increment with the base, instead of merely suffixing it, has arisen from the euphonic tendencies of the language.

I have no doubt that the suffixed particle which constitutes the Telugu inflexional increment was originally *ti*, not *ṭi*—the dental, not the lingual. This would account for the circumstance that *ṭ* alone follows words of which the final consonant is *r* or *l;* for on the addition of the dental *t* to *r* or *l* both consonants dialectically coalesce and become *ṭ;* the hard cerebral being regarded as euphonically equivalent to the two soft letters. In no case in Telugu is there a double *ṭ* in the inflexional increment. *tolli*, antiquity, forms its inflexion not in *tolṭi* or *tolliṇṭi*, as might have been expected, but in *toṇṭi*. Here, however, it is not the increment that is euphonised, but the final *l* of the base. Compare the Tamil *tondru*, antiquity, from the root *tol*. *ti* is evidently the equivalent of the Tamil *dru*, an euphonised form of *du*. The dental *ti* is used instead of the cerebral *ṭi*, as the inflexion of nouns ending in a pure vowel or in *yu* after a pure vowel—*e.g.*, *vâyu*, the mouth, inflexion *vâti; chê*, the hand, inflexion *chêti*. This circumstance proves that it was the dental *ti* which was originally used in all cases. The dental *t*, on being appended to consonants, changes naturally into the lingual; whereas the lingual rarely, if ever, changes into the dental. If we now conclude, as I think we undoubtedly may, that the Telugu inflexion was originally *ti*, not *ṭi*, this inflexional increment may at once be connected with the Telugu neuter demonstrative, *adi*, in the same manner as the Canarese *ad* and the Tamil *attu* are connected with the Tamil-Canarese neuter demonstrative *adu*. Though the identification of the inflexion and the neuter singular demonstrative could not easily be established from Telugu alone, or from any one dialect alone, yet the cumulative argument derived from a comparison of all the dialects has great force. An important link of evidence is furnished by the inflexion which follows.—

(4.) *The inflexional increment 'attu' or 'attru'* (*arru*).—All Tamil nouns which end in *am*, whether Sanskrit derivatives or pure Tamil roots, reject *am* in the oblique cases in the singular, and take *att-u* instead; and it is to this increment that the various case-signs are suffixed—*e.g.*, the locative case-sign *il* is not added to *âram* depth, but to the inflexional base *âr-attu*, so that in the depth is not *âram-il*, but *âr-att-il*. This rule admits of no exception in the ordinary dialect of the Tamil; but in the poetical dialect, which represents more or less distinctly an older condition of the language, *attu* is sometimes left unused, and the case-sign is added directly to the crude base—*e.g.*, instead of *kay-attu-kku*, to the depth (from *kayam*, depth), *kaya-kku* is used in the Chintâmaṇi. When the increment *attu* is not followed by any sign of case, but by another noun, like the other inflexion *in*, and like the corresponding Telugu inflexion *ṭi*, it has ordinarily the force either of the genitive or of an adjective, sometimes that of a locative, which is perhaps the first use to which it was put—*e.g.*, *kuḷ-attu mîn*, may mean as a genitive, the fish of the tank, as a locative, the fish in the tank, or as an adjective, tank fish. This inflexion, like *ad* and *ar* in Canarese, and *ṭi* or *ti* in Telugu, is used in connection with the singular alone. *am*, the formative of the base, which is used only by the nominative in the singular, is retained in the plural, not in the nominative only, but in all the oblique cases. To it the sign of plurality is appended, and the case-sign follows the sign of plurality—*e.g.*, *maraṅgaḷil* (*maramgaḷ-il*), in trees.

There are in Tamil a few naturally plural (neuter) pronominals and nouns of relation (*e.g.*, *avei*, those (things); *sila*, few; *pala*, many; *ellâ*, all; compare Mal. *silava*, *palava*, *ellâva*) which receive in their oblique cases the inflexional increment *arru*, pronounced *attru*. Thus, from *ellâm*, all, which is properly *ellâ-v-um* or *ellâ-um* (*um* being the conjunctive and intensitive particle 'even,' and *ellâ-um* or *ellâm*, signifying even all, all together), the locative which is formed by the Tamil is *ellâvattrilum* (*ellâ-(v)-attr'-il-um*), in all, literally, even in all. So also *avei*, they (neuter), forms its accusative not by adding *ei*, the accusative case-sign, to *avei*, but by inserting *attru*, and adding *ei* thereto—*e.g.*, *avattrei* (*av-attr-ei*), them; in which instance *ei* (for *a*), the sign of the plural, is rejected, and its place is supplied by *attru*, the inflexional increment of this class of plurals.

It is evident that the Tamil increments, *attu* and *attru*, are virtually identical. The difference in use is slight, and in pronunciation still slighter; and in general *attru* is pronounced exactly like *attu* by the vulgar. We may therefore conclude that they are one and the same, and on examining Telugu we find additional confirmation of their identity. In Telugu, *avi*, they (neuter), answering to the Tamil *avei*, forms its inflexion in *vâṭi* (for *avaṭi*). This Telugu (supposititious) *avaṭi* is evidently identical with the Tamil *avattru*. The *ṭi* of this inflexion is certainly the same as the *ṭi* of Telugu nouns substantive: and if there is no difference in Telugu between the *ṭi* which forms the inflexional increment of neuter singular nouns and demonstratives and the plural inflexion *ṭi* of such words as *vâṭi*, we may also conclude that there is no real difference between the singular *attu* and the plural *attru* of the Tamil.

Whence did the **r** which is included in *a***rr***u* or *attr-u* take its rise? We see its origin, I think, in Canarese; for in the ancient dialect *ar* or *r* forms the inflexional increment of every one of the plural pronominals which take *a***rr***u* in Tamil—*e.g.*, *avara* (corresponding Tam. *ava***rr***u*), of those things; *ellavara* (Tam. *ellâva***rr***u*), of all things; *kelavara* (Tam. *silava***rr***u*), of some (things). The Canarese *r* is probably, as we have seen, derived from, and originally identical with, *d*, or *t*; and hence Tamil in doubling **r** gives it the sound *ttr*. Thus, not only the Tamil increment *att-u*, but also *a***rr***-u*, seems to be derived from the same origin as the Canarese *ad* or *ar*, and the Telugu *ṭi*—viz., from the neuter singular demonstrative. Both these inflexions have been formed also by the same process; for *a***r**, when doubled, becomes *a***rr***-u* (*attr-u*), as naturally as *ad*, when doubled, becomes *att-u*; and in each case the doubling arises from the adjectival use to which the suffixed pronoun is put. It is a recognised rule of Tamil that when a noun ending in *d-u* is used adjectivally, the *d-u* may either become *d-in* or *tt-u*—*e.g.*, from *erud-u*, an ox, is formed either *erud-in* or *erutt-u*, of an ox. So also *ad-u*, it, which is now generally inflected by the addition of *in*, seems to have been inflected formerly as *att-u*. *adu* is vulgarly pronounced in the oblique cases as *attu* by the bulk of the northern Tamilians. The majority of the natives of Madras, for instance, use *attei* (*attu-ei*) as the accusative of *adu*, that, instead of *adei*; and in the neuter singular pronominal suffixes to the verb the same pronunciation is not only commonly heard, but is often written—*e.g.*, instead of *irukki***r***adukku*, to its being (the dative of *iru-kkir-adu*, it is, the being, or that which is), Madras Tamilians write *irukki***r***attukku*; in which compound *attu* is evidently used as the neuter demonstrative singular instead of *adu*. It is also deserving of notice, that the feminine singular suffix of a large class of appellative nouns, which is *di* or *adi* in Telugu, and which has been shown to be identical with the neuter demonstrative, is in Tamil *tti* or *atti*. I explain in this way the Tamil neuter singular preterites in *ttru*, like *âyittru* (*âyi***rr***u*), it becomes. This was *âyidadu*, which was abbreviated into *âyiddu* = *âyittu* (compare the corresponding change in Canarese), and this was euphonised into *âyittru*.

Two instances will suffice to illustrate the identity of the Tamil *attu* and the Canarese *ad*, and thus supply the only link that is wanting to the perfect identification of *attu* with the Telugu *ti*, and of both with *adu.* The Tamil *pûrv-att-il,* in ancient times, is compounded of *pûrv-am* (Sans. deriv.), antiquity, *att-u,* the inflexional increment, and *il,* the sign of the locative. Compare this with the corresponding Canarese *pûrv-ad-alli,* in which it is evident that *ad* is used in the same manner as *att-u,* and perfectly agrees with it in signification. Again, the Tamil *âyirattondru,* a thousand and one, is formed from *âyiram,* a thousand (the inflexion of which is *âyir-attu*), and *ondru,* one. When this is compared with the corresponding Canarese word *sâvirad-ondu,* from *sâvira,* a thousand (equivalent to the Tamil *âyira*)—inflexional form *sâvir-ad*—to which *ondu,* identical with *ondru,* is appended, it is evident that the Canarese increment *ad'* and the Tamil *att'* are one and the same; and also that in this instance the Canarese *ad'* is used for precisely the same purpose as the Tamil *att',* viz., as an inflexional increment with an adjectival signification.

Dr Gundert takes the Tam. **arru** (*attru*) to arise from the combination of *an-ttu,* and thinks this supposition in favour of his derivation of Can. *ar* from *an.* (See "Inflexional Increments" *ad* and *ar.*) He also thinks the Tel. *ṭi* agrees with it, as originally representing **rr** (*ttr*). I still think the view I have taken preferable. *an* = *am* being probably a neuter singular demonstrative, and *ttu* = *du* = *adu* being the same, *an-ttu* would be a doubling of two particles having precisely the same force, and therefore abnormal. The union of *attu* and *in, attin,* would not be abnormal, the particles having originally a different meaning (*attu,* demonstrative pronoun; *in,* probably sign of locative). Besides, I doubt whether *an-du* would ever become *an-ttu* and then **arru** (*attru*). It seems contrary to the euphonic laws of the language. These particles would naturally coalesce into *andu.* In Telugu we have a particle formed apparently in this very manner from the union of *an* with *du,* viz., the sign of the locative; but this is not *attru* or *ṭi,* as according to the theory referred to it ought to be, but *andu.* (See "The Locative.")

(5.) *The formation of the inflexion by means of doubling and hardening the final consonant.*—Tamil nouns ending in *ḍ-u* and **r**-*u* form the basis of their oblique cases by doubling the final *ḍ* and **r**: and the doubled *ḍ* becomes by rule *ṭṭ,* and the doubled **r**, *ttr* (though spelled **rr**)—*e.g.,* from *kâḍ-u,* a jungle, is formed *kâṭṭ-(u)-kku,* to a jungle; from *â***r**-*u,* a river, *âttr-il* (*â***rr**-*il*), in a river. This inflexion, like all others, is supposed by Dr Gundert to have been originally a locative. I am doubtful of the propriety of this theory in this instance, and prefer the following explanation.

This doubling of the final consonants of such nouns is to be regarded, I think, as a sign of the transition of the meaning of the first noun to the succeeding one, just as when intransitive or neuter verbs ending in *ḍ-u* or **r**-*u* acquire by doubling their vowels a transitive signification—*e.g.*, from *ôḍ-u*, to run, is formed *ôṭṭ-u*, to drive; from *têr-u*, to become clear, comes *têttr-u* (*têrr-u*), to clarify, to comfort. Properly speaking, therefore, this doubling of the final is an adjectival formative, rather than an inflexional or case-sign basis; but in this, as in many other cases, the same form appears to be used in two different connections, in consequence of the case-sign which is appended to the doubled final having originally been a noun, and still retaining in compounds the force of a noun.

In Telugu the final consonant of nouns of this class is hardened, but not doubled, to form the inflexion or basis of the oblique cases—*e.g.*, the inflexion of *êr-u*, a river, is not *êṭṭi* (*êrri*), but *êṭi*, of a river; and that of *nâḍu*, a country, is *nâṭi*, of a country. In some instances Telugu corresponds more closely to Tamil in forming the inflexion of nouns in **rr** by changing that into **r***t*—*e.g.*, *a***rr***u*, the neck; inflexion of the same *a***r***ti*. If we regarded Telugu alone, we should consider these examples, not as instances of the doubling of a final *ḍ* or **r**, but rather as instances of the incorporation of *ṭi*, the usual inflexional suffix, with those finals; and we should suppose this view to be confirmed by the circumstance that Telugu does not, like Tamil, double the final *ḍ-u* or **r**-*u* of intransitive verbs on converting them into transitives, but adds a formative *chu*. Nevertheless, the Tamil rule is so clear and express, and so evidently founded upon grammatical reasons, and the Telugu words in question, *nâḍi*, &c., so exactly agree with the Tamil, that we cannot but recognise in them the operation of the same principle, though somewhat disguised. In other and parallel instances, though the Telugu hardens, it does not double—*e.g.*, from *pâḍ-u*, Tam. and Tel. to sing, Tamil forms *pâṭṭ-u*, a song, Telugu *pâṭ-a*. The final *i* of such Telugu inflexions as *nâṭi*, of a country (from *nâḍ-u*), instead of *nâṭ-u*, which Tamil would lead us to expect, is owing, I have no doubt, to the influence of *ṭi*, which is the ordinary suffix of the inflexion of neuter nouns.

(6.) *The inflexional increment 'i.'*—The inflexion of the plural of the Telugu epicene demonstrative pronoun consists in *i*—*e.g.*, *vâru* (from *avaru*), those persons; inflexion *vâri*, of them, their. The final *u* of *vâr-u* is merely euphonic, but the *i* of *vâri* is certainly an inflexional increment; and possibly the final *i* of the singular masculine demonstrative inflexional *vâni* is not to be regarded as a portion of *ni*, the ordinary inflexional increment of Telugu masculine nouns, but is identical with the final *i* of *vâri*. A small class of Telugu nouns form their singular inflexion also in *i*—*e.g.*, *kâl-i*, of a foot, *têr-i*, of a car. What is the origin of this *i*? I think we are guided to a true idea of its origin by comparing it with the possessive pronoun *vâridi*, Tel. that which is theirs, which in Ku also is *êvâridi*. When *vâridi* is compared with the Tamil possessive *avaradu*, the meaning of which is exactly the same, we see that in each language the termination is that of the neuter demonstrative pronoun, which is *adu* in Tamil, *adi* in Telugu; and we also see that the penultimate *i* of *vâridi* is derived by attraction, according to Telugu usage, from the succeeding *i*, which is that of the neuter demonstrative singular *adi*. The final *i* of *vâri* may therefore be regarded as an abbreviation of *adi*, or at least as derived from it.

(7.) *Telugu plural inflexional increment in 'a.'*—In Telugu *a* constitutes the plural inflexion of most colloquial pronominals, and of all substantive nouns without exception. *l-u*, properly *l*, is the pluralising particle of all neuter nouns in Telugu, and of the majority of rational ones. The inflexion is effected by changing this *l-u* into *la*, or to speak more correctly, by suffixing *a* to *l*—the final vowel of *lu* being merely euphonic; and it is to this incremental *a*, as to *ni* and *ṭi*, the singular inflexions, that all the case-signs are appended—*e.g.*, *kattulu*, knives; inflexion *kattula;* instrumental *kattula-chêta*, by knives. I have no doubt that this inflexional increment *a* is identical with *a*, one of the Tamil-Canarese signs of the genitive, of the use of which as a genitive, in the singular as well as in the plural, we have an illustration even in Telugu, in the reflexive pronouns *tan-a*, of self, *tam-a*, of selves. This increment also, therefore, is to be regarded as a genitive in origin, though in actual use merely an inflexion; and I have no doubt that each of the Dravidian inflexions proceeds from some case-sign.

Before leaving this subject, I should briefly refer to one which bears some relation to it, viz. :—

Euphonic links of connection between the base and the inflexion, the base and the case-signs, or the inflexion and the case-signs.

In Tamil the dative case-sign *ku* is generally preceded by an euphonic *u*, and through the influence of this *u* the *k* is doubled. Thus, from *avan*, he, is formed not *avanku*, to him, but *avanukku* (*avan-u-kku*). The personal pronouns, both in the singular and in the plural, make use of an euphonic *a* in this connection, instead of *u*—*e.g.*, from *nân* (or rather from a weakened form, *ên*), *I*, is formed the inflexion *en;* and this takes as its dative not *enku* or *enukku*, to me, but *enakku* (*en-a-kku*). In the higher dialect of Tamil the dative case-sign *ku* is often directly attached to the noun, especially in those instances in which the noun terminates in a liquid or semi-vowel—*e.g.*, we find in that dialect not *avarukku* (*avar-u-kku*), to them, but *avarku*. In ancient Canarese also, the dative case-sign was invariably attached in this manner. In Malayâlam the personal pronouns require the insertion of an euphonic vowel, as in Tamil, between the inflected base and the case-sign. Thus, to thee, is *enikk'*, *inikk'*, *enakk'*, *ninakk'*, or *niṇakk'*. To us, *namukku, namakku.* Some of these forms are rarely used.

Whenever concurrent vowels meet in Tamil *v* and *y* are used, as has already been shown, to prevent hiatus; and accordingly they are used between the final vowel of nouns and those inflexions or case-signs which begin with vowels—*e.g.*, *naḍuvil* (*naḍu-(v)-il*), in the middle; *vaṛiyil* (*vaṛi-(y)-il*), in the way. Compare this with the use of *v* for a similar purpose in Magyar—*e.g.*, from *lô*, a horse, and *at*, the sign of the objective case, is formed not *lôat*, but *lôvat*, precisely as would be done in Tamil. *v* and *y* are used by Canarese in the same manner as by Tamil; but in Telugu, as has already been shown, *n* is used as a preventive of hiatus instead of *v*.

The way has now been prepared for the investigation of the Dravidian oblique cases, and of the signs of case properly so called.

The Accusative or 'Second' Case.—In the Indo-European languages the case-sign of the accusative of neuter nouns is identical with that of the nominative case. This identity has arisen, I conceive, not from the nominative being used as an accusative, but *vice versâ* from the accusative being used as a nominative. The accusative case-suffix is a sign of passivity, or of being acted upon; and it appears to have been suffixed to masculine and feminine nouns to denote that in that instance they were to be regarded not as agents, but as objects. Subsequently, I conceive, it was adopted, because of this signification, as a general characteristic of the neuter, objective, or dead class of nouns, and so came to be used as the nominative, or normal case-ending of nouns of that class.

In the Dravidian languages, on the other hand, that which was in its origin a formative termination of abstract neuter nouns, seems to have been adopted as an accusative case-sign. The old Canarese accusative case-sign *am* seems to be identical with, and is probably derived from, the *am* which is so largely used as a formative by Dravidian neuters. Notwithstanding this, the use of the nominative, or rather of the simple, unformed base, as the accusative of neuter nouns, is the ordinary and almost universal colloquial usage of Tamil-Malayâlam, and is often found even in classical compositions. The accusative case-termination may be suffixed whenever it appears to be desirable to do so, either for the sake of euphony or to prevent ambiguity; but it is rarely employed except when it is required for those purposes. When this case-termination is used without necessity, it sounds stiff and unidiomatic; and this is one of the peculiarities by which the Tamil of foreigners is marked. Tamil-Malayâḷam masculine and feminine nouns and their corresponding pronouns invariably take the accusative case-suffix when they are governed by active verbs. This probably proceeds from the principle that it is more natural for rational beings to act than to be acted upon; and hence when they do happen to be acted upon—when the nouns by which they are denoted are to be taken objectively—it becomes necessary, in order to avoid misapprehension, to suffix to them the objective case-sign. On the other hand, the difference between the nominative and the accusative of neuter nouns is often allowed to pass unnoticed, because such nouns, whether they act or are acted upon, are alike destitute of personality and inert. Whether the accusative is used as the nominative, as in the Indo-European languages, or whether, as is often the case in the Scythian tongues, the nominative is used for the accusative, the principle involved appears to be one and the same. In Telugu the use of the nominative for the accusative is confined to things without life. In the case of irrational animals, as in that of rational beings, the accusative must be expressed. As far as things without life are concerned, Telugu adheres to the ordinary Dravidian rules. The dialect of the Tudas uses the nominative for the accusative and genitive in the case of all nouns, except the personal pronouns. The use of the nominative of neuter nouns for the accusative is not unknown to the North Indian vernaculars, and is one of those particulars in which those vernaculars appear to have participated in Dravidian or non-Aryan influences.

(1.) *Accusative case-signs ei, e,* and *a.*—The only sign of the accusative which Tamil recognises is *ei*, which is suffixed to both numbers and to all genders; though, as has been mentioned, the accusative of neuter nouns is often identical with the nominative or base. Examples, *avan-ei*, him, *avaḷ-ei*, her, *ad-ei*, it. The accusative case-sign of Malayâḷam is *e*, which evidently represents the Tamil *ei*. In ancient Malayâḷam, Dr Gundert says, *a* is often used instead. Canarese ordinarily uses either *a* or *annu* as its accusative case-sign; but in some instances (*e.g.*, *nanna*, me, *ninna*, thee), *a* seems to have been converted into *na*. This *a* seems to be equivalent to the Malayâḷam *e* and the Tamil *ei*, into which the Canarese short *a* is often found to change by rule.

The Tamil-Malayâḷam accusative case-sign *e* or *a* may be compared with *he* or *e*, the dative-accusative of Hindi pronouns; with the Gujarâthi dative-accusative singular *e*; and with the preponderance of the vowel *e* which is observed in the dative-accusatives of the Bengali and Sindhi. Compare also the Brahui dative-accusative *ne* or *e*, and

*

the Malay *e*. On pushing the comparison amongst the Scythian tongues, not a few of their accusative case-signs are found to resemble the Tamil accusative. Thus the Wotiak accusative is formed by adding *â* to the root—*e.g.*, *ton*, thou, *ton-â*, thee. The Turkish accusative is *î* or *yî*; the Mongolian *î* after a consonant: *djî*, instead of the Turkish *yî*, after a vowel. The Turkish *î* is doubtless a softened form of the Oriental Turkish accusative case-sign *nî*, from which it has been derived by the same process by which the Turkish dative case-sign *eh* or *yeh* is undoubtedly derived from the old Oriental Turkish *gâ* or *ghâh*. It would therefore appear that the Scythian accusative originally contained a nasal; and in accordance with this supposition we find in the Calmuck pronouns an accusative case-sign corresponding to the Oriental Turkish *nî*—*e.g.*, *bida-nî*, us, from *bida*, we, and also *na-maï*, me, and *dzi-maï*, thee, from the bases *na* and *dzi*. With this we may again compare the Brahui dative-accusative *ne* or *e*. *nî* being evidently the basis of the Turkish and Mongolian sign of the accusative, if the Dravidian *ei* or *e* be allied to it (though this can hardly be regarded as probable), this *ei* or *e* must originally have been preceded or followed by a nasal; and in investigating the other Dravidian accusative case-signs we shall discover some reasons for surmising this to have been actually the case.

(2.) *Accusative case-signs am, annu, anna, nu, &c.*—*am* is the characteristic sign of the ancient Canarese accusative, and is used in connection with nouns and pronouns alike—*e.g.*, *avaḷ-am*, her. The more modern form of the Canarese accusative is *annu*—*e.g.*, *avaḷ-annu*, her; and this *annu* is evidently identical with the older *am*. *am* has in other instances besides this evinced a tendency to change into *an*; for 'he' is *avam* in ancient Canarese, though *avan* in Tamil. The change of the old Indo-European *m*, the sign of the accusative in Latin and Sanskrit, into the Greek ν is also a parallel case. The ancient Canarese case-sign *am* no sooner changed into *an*, than it would irresistibly be impelled to euphonise *an* by the addition of *nu*. Even in Tamil, *maṉ*, earth, is commonly pronounced *maṉṉu*, and the corresponding Telugu word is *mannu* by rule. Hence we seem to be quite safe in deriving *annu* directly from *an*, and *an* from *am*. Another form of the Canarese accusative case-sign is *anna*, instead of *annu*, or simply *nna* or *na*—*e.g.*, *na-nna*, me. The final *u* has in this instance been changed into *a*, through the attractive force of the primitive *an*; or perhaps the entire euphonic appendage *nu* has been rejected, and the original case-sign *an* been softened to *a*, whilst the final *n* of the base has been doubled to augment or express the objectivity of the signification.

The Tuḷu accusative case-sign is *nu* or *n'*, which is evidently identical with the case-signs of the Telugu and Canarese. Compare the various accusatives of 'this'—old Can. *idam*, modern Can. *idannu;* Tuḷu *unden;* Tel. *dîni*. Probably the whole of these case-signs are altered forms of the old Can. *am;* and this particle, as has already been suggested, under the head of the nominative, appears to have been originally a singular neuter demonstrative pronoun. When the Gônd accusative differs from the dative it is denoted by *ûn*.

In Telugu the neuter accusative is often the same as the nominative, as in the other Dravidian dialects; but when the noun denotes animals, or things possessed of life, whether rational or irrational, the accusative must be expressed by the addition of a sign of case. The accusative case-sign may optionally be suffixed, as in Tamil, to nouns denoting things without life; but whether the noun denote a thing without life, or a being possessed of life, whether it be singular or plural, the sign of case must be suffixed to the inflexion, genitive, or oblique case basis, not to the nominative. When the inflexion is the same as the nominative, the noun to which the case-sign is attached is still regarded as the inflexion, so that in theory the rule admits of no exceptions. The sign of the accusative in Telugu is *nu* or *ni*. When preceded by *i* it is *ni*—*e.g.*, *iṇṭi-ni*, *dom-um;* where it is preceded by any other vowel it is *ṇu*—*e.g.*, *biḍḍa-nu*, *puer-um*. A similar *ni* or *na* is used in Telugu (but not so systematically as the corresponding *in* in Tamil) as an euphonic inflexional increment; and *na* or *ni* is also a sign of the locative in Telugu. Probably those locative and genitive suffixes were originally, and are still to be regarded, as one and the same; but the sign of the accusative, though nearly identical in sound, proceeds apparently from a different source. Comparing it with the Canarese, and especially with the Tuḷu, accusative *nu* or *n'*, we can scarcely avoid the conclusion that, though in sound it is identical with the ordinary inflexional augment, it is to be regarded as a relic of the Canarese accusative case-sign *annu* or *am*. The suffixes of the accusative of the Telugu personal pronouns can be explained on this supposition alone. The inflexions of those pronouns are essentially different from their accusatives, and incapable of being confounded with them; and the accusatives of those pronouns take of necessity, and not merely for euphony, the nasal suffixes *nu* or *nnu* in the singular, and *mu* or *mmu* in the plural. Thus, whilst *nâ*, of me, is the inflexion of *nênu*, I, its accusative is *nanu* or *nannu*, me; the accusative of the second person is *ninu* or *ninnu*, thee, and their plurals are *mamu* or *mammu*, us, *mimu* or *mimmu*, you, whilst the inflexions of those plurals are *mâ* and *mî*. When these accusatives are compared with the Canarese and

Tuḷu, especially with *yanan'*, me, and *ninan'*, thee, in the latter, their virtual identity, and therefore the origin of them all from the ancient Canarese *am* can scarcely be doubted.

We may now proceed to compare this accusative case-sign *am*, *an*, *annu*, *nu*, or *na*, with the Gujarâthi dative-accusative *ne*, with the Panjâbi *nu* or *num*, and also with the Brahui *ne* or *e*, and the Turkish and Mongolian *nî* or *î*. In the Finnish tongues the greater number of singular accusatives are formed by suffixing *en*, *an*, &c., which are also used as signs of the genitive : in the plural there is rarely any difference between the nominative and the accusative. Ascending further towards the source of the Scythian tongues, we find in the language of the Scythian tablets at Behistun an unquestionable link of connection with the Dravidian. The pronoun of the second person singular in that language is *nî*, thou, of which *nin* is the accusative; and when this is compared with the Tuḷu *nin-an'*, thee, we cannot fail to be struck with the closeness of the resemblance.

We should also notice the extensive use of *m* or *n* as an accusative case-sign in the languages of the Indo-European family. In Sanskrit, Latin, and Gothic, *m* predominates, in Greek *n*; but these consonants are virtually identical, like the *m* of the ancient Canarese, and the *n* of the modern. A similar form of the accusative being extensively prevalent, as we have seen, in the Scythian tongues, it would be unreasonable to derive the Dravidian case-sign from the Indo-European. In this instance it would be safer to conclude that both families have retained a relic of their original oneness.

If, as appears highly probable, the old Dravidian accusative in *am* is identical in origin with the *am* which is used as a sort of nominative neuter, or rather neuter formative, and if this *am* was originally a demonstrative pronoun, formed from the demonstrative base *a*, we seem to find in the Dravidian languages, not only a relic of their original relationship with other families of tongues now widely divergent, but an index to the original meaning of the neuter accusative case-sign *m* or *n*, wherever found, and an explanation of the identity of the singular neuter accusative case-sign in so many Indo-European languages with the singular nominative case-sign *am*. Being a formative of neuter nouns, a class of nouns which more commonly denote things that are acted upon than things that act, it would naturally come to be used as an accusative case-sign—that is, as a sign of objectivity.

It only remains to inquire whether the Tamil-Malayâḷam accusative case-sign *ei*, *e*, or *a*, cannot be connected with the Canarese *am*, *annu*, and *na*. On comparing the ancient Canarese accusative *ninnam*, thee, with the more modern *ninna*, it can scarcely be doubted that the latter is derived from the former by the ordinary process of the softening away of the final nasal. Through this very process the final *am* of many substantive nouns has been softened to *a*—*e.g.*, *maram*, ancient Can. a tree, *mara* or *mara-vu*, modern Can. If, then, the sign of the accusative in *ninna*, thee, is not *na*, but *a* (instead of *am*), as is probably the case, there cannot be any difficulty in deriving from it the Tamil accusative case-sign *ei*, for the change of *a* into *ei* takes place so frequently that it may almost be considered as a dialectic one—*e.g.*, compare old Tamil *ila*, not, with the modern Tamil *illei*.

(1.) *The Instrumental or 'Third' Case, properly so called.*—Different particles are used by different Dravidian dialects as suffixes of the instrumental case. In Telugu the most classical instrumental is identical with the inflexional locative, and consists in changing *ṭi* or *ti*, the inflexion, into *ṭa* or *ta*—*e.g.*, *râ-ta*, with a stone, from *râ-yi*, a stone, the inflexion of which is *râ-ti*. This form of the instrumental was probably a locative in its original signification, and at all events it is identical with an old form of the locative—*e.g.*, *iṇṭa*, in a house, from *illu*, a house, of which the inflexion is *iṇṭi*. The more commonly used instrumental of Telugu is formed by the addition to the inflexion of any noun of *chê* or *chêta*, which is itself the instrumental form of *chê-yi*, the hand, signifying by the hand (of)—*e.g.*, *nippu-chêta*, by fire, literally by the hand of fire. The inflexion, or genitive, without the addition of any special suffix, is also occasionally used in Telugu, as in High Tamil, to denote the instrumental case, as well as the ablative of motion, and the locative. The particle *na* is also sometimes suffixed to neuter nouns to denote all three ablatives.

The old Canarese instrumental suffix *im* is evidently identical in origin with *in*, the suffix of the Tamil ablative of motion, originally a locative. It has already been seen how easily *m* changes into *n*: and both in Canarese and in Tamil there is so close a connection between the ablative of motion and the instrumental, that the case-sign of the one is very often used for the other, especially by the poets—*e.g.*, *vâḷ-in âya vaḍu*, Tam. a wound inflicted by a sword, not from a sword. In Canarese also the ablative of motion is denoted more frequently by the suffix of the instrumental than by its own suffix. Through a similar tendency to confound these cases, the case-sign of the instrumental has disappeared from Latin, Greek, &c., and the sign of the ablative has come to be used instead. Even in English, by, originally a locative (*e.g.*, close by), is used at present to form the ablative, or more properly the instrumental.

The instrumental case-sign in modern Canarese is *inda*, evidently an euphonised form of *an*, as are also the old Canarese suffixes *indam* and *inde.* The instrumental suffix of the Tuda is *edd.* Dr Pope connects this with *erd,* past tense of *er,* to be; but as he states that *end* is sometimes used instead of *edd,* I should prefer to consider *edd* derived from *end* by the same process by which *ondu,* one, in the other dialects, has become *odd* in Tuda, and *end,* identical with the Canarese *inda,* used by the Tudas' Baḍaga neighbours. The instrumental case-sign of the Tuḷu is *ḍ'du,* which Dr Gundert derives from a locative noun *eḍe* = *iḍei,* Tam. a place, to which the oblique case-sign or inflexion *du,* answering to the Canarese *da,* is added. I suspect the Tuḷu *ḍ'du* has the same connection with the Canarese *inda* as the Tuda *edd* appears to have.

In Tamil and Malayâlam the suffix of the instrumental is *âl;* in High Tamil *ân* also. *âl* is the case-sign of the ablative or instrumental in Gônd, though in Telugu, which is spoken between the Tamil country and the country of the Gônds, a different case-sign is used. This suffix *âl* may possibly be derived from, or allied to, *kâl,* Tam. a channel. In some dialects channel is a compound word (Tam. *kâl-vây;* Tel. *kâlava;* Can. *kâlive*), and the only meaning of *kâl* is a foot. This meaning is contained in Tamil, but that of a channel, which Tamil contains also, suits better the supposed use which is made of *kâl,* as a sign of the instrumental case. *kâl* may have lost its initial *k* in the same manner as *kaḷ* or *gaḷ,* the neuter sign of plurality, is known to have done in Telugu and Tuḷu, in which it has become *l-u,* by corruption from *kal-u* or *gal-u.* Compare also the corruption of *avargaḷ* to *âḷ* in the colloquial Tamil *avâḷ,* they. Here both *g* and *r* have disappeared. Compare also the disappearance of *k* from the Canarese *kammâranu* instead of *karmakâranu.*

Dr Gundert's theory respecting the origin of *âl* or *ân,* as a sign of the instrumental, is that it is a verbal noun from *â-gu,* to become, with the meaning, he supposes, of 'being also there,' or 'being along with it.' *âgal* is the shape this supposed verbal noun takes in Tamil, but as the root of the verb is simply *â,* we may suppose *âl* to be an earlier form of *âgal.* *âl* would readily change to *ân,* as the *il* of *âgil,* Tam., if it become, is changed poetically into *âyin,* and as *il,* the sign of the locative, becomes in the ablative of motion either *il* or *in.* Dr Gundert considers this *âl* identical with the Tuḷu *lâ,* which serves as a conjunctive particle in all the significations of the Tamil *um,* and. In both Tamil and Malayâlam *kâl,* meaning a place, is used as a locative case-sign, for which purpose in the latter it is sometimes shortened into *kal.* It would therefore appear that *âl* was originally different from *kâl.* If *âl* be identical with the Tuḷu *lâ,* it would appear to have had originally the meaning of a social or conjunctive, rather than that of an instrumental. In Sanskrit the instrumental has the force also of a social, but this is not so in the Dravidian languages, in which the social case-signs differ from those of the instrumental. Perhaps the Tamil-Malayâlam particle *âl* has the force of a social or conjunctive when used as the formative particle of the subjunctive mood; but if the instrumental *âl* of Tamil and Malayâlam nouns be really identical with *âgal*, I should prefer to explain it, in this connection, as having the force of 'arising from,' 'in consequence of;' which is a meaning *âgal* would naturally acquire. May it be supposed that *âl* is a lengthened form of the demonstrative base *al*, that, there, and that its use as a sign of the instrumental is to be illustrated by the parallel case of the use of *il*, here, as a sign of the locative? A shortening or lengthening of the included vowel (especially the latter) is not unusual. Thus *kal* and *kâl* are alternative signs of the locative in Malayâlam.

In the Indo-European family of languages there are no signs of the instrumental case which at all resemble those that we have noticed in the Dravidian family. The only analogies which I have noticed (and probably they are illusory) are those which exist between the case-sign of the Tamil-Malayâlam and the corresponding case-signs of the Finnish tongues. Compare *âl* with the instrumental suffix of the Magyar, which is *al* in the singular, *el* in the plural; and with *alla*, *ella*, &c., the instrumental suffixes of the Finnish proper, and which are euphonically augmented forms of *al* and *el*.

A secondary or periphrastic mode of forming the instrumental case, which obtains in the Dravidian languages, as also in the northern vernaculars, is by means of the preterite verbal participle of the verb to take, and the accusative or abstract nominative of any noun—*e.g.*, *kattiyei (k) koṇḍu*, Tam., with a knife, literally having taken a knife: compare the corresponding Bengali *churi diyâ*, with (*i.e.*, having taken) a knife. Various participles besides *koṇḍu* are used instead of the instrumental in Tamil and Malayâlam, as knowing, doing, seeing, considering, putting, saying, &c.; but *koṇḍu*, taking, is the one most commonly used. This has arisen from the repugnance of the Dravidian (as of the Scythian) languages to continue to make use of any inflexional form after it has ceased to express its original meaning, and has become a mere technical sign. When that has taken place, as in the instance of the Tamil *âl*, those languages are often found to abandon the old form, or let it fall gradually into disuse, and to adopt some word or phrase instead which has a distinct meaning of its own, and the use of which recommends itself at once to the intelligence of the speaker.

(2.) *The Conjunctive or Social Case.*—Dravidian grammarians have arranged the case system of their nouns in the Sanskrit order, and in doing so have done violence to the genius of their own grammar. The Dravidian ablative of motion and the locative are evidently one and the same case, though represented as different by grammarians, in deference to Sanskrit precedents; and the Dravidian social ablative, as some have called it, or rather, as it should be termed, the conjunctive case, though it takes an important position in the Dravidian languages, has been omitted in each dialect from the list of cases, or added on to the instrumental case, simply because Sanskrit knows nothing of it as separate from the instrumental. The conjunctive, or social, stands in greater need of a place of its own in the list of cases in these languages than in Sanskrit, seeing that in these it has several case-signs of its own, whilst in Sanskrit it has none.

The instrumental is best rendered in English by the preposition by, by means of; the force of the conjunctive is that of the preposition 'with,' in the sense of the Latin *cum*, or together with. Sometimes the English preposition 'with' is used in either sense—*e.g.*, I cut it *with* a knife, I went *with* him; but in the Dravidian languages the former 'with' would be represented by the sign of the instrumental case, the latter by that of the conjunctive—*e.g.*, *katti-(y)-âl*, Tam. by a knife, *avan-ôḍu*, with him. Though Sanskrit and the Indo-European languages generally are destitute of this case, Latin evinces a tendency towards it in such forms as *nobiscum*. Whilst most of the Scythian tongues have a regularly formed conjunctive case equally with the Dravidian; and *den*, the conjunctive case-sign of Calmuck, may even be compared (though doubtless the resemblance is accidental) with the Tamil conjunctive case-sign *uḍan*.

The Tamil and Malayâlam conjunctive case-signs are *oḍu* and *ôḍu* (when emphasised, *ôḍê*); also *uḍan*. *ôḍu* is evidently a lengthened form, probably a verbal noun, from *oḍu;* and the root meaning of *oḍu*, as is apparent from its derivative *oṭṭu*, adhesion, is to touch, or rather to touch so as to adhere. The particle *oḍu*, or *ôḍu*, thus denotes the closest kind of junction, and is appropriately used as the sign of the conjunctive case. *Uḍan* or *uḍanê*, the other sign of the case in Tamil, is pronounced *oḍan;* and in the Canarese *oḍanê*, the initial *o* is written as well as heard. The final *an* being one of the ordinary formative particles of Tamil nouns, it appears probable that the root is *oḍ';* and if so, *uḍan* and *oḍane* are identical in origin, as in use, with *oḍu* and *ôḍu*. *Uḍan* is still used poetically as a noun signifying conjunction, and commonly as an adjective with the meaning of joint—*e.g.*, *uḍan-*

pangâḷi, Tam. a joint sharer; as an adverb, *uḍanê* means immediately. The Tamil verb *toḍu*, to touch, with its derivative *toḍar*, to follow, seems to me to be closely allied to *oḍu*, to adhere to.

The Telugu conjunctive case-sign is *tôḍu*, of which *tô* is an abbreviated form. This *tôḍu* appears to resemble the Tamil *ôḍu*, and the Tel. adverb *tôḍanu*, *tôḍenê*, at once; it still more closely resembles the Tam.-Can. *oḍanê*. The resemblance, however, does not amount to identity; for if the Telugu words into which *tôḍu* enters in various shapes are compared, it will be found that the Tel. *tôḍu* is identical, not with the Tamil *ôḍu*, but with *tôṛa* (as in *tôṛamei*, companionship), the radical form of which is doubtless *toṛ-u*, a verb, of which the original meaning, probably 'to be together with,' survives in Tamil only in the verbal nouns *toṛudi*, a collection, and *toṛu*, a cow-stall. I quite agree with Dr Gundert in thinking that *oḍu* and *toṛu* cannot be identified; but I still think them allied, through their common point *toḍu*. The Tamil *ôḍu* and the Tel. *tôḍu* (the lengthened forms of *oḍu* and *toḍu* = *toṛu*) are certainly not identical, and yet it is difficult to suppose the resemblance between them altogether accidental. I admit, however, that different postpositions for the different signs of case may be freely selected for use in the various dialects, just as Tamil and Malayâlam use *il*, here, house, as the sign of the locative, whilst Tel. prefers *lô* = *uḷ*, within.

Tuḷu has a case, which Brigel, in his "Tuḷu Grammar," calls the communicative, which is used with some of the meanings of a dative, but which on the whole seems to have more of the force of a conjunctive. The case-sign is *ḍa* or *ṭa*, and this particle seems naturally to connect itself, both in sound and signification, with *oḍu*, the Tam.-Mal. sign of the conjunctive.

The Dative or 'Fourth' Case.—In the North Indian dialects one and the same postposition or suffix is used more or less regularly as a sign of case both by the dative and by the accusative. In the Dravidian languages, with the exception of the Gônd, not only is the difference between the dative and the accusative essential and strongly marked, but there is less discrepancy amongst the various Dravidian dialects with respect to the particular suffix used to denote the dative, than with respect to any other case-sign. The accusatives, instrumentals, ablatives, and genitives, of the various dialects, exhibit material differences; but in all the dialects of this family—in the rudest as well as in the most polished—there is but one suffix of the dative.

The dative is formed in Tamil by suffixing *ku* (in construction *kku*); in Malayâlam *kku;* in Telugu *ku* or *ki*, according to the nature of the preceding vowel—*i.e.*, *ki* after a word ending in *i*, *ku* in all other connections; in old Canarese *ge* or *ke;* in the modern dialect *ge* or *kke,* and in construction *ige;* Tuḷu, *ku, gu, k', g';* Tuda, *k* or *g,* generally the latter. From a comparison of these forms it is obvious that the guttural *k* or *g* (generally followed by a vowel) constitutes the most essential part of this suffix; and that, as the vowel seems to have been added chiefly for the purpose of helping the enunciation, it is of little moment what vowel in particular appears to be used for this purpose.

In the primitive Indo-European tongues we discover no trace of any such dative suffix or case-sign as the Dravidian *ku;* but *kô,* the dative-accusative of the Hindi (in Bengali *kê,* in Sindhi *khê*), resembles the Dravidian *ku* so much that it seemed to me highly probable that some relationship existed between them. Two recent writers, however, seem to have proved that the Gaurian *kô* has been derived from Sanskrit; and if this be the case, its relationship to the Dravidian *ku* cannot be maintained. Dr Trumpp, in his "Sindhi Grammar," derives the Sindhi *khê* and the Bengali *kê* from the Sanskrit locative *kr'tê,* for the sake of, in regard to. This form became in Prakrit first *kitê,* then *kiê.* It was then contracted into *kê,* which in Sindhi, by reason of the elided *r,* became *khê.* He derives the Hindi and Hindustani form of this postposition *kô* by a similar process from the Sanskrit *kr'tam,* which is used adverbially with the same signification as the locative *kr'tê.* In Prakrit, and still more in the modern dialects, the neuter is changed into the masculine. In accordance with this rule, we have first *kitô,* then *kiô,* and then the more modern contracted form *kô.* He thinks *kôm* and *kaum* formed from *kô* by the addition of an euphonic *anusvâra,* to which the modern tongues have taken a great fancy. Dr Trumpp argues also that the fact that the Arian vernaculars, which border immediately on the Dravidian idioms, have not adopted the use of *kô* as a sign of the dative, shows that it is improbable that the dialects more to the north have been indebted for this form to the Dravidian idioms.

Mr Beames, in his "Comparative Grammar of the Modern Aryan Languages of India" (Introduction, p. 48), attributes to the *kô* of the Hindi, &c., a different origin; but the origin he assigns to it is as distinctively Sanskritic, and equally far removed from relationship to the Dravidian case-sign. He says, "It is demonstrable from actual written documents that the modern Hindu *kô* is a pure accusative or objective, and was in old Hindu *kauṉ,* which is the usual and regular form of the Sanskrit *kam,* the accusative of nouns in *kah;* so that there does not appear to be the slightest reason for connecting it with anything but the cognate forms in its own group of languages." Though the derivation of the Hindi *kô* from the Dravidian *ku* cannot now be maintained, it does not follow that the Dravidian form must be supposed to be derived from the Hindi one. The Dravidian *ku*, being found in every dialect of the family, however cultivated or however rude, has an antiquity of its own, greatly surpassing that of the change of *kaun* into *kô* in Hindi. Probably none of the written documents referred to by Mr Beames can pretend to an antiquity equalling that of the Syrian Christian inscription, in the Tamil of the period, on the Malabar coast, which has been ascertained to have been written in 774 A.D., and in which we find *ku* used as a dative (*e.g.*, *nagarattu*KKU, to the city) precisely as it would be at the present day. All that can be said is that this resemblance of *kô* to *ku* is one of those cases of remarkably close resemblance which do not amount to, but which might readily be mistaken for, relationship.

The Singhalese dative is *ghai;* in the Oraon, a Dravidian dialect strongly tinctured with Kolarian elements, it is *gai;* in Tibetan *gya;* in the language of the Bodos, a Bhutân hill tribe, it is *kho*, nearly identical with the Hindi. The suffix of the dative in the various languages of the Turkish family seems closely to correspond to the Dravidian dative. The forms of this suffix found in the Oriental Turkish are *ke*, *ka*, *ge*, *ga*, *ghah*, and also *a*. The Osmanli Turkish dative is *yeh* or *eh*, the initial *k* or *g* of the older dialect having been softened into *y*, and then discarded. The Manchu *de* and the Mongolian *dou* are possibly allied to the Tatar *ke;* for it has already been remarked that the change of *k* into *t* or *d*, or *vice versâ*, is not an uncommon one in this group of tongues, and that even amongst sister dialects belonging to the same family or sub-genus, the pluralising particle in one dialect is *ek*, and in another *et*. In the Finnish family of languages the Turko-Dravidian dative re-appears; though the Finnish proper has *le*, not *ke*. In the Irtish and Surgutish dialects of the Ostiak the suffix of the dative is *ga*, corresponding to the Oriental Turkish *ga* or *ge*. The ordinary Ostiak has also *a*, softened, as in the Oriental Turkish itself, from *ga*. Compare also the Mordvin *adessive* suffix *va* or *ga*. The Cheremiss illative, which denotes motion into a place, is *śka*, *ske*, &c., but in adverbs and certain postpositions this is replaced by *ke*, *ka*, &c., signifying direction. The origin of this particle is considered identical with that of the particle *ke* or *ge*, which is used to form a social ablative. The syllable *ka* or *ki* is also a part of the case-sign of the ordinary ablative and the superlative. The Japanese sign of direction is *ve*, *he*, *ye*, *e*—*e.g.*, *Yedo-ve*, Yedo-wards.

Interesting and remarkable analogies have been brought to light by the Scythian tablets of Behistun. We learn from those tablets that a dative suffix which is almost identical with the Dravidian, and also with the Turkish and Ostiak, was used by the oldest Scythian dialect of Central Asia of which any remains are extant. The dative case sign or suffix which is most largely used in the Scythic tablets is *ikki* or *ikka*. Mr Norris noticed the resemblance of this suffix to the Magyar genitive-dative *nek* and the Telugu genitive postposition *yokka;* but its resemblance to the dative suffix of the Telugu and of the other Dravidian dialects is still closer. The Tamil *ku* becomes, as we have seen, *akku* or *ukku* in construction; the Canarese *ge* becomes *ige;* and the Malayâlam *ukku* or *kku* becomes *ikku;* * which last form of the suffix is identical with the Scythian of Behistun. Compare, *e.g.*, the cuneiform Scythian *nî-ikka* or *nî-ikki*, to thee, with the corresponding Malayâlam *nina-kku*, the Telugu *nî-ku*, and the Tuḷu *ni-kk'*.

It has thus been shown that the principal languages of the Scythian family accord very exactly with the Dravidian languages in the use of *ka, ki, ku*, or some related particle, as the suffix of the dative. It may be noticed also, that in the language of the Malays there is a prefix, *ka*, which signifies 'towards.' 'To a place,' however, in Malay, is *datañ*. It is difficult to determine whether the Finnish dative suffix *le* has any connection with *ke*. It certainly seems to resemble much more closely the Tibetan, Pushtu, and Marâṭhi dative suffix *lâ*—which *lâ* is evidently equivalent to the New Persian *ra*. Compare, *e.g.*, the Marâṭhi *tu-la*, to thee, thee, with the corresponding Persian *to-ra*.

Malayâlam alone of all the Dravidian dialects appears to possess two suffixes of the dative, viz., *kku*, which is the suffix most largely used, and *innu, nu*, or *u*, which is occasionally used in the dative singular only. This *innu* is evidently a compound form, and seems to be euphonised and softened from *in-ku*. Tamil is fond of adding to the base of nouns which are to be declined the euphonic increment *in* (originally a locative), before suffixing the signs of case. The same practice prevails in Malayâlam also. Consequently, this exceptional Malayâlam dative is not *inna*, but *nu*, or simply *u;* and the doubled *n* which sometimes precedes it (*e.g.*, *avannu*, to him) may only be an euphonic compensation for the loss of the *k*. The *k* or *g* of *ka* or *ga* has been softened away in some dialects of the Turkish and Ostiak, precisely as I suppose it has been in Malayâlam. Dr Gundert prefers to derive this peculiar dative case-sign *innu* from the possessive case-sign *inadu*. The Malayâlam *endre*, my, is, I doubt not, to be resolved into

---

* The final vowel of such forms in Malayâlam is extremely short. Dr Gundert always uses an apostrophe instead—*e.g.*, *kk'*. In poetry the final vowel is written *u*.

enadu, and therefore *marattindre*, of a tree, into *marattinadu*. This *marattindre* again may have been softened into *marattinu*, just as the Mal. *ninnu*, standing, *innu*, to-day, are softened from the Tam. *nindru* and *indru*. Dr Gundert supposes, therefore, that in this form of the dative we have a relic of the possessive. He is doubtful, however, himself of the validity of this explanation, as *nu* is as common in old Malayâlam as *nnu*—*e.g.*, *avanu*, to him, as well as *avannu*. Here he thinks it most probable that the *ku* has been simply dropped. If the expression "softened away" were used instead of dropped, this explanation would be equivalent to mine, which is that *innu*, being a dative, is more likely to be a softened form of *inku*, which is in itself a true dative, than that it should be a softened form of *inadu*, which is in itself a possessive.

Can a purely Dravidian origin be discovered for the Dravidian dative case-suffix *ku?* The locative suffixes *il* and *in* can be explained *ab intra;* but I doubt whether *ku* is capable of an *ab intra* explanation. The only suggestion I can offer is as follows:—Looking at such nouns of direction as *vadakku*, north, and *kiṛakku*, east, we find the final *ku*, though a dative or directive in signification, indistinguishable in form from the *ku* which is one of the commonest formatives of verbal nouns, and from the *ku*, possibly the same *ku*, which is a sign of futurity in the oldest form of the Tamil verb. Can it be that in all three connections the *ku* is the same, and that the root idea in each case was transition? This does not explain how *ku* came to mean transition; but it may indicate the direction in which inquiry may be made.

The Ablative of Motion or 'Fifth' Case.—This case appears to have been included in the list of cases by Dravidian grammarians out of deference to the grammatical principles of the Sanskrit. It is true that if we look at the construction and meaning of a Dravidian sentence, the *signification* of an ablative of motion will be found to exist, and it will be found to be expressed much more clearly even than in Sanskrit; but a distinction is to be drawn between the existence of a case and the existence of a case-sign, or regular technical suffix of case. The Dravidian languages have undoubtedly an ablative of motion, and a great many other ablatives besides; but I doubt whether they have any case-suffix which belongs exclusively to the ablative of motion.

On comparing the suffixes of the ablatives of motion (which are also used sometimes in an instrumental sense) with those of the locatives in the various dialects of this family, no real difference is apparent between the one class and the other, or at least no adequate reason appears for regarding them as distinct and independent suffixes; for whatever difference does exist is to be attributed, not to the signs of case, but to the verbs or verbal participles which are annexed to them. The object of the ablative of motion is to furnish an answer to the question, *whence?* and this answer is obtained in the Dravidian tongues, by suffixing to a noun of place the sign of the locative, and annexing to that sign a verb of motion. By this means the locative is converted into what is called the ablative, without changing its case-suffixes, and the idea of change of place is thus naturally and necessarily educed. Native Tamil grammarians appear to hold that *il*, the ordinary suffix of the ablative, and *il*, the most largely used sign of the locative in the colloquial dialect, though written and pronounced alike, are different particles with different significations. I am persuaded, however, that this view is erroneous; and that a natural system of case classification would determine that the Dravidian languages have no ablative, properly so called, but only a variety of locative and instrumental suffixes, which are capable of becoming ablatives by the addition of appropriate verbs.

In Tamil, the suffixes which are used in forming the 'fifth' case, or ablative of motion, are *il* and *in*. *il* (Tel. *illu*) signifies by itself a house, a place—*e.g.*, *kô-(v)-il*, a temple, God's house; its primitive meaning, however, appears to have been 'here,' 'in this place;' and it is therefore well suited for becoming a sign of the locative. Accordingly it has a place in the list of locative suffixes, as well as in those of the ablative; and in the colloquial dialect it is used as a sign of the locative far more frequently than any other particle. The other suffix, *in*, is identical, I conceive, with *im*, the old Canarese sign of the instrumental: it is used as an instrumental in Tamil also; but probably both *im* and *in* were previously locative suffixes. In old Canarese the proper suffix of the ablative is *attaṇim* (other forms of which are *attaṇindam* and *attaṇinde*), which is itself formed from the demonstrative adverb *aṭṭaṇa* (identical with *attal-u* or *atta*, there, or *attal*, that side), by the addition of *im*, the old instrumental suffix, meaning originally 'here,' from which *inda*, the more modern suffix, is derived; and this *inda*, though the ordinary sign of the instrumental, is also ordinarily used, with the addition of a verb of motion, as the sign of the ablative.

Whilst I think that not only *il*, but also *in* and *im* were originally locative suffixes, it is more difficult to determine whether *il* and *in* were originally identical in sound and signification, as well as in application. In every instance in which *il* is used in Tamil, *in* may be substituted for it poetically; and it is almost exclusively by the poets that *in* is used. Moreover, in Telugu, *illu*, a house, identical with *il*, is euphonised into *in*, in the inflexion *inṭi*, of a house. On the other hand, if we regard *in* as originally a locative, it will be found to have a far wider range of analogies than *il*, and may therefore be surmised to have sprung from a different root. In Finnish and Magyar we find *an*, *en*, and still more frequently *in*, used as signs of the locative. Even in Sanskrit we find *in* used as a locative case-sign of pronouns of the third person—*e.g.*, *tasmin*, in him; and though this *in* is supposed to have been euphonised from *i*, yet in the Latin locative preposition *in* and the Greek ἐν, corresponding to the Sanskrit *ni*, we find the existence of a remarkable analogy. *il*, on the other hand, has no apparent affinities out of the pale of the Dravidian family.

It seems probable that *in*, one of the signs of the locative in Tamil, is identical with *in*, a sign of the genitive, or inflexional increment, in Tamil-Canarese; and if so, a new and very wide range of affinities is disclosed, as will be seen when the case-signs of the genitive are inquired into.

The Tamil *il* and *in* agree in this, that when they are used as suffixes of the ablative, they both require to be followed by verbs of motion. In the spoken dialect of the Tamil, the verb of motion is preceded by the verbal participles *nindru*, standing, or *irundu*, being. The use of these participles strengthens the supposition that *il* and *in* are properly to be regarded as locatives. In the higher dialect, however, they are ordinarily dispensed with, and *il* or *in* is followed by a verb of motion alone—*e.g.*, *malei-(y)-in viṛum aruvi*, the cataract which falls from the mountain. In this expression the idea of "motion from a place" is plainly implied in the aoristic relative participle *viṛum*, which falls; and hence *in*, whatever it may have been in origin, acquires the force of a sign of the ablative of motion.

In Canarese the compound ablative suffixes *attaṇim* and *deseyinda* are not so commonly used as *inda*, the terminal member of the second compound suffix; and though *inda* is described to be the sign of the instrumental, I have no doubt that it is identical with *im* and *in*, and a locative in origin. The first member of the Can. compound *dese*, means a point of the compass (Sans. *diś*, Tam. *tiśei*). *inda* is not only used by itself to form the ablative, but is also allied to *alli* or *illi*, the sign of the locative, for the purpose of denoting the ablative. Compare the Canarese *allinda* or *illinda*, from, with the corresponding Tamil compound *il-irundu* or *il-nindru*. In Telugu the particle *na*, which corresponds to the Tamil *in* and the old Canarese *im*, is more distinctively a locative than an ablative of motion. This particle is *ni* after *i*; and if this is its normal form it may at once be identified with the Tamil *in*. The Telugu ablative of motion is ordinarily formed by means of the verbal participle *nuṇḍi* or *nuñchi* alone, without the aid of any such suffix as *na* or *ni*, *il* or *in*; consequently this ablative seems to have still less of the character of an independent case than in Tamil. On further examination, however, it comes into accordance with the Tamil ablative. *nuṇḍi* or *nuñchi* is regarded by Mr Clay, and I think correctly, as formed from *uṇḍi*, having been, the past participle of *uṇḍu*, to be, to which is prefixed the *n* of the locative case-sign, the full form of which is *na* or *ni*. Thus *paralôkamu-nuṇḍi vachchenu*, he came from heaven, should be divided *paralôkamu-n'-uṇḍi vachchenu*; literally, "he, having been in heaven, came." *uñchi* is not found in the classics in this connection, and being the past participle of a transitive verb derived from the same root (meaning to place), its use as the suffix of the ablative of motion would be somewhat inappropriate. On the other hand, the use of *uṇḍi* in this connection is perfectly in accordance with the use in the Tamil ablative of motion of the corresponding form *irundu*, having been, or *nindru*, having stood, to which also *in*, the true case-sign, originally a case-sign of the locative, must be prefixed.

The Tuḷu ablative of motion, which is also used as an instrumental, is *ḍ'du* or *ḍ'd'*. The corresponding form of the Tuda is *edd*, which is also pronounced *end*; and as this is probably identical with the Canarese *inda*, it seems possible that the Tuḷu *ḍ'd'* may have had the same origin.

The Genitive or 'Sixth' Case.—The genitive or possessive case is formed in the Dravidian languages in various ways, and by means of various suffixes, each of which requires to be examined separately. The Tuda dialect uses the nominative for the genitive, as for the accusative.

(1.) *The abbreviated pronominal genitive.*—The personal pronouns of the Tamil form their inflexion, or ordinary genitive, by shortening the included vowel of the root—*e.g.*, *nî* (properly *nîn*), thou, *nĭn*, thy; *nâm*, we, *năm*, our. This shortened form has the force of a genitive in Tamil without any suffix or addition whatever, though it is often strengthened by the addition of a suffix in the other dialects—*e.g.*, in Canarese it requires to have a genitive suffix appended to it, and of itself it is merely an inflexional basis. In the Scythian of the Behistun tablets the nominative of the pronoun of the second person is long—viz., *nî*, whilst the inflexional form and enclitic possessive *nĭ* is short, precisely as in Tamil-Canarese.

We shall best, I think, understand the origin and force of this peculiar form of the genitive of personal pronouns, by considering it as a pronominal adjective. Every Dravidian noun of quality or relation becomes an adjective on being prefixed to a noun-substantive for the purpose of qualifying it; and ordinarily the only changes which it undergoes on becoming an adjective are such petty euphonic changes as are intended to facilitate the combined enunciation of the two words. The change in the quantity of the personal pronoun to which I have now referred, appears to have this origin. I regard it as simply euphonic, and euphony is certainly promoted by this conversion of a long vowel into a short one prior to the addition of the case-suffixes, or of the governing substantive. We find apparently a similar euphonic shortening of the quantity of the vowel of the root, on the conversion of the abstract noun into an adjective. See the section on "Numerals"—*e.g.*, *âru*, Tam. six, *ărubadu*, sixty; *ēṛu*, seven, *ĕṛubadu*, seventy. There is room, however, as we shall see, for supposing that the process which has actually taken place may have been the reverse of this—viz., that the shorter form of these numerals is the radical one, and that the longer has been euphonically lengthened.

(2.) *The neuter inflexional genitive.*—The neuter inflexions *attu*, *attru*, *ṭi*, *ti*, &c., are largely used in forming the genitive in Tamil and Telugu.

The various suffixes which are used to form the inflexion were originally, I conceive, signs of the locative case: but in process of time they have come to convey more commonly either a possessive or an adjectival signification, according to the connection; and in many cases, as has been shown, they have shrunk into inflexional increments of the base, or have become mere euphonic links of connection between the base and the case-suffix. Dr Trumpp considers the inflexion or formative of the North Indian vernaculars originally a genitive. The inflexion which is now under consideration is in Tamil *attu*, and is used by the singular of neuter nouns alone. *aṟṟu*, pronounced *attru*, is occasionally used by neuter pronominal plurals. The same inflexion —for I believe I have shown it to be the same—is in Telugu *ṭi* or *ti*.

The inflexional suffixes being, as I conceive, first locative then possessive suffixes in their origin, their adjectival use naturally flowed from their use in forming possessives. There is sometimes little difference in signification between the locative, the genitive, and the adjective; and in several languages besides the Dravidian the adjectival formative either appears to have been derived from the possessive suffix, or to be identical with it. Thus, as we have already shown, in Tamil, it matters little whether *kuḷattu mîn* (from *kuḷam*, a tank, and *mîn*, fish) be translated adjectivally tank fish, or genitively the fish of the tank, or locatively the fish in the tank. The adjectival rendering is ordinarily the more natural one, but if a few words be added to the compound expression, so as to bring out the full force of the inflexional suffixes, it will be evident that those suffixes must have been signs of case originally, and that their adjectival use is secondary to their use as signs of the possessive or locative. Thus, when we say in Tamil, *i-(k)-kuḷattu mîn perugittru*, to render the sentence, this tank fish has increased, would not only be barbarous, but would partly fail to express the meaning, which is, the fish of this tank have increased. In this instance it is evident that the suffix *attu* is used as a sign of the genitive, though capable of acquiring in certain connections the force of an adjectival formative. This same suffix *attu* has sometimes in Tamil and Malayâlam the force of a sign of the locative, properly so called, like the corresponding inflexional suffixes in Telugu; and when used as a suffix of the locative, it is governed by a verb, not by a noun; from which it is certain that it must be regarded as a case-suffix in origin. It is here to be noted that though *attu* may have had at first a locative signification, yet, in such phrases as those given above, it is clear that it is not used as a locative. It has a locative signification only when the governing word is a verb. In these instances the governing word is a noun; *attu* is therefore used as a possessive.

Max Müller appears to derive the genitive from the adjective, not the adjective from the genitive. He says ("Lectures," p. 110), "It can be proved etymologically that the termination of the genitive is, in most cases, identical with those derivative suffixes by which substantives are changed into adjectives."

I have already mentioned the connection which subsists between the inflexional suffix *attu* and *adu*, it, the neuter singular demonstrative pronoun. It is deserving of notice in this place that *adu* (the very same demonstrative, I doubt not) is one of the recognised suffixes of the possessive case in Tamil, and is occasionally used as a possessive in the other dialects also. Thus we may say in Tamil either *marattu (k)-koppu* (from *maram*, a tree, and *koppu*, a branch), the branch of a tree, or *marattinadu koppu* (*mar'-attin-adu*). *maramadu* may also be used, though not in ordinary use, because ineuphonic; but the possessive case-sign *adu* is quite as frequently suffixed to the crude form of the noun, or the nominative, as to the oblique form—*e.g.*, *vâṛei-(y)-adu paṛam*, the fruit of the plantain, is as common as *vâṛei-(y)-in-adu paṛam*, and is even more elegant.

I have no doubt of the identity of the *adu* of *vâṛei-(y)-adu* and the *attu* of *marattu* in origin. The old crude base of *maram*, a tree, is *mara*, as found in Canarese, the final *am* or *m* being a formative; and on *adu*, the sign of the possessive (originally a demonstrative), being added to *mara*, we shall have *maradu*, of a tree (in Canarese *marada*);

of which the *d* has only to be doubled (as it is colloquially by the Tamil people, many of whom say *attu* for *adu*), when the word becomes *marattu*, the very form in which we now find it. In old Canarese we find this form *attu* alternating with *adu* and *atu* in the possessives of the personal pronouns—*e.g.*, instead of *ninnadu*, thine, we sometimes find *ninatu* or *ninattu*. In Telugu, the inflexional suffixes *ṭi* and *ti* are used without any additional particle as signs of the possessive or genitive even more frequently than in Tamil. The postposition *yokka* is but seldom added to it, and needs not ever be added. In Telugu also the connection subsisting between this suffix and the neuter demonstrative pronoun is still more obvious than in Tamil. *adi*, it, is systematically suffixed in Telugu to nouns and pronouns, to convert them into possessives (*e.g.*, *vâridi*, their or theirs), and the relation subsisting between *adi* (or *di*, as it is in some instances) and *ṭi* or *ti* is very close. In Canarese the corresponding particles *ad* and *ar*, though used as inflexional increments of the base, prior to the addition of several of the signs of case to certain classes of nouns, have not now of themselves a possessive signification. Their present use is purely euphonic, and does not contribute to grammatical expression. Nouns in which *ad* and *ar* are introduced form their possessives in *ada* and *ara;* and in these forms the final *a* is that which contains and conveys the possessive signification. *ad* and *ar* have only the same incremental or euphonic force in *ad-a* and *ar-a*, that *in* has in *in-a*, which is a corresponding Canarese possessive.

(3.) *The neuter demonstrative genitives.*—*adu*, it, and its euphonically lengthened equivalent *âdu*, are often used, especially in classical Tamil, as signs of the possessive, and they are ranked by native grammarians amongst genitive case-signs. *adu* is the neuter singular demonstrative (derived from *a*, the remote demonstrative base, and *d*, the sign of the neuter singular). Its meaning when standing alone is invariably that of a demonstrative pronoun, but by usage it has acquired the signification of a genitive or possessive, when annexed to any noun as a suffix. *avan-adu* is literally 'he + that,' that is, 'he + that which belongs to him,' but by usage it means 'his property,' his. This use of *adu*, as a possessive suffix, is derived from its use as the formative of nouns of possession.

By the addition of this demonstrative to any noun or pronoun (generally it is added to the inflexion—in the case of pronouns it is always to the inflexion that it is added) a compound noun of possession or relation is formed, which, like all Dravidian nouns of relation, is capable of being used as an adjective; and it seems to have been the use of nouns with this termination as possessive adjectives which has led to *adu* and its equivalents being regarded as signs of the possessive case. The noun to which *adu* is appended may be used, and often is used, without any addition or modification, as the nominative of a verb or of a sentence. Thus, *enadu*, Tam. (from *en*, my, and *adu*, that), signifies properly that (which is) mine; and this compound possessive may either be used adjectivally—*e.g.*, *enadu kei*, my hand, literally the hand that is mine (in which instance *adu* is called by grammarians a genitive case-sign); or it may be used as a possessive noun, and as such it becomes the nominative of a verb—*e.g.*, *enadu pôyittru*, mine (or my property) is gone. Thus *adu*, which at first meant 'that,' became secondly the formative of a possessive noun (*avan-adu*, that which is his, literally he + that), thirdly the formative of a possessive adjective (*avan-adu*, his), and lastly a sign of the possessive case generally, signifying 'of' or 'belonging to.' Another reason for regarding the genitive case-sign *adu* as originally and properly the formative of a noun or adjective of possession, is that it cannot be followed indiscriminately by any kind of noun, but by neuter nouns alone, and properly by the neuter singular alone. Thus we may say *enadu kei*, my hand, but not *enadu keigaḷ*, my hands; except indeed in the colloquial dialect, in which the singular is used for the plural more frequently than in the higher dialect or by the poets.

The higher dialect would prefer in this instance *ena keigaḷ*—*ena* instead of *enadu*—*i.e.*, *mea*, instead of *meum*. *adu* is not only a formative, therefore, but is distinctively a neuter singular formative, employed to give a possessive signification to the noun to which it is suffixed. Like all other nouns, these possessive nouns in *adu* are capable of being used as adjectives, by being prefixed without alteration to other nouns; and when so prefixed, *adu* came to be used and regarded as a possessive case-sign. This explanation seems to account for all the phenomena, and therefore is probably the true explanation. In Malayâlam, this use of *adu* as a possessive case-sign, though common in the ancient poetry, has nearly disappeared from the popular dialect. It is scarcely discernible except in *tanadu*, *enadu* (from which come *tandre* and *endre*, its, my). The old Canarese possessive pronouns, answering to the Tamil *enadu*, &c., are *ennadu*, *ninnadu*, *tannadu*, mine, thine, its. These take also the shape of *ninatu*, &c., and also *ninattu*, &c.

A similar use of the neuter singular of the demonstrative as a possessive suffix obtains in Telugu also—*e.g.*, *nâdi*, mine, literally that (which is) mine, from *nâ*, my, and *adi*, that, a form which is exactly equivalent to the Tamil *enadu*. Telugu uses a similar suffix to form a plural possessive to correspond with *enadu* or *nâdi*, viz., *vi*, which bears the same relation to *avi*, those (things), which *di* does to *adi*, that (thing)—*e.g.*, *vârivi*, theirs or the (things which are) theirs. In this respect Telugu acts more systematically than spoken Tamil. It is not so fond, however, of using these possessive nouns adjectivally as the Tamil, and therefore *di* and *vi* have not in Telugu come to be regarded as case-signs of the genitive. The Canarese and the Tamil not only form neuter possessive nouns and adjectives by adding to them the neuter demonstrative, but they form also masculine and feminine possessives, or possessive appellatives, of both numbers, by adding the masculine and feminine formatives to the genitive case or inflexion of nouns and pronouns. In the Tuda dialect, *ad*, the demonstrative base, appears sometimes to be added to the first of two nouns, when it is used adjectivally. All the Dravidian dialects agree in appending the demonstrative possessive suffixes to the inflexion, not to the nominative, as a general rule, wherever the nominative differs considerably from the inflexion. When nouns receive in Tamil a double inflexional increment—*e.g.*, *attu* and *in* (in combination *attin*), the possessive suffix is added to this double increment—*e.g.*, *mar'-attin-adu koppu*, the branch of a tree.

(4.) *The possessive suffix 'in,' and its varieties.*—*in* in Tamil and *ni* in Telugu, and corresponding particles in the other dialects, are not only used as inflexional augments of the base and euphonic bonds of connection between the base and the case-signs, but also as suffixes of the possessive and as adjectival formatives. I have no doubt that *in* and *ni*, of themselves and originally, were locative suffixes, and that every other use to which they have been applied grew out of their use as signs of the locative. As Max Müller says (p. 229), "A special case, such as the locative, may be generalised into the more general genitive, but not *vice versâ*." Native Tamil grammarians do not include *in* amongst their case-signs, but describe it as a formative augment or adjectival increment alone: but on comparing its use in Tamil with its use in the other dialects, I am convinced that it was originally a sign of the locative, then adopted as a sign of the genitive, and that it is still to be regarded, notwithstanding its other uses, and its probable origin, as one of the most characteristic of the genitive suffixes.

In Tamil, of all genitive suffixes, *in* is that which is most frequently used. *attu* is used in the neuter singular alone, and *aṟṟu* (*attru*) in the neuter plural alone; but *in* is used in connection with both numbers and with all genders. A similar use of *in* appears in the Malayâlam. In Canarese, on the other hand, *in* is used only as an inflexional augment, not as a sign of case. One of the so-called declensions of the Canarese is said by grammarians to take *ina* as its genitive case-sign; but in this instance the final *a* is the real sign of the genitive, as it invariably is in Canarese; and this genitive *a* is found to be preceded by various euphonic increments—*in*, *ad*, *ar*, or *v*, according to circumstances. Doubtless the *in* of *in-a*, like the Tamil *in*, was a sign of the locative originally, then of the possessive; but it has long ceased to contribute to grammatical expression, and therefore cannot now be regarded as a sign of case. In Telugu, *na* or *ni*, the dialectic equivalent of *in*, is used as a possessive suffix, as in Tamil, though not so frequently. The only difference in principle is that *ni* is used in Telugu in connection with the singular alone, and might be called a genitive singular case-sign, if the Telugu stood in an isolated position; whereas in Tamil it is used in connection with plural nouns as frequently as with the singular. In Ku, which has special resemblances to the Telugu, *ni* constitutes the inflexion (in reality the genitive) of all classes of nouns, whether singular or plural, precisely like the Tamil *in*. The Gônd uses as genitive case-signs *na* and *nâ*, *da* and *â*—forms which are probably allied one to another, as well as to the Brahui *nâ*, and to the Telugu and Gônd *ni* and the Tamil *in*.

Though *in* is not regarded by Tamil grammarians as a sign of the genitive, yet when those particles which are regarded as genitive case-signs are suffixed to any noun, *in* is ordinarily inserted between the noun and those case-signs; so that all auxiliary or additional particles are appended to this incremental *in*, not to the noun itself—*e.g.*, from *adu*, it, is formed not *ad'-uḍeiya*, but *ad'-in-uḍeiya*, of it; from *tambi*, a younger brother, is formed not *tambi-(y)-adu*, but more commonly *tambi-(y)-in-adu*, of a younger brother: and this rule seems to indicate that *in*, whatever its origin, has acquired more of the force of a genitive case-sign than the genitive particles which have subsequently been suffixed to it. The same inference is still more clearly deducible from the circumstance that in a large number of instances, both in the singular and in the plural, each of the case-suffixes in succession is appended, not to the crude form of the noun, but to the increment *in*. These case-suffixes are not mere postpositional fragments, but were, or are still, nouns of relation; and *in*, the particle by which they are united to the base, serves as a bond of connection, in virtue, as I conceive, of its signification as a suffix of the genitive. Thus, in the colloquial Tamil *kalliniḍattil* (*kal(l)-in-iḍattil*), in a stone, *iḍattil*, the local ablative or locative suffix, literally means 'in the place;' and this suffix evidently requires, or at least desires, the possessive *in* (with the signification 'of') to connect it with the base. Hence *kal(l)-in-iḍattil* literally signifies 'in the place of (or occupied by) a stone.'

The adjectival meaning of *in*, though not its only or original meaning, is one which is recognised by native grammarians, and which they prove by examples—*e.g.*, *ponnin* (*pon*(*n*)-*in*) *kuḍam*, a golden vessel. This adjectival use of *in* is not only allied to, but is derived from, its use as a suffix of the genitive, and in the illustration which has now been adduced it is evident that *ponnin kuḍam*, might be rendered with equal propriety, a vessel of gold. It will be found also in the Indo-European analogies which will presently be adduced, that the similarity or identity of the adjectival formative and the genitive case-sign which is apparent in this instance, has a wider range than that of the Dravidian languages. There is another particle resembling *in*—viz., *am*, with its equivalent *an*, which is occasionally used in Tamil for both those purposes, and, like *in*, it is sometimes appended to the noun itself, and sometimes to the neuter inflexion. We see this fusion of the adjectival and the genitive signification of *am* in such forms as *âlam* (*âl'-am*) *pû*, the banyan flower, or the flower of the banyan, and *âttraṅ karei* (*âttru*, the inflexion of *âru*, a river), the river-bank, or the bank of the river. The same adjectival formative is much used in Malayâlam also—*e.g.*, *mal'-am puli* (*mala-am puli*), a mountain tiger, or a tiger of the mountain, a royal tiger. The final *m* of *am* changes by rule into the nasal which corresponds to the first consonant of the word which follows it and with which it is compounded. Hence it changes into *n* when followed by a dental—*e.g.*, *panan-dôppu* (*panei-am-tôppu*), a palmyra tope. It must not be supposed, however, that we have here to deal with *an*, the formative suffix of many Tamil nouns. In such words as *adarku*, Tam. to it, for *adan-ku*, *am* is not considered a sign of case or even as an inflexional increment, but (as we have already seen in the section on "The Inflexional Increment") as a formative suffix, found in the nominative (though rarely), as well as in the oblique cases. *am* and *an* agree in this, that both are used as formative particles of nouns. *am*, however, is also used as a genitival or adjectival suffix in Tamil, whereas *an* is not. *am* and *an* are, I believe, identical in origin ; so also another pair of particles *in* and *im* (the latter the Canarese form). *am* and *an* I regard as demonstrative pronouns ; *in* and *im* as related to or derived from *il*, here, a house, the locative case-sign.

We have now to inquire whether any trace of the genitive case-sign or adjectival formative in *in*, *ni*, *am*, or any related form, can be found beyond the circle of the Dravidian dialects. Of all the North Indian vernaculars the Gujarâthi is the only one which contains a form of the genitive resembling that which we have been examining. That language has a genitive suffix in *n* (*nô*, *nî*, *nun*), which somewhat resembles the Telugu *ni*, *nu*, &c. In the language of the Bodos, a Himalayan tribe, the pronominal genitive is regularly formed by suffixing *ni*—*e.g.*, *aṅ-ni*, of me, *naṅ-ni*, of thee, *bi-ni*, of him. In Sanskrit the *n* which precedes the *ah* or *as*, of certain genitives, is undoubtedly euphonic; but both in Sanskrit and in other members of the Indo-European family, we may observe distinct traces of the adjectival or genitival use of a particle of which the consonant *n* is the most essential element. With the Dravidian particle compare *an-a*, the Sanskrit adjectival formative, and *an*, the suffix of appellatives; the Greek possessive suffix ων; the adjectival use of ιν in Greek words like λίθ-ιν-ος, and of *en*, in the Germanic wood*en*; and also *in*, the Sanskrit suffix of agency, which is preserved in the adjectives of the New Persian. These forms look as if they were reciprocally related; and possibly also there may be some ulterior relationship between them and the Tamilian *in*. There are traces in the Indo-European family of languages themselves of the use of *in* as a distinctively genitival suffix. The Celtic forms its genitive systematically by means of *n*, *an*, *en*, &c.: nor is it the genitive plural only of the Celtic dialects which uses this case-sign (as in the Sanskrit family), but it is employed to form the genitive singular also. It should be noticed too that in the ancient Egyptian *n* (alternating with *m*) was used to express all case relations, but particularly that of the genitive. Compare also the Sanskrit genitive or possessive *mama* (*ma-ma*), of me, my, with the Zend *mana*, the Old Persian *manâ*, and the Gothic *meina*, mine, *theina*, thine, *seina*, his; in each of which examples the final *na*, or its Sanskrit equivalent *ma*, resembles the Dravidian *in* or *ni*, not only in sound, but also in the union of an adjectival signification with that of the possessive or genitive case. The Lithuanian goes further than any other Indo-European tongue in resemblance to the Tamil in this point, for it not only uses *n* as a sign of the pronominal possessive (of the first person), but it adopts this genitival *man* as the inflexional base of all the rest of the oblique cases of the same pronoun.

In the languages of the Scythian stock we find a large number of still more essential analogies with the Dravidian genitival suffix *in* or *ni*. Compare both with the Dravidian and with the Indo-European possessives the Mongolian and Manchu *mini* (*mi-ni*), of me, my; and the Mongolian *tchini* and the Manchu *sini* (*si-ni*), of thee, thy. In the languages of the Finnish family, the prevailing form of the genitive is that which corresponds to the Dravidian: it is *n*, *an*, *en*, *un*, &c., not only in pronominal inflexions, but universally. Thus in Mordvin and Cheremiss, the genitive is formed by suffixing *n* or *en*—*e.g.*, *kudo*, a house, *kudo-n*, of a house. The genitive plural of the Mordvin is *nen*, possibly a reduplication of *n*, intended to symbolise the plural—*e.g.*, *kudot-nen*, of houses. The Lappish genitive takes *n* or *en* in the singular, and *i* in the plural. *ê* forms the ordinary possessive suffix of the Magyar. The Finnish proper forms the genitive by suffixing *n*, *un*, *in*, *an*, &c.—*e.g.*, *minä* (*min-ä*), I, *min-un*, of me, my.

The prevailing form of the genitive in the Tatar or High Asian families, corresponds to *nen*, the reduplicated suffix of the Mordvin plural, and to its equivalent reduplication in the old Scythian of the Behistun tablets; but whilst the reduplicated suffix is very frequently used, it systematically alternates with the simpler suffix *un* or *in*. The Oriental Turkish forms its genitive by suffixing *ning* or *nin*, or *nîng* or *nîn*. In the Ottoman Turkish the initial nasal is only occasionally used: the genitive plural is uniformly *uṉ*; the singular takes *uṉ* or *nuṉ*, according as the noun to which it is suffixed ends in a consonant or in a vowel. In the Mongolian, the sign of the genitive is *ü* after the consonant *n*; after every other consonant, *ün*; and after a vowel, *in* or *yin*. The personal pronouns, as has already been observed, form their possessive by suffixing *nu* or *ni*—*e.g.*, *mi-mu*, or *mi-ni*, my. Compare the Mongolian *köl-ün*, of the foot, with the ordinary Tamil genitive of the corresponding noun *kāl-in*, of the foot. The Calmuck dialect of the Mongolian forms its genitive by suffixing *u* or *i* to nouns ending in *n*, and *in* or *yin* to all other nouns. The Tibetan postfixes in like manner *i* or *yin*. The Manchu makes much use of a possessive relative suffix *ngge*, or *ningge*, signifying 'which has;' but it also forms genitives, properly so called, by suffixing *ni* or *i*. In Japanese *ni* is used generally as a sign of relation, with a still wider variety of meanings than the Tam. *in*. *no*, however, is the ordinary sign of the possessive, and is also used in the formation of adjectives.

In the language of the Scythian tablets of Behistun, the genitive was ordinarily formed by suffixing *na*: the first personal pronoun formed its genitive by suffixing a reduplicated form of this particle, *ni-na*—*e.g.*, *hu-ni-na*, of me; whilst the genitive plural was generally formed by means of the addition of *inna*, probably softened from *ni-na*. The nearest direct resemblance to the Behistun-Scythian genitival *na*, is the Brahui *nä*, and the Gônd *nä* or *ä*. This interesting record of the speech of the ancient Scythians, furnishes us, I think, with a clue to the origin of *nuṉ* or *niṉ*, the Tatar genitive suffix. In the Tatar tongues *nuṉ* is interchangeable with and equivalent to *uṉ*; and *un* or *in* is also interchangeable with *ni* or *nu*; in Mongolian, *yin* and *un* are suffixed to substantives, *ni* to the personal pronouns. It appears from the Behistun tablets that *na*, the ordinary genitive suffix, was sometimes euphonically changed into *ni-na*, and that this again was softened into *inna*. I conceive that the Tatar *uṉ* was in this same manner, by the reduplication of the nasal, converted into *nuṉ*; which in Manchu became *ngge* or *ningge*. Possibly also *ni* or *nu* was nasalised by the addition of a final *n* or *ng*, of the use of which we have an instance in point in the final euphonic *n* of the first and second personal pronouns in most of the Scythian languages. A parallel instance of the reduplication of a nasal is apparent in Telugu itself, in the conjunctive or copulative particle. This particle is *um* in Tamil, *û* in Canarese, and *u* in Telugu; but this Telugu *u* becomes euphonically *nu*, and by reduplication *nunnu* in particular instances.

(5.) *The genitival suffix 'a.'*—This sign of the genitive or possessive claims to be regarded not only as the most distinctively Dravidian suffix, but as the sole original one. It is little used in modern Tamil, though placed first in the list of genitive case-signs by Tamil grammarians; but if we take all the Dravidian idioms into consideration, in several of which it is the only sign in use, we shall find it more largely used than any other suffix of the genitive—a proof of the accuracy of the Tamil classification.

I conceive this suffix to be identical with *a*, the formative of the most frequently used Dravidian relative participle (see "The Verb"), but totally distinct in origin from *a*, the neuter particle of pluralisation which has already been investigated.

In Canarese *a* is the only sign of the genitive which is ever used. It is sometimes euphonically lengthened to *â*, as the Tamil *adu*, of which the same *a* forms the most essential part, is sometimes lengthened to *âdu*. *a* is sometimes preceded by an euphonic consonant, which is inserted between it and the base, to form a link of connection between them, viz., by *v* or *y*, the use of which is purely of an euphonic nature, and by *in*, *ad*, or *ar*, which are inflexional increments of the base, and old petrified locatives or genitives—*e.g.*, *guru-(v)-a*, of a priest; *kuri-(y)-a*, of a sheep; *kus-in-a*, of a child; *mar-ad-a*, of a tree; *ad-ar-a*, of that (thing), or of it. When this genitive *a* is added to the abbreviated inflexional form of the Canarese personal pronouns, the final nasal of those pronouns is doubled—*e.g.*, *nanna* (from *nân*, I), of me; *namma* (from *nâm*, we), of us. A comparison of these forms with the Tamil and Tuḷu *nama*, of us, our, proves that the doubling of the final nasal arises from an euphonic source. *a* forms the genitive suffix not only of the singular of Canarese nouns and pronouns, but also of the plural, whether the noun belongs to the rational or to the irrational class—*e.g.*, *avar-a*, of them (epicene), *avugaḷ-a*, of them (neuter). These examples prove that *a* is the true Canarese genitive case-sign: and it is also to be noted that this case-sign is never used, like *in* in Tamil, as the common fulcrum of the suffixes of all the oblique cases, but is used solely as a case-sign of the genitive.

In Tuḷu *a* is the only sign of the genitive, as in Canarese. The only difference is that in the plural *a* is weakened to *e*. In many instances in singular nouns *a* is preceded by *d* or *t*; but this consonant is merely the equivalent of the Canarese *ad* or *d*, which has already been referred to; and in the genitive of the personal pronouns *a* is preserved purer in Tuḷu than in Canarese. Thus, instead of the Canarese *nanna*, of me, the Tuḷu has *yan-a* (= *nan-a*), and instead of *ninna*, of thee, it has *nin-a*. The language of the Kotas of the Nilgherry Hills forms all its genitives by suffixing *a*.

In Telugu *a* forms the plural inflexion or genitive of all substantive nouns without exception. *lu*, the pluralising particle, is changed into *la*; and as the *u* of *lu* is added merely to facilitate enunciation, and *l* alone constitutes the suffix of the plural, it is evident that the *a* of *la* is a suffix of case. As the plural inflexion, *a* constitutes the fulcrum to which the other case-signs, or suffixes of the oblique cases, are added; and as the genitive plural, it expresses the signification of the genitive, without any auxiliary or additional particle. The Telugu personal pronouns use their crude bases adjectivally as their inflexion and genitive. The pronouns of the third person, or the demonstratives, generally form their genitives, both in the singular and in the plural, by adding *i* to the root: in the singular a few of them suffix *ni*, as is done by the greater number of nouns in the singular. One of the Telugu pronouns uses *a*, both in the singular and in the plural, as the sign of the genitive, in complete accordance with the Canarese and Tuḷu. The genitive of the reflexive pronouns *tân-u*, self, *tâm-u*, selves, is formed in Telugu by shortening the quantity of the radical vowel and suffixing *a*, as in Canarese—*e.g.*, *tan-a*, of self, *tam-a*, of selves. The adjectival *a* of some Telugu substantives is evidently identical with this genitival *a*—*e.g.*, *ûr-a kavi*, a village poet, or a poet of the village.

In Tamil, though *a* is placed first in the list of genitive suffixes, it is now less used than any other sign of the genitive, and indeed is used only as the classical genitive of the personal and reflexive pronouns—*e.g.*, *nam-a*, our (from *nâm*, we), like the Sanskrit *mama*, my, and *tava*, thy. It is difficult, indeed, to determine whether this suffix has retained in Tamil any genitival signification whatever. Whether it be attached to a singular or to a plural pronoun, it must be followed by, and be in agreement with, a neuter plural noun; and this circumstance would lead to the conclusion that in Tamil it is used as a suffix of plurality, not as a sign of the genitive. On this supposition, in the words *ena keigaḷ*, my hands, *ena* would signify not *mei*, of me, but *mea*, (the things that are) mine. It would be a pronominal adjective or possessive plural, not a genitive; and the fact that *a* is largely used in classical Tamil as a sign of the neuter plural (*e.g.*, *sila*, few, literally a few things; *pala*, many, literally many things), shows that this supposition would be a very natural one.

On the other hand, *a* was classed with genitive suffixes by the most ancient Tamil grammarians, and those grammarians, who were remarkably well acquainted with the principles of their own language, were perfectly aware that *a* was also a sign of the plural of "irrationals." Moreover, though it is stated by Tamil grammarians that the genitive in *a* must always be in agreement with a plural noun, yet they admit that the noun with which it agrees is sometimes singular in form though plural in signification—*e.g.*, the expression *nun-a śîr'aḍi*, thy small foot, occurs in the Chintâmaṇi. They say that foot is here used for feet, and this is certainly true; but it does not follow that *nun-a* is determined thereby to be a plural, for the use of the singular with a plural signification, yet with the declensional and conjugational forms of the singular, is a fixed usage of these languages. I think, therefore, that we may confidently regard this *nun-a* as an illustration of the use of *a*, even in Tamil, in connection with the singular. In Tamil, it is true, *a* is ordinarily followed by the neuter plural alone; but in Canarese and Telugu it may be followed by any gender or number; and the *a* of the Tamil *tan-a*, of self, is evidently identical with that of the corresponding Telugu *tan-a;* whilst the *a* of *nam-a*, of us, our, is evidently identical with the Canarese *namm-a*. Hence, as the one *a* is unquestionably a genitive, so must the other have been originally; and thus we are led to the supposition that the Tamil rule which requires *a* to be followed by the neuter plural is merely a secondary, recent, dialectic peculiarity, which has arisen from the influence of its accidental resemblance to the sign of the plural of irrationals. This peculiarity of the genitival *a* in Tamil may be compared with the somewhat parallel case of the use in Hindustani of one possessive suffix rather than another, according to the gender of the noun which follows and governs that to which it is suffixed. Though in grammatical Tamil *a* is always followed by the plural, yet the vulgar in the rural districts commonly use it without discrimination of number, as in Canarese and Telugu. Thus, they will say *nama* (or more commonly, as in Canarese, *namma*) *ûr*, our village; and this confirms the supposition that in Tamil, as in the other dialects, the original use of this *a* was simply that of a suffix of the genitive. In the Ho, a Kôlarian dialect, *a* is a common possessive suffix; and it is also, as in Tamil, an adjectival formative.

We have now to inquire whether there is any other language or family of languages with which this genitive suffix appears capable of being affiliated. There is no direct Scythian analogy for it, and the only affinities which I have observed are Indo-European. The most direct and reliable Indo-European analogy is that which is presented by the personal pronouns, which in some of the Indo-European dialects have a possessive in *a* strongly resembling this Dravidian possessive. If we look only at the Gothic *meina*, my, *theina*, thy, *seina*, his or its, we should naturally conclude the sign of the possessive in these words to be, not *a*, but *na* (answering to the old Scythian and Brahui *na*, and to the Telugu *ni*); but on comparing the forms which this sign of the possessive assumes in various languages, it appears probable that *a* alone conveys the signification of the possessive; and that the nasal which precedes it in the Sanskrit *mama*, the Zend *mana*, and the Gothic *meina*, may merely have been inserted euphonically for the purpose of keeping the contiguous vowels pure. Compare *mama*, Sans. my (from *ma*, I), with *tava*, thy (from *tva*, thou); and especially compare the Gothic *theina*, *seina*, with the corresponding Lithuanian possessives *tava-s*, *sava-s*. In these instances *v* euphonic is used as the equivalent of *n*. The Indo-European pronominal possessive in *a* is exceptional; for the primitive languages of that family evince an almost perfect agreement in the use of *as*, or some closely related form, as the sign of the genitive singular, and of *sâm* or *âm* as the sign of the genitive plural. In the later Teutonic dialects, however, a genitive case-sign in *a* becomes exceedingly common, and is found in the plural as well as in the singular. Thus in the Frisian all plural substantives and such singulars as end in a vowel form their possessive by suffixing *a*; in the Icelandic all plurals and all masculine and neuter singulars use *a* as their case-sign; and in the Anglo-Saxon all plurals. Though the oldest Gothic possessives accorded with the ordinary Sanskrit forms *as* and *âm*, yet the resemblance between the possessives of some of the Teutonic vernaculars and the Dravidian possessive is deserving of notice. The use of *a* as a sign of the possessive by all *plural* substantives in Telugu is especially remarkable. Has the Dravidian *a* under consideration been softened from *as* (of which, however, there is not the smallest trace or analogical probability), or has it been softened from *na*, the old Scythian suffix? The latter supposition, though unsupported by evidence, is not an improbable one in itself; for we have seen that the Gônd *nâ* alternates with *â*, the Scythian *ni-na* with *inna*, the Turkish *nuṉ* with *unu*.

(6.) *The Malayâlam genitive singular suffix 're' or 'de.'*—In most cases this Malayâlam genitive takes the shape of *indre* or *inde*, of which *in* is the genitival suffix and inflexional increment, which has already been described. In *en-de*, my, the inflexional base is of itself a genitive, and the addition of *in* is not required; hence it appears that *de* or *dre* is an auxiliary genitive suffix, like the *adu* which is so often added to *in* in Tamil, and is probably from the same origin. This suffix is written **r**e; but it is always added to *n*, and when it is thus added, the compound is regularly pronounced, not as *n***r***e*, but as *ndre* or *nde*. Neither the Tamil nor the Malayâlam possesses any other method of producing the sound which is indicated by these letters (a peculiarly euphonic *nd*), but that of conjoining the final *n* of those languages and the hard **r**; which, when pronounced in combination, have the sound of *ndr*, or, as some pronounce it, *ndz*, or more commonly still, *nd*. Thus, from *en*, to say, and *du*, the regular formative of the preterite participle, the Canarese forms *endu*, saying, or having said; and this in Tamil is written *en***r***u*; but it would be erroneous to suppose **r***u* to be the sign of the preterite in Tamil instead of *du*, for *en***r***u* is intended to be, and is pronounced, *endu* or *endru*, nearly as in Canarese.

Hence some analogies to the Malayâlam **r***e* (in reality *de*), which might be suggested, appear at once to be illusory. The Malayâlam **r***e* was connected by Dr Stevenson with the Canarese genitive *ra*. It has been shown that *a*, not *ra*, is the genitive suffix of the Canarese, and that the *r* which precedes it is properly *ar*, an inflexional increment (like *ad* and *in*), which is inserted between the root and the case-signs of three cases, besides the genitive, of certain classes of nouns. The Malayâlam **r***e* (*de*), on the other hand, is suffixed exclusively to the genitive, and no other suffix of case is ever appended to it. Nevertheless, as I connect *de* with the Tamil *adu*, it, and as with this I connect also the Canarese *ad* and its hardened form *ar*, it may be admitted that in this modified and remote manner the Malayâlam and the Canarese forms are allied.

Still more illusory is the apparent resemblance of this Malayâlam **r***e* or *de* to the adjectival possessive suffixes of the Hindustani personal pronouns *râ* and *rî* (*e.g.*, *mêrâ*, meus, *mêrî*, mea), to the corresponding New Persian inflexion *râ* (*e.g.*, *to-râ*, thy, thee), and to *ra*, the Gothic genitive plural suffix of the personal pronouns (*e.g.*, *unsara*, our, *izvara*, your), from which the final *r* of our English *our* and *your* has been derived. The Hindustani *r* is supposed by Bopp to be derived from *d*; *mêrâ*, meus, being derived from the Sanskrit *madîya*, my; but I cannot suppose that the Malayâlam form has any connection whatever with the Hindustani and the Persian, except, indeed, on the supposition that the *d* of the Tamil demonstrative neuter singular, *adu*, is remotely connected with the formative *d* of the Sanskrit possessive adjective.

The Malayâlam *de*, like the Tamil *adu*, is used as a genitive suffix of the singular alone, a confirmation of the opinion that it is derived from *adu*, which in its original signification is the neuter singular of the demonstrative. In the genitive plural, the Malayâlam uses *uḍe*, answering to the colloquial Tamil *uḍeiya* (from *uḍei*), belonging to, of. Compare the Malayâlam *enre*, *endre*, or *ende*, of me, with the corresponding Tamil *enadu*, of me, that which is mine. The Malayâlam possessive noun mine, or that which is mine, is *endredu*, from *en-de*, my, and *adu*, it, corresponding to the Tamil *enadu*. This latter *enadu*, however, is not the genitive *enadu*, my, with which I have compared *en-dre*, but a possessive noun in the nominative case; and though I suppose the Malayâlam *de* to be itself a corruption from *adu*, it, yet the demonstrative suffix would be appended a second time, on the origin and true meaning of *de* being forgotten. We see illustrations of this repetition of an ancient suffix in many languages—*e.g.*, *malei-(y)-in-in*, High Tam. from a mountain; and this very demonstrative *adu*, it, is twice used in the Tamil negative participial noun *illâdadu*, the thing which is not; in which the first *d*, though a representative originally of the neuter singular demonstrative, has lost its proper signification, and become a mere euphonic link of connection, or technical sign, in consequence of which *d* requires to be repeated.

(7.) *Auxiliary suffixes of the genitive in Telugu and Tamil.*

(i.) In Telugu, *yokka*, or *yoka*, is sometimes appended to the inflexion, or natural genitive, as an auxiliary suffix of case—*e.g.*, from the ordinary possessive *nâ*, my, is formed optionally the equivalent form *nâ-yokka*, my, of me. This suffix is rarely used, and seems foreign to the idiom of the language; no other pure Dravidian dialect possesses any suffix resembling it. A suffix somewhat resembling *yokka* is found in the Râjmahal and Ûrâon languages, which contain an overwhelming preponderance of Kôl elements, though formed probably upon a Dravidian basis. The possessive suffix of the Râjmahal is *ki*, that of the Ûrâon *ghi*. If these particles are at all connected with the Telugu *yoka*, which seems doubtful, we should be warranted in connecting the whole with the ordinary possessive or adjectival suffix of the Hindustani, the feminine of which is *kî* (masculine *kâ*), and through that suffix with the formative *ka* of the Sanskrit possessive adjectives *mâmaka*, my, *tâvaka*, thy, *asmâkam*, of us, our, &c. A closer analogy to *yoka* is that of the dative postfix of the Mikir, which is *yok* or *ayok*.

(ii.) In Tamil, *uḍeiya* is commonly appended to the inflexion of nouns and pronouns as an auxiliary possessive suffix. *uḍeiya* (*uḍei-(y)-a*), means belonging to, or, literally, which is the property of, and is derived from the noun *uḍei*, property, possession, by the addition of *a*, the sign of the relative participle, on the addition of which to any noun it is converted into an adjective. Thus, *en-uḍeiya kei*, my hand, means literally the hand which is my property, for *en* of itself signifies my. Through usage, however, there is no difference in signification, or even in emphasis, between *en* and *en-uḍei-(y)-a*. The Malayâlam dispenses with *ya* or *a*, the sign of the relative participle, and uses *uḍe* (in Tamil *uḍei*), the uninflected noun itself, as its auxiliary suffix of the genitive. This suffix is still further mutilated in modern Malayâlam into *ḍe*—*e.g.*, *putrî-ḍe*, of a daughter. *uḍeiya* is very largely used as an auxiliary genitival suffix in colloquial Tamil, and in some grammars written by foreigners it is classed with the signs of the genitive; but, properly speaking, it is not a case-sign, or suffix of case at all, but the relative participle of an appellative verb used adjectivally, and it is to be compared not with our preposition *of*, but with the phrase, belonging to.

Locative or 'Seventh' Case.—Dravidian grammarians state that any word which signifies 'a place' may be used to express the locative. In each dialect, however, some words or postpositions are so frequently and systematically used for this purpose that they may be regarded as distinctively locative suffixes.

In Tamil, *kaṇ*, an eye, which has also the signification of a place, is given in the grammars as the characteristic suffix of the locative. As a verbal root, *kaṇ* means to see: its secondary signification was, look! its third, there; its fourth, a place: and in consequence of the last meaning it came to be used as a sign of the locative. It is very rarely used, and the use of *kâl* (in Malayâlam *kal*), which stands next in the list in the Nannûl, is still more rare. I have no hesitation in saying that the most distinctive sign of the Tamil locative is *il*, a house, a place—literally, this place, here. In colloquial Tamil the most commonly used sign of the locative is *iḍattil*, a compound suffix, which is derived from *iḍam*, the ordinary word for a place, *attu*, the inflexion or basis of the oblique cases (*iḍ'-attu*), and *il*, an older, purer word for a place, which is added to *iḍ'-attu* (*iḍ'-att'-il*), as the real sign of the locative, with the meaning of our preposition *in*. The signification of the whole suffix is literally, in the place of, or in the place occupied by; but it is evident that what really distinguishes the locative in this compound is *il*, in—the suffix of a suffix; and that the meaning which the entire compound receives in actual use is simply *in*. In the lowest patois of colloquial Tamil, the locative suffix which is most used is *kiṭṭa*, near, the infinitive of a verb.* The higher dialect of the Tamil uses also *uḷ* and *uṛi*, within, among, as signs of the locative.

The ancient Canarese generally used *ôḷ*, corresponding to the Tamil *uḷ*, as its locative suffix; whilst the modern dialect uses *alli* or *illi*, a form which answers to the Tamil *il*. *alli* is properly a noun of place, formed from the remote demonstrative *a*; and its fellow is *illi*, formed from *i*, the proximate demonstrative. These words mean literally that place and this place, or there and here, and their use as locative suffixes appears to betoken a later state of the language than the use of *il* and *uḷ* in Tamil, and of *ôḷ* in Canarese. The locative suffix of the Tuda is *uḷch* or *orzh*, which seems to be simply the Tamil *uḷ* rudely pronounced. *r* and *l* seem generally to become *rzh* in this dialect.

In Telugu the sign of the locative most commonly used is *lô*; another form frequently employed is *andu*. *lô* is more intensely locative in its signification than *andu*; it means within, and is obviously identical with the Canarese *ôḷ* and the Tamil *uḷ*. *andu* means simply 'in,' and, like the Canarese *alli*, is properly a noun of place. I consider *andu*, the adverbial noun, there, identical with *andu*, the sign of the locative. It is evidently formed from *a*, the remote demonstrative, with the addition of a formative *d*, whilst *indu*, the correlative adverb of place, is derived from *i*, the proximate demonstrative. The Canarese also possesses adverbs corresponding to these, viz., *anta* and *inta*, *antalu* and *intalu*, but uses them chiefly to express comparison, like our adverb *than*. The Telugu locative suffix *andu* (meaning on or in) bears some apparent resemblance to the Sanskrit *antar*, among, but this resemblance is illusory; for *andu* is derived from *a*, that, by the addition of the neuter formative *du*, which becomes euphonically *ndu*, and corresponds not to the Sanskrit, but rather to *anda*, that, the demonstrative adjective of the Tamil. The Tuḷu locative suffix is *du* or *ḍ'*, *tu* or *ṭ'*,

---

* I cannot forbear noticing the remarkable (though probably accidental) resemblance between the double meaning of *il* in Tamil and of *in* in Latin. Each is used as a locative suffix with the meaning of 'in;' and each is used also as a particle of negation. The Latin *in* not only means 'in,' but has also the additional meaning of 'not' in such compounds as *indoctus* (like the Gothic *un* and the Greek and Sanskrit *a* or *an* privative); and in like manner the Tamil *il* means not only 'in,' but also 'not.' Moreover, as the Latin *in* privative is *an*, *un*, in some other dialects, so the Tamil *il*, not, takes also the shape of *al*, with a very slight difference, not in the meaning, but only in the application. Dr Gundert suggests that possibly *il* is merely the equivalent of *uḷ*, meaning existence, and that the negative power of *illa* rests in the final *a*. I have shown, however, that this *a* is the pluralising particle of the neuter plural. See "Neuter plural suffix in *a*." The neuter singular is *il-du*, *indṛu*, the thing that is not.

which Dr Gundert conjectures may be derived from *uḍu*, equivalent to *uḷ*, Tam. within, *ôḷ*, Old Canarese, or from *eḍe*, equivalent to Tam. *iḍei* or *iḍam*, place. The nature of the initial vowel of the Tuḷu suffix seems difficult to ascertain. The *ḍ* is sometimes preceded by *o*, sometimes by *a* or *e*; and sometimes it is obliterated, as in *keiṭ*, in the hand, a form which suggests Telugu analogies. On the whole it seems to me most likely that the Tuḷu locative *ḍu* or *ṭu* has sprung from the same origin as the Can. *alli* and the Tel. *andu*, viz., the adverb of place *there*, one form of which in Tuḷu is *aḍe*, thither (corresponding to *iḍe*, hither, and *oḍe*, whither).

In Telugu the postposition *na*, which becomes *ni* after *i*, is used as a locative suffix in connection with neuter nouns. *ni* (and hence its equivalent *na* also) is evidently identical with *in*, the sign of the ablative of motion in High Tamil, which I have supposed to be properly a sign of the locative; and probably this *in* is the origin of *in*, the Tamil, and *ni* and *na*, the Telugu, genitival or inflexional suffixes. The genitive is more likely to be derived from the locative than the locative from the genitive. With this Telugu locative *na* we may compare the Ostiak locative *na*, *ne*, the Finnish and Magyar *an* and *en*, and especially the Japanese locative *ni*—*e.g.*, *Yedo-ni*, in or at Yedo.

In Telugu, and in the higher dialect of Tamil, the inflexion or basis of the oblique cases, which has generally the force of a genitive, is sometimes used to denote the locative also. This is the case in Tamil only in those connections in which it is governed by a verb, expressed or implied. In Tamil the inflexion which is chiefly used in this manner is *attu*—*e.g.*, *nilattu*, upon the earth. The Malayâlam uses *attu* in a similar manner; and in Telugu a corresponding change from *ti* to *ta* converts the inflexion or obsolete genitive into a locative —*e.g.*, *iṇṭi*, of a house, *iṇṭa*, in a house. The same inflexion in *ta* denotes the instrumental in Telugu, as well as the locative—*e.g.*, compare *chêti*, of a hand, with *chêta*, by a hand; but this form seems to have been a locative originally. This fusion of the meaning of the genitive and locative suffixes corresponds to a similar fusion of the signs of those cases which a comparison of the various Indo-European tongues brings to light. The genitive and locative case-signs are often identical in the Finnish family of languages also. Bearing this in mind, we may conclude that *in* or *ni*, one of the most common inflexional increments in all the dialects; *in*, one of the Tamil possessive and adjectival suffixes; *in*, the sign of the Tamil ablative of motion; and *im*, the Canarese sign of the instrumental, with the various shapes they take, were all originally locatives, and identical with *il*, which we have seen is so exceedingly common as a locative suffix, with the original meaning of *here*.*

In all the Dravidian idioms the locative suffixes are used like our *than*, to express comparison. Sometimes the locative alone is used for this purpose: oftener the conjunctive particle is added to it—*e.g.*, *il-um*, in Tamil, *lô-nu*, in Telugu, which compound has the signification of our *even than*.

The Vocative or 'Eighth' Case.—In the Dravidian languages there is nothing which properly deserves to be styled a suffix or case-sign of the vocative. The vocative is formed merely by affixing or suffixing some sign of emphasis, or in certain instances by suffixing fragments of the personal pronouns. The most common vocative in Tamil is the emphatic *ê*, which is simply appended to the noun. Sometimes, also, the vocative is formed by substituting *â* for the formative of gender—*e.g.*, from *kartan*, Lord, is formed *kartâ*, O Lord; by converting the final vowel into *ây* (a fragment of the old pronoun of the second person singular)—*e.g.*, from *tangei*, sister, is formed *tangây*, O sister; or by lengthening the vowel of the pluralising particle—*e.g.*, from *pâvigal̥*, sinners, is formed *pâvigâl̥*, O sinners. Sometimes, again, especially in poetry, rational plurals are put in the vocative by appending to them *îr*, a fragment of *nîr*, you—*e.g.*, *ellîr*, literally *ell-îr*, all ye. Both in Tamil and Malayâlam the vocative is often formed by lengthening the final vowel of the nominative—*e.g.*, *tôr̥i*, female friend, voc. *tôr̥ê*. This usage prevails also in Japanese.

In the Indo-European languages the nominative is often used for the vocative, and what appears to be a vocative case-ending is often only a weakened form of the final syllable. In the Dravidian languages, in like manner, the crude root, deprived of all increments, is often used as the vocative.

In Telugu the vocative singular is ordinarily formed by lengthening the final vowel of the nominative (and all Telugu words end in some vowel), or by changing the final *u* into *a* or *â*. *ara* or *arâ*, from the same root as the Tamil pronominal fragment *îr* (viz., *nîr*, ye), is post-

---

* Can. and Tel. agree in using *al* as the base of a remote demonstrative. Can. uses the corresponding *il* (*illi*), here, as a proximate demonstrative, but does not give to it the meaning of house. Tel. gives to *il* the meaning of house (*ilu*, *illu*), but does not use it as a proximate demonstrative. The demonstrative meaning of *il*, which has disappeared from the Tel. *il-u*, house, is retained, however, in the longer form *ilâgu*, in this manner. The radical element in *il*, here, is the proximate demonstrative root *i*, this, and this would seem to be the origin also of the Indo-European locative *i*. "This short *i*," says Max Müller (p. 227), speaking of the Sanskrit locative *i* in *hrid-i*, in the heart, "is a demonstrative root, and in all probability the same root which produced the preposition *in*."

fixed as the vocative of masculine-feminine plurals. In addition to these suffixes, various unimportant vocative particles, or particles of exclamation, are prefixed to nouns; some to one number only, some to both. In Canarese the vocative is ordinarily formed by appending *â*, by lengthening the final vowel of the nominative, or by adding *e* or *ê*. Masculine-feminine plurals form their vocative not only by means of *e* or *ê*, but also by suffixing *ira* or *irâ*, from the same source as the Telugu *arâ*—viz., the old *nîr* or *îr*, ye. Such being the origin and character of the Dravidian signs of the vocative, it is evident that we cannot expect to find allied forms in any other family of languages.

Compound Case-signs.—As in the Hungarian and other Scythian tongues, and in some of the languages of the Eastern islands, so in Dravidian, two or more case-signs are occasionally compounded together into one. We have already noticed the custom of annexing the various signs of the oblique cases to the inflexion or sign of the genitive; but other combinations of case-signs are also in use. Thus, there is a combination of the dative and locative—*e.g.*, *vîṭṭukkuḷ* (*vîṭṭu-kk'uḷ*), colloquial Tam. within the house, in which the locative *uḷ* is combined with the dative or directive *kku*, for the purpose of intensifying *in*, and educing the meaning of 'within.' The higher dialect would in this instance prefer *vîṭṭuḷ*, the simple locative; but *vîṭṭu-kkuḷ* is also idiomatic. The ablative of motion in each of the Dravidian dialects is generally a compound case, being formed of the locative and a verbal participle, or even of two locatives—*e.g.*, *mane-(y)-ill-inda*, Can. out of the house, from *illi* or *alli*, the sign of the locative, and *inda*, a sign of the instrumental, which is used also as a sign of the ablative, but which was, I conceive, a locative originally, and identical with *im*, the Canarese form of the Tamil *in*.

Such compounds may indeed be formed in these languages at pleasure, and almost *ad infinitum*. Another instance of them in Tamil is seen in the addition of the dative to the locative (*e.g.*, *il-ku*, *iḍattil-ku*), to constitute the locative-directive, which is required to be used in such expressions as, I sent *to* him. The Malayâlam *inikkuḷḷa* (*in-i-kk'* and *uḷḷa*), my, is a compound of the dative of the personal pronoun (which is itself a compound), and a relative participial form of *uḷ*, within; in colloquial Tamil, also, a similar form is used as a possessive.

Possessive Compounds.—The Dravidian languages are destitute of that remarkable and very convenient compound of nouns and pronominal suffixes with a possessive signification which is so characteristic of the Turkish, Finnish, and other Scythian families. See Castren's "Dissertatio de Affixis Personalibus Linguarum Altaicarum."

In Hungarian they form the following compounds of *ur*, master, with the pronominal fragments, used as possessives :—

ur-am,	my master.	*ur-aim*,	my masters.
ur-ad,	thy master.	*ur-aid*,	thy masters.
ur-a,	his master.	*ur-ai*,	his masters.
ur-un-k,	our master.	*ur-ain-k*,	our masters.
ur-at-ok,	your master.	*ur-ait-ok*,	your masters.
ur-ok,	their master.	*ur-ai-k*,	their masters.

These compounds are regularly declined like uncompounded nouns, in the usual way : *e.g.*—

uramnak (*ur-am-nak*), to my master.
urunknak (*ur-un-k-nak*), to our master.
uraimnak (*ur-aim-nak*), to my masters.
urainknak (*ur-ain-k-nak*), to our masters.

The absence of possessive compounds of this nature in the Dravidian languages, notwithstanding their agreement with the Scythian group in so many other points, is remarkable : it is the only point in which any structural difference of a generic or class type appears to exist. In all the Dravidian languages the possessive pronouns are prefixed to nouns, as in the Indo-European tongues, never postfixed, as in the Scythian. There is a class of words in the Dravidian languages compounded of a noun and a personal suffix, called conjugated nouns, or appellative verbs. See the section in which these are explained. That class of words, though it resembles, is not identical with, the Scythian possessive compounds. It is identical, however, with the predicative compounds of the Scythian languages.

SECTION III.—ADJECTIVES, OR NOUNS USED ADJECTIVALLY.

The difference between the Indo-European languages and those of the Scythian group with respect to the formation and use of adjectives, is very considerable.

The agreement of adjectives with the substantives which they qualify, in gender, number, and case, forms an invariable characteristic of the languages of the Indo-European family ; whilst in the Scythian languages adjectives have neither number, gender, nor case, but are mere nouns of relation or quality, which are prefixed without alteration to substantive nouns. In this particular the Dravidian languages present no resemblance to the Sanskrit, or to any other member of the

Indo-European stock, but are decidedly Scythian in character. Dravidian adjectives, properly so called, like those of the Scythian tongues, are nouns of quality or relation, which acquire the signification of adjectives merely by being prefixed to substantive nouns without declensional change; and, in virtue of that acquired signification, they are called by Tamil grammarians *uri chol*, qualitative words. Participles of verbs, and nouns with the addition of participial formatives, are also largely used as adjectives in the Dravidian, as in the Scythian, family. Such being the simplicity of the construction of Dravidian adjectives, it will not be necessary to occupy much time in the investigation of this department of grammar. It may suffice to state, *seriatim*, the various modes in which nouns or verbs are used as adjectives, and the formative or euphonic modifications which they undergo on being prefixed to the substantives which they qualify: nor will it be necessary to state *all* the modifications which are discoverable in each dialect, but only those which appear to be most characteristic, or which are peculiarly worthy of remark.

1. The majority of adjectives in all the Dravidian dialects are nouns of quality or relation, which become adjectives by position alone, without any structural change whatever, and without ceasing to be, in themselves, nouns of quality. Thus, in the Tamil phrases *pon aridu*, gold (is) scarce, and *pon muḍi*, a golden crown, *pon*, gold, is precisely the same in both instances, whether used as a substantive in the first, or as an adjective in the second. In a similar manner, in English and the other modern Indo-European dialects, the same word is often used as a noun in one connection, and as an adjective, without addition or change, in another connection—*e.g.*, gold is more ductile than silver; a gold watch. Whilst adjectival nouns of this class undergo in the Dravidian languages no structural change, their combination with the nouns to which they are prefixed is facilitated in certain instances by unimportant euphonic changes, such as the assimilation of the final consonant of the adjective and the initial consonant of the substantive, in accordance with the requirements of Dravidian phonetics (*e.g.*, *por chilei* (for *pon śilei*), a golden image); the softening, hardening, or doubling of the initial of the substantive; or the optional lengthening of the included vowel of the adjectival noun, to compensate for the abandonment of the euphonic final *u*—*e.g.*, *kâr*, black, in place of *karu*, or *vice versâ*. These changes are purely euphonic; they differ in the different dialects, and they contribute to grammatical expression only in so far as they serve to indicate the words which are to be construed together as adjective and substantive. It is only on the ground of the repugnance of the Dravidian ear to certain classes of concurrent sounds

that the changes referred to are required by Dravidian rules; and in the majority of instances nouns sustain no change whatever on being used adjectivally.

In the poetical dialects, adjectival formatives are less used than even in the colloquial dialects; and it is generally the crude ultimate form of the noun of quality which performs the functions of the adjective in classical compositions. Thus, whilst *nalla*, good, and *pala*, many, are commonly used in spoken Tamil, the higher idiom prefers, and almost invariably uses, the crude nouns of quality and relation *nal* and *pal*—*e.g.*, *nal vaṛi*, the good way, and *pan* (for *pal*) *malar*, many flowers.

2. Sanskrit derivatives (neuter nouns of quality) ending in *am* in Tamil, and in *amu* in Telugu, become adjectives when prefixed to other nouns by rejecting the final *m* or *mu*—*e.g.*, *subam*, goodness, and *dinam*, a day, become *suba dinam*, a good day. This, however, is in imitation of a Sanskrit rule, and it flows from the circumstance that when two Sanskrit nouns are formed into a compound, the crude form of the first of the two nouns is used instead of the nominative—*subha* instead of *subham*.

Pure Dravidian nouns ending in *am* or *amu* rarely become adjectives in this manner; and when they do, it may be suspected that it is through imitation of Sanskrit derivatives. In Telugu, final *amu* is sometimes hardened into *ampu*—*e.g.*, from *andamu*, beauty, is formed *andapu* or *andampu*, beautiful. In Tamil, when a noun of this class is used as an adjective, *am* is generally rejected, and *attu*, the inflexion, suffixed instead—*e.g.*, from *puram*, externality, is formed *purattu*, external. Sometimes also Tamil deals in this manner with Sanskrit derivatives, converting them into adjectives by means of the inflexional *attu;* but in all instances of nouns ending in *am* or *amu*, the most common method of using them adjectively is that of appending to them the relative participle of the verb *to become* (*âna*, Tam., *ayana*, Tel., or *âda*, Can.), without any change, whether structural or euphonic, in the nouns themselves.

3. Many Tamil nouns ending in *ś-u*, *ḍ-u*, *ṇḍ-u*, or *r-u*, double their final consonants when they are used as adjectives, or when case-signs are suffixed to them—*e.g.*, compare *nâḍ-u*, Tam. the country, with *nâṭṭ-u vaṛakkam*, the custom of the country, or *nâṭṭ-il*, in the country. (See the "Inflexional Increments.") From the corresponding Telugu *nâḍ-u*, the country, is formed *nâṭi*, of the country. In these instances the final consonant of the root is doubled and hardened (or in Telugu hardened only), for the purpose of conveying the signification of an

adjective; but in another class of instances the root remains unchanged, and it is the consonant of the formative addition that is doubled.

When Tamil nouns ending in the formative *mbu* are used adjectivally, *mbu* changes into *ppu*—*e.g.*, from *irumbu*, iron, and *kôl*, a rod, is formed *iruppu* (*k*)*kôl*, an iron rod. A similar change sometimes takes place in Telugu, in which *inumu*, iron, becomes *inupa*—*e.g.*, *inupa pette*, an iron box. Tamil nouns ending in the formative *ndu* and *du* change in the same manner to *ttu* on being used as adjectives—*e.g.*, compare *marundu*, medicine, and *erudu*, an ox, with *maruttu* (*p*)*pei*, a medicine-bag, and *eruttu* (*p*)*podi*, an ox-load. More rarely, nouns ending in the formative *ngu* change into *kku* both in Tamil and Malayâlam—*e.g.*, *kurakku-*(*p*)*-paḍei*, a monkey army, from *kurangu*, a monkey. These changes precisely resemble those which neuter or intransitive verbs ending in *d-u* or **r**-*u* (or with the formative additions of *mb-u*, *ng-u*, *nd-u*, &c.) undergo on becoming active or transitive, and a similar principle is in each instance apparent in the change; for when nouns of quality are prefixed to other nouns adjectivally, there is a transition of their signification to the nouns which they are intended to qualify, which is analogous to the transition of the action of a transitive verb to the object which it governs. (See "Roots," and also "The Verb.")

4. Each of the inflexional increments, or petrified case-signs, is used for the conversion of substantives into adjectives. These are *in* in Tamil and *ni* in Telugu, *attu* in Tamil and *ṭi* or *ti* in Telugu. In those instances in which *in* in Tamil and *ni* in Telugu are used as adjectival formatives, their use is optional—*e.g.*, in Telugu we can say either *tella*, white, or *tella-ni;* and in Tamil either *niṛal*, shady (literally *shade*, a noun used adjectivally), or (but in the poetical dialect only) *niṛal-in*. So also we may say either *mara* (*k*)*koppu*, Tam. the branch of a tree, or *mar'-attu* (*k*)*koppu*. In Tamil, *am*, an inflexional increment which is apparently equivalent to *in*, is often used as an adjectival formative—*e.g.*, *panan dôppu* (*panei-am tôppu*), a palmyra tope. The same formative is used in Malayâlam also—*e.g.*, *malam pâmbu* (*mala-am pâmbu*), a rock-snake.

It has been shown that the inflexions or inflexional augments *attu* and *ṭi* are in reality locative or possessive case-signs, and that they are used to convert substantives into adjectives through the relation subsisting between possessives—*e.g.*, of gold—and adjectives—*e.g.*, golden. In consequence of the frequency of their use in this connection, they have come to be appended even to adverbial forms for the purpose of giving to them an adjectival meaning. Thus, from *monna*, Tel. before, is formed the adjective *monna-ṭi* (*e.g.*, *monna-ṭi tîrpu*, the former decision); and in Tamil, from *vaḍakku*, north (perhaps originally a dative), is formed the adjective *vaḍakk'-att-u*, northern (*e.g.*, *vaḍakkattiyân*, a northerner). In these and similar instances it is plain that the so-called adverbs are in reality only nouns used adverbially.

5. Relative participles of verbs, and nouns of quality converted into relative participles by the addition of participial formatives, are largely used as adjectives in all the Dravidian languages. Much use is made of relative participles as adjectives by the languages of High Asia; and in Japanese also participial forms of the verb are used as adjectives. It often happens that the same root is used, or at least is capable of being used, both as a verb and as a noun; and hence, in many instances of this kind in the Dravidian languages, two methods of forming adjectives are practicable, viz., either by prefixing the noun to the substantive which we wish to qualify, or by using one of the relative participles of the related and equivalent verb. The colloquial dialect of Tamil prefers the latter method: the former is preferred by the poets on account of its greater simplicity and brevity. Thus, in Tamil either *uyar*, height (adjectivally 'high'), or the relative participle *uyarnda*, high, literally 'that was high' (from *uyar*, considered as a verb signifying 'to be high'), may be used to express high or lofty—*e.g.*, *uyar malei* or *uyarnda malei*, a lofty hill: but *uyar* would be preferred in poetical compositions, whilst *uyarnda* is better suited to prose and colloquial purposes, and is consequently the form which is commonly used by the Tamil people.

6. The past verbal participle of Telugu verbs is sometimes used adjectivally in Telugu; hence when Sanskrit neuter nouns in *am* are used as adjectives, *ayi*, 'having become' (the verbal participle), is often annexed to them instead of *ayi-na* (Tam. *âna*, Can. *âda*, that became, that is (the relative participle). It seems evident, therefore, that the final *i* of many Telugu adjectives may be explained as identical with the *i* by which the past participles of verbs are formed—*e.g.*, *kindi*, low, from *kinda*, below—*e.g.*, *kindi illu*, the lower part of the house. The addition of the same *i* (if it be the same) converts substantives also into adjectives—*e.g.*, from *kûn-u*, a hump, is formed *kûni*, hump-backed. (See "Inflexional Increments," 7, *i*; and "The Verb: Nouns of Agency.")

7. A very numerous class of Dravidian adjectives is formed by the addition to crude nouns of quality of the suffixes of the relative participles, more or less modified. *Uyarnda* is a perfectly-formed preterite relative participle, comprising, in addition to the verbal root,

nd, the sign of the preterite tense, and *a*, the sign of the relative; and though the idea of time is in this connection practically lost sight of, yet that idea is included and expressed. On the other hand, in the class of words now to be considered, the signs of tense are modified or rejected to correspond with their use as adjectives, and the idea of time is entirely merged in that of relation. It is words of this class which are commonly adduced by grammarians as specimens of qualitative words, or *adjectives;* and, if the name can correctly be used at all in the Dravidian family of tongues, it is to this class that it is applicable. I am convinced, however, that it is more correct to regard these words simply as relative participles; and I class them under this head, immediately after the investigation of the noun, because in most instances the root to which the relative signs are suffixed is used by itself, not as a verb, but only as a noun of quality or relation, or as an appellative.

(1.) Many Tamil adjectives of this class are formed by the addition of *iya* to the root—*e.g.*, *periya*, great, *śiriya*, small. The roots of these words are *per-u* and *śir-u;* and as *u* is merely a help to enunciation, I do not say that *u* is changed into *i*, but prefer to say that *iya* is added to the root. I have no doubt that we shall be able to explain each part of this addition grammatically, without having recourse to arbitrary mutations. These adjectives are simply the relative participles of "conjugated nouns." *Iya* (*i-y-a*) is compounded of *i*, a sign of the preterite tense, and *a*, the sign of the relative participle, with the addition of *y* inserted euphonically. In Telugu, the past participle alone is often used adjectivally without the suffix of the relative, as we have already seen; and the *i* with which that participle terminates explains the *i* which precedes the final *a* of such Tamil adjectives as *peri-(y)-a*. *i* is the sign of the verbal participle, and the addition of *a* or *ya*, transforms it into a relative participle. In classical Tamil compositions, *iya* is generally used instead of *ina*, as the sign of the preterite relative participle of ordinary verbs—*e.g.*, *paṉ-ṉiya*, instead of *paṉṉina*, that made. When the same suffix is added to a noun of quality like *per-u*, great, it converts it into a relative participle, which, with the form of the preterite, contains in it no reference to time, and which may therefore be called an adjective. The suffix *iya* being somewhat archaic, readily loses the idea of time, whereas that idea is firmly retained by *ida*, *ina*, and the other preterite relative suffixes which are in ordinary use.

A good illustration of the adjectival use of *iya* is furnished by the very roots to which we have referred, viz., *peru*, great, *śiru*, small. When these roots are regarded as verbs, their preterite relative participles are *perutta*, that was or became great, *śirutta*, that was or became small; in which participles the ideas of time and change are always included: whereas, when *peru* and *śiru* are regarded as nouns of quality, they are adapted for general use as adjectives by having *iya* suffixed to them—*e.g.*, *periya*, *śiriya* (*per'-iya*, *śir'-iya*). In this shape they mean simply great and small, without any reference to time; and in consequence of *iya* being so purely aoristic, adjectives of this mode of formation are largely used. *periya*, great, *koḍiya*, cruel, may properly be styled adjectives, seeing that they are used as such; but it is a mistake to regard *periya-(v)-an*, or *periya-n*, a great man, *koḍiya-n*, a cruel man, and similar words, as adjectives. They are compounds of adjectives and suffixes of gender; and are properly appellative nouns, as has been shown under the head of "Gender," and as appears from the manner in which they are used. It is remarkable that *a* or *ia* is postfixed in Kôl also to many adjectives; and that the same participle is a sign of the possessive, as *a* is in Dravidian.

(2.) Some adjectives are formed by simply suffixing *a*, the sign of the relative participle, without the preterite *i*, or any other sign of tense whatever—*e.g.*, *nalla*, Tam. good; *doḍḍa*, Can. great; *pedda*, Tel. great. The examples here given may be, and doubtless are, derived from preterite relative participles (*nalla** from the High Tamil *nalgiya*, and *doḍḍa* from the ancient Canarese *doḍḍida*); but in some instances, *a*, the sign of the relative participle, is appended directly to nouns, without borrowing any portion of the sign of the preterite. We have an instance of this even in colloquial Tamil, viz., *uḍeiya* (*uḍei-(y)-a*), the ordinary colloquial suffix of the genitive, which literally signifies that belongs to, that is the property of, from *uḍei*, property, to which *a*, the sign of the relative participle, is simply suffixed. This mode of forming adjectives from substantives by directly suffixing *a* is very common in the classical dialect of the Tamil, especially in connection with substantives ending in *ei* or *î*—*e.g.*, from *malei*, a hill, comes *malei-(y)-a*, adj., hilly, or of a hill; from *śunei*, a spring, comes *śunei-(y)-a*, that relates to a spring. So also from *tî*, evil, is formed

* *Nalla* is generally considered to be a primitive word, and a *bonâ fide* adjective; but if *keṭṭa*, bad, is admitted to be a relative participle, from *keḍ-u*, to become bad, it is reasonable to suppose that *nalla*, good, has also some such origin. Accordingly we find a root, *nal*, goodness, which is capable of being used adjectivally, and then signifies good, and the verb *nalg-u*, to be bountiful, to be good. The preterite relative participle of this verb is *nalgiya*, that was or is bountiful; and from this, I believe, the much-used adjective *nalla*, good, has been derived.

tî-(y)-a, adj., evil. The circumstance that in most of these examples the signification of the genitive is as natural as that of the adjective, shows how intimately the genitive and the adjective are allied. Nevertheless, as used in these examples, I regard *a* as an adjectival termination, rather than as a sign of the genitive, and as acquiring this force from its being the sign of the relative participle. Indeed, I would define these qualitative words (*malei-(y)-a*, &c.) to be the relative participles of appellative verbs. See that class of words investigated in the section on "The Verb."

This usage, perhaps, explains the origin of the Tamil adjectives *pala*, many, and *sila*, few, viz., from the roots *pal* and *sil* (which are used in their crude state in the poets), and *a*, the sign of the relative participle. It is true that these words are also regarded as neuters plural; and that in some instances they are correctly so regarded appears from the phrase *palavin* (*pala-v-in*) *pâl*, the Tamil designation of the neuter plural, literally the gender of the many (things). But when we look also at such phrases as *pala araśar*, many kings—phrases of constant occurrence, not only in the colloquial dialect, but in the classics—the *a* of this latter *pala* appears to be used, not as a suffix of the neuter plural, or as a sign of plurality of any sort, but as a sign of the relative participle, by the use of which *pal-a* becomes an adjective.

(3.) Many adjectives of this class are formed by the addition to nouns of quality of the sign of the relative participle of the future or aorist, which is *um* in Tamil — *e.g.*, *per-um*, great. Native grammarians suppose this adjective to be derived from the abstract noun *perumei*, greatness, by the rejection of the final *ei*, and to all other adjectives of this class they attribute a similar origin. *mei*, however, not *ei*, is the suffix by which abstract nouns are formed (*vide* "The Verb"), and as such it is one and indivisible. It is much better to derive *perum* from *per'*, the uneuphonised form of the root *peru*, greatness, great, and *um*, the ordinary relative participle of the aorist, in the same manner as *periya* has been seen to be derived from *per* and *iya*, the relative participle of the preterite. *um* is ordinarily called the relative participle of the future, but this future will be shown, in the part on "The Verb," to be properly an aorist, and as such to be used very indeterminately with respect to time. *Viṇṇil minaṅg-um śuḍar*, Tam., means, not the stars that will shine in the sky, but the stars that shine in the sky, this tense being especially fitted to denote continued existence; and in consequence of this looseness of reference to time, *um*, the sign of the relative participle of this tense, is better fitted even than *iya* to be suffixed to nouns of quality as an adjectival formative. Hence *perum*, literally that is, was, or will be great, is a more expressive and more classical word for great than *periya*. It has already been shown, in the part on "Sounds," that *peim*, Tam. green, is not a distinct form of adjective, but is softened from *paśum* (*payum*) by a dialectic rule, whilst *paśum* is derived regularly from *paś-u*, greenness, green, and *um*, the particle which is now under consideration.

8. Dravidian nouns of every description may be used adjectivally by appending to them the relative participles of the verb signifying to become, which are in Tamil *âna* and *âgum* (also *uḷḷa*, an equivalent word), in Telugu *agu* and *ayina* (pronounced *aina*), in Canarese *âda*—*e.g.*, *uyarvâna* (*uyarv'-âna*), Tam. lofty, literally that was or has become high or a height. This mode of forming adjectives is especially used in connection with Sanskrit derivatives, on account of their greater length and foreign origin. Such adjectives, however, are phrases, not words; but they were at one time incorrectly classed amongst adjectives by Europeans who treated of Dravidian grammar.

I may here also again remark, that certain words have been styled adjectives by some European writers, which in reality are appellative nouns, not adjectives, and which acquire the force of adjectives merely from the addition of the relative participles of the verb to become, which have been referred to above. Thus, the Tamil words *nallavan*, a good (man), *nallavaḷ*, a good (woman), *nalladu*, a good (thing), are appellative nouns formed by the suffix to a noun of quality of the formatives of the three genders; and the addition of *âna*, that has become, to any of these words, though it constitutes them adjectives in effect, leaves them in grammatical form precisely what they were before. *Bonus* may either qualify another noun—*e.g.*, *bonus vir*, when it is an adjective, or it may stand alone and act as nominative to a verb, when it is a qualitative noun—*e.g.*, *bonus virtutem amat*. The Tamil *nallavan*, a good (man), can only be used in the latter sense, and therefore is not an adjective at all.

Comparison of Adjectives.—In all the Dravidian dialects, comparison is effected, not as in the Indo-European family, by means of comparative or superlative particles suffixed to, and combined with, the positive form of the adjective, but by a method closely resembling that in which adjectives are compared in the Semitic languages, or by the simpler means which are generally used in the languages of the Scythian group. When the first of these methods is adopted, the noun of quality or adjective to be compared is placed in the nominative, and the noun or nouns with which it is to be compared are put in the locative and prefixed. It is generally stated in Tamil grammars that it is the ablative of motion which is thus used; but I am persuaded that even when the case-sign is that of the ablative of motion, the signification is purely that of the locative, and that in Tamil *il* and *in* have in this connection the meaning of *in* (*i.e.*, are locatives), rather than that of *from*—*e.g.*, *avattr'-il idu nalladu*, Tam. this is better than those, literally in those things this is good.

The conjunctive particle *um*, and, even, is often added, especially in the colloquial dialect, as an intensive—*e.g.*, *avattr'-il um idu nàlladu*, Tam. this is better than those, literally even in those this is good. Very frequently the noun with which comparison is to be made is put in the dative instead of the locative. Sometimes, again, comparison is effected by means of an auxiliary verb. The noun with which comparison is to be made is put in the accusative; it is followed and governed by the subjunctive or infinitive of a verb signifying to see, to show, or to leave; and the phrase is concluded by the subject of the proposition, with the adjective to be compared. Thus, in Tamil we may say *adei-(p)-pârkkilum idu nalladu*, literally even though looking at that this (is) good, or *adei viḍa idu nalladu*, quitting that this (is) good, *i.e.*, this is so good as to induce one to abandon that. Such modes of comparison, however, are stiff, cumbrous, and little used except by Europeans; and in the Dravidian dialects, as in those of the Scythian group, direct comparison of one thing with another is ordinarily left to be understood, not expressed. The effect which is aimed at is secured in a very simple manner by prefixing to the positive form of the adjective some word signifying much or very, or by appending to the subject of the proposition a sign of emphasis, or a word signifying indeed—*e.g.*, *id-ê* (or *idu tân*) *nalladu*, Tam. THIS indeed is good. In Telugu and Canarese the conjunctive particles *u* and *û* are not necessarily required to help forward the former method of comparison, like the Tamil *um*, nor is this particle generally used in the higher dialect of the Tamil itself. The Canarese makes use also of the particles *anta* and *inta, antalu* and *intalu* (which, in their origin, are compounds of locatives and demonstratives), to assist in effecting comparison.

In all these dialects the superlative is generally expressed by means of prefixed adverbs signifying much or very, or by the very primitive plan of doubling of the adjective itself—*e.g.*, *periya-periya*, very great, literally great-great. If greater explicitness is required, the method by which it is effected is that of putting the objects with which comparison is made in the plural and in the locative case. Thus, the phrase, the tiger is the fiercest animal, would be expressed in Tamil as follows: —*vilaṅgugaḷil vêṅgei koḍidu*, amongst animals (literally in animals) the tiger is the cruel one. Sometimes, for the purpose of increasing the intensity of the superlative signification, the adjectival noun *ellā*, all, is prefixed to the plural noun which denotes the objects compared—*e.g.*, in (*i.e.*, amongst) all animals the tiger is cruel.

It is evident that the modes of forming the comparative and superlative degrees of adjectives which have now been described, differ greatly and essentially from those which characterise the Indo-European family of tongues. If Dravidian adjectives had ever been compared like those of the Sanskrit, it is inconceivable that so convenient and expressive a plan should so completely have been abandoned. The Dravidian modes of comparison agree, up to a certain point, with those of the Semitic tongues; but they are in most perfect accordance with the Turkish method, and with the modes of comparison which are employed in the languages of Tatary generally.

Robert de Nobilibus and the Jesuit writers endeavoured to naturalise in Tamil the Sanskrit superlative particle *tama*, but the Tamil adhered resolutely to its own idiom, and the attempt failed.

Postpositions.—It has already been stated that all the Dravidian postpositions are, or have been, nouns. When suffixed to other nouns as postpositions, they are supposed to be in the locative case; but they are generally suffixed in their uninflected form, or in the nominative; and the locative case-sign, though understood, is rarely expressed. It seems quite unnecessary to enter into an investigation of the postpositions in a work of this kind, inasmuch as they are sufficiently explained in the ordinary grammars, and are to be regarded simply as nouns of relation.

COMPARATIVE PARADIGM OF A NEUTER DRAVIDIAN NOUN.

Eng. a tree.—Tam. *maram;* Mal. *maram;* (Tel. *gurramu*, a horse);* Can. *mara;* Tuḷu, *mara;* Coorg, *mara.*

	Tamil.	Malayâlam.	Telugu.	Old Canarese.	Tuḷu.	Coorg.
Singular.						
Nom. a tree	*maram.*	*maram.*	*gurramu, gurram.*	*maram.*	*mara.*	*mara.*
Acc. a tree	*maratte, marattinei.*	*marattine, maratte.*	*gurramunu, gurrânni, gurram.*	*maramam, maravam, maranam.*	*maronu.*	*marat'na.*
Instr. by a tree	*marattâl, marattinâl, marattinân.*	*marattâl.*	*gurramuna, gurrâna.*	*maradim, maradindam.*	*maroḍ'du* (also conj. and ablat.)	*maratiñji.*
Conj. with a tree	*maramoḍu, marattôdu, marattinoḍu.*	*marattôḍu.*	*gurramutô.*	...	do.	...
Dat. to a tree	*marattirku.*	*marattinnu.*	*gurraminaku, gurrânaku.*	*marake, marakke.*	*maroku.*	*marakk'.*
Com. to or with a tree	...	...	...	...	*maraṭa.*	...
Ablat. from a tree	*marattin.*	*marattilninnu.*	*gurramunuṇḍi.*	*maradattaṇim.*	*maroḍ'du* (also instr. and conj.)	...
Gen. of a tree	*marattinadu, marattinâdu* (before a singular). *marattina* (before a plural).	*marattindre, marattinuḍe.*	*gurramu, gurramuyokka.*	*marada, maradâ.*	*marata.*	*marat'ra.*
Loc. in a tree	*marattinkaṇ, marattil, marattinil.*	*marattil.*	*gurramandu, gurramunandu.*	*maradoḷ, maradôḷ.*	*maroṭu.*	*marat'l'.*
Voc. O tree!	*maramê.*	*maramê.*	*gurramâ.*	*mara, marâ, marame.*	*marâ.*	...

	PLURAL.						
Nom.	trees . . .	*maraṅgaḷ.*	*maraṅṅaḷ.*	*gurramulu, gurrâlu.*	*maragaḷ, maraṅgaḷ.*	*marokuḷu.*	Neuter nouns have no plural in this dialect.
Acc.	trees . .	*maraṅgaḷei, maraṅgaḷinei.*	*maraṅṅaḷe.*	*gurrumulanu, gurrâlanu.*	*maragaḷam.*	*marokuḷen'.*	
Instr.	by trees .	*maraṅgaḷâl, maraṅgaḷinâl (ân).*	*maraṅṅaḷâl.*	*gurramulandu.*	*maragaḷim.*	*marokuḷed'd'* (also conj. and ablat.)	
Conj.	with trees .	*maraṅgaḷôdu, maraṅgaḷinoḍu.*	*maraṅṅaḷôḍu.*	*gurramulatô, gurrâlatô.*	...	do.	
Dat.	to trees . .	*maraṅgaḷirku.*	*maraṅṅaḷkku*	*gurramulaku, gurrâlaku.*	*maragaḷge.*	*marokuḷeg'.*	
Com.	to or with trees	...	...	...	...	*marokuḷeḍa.*	
Ablat.	from trees .	*maraṅgaḷin.*	*maraṅṅaḷilninnu*	*gurramulanuṇḍi.*	*maragaḷattaṇim.*	*marokuḷed'd'* (also instr. and conj.)	
Gen.	of trees .	*maraṅgaḷinadu* (before a singular). *maraṅgaḷina* (before a plural).	*maraṅṅaḷuḍe.*	...	*maragaḷa.*	*marokuḷe.*	
Loc.	in a tree . .	*maraṅgaḷinkaṇ.*	*maraṅṅaḷil.*	*gurramulandu.*	*maragaḷoḷ, maragaḷôḷ.*	*marokuḷeḍ'.*	
Voc.	O trees ! . .	*maraṅgaḷê.*	*maraṅṅaḷê.*	*gurramulârâ.*	*maragaḷir, maragaḷirâ.*	*marokuḷê.*	

* The declension of the noun *mânu*, properly *mrânu*, a tree, is so irregular in Telugu that I have been obliged to select another word.

PART IV.

THE NUMERALS.

In the Dravidian languages each of the cardinal numbers presents itself to us in a twofold shape. The first and probably the more primitive form is that of numeral adjectives; the second and more largely used is that of numeral substantives, or neuter nouns of number. The numeral adverbs (twice, thrice, &c.), and also the distributive numerals (by twos, by threes, &c.), are formed from the numeral adjectives; whilst the ordinal numbers (second, third, &c.) are formed from the abstract numeral nouns.

In the colloquial dialects the neuter nouns of number are often used, without change, as numeral adjectives—*e.g.*, in Tamil, we may say *iraṇḍu peyar*, two persons, though *iru peyar*, or the still more classical appellative noun *iruvar*, might have been expected to be used. This use of the numeral substantive instead of the numeral adjective is not ungrammatical, but is in accordance with the characteristic Dravidian rule that every noun of quality or relation, though in itself neuter and abstract, becomes an adjective by being prefixed to a substantive noun in direct apposition. The numeral noun *ondru*, Tam., *okaṭi*, Tel., one, is the only numeral which is never used in this manner, even in the colloquial dialects, except in Canarese; the adjectival numerals, *oru*, *oka*, &c., being invariably prefixed to substantive nouns as numeral adjectives: the same forms are employed also as indefinite articles. In Canarese alone the abstract neuters are used freely as numeral adjectives—*e.g.*, *ondu hei*, one hand. The abstract or neuter nouns of number are sometimes elegantly postfixed, instead of being prefixed, to the substantive nouns which they are intended to qualify—*e.g.*, instead of *nâl' erudu*, Tam. four oxen, we may say not only *nâng' erudu* (using the noun of number *nângu*, instead of the numeral adjective *nâlu*), but also *erudu nângu*, a phrase which literally means a quaternion of oxen. This phrase affords an illustration of the statement that the Dravidian nouns of number are properly abstract neuters.

The primitive radical forms of the Dravidian numerals will be found to be those of the numeral adjectives, corresponding to the oblique case or inflexion of ordinary nouns. In investigating the numerals one by one, it will be seen that the neuter or abstract nouns of number have been formed from the shorter and simpler numeral adjectives by the addition of neuter formatives and euphonic increments, or by the lengthening of the root-vowel. It is, therefore, the numeral adjectives of the Dravidian languages, not their numeral nouns, which are to be compared with the numerals of other families of languages. The compound numbers between ten and twenty, and especially the higher compounds (twenty, thirty, two hundred, three hundred, &c.), afford much help towards ascertaining the oldest forms of the Dravidian numeral roots; seeing that the numeral adjectives which are employed in those compounds exhibit the numerals in their briefest, purest, and most ancient shape.

It is the adjectival form of the numerals which is used in forming appellative nouns of number, such as *iruvar* (*iru-*(*v*)-*ar*), Tam. two persons. The basis of this word is not *iraṇḍu*, the noun of number two, but the numeral adjective *iru*, with the addition of *ar*, the usual suffix of the epicene or masculine-feminine plural. In the colloquial dialects, adjectival or appellative nouns of number are formed in this manner from the first three numeral adjectives alone—*e.g.*, *oruvan*, Tam. one person (masc.), *unus; orutti*, one person (fem.), *una; iruvar*, two persons; *mûvar*, three persons (both epicene); but in the higher or poetical dialects, almost all the numeral adjectives are converted in this manner into appellative nouns. From these circumstances it is evident that the Dravidian numeral adjectives are to be regarded as the only essential portion of the roots of the numeral substantives, and probably as the very roots themselves.

One.—Two forms of the numeral substantive *one* are found in the Dravidian languages, which will appear, I think, to be allied. The first, *oru*, is that which is used in all the dialects except the Telugu; the latter, *oka*, is used as a numeral in the Telugu alone.

1. The basis of the first and most commonly used form of this numeral is *or*, to which *u* is added for euphonisation; and this constitutes the numeral adjective *one*, in all the dialects which make use of this base. *or-u*, in colloquial Tamil, becomes *ôr* in the poetical dialect; the essential vowel *o* being lengthened to *ô* to compensate for the rejection of the euphonic addition *u*. *or* is also known. The adjectival form used in Tuḷu is *or* (*ori*, one person, *ora*, once), in Ku, *ra;* with which the Behistun numeral adjective *irra* or *ra* may be compared. The Canarese numeral adjective is identical with the Tamil, though its true character is somewhat concealed. Instead of

oruvan, Tam., *unus*, Canarese has *obban-u*, and instead of *oruvaḷ*, *una*, *obbaḷ-u*. Ancient Canarese, however, uses also *orbam* for the former, and *orbaḷ* for the latter; the base of which, *or*, is the numeral root, and is identical with the Tamil *or-u* or *ôr*. The abstract neuter noun 'one,' meaning literally, one thing, or unity, is in Canarese and Coorg *ondu;* in grammatical Tamil, *onṟu* (pronounced *ondru* or *ondu*, and in vulgar Tamil, *oṉṉu*); in Telugu (one of its two words), *oṇḍu;* in Malayâlam, *onn';* in Tuḷu, *onji;* in Gônd, *undî;* in Tuda, *odd;* in Ûrâon, *ûntâ*. *or* being the adjectival form of this numeral, it claims by rule to be the representative of the crude root, as well as the basis of the abstract or neuter nouns of number signifying one or unity, which are used in the various dialects. It remains to be seen whether the derivation of each of those nouns of number from *or* can be clearly made out.

At first sight the Tamil *ondru* and the Canarese *ondu*, and especially the Malayâlam *onn'*, appear to resemble the most common form of the Indo-European numeral 'one,' which is in Latin *un-us* (in an older form, *oin-os*); in Greek, *ἕν*; in Gothic, *ain'-s*. In the Koibal, a Samoïede dialect, there is a similar word for one—viz., *unem;* and we find in the Tungusian *um*, in Manchu *emu*. Even in Sanskrit, though *êka* is invariably used for one, a form has been noticed which appears to be allied to the first numeral of the Western languages—viz., *ûna-s*, less, which is prefixed to some of the higher numerals to express diminution by one (*e.g.*, *ûnavinshati*, nineteen), like the corresponding prefix *un* in the Latin *undeviginti*. It would be an interesting circumstance if the Malayâlam *onn'* and the Latin *un-us* were found to be allied; but the resemblance is, I believe, altogether illusory, and vanishes on the derivation of *onn'* from *or* being ascertained. It is reasonable to suppose that the numeral adjective of the Tamil, *oru*, and its numeral noun *onṟu*, must be closely related. Now, whilst it is impossible, I think, on Dravidian principles to derive *oru* from *onṟu*, it will be shown that the derivation of *onṟu* from *oru* is in perfect accordance with Dravidian rules; and if the Malayâlam *onn'* be simply an euphonised form of the Tamil *onṟu*, as it certainly is, every idea of the existence of a connection between any of these forms and the Latin *un-us* will have to be abandoned.

It was shown in the section on "Sounds" that the Dravidian languages delight to euphonise certain consonants by prefixing nasals to them. If the *r* of *oru* is found to have been converted in this manner into *nr*, the point under discussion will be settled. What analogy, then, is there for this conversion? *mûru*, Can. three, has through this very process become in Tamil *mûnṟu* (pronounced *mûndru*, *mûṇḍu*, or *mûṉu*); in Malayâlam, *mûnn'*. Again, *kiṟu*, the verbal suffix denoting present time in Tamil, has become in the poetical dialect *kin***r***u*, pronounced *kindru;* and this, in the Malayâlam present tense is found to be still further softened into *kunnu*, and even *unnu*. In these instances we perceive that very euphonic alteration by which *oru* has become progressively *on***r***u*, *ondru*, *ondu*, *oṇṇu*, and *onn';* and thus the derivation of *onn'* from *oru* is found to be strictly in accordance with analogy.

It may be objected that the illustrations which have been given above exhibit a change of the hard **r** into *ndr*, whereas the *r* of *oru* is the soft medial; and that, therefore, the analogy, though very remarkable, is not complete. I answer that, though the *r* of our present Tamil *oru* is certainly the medial semi-vowel, not the hard **r**, yet originally the hard **r** must have been the very **r** employed. This appears from the Tamil adjective, odd, single. That adjective is *o***rr***ei* (pronounced *ottrei*); and it is derived from the numeral adjective, one. It has been derived, however, by the usual process of doubling the final consonant, not from *or-u*, but from *o***r**-*u*—evidently a more ancient form of the word, in which the *r* was the hard rough **r**—that very **r** which is usually euphonised into *ndr*. It is not an uncommon thing for **r** and *r* to be thus interchanged—*e.g.*, there are two words for black, *karu* and *ka***r***u*. They differ slightly in some of their meanings, but there can be no doubt that they are identical in origin.

It appears, therefore, that the origin which I have ascribed to *onru* is in complete accordance with analogy. Moreover, if the *n* of *ondru*, *ondu*, or *onn'*, were part of the root of this numeral, the *du* which is suffixed to it could only be a neuter formative; and in that event *on* should be found to be used as the numeral adjective. *on*, however, is nowhere so used; and therefore both the use of *or-u*, instead of *on*, as the numeral adjective, and the existence of the derivative *o***r**(**r**)*ei* (*ottr-ei*), single, seem to me to prove that the root of this numeral must have been *or*, not *on*.

It may be said that the instances I adduced of the euphonisation of **r** into *ndr* are capable of two explanations. I shall, therefore, adduce some examples to which this objection cannot be made. Can. *karu*, a calf, becomes in Tamil *kan***r***u*, pronounced *kandru*. This is vulgarised in colloquial Tamil to *kaṇṇu*, and in Malayâlam becomes *kann'*. Yet it is certain that the root was *kar* and that there was no nasal in it originally, because the Tamil adjectival form, which is always the oldest, rejects the nasal and goes back to the original **r**, which it doubles by rule. Thus *kandru* becomes adjectivally *kattr-u*—*e.g.*, *kattr-â*, a cow which has a calf. Compare this with *âṭṭei*, annual, from *âṇḍu* (*yâṇḍei*, when), a year, from which it is clear that *âṇḍu* was originally *â-ḍu*. (See "Euphonic Nunnation.") Tamil itself also furnishes us with instances of the euphonic change of **r** into *ndr*, with respect to which it cannot be doubted which was the original form, and which the derived. Compare *ku***r***u-gu*, to become small, and *kundru*, the same, also a small hill. It is evident that *ku***r̄***u* was the older form, from the circumstance that it is from it that all the verbal nouns are derived—*e.g.*, *ku***r***ei*, deficiency; *ku***rr***am* (*kuttram*), a fault; *ku***r***il*, a short letter; *ku***r***i*, a mark. I do not think it can be proved that *ndr*, from *n* or *m*, ever changes in Tamil into **r**. *ondru*, one, may therefore be derived from *or-u*, but *oru* cannot, I think, be derived from *ondru*. Dr Gundert considers *ondru* an euphonised form of *on*, with the addition of *du*, the neuter formative, and that *on* and *or* are equivalents, being both verbal nouns from *o*, to be one. It is quite true that such a verb as *o* exists, that *n* or *an*, alternating with *am*, is used as a formative by many nouns, and that *n* sometimes changes into or alternates with *r* or **r**—*e.g.*, Mal. *uḷan* = *uḷar*, being, birth; also Tam. *pin*, after, another shape of which is *pi***r**, in *pi***r̈***agu*, after. I think it also quite possible that the reason why *o***r***u* was nasalised into *ondru*, and *mû***r***u*, three, into *mûndru*, was that *du*, the formative neuter particle, had been affixed to them, in consequence of which *o***r***-du* became *ondru*, and *mû***r***-du*, *mûndru*, just as we see that *ir*, two, by the addition of the neuter formative *ḍu*, became *iraḍu* and then *iranḍu*. On the other hand, whilst I admit that each step of this process would be a natural and easy one, it appears to me that a comparison of the various forms of the numeral *one*, found in different connections in the different dialects, and of the uses to which they are put, show that the view I have taken is in better accordance with the process that has actually taken place.

ondru is used as a verb also in Tamil, meaning to unite, neuter, the transitive form of which is *o***rr***u* (*ottru*). *ondri* is an adjectival form meaning single.

After the above was written I found the same view of the origin of *ondu* stated in a paper by Mr Kittel in the *Indian Antiquary* for January 1873. Mr Kittel says, "When the affix *du* is joined to a short monosyllabic root with final *r*, the root in this case being *or*, this liquid is sometimes changed into the *bindu* (*m* or *n*); *n* or *du* thus becomes *on-du*, or in Tamil *on-dru*, in the manner I have stated."

Though *or*, in its primitive, unnasalised shape, is not now found in the cultivated Dravidian dialects as the first abstract neuter noun of number for one or unity; yet it appears in one of the ruder dialects of the family—viz., in the Rajmahâl; in which the numeral noun one is *ort*, which is evidently formed directly from *or*. If it be true, as has been asserted, that the Rajmahâl *ort* is appropriated to human beings, it must be identical with the Tamil *orutt-an*, one man, *orutt-i*, one woman; the *tt* of which is a formative, and is derived from the pronoun of the third person. *ondong* (answering to the Dravidian neuter noun *ondru*) is said to be another Rajmahâl word for one. Compare also the Brahui *asit*, one, of which *as*, the crude root. seems to bear as close an analogy to *or-u* as *mus*, the crude root of *musit*, the Brahui for three, undoubtedly does to the Canarese *mûr-u*. If in the latter case the *s* and *r* are mutually convertible, it cannot be considered improbable that *asit* and *art*, and consequently *as* and *or*, bear a similar relation one to the other.

2. Telugu makes use of two numerals signifying 'one.' One of these, *oṇḍu*, is identical with the *ondru*, *ondu*, *onn'*, &c., of the other dialects. From *oṇḍu* is formed also an adjectival numeral, *oṇṭi*, identical with the Tamil *ondri* (vulgarly *oṇḍi*), single. Compare Tel. *oṇṭigâḍu*, a single man, with the corresponding Tam. *ondrikkâran*. The other numeral, which is much more largely used in Telugu, is *okaṭi* (*oka-ṭi*). The basis of this numeral seems at first sight to be essentially different from that which is used in the other Dravidian dialects. There would be nothing extraordinary in the discovery in any language or family of languages of two roots for *one*. This would naturally arise from the very concrete character of this numeral, and the variety of uses to which it is put. Even in Sanskrit we find both *êka* and *prathama*. Two is also represented in Latin by *duo*, *ambo*, and the participial *secundus*. The Telugu neuter noun of number for one, *okaṭi*, means literally one thing, of which the adjectival form is *oka*, sometimes *okka*. *okaṭi* is formed from *oka* by the addition of the neuter and inflexional formative, *ṭi*; and by annexing the usual masculine and feminine suffixes, the Telugu forms *okanḍu* or *okaḍu*, one man, and *okate*, one woman. *oka* being found to be the crude root of this numeral, we have now to inquire into its affinities. Is the Telugu *oka* derived, as has sometimes been supposed, from the Sanskrit *êka*, one? It seems not improbable that the Telugu word has some ulterior connection with the Sanskrit one, to which it bears so great a resemblance; but it is impossible to suppose it to have been directly derived from the Sanskrit, like the Bengali *ok*, or even the Persian *yak*; for the Telugu has borrowed, and occasionally uses, the Sanskrit numeral *êka*, in addition to its own *oka*; and it never confounds *oka* with *êka*, which Telugu grammarians regard as altogether independent one of another. It will be seen also that the root of *oka* is probably Dravidian, and that words closely analogous to it are used in the Finnish languages, by which they cannot be supposed to have been borrowed from the Sanskrit. Thus, the numeral one is in Votiak *og*, *odyg*; in

Samoïede, *okur*, *ockur*, *ookur*; in Vogul, *ak*, *akv*; in Magyar, *egy*; in Lappish, *akt*; in Finnish, *yht* and also *yxi* (*yk-si*); in Cheremiss, *ik*, *iktä*. In the sub-Himalayan languages, we find *ako* in Miri, *akhet* in Naga, and *katka* in Kuki. In the Scythian of the Behistun tablets, in which we find the oldest extant specimen of the Scythian languages, the numeral for one is *kir*, and the numeral adjective derived from it *irra* or *ra*. These analogies to the Telugu *oka*, combined with analogies to the ordinary Dravidian *or*, show that *oka* has not necessarily, or even probably, been derived from the Sanskrit *êka*; and if the two roots *oka* and *êka* are allied, as they appear to be, it must be in consequence of the relation of the Sanskrit, the Dravidian, and the Scythian families to an earlier form of speech. It deserves notice that *ra*, the Behistun numeral adjective, seems identical with *ra*, the numeral adjective of the Ku, a Dravidian dialect. In the Turkish, 'one' is represented by *bir*, which seems to be allied rather to the Persian *bâr* in *bâri*, once (and ulteriorly to the Sanskrit *vâr*, time), than to the Tamil *or*. The Caucasian numerals for 'one' exhibit a closer resemblance to the Dravidian—viz., Lazian *ar*, Mingrelian *arti*, Georgian *erthi*; and it may be noticed that as in the Dravidian *or*, one, *ir*, two, so in those Caucasian dialects, *r* forms an essential part of both those numerals.

Are the Tamil *or* and the Telugu *oka* related? I think there can be little doubt of their relationship, though there are several links in the chain which cannot be made out to my satisfaction. There is a verbal root in Tamil, *o*, which has been supposed to mean, to be one. *on* and *or* (*ondru* and *oru*) are supposed by Dr Gundert to be verbal nouns from this *o*. An undoubted derivative of *o* in Tamil and Malayâlam is *okka*, which in Malayâlam and the Tamil of the extreme south means 'altogether,' 'all' (compare Mordvin *wok*, all); and this is supposed by Dr Gundert to be identical with the Telugu *oka*, one. Every step in this process, with one exception, is encumbered with difficulties. It is not clear to me that *o*, the Tamil verbal root, ever means to be one; its ordinary meaning is to be like or suitable—*e.g.*, *okkum*, it will be like. It is also not clear to me that *on* and *or* are derived from the verbal root *o*. On the contrary, the verbal root *o* may have been softened from the noun *or*. The word used for 'one' must surely in every language have been a noun from the very first, not a derivative from a verbal root of wider meaning. *okka*, the infinitive, means not 'one,' but 'altogether.' My chief difficulty, however, is that the *kka* of *okka* is the formative of the Tamil infinitive, the root being *o*, not *ok*; so that it is very difficult to see how this Tamil infinitive got turned into an adjectival noun in Telugu without losing or changing its formative. Notwithstanding these difficulties, we can scarcely avoid concluding that the Tamil *okka* and the Telugu *oka* must somehow be allied. If we suppose *okka* to have been taken to mean 'all in one,' which no doubt is a meaning it sometimes has, we may see how the Telugu may have selected its root for use as a numeral. It would then convert the verbal root *o* into a noun by the addition of *ka*, an ordinary adjectival formative. *o-ka*, the Telugu adjectival noun, would then resemble *o-kka*, the Tamil infinitive, in sound, though it would be differently derived. It is especially noticeable that Telugu had already at its disposal the ordinary numeral *oṇḍu;* it is probable, therefore, that *oka* was used at first with a slightly different meaning. The root *o* seems sometimes to be used instead of *ondu* or *oru* in Canarese, in such a manner as seems at first sight to confirm the supposition that *o* meant originally to be one—*e.g.*, *okkaṇṇanu*, a one-eyed man. On the other hand, when we compare this with Can. *obbanu*, one person, which is clearly a softened form of *orbanu* (Tam. *oruvan*), it appears that we have here to deal merely with the ordinary numeral *or-u*. It is noticeable here, too, that this *o* doubles the following consonant, from which it appears that it was originally followed by a consonant, evidently *r*.

Dravidian Indefinite Article.—The Dravidian numeral adjectives *oru* and *oka* are used, like similar numerals in most languages, as a sort of indefinite article. The Turkish uses *bir*, one, in a similar manner; and a corresponding usage prevails in the modern European languages, as well as in the colloquial dialects of Northern India. The only thing which may be considered as distinctive or peculiar in the use of the Dravidian numeral adjective one, as an indefinite article, is the circumstance that it is not used in the loose general way in which in English we speak of a man, or a tree, but only in those cases in which the singularity of the object requires to be emphasised, when it takes the meaning of a certain man, a particular kind of tree, or a single tree. Europeans, in speaking the native languages, make in general too large and indiscriminate a use of this prefixed numeral, forgetting that the Dravidian neuter noun, without prefix or addition, becomes singular or plural, definite or indefinite, according as the connection requires.

Two.—The abstract or neuter noun of number signifying two or duality is in Canarese *eraḍu*, in Tamil *iraṇḍu*, in Telugu *reṇḍu*, in Tuḷu *raḍḍ'*, in Malayâlam *reṇḍ-u*, in old Malayâlam, as in Tamil, *iraṇḍu*, commonly pronounced *reṇḍu*, in Coorg *daṇḍu*, in Gônd *rend* or *ranu*, in Seoni Gônd *rund*, in Tuda *edd*. The Singhalese word for double is *iruṇṭata*. The change of the *iraṇḍu* of the Tamil and the *eraḍu* of the Canarese into *reṇḍu* in Telugu is analogous to the change of the Tam. *irâ*, night, into Tel. *rê*. In all the Dravidian dialects the corresponding numeral adjective is *ir*, with such minor modifications as euphony dictates. This numeral adjective is in Tamil *iru;* in the higher dialect *îr*, the increase in the quantity of the radical *i* compensating perhaps for the rejection of the final euphonic *u*. *ir* is also found. The *r* which constitutes the radical consonant of *ir* is the soft medial semi-vowel, and it evinces, in consequence of its softness, a tendency to coalesce with the succeeding consonant, especially in Canarese and Telugu. Thus, for *iruvar*, Tam. two persons (Tuḷu, *irvar*), the modern Canarese uses *ibbar-u* (ancient dialect, *irvar*), and the Telugu *iddar-u*. Instead, also, of the correct *irunûru*, two hundred, of the Tamil, both the Telugu and the Canarese have *innûru;* and the Canarese word for twenty is *ippattu*, instead of *irupattu*, which would be in correspondence with the Tamil *irubadu* and the Telugu *iruvei*.

In the Canarese neuter noun of number *eraḍu*, two, *e* is used instead of *i* as the initial vowel; but in this point the Canarese stands alone, and in all the compound numerals, even in the Canarese, the *i* reappears. Were it not for the existence of the numeral adjective *ir-u* or *ir*, we might naturally suppose the *i* of the Tamil *iraṇḍu* and of the obsolete Canarese *iraḍu* to be, not a component element of the root, but an euphonic prefix, intended to facilitate pronunciation. *i* is very commonly so prefixed in Tamil—*e.g.*, the Sanskrit *râjâ* becomes in Tamil *irâśâ*. This supposition with respect to the euphonic character of the *i* of *iraṇḍu* might appear to be confirmed by the circumstance that it disappears altogether from the numeral nouns of the Telugu, the Malayâlam, and several other dialects. The existence, however, of the numeral adjective *iru* or *ir*, in every one of the Dravidian dialects, and its use in all the compound numbers (such as twenty and two hundred), suffice to prove that the *i* of the Tamil-Canarese numeral noun *iraḍu* is not merely euphonic, but is a part of the root itself, and that *iraḍu*, the neuter noun of number, has been formed from *ir* by the addition of a formative suffix. A comparison of the various forms shows clearly that *ir*, euphonised into *iru*, was the primitive form of the numeral adjective two; and we have now only to inquire into the characteristics of the numeral noun.

The Canarese *eraḍu* (or rather *iraḍu*, as it must have been originally) appears to be the earliest extant form of the noun of number. The Tamil is *iraṇḍu*, *ḍ* having been euphonically changed to *ṇḍ*. Though there is a nasal in the Tamil word which is now in use, the Tamil noun-adjective *double* bears witness to the existence of an earlier form, which was destitute of the nasal, and which must have been identical with the Canarese. The Tamil word *iraṭṭ-u*, double, is formed directly from *iraḍ-u*, by the doubling of the *ḍ*, as is usually done when a noun is converted into an adjective; and the euphonic change of *ḍḍ* into *ṭṭ* is according to rule. *du* or *ḍu* is a very common termination of neuter nouns, especially of appellative neuters, in all the Dravidian languages. Thus, from the root *kiṛa*, Tam. old, is formed *kiṛaḍu*, that which is old. The *ṇ* which is inserted before *ḍ* in the Tamil *iraṇḍu* is evidently euphonic, and is in perfect accordance with the ordinary phonetic usages of the Dravidian languages. In Telugu every word ending in *ḍu* receives in pronunciation an obscure nasal, whether it has a place in the written language or not; and there are many instances in Tamil also of the insertion of this nasal before a final *ḍu* for the sake of euphonisation, when it is quite certain that there was no such nasal originally in the word in which it is found—*e.g.*, *âṇḍu*, there, *îṇḍu*, here, and *yâṇḍu*, where, are euphonised forms of *âḍu*, *îḍu*, and *yâḍu*. Compare also *karaṇḍi*, a spoon, Tam., with the more primitive Telugu *gariṭe*. The Tamil noun of number signifying two must, therefore, have been *iraḍu* originally. In the Gônd *ranu*, the *ḍ* of *iraṇḍu* has disappeared altogether, a change which is in accordance with the Malayâḷam corruption of *ondu*, one, into *onn'*. The Ûrâon word for two, *enotan*, is probably Dravidian. In Ûrâon, *otan* (from the Hindi *gotan*) is a suffix of each of the first three numerals; consequently *en* is to be regarded as the Ûrâon root; and this seems to be analogous to the Dravidian *er*.

I have little doubt that the root of the Dravidian word is native, not foreign, though it is difficult now to identify it with certainty. I can scarcely agree with Dr Gundert in connecting it with the root of *iruḷ*, darkness, *irâ*, night, a root which also, he thinks, appears in *îr*, to saw. If we consider the latter verb, however, with its derivatives, apart from its supposed connection with *iruḷ*, darkness, it may be found to supply us with the true root. *Îr* means not merely to saw, but still more frequently to pull asunder, to split; and from division into two by the act of pulling asunder, *ir*, *îr*, the word for two, may have been derived. The radical form of *îr*, two, was doubtless short, *ir;* but the earliest shape of *îr*, to pull asunder, may also have been short, as monosyllables ending in consonants seem generally to have been. There is another root common to all the Dravidian languages, *ir*, to be; but this seems to be quite independent both of *ir*, dark, and of *ir*, two.

I find that Mr Kittel, also, in the *Indian Antiquary* for January 1873, derives the Dravidian word for two from *îr*, to split, especially to split off a branch; whilst *or*, one, he considers to mean a unit without a branch. It seems to me, as I have already mentioned, probable that the word for one was originally a noun, and that the verbal meaning to coalesce, to resemble, was a secondary development. The case, however, does not seem to me quite so clear with respect to the origin of the word for two. On the whole, the concrete seems to me likely to have been older than the abstract; that is, the noun or adjective two would, I think, naturally come into use earlier than the verb to separate into two, to split.

There are no analogies to *ir*, two, in any of the Indo-European languages, and I am doubtful whether any real analogies to it are discoverable even in the Scythian group, except perhaps in the Caucasian. The Brahui vindicates its claim to be regarded as in part Dravidian, or at least as the inheritor of an ancient Dravidian element, by the close affinity of its second and third numerals to those of the Dravidian tongues. In Brahui, two is *irat;* and when this word is compared with the Brahui *asit*, one, and *musit*, three, it is evident that in each of these instances the final *it* or *at* is a formative suffix which has been appended to the root. Consequently *ir*, the root of *ir-at*, seems absolutely identical with the Dravidian *ir*. Even the Brahui formative evinces Dravidian affinities—*e.g.*, compare *irat* with the Canarese noun of number *eraḍu*, and especially with the Tamil derivative *iraṭṭ-u*, double.

The nearest analogies to the Dravidian *ir* which I have noticed in other families of tongues are in the Caucasian dialects—*e.g.*, in the Georgian *ori;* in the Suanian (a dialect of the Georgian) *eru* or *ieru;* in the Lazian *zur;* and in the Mingrelian *shiri:* compare also the Armenian *ergov;* the Chinese *arh* or *âr*. In the Samoïede family of tongues, several words are found which bear at first sight some resemblance to the Dravidian *ir*. These are *sit, side*, and especially *sire* or *siri*. It seems improbable, however, that the Dravidian *ir* arose from the softening off of the initial *s* of these words; for in the Finnish family this same *s* appears as *k;* whence two is in some dialects of that family *kit;* in Magyar *ket, ketto;* and in Lappish *quekt*. It has also been shown that an initial *k* is a radical element in the majority of the Scythian words for two; and hence, though the Mongolian *kur-in* (for *kuyar-in*), twenty, becomes in Manchu *or-in*, in Turkish *igir-mi*, we cannot venture to compare this Manchu *or* with the Dravidian *ir* or *er;* for it is certain that the latter was never preceded by *k*, or any other consonant, so far back as the Dravidian languages can be traced.

Three.—The neuter noun of number signifying three or a triad is in Canarese *mûru;* in Telugu *mûḍu;* in Tamil *mûnṟu* (pronounced *mûndru*, *mûndu*, and *mûṇu*); in Coorg *mûndu;* in Malayâḷam *mûnn';* in Tuḷu *mûji* (*j* in Tuḷu regularly represents ṟ; com. *âji*, six, with *âṟu* in the other dialects); in Gônd it is *mûnd;* in Tuda *mûd;* in Ûrâon *man-otan*.

The numeral adjective three, which is employed in three persons, thirty, three hundred, and similar compounds, is either *mû* or *mu*. The long *mû* is found in the Tamil, Tuḷu, and Canarese epicene nouns *mûvar*, *mûvar-u*, three persons, and in the Canarese *mûvattu*, thirty. The shorter form, *mu*, is used in three hundred, which in every one of the Dravidian dialects is *mûnnûru* (Tuḷu *munnûdu*); and we see it also in the Tamil *muppattu*, and the Telugu *mupphei*, thirty, and in the Telugu *muggur-u*, three persons. The primitive and most characteristic form of the neuter noun of number is evidently that of the Canarese *mûr-u*, from which it seems clear to me that the Tamil *mûnr-u* (*mundr-u*) has been derived, by the same nasalising process as that by which *oru*, one, was converted into *onru*. I do not think it probable, with Dr Gundert, that *muru* was altered from *mundru*.

It was shown in the section on "Sounds," that the Tamil *r* is often changed into *d* in Telugu: hence *mûr-u* and *mûḍ-u* are identical; and it is more probable that *mûḍ-u* has been altered from *mûr-u*, than that *mûr-u* was altered from *mûḍ-u*. *s* and *r* evince in many languages a tendency to interchange, generally by the hardening of *s* into *r*; consequently the Brahui *mus* (*mus-it*), three, seems closely allied to the Canarese *mûr*, and still more closely to the Tuḷu *mûji*.

The vowel of *mûr-u* was, I have no doubt, originally short, but it is doubtful whether the *r* of *mûr-u* should be considered as a formative or as a part of the ancient root. On the whole, it seems probable that the *r* is radical. The final consonants of *âru*, Tam. six, and of *ēṟu*, seven, belong unquestionably to the roots of those numerals. Moreover, when we compare *mun-nûru*, three hundred (the same in all the dialects), with *in-nûru*, two hundred, in Telugu and Canarese, and when it is remembered that the latter has certainly been softened from *ir-nûru* (in Tamil *iru-nûru*), it seems to be probable that *mun-nûru* has been formed in a similar manner from *mur-nûru*, and consequently that *mur*, not *mu*, was the original root of this numeral. The same conclusion is indicated by a comparison of the Telugu *iddaru*, two persons, and *mugguru*, three persons. It seems probable, therefore, that *mu* originally was followed by a consonant; and the softening off of this consonant would naturally account for the occasional lengthening of *mu* into *mû*.

I have not been able to discover any analogy to this numeral either in the Scythian or in the Indo-European tongues. The only extra-Indian resemblance to it is that which is found in the Brahui; and this circumstance is a striking illustration of the existence in the Brahui of a Dravidian element. The total absence of analogy to the Dravidian *mur* in other families of languages leads me to conclude that it must have been derived directly from some Dravidian verbal root. The Latin *secundus* is undoubtedly derived from *sequor;* and Bopp connects the Indo-European *tri,* three, with the Sanskrit root *tṛ*, to pass over, to go beyond, signifying that which goes beyond two. If this derivation of *tri* be not regarded as too fanciful, a somewhat similar derivation of *mur* from a Dravidian verbal root may easily be discovered. There are two verbal roots which present some points of resemblance—viz., *mîṟu,* to go beyond, to pass, and *mâṟu,* to change. The nearest root, however, is *muṟu* (*muṟugu,* Tam.), to turn, from which comes the verbal noun *muṟei,* a turn, a succession, repetition.

Dr Gundert derives *mûndru* from *mu,* the radical portion of *mun,* before. The root *mu* appears in various compounds with the meaning of before, ancient; as also *mû,* a lengthened form of the same root. Both *mu* and *mû* mean before, and both *mu* and *mû* mean three. The identity of the two words seems therefore very probable. It is not clear to me, however, how a word meaning before, came to be used for the numeral three. This word is used in its proper sense as the basis of the Dravidian ordinal number 'first,' which is *mu-dal* in Tam., *mo-dalu* in Tel., *mo-dal* in Can.; and it is difficult to suppose that the same root should be used also in an improper sense to denote another numeral. Mr Kittel derives *mûndru* from *mu,* but interprets *mu* as meaning to advance, grow, a further advance. This is ingenious, but I cannot find any authority for this meaning. *mudu* means not growth, as he represents, but priority, age, ripeness. A secondary word, *muttru,* means completeness. He considers *mûṟu,* Can., a secondary form of the root *mu* or *mû; ṟu,* he says, being frequently used to produce such forms. On the contrary, a final *ṟu,* which is not radical, seems to me very rare.

The neuter formative *du* seems to be contained in various shapes in the first three numbers, *ondru, iraṇḍu, mûndru,* and also, as will be seen, in *eindu,* five. *ḍu* is equivalent to *du,* and with the addition of the nasal becomes *ṇḍu. ondru* points to an older *or-du; irandu* to *ir(a)-du;* and *mûndru* to *mûṟdu,* or, as the scholars whose opinions are mentioned above think, to *mû-du.*

Four.—The Dravidian noun of number signifying four, or a quaternion, is in Canarese *nâlku;* in Coorg *nâlu;* in Telugu *nâlugu;* in Tuḷu *nâl'*; in Malayâḷam *nâl, ṉâṅgu;* in Tamil *nâlu, nânku;* in Tuda *nânk';* in Gônd *nâlu;* in Ûrâon *nâkh-otan.*

The adjectival or crude form of this numeral is *nâl* or *nal.* In Tamil it is *nâl-u,* in some Telugu compounds *nal;* and this adjectival form is often used as a noun of number, instead of *nâlku,* &c. In composition *nâl* undergoes some changes. The quantity of the included vowel, which is long in all the rest of the dialects, is short in Telugu compound numbers—*e.g.*, compare the Tamil *nâṟpadu*, the Canarese *nâlvattu*, and the Malayâḷam *nâlpadu*, forty, with the Telugu *nălubhei;* and the Tamil *nân-nûṟu* and the Canarese *nâl-nûṟu*, four hundred, with the Telugu *năn-nûru*.

The final *l* also is subject to change. In Tamil it is changed into ṟ before *p*, as in *nâṟpadu*, forty; and before *n* it is assimilated and becomes *n*, in both Tamil and Telugu—*e.g.*, *nânnûṟu* (in the one), and *nannûru* (in the other), four hundred; in Coorg, *nâ*. These changes of *l*, however, are purely euphonic. It is evident from a comparison of the above forms, that *nâl* (or, as the Telugu seems to prefer it, *năl*) was the primitive shape of this numeral; to which *ku* or *gu* was subsequently added as a formative, in order to constitute it a neuter noun of number. This formative *ku* (pronounced *gu*) is a very common one in the Dravidian languages—*e.g.*, *nan-gu*, Tam. goodness, from *nal* (=*nan*) good. The only numeral to which *ku* or *gu* is appended is *nâl*. The *g* which appears in Telugu in the rational plurals, such as *âru-guru*, six persons, is not to be confounded with this formative *gu*. In such connections Tamil uses *v* euphonic instead of *g* (*e.g.*, *aṟu-(v)-ar*), which proves that *g* does not add to the grammatical expression, but is merely euphonic. Even in Telugu *âruvur-u* may be used instead of *ârugur-u*.

The change of *l*, in Tamil, into *n*, before the *k* of this appended formative, *ku*, is an euphonic peculiarity which requires to be noticed. In modern Tamil, *l* in this conjunction would be changed into ṟ; but the change of *l* into *n*, before *k* or *g*, which we find in the Tamil noun of number *nân-gu*, is one which, though now uncommon, appears to have been usual at an earlier period of the history of the language—*e.g.*, compare *Paṅ-guni*, the Tamil name of the month March–April, with the Sanskrit name of that month, *Phalguna*, from which it is known to have been derived. This change of *l* into *n*, in *nân-gu*, must have been made at a very early period, seeing that we find it also in the Tuda *nânk'*.

nangu in Tam. (from *nal*) means goodness, beauty; *naṅgu*, in Mal. beauty. In Can. *nal* is good; *nali*, pleasure, as a verb, is to love. This is the meaning of *naḷ* in Tam., doubtless another form of *nal*—*e.g.*, *naṉbu*, love; Tel. *naluvu*, beauty. One of the meanings of *nal* in poetical Tamil is liberal, plentiful, abundant. Comparing this with the use of *nâl*, four, for many, general, &c., may we venture to assume that we have here the origin of the name of this numeral? Mr Kittel says that "the idea of evenness seems to have guided the Dravidians in the formation of this word." I cannot find 'even,' however, amongst the meanings of *nal* in any of the dialects. If this meaning existed, it would suit very well the purpose for which it is used.

In the entire family of the Indo-European languages there is not one language which contains a numeral signifying four, which in the smallest degree resembles the Dravidian *nâl*. Here the Brahui also fails us; for it is only in the first three Brahui numerals that we find traces of Dravidian influences, and the rest of the numerals of that language, from *four* to *ten* inclusive, are of Sanskritic origin. Though other analogies fail us, in this instance Ugrian affinities are more than usually distinct. The resemblance between the Finnish tongues and the Dravidian, with respect to the numeral *four*, amounts almost to identity, and can scarcely have been accidental. Compare with the Dravidian *nal*, the Cheremiss *nil;* the Mordvin, *nile, nilen;* the Vogul *nile;* the Ostiak *nel, nil, njedla, nieda, njeda;* the Finnish proper *neljâ;* the Lappish *nielj, nelje, nellâ;* the Magyar *nêgy* (pronounced *neidj*). The root of all these numerals is evidently *nil* or *nel*, the resemblance of which to the Dravidian *nâl* or *nal* is very remarkable. The Magyar *nêgy* seems to have lost the original *l*, through the tendency, inherent in the Finnish idioms, to regard *l* and *d* as interchangeable. The Ostiak *njedla* or *nedla*, in which *d* and *l* form but one letter, a cerebral, constitutes apparently the middle point of agreement.

Five.—The Dravidian numeral noun five is in Canarese *eid-u* or *ayd-u;* in Telugu *eid-u;* in Tamil ordinarily *eind-u*, occasionally, especially in the colloquial dialect, *añj-u;* in Coorg *anji;* in Malayâḷam *añju;* in Tuḷu *ein';* in Tuda *ütsh* or *ûj*. The Gônd has *seighan* or *seiyan*, a word which is derived like *sârûn*, six, from the use of *s* as an euphonic prefix; *eiyan* is to be regarded as the correct form of the Gônd numeral. The Ûrâon, and other rude dialects of the North Dravidian family, exhibit no analogy to any of the Dravidian numerals above four. In Telugu compounds, the word for five is not *eid-u*, but *ên-u*—*e.g.*, *padihên-u*, fifteen. In this case the medial *h* is purely euphonic, and used for the prevention of hiatus, as in the parallel instances of *pada(h)âru*, sixteen, and *padi(h)êḍu*, seventeen. The Telugu possesses, therefore, two forms of five, *eid-u* and *ên-u;* and the Tamil *eindu* shows how *eidu* may have been converted into *ênu*, viz., by the insertion of an euphonic nasal and the subsequent assimilation to it of the dental.

The numeral adjective five is in most of the Dravidian dialects *ei*, in Telugu and Tuda *ê*. In Tamil, and also occasionally in Canarese, *ei* is in combination converted into *ein* or *eim* (in Coorg *im*) by the addition of an euphonic nasal. Thus fifty (five tens) is in Canarese *eivatt-u*, in Tamil *eimbad-u* (*eim-pad-u*), in Telugu *êbhei* (*ê-bhei*), in Tuḷu *eiva*. Five hundred is in Canarese *ein-nûr-u*, in Tamil *eiñ-ñûru*, in Telugu *ê-nûr-u*, in Tuḷu *einûdu*. We see the numeral adjective five, and the noun of number five, in juxtaposition in the Tamil *ei-(y)-eind-u*, five times five. *ei* remains also in its pure, unnasalised form in the Tamil *eivar* (*ei-(v)-ar*), five persons. The nasal *n* or *m*, which follows *ei* in the compounds *eimbad-u*, fifty, and *eiññjûr-u*, five hundred, is not, I believe, to be confounded with the *n* of the Tamil *eind-u*, or the Telugu *ên-u*, but proceeds from a different source. It is an adjectival increment; and is added by rule, not only to this numeral adjective *ei*, five, but to many similar words which consist of a single syllable, of which the final is a long open vowel, when such words are used adjectivally. Thus we find in Tamil not only such compounds as *eindiṉei* (*ei-n-tiṉei*), the five conditions, and *eimbulan* (*ei-m-pulan*), the five senses; but also *keinnoḍi* (*kei-n-noḍi*), a snap of the finger, and *keimbeṉ* (*kei-m-peṉ*), a widow. This adjectival euphonic addition seems to be an abbreviation of *am* or *an*, and is probably identical with the inflexional increment. See the section on "Nouns: Inflexion." What appears to me to prove that *eim* is not the root of *eindu*, but only an euphonic form of *ei*, is the circumstance that it is found only before words beginning with hard consonants and nasals. Before vowels and semi-vowels it is invariably *ei*. It may be doubted whether the Tamil-Canarese *ei* or the Telugu *ê* is the better representative of the original numeral; but the evidence of the various dialects preponderates in favour of *ei*.

A remarkable resemblance must have been noticed between the Sanskrit *pañchan*, five (in Tamil *pañja*) and the Tamil and Malayâḷam *añju*. It has already been mentioned that *ei* or *eindu* is the ordinary form of this word in Tamil. The shape in which the word is perhaps most commonly used in the colloquial dialect is *añju*, and this form of the word is occasionally, but rarely, used in the classics. So rare is its use in correct Tamil, that it is not given at all in the "Nannûl," the classical Tamil grammar, or in any of the classical Tamil dictionaries. It is found, however, in the "Kuraḷ," which is a clear proof of its right to a place in the language. The ordinary use of *añju* or *añchu* in Malayâḷam and colloquial Tamiḷ, and its occasional use in poetical Tamil, have naturally led some to suppose that *anju*, not *eindu*, *eiḍu*, *ei*, was the original form of this numeral, and that it was derived from the Sanskrit *pañchan* by the easy process of the softening away of the first consonant. Instead, however, of this supposition being confirmed by a comparison of the various Dravidian idioms, and of the various forms under which this numeral appears, as would be the case if the analogy were real, it appears to me to be dissipated by comparison, like the apparent analogy which has already been observed between the Malayâḷam *onn'*, one, and the English *one.*

The primitive radical form of the Dravidian numeral five is, as we have seen, *ei* or *ê*, as appears from its use as a numeral adjective. The abstract or neuter noun of number is generally formed from the numeral adjective by the addition of some formative. The formative suffix which is added to *ir-u*, two, is *ḍu;* and by the addition of *d-u*, a still more common shape of the formative, *ei* becomes *ei-du*, five, or five things; which is in itself a neuter noun, though, like all such nouns, it is capable of being used without change as an adjective. This suffix *d-u* is an exceedingly common formative of neuter appellative nouns in the Dravidian languages, particularly in Tamil; and is doubtless borrowed from, or allied to, the final *d-u* of *ad-u*, it, the neuter singular of the demonstrative pronoun. *eid-u*, the numeral noun of both the Canarese and the Telugu, is evidently the original and most regular form of this word. *eid-u* could not, I believe, have been corrupted from *anj-u*, or even from *eind-u*, but the corruption of *eind-u* and *añj-u* from an original *eid-u* will be shown to be in perfect accordance with usage.

The first change was from *eid-u* to *eind-u*, by the insertion of an euphonic nasal, as in the former instances of *iraḍ-u*, two, changed into *iranḍ-u*. This euphonic insertion of *n* after certain vowels is so common in Tamil, that it may almost be regarded as a rule of the language; and hence preterite participles which end in Canarese in *ed-u*, always end in Tamil in *n-du*—*e.g.*, compare *aled-u*, Can. having wandered, with *aleind-u*, Tam. When *eidu* had been changed into *eind-u*, Tamil usages of pronunciation facilitated a further optional change into *eiñj-u*, or *añj-u*. It is a rule of colloquial Tamil that when *nd* is preceded by *ei* or *i*, it is changed in pronunciation into *ñj*. This change is systematically and uniformly practised in the colloquial dialect, and it has occasionally found its way into the classical and poetical dialect also.

Moreover, in changing *eind* into *eiñj*, there is a further change of the vowel from *ei* to *a*, in consequence of which *einj* becomes *anj*. This change almost always takes place in Malayâḷam, and also in the pronunciation of the mass of the people in Tamil. Thus, *pareindu*, Tam. having spoken, becomes in Malayâḷam *parañña;* and in this instance we see illustrated the change both of *ei* into *a*, and of *nd* into *ñ;* consequently the perfect regularity of the change of *eind-u*, five, into *añj-u*, is established. Where the Malayâḷam does not change *nd* into *ñj*, it changes it into *nn*—*e.g.*, *naḍandu*, Tam. having walked, is in Malayâḷam *naḍannu.* This illustrates the process by which *eind-u* became *ein-u* in Tuḷu, and *ên-u* in the Telugu compound *padi(h)ên-u,* fifteen. It is thus evident that the apparent resemblance of the Dravidian *añju* to the Sanskrit *pañchan* is illusory. It disappears on examination, and the slight resemblance which does exist is found to arise from the operation of Dravidian principles of sound. Consequently *ei* or *ê* must be regarded as the sole representative of the Dravidian numeral, and with this it is evident that neither *pañchan,* nor any other Indo-European form has any analogy whatever. The Sanskrit *pañcha* is used in the Dravidian languages in Sanskrit compounds, but it is never confounded with *eindu* or *añju* by native scholars.

In some of the Finnish tongues the word for five has some slight resemblance to the neuter Dravidian numeral *eid-u.* The Vogul is *ät;* the Ostiak *vet* or *vuet;* the Magyar *öt* (pronounced somewhat like *êt*). This resemblance, however, seems purely accidental, for the final *t* of the Ugrian word for five appears to be radical, whereas the final *d* of the Dravidian noun of number *eid-u* is simply a neuter formative. The Chinese *u* may perhaps be compared with the Dravidian numeral adjective *ei.*

Dr Gundert, in his private communication to me, and more fully in the *Journal of the German Oriental Society* for 1869, advocates the derivation of the Dravidian word for five from the Sanskrit *pañcha.* After arguing that the Dravidian *padi,* ten, is derived from the Sanskrit *paṅkti,* a row, a row of fives, ten, he proceeds to say—"If now the Sanskrit root *pañch* serves, by means of the word *paṅkti* derived from it, for denoting ten, it is very probable that five also is derived from the same word. In Canarese an initial *p* is regularly changed into *h,* which the other dialects readily reject. The Canarese *hañchu,* to divide, seems thus to show that the Tam. and Mal. *añju* (five) is only a far-advanced *tadbhava* of *pañcha.* One feels further inclined to derive the Sanskrit *amśa,* a portion, from the aforesaid *pañchu, añju,* as a Sanskritising of a popular word." I confess I dô not feel convinced. I have gone over each step of the ground again, and can find no flaw in the evidence from which I conclude that *ei* is the oldest form of the Dravidian numeral; and as that is the form we are always brought back to, it seems to me safest to accept it as the point from which we should start.

What appears to be the radical meaning of *ei?* In some languages the word used to signify five properly means a hand, or is derived from a word which has that meaning,—the number of fingers in each hand being five. In Lepsius's opinion, the word for ten, which is used in all the Indo-European dialects, had its origin in the Maeso-Gothic *tai-hun*, two hands. Applying this principle to the Dravidian languages, *ei*, five, might be presumed to be derived from *kei*, Tam. a hand, by the process of the softening away of the initial consonant. On the other hand, there is no evidence of this process having taken place in this instance, or of *ei* having ever been preceded by *k* or any other consonant. Though this origin of the word fails us, we need not go out of the Dravidian languages for a derivation; and it is increasingly probable, after the first few numerals have been left in the mystery in which they were found, that each higher numeral in succession has been derived from a Dravidian root. It is admitted that the roots of six, seven, eight, and nine are Dravidian; why should we have to look to Sanskrit for the root of five alone? The Tamil root *ei*, which is identical in form with that of the numeral for five, gives a meaning which is as appropriate as we could wish. The abstract noun formed from this root is *eimei*, another form of which is *eidu*, the meaning of which is, close juxtaposition without contact, separation by slight intervening spaces, like growing stalks of corn or the laths on a roof, or like the fingers of the hand held up and expanded for the purpose of denoting the number five by signs. This word *eidu* is formed from *ei* by the addition of the neuter formative *du*, precisely as the Tel.-Can. *eidu*, five, appears to me to have been formed; and the identity of the two words in composition and shape, and their close resemblance in meaning, are certainly remarkable.

I find that Mr Kittel (*Indian Antiquary* for January 1873) agrees with me in considering the Dravidian word for five independent of the Sanskrit *pañchan*. He says—"*aydu* is *ay* + *du*, *ayndu* is *ay* + *bindu* + *du*. *añju* too *ai* + *bindu* + *du*, the *du* having become *ju*. Conf. 'One.'" Mr Kittel writes the word as *ay*, this being one of the ways in which the word is written in Canarese. *ei* is more common even in Canarese, and the only form used in the other dialects. He goes on to say—"The rule is, that when to certain long roots, for instance *miy* (*mî*) and *bey* (*bê*), *du* is joined, the root is shortened and the *bindu* put between (*mindu*, *bendu*). This rule may also explain the short *u* in this case before the *bindu* in *añju*. Wherever the *du* is again dropped, and at the same time the *bindu* is retained, the theme is optionally *añ* or *aỹn*, *ayn*, *aym*." Mr Kittel's illustrations are from Canarese, but the same tendency has been shown to exist in Tamil also, in connection with the formation of the preterites of verbs. (See Roots, p. 112.) In Tam. *vê*, to be burned, becomes by this rule *vendu*, having been burnt. *mî*, to bathe, Can., is not in Tamil, except perhaps under the shape of *nîndu*, to swim. The derivation of *eidu*, five, from *aydu*, Can. to obtain, given by Mr Kittel, does not appear to me satisfactory. This word *aydu* is in classical Tamil *eydu*, with the same meaning, to arrive at, to obtain. *ey* in Tam., like *isu* in Can., means to throw; but I do not find in either of these words any trace of the meaning which is necessary for Mr Kittel's explanation, viz., "the counting of the fingers of one hand, forming a going or one turn, a turn."

Six.—In all the Dravidian dialects, the difference found to exist between the neuter noun of number six and the numeral adjective is extremely small. The numeral noun is *âru* in Tamil, Telugu, Canarese, and Malayâḷam, and *âr* in Tuda; in Gônd *s-ârûn.* In Tuḷu it is *âji*, a form which bears the same relation to *âru* that *mûji*, Tuḷu, three, does to the Canarese *mûru.*

The numeral adjective differs from the noun of number with respect to the quantity of the initial vowel alone, and in some cases even that difference does not exist. In all Tamil compounds in which *âr-u* is used adjectivally, it is shortened to *ăr-u*—*e.g.*, *arubadu*, sixty. The vowel is short in the Canarese *aravattu*, the Tuḷu *ajipa*, and the Telugu *aruvei*, sixty; whilst it is long in the higher compound *ârunuru*, Can., *âjinûdu*, Tuḷu, and *ârnûru*, Tel., six hundred. In Tamil it is short in six hundred, but long, as in the other dialects, in six thousand. The adjectival form of the numerals may, as I have already said, be regarded as the original, and the form of the abstract noun of number, where any difference exists between it and the adjectival numeral, as a secondary form. *aru*, therefore, not *âru*, seems to be the primitive shape of the Dravidian word for six. The numbers two and five take the formative *du*; 'one' also probably takes the same formative; 'four' takes *hu.* Six and seven, on the other hand, form nouns of number, not by means of the addition of a formative particle, but by the lengthening of the included vowel. Mr Kittel notices that one of the meanings of *âru* in old Canarese is to be strong, or to strengthen, and infers that "the numeral seems, therefore, to convey the idea of addition; a further addition." This is one of the meanings given to *âru* in the "S'abdamaṇidarpaṇa" (Kittel's edition), the other being the common Dravidian one of drying up. This *âru*, however, like the numeral *âru*, seems to point back to an older *aru*, and *aru* gives no meaning like this in any of the Dravidian dialects. Its root-meaning seems to be to break off as a string. Hence as a verbal noun it would most naturally mean severance, a section. The connection between this meaning and that of six is not very clear, but still a connection must exist somehow, for it seems to me nearly certain that this *aru* is the root. The idea of the old Dravidians may perhaps have been, that with the number six, which was the first of the numbers requiring to be reckoned on the second hand, a new section of numerals commenced.

No analogy whatever can be traced between this Dravidian numeral and any word for six that is contained in the Indo-European languages; and no trustworthy Scythian analogies are discoverable. In Magyar six is *hat;* in the Turkish languages *âlty, âlte,* &c. It may be supposed to be possible that the first syllable of the latter word, *âl,* is allied to the Dravidian *âr*, in virtue of that interchange of *l* and *r* which is so common in the Scythian tongues. It may be conceived, also, that the Turkish *alt* and the Magyar *hat* are allied. I have no faith, however, in these indistinct resemblances of sound; for the Magyar *hat* seems originally to have had a hard initial consonant. *kot* is the corresponding numeral in Lappish, and *kuut, kuusi* in Finnish, in Cheremiss *kut;* whereas there is no reason to suppose that the Dravidian *âr* ever commenced with a consonant; nor do I suppose it very likely that in the rude Scythian tongues, in which even the numerals of cognate dialects differ from one another so widely, any real analogy with the Dravidian numerals above four would be discoverable. As I have already remarked in the introduction, "Affiliation of Dravidian Languages," the numerals of every family of languages in the Scythian group differ so widely from every other as to present few points of resemblance.

Seven.—The Dravidian noun of number seven is *êṛ-u* in Tamil and Malayâḷam, *êḷ-u* in Canarese, *êḷ'* in Tuḷu, *êḍ-u* in Telugu. These differences are in accordance with the rule that the Tamil deep, liquid, semivowel *ṛ* becomes *ḍ* in Telugu, and *ḷ* in Canarese. In the Tuda this numeral is *êlzh;* in Mahadeo Gônd, *y-ênû* or *y-êtû;* in Seoni Gônd, *êro.* A Tamil poetical form is *eṛumei.*

The numeral adjective seven, which is used in the compound numbers seventy, seven hundred, &c., exhibits a few trivial differences from the noun of number. In Tamil, *êṛ-u* is shortened to *eṛ-u* when used adjectivally, like *âr-u,* six, which is similarly shortened to *ar-u.* In Tuḷu, seventy is *eḷpa,* seven hundred *êḷ'nûdu.* In Canarese, seventy is *eppattu,* in which not only is *ê* shortened to *e,* but the radical consonant *ḷ,* answering to the Tamil *ṛ,* has been assimilated to the initial consonant of the succeeding word. In *êḷnûru,* Can. seven hundred, this assimilation has not taken place. In Telugu, the *ḍ* of *êḍ-u* does not appear to be very persistent. In *êḷnûru,* seven hundred, *ḍ* becomes *ḷ* as in the Canarese; and in *ḍebhei,* seventy (for *eḍubhei*), the initial vowel *e* has been displaced, as that of *renḍu,* two, according to a peculiar usage of the Telugu, which was explained in the section on "Sounds." This displacement of the initial vowel shows that the *e* of the supposititious *edubhei* was short, as in the corresponding Tamil and Canarese compounds. As in the case of the other numerals, the short form *eṛu* is to be regarded as the original: this in Tamil means, to rise. *êṛu*, its verbal noun, would mean a rising or increase—an appropriate meaning for the second numeral in the new section of five fingers.

It cannot be determined with perfect certainty which of the three consonants *ṛ*, *ḍ*, or *ḷ* was the primitive one in this numeral; but as the Tamil *ṛ* changes more easily into *ḷ* or *ḍ* than either of those consonants into *ṛ*, and could also be changed more easily than they into the *n* of the Gônd, possibly *ṛ*, as in Tamil, is to be regarded as the primitive form of this consonant, from which *ḍ* and *ḷ* were derived. It is more probable, however, that *ḷ*, *ḍ*, and *ṛ* are to be regarded merely as different modes of representing in writing one and the same primitive sound.

No resemblance to this Dravidian numeral is to be found in any of the Indo-European languages; and the slight apparent resemblances which may perhaps be traced in some of the Scythian tongues are not trustworthy. Compare with the Telugu *êḍ-u*, the Turkish *yedi;* the Turkish of Yarkand *yettah* (the root of which appears in the Ottoman Turkish *yet-mish*, seventy); and the Magyar *het*. In Armenian, seven is *yotn*, in Tahitian *hetu*. The *h* of the Magyar numeral and the *y* of the Turkish may be identical; but both have been derived from a harder sound, as will appear on comparing the Magyar *het* with the Lappish *kietya*, and with the corresponding Finnish *seit* in *seitsemän*.

Eight.—The Tamil numeral noun *eṭṭu*, eight, bears a remarkable resemblance to the corresponding numeral of the Indo-European family, which is in Latin *octo*, in Gothic *ahtau*. It especially resembles *aṭṭa*, the manner in which *ashṭan*, Sans. eight, is written and pronounced in classical Tamil, in which it is occasionally used in compounds; hence it has naturally been supposed by some that the Tamil *eṭṭu* has been derived from, or is identical with, this Sanskrit derivative *aṭṭa*. It will be found, however, that this resemblance, though so close as to amount almost to identity of sound, is accidental, and that it disappears on investigation and comparison, even more completely than the resemblance between *onn'* and *one*, *añju* and *pancha*.

The Dravidian noun of number eight is in Tamil *eṭṭu*, in Malayâḷam *eṭṭ-u*, in Canarese *eṇṭ-u*, in Telugu *enimidi* or *enmidi*, in Tuḷu *eṇma*, in Gônd *anumâr* or *armur*, in Tuda *eṭṭ*, in Mâdi *ermadi*. The corresponding numeral adjective, which should by rule exhibit the primitive form of the word, is *eṇ*. In Tamil *eṇ* is used adjectivally for eight in all compound numerals—*e.g.*, *eṇ-badu*, eighty, *eṇ-nûṛu*, eight hundred, as also in miscellaneous compounds, such as *eṇ-kaṇan*, he who has eight eyes, Brahmâ. The same form is used adverbially in *eṇ-êṛu*, eight times seven. In Canarese, in which the numeral noun is *eṇṭu*, *eṇ* is used as the numeral adjective in *eṇvar-u*, eight persons (Tam. *eṇmar*); whilst in *embattu*, eighty, *n* is changed into *m* through the influence of the labial initial of the second member of the compound. In *eṇṭu-nûru*, eight hundred, the numeral noun is used adjectivally instead of the numeral adjective. The Tuḷu numeral substantive is *eṇma*. The adjectival form of this numeral, as apparent in *enpa*, eighty, is simply *eṇ*, as in Tam., Can., Mal., from which it is evident that *ma* is not a part of the root, but an addition to it, which from its resemblance to *me*, the formative of abstract nouns in Tuḷu and Canarese (*mei* in Tam.), and especially to *ma*, the same formative in Mal., may be concluded to be identical with it. *eṇma* would thus mean eight-ness. *eṇmei* is found in Tamil, but only with the meaning of poverty, from *eḷ*, poor. I am indebted for this Tulu derivation to Mr Kittel. I had previously been inclined to connect *ma* with *pa*, *ba*, &c., contractions of *patta*, ten, in consequence of the resemblance of the Tuḷu *eṇma* to the Telugu *enimidi*, the *midi* of which must be from *padi*, ten.

The Telugu noun of number *enimidi*, though it closely resembles the Tuḷu *eṇma*, appears to differ considerably from the Tamil *eṭṭu*, and the Canarese *eṇṭu*; but the difference diminishes when the numeral adjectives are compared. The Telugu numeral adjective used in *enabadi* or *enabhei*, eighty, is *ena*, which is almost identical with the Tamil-Canarese *eṇ*. There is a poetical form of this word, *enb'adi*, the *eṇ* of which seems quite identical. It is no objection to this that the Tel. *n* is dental, whilst that of the Tamil-Canarese is lingual, for this is of very common occurrence; comp. Tel. *ennu*, to count, with the Tam. *eṇṇu* or *eṇ*. In *enamanḍru* or *enamaṇḍugur-u*, eight persons, and *enamannûru*, eight hundred, the *m* of *enimidi*, eight, evinces a tendency to assume the place of an essential part of the root. It will be shown, however, that *miḍi* is not a part of the root of this numeral, but an addition to it; and consequently *eṇ* or *en*, without the addition of *m*, may be concluded to be the true numeral adjective, and also the root itself. Thus, the apparent resemblance of the Tamil *eṭṭu* to the Sanskrit derivative *aṭṭa* (euphonised from *ashṭa*) disappears as soon as the various forms under which it is found are compared.

The primitive form of the neuter noun of number derived from *eṇ* is evidently that which the Canarese has retained, viz., *eṇṭu*, which is directly formed from *eṇ* by the addition of *ṭu*, the phonetic equivalent of *ḍu* or *du*—a common formative of neuter nouns, and one of which we have already seen a specimen in *eraḍu*, two, and *eindu*, five. The Tamil *eṭṭu* has been derived from *eṇṭu* by a process which is in accordance with many precedents. It is true that in general Tamil refrains from assimilating the nasal of such words as *eṇṭu*, and oftentimes it inserts a nasal where there is none in Canarese—*e.g.*, *iraṇḍu*, Tam. two, compared with the Canarese *eraḍu*; still this rule, though general, is not universal, and is sometimes reversed. Thus, *peṇṭe*, Can. a hen (in modern Canarese *heṇṭeyu*), has in Tamil become *peṭṭei*—a change exactly parallel to that of *eṇṭu* into *eṭṭu*.

Much difficulty is involved in the explanation of *enimidi*, the Telugu noun of number which corresponds to *eṭṭu* and *eṇṭu*. *eni*, *enu*, *ena* or *en* (*enabadi*, *enubadi*, *enbadi*, eighty) is evidently identical with the Tamil-Canarese *eṇ*: but what is the origin of the suffix *midi*? This *midi* becomes *ma* in some instances—*e.g.*, *enama-ṇḍru*, eight persons; *enamannûru*, eight hundred; and the Tuḷu noun of number eight is *eṇma*. Shall we consider *midi* to be synonymous with *padi*, ten, and *enimidi*, eight, to be a compound word, which was meant to signify two from ten? It will be shown under the next head that in the Telugu *tommidi*, nine, *midi* is without doubt identical with *padi*, ten. If so, there would seem to be a valid reason for supposing that the *midi* of *enimidi*, eight, is also derived from the same source, and appended to *en* with the same intent. It will be shown in our examination of the Dravidian numeral ten that *padi* has become greatly corrupted in compounds, especially in Telugu; in which the second syllable has disappeared in compounds above twenty. If *midi*, identical with *padi*, were liable to a similar corruption, as is probable enough, we may see how *enimidi* would be softened into *enama* (in *enamaṇḍru*, *enamannûru*), and also into *eṇma* in Tuḷu. It is a characteristic of the Scythian languages that they use for eight and nine compounds which signify ten minus two and ten minus one. In some instances an original uncompounded word is used for eight; but nine is always a compound. The Dravidian word for nine is, I have no doubt, formed in this very manner; and this seems to be also a rational explanation of the origin of the Telugu word for eight. On the other hand, in the Tamil-Canarese idioms, *eṇ* by itself is used to signify eight, without any trace of the use in conjunction with it of the word *pattu* or *padi*, ten. It is also deserving of notice that in the Telugu *enabhei*, eighty, the second member of *enimidi* has disappeared. *enabhei* is of course for *enabadi*, but if *enimidi* is eight, eighty ought to be *enimidibadi*. The use of *ena* or *en* alone in the numeral eighty shows that *ena* or *en* alone, without *midi*, means eight.

It is difficult to determine whether the disuse of ten as a component element in the numeral eight of the Tamil and Canarese is to be regarded as a corruption, or whether the use of ten by the Telugu in the construction of eight is itself a corruption, arising from the influence and attraction of the principle which was adopted in the formation of the next numeral, nine. On the whole, I consider the latter supposition the more probable, and therefore regard the Tamil-Canarese *eṇ* (in Telugu *en* or *ena*) as the primitive shape of this Dravidian numeral.

Max Müller supposed *en* must be identical with *er*, properly *ir*, two. Mr Clay's theory respecting the origin of the Telugu *enimidi* is almost identical with this. He supposes the *eni* of this word to be derived from *el*, in *elli*, Tel. to-morrow, or next day, and this he supposes to be an old word for two. In this way he would bring out the meaning which is apparently required by *enimidi*—viz., two from ten. This derivation seems very plausible, but unfortunately I can find no trace of *el* having ever meant two. *elli* is evidently identical with the Tuḷu *elle*, to-morrow, and apparently identical also with *el*, Tam. a day (root-meaning, a limit, a term), so that its use in Telugu and Tuḷu to denote to-morrow seems analogous to the use of *nâḷei* in Tamil, which is used to mean to-morrow, but of which the real meaning is simply a day. Compare the formation of *ell-uṇḍi*, Tel. the day after to-morrow, with that of the Tamil *nâḷei-nindru*, the same, literally, waiting over to-morrow. I have already shown that the *midi* of *enimidi* disappears altogether in *ena-badi*, eighty, and that the *en* or *ena*, which in that word represents eight, is probably identical with the Tam.-Can. *eṇ*. I feel constrained therefore to adhere to the explanation I have given.

eṇ has no resemblance to any numeral belonging to any other language, whether Indo-European or Scythian; and it cannot, I think, be doubted, that it was first adopted into the list of numerals by the Dravidian people themselves. We have not to go far to seek for a derivation. *eṇ* is a primitive and very common Dravidian root, signifying either to reckon or a number, according as it is used as a verb or as a noun. As a verb, it is in Tamil *eṇ* (vulgarly *eṇṇu*), in Telugu *enn-u*, in Canarese *eṇ-usu*. We have an instance of its use as a noun in *eṇ-śuvaḍi*, Tam. a book of arithmetic, literally a number book. After the Dravidians of the first age had learned to count seven, they found they required a higher numeral, which they placed immediately above seven and called *eṇ*, *the* number—an appropriate enough term for perhaps the highest number which they were then accustomed to reckon. A similar mode of seizing upon a word which denotes properly a number or any number, and using it restrictively to denote some one number in particular—generally a newly-invented, high number—is found in other languages besides the Dravidian. Thus, in Lappish, *lokke*, ten, means literally a number, from *lokket*, to count.

Compare the origin of the Aryan word for nine, *navan*, literally the new (number).

Nine.—In all the Dravidian idioms the numeral nine is a compound word, which is used indifferently and without change as a noun of number and as a numeral adjective.

The second member of the compound numeral nine is identical with, or evidently derived from, the numeral ten, the differences between it and that numeral being such as can be accounted for by the phonetic tendencies of the various Dravidian dialects.

The principal forms which this numeral assumes are the following:—in Tamil it is *onbad-u*, in Malayâḷam *ombadu*, in Canarese *ombhattu*, in Coorg *oyimbadu*, in Telugu *tommidi*, in Tuḷu *ormba*, in Tuda *onpath'*, in Kota *ormpatu;* in each of which instances the second member of the compound plainly represents ten. In Gônd, nine is said to be *anmu*. A word for nine in poetical Tamil is *toṇḍu;* this means also old. It is a curious circumstance that, whilst the Sanskrit word for nine means the new (number), one of the Dravidian words for nine means the old (number). Another word for nine in poetical Tamil is *onbân*, in which *pân* represents ten.

In ordinary Tamil, ten is *patt-u;* nine is *onbad-u* (*on-pad-u*, euphonically *on-badu*); and not only is it evident that *patt-u* and *pad-u* are allied, but the resemblance becomes identity when *pad-u*, the second member of *onbad-u*, is compared with the representative of ten in *irubad-u*, twenty—literally twice ten—and similar compound numerals. Moreover, *onbad-u* itself becomes *onbatt-u* when used adverbially—*e.g.*, *onbatt'-êṛ-u*, nine times seven. In ancient Canarese, ten was *patt-u*, as in Tamil. In modern Canarese it changes by rule into *hatt-u;* nevertheless the original labial retains its place in the compounds *ombhatt-u*, nine, and *embatt-u*, eighty; from which it is evident that in Canarese nine is formed from ten, by means of an auxiliary prefix, as in Tamil. In Telugu alone there is some difference between the word which separately signifies ten and the second member of *tommidi*, the compound numeral nine. Ten is in Telugu *padi*, whilst nine is not *tompadi* or *tombaḍi*, but *tommidi;* and nine persons is *tommaṇḍugur-u*. It can scarcely be doubted, however, that *tommidi* has been euphonised from *tombadi*. In the other compound numerals of the Telugu (twenty, thirty, &c.), in which *padi* forms of necessity the second member, the corruption of *padi* into *bhei* or *vei* is still greater than in the instances now before us. It may be regarded, consequently, as certain that the second member of the Dravidian word for nine is identical with the word for ten. We have, therefore, now to inquire only into the origin and signification of the first member of the compound.

In the Tamil *onbadu*, *on* is the auxiliary prefix by which *padu* is specialised, and we have the same prefix in the poetical form, *onbân*. *on* is in Malayâḷam and Canarese *om*, in Coorg *oyim*. This *on* has been supposed to be identical with the first portion of the Tamil *ondru*, one (in Canarese and Coorg *ondu*, in Telugu *oṇḍu*, in Malayâḷam *onn'*, in Tuḷu *onji*); and Dr Gundert (in his private communication to me) expresses himself in favour of this supposition. In Tuḷu, nine is *ormba*, in the Kota dialect *ormpatu*, in each of which forms we cannot but recognise a development of the ordinary Dravidian *or*, one, from which the compound word for nine will take the very appropriate meaning of one from ten. The supposition that the *on* and *om* of the Tam.-Can. words for nine has the same origin as the Tuḷu, &c., and is used to express the same meaning, has certainly much to recommend it. As *padin-ondru*, Tam. eleven, means one added to ten, so *on-badu*, nine, might naturally be taken to mean one from ten, or one before ten. There are some difficulties, however, in the way of this supposition. I can find no distinct trace of the syllable *on*, standing alone, having ever stood for one. The form we always find, or to which we are always obliged to come back, is *or* or *oṟ*. But another and greater difficulty comes to view when we compare the Tamil *on'-badu* with the Telugu *tom-midi*. We have here a prefix beginning with *t*, which points to the possibility of the Tamil *on* having originally been *ton*, and the Canarese *om* having been *tom*. What is still more worthy of notice is, that in the higher numbers, even in Tamil, into which nine enters, *on* is represented by *ton* (or its equivalent *toḷ*)—*e.g.*, *toṇṇûṟu*, ninety, *toḷḷâyiram*, nine hundred. In Telugu we find *tom* not only in *tom-midi*, nine, but in *tom-bhei* or *tom-badi*, ninety, and *tomma-nnûṟu*, nine hundred. In Canarese we find the same prefix in *tom-bhattu*, ninety, though nine is *ombhattu*, and nine hundred is *ombhaiyi-nûru*. In Coorg, nine is *oyim-badu*, whilst ninety, *ttonûru*, follows the Tamil, and nine hundred, *ombei-nûru*, the Canarese. The Tuḷu word for ninety is *śonpa*, in which *śoṇ* evidently stands for the *tom* or *toḷ* of the other dialects: nine hundred is *ormba nûdu*. The Tuda word is *ênpath*. Even in Tamil a poetical form for nine has an initial *t*. This is *toṇḍu*, of which we cannot doubt that the first portion, *toṇ*, is allied to the *tom* of the other dialects. The original shape of this prefix must have been *toḷ*. The final *l* is changed into a nasal, according to a well-recognised Dravidian law of sounds, not only when followed by a nasal, but even when followed by certain hard consonants. *eḷ* + *ney*, sesame oil, becomes *eṇṇey*; *kal* + *malei*, stony hill, *kanmalei*. So also *śel* + *du*, having gone, becomes *śendru*; and *koḷ* + *du*, having taken, *koṇḍu* (the latter becomes more completely nasalised in the Tuḷu equivalent *koṇ* and the Telugu *konu*). Hence from *tol*, old, before, with the neuter formative *du*, comes *tondru*, antiquity; and from *toḷ*, an alternative form of the same root, comes *toṇḍu*, the word under consideration, meaning also antiquity, priority, but containing amongst its many meanings that of nine. The Telugu *tom* appears to have been derived from *tol*, not *toḷ*, though both forms were doubtless identical originally; and in Telugu the meaning, first, before, is more distinctly developed than in Tamil—*e.g.*, *toli-vâramu*, the first day of the week; *tol-nâḍu*, the day before. This gives us a satisfactory explanation of the prefix by which in Telugu nine, in Tamil and Malayâḷam ninety and nine hundred, in Canarese ninety, are formed. It properly means the number standing next in order *before* the number to which it is prefixed. Thus in Telugu nine means the number before ten; in Malayâḷam, Tamil, and Coorg, ninety means the number before a hundred; and in Malayâḷam and Tamil nine hundred means the number before a thousand. The word for nine sometimes found (as has been mentioned) in poetical Tamil, *toṇḍu*, means properly before; but, as used, it signifies, like the Telugu word for nine, the number before ten. When the Telugu, Tuḷu, and Canarese numbers for ninety are compared with the Tamil, Malayâḷam, and Coorg, we are struck with the greater regularity of the latter compounds. The Telugu *tom-bhei* and the Canarese *tom-bhattu* are meant to denote nine tens; but *tom*, the prefix used to denote nine, does not properly mean nine at all, but is only the first part of the numeral nine, which is itself a compound. The Telugu and Canarese compounds for nine hundred, *tommannûru* and *ombhayi-nûru*, are formed on the same plan, but with a fuller representation of both parts of the number nine, which they adopt as their first member. The Tuḷu word for ninety, *śoṇpa*, is very curiously constructed. Comparing it with *eḷpa*, seventy, and *eṇpa*, eighty, it seems evident that *pa* means ten; but *śoṇ*, the first part of the word, finds no place, as the corresponding Telugu and Canarese particles do, in the Tuḷu word for nine. It appears to be the equivalent of the *tol*, *ton*, and *tom* of the other dialects, the meaning of which is, before; but in order to bring out the meaning of ninety, this particle should have been prefixed to a hundred, like the Tam.-Mal., not to ten. In Tamil and Malayâḷam, on the other hand, the composite numeral nine is altogether lost sight of in the construction of the compounds ninety and nine hundred, and these compounds are formed in perfect accordance with rule by prefixing *toḷ*, before, to the word a hundred, to form ninety, and the same *toḷ* to a thousand, in order to form nine hundred. In these instances *toḷ* is used in its proper original signification of before, without any reference to the use of the same prefix (if indeed it be the same that is used in Tamil, as it certainly is in Telugu), to form nine. We should naturally expect to find the Tamil-Canarese word for nine formed in the same manner, and by means of the same prefix, as the Tamil and Malayâḷam words for ninety and nine hundred; and if we could suppose the oldest form of the Tamil nine to have been *ton-badu*, and that of the Canarese *tom-bhattu*, corresponding to the Telugu *tom-midi*, this would have been the case. As it is, we must consider it possible that the prefix of the Tamil-Canarese word for nine may be a representative of the word for one; though the reasons why we should prefer to derive the Tamil *on* and the Canarese *om*, like the Telugu *tom*, from *tol* or *toḷ*, before, with the initial *t* softened away, seem to me still weightier.

The native Tamil grammarians derive the prefix *toḷ*, in the words for ninety and nine hundred, directly from *onbadu*, the word for nine. First, they say, the *badu* of *onbadu* is lost; then *on* is changed into *ton;* then this is changed into *toḷ*. (See "Nannûl.") The plan of deriving anything from anything was evidently not unknown to the ancient grammarians of the Tamil country.

It seems scarcely necessary now to add, that there is no affinity whatever, as some have surmised, between the initial portion of the Tamil *onbadu* and the Greek *ἐννέα*, the Sanskrit form of which is *navan*. The Manchu *onyan*, nine, has not only some resemblance to the Dravidian word, but seems to be a compound formed on similar principles. Nevertheless the ultimate component elements of the Manchu word—*emu*, one, and *juan*, ten—have no resemblance whatever to the Dravidian.

Ten.—In all the Dravidian languages the words used for ten are virtually the same; in Tamil *patt-u*, in modern Canarese *hatt-u*, in the ancient dialect *patt-u*, in Tuḷu *patt'*, in Telugu *padi*, in Tuda *pattu*, in Gônd *pudth*. In those Tamil compound numerals in which ten is the second member—*e.g.*, *irubadu*, twenty, *pattu* becomes *padu* (euphonically *ppadu* or *badu*), which is in close agreement with the Telugu *padi*. In Tamil poetry we sometimes find *pân* (euphonically *bân*), instead of *pattu*, as the second member of such compounds—*e.g.*, *onbân*, nine, *irubân*, twenty. This may possibly be an euphonically lengthened form of *pan*, equivalent to *pad-u*.

In the Tamil compound numerals under twenty, in which ten constitutes the first number, nineteen is *patton-badu*, the first portion of which, when compared with the last, appears to be an adjectival form of *padu*, seeing that the word used for ten in all the other compounds is certainly adjectival. Twelve is *pannirandu*, the first portion of which, *pan*, is either an abbreviation of *padin*, the adjectival form of ten in general use, or is identical with *pan*, the supposititious radical form of *pân*, the poetical word for ten mentioned above. In all the other compound numerals in Tamil, the first portion representing ten is *padin*, which is formed from *pad-u*, the radical form, and *in*, the adjectival formative—a particle which is much used, as we have seen, as a locative and ablative case-sign, as a sign of the possessive, and still more frequently as an inflexional increment. The addition of *in* converts a noun into an adjective. (See "Nouns.") *padin* is the form of the word for ten which enters most commonly into other compounds—*e.g.*, *padinmar*, ten persons, *padinmaḍangu*, tenfold. The Malayâḷam forms are identical with those of the Tamil, with the exception of the word for twelve, *pandireṇḍu* or *pandrendu*, in which the *pan* of Tamil and the other dialects is represented by *pand*.

The Telugu simple numeral *padi*, ton, is evidently identical with the Tamil *padu* (the root form of *pattu*), just as *adi*, Tel. it, is evidently identical with *adu*, Tam. In the compounds under twenty, *padi* undergoes more changes than the corresponding Tamil word. In eight and nine it becomes *midi;* in the numbers above ten, *padi*, *pada*, *pad*, or *padd*, with the exception of twelve, which is *panneṇḍu* (*panneṇḍu*); compare *panniddara*, twelve persons, and nineteen, which is *pandommidi* (*pan-tommidi*). The *pan* of the Tamil compound here appears twice. In the compounds from twenty upwards, in which ten is the second member of the compound, and is a numeral noun, *padi* is materially changed. In twenty and sixty it is altered to *vei*, in thirty to *phei*, in seventy to *bbhei*, and in the other numbers to *bhei*. This change is effected by the softening of the *d* of *padi*, after which *pa-i* or *ba-i* would naturally become *bei*, and then *vei*.

In Canarese, ten is *hattu*, by the change of *p* into *h*, which is usual in the modern dialect; in the ancient dialect, as in Tamil and Malayâḷam, it is *pattu*. In the compound forms between ten and twenty, in which ten is used adjectivally, and is the first portion of the word, *pattu* is generally represented by *padin*, as in Tamil. The exceptions are eleven and twelve, in which *pad* is replaced by *pan*—*e.g.*, *pannoṇḍu*, *panneraḍu*. Before one thousand in old Canarese we find *payin* instead of *pan* or *padin*. In the compounds above twenty, in which ten holds the second place, *pattu* (*hattu*) becomes *bhattu* or *vaṭtu*, or remains *pattu*, according as euphony requires. The difference between Canarese and Coorg, with respect to ten and the numerals into which ten enters, are so slight, that only one need be mentioned. In the numbers from thirteen to eighteen inclusive, *pattu* is represented in Coorg, not by *padin*, but by *padun*, which is evidently an equivalent form. The Tuḷu uses *patt'* for the noun of number, and *patt'*, *pad*, *pad'n*, and *pâd'n*, as the numeral adjective. In twenty and upwards, *patt'* becomes *pa*, *va*. In compounds like *irvatonji*, twenty-one, the *tt'* of *patt'* is represented by *t*. In *pâd'nêḽ'*, seventeen, we find an euphonic lengthening of the vowel of *patt'*, the only thing resembling which, in any of the dialects, is the poetical Tamil *pân*.

Dr Gundert (in the private communication already referred to) suggested the possibility of the Dravidian word for ten, *padu* or *padi*, being directly derived from the Sanskrit *paṅkti*, and more recently (in the *German Oriental Society's Journal* for 1869) he has advocated this derivation in more decided terms. "The word for ten," he says, "which Caldwell derives from a Dravidian root, *pad*, is nothing but a *tadbhava* from *pankti* (Sans.), a row of fives, ten. From this first we have the *tadbhava pandi* (Tam.), a row of guests, then *pandu*, ten (still retained in the Mal. *pand-iru*, twelve). It bears also further abbreviation in *padu*, *padi*, *pei* (in Tamil also *pani*, properly *panni*), whilst it is found lengthened again by the suffix of the neuter termination *tu* (Tam. *pattu*, from *pad-tu*)."

It seems, I admit, more reasonable that the Dravidians should have borrowed their word for ten from their Aryan neighbours than that they should have borrowed from them their word for five. Ten being not only a higher number, but one that could not fail soon to acquire a special value in calculation, it would not surprise us to find the word for this number borrowed by a less cultured people from a more cultured. On the other hand, the word used in all the Dravidian languages for a hundred is native; one of the Telugu words for a thousand is native; and it is only the words for the high abstract numbers, a *lakh* and a *crore*, that are invariably borrowed from the Sanskrit. If so, the possibility of the Dravidian word for ten having been borrowed from the Sanskrit is met by the improbability of this being done by people who could invent words of their own for a hundred and a thousand. Besides, if the Dravidians felt any temptation to borrow from the Sanskrit its word for ten, they would naturally, as it seems to me, have chosen *daśan*, the word which they found in constant use, instead of *paṅkti*, a derivative from *pañcha*, five, denoting ten in certain compounds only (*e.g.*, *paṅkti grîva*, one who has ten necks, *Râvaṇa*), but generally meaning merely a row. *paṅkti* is sometimes used in Telugu without alteration in *tatsama* compounds with the meaning of ten; but the *tadbhava panti*, which is somewhat nearer the Dravidian word for ten in appearance, has never this meaning, but only means a row. In Tamil, the *tatsama paṅkti* is unknown; but there are two *tadbhavas*, *pandi* and *patti*, both signifying a row, of which the former generally means a row of guests. No trace of the meaning of ten adheres to either of these words, nor are *padu* or *padi* ever supposed by native scholars to be derived from *paṅkti*, or connected with its *tadbhavas*, *pandi* or *patti*, notwithstanding the fondness of native scholars for deriving everything they can from Sanskrit. The two words are kept carefully separate in pronunciation and usage, and, as far as appears, it was only in its secondary meaning of a row that the old Dravidians thought fit to borrow the Sanskrit word. Dr Gundert's strongest point is the use of *pand* for ten in *pandiren̤ḍu*, the Malayâḷam word for twelve. The strength of this point seems to me, however, a good deal diminished when we compare the word he refers to, *pandirendu*, Mal., with *panniraṇḍu*, Tam., *pannen̤ḍu*, Tel., *panneraḍu*, Can., and especially with the Tuḷu *pad'râḍ'* (for *pad'raḍḍ'*), in which latter word the *n* of the other dialects has altogether disappeared. Compare also the Canarese *pannondu*, eleven, with the *padinondru* or *padinonn'* of the Tamil and Malayâḷam, and especially with the *pattonji* of the Tuḷu. When we find the *pan* which represents ten in the word for eleven in one of these dialects resolving itself in two other dialects into *padin* (from *padu* and *in*), and in one coming back bodily to *patt'*, it is but reasonable to suppose that the *pan* of the word for twelve has also originated in this way; and if this explanation holds good for *pan*, it will also, as appears, hold good also for *pand*, which is, after all, a little nearer *padin* than *pan* itself is. Even on the supposition of *pan* being, not a corrupted form of *padin*, but an old equivalent of *pad-u* (surviving in Tam. *iru-bân*, twenty, possibly lengthened from *pan* *), it would not be necessary for us to look to the Sanskrit *paṅkti* for an explanation of it, for *pan* might very well be supposed to have the same relation to *padu* or *padi* that *am* or *an*, the obsolete demonstrative pronoun, has to *adu* or *adi*, the forms now in use in Tamil and Telugu respectively. I prefer, notwithstanding this, deriving the *pan* of the various words for eleven and twelve from *padin*, and would give the same explanation to the *pand* of the Malayâḷam word.

Though I am not prepared to accept the derivation of the Dravidian *padu* or *padi* from *paṅkti*, yet I admit the difficulty of deriving this word satisfactorily from a Dravidian root. It is to be remembered, however, that it is equally, if not more, difficult to determine the root

---

* Native Tamil grammarians consider the final *ân* of the poetical *irupân* (pronounced *irubân*), twenty, &c., as a poetical expletive. I should prefer calling it a poetical formative. The fact, however, that they consider *p* the only representative of ten in such words, shows that the supposition that *pân* sometimes stood for *padu* or *pattu* at an ancient period, must be advocated with caution.

of the Sanskrit *daśan*. If the final *du* or *di* of *padu* or *padi* is a neuter formative, as it may be concluded to be from the analogy of so many other numerals, we have to look for a verbal root like *pa*, from which *padu* or *padi* would naturally be derived. *pa* is not now found standing alone as a verbal root, even in Tamil, but there is a large number of roots extant of which *pa* is the base (*pad*, *pan*, *pam*, *pay*, *par*, *pal*, with lengthened, specialised forms of the same), the generic meaning of which is extension, increase, multiplication; and possibly *pa-du* (or *pa-n*) may be derived from this base. I may suggest also an alternative derivation—viz., from *pag-u*, to divide. The classical Tamil grammars teach that *pattu* may, in certain connections, be written *paḥdu*—*e.g.*, *oru paḥdu*, one ten, *iru paḥdu*, two tens.* The use of this *ḥ*, which is the peculiar Tamil letter called *âydam*, and a sort of guttural, is generally considered pedantic (see "Sounds: Alphabet"), but in this instance it may be supposed to represent an original guttural consonant, which could only have been *k* or *g*. This would give us *pag-u*, to divide, as the root of *paḥdu*, and *pahdu* would then correspond to the ordinary derivative from this root *pagudi*, a portion (classical Tam. *pâl*, *pâttru*, *pânmei*), a division. The meaning the word would then convey would suit the purpose to which the numeral ten is put exceedingly well. Another and very common corruption of *pagudi*, a division, is *pâdi*, half.

Since the above was written I have seen Mr Kittel's paper on the Dravidian numerals, in the *Indian Antiquary* for January 1873. His remarks are as follows:—

"10. *pattu*, *pandu*, *pannu*, *padin*, *padu*, *padi*, *payin*, *pay*, *pa* [root], *pattu* [Can.], *parru*, pronounce *pattu* [Tam. to be pronounced *pattru*], to come together, join; a joining or combination of all the ten fingers."

To this he appends the following note:—

"The first three forms are quite regular—*i.e.*, *par* + *tu* (*tu* = *du*, conf. *ottu* under No. 1), *par* + *du* (= *pandu*, see No. 1). The single *d* in the three subsequent forms at first sight looks strange; but all difficulty is removed when considering the form *pa* in the end [beginning]. This *pa* is unchangeable, whereas the liquid *r* falls under the rule of S'ithilatva (cf. No. 4)—*i.e.*, the rule that in many cases a liquid before *k*, *g*, *d*, is so slightly sounded that no double consonant is formed, and accordingly has simply been dropped, so that *pa* + *du* (*di*)

* This explains the peculiar word for ten, in what is styled ancient Tamil, which we find in Dr Hunter's "Comparative Dictionary." This is *orupakadu* (so also *onbakadu*, nine, and *irupakuda*, twenty), the meaning of which, when the words are separated, is *oru paḥdu*, one ten.

has remained: *ede*, *erde*, breast; *baduku*, *barduku*, life [class. coll. Can.] *d* appears twice in the form of *y*; see under No. 3, and compare the *j* (a known cognate of *y*) under Nos. 1 and 5 [Tuḷu]. We add that *paṅkti* [Sans.], when meaning the number 10, is a *tadbhava* of the Dravidian *pattu*, just as *muktâ* [Sans.], pearl, is a *tadbhava* of *muttu*, and *sukti* [Sans.], a curl, a *tadbhava* of *suttu*."

Doubtless *pattu* could have been regularly derived in the way Mr Kittel describes, yet I am unable to accept this derivation; for, as a matter of fact, I can find no trace of *r* in the words for ten in any of the Dravidian dialects. *pattu*, in Canarese, is *paṟṟu* (pronounced *pattru*) in Tamil, and *paṭṭu* in Telugu. *paṟṟu*, Tam., means, it is true, to unite, to solder, to adhere, &c., but its radical meaning is to grasp. Metaphysically it means attachment. I consider it a secondary theme, of which the primitive form is *paṟ'*, which, from a comparison of the related secondary themes in Tamil—*paṟi*, intrans. to escape, *paṟi*, trans. to pluck, *paṟa*, to fly, *paṟei*, to utter a sound—must have meant to move rapidly. It is noteworthy that Mr Kittel, so far from considering *pattu*, Drav. to be a *tadbhava* of *paṅkti*, Sans., turns the tables on Sanskrit by representing *paṅkti* itself to be a *tadbhava* of *pattu*.

A Hundred.—In all the Dravidian dialects this word is *nûṟ-u*. Telugu, in addition to *nûṟ-u*, has *vanda*. In Tuḷu, *nûṟ-u* becomes *nûdu*, which is an illustration of the tendency of that dialect to soften down the hard **ṟ** of the other dialects into *d* or *j*.

I have not been able to discover any resemblance to *nûṟ-u* in any other family of tongues. In no two Scythian stems do we find the same word used to express this high number; nor indeed amongst such rude tribes could we expect to find it otherwise. One and the same word for hundred, slightly modified, is used in every language of the Indo-European family, a remarkable proof of the unity and ancient intellectual culture of the race; and the Finnish word for a hundred, *sata*, has evidently, like some other Finnish words, been borrowed from that family of tongues.

In Telugu and Malayâḷam, *nûru*, *nûṟu*, ashes, powder, is identical with *nûru*, *nûṟu*, a hundred. In Tamil, ashes, to reduce to ashes, is *nîṟu*, pronounced nearly like *nûṟu*. The word is written both with *î* and with *û* in Tel. and Mal.; so that the difference in Tamil between *nîṟu*, ashes, and *nûṟu*, a hundred, resolves itself into a mere question of pronunciation. There cannot be any doubt that we have here the origin of the Dravidian word for a hundred. Dust, powder, would naturally appear to a primitive race an appropriate name for a number which must have seemed to them innumerable.

A Thousand.—The Dravidian words for thousand are *âyiram*, Tam.

and Mal.; *sâvira*, and also *savara*, Can.; *vêlu*, Tel.; *sâra*, Tuḷu. *sâvira* or *savara*, and *sâra*, are evidently identical; and we may safely derive both from the Sanskrit *sahasra*. The Tamil *âyiram* also is an old corruption of the Sanskrit. Dr Gundert derives it thus: *sahasram*, *sahasiram*, *a-a-yiram*, *âyiram*. *À priori* we might have expected to find the Dravidian languages borrowing from the Sanskrit a word for expressing this very high numeral. The Telugu word for thousand, *vêl-u*, is a purely Dravidian word, and is the plural of *veyi* or *veyyi* (*veyu-lu*); *vê* is also used. I am inclined to connect this word with the root *ve*, to be excessive, to be hot, harsh, &c.

ORDINAL NUMBERS.—It is unnecessary in this work to devote much attention to the ordinal numbers of the Dravidian languages, seeing that they are formed directly, and in the simplest possible manner, from the cardinal numbers, by means of suffixed verbal participles or participial forms. The only exception is that of the first ordinal, viz., the word signifying first, which in most of the Dravidian languages, as in the Indo-European, is formed, not from the cardinal number one, but from a prepositional root. In the Canarese and Malayâḷam, the numeral one itself is the basis of the word used for first. The base of the first ordinal in Tamil and Telugu is *mudal*, a verbal noun signifying priority in time or place, or a beginning. This, like all other Dravidian nouns, may be used adjectivally without any addition or change; and therefore *mudal* alone, though signifying a beginning, is often used as an ordinal number in the sense of first. More frequently, however, it receives the addition in Tamil of *âm*, which is the usual suffix of the ordinal numbers, and is in itself an aoristic relative participle of the verb *âg-u*, to become. When *mudal* is used in Telugu without the usual ordinal or participial suffix, it requires to be put in the inflected form—*e.g.*, not *modal*, but *modaṭi*. The verbal noun *mudal* is connected with the postposition *mun*, Tam. before; so that there is the same connection between the ordinal number first in the Dravidian languages, and the postposition before, which is observed to exist in the Indo-European languages between the preposition *pra*, Sans. before, and *prathama*, πρῶτος, &c., first. Though the Tamil *mun*, before, is allied to *mudal*, first, yet neither of those words exhibits the ultimate root. The *n* of *mun* appears in the verb *mundu*, Tam. to get before; but it does not appear to have had any place in *mudal*, of which *dal* is a formative termination belonging to a numerous class of verbal nouns, and *mu* alone is the root. *mudal*, though itself a verbal noun, is also used as the root of a new verb, signifying to begin. I have no doubt that all these words and forms spring from *mu* as their ultimate base. *mu* is evidently a word of relation, signifying, like the Sanskrit *pra*, priority; and with it I connect *mû*, Tam. to be old, properly *mu*, as found in *mudu*, antiquity, this also being a species of priority, viz., priority in time. In all the Dravidian idioms, the other ordinal numbers, from two upwards, are formed directly from the cardinal numbers by the addition of formative suffixes. The same suffix is added to every numeral in succession, without change either in the cardinal number or in the suffix itself.

The ordinal suffix of the grammatical Telugu is *ava*, which is instead of *aga*, from *agu*, to become, the *g* of which verb is generally changed into *v*—*e.g.*, *mûḍava*, third: Canarese adds *anê* to the cardinal numbers—*e.g.*, *mûranê*, third: the ordinal of the Tamil is formed by adding *âm* to the cardinal—*e.g.*, *mûndrâm*, third. The clear and certain origin of the Tamil suffix *âm* from *âgum*, poetically and vulgarly *âm*, the aoristic relative participle of *âgu*, to become, illustrates the origin of the suffixes of the Telugu and Canarese, which, though considerably changed, are undoubtedly identical with the Tamil in origin.

The adverbial forms of the Dravidian numerals are formed by means of another class of suffixes from the same auxiliary verb *âgu*, to become. In this instance the suffixes which are used by Tamil, *âvadu*, &c., are neuter participial nouns used adverbially. Oftentimes, however, adverbial numerals are formed by the addition of nouns signifying succession, &c., to the cardinal or ordinal numbers—*e.g.*, *iru-muṛei*, Tam. twice, literally two times.

The multiplicative numbers, as has already been stated, are the same as the numeral adjectives.

Affiliation.—It only remains to inquire what evidence respecting the affiliation of the Dravidian family of tongues is furnished by the preceding investigation of the numerals of that family.

The evidence is not only decidedly opposed to the supposition that the Dravidian languages are derived from the Sanskrit, but also, so far as it goes, seems inconsistent with the supposition of the descent of those languages from the Aryan family. Even if we accepted Dr Gundert's theory that the words for five and ten are Sanskrit *tadbhavas*, that would only prove that the less cultured people had borrowed certain words from the more cultured. Borrowing something from a friend is one thing, being related to him is another. An ultimate relationship of some sort between the Dravidian languages and those of the Indo-European family may perhaps be deduced, or at least guessed at, from other departments of the grammar; but on this point, as it appears to me, the numerals are silent. The only resemblance I can find between the Dravidian numerals and those of any Indo-European language (excluding for the present the debated five and ten), is the resemblance of the Telugu *oka*, one, to the Sanskrit *êka*, as well as to the Ugrian *og*, *ak*, and *okur;* and in that instance it seems possible that the Sanskrit itself may have inherited a Scythian numeral, the numeral for *one* of the Greek, Gothic, Celtic, &c., being derived from a different base. All the other numerals of the Indo-European languages can be traced to the same forms, and are virtually identical; and hence, when we find in the Dravidian numerals, as I think we do, no resemblance to those of the Indo-European tongues, with the exception of the abnormal Sanskrit *êka*, we seem to be compelled to conclude that the Dravidian languages cannot be Indo-European.

On the other hand, a comparison of the Dravidian numerals with those of the Scythian tongues appears to establish the fact of the existence of Scythian analogies in this department, as in many others, of the grammar of the Dravidian family. The resemblance between the Dravidian one and four, especially the latter, and the corresponding numerals in the Finno-Ugrian languages, is so remarkable, that we may almost regard those numerals as identical. The same statement applies to the word for 'one' which is found in the Scythian version of Darius's cuneiform inscriptions at Behistun. The numeral four, and the other numerals above one, are not contained in that unique relic of the ancient Scythian speech of Central Asia; and in this case the negative argument proves nothing. Professor Hunfalvy doubts the relationship of the Dravidian word for 'one' to that in the Finno-Ugrian languages. He shows that the resemblance of the Votiak *og*, one, to the Telugu *oka*, diminishes considerably when it is compared with the Finnish *yht* (*yksi*); but he refrains from showing that there is any similar diminution of resemblance in the case of the Dravidian numeral four, the identity of which with the Finno-Ugrian word he must, I think, have admitted. The fact that the Dravidian word for four, which seems not only to resemble, but to be identical with, the Finno-Ugrian word, cannot be explained, as most of the Dravidian numerals can, by derivation from a Dravidian root, seems to me to add weight to the supposition that this resemblance can scarcely be regarded as fortuitous. It may perhaps be thought that the resemblance of only two numerals at most (one and four), out of ten, cannot be considered to prove much; but it is to be borne in mind that this resemblance is all, or nearly all, that is generally observed in the Scythian languages themselves between the numerals of one family of languages and those of other families belonging to the same group. Where the arithmetical faculty is not strongly developed, words of number are formed slowly and irregularly, and are easily changed or forgotten.

DRAVIDIAN NUMERALS IN THE FIVE PRINCIPAL DIALECTS.

	Tamil.	Malayâḷam.	Telugu.	Canarese.	Tuḷu.
One	*ondru ; oru, ôr.*	*onnu ; oru, ôr.*	*okaṭi, oṇḍu ; oka.*	*ondu ; or.*	*oñji ; or.*
Two	*iraṇḍu ; iru, îr.*	*reṇḍu ; iru, îr.*	*reṇḍu ;* (iddaru).	*eraḍu ; ir.*	*raḍḍu ; ir.*
Three	*mûndru ; mû, mu.*	*mûnnu ; mû, mu.*	*mûḍu ;* (mugguru).	*mûru ; mû, mu.*	*mûji ; mû, mu.*
Four	*nâlu, nãngu ; nâl.*	*nâl, naṅgu.*	*nâlugu ; nalu, nala, nal.*	*nâlu, nâlku ; nâl.*	*nâlu ; nâl.*
Five	*eindu, añju ; ei.*	*añju ; ei.*	*eidu, ênu ; ê.*	*eidu ; ei.*	*einu ; ei.*
Six	*âru ; aru.*	*âru ; aru.*	*âru ; aru.*	*âru ; ara.*	*âji ; âj, aji.*
Seven	*êṛu ; eṛu.*	*êṛu ; eṛu.*	*êḍu ; êḷ, ḍe.*	*êḷu ; e.*	*êḷu ; êḷ.*
Eight	*eṭṭu ; eṇ.*	*eṭṭu ; eṇ.*	*enimidi, enmidi ; ena.*	*eṇṭu ; eṇ.*	*eṇma ; eṇ.*
Nine	*onbadu, onbân, toṇḍu ; onbattu, toḷ.*	*ombadu ; toḷ.*	*tommidi ; tommaṇḍu, tomma.*	*ombhattu ; ombhayi, tom.*	*ormba ; soṇ.*
Ten	*pattu ; pân, padu, padin, pan.*	*pattu ; padin, (pand').*	*padi ; pada, pan, pei, bhei, vei.*	*pattu, hattu ; bhattu, vattu, padin, padi, pan.*	*pattu ; pâd', padu, padun, vat, pa, va.*
Hundred	*nûru.*	*nûru.*	*nûru.*	*nûru.*	*nûdu.*

PART V.

THE PRONOUN.

Much light is thrown by the pronouns on the relationship of languages and families of languages; for the personal pronouns, and especially those of the first and second person singular, evince more of the quality of permanence than any other parts of speech, and are generally found to change but little in the lapse of ages. They are more permanent even than the numerals, the signs of case, and the verbal inflexions; and though, like everything else, they are liable to change, yet their connections and ramifications may be traced amongst nearly all the languages of mankind, how widely soever sundered by time or place. In some instances the personal pronouns constitute the only appreciable point of contact or feature of relationship between languages which appear to have belonged originally to one and the same family, but which, in the lapse of time and through the progress of mutation, have become generically different. This remark especially applies to the pronouns of the first person, which of all parts of speech appears to be the most persistent. A remarkable peculiarity of the Japanese is the absence of personal pronouns, properly so called. Usage alone determines which of the three persons is denoted; as in English, it is usage that determines that 'your servant' means I, and 'your honour,' you.

SECTION I.—PERSONAL PRONOUNS.

1. Pronoun of the First Person Singular.

Comparison of Dialects.—Our first inquiry must be, what appears to have been the primitive form of this pronoun in the Dravidian languages? A comparison of the forms it assumes in the different dialects may be expected to throw much light on this question. It will be well to exhibit the facts of the case first, with only such explanations as seem to be necessary, reserving to the end the consideration of the inferences which the facts appear to establish.

I must here remind the reader of what I have said in the Introduction respecting the relation subsisting between the classical and colloquial dialects of the principal Dravidian languages. There is a presumption in favour of the antiquity of words and forms found in the literature of those languages, especially when found in the grammars and vocabularies, which are at least seven or eight hundred years old, and are regarded as works of authority; but on the whole it is safer to regard those words and forms, not as necessarily more ancient, but only as probably more ancient, and certainly more classical. In citing those dialects, therefore, I shall cite them, not, as has generally been done, under the names of the ancient and the modern dialects, but as the classical and the colloquial.

It will be seen that in all cases I compare, not only the nominatives of the personal pronouns found in the various dialects, but also the inflexional bases of the oblique cases and the pronominal terminations of the verbs. The base of the oblique cases of the pronoun of the first person in the Indo-European languages seems altogether unconnected with the base of the nominative. In the Dravidian languages it is evident that the nominative and the inflexions of this and of all pronouns are substantially the same. Differences, it is true, are apparent, but they are comparatively insignificant, and are generally capable of being explained. Where the inflexion differs from the nominative, but agrees with the verbal endings, we may reasonably suppose the inflexion a better representative than the nominative of the oldest shape of the pronoun. In most of the dialects, the included vowel of each of the personal pronouns is long in the nominative, short in the inflexion. In such cases, the inflexion might be supposed to be an abbreviation of the nominative, made for the purpose of enabling the base to bear the weight of the case-signs. On the other hand, as in the Dravidian languages the nominative of the personal pronouns is only used when it is emphatic, the lengthening of the included vowel of the nominative may be regarded merely as a result of emphasis. On the whole, the latter supposition seems preferable. (Compare the lengthening of the vowel of several of the numerals, when used not as adjectives, but as substantives.) It seems desirable also to compare the plural forms of this pronoun with the singular. The mode in which the personal pronouns are pluralised will be explained under a separate head; but the plural forms themselves will be cited here, for the sake of the light they may be expected to throw on the initial consonant and included vowel of the singular. In all cases it will be found that the ultimate base of the singular and that of the plural are identical.

Unlike the Indo-European tongues, as best represented by the Vedic

Sanskrit, in which the plural of the first person has the force of 'I and they,' and that of the second person 'thou and they,' the plurals of the Dravidian languages seem to be simply the singulars with the addition of suffixes denoting plurality. The reader is requested to remember (see note on Transliteration, preceding Sounds) that in most of the Dravidian dialects *y* has come to be pronounced before initial *e*—*e.g.*, in Tamil, *en*, my, is pronounced *yen*. This *y* (and the corresponding *v* or *w* before *o*) has frequently made its appearance in the transliteration into the Roman character of words commencing with *e*, and sometimes even in cases where a comparison of dialects was the object in view. No notice will be taken of this euphonic *y* of pronunciation in the following analysis. I cite each word as it is written by the best classical writers, believing that the written form of the word best represents the manner in which it was actually pronounced when the language was first committed to writing. If *y* appears anywhere in this analysis, it is because in that instance *y* has a place in the written language, and appears to be radical.

In colloquial Tamil the nominative of the pronoun of the first person singular is *nân*: in classical Tamil it is *yân* or *nân*, more commonly the former. The "Nannûl," the most authoritative grammar of this dialect (the date of which cannot, I think, be later than the eleventh century), gives both forms, *yân* or *nân*, but always places *yân* first. This proves nothing, I think, respecting the relative antiquity of the two forms; it only proves that *yân* was regarded by the author of the "Nannûl," as it is still regarded, as more elegant than *nân*. The inflexion of this pronoun in both dialects is *en*. It is here apparent, and will be seen in all the other dialects also, that the included vowel vibrates between *a* and *e*. The personal terminations of the verbs are *ên* in the colloquial; and *en* and *ên*, and occasionally *an*, in the classical dialect. (I omit all consideration of those forms of the Tamil verb which, though regarded by native grammarians as belonging to the first person singular and plural, are in reality impersonal.) The corresponding plurals are—nom. colloquial, *nâm*, *nâṅgaḷ*; classical, *yâm* or *nâm*: inflexion, coll. *nam*, *eṅgaḷ*; class. *em*, *nam*. The nom. *yâm* is more common in the classics than *nâm*; but in the inflected forms *nam* is regarded as nearly, if not quite, as elegant as *em*—*e.g.*, *namar* = *emar*, our party, *nostrates*. In the classical compound *elâm*, all we, corresponding to *elîr*, all you, the plural nom. is *âm*. Personal terminations of the verb—coll. *ôm*; class. *em*, *êm*, *am*, *âm*, *ôm*.

At first sight we might suppose *nam* and *nem* to be the pronominal terminations of the class. Tam. *naḍandanam*, *naḍandanem*, we walked, and of many similar verbs and conjugated nouns—nouns with which a pronoun is combined (see "Classification of Dravidian Verbs," "Appellative Verbs or Conjugated Nouns"); but the *n* of these terminations is merely euphonic, and is used to prevent hiatus. When it is omitted, the vowels which it had kept separate coalesce—*e.g.*, *naḍanda-am* becomes *naḍandâm; naḍanda-em, naḍandêm.* The termination *ôm* is the only one now used in the colloquial dialect. This could not well have been derived from *êm*, but would spring naturally enough from *âm*. Of this we have an illustration in the fact that *âm*, contracted from *âgum*, or *â-um*, it is so, yes, is sometimes written, as well as pronounced, *ôm*. Moreover, whilst many instances of the change of *a* into *e* or *ei*, and also *o*, can be adduced, I do not know any of the converse of this.

In Malayâḷam the nominative is *ñân* (the initial *ñ* of which is the nasal of the palatals, pronounced like *ni* in onion). The inflexion is ordinarily *en*, as in Tamil; but in the dative *inikk'* is often used, as well as the more regular *enakk'* and *enikk'*. *en* is here altered to *in*, a form which I do not find in any of the other cultivated Dravidian dialects. The verb in ordinary Malayâḷam is destitute of personal terminations; but in the poetry an inflected form is frequently used, in which the termination representing this pronoun is *ên*, as in Tamil. In conjugated nouns the personal termination, as *an* or *ên*—*e.g.*, *aḍiyan* or *aḍiyen*, I (thy) servant; plural nom. *nâm*, *nôm*, *nammaḷ*, *ñaṅṅaḷ*, *nummaḷ*; inflex. *ñaṅṅaḷ*, *eṅṅaḷ*, *em*, and also *nô*, *nôm*, *nom*, *num*. Personal terminations of verb (in the poets), *ôm*. The shortness of the included vowel of *ñaṅṅaḷ*, and the ordinary use of this form, rather than of *eṅṅaḷ*, as the inflexion, are noticeable peculiarities in the Malayâḷam plural. Another peculiarity is the occasional use of *nôm* instead of *nâm*, answering to the *ôm* which forms the personal termination of the verb in poetical Malayâḷam and colloquial Tamil.

In colloquial Canarese the nominative of this pronoun is *nânu*, nearly as in Tamil, the inflected form of which, as seen in all the oblique cases, is *nan'*. The crude form of this pronoun *nâ* is also used as a nominative. This is a peculiarity of Canarese and Telugu; but the use of *nî*, the crude form of the pronoun of the second person, instead of *nînu*, has its counterpart in Tamil, in which *nî* is the only form of the nominative known. In the classical dialect, or what is commonly called "Old Canarese," the nominative is *ân*, *yân*, or *âm*; the inflexion, *en*, is identical with that of the Tamil in both its dialects. The pronominal terminations of the first person singular of the verb are *enu*, *ênu*, and *ẹne* in the colloquial dialect, and *en* in the classical. It is deserving of notice that the final *u* or *nu* of the personal terminations, as of the isolated pronouns, is frequently dropped in the colloquial dialect. The personal termination of this person of the verb, when *nu* is dropped, becomes *e*, with which the Tuḷu termination may be compared. Plurals: nominative, coll. dial. *nâvu;* class. dial. *âm, âvu;* inflexion, coll. *nam;* class. *em.* Personal terminations of verb: coll. *evu, êvu,* and *êve;* class. *evu.* *evu* is as clearly a softened form of *em* as *âvu* of *âm.*

In colloquial Telugu the nominative of this pronoun is *nênu:* the crude *nê* may also be used, like *nâ* in Canarese. In the classical dialect, *ênu* is preferred, and this is sometimes represented by *ê* alone. *nênu* takes *nâ* for its inflexion in all cases except the accusative (*nanu* or *nannu*), in which it is *nan'*, as in colloquial Canarese. It appears from this that the vowel of the pronominal base librates between *a* and *e*, but that *e* is probably to be regarded as the more ancient, as well as the more elegant form, in so far as Telugu usage is concerned. The verbal inflexions of the Telugu retain only the final syllable of the nominative of each of the pronouns—viz., *nu* or *ni* after *i* (from *nênu,* I); *vu* or *vi* after *i* (from *nîvu,* thou); and *ṅḍu* (from *vâṅḍu,* he). Plurals: nominative, coll. *mêmu, manamu;* class. *êmu;* inflexions, *mâ, mam, mana;* personal termination of verbs, *mu,* or *mi* after *i.* The most essential part of the personal pronouns has been dropped, we see, in the verbal inflexions of the Telugu, the fragments which have been retained being probably merely formatives, or at most signs of number and gender. Of the same character is the *ru,* or *ri* after *i,* which forms the personal termination of the second person plural and the third person epicene plural. It represents merely the *ar* by which epicene nouns are pluralised.

The Tuḷu nominative is *yân';* inflexion, *yen'.* This is the only instance in any of these dialects in which *y,* the initial letter of the nominative, appears in the inflexion in writing. In classical Canarese and Tamil the inflexion is written *en,* though pronounced *yen.* The personal termination of the verb is *e* (compare the colloquial Canarese verbal termination *e,* and the classical Telugu nominative *ê*). This *e,* Mr Brigel informs us, is pronounced nearly like *a* in man; whilst the *e* which forms the termination of the third person masculine of the verb is pronounced pure. Plurals: nominative, *nama, yenkaḷu;* inflexion, *nam', yenkuḷ'.* The included vowel of *nama* is short in the nominative, as well as the inflexion. The only instance of this in the other dialects is *nammaḷ,* one of the Malayâḷam nominatives, and its related *ñaṅṅaḷ.* Personal termination of the verb, *a.* The personal terminations of the first person plural and the third person neuter plural (both *a*) are alike, which is a remarkable peculiarity of this dialect.

The Tuda nominative is *ân* (*â* is pronounced in Tuda like the English *aw*); inflexion, *en;* personal termination of verb, *en, eni, ini;* plural nom. *âm* or *ôm*, also *êm;* inflex. *em* (the nominative *âm* is also used, according to Dr Pope, like an inflexion). Mr Metz writes this not *âm*, but *am*, which is more in accordance with analogy. Personal terminations, *emi, imi.* In the dialect of the Kotas, according to Mr Metz, the nominative singular is *âne;* inflexion, *en;* plural nom. *âme, ême*, and also *nâme;* inflex. *em, nam;* personal terminations, singular, *e*, as in Tuḷu; plural, *ême* and *eme.*

In Gônd the nominative is *annâ;* inflexion, *nâ;* plural, *ammâṭ;* inflexion, *mâ.* Personal terminations of the verb: singular, *ân* or *na;* plural, *âm, am*, or *ôm.* In the Ku or Khond the nominative singular is *ânu*, as in classical Canarese; inflexion, *nâ*, as in Telugu and Gônd (Dr Hunter's lists, *ânu;* inflex. *nânde*); plural nom. *âmu;* inflex. *mâ;* also *âju;* inflex. *ammâ.* Personal terminations of verb: singular, *in* or *iñ* (*mâin*, I am), or *e* (*mâsse*, I was); plural, *âmu.*

In the Brahui the nominative is *î;* but in the oblique cases (*e.g.*, *kanâ*, of me; *kane*, me, to me) the pronominal base is *ka* or *kan*, a root which seems to be totally unconnected with the Dravidian *nân* or *yân*, and which is to be compared rather with the Cuneiform-Scythian, Babylonian, and Gujarâthi *ku, hu*, &c. The plural of the first person, *nan*, is on the whole in accordance with the Dravidian pronoun. The verbal inflexion of the plural is *en*—*e.g.*, *aren*, we are.

In the Rajmahâl dialect, I is *en;* mine, *ongki;* we, *nam, om;* our, *emki, nâm-ki.* Ûrâon, I, *enan;* mine, *enghi;* we, *em* (Dr Hunter, *en*); our, *emhi.*

We have now to determine, if possible, from a consideration of the facts elicited by this comparison, what was the primitive form of the Dravidian pronoun of the first person. In the first edition, I said, "The weight of evidence seemed to be in favour of our regarding *nân*, the Tamil nominative, as the best existing representative of the old Dravidian nominative of this pronoun, and *nâ*, the crude form of the Canarese, as the primitive unmodified root." In coming to this conclusion, I was much influenced by the extra-Dravidian relationships of this pronoun, which, as will be seen hereafter, are strongly in favour of *nân*, as against *yân.* Viewing the question, however, from a purely Dravidian point of view, the conclusion I arrived at did not seem to me quite satisfactory; and the passage cited above had hardly been printed ere I wished I had decided in favour of *yân.* I did not suppose, however, that when we arrived at *nân* (or *yân*), the earliest organic development of this pronoun, we had reached a point in its history beyond which we could not go; for it seemed to me, and still seems, probable that the final *n* is only a formative, denoting the singular number, and that the initial *n* (corresponding as it does with the initial *n* of the pronoun of the second person) is another formative, denoting in some way personality; whilst it is by means of the included vowels (*a* and *i*) alone that the pronoun of the first person is to be differentiated from that of the second. In consequence of this, I thought I could recognise in those included vowels (*a* and *i*) the very earliest shape of the Dravidian pronoun.

Dr Gundert considers *yân* as probably older than *nân*. This is also Dr Pope's view, though in his "Outlines of Tuda Grammar," p. 5, he says, very truly, I think, "The original form of the Dravidian pronoun of the first person is uncertain." The late Mr Gover, in a paper on the "Dravidian Pronoun," of which he was so kind as to send me a privately printed copy, advocated *yân* as against *nân*, but further on rejected the *y* also, as probably not primitive, and adopted *ân* or *ên* as the real base. It was necessary to his theory to regard the final *n* as primitive, being derived, as he supposed, from the *m* of the Aryan *ma* (changed first, he thought, to *na*, and then to *an*). Dr Pope seems to concur in Mr Gover's view of both of the initial letters and of the final *n* (though for a different reason), when he says in his "Outlines," p. 5, "I would compare *ân* with the very ancient Sanskrit *aham*." I conclude that both Dr Pope and Mr Gover may be cited, not only in favour of *yân*, as against *nân*, but also in favour of *ân*, as against *yân*.

This latter point may be considered first. Which is to be regarded as the older form, *yân* or *ân*? A change of *yân* into *ân* seems to me much easier and more natural than a change of *ân* into *yân*. But in this instance we are not left to mere abstract probabilities; parallel cases can be adduced, and that from the list of pronouns and pronominals. The Tamil *âr*, who? epicene plural, has undoubtedly been softened from *yâr*, and that from *yâvar*; and this is quite certain, because both the changed form and the unchanged are still in daily use; the only difference is, that the older form is considered more elegant. We have another instance in *âṇḍu*, Tam. a year, which is properly *yâṇḍu*, when? a year, from the same interrogative base *ya*. *yâṇḍu* is the form of this word invariably used in inscriptions of any antiquity. The ease with which *ya* would change into *a* may be concluded also from the ease with which it has changed into *e*, an instance of which we have in the change of the interrogative pronoun already cited, *yâvar*, not only into *yâr* and *âr*, but also into *evar*. It is evident from these facts that *y* is a particularly changeable letter, and therefore that *ân* may safely be regarded as a softened form of *yân*.

The next point to be considered is, what is the relationship of *yân* to *nân*? I refer here to the initial consonant alone, not to the difference between the Tamil *nân*, *yân*, and the Telugu *nênu*, *ênu*. That difference consists in the included vowel, and will be considered afterwards. As I have already said, it appears to me now that *yân* is probably older than *nân*, but *nân* also I consider as of great antiquity. It is quite clear that there is a tendency in the Dravidian dialects, especially in Tamil and Malayâḷam, to convert *y* into *n*. Several words which begin with *n* or *ñ* in Tamil begin with a vowel in other dialects. Comp. Tam. *nîndu*, to swim, with Tel. *îdu;* Tam. and Mal. *naṇḍu* or *ñandu*, a crab, with the Tel., Can., and Tuḷu *eṇḍi*, *eṇtri*, *yandri*. In these cases, however, it cannot be determined with certainty whether the initial *n* of the Tamil may not have been radical. Clearer evidence might perhaps appear to be furnished by the relative participles of the preterite Tamil verb, which may take either *y* or *n*—*e.g.*, *śolliya* or *śonna* (for *śollina*), that said; with respect to which it might be concluded that *y*, being considered more elegant, is also more ancient. This, however, seems to me doubtful, seeing that the use of *n*, as in this case, to prevent hiatus, is capable of being traced back to a very early period in the history of the language. The only instances of the change of *y* into *n* that are quite reliable are those that are seen in Sanskrit *tadbhavas*. The Sanskrit *yuga*, a yoke, is ordinarily in Tamil *nugam*, sometimes *ugam*. The Sanskrit *Yama*, the god of death, though ordinarily *yaman*, is also found, especially in the poetry, as *ñaman*, *naman*, and *eman*.* Here we have indubitable instances of the changeableness of *y*. It is evidently liable both to be hardened into *n*, and also to be softened away into a vowel. We see therefore the possibility of a primitive Dravidian *yân* changing on the one hand into *nân*, and also on the other into *ân* or *ên*. What seems to raise the possibility in this case into a probability is the circumstance that the *en*, which forms the only inflexion of this pronoun in the classical dialects of Tamil and Canarese, could much more easily be weakened from *yân* than from *nân*. This is partly in consequence of *y* being more easily softened away than *n;* partly in consequence of the peculiar tendency in the Dravidian languages to pronounce *y* before *e*, so that *en* would naturally be pronounced *yen*, and would therefore naturally connect itself with *yân*. It is curious also that *yâ* seems to have a special tendency of

* Dr Pope points out that the English 'anchor' has become in Tamil *naṅgkuram* or *naṅgkûram*.

its own to change into *e*, as we have seen in the case of the interrogatives—*yâvar*, Tam. who? which becomes *evar; yâṅgu*, where? which becomes *eṅgu*. The change of *ya* (short) into *e* in Tamil may also be illustrated from Sanskrit *tadbhavas*. *yantra*, a machine, becomes *endiram; yajamâna*, a sacrificer, a master, *eśamân*. There is an ulterior tendency in Tamil to change *a* into *e*, which will be illustrated further on, in considering the included vowel of this pronoun. The change of *yân* into *nân* would be facilitated if we should take the Malayâḷam *ñân*, as I think we fairly may, as the middle point. If *y* were usually pronounced with a slightly nasal sound, it would naturally become *ñ;* and this would naturally harden in some instances into the *n* of the dental series, possibly even into *ṅ* and *m*.

We have seen in the course of our comparison of the different Dravidian dialects that the initial *n* or *ñ* of *nân, nênu, ñân*, has entirely disappeared in the verbal inflexions. The final *n*, whatever its origin, has shown itself more persistent; though it also, as we shall see, sometimes disappears; but in none of the dialects has the initial *n* or *ñ*, or any relic of it, been retained in the personal terminations of the verb. I think it unsafe, however, to conclude from this, or from any of the facts mentioned, that the initial *n* of *nân* is of modern origin. *nân* may have been altered from *yân*, as I think it was, and yet the alteration may have taken place at so early a period, and both forms may have continued so generally in use, that the question to be considered is not so much, which is ancient, and which is modern? as, which is to be regarded as the best representation of the primitive form of the word? It would not be correct to say that the initial *n* is not contained in any of the old forms, or that it has disappeared from every ancient dialect. *nân* is represented, as we have seen, as alternating with *yân* in the most authoritative grammar of the classical Tamil; and whilst the singular inflexion is always *en*, the plural may be either *em* or *nam*. *nam* is found in Tamil compounds of high antiquity, like *nambi* (comp. *embi*), lord, literally, our lord. *nâ* or *nan* is the inflexion of the singular in Telugu, colloquial Canarese, Ku, and Gônd. In Malayâḷam *ñân* is the most common form of the nominative, though *yân* also is known, and the *ñ* of *ñan* is lost in the inflexion. In Tuḷu the plural is *nama*. The Telugu plural *mêmu* has plainly been derived from *nêmu*. These deep-seated traces of the use at one time of a nominative in *nân*, contemporaneously with one in *yân*, in the dialects of people so long and so widely separated from one another as the Ku and the Tamil, the Gônd and the Malayâḷam, seem to carry us back to an antiquity far greater than that of any of the so-called ancient dialects. The classical compositions commonly called ancient carry us back not much more than a thousand years; but we must go back perhaps three times that period before we reach the time when the ancestors of the existing Tamilians lived side by side in the plains of Northern India with the ancestors of the existing Gônds. At that time, whenever it was, *nân* may be concluded to have been in use as well as *yân;* but even then *nân* appears to have been a secondary form; *yân*, the more characteristic and authoritative. An excellent illustration of the admissibility of this hypothesis may be derived from Sanskrit. It is commonly asserted, and may perhaps be admitted to be a fact, that the Vedic *asme*, we, is older than *vayam*, the corresponding word in use in the later literature. The use of *asmê* in the Vedas is one argument for its antiquity; another and still better is its appearance in Greek in the shape of ἄμμες. But we must not too hastily assume that, because *vayam* appears in the later Sanskrit literature, whilst *asmê* is found in the earliest, *vayam* is therefore a modern corruption; for we find (*va* or *vê*) the base of this form not only in the Zend *vaêm*, but also in the Gothic *veis* (English, *we*); and this carries us back to the period—a period of unknown antiquity—when the Teutonic tribes had not yet left their early seats in the East. The reappearance in the plural, in the Pâli-Prâkrit *tumhê*, you, of the *tu* out of which the *yu* of *yushme* and *yûyam* was corrupted, after it had wholly disappeared from every other form of Aryan speech, is another case in point, as tending to prove that an old form may be retained in existence, and, to a certain extent, in use, long after another form has supplanted it in popular favour. The antiquity of one form is evidently therefore no valid argument against the antiquity of another.

In a discussion of this kind, it should not be forgotten that the pronouns of the first and second person in all the Dravidian dialects are evidently formed on the same plan. They have been exposed to the same influences, and have changed in nearly the same degree. Dr Pope ("Outlines of Tuda Grammar"), who considers the initial *n* of *nân*, I, a late addition, thinks the initial *n* of *nîn* (or *nî*), thou, undoubtedly radical. If, then, *n* is to be regarded as undoubtedly radical in *nî*, though it disappears in most of the inflexions, and in the personal terminations of all the verbs, and though even the nominative becomes *î* in Tuḷu and *îvu* in poetical Telugu, may we not conclude that the initial *n* of *nân*, I, though not radical (I have never claimed for it that distinction), carries us back to a period in the history of the language beyond which we can do little more than guess our way?

What was the included vowel of the primitive Dravidian pronoun? We have only to choose, I think, between *a* and *e*. *ô* is found in the plural in some connections in Tamil and Malayâḷam, but it is derived, as I think I have shown, from the *â* of *âm*. The *i* which makes its appearance in a solitary instance in Malayâḷam is quite exceptional, and seems to be the result of attraction. *en*, which occupies so important a place in almost all the dialects, both in the inflexion and in the verbal terminations, seems to point to a nominative in *ên*, the best representative of which is the classical Telugu *ênu*. On the other hand, in the greater number of the dialects, including both the cultivated dialects in Southern India and the uncultivated dialects in the hills in Northern India, the nominative is *nân* or *ân*. *a*, I think, is to be preferred, on account of the existence of a tendency in almost all languages, and particularly in the Dravidian, to weaken *a* into *e*, whilst I cannot discover any distinct trace of the existence of the contrary tendency. The tendency of the Tamil to weaken *a* into *e* may best be illustrated by Sanskrit derivatives, inasmuch as in these cases we know which vowel was the original and which was the corruption. Some have been quoted already, as showing the tendency of *ya* in particular to change into *e*; but the following examples, in connection with other consonants, may be added—*e.g.*, *japa*, Sans. prayer, Tam. *śebam*; *bala*, Sans. strength, Tam. *belam*. This tendency shows itself in the pronunciation of many Sanskrit words used in Tamil in which the vowel remains unaltered in writing. I should add that Dr Gundert appears to consider not *ya*, but *ye*, euphonised to *yê*, the primitive form of this pronoun. He admits, however, that *e* is only another form of *a*.

What is the origin of the final *n* of *yân*, *nân*, &c.? Whatever be its origin, it seems to me certain that it is not radical. It is more persistent than the initial *n*, but in the plural it is uniformly rejected, and *m* (probably from the copulative *um*), the sign of plurality distinctive of the personal pronouns, used instead. This sign of plurality is not added to *n*, as it would have been if *n* had been regarded as a part of the root, or even as a help to the expression of the idea of personality, but substituted for it. If we compare *nân*, I, with *nâm*, we, *nîn*, thou, with *nîm*, you, *tân*, self, with *tâm*, selves, it is evident that the final *n* is a sign of the singular number, and the final *m* a sign of the plural. The pronominal base is evidently the same in both numbers; and the certainty of this is not affected by any question that may arise as to the shape of the oldest form of the pronominal base. If we regard *yân* as more primitive than *nân*, the conclusion we come to must be the same, the plural of *yân* being *yâm*. This appears to prove that *nâ* (or *yâ*) denotes either I or we, according to the singularity or plurality of the suffixed particle (*nâ* + *n* = I alone;

nâ + *m* = I's (egoque) we); and that the final *n* of *nân*, no less than the final *m* of *nâm*, is a sign, not of personality, but merely of number.

Is the final *n* of *nân* a sign of gender as well as of number? Is it a sign of the masculine singular, and connected with *an* or *n*, the ordinary masculine singular suffix of the Tamil? The pronouns of the first and second persons are naturally epicene, but it is not unusual in the Indo-European languages to find them assuming the grammatical forms of the masculine. Thus in Sanskrit the terminations of the oblique cases of the pronouns of the first and second persons, are those which are characteristic of the masculine gender. I am not inclined, however, to adopt this explanation of the origin of the final *n* of the Dravidian personal pronouns. I am not satisfied, either, with the supposition that this final *n* is merely euphonic, like the final nasal of the Tatar *man̄*, I. The explanation which appears to me to suit the facts of the case best is, that this *n* is identical with the *an*, alternating with *am*, which is so largely used, especially in Tamil and Malayâḷam, as a formative of neuter singular nouns—*e.g.*, *ur-an*, Tam. strength = *ur-am*. It would thus accord in use (possibly in part even in origin) with the final *am* of the nominative of the Sanskrit personal pronouns, *ah-am*, I, *tv-am*, thou, *svay-am* (*sva-m*), self (compare Greek ἐγών), which is evidently a formative, and identical with one of the most common nominative and accusative singular neuter case-signs. (See "The Noun: the Nominative.") Compare the optional use of *m* instead of *n*, as the final consonant of the pronoun of the first person in classical Canarese—*e.g.*, *âm*, I, instead of *ân*. So also the same dialect has *avam* for he, instead of *avan*.

am, the formative of the nominative of the Sanskrit pronouns, is used not only by the singulars, but, in later Sanskrit at least, by the plurals—*e.g.*, *vayam*, we, *yûyam*, you; but properly these plurals are to be regarded as abstract neuter singulars in form, though plurals in signification. The Dravidian formative *am* or *an* is exclusively singular.

Whatever be the origin of the final *n* in question, it must have had a place in the personal and reflexive pronouns from a very early period, for we find it in the Brahui *ten*, self (compare Dravidian *tân*), and in the Ostiak *nyn*, thou (compare Dravidian *nîn*). This throws light on the probability of the supposition I advanced with regard to the initial *n* of *nân*—viz., that though *nân* was apparently derived from *yân*, the date of its origin might be far earlier than that of any portion of the literature which is written in what are sometimes called the ancient dialects.

If, as we have seen, *nâ* or *yâ* is to be regarded as the primitive form of the Dravidian pronoun of the first person, and the final *n* as merely a sign of number, it might appear extraordinary that in the pronominal terminations of the verb the initial *n* (or *y*) should have invariably and altogether disappeared, whilst the first person singular should be represented, either by the final *n* alone, or by the fragmentary vowel *e* alone. Similar anomalies, however, are discoverable in other languages. In Hebrew, *anachnu*, we, from *anach* (in actual use *anôkî*), I, with the addition of *nu*, a sign of plurality, is the full form of the plural of the pronoun of the first person; yet in the verbal terminations *anachnu* is represented solely by *nu*, the final fragment, which originally was only a suffix of number. But we need not go beyond the range of the Dravidian languages themselves for an illustration. We are furnished with a perfectly parallel case by the Telugu. The pronoun of the second person singular in Telugu is *nîvu*, thou, from *nî*, the radical base, and *vu*, an euphonic addition. This *vu* is of so little importance to the expression of the idea of personality, that it totally disappears in all the oblique cases. Nevertheless, it forms the regular termination of the second person singular of the Telugu verb, and it has acquired this use precisely like the *n* which forms the ordinary termination of the first person singular of the Dravidian verb, simply from the accident of position, seeing that it is not even a sign of number, like the *n* of the first person, much less of personality, but is merely an euphonisation.

Supposing *nâ*, *yâ*, or *â*, to be the primitive form of the Dravidian pronoun of the first person, and *nî*, *yî*, or *î* (as we shall presently find it to be) the corresponding form of the pronoun of the second person, it seems evident that the only essential difference between the two consists in the difference between the two vowels *a* and *î*. We seem to be able also to trace back these pronouns historically to the same two vowels. The initial consonant, whatever be the consonant used, seems to be the common property of both pronouns and the means by which their personality is expressed, whilst the annexed *a* restricts the signification to the first person, or that of the speaker; *i*, to the second person, or that of the person addressed. Some resemblance to this arrangement may be noticed in the personal pronouns of the Hebrew, in which I is *an-ôkî;* thou, *an-tâ* (corrupted into *at-tâ*). The method adopted by the Dravidian languages of expressing the difference between the first person and the second by means of the vowels *a* and *i*, does not appear to be the result of accident. It is probably founded on some ultimate principle, though it may be difficult or impossible now to discover what that principle is. If the pronominal bases, *a* and *i*, be considered as identical with *a* and *i*, the demonstrative bases, an idea which would suit the signification, and which is corroborated by the circumstance that *u*, the next vowel in order, is also a demonstrative, we are met by the apparently insurmountable difficulty that in all the Dravidian tongues, and (as far as the use of these demonstrative vowels extends) in all the tongues of the Indo-European family also, *a* is not the proximate, but the remote, demonstrative; and *i* is not the remote, but the proximate; whilst *u* is used in Tamil as an intermediate between these two. If this supposition had been well grounded, we should have expected to find *î* mean I, and *â*, thou. But what we actually find is that *â* means I, and *î*, thou. In Tamil, *avviḍam*, literally that place, is occasionally used as a polite periphrasis for you, and *ivviḍam*, literally this place, as a courtly periphrasis for we. So in Malayâḷam, *addêham*, literally that body, is sometimes used for thou, and *iddêham*, literally this body, for I. *aṅgu*, thither, means also, in Malayâḷam, to thee, to you; *iṅgu*, hither, to me, to us. This use of the demonstrative vowels is exactly the reverse of the use to which we find *a* and *i* put in the personal pronouns in all the Dravidian dialects. It seems useless, therefore, to look to the existing demonstrative bases for the origin of the *â* of *nâ*, I, and the *î* of *nî*, thou.

Is any weight to be attributed to the circumstance that *a*, being the easiest and most natural of all vowel sounds, has the first place in all lists of vowels, whilst *i*, being the next easiest vowel sound, stands second? The first vowel sound would thus be taken to represent the first person, whilst the second person would be represented by the second vowel sound. If this theory had anything to support it beyond its plausibility, it would take us very far back indeed into the history of the origin of human speech. It is remarkable, however, that this theory seems to receive confirmation from the Chinese, which exhibits probably the oldest stage of human speech of which any written records survive. According to Mr Edkins, the oldest forms of the first two pronouns in Chinese were *a* and *i*. I may add, that the most peculiar and distinctive, possibly the most ancient, of the Dravidian demonstratives—the demonstrative which denotes in Tamil, Malayâḷam, Canarese, something intermediate between *a* and *i*—was *u*. We thus find the whole of the first three simple vowels utilised, *a* = I; *i* = thou; *u* = he, she, it.

Extra-Dravidian Relationship.—We now enter upon a comparison of *a*, *ya*, or *na*, the Dravidian pronoun of the first person, with the pronouns of the same persons which are contained in other families of tongues, for the purpose of ascertaining its relationship. As *nâ* constitutes the personal element in *nâm*, we, as well as in *nân*, I (and it is the same with *ya* and *a*, the verbal forms), it is evident that our comparison should not be exclusively restricted to the singular, but that we are at liberty to include in the comparison the plurals of this pronoun in the various languages which are compared; for it is not improbable *à priori* that some analogies may have disappeared from the singular which have been retained in the plural. It is also to be remembered that we are not obliged to restrict ourselves to comparing the pronouns of other families of languages with the Dravidian *ya* alone. *ya* may be older than *ña*, *na*, or *a;* yet each of these is old enough for any comparison that can be instituted.

All pronouns of the first person singular that have been used at any time in Asia, Europe, or Northern Africa, whether it be in connection with the Indo-European, the Semitic, or Scythian family of tongues, can more or less distinctly be traced back, I believe, to two roots. Each of those roots has been preserved in Sanskrit, and in the more primitive members of the Indo-European family; one (*ah*) in the nominative, the other, and by far the more widely prevalent one (*ma*), in the oblique cases. In order, therefore, to investigate the affiliation of the Dravidian pronoun of the first person, it will be necessary to extend our inquiries over a wider area than usual.

1. *Semitic Analogies.*—The Semitic pronoun presents some remarkable analogies to the Dravidian. This will appear on comparing the Dravidian *nâ* with the corresponding Hebrew *anî*, with the prefix *an* of the Hebrew *anôkî*, of the Egyptian *anuk*, and of the Babylonian *anaku*, *ânaka*, or *anku*, and especially with the Jewish-Syriac *anâ*, the Christian-Syriac *eno*, and the Æthiopic and Arabic *anâ*. The plural of the Aramaic *anâ* is formed by suffixing *n* (the final consonant of *în* or *ân*): we may therefore compare the Tamil *nâm*, we, with the Aramaic plural *anân*, and also with the Egyptian plural *anen*.

Notwithstanding this remarkable resemblance between the Semitic pronoun and the Dravidian, it is doubtful whether the resemblance is not merely accidental. The Semitic initial syllable *an*, in which the resemblance resides, is not confined to the pronouns of the first person. We find it not only in *ana* (from *anah*, and that again from *anaḥ*), I, but also in the Arabic and Old Hebrew *antâ* and the Aramaic *ant*, thou (Egyptian, *en-tek*, *en-ta*). The prefix being precisely the same in both cases, the pronoun of the second person seems to have as good a claim to it as that of the first. It does not seem, moreover, to be an essential part of either pronoun; for we find a similar prefix in the third person in some of the Semitic dialects—*e.g.*, in the Egyptian *entuf*, he, *entus*, she, and the Chaldaic and Hebrew suffix *enhu*, he. Moreover, the alliance of the Semitic pronouns of the first and second persons with the Indo-European comes out into more distinct relief when this prefix is laid aside. When the initial *an* is removed from the pronoun of the first person, we cannot doubt the connection of the remaining syllable (*oki, ah, aḥ, uk, aku,* or *ak*) with the Sanskrit *ah,* the Gothic *ik,* and the Greek-Latin *eg;* and it is equally evident that when *an* or *en* is rejected from the pronouns of the second person (*antâ, anti, ant, entek, enta*), the *ta, ti, te,* or *t,* which remains, is allied to the Sanskrit and Latin *tu.*

It has sometimes been supposed that this Semitic prefix *an* is simply euphonic—a sort of initial *nunnation* like that which is admitted to exist in the Talmudic *ìnhû,* he, when compared with the ordinary and undoubtedly more ancient Hebrew *hû.* On this supposition, it is allied, in nature and origin, to the euphonic suffixes or *nunnations* which may be observed in the Greek ἐγώ-νη, in the Finnish *mi-nâ,* I, and in the final nasal of the North Indian *maiñ,* I, and *taiñ* or *tuñ,* thou. If this be the origin of the Semitic prefix *an,* it must certainly be unconnected with the Dravidian *nâ* or *anâ.*

Sir H. Rawlinson supposes *an* to be a particle of specification, a sort of definite article; and he also considers it to be identical with *am,* the termination of the Sanskrit personal pronouns *ah-am,* I, *tv-am,* thou, *va-y-am,* we, *yû-y-am,* you. The only difference, he says, is that the particle is prefixed in the one family of languages, and suffixed in the other, with a change of *m* into its equivalent nasal *n.* I have already stated that I regard the Sanskrit termination *am* as the ordinary termination of the nominative of the neuter singular, and as used instead of the masculine and feminine, simply because of the intense personality which is inherent in the first and second personal pronouns, especially in their nominatives, and which renders the terminations distinctive of those genders unnecessary.

I have also stated that I regard it as probable that the terminal *n* of the Dravidian personal pronouns is identical with the formative *an* or *am* of many Dravidian neuter singular nouns, and possible that it is identical also with the Sanskrit nominative-accusative neuter case-sign *am,* which has found its way, as it appears to me, into the nominatives of the Sanskrit pronouns *ah-am,* &c. If the initial *an* of the Semitic languages is allied to the final *am* of the Sanskrit *aham,* then it may possibly be allied also to the final *n* or *an* of the Dravidian pronouns *nâ-n,* I, *nî-n,* thou, *tâ-n,* self. On the whole, however, it appears to me more probable that the resemblance between the Semitic and Dravidian languages on this point, though deserving of notice, is altogether accidental.

2. *Indo-European Analogies.*—It has already been remarked that there appear to be but two pronouns of the first person singular known

to the Indo-European family of tongues, as to the Semitic and Scythian, one of which appears in the nominative of the older Indo-European languages, the other in the oblique cases. The nominative of this pronoun is *ah-am* in Sanskrit, *ad-am* in Old Persian, *az-em* in Zend, *eg-o* in Latin and Greek (*ἐγών = aham*), *ik* in Gothic, *ih* in the Old German, *az* in the Old Slavonic, *asz* in Lithuanian, and *gâ* in Bohemian. We find substantially the same root in the Semitic *âh*, *aḥ*, *uk*, *aku*, *ôkî*, &c., and in several languages of the Malayo-Polynesian group—*e.g.*, Malay *âkû*, Tagala *aco*, Tahitian *au*. Dr Pope, in his "Outlines of Tuda Grammar," p. 5, says, "This is not the place for a full discussion of the subject, but I would compare *ân* with the very ancient Sanskrit *aham*." I regret that I am not acquainted with Dr Pope's reasons for supposing *ân* connected in some way with *aham*. If he had restricted the connection to the final *n* of the one and *am* of the other, on the ground of their being nearly identical in use, and possibly identical in origin, I should be quite prepared, as has already been seen, to agree; but if, as I fancy, he connects *â* also, and therefore *yâ* and *nâ* with *ah* (the earliest shape of which—probably *agh*—seems to have been a decided guttural), in that case I must dissent. The existence of some connection between the Dravidian pronoun and the Indo-European may be suspected, if it be not capable of being clearly proved; but it is between the Dravidian pronoun and the base of the Indo-European oblique cases, not between the Dravidian pronoun and the Indo-European nominative, that the connection, whatever it be, appears to me to subsist. Mr Gover, in his privately printed paper already referred to, stated that he was at first inclined to identify *ân* with *aham*, but on further consideration preferred to connect it with the oblique form *ma*. His mode, however, of doing this (*ma* = *na* = *ana* = *ân*) seems to me needlessly roundabout, besides being vitiated, as I think, by beginning at the wrong end. It is not the final *n* of *ân* (*yân* or *nân*), which is only a sign of the singular number, not an expression of personality, but the initial *n*, which takes also the shape of *y* or gets lost altogether, that is to be compared with the *ma* of the Aryan tongues.

The oblique cases of the pronoun of the first person singular in the Indo-European family are formed from a totally different base from that of the nominative, and of this oblique base perhaps the best representative is the Sanskrit *ma*. *m* forms the most prominent and esential portion of *ma*; and this *m* is followed either by *a* or by some vowel which appears to have been derived from it. In the oblique cases of Sanskrit, this pronoun has the form of *ma*, whenever the nature of the succeeding syllable allows *a* to remain unchanged—*e.g.*, *ma-yi*, in me, *ma-ma*, of me. In the secondary forms of the dative and the genitive it becomes *mâ*. In Zend and Old Persian, *ma* preponderates, whilst compounded and abbreviated vowels appear in the Zend dative-genitives *mê*, *môi*; and a pronominal base in *ama* is found in some of the Old Persian prepositional compounds. In the Greek μέ, ἐμέ, μοί, μοῦ, &c., the vowel which is employed librates between *e* and *o*, each of which is naturally derived from *a*; whilst the initial *e* of ἐμέ is in accordance with the tendency of Greek to prefix a vowel to certain words beginning with a consonant—*e.g.*, ὄνομα for νῶμα. Latin has *me*, except in the dative, which is *mihi*. Gothic has *mi* and *mei* (gen. *meina*). Lithuanian uses *man* as the basis of its oblique cases; though possibly the final *n* of this form belongs properly, like the *n* of Gothic, to the sign of the genitive.

In the pronominal terminations of the verb in the Indo-European languages, the first person singular almost invariably makes use of this oblique pronominal base, in preference to the base of the nominative, with such modifications as euphony may require. The termination of the first person singular is *mi* or *m* in Sanskrit and Zend, in all primary and secondary verbs. We have the same ending in Greek verbs in μι, and in the μαι of the middle voice; in the *m* of the Latin *sum* and *inquam*, in the Lithuanian *mi*, in the Polish *am*, in the Armenian *em*, in the New Persian *am*. It becomes *m* in the old High German *gâm*, I go; *tuom*, I do; and *bim* or *pim* (Sans. *bhavâmi*), I am, converted in modern German to *bin*.

On comparing the pronominal terminations of the Indo-European verb, it is evident that the preponderance of use and authority is in favour of *mi*, and that *m* has been derived from *mi* by abbreviation. It seems equally clear, however, that *mi* itself has been derived from *ma*, the normal base of the oblique cases; for in all languages *a* evinces a tendency to be converted into some weaker vowel, *i*, *e*, or *o*; whereas no instance is adducible of the opposite process. Perhaps the best illustration of the regularity of this change from *ma* to *mi* is that which is furnished by the Esthonian, a Finnish dialect, in which each of the personal pronouns has two forms, the one primitive, the other euphonised—*e.g.*, *ma* or *minna*, I; *sa* or *sinna*, thou.

The question of the relative antiquity of the nominative base *agh* and the inflexional base *ma* does not appear to me to be one of any great importance, both bases, as we have seen, being of immense antiquity. Still, if any considerable difference in age exists, I am inclined to consider *ma* as the older. Children learn to say 'mine' long before they discover the meaning and use of I; and it may have been the same in the childhood of nations. *ma*, the base of mine, may probably claim to be one of the oldest shapes of the pronoun of the first person now discoverable in the world.

We have now to inquire whether any analogy is discoverable between the Dravidian *na*, *ya*, or *a*, and the ultimate Indo-European base *ma*. I do not seek for traces of the *derivation* of the one from the other. The only admissible idea, as it appears to me, is that of *analogy*, or remote relationship. Before proceeding further in the inquiry, it is desirable that we should ascertain what changes the *m* of *ma* sustains in the Indo-European languages themselves. It appears certain that *ma* changes into *na* and *va*, and probable that it changes also into *a*.

(1.) The *m* of *ma* often changes in the Indo-European languages into *n*. The final *m* of the first person of Sanskrit and Latin verbs (the abbreviation and representative of *mi* or *ma*) has in some instances degenerated into *n* in Greek—*e.g.*, compare the Sanskrit *âsam*, I was, and the corresponding Latin *eram*, with the Greek *ἦν*; and *adada-m* with *ἐδι-δω-ν*. We see a similar change of *m* into *n*, on comparing the modern German *bin*, I am, with the old High German *bim* or *pim*; and the Persian *hastam*, I am, with the Beluchi *hastjan*. Compare also the Laghmani *pâkan*, I go.

The *n* which constitutes the initial and radical consonant of the plural of the pronoun of the first person in many of the Indo-European languages is evidently, like the final *n* of the singular terminations referred to above, derived from an older *m*. One of the oldest forms of the plural of this pronoun, if not the very oldest, is that which is employed in the verbal inflexions, and which in Sanskrit is *mas* (Vedic-Sanskrit *masi*), in Latin *mus*, in Greek *μεν* (for the more ancient and more correct Æolic *μες*): the most natural explanation of which pronominal ending is to consider it as derived from *ma*, the old first person singular, by the addition of *s*, the sign of plurality. The *m* of this primeval *mas* often becomes *n*—*e.g.*, in the Latin *nos*, the Celtic *ni*, the Greek *νῶι*; and also in the Sanskrit secondary forms *nas* and *nau*, the Zend *nô*, and the Old Slavonic *na*. This *n* is evidently a weakening of *m*, and represents the personality of the pronoun of the first person, irrespective of the idea of number; which is expressed, I conceive, by the subsequent portion of the word.* It is

* It has been suggested by Sir H. Rawlinson that the Sanskrit *nas*, the Latin *nos*, and the Greek *νῶι* (like the *nu* of the Hebrew *anachnu*), were originally signs of plurality, which have made themselves independent of the bases to which they were attached. I am unable, however, to adopt this view; for the *n* of these forms naturally interchanges with *m*, and evidently conveys the idea of personality; and the *s* of the Latin *nos* (as of the corresponding *vos*) seems more likely to be a sign of plurality than an abbreviation (as Bopp conjectures it to be) of the syllable *sma*.

remarkable that in Welsh, whilst the absolute forms of the personal pronouns I and we, are *mi* and *ni* respectively, in the personal terminations of the verb *m* and *n* are often found to change places, so that the first person singular comes to be represented by *n*, and the corresponding plural by *m*—*e.g.*, *gwelwn*, I saw; *gwelem*, we saw. Something similar has been observed in the Greek ἐδίδουν, compared with the plural of the same, ἐδίδομεν; but the use of *n* in the singular and *m* in the plural, in verbal terminations, is much more systematic in the Welsh and its related dialects than in Greek. The Irish generally differs from those dialects in this particular—*e.g.*, compare Irish *cairim*, I love, with the Welsh *carwn*. Welsh verbs of the first person, ending in *n* in the singular and *m* in the plural, bear a remarkable resemblance to the Tamil singular *ên*, plural *êm* or *ôm*. Mr Gover too hastily, as I think, concluded these forms to be identical; but in Welsh the pronoun is represented by the final consonant, *m* or *n*, both derived from the *m* of the primeval *ma*; whilst in Tamil the final *n* and *m* are merely signs of number, and the personality of the pronoun is represented by the preceding vowel alone. However this may be, it is perfectly clear that *m* evinces, in the Indo-European languages, a tendency to change into *n*, and that this tendency is specially apparent in the changes the pronoun of the first person has undergone. In Old Slavonic, the nominative plural retains the probably primitive *m*, whilst *n* replaces *m* in all the oblique cases of the plural—*e.g.*, nom. *my*, acc. *ny*, dat. *na-mu*, instr. *na-mi*. The dual 'we,' too, has *vê* for its nominative, *na-ma* for its accusative, dative, and instrumental. The genitive and locative plural is *na-su*, dual *na-ju*. Sometimes the *m* changes into *n* in the singular, whilst it remains unchanged in the plural; sometimes it changes in the plural and remains unchanged in the singular. No principle seems to be involved in this diversity, for both changes may be observed in one and the same language. This is especially observable in Welsh, in which the absolute pronouns are *mi*, I, and *ni*, we, whilst in the verbal terminations, I love is *carwn*, we love, *carem*. Compare also the change from *m* in the nominative to *n* in the oblique cases in the Old Slavonian—*e.g.*, *my*, we, *ny*, us. The chief point to which I call attention is the fact that the change from *m* into *n* is one which readily takes place in this family of languages.

(2.) This *m* changes also into *v*. *v* alternates with *n* as the initial and radical consonant of the plural of the first person in several Indo-European languages; and this *v*, I conceive, is merely a softened form of *m*. It was shown in the part on "Sounds" that, in the Dravidian languages, wherever *n* and *v* are found to alternate, we have reason to conclude that both are derived from, or represent, an older *m*; and the rule appears to hold equally good in regard to the Indo-European languages. When we find in Sanskrit the nominative plural *vayam* (from *va* and the neuter formative *am*), we, and at the same time *nas*, which is optionally used for the accusative, genitive, and dative plural of the same pronoun, we cannot avoid coming to the conclusion that both the *na* of *nas* and the *va* of *vayam* are derived from a more primitive *ma*. This idea is confirmed by finding *n* and *v* in exactly the same connections in Zend. Compare the Old Slavonic plural *mes*, we, with the Gothic *veis*, and especially the Old Slavonic dual *ve*, we two, with the accusative of the same, *na*, us two. In the Lithuanian dual, *v* alternates, not with *n*, but with *m*—that is, with what appears to be the more primitive consonant. The nominative-accusative masculine may be either *ve-du* or *mu-du*. In the personal endings of the Old Slavonic verb, *ve* represents the first person dual; in Lithuanian, *va*; whilst the plural proper ends in *mu* in the former language, and *me* in the latter.

(3.) The *m* of the pronoun of the first person disappears sometimes altogether, so that *ma* changes into *a*. This is the only reasonable explanation that has been given of the origin of the Vedic *asmê*, we = ἄμμες. When this is compared with *yushmê*, you = ὕμμες, it is evident that *smê*, whatever its origin, is in use simply a sign of the plural, and that as the *yu* (= *tu*) of *yushmê* represents the singular thou, so the *a* of *asmê* must represent the singular I. This being the case, *a-smê* must be equivalent to *ma-smê*. This seems to be the best explanation also of the *â* of the Sanskrit dual *âvâm*, we two, probably derived, some think, from *ma*, I, and *dva*, two. We find the *a* of the plural *asmê* itself similarly lengthened in the Bengali *nâmi*, modern Bengali *âmi*. (See "Pluralisation of Pronouns.")

The same pronominal root *m* changes also in the Scythian tongues, as will be seen, to *n* and *ng*, and even to *b*; but at present we have to deal exclusively with the changes that take place in the Indo-European tongues.

Can we now infer the existence of any relationship between the Dravidian pronominal base and the Indo-European? Is the Dravidian *ya*, varying to *ñ* or *n*, on the one hand, and *a* on the other, connected in any way with the Indo-European *ma*, varying to *na* on the one hand, and on the other to *va*, and possibly also to *a*? I think we are warranted in inferring the existence of some connection. It is more difficult, as it appears to me, to suppose that these two series of words, belonging to the earliest requirements of human speech, identical in meaning, and so nearly alike in form, were from the beginning independent of one another, than that an ultimate relationship of some kind existed between them. If we were at liberty to compare the Dravidian *na* directly with the Indo-European *ma*, no room for doubt could exist—*ma*, as we have seen, being proved to change into *na*. And even though we are obliged to be suspicious of the credentials of the Dravidian *na*, and to prefer *ya* as probably a better representative of the very oldest form of the word, yet we are not altogether precluded thereby from making the comparison under consideration, the antiquity of *na* being almost as great as that of *ya*, just as the Indo-European *na*, *va*, and *a* must be almost as ancient as *ma*. *ya*, it is true, is not one of the shapes the primeval *ma* is found to have assumed within the circle of the Indo-European tongues; but as *ma* is not confined to that family, but is the common property also of the languages of the Scythian group, in which it will be found to have sustained a set of changes peculiar to them, it does not seem unreasonable to suppose that *ya*, varying to *ña*, may have been the shape it first assumed amongst the early Dravidians.

3. *Scythian Analogies.*—When we examine the personal pronouns of the Scythian group of tongues, some independent and very interesting analogies to the Dravidian pronoun are brought to light.

The pronominal root which constitutes the basis of the oblique cases in the Indo-European languages, is adopted in the languages of the Scythian family, not only in the oblique cases, but also in the nominative itself. Whilst in both families the oblique cases are substantially the same, the Indo-European uses as its nominative the base in *ah*, the Scythian the base in *ma*. There are a few languages even in the Indo-European family in which *ma* has found its way into the nominative—*e.g.*, the Celtic has *mi*, the New Persian *mañ*, the North Indian vernaculars *maiñ*. In some cases, also, especially in the later dialects of this family, the accusative has come to be used instead of the nominative, in violation of ordinary grammatical rules. Thus, the Singhalese *mama*, the Kavi *mami*, and the Cuneiform Persian *mâm*, are probably accusatives in their origin, like the Italian *mi* and the French *moi*. On the other hand, we are met by one, and only one, exceptional case in the Scythian tongues. The Scythian of the Behistun inscriptions makes use of *hu* as its nominative; but in *mi*, the corresponding possessive suffix, the ordinary Scythian base reappears.

(1.) The nominative (as well as the oblique cases) of the first personal pronoun in all existing languages of the Scythian group is derived from a base in *ma*; and it will be shown that this *ma* not unfrequently comes into perfect accordance with the Dravidian pronoun, by changing into *nga* and *na*. In those languages *ma* is very generally euphonised or nasalised by the addition of a final *n*, or of an obscure nasal resembling the Sanskrit *anusvâra;* in consequence of which, not *ma*, but *mañ*, may be stated to be the normal form of the Scythian pronoun, and this bears a closer resemblance than *ma* to the Dravidian *nân*. The addition of this euphonic nasal is not unknown even to the Indo-European languages. It may be seen in the Persian *man*, the Sindhian *mân*, and the Belûchî *menik;* and a similar inorganic addition is apparent in the old Greek ἐγώνη, as also in τύνη. This nasal is much more common, however, and more characteristic in the Scythian tongues. On examining the Turkish family of tongues, we find *men* in Oriental Turkish; *mân* in Turkoman; *mâm* in Khivan; *ben* (*m* degraded to *b*) in Ottoman Turkish. In the Finnish family, the Finnish proper has *minâ;* the Lappish *mon;* the Esthonian *ma* or *minna;* the Mordvin and Votiak *mon;* the Ostiak *ma* (dual *mîn*, plural *men*); the Magyar *ên*. The Samoïede dialects have *man*, *mani*. In both Mongolian and Manchu the nominative of this pronoun is *bi;* but this is evidently corrupted from *mi* (like the Ottoman *ben*, from the Oriental or Uigur *men*); and it is *mi*, with a final nasal, which forms the basis of the oblique cases. In both languages the genitive is *mi-nu* or *mi-ni;* and the dative is *men-dou* in Mongolian, *min-de* in Manchu.

It is evident from the above comparison that the true and essential representative of this pronoun in the Scythian tongues is *ma*. In many of those idioms *ma* still retains its place unchanged, or may optionally be used instead of the later *man*. The Mingrelian has *ma*, the Suanian *mi*, the Lasian *ma*, the Georgian *me*. The Finnish has both *me* or *ma* and *minâ*, and also *mia;* the Ostiak both *min* and *ma*.

It is found also in those languages in which *man* constitutes the isolated pronoun that *m* is used as its equivalent in the personal terminations of the verbs, and generally in all inflexional compounds. We see this usage illustrated in the colloquial languages of Northern India and in Persian. For example, whilst *man* is the nominative of the Persian pronoun, the basis of the oblique cases is not *man*, but *ma* (*e.g.*, *ma-râ*, me, of me); and the pronominal ending of the verb in the first person singular is *m*. In a similar manner, in the Turkish family of languages, *m* is used in composition as the equivalent of *man* or *men*. Thus, in Oriental Turkish, whilst *men* is retained in the present tense—*e.g.*, *bôlâ-men*, I am—the preterite is contented with *m* alone—*e.g.*, *bôldî-m*, I was.

The same suffix is used to denote the first person singular in most of the Scythian possessive compounds, a class of words which is peculiar to the Scythian family—*e.g.*, Turkish *bâbâ-m*, my father, from *bâbâ*, father, and *m*, the representative of the first person singular. In the Magyar also, though the isolated pronoun of the first person singular is *ên*, yet *m* is used instead of *n* in the possessive compounds and "objective" inflexional terminations—*e.g.*, from *atya*, father, is formed the possessive compound *atya-m*, my father; and the first person singular of "objective" verbs ends in *m*—*e.g.*, *szeretem*, I love (some one). It is also to be noticed, that whilst the Magyar has *ên* as the singular of the isolated pronoun, its plural is *mi* or *mink;* the former of which is evidently pluralised from *ma* or *me*, the latter from *min*.

(2.) It was shown that the initial and radical *m* of the Indo-European pronoun was occasionally converted into *n*: we have now to show that a similar change from *m* to *n* is apparent in the Scythian languages also, and that in some of those languages *n* has become as distinctive of the first person as in the Dravidian family itself. In Finnish, though the isolated form of this pronoun is *ma* or *minâ*, yet in all inflexional additions and compounds *m* is represented by *n*—*e.g.*, from *isâ*, father, is formed *isâ-ni*, my father, and from *ôl*, to be, is formed *ôl-en*, I am. This final *n* is not derived from the euphonic *n* of *minâ;* but from a direct conversion of *m* into *n;* for though we see the same euphonic addition of *n* in *sinâ* (from *se* or *sia*), thou, yet we have *t* alone (the equivalent of *s*) in *ôl-et*, thou art. *n* has, therefore, become in Finnish, as in Dravidian, the ordinary sign of the first person singular of the verb; though there is this difference, that in Dravidian the *n* is the final *n*, which is distinctive only of numbers, whereas the Finnish *n* seems to be derived by conversion from an older *m*, the initial *m* of *ma*.

The Magyar *ên*, I, appears to be still more nearly allied to the Dravidian pronoun; and in this case *n* is certainly derived from *m*, for whilst *n* is found in the nominative, *m* is used instead in all possessive compounds and verbal inflexions. With the Magyar nominative *ên*, compare the Tamil-Canarese *ên* or *en*. May we also compare *ân*, I, in the Lar, a Sindhian dialect? A similar form of this pronoun is found in the Mordvin, another idiom of the Finnish or Ugrian family, in which, whilst *mon* is the isolated nominative, *an* is used instead in verbal inflexions—*e.g.*, *paz-an*, I (am) the Lord.

In the Olet or Calmuck dialect of the Mongolian tongue, there are distinct traces of the same change of *ma* into *na;* and in this instance the *n* appears, not as the final, but as the initial, and is therefore in more perfect accordance with the *n* of the Dravidian pronominal base. The nominative of this pronoun in Calmuck is *bi* (from *mi*), and the same base appears in the genitive *mini;* but the rest of the oblique cases are formed, not from *bi* or *mi*, but from *nad* or *na*—*e.g.*, *na-da*, to me, *na-da-edze*, from me, and also *na-maï*, me. We here discover the existence of a pronominal base in *na* (probably derived from *ma*), which is in remarkable agreement with one of the forms of the Dravidian base.

In a few of the Scythian languages, the isolated pronoun, including its nominative, seems to be almost identical with that of the Dravidian family—*e.g.*, *na* in the Quasi Qumuk, a Caucasian dialect; and *ne* in Motor, a dialect of the Samoïede; *na* or *nai* in Corean; *ne* or *ni* in Basque. In the East Asian languages, *gn* or *ng* (which are pronounced alike) are often found to take the place of *n*. Sometimes *n* and *gn* alternate in the same language, like *n* and *ñ* in Tamil-Malayâḷam. The Canton Chinese is *ngo*; the Mandarin, *wo*. Old Chinese forms, according to Mr Edkins, are *nga*, *ga*, *go*, *kan*, *a*. The analogy of the pronoun of the second person would seem to show that *a* was the oldest form of all. Compare Burman, *nâ* or *ngâ*; Tibetan, written *nâ*, colloquial *gnyâ* ('mine,' written *naki*, *nayi*, colloquial *gnay*); Tetenge, an Assam dialect, *ne*; Mikir, *ne*; Khari Naga, *ni*. The Burman *ngâ* prevails in the languages of the sub-Himalayan tribes. A very common form among those tribes, and those of the north-eastern frontier, including also the Kôls of Central India, ends in *ng*—*e.g.*, *ang*, *ung*, *ing*, *aing*. I am not clear, however, as to the nature of the relationship of the latter forms to *ma*, *nga*, and *na*, the High Asian group, with which the Dravidian (and also the Indo-European) pronoun seems to stand in closer connection. I feel, however, on tolerably firm ground in comparing the Tibetan *nâ*, I, colloquial *nga*, with the Malayâḷam *ñâ*; and if so, the Chinese *ngo*, especially when examined in the light of the Chinese *ni*, thou, may also be allowed to claim kindred. We may here, too, compare the Australian pronouns of the first person—viz., *nga*, *nganya*, I; its dual, *ngalee*, we two; and the plurals *ngadlu* and *nadju*, we.

(3.) A few traces of the softening of *na* or *nga* to *ya* and *a*, or at least of the use of *ya* and *a* instead of *nga* and *na*, may also perhaps be discovered in the East Asian languages. Thus the Sgau-Karen is *yâ*, *yâh*; the Pwo-Karen *yer*; the Manyak *â*. The Pekin Chinese *wo* may also be compared.

On the whole, we seem to have reason to conclude that the various forms which the pronoun of the first person singular assumes in the Scythian group of languages, and which we have now compared, are identical. Possibly, also, we may see reason to conclude that the Scythian forms (*ma*, *na*, *ba*, *nga*, *ya*) have had a common origin with the Indo-European (*ma*, *va*, *na*, and *a*). The Dravidian *ya*, *na*, *a*, bear so close a resemblance to the pronouns of both groups (especially, as we have seen, to the Scythian), that we seem to be justified in regarding them as related to both in common. If this be admitted, we seem to be justified in arriving at the conclusion that one and the same pronoun of the first person, probably *ma*, was the common property of the whole Japhetic family prior to the separation of the Indo-European tribes from the Scythian. The conclusion arrived at by Professor Hunfalvy (in his paper on the study of the Turanian languages, read at the International Congress of Orientalists, 1874) is substantially similar. He notices the resemblances between the Aryan and Turanian languages with regard to the personal pronouns, and then says that, "considering this fact, he is inclined to suppose that a stage of language anterior to both classes must have existed." He thinks he sees also in certain single words, as *papa*, *mama*, &c., visible remains of that ancient form of speech.

2. Pronoun of the Second Person Singular.

Comparison of Dialects.—Our first inquiry, as with respect to the pronoun of the first person singular, must be what appears to have been the primitive form of this pronoun.

In Tamil, *nî*, which is properly the crude base, is invariably used as the isolated nominative, instead of *nîn*—the form which would correspond by rule to *nân*, the nominative of the first person singular. That *nîn* originally constituted the nominative even in Tamil, appears from this, that the oblique cases in the higher dialect agree in using *nin* as the base to which the case-suffixes are attached. *un* is occasionally used as the inflexion in the classics, always in the colloquial dialect. Another form which is occasionally used in the classics is *nîy*, in which the final *y* appears to bear the same relation to *n* as the initial *n* of *yân* or *nân* of the first person—that is, it has either been softened from *n*, or is the primitive letter from which *n* was hardened. This final *y* appears also in *ây* and *ôy*, two of the personal terminations of verbs and conjugated nouns. The final *n* of this pronoun, though it is generally lost altogether in the nominative, and is only represented occasionally by *y*, is invariably retained in the inflexional base, in which it is the initial *n* that becomes liable to alteration. When the initial vowel is retained, the included vowel is either *i* or *u* (*nin* or *nun*), generally the former, but when it is discarded, *u* (*un*) is the only vowel in use. The inflexions now described are *nin*, *nun*, *un*. In the personal terminations of the Tamil verb, this pronoun is represented by the suffixes *ây*, *ôy*, *ei*, or *i*; from each of which suffixes the final *n*, as well as the initial, has disappeared. In the poetical dialect of the language, the initial *n* at first sight appears to have retained its place in such forms as *naḍandanei,* thou didst walk, and in the corresponding plural *naḍandanîr*, ye walked; but the *n* of these pronominal terminations (*nei* and *nîr*) is merely euphonic (as in similar terminations of the first person of the verb already mentioned), and is inserted for the purpose of keeping separate the contiguous vowels of *naḍanda-ei* and *naḍanda-îr.*

The root of the verb is regularly used in Tamil as the second person singular of the imperative, without any pronominal suffix, and even without any euphonic addition; but the second person plural of the imperative in the colloquial dialect is formed by the addition of *um*, which is probably identical with the *um* or *m* which constitutes the normal sign of plurality in Dravidian pronouns, and is probably in itself the copulative 'and' or also. (See the pronoun of the first person.) Compare this with the optional addition of *mu* to the root in Telugu to form the imperative singular. Properly *mu* forms an honorific singular, and is therefore to be regarded, like the Tamil *um*, as a plural in original signification. In the higher dialect of Tamil, *ây* and *îr*, the ordinary representatives of these pronouns in the verbal inflexions, are often added to the root to form the singular and plural imperative—*e.g.*, *kêḷây,* hear thou, *kêḷîr*, hear ye. These forms appear at first sight to be identical with *kêḷây̆,* thou hearest not, and *kêḷîr*, ye hear not; but they are not really identical, as Beschi supposed, for it will be shown in the section on the "Negative Verb" that *a*, probably a relic of *al*, not, is an element in all negative forms; though in these, and in some other instances, it has been absorbed in the succeeding long vowel.

Beschi, in his Grammar of the High Tamil, represents *di* as being used occasionally by the Tamil poets as a suffix of the second person singular of the imperative; and if this representation were correct, it would be necessary to regard *di* as a pronoun, or as the fragment of a pronoun, of the second person singular. It is founded, however, on an error; for the word which Beschi cites in proof (*âdi,* become thou, from *âgu,* abbreviated into *â,* to become) is not really an imperative, but is the second person singular of the preterite; and *di* is compounded of *d*, the sign of the preterite tense, and *i*, the usual fragment of *nî*, thou. *Âdi* means properly thou hast become, and it is used as an imperative by the poets alone to convey an emphatic prediction of a result which is regarded as already certain. We find the same suffix in such poetical preterites as *varu-di* (for *vandây̆*), thou camest, and *keḍu-di* (for *keṭṭây̆*), thou art ruined.

The plural forms of this pronoun in Tamil are as follows:—nom.

nîr, nîyir, nîvir, nîṅgaḷ; inflexion, *num, um, uṅgaḷ. nin*, the singular poetical inflexion, does not become *nim* in the plural, as might be expected, and as we find it in Canarese, but only *num*. Personal terminations of the verb, *ir, îr*. Tamil grammarians give *min* (*e.g.*, *keṇmin*, hear ye) as one of the signs of the second person plural in the imperative. The nature of this form will be considered in the section on the "Pluralisation of the Personal Pronouns."

In Malayâḷam the nominative is *nî*, as in Tamil in both dialects; the inflexion *nin*, as in classical Tamil—*e.g.*, *ninakk'*, to thee; plurals, nom. *nîṅṅaḷ, niṅṅaḷ;* inflexion *niṅṅaḷ*, also in the poets *nim* (*e.g.*, *nimmôḍu*, with you), from the obsolete nom. *nîm*.

The Tuḷu nominative singular is *î* (comp. Tel. *îvu*, from an obsolete *î*); inflexion *nin'*—*e.g.*, *nina*, thy. In *nikk'*, to thee, the inflexion is *ni*. Verbal termination *a;* plurals, nom. *îr* (chiefly used as an honorific singular, like *nîr* in colloquial Tamil), also *nikuḷu;* inflexions *îr'* and *nikuḷ';* verbal ending *ar*.

In Canarese, the nominative of this pronoun in the colloquial dialect is *nîn-u*, classical *nîn;* but the crude form *nî* is often used instead of *nîn-u*, as is always the case in Tamil. In both dialects the inflexion in *nin*—*e.g.*, *ninna*, thy. In the personal terminations of the verb this pronoun is much changed in all the Dravidian dialects. It not only loses its initial *n*, like the pronoun of the first person, but its final *n* also disappears. Generally nothing remains in the verbal inflexions but the included vowel (probably the primitive pronominal base), and that also is more or less modified by use. In the colloquial Canarese verb it appears as *i, î, îye*, and *e;* in classical Canarese *ay* only, closely resembling the Tamil *ây*. Plurals, nom. coll. *nîvu;* class. *nîm;* inflexion in both *nim*—*e.g.*, *nimma*, your. Verbal terminations, coll. *iri, îri, ari;* class. *ir*. This *ir* is identical with one of the classical Tamil terminations.

The Telugu nominative is *nîvu*, expanded from *nî* by the addition of the euphonic particle *vu*. *nîvu*, Tel. thou, is identical in form, though not in meaning, with the modern Canarese plural of the same pronoun—viz., *nîvu*, you. *nî*, the crude form, is also used, as in the other dialects. In the oblique cases, Telugu rejects the euphonic addition of *vu*, and uses *nî* as its inflexional base, and also as its possessive. The objective alone follows the example of the other dialects in abbreviating the included vowel, and appending a final nasal. That case is *nin-u* or *nin-nu*, and is evidently formed from a nominative *nîn-u*. In the higher dialect of Telugu, *îvu*, from an obsolete nominative *î*, identical with the Tuḷu, is occasionally used instead of *nîvu*. The Telugu plural of this pronoun has *mîru* as the nominative, *mî* as the inflexion, and *mimu* as the accusative. Both *mîru* and *mimu* indicate a base in *mî*, from which they have been formed by the addition of signs of plurality; and *mî* bears the same relation to the *nî* of the other dialects that *mâ*, the Telugu plural of the first person, does to the ordinary Dravidian *nâ*. How this change from *n* to *m* has taken place will be inquired into under the head of "The Plurals." The plural in the higher dialect is *îru*. In the personal terminations of the verb, Telugu rejects every portion of the pronominal root, and employs only the euphonic addition *vu* or *vi*.

The Tuda nominative is *nî*, inflexion *nin*, personal termination of verb *i* or *e*. Plural nominative *nima*, inflexion *nim*, personal termination of verb *i* or *e*, as in singular. In the dialect of the Kotas, the nominative is *nî*, inflexion *nin*, personal termination of verb *i*. Plural nominative *nîme* (also *nîve*), inflexion *nim*, personal termination of verb *iri*, *îri*.

In Gônd, the nominative singular is *immâ*, which is evidently an older form of the plural used as the honorific singular. The inflexion is *ni* (*niwa*, thy), personal termination of verb *ni* or *i*. Plural nominative *immâṭ*, inflexion *mî*, as in Telugu; personal termination of verb *îṭ*. The personal terminations of the first and second person singular in Gônd require a little consideration. In both persons the initial *ṉ* of the isolated pronoun seems to hold its ground in some of the tenses in a manner which is not observed in any other dialect—*e.g.*, *âyâtônâ*, I am becoming, *âyâtônî*, thou art becoming. In some other tenses (*e.g.*, imperfect *ânḍân*, I became, perfect *âttân*, I have become), the termination of the first person resembles that in use in most of the other dialects. In the second person (*ândî*, *âttî*), the *n*, whatever its origin, disappears altogether, and is replaced by the ordinary Dravidian *i*. I prefer, therefore, to regard the *n* of the first and second persons, in these tenses, as the *n* of the pronoun of the third person singular, *ôn*, he, forming, when added to the root, a participial noun. *âyât-ôn-â* would then mean, I am one who becomes; *âyât-ôn-î*, thou art one who becomes. If this view is correct, nothing can be observed in these forms differing in reality from those in the other dialects.

The Ku pronoun corresponds on the whole to the Telugu. Nominative singular *înu*, inflexion *nî*, personal termination of verb *i*; plural nominative *îr-u*, inflexion *mî*, personal termination of verb *êru*, *âru*.

The Rajmahâl nominative singular is *nin*, inflexion *nin*; plural *nina*, inflexion *nim*. Ûrâon nominative singular *nîen*, inflexion *nîen*; plural nominative *âsu*, inflexion *âss'*.

The Brahui nominative is *nî*, as in most of the Dravidian dialects, inflexion *nâ*; plural nominative *num*, one of the inflexions of the plural in classical Tamil; inflexion *num* (*numâ*, your); verbal termination *ri*, as in many of the Dravidian dialects (compare *aren*, we are, *areri*, you are).

See the "Table of Pronouns" of the second person for the forms found in the minor dialects of Central India.

We have now to consider the conclusion to be drawn from the comparison made above. We found three forms of the pronoun of the first person singular, *nân*, *yân*, *ân*, each of which claimed to be the best representative of the original form; and of these, *yân* seemed to carry with it most authority, and to be probably the source from which *nân* on the one hand, and *ân* on the other, were derived. With regard to the pronoun of the second person singular, there are only two forms (*nîn*, *în*) whose relative antiquity we are called upon to decide. No claim can be set up in behalf of *yîn* as a pronoun of the second person to correspond with the *yân* of the first person. If such a form ever existed, I can find no trace of it now left. The final *n* of *nîn* or *în* (as of *nân*, *yân*, *ân*) has already been ascertained to be merely a sign of the singular number. In the plural it is replaced by *m*, the sign of plurality, or *r*, *ir*, a relic of *ivar*, they (prox.) This final *n* of the singular may, therefore, be dismissed from our consideration at once. On comparing *nî* and *î*, with *nâ* and *â*, it seems evident that if the initial *n* of *nân* did not belong to the root, but was a product of nasalisation, the initial *n* of *nîn* cannot safely be regarded as radical. If *nâ* was derived from a more primitive *yâ* or *â*, it seems evident that *nî* must have been derived from a more primitive *î*. The initial *n* of *nî* must be identical with the initial *n* of *nâ*. Whatever the origin of the one may be, the origin of the other must be the same. Just as the initial *n* of *nâ* disappears from all the verbal terminations of the first person, so the initial *n* of *nî* disappears from all the verbal terminations of the second. If this initial *n* had been radical, it would have retained its place more or less firmly in the verbal inflexions, like the *m* of the Indo-European first person, and the *t* or *s* of the second person of the same. As the initial *n* has disappeared so completely from the Dravidian verbal inflexions, though it sometimes retains its place as the inflexional base of the oblique cases, I conclude that it is not radical, and that we are to consider *î* more primitive than *nî*. Still the antiquity of the initial *n* of *nî* must be enormously great—almost equal to that of *î* itself, seeing that we find it, as we shall presently see, in the Scythian of Behistun, and even in Chinese, in both of which the pronoun of the second person is *ni*. It is *ni* also in Bornu, a language of Central Africa.

Even when looking at the Dravidian dialects alone, we cannot suppose *nî* much later in origin than *î*. Whatever be the relative antiquity of *nî* and *î*, I consider the vowel, not the consonant, as the real pronominal base. The only question that remains, therefore, is, what is to be regarded as the oldest shape of this vowel? We find *i*, *u*, and also, but more rarely, *a* and *e*. The last two may be left out of account. The vowels most generally used are *i* and *u*. In the verbal terminations *i* has driven *u* out of the field altogether. On the whole, there seems to be more in favour of the antiquity of *i* than of that of *u*, though it must be admitted that *u* changes more readily in Dravidian speech to *i* than *i* to *u*—*e.g.*, *puli*, Tam. a tiger, becomes in the pronunciation of the vulgar *pili*; *mun*, before, becomes *min*, &c. It will be seen that generally in the Indo-European languages the vowel of the pronoun of the first person is *u*, whilst in the Scythian languages it is *i*. Possibly at the outset there was no very sharp line of distinction between these two sounds. At all events, we cannot safely venture to draw any such sharp line of distinction now between the *i* and *u* of the pronoun of the second person in the Dravidian tongues, both vowels being retained, in some connection or another, in most of the dialects. Thus in poetical Tamil we find both *nin* and *nun* as the singular inflexion of the pronoun; in the plural we find *num* and *uṅgaḷ*, but not *nim*, though the nominative *nîṅgaḷ* must be considered as the representative of an older *nîm*.

Extra-Dravidian Relationship.—It has been shown that the Dravidian pronoun of the first person has affinities with each of the great Japhetic groups, with some special Scythian affinities. It will be found that the relationship of the pronoun of the second person is less extensive, but more distinctive; it is more specifically Scythian, or at least non-Aryan.

Throughout the Scythian, as well as the Indo-European group, the most prevalent form of the pronoun of the second person singular is that which is formed from the consonant *t* (*e.g.*, *tu*), or its euphonised equivalent *s* (*e.g.*, *σύ*); and the only other form found in any family of either of those groups is that which is built upon the consonant *n*, and of which the Cuneiform Scythian, the Chinese, and the Dravidian *ni* is the best representative. These roots appear to have been always independent of one another. I cannot discover any reliable trace of a connection between them, or of a gradual change in any instance of the one form into the other.

In order to place this point in a clear light, it is desirable, in the first place, to trace out the connections and alliances of the pronominal root *tu*. It has been conjectured that this pronoun had its origin in the demonstrative base *t*; but the investigation of this point is beyond our purpose, which is merely that of tracing its relationship. In Sanskrit the pronoun of the second person singular is *tva-m;* in Zend *tû-m,* and also *thw',* as included in the accusative *thwâ,* thee. Connected with the Sanskrit *tva,* there is a simpler form, *ta,* which is apparent in *tava,* thy; and we have analogies to this in the Kavi *ta* and the Semitic *ta* (included in *antâ,* thou). The Semitic *tâ* is changed in the inflexions to *kâ,* a change which resembles that of the Kavi, which has *ta* as its nominative and *ko* as its possessive. Bopp supposes that *yu,* the base of the most common form of the plural of this pronoun, is derived from *tu,* and that *va,* the base of the Sanskrit secondary plural *vas* and of the Latin *vos,* is derived from *tva.* *v,* however, is more frequently derived from *m* than from any other letter, of which we have seen an instance in the change of the *ma* of the first person into *va* in *vayam.* It is not very easy to explain how *t* became *v* and *y.* *tva-m* becomes *tuva-m* in Old Persian; and from *tu* (itself derived from *tv*) proceeds the Sanskrit dative *tu-bhayam,* the base of which is allied to, or identical with, the Latin, Armenian, and Pehlvi *tu;* the Æolic and Doric *τύ*; the Persian, Afghan, and Singhalese *tu;* and the Gothic *thu.* The *th* of the Gothic and Zend seems to point out the path by which the Old Greek *τύ* was converted into *σύ.* Mr Edkins, in his "China's Place in Philology," has suggested another origin for *yu.* He supposes it may be connected with *ni* or *nu,* the Chinese pronoun of the second person, of which *i* or *u* was, he thinks, the primitive form. If this supposition should be correct, *yu* will then be the Indo-European equivalent, not only of the Chinese *ne* or *nu,* but of the Dravidian, which also is *ni* or *nu*—*ni* in the nominative, *nu* (*nu-n*) in the oblique.

In the personal terminations of the verbs, in Sanskrit and most other languages of the same family, the earlier *t* of the ordinary form of this pronoun has very generally been weakened into *s* in the singular, whilst in most of the plural terminations, *t,* with some trivial modifications, and with a sign of plurality annexed, has succeeded in retaining its place. In our investigation of the pronoun of the first person, it was found that *ma* was converted in the personal terminations of the verb into *mi,* and still further weakened into *m:* so also *su* (for *tu*) generally becomes *si* in the verbal terminations; and *si* in like manner afterwards becomes *s.*

In the Scythian group of tongues, the pronoun of the second person in general use is substantially the same as in the Indo-European—another evidence of the primeval identity of both groups; but in the Scythian tongues the weaker *s* has obtained wider prevalence than the older *t;* and the vowel by which *s* is enunciated is more frequently *i* or *e*, than *u* or *a*. The Magyar has *te* in the singular, *ti* or *tik* in the plural, with which we may compare the Armenian *tu*, thou, and *tuk*, you. The Mongolian *tchi* or *dzi*, thou, exhibits the progress of *ti* towards softening into *si*. In Finnish proper, the isolated pronoun of the second person singular is *se* or *sina;* but *t* retains its place in the plural, and the personal termination of the verb even in the singular is *t*.

The chief peculiarity apparent in the Scythian form of this pronoun is, that it has generally been euphonised by the addition of a final nasal, the consonant *n*, precisely in the same manner as the pronoun of the first person singular. In the older Greek, τύνη and τούν correspond to ἐγώνη and ἐγών; and in like manner, in the languages which belong to the Scythian group, or which have been subject to Scythian influences, where the pronoun of the first person is found to be nasalised, the pronoun of the second person generally exhibits the same feature. In the vernaculars of Northern India we see this euphonic addition to the pronoun of the second person in the Hindi, Panjabi, and Sindhi *tuñ*, and in the Marâṭhi and Gujarâthi *tûñ*. In some of those idioms, especially in the Gujarâthi and Panjabi, the euphonic nasal appears in the oblique cases as well as in the nominative, but more commonly it is found in the nominative alone.

In the Turkish family of tongues, *sin* or *sen* is the usual form of the pronoun of the second person singular. The *n* retains its place in the oblique cases, but is lost in *siz*, the plural. Compare also the Georgian *shen*, the Samoïede *tan*, *tani*, the Lappish *don*, the Votiak and Mordvin *ton* (plural *tin*), and the Finnish *sinâ*, which alternates with *se*, *sia*, and *sie*. The euphonic origin of this *n* is most evident in the Esthonian dialect of the Finnish, which uses indifferently *sa* or *sinna* for the second person, and *ma* or *minna* for the first. In the Mongolian and Manchu, *n* appears in the oblique cases only. In Mongol the nominative is *tchi*, in Manchu *si;* but the genitive in the former is *tchini*, in the latter *sini*, and the corresponding datives are *tchim-dou* and *sin-de*. In Calmuck the nominative is *dzi* or *dzima*, genitive *dzini*, dative *dzimadou*, accusative *dzimaï*. In the pronouns of this language we may observe several instances of *m* being used as an euphonic, instead of *n*.

It is evident that there is no resemblance whatever between any of the pronouns compared above and the Dravidian *nî*. The final *nâ* of the Finnish *sinâ*, and its equivalent, the final νη of the Greek τύνη, are separable, euphonic, inorganic additions, and can have no real connection with *nî*, which is an ultimate root. It will be necessary for us therefore to go further in search of a really trustworthy analogy.

We have seen that the Indo-European and Scythian *m*—the initial of the pronoun of the first person—was probably the origin of the *n* of the Dravidian *nâ*. Is it possible that the radical *t* of the pronoun of the second person in both those families of tongues was changed in like manner into *n*, so as that *tu* or *ti* was the origin of the Dravidian *nî*? I think not. This is supposed by Castrén, a very high authority, to be the history of the *n* by which the second person singular is often represented in the personal affixes of the Finnish and Turkish families. It may also be mentioned here, that a change of *t* into *n* is not quite unknown even in the Indo-European languages. It is somewhat frequently found to take place in Pali—*e.g.*, *tê*, they, masculine, becomes optionally *nê*; *tâ*, they, feminine, becomes *nâ*; and *tâni*, they, neuter, becomes *nâni*. In Sanskrit also, *êtam*, him, is sometimes changed into *ênam*. There is no evidence, it is true, that the *n* now under consideration—the initial *n* of the Dravidian *ni*—arose from any such process of change. That it proceeded from an older *t* would be a wholly gratuitous assumption, in so far as the internal history of the Dravidian languages is concerned. It would be more in accordance with precedent, indeed, to regard it as a mere nasalisation. Yet when we carry our inquiries a step further, and bring to view a pronoun with *n*, not *t*, in some of the oldest languages of the Scythian group, whilst on the one hand we shall find that the resemblance of this Scythian pronoun to the Dravidian amounts to identity, on the other hand we shall possibly find it allied, by a deep-seated, underground relationship, to the ordinary pronoun with *t*, so that it must always remain doubtful whether these are not two Japhetic bases of the pronoun of the second person, *tu* and *ni*, originally independent, like *ah* and *ma* of the first, or whether *tu* did not change into *nu*, and that to *ni*, at some early period, now unknown, before the isolation of the Dravidians, and even before the isolation of the Chinese, from the rest of the Japhetic race.

I must first endeavour to establish the first point now mentioned, viz., that traces will be found in various languages of the Scythian group of the existence of a pronoun of the second person, apparently identical with, and certainly allied to, the Dravidian *nî*.

I begin with the most ancient analogy which is capable of direct proof, viz., the pronoun of the second person in Chinese. This is *ni*, precisely as in the Dravidian idioms. The plural is *ni-men* (compare *wo-men*, we, *t'a-men*, they); Old Chinese *ngi*, *nu*, *yu*, *u*. Mr Edkins thinks the oldest form of all was *i*, to which *n* was prefixed. The same *ni* appears in some of the dialects of the nomad tribes of the western frontier of China, towards Tibet—*e.g.*, Gyâmi and Horpa. The plurals in Gyâmi are *ni-me*; in Horpa, *ni-ni*. The Tibetan itself, though agreeing so closely as regards the first person, seems to present no analogy in the second. In the dialects of Barma, the prevailing form of the word is *nang;* in the Karen dialects *nah, ner, nâ.* The Manyak, a dialect of the same stock, which has *â* for the first person, has *nô* for the second. All the analogous forms of Eastern Asia rest upon the Chinese; and the antiquity of the Chinese language and literature is so great, that the identity of the Chinese pronoun of the second person with the Dravidian is a point of great interest and importance. The next analogy I adduce is one which I regard as almost equally remarkable and decisive, viz., the pronoun of the second person in the Scythian tablets at Behistun. This is *nî*, precisely as in the Dravidian idioms; and the possessive which is used in compounds is *nĭ*, which is identical with the similarly abbreviated basis of the Dravidian oblique cases of this pronoun. The plural of this pronoun is, unfortunately, unknown. The personal termination of the verb is not *ni*, but *nti*, which I suspect to be a compound of *ni* and *ti*, like the *antâ, anti*, of the Semitic languages. I have given the Brahui a place amongst the Dravidian dialects, but I refer to it here again on account of its centrical geographical position. The Brahui pronoun, as we have seen, is *nî* (plural *num*), the identity of which, both with the Dravidian, properly so called, and with the Behistun and Chinese, cannot, I think, be doubted. It is a remarkable circumstance, and very difficult to explain, that in the Kanuri, a language of Bornu, in Central Africa, together with several other Scythian peculiarities, the pronoun of the second person is *ni*.

The antiquity of the Dravidian pronoun of the second person is thus clearly proved, and this proof of its antiquity entitles us to regard as real certain resemblances to it which otherwise might be thought to be accidental. In the Ostiak, the most Dravidian of the Finnish dialects, in that compound of nouns with possessive suffixes which is so characteristic of the Scythian group, the first personal pronoun is represented by *m*, the second by *n*—*e.g.*, *ime-m*, my wife; *ime-n*, thy wife. In the Syrianian, another Finnish idiom, the second person of the verb, both singular and plural, is formed by annexing a pronoun of which *n* is the initial and radical—*e.g.*; *kery-n*, thou hast done (from *kery*, to do), *kery(n)nyd*, you have done. In *nyd*, you, we see indications of a singular *ny*, thou, which has been pluralised, as is usual in these languages, by suffixing to it *d* or *t*.

In addition to the allied forms discoverable in these compounds, we find in the Ugrian tongues several instances in which the isolated pronoun of the second person, which is used as a nominative, is plainly allied to the Dravidian. In the Ugro-Ostiak, or that dialect of the

Ostiak which is treated of in Castrén's Grammar, thou is *neṇ;* you two, *nîṇ;* you (indefinitely plural), *nen.* Here *ne* or *ni* constitutes the pronominal base, and the final *n* of the singular *neṇ* is a formative or euphonic addition like that which has converted the Dravidian *nî* into *nîn.* The strong pronunciation of this Ostiak final *n* reappears, as we shall see, in Turkish. In other Ostiak dialects we find *num* and *ma,* and also (which is more deserving of notice) *nyn,* with a plural *nynt.* In Vogul we find analogies which are no less remarkable than the above—*e.g., nei, ny, nan, nyngi,* and *nank.* Compare also the Vogul plurals *nen* and *non.*

In the Finnish proper, the only trace of this pronoun which we observe is one which, but for the existence of such express analogies in other members of the family, we should probably have overlooked. In the plural of the second person of the Finnish verb (*e.g., olette,* ye are, pluralised from *olet,* thou art), the suffixed pronoun corresponds to that of which *t* or *s* is the initial; but in the possessive compounds, in which we should expect to find precisely the same form, we find instead of it a plural possessive of which the initial and radical is *n.* Thus, the expression thy hand, being *kâtes,* we should expect to find your hand, *kâtesse,* or, more primitively, *kâtette,* like the corresponding Magyar *kezetek* (from *tek,* you, another form of *te*), whereas the form actually used in Finnish is *kâtenne.* It thus appears that two pronouns of the second person retain their place in the Finnish; one, the singular of which is *si,* or more properly *ti,* the plural *te;* and another, hidden in the ancient compounds, the plural of which is *ne,* and of which, by dialectic rules, the singular must have been *ni.*

Even in Turkish, we shall find traces of the existence of a similar pronoun. In the possessive compounds, the second person singular is not represented, as we should have expected it to be, by *sen,* as the first person singular is by *m;* but *ṅ* or *ng* is used instead (a nasal which corresponds to that of the Ostiak *neṇ*)—*e.g., bâba-ṅ,* thy father; and as the final *m* of *bâbâ-m* is derived from *mî* or *me,* I, we seem to be obliged to deduce also the final *n* of *bâbâ-ṅ* from an obsolete *ṅi* or *ṅe,* thou, which is allied to the corresponding forms that have been pointed out in other Scythian tongues. We find this possessive *ṅ* or *ng* not only in the Osmanli Turkish, but even in the Yakute, the Turkish of Siberia.

The same *ṅ* makes its appearance in the personal terminations of the Turkish verb. *sen* is more commonly used than *ṅ;* but *ṅ* is found as the representative of the second person in those verbal forms which must be considered as of greatest antiquity—*e.g.,* in the preterite of the auxiliary substantive verbs, *îdum,* I was, *îduṅ,* thou wast, *îdî,* he was. In the Oriental Turkish the forms corresponding to these are *bôldîm, bôldûṅ, bôldî;* and the same termination of the second person singular—the nasal *ṅ*—appears in all the preterites of that language. We may compare also the plural forms of this pronominal suffix. The Turkish pronouns are pluralised by changing the final formative *n* into *z*, or rather by adding *z* to the crude base. Thus, we is *biz* (for *miz*), and you is *siz.* In possessive compounds *i* changes into *u;* and hence our father is *bâbâ-muz.* In the same manner, your father is *bâbâ-ṅuz,* indicating a supposititious, isolated pronoun, *ṅiz,* you, corresponding to *miz,* we. Whilst *u* is used instead of *i* in Osmanli Turkish, the older and more regular *i* retains its place in the Oriental Turkish—*e.g.*, *uzû-ṅîz,* you yourselves; in which you is *ṅîz* or *ngîz,* and from which, when *z*, the sign of plurality, is rejected, we deduce the singular *ṅî* or *ngî.* The same mode of forming the plural termination of the second person appears in all regular Turkish verbs—*e.g.*, compare *ḳôrḳdu-ṇuz,* ye feared, with *ḳôrḳdu-ṅ,* thou feardest. We see it also in the imperative *ḳôrḳdu-ṅuz,* fear ye. In all these instances, I consider the Turkish *ṅ* or *ng* to be dialectically equivalent to the Finnish *n;* and the pronominal root which is thus found to underlie so many Turkish and Ugrian compounds of the second person looks as if it might be regarded as identical with the Dravidian, Chinese, and Behistun-Scythian pronoun. Even the libration between *i* and *u*, which we noticed in considering the Dravidian forms of this pronoun, meets us again in Turkish.

In the Himalayan dialects, we can scarcely fail to see Dravidian analogies in the Dhimal *nâ*, in the Miri *no*, in the Garo *nââ;* and in the *n* which forms the first and most essential radical of the pronoun of the second person in all the rest of the Lohitic dialects.

Compare also the pronouns of the second person in various Australian dialects—*e.g.*, *ninna, nginnee, nginte;* the duals, *niwa, nura;* and the plural *nimedoo.*

On a comparison of the various forms of this pronoun which have been adduced above, it must be evident that the affinities of the Dravidian *nî* are almost wholly Scythian; and this important circumstance, taken in conjunction with the predominance of Scythian influences over Indo-European in the formation of the first personal pronoun, tends to show that the Dravidian languages stand in closer relationship to the Scythian class of tongues than to the Indo-European.

3. The Reflexive Pronoun 'Self.'

The Dravidian pronouns of the third person are, properly speaking, demonstratives, not personal pronouns; and they will, therefore, be investigated under a subsequent and separate head. The pronoun which is now under consideration is entitled to a place amongst personal pronouns, because it possesses all their characteristics, and is declined precisely in the same manner. It corresponds in meaning to the Sanskrit *svayam*, to the defective Greek ἵ and the Latin *sui*, *sibi*, *se*; with a range of application which is more extensive than theirs. It may almost, indeed, be regarded as a pronoun of the third person, seeing that, when it stands alone as the nominative of a verb, the verb with which it agrees must always be in the third person.

In Tamil the nominative singular of this pronoun is *tân*: the plural of which (by the usual pronominal change of *n* into *m*) is *tâm* (*tâṅgaḷ*); and the inflexion, or basis of the oblique cases (which, taken by itself, has the force of a possessive), is formed, as in the case of the other personal pronouns, by simply shortening the included vowel—*e.g.*, *tăn*, of self, *sui*, or (adjectivally) *suus, sua, suum*. In all its cases and connections *tân* is found to be more regular and persistent than any other pronoun. The Canarese nominative is *tân* in the ancient, *tân-u* in the modern dialect: the inflexion is formed, as usual, by the shortening of the included vowel; and the crude root *tâ* (without the formative *n*) is sometimes used instead of *tân-u*, just as *nâ*, of the first person, and *nî*, of the second, are occasionally used instead of *nân-u* and *nîn-u*. In Telugu the reflexive pronoun is more regularly declined, and is more in accordance with the Tamil-Canarese, than any other pronoun of the personal class. The nominative is *tân-u*, the inflexion and possessive *tăn-a*, the plural nominative *tâm-u*. *târ-u* may be used instead of *tâm-u*. This appears to be a contracted form of *tamar-u*, a form also used in poetical Tamil, and meaning they who belong to one's-self. *tâ* may be used at pleasure, as in Canarese, for *tân-u*. A similar regularity of formation and of declension is apparent in all the Dravidian dialects, so that further comparison of the forms of this pronoun seems to be unnecessary. The root or base is evidently *tâ* or *ta*, self. The final *n* of the singular, though only a sign of the singular number (like the final *n* of *nâ-n*, I, and *nî-n*, thou), is one of great antiquity, for we find it even in the Brahui—*e.g.*, the nominative singular is *tenat* (compare with this the inorganic *t*, which is suffixed to the personal pronouns in Gônd); genitive *tena*, dative *tene*. *tân*, self (like *nân*, I, and *nîn*, thou), is of no gender.

The use of this pronoun agrees, on the whole, with the use of the corresponding Indo-European reflexive. When not itself used as the nominative of a sentence, it always agrees with the principal nominative and with the governing verb, that is, with that verb which is in agreement with the principal nominative. It is also used as an emphatic addition to each of the personal and demonstrative pronouns, like the

Latin *ipse*, the Sanskrit *svayam*, or the English self, in the compounds myself, yourself, &c.—*e.g.*, we say in Tamil *nân-tân*, I myself; *nî-tân*, thou thyself; *avan-tân*, he himself; *avaḷ-tân*, she herself; *adu-tân*, itself or that itself; and *tâm*, the plural of *tân*, is in like manner appended to the plurals of each of those pronouns and demonstratives. The reduplicated form of the inflexion, *tat-tam*, for *tam-tam*, is used to mean 'theirs respectively.' The Sanskrit *svayam* is indeclinable; the Dravidian *tan* is regularly declined, which is a difference worthy of notice. *tân* acquires also an adverbial signification by the addition of the usual adverbial formatives—*e.g.*, *tânây* (for *tân-âgi*), Tam., of myself, of yourself, or spontaneously; and when appended to nouns of quality or relation its use corresponds to that of our adverbs really, quite, &c.—*e.g.*, *mey tân*, Tam., it is really true, *śari tân*, quite right. In most of the above instances *t* is a sonant, and is pronounced like soft *th* or *d*.

One use to which the reflexive is put is peculiar to these languages—viz., as an honorific substitute for the pronoun of the second person; and in this connection either the singular, the plural, or the double plural may be used, according to the amount of respect intended to be shown. When used in this manner, it is not annexed to, or compounded with, the pronoun of the second person, but is used alone: and though, when it stands alone, it generally and naturally denotes the third person, yet when thus used honorifically for the second person, the verb with which it is connected receives the pronominal terminations, not of the third person, but of the second. This use of *tân* as an honorific pronoun of the second person, illustrates the possibility, if not the probability, of the ultimate origin of the Indo-European pronoun *tu*, thou, from a demonstrative base.

A very interesting class of Dravidian words, the nature of which has generally been overlooked, has originated from the honorific use of the reflexive pronoun. Its inflexion, or possessive, has been prefixed honorifically to most of the pure Dravidian words which denote parents and other near relations, in a manner which somewhat resembles our modern periphrasis, Her Majesty, your worship, &c. In general the plural *tam* has been used in this connection instead of the singular *tan*, as a prefix of greater honour. In some instances also the crude base *ta* has been used as the first member of the compound instead of the regularly organised *tam*. This class of compounds especially abounds in Tamil, in which also *em* and *nam*, our, and *um*, your, are optionally used in poetry instead of *tam* or *ta*, with the same honorific signification. The following illustrations are from Tamil alone. In the other dialects (except Malayâḷam, which here is in agreement with Tamil), some of the most interesting of these compounds are unknown, or the different members of the compound have become so corrupted that it is more difficult to identify them than in Tamil.

tambirân (Mal. *tamburân*), God, lord, the abbot of a Saiva monastery: the nearest English is his lordship; from *tam*, used honorifically, and *pirân*, lord (probably a derivative from the Sans. *pra*, before). *embirân*, our lord, and *umbirân*, your lord, are also used. *pirâṭṭi*, *tambirâṭṭi*, lady. Comp. *emberumân* (*em*, our, *perumân*, great person), our lord, literally our great one, a title common in poetry and in inscriptions; (fem. *perumâṭṭi*, lady.)

tagappan, father; from *tam*, used honorifically, and *appan*, father. This word is sometimes pronounced by Brahmans in the ancient manner, *tamappan;* in Malayâḷam it is both *tagappan* and *tammappan:* nearest English, his fatherhood.

tandei, father, his fatherhood; a more classical word than *tagappan*, yet almost as common (Can. *tande*, Tel. *taṇḍri*, Mal. *tanda*). There can be no doubt that the first portion of this word is the honorific reflexive *tam*, seeing that we find also in the Tamil poets *endei* (*em*), *nandei* (*nam*), our father; and *undei* (*um*), *nundei* (*num*), your father. Comp. also *mundei*, ancestor, first father, from *mun*, before. It is difficult to explain *tei* (*dei*), the second member of the compound. It is plain that it means father; but the only word for father at all resembling it in Tamil is *attan*, father (also *âttan*, a superior person; comp. *attei*, *âttâl*, mother). If the *tei* of *tandei*, &c., is connected with this word, it must have come from an older abstract form, *attei*, meaning either father or mother, according to the connection (as *tannei*, mother, elder sister, is also used in the poets for elder brother); and this word *attei* we might possibly derive from the verbal root *attu*, to join, to lean upon. (See "Glossarial Affinities, Sanskrit and Scythian.")

tây, mother, her maternity; from *ta*, the base of *tam*, used honorifically, and *âyi*, mother (*ta-âyi*); Can. *tâyi*. *âyi*, mother, matron, lady, is a more classical word than *tây*, though retained in many compounds in daily use. Another form is *ây* (Tam.) This is identical in sound with a verbal root signifying to select; but it is difficult to suppose that select, pretty, can have been the original meaning of one of the most ancient patriarchal Dravidian words for matron, mother. Another and perhaps more probable derivation is from *â*, ancient Tam., cow, from which *âyi*, fem., would naturally be formed, with the meaning of mistress of the cows. Comp. *duhitṛi*, Sans., a daughter, literally a milkmaid. *âchchi*, matron, is a South Malayâḷam form for *âyi*. *âyar*, Tam.-Mal. the epicene plural of this word, is a common poetical epithet for cowherds.

tammei, mother; from *ta*, honorific for *tam*, and *ammei*, an honorific word for mother, matron (also *amman*, *ammâ*, *ammâḷ*).

tannei, mother; from *ta*, honorific, and *annei*, an honorific word for mother, probably identical in origin with *ammei*. This word means not only mother, but also both elder sister and elder brother.

tameiyan, elder brother, his eldership; from *tam*, used honorifically, and *eiyan* (sometimes *ayan*), a senior or elder, and therefore meaning also father, elder brother, or *guru*. Another very common word for elder brother is *aṇṇan*, *aṇṇal*, from *aṇṇu*, to resort to, to lean upon (Tel. *anna*, Can. *aṇṇa*). Comp. *tammun* (poetical), an elder brother, from *tam* and *mun*, before, his precedence-ship.

tamakkei, elder sister, her eldership; from *tam* and *akkei*, elder sister (also mother). The ordinary Tamil forms are *akkâ* and *akkâḷ*.

tambi, younger brother; from *tam*, honorific, and *pi*, a word or portion of a word of doubtful origin and meaning. The Telugu *tammuḍu* and the Canarese *tamma* throw no light on the meaning of *pi* (Mal. both *tambi* and *tambân*). Comp. with *pi*, *peidal*, Tam. and Mal., a boy, literally that which is fresh and green. The most probable explanation, though one which is not free from difficulty, is that *pi* is for *pin*, after. Comp. *tammun*, Tam., from *tam* and *mun* before, a poetical word for elder brother. *tambi* is explained by the native lexicographers as meaning *pin-pirandôn*, he who has been born afterwards. They also give *pinnôn*, he who is after, as a synonym for *tambi*, and *pinnei*, the corresponding feminine or neuter abstract, as a synonym for *tangei*, younger sister. Probably *pi* was the primitive shape of *pin*, as *mu* was certainly the primitive form of *mun*; still it is difficult to see how the formative *n* (changing to *r* in *piṟagu*, after), which was retained in *mun* when used as the final member of a compound, happened to be omitted altogether from *pin*. Equivalent forms of this word in poetical Tamil are *embi*, our younger brother, *umbi* and *numbi*, your younger brother; probably also *nambi* (which see) is to be regarded as another form of the same word.

tangei, younger sister; from *tam*, used honorifically, and *kei*, a word of doubtful origin (Mal. *tanga*, Can. *tangi*, Coorg *tange*). It would seem from the Tamil poetical word *nangei*, a lady, that *kei* does not mean one that is young, or one that comes afterwards, as I have supposed the *pi* of *tambi* to mean, but must have had a meaning in some way suitable to be applied to women in general (*mangei*, a girl, looks as if it included the same *kei*); yet, on the other hand, we find in the Tamil poets this very word *kei*, in the shape of *keiyei*, an abstract noun, used as a synonym for *tangei*, a younger sister. This appears to settle the question as regards the *meaning* of *kei*; but the *origin* of the word continues doubtful. It cannot be connected with *keimmei*, *keimben*, Tam., a widow, that word being most naturally derived from *kei* (another shape of which is *kaśu*), to be bitter; hence also the noun *kei*, adversity. We seem, therefore, to be obliged to fall back on *kei*, a hand, in the sense of a help, a handmaid, and to explain *tangei* as meaning her handmaidenship *—a meaning which suits well the position a younger sister would naturally have assigned to her. The corresponding Telugu word *chellelu*, younger sister, includes the meaning of playful, petted.

nambi, a title of inferior priests, meaning probably, like *tambi*, younger brother (which see). Comp. *nambûri*, properly *nambûtiri*, the title of a class of Malayâḷam Brahmans. Comp. also Telugu *tammali*, a petty priest.

I notice in Coorg two instances of *tam* used honorifically, which are not in Tamil—viz., *tammâvu* father-in-law, from *tam* and *mâvu* (Tam. *mâman*), the same, and *tammâvi*, mother-in-law, from *tam* and *mâvi* (Tam. *mâmi*), the same.

Another remarkable use of the reflexive pronoun is the adoption of its possessive, or inflexional base, *tan*, of self, or self's, as the base of the abstract noun *tan-mei* or *tanam*, quality or nature, literally selfness. *tanam* is the form of this word used in Telugu. Tamil uses both *tanam* and *tanmei*; but the latter can stand alone, whilst *tanam* is used only in compounds. *mei* is the regular formative of Tamil abstracts; like our English *nes*, the Latin *tass*, or the Sanskrit *twam*. *tanmei* is identical in meaning with the Sanskrit *tatvam*, nature, property, which is derived from *tad* or *tat*, that, and is possibly allied to it in origin, though indirectly.

* Compare with this meaning of a younger sister the name of spinster, which is applied by ourselves to unmarried females; and also the derivation attributed to *duhitṛi* (*duhitar*), Sans. daughter, viz., a milkmaid, the milkmaid of the family.

tâ or *ta*, the base of the Dravidian reflexive pronoun, has no connection with, or resemblance to, any other pronoun of this family of languages, though it is unquestionably a pure Dravidian root. If we look at its meaning and range of application, it must, I think, have originated from some emphatic demonstrative base; and it will be found that there is no lack, either in the Indo-European or in the Scythian family, of demonstratives closely resembling *ta* or *ta-n*. We see examples of this resemblance in the Sanskrit *tat*, that (from *ta*, the demonstrative base, and *t*, the sign of the neuter singular); in *tadâ*, then, at that time; and also (with the *t* weakened into *s*) in *sah*, he, *sâ*, she. The reflexive pronouns of this family, *sva*, *se*, &c., are probably derived from the same base, though considerably altered. Compare also the old Greek article, which is properly a demonstrative pronoun, *τός*, *τή*, *τό*, and the corresponding German *der*, *die*, *das*. We find the same or a similar demonstrative (with an annexed nasal, as in the Dravidian *tan*) in the Doric *τῆν-ος*, he, that, which is the form from which the Æolian *κῆν-ος*, and the later Greek *ἐ-κεῖν-ος*, is supposed to have been derived (by a change similar to that by which the Hebrew pronominal suffix *kâ* was derived from *tâ*). The resemblance between *τῆν* and *tân* is certainly remarkable; and may not this Dravidian reflexive pronoun, which is used honorifically as a pronoun of the second person, throw some light on that curious indeclinable Greek word which is sometimes used as a form of polite address, viz., *τᾶν* or *ὦ τᾶν*, Sir, My good friend, &c., and which has been derived by some etymologists from *τῆν-ος*, by others from an obsolete vocative of *τύ* or *τύνη*?

The same demonstrative base, with a similar final *n*, appears also in the Old Persian *tan's* (for *tana-s*), he; and in the Scythian tongues we find it, either nasalised or pure, in the Finnish remote demonstrative *tuo*, and the proximate *tama;* in the Lappish *tat*, he, *tan*, of him (root *ta*)*;* and in the Ostiak remote demonstrative *toma*, and proximate *tema*. The reflexive pronoun is used by the Seoni Gônd both as a reflexive and as a demonstrative. Thus, in the "Song of Sandsumjee," in Dr Manger's paper (*Journal of the Bengal Asiatic Society*), *ten* means him (not *se*, but *illum*)*;* *tunna*, his; and *tâne*, her and it. The reflexive signification also appears in the same song in *tunwa* (Tam. *tan*), *suus-a-um*. This seems to indicate that *tâ* was originally a demonstrative. Even in Tamil we find, I think, a distinct trace of the demonstrative signification of the reflexive *ta* still surviving in the use in poetry of the oblique cases of *tân*, *tâm*, instead of the oblique cases of the nouns to which they belong, in a manner similar to the use of *adu*, it, with its cases—*e.g.*, *marandanei* (*tanei*, the accusative of *tân*) *(k)kaṇḍên,* I saw the tree, instead of *maramadei,* the other poetical form, or the colloquial *marattei.* (See the Noun—inflexional formative *am.*)

The strongest argument, perhaps, for considering the Dravidian *ta* or *tân,* self, to be allied to the Sanskrit-Scythian demonstrative *ta,* is the circumstance that *tan,* the inflexional base of *tân,* is used, as has been already mentioned, in the formation of the word *tanmei* or *tanam,* quality, selfness, in precisely the same manner as the Sanskrit *tad,* that, which forms the basis of the corresponding Sanskrit word *tatvam,* quality, quiddity, thatness. The Dravidian word may have been, and probably was, framed in imitation of the Sanskrit (for so abstract a term is necessarily of late origin), but it cannot have been directly derived from the Sanskrit word. It seems very probable that both bases are remotely allied; and if they are so allied, their alliance carries us back to a very remote period; for whilst the Dravidian reflexive pronoun retains the original demonstrative *t,* the corresponding reflexive in every one of the Indo-European tongues (*sva, se,* &c.) had already allowed *t* to be weakened into *s,* before those tongues separated from the parent stem.

4. Pluralisation of the Personal and Reflexive Pronouns.

I class the plurals of these pronouns together because they are formed from the same pronominal bases as their singulars (which have already been investigated), and because they are all formed on one and the same plan, viz., either by the addition of a pluralising particle (generally *m*) to the pronominal base, or by the substitution of that particle for the singular formative. Exceptions exist, but they are few and unimportant.

Comparison of Dialects.—In the classical dialect of Tamil, the plurals of the personal and reflexive pronouns (*nân,* I; *nî,* thou; *tân,* self) are *yâm* or *nâm,* we; *nîr, nîyir,* or *nîvir* (instead of the more regular *nîm*), you; and *tâm,* selves. In the colloquial dialect a double plural has got into extensive use, which is formed by the addition to the classical plurals of *gaḷ,* the sign of plurality which especially belongs to the class of irrationals. In consequence of the existence of these two sets of plurals, a difference in their use and application has gradually established itself. The classical or pure and simple plurals are now used in the colloquial dialect as honorific singulars; whilst the double plurals—*nâṅgaḷ* (*nâm-gaḷ*), we; *nîṅgaḷ* (*nîm-gaḷ*), you; and *tâṅgaḷ* (*tâm-gaḷ*), selves—are used as the ordinary plurals. A double plural has crept into Telugu also—*e.g., mîralu* (for *mîru*), you, *vâralu* (for *vâru*), they. Another point of difference between *nâm* and *nâṅgaḷ*, the two Tamil plurals of the first personal pronoun, will be inquired into under a subsequent head. The formation of these secondary double plurals of the Tamil and Telugu is in harmony with a usage which is observed in some of the Gaurian languages. Of the Oriya, Mr Beames writes (*Indian Antiquary* for October 1872):—"The plural of *mu*, I, is *amhe* (pronounced *ambhe*), and that of *tu*, thou, is *tumhe* (*tumbhe*); but as the learned have taken *ambhe* and *tumbhe* into use as equivalents for I and thou, they have had to make fresh plurals, *ambhemâne*, *tumbhemâne*. Din Krishna (a poet who lived at the close of the fifteenth century) uses only the two first (*ambhe*, and *tumbha*), and always in their proper ancient signification. The same process is observed in the Turkish. In that language *ben*, I, is regularly pluralised into *biz*, we; and *sen*, thou, into *siz*, you; but those plurals are sometimes pluralised over again by the addition of *ler*, the ordinary suffix of plurality—*e.g.*, *biz-ler*, we, *siz-ler*, you.

In the verbal inflexions the initial consonant of each of the pronominal plurals (as of the corresponding singulars) disappears; and the pronoun is represented solely by the included vowel and the sign of plurality. The personal termination of the first person plural in the colloquial dialect is *ôm*; in the classical dialect *am*, *âm*, *em*, *êm*. The termination of the second person plural is *îr* or *ir*, the representative of *nîr*. The reflexive pronoun *tâm*, selves, has no place in the verbal inflexions. Of the three High Tamil or classical plurals which have been mentioned—*nâm*, *nîr*, and *tâm*—two form their plurals by substituting *m* for the final *n* of the singular, or by adding *m* to the crude root. This I consider to be the regular method of pluralising the personal pronouns; and the use of *nîr*, you, instead of *nîm*, is an abnormal exception. This appears on comparing it with *nîṅ-gaḷ*, the corresponding plural in the colloquial dialect, which is formed from *nîm*—the plural that is required by rule, and which is found in classical Canarese. It also appears from the circumstance that *nîr* is not the base of the oblique cases of the plural of this pronoun in any dialect of the Tamil. *m* constitutes the sign of plurality instead of *r* in the oblique cases of *nîr*, precisely as in those of *nâm*, we. *nâm* is represented in the oblique cases in the classical dialect by *nam* and *em*; and by *nam* and *eṅgaḷ* (*em-gaḷ*) in the colloquial dialect. In like manner, the oblique cases of the plural of the second personal pronoun are *um* and *num* in the higher dialect; and *uṅgaḷ* (*um-gaḷ*) in the colloquial. *nin*, the abbreviation of *nîn*, being used in the classics as the inflexion of the old singular, we should have expected to find the corresponding *nim* (from *nîm*) in the plural: but in the oblique cases *i* has given place to *u*.

The final *n* of *nân*, *nîn*, *tân*, may be omitted in the nominative in several of the Dravidian dialects, but the final *m* of the plurals (though softened in colloquial Canarese to *vu*) is never omitted. The reason is that the singular might often be taken for granted, or would appear sufficiently from the context, whilst, if the plural were meant, it was more necessary that it should be distinctly expressed.

In Canarese the plurals of all the personal pronouns are formed in the classical dialect with perfect and beautiful regularity—*e.g.*, *ân*, I, *âm*, we; *nîn*, thou, *nîm*, you; *tân*, self, *tâm*, selves. In the oblique cases the included vowel is shortened as usual; and the only other change which takes place is in the weakening (as in Tamil) of the radical *a* of the nominative of the first person into *e* in the oblique cases—*e.g.*, *emma*, our. In this particular, *namma*, the form which has survived in the colloquial dialect is more regular, and probably more ancient. The colloquial dialect substantially agrees with the classical, the chief difference consisting in the softening, in the nominatives alone, of the final *m* into *vu*—*e.g.*, *nâvu*, *nîvu*, and *tâvu*, instead of *nâm*, *nîm*, and *tâm*. In the personal terminations of the verb, the modern dialect uses *êve*, *evu*, and *êvu*, as representatives of *nâvu*, we; the *e* of which forms corresponds to *ên*, the termination of the Tamil singular. This final *vu* of the modern Canarese is not euphonic, like the *vu* of the Telugu singular, *nî-vu*, thou; but is softened from, and is the representative of, an older *m*. Though *m* is the true sign of the plural of the second person, as of the other personal pronouns, *r* is used instead in all the Canarese verbal terminations, as in those of all the other dialects. The ancient Canarese uses *ir*, the modern *iri* and *îri*.

In Telugu the second personal pronoun is pluralised in the nominative by *r* instead of *m*—*e.g.*, *mîr-u*, higher dialect *îru*, you; and in Telugu, as in all the other Dravidian dialects, *r* invariably forms the plural of the terminations of the second person of the indicative mood of the verb. It will be seen, however, in the sequel that there are indications in Telugu that the use of *r* in the nominative plural of the pronoun is abnormal.

The *m* which constitutes the pronominal sign of plurality in Telugu is not softened into *vu* in the termination of the first person plural of the verb, as in Canarese. That termination is *amu*, *âmu*, *emu*, *êmu*; and in the preterite it takes the shape of *imi*, through the influence of *ti*, the preterite formative. The plural of the second person is represented by *âru*, *îri*, *eru*, *êru*, *uru*, and *ru*; of which *r*, the pluralising suffix of *mîru*, you, is the only essential element. Telugu differs from Tamil-Canarese in occasionally using *târ-u*, softened from *tamar-u*, instead of *tâm-u*, as the nominative plural of the reflexive pronoun.

This irregularity, however, like that of the pluralisation of the second personal pronoun by means of *r* instead of *m*, disappears in the oblique cases; the plural inflexion or possessive of this pronoun being *tam-a*, in Telugu, as in the other dialects. *tamar-u* is properly a possessive noun. The Telugu plurals *mêm-u*, we, and *mîr-u* (or *mîralu*), you, present some peculiarities which require to be investigated.

In common with their singulars, the inflexions of these pronouns reject altogether the final consonant—the sign of number—and retain the long included vowel of the nominative unaltered. Thus, the inflexion or possessive of *mêmu* is *mâ*, and that of *mîru*, *mî*—corresponding to the singular inflexion *nâ* and *nî*. The objective case, however, follows the rule of the Tamil and Canarese—*e.g.*, *mamu* or *mammu*, us, *mimu* or *mimmu*, you. It may, therefore, be concluded that the mode in which the inflexions *mî* and *mâ* are formed is irregular and of comparatively late origin; and that in Telugu, as in the other dialects, *m* is to be regarded as the ancient and regular sign of the plural of the personal pronouns.

The chief peculiarity of these pronouns (*mêm-u* and *mîr-u*) in Telugu, is the change of the initial *n* into *m*. How is it to be accounted for that the Telugu plurals have *m* as their initial, instead of *n*?—*mêm-u* and *mîr-u*, instead of *nêm-u* and *nîm-u* or *nîr-u*—the sign of plurality prefixed, instead of being suffixed? I believe that this *m* is not to be considered as the representative of an older pronominal root; but that it is merely the result of the euphonic attraction of the final *m*, which constitutes the regular sign of plurality. If the plural of the Telugu first person alone had *m* for its basis, we might possibly suppose that *m* to be radical and primitive, on account of *m* being, as we have seen, the basis of the corresponding Scytho-Sanskrit pronoun; but we find the same initial *m* in the plural of the Telugu second person also. Now, as it can scarcely be doubted that *nî*, the singular of that pronoun (agreeing as it does with the Behistun-Scythian and the Chinese, as well as with many of the Finnish forms) faithfully represents the earliest organised form of the Dravidian pronoun of the second person, it seems evident that *mîm* (the supposititious nominative from which the objective *mim-mu* has been derived) must have been altered from *nîm*. We may, therefore, conclude that the same process must have taken place in the pronoun of the first person also. Telugu is more addicted to harmonic changes than any other Dravidian dialect. It alters both vowels and consonants for harmonic reasons so frequently, that the change from *nêm-u* to *mêm-u*, and from *nîm-u* to *mîm-u*, would be thought by Telugu people a very natural and easy one. It occasionally drops also the initial *n* or *m* of these words.

We have seen that the first person forms its plural in all the Dravidian idioms, properly so called, by changing the final formative of the singular *n* into *m;* and that the second person originally formed its plural in the same manner—viz., by substituting *m* for *n*, though the verbal endings and the nominative of the isolated pronoun in some of the dialects are now found to prefer *r*. We have seen that the reflexive pronoun also forms its plural by discarding *n* and annexing *m*. Consequently we are now entitled to regard *m* as the most regular and ancient sign of plurality used by the Dravidian personal pronouns.

Origin of Pluralising Particles. (1.) *Origin of 'r.'*—We have already seen, under the head of the "Pluralisation of Nouns," that the epicene plural of the Dravidian languages is *ar* or *ir;* and that the *a* and *i* of *ar* and *ir* are probably the remote and proximate demonstrative bases, *a* and *i*, to which *r*, a sign of plurality, has been appended. *ar* and *ir*, we have seen, may be regarded as equivalent to the more fully developed *a(v)ar*, *i(v)ar*, those people, these people. But how has a termination which is naturally appropriate to the third person only found its way into the second? In this manner, I apprehend. *nîr*, Tam. you, takes also, as we have seen, in the Tamil classics, the form of *nîvir*, and *nîyir*, and in this instance I have no doubt that the more classical form is also the more ancient. *nî-(y)-ir* or *nî-(v)-ir* will thus mean thou + they, and this compound will naturally acquire the signification of you. The Sanskrit *yushmê*, you (*yu* + *smê* = thou + they), is supposed to have a similar origin. The Tamil word, however, is still more suitable than the Sanskrit one to express the meaning required. *ir* in Tamil means not, as the Sanskrit *smê* is supposed to do, they, indiscriminately, without reference to the distance or proximity of the persons referred to, but, they who are standing nearer than certain other people. It means not those people, but these people. The Tamil *nî-(v)-ir* means, therefore, thou + these people; and this supplies us with a more suitable origin for the word used for 'you' than is to be found in Sanskrit, or, I believe, any other language. An alternative explanation is that the *ir* of the plural pronouns is identical in origin with *ir*, two. On this supposition *nîyir*, *nîvir*, *nîr*, would mean 'two thous,' and would have been used first as a dual, then as a plural.

(2.) *Origin of 'm.'*—Can the origin of *m*, the most distinctive sign of the plural of the Dravidian personal and reflexive pronouns, be discovered? It is only in the event of our being unable to discover its origin in the Dravidian languages themselves, that it will be desirable or necessary for us to seek for it elsewhere. It will be found, I think, to be capable of satisfactory explanation. It appears to me to have been derived from *um*, the conjunctive or copulative particle of almost all the Dravidian dialects. Being a conjunctive it is used for conjoining person to person—that is, for pluralising. (See "The Plural Imperative.") This particle is *um* in Tamil and Malayâḷam, *um* or *am*, more commonly *um*, in classical Canarese, *û* in colloquial Canarese, *u* in Telugu. The Telugu particle takes euphonically the shape of *yu* or *nu*, according to the preceding vowel, but in itself it is simply *u*, and identical with the Tamil-Malayâḷam-Canarese *um*, the *m* of which appears to be the ordinary formative *m* of neuter nouns. *u* is best explained as the intermediate demonstrative base *u*, correlative to the remote demonstrative base *a* and the proximate *i*. Tuḷu stands alone in using *lâ* as its copulative particle. Whatever be the origin of *um*, its use as a copulative particle is of very great antiquity. Like the Latin *que*, it is incapable of being used separately, and is agglutinated to the word it qualifies. On the supposition of the final *m*, which constitutes the sign of plurality in Dravidian pronouns, personal and reflexive, being a relic of the copulative *um*, *nâm*, we, and *nîm*, you, resolve themselves into *nâ-um*, I-and, *egoque*, and *nî-um*, thou-and, *tuque*. This view is corroborated by the extensive use which is avowedly made of this very *um* in the formation of Tamil distributive and universal nouns and pronouns. Thus, *evanum*, every one, *quisque; engum*, everywhere, *ubique;* and *epporudum*, always, every time; are unquestionably derived from *evan*, who, *engu*, where, and *epporudu*, what time, with the addition in each instance of the conjunctive particle *um*, and; so that the compound pronoun 'every one' is regularly expressed in Tamil, like *quisque* in Latin, by 'who, and—'; everywhere, like *ubique*, by 'where, and—'; always, by 'what time, and—.' In the same manner *um* is annexed as an auxiliary to some affirmative universals for the purpose of widening their application—*e.g.*, *ellâ-(v)-um*, Malayâḷam, all, literally 'all and—,' from *ellvâ*, all, and *um*, and. This form is abbreviated in Tamil into *ellâm;* which is regarded and treated by grammarians as a neuter plural. The corresponding epicene plural is *ellâr-um*, all persons. In Tamil poetry *elâm* is regarded as a plural of the first person, meaning all we, in which *âm* probably represents *âm*, we. If then the addition of *um*, abbreviated to *m*, undoubtedly constitutes pronominal distributives and universals, may not the sign of plurality which is employed by the personal pronouns be an abbreviation of the same *um?* In poetical Tamil, personal verbs are sometimes pluralised by the addition of *um*—*e.g.*, *śeygu*, I will do; *śeygum* (*śeyg'-um*), we, ye, they will do. So also *śeygum vandêm*, we have done (so and so) and come. Here *śeygu* is an old future or aoristic verbal participle, capable of being used also as a finite verb, and we find that by the addition of *um* it is pluralised, so as to correspond with the more fully expressed plural *vandêm*, we came. In the same dialect of Tamil *śeydu* (which in the modern colloquial dialect means having done) is sometimes used in the sense of I did, and *śeyd-um* in the sense of we did. We have here distinct and evidently very ancient traces of the use of *um* as a sign of personal plurality. This use of *um* appears still more distinctly in the second person plural of the imperative of Tamil verbs in the colloquial dialect, which is much used as an honorific singular—*e.g.*, *kêḷ* (the root used as the first person singular imperative), hear thou; *kêḷum*, hear ye. This form has been still further vulgarised by the addition of *gaḷ*, the sign of plurality belonging to irrational nouns—*e.g.*, *kêḷuṅgaḷ*, hear ye. Compare the Telugu honorific singular (properly a plural) *rammu*, come ye, the regular singular of which is *râ*, come thou. Neither the Tamil *um* of the second person imperative, nor the corresponding Telugu *mu* or *urnu*, can be satisfactorily explained by identifying it with the Tamil *um*, the inflexion of the pronoun of the second person plural. It is best explained by identifying it with the *um* by which that inflexion *um* itself (from *nîm*), together with the other plurals of the personal and reflexive pronouns, was originally pluralised.

A parallel instance of the use of a copulative conjunction as a sign of plurality appears in Ostiak, in which the sign of the dual (*ga*, *ka*, *gai*, &c.) is derived by Castrén from *ka* or *ki*, also.

Extra-Dravidian Relationship.—We now proceed to inquire whether final *m*, the distinctive Dravidian plural of the personal pronouns, forms the plural of this class of words in any other family of languages.

m having a tendency to be weakened into *n* (of which there are many examples in the terminations of Tamil nouns), and *m* and *n* being generally equivalent nasals, the use of a final *n* as a sign of the plural of pronouns may possibly be equivalent to that of *m*. If so, we may adduce as examples of plurals resembling the Dravidian the Brahui *nan*, the Chaldee *anân*, and the Ostiak *men*, we; as also the Persian *tan*, you. A slight trace of the use of *m* as a sign of the plural may be noticed in the Beluchi *mimiken*, we, when compared with *menik*, I. In the Ostiak, a Finno-Ugrian dialect, the first person plural of the verb terminates in *m*, whilst the plural of the corresponding pronoun terminates in *n*. On comparing the Finnish proper *olen*, I am, with *olemme*, we are, we are struck with their resemblance to the Dravidian rule. The resemblance, however, is illusory; for the *m* of the Finnish *me* is a sign of personality, not of plurality. *me*, we, is the plural of *ma*, the old Finnish I; of which *na* (from which the *n* of *olen* arises) is, as I have shown, an euphonic modification. We can scarcely indeed expect to find in the pronouns of the Scythian languages any sign of plurality perfectly corresponding to that of the Dravidian *m* ; for in those languages the personal pronouns are generally pluralised by a change of the final vowel, not by any change or addition of consonants—*e.g.*, Manchu *bi*, I, *be*, we ; Magyar *te*, thou, *ti*, you ; Ostiak and Finnish *ma*, I, *me* (or *men*), we.

I have reserved till now the consideration of a series of remarkable analogies which run through the whole of the Indo-European family of languages, and which are found also in the Gaurian or North Indian vernaculars. In those languages we find very frequent use of *m* in the plurals of the personal pronouns, in which it either constitutes the final consonant, or occupies a place of evident importance ; and this *m* in some instances appears to replace a final *n* or *ṅ* which is used by the corresponding singulars.

In the vernaculars of Northern India we find the following instances of the use of *n* or *ṅ* in the singular and *m* in the plural. Hindi *maiṅ*, I ; *ham*, we ; *tû*, *tûṅ*, or *taiṅ*, thou ; *tum*, you. Gujarâthi *huṅ*, I ; *hame*, we ; *tûṅ*, thou ; *tame*, you. Marâṭhi, *tûṅ* thou ; *tumhi*, you. In Bengali and Oriya *ṅ* disappears from the terminations of the singulars, but in the plural *m* retains its place as in the other dialects—*e.g.*, Bengali *toma* or *tumi*, the inflexional base of the plural of the second person ; and Oriya *tumbha*, the base of the double plural, *tumbhamâne*. The same distinctive *m* appears in the Pâli-Prâkrit, the stock from which the Gaurian vernaculars radiated, in *tumhe*, you, *amhe*, we. Compare also the New Persian *shumâ*, you, and the final *m* of *hastêm*, we are. I quote the following from an article by Mr Beames in the *Indian Antiquary* for November 1872 :—"*hâm*, plural of personal pronoun, first person ; Hindi, *ham*. This is a peculiarly instructive form. The origin of this word in all the seven languages (of Northern India) is the Prâkrit *amhê*. The Oriya, with its usual fondness for archaisms, still retains this form almost unchanged in *âmbhe*, where the *b* is merely the natural thickening of the pronunciation after *m*. Hindi has thrown the *h* backwards to the beginning of the word, making *hamê*. In *hâm* we have the tendency, natural to Bengali, towards lengthening the short vowel, so that this form may be regarded as transitional between middle Hindi and the modern Bengali *âmi*."

Similar and very striking analogies meet us in Greek. Compare the singulars ἐγών and τούν, ἐγώνη and τούνη, with the plurals ἡμεῖς and ὑμεῖς. This resemblance, too, is strengthened when the vowels of the Greek plurals are compared with some of the corresponding Dravidian ones—*e.g.*, compare ἡμ-εῖς with the Telugu *êm-u*, we ; and ὑμ-εῖς with *um*, which is the base of the oblique cases of the Tamil plural of the second person. It also deserves to be noticed, that in the Greek, Persian, Gaurian, &c., *m* is not used indiscriminately by all nouns, or even by all pronouns, as a sign of plurality in general, but is invariably restricted to the pronouns of the first and second person—a usage which precisely accords with that of the Dravidian languages.

A strong case for regarding the *m* of the above-mentioned Aryan idioms as closely allied to the *m* which constitutes the most distinctive sign of the plural of the three personal pronouns in the Dravidian family (in Canarese, *âm*, we; *nîm*, you; *tâm*, selves) has now been established. I do not wonder, therefore, that the late Mr Gover (in a privately-printed paper on the Dravidian personal pronouns) considered that there was "no possible doubt as to their real and intimate connection;" or that Dr Pope, in his "Outlines of the Tuda Grammar" (p. 5), should have said, though with hesitancy, "Nor can I think it clear that *ôm* (Tuda, we) is not related to the Sanskrit *vayam*, or to the Greek ἡμ-εῖς or ἄμμες, and Vedic *asme*." The evidence of relationship appears to me to be weakened by this reference to *vayam*. We have already seen that the *am* of *vayam* is properly a sign of the neuter singular, constituting *vayam*, we, like *yûyam*, you, an abstract noun—plural, indeed, in signification, but singular in form. It has been seen, also, that the same *am* appears in *aham*, I; *tvam*, thou; and *svayam*, self. When *vayam* and *yûyam* are set aside as not really related to the Dravidian forms, the probability of the existence of a real relationship between the Dravidian *âm*, *yâm*, we, and the Græco-Vedic ἄμμ-ες, *asm-e*, and still more between the Dravidian *âm* and the Bengali *hâm*, *âmi*, becomes, I admit, very great; so also the probability of a relationship between *um*, the Dravidian oblique form of you, and the Græco-Vedic ὔμμ-ες, *yushm-e*, and the *um* of the Hindi *tum*. I feel still, however, obliged to say, as I said in the first edition, that, on a more extended comparison and on closer consideration, this resemblance appears to me first to diminish and then to disappear. The more it is examined, the more the difficulties in the way of its reception appear to increase. Perhaps, indeed, no better illustration could be found of the danger of confiding in apparent resemblances, however close and exact, and of the necessity of tracing words back to their earliest shapes before concluding that resemblances imply relationship.

We have seen that the plural *m* of the Dravidian personal pronoun resolves itself most naturally into *um*, the Dravidian conjunctive particle, and, also. What is the history of the plural *m* of the Græco-Gaurian personal pronouns? How far soever we trace back the Dravidian *m*, it is found to sustain no change, and to exhibit no signs of being descended from anything extrinsic to itself. On the other hand, though the *m* of the Greek and Gaurian presents itself to us simply as *m* in these languages; yet on carrying our comparison a few stages further back, and inquiring into its origin and history, we find it losing its simplicity, and presenting itself to us as only one member in a composite formative, to which the Dravidian *m* bears no resemblance.

ἡμεῖς and ὑμεῖς, as is well known, are not the oldest forms of the Greek plurals. For ἡμεῖς, the Doric and Æolic dialects have ἄμες, ἄμμες, and ἄμμε; for ὑμεῖς they have ὔμες, ὔμμες, and ὔμμε; of which forms the oldest and most reliable appear to be ἄμμες, or its uninflected type ἄμμε and ὔμμες or ὔμμε. In like manner the Gaurian forms of the plurals of the personal pronouns are not the oldest forms of these plurals we have to deal with. The Hindi *ham*, the Gujarâthi *hame*, the old Bengali *hâm*, the modern Bengali *âmi*, the Oriya *âmbhe*, are all derived from the Prâkrit *amhe*. The Greek ἄμμε and the Prâkrit *amhe* are evidently identical; but what is the origin of both? In Zend the *m* and *h* of the Prâkrit *amhe* change places, so that *ahme* may have been an older form. The plural nominative in Zend is *vaem*, answering to the later Sanskrit *vayam;* but all the oblique cases are built upon *ahma* (pointing to a nominative *ahme*)—*e.g.*, ablat. *ahmat* (Sans. *asmat*). Already the Dravidian *m* is losing its resemblance to the Aryan; but when we come to the next stage, the Vedic-Sanskrit *asme* (*a* + *sme*), the fountain-head of all these pronominal forms, the resemblance appears almost wholly to vanish. The Aryan genealogical tree is very clearly made out: *asme*, *ahme*, *amhe*, ἄμμε, ἀμμί-ες = ἡμεῖς; *âmbhe*, *hame*, *ham*, *hâm*, *âmi*. In the Dravidian languages, on the other hand, even if we trace our way back to the time when the Tamilians and the Khonds were still one people, inhabiting the same districts and speaking the same tongue—a time earlier by many ages than the degradation of the Prâkrits into the modern Gaurian vernaculars—we still find an unvarying *m* (irresoluble except into *um*) used for the pluralisation of the personal pronouns.

In like manner, on comparing ὔμμες or ὔμμε, you, with the Zend *yûshem* (in the oblique cases *yusma* or *yûsma*), and with the Vedic-Sanskrit *yushme* (for *yusme*), it is equally obvious that *yusme* is the root of the whole. *yusme*, you, the plural of *tu*, thou, has probably been softened from *tusme* = *tu-sme* (as *asme* from *masme* = *ma-sme*); and this supposititious *tusme* (weakened into *tuhme*, like *asme* into *ahme*) becomes a reality when we turn to the Prâkrit *tumhe*, you, from which comes directly the Gaurian *tumhi*, *tumbha*, *tame*, *tum*, &c. Compare also the New Persian *shumâ*.

When we find that the Dravidian *m* or *um* is to be compared, not with the apparently identical *m* of the Gaurian *ham* and *tum*, but with the Vedic-Sanskrit *sme* of *asme* and *yushme*, it is evident that the improbability of *m* or *um* being identical with *sme*, or nearly related to it, becomes very great. This improbability increases when the uses of *sme* and those of *m* are compared.

sme is a compound consisting of two members, *sma* and *e*, of which *e* alone is characteristic of the plural. *sma*, which contains the *m* that has been supposed to be connected with the Dravidian sign of plurality, is a particle the origin of which is doubtful, and the force of which is still more doubtful. When used as an isolated particle, it gives to the present tense of verbs a species of past signification. Its use in the inflexion of pronouns, when inserted between the pronominal base and the signs of case and number, suggests the idea that it was originally a pronoun of the third person, meaning, perhaps, self or the same, which came to be added on occasionally to the other pronominal bases for the purpose of imparting additional emphasis. We find a somewhat similar use in Tamil of *tan*, *tam*, the inflexion of the reflexive pronoun self, selves, which is occasionally, especially in poetry, inserted between nouns and their case-signs. The *e* of *sme* is the ordinary sign of the nominative plural of pronominals of the class of *sme*, all, and has obviously no resemblance to the Dravidian *m*; and the *sma* into which the *m* of *sme* resolves itself, whatever be its origin, seems to resemble it as little.

It is also worthy of notice, that *sma* makes its appearance not only in the inflexion of the plurals of the personal pronouns, but also in the singular. It is used in the plural alone in connection with the pronouns of the first and second persons in Sanskrit; but Bopp recognises it in the singular also in Zend in *thwahmî*, in thee, and more doubtfully in Gothic and Latin; and there can be no doubt of its use in the singular of the personal pronouns in the Prâkrit (which may be defined as early colloquial Sanskrit), in *mamasmi* or *mamammi*, in me, and *tumasmi* or *tumammi*, in thee. Bopp supposes this use of *sma* in singular pronouns to be of late origin, and to have arisen from imitation of the plurals; but as the reason why *sma* was used in the inflexion of pronouns has only been guessed at, and is not certainly known, there is no proof that the plural has a better right to it than the singular. But however this may be, it is evident that its resemblance to the Dravidian *m*, which is used in the inflexion of the personal pronouns in the plural alone (never in the singular), has become less and less. The resemblance, as it appears to me, wholly vanishes when it is found that, whilst this use of *m* as a sign of plurality is absolutely restricted in the Dravidian languages to the pronouns of the first and second persons and the reflexive 'self,' in Sanskrit, and more or less distinctly in the other Aryan languages, *sma* makes its appearance (in three of the cases in the singular) in the inflexion of the pronouns of *the third person,* including the demonstrative, the relative, and the interrogative pronouns. Nothing could be further than this from the Dravidian use; and nothing also, I think, could show more clearly that the *sma* of *asme* and *yushme* cannot safely be regarded as in any sense a sign of the plural.

Twofold Plural of the Dravidian Pronoun of the First Person.—The ordinary plural of the Dravidian first personal pronoun is constantly used, not only as a plural, but also as an honorific singular, precisely as the royal and editorial 'we' is used in English; and the plural of every other Dravidian pronoun may optionally be used as an honorific singular in the same manner. It is not, however, this twofold signification or use of the same pronoun to which I now refer; but the existence of two pronouns of the first person plural, which differ from one another in signification almost as much as the plural and the dual of other languages. In all the Dravidian dialects, with the exception of Canarese, there are two plurals of the pronoun of the first person, of which one denotes, not only the party of the speaker, but also the party addressed, and may be called *the plural inclusive;* the other excludes the party addressed, and denotes only the party of the speaker, and may be called *the plural exclusive.* Thus, if a person said "We are mortal," he would naturally use the 'we' which includes those who are spoken to, as well as the speaker and his party, or *the plural inclusive:* whilst he would use the *plural exclusive,* or that which excludes the party addressed, if he wanted to say "*We* are Hindus; *you* are Europeans."

There is a similar distinction between the two plurals of the first person used in the Marâṭhi and the Gujarâthi—*e.g., hame* in Gujarâthi means we—the party speaking; whilst *âpane* means we—the party speaking, and you also who are addressed. There is no connection between the particular pronominal themes used for this purpose in Northern India and in the languages of the South; but the existence of so remarkable an idiom in the North Indian family, as well as in the Southern, seems to demonstrate the existence in the Northern family of an ancient under-current of Dravidian, or at least of non-Aryan influences. The idiom in question is a distinctively Scythian one, and is one of those points which seem to connect the Dravidian family with the Scythian group. There is no trace of this twofold plural in Sanskrit, or in any of the languages of the Indo-European family, but it is found everywhere in Central Asia. Thus Manchu has *mû,* we—of the one party, and *be,* we—the whole company. Mongolian has a similar idiom. This peculiarity is found also in the northern dialect of the Chinese. In that dialect, *tsa-men,* we, includes the persons addressed, whilst *wo-men*, we, does not. It is remarkable that it is found also in the Polynesian languages, in many of the languages of America, and also in those of the Australian tribes.

All the Dravidian languages do not use precisely the same plural pronouns as *inclusive* and *exclusive* plurals. The colloquial Tamil (with which the Malayâḷam agrees) forms the plural exclusive from *nâm*, the ordinary and regular plural, by the addition of *gaḷ*, which is properly a neuter sign of plurality; by which addition *nâm* becomes *nâṅgaḷ* in Tamil, *ñaṅaḷ* or *ñaṅṅaḷ* in Malayâḷam. The corresponding plural in Tuḷu is *enkuḷu*. Telugu, on the other hand, uses *mêm-u* (answering not to the Tamil *nânggaḷ*, but to *nâm*) as its plural exclusive; and as this is the simplest form of the pronoun, it seems better suited to this restricted use than the reduplicated form. Telugu, though differing from Tamil in this point, agrees with Tamil in using *mêmu* as its honorific singular; and this use of the plural exclusive in Telugu as an honorific is more in accordance with philosophical propriety than the Tamilian use of the plural inclusive for this purpose; for when a superior addresses inferiors, it is evidently more natural for him to make use of a plural which excludes those whom he addresses, than one in which they would be included together with himself. Ku agrees with Telugu, and uses *âm-u* (identical in origin with the Tamil *yâm*, *nâm*) to express the restricted signification which Tamil gives to *nâṅgaḷ*. Its plural inclusive is *âju*, the oblique form of which is *ammâ*; and the Telugu plural which corresponds to *âju* (but which in meaning corresponds to *nâm*) is *manam-u*, the base and inflexion of which is *mana*. *manam-u* is probably derived from *mâ*, the inflexional base of *mêmu*, with an euphonic addition, or possibly with a weakened reduplication.

I have now gone over the ground traversed in my first edition, with such additions and corrections as recently-published grammars have enabled me to make. The results are exhibited, for convenience of comparison, in the accompanying table. In this list, I include only those dialects which have been carefully studied, and of which grammars have been published. The pronouns of the first person contained in the Rajmahâl and Ûrâon are exhibited in a separate list, together with those found in Dr Hunter's lists of words contained in the rest of the Central Indian dialects. It is obvious, however, that it would be unsafe to deduce any inference, except one of the vaguest kind, from lists of isolated words collected by persons who had little or no real acquaintance with the dialects to which they belonged. We tread on firmer ground when we compare with one another dialects which have attained to the dignity of possessing published grammars.

DRAVIDIAN PRONOUN OF THE FIRST PERSON.

	SINGULAR.			PLURAL.		
	Nominative, "I."	Inflexion, *i.e.*, inflexional basis of "my," "me," &c.	Pronominal terminations of the Verb.	Nominative, "We."	Inflexion, *i.e.*, inflexional basis of "our," "us," &c.	Pronominal terminations of the Verb.
Tamil . .	*yân, nân.*	*en.*	*en, ên ; an.*	*yâm, nâm, nâṅgaḷ.*	*em, nam, eṅgaḷ.*	*am, âm, em, êm, ôm.*
Malayâḷam .	*ñân.*	*en ; in.*	*ên.*	*nâm, nôm, nammaḷ, nummaḷ, ñaṅgaḷ.*	*em, nô, nôm, nom, num, eṅgaḷ.*	*ôm.*
Telugu . .	*ên-u, ê, nên-u, nê.*	*nâ, nan'.*	*nu, ni, vu, vi.*	*êm-u, mêm-u, manam-u.*	*mâ, mam', mana.*	*mu, mi.*
Canarese. .	*yân, ân, nân-u, nâ.*	*en, nan'.*	*en, en', ên-u, êne, e.*	*âm, âv-u, nâv-u.*	*em, nam.*	*ev-u, êv-u, êv-e.*
Tuḷu . . .	*yân'.*	*yen', yena.*	*e.*	*yenkuḷu, nama.*	*yenkuḷe, nama, nam.*	*a.*
Coorg. . .	*nan'.*	*en.*	*i, e, u.*	*nanga, enga.*	*enga.*	*a, i, u.*
Gônd . . .	*annâ.*	*nâ.*	*ân, na.*	*ammâṭ.*	*mâ.*	*âm, am, ôm.*
Ku . . .	*ân-u.*	*nâ.*	*in, iñ, e.*	*âm-u, âj-u.*	*mâ, ammâ.*	*âm-u.*
Tuda . . .	*ân.*	*en.*	*en, eni, ini.*	*âm, ôm, êm.*	*am ; âm ?*	*emi, imi.*
Kôta . . .	*âne.*	*en.*	*e.*	*âme, nâme,ême.*	*em, nam.*	*eme, ême.*
Rajmahâl .	*en.*	*on ?*		*nam, em, om ; en ?*	*em, nâm.*	
Ûrâon . .	*en.*	*en.*		*em, nâm.*	*em.*	

DRAVIDIAN PRONOUN OF THE SECOND PERSON.

	SINGULAR.			PLURAL.		
	Nominative, "Thou."	Inflexion, *i.e.*, inflexional basis of "they," "thee," &c.	Pronominal terminations of the Verb.	Nominative, "You."	Inflexional basis of "your," &c.	Pronominal terminations of the Verb.
Tamil	*nî, nîy.*	*nin, nun, un.*	*ây, ôy, ei, i.*	*nîr, nîgir, nîvir, nîṅgaḷ.*	*num, um, uṅgaḷ.*	*ir, îr; min?*
Malayâḷam	*nî.*	*nin.*		*niṅṅaḷ, nîṅṅaḷ.*	*niṅṅaḷ, nim.*	
Telugu	*nîv-u, nî, îv-u.*	*nî, nin'.*	*vu, vi.*	*mîr-u, îr-u.*	*mî, mim'.*	*ru, ri.*
Canarese	*nîn, nî, nîn-u.*	*nin.*	*ay; i, î, îye, e.*	*nîm, nîv-u.*	*nim.*	*ir, iri, îri, ari.*
Tuḷu	*î.*	*nina, ni.*	*a.*	*nikuḷu, îr'.*	*nikuḷe, îre.*	*ar'.*
Coorg	*nin'.*	*nin.*	*iya.*	*ninga.*	*ninga.*	*ira.*
Gônd	*immâ.*	*ni.*	*ni, i.*	*immâṭ.*	*mî.*	*ît.*
Ku	*în-u.*	*nî.*	*i.*	*îr-u.*	*mî.*	*êr-u, âr-u.*
Tuda	*nî.*	*nin.*	*i, e.*	*nima.*	*nim.*	*i, e.*
Kôta	*nî.*	*nin.*	*i.*	*nîme, nîve.*	*nim.*	*iri, îri.*
Rajmahâl	*nina, nin.*	*nin.*		*nima; nina?*	*nim.*	
Ûrâon	*nin, nîen.*	*nin, nîen.*		*nim; âs-u?*	*nim; âss'?*	
Brahui	*nî.*	*nâ.*		*num.*	*num.*	*ri.*

PRONOUN OF THE FIRST PERSON IN SEVENTEEN DIALECTS OF CENTRAL INDIA.

Dr Hunter's "Comparative Dictionary."

	Singular.		Plural.	
	"I."	"Mine."	"We."	"Our."
Ho (Kol)	*îng.*	*inya.*	*álle, ábú.*	*alléa, abúá.*
Kol (Singbhúm)	*aing.*	*iyan.*	*áling, ále.*	*alle-á.*
Santáli	*ing, inge.*	*ting ; ing-reá.*	*áling, álang ; ále, ában.*	*tálnig ; tále, taban (alleá ?)*
Bhúmij	*ing.*	*inya.*	*ále.*	*ábusa-ban.*
Mundala	*ing.*	*jhátaná.*	*állege.*	*ahuá-tana.*
Gayeti	*nana.*	*idana, awá.*	*mamad.*	*idana, awa.*
Rutluk	*nan-na.*	*náwá.*	*caret.*	*mawa.*
Naikude	*an.*	*anet.*	*ále (?)*	*ámed.*
Kolami	*an.*	*aneten.*	*anandun.*	*anet.*
Mádi	*nanna, nan.*	*náwá.*	*mam.*	*mawa, adunawaná.*
Mádia	*ana.*	*caret.*	*caret.*	*caret.*
Kuri	*in (ing ?)*	*ing.*	*ále.*	*nan.*
Keikádi	*nanu.*	*namtu.*	*nang.*	*caret.*
Sávara	*gná.*	*gnánate.*	*mo-ni.*	*moni-nate.*
Gadaba	*nai-sa.*	*noinyo.*	*ne-yam.*	*niyyino.*
Yerukala	*ná-nu.*	*nungudedi, namburudu.*	*nama, nam-buru.*	*namburudu.*
Chentsu	*há-me, há-mi.*	*hamár.*	*hame.*	*hamár.*

PRONOUN OF THE SECOND PERSON IN SEVENTEEN DIALECTS OF CENTRAL INDIA.

DR HUNTER'S "COMPARATIVE DICTIONARY."

	SINGULAR.		PLURAL.	
	"Thou."	"Thine."	"Ye."	"Your."
Ho (Kol)	*um.*	*umma.*	*áppe.*	*appéa.*
Kol (Singbhúm)	*um (ám ?)*	*ummá.*	*ape (?)*	*appea.*
Santáli	*ám, umge.*	*tám ; ám-rea (ámi ?)*	*aben ; ápe.*	*taben ; tápe (appe ?)*
Bhúmij	*ám (am ?)*	*ummá.*	*ápe (?)*	*(áppe, tápe ?)*
Mundala	*ám (am ?)*	*ámá-tana.*	*inkoghi.*	*ápiá-tana.*
Gayeti	*ime.*	*niwá.*	*im.*	*ida-wonan.*
Rutluk	*imá.*	*niwá.*	*caret.*	*miwa.*
Naikude	*niwa.*	*inet.*	*ápe (?)*	*imed.*
Kolami	*niwa.*	*ineten.*	*niwa.*	*yeinnaton.*
Mádi	*nima.*	*niwa.*	*mirad.*	*miwa, aduniwand.*
Mádia	*caret.*	*caret.*	*caret.*	*caret.*
Kuri	*am.*	*áma.*	*ápe.*	*caret.*
Keikádi	*ninu.*	*nimtu.*	*ne*	*miwa.*
Sávara	*aman.*	*ammanate.*	*aman.*	*ammanate.*
Gadaba	*no.*	*nenne.*	*pen.*	*caret.*
Yerukala	*ni-nu.*	*ningaḍeo, ninaḍidi.*	*ning-alu, avaru.*	*ningalide, nine-buḍudu.*
Chentsu	*yi-ke, tu-myi, tu.*	*thor.*	*te, tu-myi.*	*thor.*

SECTION II.—DEMONSTRATIVE AND INTERROGATIVE PRONOUNS.

It is very difficult to treat the demonstrative and interrogative pronouns of the Dravidian family separately. The bases are different, but they are built up on those bases in precisely the same manner, and obey one and the same law, so that what is said about the one class may be regarded as said about the other also. I shall discuss them separately as far as possible, but it will often be necessary to treat them together.

1. Demonstrative and Interrogative Bases.

1. *Demonstrative Bases.*—The Dravidian languages, like most other primitive uncompounded tongues, are destitute of pronouns (properly so called) of the third person, and use instead demonstratives signifying this or that, with the addition of suffixes of gender and number. In these languages 'he,' means literally that man; 'she,' that woman; and 'they,' those persons or things. The interrogatives are formed in the same manner by the addition of suffixes of gender and number to an interrogative base signifying 'what.'

The words which signify man and woman have gradually lost the definiteness of their original signification, and shrunk into the position of masculine and feminine terminations. They are no longer substantives, but mere suffixes or signs of gender; and are so closely incorporated with the demonstrative bases that it requires some knowledge of the principles of the language to enable us to separate them. In comparison, therefore, with the Turkish and Ugrian languages, in which there is but one pronoun of the third person, the Dravidian languages, which possess a great variety, appear to considerable advantage. Nevertheless, the speech of the Dravidians appears to have been originally no richer than the other Scythian idioms; and to have at length surpassed them only by the Aryanistic device of fusing that-man, that-woman, that-thing, into single euphonious words. The signification of man and woman still shines through in the masculine and feminine terminations; but no trace remains of the words by which a thing and things were originally expressed, and which are now represented only by *d*, the sign of the neuter singular, and *a*, that of the neuter plural.

Four demonstrative bases are recognised by one or another of the Dravidian dialects, each of which is a pure vowel—viz., *a*, the remote *i*, the proximate, and *u*, the medial demonstrative; together with *ê*, which is the suffix of emphasis in most of the dialects, but is a demonstrative in Ku. The first two—viz., *a*, the remote, and *i*, the proximate demonstrative—are the most widely and frequently used. The medial *u* is occasionally used by the Tamil poets, more frequently in classical Canarese and in Tuḷu, to denote a person or object which is intermediate between the remote and the proximate; and it will be found that it has ulterior affinities of its own. *ê*, the ordinary Dravidian suffix of emphasis, is used as a demonstrative in Ku alone—in addition however to *a* and *i*—*e.g.*, *êvâru*, they. It appears also in the Ûrâon *êdah*, this, the correlative of *hûdah*, that. The use of *ê* being chiefly emphatic, I refer the reader, for an account of it, to a subsequent head. The ordinary demonstratives of the Dravidian dialects are the simple short vowels *a*, *i*, and *u*; and it will be found that every other form which they assume is derived from this by some euphonic process.

2. *Interrogative Bases.*—There are two classes of interrogatives in the Dravidian languages—viz., interrogative pronouns or adjectives, such as, who? which? what? and syntactic interrogatives, such as, is it? is there? Interrogative pronouns and adjectives resolve themselves in the Dravidian tongues into interrogative prefixes, resembling the demonstrative prefixes already considered, by suffixing to which the formatives of number and gender we form interrogative pronouns. The interrogative particle itself, when simply prefixed to a substantive, constitutes the interrogative adjective what?

(*a.*) The most common interrogative prefix is the vowel *e*. In all the Dravidian dialects this prefix is used in the formation of pronominals, in precisely the same manner as the demonstrative bases *a* and *i*. It forms one of a set of vocalic prefixes (*a*, *i*, *u*, and *e*), which occupy one and the same position, obey one and the same law, and differ only in the particular signification which is expressed by each. The unity of principle pervading these prefixes will be clearly apparent from the subjoined comparative view. The forms which are here exhibited are those of the Tamil alone; but in this particular all the dialects agree on the whole so perfectly with the Tamil, and with one another, that it is unnecessary to multiply examples. I exhibit here an alternative (probably an older) interrogative base in *yâ*, which will be inquired into further on.

	Proximate Demonstrative *i*.	Remote Demonstrative *a*.	Intermediate Demonstrative *u*.	Interrogative *e* or *yâ*.
Mas. sing.	*ivan*, hic.	*avan*, ille.	*uvan*.	*evan* or *yâvan*, quis ?
Fem. do.	*ivaḷ*, hæc.	*avaḷ*, illa.	*uvaḷ*.	*evaḷ* or *yâvaḷ*, quæ ?
Neut. do.	*idu*, hoc.	*adu*, illud.	*udu*.	*edu* or *yâdu*, quid ?
Epic. plu.	*ivar*, hi, hæ.	*avar*, illi, illæ.	*uvar*.	*evar* or *yâvar*, qui ? quæ ?
Neut. do.	*ivei*, hæc.	*avei*, illa.	*uvei*.	*evei* or *yâvei*, quæ ?

I need not call attention to the beautiful and philosophical regularity of this quadruple set of remote, proximate, and intermediate demonstratives and interrogatives. In no other language or family of languages in the world shall we find its equal, or even its second. In addition to which, the circumstance that the demonstrative vowels are not only used in these languages with an invariable and exact discrimination of meaning which is not found in the Indo-European tongues (with the solitary and partial exception of the New Persian), but are also associated with a corresponding interrogative vowel of which the Indo-European tongues are totally ignorant, tends to confirm the supposition which I have already expressed, that the Dravidian family has retained some Præ-Sanskrit elements of immense antiquity; and, in particular, that its demonstratives, instead of being borrowed from Sanskrit, represent those old Japhetic bases from which the demonstratives of Sanskrit itself, as well as of various other members of the Indo-European family, were derived.

(*b*.) The other interrogative base of the Dravidian languages is *yâ*. *yâ* is not used at all in Telugu, but is largely used in Canarese, and somewhat more rarely in Tamil. Probably there was originally only one interrogative base, and if so, it must have been *yâ*, and *e* must have been corrupted from it. The process by which *yâ* became *e* is tolerably clear. *a* evinces a tendency to be weakened into *e*. (See "Part I., Sounds.") We have seen an illustration of this in the circumstance that the Sanskrit *yama*, the name of the god of death, becomes in Tamil *ema(n)*, pronounced *yema(n)*. In Tuḷu, *yâr*, who, becomes *yêr'*. This is a considerable step towards *e*. Then, also, *e* is commonly pronounced as *ye*, and *ê* as *yê*; and in Telugu this *y* is frequently written, as well as heard. This would facilitate the omission of the *y* in writing, when *yâ* came generally to be weakened into *yê*.

ê alone would in time have the same force as *yê*, and would come to be regarded as its equivalent. The long form *ê* still survives in the Malayâḷam *êvan*, *êvaḷ*, he, she, for *evan*, *evaḷ*; and in the Tamil and Malayâḷam *êdu*, and the Telugu *êdi*. In Telugu *ê* sometimes directly corresponds to the Tamil *yâ*—*e.g.*, compare *yâṇḍu*, Tam. where, when, a year (nasalised from *yâḍu*), with the Telugu *êḍu*, where, *êḍi*, a year. We see also this long interrogative *ê* in the Telugu *êla*, how, in what manner, compared with *âla*, *îla*, in that manner, in this manner.

There is a remarkable change in Canarese of the interrogative *yâ* into *dâ*. We may say either *yâvan-u* or *dâvan-u*, what man? *yâvaḷ-u* or *dâvaḷ-u*, what woman? *yâvadu* or *dâvadu*, what thing? So also the crude interrogative is *yâva* or *dâva*, who, which, what? In Tuḷu we find the same *dâ*, which? alternating with *vâ* and *vôva*; also *dâṇe*, what? *dâye*, why? In these instances the analogy of the other dialects leads me to conclude *yâ* to be the older and more correct form of the interrogative base. In *yêr*, who? *yâ* appears as *yê*, which is a very trifling change. The Gônd interrogative *bâ* and *bô* appear to be hardened from *yâ*, like the Tuḷu *vâ*.

In High Tamil, *yâ* is not only prefixed adjectivally to substantives (like *a*, *e*, and *e*)—*e.g.*, *yâ-(k)kâlam*, what time? but it is even used by itself as a pronoun—*e.g.*, *yâ-(ś)śeydây*, what hast thou done? It forms the basis of only one adverbial noun—viz., *yâṇḍu*, Tam. when? a year, a correlative of *âṇḍu*, then, and *îṇḍu*, now. The only use to which *yâ* is put in the colloquial dialect of Tamil, is that of forming the basis of interrogative pronouns; a complete set of which, in Tamil as well as in Canarese, are formed from *yâ*—*e.g.*, *yâvan*, *quis?* *yâvaḷ*, *quæ?* *yâdu*, *quid?* *yâvar*, *qui*, *quæ?* *yâvei*, *quæ?* The Canarese interrogative pronouns accord with these, with a single unimportant exception. The neuters, singular and plural, of the Canarese are formed from *yâva*, instead of *yâ*—*e.g.*, *yâvadu*, *quid?* (for *yâdu*,) and *yâvavu*, *quæ?* (for *yâva*.) This additional *va* is evidently derived by imitation from the euphonic *v* of *yâvanu*, he, and its related forms; but it is out of place in connection with the neuter, and is to be regarded as a corruption. In Tamil, a peculiar usage with respect to the application of the epicene plural *yâvar*, *qui*, *quæ*, has obtained ground. It is largely used in the colloquial dialect, with the signification of the singular as well as that of the plural, though itself a plural only and epicene; and when thus used, *yâvar* is abbreviated into *yâr*—*e.g.*, *avan yâr*, who is he? (literally he who;) *avaḷ yâr*, who is she? *yâr* has also been still further corrupted into *âr*, especially in compounds.

1. *Demonstrative and Interrogative Pronouns.*—The original character of the demonstrative bases, like that of the interrogative, is

best exhibited by the neuter singular, the formative of which does not commence with a vowel, like *an* and *aḷ* (Tamil), the masculine and feminine suffixes, but consists in a single consonant, *d*, followed by an enunciative vowel—that is, a vowel intended merely as a help to enunciation. This vowel is *i* in Telugu, a very short *u* in the other languages. The remote and proximate neuter singulars are in Telugu *adi*, *idi*, that (thing), this (thing); the interrogative *êdi*, what (thing); in Tamil, Malayâḷam, and Canarese they are *adu*, *idu* (with the intermediate *udu*), and *edu*. In Gônd the demonstratives are *ad*, *id*. The anomalous forms of the Tuḷu and the Tuda will be considered further on.

d having already been shown to be the sign of the neuter singular used by pronominals and appellatives, and there being no hiatus between *a*, *i*, or *u* and *d*, and therefore no necessity for euphonic insertions, it is evident that the *a*, *i*, and *u* of the neuter singulars cited above constitute the purest form of the demonstrative bases. The suffixes which are annexed to the demonstrative bases *a*, *i*, and *u*, for the purpose of forming the masculine and feminine singulars and the epicene and neuter plurals, commence with a vowel. Those suffixes are in Tamil *an* for the masculine, *aḷ* for the feminine, *ar* for the epicene plural, and *ei* or *a* for the neuter plural; and *v* is the consonant which is most commonly used to prevent hiatus. The following, therefore, are the demonstrative pronouns of Tamil—viz., *avan*, ille; *ivan*, hic; *avaḷ*, illa; *ivaḷ*, hæc; *avar*, illi; *ivar*, hic; *avei*, illa; *ivei*, hæc. To these must be added the intermediates *uvan*, *uvaḷ*, *udu*, *uvar*, *uvei*, which do not admit of being translated by a single word. I quote examples from Tamil alone, because, though different formatives of number and gender are sometimes annexed in the other dialects, those differences do not affect the demonstrative bases. The anomaly which will be noticed in the case of Tuḷu will be found, when examined, to be only apparent. All the above suffixes of gender have already been investigated in the section on "The Noun." The mode in which they are annexed to the demonstrative bases is the only point which requires to be examined here.

The demonstrative bases being vocalic, and all the suffixes, with the exception of the neuter singular, commencing with a vowel, some euphonic consonants had to be used to keep the concurrent vowels separate and pure. *v*, though most frequently used to prevent hiatus, is not the only consonant employed for this purpose. The Ku being but little attentive to euphony, it sometimes dispenses altogether with the euphonic *v*, and leaves the contiguous vowels uncombined—*e.g.*, *ââñju*, he; *ââlu*, she. Even Tamil sometimes combines those vowels instead of euphonically separating them—*e.g.*, *yâvar*, who? is commonly abbreviated into *yâr*; and this is still further softened to *âr* in the colloquial dialect.

In the higher dialect of Tamil, *n* is often used euphonically instead of *v*, especially in the personal terminations of the verbs. Thus, instead of *irundân* (for *irundavan*), he was, the poets sometimes say *irundanan;* and for *irundava*, they (neuter) were, the form which we should expect to find used, *irundana* is universally used instead. This euphonic *v* has in some instances come to be regarded as an integral part of the demonstrative itself. In the nominative plural of the Gônd neuter demonstrative, the final and characteristic vowel *a* has disappeared altogether, without leaving any representative—*e.g.*, *av*, those (things); *iv*, these (things). In the oblique cases *a* is represented by *e*. In Telugu, though the nominatives of the neuter plural demonstratives *avi* and *ivi* use *v* merely as an euphonic, yet in the oblique cases, the bases of which are *vâ* and *vî*, the demonstrative vowels have got displaced, and *v* stands at the beginning of the word, as if it were a demonstrative, and had a right *per se* to be represented. In the masculine singulars *vâḍu*, ille; *vîḍu*, hic; and in the epicene plurals *vâru*, illi; *vîru*, hi, *v* euphonic has advanced a step further, and assumed the position of a demonstrative in the nominative as well as in the inflexion. That this *v*, however, is not a demonstrative, and that the use to which it is put in Telugu is abnormal, is shown by the fact that in *dâ* and *dî*, the inflexions of *adi* and *idi*, illud and hoc, the neuter singular demonstratives of the Telugu *d*, though certainly not a demonstrative, nor even euphonic, but simply a sign or suffix of neuter singularity, has been advanced to as prominent a position (by a similar euphonic displacement) as if it belonged to the root. Compare especially the corresponding Telugu interrogative.

In Tuḷu the proximate neuter singular demonstrative is *indu* or *undu*, the remote *avu*. *indu* and *undu* correspond to the Tamil proximate *idu* and intermediate *udu:* the only difference consists in the nasalisation of the *d*. *avu*, the remote demonstrative, though a neuter singular, is identical in form with the Canarese *avu*, they (neuter). The *v* of *avu* seems to be merely euphonic, as it disappears altogether in the plural, which is not *avukuḷu*, but *eikuḷu* (*avu* = *ayu* = *ei*). The corresponding masculine pronoun is *âye*, he, in which *y* is used euphonically where *v* would have been used in Tamil. In the feminine *âḷ'*, she (Tam. *avaḷ*), even the *y* has disappeared, and the two contiguous vowels have coalesced. The proximate pronouns of the Tuḷu masculine and feminine singular and plural present several peculiarities. *imbe*, he (*hic*), corresponds to the Tamil *ivan*, the Old Canarese *ivam*. The euphonic *v* of those languages seems to have been hardened into *m*, and this *m* to have become *mb*. The plural of the same is *mêr'* (the remote is *âr*, for *avar*). The feminine proximate she (hæc) is *môḷ'*, the plural of which is *môkuḷu*. *mêr* stands for *ivar* = *imar*, and *môḷ'* for *ivaḷ* = *imaḷ*. Compare the apparent disappearance of the demonstrative bases *i* and *a* in the Telugu *vîru* and *vâru*, they, proximate and remote, for *ivar* and *avar*. See also "The Noun," epicene plural, in *mâr*. The same peculiarity appears in the Tuḷu demonstrative adverbs. *avuḷu*, there, corresponds with similar words in the other dialects (Can. *alli*); but *mûḷu*, here, presents the same peculiarity as *môl*, hæc.

In the Tuda dialect the pronoun of the third person is the same for both numbers and for all three persons, like the Sanskrit reflexive pronoun *svayam*. *atham* represents everything of which 'that' can be predicated; *itham* is the equivalent for this. With *atham*, *itham*, compare the Telugu *ataḍu*, *atanu*, *âtaṅdu*, *âtaḍu*, *itaḍu*, *itanu*, *îtaḍu*, *îtanu*; the Old Canarese singular masculines *âtam*, *îtam*, *ûtam*. The final *am* of the Tuda is occasionally dropped.

Tamil possesses a complete set of abstract demonstrative and interrogative nouns of perfect regularity and great beauty. I class them here (for convenience of comparison) with demonstrative and interrogative pronouns; but they are in reality nouns, expressing abstractly the ideas that are embodied in the pronouns in a concrete shape. They consist of the demonstrative and interrogative vowel bases (*a*, *i*, *u*, *e*), with the addition of *mei*, the ordinary formative of abstract nouns, which we have already noticed in *tan-mei*, nature, literally self-ness, in the section on the reflexive pronoun *tân*. The initial consonant of *mei* is doubled by rule after the demonstrative and interrogative vowels. The words referred to are *immei*, this-ness; *ammei*, that-ness; *ummei*, an intermediate position between that-ness and this-ness; *emmei*, what-ness. In use, the words chiefly denote the different states of being or births. *immei*, the present state or birth, is the only word of the set in common use; the rest are found only in the poets. *ammei* (common equivalent *maṟumei*, other-ness) denotes the future birth; *ummei*, the birth before the present; *emmei*, what birth? generally found with the addition of *um*, and so as to give the meaning 'in whatsoever birth.'

We have seen that the neuter singular of the demonstrative and interrogative pronouns, properly so called, is formed by the addition of the neuter formative *d* to the vowel bases *a*, *i*, *u*; *e* or *yâ*.

There are traces also of the existence of two classes of pronouns formed by means of the addition to the same vowel bases of *m*, the equivalent of which is *u*, or of *l*. Pronominals ending in *l* are used chiefly as adverbs of place and mode. There are exceptions, however —*e.g.*, *alla*, Tel., that, has the force of an adjective (*alladi*, that thing). See Adverbs : formative *l*, *ḷ*. The demonstrative pronouns and pronominals ending in *m* or *n* are not free from doubt: I shall, therefore, adduce first the interrogatives belonging to this class, about which no doubt can be entertained.

Each of the dialects possesses a neuter interrogative pronoun, formed from the interrogative base *e* or *ê*, and the neuter formative *n* or *m*. This formative is more abstract than *d*, but less so than *mei*. *ed-u* means which? *en*, what? In Tamil we find *en*, what? from which is formed the singular appellative *ennadu*, what thing? and the plural *eṉna*, what things? *en* is also lengthened into *ên*, the ordinary meaning of which is why? Though *enna* is properly a plural neuter, it has come to be used also as a singular, and is even turned colloquially into a singular neuter noun, *ennam*—*e.g.*, *ennamây*, how? Malayâḷam uses *ên*, like Tamil, meaning what? rather than why? but does not use *en;* instead of this we have *endu*, what? which, however, is probably the Malayâḷam shape of the Tamil *ennadu* = *en-du*. In Canarese *ênu* is not a mere interrogative particle, but a regularly declined interrogative pronoun, like the vulgar Tamil *ennam*. We have substantially the same word in the Telugu *êmi*, what? why? *êmi* bears the same relation to *êdi*, Tel. what (thing)? that *en* in Tamil bears to *edu*. The only difference is in the use of the more abstract *n* or *m* as a neuter formative, instead of *d*, which gives more distinctly the sense of the neuter singular. In the compound word *êmô*, Tel., I know not what (Tam. Mal. Can. *ênô*), from *êm* and *ô*, the particle of doubt, we see that *êmi* is a secondary form of *êm;* and by the help of Tamil we are able to trace this *êm* back to the shorter form *em*. *êni*, which I consider the equivalent of *êmi*, is used in the conjugation of Telugu verbs as a conditional particle; properly it implies a question.

We now return to the demonstratives which appear to be formed from the demonstrative vowels *a*, *i*, *u*, with the addition of *m* or *n*. *am*, that, appears to survive in the *am* which is used so largely as a formative by neuter nouns in Tamil and Malayâḷam; and possibly also in *am*, which seems to be the oldest sign of the Dravidian accusative case. In each of these instances *an* is often used instead of *am*. See the sections treating on these formatives and case-signs in Part III., "The Noun." *im* shows itself in the Canarese sign of the ablative case, originally a locative, and in the corresponding Tamil *in*, with which *il* corresponds. The primitive meaning seems to be this place, here, and hence, a place, a house. Both *al* and *il* appear also in verbal derivatives, especially in Tamil, in which, *e.g.*, the number of nouns derived from verbal roots which take *al* or *il* as their formative, is almost as large as those which take *am* or *an*. Dr Gundert derives from *am* or *im* the Tamil demonstrative adjectives *anda*, that, *inda*, this; and I presume would attribute the same origin to the Telugu and Canarese adjectives *anta*, *inta*, &c., which are more or less demonstratives in meaning. On the whole, however, I still prefer to regard these forms as nasalised from *ad'*, that, *id'*, this. We had an instance of this nasalisation before us just now in the Tuḷu pronoun *indu*, *undu*, this (thing), which must be identified with the *idu*, *udu* of the other dialects. On the other hand, I have no doubt of the origin of *inda*, the Canarese sign of the ablative, from *im;* and the Tamil adverbial nouns *andru*, *indru*, *endru*, that day, to-day, what day, seem to be formed either from *am*, *im*, *em*, or from *al*, *il*, *el*. See the Demonstrative and Interrogative Adverbs.

A very interesting inquiry remains. Is *um*, the Tamil-Malayâḷam particle of conjunction, and, even (Tel. *u*, classical Can. *um*, *am;* coll. Can. *û*), to be regarded as a demonstrative pronoun, formed from *u*, the intermediate demonstrative base, and the formative *m*, corresponding in origin to the demonstrative *am* and *im*, and also to the interrogative *em*, considered above? That this is the origin of *um* is one of the most ingenious of the many ingenious suggestions contained in Dr Gundert's communication. In his Malayâḷam dictionary he prefers to derive *um* from *u*, the supposed root of the verbal noun *uyar*, height, with the meaning of above. In classical Canarese *am* is sometimes used as the equivalent of *um;* and this seems to connect the particle at once with the demonstratives. In Tamil poetry we find an adverbial demonstrative of place, *umbar*, with the meaning of the intermediate demonstrative *u*, the correlatives of which are *ambar*, that place, *imbar*, this place, and *embar*, which place? *umbar* means literally a place intermediate between two other places; but it is remarkable that it is also used in a secondary sense to signify on, upon, above, and even *uyar*, height. We thus get for *um*, the conjunctive particle, the meaning above, which is one that suits it exceedingly well, without any inconsistency with its ultimately demonstrative origin. *um* at the end of verbs changes occasionally in the Tamil poets to *undu*, which reminds one of the *undu*, this (thing), and also yes, of the Tuḷu.

2. *Demonstrative and Interrogative Adjectives.*—When the demonstrative bases *a* and *i* are simply prefixed to substantives, they convey the signification of the demonstrative adjectives that and this. When prefixed, they are indeclinable; but on thus prefixing them to substan-

tives, either the initial consonant of the substantive is euphonically doubled—*e.g.*, *annâḷ* (*a-(n)-nâḷ*), Tam. that day; or if this euphonic doubling is not resorted to, the demonstrative vowels are lengthened. Tamil invariably adopts the former plan: the latter is more common in Malayâḷam and Canarese. When the substantive commences with a vowel, and *v* is inserted as usual to prevent hiatus, Tamil, by a dialectic rule of sound, doubles this *v*, as if it were regarded as an initial consonant—*e.g.*, when *ûr*, Tam. a village, receives this prefix, it becomes not *avûr* (*a-(v)-ûr*), but *avvûr*. The origin of this doubling of the initial consonant of the word to which the demonstrative vowel is prefixed, is to be ascribed to the emphasis which is necessarily included in the signification of the demonstrative. Through this emphasis *a* and *i* assume the character, not of ordinary formatives, but of qualifying words; and the energy which they acquire influences the initial consonant of the following substantive, which is no longer an isolated word, but the second member of a compound. In the same manner and from a similar cause, when Sanskrit words which commence with *a* privative are borrowed by Tamil, the consonant to which *a* is prefixed is often doubled, at least in the colloquial dialect—*e.g.*, *aññânam* (*a-(ñ)-ñânam*), ignorance.

The occasional lengthening of the demonstrative vowels, when used adjectivally, in Malayâḷam, Canarese, and the other dialects (without the doubling of the succeeding consonant), is merely another method of effecting the same result. The emphasis which is imparted in this manner to the demonstrative, is equivalent to that which the doubled consonant gives; and hence when the demonstrative vowels are lengthened, from *ă* and *ĭ* to *â* and *î*, the succeeding consonant always remains single. The fact that the demonstrative vowels are short in the pronouns of the third person in each of the Dravidian dialects without exception, shows that those vowels could not originally have been long, and that the use of long *â* and *î* as adjectival prefixes, instead of *a* and *i*, is owing to emphasis. Some curious illustrations of the lengthening of a vowel through emphasis alone, are furnished by the common speech of the Tamil people—*e.g.*, *adigam*, much, large—a word which is borrowed by Tamil from Sanskrit—when it is intended to signify very much, is colloquially pronounced *adîgam*. Similar instances might be adduced from each of the colloquial dialects.

The only peculiarity which requires notice in the use of the interrogative prefix *e*, is the circumstance that it is occasionally lengthened to *ê*, precisely as *a* and *i* are lengthened to *â* and *î*. In Tamil this emphatic lengthening is very rare. It is found only in the neuter singular interrogative pronoun *edu*, what or which (thing?) quid?

which sometimes, especially in composition, becomes *êdu;* and in the interrogative *en*, what, why? which is ordinarily lengthened to *ên*. In Malayâḷam *êdu* and *ên* have entirely displaced *edu* and *en*. In Telugu also this increase of quantity is common. It appears not only in *êmi* and *êla*, why? but is often used as the interrogative prefix, where Tamil invariably has short *e*. Thus, whilst Tamil has *evvidam*, what manner? how? Telugu says either *evvidhamu* or *êvidhamu*. So also, whilst Tamil occasionally only uses *êdu*, quid, instead of the more classical *edu*, the corresponding interrogative of Telugu is invariably *êdi*, and its plural *êvi*. On the other hand, the Telugu masculine interrogative pronoun *evvaḍu*, quis? preserves the same quantity as the Tamil *evan;* and even when the prefix is used adjectivally, it is sometimes *e* (not *ê*) as in Tamil—*e.g.*, *eppuḍu*, what time? when? and *epuḍu*, *epḍu*, in poetry, but not *êpuḍu*. In the Tuḷu interrogatives of time, *ê* is the interrogative base; in those of place—*e.g.*, *ôḷu*, where (pronounced *wôḷu*), *ê* is replaced by *ô*.

In addition to the use of the simple vowels *a*, *i*, and *e*, and their equivalents *â*, *î*, and *ê*, as demonstrative and interrogative adjectives, much use is also made in Tamil of a triplet of adjectives derived from the above. The simple vowels may be styled merely demonstrative prefixes. The adjectives referred to may be called by right demonstrative adjectives. They are *anda*, that, *inda*, this, *enda*, which? or what? —*e.g.*, *anda maram*, that tree, *inda nilam*, this land, *enda âḷ*, which person? These demonstrative and interrogative adjectives are unknown to the other dialects of the family. They are unknown even in Malayâḷam, and in the higher dialect of Tamil itself they are unused. They appear to have been developed in Tamil subsequently to the separation from it of Malayâḷam, and subsequently to the first beginnings of its literary cultivation. We find demonstrative and interrogative adjectives similar to these in form, and probably in origin, but differing somewhat in meaning, both in Telugu and in Canarese. The Tamil *anda*, *inda*, *enda*, mean simply that, this, which? the parallel Telugu and Canarese words have the meaning of such, like that or this, so much, &c., and are used more like adverbs than like adjectives. They are in both languages *anta*, *inta*, *enta*, with a few dialectic differences of no importance. Connected with these is the Tam.-Mal. adjective *inna*, such and such—*e.g.*, *inna ûr*, such and such a town. There is no corresponding adjective derived from *a*. The final *a* of all these adjectives is clearly identical with the *a* which is one of the most common formatives of the relative participle, and the most common case-sign of the possessive, by means of which also so many adjectives are formed. The first part of these words (*and'*, *ant'*, &c.) has been considered above under the head of "Demonstrative Pronouns."

I should here add the Telugu triplet of adjectives *iṭṭi*, *aṭṭi*, *eṭṭi*, this like, that like, what like? Also the Canarese triplet, with a signification partly adjectival, partly adverbial, *initu*, *anitu*, *enitu*, this much, that much, how much? With this is connected the Telugu set of secondary pronouns, *indaru*, so many people, *inni*, so many things, with their corresponding remote and interrogative forms, *andaru*, *anni*; *endaṛu*, *enni*.

The demonstrative and interrogative bases *il*, *al*, *el* are used, as has been mentioned, almost exclusively as adverbs. One of them makes its appearance in Telugu as an adjective, viz., *alla*, that (*e.g.*, *alladi*, that thing). Both in Tamil and Malayâḷam the demonstrative pronouns *adu*, *idu* are often used instead of the demonstrative adjectives *a*, *i*, *anda*, *inda*, in Tamil, and *â*, *î* in Malayâḷam—*e.g.*, *adu kâriyam*, Tam. that matter, *adu poṛudu*, Mal. that time. This usage illustrates the manner in which I suppose *anda*, &c., to have been derived from *adu*, &c.

3. *Demonstrative and Interrogative Adverbs.*—All Dravidian adverbs, properly speaking, are either nouns or verbs. Adverbs of manner and degree are mostly infinitives or gerunds of verbs. Adverbs of place, time, cause, and other relations are mostly nouns. Some of those adverbial nouns are indeclinable, and those of them which are capable of being declined are rarely declined. Whether declined or not declined, they have generally the signification either of the dative or of the locative case. The latter is the more usual, so that words literally signifying that time, what time? really signify at or in that time, at or in what time? Any noun whatever, conveying the idea of relation, may be converted into a demonstrative or interrogative adverb by simply prefixing to it the demonstrative or interrogative vowels.

There is a class of words, however, more nearly resembling our adverbs, formed by annexing to the demonstrative and interrogative vowels certain formative suffixes. The suffix is not of itself a noun, like the second member of the class of words mentioned above. It is merely a formative particle. But the compound formed from the union of the vowel base with the suffixed particle is regarded as having become a noun, and is treated as such, though in signification it has become what we are accustomed to call an adverb. A comparison of the demonstrative and interrogative adverbs of the various dialects shows that the same, or substantially the same, word is an adverb of place in one dialect, an adverb of time in another, an adverb either of place or of time, as occasion may require, in a third, and an adverb of mode or of cause in a fourth. It seems best therefore to arrange them, not in the order of their meanings, but in the order of the different suffixes by means of which they are formed.

(1.) *Formative k, g, ṅ.*—Tam. *iṅgu, îṅgu; aṅgu, âṅgu; eṅgu, yâṅgu*, here, there, where? Can. *îga, âga, yârâga*, now, then, when? *hîge, hâge, hyâge*, in this manner, in that manner, in what manner? *yâke*, why? Gônd, *hoke*, thither, *hike*, thither, *haga, aga*, there, *iga*, here, *baga*, where? *inga*, now.

I consider the Tamil *aṅgu*, &c., nasalised from *agu*. The primitive unnasalised form is seen in the Canarese and Gônd. The change of the *gu* of the other dialects into *ngu* in Tamil is exceedingly common. The resemblance between the Gônd *iga*, here, and the Sanskrit *iha*, here, is remarkably close; yet there is no appearance of the Gônd word having been borrowed from the Sanskrit one. The demonstrative base *i* is, as we have seen, the common property of the Indo-European and the Dravidian languages; but though *iga* seems to bear the same relation to *iha* that *eg-o* bears to *ah-am*, yet the Dravidian formative *k, g, ṅg*, by suffixing which demonstrative vowels become adverbs of place and time, and so many nouns are formed from verbs, does not seem to have any connection with the merely euphonic *h* of *iha*. Comp. Mongolian *yago*, what?

(2.) *Formative ch, j, ñ.*

The only instances of this are in Tuḷu. *iñchi, añchi, oñchi*, hither, thither, whither? *iñcha, añcha, eñcha*, in this, that, what manner? In Tinnerelly, in the southern Tamil country, *iṅgê*, here, is vulgarly pronounced *iñje*.

(3.) *Formative ṭ, ḍ, ṇ.*

Tamil (classical dial.) *îṇḍu*, here, in this present life, in this manner; *âṇḍu*, there (vulgarly, but erroneously used for *yâṇḍu*, a year); *yâṇḍu*, where? when? a time, a year. *âṭṭei*, annual, should be *yâṭṭei*. *ivan, avan, evan*, here, there, where? Telugu, *iṭa, aṭa, eṭa*, here, there, where? *iṭu, aṭu, eṭu*, in this, that, what manner? *îḍa, âḍa, êḍa*, here, there, where? From *êḍa*, with the secondary meaning 'when,' comes *êḍu*, a year. Tuḷu, *iḍe, aḍe, oḍe*, hither, thither, whither? We see now that the primitive, unnasalised form of the Tamil *yâṇḍu* must have been *yâḍu*, formed regularly from *yâ + ḍu*, like *edu*, which? from *e + du*.

(4.) *Formative t, d, n*, also *ndr*.

Tamil, *indru, andru, endru* (secondary forms, *ittrei, attrei, ettrei*); Canarese, *indu, andu, endu;* Malayâḷam, *inn', ann', enn';* Tuḷu, *ini, âni, êni*. In each case the meaning is the same—viz., this day, that day, what day? or now, then, when? In the Telugu, *indu, andu, endu,* we have evidently the same triplet of words. The only difference is that they are used as adverbs of place, not, as in the other dialects, as adverbs of time. They are used to mean, in this, that, what place—*i.e.*, here, there, where? *indu* and *andu* have acquired the special meaning of, this life and the next, here and hereafter, like the Tamil, *immei, ammei;* and *andu,* there, is commonly used as the sign of the locative case, like the Canarese *alli.* In all the dialects these adverbs are declinable. In form they are simply nouns. It appears on the whole most probable that these words have been nasalised from the pronouns *idu, adu, edu.* There is a peculiarity in the Tamil form of these words, consisting in this, that *ndr* suggests the idea that *andru* is formed from *al,* that, like the corresponding *andru,* not, it is not (from *al,* not + *du*), or *endru,* classical Tam. the sun (from *el,* the sun, time + *du*); but the testimony of the other dialects does not confirm this idea. As, however, in Tamil *endru* (the sun) is formed from *el,* so another *endru* is formed from *en*—viz., *endru,* having said, which is from *en* + *du.*

(5.) *Formative mb.*

Tamil-Malayâḷam, *imbar, ambar, embar,* here, there, where?

The formative *mb* is as commonly used in the formation of derivative nouns as *ng,* but the demonstrative adverbial nouns formed from *mb* are now obsolete. They survive in poetry alone. The final *ar* is the equivalent of *al.* Strange to say, there is an interrogative in Mongolian which looks almost identical with this, *yambar,* what? This might be supposed to be a mere accident were it not that the Mongolian *yambar* is formed from the interrogative base *ya,* which is also the true, primitive Dravidian base. This base appears also in the Mongolian *yage,* what?

(6.) *Formative l, ḷ.*

Canarese, *illi, alli, elli,* here, there, where? In Telugu *il,* the proximate, is not used as a demonstrative, but survives in *ilu, illu,* a house, the root-meaning of which appears to be this place, here. The longer form of this word, however, is used demonstratively—*e.g., îlâ,* in this manner; *ala,* there, *âlâ,* in that manner; *elli,* where? *elli* is used also to mean to-morrow (in Tuḷu *elle* is to-morrow); *êla, êlâ,* in what way? These words show that *l* holds an important place amongst the demonstrative and interrogative formatives. In some Tuḷu adverbs *l* is replaced by the lingual *ḷ*—*e.g., mûḷu, avaḷu, ôḷu,* here, there, where?

The existence in Tamil of demonstratives and interrogatives formed from *l,* like those we find in Telugu and Canarese, is by no means certain, but traces of them, particularly of the interrogative *el,* may, I think, be discovered. *el* is not now used directly as an interrogative, but there are many words formed from *el,* the meanings of which seem to me to pre-suppose the existence of a primary interrogative sense. Compare *yâṇḍu,* Tam. a year, primarily where? when? also Tel. *êḍu,* a year, primarily where (*êḍa*)? I shall here set down the various meanings of the Tamil *el* in what appears to me to be the order of their growth. It will be found, I think, that they include the words for 'a boundary,' and for 'all,' not only in Tamil, but in all the Dravidian dialects.

(1.) What, where, when? as in Canarese and Telugu (supposititious meaning).

(2.) A period of time, a day, to-morrow (compare Telugu and Tuḷu), the sun (the cause of day), night (that being also a period of time). Other forms of this word are *elvei, êlvei,* time, a day; *elli, ellavan, endru* (*el* + *du*), *endravan,* the sun. The meaning of the sun appears in *erpâḍu,* properly *el-pâḍu,* sun-set. *elli* means night, as well as the sun.

(3.) A boundary. This in Tamil is *ellei,* old Tamil *elgei* (*gei,* a formative of verbal nouns). This word means in Tamil, not only a boundary, but also a term, time, the sun, end, the last. There appears to me no doubt of the identity of this word with meaning No. 2. The meaning of boundary is derived from that of termination. Compare the poetical compound *ellei-(t)-tî,* the last fire, the fire by which the world is to be consumed.

(4.) All. This stage of development is more doubtful, but I find that Dr Gundert agrees with me here, at least as to *el,* the first part and base of the word meaning a boundary. I explain *el* to mean 'whatever is included within the boundary,' everything up to the last. Dr Gundert thinks *ell-â* a negative, meaning boundless. This would be a very natural derivation for a word signifying all, but I am obliged to dissent, as I find no trace of this *â* of negation in any of the older poetical forms of this word in Tamil—*e.g., el-âm,* all we, *el-îr,* all ye. The colloquial word *ellâm* (properly *ellâvum*) is not to be confounded with the classical word *elâm,* all we. It does not contain the meaning of 'we.' The *â* of *el(l)-â-(v)um* is the abbreviated relative participle of *âgu,* commonly used as a connective or continuative link, and meaning properly 'that which is.' *um* is added in Tamil to give the word a universal application. This use of *um* confirms me in the idea that *el,* all, is identical not only with *el,* a boundary, but with *el,* what? The latter and primitive meaning seems to me to shine through that of a boundary, and to throw light on that of all. Just as *evâṇ-um,* who—and, means whosoever, so if *el* were originally an interrogative, *el(l)-â-(v)um* would naturally be used to mean whatsoever, all. The Tamil *ellavan*, the sun, from *el*, when? time, is a singular noun. Pluralise it, and we get *ellavar*, which is a classical Tamil form of the word all. We may safely, therefore, I think, conclude that these words are identical.

The traces we find in Tamil of the existence of demonstratives in *il* and *al* are more indistinct than those of the interrogative *el;* but if an interrogative *en*, *ên*, pointed to the existence of the corresponding demonstratives *in*, *im*, *an*, *am*, we may reasonably regard the existence of *il* and *al* as testified to by the existence of *el*.

We find *il* in the locative case-sign alternating with *in*, and meaning also 'house;' also, I think, in verbal nouns ending in *il*, such as *kaṭṭ-il*, a cot, *vaṇḍ-il*, a wheel, a cart. *al* we find in a still larger class of verbal nouns, such as *kaḍ-al*, the sea, in which *al* seems to be equivalent to *am* and *an* (*e.g.*, *âṛ-am*, depth, *kaḍ-an*, debt). The most conclusive illustrations of the use in Tamil of *il* and *al* as demonstratives, and of *el* as an interrogative, would be furnished by *indru*, *andru*, *endru*, this day, that day, what day? if we could be sure that they are formed from a base in *l*, and not from one in *n* or *m*. The peculiar combination *ndr* could be derived from either. Thus, *en* + *du*, having said, becomes *endru*, and equally also *el* + *du*, the sun, becomes *endru*. Considering the identity of *endru*, the sun, with *el*, the sun, time, a day, to-morrow, it seems to me probable that *endru*, what day? must be the same word, and if so, *indru* and *andru*, this day, and that day, will become representatives, not of *in* and *an*, but of *il* and *al*, and the original existence of demonstratives in *il* and *al* will then be placed beyond the reach of doubt. *andru* in Tamil, though derived from *al*, might possibly become *andu*, *annu*, in the other dialects. On the whole, however, the evidence of those dialects is unfavourable to this supposition.

The Dravidian negatives *il* and *al* bear a strong apparent resemblance to demonstratives. *il* negatives existence (there is not such a thing); *al* negatives attributes (it is not so and so). *al*, Tam. as a verbal root, means to diminish, and as a noun, means night (*alli*, night, a night flower). No similar extension of the idea of negation seems to proceed from *il*. *il* and *al* resemble demonstratives not only in sound, but in the structure of the derivatives formed from them. Compare *andru*, it is not, with *andru*, that day; *indru*, there is not, with *indru*, this day. I am unable, however, in this matter, to go beyond resemblance and conjecture. No connection between the demonstrative and negative meanings of *il* and *al* seems capable of being historically traced.

Affiliation of Demonstrative Bases: Extra-Dravidian Affinities.—There is only a partial and indistinct resemblance between the remote *a*, proximate *i*, and medial *u*, which constitute the bases of the Dravidian demonstratives, and the demonstratives which are used by the languages of Northern India. In Bengali and Singhalese, *ê* is used as a demonstrative; in Marâṭhi *hâ*, *hî*, *heṅ*: in Hindustani we find *vuh*, that, *yih*, this; but in the oblique cases the resemblance increases—*e.g.*, *is-kô*, to this. *i* is used as the proximate demonstrative in the North Indian languages more systematically than *a* or any corresponding vowel is used as the remote—*e.g.*, Marâṭhi *ikaḍe*, here; Hindi *idhar*, hither; Mar. *itake*, so much. The Sindhi proximate is *hî* or *hê*. In the Lar dialect, *h* is commonly dropped, and the base is seen to be *î*, as in the Dravidian tongues. The remote in Sindhi is *hû* or *hô*; in Lar *û* or *ô*.

A general resemblance to the Dravidian demonstrative bases is apparent in several of the Himalayan languages—*e.g.*, Bodo *imbe*, this, *hobe*, that; Dhimal *î*, *û*; Ûrâon *êḍah*, *hûdah*. The Rajmahâl *êh* and *âh* are perfectly identical with the Dravidian demonstratives, and form another evidence of the Dravidian character of a portion of that idiom. The connection which appears to subsist between the Dravidian medial demonstrative *u* and the *û* of the Ûrâon and Dhimal is deserving of notice. Perhaps the Dravidian medial *u* (Dhimal *û*, Ûrâon *hûdah*) may be compared with the Old Hebrew masculine-feminine pronoun of the third person, *hû*; and thus with the Old Persian remote demonstrative *hauva*, of which the first portion appears to be *hu*, and the second *ava*,—which *ava* forms the base of the oblique cases. It may also be compared with the *u* or *o* which forms the remote demonstrative in some of the Scythian languages—*e.g.*, Finnish *tuo*, that, *tâma*, this; Ostiak *toma*, that, *tema*, this. Compare also the Hind. *vuh*, that; Bodo *hobe*. The Magyar demonstratives are more in accordance with the Dravidian *a* and *i*—*e.g.*, *az*, that, *ez*, this. The demonstratives of the other languages of the Scythian family (*e.g.*, the Turkish *bou*, that, *ol*, this) are altogether destitute of resemblance.

When we turn to the languages of the Indo-European family, they appear in this particular to be closely allied to the Dravidian. Throughout that family both *a* and *i* are used as demonstratives; though not to so large an extent, nor with so perfect and constant a discrimination between the remote and the proximate, as in the Dravidian family. In Sanskrit *a* is used instead of the more regular *i* in most of the oblique cases of *idam*, this; and the correlative of this word, *adas*, means not only that, but also this. Nevertheless, *a* is more generally a remote than a proximate demonstrative, and *i* more generally a proximate than a remote. In derived adverbial words *i* has always a proximate force; but *ta,* the consonantal demonstrative, is more generally used than *a.* The following are examples of each vowel:— *i-ha,* here; *i-dânîm,* now; *ta-dânîm,* then: also *i-ti,* so, this much; *a-tha,* so, thus, in that manner. *i,* the proximate demonstrative root, is in all probability identical with *i,* the sign of the locative in such words as *hrid-i,* heart. Probably, also, we see the same root in the preposition *in.* We may compare the Old Persian *avadâ,* thither, in that direction; and the corresponding proximate *i-dâ,* hither, in this direction. The resemblance between the bases of these forms, notwithstanding the irregularity of their application, and the Dravidian remote and proximate demonstrative bases, seems to amount to identity. All irregularity disappears in the New Persian, which in this point accords as perfectly with the Dravidian languages as if it were itself a Dravidian idiom. Its demonstratives are *ân,* that, *în,* this. These demonstratives are adjectival prefixes, and naturally destitute of number; but when plural terminations are suffixed, they acquire a plural signification—*e.g., ânân,* those (persons), *înân,* these (persons). The same demonstratives are largely used in modern Turkish, by which they have been borrowed from Persian. *ân* and *în* are undoubtedly Aryan demonstratives. This is apparent when we compare *ân* with the Zend *aêm,* that, and that again with the Sanskrit *ayam;* but *în* is still more clearly identical with the Zend *îm,* this. The same *îm* constitutes the accusative in Vedic Sanskrit (and is also identical with *iyam,* the masculine-feminine singular of the Old Persian, and the feminine of Sanskrit); but in Zend *îm* is the nominative, not the accusative, and it is to this form that the New Persian is most closely allied. The demonstrative base *i* (without being restricted, however, to a proximate signification) appears in the Latin *is* and *id,* and in the Gothic *is;* and the Dravidian and New Persian distinction between the signification of *a* and that of *i,* has been re-developed in our English that and this. Whilst the New Persian *ân* and *în* are closely connected with Sanskrit and Zend demonstratives, it does not follow that they are directly derived from either the one tongue or the other. On the contrary, the exactness with which the Persian discriminates between the remote and the proximate, leads me to conclude that it has retained more faithfully than either of those languages the primitive characteristics of the Præ-Sanskritic speech. If so, instead of supposing the Dravidian dialects to have borrowed their demonstratives, which are still purer than the Persian, from Sanskrit (which are irregular and greatly corrupted), it is more reasonable to suppose that the Dravidian demonstrative vowels retain and exhibit the primæval bases from which the demonstratives of the Sanskrit and of all other Indo-European tongues have been derived.

Affiliation of Interrogative Bases: Extra-Dravidian Relationship.—There seems to be no analogy between either *e* or *yâ* and any of the interrogative bases of the Indo-European family. Both in that family and in the Scythian group, the ordinary base of the interrogative is the guttural *k*—*e.g.*, Sanskrit, *kim*, what? The same base appears in the Sanskrit interrogative initial syllables *ka-*, *ki-*, *ku-*, which correspond to the Latin *qu-*, the Gothic *hva-*, and the English *wh-*. We find the same base again in the Turkish *kim* or *kîm*, who? what? in the Magyar *ki*, who? plural *kik;* and in the Finnish *kuka* (root *ku*). I am unable to suppose the Dravidian *yâ* derived from the Sanskrit and Indo-European *ka.* I see nowhere else any trace of a Sanskrit *k* changing into a Dravidian *y.* It would be tempting, but unsafe, to connect *ka-t* (Sans.) with *yâ-du* (Tam.) which?

In the absence of a real relative pronoun, the interrogative is used as a relative in many of the Scythian languages. The base of the Sanskrit relative pronoun *ya* (*yas*, *yâ*, *yat*), bears a close apparent resemblance to the Dravidian interrogative *yâ*. The Sanskrit *ya*, however, like the derived North Indian *jô*, and the Finnish *yo*, is exclusively used as a relative, whereas the Dravidian *yâ* is exclusively and distinctively an interrogative.

It has been conjectured that the Sanskrit *ya*, though now a relative, was a demonstrative originally; and if (as we shall see that there is some reason for supposing) the Dravidian interrogatives *e* and *a* were originally demonstratives, it may be supposed that *yâ* was also a demonstrative, though of this no direct evidence whatever now remains. If *yâ* were originally a demonstrative, the connection which would then appear to exist between it and the Sanskrit relative would require to be removed a step further back; for it is not in Sanskrit that the relative *ya* has the force of a demonstrative, but in other and more distant tongues—viz., in the Lithuanian *yis*, he; and in the Slavonian *yam*, and the Zend *yim*, him.

Emphatic ê.—It has been seen that in Ku *ê* is used as a demonstrative—*e.g.*, *êvâru* (*ê-(v)-âr*), they; and this may be compared with the demonstrative *ê* of the Sanskrit *êtat*, this (neuter), and the corresponding Zend *aêtat.* In the other Dravidian dialects, however, *ê* is not used as a demonstrative, but is postfixed to words for the purpose of rendering them emphatic. The manner in which *ê* is annexed, and the different shades of emphasis which it communicates, are precisely the same in the various dialects, and will be sufficiently illustrated by the following examples from Tamil. When *ê* is postfixed to the subject of a proposition, it sets it forth as the sole depositary of the quality predicated—*e.g.*, *kalvi-(y)-ê śelvam*, learning (alone is) wealth; when postfixed to the predicate, it intensifies its signification—*e.g.*, *kalvi śelvam-ê*, learning is wealth (indeed). When postfixed to a verb or verbal derivative, it is equivalent to the addition of the adverb truly, certainly—*e.g.*, *alla-(v)-ê* (certainly) not. In the colloquial dialect, it has often been annexed to the case-terminations of nouns without necessity, so that it has sometimes become in that connection a mere euphonic expletive; in consequence of which, in such instances, when emphasis is really required by a sign of case, the *ê* has to be doubled—*e.g.*, *ennâlêyê* (*ennâl-ê-(y)-ê*), through me (alone). In Tuḷu, emphatic *ê* becomes euphonically, not only *y*(*ê*) and *v*(*ê*), as in Tamil, after certain vowels, but also *n*(*ê*). *ê*, however, is always to be regarded as the sign of emphasis. The same sign of emphasis forms the most common vocative case-sign in the various Dravidian dialects, the vocative being nothing more than an emphatic enunciation of the nominative. Compare with this the use of the nominative, with the addition of the definite article, as the vocative in Hebrew and in Attic Greek. The Persian *ê* of supplication may also be compared with it.

Some resemblance to the use of *ê* as a particle of emphasis may be discovered in the Hebrew '*he* paragogic,' which is supposed to intensify the signification of the words to which it is annexed. The '*he* directive' of the same language is also, and not without reason, supposed to be a mark of emphasis. A still closer resemblance to the emphatic *ê* of the Dravidian languages is apparent in Chaldee, in which *â* suffixed to nouns constitutes their emphatic state, and is equivalent to the definite article of many other languages. The Persian *ê* of particularity, the *ê* of ascription of greatness, &c., in addition to the *ê* of supplication, which has already been referred to, probably spring from a Chaldaic and Cuthite origin, though each of them bears a remarkable resemblance to the Dravidian emphatic *ê*.

Honorific Demonstrative Pronouns.—I have deferred till now the consideration of a peculiar class of honorific demonstratives, which are found only in Telugu and Canarese, and in which, I think, Aryan influences or affinities may be detected. In all the Dravidian dialects the plural is used as an honorific singular when the highest degree of respect is meant to be expressed; but when a somewhat inferior degree of respect is intended, the pronouns which are used by the Telugu are *âyana*, he, ille, and *âme*, she, illa; with their corresponding proximates *îyana*, hic, and *îme*, hæc. These pronouns are destitute of plurals. When a little less respect is meant to be shown than is implied in the use of *âyana* and *îyana*, and of *âme* and *îme*, Telugu makes use of *atadu*, ille, *âse*, illa, with their corresponding proximates *itadu* and *ise*; *atanu* and *itanu* are also used, also the longer forms *âtanu*, *âtadu*, &c. Here Canarese agrees with Telugu—*e.g.*, *âtanu*, ille, *îtanu*, hic (class. Can. *âtam*, *îtam*). The Canarese feminines *âke*, illa, *îke*, hæc, do not appear so perfectly to accord with the Telugu *âse*, *îse*. Both the above sets of Telugu pronouns are destitute of plurals, but both are pluralised in Canarese—*e.g.*, *âtagaḷu*, *îtagaḷu*, those and these men; *âkeyar*, *îkeyar*, those and these (women). The Tuda *atham*, he, she, it, appears to be allied to the pronouns now referred to. I consider it to be a neuter singular, synonymous with *adu*, the neuter singular of the Tamil-Canarese, and used corruptly for the masculine and feminine, as well as for the neuter.

An Aryan origin may possibly be attributed to some of these words, especially to *âyana*, *îyana*, *âme*, *îme*; and this supposition would account for the circumstance that they are found in Telugu only, and not in any other dialect of the family (except the Tuḷu *âye*, he, is to be regarded as a connected form): it would also harmonise with their use as honorifics. Compare *âyana* with the Sanskrit masculine *ayam*, ille, and *îyana* with the Sanskrit feminine, and the Old Persian mas. fem. *yam*, hic, hæc. *âme*, illa, and *îme*, hæc, the corresponding feminine pronouns of the Telugu, may be compared not only with the plurals of the Sanskrit pronoun of the third person (*ime*, mas., *imâh*, fem., *imâni*, neut.), but also with *amum* and *imam*, him, which are accusative singulars, and from which it is evident that the *m* of the plural forms is not a sign of plurality, but is either a part of the pronominal base, or an euphonic or formative addition. Bopp considers it to be the former, but Dravidian analogies incline me to adopt the latter view, and the *m* of these forms I conceive to be the ordinary neuter formative of Dravidian, and especially of Tamil, nouns, whilst the *v* seems to be merely a softening of *m*. *me* is a common suffix of Telugu neuter nouns.

When the Telugu masculine of respect *âtadu*, *âtanu*, and the corresponding Canarese honorific *âta-nu*, are scrutinised, it is evident that in addition to the vocalic demonstrative bases, *a* and *i*, which are found in Dravidian demonstratives of every kind, the *ta* which is subjoined to *a* and *i*, possesses also somewhat of a demonstrative or pronominal signification. It cannot be regarded like *v*, as merely euphonic; and its restriction to masculines shows that it is not merely an abstract formative, as the *k* of the feminine *âke* may be presumed to be. It can scarcely be doubted, I think, that the affinities of this *ta* are Aryan; for we find in all the Aryan languages much use made of a similar *ta*, both as an independent demonstrative, and as an auxiliary to the vocalic demonstrative. *ta-d*, Sans. that, is an instance of the former; whilst the secondary or auxiliary place which *ta* or *da* occupies in the Sanskrit *êtad* (*ê-ta-d*), this, and *adam*, *adas* (*a-da-m*, *a-da-s*), this, or that, is in perfect agreement with the Telugu and Canarese *â-ta-nu*, *â-ta-ḍu*. The final *e* of *âse*, *îse*, *âme*, *îme*, *ûke*, *îke*, is equivalent to the Tamil *ei*. *e* or *ei* is an ordinary termination of abstracts in these languages, and a suitable one, according to Dravidian notions, for feminine honorific pronouns.

Syntactic Interrogatives, â and ô.—The interrogative prefixes *e* and *yâ* are equivalent to the interrogative pronouns and adjectives, who? which? what? &c. Another interrogative is required for the purpose of putting such inquiries as are expressed in English by a change of construction—*e.g.*, is there? is it? by transposition from there is, it is. This species of interrogation is effected in all the Dravidian languages in one and the same manner, viz., by suffixing an open vowel to the noun, verb, or sentence which forms the principal subject of interrogation; and in almost all these languages it is by the suffix of *â* or *ô* alone, without any syntactic change, or change in the collocation of words, that an interrogative verb or sentence differs from an affirmative one—*e.g.*, compare the affirmative *avan tandân*, Tam. he gave, with *avan tandân-â?* did he give? and *avan â tandân?* was it he that gave? compare also *adu ûr*, that is a village, with *adu ûr-â?* is that a village? This interrogative is never prefixed to nouns or pronominals, or used adjectivally; but is invariably postfixed, like an enunciated or audible note of interrogation.

ô is used instead of *â* in Malayâḷam, in which the interrogative use of *â* is almost unknown. *â* seems to survive only in *idâ* (Tam. *idô*) lo, literally what is this? *ô* is used occasionally in Tamil also as a simple interrogative; but its special and distinctive use is as a particle expressive of doubt. Thus, whilst *avan-â* means is it he? *avan-ô* means can it be he? or, I am doubtful whether it is he or not. *ô* is postfixed to words in precisely the same manner as *â*, and is probably only a weakened form of it, in which, by usage, the interrogation has been softened into the expression of doubt. It has acquired, however, as a suffix of doubt a position and force of its own, quite independent of *â*; in consequence of which it is often annexed even to interrogative pronouns—*e.g.*, *evan-ô*, Tam. I wonder who he can be; *enna*(*v*)-*ô*, what it may be I know not—compound forms which are not double interrogatives, but which consist of a question *evan*, who? or *enna*, what? and an answer *ô*, I am doubtful, I know not, there is room for further inquiry. In Tuḷu, in addition to the use of *â* and *ô*, as in the other dialects, *ê* (euphonically (*v*)*ê* or (*n*)*ê*) is used syntactically as an interrogative. This *ê* is doubtless identical with the *ê* of emphasis in origin. The use of *â* or *ô* as an interrogative suffix does not seem to have any counterpart in any language either of the Scythian or of the Indo-European family. It is altogether unknown to Sanskrit; and Cashmirian is the only non-Dravidian tongue in which it is found.

I am inclined to consider *â*, the ordinary Dravidian interrogative, as derived from, or at least as allied to, *a* or *â*, the remote demonstrative of the same family. The quantity of that demonstrative *a* is long or short, as euphonic considerations may determine; and though the interrogative *â* is always long in Tamil, yet in consequence of its being used as a postfix, it is pronounced long by necessity of position, whatever it may have been originally. In Telugu it is generally short; always so in poetry. Hence the question of quantity may, in this inquiry, be left altogether out of account. The only real difference between them is the difference in location; *a* demonstrative being invariably placed at the beginning of a word, *a* interrogative at the end of it. If the interrogative *a* were really connected with *a* the demonstrative, we should expect to find a similar connection subsisting between *e* or *ê*, the adjectival interrogative, and some demonstrative particle, with a similar interchange of places; accordingly this is found to be the case, for *ê* is not only the ordinary sign of emphasis in all the Dravidian tongues, but it is used in Ku as an adjectival demonstrative; and it is curious that in this instance also there is a change of location, *ê* emphatic being placed at the end of a word, *e* interrogative at the beginning. *ô* would naturally be derived from *â*, as in the change of *yâm*, we, Tam. into *ôm*, in the pronominal terminations of the Tamil verb.

A similar change in the position of particles, to denote or correspond with some change in signification, is not unknown in other tongues. Thus in Danish, the article *en* has a definite sense in one position, and an indefinite in another—*e.g.*, *en konge*, a king, *kongen*, the king. But it is still more remarkable, and more corroborative of the supposition now advanced, that in Hebrew, one and the same particle, *he* (for it must be regarded as one and the same, and any difference that exists seems to be merely euphonic), imparts emphasis to a word when postfixed to it, and constitutes an interrogative when prefixed. Even in English the interrogative is founded upon the demonstrative. 'That?' differs from 'that' only in the tone of voice with which it is pronounced.

Distributive Pronouns.—In all the Dravidian tongues distributive pronouns are formed by simply annexing the conjunctive particle to any of the interrogative pronouns. Thus, from *evan*, who? by the addition of *um*, and, the conjunctive or copulative particle of the Tamil is formed, viz., *evanum*, every one, whosoever (literally who?-and); and from *epporudu*, when? is formed in the same manner *epporudum*, always (literally when?-and). In Canarese similar forms are found, though not so largely used as in Tamil—*e.g.*, *yâvâgalû* (*yâ-âgal-û*), always; and in Telugu *u* (the copulative particle which answers to the Tamil *um* and the Canarese *u*) is used in the same manner in the formation of distributives—*e.g.*, *evvaḍunu* (*evvaḍu-(nn)-u*), every one, *eppuḍunnu* (*eppuḍu-(nn)-u*), always.

SECTION III.—RELATIVE PRONOUNS.

I give this heading a place in the book solely for the purpose of drawing attention to the remarkable fact that the Dravidian languages have no relative pronoun, a participial form of the verb being used instead.

Instead of relative pronouns, they use verbal forms which are called by English grammarians relative participles; which see in the part on "The Verb." All other words which correspond either in meaning or in use to the pronouns of other languages will be found on examination to be nouns, regularly formed and declined.

PART VI.

THE VERB.

The object in view in this part of the work is to investigate the nature, affections, and relations of the Dravidian verb. It seems desirable to commence with some general preliminary remarks upon its structure.

1. A large proportion of Dravidian roots are used indiscriminately, either as verbs or as nouns. When case-signs are attached to a root, or when, without the addition of case-signs, it is used as the nominative of a verb, it is regarded as a noun: the same root becomes a verb without any internal change or formative addition, when the signs of tense (or time) and the pronouns or their terminal fragments are suffixed to it. Though, abstractly speaking, every Dravidian root is capable of this twofold use, it depends upon circumstances whether any particular root is actually thus used; and it often happens, as in other languages, that of three given roots one shall be used solely or generally as a verbal theme, another solely or generally as the theme of a noun, and the third alone shall be used indiscriminately either as a noun or as a verb. Herein also the *usus loquendi* of the various dialects is found to differ; and not unfrequently a root which is used solely as a verbal theme in one dialect, is used solely as a noun in another.

2. The inflexional theme of a Dravidian verb or noun is not always identical with the crude root or ultimate base. In many instances formative or euphonic particles (such as *vu*, *ku*, *gu* or *ṅgu*, *du* or *ndu*, *bu* or *mbu*) are annexed to the root,—not added on like isolated post-positions, but so annexed as to be incorporated with it. (See Part II., "Roots.") But the addition of one of those formative suffixes does not necessarily constitute the root to which it is suffixed a verb: it is still capable of being used as a noun, though it may be admitted that some of the roots to which those suffixes have been annexed are more frequently used as verbs than as nouns.

3. The structure of the Dravidian verb is strictly agglutinative.

The particles which express the ideas of mood and tense, transition, intransition, causation, and negation, together with the pronominal fragments by which person, number, and gender are denoted, are annexed or agglutinated to the root in so regular a series and by so quiet a process, that generally no change whatever, or at most only a slight euphonic change, is effected either in the root or in any of the suffixed particles. (See this illustrated in "Roots.")

4. The second person singular of the imperative may perhaps be considered as an exception to the foregoing rule. The crude theme of the verb, or the shortest form which the root assumes, and which is capable of being used also as the theme of a noun, is used in the Dravidian languages, as in many others, as the second person singular of the imperative; and the ideas of number and person and of the conveyance of a command, which are included in that part of speech, are not expressed by the addition of any particles, but are generally left to be inferred from the context alone. Thus, in the Tamil, sentences *aḍi viṛundadu*, the stroke fell; *ennei aḍi-ttân*, he struck me; and *idei aḍi*, strike thou this; the theme, *aḍi*, strike, or a stroke, is the same in each instance, and in the third illustration it is used without any addition, and in its crude state, as the second person singular of the imperative.

5. As the normal Dravidian noun has properly but one declension, so the normal Dravidian verb has properly only one conjugation and but very few irregular forms. It is true that grammarians have arranged the Dravidian verbs in classes, and have sometimes styled those classes conjugations; but the differences on which this classification is founded are generally of a trivial and superficial character. The structure of the verb, its signs of tense, and the mode in which the pronouns are suffixed, remain invariably the same, with such changes only as euphony appears to have dictated. Consequently, though class differences exist, they are hardly of sufficient importance to constitute different conjugations. When I speak of the normal Dravidian nouns and verbs I mean those of the more highly cultivated dialects, Tamil, Malayâḷam, Canarese, and Telugu. The Tuḷu and Gônd verbs will be found exceptionally rich in moods and tenses.

Such is the simplicity of the structure of the normal Dravidian verb, that the only moods it has are the indicative, the infinitive, the imperative, and the negative, and that it has only three tenses, the past, the present, and the aorist or indefinite future. There is reason to suspect, also, that originally it had no present tense, but only a future and a past. The ideas which are expressed in other families of languages by the subjunctive and optative moods, are expressed in all the members of the Dravidian family, except in Tuḷu and Gônd, by means of suffixed particles; and the imperfect, perfect, pluperfect, future perfect, and other compound tenses, are expressed by means of auxiliary verbs. In these respects the normal Dravidian verb imitates, though it does not equal, the simplicity of the ancient Scythian verb. The modern Turkish has, it is true, an extraordinary number of moods—conditionals, potentials, reciprocals, inceptives, negatives, impossibles, &c., together with their passives, and also a large array of compound tenses; but this complexity of structure appears to be a refinement of a comparatively modern age, and is not in accordance with the genius of the Oriental Turkish, or Tatar properly so called. Remusat conjectures that intercourse with nations of the Indo-European race, some time after the Christian era, was the occasion of introducing into the Turkish language the use of auxiliary verbs and of compound tenses. "From the extremity of Asia," he says, "the art of conjugating verbs is unknown. The Oriental Turks first offer some traces of this; but the very sparing use which they make of it seems to attest the pre-existence of a more simple method."

All the Dravidian idioms conjugate their verbs, with the partial exception of Malayâḷam, which has retained the use of the signs of tense, but has rejected the pronominal terminations, except in the ancient poetry. Nevertheless, the system of conjugation on which most of the Dravidian idioms proceed is one of primitive and remarkable simplicity.

Tuḷu and Gônd verbs possess more complicated systems of conjugational forms, almost rivalling those of the Turkish in abundance. Tuḷu has a perfect tense, as well as an imperfect or indefinite past. It has conditional and potential moods, as well as a subjunctive. Tamil has but one verbal participle, which is properly a participle of the past tense, whilst Tuḷu has also a present and a future participle. All these moods, tenses, and participles have regularly formed negatives. I do not refer here to the pluperfect and second future, or future perfect tense, of Tuḷu, these tenses being formed, as in the other dialects, by means of the substantive verb used as an auxiliary.

Gônd has all the moods, tenses, and participles of Tuḷu, and in addition some of its own. It has an inceptive mood. Its imperfect branches into two distinct tenses, an imperfect, properly so called (I was going), and a past indefinite (I went). It has also a desiderative form of the indicative—that is, a tense which, when preceded by the future, is a subjunctive, but which when standing alone implies a wish.

On comparing the complicated conjugational system of the Gônd with the extreme and almost naked simplicity of the Tamil, I conclude that we have here a proof, not of the superiority of the Gônd mind to the Tamilian, but simply of the greater antiquity of Tamilian literary culture. The development of the conjugational system of Tamil seems to have been arrested at a very early period (as in the parallel, but still more remarkable, instance of the Chinese) by the invention of writing, by which the verbal forms existing at the time were fossilised, whilst the uncultured Gônds, and their still ruder neighbours the Kôls, went on age after age, as before, compounding with their verbs auxiliary words of time and relation, and fusing them into conjugational forms by rapid and careless pronunciation, without allowing any record of the various steps of the process to survive.

The Dravidian languages do not make a distinction, as the Hungarian does, between subjective and objective verbs. In Hungarian, 'I know,' is considered a subjective verb; I know (it, them, something), an objective verb. A like distinction is made by the Bornu or Kanuri, an African language, but not by any of the Dravidian dialects.

6. The Dravidian verb is as frequently compounded with a noun as the Indo-European one; but the compound of a verb with a preposition is unknown. An inexhaustible variety of shades of meaning is secured in Sanskrit and Greek by the facility with which, in those languages, verbs are compounded with prepositions; and the beauty of many of those compounds is as remarkable as the facility with which they are made. In the Scythian tongues, properly so called, there is no trace of compounds of this kind; and though at first sight we seem to discover traces of them in the Dravidian family, yet when the component elements of such compounds are carefully scrutinised, it is found that the principle on which they are compounded differs widely from that of Indo-European compounds. The Dravidian preposition-like words which are most frequently compounded with verbs are those which signify over and under, the use of which is illustrated by the common Tamil verbs *mêr-koḷ*, to overcome, and *kîḻ-(p)paḍi*, to obey. Dravidian prepositions, however (or rather, postpositions), are properly nouns—*e.g.*, *mêl* (from *mi-(y)-al*), over, literally means over-ness, superiority; and *mêl-koḷ* (euphonically *mêr-koḷ*), to overcome, literally signifies to take the superiority. These and similar verbal themes, therefore, though compounds, are not, after all, compounds of a preposition and a verb, but are compounds of a noun and a verb; and the Greek verbs with which they are to be compared are not those which commence with *περί*, *κατά*, *ἀνά*, &c., but such compounds as *πολιορκέω*, to besiege a city, literally to city-besiege; *ναυπηγέω*, to build a ship literally to ship-build. In such cases, whether in Greek or in Tamil,

the first member of the compound (the noun) does not modify the signification of the second (the verb), but simply denotes the object to which the action of the verb applies. It is merely a crude noun, which is used objectively without any signs of case, and is intimately combined with a governing verb.

Dravidian verbs acquire new shades of meaning, and an increase or diminution in the intensity of their signification, not by prefixing or combining prepositions, but by means of auxiliary gerunds, or verbal participles and infinitives—parts of speech which in this family of languages have an adverbial force—*e.g.*, *mundi* (*p*)*pônân*, Tam. he went before, literally having-got-before he went; *śuṟṟi* (*śuttri*) (*p*)*pônân*, he went round, literally rounding he went; *tâṛa* (*k*)*kudittân*, he leaped down, literally so-as-to-get-down he leaped. A great variety of compounds of this nature exists in each of the Dravidian dialects. They are as easily made, and many of them are as beautiful, as the Greek and Sanskrit compounds of prepositions with verbs. See especially Dr Gundert's "Malayâḷam Grammar."

SECTION I.—CLASSIFICATION.

1. Transitives and Intransitives.

Dravidian grammarians divide all verbs into two classes, which are called in Tamil *piṟa vinei* and *tan vinei*, transitives and intransitives, literally outward-action words and self-action words. These classes correspond rather to the *parasmai-padam* and *âtmanê-padam*, or transitive and reflective voices, of the Sanskrit, than to the active and passive voices of the other Indo-European languages.

The Dravidian *piṟa vinei* and *tan vinei*, or transitive and intransitive verbs, differ from the *parasmai-padam* and *âtmanê-padam* of the Sanskrit in this, that instead of each being conjugated differently, they are both conjugated in precisely the same mode. They differ, not in their mode of conjugation, but in the formative additions made to their themes. Moreover, all *piṟa vinei*, or transitive verbs, are really, as well as formally, transitives, inasmuch as they necessarily govern the accusative, through the transition of their action to some object; whilst the *tan vinei*, or intransitive verbs, are all necessarily, as well as formally, intransitives. The Dravidian transitives and intransitives closely resemble in force and use, though not in shape, the objective and subjective verbs of the Hungarian. The Hungarian objective verbs, like the Dravidian transitives, imply an object—an accusative expressed or implied—*e.g.*, *szeretem*, I love (some person or thing); whilst the

Hungarian subjective verbs, like the Dravidian intransitives, neither express nor imply an object—*e.g.*, *szeretek*, I love—*i.e.*, I am in love.

In a large number of instances in each of the Dravidian dialects, including entire classes of verbs, there is no difference between transitives and intransitives, either in formative additions to the theme, or in any structural peculiarity, the only difference is that which consists in the signification. Thus in Tamil, all verbs of the class which take *i* as the sign of the past participle are conjugated alike, whether they are transitives or intransitives—*e.g.*, from *paṇṇ-u*, trans. to make, are formed the three tenses (first person singular) *paṇṇu-giṟ-ên*, I make, *paṇṇ-i-(n)-ên*, I made, and *paṇṇu-v-ên*, I will make; and in like manner from *pêś-u*, intrans, to talk, are formed, precisely in the same manner, the corresponding tenses *pêśu-giṟ-ên*, I talk, *pêś-i-(n)-ên*, I talked, and *pêśu-v-ên*, I will talk. In a still larger number of cases, however, transitive verbs differ from intransitives, not only in signification and force, but also in form, notwithstanding that they are conjugated alike. The nature of the difference that exists and its rationale are more clearly apparent in Tamil than in any other Dravidian dialect; my illustrations will, therefore, chiefly be drawn from the Tamil.

There are three modes in which intransitive Tamil verbs are converted into transitives.

1. Intransitive themes become transitive by the hardening and doubling of the consonant of the appended formative—*e.g.*, *peru-gu*, to abound, by this process becomes *peru-kku*, to increase (actively), to cause to abound. Transitives of this kind, which are formed from intransitives in actual use, are often called *causals*, and they are as well entitled to be called by that name as many causal verbs in the Indo-European tongues; but as there is a class of Dravidian verbs which are distinctively causal (and which are formed by the annexing to the transitive theme of a causal particle—*e.g.*, *paṇṇuvi* (*v-i*), Tam. to cause to make, from *paṇṇu*, to make), it will contribute to perspicuity to regard the whole of the verbs of which we are now treating simply as transitives, and to reserve the name of *causal verbs* for the double transitives referred to. When transitives are formed from intransitives by doubling the consonant of the formative, there is no change in any of the signs of tense, or in the mode in which those signs are added; and the hardened formative appears in the imperative, as well as in the other parts of the verb. The nature of these formatives has already been investigated in Part II., on "Roots;" and it has been shown that they are generally either euphonic accretions, or particles of specialisation, which, though permanently annexed to the base, are not

to be confounded with it. I subjoin a few illustrations of this mode of forming transitives by the doubling and hardening of the consonant of the formative.

(1.) *gu*, or its nasalised equivalent *ṅgu*, becomes *kku*—*e.g.*, from *pô-gu*, to go (in the imperative softened into *pô*), comes *pô-kku*, to drive away; from *aḍa-ṅgu*, to be restrained, comes *aḍa-kku*, to restrain.

(2.) *śu* becomes *chchu*—*e.g.*, from *aḍei-śu*, to be stuffed in, comes *adei-chchu*, to stuff in, to stick on.

(3.) *du*, euphonised into *ndu*, becomes *ttu*—*e.g.*, from *tiru-ndu*, to become correct, comes *tiru-ttu*, to correct.

(4.) *bu*, euphonised into *mbu*, becomes *ppu*—*e.g.*, from *nira-mbu*, to be full, comes *nira-ppu*, to fill.

When intransitives are converted into transitives in this manner in Telugu, *gu* or *ngu* becomes, not *kku* as in Tamil, but *chu*—a difference which is in accordance with dialectic rules of sound. Thus from *tû-gu*, or euphonically *tû-ṅgu*, to hang, to sleep, comes *tû-chu*, or euphonically *tû-ñchu*, to weigh, to cause to hang (Tam. *tû-kku*). Telugu also occasionally changes the intransitive formative *gu*, not into *chu*, the equivalent of *kku*, but into *pu*—*e.g.*, from *mêy*, to graze, comes *mê-pu*, to feed; and as *ppu* in Tamil is invariably hardened from *bu* or *mbu*, the corresponding Telugu *pu* indicates that *bu* originally alternated with *gu*; for the direct hardening of *gu* into *pu* is not in accordance with Dravidian laws of sound. This view is confirmed by the circumstances that in Telugu the use of *pu* instead of *chu* (and of *mpu* instead of *ñchu*) is in most instances optional, and that in the higher dialect of Tamil the formative *pp* sometimes supersedes *kk*—*e.g.*, the infinitive of the verb 'to walk' may in that dialect be either *naḍa-kka* or *naḍa-ppa*. It is obvious, therefore, that these formative terminations are mutual equivalents.

If the transitive or causal *p* of such verbs as *nira-ppu*, Tam. to fill, *mê-pu*, Tel. to feed, were not known to be derived from the hardening of an intransitive formative, we might be inclined to affiliate it with the *p*, which is characteristic of a certain class of causal verbs in Sanskrit—*e.g.*, *jîvâ-p-ayâmi*, I cause to live, *jñâ-p-ayâmi*, I make to know. It is evident, however, that the resemblance is merely accidental, for etymologically there is nothing of a causal nature in the Dravidian formatives; it is not the formative itself, but the *hardening* of the formative which conveys the force of transition; and on the other hand, the real sign of the causal in Sanskrit is *aya*, and the *p* which precedes it is considered to be only an euphonic fulcrum.

It has already been shown (in "Roots") that the various verbal formatives now referred to are used also as formatives of nouns, and that when such nouns are used adjectivally, the consonant of the formative is doubled and hardened, precisely as in the transitives of verbs —*e.g.*, *maruttu*, medicinal, from *marundu*, medicine; *pâppu*, serpentine, from *pâmbu*, a snake. When nouns are used to qualify other nouns, as well as in the case of transitive verbs, there is a transition in the application of the meaning of the theme to some other object; and the idea of transition is expressed by the doubling and hardening of the consonant of the formative, or rather by the forcible and emphatic enunciation of the verb of which that hardening of the formative is the sign. There is something resembling this in Hebrew. The doubling of a consonant by *Dagesh forte* is sometimes resorted to in Hebrew for the purpose of converting an intransitive verb into a transitive—*e.g.*, compare *lâmad*, he learned, with *limmêd*, he caused to learn, he taught.

2. The second class of intransitive verbs become transitives by the doubling and hardening of the initial consonant of the signs of tense.

Verbs of this class are generally destitute of formatives, properly so called; or, if they have any, they are such as are incapable of change. The sign of the present tense in colloquial Tamil is *giṟ*; that of the preterite *'d*, ordinarily euphonised into *nd*; and that of the future, *b* or *v*. These are the signs of tense which are used by intransitive verbs of this class; and it will be shown hereafter that they are the normal tense-signs of the Dravidian verb. When verbs of this class become transitives, *giṟ* is changed into *kkiṟ*, *d* or *nd* into *tt*, and *b* or *v* into *pp*. Thus, the root *śêr*, to join, is capable both of an intransitive sense—*e.g.*, to join (a society)—and of a transitive sense—*e.g.*, to join (things that were separate). The tense-signs of the intransitive remain in their natural condition—*e.g.*, *śêr-giṟ-en*, I join, *śêr-nd-ên*, I joined, *śêr-v-ên*, I will join; but when the signification is active or transitive —*e.g.*, to join (planks), the corresponding parts of the verb are *śêr-kkiṟ-ên*, I join, *śêr-tt-ên*, I joined, *śêr-pp-ên*, I will join. The rationale of this doubling of the first consonant of the sign of tense appears to be exactly the same as that of the doubling of the first consonant of the formative. It is an emphasised, hardened enunciation of the intransitive or natural form of the verb; and the forcible enunciation thus produced is symbolical of the force of transition by which the meaning of the transitive theme overflows and passes on to the object indicated by the accusative. In verbs of this class the imperative remains always unchanged; and it is the connection alone that determines it to a transitive rather than an intransitive signification.

It should here be mentioned, that a few intransitive verbs double the initial consonant of the tense-sign, and that a few transitive verbs leave the tense-sign in its original, unemphasised condition. Thus, *iru*, to sit, to be, is necessarily an intransitive verb; nevertheless, in the present tense *iru-kki***r***-ên*, I am, and in the future *iru-pp-ên*, I shall be, it has made use of the ordinary characteristics of the transitive. So also *paḍu*, to lie, though an intransitive, doubles the initial consonant of all the tenses—*e.g.*, *paḍu-kki***r***-ên*, I lie, *paḍu-tt-ên*, I lay, *paḍu-pp-ên*, I shall lie. On the other hand, *î*, to give, to bestow, though necessarily transitive, uses the simple, unhardened, unemphatic tense-signs which are ordinarily characteristic of the intransitive—*e.g.*, *î-gi***r***-ên*, I give, *î-nd-ên*, I gave, *î-v-ên*, I will give. These instances are the result of dialectic rules of sound, and they are not in reality exceptions to the method described above of distinguishing transitive and intransitive verbs by means of the hardening or softening of the initial consonant of the tense-signs. Besides, this anomalous use of the transitive form of the signs of tense for the intransitive is peculiar to Tamil. It is not found in Telugu or Canarese.

3. A third mode of converting intransitives into transitives is by adding a particle of transition to the theme or root. This particle is *du* in Canarese, and *ttu* (in composition *tu* or *du*) in Tamil, and may be regarded as a real transitive suffix, or sign of activity. We have an instance of the use of this particle in the Canarese *tâḷ-du*, to lower, from *tâḷ-u*, to be low, and the corresponding Tamil *tâṛ-ttu*, to lower, from *tâṛ* or *tâṛ-u*, to be low. When the intransitive Tamil theme ends in a vowel which is radical and cannot be elided, the transitive particle is invariably *ttu*—*e.g.*, *paḍu-ttu*, to lay down, from *paḍu*, to lie. It might, therefore, be supposed that *ttu* is the primitive shape of this particle; but on examining those instances in which it is compounded with the final consonant of the intransitive theme, it appears to resolve itself, as in Canarese, into *du*. It is always thus compounded when the final consonant of the theme is *l* or *ḷ*, *ḍ* or **r**; and in such cases the *d* of *du* is not merely placed in juxtaposition with the consonant to which it is attached, but is assimilated to it, or both consonants are euphonically changed, according to the phonetic rules of the language. Thus *l* and *du* become **rr**-*u* (pronounced *ttr-u*)—*e.g.*, from *suṛal*, intrans., to be whirled, comes *suṛa***rr***-u* (*suṛattr-u*), trans., to whirl. *ḷ* and *du* become *ṭṭu*—*e.g.*, from *mîl*, to return, comes *mîṭṭ-u*, to cause to return, to redeem. From these instances it is clear that *du*, not *ttu*, is to be regarded as the primitive form of this transitive suffix.

What is the origin of this transitive particle, or sign of activity, *ttu* or *du*? I believe it to be identical with the inflexion or adjectival formative, *attu* or *ttu*, which was fully investigated in Part III., "The Noun," and of which the Canarese form is *ad'*, the Telugu *ṭi* or *ti*.

There is a transition of meaning when a noun is used adjectivally (*i.e.*, to qualify another noun), as well as when a verb is used transitively (*i.e.*, to govern an object expressed by some noun in the accusative); and in both cases the Dravidian languages use (with respect to this class of verbs) one and the same means of expressing transition, viz., a particle which appears to have been originally a neuter demonstrative. Nor is this the only case in which the Tamil transitive verb exhibits the characteristics of the noun used adjectivally, for it has been shown also that the doubling and hardening of the consonant of the formative of the first class of transitive verbs is in exact accordance with the manner in which nouns terminating in those formatives double and harden the initial consonant when they are used to qualify other nouns. Another illustration of this principle follows.

4. The fourth (a distinctively Tamil) mode of converting intransitive verbs into transitives consists in doubling and hardening the final consonant, if ḍ or **r**. This rule applies generally, though not invariably, to verbs which terminate in those consonants; and it applies to a final *ṇḍ-u* (euphonised from *ḍ-u*), as well as to *ḍ-u* itself. The operation of this rule will appear on comparing *vâḍ-u*, to wither, with *vâṭṭ-u*, to cause to wither; *ôḍ-u*, to run, with *ôṭṭ-u*, to drive; *tiṇḍ-u*, to touch, with *tîṭṭ-u*, to whet; *mâ***r***-u*, to become changed, with *mâ***rr***-u* (pronounced *mâttr-u*), to change. The corresponding transitives in Telugu are formed in the more usual way by adding *chu* to the intransitive theme—*e.g.*, *mâ***r***u-chu*, to cause to change, *vâḍu-chu*, to cause to wither. Tamil nouns which end in *ḍ-u*, *ṇḍ-u*, or **r***-u*, double and harden the final consonant in precisely the same manner when they are placed in an adjectival relation to a succeeding noun—*e.g.*, compare *kâḍ-u*, a jungle, with *kâṭṭ-u vaṛi*, a jungle-path; *iraṇḍ-u*, two, with *iraṭṭu nûl*, double thread; *â***r***-u*, a river, with *â***rr***u* (pronounced *âttru*) *maṇal*, river sand. Thus we are furnished by words of this class with another and remarkable illustration of the analogy which subsists in the Dravidian languages between transitive verbs and nouns used adjectivally.

2. Causal Verbs.

There is a class of verbs in the Dravidian languages which, though generally included under the head of *transitives*, claims to be regarded distinctively as *causals*. These verbs have been classed with transitives both by native grammarians and by Europeans. Beschi alone places them in a class by themselves, and calls them *êval vinei*, verbs of command—*i.e.*, verbs which imply that a thing is commanded by one person to be done by another. *Causals* differ from transitives of the ordinary character, as well as from intransitives, both in signification and in form. The signification of intransitive verbs is confined to the person or thing which constitutes the nominative, and does not pass outward or onward to any extrinsic object—*e.g.*, *pô-gir-ên*, I go. The signification of transitive or active verbs, or, as they are called in Tamil, *outward action-words*, passes outward, to some object exterior to the nominative, and which is generally put in the accusative—*e.g.*, *unnei anuppu-gir-ên*, I send thee: and as to send is to cause to go, verbs of this class, when formed from intransitives, are in some languages, appropriately enough, termed causals. Hitherto the Indo-European languages proceed *pari passu* with the Dravidian, but at this point they fail and fall behind; for if we take a verb which is transitive of necessity, like this one, to send, and endeavour to express the idea of causing to send, *i.e.*, causing one person to send another, we cannot by any modification of structure get any Indo-European verb to express by itself the full force of this idea: we must be content to make use of a phrase instead of a single verb; whereas in the Dravidian languages, as in Turkish and other languages of the Scythian stock, there is a form of the verb which will express the entire idea, viz., the causal—*e.g.*, *anuppu-vi*, Tam. to cause to send, which is formed from *anuppu*, to send, by the addition of the particle *vi* to the theme. Transitives are in a similar manner converted in Turkish into causals by suffixing a particle to the theme—*e.g.*, *sev-dur*, to cause to love, from *sev*, to love; and *âtch-û*, to cause to work, from *âtch*, to work.

There is a peculiarity in the signification and use of Dravidian causal verbs which should here be noticed. Indo-European causals govern two accusatives, that of the person and that of the object—*e.g.*, I caused him (acc.) to build the house (acc.); whereas Dravidian causals generally govern the object alone, and either leave the person to be understood (*e.g.*, *vîṭṭei (k)kaṭṭuvittên*, Tam., I caused to build the house (or, as we should prefer to say, I caused the house to be built); or else the person is put in the instrumental—*e.g.*, I caused to build the house, *avanei (k)koṇḍu*, through him, or employing him; that is, I caused the house to be built by him. Double accusatives are occasionally met with in classical compositions in Tamil, and are not uncommon in Malayâḷam. Dr Gundert quotes the Malayâḷam phrase *avane Yama-lôkam pûgichchu*, he caused him to enter the world of Yama—to die; but in all such instances, I think, Sanskrit influences are to be suspected.

Though the Dravidian languages are in possession of a true causal—formed by the addition of a causal particle—yet they sometimes resort to the less convenient Indo-European method of annexing an auxiliary verb which signifies to make or to do, such as *śey̆* and *paṉṉ-u* in Tamil, *mâḍ-u* in Canarese, and *chêy-u* in Telugu. These auxiliaries, however, are chiefly used in connection with Sanskrit derivatives. The auxiliary is annexed to the infinitive of the principal verb.

Tamil idiom and the analogy of the other dialects require that causals should be formed, not from neuter or intransitive verbs, but from transitives alone; but sometimes this rule is found to be neglected. Even in Tamil, *vi*, the sign of the causal, is in some instances found to be annexed to intransitive verbs. This usage is not only at variance with theory, but it is unclassical. In each of those cases a true transitive, derived from the intransitive in the ordinary manner, is in existence, and ought to be used instead. Thus, *varu-vi*, Tam., to cause to come, is less elegant than *varu-ttu;* and *naḍa-ppi*, to cause to walk, to guide, than *naḍa-ttu*.

The use of the causal, instead of the active, where both forms exist, is not so much opposed to the genius of the other dialects as to that of Tamil. The use of one form rather than another is optional in Telugu and Canarese; and in some instances the active has disappeared, and the causal alone is used. Thus *ra-(p)-piñchu*, or *râ-viñchu*, to cause to come, the equivalent of the Tamil *varu-vi*, is preferred by Telugu to a form which would correspond to *varu-ttu;* and instead of *âkk-u*, Tam., to cause to become, to make, which is the active of *âg-u*, and is formed by the process of doubling and hardening which has already been described, Telugu uses the causal *kâv-inchu*, and the Canarese the corresponding causal *âg-isu*.

One and the same causal particle seems to me to be used in all the Dravidian dialects, with the exception of Tuḷu and Gônd. It assumes in Tamil the shapes of *vi*, *bi*, and *ppi;* in Telugu, *iñchu* and *piñchu;* in classical Canarese, *ichu;* in the colloquial dialect, *iśu*. It seems difficult at first sight to suppose these forms identical; but it will be found, I think, in every case that the real form of the causal particle is *i* alone, and that whatever precedes or follows it pertains to the formatives of the verb.

I begin with Telugu, which, in regard to this point, will be found to throw light on the rest of the dialects. In Telugu, causal verbs end either in *iñchu* or *piñchu*—*e.g.*, *chêy-iñchu*, to cause to do, from *chêy-u*, to do; *pili-piñchu*, to cause to call, to invite, from *pilu-chu*, to call. *ñchu*, the final portion of *iñchu* or *piñchu*, has first to be explained. *ñchu* (pronounced. *ntsu*) is a nasalised form of *chu*, which is a very common formative of Telugu verbs. When *chu* follows *i*—*i.e.*, when the base to which it is attached ends in *i*, it is invariably euphonised or nasalised into *ñchu*—*e.g.*, *jayi*, a Sanskrit derivative, though not a causal, ends in *i*; hence the Telugu verb formed from it is *jayi-ñchu*, to conquer; and hence also, as the causal verb in Telugu is formed by affixing the particle *i* to an ordinary verbal root, all such causal verbs end in *iñchu*. *ichu* is to be regarded as the original form, and *ichu* is compounded of the causal particle and the affix *chu*.

What is this *chu*? We have already shown, in the section on "Formative Additions to Roots," that the Telugu *chu* is a verbal formative, identical in origin with the Tamil *kku*. The formative *kku* of Tamil is affixed to the verbal base of causals, as to various other classes of verbal bases, before adding the *a* which forms the sign of the infinitive. It is also affixed to the base before adding *um*, the sign of the indefinite future; and the identity of this Tamil *kku* with the Telugu *ñchu* will appear as soon as the Tamil infinitive is compared with the Telugu—*e.g.*, comp. *śeyvi-kka*, Tam. infinitive, to cause to do, with the Telugu *chêyi-ñcha; aṟeippi-kka*, Tam. infinitive, to cause to call, with the Telugu *pilipi-ñcha*. Comp. also an ordinary transitive verb in the two languages—*e.g.*, *maṟa-kka*, Tam. infinitive to forget, with the Telugu *maṟa-cha*. It thus appears that the *ch* or *nch* of the Telugu is as certainly a formative as the *kk* of the Tamil. Even in the vulgar colloquial Tamil of the extreme southern portion of the Tamil country *kk* systematically becomes *ch*. Thus *maṟakka*, the word just mentioned, is *maṟacha* in the southern patois, precisely as in Telugu. The chief difference between Tamil and Telugu with respect to the use of this formative is, that it is used by two parts of the Tamil verb alone (the infinitive and the neuter future), whereas in Telugu it adheres so closely to the base that it makes its appearance in every part of the verb.

What is the origin of the *p* which often appears in Telugu causal verbs before *inchu*? The causal formed from *viḍuchu*, Tel. to quit, is not *viḍiñchu*, but *viḍipiñchu*, to release. This *p* shows itself, not in all causals, but only in those of verbs ending in the formative *chu*, and it is a peculiarity of that class of verbs that *ch* changes optionally into *p*. Their infinitives may be formed by adding either *pa* or *cha* to the base. On the causal particle *i* being affixed to such verbs, *ch* changes by rule into *p*: thus, not *pili-ch-iñchu*, to cause to call, but *pili-p-iñchu*. This preference for *p* to *ch* before another *ch* looks as if it had arisen from considerations of euphony. But however this may be, *p* is frequently used in Telugu in the formation of verbal nouns, where such considerations could hardly exist—*e.g.*, *maṟap-u*, forgetfulness, from *maṟa-chu*, to forget (Tam, *maṟappu*); *teṟa-pa*, an opening, from *teṟa-chu*, to open (Tam. *tiṟappu*). This formative is sometimes doubled in Telugu—*e.g.*, *tepp-inchu*, to cause to bring, from *techch-u*, to bring. In Tamil *p* is always doubled, except after nasals or *ṛ*. Though the use of this hardened form of *p* is rare in Telugu, yet its existence tends still further to identify the Telugu causal with the Tamil.

Certain verbs in Telugu, ordinarily called causals (ending in *chu*, *ñchu*, *pu*, *mpu*, &c., without a preceding *i*), are to be regarded not as causals, but simply as transitives—*e.g.*, *viḍuchu*, *viḍupu*, to cause to quit; *vañchu*, to bend; *lêpu*, to rouse. They are formed, not by annexing *vi* or *i*, but by the doubling and hardening of the final consonant of the formative (*e.g.*, compare *lêpu*, to rouse, with the corresponding Tamil *eṛuppu*, the transitive of *eṛumbu*); and the verbs from which they are so formed are not actives, but neuters. Instead, therefore, of saying that *tîr-u*, to end, forms its causal either in *tîr-chu* or *tîr-piñchu*, it would be more in accordance with Tamil analogies to represent *tîr-u* as the neuter, *tîr-chu* as the transitive, and *tîr-piñchu* as the causal. It is of the essence of what I regard as the true causal that its theme is a transitive verb—*e.g.*, *kaṭṭ-iñchu*, to cause to build, from *kaṭṭ-u*, to build.

In Canarese, causal verbs are formed by suffixing *iśu*, or rather *i-śu*, to the transitive theme—*e.g.*, from *mâḍu*, to do, is formed *mâḍ-i-śu*, to cause to do. This causal particle *i-śu* (in the classical dialect *i-chu*) is annexed to the theme itself before the addition of the signs of tense, so that it is found in every part of the causal verb, like the corresponding Telugu particle *i-ñchu*, with which it is evidently identical. It has been shown that the Telugu *i-ñchu* has been nasalised from *i-chu* (the phonetic equivalent of the Tamil *i-kku*); and now we find this very *i-chu* in classical Canarese. The change in colloquial Canarese from *i-chu* to *i-śu* is easy and natural, *ś* being phonetically equivalent to *ch*, and *chu* being pronounced like *tsu* in Telugu.

An additional proof, if proof were wanting, of the identity of the Canarese *i-śu* with the Telugu *i-ñchu*, is furnished by the class of derivative verbs, or verbs borrowed from Sanskrit. Sanskrit derivative verbs are made to end in *i* in all the Dravidian dialects (*e.g.*, *jay-i*, to conquer); and those verbs invariably take in Telugu, as has been said, the formative termination *ñchu*—*e.g.*, *jayi-ñchu*. The same verbs invariably take *i-śu*, or *yi-śu*, in Canarese. Thus from the Sanskrit derivative theme, *dhari*, to assume, Telugu forms the verb *dhari-ñchu*, the Canarese equivalent of which is *dhari-śu*, Tamil infinitive *tari-kka*. These verbs are not causals; but the use which they make of the formative *ñchu* or *śu*, preceded by *i*, illustrates the original identity of the Canarese causal particle *i-śu* with the Telugu *i-ñchu*, and of both with the Tamil *i-kku*. Generally the older and harsher sounds of

Canarese have been softened by Tamil; and in particular, the Canarese *k* has often been softened by Tamil into *ś* or *ch*; but in the instance of the formative annexed to the causative particle, exactly the reverse of this has happened; the Tamil *kk* having been softened by the Canarese into *ś*. Canarese, like Telugu, does not so carefully discriminate between transitive and causal verbs as Tamil. The true causal of Tamil is restricted to transitive themes; but Canarese, notwithstanding its possession of transitive particles (*e.g.*, compare *nera-hu*, to fill, with *neri*, to be full, and *tiru-pu*, to turn (actively), with *tiru-gu*, to turn (of itself), often annexes the causal particle *i-śu* to intransitive themes—*e.g.*, *ōḍ-i-śu*, to cause to run (Tam. *ōṭṭ-u*), from *ōḍ-u*, to run. In Japanese, causative verbs are formed by affixing *si* to the root. *si* means to do.

We now return to consider the causal particle of Tamil, instead of beginning with it. *vi* is generally supposed to be the causal particle of Tamil, hardening in certain connections into *bi* or *ppi*. In the first edition I adopted this view in substance, though regarding *i* alone as the causal particle in Telugu and Canarese, but preferred to consider *bi*, rather than *vi*, the primitive form, seeing that *v* does not readily change into *b* in Tamil (though *v* in Tamil often becomes *b* in Canarese—*e.g.*, *vā*, Tam. to come = Can. *bā*), whilst *b* would readily soften into *v* on the one hand, or harden into *pp* on the other. On reconsideration, however, it seems to me better to regard *i* alone as the causal particle of Tamil, as of Telugu and Canarese, provided only the *v*, *b*, or *pp*, by which it is always preceded, be found capable of some satisfactory explanation.

A clue to the right explanation seems to be furnished by the use of *p* instead of *ch* in Telugu. *kk* in Tamil answers to *ch* in Telugu, and we find the Tamil *kk* changing optionally in classical Tamil into *pp*, precisely in accordance with Telugu usage. Instead of the infinitive *naḍa-kka*, to walk, *naḍa-ppa* may also be used. On comparing the Tamil *naḍakka*, to walk, with the Telugu *naḍucha*, and the Tamil *naḍappikka*, to cause to walk, with the Telugu *naḍipiñcha*, we find them substantially identical. No difference exists but such as can be perfectly explained either by the change of *kk* into *ch*, nasalised into *ñch* after *i* as already mentioned, or by the "harmonic sequence of vowels" explained in "Sounds." The *p* preceding *i* has clearly the same origin, and is used for the same purpose in both dialects. As it is certainly a formative in Telugu, it must be the same in Tamil; and accordingly we find it actually used as a verbal formative in the classical Tamil infinitive *naḍappa*, to walk, as mentioned above. It will be seen hereafter that *a* alone is the sign of the infinitive, and that whatever precedes it belongs to the verbal theme, or its formative. This circumstance might explain the *pp* of the Tamil causals ; but it is necessary to go a little further in order to be able to explain the *v* or *b* which alternates with *pp*. The most common formative of Tamil causals is *vi*—*e.g.*, *varu-vi*, to cause to come ; the next is *ppi*—*e.g.*, *paḍi-ppi*, to cause to learn. The remaining form is *bi*, used only after nasals—*e.g.*, *en-bi*, to cause to say, to prove, from *en*, to say, *kâṇ-bi*, to show, from *kâṇ*, to see. There is no doubt that neither the *b* of *bi* nor the *pp* of *ppi* can have been inserted merely for euphony. *v* before *i* (as in *vi*) *might* be merely euphonic ; but this is rendered improbable by the circumstance that *vi* is added, not only to verbs ending in vowels, but also to certain verbs ending in consonants (*y* and *ṛ*)—*e.g.*, *śey-vi*, to cause to do, from *śey*, to do. Telugu and Canarese add *i* nakedly to the base (*e.g.*, *chêy-iñchu*, from *chêy-u*, *gêy-isu*, from *gêy-u*). We have an instance of the use of *vi* after the soft, deep *ṛ* in Tamil, as well as after *y*, in *vâṛ-vi*, to cause to flourish, from *vâṛ*, to flourish. *vi* is almost always used after *u* (*e.g.*, *kaṭṭu-vi*, to cause to build), but in some instances *ppi* is used by rule after *u*—viz., where *u* is preceded by a short vowel and a single consonant—*e.g.*, *eḍu-ppi*, to cause to take up, to erect, from *eḍu*, to take up.

The Tamil future tense-signs seem to throw light on the formatives to which the causal particle *i* are affixed. It is remarkable, at all events, that those three signs, *v*, *b*, *pp*, are identical with the formatives of the causal verb, in what way soever this identity may be accounted for, so that if we know which of those three signs is used by any verb in the formation of its future tense, we know at once how the causal of the same verb is formed. Compare *varu-v-ên*, I will come, with *varu-v-i*, to cause to come ; *eḍu-pp-ên*, I will take up, with *eḍu-pp-i*, to cause to take up, to erect ; *paḍi-pp-ên*, I will learn, with *paḍi-pp-i*, to cause to learn, to teach. This rule applies also to verbal roots ending in consonants—*e.g.*, compare *vâr-pp-ên*, I will pour, with *vâr-pp-i*, to cause to pour, to cast ; *vâṛ-v-ên*, I will flourish, with *vâṛ-v-i*, to cause to flourish ; *kâṇ-b-ên*, I will see, with *kâṇ-b-i*, to cause to see, to show. Tamil admits of the use of a double causal—that is, of a verb denoting that one person is to cause another to cause a third person to do a thing. In this case also the new causal agrees with the future of the first causal, on which it seems to be built. Compare *varu-vi-pp-ên*, I will cause to cause to come, with *varu-vi-pp-i*, to cause to cause to come.

The explanation of this curious coincidence seems to be that the Tamil future was originally a sort of abstract verbal noun, which came to be used as a future by the addition of pronominal signs, whilst the same abstract neuter noun was converted into a causal (as we have seen was probably the case also with Telugu causals in *p-i-ñchu*) by the addition to it of the causal particle. The addition of the causal particle in all cases in Canarese to the verbal root would seem to indicate an older and simpler period of Dravidian speech. Tuḷu forms its causal verbs in a somewhat different manner from the other Dravidian dialects—viz., by suffixing â instead of *i* to the verbal theme, or sometimes *ḍu*, and then adding the signs of tense—*e.g.*, from *maḷp-u*, to make, is formed *maḷp-â-vu*, to cause to make, from *naḍapu*, to walk, *naḍapuḍu*, to cause to walk. This â of the Tuḷu resembles the Hindustani causal—*e.g.*, *chal-wâ-nâ*, to cause to go, from *chal-nâ*, to go; and as the Hindustani causative particle *wâ* has probably been derived from the Sanskrit *aya* or *p-aya*, the Tuḷu â might possibly be supposed to proceed from the same or a similar source. In Gônd *ha* or *h* is the causal particle, and is added to the present participle of transitive verbs, not to the theme.

Origin of the Dravidian Causal Particle '*i*.'—The oldest form of the Indo-European causative particle is supposed to be the Sanskrit *aya* (with *p* prefixed after a root in *â*). *aya* becomes *i* in old Slavonic, and the apparent identity between this *i* and the Dravidian *i* is noteworthy. Notwithstanding this, it does not seem to me either necessary or desirable to seek for the origin of Dravidian particles out of the range of the Dravidian languages, if those languages themselves provide us with a tolerably satisfactory explanation. The Dravidian causative particle *i* may be supposed to have been derived from *î*, to give. This *i* is short in various portions of the Telugu verb. The crude base is *i-chch-u*, the infinitive *î-va* or *i-vva*. The Canarese *îsu* also, the causal of *î*, seems to be formed, not from *î*, but from *i* (*i-isu* = *îsu*). In nearly all cases in the Dravidian languages the short vowel seems to be older than the long one. The meaning of 'give' seems tolerably suitable for a causal particle; but we find it developing into a still more appropriate shape in Telugu, in which *î* is used after an infinitive to mean to let, permit, &c.—*e.g.*, *pô(n)-î*, let it go, from *pô*, to go, literally give it to go. In Canarese also *î-su*, the causal of *î*, is used in the same sense of to let, permit, &c., as the original verb itself in Telugu—*e.g.*, *pôgal-îsu*, permit to go. It is remarkable also that in Canarese the corresponding and more common word *koḍu*, give, is used in the same manner as a permissive or causal—*e.g.*, *mâḍa koḍu*, permit (him) to do.

3. Frequentative Verbs.

There is a class of verbs in all the Dravidian languages that have sometimes been called iterative or frequentative. The following are

Tamil examples : *minuminu-kku*, to glitter, from *min*, to shine ; *veḷu-veḷu-kku*, to whiten, from *veḷu-kku*, to be white, root *veḷ*, white ; *mura-mura-kku*, to murmur, *muṇamuṇa-kku*, to mutter, *kirukiru-kka*, to be giddy. It does not seem to me, however, necessary to enter into the examination of these and similar words, seeing that there is no peculiarity whatever in the mode in which they are conjugated, the iterative meaning resides in the root alone, and is expressed by the device, in common use in all languages, of doubling the root. Compare Latin *murmuro, tintinno*, &c. In Tuḷu, however, there is a form of the verb rightly called frequentative. It is formed by inserting *ê* (probably the particle of emphasis) between the base and the personal signs, whereupon a new verbal base is formed, which is regularly conjugated —*e.g.*, *maḷpêve* (*maḷpu* + *ê* + (*v*)*e*), I make again and again.

4. Intensive Verb.

This form of verb is also found only in Tuḷu. Compare *maḷpuve*, I make, with *maḷtruve*, I make energetically ; *kêṇuve*, I hear, with *kêṇḍruve*, I hear intensely ; *bûruve*, I fall, with *bûrḍuve*, I fall heavily.

5. Inceptive Verb.

We find a fully developed inceptive or inchoative form of the verb in Gônd alone. It is formed by annexing the signs of person and tense, not to the base, as in the case of the ordinary verb, but to the infinitive.

6. The Passive Voice.

Each of the primitive Indo-European languages has a regular passive voice, regularly conjugated. The Sanskrit passive is formed by annexing the particle *ya* (supposed to be derived from *yâ*, to go), to the verbal theme, and adding the personal terminations peculiar to the middle voice. Most of the languages of the Scythian family also form their passives by means of annexed particles. In order to form the passive, the Turkish suffixes to the verbal theme *il* or *îl*; the Finnish *et*; the Hungarian *at, et, tet*; and to these particles the pronominal terminations are appended in the usual manner. Japanese has a passive voice, the form of which is active. The Dravidian verb is entirely destitute of a passive voice, properly so called, nor is there any reason to suppose that it ever had a passive. None of the Dravidian dialects possesses any passive particle or suffix, or any means of expressing passivity by direct inflectional changes ; the signification of the passive voice is, nevertheless, capable of being expressed in a variety of ways.

We have now to inquire into the means adopted by the Dravidian languages for conveying a passive signification; and it will be found that they correspond in a considerable degree to the means used for this purpose by the Gaurian vernaculars of Northern India, which also are destitute of a regular passive voice. In the particulars that follow, all the Dravidian dialects (with the exception of the Gônd) agree: what is said of one holds true of all.

(1.) The place of a passive voice is to a large extent supplied by the use of the neuter or intransitive form of the verb, somewhat as in Japanese. This is in every dialect of the family the most idiomatic and characteristic mode of expressing the passive; and wherever it can be used, it is always preferred by classical writers. Thus, it was broken, is ordinarily expressed in Tamil by *uḍeindadu*, the preterite (third person singular neuter) of *uḍei*, intransitive, to become broken; and though this is a neuter, rather than a passive properly so called, and might literally be rendered, 'it has come into a broken condition,' yet it is evident that, for all practical purposes, nothing more than this is required to express the force of the passive. The passivity of the expression may be increased by prefixing the instrumental case of the agent—*e.g.*, *ennâl uḍeindadu*, it was broken by me, literally it came into a broken condition through me.

(2.) A very common mode of forming the passive is by means of the preterite verbal participle of any neuter or active verb, followed by the preterite (third person singular neuter) of the verbs to become, to be, to go, or (occasionally) to end. Thus, we may say either *mugindadu*, it is finished, or *mugind' âyittru*, literally, having finished it is become. This form adds the idea of completion to that of passivity: not only is the thing done, but the doing of it is completed. Transitive or active verbs which are destitute of intransitive forms may in this manner acquire a passive signification. Thus *kaṭṭ-u*, to bind or build, is necessarily a transitive verb, and is without a corresponding intransitive; but in the phrase *kôvil kaṭṭi âyittru*, the temple is built, literally, the temple having built has become, a passive signification is acquired by the active voice, without the assistance of any passive-forming particle. *pôyittru*, it has gone, may generally be used in such phrases instead of *âyittru*, it is become.

Verbal nouns, especially the verbal in *dal* or *al*, are often used in Tamil instead of the preterite verbal participle in the formation of this constructive passive—*e.g.*, instead of *śeÿd' âyittru*, it is done, literally, having done it has become, we may say *śeÿdal âyittru*, which, though it is used to express the same meaning, literally signifies the doing of it has become—*i.e.*, it has become a fact, the doing of it is completed.

The Dravidian constructive passives now referred to require the third person neuter of the auxiliary verb. The force of the passive voice will not be brought out by the use of the masculine or feminine, or by the epicene plural. If those persons of the verb were employed, the activity inherent in the idea of personality would necessitate an active signification; it would tie down the transitive theme to a transitive meaning; whereas the intransitive relation is naturally implied in the use of the action-less neuter gender, and therefore the expression of the signification of the passive (viz., by the intransitive doing duty for the passive) is facilitated by the use of the third person neuter.

A somewhat similar mode of forming the passive has been pointed out in the Hindustani and Bengali—*e.g.*, *jânâ yây*, Beng. it is known, literally, it goes to be known. *jânâ* is represented by some to be a verbal noun, by others to be a passive participle; but, whatever it be, there is some difference between this idiom and the Dravidian one; for in the corresponding Tamil phrase *terind' âyittru*, it is known, *terind-u* is unquestionably the preterite verbal participle of an intransitive verb, and the phrase literally means 'having known it is become.' *terindu pôyittru*, literally, having known it is gone, conveys the same signification. It is remarkable, however, that a verb signifying to go should be used in the Dravidian languages as a passive-making auxiliary, as well as in the languages of Northern India.

Occasionally Dravidian active or transitive verbs themselves are used with a passive signification, without the addition of any intransitive auxiliary whatever. Relative participles and relative participial nouns are the parts of the verb which are most frequently used in this manner —*e.g.*, *eṛudina śuvaḍi uṇḍu; achch' aḍitta pustagam vêṇḍum*, Tam. I have a written book; I want a printed one. In this phrase both *eṛudina*, written, and *achch'-aḍitta*, printed, are the preterite relative participles of transitive themes. The former means literally 'that wrote,' yet it is used passively to signify 'written;' and the latter means literally 'that printed or struck off,' but is used passively as equivalent to 'that is printed.'

The relative participial noun, especially the preterite neuter, is oftentimes used in the same manner—*e.g.*, in *śonnadu pôdum*, Tam. what was said is sufficient, *śonnadu*, literally means 'that which said;' but the connection and the usage of the language determine it to signify passively that which *was* said; and so distinctively in this case is the passive sense expressed by the connection alone, that the use of the more formal modern passive, *śolla-(p)paṭṭadu*, would sound awkward and foreign. *endra*, Tam., *anêde*, Tel., that is called, literally that spoke, is another very common instance of the same rule. *Iyêśu enbavar*, Tam., signifies literally, Jesus who speaks; but usage determines it to mean he who is called Jesus.

The mode of expressing the passive adopted by Tuḷu is on the whole similar to this. The perfect active participle is used for the passive in this manner, but the pronoun is repeated at the end—*e.g.*, *âye nindi-s'dinâye âye*, he is one who has despised, meaning, he is one who has been despised. (The corresponding Tamil would be *aran nindittavan avan.*)

(3.) The passive is formed in Gônd in a manner peculiar to that language, viz., by the addition of the substantive verb I am to the participle of the active voice. In the other Dravidian dialects this is the usual mode in which the perfect tense is formed. In Tamil, *nân aḍitt' irukkirên*, I am having beaten, means I have beaten. The corresponding Gônd expression *ana jisi aiâtona*, means I am beaten. This corresponds to the modern English mode of forming the passive, as in this very expression, I am beaten; but still more closely to the mode adopted by New Persian, in which the same form of the verb has an active meaning when it stands alone, and a passive meaning when followed by the substantive verb.

(4.) The verb *uṇ*, to eat, is occasionally used in the Dravidian languages as an auxiliary in the formation of passives. It is invariably appended to nouns (substantives or verbal nouns), and is never compounded with any part of the verb—*e.g.*, *aḍi uṇḍân*, he was beaten, or got a beating, literally he ate a beating; *paḍeipp' uṇḍên*, I was created, literally I ate a creating. The same singular idiom prevails also in the Gaurian or North Indian vernaculars. The particular verb signifying to eat used in those languages differs indeed from the Dravidian *uṇ;* but the idiom is identical, and the existence of so singular an idiom in both the northern and the southern family is deserving of notice. It is remarkable that the same peculiar contrivance for expressing the passive is found in Chinese, in which also to eat a beating, means to be beaten.

(5.) Another mode of forming the passive used in each of the modern cultivated colloquial dialects of the Dravidian family, except Tuḷu, is by means of the auxiliary verb *paḍ-u*, to suffer, to experience, which is annexed to the infinitive of the verb signifying the action suffered—*e.g.*, *kolla-(p)paṭṭân*, Tam. he was killed, literally, he suffered a killing. It is also annexed to nouns denoting quality or condition—*e.g.*, *veṭka-(p)pâṭṭân*, he was ashamed, literally, he suffered or experienced shame. The ultimate base of a verb is sometimes used instead of the infinitive or verbal noun in construction with this auxiliary, in which case the base is regarded as a noun—*e.g.*, instead of *aḍikka-(p)paṭṭân*, we may say *aḍi paṭṭân*, he was beaten, or literally he suffered a beating; and where this form can be used, it is considered more idiomatic than the use of the infinitive.

It is evident that this compound of *paḍ-u*, to suffer, with an infinitive or noun of quality, is rather a phrase than a passive voice. It is rarely found in the classics; and idiomatic speakers prefer the other modes of forming the passive. *paḍ-u* is often added, not only to active, but also to neuter or intransitive verbs; but as the intransitive expresses by itself as much of a passive signification as is ordinarily necessary, the addition of the passive auxiliary does not alter the signification—*e.g.*, there is no difference in Tamil between the intransitive *teriyum*, it appears, or will appear, and *teriya (p)paḍum;* or in Telugu between *teluśunu* and *teliya baḍunu*, the corresponding forms. In ordinary use, *paḍ-u* conveys the meaning of continuous action or being, rather than that of passivity—*e.g.*, *irukka-(p)paṭṭa* (Tam.) is vulgarly used for *irukkira*, that is; and I have heard a Tamilian say, *nân nandrây śâppiḍa-(p)paṭṭavan* (Tam.), meaning thereby, not I have been well eaten, but I have been accustomed to eat well. The Dravidian languages, indeed, are destitute of passives properly so called, and, therefore, resist every effort to bring *paḍ-u* into general use. Such efforts are constantly being made by foreigners, who are accustomed to passives in their own tongues, and fancy that they cannot get on without them; but nothing sounds more barbarous to the Dravidian ear than the unnecessary use of *paḍu* as a passive auxiliary. It is only when combined with nouns that its use is thoroughly allowable.

7. The Middle Voice.

In none of the Dravidian dialects is there a middle voice, properly so called. The force of the middle or reflective voice is expressed constructively by the use of an auxiliary verb—viz., by *koḷ*, Tam. to take (Tel. *kon-u;* Tuḷu, *koṇu* and *oṇu*)—*e.g.*, *paṇṇi-(k)koṇḍên*, I made it for myself, literally, I made and took it. This auxiliary sometimes conveys a reciprocal force rather than that of the middle voice—*e.g.*, *pêśi-(k) koṇḍârgaḷ*, Tam. they talked together; *aḍittu-(k)koṇḍârgal*, they beat one another. The same usage appears in the other dialects also.

8. The Negative Voice.

Properly speaking, the Dravidian negative is rather a mood or voice than a conjugation. All verbal themes are naturally affirmative, and the negative signification is expressed by means of additions or changes. Nevertheless, it will conduce to perspicuity to inquire now into the negative mood or voice, before entering upon the consideration of the pronominal terminations and tenses.

The regular combination of a negative particle with a verbal theme is a peculiarity of the Scythian family of tongues. Negation is generally expressed in the Indo-European family by means of a separate particle used adverbially; and instances of combination like the Sanskrit *nâsti*, it is not, the negative of *asti*, it is, are very rare; whereas, in the Scythian languages, every verb has a negative voice or mood as well as an affirmative. This is the case also in Japanese. The Scythian negative voice is generally formed by the insertion of a particle of negation between the theme and the pronominal suffixes; and this is as distinctive of the Dravidian as of the Turkish and Finnish languages. Different particles are, it is true, used in the different languages to express negation; but the mode in which such particles are used is substantially the same in all.

In general, the Dravidian negative verb has but one tense, which is an aorist, or is indeterminate in point of time—*e.g.*, *pôgên*, Tam. (*pôvanu*, Tel., *pôgenu*, Can.), I go not, means either I did not, I do not, or I will not go. The time is generally determined by the context. Ku, Gônd, and Tuḷu use the negative more freely. In Ku there is a negative preterite as well as a negative aorist; and in Tuḷu and Gônd every tense of every mood has its appropriate negative verb. Malayâḷam has three negative tenses—the present, the past, and the future—*e.g.*, *pôgâ-(y)-unnu*, I go not; *pôgâ-ññu*, went not; *pôgâ-(y)-um*, will not go. In the other dialects there is only one mood of the negative in ordinary use, viz., the indicative. If an infinitive and imperative exist, it is only in classical compositions that they appear; and they are ordinarily formed by the help of the infinitive and imperative of the substantive verb, which are suffixed as auxiliaries to the negative verbal participle—*e.g.*, *śeyyâd'-iru*, Tam. do not thou, literally, be thou not doing. In Telugu a prohibitive or negative imperative is in ordinary use even in the colloquial dialect.

In the Dravidian negative voice, as in the affirmative, the verbal theme remains unchanged; and in both voices the pronominal terminations are precisely the same. The only point, therefore, which it is necessary to investigate here is *the means whereby the idea of negation is expressed.*

The Tamil-Telugu-Canarese negative is altogether destitute of signs of tense: it is destitute, not only of the signs of present, past, and future time, but even of the sign of the aorist; and in Tamil and Canarese the pronominal suffixes are annexed directly to the verbal theme. Thus, whilst the present, past, and future tenses (first person singular) of the affirmative voice of the Tamil verb *vâṛ*, to flourish, are *vâṛ-gir-ên, vâṛ-nd-ên, vâṛ-v-ên;* the corresponding negative is simply *vâṛ-ên*, I flourish not—literally, as appears, flourish-I,—without the insertion of any sign of time between the theme and the pronoun.

What is the rationale of this negative? The absence of signs of tense appears to contribute to the expression of the idea of negation: it may at least be said that it precludes the signification of the affirmative. In consequence of the absence of tense-signs the idea expressed by the verb is abstracted from the realities of the past, the present, and the future: it leaves the region of actual events, and passes into that of abstractions. Hence, this abstract form of the verb may be supposed to have become a negative mood, not by a positive, but by a negative process,—by the absence of a predicate of time, not by the aid of a negative particle. Is this to be accepted as the rationale? If we examined only Tamil and Canarese, we might be satisfied with this explanation; for in the various persons of the negative voice in both languages there is no trace of the insertion of any negative particle; and though the vowel *a* has acquired a predominant and permanent place in the verbal and relative participles, we should not feel ourselves warranted in considering that vowel as a particle of negation, without distinct, trustworthy evidence from some other source.

The only peculiarity in the personal forms of the Tamil negative is the invariable length of the initial vowel of the pronominal terminations. Thus the initial *a* of the neuter singular demonstrative being short, we should expect the Tamil of 'it flourishes not' to be *vâṛ-adu;* whereas it is *vâṛ-âdu* or *vâṛ-â*. This increase of quantity might arise from the incorporation and assimilation of some inserted vowel; but we might also naturally suppose it to be merely lengthened euphonically for the sake of emphasis. The corresponding vowel is short in Telugu. In the Canarese negative we miss even this lengthening of the initial vowel of the pronominal terminations—*e.g.*, we find invariably *bâḷ-adu*, instead of the Tamil *vâṛ-âdu*. In the verbal and relative participles in both languages the vowel *a* is inserted between the theme and the formative, and this *a* is invariably short in Canarese and long in Tamil—*e.g.*, *bâḷ-a-de*, Can. not having lived, or without living; Tam. *vâṛ-âdu* or *vâṛ-â-mal*, without living. The verbal noun in Tamil is *vâr-â-mei*, the not living. The relative participle that lived or lives not, is in Canarese *bâḷ-a-da*, in Tamil *vâr-â-da*. In these instances, if euphony alone had been considered, *u*, the ordinary enunciative vowel, would have appeared where we find *a:* it may, therefore, be concluded that *a* (euphonically *â* in Tamil and Malayâ-ḷam) has intentionally been inserted, and that it contributes in some manner to grammatical expression.

It will be found that light is thrown upon this subject by Telugu. The pronominal terminations of the negative voice of the Telugu are identical with those of the present tense of the affirmative. In Tamil and Canarese the pronominal terminations of the verb commence with a vowel; but in Telugu verbs the pronoun is represented by the final syllable alone, and that syllable invariably commences with a consonant. Hence, if no particle of negation were used in the conjugation of the Telugu negative voice, the pronominal suffix would be appended directly to the verbal theme, and as every Telugu theme terminates in the enunciative *u*, that *u* would not be elided, but would invariably remain. What then is the fact?

On examining the Telugu negative, it is found that the vowel *a* invariably intervenes between the theme and the pronominal suffix; and as the final enunciative *u* of the theme has been elided to make way for this *a*, it is evident that *a* is not an euphonic insertion, but is a particle of negation. Compare *chêy-a-nu*, Tel. I do not, with Tamil *śey(y)ên; chêy-a-vu*, thou dost not, with Tamil *śey(y)-ây; chêy-a-mu*, we do not, with Tamil *śey(y)-ôm; chêy-a-ru*, you do not, with Tamil *śey(y)îr*. From this comparison it cannot be doubted that *a* is regularly used in Telugu as a particle of negation. We find the same *a* used in Telugu, as in Canarese and Tamil, in the negative verbal participle—*e.g.*, *chêy-a-ka*, without doing; in the relative participle—*e.g.*, *chêy-a-ni*, that does not; and in the verbal noun—*e.g.*, *chêy-a-mi*, the not doing. In each of these participials *a* is used in the same manner by the Canarese, and *â* by the Tamil: and that those vowels are not euphonics or conjunctives, but signs of negation, even in Tamil-Canarese, is now proved by the evidence of Telugu, in which a similar *a* is used, not only by the participles, but by all the personal forms of the verb.

The Telugu verb 'to go' forms its ordinary negative, it is true, without any trace of this vowel of negation—*e.g.*, *pônu*, I go not, *pôvu*, thou goest not. This, however, is only an apparent irregularity, for the classical forms are *pôv-a-nu* and *pôv-a-vu*. The lengthening of the included *a* of *kânu*, I become not, is in accordance with the Telugu law of displacement, *kânu* being instead of *ak-a-nu* or *ag-a-nu*, the equivalent of the Tamil *âgên*. We have thus arrived at the conclusion that *a* is the sign of negation which is most systematically used by the

Dravidian languages in the formation of the negative voice of the verb. It has, it is true, disappeared from the conjugated forms of Tamil and Canarese; but the analogy, not only of the Telugu personal forms, but also of the Tamil and Canarese participles and participial nouns, shows that it must originally have been the common property of all the dialects. The negative *a*, being succeeded in Tamil and Canarese by the initial vowel of the pronominal suffix, appears gradually to have got incorporated with it; and an evidence of this incorporation survives in the euphonic lengthening of the pronominal vowel in Tamil.

The negative particle of the Tuḷu is *ijji*, answering to Tam. *illei*, Mal. and Can. *illa*. Most of the tenses of the Tuḷu negative verb are formed by annexing to the temporal particles of the verb *j*, the abbreviation of this *ijji*, with such enunciative vowels as euphony is supposed to require. The negative of the future tense appears to be formed from *a*, the particle used in the other dialects. Comp. *maḷ-puji*, I do not make, *maḷt'diji*, I have not made, with *maḷpaye*, I shall not make, and the conditional form *maḷt'dvaye*, I should not make. Gônd inserts the negative particles *hille* or *halle* (Drav. *ille* or *alle*) between the pronoun and the verb, without abbreviation. This crude use of the form has doubtless come down from a high antiquity, as we shall find that *al* is sometimes used in a somewhat similar manner by the Tamil poets.

It is desirable now to inquire into the participial and imperative formatives of the negative verb. The negative verbal participle of Tamil is formed by suffixing *â-du* or *â-mal*—*e.g.*, *śey*(*y*)-*â-du* or *śey*(*y*)-*â-mal*, not doing, or without doing. In the highest and lowest Tamil *mei* is used as the formative of this participle instead of *mal*—*e.g.*, *vaṛuv-â-mei*, without slipping. *mei* constitutes the ordinary termination of abstract nouns, and is added both to crude roots and to the relative participles of verbs—*e.g.*, *tâṛ-mei*, lowness, humility; *irukkindr-a-mei*, a being or the being. The formative termination of negative verbal nouns is identical with this abstract *mei;* and *mal*, the participial formative, is evidently equivalent to it. Probably also it is the original form; for, on the whole, it is more likely that a final *l* should have been softened away than added. The verbal noun of the Telugu negative verb ends in *mi*, which is virtually the same as *mei*. The other Tamil termination of negative verbal participles, *du*, is an ordinary formative of neuter nouns of quality. The corresponding Canarese termination is *de;* and in Tamil *du*, with a subsequent emphatic *ê*, is commonly used as a negative imperative or prohibitive—*e.g.*, *śey*(*y*)-*â-d-ê*, do not thou,—a proof that the negative verbal participle in *du* or *de* is properly a verbal noun. The relative participle of the negative verb in each of the dialects, except Telugu, is formed by suffixing *a*, the sign of the relative, to the verbal participle in *d-u*, eliding as usual the enunciative *u—e.g.*, *śey(y)-â-da*, Tam., *gêy-a-da*, Can., that does or did not. Many additional forms are constructed by the addition of the various tenses and participles of the substantive verb, and it is by the help of that verb that the negative imperative and negative infinitive in both Canarese and Tamil are ordinarily formed. The negative relative participle of Telugu is formed by adding *ni*, instead of the usual relative *a*, to the negative particle—*e.g.*, *chêy-a-ni*, that does or did not. This *ni* is one of the Telugu inflexional increments, and is also used as a particle of conjunction, as will be seen under the head of the "Relative Participles."

Mr A. D. Campbell, in his "Telugu Grammar," states that the negative verbal particle of the Telugu is formed by suffixing *ka* to the infinitive of the affirmative voice; and that the prohibitive is formed in like manner by suffixing *ku* or *ka* to the infinitive [*ka* is not so used], with the ordinary addition of *mu* or *mo*. In consequence of this representation, Dr Stevenson was led to consider *ku* as a Telugu sign of negation, and to search for allied or equivalent particles in other Indian languages. The comparison of the negative verbs in the various Dravidian dialects which has just been made proves that this representation is inaccurate, and that the *a* to which the *ka* and *ku* aforesaid are suffixed is not the *a* which forms the sign of the infinitive, but the negative particle *a*. The suffixes of the forms in question, therefore, are not *ku* or *ka*, but *a-ku* and *a-ka;* and thus *chêy-a-ka*, without doing, or not having done, and *chêy-a-ku*, do not, come into harmony with the other Telugu forms, viz., *chêy-a-ni*, that does not, *chêy-a-mi*, the not doing; and also with the negative participles and verbals of the other dialects.

The *a* of the Telugu imperative and negative verbal participle being undoubtedly the sign of negation, it only remains to inquire into the origin of the *ka* or *ku* which is suffixed to it. The participial suffix *ka* is evidently used in Telugu for the same purposes as the Tamil suffixes *du*, *mal*, and *mei*, and the Canarese *de*. Those suffixes, though used by verbal participles, are undoubtedly to be regarded as formatives of verbal nouns. I consider *ka* also as proceeding from a similar origin; for in Telugu many verbal nouns are formed in this very manner by adding *ka* to the root—*e.g.*, *nammi-ka*, confidence, from *nammu*, to confide; and *kôri-ka*, hope, from *kôru*, to hope. This *ka* is *kkei*, in Tamil (*e.g.*, *nambi-kkei*, confidence), and *ge* or *ke* in Canarese: it is a very common formative of verbal nouns, and is equivalent in use to the formatives of which *d* or *t*, *b* or *p*, is the initial. When we compare Telugu derivative nouns ending in *ka* (*e.g.*, *teliyi-ka*, semblance, from *teliyu*, to appear) with the negative verbal participles of the same language, which invariably end in *ka* (*e.g.*, *teḷiy-a-ka*, not seeming), it is evident that the particle *ka* is not that by which the difference in meaning is expressed. The *a* which precedes *ka* is evidently the seat of the difference. In those cases in which the derivative noun and the negative participle are absolutely identical in sound and appearance, the negative *a* has been absorbed by the preceding long *â* of the root. This is the cause of the similarity between *râka*, a coming, and *râka*, not or without coming, the latter of which is for *ra-a-ka*.

In the dialect of the Kotas of the Nilgherry Hills, *p* appears to be used as the formative suffix of the negative verbal participle instead of the Telugu *k* and the Tamil-Canarese *d*—*e.g.*, *hôgâ-pe*, without going, corresponding to the Canarese *hôgade*, and the Telugu *pôvaka*. This is in accordance with a rule often already noticed, viz., the interchangeableness of *k* and *p* in the formatives of verbs and nouns. The Telugu prohibitive suffix *ku* is, I conceive, substantially identical with *ka*, the suffix of the verbal participle, just as *dê*, the colloquial Tamil prohibitive, is identical with *du*, the negative verbal participle in the same dialect. Dravidian imperatives are in general nothing but verbal nouns pronounced emphatically. Hence, the Tamil *śey(y)-â-dê*, do not thou, is simply *śey(y)-â-du*, doing not, with the addition of the emphatic *ê*; and the Telugu *chêy-a-ku*, do not thou, is in like manner, I conceive, identical with the verbal participle *chêy-a-ka*, doing not, or without doing, with an emphasis understood.

There is in classical Tamil a prohibitive particle which nearly corresponds to this Telugu prohibitive, viz., *arka*—*e.g.*, *śey(y)-arka*, do not. It is used in connection with both numbers and every gender; and I believe that it is by usage only that the corresponding Telugu form is restricted to the second person singular; for when we compare the Tamil *śey(y)-arka* and the Telugu *chêy-a-ku*, we can scarcely doubt that they are substantially identical. What is the origin of this Tamil prohibitive suffix *arka*? It is derived from *al* (pronounced *ar* before *k*), the particle of negation, the origin of which from the negative base *a* will presently be shown, and *ka*, which is identical with *ka* or *ga*, a sign of the Tamil infinitive, optative, or polite imperative, apparent in such words as *vâṛ-ga*, may (he, thou, you, they, &c.) flourish. This infinitival, participial, or imperative form appears to have been originally a verbal noun.

We should here notice the prohibitive particle of Gônd, viz., *manni* or *minni*. This is not suffixed to the verb, but prefixed, like the Latin *noli.* *manni* closely resembles the Tamil suffix *min*, in such words as *śey(y)an-min*, do not ye; but the resemblance is purely accidental, for the prohibitive particle of *śey(y)an-min* is *an* euphonised from *al*, and *min* is not, as Beschi supposed, a prohibitive particle at all, but is a sign of the second person plural of the imperative, and as such is systematically used in the higher dialect by the imperative of the affirmative voice, as well as by the prohibitive—*e.g.*, *poṟu-min*, bear ye. This in Malayâḷam is *vin*, *pin* (see the imper. of the affirmative). In poetical Tamil also *aṟpin* (*al-pin*) is occasionally used instead of *an-min*. There is also a plural form of this, *aṟpîr*. Possibly the Gônd prohibitive, *manni*, may be connected with the Hindustani *mat* and the Sanskrit *mâ*, or, but very remotely, with the Turkish particle of negation *me* or *ma*, which is used like the Dravidian *a* in the formation of the negative voice of the verb. *manni* resembles *inni*, the prohibitive particle of the Scythian tablets of Behistun.

Origin of 'a,' the Dravidian Negative Particle.—We have seen that *a* is the sign of negation in Dravidian negative verbs, and that it is inserted between the theme and the signs of personality and other suffixes to form the negative voice. Has this *a* any connection with the alpha privative of the Indo-European tongues? I think not, though this would seem a more natural use of the alpha privative than that of forming the temporal augment in Sanskrit and Greek, according to Bopp's theory. There is no trace of alpha privative or any equivalent privative *pre*-fix in the Dravidian languages; and its place is supplied by some *post*-fixed relative participle or verbal noun formed from *il* or *al*—*e.g.*, from *nêr*, Tam. straight or straightness, is formed *nêr-inmei* (*il-mei* euphonised), crookedness, want of straightness.

The negative *a* of the Dravidian negative verb is, I have no doubt, equivalent to *al* or *il*, the ordinary isolated particle of negation. This very sign of negation is sometimes used by the Tamil classics instead of *a* in verbal combinations—*e.g.*, *aṟi(g)-il-îr*, you know not, takes the place of the more common *aṟi-(y)-îr:* compare also *ninei-(y)-al-â*, not considering; *śey(g)-al-âdâr*, they will not do, or they who will not do. In all these examples the *al* is evidently the isolated negative particle. There cannot be any doubt whatever of the negative force of *al* in the negative appellatives, which are formed from *al-an* or *il-an*, he is not, combined with verbal roots—*e.g.*, *pês-al-êm*, we speak not, *uṇḍ-il-ei*, thou eatest not or hast not eaten. Compare also *mâttralan* (*mâṟṟalan*), Tam. and Mal. an enemy, from *mâttru* + *al* + *an*, he who cannot be changed. Dr Gundert derives this from *mattrâ* + *uḷ* + *an*, he who is + unchangeable. In the ordinary negative form, *mâttrân*, Tam. and Mal. an enemy, the idea of negation is expressed by *â;* but in *mâttra-*

alan I have no doubt we have the negative particle *al.* Gônd regularly forms its negative voice by suffixing *halle* or *hille,* a barbarous euphonisation of the more correct *alle* or *ille;* and the dialect of the Kotas makes a similar use of the particle *illa.* This particle is also systematically used in forming the prohibitive, or negative imperative, of poetical Tamil, in which connection *al* is ordinarily lengthened to *âl* or *êl*—*e.g.*, *śel-êl,* go not, *muni-(y)-êl,* be not angry. But it is also, as we have seen, often retained unchanged—*e.g.*, *śey(y)-ar-ka* (*ar* for *al*), do not, and *śey(y)-an-min* (*an* for *al*), do not ye. In modern colloquial Tamil, *illei* (for *illa*) is commonly subjoined to the infinitive of the affirmative verb to form an aoristic negative—*e.g.*, *vara-(v)-illei* (I, thou, he, &c.), did not, do not, or will not come. This form, though very common, is not classical, and has arisen from the tendency which compounds evince to break up in process of time into their component elements.

It is evident that *a,* the sign of negation in the Dravidian negative verb, and *al,* the isolated negative particle, are substantially identical. The use of *al* instead of *a* in various verbal combinations in classical Tamil seems to me to prove this point. It remains, however, to endeavour to ascertain which is the older form. Has *a* been softened from *al?* or is *al* a secondary form of *a?* There are several parallel instances of the apparent disappearance of a final *l*—*e.g.*, *dal,* the formative of many verbal nouns in Tamil, is represented by *ta* in Canarese and Telugu. Thus *muri-dal,* Tam. a breaking, is in Can. *mura-ta; śey-dal,* Tam. a doing, is in Tel. *chê-ta.* The infinitive is *al* or *a* in Canarese, *a* alone in Tamil. We have seen also that the Tamil suffix of the negative verbal noun may be either *mal* or *mei.* None of these instances, however, is decisive; as it may be supposed, and is I think probable, that a final *l,* answering to a final *m, n,* or *r,* was annexed to many verbal nouns in process of time for the purpose of making them more distinctive. In those instances, therefore, *a* may be the primitive shape, *al* the secondary. The same explanation seems to be the most satisfactory mode of accounting for the double form of the negative particle. I regard *a* as the original shape of that particle —the primitive negative base—answering to *a,* the primitive demonstrative base, and *al* as the more fully developed form of the negative —a negative noun—answering to the demonstrative nouns *am, ad, al,* &c. I refer in this only to the resemblance in form between the demonstrative and the negative bases and nouns; but perhaps we may now venture to go a step further, with Dr Gundert, and derive the negative meaning itself from the interrogative, and ultimately from the demonstrative. He says (in his private communication to me), "I believe the [remote demonstrative] pronoun *a* forms the [particle of negation in the] negative verb; just as this *a* in its interjectional [syntactic] form has the signification of a question. From the meaning of a question comes the meaning of negation. *adu varum-â?* will it happen? = it will never happen." In the colloquial dialect of the Tamil, at least, it is certain that the idea of negation is very often expressed by putting a question. It is at once a poetical and a vulgar usage.

I am unable, however, to agree with Dr Gundert when he proceeds to say that he does not consider *al* a negative in itself, but only a negative when followed by the negative particle *a*, as in the words *alla*, &c. Whether *al* may or may not have been a demonstrative in origin, as I think it probably was, yet, when used as a particle of negation, it seems to me certain that it is a negative of itself without any addition, and that the added vowels *a*, &c., are merely enunciative. This applies with equal force to the corresponding negative particle *il*. The following words in Tamil seem to me to prove that *al* and *il* have of themselves the full force of negatives. Al:—*andru* (*al-du*), it is not; (class. Can. *altu*, Tuḷu, *att'*); *anmei* (*al-mei*), not-ness, negation; *al-gu*, to become less. *al*, darkness. *al-vaṛi*, a grammatical term, absence of inflexion. Il:—*indru*, it is not; *inmei* (*il-mei*), not-ness, non-existence. *ili*, one who has nothing; *il-porul* (*poruḷ*, thing), non-existence, &c., the thing that is not.

Whatever opinion we entertain respecting the derivation of *al* from *a*, the widely extended affinities of *al*, *âl*, or *êl*, the prohibitive or negative imperative particle, are deserving of notice. Compare the Sanskrit prohibitive particle *alam*, no, not, which looks as if it were derived from the Dravidian *al*. The prohibitive particle of the Sântâl, a Kôl dialect, is *âlâ*; the Finnish prohibitive also is *âlâ*; the Ostiak *ilâ*; and we find a similar prohibitive particle even in Hebrew—viz, *al*; Chaldee, *lâ*.

9. Appellative Verbs, or Conjugated Nouns.

In some languages of the Ugrian group the pronominal terminations of the verbs, or those pronominal fragments in which verbs commonly terminate, are suffixed directly to nouns; which nouns become by that addition denominative or appellative verbs, and are regularly conjugated through every number and person—*e.g.*, from the noun *paz*, the Lord, the Mordvin forms *paz-ân*, I am the Lord; and from the possessive *paz-an*, Lord's, it forms *paz-an-ân*, I am the Lord's. Adjectives being merely nouns of quality in the Scythian languages, every rule which applies to nouns applies to adjectives also. In the New Persian, possibly through the influence of the conterminous Scythian languages, there is a similar compound of a noun or an adjective with the verbal terminations—*e.g.*, *merd-em*, I am a man, from *merd*, a man, and *em*, the contracted form of the substantive verb I am. This class of compounds resembles, but is not identical with, the class of possessive compounds described in p. 202; that class is not found in the Dravidian languages.

The agreement between the Dravidian languages and those of the Ugrian family with respect to the formation of appellative verbs of the character referred to is very remarkable, and has been admitted to be very remarkable by Professor Hunfalvy, though in other particulars he fails to see much resemblance between the Finno-Ugrian and the Dravidian languages. Any Dravidian noun and any adjective may be converted into a verb in the more ancient dialects of each of the Dravidian languages, and in some connections even in the colloquial dialects, by simply suffixing to it the usual pronominal fragments; and not only may nouns in the nominative case be thus conjugated as verbs, but even the oblique case-basis, or virtual genitive, may in classical Tamil, as in Mordvin, be adopted as a verbal theme. Tamil grammarians call the verbs here described *vinei-(k)kuṟippu*, literally verbal signs; and they have, not inappropriately, been styled conjugated nouns by an English writer on Tamil Grammar: but I think the best name is that which was given them by Beschi—viz., appellative verbs or conjugated appellatives.

Appellative verbs are conjugated through every number and person, but they are restricted to the present tense; or rather, they are of no tense, for the idea of time is excluded from them. Thus, from *kôn*, Tam. a shepherd or king, may be formed *kôn-en*, I am a king, *kôn-ei*, thou art a king, *kôn-em*, we are kings, *kôn-ir*, ye are kings. So also we may annex to the crude base the oblique or genitival formative *in*, and then from the new constructive base *kôn-in*, of the king, or the king's, we may not only form the appellative nouns, *kôn-in-an*, he who is the king's, *kôn-in-ar*, they who are the king's (each of which may be used also as an appellative verb, which signifies he is the king's, or they are the king's), but we may also form the more distinctively verbal appellatives, *kôn-in-en*, I am the king's, *kôn-in-em*, we are the king's, &c. This use of the oblique or inflexion as the basis of appellative verbs is a peculiarity of classical Tamil; but the formation of appellative verbs from the nominative or crude base of nouns is common to the whole Dravidian family. Thus, in Telugu (in which the vowel of the pronominal termination varies by rule in accordance with the preceding vowel), from *sêvakuḍu*, a servant, or *kavi*, a poet, we form the appellative verbs *sêvakuḍa-nu*, I am a servant, *kavi-ni*, I am a poet; *sêvakuḍa-vu*, thou art a servant, *kavi-vi*, thou art a poet. In the plural, Telugu has allowed the base of the noun (to which the pronominal terminations are affixed) to be pluralised, apparently from having forgotten that the plural sign of the pronominal termination was sufficient of itself—*e.g.*, it says *sêvakula-mu*, we are servants; whereas in Tamil the difference between *aḍi-(y)-ên*, I am (your) servant, and *aḍi-(y)-êm*, we are (your) servants, appears in the pronominal terminations alone; and the plan of denoting the plural which the Tamil has adopted is evidently more in accordance with the true theory of the appellative verb. The Malayâḷam singular *aḍiyan* or *aḍiyên* agrees with the Tamil, but the plural *adiyaṅṅaḷ* bears marks of corruption. The classical Tamil words *el-âm*, all we, *el-îr*, all ye, belong to this class.

The Telugu appellative verb is destitute of a third person except in the neuter singular. It is obliged to be content with placing the isolated pronoun of the third person and the substantive noun in apposition, with a substantive verb understood—*e.g.*, *vâḍu kavi*, he (is) a poet. Tamil is in this particular more highly developed, for its appellative verbs are freely conjugated in the third person in each gender and number, by suffixing the final fragment of the pronoun—*e.g.*, from *nal*, goodness or good, is formed *nal(l)-an*, he is good, *nal(l)-aḷ*, she is good; *nal(l)-adu* or *nan-dru* (for *nal-du*), it is good, *nal(l)-ar*, they (epicene) are good, *nal(l)-ana*, or *nal(l)-a*, they (neuter) are good. The neuter singular in Tamil may appear to take a variety of forms; but on examination those various forms will be found to be identical, and the apparent differences which exist are owing either to the euphonic union of the final *du* with some previous consonant, or to its euphonic reduplication. The third person neuter, singular and plural (and occasionally the third person masculine and feminine also), of every species of Dravidian verb, is often used not only as a verb, but also as a verbal or participial noun. Its primary use may have been that of a participial noun, and its use as a verb may be a secondary one; but at all events, the two uses are found to be interchangeable—*e.g.*, *irukkiradu*, means either it is, or that which is, or the being, according to the context. It is especially with relation to appellatives that this twofold use of the forms of the third person must be borne in mind; for in the third person (singular and plural, masculine, feminine, and neuter) there is no difference whatever in spelling or pronunciation between appellative verbs and appellative nouns, and it is the context alone that determines which meaning is the correct one. Generally the appellative verb is more commonly used in the classical dialect, and the noun in the colloquial dialect; but to this there are exceptions, and (*e.g.*) *nalladu* more frequently signifies in the colloquial dialect 'it is well' than 'that which is good'—that is, it is used more frequently as an appellative verb than as an appellative noun. It is certain, however, that the appellative verb, whatever person or gender it takes, is used more largely in the higher dialect of the Tamil than in the lower; and its brevity and compression render it peculiarly adapted for metaphorical use.

Adjectives are formed into appellative verbs as well as nouns; but as the Dravidian adjective is merely a noun of quality used adjectivally, the difference is more in terms than in reality—*e.g.*, *oḷi-(y)-ei*, Tam. thou art bright, is literally thou art brightness; and *ini-(y)-ei*, thou art sweet, is thou art sweetness. Appellative verbs are formed from adjectives, or nouns of quality, not only in the cultivated Dravidian dialects, but even in Ku, which is spoken by an uncultured race —*e.g.*, *negg-ânu*, Ku, I am good, *negg-âmu*, we are good.

When nouns of quality are used as the bases of appellative verbs or nouns, they are generally adopted in their crude shape, as in the instances which have just been cited; but in many cases we find the particle *iya* intervening between the crude base and the pronominal termination or sign of gender—*e.g.*, *koḍ-iya-n* (as a verb), he is cruel; (as a noun) one who is cruel, or a cruel man; *val-iya-n*, a strong man, or he is strong, &c. This is the same particle which we have already seen to be used as an adjectival formative—*e.g.*, *val-iya*, strong, *per-iya*, great, *śir-iya*, little, &c., and I have stated that I conceive words like these to be relative participles. *i* is identical with the *i* of the past verbal particle, which is often used in Telugu as an adjectival formative without any addition; and the final *a* is the sign of the relative, which is kept separate from *i* by an euphonic *y*. *iya* is therefore the formative of the relative preterite participle, and *val-i-(y)-a*, strong, means properly that which was strong. But though the form of the preterite tense is employed, the signification (as often happens, especially in the case of relative participles) is aoristic, or without reference to time. This being the origin, as I conceive, of such forms as *val-iya*, an appellative noun like *val-iya-n*, a strong man, is in reality a participial noun, signifying he who is strong, and so of the other genders; and this explanation brings such forms into perfect harmony with other parts of the Dravidian conjugational system, for participial nouns are regularly used in these languages as verbs.

In some instances *a*, the sign of the relative participle, is dispensed with, and the pronominal signs or signs of gender are elegantly suffixed to *i*, the sign of the verbal participial—*e.g.*, *peri-du*, Tam. it is great, or that which is great, instead of *peri-(y)-a-du*. On the other hand, in another class of instances, *i* disappears, and *a* alone remains. Words of this class, when deprived of their signs of gender, are commonly called adjectives, and undoubtedly it is as adjectives that they are used; but, looking at their construction and force, I should term them relative participles of appellative verbs. In the words referred to, *a*, the sign of the relative participle, is directly annexed to crude substantive roots—*e.g.*, *uḍei-(y)-a*, belonging to, more literally which is the property of. *malei-(y)-a*, hilly, literally which is a hill; *tî-y-a*, evil, literally which is evil. As *uḍei-(y)-an*, considered as a noun is certainly an appellative, signifying he who owns, a proprietor; and as the same word is used poetically as an appellative verb when it signifies he is the owner, it seems evident that the proper light in which to regard *uḍei-(y)-a* (and every similar word) is to consider it as the relative participle of an appellative verb used adjectivally.

SECTION II.—CONJUGATIONAL SYSTEM.

Mode of Annexing Pronominal Signs.—The persons of the Dravidian verb, including the related ideas of gender and number, are formed by suffixing the personal or demonstrative pronouns, or their fragmentary terminations, to the signs of tense. The change which the pronouns undergo when they are appended to verbs as signs of personality have already been exhibited in the section on "The Pronoun." They consist chiefly in the softening away of the initial consonant; but in a few instances the final consonant has also been softened away, and nothing left but the included vowel. In Telugu, *nî-vu*, the pronoun of the second person singular, has lost both its radical initial and its formative final; and in the personal terminations of the verb it is represented only by *vu*, an euphonic addition.

In the Indo-European languages the personal signs of the verb are formed by suffixing pronominal fragments to the root; and those fragments are disguised in a still greater degree than in the Dravidian languages, not only by frequency of use and rapidity of enunciation, but also by the love of fusing words and particles together, and forming them into euphonious compounds, which distinguishes that family of tongues. Sometimes one dialect alone furnishes the key to the explanation of the inflexional forms which are apparent in all. Thus the origin of *unt* or *ant*, the sign of the third person plural in the various Indo-European languages (*e.g.*, *fer-unt*, *φέρ-οντι*, *bharanti*, &c.), is found in Welsh alone, in which *hwynt* is a pronoun of the third person plural.

The various changes which the Dravidian pronouns undergo on

being used as the pronominal signs of verbs have already been stated in order. In Telugu, and partly also in Canarese, the pronominal terminations vary according to the tense; but this arises from the operation of the law of harmonic sequences (see "Sounds"), by which a vowel is affected by a preceding vowel, and changed so as to harmonise with it. What requires here to be investigated is simply the mode in which the pronominal signs are attached to the Dravidian verb.

1. The pronominal signs of the Dravidian verb are suffixed, not prefixed. The primitive Turanian verb seems to have been destitute of pronominal terminations altogether. The pronoun was neither prefixed nor affixed, but had a position of its own as a separate word. This continues to be the case with the most distinctively Turanian languages; but in the Buriat dialect of the Mongolian, and in the Tungusian idiom, spoken near Njertschinsk in Siberia, personal terminations have recently been added to the verb. In Turkish, Finnish, and Hungarian, as in the primitive Indo-European languages, the pronouns have been compounded with the verb, and have dwindled down to pronominal terminations. In the modern Indo-European vernaculars, most of the verbs have lost their old pronominal terminations, and the pronouns which are used as nominatives to verbs are usually isolated and placed first. Thus, instead of love-I, in accordance with the ancient *am-o*, we have learnt to say I love,—an alteration of position which produces no change in meaning. In the Semitic languages a change in the position of the pronoun from the termination of the verb to its commencement produces an important change in grammatical signification: the position of the pronouns or pronominal fragments determines the tense. When the pronominal fragments are prefixed, the tense of the verb is regarded as future or aoristic: it is regarded as past when they are suffixed. Prefixing the pronominal fragments appears to denote that the action of the verb has, as yet, only a subjective existence in the mind of the speaker or agent—*i.e.*, it is future; suffixing them may denote that the action of the verb has already acquired an objective existence, apart from the will or wish of the speaker or agent—*i.e.*, it is past.

No peculiarity of this kind characterises the Dravidian languages. The tenses are formed, not by means of the position of the pronouns, but by particles or signs of present, past, and future time suffixed to the theme; and the personal signs, as in the Turkish and Finnish families, are suffixed to the signs of tense. The only exception to this rule is that which forms the most characteristic feature of Malayâḷam —a language which appears to have been originally identical with

Tamil, but which, in so far as its conjugational system is concerned, has fallen back from the inflexional development reached by both tongues whilst they were still one, to what appears to have been the primitive condition of both—a condition nearly resembling that of the Mongolian, the Manchu, and the other rude primitive tongues of High Asia. In ancient times, as may be gathered from Malayâḷam poetry, and especially from the inscriptions preserved by the Syrian Christians and the Jews, the pronouns were suffixed to the Malayâḷam verb, precisely as they still are in Tamil. At present, the verb is entirely divested, at least in the colloquial dialect, of signs of personality; and with the pronouns the signs of number and gender also have necessarily disappeared; so that the pronoun or nominative must in every instance be separately prefixed to the verb to complete the signification, and it is chiefly by means of this prefixed pronoun that a verb, properly so called, is distinguished from a verbal participle. Though the personal signs have been abandoned by the Malayâḷam verb, the signs of tense or time have been retained, and are annexed directly to the root as in the other dialects. Even in modern English some persons of the verb retain archaic fragments of the pronominal signs (*e.g.*, *lov*est, *lov*eth); but in modern Malayâḷam every trace of those signs has disappeared. Thus, whilst we should say in Tamil *aḍittên*, I beat; *aḍittây*, thou didst beat; *aḍittân*, he beat; Malayâḷam uses in these and all similar cases the verbal participle *aḍichu* (for *aḍittu*), having beaten, with the prefixed pronouns I, thou, he, &c.—*e.g.*, *ñân aḍichu*, I beat; *nî aḍichu*, thou didst beat; *avan aḍichu*, he beat. Though the pronominal signs have been lost by the Malayâḷam verb, they have been retained even by the Tuda; and notwithstanding the comparative barbarity of the Gônds and Kus, their conjugational system is peculiarly elaborate and complete.

2. Another peculiarity in the manner in which the personal signs are suffixed in the Dravidian languages consists in their annexation, not directly to the root, as in the Indo-European family, but to the temporal participles. The first suffix to the root in the affirmative voice is that of the sign of tense, then follows the suffix of personality. Every pure Dravidian affirmative verb is compounded of three elements, which are thus arranged and named by Tamil grammarians, viz. (1) the *pagudi* (*prakṛiti*, Sans.), or root; (2) the *iḍei nilei*, or medial particle, *i.e.*, the sign of tense; and (3) the *vigudi* (*vikṛiti*, Sans.), the variation or differentia, *i.e.*, the pronominal termination. When the signs of tense are attached to the theme, some euphonic changes take place (not in the theme, but in the signs themselves), which serve, as has been shown, to distinguish transitive verbs from intransitives.

Other euphonic changes also take place in accordance with Dravidian laws of sound, which will be inquired into when those signs of tense are one by one examined. The changes which take place in the pronominal signs when they are annexed to the signs of tense have already been stated in the section on "The Pronoun."

In the Indo-European languages we meet, I think, with no instance of the annexation of the pronominal signs to the participles, *i.e.*, to the combination of the root with the signs of tense. I know of no instance of the use of any form like *amant-o*, instead of *am-o*, to signify I love. This, however, is the method which is invariably employed in the Dravidian languages, and which constitutes an essential element in the family likeness by which they are pervaded. It is also distinctive of Turkish. Thus, the Turkish *ôlûrsen*, thou art, is formed from *ôlûr*, being, the present participle of the verb *ôl*, to be, with the addition of the pronoun *sen*, thou. So also the Oriental Turkish *bôlâmen*, I am, is formed from *bôlâ*, being (theme, *bôl*, to be), and the pronominal suffix *men*, I.

An important difference generally found to exist between the Dravidian languages and the Gaurian vernaculars should here be stated. In the languages of Northern India the present tense of a verb is ordinarily formed by annexing the substantive verb to its present participle—*e.g.*, *karitechi*, Beng. (*karite-âchi*), I am doing, instead of I do. In Telugu, perhaps through the influence of the North Indian vernaculars, a similar usage prevails; but it is found in the present tense only; it may readily be dispensed with; and the simpler usage, which accords with that of all the other Dravidian dialects, is undoubtedly the more ancient. In Tamil and Canarese this use of the substantive verb, as an auxiliary in the formation of the present tense, is unknown: it is used as an auxiliary only in the formation of the compound preterite and future tenses. Malayâḷam occasionally uses the substantive verb in a similar manner to Telugu, but with a somewhat different signification. In Telugu *naḍuchutunnânu*, I walk (from *naduchu-tu*, walking, and *unnânu*, I am), has simply the meaning of the present tense, and is equivalent to the simpler form *naḍuchutânu*, answering to the Tamil *naḍakkirên*, and the Canarese *naḍeyuttêne;* but in Malayâḷam, whilst *ñân naḍakkunnu* means I walk, *ñân naḍakkunnuṇḍa* has generally an emphatic sense—*e.g.*, I am really walking. Tamil has a form precisely resembling this.

3. It is a peculiarity of Telugu that the third person of the preterite is sometimes left altogether destitute of the signs of time, person, number, and gender; and this peculiarity applies also to the third person of the aorist. Thus, whilst *uṇḍitini*, I was, and *uṇḍitivi*, thou

wast, are supplied with the usual signs of tense and person, the third person of the same tense is simply *uṇḍe-nu*, he, she, or it was, or they were, without distinction of number or gender, and without even the particle *ti*, which constitutes the usual sign of the preterite. The aorist third person, with a similar absence of distinction, is *uṇḍu-nu*; and in both cases the final *nu* is merely a conjunctive suffix, like the corresponding Tamil *um*. Sometimes even the aorist formative *nu* is discarded, and the root alone is used as the third person singular. Thus (he, she, or it) falls or will fall, may either be *paḍu-nu*, or simply *paḍu*. The usage of poetical Tamil occasionally agrees with that of the Telugu with respect to the neuter gender, both singular and plural, especially in connection with the negative voice of the verb—*e.g.*, *śey(y)-â*, it will not do, is often used for *śey(y)-âdu*.

A usage similar to this prevails in many languages which are widely different one from the other. Thus, the New Persian uses for the third person singular of the preterite *the contracted infinitive*, as grammarians style it—an abstract verbal noun, which may be regarded as the theme of the verb. The Hebrew third person masculine of the preterite tense is also a verbal noun, without pronominal addition. We see a similar peculiarity in the third person of the *present* tense of the verb in some languages—*e.g.*, compare the three persons of the present tense of the Turkish substantive verb, *ôlûrum*, I am; *ôlûrsen*, thou art; *ôlûr*, he is. Compare also the Armorican *kanann*, I sing; *kanez*, thou singest; *kan*, he sings. Compare with these examples the Hungarian *ismerek*, I know; *ismersz*, thou knowest; and *ismer*, he knows.

4. There are traces in ancient Tamil and Canarese of the existence of a very primitive system of conjugation. A form of the verb is occasionally used by the poets, which must have come down from a period of great antiquity. In High Tamil, *śeydu* (*śey-du*), which is now the preterite verbal participle, may be used for the preterite tense of the finite verb in all persons in the singular, and *śeydum* (*śey-d'-um*) (the same form with the addition of the conjunctive *um*, used as a pluralising particle), for all persons in the plural. A somewhat similar form may be used for the future, by means of the addition of *ku* or *gu* to the root, instead of the sign of the preterite, *du*. *śey-gu* is used to mean I will do; *śey-g'-um*, we will do. The use of this form is not extended to the other persons so widely as that of *śeydu*, an irregularity which shows that it had become nearly obsolete when it received a place in written compositions. The *um* of the aoristic future in modern Tamil is restricted to the neuter gender, but it is used for both numbers indiscriminately. The *gu* and *gum* of poetical Tamil is found

also in classical Canarese in the form of *gum* or *kum*, in which it has a wider range of application than in Tamil. In classical Tamil its use is confined to the first person; in classical Canarese it is used indiscriminately for all persons—*e.g.*, *avar mâḍugum*, they do. *ku* also survives in Canarese—*e.g.*, *kê-ku* (Tam. *veṇḍ-um*), must. It would appear, therefore, that the Dravidian verb was originally uninflected; and this may partly account for the circumstance that Malayâḷam so readily lost the inflexions which, in common with Tamil, it had acquired. The period when the Dravidian verb was uninflected must have been long prior to the separation of the present tongue into dialects, in all which, even in the rudest, a system of inflexions has been developed. The retention of traces of the ancient verb in Tamil and Canarese, and partly also, as noticed in the previous paragraph, in Telugu, seems to prove the great antiquity of the literary culture of the Dravidian languages.

5. The Dravidian verb, as now inflected, like the verb of many other languages, does not distinguish the genders of either the first person or the second, whether singular or plural; but in the third person it marks all existing distinctions of gender with peculiar explicitness and minuteness. Thus, without the use of isolated pronouns, and employing the inflexions of the verb alone, we can say in Tamil *varugirân*, he comes; *varugirâḷ*, she comes; *varugiradu*, it comes; *varugirâr*, they (men and women) come, or honorifically he comes; *varugirârgal*, they (men and women) come; *varugindrana*, they (things) come.

Formation of the Tenses.—Most of the Dravidian tenses are formed from participial forms of the verb: an inquiry into the participles is, therefore, a necessary preliminary to an inquiry into the tenses. Dravidian verbs have two species of participles, one of which, (called *relative participles*, because they include the signification of the relative pronoun), will be inquired into in a subsequent part of this section; the other, commonly called *verbal participles* or *gerunds*, and which are now to be considered, constitute the bases on which the tenses are formed. The *forms* which are assumed by the verbal participles will be inquired into in connection with the signs of tense, from the consideration of which they cannot be severed. I content myself here with some general remarks on the signification and force of this class of words.

Verbal Participles, their Signification and Force.—In ordinary colloquial Tamil there is but one verbal participle, that of the past tense. In Malayâḷam and in classical Tamil there is a verbal participle of the future tense as well as of the past. In Canarese and Telugu there is a verbal participle of the present and of the past. In Tuḷu there are three verbal participles, that of the present (or future), that of the imperfect past, and that of the perfect. In this particular, therefore, colloquial Tamil may be considered as the poorest of the Dravidian dialects. Properly speaking, the words which are called *verbal participles* are not *participles* at all, seeing that they do not *participate* in the nature of adjectives, as all the Indo-European participles do. They have somewhat of the signification of gerunds, inasmuch as in addition to the idea of time, they include more or less of the idea of cause. Nevertheless, as each of the Indo-European participles is commonly used also as a gerund, without losing the name of a participle, and as the gerund in *do* (to which alone, amongst Latin gerunds, the Dravidian participles have any resemblance) has a very restricted application, it appears advisable, after all, to style these words participles instead of gerunds,—or more fully *verbal participles*, to distinguish them from what are called *relative participles.*

The following sentences will illustrate the force of the Dravidian verbal participles :—

1. *Present Verbal Participle.*—This verbal participle, though unknown in Tamil and Malayâḷam, is commonly used both in Canarese and in Telugu. I quote the illustration which follows from Canarese. "Vikramârka, punishing the wicked and protecting the good, reigned over the kingdom." Here the English words 'punishing' and 'protecting' are participles of the present tense, used gerundially; and the Dravidian words which they represent (in Canarese, *sikshisuttâ* and *rakshisuttâ*) have precisely the same force. In this respect only there is a difference between them, viz., that the English participles are capable of being used also as adjectives, whereas the Dravidian words, though called participles, cannot be used adjectivally, or in any other way than that here exemplified.

2. *Preterite Verbal Participle.*—" Sâlivâhana, having killed Vikramârka, assumed supreme power." Though the English participle 'having killed,' which is here used, is a compound one (being formed from the present participle having, and the passive participle killed), its signification is that of a simple, uncompounded participle of the past tense, and the Dravidian word which it represents (*kondru*, Tam., *kondu*, Can.) is also a preterite active verbal participle. In this instance, neither the English participle nor the Dravidian one is capable of being used as an adjective. In reality, they are both preterite gerunds or gerundials, though they retain the name of participles as a matter of convenience.

In those Dravidian dialects in which there is a present, as well as a preterite, verbal participle (as in Canarese and Telugu), the present is used to express subordinate actions which are contemporaneous with that which is denoted by the principal and finite verb; whilst the preterite expresses subordinate actions which are antecedent in point of time to the principal action. In Tamil, the preterite participle is used to express all subordinate actions, whether simultaneous with the main action or antecedent to it; but though that participle is always a preterite in form, it possesses the force of a participle of the present tense when the connection requires it. In each of the dialects and in every connection, the nominative of the final governing verb is the nominative of all the subordinate verbal participles.

The Dravidian verbal participles may be compared with the Sanskrit indeterminate past participle in *twâ—e.g.*, *kṛitwâ*, having done. Like that participle they are indeclinable and indeterminate. One of the chief peculiarities, however, of these verbal participles is, that they have a continuative force, dispensing altogether with the use of conjunctions. In the Dravidian languages, though nouns and pronouns are united by means of conjunctions, finite verbs are never so united. In every sentence there is but one finite verb, which is the last word in the sentence, and the seat of government; and all the verbs which express subordinate actions or circumstances, whether antecedent or contemporaneous, assume an indeterminate, continuative character, as verbal participles or gerundials, without the need of conjunctions or copulatives of any kind; so that the sense (and more or less the time also) waits in suspense for the authoritative decision of the final governing verb. Hence those participles might properly be called continuative gerundials. Tamilian grammarians class them, together with infinitives and subjunctives, as *vinei echcham*, verb defects, or verbal complements—*i.e.*, words which require a verb to complete the sense.

It is a peculiarity of these languages that when a series of verbal participles constitutes a relative clause in a sentence, antecedent to a noun to which the relative clause relates, the last of the verbal participles alone is converted into a relative participle. All the rest remain in form verbal participles or gerunds. So also in the Scythian languages. "The Turanian," says Mr Edkins, "in describing a succession of events gives to his verbs the form of gerunds, and adds to them, when needed, the case suffixes,"—converting the gerund thereby into a relative participle, as in Tamil, &c. The rationale of the process seems to be that in both families of tongues the gerund is treated as a noun, and must have been a verbal noun in origin.

1. *The Present Tense.*—It may be stated generally that the present tense of the Dravidian verb is formed by suffixing the pronominal

as signs to the present verbal participle, with such trivial changes only euphony requires. The exceptions to this general rule are as follows :—

(1.) In poetical Tamil the tenses are sometimes formed by suffixing the pronominal terminations to the relative participles, instead of the gerunds or verbal participles—*e.g.*, *naḍanda(n)an* (equivalent to the colloquial *naḍanda(v)an*), he walked, literally a man who walked. In such instances a verbal or participial noun is used with the force of a verb. This is not an uncommon usage in other languages also; and in colloquial Tamil the third person neuter of the verb, both singular and plural, is certainly a verbal noun in its origin, though used with the force of a verb—*e.g.*, *naḍandadu*, it walked, literally means a thing which walked; and the plural *naḍanda(n)a*, means literally things which walked. A peculiarity of the poetical dialect is the extension of this usage to each person of the verb—*e.g.*, *naḍanda(n)en*, I walked, literally, I who walked; *naḍanda(n)am* or *naḍanda(n)em*, we walked, literally we who walked. This mode of forming the tenses has been developed from the Dravidian custom of using participial and verbal nouns as the conjugational bases of verbs, and, so far, is in accordance with the genius of the language; but it has a constructive, artificial look, and it is an exception to the mode which prevails throughout all the other dialects of the family, whether colloquial or classical.

(2.) Tamil and Malayâḷam have, properly speaking, no present verbal participle, but only a particle denoting present time, which is suffixed to the theme of the verb, and to which, in Tamil, the pronominal signs are then suffixed for the purpose of forming the present tense. The combination, however, of the root and the particle of present time, forms virtually a present participle. I think it may, therefore, be assumed that the Tamil-Malayâḷam had a verbal participle of the present tense at a former period, which has now become obsolete, except in combination with the personal terminations, when it constitutes the present tense of the verb.

(3.) In the ancient or classical dialect of Canarese there is another exception to the general rule. In the colloquial dialect the present tense is formed regularly from the present participle; but the present tense in the classical dialect is altogether unconnected with that participle, or at least is only very distantly related to it. The sign of the present participle is *ute*, &c., whilst that of the present tense is *dap*—*e.g.*, *bâḷute*, living, *bâḷdapem*, I live.

(4.) The Telugu usage of employing the substantive verb in a modified form (viz., *unnânu*, I am, *unnâvu*, thou art, &c.) as an auxiliary in the formation of the present tense, can scarcely be called an exception to the general rule specified above; for this auxiliary is annexed to the present verbal participle, which is closely allied to that of Canarese; and its use in this connection is only a refinement, not a necessary element in the formation of the present tense.

These real or apparent exceptions being disposed of, it remains to inquire into the formation of the present verbal participles in the various dialects.

Formation of the Present.—In both the classical and colloquial dialects of Canarese the verbal participle of the present tense is formed by adding to the verbal root a particle, of which *ut* is the most essential portion—*e.g.*, coll. Can. *bâl-uta*, living; *ond-utta*, joining; *mâḍ-uttâ*, making: class. Can. *ôd-ute*, reading; *iḷi-(y)-utte*, descending; *kaṭṭ-uttu*, tying; *geyutum* (*geyuttum*, *geyyutum*), doing. The final vowel of this particle *ut* assumes various shapes, and is elided before the initial vowel of the pronominal signs in the formation of the present tense in the colloquial dialect (*e.g.*, comp. *mâḍ-utta*, doing, with *mâḍ-utt'êne*, I do). It may, therefore, be concluded that it is simply enunciative; and as *u* is the vowel most commonly used as a help to enunciation in all the dialects, the primitive shape of this particle must have been *utu*. I have no doubt that Mr Kittel is correct in identifying this *utu* with *udu*, the intermediate demonstrative pronoun of the Tamil and Canarese, used as a proximate demonstrative in Tuḷu. Another form of *udu* in classical Canarese is *ûtam*. *utu*, with the meaning of 'this,' would very naturally come to be used as a sign of present time in the formation of a participle of the present tense. It will be seen, in considering the preterite tense, that the *d* which constitutes the sign of past time is probably a relic of *adu*, the remote demonstrative 'that.' Probably the *um* of *utum* is the ordinary conjunctive *um*, used for the purpose of more distinctly emphasising the time.

It is more difficult to explain the origin of the sign of present time used in the formation of the present tense in Old Canarese. The present tense in that dialect is not formed from the present participle. That participle is, as we have seen, substantially the same in both dialects; and in the colloquial dialect the present tense is formed by affixing to this participle the personal terminations. The ancient dialect, on the other hand, makes no use of its present participle in forming its present tense, but forms that tense by inserting the particle *dap* between the verbal root and the pronominal fragments. The colloquial Canarese *bâḷuttêne*, I live, is formed from the colloquial and classical present participle *bâlutte*; but the corresponding form in classical Canarese is *bâḷdapem*, in which present time is represented by *dap*. What is the origin of this particle? Mr Kittel (in a private communication with which he has favoured me) regards *dap* as being properly *dapa*, and *dapa* as consisting of *da + apa*. This *apa* he considers identical with *aha*, the future participle of *ahu* (in coll. Can. *âgu*), to become; *da* he regards as the sign of the past tense. Hence *mâḍi + da + apa + em* (*mâḍidapem*) would mean 'having made I shall be.' This form, therefore, was properly a second future. He traces its origin to the custom of replying to a command by an answer in the past tense—*e.g.*, you say to some one, Come! and the reply is, I came—*i.e.*, I come. The fact that this form was originally a second future, accounts, he thinks, for the introduction at length into the modern or colloquial dialect of a present tense distinctively denoting the present, being formed from the present participle in use in both dialects. This explanation is certainly very ingenious, and seems to me satisfactory. It will be shown further on that one of the forms of the present in Tamil makes use of a participle of the verb *â* (*âgu*), to become, and that most of the Dravidian presents were formed from futures. It will also be shown that the use of *d*, the ordinary sign of the preterite in all the dialects, was not originally restricted to that tense so absolutely as it is now.

The present verbal participle of Telugu is ordinarily formed by adding *chu* (pronounced *tsu*) to the theme of the verb. In the colloquial dialect *tu* is used instead of *chu;* and though it is possible that *chu* may be the original, and *tu* (from *tsu*) the corruption, yet it would be more in accordance with analogy to derive *chu* from *tu;* and this *tu* so nearly resembles the Canarese *uta* or *ute*, that we may safely conclude both forms to have been originally identical. Probably also *du*, the particle which in most instances is inserted as a sign of tense between the verbal theme and the pronominal terminations of the Telugu aorist, springs from the same origin as *tu*. *chunnu* or *tunnu*, the ordinary termination of the participle of the present tense in grammatical Telugu, is a compound form derived from *chu* or *tu*, the real and only sign of present time in this language, and *unnu*, a participle of the substantive verb *uṇḍu*, to be, used as an auxiliary.

The Tuḷu participle of the present tense is also used for the future as well as for the present, and was probably a future originally. The sign of the present used in the present tense of the verb is *v*, which is identical with the Tamil-Canarese sign of the future.

The sign of present time used by the Tamil and Malayâḷam, differs considerably from that of the Telugu-Canarese. The present tense in Tamil is formed by suffixing *gir-u*, *gindr-u*, or *â-nindr-u*, to the verbal theme, to one or other of which particles the pronominal signs are annexed. *â-nindr-u* is a compound form, which is rarely used even by the poets, and is derived, I conceive, from *â*, the ultimate base of *â-gu*, to become (and which is not unfrequently used in this shape in the poets), and *nindr-u*, standing, abiding, continuing; root, *nil*, to stand. The meaning of the compound seems to be continuing to become—*e.g.*, *tâṛânindrân* (*tâṛ-â-nindr'-ân*), he is low, he is humble, literally, he *continues* to *become* low or humble. Documentary evidence is forthcoming of the accuracy of my supposition that the *â* of *ânindru* was a representative of *âgi*. In an Old Tamil inscription (774 A.D.) in the possession of the Syrian Christians on the Malabar coast, I find *âyi-nindru* instead of the *â-nindru* which has been universally used in later times. *âgi* is often softened into *âyi* even in modern Tamil, then into *ây*, and then into *â*.

The other particles of present time, *gi***r**-*u* and *gindr-u*, are in more common use, especially the former—*e.g.*, *varu-gi***r**-*ân*, or *varu-gindr'-ân*, he comes. The only difference between them is that *gindr-u* is considered more euphonious and elegant than *gi***r**-*u*, and more suitable, in consequence, for poetry and elevated prose. I have no doubt that they are identical in origin, and that the one is either an euphonised or a corrupted form of the other. In some connections *gi***r**-*u* and *gindr-u* are changed by dialectic rules of euphony to *kki***r**-*u* and *kkindr-u*—viz., when they are attached to roots consisting of two short syllables (like *paḍu*, to lie; *iru*, to be; *naḍa*, to walk), the final vowel of which is regarded as a part of the root, and is incapable of being elided. It is a rule of the language that if in such cases the sonants *g*, *d*, *b*, immediately follow, they shall be hardened, that is, converted into the corresponding surds *k*, *t*, and *p*; and in Tamil the only method of hardening sonants is by doubling them,—for it has already been shown that in this language the same consonant is a sonant when single and a surd when doubled. Hence we say in Tamil not *iru-gi***r**-*ên*, I am, but *iru-kki***r**-*ên*. A similar result follows in another and more numerous class of instances from a different cause. It has been shown in a former part of this section that transitive or active verbs are in many instances made to differ from intransitives by the hardening and doubling of the initial consonant of the sign of tense. In such cases *gi***r**-*u* and *gindr-u* become (not for the sake of euphony merely, but as a means of grammatical expression) *kki***r**-*u* and *kkindr-u*.

Malayâḷam uses the same sign of tense somewhat modified: the sign of present time in Malayâḷam is *unnu* or *kkunnu*, suffixed to the verbal theme. The older dialect of Malayâḷam has generally *innu*, especially in connection with the negative verb—*e.g.*, *varâ-(y)-innu*, comes not. Where Tamil would use *gindru*, Malayâḷam omits the *g*. When Tamil doubles the *g* and says *kk*, Malayâḷam uses *kk* also. The Malayâḷam *innu* is clearly a softened and euphonised form of the Tamil particle. The Tamil compound sound *ndr* is constantly converted into *nn* in Malayâḷam—*e.g.*, *ondru*, Tam. one, is in Malayâḷam *onn'*, and *mûndru*, Tam. three, is in Malayâḷam *mûnn'*. Even in vulgar colloquial Tamil the same or a similar tendency appears: *ondru*, one, being commonly pronounced *oṇṇu*, and *mûndru*, three, *mûṇu*. The Tamil *gindru* and *kkindru* would, therefore, naturally and dialectically be converted in Malayâḷam to *ginnu* and *kkinnu*. The next point is the softening away of the *g* of *ginnu*. This has arisen from the circumstance that in Tamil *g* is pronounced in the middle of a word so softly as to be little more than an indistinct guttural breathing; in consequence of which, it is used to represent the *h* of Sanskrit, and in the colloquial dialect it is often discarded altogether —*e.g.*, *pôgirên*, I go, is commonly pronounced *pô-rên*; and *varugirân*, he comes, *varu-rân* or *vâ-rân*. Hence *ginnu* (from *gindru*) would naturally become in Malayâḷam *innu*. The only remaining difference is between the *i* of *innu* and the *u* of *unnu*; but this presents no difficulty, for even in Tamil *i* is very often pronounced as *u* by the vulgar, and we have seen that in Malayâḷam also *innu* is more classical than *unnu*.

The identity of the Malayâḷam sign of the present tense with that of Tamil, cannot be doubted. Sometimes in Malayâḷam poetry the pronominal signs are suffixed to the signs of tense, as in Tamil; and in that connection the identity of the signs of tense is clearly apparent—*e.g.*, compare *aḍikkindrân* (*aḍi-kkindr-ân*), Tam. he beats, with the corresponding form in poetic Malayâḷam *aḍikkunnân* (*aḍi-kkunn'-ân*). *A priori* it might have been supposed that the Malayâḷam *unnu* or *kkunnu* was related to *chunnu* or *tunnu*, the sign of the present participle in Telugu. The resemblance, however, is altogether illusory; for the Malayâḷam particle is derived from the Tamil *gindru* or *kkindru*, whilst the Telugu *chunnu* is compounded of *chu*, the real sign of present time, and *unnu*, a participle of *uṇḍu*, to be; which participle is in Malayâḷam *uṇḍ'*.

I have said that I believe the Tamil *gir-u* and *gindr-u* were identical in origin, and that the one is merely an euphonised or corrupted form of the other. Which is the original form? and which the euphonised or corrupted? There are many instances of **r** being euphonised in Tamil into *ndr*—*e.g.*, *kundru*, as a verb, 'to become small,' as a noun, 'a small hill,' must be a secondary form of *kur-u*, small, a form of the root which constitutes the basis of a large number of words, such as *ku**rr**am*, a fault. The change of *ndr* into **r** is not so easy, nor can I find any instances of it which are free from doubt. Still such a change may be suspected to have taken place in several instances, one of which is *indru*, now, to-day. A secondary form of *indru* in Tamil is *i**rr**ei* (pronounced *ittrei*), and this seems to point to *il-tei*. *l* + *t*, sometimes became *ndr* in Tamil, and sometimes in the poets skrinks into **r**. Thus *śel-tal*, the verbal noun of *śel*, to go, is changed to *śê**r**al* in the "Nannûl," the Tamil classical grammar. In this case, however, there is also a lengthening of the preceding vowel. If we may suppose *il-tu* to have become, on the one hand, *indru*, and on the other, perhaps at a latter period, *i**r**u*, we arrive at the best explanation which has been given of *gindru* or *gi**r**u*, the Tamil sign of present time. Dr Granl, I believe (in his "Outlines of Tamil Grammar"), was the first to suggest the origination of this sign from *k* = *g*, a sign of the future in poetical Tamil, and *indru*, now. His idea appears to have been that Tamil was originally without a present tense, and that the present was a new secondary tense, formed from the future by the addition of a sign of present time. *kindru* was thus = *k-indru* (then *ki**r**u*). The same view seems to have been adopted, or independently arrived at, by Dr Gundert. The fact that the form of this particle retained in Malayâḷam is *unnu* (in older compositions often *innu*) would seem to prove that *kindru*, not *ki**r**u*, was the form in use in Tamil prior to the final separation from Tamil of the Malayâḷam, and, therefore, not only the more classical form in Tamil, as it is admitted to be, but also the more ancient. This fact, though it does not prove the derivation of *kindru* from *k-indru*, yet favours that supposition.

The present tense is seldom used in Tamil poetry, and I have never found it in inscriptions, though the past and future and combinations of both abound. In the talk of the common people, though the present tense is freely used, yet the grammatical signs of the present, *gi**r**u*, &c., are generally omitted. They say *vêgudu*, it burns, instead of *vêgu-(gi**r**)-adu*. It would seem, consequently, that the inflexional forms of the present tense are not very deeply rooted in the language.

In the language of the Tudas the present and future seem to be identical, and the sign of time seems to be *k* or *g*—*e.g.*, *pôkeni*, I go, *pôkemi*, we go; *ershken* (*ersh-k-en*), I am, *ershkimi*, we are (*rsh* for *r*). In the second and third persons the *k* seems to be softened into *ch*—*e.g.*, *ershchi*, he or they are. In the language of the Kotas, *p* seems to replace *k*—*e.g.*, *hôgape*, I go, *hôgapême*, we go. In the third person, however, singular and plural, *k* asserts its place—*e.g.*, *hôgako*, he or they go.

The Tuda *k* of the first person and the Kota *k* of the third seem naturally to connect themselves, not only with the *gu* of the Old Tamil, but with the *kum* or *gum* of the Old Canarese aorist—*e.g.*, Old Tamil *śey-gu*, I do or will do; Old Canarese *mâḍu-gum* (I, he, they, &c.), do. The *p* of the Kota present is evidently connected with *dap*, the Old Canarese sign of the present tense, but still more nearly related to the *v*, *b*, or *p* of the Tamil-Malayâḷam-Canarese future. In some Kota verbs *k* is the sign of the present tense, as in Tuda—*e.g.*, *vindkene* (*vind-k-ene*), I ask, *vindkeme*, we ask. In some, both letters seem to be mixed, as in *ettakepe*, I raise up, I build, of which the past tense is *êttape*.

2. *The Preterite Tense.*—The mode in which a language forms its preterite constitutes one of the most distinctive features in its grammatical character, and one which materially contributes to the determination of the question of its relationship. In the Semitic languages past time, or the objective reality of past events, is denoted by placing the verbal theme first, and suffixing to it the sign of the personal agent. In the primitive Indo-European languages, the preterite appears to have been most commonly formed by means of the reduplication of the root or verbal theme; but this reduplication has in many instances been so softened and euphonised, that it has dwindled into the mere use of a different vowel in the preterite from that which appears in the root. The Indo-European preterite was also frequently formed by means of a prefixed temporal augment; a prefix which Bopp considers to be identical with 'alpha privitive,' but which is supposed by Meyer to be identical with *a*, a relic of the auxiliary verb to have, which is still prefixed to verbs in the Celtic languages as a temporal augment—*i.e.*, as a sign of past time. In a large proportion of the verbs in the modern Teutonic tongues, in the modern Persian, in the Turkish and Finnish families of languages, in the vernacular languages of Northern India, and, with a few exceptions, in the Dravidian languages, the preterite is formed by suffixing to the verbal theme a particle, sometimes a consonant, sometimes a vowel, which is significant of past time.

The Dravidian preterite tense is ordinarily formed, like the present, by annexing the pronominal signs to the preterite verbal participle. It is in that participle that the idea of past time resides: by it alone that idea is expressed. The changes that are made when the pronominal signs are added will be shown to be euphonic merely, not structural; and in Malayâḷam (in which the pronominal signs have ceased to be annexed), that part of speech which corresponds to the Tamil preterite verbal participle expresses by itself the past tense of the verb. Consequently, an inquiry into the Dravidian preterite tense resolves itself into an inquiry into the formation of the preterite verbal participle. The preterite verbal participle is used in Tamil with a wider range of signification than in any other dialect, though its proper and inherent meaning is that of the preterite alone. Tamil, being destitute of a present verbal participle, uses the preterite verbal participle instead, in consequence of which, in a Tamil sentence, the question of time is in abeyance till it is determined by the tense of the final governing verb. This is more or less the case in all the dialects. Where there is a present participle as well as a preterite, the present is used to denote simultaneous actions, the preterite successive actions; but it is the final verb which determines whether those actions, whether simultaneous or successive, belong to the present, the past, or the future. This indeterminateness of time in Tamil applies to the verbal participle alone, not also to the preterite tense of the finite verb, which is restricted in Tamil to the expression of past time, precisely as in other languages.

We have now to inquire particularly into the Dravidian methods of forming the preterite. They divide themselves into two—(1.) by reduplication of the final consonant; and (2.) by suffixing a sign of past time.

1. The Formation of the Preterite by Reduplication of the Final Consonant.—This mode of forming the preterite is adopted by a very small number of verbs in each of the Dravidian dialects; but its existence cannot be doubted, and it is a mode which is as interesting as it is remarkable. In the Indo-European languages, when the preterite is formed by means of reduplication, it is the root which is doubled, or at least the first syllable of the root; but in the Dravidian dialects the reduplication is that of the final consonant alone. The verbal themes which form their preterites in this manner are those which end in *ḍ-u, g-u*, or **r**-*u*, preceded by a single short vowel—*e.g.*, in classical Tamil *paḍ-u*, to suffer; *pug-u*, to enter; and *pe***r**-*u*, to obtain —the preterites of which are *paṭṭ-ên*, I suffered; *pukk-ên*, I entered; and *pettr-ên*, I obtained. In each of the above examples the final consonants—*ḍ, g*, and **r**—are doubled, and being thus doubled, are converted by rule into the corresponding surds *ṭṭ, kk*, and **rr** (pronounced *ttr*). Whilst the above and similar verbs form their preterites in this manner in the classical dialect of Tamil, in the modern colloquial dialect some of those very verbs have adopted the more ordinary method of denoting past time by means of a suffixed particle or consonant. Thus *pukk-ên*, I entered, has been superseded in the modern

dialect by *pugu-nd-ên*, and *nakk-ên*, I laughed, by *nagei-tt-ên*. Canarese forms the preterites of this class of verbs in exact agreement with classical Tamil—*e.g.*, *nakk-anu*, he laughed, from *nag-u*, to laugh; and Telugu, though less systematic in this point, exhibits the operation of the same rule, especially in the relative participles of the preterite. This Dravidian reduplication differs materially in form from that of the Indo-European languages, but it appears to proceed from a similar principle, and it constitutes, so far as it goes, an interesting point of resemblance between the two families.

2. The Formation of the Preterite by Suffixing some Particle or Sign of Past Time.—This, with the exception of the very few verbs included in the previous class, is the method of forming the preterite which is invariably adopted by the Dravidian languages, and which may be regarded as their characteristic mode. For the purpose of thoroughly investigating this subject, it will be desirable to inquire into the practice of each dialect *seriatim*.

(1.) *The Canarese Preterite.*—The most characteristic Canarese preterite is formed by annexing *d* (euphonically *d-u*) to the verbal theme. This addition constitutes the preterite verbal participle—*e.g.*, *iḷi-d-u*, having descended, *nuḍi-d-u*, having spoken; to which the pronominal terminations are suffixed to form the preterite tense—*e.g.*, *iḷi-d-enu*, I descended, *nuḍi-d-i*, thou saidst. All verbal themes (both in the classical and in the colloquial dialect, and whether transitive or intransitive) which end in *i* or *e*, form their preterites in this manner, together with many themes ending in *u*. All the apparent irregularities that exist are merely modifications of the *d* in question. Thus, sometimes *t* is substituted for *d*—*e.g.*, *aritanu*, he knew, instead of *aridanu* (corresponding to the Tamil *arindân*); sometimes the *d* of the preterite combines with the final consonant of the root, and converts it into *dd* or *tt*—*e.g.*, *iddanu*, he was, instead of *irudanu* (Tam. *irundân*); *eddu*, having risen, instead of *eḷudu* (Tam. *eṛundu*); *uttu*, having ploughed, instead of *uḷudu* (Tam. *uṛudu*); *nintu*, having stood, instead of *niludu* (Tam. *nindru*).

Another Canarese preterite is formed by suffixing *i* to the crude verbal theme—*e.g.*, *mâḍ-i*, having done, from *mâḍ-u*, to do. Between this *i* and the pronominal terminations, *d* is inserted in the formation of the preterite tense—*e.g.*, *mâḍ-i-(d)-enu*, I did, *bâḷ-i-(d)-anu*, he lived. This mode of forming the preterite characterises most verbs ending in *u* in the modern dialect. The final *u* of such verbs is merely euphonic, not radical, and is elided on *i* being annexed; and the *d* which is inserted between *i* and the pronominal signs, though possibly identical in origin with the *d* which constitutes a sign of the preterite, is merely euphonic in so far as the use to which it is now put is concerned.

In a considerable number of instances the formation of the preterite in *i* appears to be a modern corruption. Intransitive verbal themes ending in *u* form their preterite in *d* in the classical dialect; and it is in the colloquial dialect alone that *i* forms their preterite—*e.g.*, instead of *bâḷ-i* (coll.), having lived, the classical dialect has *bâḷ-d-u;* and as the classical dialect is undoubtedly more authoritative and probably also more ancient than the colloquial, *d* or *d-u* may be considered as the legitimate form of the preterite of this class of verbs. This conclusion is confirmed by the analogy of Tamil, in which the corresponding verbal theme forms its preterite verbal participle by suffixing *nd*, an euphonised form of *d*—*e.g.*, *vâṛ-nd-u*, having flourished, which is the equivalent, not of the modern Canarese *bâḷ-i*, but of the ancient *bâḷ-d-u*.

How is this diversity in the formation of the preterite to be accounted for? Can *i* have been derived in any manner from *d?* An argument in favour of this supposition may be deduced from the circumstance that the classical *bâḷ-d-en*, I lived, which is in perfect dialectic agreement with the Tamil *vâṛ-nd-ên*, has in the colloquial dialect become *bâḷ-i-d-enu*. Even in the ancient dialect itself, though this *i* is generally unknown, it makes its appearance in the preterite relative participle, which may be *bâḷ-i-d-a*, that lived, as well as *bâḷ-d-a*, though the corresponding Tamil is always *vâṛ-nd-a*. If we could form a judgment, therefore, from these instances alone, *i* would seem to have come into existence as a vocalic bond of connection between the root and the sign of the preterite.

The future, both in Canarese and in Tamil, often makes use of *u* as a bond of union between the verbal root and *v*, the sign of tense—*e.g.*, *bâḷ-u-v-enu*, coll. Can., and *vâṛ-u-v-ên*, coll. Tam. I shall live, instead of the ancient and more correct *bâḷ-v-en*, Can., and *vâṛ-v-ên*, Tam. In this case the *u* is certainly euphonic, though it has not come to be used, as *i* has, to express grammatical relation, or in lieu of the sign of tense which it is employed to euphonise. If we had to account for the insertion of *i* before *d* in such instances only as have been mentioned, we might be content with the supposition of its euphonic origin; but the use of *i* as a sign of the preterite has a much wider range. All transitive verbs ending in *u*, both in the classical dialect of Canarese and in the colloquial, form their preterite verbal participles by suffixing *i;* and there is nothing to show that those verbs ever formed their preterites in any other manner. A very large number of verbs of this class form their preterites in Tamil also by suffixing *i;* and in Telugu the preterite is formed by suffixing *i* to the root, not of one class of verbs only, but of all, with the exception of the small class of reduplicative verbs.

This statement applies, it is true, to the preterite verbal participle of Telugu, not to the preterite tense of the verb, which generally suffixes or inserts, as a tense-sign, some additional consonant or particle; but in Malayâḷam the preterite verbal participle constitutes by itself the preterite tense, without the addition of any pronominal signs; and in that dialect *i* is the only sign of past time which is used by a large number of verbs. Thus *pâḍi*, which means having sung in the other dialects, signifies in Malayâḷam (he, she, or it) sang; *i* is, therefore, in that dialect a distinctive sign of the preterite in the class of verbs referred to; and it is to be remembered that the addition of the pronominal terminations, though the means of expressing personality, effects no change in the means whereby time is expressed. The extent and prevalence, therefore, of the use of *i* as a sign of the preterite seems to forbid our supposing it to have been in all cases derived from an euphonisation of *d;* and as *d*, on the other hand, cannot have been derived from *i*, it appears probable that *d* and *i* are distinct and independent signs of past time.

Of these two signs of past time *d* is to be considered, if not the older, yet at least the more prevalent and more characteristic. We have seen that in many instances in which the colloquial Canarese has *i*, the classical dialect and Tamil have *d*. Not in those instances only, but universally, Telugu uses *i* as the sign of the preterite; but the great antiquity of the grammatical forms of Tamil and Old Canarese precludes the supposition that their most characteristic sign of past time has been borrowed from that of Telugu. In addition to which, it will be shown that in Telugu itself there are traces of the existence of an old sign of the preterite agreeing with that of Tamil and classical Canarese. It would, therefore, appear that two modes of forming the preterite being in existence, one in *d*, another in *i*, the latter form has in many instances, particularly in Telugu, superseded the former; and the prevalence of *i* in Telugu and Gônd would seem to prove that this form must be one of great antiquity.

In the Indo-European family of languages we find similar interchanges amongst the signs of past time; and though in some instances one form or mode may have been derived from another, yet this cannot have been the case uniformly—*e.g.*, the *weak* Germanic conjugations cannot have been corrupted from the *strong*, or *vice versâ;* though it seems certain that the strong method of forming the preterite was more ancient than the weak, and though it is also certain that the former mode has in very many instances been superseded by the latter.

What is the origin of the *d* which is inserted in Canarese between *i* and the pronominal terminations, and also between *i* and the sign of the relative participle? It appears to be used (whatever be its origin) merely for the purpose of preventing hiatus between concurrent vowels—*e.g.*, *mâḍi-(d)-enu*, I did, *mâḍ-i-(d)-a*, that did. Hiatus is generally prevented in the Dravidian languages by the insertion of a nasal, or of one of the semi-vowels *y* and *v*; and it seems extraordinary that *d* should be used for this purpose. It is true that in some of the inflexions of Canarese nouns—*e.g.*, *mara-d-a*, of a tree, *d* might seem to be used euphonically; but it has been shown in the section on "The Noun" that that *d* is the remnant of a neuter demonstrative, and is used as an inflexional increment; it is not, therefore, a precedent for the use of *d* for the prevention of hiatus merely. Possibly the use of this *d* by the Canarese verb may thus be accounted for: a consonant for preventing hiatus between the sign of the preterite and the subsequent signs of personality and relation being required, Canarese preferred using for this purpose a sign of the preterite which still survived. Thus *d* was not a new invention, but an old particle used for a new purpose, and placed in a position in which it would not have appeared but for the use to which it had already been put.

(2.) *The Tamil Preterite.*—The preterite is ordinarily formed in Tamil, as in Canarese, in two ways—viz., by suffixing either *d* or *i* to the verbal theme. In the former case, *d* itself is more rarely used than some euphonisation of it or related consonant; but such secondary forms invariably resolve themselves into *d*. Thus, when a theme with *l* as its final letter is followed by *d* as the sign of the preterite, the compound becomes *ndr*—*e.g.*, the preterite verbal participle of *pôl*, like, is not *pôl-d-u*, but *pôṅ-dr-u.* Sometimes, however, when *d* follows *l*, the compound becomes **rr**, pronounced *ttr*—*e.g.*, from *kal*, to learn, comes, not *kal-d-u*, but *ka***rr***-u* (*kattr-u*), having learned (Can. *kali-d-u*). *ḷ* followed by *d* becomes *ṇḍ*—*e.g.*, from *mâḷ*, to die, comes *mâṇḍ-u*, having died. Sometimes, however, when *d* follows *ḷ*, the compound becomes *ṭṭ*—*e.g.*, from *kêl*, to hear, comes *kêṭṭ-u*, having heard. These and similar combinations are merely instances of euphonisation, in accordance with the fixed phonetic rules of the language; and in each case it is in reality *d* alone which constitutes the sign of past time. In some verbs the primitive *d* still remains unchanged and pure—*e.g.*, *uṛu-d-u*, having ploughed, from *uṛu*, to plough; or with a conversion of the dental *d* into the cerebral *ḍ*—*e.g.*, *kaṇ-ḍ-u*, having seen, from *kâṇ*, to see.

The euphonisation of *d* which occurs most frequently, and is most characteristic of Tamil, is its conversion into *nd*. This conversion takes place without phonetic necessity, and solely through that fondness for nasalisation which is so deeply inherent in Tamil and Telugu, especially in Tamil, and by means of which the formatives *gu*, *du*, and *bu* have so generally been changed to *ṅgu*, *ndu*, and *mbu*. In the majority of cases in Tamil in which *d* (preceded by a vowel or semi-vowel) once formed the sign of the preterite, it has been nasalised into *nd;* whilst Canarese, wherever it has preserved the primitive *d*, has preserved it un-nasalised and pure. Thus whilst the Tamil preterite of *iru*, to be, is *iru-nd-ên*, I was, the corresponding Canarese is *iddenu* (for *iru-d-enu*); and whilst the preterite of the Tamil verb *vâṛ*, to flourish, is *vâṛ-nd-ân*, he flourished, the equivalent in classical Canarese is *bâḷ-d-am*. The higher dialect of Tamil retains some traces of the primitive un-nasalised purity of this sign of the preterite—*e.g.*, *viṛu-nd-u*, having fallen, from *viṛu*, to fall, is occasionally written by the poets *vîṛ-d-u*. (*vîr* is phonetically equivalent to *viṛu*.) It is curious to notice the progress of nasalisation which is apparent in this verb on comparing the Canarese *biddu* (for *biḷ-du*), the High Tamil *vîṛdu*, the modern Tamil *viṛundu*, and the Malayâḷam *vîṇu*.

Another change which *d* undergoes in Tamil consists in its being hardened and doubled in certain cases, so as to become *tt*. This happens to *nd* as well as to *d*,—a clear proof of the development of the former from the latter; and when the *d* of *nd* is doubled, the nasal entirely disappears. Just as the doubled form of *ṅg* is *kk*, and that of *mb*, *pp*, so the doubled form of *nd* is *tt*. In some instances this change is merely euphonic—*e.g.*, *paḍu*, to lie, an intransitive verb, takes for its preterite, not *paḍu-d-ên* or *paḍu-nd-ên*, but *paḍu-tt-ên*, I lay. Such cases, however, are rare, and in general the use of *tt* as a sign of the preterite instead of *d* or *nd*, is a means of distinguishing transitives or active verbs from intransitive—*e.g.*, the *tt* of *tâṛ-tt-ên*, I lowered, is formed by the doubling and hardening of the *nd* (the equivalent of *d*) of the corresponding intransitive *tâṛ-nd-ên*, I became low. See the further explanation of this subject under the head of "The Classification of Verbs."

The second mode of forming the preterite in Tamil, as in Canarese, is by suffixing *i* to the verbal theme. The themes which form their preterite in this manner are those which terminate in *u* euphonic, and of which the radical portion consists either in one long syllable or in two syllables, whether short or long. In this connection, as in prosody, a vowel which is long by position is equivalent to one which is naturally long. The following are examples of the classes of verbs which take *i* for their preterite :—(long syllable) *pâḍu,* to sing; (long by position) *paṇṇ-u,* to make; (two short syllables) *eṛud-u,* to write; (one syllable short, and one long by position) *tirupp-u,* to turn. All verbs of which the final consonant is a liquid semi-vowel (*l, ḷ, r, ṛ,* not *v* or r), whatever number of syllables they may contain, form their preterite by means of *d* or some of its modifications: such verbs are therefore exceptions to the above rule.

Even in the class of Tamil verbs which take *i* as their preterite suffix, there are traces of the prevalence of *d* at a more ancient period. Thus, whilst 'thou didst go' is in the ordinary dialect *pô-(n)-ây* (properly *pôg-i-(n)-ây,* from *pô,* or *pô-gu,* to go), in the poets *pô-d-i* is sometimes used instead; so instead of *â-(n)-ây* (for *âg-i-(n)-ây,* from *â-gu,* to become), thou becamest, the poets sometimes use *â-d-i.* In these instances Canarese also, even in the colloquial dialect, says *pôdi* and *âdi.* Even *nd* is sometimes *d* only in Tamil poetry—*e.g., varu-d-i,* thou camest, is found instead of the more modern *va-nd-ây* (for *varu-nd-ây*); and it is evident that this form, *varu-d-i,* exactly corresponds to the forms quoted above, *pô-d-i* and *â-d-i.*

Notwithstanding, therefore, the prevalence of *i* as a sign of the preterite in Tamil, as in Canarese (though in a less degree than in Canarese), there seems to be some reason for regarding it as an innovation, or at least as a less characteristic and less widely used sign than *d.* *n* is inserted in Tamil (as *d* in Canarese) between the *i* which constitutes the sign of the preterite of certain classes of verbs and the pronominal terminations, and also between the sign of the preterite and the sign of the relative participle—*e.g.*, from *pâḍ-i,* having sung (the preterite verbal participle of *pâḍ-u,* to sing), is formed *pâḍ-i-(n)-ân,* I sang; *pâḍ-i-(n)-ây,* thou didst sing; *pâḍ-i-(n)-ân,* he sang: so also *pâḍ-i-(n)-a,* the relative participle, that sang. Whatever be the origin of this *n,* it cannot be doubted that its *use* in Tamil is at present wholly euphonic; and this statement applies also to the use of the same *n* in the preterite relative participle of Telugu. It in no respect contributes to the expression of grammatical relation; and when used by the relative participle in Tamil, it may optionally and elegantly be changed into *y,* which is one of the semi-vowels that are systematically used for the prevention of hiatus—*e.g.,* instead of *pâḍi(n)a,* that sang, we may write with still more perfect propriety *pâḍi(y)a.* Probably *y* is in this connection older than *n.* (See "Sounds.") We see a parallel use of *n* in the Turkish verb, in the frequent insertion of an euphonic *n* between the theme and the infinitival particle, and also between the theme and the sign of the passive. The most weighty argument in confirmation of the euphonic origin of the Tamilian *n* in question is derived from the use of *n* as an euphonic fulcrum, or means of preventing hiatus in the Dravidian languages generally, and even in connection with another part of the Tamil verb. Thus, in the classical plural neuter of the present tense, *varugindrana* (*varu-gindr-ana*), they (things) come, the *n* of the pronominal termination *ana* is undoubtedly equivalent to the *v* of the isolated plural neuter *avei* (for *ava*); and is used merely for the euphonic prevention of hiatus between the first *a*, or the demonstrative vowel, and the final *a*, or the sign of the neuter plural. (*a*(*n*)*a* or *a*(*v*)*a* is equivalent to *a-a*.) Native Tamil grammarians consider *in*, not *i*, the sign of the preterite; but as *i*, never *in*, is the form used by the preterite verbal participle, it is evident that they have given too important a place to what is at present at least a merely euphonic letter.

If Tamil and Telugu alone were concerned, we should perhaps be justified in considering the purely euphonic origin of the *n* in question to be a settled point; but a difficulty arises on comparing those languages with Canarese. Wherever Tamil and Telugu use *n* in the formation of the preterite tense and the preterite relative participle, there Canarese, as has been observed, uses *d*—*e.g.*, *mâḍi-*(*d*)*-enu*, I did, not *mâḍi-*(*n*)*-enu;* and *mâḍi-*(*d*)*-a*, that did, not *mâḍi-*(*n*)*-a*. Now, though this *d* of the Canarese is certainly euphonic in its present use, it has been shown that there is reason for suspecting it to be derived from *d*, the old sign of the preterite; and if this supposition be correct, it would follow that the Tamilian *n*, which corresponds so perfectly to the Canarese *d*, may be derived from the same source as *d*, and euphonically altered from it. The *n* of the Tamil preterite, therefore, as well as the *d* of the Canarese, may testify to the primitive universality of the use of *d* as a sign of past time. Whether *d* (= *n*) was originally a sign of the preterite or not, the conversion of *d* into *n* in this connection, viz., in the preterite tense, and especially in the preterite relative participle, is analogous to the change of *ta* or *da* to *na* in the past participle of the Indo-European tongues, especially in German, from which the final *n* of our own past participles (such as 'fallen') has been derived.

(3.) *The Malayâḷam Preterite.*—The Malayâḷam preterite is substantially the same as the Tamil; the only real difference consists in the disuse in Malayâḷam of the pronominal terminations. The sign of past time is invariably the same in each Dravidian language, with only such modifications of sound as are dialectic and regular. That which constitutes the preterite verbal participle in Tamil is in Malayâḷam the preterite tense of the verb—*e.g.*, *naḍandu* in Tamil signifies having walked; the corresponding Malayâḷam word *naḍannu*, means (he, she, it, or they) walked. Some confusion has been introduced in Malayâḷam books by writing the preterite *verbal* participle *naḍanna*, having walked, as if it were identical with the preterite relative participle *naḍanna*, that walked. The rendering of the sound of the latter word is correct, the final *a* being the sign of the relative participle in all the Dravidian languages, and, as I conceive, identical in origin with *a*, the sign of the genitive. *naḍanna*, that walked, is therefore identical with the Tamil *naḍanda*. On the other hand, the final *a* of the preterite *verbal* participle ought either to have been *u*, corresponding to the Tamil *naḍandu*, having walked, or, being a very short vowel, merely enunciative and euphonic, it should have been elided (as it is when followed by another vowel), after the fashion employed in North Malabar, in which this word is written *naḍann'*. In Dr Gundert's Malayâḷam Grammar and Dictionary, the short *u* is denoted by *ų*, in accordance with Lepsius's system of transliteration. This mode of rendering the latter has also been adopted in Brigel's "Grammar of the Tuḷu," in which language the short enunciative *ų* has acquired a very prominent place. It is to be hoped, therefore, that this blemish in Malayâḷam orthography, as Dr Gundert terms it, will now disappear.

(4.) *The Telugu Preterite.*—In Telugu all preterite verbal participles, without exception, are formed by adding *i* to the theme. Even those verbs which form their preterites by suffixing *d* or some modification of it in Tamil, Canarese, and Malayâḷam, form their preterites in Telugu by suffixing *i*—*e.g.*, *koṇ-ḍu*, Tam. and Can., having bought, is in Telugu *kon-i*, and *kaṇ-ḍu*, Tam. and Can. having seen, is *kan-i*. Notwithstanding the universality of this rule, there are traces even in Telugu of the use of a particle corresponding to the *d* of the other dialects as a sign of past time. Though the preterite verbal participle never takes any suffix but that of *i*, some parts of the preterite tense of the verb in the higher idiom of the language (viz., the first and second persons both singular and plural) insert the particle *ti* between the *i* of the verbal participle and the pronominal terminations. It cannot be doubted, I think, that this *ti*, which is found nowhere but in the preterite, is allied to the *d* which is inserted in the same place in the Canarese preterite. Thus, whilst both in Canarese and in Telugu the preterite verbal participle of *âḍ-u*, to play, is *âḍ-i*, having played, in both dialects *ti* or *d* is suffixed to *i* before adding the personal terminations—*e.g.*, compare Can. *âḍ-i-d-enu*, I played, Tel. *âḍ-i-ti-ni*. It has already been shown to be probable that the *d* thus inserted by the Canarese, though now used to so large an extent euphonically, was originally a sign of the preterite, identical with the *d* which is still used for that purpose by many verbs. This view derives confirmation from Telugu, in which the corresponding *ti* does not appear to be used euphonically at all, and certainly is not used for the prevention of hiatus; for there is no hiatus and no necessity for an euphonic insertion between the aforesaid *âḍi* and *ni*, the pronominal fragment, or in the second person between *âḍi* and *vi*. It therefore follows that we must regard *ti* as a sign of past time, subordinate indeed to *i*, and unused in the third person of the preterite, but immediately allied to *d*, the past tense-sign of Tamil and Canarese, and testifying to the existence of a time when *d*, or its equivalent *t*, was one of the signs of the preterite in Telugu as in the other dialects. In some Telugu verbs, *ti* is combined in such a manner with the final consonant of the theme, as to prove beyond doubt its identity in origin and force with the Tamil *d*—*e.g.*, *chês-ti-ni*, Tel. I did (for *chêsi-ti-ni*), is evidently equivalent to the Tamil *śey-d-ên;* and *koṉ-ṭi-ni*, I bought (for *koni-ti-ni*), is equivalent to *koṉ-ḍ-ên*. So also when *ê*, the Telugu conditional particle, answering to the Tamil *âl*, is suffixed to the preterite tense of a verb for the purpose of giving to it the meaning of the subjunctive, it appears evident that the ancient sign of the preterite of the Telugu must have been, not *i*, but *ti* or *t*—*e.g.*, compare the Telugu *chêst-ê*, if (I, thou, he, &c.) did or do (abbreviated from *chêśi-t-ê*), with the Tamil *śeyd-âl*. It may be mentioned as a singular coincidence that in Mongolian the gerund *du* has been modernised into *ju*, and that again has been changed colloquially into *ji*.

We have seen that Tamil inserts *n* between the preterite verbal participle and the pronominal terminations in many instances in which *d* is used for this purpose in Canarese. The colloquial dialect of Telugu makes much use of *na* in the same connection—*e.g.*, *âḍ-i-(n)-ânu*, I played (answering to the Tamil *âḍ-i-(n)-ên*), instead of the more elegant and probably more ancient *âḍ-i-ti-ni*. Compare *ay-i-(n)-ânu*, Tel. I became, *â-(n)-ên*, Tam. (for *âg-i-(n)-ên*), and *â-(d)-enu*, Can. (for *âg-i-(d)-enu*). On the whole, it may be concluded that the Telugu agrees with the other dialects in exhibiting distinct and deep-seated traces of the ancient use of *d* or *t* as a sign of the preterite, notwithstanding the universal prevalence in Telugu at present of the use of *i*, as the sign of the preterite verbal participle.

I may here take occasion to guard against an illusory resemblance to which my attention was once called, viz., the resemblance which subsists between the Telugu preterite verbal participle *veichi*, having placed, and the corresponding Tamil participle *veittu*, which is vulgarly pronounced *veichi*. The *tt* of the Tamil *vei-tt-u*, being simply the hardened and doubled form of *d*, is the ordinary sign of the preterite;

and if there were any real alliance between *tt-u*, through its provincial pronunciation, and the Telugu *ch-i*, we should undoubtedly have here an instance of the use of *tt*—*i.e.*, of *d*—in modern Telugu as well as in Tamil, as a sign of the preterite verbal participle, and consequently of past time. The resemblance, however, is illusory. The *ch* of the Telugu *veichi* corresponds, not to the *tt* of the Tamil *veittu*, but to the *kk* which constitutes the formative of so many verbs and nouns in Tamil. *kk* makes its appearance in the infinitive of this very verb, viz., *vei-kk-a*, to place, the Telugu of which is *vei-ch-a*. *kk* is vulgarly pronounced *ch* in the southern part of the Tamil country, and the same pronunciation universally obtains in Telugu. The imperative or theme of this verb in Telugu is not *vei*, as in Tamil, but *veich-u* (with the addition to *vei* of the formative *ch-u*, which is equivalent to the Tamil *kk-u*); and from this *veich-u*, the preterite verbal participle *veich-i*, is regularly formed, in this as in all other cases, by the addition of *i*. If the corresponding Tamil verb formed its preterite in the same manner, its verbal participle would be *vei-kk-i*, not *vei-tt-u*. A case in point in illustration of this is the Tamil *tû-kk-u*, to lift, to weigh (Tel. *tû-ch-u*), the preterite verbal participle of which is *tû-kk-i* (Tel. *tû-ch-i*).

(5.) *The Tuḷu Preterite.*—The Tuḷu preterite, like that of Gônd, divides itself into two tenses, an imperfect and a perfect, each regularly inflected. The *imperfect* tense is that which corresponds to the ordinary preterite of the other dialects, and is formed in substantially the same manner by suffixing to the root either the ordinary Dravidian *t* or *d*, or the *i*, which is still more commonly used in several dialects. Compare Tuḷu *itte*, I was, with *iddenu*, Can.; *irundên*, Tam.: Tuḷu *kênḍe* (*kêṇ'* for *kêḷ*) with *kêṭṭen* (*kêḷ-ṭên*), Tam.; *kêḷidenu*, Can. *i* appears in *bûriye*, I fell, from *bûru*, to fall (Tam. *viṛu*, *vîṛ*). The *perfect* tense seems to be formed by suffixing an additional *d*, with such euphonic changes as the dialect requires. Compare *itte*, I was, with *itt' de*, I have been.

(6.) *Preterites of Minor Dialects.*—It is difficult to make out the Tuda preterite. *th* appears to be the sign of the past, corresponding to the Tamil and Canarese *d*—*e.g.*, compare *âḍ-k-en*, I dance, with *âḍ-th-b-ini*, I danced. This *th* is written *ch* by Mr Metz—*e.g.*, *bindch-pini*, I asked; and, according to him, the same *ch* appears alike in the present and the past, in each person except the first. Dr Pope inserts *th* before *ch* in the past—*e.g.*, *âḍ-th-chi*, danced. In the Kota dialect the past seems to be represented by *si*—*e.g.*, compare *hôgape*, I go, with *hôsipe*, I went. In this it does not stand alone, as will be seen. In Gônd, *si* or *ji*, apparently softened from *ti*, forms the verbal participle of the preterite; but the perfect tense is formed by suffixing *tt*—*e.g.*, *kei-tt-ân*, I have called; *kei-si*, having called. In Seoni Gônd, also, the preterite or conjunctive participle suffixes *si*—*e.g.*, *wunk-si*, having spoken; but the past participle is formed by suffixing *tûr*—*e.g.*, *wunk-tûr*, spoken; and the past tense simply suffixes *t*—*e.g.*, *wunk-t-an*, I spoke, *wunk-t-i*, thou didst speak. An imperfect or progressive tense is formed by inserting *und* or *nd*, apparently the substantive verb, between the root and the pronominal terminations.

These instances tend to confirm the supposition that *d*, or some modification of it, is, if not the only, yet at least the most ancient and characteristic sign of the Dravidian preterite.

Origin of the Dravidian Signs of Past Time.

1. The most probable conjecture I can offer respecting the origin of *i*, is one which would confirm the supposition of its secondary character. I conceive it to have been originally a vowel of conjunction, employed for the purpose of euphonically connecting the verbal theme and the true sign of past time, *d* or *d-u*. Where the theme terminated in a hard consonant, euphony would require some such vocalic bond of connection—*e.g.*, the Old Canarese *bâḷ-d-en*, I lived, is undoubtedly somewhat harsh to an ear that is attuned to Dravidian phonetics; and it was natural that it should be softened, as it has been in modern Canarese, into *bâḷ-i-d-enu*. We see a precisely similar euphonic insertion of *i* in the Latin *dom-i-tus* (instead of *dom-tus*), tamed, and the Sanskrit *pîḍ-i-tah* (instead of *pîḍ-tah*), pressed. Subsequently we may suppose the true preterite *d* to have gradually dropped off; whilst *i* remained, as being the easier sound, with the adventitious signification of the preterite. There are many instances in all languages of euphonic additions coming to be used instead of the parts of speech to which they were attached—*e.g.*, in the Telugu verb, *vu* is used to represent the second person singular of the pronoun instead of *nî*, thou, though *vu* was originally only an euphonic addition to *nî*, by which it was converted into *nîvu*.

It deserves notice that wherever *i* is used in Canarese or in Tamil, instead of *d*, as a sign of the preterite, the use of *d* would in that instance be harsh and uncouth; and that on comparing the Tamil verbs which form their preterite in *i* with those that suffix *d*, no reason but euphony can be alleged why the one suffix should be employed rather than the other; consequently euphonic causes must at least have helped the development of *i*. This supposition of the origin of *i* from the vocalic conjunction of *d* with the verbal theme, would also account for the circumstance that wherever *i* is followed by a vowel (whether the initial vowel of the pronominal terminations, or the *a* which constitutes the sign of the relative participle) it picks up again the *d* which it had gradually lost, and uses it as an euphonic bond of conjunction, either in its original shape of *d*, as in Canarese, or in its nasalised shape of *n*, as in Tamil and Telugu. The manner in which *ti* is separated from the theme in some Telugu preterites—*e.g.*, *kon-i-ti-ni* (*koṇ-ṭi-ni*), I bought, confirms this supposition of the euphonic origin of *i*.

2. *d*, the more characteristic sign of the Dravidian preterite, presents many interesting resemblances to corresponding signs of past time in various Indo-European and Scythian languages.

It may have an ulterior, though remote, connection with *t* or *ta* (alternating with *na*), the ordinary suffix of the Indo-European passive participle—*e.g.*, *jñâ-ta-h*, Sans. known; Greek *γνω-τό-ς*; Latin (*g*)*nô-tu-s*: *bhug-na-s*, Sans. bent; Gothic *bug-a-n*(*a*)*s*. In Gothic this suffix is *d* or *t*; in New Persian invariably *d*. In Sanskrit the participle which is formed from *ta* is in general distinctively passive; but a few traces exist of a preterite signification, only, however, in connection with neuter verbs—*e.g.*, *ga-ta-s*, one who went; *bhû-ta-s*, one who has come into being. A preterite signification predominates also in the active participles formed by suffixing *tavat* (derived from the passive *ta*)—*e.g.*, *kṛi-tavat*, was making, and in the indeterminate past participle, or gerund, which is formed by suffixing *tvâ*—*e.g.*, *kṛi-tvâ*, having made or through making.

Though there may possibly be some ultimate connection between the preterite *d* of the Dravidian languages and the passive (and secondary preterite) *t* of the Sanskrit, the use of this *d* as a sign of the preterite is too essential a characteristic of the Dravidian languages, and too rare and exceptional in Sanskrit to admit of the supposition that the former borrowed it from the latter.

The *l* which constitutes the sign of the preterite in Bengali has been supposed by Professors Max Müller and Bopp to be derived from the past participial *t* of the Sanskrit—*e.g.*, *karilâm*, I did, is derived by them from *karita*, Sans. done, followed by the personal termination *âm*. This supposition is confirmed by the conformity of *karilâm* to the New Persian *kardem*, I did, and by the use in Marâṭhi of a similar preterite in *l*, which is supposed to be derived in like manner from the Sanskrit passive participial *t*—*e.g.*, *mî kelo-m*, I did, *mîn gêlô-n*, I went. The interchange of *ḍ* and *l* is of frequent occurrence; and possibly the Sanskrit *t* may have become *d* or *ḍ* before it was corrupted into *l*. There is no proof of this, however, and the *l* which is used as the equivalent of *t* or *d* in the formation of the Slavonian preterite *byl* (Pers. *bûd*, Sans. *bhûtas*), he was, shows that *t* may have passed into *l* immediately, without the middle point of the cerebral *ḍ*.

Whether the preterite *l* of the Bengali and Marâṭhi is derived directly from the Sanskrit passive participial *t*, or whether it has descended from some old vernacular of Northern India, it is interesting to notice the fact of the conformity in this important particular between the Dravidian languages and those of the Gaurian family. We should notice, however, this important difference between the two, that whilst the Gaurian preterite *l*, in so far as it is derived from the Sanskrit, appears to be only a secondary constructive preterite, the Dravidian *d* exhibits no trace whatever of connection with any passive participle.

In the New Persian, *d* invariably forms the sign of the preterite—*e.g.*, *bû-d-em*, I was; *bur-d-em*, I bore. The participle which constitutes the verbal theme in Persian, and which has a formative that is passive in Sanskrit, has an active as well as a passive-preterite signification—*e.g.*, *burdeh* means either borne or having borne, according to the context. The preterite tense has in Persian been developed out of a passive participle; and this appears to have happened through the influence of the past time which is inherent in the perfect passive. In Gothic and in the modern Teutonic tongues, *d* is used in connection with a large class of verbs to denote the preterite; but this *d* has been shown to be a relic of *did*, and this again to be reduplication of the root *do*. Consequently the *d* of *loved* cannot really be related to the *t* of the Sanskrit and Persian, still less with the *d* of the Dravidian preterite, though all three might naturally be supposed to be identical.

The formation of the preterite by suffixing *d* prevails also in the Turkish and Ugrian tongues. *d* is the sign of past time used by Turkish—*e.g.*, compare *sever-im*, I love, with *sever-d-im*, I loved; and this *d* is inserted, as in Tamil and Canarese, between the root and the pronominal signs. Compare the present *îm*, I am, with the preterite *î-d-um*, I was. Notice also *ôl-d-um*, I was, and the equivalent form in Oriental Turkish, *bôl-d-îm*. In Finnish, the preterite is regularly formed by suffixing *t*. The preterite participle from which the perfect tense is formed terminates in *ut*, *yt*, *et*, &c.—*e.g.*, *oll-ut*, having been, from the theme *ol*, to be. The Hungarian forms its preterite in a similar manner—*e.g.*, the preterite participle of *le-nni*, to become, is *le-tt*, having become; and from this is regularly formed the perfect *le-tt-em*, I have become. It especially deserves notice, that these Turkish, Finnish, and Hungarian signs of the preterite are totally unconnected with the passive participle. They are signs of past time, not of passivity; and as such they are suffixed to all indicatives, whether active or neuter, and are appended, in addition to the sign of passivity, to passive forms, only when those passives are also preterites.

In this particular, therefore, the analogy between the Dravidian preterite and the Turko-Ugrian is closer and more distinctive than the Indo-European analogies which have been pointed out. As regards use, indeed, whatever be, or be supposed to be, the origin of each, it may be said to amount to identity.

The Dravidian languages being so highly cultivated, and having been cultivated from so early a period, we should be prepared to expect that in developing their inflexional forms they availed themselves, as far as possible, of words or particles which they had already in use, instead of borrowing the inflexional particles of their neighbour. May it not be practicable, therefore, to discover the origin of *d*, the Dravidian sign of the preterite, in the Dravidian languages themselves?

Dr Granl (in his "Outlines of Tamil Grammar," p. 42) says, "The verbal form in *du* (*e.g.*, *śeydu* = *śey-adu*, perhaps 'something endowed with what the root *śey* signifies, *i.e.*, something doing') originally seems to have been used for all the forms of the finite verb in the singular (*nân śeydu*, I doing, *nî śeydu*, thou doing, &c.), and *śeydum* (*śeydu-um*), in the plural (*nâm śeydum*, *nîngaḷ śeydum*, &c. *śeydu* in the sense of I did, and *śeydum* in the sense of we did, are still found in the ancient dialect). Probably the personal affixes were added later, *śeydu ên* = *śeydên*, I did, &c. In Malayâḷam the personal affixes are not yet used in prose." It would have been more correct to have said the personal affixes have *ceased* to be used in Malayâḷam prose, for we find them in the prose of ancient inscriptions; but he is quite right in what he says respecting the occasional use of the uninflected forms *śeydu* and *śeydum* in the Tamil poets. *śeydu* is used both for the preterite and the future, but at present only in the first person singular, and *śeydum* in the plural—*e.g.*, *śeydu*, I did, or will do, *śeydum*, we did, or will do. Dr Granl's identification of the *d*, which is the sign of the preterite, with the *d* which denotes the neuter singular in *adu*, *idu*, that, this, in Tamil, and *adi*, *idi*, in Telugu, is very ingenious. This *d* is used largely in the formation of verbal nouns, and might easily be turned to account for the purpose of denoting the present-future; but it is not so easy to see how it came to be used as the sign of the preterite, the most distinctive of Dravidian tenses. In the Tamil conditional *śeyd-âl*, if (one) does, or did, *śeydu* appears to express the meaning of 'doing' irrespective of time. In some connections, however, it will be seen that this conditional form connects itself distinctively with the past. (See "The Conditional.") Every difficulty would be removed if we supposed the particle originally appended to the root to have been, not simply *du*, but *adu*, the remote demonstrative that. It has been seen that *ute*, the sign of the present in Canarese, is probably *utu*, this. There is something very enticing in the supposition of the origin of one of the present tenses of the Dravidian verb from the demonstrative 'this' and of that of the most distinctive form of the past from 'that.' The chief difficulty in the way of this supposition, as far as the preterite is concerned, is the fact that the *a* of *adu* does not survive. It might be answered that this vowel might easily be lost after the reason for its use had ceased to be perceived. True; but in this case another vowel, *i*, has asserted a place for itself instead of *a*, being used euphonically in Canarese before *d*, and used by itself in Tamil, Malayâḷam, and Telugu as a sign of the preterite; and if *i* is used demonstratively, or is a relic of a vowel used demonstratively, the preterite must have been formed by the addition to the root of 'this,' not 'that,' which is very unlikely. All that can safely be concluded, therefore, is that the *d* of the Dravidian preterite was probably in its origin a neuter singular formative, converting the verbal root to which it was attached into a verbal noun; not into an abstract verbal noun, such as the future seems to have been formed from, but into a concrete or conjugated noun, in which the action of the verb was arrested and localised. If this supposition should be accepted, it will follow that an agreement, up to a certain point, will be discovered to exist between the Dravidian languages and the Sanskrit and Persian. A demonstrative letter or particle will be found to be made use of in both classes of languages for substantially the same purpose. In one it is used to denote the preterite, in the other to form a passive participle capable of being used as a preterite. What renders it more remarkable is that this demonstrative letter or particle is *t* or *d* in both. The *di* of the Turkish preterite (*sever-di-m*, I loved) is regarded by Max Müller ("Lectures," p. 324) as the relic of a possessive pronoun. "Paying belongs to me," he says, "equals I have paid"—*i.e.*, I have or possess paying. Is the preterite *d* of Tamil also a possessive? It *might* take this force, seeing that whilst *adu* is a demonstrative, meaning that or it, it is also a possessive meaning of—*e.g.*, *adu enadu*, that is mine. On the other hand, I can discover no trace of a possessive signification in the Tamil preterite. It does not seem to get beyond a demonstrative meaning.

It is remarkable that the Mongolian has a gerund, formed by affixing *d*, which is used precisely in the same manner as the Dravidian *d-u*—*e.g.*, *onad*, riding, from *onihu*, to ride. This seems to be connected in some way with the Turkish preterite *d* or *di*, if not also with the Dravidian *d*, the Sanskrit *t*, and the Persian *d*. The Mongolian has another gerund in *ji*, which Mr Edkins thinks is derived from *d*, the Mongol *j* having *d* for its equivalent. So also as we have seen, the Tamiḷ *du* becomes *śi* in Telugu. The Japanese gerund in *te* nearly agrees in form and use with the Mongol—*e.g.*, *aghete*, lifting up, from *aghe*, to lift up. The Japanese preterite tense also is formed by affixing *ta* (apparently a modification of the gerund *te*)—*e.g.*, *mita*, saw, from *mi*, to see.

3. *The Future Tense.*—The preterite tense of the Dravidian verb is generally formed from the preterite participle by suffixing the pronominal terminations, but the future is generally formed, not from a future participle, but by suffixing to the verbal theme some particle which is regarded, whatever its origin may have been, as a sign of future time, and adding to that particle the pronominal terminations. Generally these languages are destitute of a future participle. The exceptions are Malayâḷam and classical Tamil, in both of which there is a participle of the future in *vân* or *pân*, and Tuḷu, in which there is a participle which may be used either for the present or the future.

In the Dravidian languages there are two future formations. One, which is called in Canarese grammars the conditional future, is found in Canarese and Telugu alone; the other, which is contained in all the dialects, inclusive of the Canarese and Telugu, is an indeterminate tense, only slightly futuric, and is called by Telugu grammarians "the aorist." It should here be observed also, that the use of the present for the future is exceedingly common in all the Dravidian dialects.

The future is the least distinctive of the Dravidian tenses. It is used to denote what is, was, or shall be habitually done, and it is generally the connection only which fixes it to a particular time. When used alone it denotes the future more commonly than any other time, and hence is called the future by grammarians. The particles by which it is expressed seem to show that originally it was a verbal noun, denoting abstractly the idea contained in the verb; and if this idea is correct it will account for its indeterminateness.

In Tamil there are several modes of forming the future, each of which has its counterpart in one or another of the other dialects. The oldest form of the future—of which a few traces only survive in the poets—was formed by adding *g* or *k* to the root, with the usual enunciative *u*—*e.g.*, *śey-gu*, I will do. This is pluralised by the addition of *um*—*e.g.*, *śey-gum*, we will do, also *śey-gum vandem*, we came in order to do, in which *śey-gum* has the force of a plural participle of the future. I have no doubt we have here the origin of the *gum* or *kum* which may be affixed to any verb in classical Canarese, to form an aorist—*e.g.*, *gêyu-gum*, he, it, they, &c., do. The sign of the future is *g*. *um*, originally a conjunctive particle, can be used either as a sign of comprehension, to give fulness to the sense, or as a sign of plurality. The connection shows in which sense it is used. In the next stage of the growth of this form of the future we find the personal terminations suffixed to *gu*, but still only in the poets—*e.g.*, *śeygên* (*śeyg'-ên*), I will do. In certain connections this *g* is hardened to *kk*—*e.g.*, *aḍeikkên*, I will obtain. In both these cases *v* would be used in the ordinary dialect instead of *g*. This *g* or *kk*, though used in a futuric sense, seems to connect itself naturally with the formative *g* or *kk*, which constitutes the ordinary formative of many verbs, and appears as such in the infinitive and the neuter future, as well as in verbal derivatives—*e.g.*, *pô-ga*, to go; *pô-gum*, it will go; *iru-kka*, to be; *iru-kkum*, it will be.

The future is ordinarily formed in Tamil, both in the poets and in the colloquial dialect, by adding *v*, *b*, or *pp* to the root, in accordance with the rule of euphony explained when treating of the causal verb. After *y*, *l*, *r*, *ṛ* and *ḷ*, *v* is generally used—*e.g.*, *śey-v-ên*, I will do; *śol-v-ên*, I will say; *śâr-v-ên*, I will lean upon; *vâṛ-v-ên*, I will flourish; *mâḷ-v-en*, I will perish. To this, however, there are exceptions in regard to roots ending in *l* and *ḷ*—*e.g.*, *kal*, to learn, becomes in the future *kaṟpên* (= *kal-ppên*), and *kêḷ*, to hear, becomes *kêṭpên*(= *kêḷ-ppên*). *v* is used after roots ending in *u* preceded by a long vowel, whether long by nature or by position—*e.g.*, *pâḍu*, to sing, becomes in the future *pâḍu-v-ên*; *anuppu*, to send, *anuppu-v-ên*. The nasals *n* and *ṇ* form their futures by suffixing *b*—*e.g.*, *en*, to say, becomes in the future *en-b-ên*, I will say; *uṇ*, to eat, becomes *uṇ-b-ên*. This *b* changes sometimes in the poets to *m*—*e.g.*, instead of *enbar*, they will say, the poets are fond of using *enmar*. Another and still more poetical form of this future verb is *enmanâr*. (See Epicene Plural, p. 138.) *b* also makes its appearance in those future participial nouns in which two *v's* would otherwise appear—*e.g.*, *varubavan*, not *varuvavan*, he who will come. All other Tamil verbs (with a few unimportant exceptions) form futures of this class by affixing *pp*—that is, by doubling *b*, which then becomes *pp* by rule—*e.g.*, *iru*, to be, becomes in the future *iru-pp-ên*; *naḍa*, to walk, *naḍa-pp-ên*; *kaḍi*, to bite, *kaḍi-pp-ên*. Of all these futuric particles or modifications of the same particle, the one most largely used in Tamil is *v*, and this is the future suffix invariably used in colloquial Canarese, and generally in the classical dialect. The Tuḷu present, originally a future, also uses *v*. I am inclined to consider these signs of the future as originally nothing more than formatives of verbal nouns. According to this supposition, *g*, the oldest sign of the future in Tamil, would naturally ally itself to *v*, *b*, and *p*. The only difference between the verbal noun and the future is that the verbal noun affixes to the *g*, *v*, *b*, or *p*, only an enunciative vowel, generally *u*, whilst the future is recognised by its affixing to the same formative letters the pronominal terminations—*e.g.*, compare *kaḍu-gu*, mustard, from *kaḍu*, to be sharp; *kuru-kku*, athwart, from *kuru*, to be short; *ari-vu*, knowledge, from *ari*, to know; *śâr-bu*, support, from *śâr*, to lean upon; *tira-ppu*, an opening, from *tira*, to open. The formatives most largely used in the formation of these verbal nouns are *v* and *pp*, just as we have seen that *v* and *pp* are the most commonly used signs of the future. That the future was originally a verbal noun will appear still more clearly when we consider the Tamil second future, or defective aoristic future, in *um* or *u*.

The Tamil future formed from *v*, *b*, or *pp*, is destitute of a relative participle, and uses instead the aorist future in *um*. Generally also, that aorist is used instead of the more distinctive future in the third person singular neuter. Thus, whilst 'he will be' is *iru-pp-ân*, 'it will be' is ordinarily *iru(kk)-um*, not *iru-pp-adu*; and forms like *iru-pp-adu* are in general used only as participial nouns. In this respect Tamil is less regular than Canarese, in which the ordinary third person neuter singular of the future tense is *iru-v-adu*. In the classical dialect of Tamil, however, we find *varu (n)a*, things that will come.

Another or second future formation of the Tamil may be called the defective aoristic future, inasmuch as its reference to future time is still less distinct and determinate than the future in *v*, and as it is ordinarily restricted to two forms, the third person singular neuter, and the relative participle. This defective future is formed by suffixing *um* to the formed theme—*e.g.*, *pôg-um*, it will go; *var-um*, it will come; *irukk-um*, it will be. The future in *um* is not considered by Tamil grammarians as distinct from, and independent of, the future in *v*, but is strangely enough considered as a part of it. Its claim, however, to be regarded as a distinct future formation is confirmed by the Malayâḷam, in which it is the form of the future in ordinary use—*e.g.*, *ñân eṛud-um*, I will write, *nî eṛud-um*, thou wilt write; the other form corresponding to the Tamil future in *v*, *b*, *pp*, is used in Malayâḷam as in Tamil, but not so commonly, except in conjunction with certain nouns—*e.g.*, *âv'ôḷam*, till (it) become, for *âgu-(v)-ôḷam* or *âgum-ôḷam*; *maripp'ôḷam*, till (it die), for *marikkum-ôḷam*. In the Tamil of prose and conversation the future in *um* is used in connection with the neuter of the third person singular alone; but in the poetry it occasionally takes a wider range of application, and is sometimes construed even with the masculine-feminine plural, as in Malayâḷam. The future in *um*, when used in Tamil as a relative participle, does not differ from the form of the same future which is used as the third person singular neuter. The forms are identical—*e.g.*, *pôg-um*, it will go, *pôg-um*, which will go; they may therefore be regarded as one.

um is added, not to the crude root of the verb, or that form which is used as the imperative, but to the formed theme, or that verbal noun which forms the basis of the infinitive, and the equivalent of which constitutes in Telugu the inflexional basis of every part of the verb. The base to which the future *um* is suffixed, may, therefore, safely be assumed to be a verbal noun, even in Tamil, though it rarely appears in a separate shape. The following instances will show the relation subsisting between the Tamil infinitive and the aoristic, impersonal future, in virtue of the formation of both on the basis of the formed verbal theme, or assumed verbal noun, in question:—compare *pôg-a*, to go, *pôg-um*, it will go; inflexional theme, *pô-gu*: *pôkk-a*, to cause to go, to get rid of; *pôkk-um*, it will get rid of; inflexional theme, *pô-kku*: *irukk-a*, to be; *irukk-um*, it will be; inflexional theme, *iru-kku*. In those cases in which intransitive verbs are converted into transitives by doubling the initial consonant of the tense-sign (*e.g.*, *vaḷar-gir-ên*, I grow, hardened into *vaḷar-kkir-ên*, I rear), the infinitive and the aoristic future of the transitive verb are formed upon the basis of a theme which terminates in the formative *kk-u* (the equivalent of which is *ch-u* in Telugu), whilst the unformed theme, or ultimate root, is the basis of the corresponding forms of the intransitive—*e.g.*, compare *vaḷar-a*, to grow; *vaḷar-um*, it will grow: theme, *valar*; with *vaḷar-kk-a*, to rear; *vaḷar-kk-um*, it will rear: theme *vaḷar-kku*. It is evident from a comparison of these illustrations, that the above *g* or *k* is no part of the sign of future time; it belongs to the formative, not to the future; the infinitive as well as the aoristic future is built upon it; and the Telugu formative which corresponds to it has a place in every part of the verb. The conclusion we thus arrive at confirms the supposition that the first Tamil future also was originally only a verbal noun, and that it is indebted to usage for its futuric meaning.

The future in *um* is altogether impersonal; no pronominal terminations are ever added to it, and in consequence it is well adapted to be used as a relative participle, the relative participles being used alike by all persons, numbers, and genders. The particle *um*, which constitutes the sign of future time, is identical in form, and is also, I believe, identical in origin and force, with *um*, the conjunctive or copulative particle of Tamil. It is also identical with *nu*, the impersonal suffix of the third person singular and plural of each gender of the Telugu aorist,—a tense which perfectly corresponds with the one now under consideration. *nu* is an euphonised form of *u*, the conjunctive particle of Telugu, corresponding to *u*, the ultimate base of the Tamil *um*; and it is probable that this particle has been chosen, both in Tamil and in Telugu, to be the characteristic sign of the aorist, because of its suitableness for conjoining the future to the present and past,—that is, for expressing the idea of continuity. This tense, it is true, frequently denotes the future; but does this only in a vague manner, and it is much more frequently used to express continuous action, or what is habitually done. Thus, *mâḍ-u pul tin(n)-um* (Tam.) is to be translated, not the ox will eat grass, but the ox eats (*i.e.*, habitually eats) grass, or grass is the ox's food.

When the relative participle of this aoristic future, coupled to a noun signifying time, is followed by a finite preterite verb, the future in Tamil takes the sense of the imperfect—*e.g.*, *nân var-um poṛudu, pôrei (k)kaṇḍên*, when I was coming (which appears to mean literally when I shall come), I saw the battle. In respect of this capacity of the aoristic future for becoming an historical preterite, it resembles the future tense of the Semitic languages.

Classical Tamil, Malayâḷam, and Telugu occasionally form this aoristic future by suffixing *u* instead of *um*—*e.g.*, *var-u*, Tam. it will come, instead of *var-um; uṇg-u*, it will eat, instead of *uṇg-um; parapp-u*, it will spread, instead of *parapp-um*. It is apparent from these illustrations that *u*, like *um*, is suffixed, not to the root or ultimate base of the verb, but to the formed verbal theme, or primitive verbal noun, which forms the basis of all forms of the future. This future in *u* is considered by native grammarians as an *al-vaṛi*, or uninflected form, and the circumstance that the *u* is sometimes elided gives colour to this idea; but as the basis is not the bare root, but that root *plus* the formative, it appears to me that to that extent at least it must be regarded as an inflected form. The *u* is probably not the merely euphonic enunciative *u*, as appears from the position it holds in Malayâḷam, but the *u* which constitutes the base of the conjunctive particle *um*. The future in *um* and the future in *u* are thus brought into agreement.

Future Verbal Participle.—There is a verbal participle of the future in use in classical Tamil, and still more largely used in Malayâḷam, which is formed by adding *vân*, *bân*, or *ppân*, either to the root or to the inflexional base of the verb. Another form found in Tamil alone, and in it but rarely, is *pâkku*. This is a verbal participle, not an infinitive, but is sometimes scarcely distinguishable from the infinitive in use—*e.g.*, Tamil, *kolla* (infin.) *eṛundân*, means he rose up to slay; and *kolvân* (fut. part.) *eṛundân*, means also he rose up to slay. It might be rendered, he rose up being about to slay; but this would be simply an awkward way of saying the same thing. The initial letter of this particle is *v*, *b*, or *pp*, according to circumstances; and those circumstances are precisely the same as those under which the sign of the future tense, already considered, becomes *v*, *b*, or *pp*. Whatever is the origin of the one sign must be the origin of the other.

The following are instances of all three initials:—*varu-vân*, being about to come; *uṇ-bân*, being about to eat; *naḍa-ppân*, being about to walk. I have not met with any instance of the change of *b* into *m* after a nasal, in connection with this particle (though it was noticed that the *b* of the future tense often changes in the poets into *m*—*e.g.*, *enbar* = *enmar*, they will say); but this change, or the equivalent one of *v* into *m*, is common in Malayâḷam, in which they would say, not *uṇ-bân*, being about to eat, as in Tamil; but *uṇ-mân*. In Malayâḷam the *v* is sometimes optionally omitted—*e.g.*, *var-ân*, instead of *varu-vân*, being about to come. *ân*, the second portion of this particle, though apparently identical with *ân*, the pronominal termination of the third person singular masculine in Tamil, has in reality no connection with it. I regard it as an euphonic or emphatic lengthening of *an*, and this as equivalent to *am*, *adu*, the ordinary formatives of Tamil neuter singular nouns. We have another instance of this change of *adu* to *an*, and then to *ân*, in *pân*, ten, which is a poetical form of *padu* or *pattu*. See "Numerals:" Ten. *iruppân*, Tam. being about to be, is therefore, I conceive, the equivalent of *iruppadu*, that which is about to be, it will be (Can. *iruvadu*).

Canarese forms its ordinary future, and the Tuḷu its present (by analogy a future), by inserting *v* between the theme and the pronominal terminations, in accordance with the first Tamil future—viz., that in *v*. This Canarese future, like the Tamil, has often an indeterminate, aoristic sense; but it is more regular than the Tamil, inasmuch as it never changes *v* into *b* or *pp*, in the modern dialect, but uses *v* as the invariable sign of future time. It is not obliged also, like the Tamil, to borrow its third person singular neuter from another formation, but forms it, like the other persons, by means of *v*—*e.g.*, *iru-v-adu*, it will be; and it has also a relative participle of its own—*e.g.*, *bâḷu-v-a* or *bâḷ-v-a*, that will live. It is richer in this respect than the other dialects. The Tuḷu future, properly so-called, must be considered as simply a verbal noun, with the affixes of the personal terminations.

The Telugu tense which corresponds to the Tamil and Canarese aoristic futures is still more distinctively an aorist than they, though with an inclination in general to the idea of futurity. By English grammarians this tense is commonly called, not the future, but the aorist. It is formed by inserting *du* between the theme and the pronominal terminations; with the exception of the third person singular masculine and feminine, and third person plural neuter, in which *nu* alone, the equivalent of the Tamil *um*, is added to the theme. Compare the Tamil *âg-um*, it will become, it will be, with the Telugu aorist *avu-nu* (he, she, it, they, neut., &c.), will become. Possibly the

Telugu aoristic formative *du* is allied to *tu*, the particle of present time. Gônd makes use of *k* as the sign of the future, in connection with the first and second persons of the verb—*e.g.*, *wunkî-k-a*, I will speak. Compare the *g* or *kk* which is sometimes used as the sign of the future by the High Tamil.

2. *The more Distinctive Future.*—In modern Canarese this constitutes the second form of the future, in consequence of being less used than the other. It is formed by inserting *iy*, or *î*, or *d*, between the theme and the pronominal signs, and lengthening the vowel which immediately follows this future particle—viz., the initial vowel of the pronoun—*e.g.*, *mâḍ-iy-ênu*, I will do, or *nuḍi-d-ênu*, I will say. In Telugu also, this future assumes a twofold form, from the optional use of two inserted particles, corresponding to the *iy* or *î*, and *d* of the Canarese. One form inserts *ê* between the theme and the pronominal terminations—*e.g.*, *chês-ê-nu*, I will do—which *ê* is optionally changed to *î*, in the third person neuter plural—*e.g.*, *chês-î-ni*, they (neut.) will do. The other form of the future, which is still more rarely used, inserts *eda*—*e.g.*, *chês-eda-nu*, I will do—except in the third person singular, and the third person neuter plural, in which *eḍi* is used instead of *eda*—*e.g.*, *chês-eḍi-ni*, they (neut.) will do.

Affinities of the Sign of the Future.—The most characteristic and most extensively used sign of the future in the Dravidian tongues, is evidently the *v* of the Tamil, Canarese, and Tuḷu. It is remarkable that in Bengali and Oriya, and also in Bhojpuri Hindi, the sign of future time is *v*, pronounced *b*—*e.g.*, *râkhiba*, Beng. I will preserve; in Oriya, *râkhibi;* in Bhojpuri Hindi, *râkhab*—and this *b* has been connected by Max Müller with the *b* or *bo* which forms the most characteristic sign of the Latin future, and which is considered to be a relic of an old substantive verb. The *d* of the Dravidian preterite seemed to have so wide a range of affinities both in Europe and Asia, that it need not be considered impossible, though I can scarcely consider it probable, that the Dravidian futuric *v* also should possess some ulterior affinities. The nearest resemblances are those of the Ugrian languages. In Finnish, *wa* or *va* is the sign of the future participle which is used as an auxiliary in the formation of the future tense—*e.g.*, *ole-va*, about to be; and the sign of the future infinitive is *van*— *e.g.*, *ole-van*, to be, to be about to be; with which we may compare the Tamil future verbal participle in *vân*. In Hungarian, the future participle is formed by suffixing *vô*—*e.g.*, *lê-vô* (Finnish *ole-va*) being or about to be. If I am right, however, in considering the Dravidian future in *v*, *b*, *p*, as a verbal noun originally, and the signs of the future as the ordinary formatives of verbal nouns, all such Indo-European and Scythian resemblances must be regarded as merely accidental.

4. Compound Tenses.—It is unnecessary to enter into an investigation of the Dravidian compound tenses, inasmuch as in all the dialects, except the Tuḷu and Gônd, they are formed in the simplest possible manner, by suffixing the various tenses of the substantive verb to the verbal participles of active verbs. Thus 'doing I was' will represent the imperfect (also 'doing I came'); 'doing-keeping' (*i.e.*, keeping a doing) 'I was,' a more continuative imperfect; 'having done I am,' the perfect; 'having done I was,' the pluperfect; 'having done I shall be,' the future perfect. The last two compound tenses are formed in this manner even in Tuḷu and Gônd.

A vast number of auxiliary verbs are used in all the Dravidian dialects, in conjunction with infinitives and verbal participles, for the purpose of expressing compound ideas; but as the use of those auxiliaries pertains rather to the idiom or syntax of the language than to the grammatical structure, and is sufficiently explained in the ordinary grammars, it would be out of place to inquire into them here. (See "Classification of Verbs.")

The Relative Participle.—It is a remarkable peculiarity of the Dravidian languages, that they have no relative pronouns whatever, and that the place of the relative pronoun is supplied by a part of the verb which is called the relative participle, or the adjective participle, a participle which is invariably followed by a noun, and preceded by the words or phrases that depend upon the relative.

The vernaculars of Northern India have relative pronouns derived from the Sanskrit relatives *yah*, *yâ*, *yad*, who, masc., who, fem., which, neut.; but of those pronouns they make little use, probably through an under-current of Dravidian, or at least of Præ-Sanskrit, influences. In those languages a sentence which contains a relative is ordinarily divided into two members; and the demonstrative pronoun which forms the nominative of the second member of the sentence, is used instead of a relative. Thus instead of saying, the man who came yesterday has come again to-day, they would prefer to say, a man came yesterday, he is come again to-day. The Dravidian languages sometimes make use of a similar idiom, but only in the hurry of conversation. They are not obliged to have recourse to any such arrangement, the signification of the relative, together with that of the definite article, being contained in, and distinctly expressed by, the relative participle of the verb. Thus they would say in Tamil, *vanda-âḷ*, the person who came, literally, the-who-came person. In like manner they might use the present relative participle—*e.g.*, *varugira âḷ*, the-who-is-coming person, or the future *varum âḷ*, the-who-will-come person.

The name given to the relative participle by Tamil grammarians, is *peyar echcham*, noun-defect, or noun-complement—*i.e.*, a word which requires the complement of a noun to complete its signification. This name is given to it because it participates so largely in the nature of an adjective that it is invariably followed by a noun, to which it stands in the relation of a relative, and which it connects with the antecedent clauses. Like other Dravidian adjectives, it undergoes no alteration on account of the number or gender of the related noun; but inasmuch as it is a verb as well as an adjective (*i.e.*, a participle participating in the nature of both parts of speech), it is capable of governing a preceding noun, equally with any other part of the verb to which it belongs—*e.g.*, *nûlei eṛudina pulavan*, Tam. the poet who wrote the book, literally, the-who-the-book-wrote poet; *kâṭṭil tirigira yânei*, Tam. the elephant that wanders in the jungle, literally, the-that-in-the-jungle-wanders elephant.

The relative suffix most largely used in the Dravidian languages is *a*, which is appended to the verbal participle or gerund, to convert it into a relative participle. Thus in Tamil, the (assumed) present verbal participle of *uṛu*, to plough, is *uṛu-gir*, ploughing; from which, by suffixing *a*, is formed the present relative participle *uṛugir-a*, that ploughs. The preterite verbal participle of the same verb is *uṛu-d-u*, having ploughed (of which the final *u* is merely enunciative), from which by the addition of the same *a*, is formed the preterite relative participle *uṛud-a*, that ploughed. When the preterite verbal participle ends, not in *d-u*, but in *i*, *n* (or more elegantly *y*) is euphonically inserted between the concurrent vowels *i* and *a*—*e.g.*, from *eṛud-i*, having written, is formed *eṛud-i-(n)-a*, or *eṛud-i-(y)-a*, that wrote. In all these particulars Malayâḷam perfectly agrees with Tamil. The future relative participle of Tamil is not formed from *a*, but terminates in *um*, and is identical with the aoristic future third person singular neuter. This is also the form of the future relative participle almost invariably used in Malayâḷam.

Canarese has in this point the advantage not only of Tamil, but generally of the other dialects; inasmuch as it forms its future relative participle by affixing the same *a*—*e.g.*, *mâḍu-v-a*, *bâl-v-a*, or *bâḷu-v-a*, which will live. On the other hand, the relative participle of the present tense in Canarese is defective, being formed by means of the relative participle of the future used as an auxiliary—*e.g.*, *bâḷ-utt-iruva*, which lives, literally, which will be living. The preterite relative participle is formed, like that of Tamil, by suffixing *a*; the only difference is, that between the final *i* of the verbal participle and the relative *a*, *d* is inserted euphonically instead of *y* or *n*—*e.g.*, *mâḍ-i-(d)-a*, which did, from *mâḍ-i*, having done. Telugu agrees with Tamil in forming its present and preterite relative participles by suffixing *a*, and in inserting *n* between the *i* in which the preterite verbal participle of that dialect invariably ends, and the relative *a*—*e.g.*, from *avu-tu-nnu*, becoming, is formed *avu-tu-nn'-a*, that becomes; and from *ay-i*, having become, is formed *ay-i-(n)-a*, that became. The suffix of the relative participle of the negative voice of the verb is *a* in Tamil, Malayâḷam, and Canarese, in Telugu it is *ni*. It is now evident that *a* may be regarded as the characteristic relative suffix of the Dravidian languages. The only exceptions are *ni*, the negative relative suffix of the Telugu; the suffix of the aoristic future relative in several of the dialects—viz., *ni* in Ku, *um* in Tamil, and *eḍu*, *eḍi*, *ê*, or *êṭi* in Telugu; and *ti* the sign of the preterite relative participle in Ku. The relative participles of Tuḷu do not appear to differ from its verbal participles.

Not only are the greater number of relative participles formed by suffixing *a*, but, as was observed in the section on "The Noun," most Dravidian adjectives also receive the same suffix. Ultimate nouns of quality or relation are capable of being used as adjectives, without any change or addition—*e.g.*, *siṟ-u*, small, *per-u*, great; but more commonly these nouns are converted into quasi relative participles, and rendered thereby more convenient for use as adjectives—*e.g.*, *siṟ-i-(y)-a*, small, *per-i-(y)-a*, great. The preterite relative participles of regular verbs are also frequently used as adjectives—*e.g.*, *uyar-nd-a*, high, literally, that was high, *tâṛ-nd-a*, low, literally, that was low. Tamil adjectives like *per-i-(y)-a*, agree so exactly with preterite relative participles like *paṇṇ-i-(y)-a* (for *paṇṇ-i-(n)-a*), which made, that they may safely be regarded as preterite relative participles in form, though unconnected with the preterite or any other tense in signification, and grammatically explained as relative participles of appellatives or conjugated nouns. Another class of Tamil adjectives receive the suffix of the future or aorist relative participle—*i.e.*, *um*, which is suffixed like *i-(y)-a*, to the crude noun of quality—*e.g.*, *per-um*, great, *paś-um*, green. There is no difference in meaning between these two classes of adjectival formatives, the use of the one rather than the other being determined solely by euphony or usage; but on the whole *um* is considered more elegant than *i-(y)-a*. (See "Adjectives," p. 208.)

Origin of the Relative Suffixes.—The Tamil aorist or future suffix *um*, has already been shown to be identical with the conjunctive or copulative particle. I regard all the other relative suffixes as originally signs of the *inflexion*, or possessive case-signs, expressing the signification of, endowed with, possessed of, having, which has, &c. In the older Scythian languages, a relative participle is used, as in the Dravidian languages, instead of a relative pronoun. Japanese also has no relative pronoun, but uses a relative participle instead in a truly Scythian manner. The existence of a family likeness in so remarkable a particular tends to show the existence of some family relationship between the Scythian group and the Dravidian. The particle which is affixed in the Scythian languages for the purpose of forming a relative participle out of a verbal participle, is identical with the sign of the possessive case. In Manchu this particle is *ngge* or *ninge* (corresponding to the Turkish *ning*); and the addition of this possessive case-sign converts the verbal participle (*i.e.*, the theme with the tense-sign attached) into a verbal adjective or relative participle, precisely as in Tamil or Canarese. Thus in Manchu, from *aracha*, written, which is the verbal participle of *ara*, to write, is formed the relative participle *aracha-ngge*, which wrote, literally the-written-having. Compare in Mongolian *bi omsihu-ne bichig*, the book I am reading, in which phrase *ne* has the same force as *a* in Tamil, being in itself a possessive, and converting the verbal participle to which it is appended into a relative participle. *bi* is I; *bichig*, book. Hence the literal meaning, as in the Tamil *nân vâśikkindr-a nûl*, is 'the I reading-having book.' The Chinese construction is similar. *Wo nien-ti shu* means the book I am reading. *ti* is the sign of the possessive, and is added to *nien*, read. The relative participle in these languages is simply the verb in the possessive case; and the fact that it has a case shows that, *pro tanto* at least, it is treated as a noun. Mr Edkins remarks:—"The Turanian intellect nominalises the verb. Every verb is looked at as a substantive." This holds true of the Dravidian languages also to a considerable extent. The Dravidian relative participle is treated, as we have seen, as a noun; and if the verbal participles had not been regarded as nouns, they could not have been converted, as they are, into relative participles by the addition of the sign of the possessive case. It will be seen also that the infinitive is a verbal noun, and that the neuter participial noun is identical with the third person singular neuter of the verb. The only light that has ever been thrown on the Dravidian relative participle is that which emanates from the non-Aryan languages of Asia.

Mr Edkins illustrates the possibility of the same form of a word being used even in the Indo-European languages, both as a preterite and as a possessive adjective, somewhat after the Dravidian style, by the use of the words 'horned' in the English 'horned cattle.' In this case, however, the *ed* is not a sign of the possessive case. The language of the Scythian tablets of Behistun has a relative suffix, *pi*, answering to the Mongolian *ki*, which is appended, as in the Dravidian languages, to the theme in the formation of relative participles.

Looking at the analogy of the Scythian languages, and at the genius of the Dravidian languages themselves, I have no doubt that *a*, which forms the most common Dravidian relative suffix, is identical with *a*, the oldest and most characteristic sign of the possessive case. The other particles also which are used as suffixes of the relative will be found to have a similar nature. Dr Gundert identifies the *a* of the relative participle with the demonstrative base *a*. But I still prefer the explanation I have given, unless, indeed, we feel warranted in going a step further, and regarding the use of *a* as a possessive as a secondary use of the demonstrative *a*.

Though the sign of the relative participle in Ku differs from that which prevails in the other dialects, yet *ni*, the sign of the aorist relative participle, is identical with the sign of the *inflexion* or possessive case, which is also *ni*. *ṇi*, the sign of the negative relative participle in Telugu, appears to bear the same relation to *ni*, a sign of the Telugu inflexion. *ti*, the sign of the preterite relative participle in Ku, is the most commonly used sign of the inflexion in Telugu; and the various suffixes of the Telugu aorist relative participle are apparently adjectival formatives, corresponding in origin to *ti*, the sign of the neuter inflexion in the same language.

Though the use of a relative participle, instead of a relative pronoun, is characteristic of the Scythian tongues, yet both the Turkish and the Finnish languages possess a relative pronoun as well. The use of such a pronoun seems foreign to the grammatical structure of those languages, and is reasonably supposed to have been imitated from the usage of languages of the Indo-European stock. It is certain that Turkish has been much influenced by Persian; and Oriental Turkish, though it has borrowed from Persian a relative pronoun, rarely uses it, and ordinarily substitutes for it an appended particle of its own, in a genuinely Scythian manner.

FORMATION OF MOODS.

The investigation of the structure of the Dravidian verb may now be considered as completed; for in each dialect of the family the verb has, properly speaking, only one mood, the indicative; and the forms which correspond to the conditional, the imperative, and the infinitive moods of other languages, are verbal nouns or compounds, rather than moods. Nevertheless, it is desirable at this point to inquire into the manner in which those moods are formed.

(1.) *The Conditional or Subjunctive.*—In most of the Indo-European languages, and even in Turkish and Finnish, the subjunctive is a regularly conjugated mood, distinct from the indicative, with pronominal terminations of its own. In the Dravidian languages the subjunctive is generally formed by simply postfixing to different parts of the verb, either a particle corresponding in meaning to *si*, or 'if,' or the conditional forms of the substantive verb, which includes the same particle, and which signifies if it be. Different particles are used for this purpose in the different dialects, and they are not in each dialect suffixed to the same part of the verb; but the principle on which they are suffixed, and the use to which they are put, are the same in all.

In Canarese the conditional particle is *re*. This is supposed by Dr Gundert to be abbreviated from *âre* (Tam. and Mal. *âru*, a way). He compares Canarese *banda-re*, when he has come, with Malayâḷam *vanna-(v)-âre*, commonly *vann'âre*, literally in the way of his having come, that is, in the event of his having come. Classical Tamil is *vanda-(v)-âru*. *re* is appended to the relative participle of the preterite, and that participle being impersonal, the condition applies, without change of form, to all persons, numbers, genders, and times—*e.g.*, *mâḍida*, that did, on receiving this suffix becomes *mâḍida-re*, if (I, thou, he, she, they, &c.) do, did, or shall do. Person, number, and gender are expressed by the prefixed pronoun, and time by the subsequent finite verb. The use of the relative participle—a form which always requires a noun to complete its signification—shows that *re*, whatever be its origin, is regarded as a noun, and that a closer rendering of the construction would be in the event of (my, your, &c.) doing, more literally in the event that (I, you, &c.) have done (so and so). Canarese adds *rû* or *âgyû* to the relative participle, instead of *re*, when the sense required is that of although. *rû* is *re* with the copulative particle *û* annexed: *âgyû* is *âgi*, having been, with the addition of the same *û*. The use of these participles is in perfect agreement with *âgilum*, &c., in Tamil.

In Tuḷu there are two forms of the conditional; one called by Mr Brigel the conditional, the other the subjunctive. The conditional is a compound tense, formed by appending *v*, the sign of the futuric present, to the perfect participle. Compare *maḷt'de*, I have made, *maḷt'dve* (*maḷt'd-v-e*), I should make. There is a negative conditional in Tuḷu, as there is a negative form of every part of the verb; and this negative conditional appears to be formed by inserting *a* as a particle of negation—*e.g.*, *maḷt'dvaye* (*maḷt'd-v-a-ye*), I should not make. The subjunctive is formed by adding the particle *ḍa*, if (corresponding to the Tamil-Malayâḷam *il*, *âl*, and apparently, like them, a locative in origin), to every person in every tense—*e.g.*, *maḷpuve*, I make; *malpuveḍa*, if I make. The negative of this form of the verb inserts the usual *j* (from the negative *ijji*) of the Tuḷu—*e.g.*, *maḷpu-jeḍa*, if I do not make.

The most essential and ancient form of the Telugu conditional consists in annexing *ina* to the ultimate conjugational base—*e.g.*, *chûch-ina*, if (I, thou, he, &c.) should see. This *ina* appears to be identical with the *in* which is used for the same purpose and in the same manner in Tamil; and as the Tamil *in* is a sign of the locative, signifying in or in the event of, so is the Telugu *ina* or *ni* apparently identical in origin with the *na* or *ni* which Telugu uses as a locative. In Telugu the various conditional particles which are in ordinary use are parts of the substantive verb, more or less regular in form, each of which is used to signify if it be. The particle commonly used for this purpose in the higher dialect is *ê-ni*, the conditional form of the verb *avu*, to be or become,—a form which corresponds to the Tamil *ây-in*, and means, as will be seen, in being—*i.e.*, in the event of being. This particle or auxiliary, *ê-ni*, is appended not to the verbal or relative participle, but to the personal terminations of the verb. It may be appended to any tense, as to any person; but whatever tense it is attached to, the time of that tense is rendered aoristic, and is determined, as in Canarese, by the connection, especially by the tense of the succeeding verb. The manner in which *êni* is postfixed in Telugu exactly corresponds to the use that is made of *âyil*, *âgil*, *âyin*, or *ânâl* in Tamil—*e.g.*, *chêsitin'-êni*, if I did or do (literally if it be (that) I did), and *chêsitim'-êni*, if we did or do, are equivalent to the Tamil *śeydên-âyin*, if I did, and *śeydôm-âyin*, if we did. Some grammarians appear to consider this particle identical with *êmi*, why, and to imply a question; but its resemblance in sound and use to the Tamil *âyin*, if it be, seems too complete to allow of this supposition.

In the colloquial dialect of Telugu, the conditional particle commonly used is simply *ê*, which is suffixed, not to any tense at pleasure like *ê-ni*, but only to the preterite, and is not appended, as *ê-ni* is, to the personal termination, but to the root of the preterite, or as I conceive it to be, the old preterite verbal participle—*e.g.*, *chêsi-t-ê* or *chêst-ê*, if (I, thou, he, &c.) did or do. This *ê* is considered by Mr Clay identical with the interrogative *ê*, interrogative forms being much used in Telugu to express the conditional. Did he do it? is equivalent to if he did it?

Another mode of expressing the conditional mood in the colloquial dialect of Telugu agrees with the Canarese in this, that the particles are suffixed to the relative participle. The particles thus suffixed are *aṭṭ-ayitê* and *aṭṭ-âyenâ;* the first part of both which compounds, *aṭṭ-u,* is a particle of relation meaning so as, as if. *ayitê* (*ayit-ê*) is the ordinary conditional of *avu,* to be, being an emphasised form of *ayi-ti,* the impersonal preterite, or old preterite verbal participle of *avu.* *âyenâ* is the interrogative form of *âyenu,* properly *ayenu,* it was, the third person of the preterite tense of *avu,* literally has it become? Telugu, like Tamil, expresses the meaning of although by adding the conjunctive particle *u* to the conditional particle *ina*—*e.g.*, *chês-ina,* if (I) do; *chês-ina-(n)-u,* although (I) do (= Tam. *śeyd-in, śeyd-in-um*).

In Tamil the most characteristic, and probably the most ancient, mode of forming the conditional mood is by affixing the locative case-signs *il* or *in* to the formed verbal theme—*i.e,* that assumed verbal noun which forms the basis of the infinitive and the aoristic defective future. Thus, from the formed theme *pôg-u,* going, is formed the infinitive *pôg-a,* to go, and *pôg-um,* it will go; and from the same base by the addition of the locative *il* or *in,* is formed the conditional *pôg-il* or *pôg-in,* if (I, thou, &c.) go. From *var-u,* coming, is formed *var-a,* infinitive, to come, *var-um,* it will come, and also *var-il* or *var-in,* if (I, &c.) come. In like manner, from *âg-u,* being, is formed the infinitive, *âg-a,* to become or be, *âg-um,* it will be, and also *âg-il,* if (I, &c.) be. *âg-in* (the equivalent of *âg-il*) has been softened into *ây-in;* and this appears to be identical in origin and meaning with the Telugu *ê-ni* referred to above, and is subjoined to the personal terminations of verbs in the same manner as *ê-ni.* This conditional *il* or *in* is undoubtedly identical with *il* or *in,* the Tamil sign of the ablative of motion, which is properly a sign of the locative, signifying in, at, or on; and of this *in,* the Telugu equivalent, in accordance with dialectic laws, is *ni,* which is also occasionally used as a locative. This being the case, the signification of *âg-il* or *ây-in* is evidently in being, *i.e.,* in the event of being; and this is equivalent to the phrase if it be. Hence *âg-il, ây-in,* and *ê-ni* are well suited to be used as conditional auxiliaries, and appended to the various personal terminations of verbs.

The second mode of forming the conditional in Tamil consists in the use of the above-mentioned conditional forms of the substantive verb, viz., *âg-il* and *ây-in* (and also a commoner form, *ân-âl*) as auxiliaries to other verbs; and when thus used they are postfixed, like the corresponding Telugu *ê-ni,* to any person of any tense—*e.g., śeydên-âgil,* if it be that I did, or if I did, literally in the (event of its) being (that) I did; *śeyvên-âgil,* if I shall do, literally in the (event of its) being (that) I shall do. This mode of forming the Tamil conditional, though not confined to the classics, is but rarely used in the colloquial dialect: it is chiefly used in elegant prose compositions.

A third form of expressing the sense of a conditional mood in Tamil is by appending the particle or noun *kâl* to the past relative participle —*e.g.*, *śêyda-(k)kâl*, if (I, &c.) do or did; *uvari olitta-(k)kâl*, if the sea should roar. The conditional form which is most commonly used by the vulgar is a corruption of this, viz., *śeydàkkâ*, or even *śeydâkki*; and the Ku conditional also is formed by appending *kka*. *kâl* being appended to a relative participle, it is evidently to be considered as a noun; and it may either be the crude Sanskrit derivative *kâl* (for *kâl-am*), time, used adverbially to signify when, a use to which it is sometimes put in Tamil; or, more probably, the pure old Dravidian word *kâl*, one of the meanings of which is a place. In the Malayâḷam locative this is abbreviated to *kal*. All nouns of place, when generalised, are capable of being used as signs of time. Hence *kâl*, a place, comes to mean when, and becomes a means of forming the conditional as readily as *il*, a place. The literal meaning, therefore, of *śeyda-(k)kâl* will be, when (I) do or did, a form which will readily take from the context a conditional force—*e.g.*, in the following Tamil stanza—"When you have done (*śeyda-(k)kâl*) a good action to any one, say not, 'When will that good action be returned?'"—it is evident that when you have done is equivalent to if you have done. The signification of when is still more clearly brought out by the use of *kâl* in connection with the future relative participle—*e.g.*, *śey(y)uṅ-kâl*, if (he, they, &c.) should do, literally when (they) shall do, or in the time when (they) shall do. This mode of expressing the conditional mood is exceedingly common in the Tamil poets.

The fourth Tamil mode of forming the conditional is by suffixing *âl* to the abbreviated preterite relative participle—*e.g.*,*śeyd-âl*, if (I, &c.) do. If we looked only at examples like *śeyd-âl*, we might naturally suppose *âl* to be suffixed to the preterite verbal participle (*śeyd-u*), the final *u* of which is regularly elided before a vowel; and this form of the conditional would then perfectly agree with the second Telugu mode—*e.g.*, *chêst-ê*. If we look, however, at the class of verbs which form their preterite in *i*, and their preterite relative participle in *n-a*, we shall find that *âl* is added to the relative, not to the verbal participle, and that the two vowels (*a* and *â*) are incorporated into one—*e.g.*, the conditional of *âg-u*, to be, is not *âg-i-âl*, but *ân-âl*, evidently from *ân-a* (*âg-i-(n)-a*), that was, and *âl*. Besides, the verbal participle must be followed by a verb or some verbal form; but *âl* is a noun, and therefore the participle to which it is suffixed must be a relative participle, not a verbal one. In colloquial Tamil, *âl* is suffixed to impersonal forms of the verb alone; but in the higher dialect *âl*, or its equivalent *êl*, may be suffixed to any person of any tense—*e.g.*, *śeydanei-(y)-êl*, if thou hast done; *śeyguvên-êl*, if I shall do. It is also suffixed to the relative participle, as I conceive *âl* is in the ordinary dialect—*e.g.*, *śeygindra-(v)-âl*, *śeyda-(v)-âl*, if (I, thou, &c.) should do. This *śeyda-(v)-âl* of the High Tamil illustrates the origin of the more common colloquial form *śeyd-âl*.

This conditional particle *âl*, whatever its origin, seems to be identical with *âl*, the sign of the instrumental case in Tamil. The best supposition respecting the origin of this particle is that of Dr Gundert, who considers it as equivalent to *âgal*, Can. when, which is literally a verbal noun from *âg-u*, to become. *âgal* is capable of becoming *âl* in Tamil, the primitive base of *âgu* being *â*. *âl* is rarely used as a sign of the conditional in the higher dialect in Tamil, in which *kâl* is generally preferred.

One form of the conditional mood is expressed by if (*e.g.*, if I do); another is expressed by though, or although (*e.g.*, though I do, or though I have done). This second form of the conditional is generally expressed in the Dravidian languages by affixing the conjunctive particle to one of the conditional particles already referred to. Thus, in Tamil, *śeyd-âl* signifies if (I, &c.) do; whilst *śeyd-âl-um* signifies though (I, &c.) do. *um*, the conjunctive or copulative particle, having the sense of even, as well as that of and—the literal meaning of this phrase is even if (I) do. The same particle *um* is affixed to the preterite verbal participle to bring out a preterite signification—*e.g.*, *śeyd-um*, though (I, &c.) did, literally even having done.

2. *The Imperative.*—In the Dravidian languages the second person singular of the imperative is generally identical with the root or theme of the verb. This is so frequently the case, that it may be regarded as a characteristic rule of the language. In a few instances in Tamil there is a slight difference between the imperative and the verbal theme; but those instances scarcely constitute even an apparent exception to the general rule, for the difference is caused not by the addition of any particle to the root, for the purpose of forming the imperative, but merely by the softening away of the formative suffix or the final consonant of the theme, for the sake of euphony—*e.g.*, *var-u*, to come, takes for its imperative *vâ*, Tel. *râ*; the plural (or honorific singular) of which is in High Tamil *vammin*, in Telugu *rammu*.

It has been shown that there is a class of Tamil verbs which form their transitives by doubling the initial consonant of the sign of tense. Such verbs also, however, use the simple unformed theme as their imperative, and, in so far as that mood is concerned, make no distinction, except in connection, between transitives and intransitives. Thus, *keḍ-u* is either spoil or be spoiled, according to the connection, whilst every other part of the verb takes a form suited to its signification—*e.g.*, the infinitive of the intransitive is *keḍ-a*, that of the transitive *keḍukk-a*. Telugu, on the other hand, generally makes a distinction between the imperative of the transitive and that of the intransitive—*e.g.*, whilst the intransitive be spoiled, is *cheḍu*, the transitive is not also *cheḍu*, but *cheruchu* (for *cheḍuchu*), a form which would be *keḍukku* in Tamil. A large number of Telugu verbs use as their verbal theme, not the ultimate root, but a species of verbal noun ending in *chu*, *pu*, or *mpu*. This accounts for the presence of *chu*, which is in itself a formative, in the imperative *cheruchu*, and not only in the imperative, but through all the moods and tenses of the Telugu verb. The Tamil uses the equivalent verbal noun (ending in *kku*) as the base of its transitive infinitive, and of the third person singular neuter of the future or aorist of its transitive—*e.g.*, *keḍukk-a*, to spoil, and *keḍukk-um*, it will spoil; but in every other part of the verb it uses the root alone (including only the inseparable formative, if there be one) as its inflexional theme. Hence it is easier to ascertain the primitive, true root of a verb in Tamil than in Telugu.

The particle *mu* or *mî*, is often added to the inflexional base of the verb, or verbal theme, to form the imperative in Telugu. The same practice obtains in Ku; and even in Tamil, *mô* is sometimes suffixed to the singular of the imperative—only, however, in the classical dialect. In Telugu, nevertheless, as in Tamil, the verbal theme is more commonly used as the imperative without the addition of any such particle; and it seems probable that *mu* or *mî*, the only remaining relic of some lost root, is added as an intensitive or precative, like the Tamil *ên*—*e.g.*, *kêḷ-ên*, Oh do hear. *aṇḍi*, which is added to the root in Telugu to form the second person plural of the imperative, is the vocative of an obsolete noun, sirs (used honorifically to mean sir); and the other signs of the same part of the verb in Telugu (*ḍi*, *uḍi*, and *uḍu* or *ḍu*), are evidently abbreviations of *aṇḍi*.

The second person plural of the imperative in Canarese is substantially identical with the second person plural of the future tense—*e.g.*, *mâḍiri*, do ye, *mâḍuviri* or *mâḍîri*, ye will do. The neuter participial noun of the future tense, it will do, or it is a thing to be done, is also optionally used for the imperative both in the singular and plural. In the classical dialect the most common plural imperative is formed by adding *im*, probably a fragment of *nîm*, the pronoun of the second person plural, to the root—*e.g.*, *bâḷ-im*, live ye, *iḷi-(y)-im*, descend ye.

Tuḷu forms its imperative from the future form of the verb in both numbers by appending *la* to the future in the singular and *le* in the plural—*e.g.*, *maḷpula*, make thou, *maḷpule*, make ye. Dr Gundert identifies this *l* with *lâ* (corresponding in meaning to the Tamil *um*), the conjunctive particle of the Tuḷu.

The imperative of the second person plural in colloquial Tamil is identical in form, and possibly in origin, with the aoristic future ending in *um*—*e.g.*, compare *śey(y)-um*, it will do, with *śey(y)-um*, do ye; *vâṛ-um*, it will flourish, with *vâṛ-um*, flourish ye. This form is used honorifically for the singular, and if this use of *um* is derived directly from the use of the same particle as a sign of the future, it would naturally have been used originally for both numbers indiscriminately. I have no doubt that the imperative second person in classical Tamil, to which we shall come presently, was originally a future; but there is some difficulty in the way of concluding the *um* of the colloquial imperative to be identical with the futuric *um*. The futuric *um* is appended, as has been shown, not to the ultimate root of the verb, but to the inflexional base, originally, I conceive, an abstract verbal noun; whereas the *um* of the second person imperative is generally appended directly to the root. This difference does not show itself in those verbs of which the unchanged root itself is used as the inflexional base, such as the two verbs *śey* and *vâṛ*, just adduced; but it appears in that large class of verbs which harden their formatives. Thus, destroy ye, is *keḍ'-um*; but, it will destroy is not *keḍ'-um*, but *keḍukk-um*: be ye is *ir-um*, but it will be is not *ir-um*, but *irukk-um*. Though, therefore, *um* may be, and I have no doubt is, the same *um* in both cases; yet in the imperative, as in the personal pronouns, it seems to be used as a sign of plurality, whilst in the future tense it conveys the meaning of the future. A connection may perhaps be traced between these meanings. *um* always appears to retain its original force as a conjunctive particle; but in the case of the pronouns (and probably in that of the second person imperative), it conjoins person to person—that is, it pluralises, whilst in the future tense of the verb (properly, as has been shown, a continuative tense), it conjoins a present or future action to the past.

The plural imperative of the classical dialect of Tamil is formed by appending to the root the particle *min*, which assumes sometimes the more fully developed, or doubly pluralised, shape of *minîr*. This particle cannot be explained from Tamil alone, but a flood of light is thrown upon it by Malayâḷam. In Malayâḷam the plural imperative is formed after the plan of the first future, both in Tamil and Malayâḷam, by appending to the root a particle which has for its initial letter *v*, *m*, or *p*, according to the connection. Compare the Tamil and Malayâḷam future participle *varu-vân*, about to come, with the Malayâḷam imperative *varu-vin*, come ye; *kâṇ-mân*, about to see, with *kâṇ-min*, see ye; *kêḷ-pân*, about to hear, with *kêḷ-pin*, hear ye. It is clear from this that the imperative is built upon the future, and indeed that it differs from it only by changing the final *ân* to *in*. The Tamil future participle uses *b* instead of *m*, after nasals; on the other hand it uses *m* alone in other connections, whereas Malayâḷam uses *v*, *m*, or *p*—*e.g.*, for the Malayâlam *kêḷ-pin*, classical Tamil uses *kêṇ-min*. A form of the negative imperative occasionally found in the Tamil poets agrees with Malayâḷam in using *p*; it is *aṟpîr* (*al-pîr*), be not. We are therefore warranted in concluding that the Malayâḷam and classical Tamil plural imperative is formed by adding *in* to the future tense, or, perhaps it may be said, by changing *ân* to *in*. This *in* (*îr*, in *aṟpîr*, as above) appears to be a relic of the plural pronoun of the second person, as I have supposed the corresponding classical Canarese *im*, to be. Whatever their origin, the Tamil and Malayâḷam *in* and the classical Canarese *im* appear to be identical.

The possibility of the future forming the basis of the imperative is well illustrated by the example of the Hebrew. Gesenius ("Hebrew Grammar") says, "The chief form of the imperative is the same that lies also at the basis of the future, and which, when viewed as an infinitive, is likewise allied to the noun."

3. *The Infinitive.*—It has been customary in Dravidian grammars, especially in Telugu, to call various verbal nouns infinitives; as the infinitive in *uṭa*, the infinitive in *aḍam-u*, and the infinitive in *êdi*. This use of terms is not sufficiently discriminative; for though each of those forms may be used with the force of a quasi infinitive in certain connections, yet the two first are properly verbal nouns, and the third is a participial noun. Each is capable of being regularly declined, and each possesses a plural. The Telugu *paḍu-ṭa*, is identical with the Tamil *paḍu-dal*, suffering; whilst the infinitive proper, to suffer, is in both languages *paḍ-a*. I have no doubt that the true infinitive was originally a verbal noun also (as in the Scythian languages it is always found to be), and this origin of the Dravidian infinitive will, I think, be proved in the sequel; but the *usus loquendi* of grammatical nomenclature requires that the term infinitive should be restricted to those verbal nouns which have ceased to be declined, which are destitute of a plural, and which are capable of being used absolutely.

In Malayâḷam the future verbal participle *vân*, *mân*, or *pân* is much used, as in classical Tamil, in a manner closely resembling the use of the infinitive. There is a true infinitive however in *a*, identical with that of the Tamil, though in less common use. The Dravidian infinitive, properly so called, is generally formed by suffixing *a* to the verbal theme. This is invariably the mode in which the infinitive is formed in Telugu—*e.g.*, *chêy-a*, to do. Ordinarily in Tamil and Canarese the infinitive is formed in the same manner; but a verbal noun is also much used in Canarese as an infinitive, with the dative case-sign understood or expressed—*e.g.*, instead of *mâḍ-a*, to do, they often say *mâḍ-al-ke* (in the colloquial dialect *mâḍ-ali-kke*), for doing, or (without the case-sign) *mâḍ-al* or *mâḍ-alu*, doing or to do. Similar constructive infinitives are often used in classical Tamil also, instead of the true infinitive in *a*—*e.g.*, *śollaṟku* (*śollal-ku*), for saying, and *śollal*, saying, with the sign of the dative understood, instead of *śoll-a*, to say. There is also another infinitive or honorific imperative in *ga* or *ya* which is much used in classical Tamil and Malayâḷam—*e.g.*, *aṟi-ga*, to know, or mayest (thou) know, *vâḻi-ya*, mayest thou flourish, a form which will be inquired into presently. Notwithstanding these apparent exceptions, *a* is to be considered as the regular and most ancient sign of the infinitive in all the Dravidian dialects except the Gônd and the Tuḷu. The Gônd infinitive is formed by appending *âlle* or *ille* to the root—*e.g.*, *hand-âlle*, to go, *ke-ille*, to call. This form of the infinitive is evidently identical with the infinitive in *al*, which is used as an infinitive, but is properly a verbal noun, in Canarese and classical Tamil. In Tamil, verbal nouns occasionally end in *il*, though *al* is much more common—*e.g.*, *vey-il*, sunshine, literally, a burning, from *vey*, to burn. Tuḷu as usual takes a course of its own, both as to the number and variety of its infinitives, and as to the formatives it uses. It has a first infinitive, a present, an imperfect, and a perfect, all formed by appending *ni* to the participles, and a second infinitive, or supine, formed by appending *ere*—*e.g.*, *bûruni*, to fall, *bûrini*, to have been falling, *bûrudini*, to have fallen; supine *bûriyere*, to fall. Each of these infinitives is furnished also with a negative, but these negative infinitives are formed by means of the infinitives of the substantive verb appended as auxiliaries to the negative participle—*e.g.*, from *bûrande*, perf. participle, having not fallen, is formed *bûrande ittini*, not to have fallen.

Professor Max Müller, noticing that the majority of Tamil infinitives terminate in *ka*, supposed this *ka* to be identical in origin with *kô*, the dative-accusative case-sign of the Hindi, and concluded that the Dravidian infinitive was the accusative of a verbal noun. It is true that the Sanskrit infinitive and Latin supine in *tum* is correctly regarded as an accusative, and that our English infinitive to do, is the dative of a verbal noun; it is also true that the Dravidian infinitive is a verbal noun in origin, and never altogether loses that character;

nevertheless, the supposition that the final *ka* of most Tamil infinitives is in any manner connected with *ku*, the sign of the Dravidian dative, or of *kô*, the Hindi dative-accusative, is inadmissible. A comparison of various classes of verbs and of the various dialects shows that the *ka* in question proceeds from a totally different origin.

The Tamil infinitive terminates in *ga* (*g-a*) only in those cases in which the verbal theme ends in a formative *gu* (*g-u*); and in many instances in which *g* appears in the infinitive (as in the verbal theme) in the ordinary dialect, *v* replaces it in the poets—*e.g.*, *nôga*, to be pained, is not so much used by the classics as *nôva*. *ppa* is also used in the higher dialect instead of *kka*—*e.g.*, *naḍappa*, to walk, for *naḍakka*. These interchanges of the formative consonant, which is the termination of the verbal theme, and to which the infinitival *a* is added, are in perfect agreement with Telugu; and from both it is apparent that *a* alone is the sign of the infinitive. Tamil verbs ending in the formative *g-u* are intransitives; and when they are converted into transitives, the formative is doubled for the purpose of denoting the increased intensity of signification. In such cases the formative *g-u* is converted into *kk-u*; and, accordingly, the infinitive of all such verbs ends in *kk-a*.

Thus, the verb *pô*, to go, takes *gu* for its intransitive formative, and hence its verbal theme is *pô-gu*; from which is formed the aoristic future *pôg-um*, it will go, the verbal noun *pôg-al*, going, and the infinitive *pôg-a*, to go. The corresponding transitive verb is *pô-kku*, to drive away (*gu* being converted into *kku*); and from this is formed in like manner *pôkk-um*, it will drive away, and also the infinitive *pôkk-a*, to drive away. In some instances the intransitive shape of the verb has no formative; and when it is converted into a transitive, the initial consonant of the tense-sign is hardened and doubled—*i.e.*, *gir* becomes *kkir*, *d* or *nd* becomes *tt*, and *v* or *b* becomes *pp*. In such instances the verbal theme on which the infinitive is constructed takes the doubled formative, *kk-u*—*e.g.*, compare *vaḷar-a*, to grow, with *vaḷar-kk-a*, to rear. This formative (*kk*), however, appears not only in the infinitive, but also in the aoristic future *vaḷar-kk-um*, it will rear. A very large number of Tamil verbs, including many transitives, have no formative termination whatever; and the infinitive of such verbs is formed by simply suffixing *a* to the root—*e.g.*, *vâṛ-a*, to flourish, and *kâṇ-a*, to see. In the event of the root of a verb of this class ending in *i* or *ei*, *y* is inserted between the root and the sign of the infinitive—*e.g.*, *ari-(y)-a*, to know; *aḍei-(y)-a*, to obtain. This *y*, however, is clearly euphonic. When an intransitive root is converted into a transitive by annexing *tt-u* to the root—*e.g.*, *tâṛ-tt-u*, to lower, the infinitive simply elides the euphonic *u*, and suffixes *a*—*e.g.*, *tâṛ-tt-a*.

From a comparison of these instances, it appears certain that *a* alone is the normal suffix of the Tamil infinitive, and that the *g* or *kk* which so often appears, belongs to the formative of the verbal theme—not to any suppositious case-sign. What then is the origin of the infinitival suffix *ga*, which is occasionally used in classical Tamil—*e.g.*, *aṟi-ga*, to know, instead of the ordinary *aṟi-(y)-a;* and *śey-ga*, to do, instead of *śey(y)-a?* This form is chiefly used as an optative, or as conveying a wish or polite command—*e.g.*, *nî aṟi-ga*, mayest thou know! It does not follow, however, from this, that it would be correct to regard it as a form of the imperative originally; for the ordinary infinitive in *a* is often used by the poets in the same manner, and not unfrequently even by the peasants. I am persuaded that the *g* of *ga* is simply the usual formative *g* or *g-u* of verbal nouns. The same formative *g* is found to be used by the poets in connection with other parts also of the very verbs which are given as examples of this rule. Thus, not only is *aṟi-ga*, to know, used instead of *aṟi-(y)-a*, but *aṟi-g-il-ir*, you know not, instead of *aṟi-(y)-il-îr*, or *aṟi-(y)-îr;* and just as *śey-ga*, to do, is used instead of *śey(y)-a*, so we find *śey-gu-v-ên*, I will do, instead of *śey-v-ên*. The *g* which makes its appearance in these instances, is in its origin the formative *g-u*, as appears by the second example; but has come to be used rather for euphony than any other cause. It is also to be noticed that the formative *gu* may be appended to any verbal root whatever, as a fulcrum to the inflexional forms, provided only that the euphony is improved by it, or that the prosody requires it. This view of the origin of the *ga* in question is confirmed by the evidence of Malayâḷam, for in that dialect *ga* is the formative of verbal nouns, answering to the Tamil *gei*—*e.g.*, *chey-ga*, a doing; and yet the very same form is used as a polite imperative—*e.g.*, *nî chey-ga* (Tam. *śey-ga*), mayest thou do! Here we see not only a verbal noun used as an imperative, but we see the infinitive of one dialect treated as a verbal noun in another. The Tamil verbal noun which directly answers to the Malayâḷam *chey-ga*, a doing, is *śeygei;* and *śey-ga* in Tamil has ceased to be used as a verbal noun, and been restricted to the use of an infinitive and imperative; but it is evident from the identity of both with the Malayâḷam *chey-ga*, that both are verbal nouns in origin. The Malayâḷam *chey-ga* is regularly declined—*e.g.*, *chey-ga(y)-âl*, through the doing. We thus come back to the conclusion that *a*, not *ga*, is the true infinitival suffix of the Tamil.

On examining the Telugu, we shall find that the only sign of the infinitive recognised by that language is *a*. The various formatives which, as we have seen, are inserted between the Tamil verbal root and the suffixes of the infinitive, form in Telugu part of the verbal theme itself, and are found not only in one or two connections, but in every mood and tense of the verb, including the imperative. In Telugu, therefore, the only difference between the imperative and the infinitive is, that the latter elides the enunciative *u* of the former, and substitutes for it its own distinctive suffix *a*. Thus, whilst the imperative of the verb to open, is in Tamil *tira*, and the infinitive *tira-kk-a;* the formative *kk* which appears in the Tamil infinitive, and which might be supposed to form part of the infinitival suffix, appears in Telugu (in its dialectically softened form of *ch*) not only in the infinitive, but also in the imperative and throughout the verb—*e.g.*, *tera-ch-a*, infinitive, to open; *tera-ch-u*, imperative, open thou. At the same time, the Telugu sign of the dative case *ku* or *ki* is never softened into *ch* in any connection; consequently, there is no possibility of connecting the Telugu sign of the infinitive with that of the dative. Moreover, the formative *ch* is often replaced, especially in the imperative and infinitive, by *p*—*e.g.*, *naḍu-p-a*, infinitive, to walk, instead of *naḍu-ch-a*, corresponding to the colloquial Tam. *naḍa-kk-a*, and the classical Tam. *naḍa-pp-a*, of which the imperative and also the theme is *naḍa*. Hence, it cannot be doubted that the Tamil *ġ* and *kk*, and the corresponding Telugu *ch* and *p*, alternating (after *i*) with *ñch* and *mp*, are merely formatives, without any special connection with the suffix of the infinitive, which is *a* alone. In most instances in Canarese the formatives referred to above are discarded altogether, and the *a* which constitutes the sign of the infinitive is suffixed to the crude verbal root. Thus, whilst the verb *ir-u*, to be, takes *iru-kk-a* for its infinitive in Tamil, the simpler and evidently more primitive Canarese infinitive is *ir-a*.

Origin of the Infinitive Suffix 'a.'—I conceive that we may safely identify this *a* with the demonstrative base. We have seen that most of the formatives of nouns were originally demonstratives, appended to nouns for the sake of emphasis. To this class belongs especially the formative *am* ($a + m$), which sometimes assumes the shape of *an* ($a + n$), and also that of *al* ($a + l$). We have seen that *al*, that, and *al*, not, appear to have been derived from *a*, *al* being the secondary form constituting the word a substantive, and *a* the primitive base. The same explanation seems perfectly to suit the infinitive in *a* or *al;* and whether the negative *a* may safely be derived from the demonstrative *a* or not, I can see no reason for thinking it improbable that the *a* which forms the suffix of the infinitive, and which is consequently to be regarded as the formative of a verbal noun, was originally identical with the demonstrative.

There cannot be any doubt, I think, that *al*, the alternative suffix of the infinitive, is a secondary form of *a*.

Use of the Infinitive.—By Tamil grammarians it is defined to be "the verbal participle common to the three tenses;" but if we look at its force and use, we shall discover, I think, conclusive reasons for regarding it as a verbal or participial noun. It is not only used as in other languages to denote a purpose or end—*e.g.*, *var-a (ś)śollu*, tell (him) to come—but also in such connections as the following:—(1.) The majority of Dravidian adverbs are infinitives of neuter verbs—*e.g.*, he knocked down, would be in Telugu *paḍa goṭṭenu*, in Tamil *viṛa (t)taḷḷinân;* in which phrases down means to fall—*i.e*, so as to fall. Through the same idiom *âg-a*, the infinitive of the verb to become (in Tel. *kâ* or *gâ*), is ordinarily added to nouns of quality to convert them into adverbs—*e.g.*, *nandr'-âga*, Tam. well, from *nandr-u*, good, and *âg-a*, to become. (2.) The infinitive is elegantly used with an imperative signification (in accordance with the Hebrew idiom), or rather as an optative, seeing that it conveys a wish rather than a command—*e.g.*, *nî vâṛ-a* (more frequently *vâṛ-g-a* or *vâṛi-y-a*), mayest thou flourish! The infinitive of the verb to be, also regularly forms an optative, or polite imperative, by being annexed to the future tense of any verb—*e.g.*, *śeyvây-âga*, mayest thou do, from *śeyvây*, thou wilt do, and *âga*, to become, literally may it be (that) thou wilt do. (3.) It is used as a kind of ablative absolute—*e.g.*, *poṛudu viḍind' irukk-a*, *ên tûngugiray*, Tam., the sun having arisen, why sleepest thou? In this instance, *viḍind' irukk-a* (literally to be—having arisen) is in the perfect tense; but *irukk-a* is not a preterite infinitive, but is the ordinary or aorist infinitive of the verb *ir-u*, to be. (4.) A series of infinitives is often elegantly used, somewhat as in Latin, to express minor actions that take place contemporaneously with the principal action—*e.g.*, they would say in Tamil *mugil eṛumba* (whilst the clouds were rising), *vânam iruḷ-a* (whilst the sky was gathering blackness), *maṛei poṛindu pey(y)a* (whilst the rain was falling abundantly), *ûrâr tiru-viṛâ naḍattinârgaḷ* (the villagers celebrated their sacred festival). (5.) The reduplication of any infinitive expresses exactly the force of the Latin gerund in do—*e.g.*, *pôg-a pôg-a*, *balaṅ koḷḷum*, vires acquirit eundo; more closely, as it goes—as it goes (literally to go—to go) it gathers strength.

These illustrations prove that the Dravidian infinitive has the force of a gerund or verbal participle, or of a verbal noun, as well as that of the infinitive properly so called. The examples adduced are all from Tamil, but parallel examples could easily be adduced from each of the other dialects.

Much use is made in Tamil of a verbal or participial noun ending in *dal*—*e.g.*, *alei-dal*, a wandering, from *alei*, to wander; *muṟi-dal*, a breaking, from *muṟi*, to break. In Canarese the final *l* of those and similar verbal nouns is unknown—*e.g.*, *ale-ta*, a wandering; *mura-ta*, a breaking. In Telugu also such nouns end in *a* alone, without *l*—*e.g.*, compare the Tamil *mêy-(t)tal*, pasturage, with the corresponding Telugu *mêt-a*; *chêt-a*, Tel. an act, with *śey-dal*, Tam.; and *naḍa-ta*, Tel. walk, conduct, with *naḍa-(t)tal*, Tam. Even in Tamil also, *naḍa-(t)tei* (Mal. *naḍa-tta*) alternates with *naḍa-(t)tal*.

It has already been stated that the verbal noun in *al*, with or without the dative case-sign, is used instead of the infinitive in *a* in both dialects of Canarese and in classical Tamil. In Gônd also, it has been shown that one of the signs of the infinitive is *âlle*, amplified from *al*—*e.g.*, *aiâlle*, to be, which is evidently identical with the Tamil verbal noun *âgal*, being—a form often used in the higher dialect as an infinitive. Now, as the Dravidian infinitive undoubtedly partakes of the character of a participial or verbal noun, and is considered by native grammarians as a verbal participle or gerund of the three tenses, as it is certain that it is intimately associated with a verbal noun in *al*, one of the most characteristic in the language, and which denotes not the abstract idea of the verb, but the act; and as *al* in other connections has been found to be amplified from *a*, we seem to be justified in coming to the conclusion that *a*, the infinitive suffix, is the basis of the *al* in question, and, consequently, that *âg-a*, to be, is simply an older and purer form of *âg-al*, being.

There is a remarkable, but probably accidental, resemblance to the Dravidian infinitive in *al*, in the Armenian, in which *l* is the infinitive suffix—*e.g.*, *ber-e-l*, to carry (compare Tam. *poṟ-al*, bearing or to bear); *ta-l*, to give (compare Tam. *ta(r)-al*, giving or to give, imperative, *tâ*).

FORMATION OF VERBAL NOUNS.

Dravidian verbal nouns divide themselves into two classes—viz., participial nouns, which are formed from the relative participle of each tense, and retain the time of the tense to which they belong, and verbal nouns, properly so called, which are always formed directly from the theme, and are indeterminate in point of time.

1. *Participial Nouns.*—The greater number of nouns of this class are formed by suffixing the demonstrative pronouns, or their terminations, to the present and preterite relative participles—*e.g.*, from *śeygiṟa*, that does (the present relative participle of *śey*, to do), is formed *śeygiṟa-(v)-an*, he that does; *seygiṟa-(v)-aḷ*, she that does, &c.

In like manner, from the past relative participle *śeyda*, that did, is formed *śeyda-(v)-an*, he that did; *śeyda-(v)-aḷ*, she that did, &c.; and by simply adding the appropriate terminations, participial nouns of any number or gender (but always of the third person only) may be made at pleasure. A similar series of future participial nouns exists, or may be constructed if required—*e.g.*, *ôduvân*, he who will read, or who is accustomed to read. The Tamil future in *v* or *p* is destitute of a relative participle; but its existence is implied in that of future participial nouns, like *pôva-du*, that which will go, and *kâṇba-(v)-an*, he who will see, and must have ended like the future relative participle of the Canarese, in *va* or *pa*. The Tamil aoristic future in *um*, though a relative participle as well as a future tense, forms no participial nouns, probably in consequence of *um* being in reality a conjunctive particle, not a true suffix of relation. Negative participial nouns of each number and gender are formed exactly like the affirmative participial nouns, by suffixing the various demonstrative terminations to the negative, instead of the affirmative, relative participle. These participial nouns are declined like other nouns; nevertheless, being parts of the verbs, they have the same power of governing nouns as the verbs to which they belong—*e.g.*, *vîṭṭei (k)kaṭṭinavanukku*, to him who built the house. In these respects all the Dravidian dialects are so perfectly agreed that it is needless to multiply quotations.

There is a peculiarity about the words used as neuter participial nouns in Tamil which requires to be noticed. Each of them is used in three different significations, viz.—as the third person neuter of the verb, as a neuter relative-participial noun, and as a verbal-participial noun. Thus *śeygiṟadu* in the first connection means it does; in the second, that which does; in the third, the doing or to do. I have termed it in the third connection "a verbal-participial noun," to distinguish it from the ordinary verbal nouns, which are formed from the theme, not from participles, and from which the idea of time is excluded. It is a verbal noun in use, though participial in origin. I am persuaded that of these three senses the original and most correct one is the last—viz., that of the verbal-participial noun; for the relative-participial noun ought by analogy to be *seygiṟa-(v)-adu*, not *śeygiṟ-adu;* and whilst it is certain that a participial or verbal noun might easily be used as the third person neuter of the verb, in accordance with the analogy of many other languages, it is difficult to see how the third person neuter of the verb could come to be used so regularly as it is as a verbal-participial noun. This species of participial noun, though neuter or without personality, includes the idea of time. It has three forms, in accordance with the present, the past, and the future tenses of the verb—*e.g.*, *śeygiṟadu*, the doing; *śeydadu*, the having done; and *śeyvadu*, the being about to do. Each of these forms may be pluralised, as far as usage permits, when it is used as the third person neuter of the verb, or as a relative-participial noun; but when used abstractly as a verbal-participial noun it is not pluralised. The participial noun formed from the future is one of the most commonly used forms of the verbal-noun in Canarese—*e.g.*, *iḷiyu-v-adu*, or *iḷivu-du*, the act of descending, from *iḷi*, to descend.

Words of this kind have sometimes been called infinitives; and it is true that they may generally be rendered in the infinitive on translating them into English—*e.g.*, *appaḍi seygiṟadu sari* (*y*) *alla*, Tam. (it is) not right to do so. But this is simply because the English infinitive itself is sometimes used as a verbal noun, and to do is equivalent to the participial noun, the doing. The phrase might be more closely rendered, the doing thus (is) not right. Verbal nouns of this class become more allied to infinitives when they are put in the dative—*e.g.*, *seygiṟadu-kku*, for the doing—*i.e.*, to do. As the pronoun *adu* becomes in construction *adan*, so *śeygiṟadan-ku*, euphonically *śeygiṟadaṟ-ku*, is more common in written compositions, and considered more elegant, than *śeygiṟadu-kku*.

Tamil and Malayâḷam alone possess an abstract relative-participial noun, expressing in the form of a declinable participle the abstract idea denoted by the affirmative verb. It is formed by appending *mei* (Mal. *ma*), the suffix of abstracts, to the present or preterite relative participle of any verb—*e.g.*, from *irukkindr-a*, 'that is' (the present relative participle of *iru*, to be), by the addition of *mei*, Tamilians form *irukkindra-mei*, being. Negative nouns of this description are also formed in Tamil by appending *mei* to the negative relative participle—*e.g.*, *irâ-mei*, the not being. These negative participial abstracts are in more common use in Tamil than the affirmatives, and are as largely used in Malayâḷam and Telugu as in Tamil. The use of the Tamil affirmative *mei* is confined to classical compositions; but the abstract appellative *nouns* which are formed by annexing *mei* to the crude verbal theme (*e.g.*, *poṟu-mei*, patience, from *poṟu*, to bear) are much used even in the colloquial dialect of Tamil, as well as in Malayâḷam and all the other dialects in a slightly altered shape. The relative-participial noun in *mei*, whilst it is declined like a noun, has the governing power of a verb; but the corresponding appellative in *mei* has the force of a substantive only.

The Tamil suffix *mei* is *ma* in Malayâḷam, *me* in Canarese, *mi* in Telugu. In several of the Scythian tongues we find a suffix used which bears a considerable resemblance to this. The suffix of the participial noun in Finnish is *ma* or *mä:* in Esthonian *ma* is the suffix of the infinitive: supines are formed in Finnish by suffixing *man:* the Turkish infinitival suffix is *mak* or *mek.* We may also compare with this Dravidian *me* or *mei,* the old Greek infinitive in *μεν,* and such nouns as *ποίη-μα, δεσ-μό-ς,* and *σχισ-μή,* each of which exhibits an old participial suffix.

2. *Verbal Nouns.*—Dravidian verbal nouns are indeterminate with respect to time, being formed, not from participles, but from the verbal root or the formed theme; and they express the act, not the abstract idea, of the verb to which they belong, and hence are called by Tamil grammarians *toṛil peyar,* nouns of operation or employment. Verbal nouns are carefully to be distinguished from verbal derivatives, or substantives derived from verbs. The latter, though derived from verbs, are used merely as nouns; whereas the verbal noun, properly so called (like the participial noun), is construed as a verb. As a noun it can be used as the nominative of a subsequent verb; and as a verb it may be preceded by a nominative of its own, and may govern a noun in case. In several Dravidian grammars written by Europeans this distinction has not been attended to; and Tamil derivative nouns like *naḍei* or *naḍappu,* walk, have been classed with verbal nouns like *naḍakkei, naḍakkudal,* and *naḍakkal,* walking. Though, however, each of these words may be translated 'walking,' the first two are simply substantives; and adjectives, not adverbs, must be used to qualify them; whereas *naḍakkudal,* the corresponding noun of operation, is a true verbal noun, and is qualified by adverbs, precisely as the verb itself, *naḍa,* to walk, would be. Thus, we can say *nîdi(y)ây naḍakkudal,* acting or walking justly; but we could not use the adverb *nîdi(y)ây* to qualify either *naḍappu* or *naḍei.* It would be necessary to qualify those words by the adjectival form *nîdi(y)âna,* there being nearly the same difference between *naḍappu* and *naḍakkudal* that there is in English between behaviour and behaving.

A verbal noun in *gei* or *kkei* is often used in Tamil—*e.g., irukkei,* the being; *śeygei,* the doing; but though this is used as a verbal noun—*e.g., appaḍi irukkei-(y)-âl,* seeing that it is so, more literally through its being so, yet the forms which are most commonly used as verbal nouns, and which have the best claim to that character, are those which terminate in *al*—*e.g., śey(y)-al,* or *śey-dal,* doing; *naḍakk-al,* or *naḍakkudal,* walking. Whether the suffix appended be *al* or *dal,* it is generally suffixed, not to the crude root, but to the formed verbal theme—*i.e.,* to that which forms the basis of the infinitive and of the aoristic future—*e.g.,* the verbal noun that is formed from *ir-u,* to be, is not *ir-al,* but *iru-kk-al,* being; and from *naḍ-a,* to walk, is formed not *na-ḍ-al*, but *naḍa-kk-al*. Notwithstanding this, *al* or *dal* is sometimes added directly to the ultimate base—*e.g.*, not only have we *pôg-al* or *pôgu-dal*, going, but also *pô-dal;* and not only *âg-al* or *âgu-dal*, becoming, but also *â-dal*. Probably, however, in these instances the right explanation is, that the formative *g* of *pô-gu* and *â-gu* has been softened by use. The *d* of *dal* is clearly a formative of the same character and force as the *g* of *gei* or *kkei;* and this is proved by the circumstance that the *d* is doubled and converted into *tt* when the verb becomes a transitive instead of an intransitive, or when euphonic considerations require—*e.g.*, comp. *kurei-dal*, intransitive, a being curtailed, with *kurei-ttal*, transitive, a curtailing. It is evident that this *d* is not intended in any way to denote the preterite tense; for the verbal noun in *dal* is as indeterminate with respect to time as that in *al* or that in *gei, kkei;* and the corresponding Telugu forms are *ṭa* and *ḍam-u*—*e.g.*, *chêyu-ṭa* or *chêsu-ṭa*, or more commonly *chêya-ḍam-u*, doing. The distinction which has been shown to exist between verbal nouns, properly so called, generally ending in *al*, and derivative nouns, furnishes, I conceive, some confirmation of the hypothesis that *al*, the Tamil suffix of verbal nouns, is a secondary form of *a*, the sign of the infinitive. It is remarkable that *l* or *al* is used also in Mongolian as a formative of verbal nouns—*e.g.*, *c'hidal*, ability, from *chidahu*, to be able.

3. *Derivative Nouns or Verbal Derivatives.*—It seems scarcely necessary to enter into the investigation of the formatives of *verbal derivatives*, or substantives derived from verbs, most of those formatives being merely euphonic, and their number in the various dialects, particularly in Tamil, being very great. It may be desirable, however, to direct the reader's attention to the more characteristic and interesting modes in which the Dravidian languages form nouns of this class.

(i.) The first class of derivative nouns (if indeed it is correct to consider them as *derivatives*) consists in those that are identical with verbal themes—*e.g.*, compare *kaṭṭ-u*, a tie, and *kaṭṭ-u*, to tie.

(ii.) Some verbal themes become nouns by the doubling and hardening of the final consonant—*e.g.*, *eṛutt-u*, a letter, from *eṛud-u*, to write; *pâṭṭ-u*, a song, from *pâḍ-u*, to sing. This is especially a Tamil method of forming derivative nouns, for some of the corresponding Telugu nouns are formed differently; and where they do resemble the Tamil, the resemblance consists only in the hardening, and not also in the doubling, of the final consonant—*e.g.*, *pâṭa*, Tel. a song, from *pâḍ-u*, to sing. Telugu differs also from Tamil in changing the final or enunciative *u* of the verbal root into *a*. Compare *âṭ-a*, play (Tam.

âṭṭ-u), from *âḍ-u*, to play. The Tamil mode of doubling, as well as hardening, the final consonant, seems most in accordance with Dravidian analogy; for it is when a sonant is doubled that it is naturally converted into a surd, and when it is not doubled, it should be pronounced as a sonant.

It is remarkable how many purposes are served by the doubling of Dravidian final consonants. (i.) It places substantives in an adjectival relation to succeeding substantives; (ii.) it converts intransitive verbs into transitives; (iii.) it forms a sign of the preterite tense; and (iv.) it forms derivative nouns from verbal themes.

(iii.) A very interesting mode of forming derivatives is that of lengthening the included vowel of monosyllabic verbal roots—*e.g.*, in Tamil, from *paḍ-u*, to suffer, comes *pâḍ-u*, suffering; from *min*, to glitter, comes *mîn*, a star. Nor is this method found only in the classics: it appears in words of the most familiar class—*e.g.*, *nâkk-u*, the tongue, from *nakk-u*, to lick. Tamil simply lengthens the root vowel in forming derivatives of this class, and leaves the final consonant unchanged; but Telugu and Canarese harden the final consonant, in addition to lengthening the root vowel—*e.g.*, from *paḍ-u*, to suffer, they form not *pâḍ-u*, but *pâṭ-u*, suffering. See the section on "Roots."

4. Abstract nouns are formed from verbal themes by suffixing *mei*—*e.g.*, *poru-mei*, endurance, from *poru*, to bear. The same suffix forms abstracts also from nouns of quality or relation and pronominals—*e.g.*, *peru-mei*, greatness, from *per-u*, great, and *tan-mei*, nature, quality, from *tan*, self, literally self-ness. This suffix is in Telugu *mi*—*e.g.*, *kali-mi*, wealth, from *kalu-gu*, to accrue.

5. Many nouns are formed from verbs in Tamil by suffixing *am*, and at the same time doubling and hardening the final consonant of the verbal theme. *ṅg* being the equivalent of *g*, *nd* of *d*, *ṇḍ* of *ḍ*, and *mb* of *b*, *ṅg* on being doubled becomes *kk*, *nd* becomes *tt*, *ṇḍ* becomes *ṭṭ*, and *mb* becomes *pp*—*e.g.*, from *tûṅg-u*, to sleep, is formed *tûkk-am*, sleep; from *tirund-u*, to become correct, comes *tirutt-am*, a correction; from *tôṇḍ-u*, to dig, comes (I think) *tôṭṭ-am*, a garden; and from *virumb-u*, to desire, comes *virupp-am*, a desire. In most instances the Telugu (and the Canarese always) rejects the final *m* of the nouns of this class—*e.g.*, *tûg-u*, Tel. sleep, instead of the Tamil *tûkk-am*. Though the final consonant, if *g*, *d*, *b* (or their equivalents), is always doubled before this *am* in Tamil and Malayâḷam, verbal themes which end in other consonants often become nouns by simply annexing *am*—*e.g.*, *uyar-am*, height, from *uyar*, to be high, *âṛ-am*, depth, from *âṛ*, to be deep. Mr Edkins connects this *m* with the *m* used in Hebrew

to form participial substantives from verbs—*e.g.*, *mishpat*, judgment, from *shâphat*, to judge. See, however, "Case-signs: the Accusative."

6. A vast number of verbal derivatives in all the Dravidian dialects, are formed by suffixing to the verbal themes those favourite and multifariously used formatives, *g*, *d*, *b*, under various modifications, and with various vowel terminations.

i. The *g* formative generally becomes in Tamil *gei*—*e.g.*, *śey-gei*, an action, from *śey*, to do; it is nasalised to *ṅgei*—*e.g.*, *kâ-(ṅ)gei*, heat, from *kây*, to burn; or it is doubled and hardened into *kkei*—*e.g.*, *paḍu-kkei*, a bed, from *paḍ-u*, to lie. The corresponding Canarese formatives are *ke* or *ge*, with not unfrequently the prefix of an euphonic *i*. The Telugu nouns which take this formative terminate in *ka* or *ki*—*e.g.*, *êli-ka*, government, from *êl-u*, to govern, and *uni-ki*, residence, from *uṇḍu*, to be, to dwell.

ii. The *d* formative is in Tamil *di*—*e.g.*, *keḍu-di*, ruin, from *keḍ-u*, to spoil. Being doubled and hardened it becomes *tti*—*e.g.*, *uṇar-tti*, sensibility, from *uṇar*, to feel, to be sensible. This *tt* is generally softened into *chi*—*e.g.*, *pugaṛ-chi* (instead of *pugaṛ-tti*, in Malayâḷam *pugaṛ-cha*), praise, from *pugaṛ*, to praise. This formative is *t* instead of *d* in Canarese and Telugu. It appears in Canarese under the forms of *ta* and *te*—*e.g.*, *hogaḷ-te*, praise, from *hogaḷ* (Tam. *pugaṛ*), to praise; *kây-ta*, producing fruit, from *kây*, to fruit. In Telugu we find *ta* or *ṭa* and *ti* or *ṭi*—*e.g.*, *alasa-ta*, fatigue, from *alay-u* (*alas-u*), to be tired; *tiṇḍ-i*, food, eating, from *tin*, to eat; *mû-ta*, a lid, from *mû-yu*, to shut; and *naḍi-ti*, conduct, from *naḍu-chu*, to walk.

iii. The *b* formative is in Tamil generally softened into *v*—*i.e.*, *vi* or *vu*—*e.g.*, *kêḷ-vi*, hearing, from *kêḷ*, to hear, and *maṟei-vu*, concealment, from *maṟei*, to conceal. In some instances, however, *b* is euphonised into *mb* (*mbu*)—*e.g.*, *vê-mbu*, the Margosa tree, from *vê-y*, to be umbrageous; *pâ-mbu*, a snake, from *pâ-y*, to spring. *b* cannot retain its proper sound before a vowel, and when single either becomes *v* or *mb*; and that the *vu* which is so common a formative in each Dravidian dialect was softened from *bu*, appears from the circumstance that when it is doubled it becomes *ppu*—*e.g.*, *naḍa-ppu*, a walking, *iru-ppu*, a being, *mû-ppu*, old age. In Telugu this formative is *vu*, *vi*, or *pu*—*e.g.*, *châ-vu*, death, from *cha-chchu*, to die (corresponding Tam. and Can. *śâ-vu*, from *śâ*); *digu-vu*, the bottom, from *dig-u*, to descend; *teli-vi*, understanding, from *teli-yu*, to know; *chêru-pu*, nearness, from *chêr-u*, to draw near; *êḍu-pu*, a weeping, from *êḍu-chu*, to cry (corresponding Tam. *aṛa-ppu*, from *aṛa*). Canarese generally uses in this connection *vu* alone—*e.g.*, *ira-vu*, a being, corresponding to the Tamil *iru-ppu*—

but sometimes it uses also *pu—e.g.*, *biḍu-vu*, or *biḍu-pu*, an open space.

7. A few derivative nouns are formed in Tamil and Malayâḷam by affixing certain particles, originally independent nouns with a meaning of their own, which in process of time have come to be used conventionally. Such derivatives would naturally be considered compounds, were it not that the meaning of the second member of the compound is more or less in abeyance. Thus by suffixing *kaṇ*, the ordinary meaning of which is 'an eye,' but which in the classics means also 'place,' and is the ordinary classical sign of the locative case, Tamil forms *iḍu-(k)kaṇ*, oppression, from *iḍ-u*, to press, also *uṟu-kaṇ*, poverty, from *uṟu*, to suffer. These words are used only in the classical dialect, but there are derivative nouns largely used in the colloquial dialect, which are formed by affixing *pâḍ-u*, a condition of being, from *paḍ-u*, to experience, and *mânam*, perhaps meaning originally likeness, from *mân-u*, to be like, but, as actually used, merely a formative suffix, without any very definite meaning of its own—*e.g.*, *kaṭṭu-(p)pâḍu*, a compact, from *kaṭṭu*, to tie; *śêr-mânam*, junction, from *śer*, to join; also *kaṭṭu-mânam*, building, from *kaṭṭu*, in the sense of 'build.' To these may be added words terminating in *agam*, house, place—*e.g.*, *vânagam* (*vân-agam*) = *vân-am* or *vân*, the sky; *veiyagam* (*vei-(y)agam*) = *vei-(y)am* or *vei*, the earth (from *vei*, to place, *vei-gu*, to rest). I have a suspicion, however, that in these cases the words end simply in *am*, and that *g* is inserted euphonically, as is certainly the case in the colloquial pronunciation of some words—*e.g.*, *andrâḍam*, daily, which is commonly mispronounced *andrâḍagam*; *lanjam* (a word borrowed from Telugu), a bribe, mispronounced *lanjagam*. Dr Gundert derives from this *agam* the Malayâḷam *nâragam*, an orange tree, literally, fragrance-holder, from *nâṟ-u*, Tam.-Mal. to be fragrant, Sans. *nâranga*.

The following will be found, I think, a complete list of Tamil derivative nouns formed by suffixing formative particles. I do not include in this list any participial nouns, whether derived from verbs or from appellatives, or any verbal nouns, properly so called, or any nouns of agency, a class of nouns which will be considered further on. The nouns in the list are derivative substantives; but there are three classes even of these which are not included—viz., nouns which are absolutely identical with verbal roots—*e.g.*, *nîḍu*, length, from *nîḍu*, to be long; nouns which are formed by doubling the final consonant of verbal roots—*e.g.*, *eṛuttu*, a letter, from *eṛudu*, to write; and nouns which are formed by lengthening the included vowel of the verbal root, without any other change—*e.g.* *mîn*, a star, from *min*, to glitter. I include in this last only that class of derivative nouns which are formed by means of an addition to the root. The addition too is not one of an independent word—in which event we should have a new compound noun—but that of a mere particle, a relic doubtless of some old independent word, but at present holding the meaner position of a suffix, either without any meaning at all, or without any definite meaning now discoverable. A very large number of the nouns belonging to this class are used also as verbs. Though verbal derivatives in origin, and still used as such, they have become also secondary verbal themes. I have excluded such nouns as far as possible, retaining only those which are either never used as verbal themes, or at least very rarely. I have preferred also nouns derived, by the addition of a formative, from older nouns, where such could be had, to nouns derived from verbs, for the purpose of keeping the list as clear as possible from verbal nouns, properly so called.

FORMATIVE.	NOUN.	ROOT.
a	*mag-a*, a child.	*mag* (pl. *makkaḷ*).
	śey(y)-a, to do; type of infinitive, probably an old verbal noun.	*śey*, to do.
â	*śur-â*, the shark.	probably *śur-u*, quick.
	viṛ-â, a festival.	*viṛ-i*, to keep awake.
i	*kar-i*, charcoal.	*kar-u*, black.
	śêr-i, a village.	*śêr*, to join.
ei	*pir-ei*, the waxing or waning moon.	*pir*, other, after; *pira*, to be born.
	tol(l)-ei, trouble.	*tol*, old.
gu	*nan-gu*, goodness.	*naḷ* (*nan*), good.
	pira-gu, afterwards.	*pir-a* (=*pin*), after.
ṅgu	*kiṛa-ṅgu*, a root.	*kiṛ-a* (=*kiṛ*), below.
	tî-ṅgu, evil.	*tî*, bad.
kku	*kiru-kku*, craziness.	*kiru-kiru*, giddy.
	koḍu-kku, a sting.	probably *koḍ-u*, crooked, cruel.
gei	*paṇḍi-gei*, a feast.	*paṇḍu*, Tam. ancient; *paṇḍu*, Tel. to be ripe, to be accomplished; ultimate root *par-u*, old.
	tiri-gei, a mill.	*tiri*, to turn.
ṅgei	*kâ-ṅgei*, heat.	*kây*, to burn.
kkei	*paru-kkei*, a pebble, a grain of rice.	*par-u*, large (=*per-u*).
	vâṛ-kkei, felicity (*il-vâṛ-kkei*, domestic life; *il*, house).	*vâṛ*, to flourish.

FORMATIVE.	NOUN.	ROOT.
śi	*pâ-śi*, moss, sea-weed.	*pâ-vu*, to spread.
ñji	*koṛu-ñji*, a shrub.	*koṛ-u*, tender (*koṛu-ndu*, a tender twig).
chchi	*iṟei-chchi*, flesh.	*iṟei*, to flow, issue.
śu	*tari-śu*, fallow land.	*tari*, to remain.
chchu	*amei-chchu*, the office of a minister.	*amei*, to settle.
śei	*poli-śei*, interest.	*poli*, to increase.
ḍi	*pada-ḍi*, chaff.	= *padar*, chaff, the same.
ṇḍi	*kaṟa-ṇḍi*, a spoon, a trowel.	= *kaṟa-ṇei*, the same.
ḍu	*kuṟa-ḍu*, pincers.	*kuṟa-ṇḍu*, to be crooked, from *kuṟ-u*, short.
	kuru-ḍu, blindness.	*kur-u*, tender.
di	*uru-di*, strength.	*ur-u*, to be strong.
ndi	*ôndi*, a lizard.	= *ôdi*, the same.
tti	*paru-tti*, cotton.	*par-u*, to expand.
du	*paṛu-du*, defect.	*paṛ-u*, old.
ndu	*maru-ndu*, medicine.	*mar-u*, sweet-smelling.
ttu	*kuru-ttu*, young shoot of palm.	*kuru*, tender.
dei	*iṛu-dei*, a lie.	*iṛ-u*, to swerve.
ndei	*kuṛa-ndei*, an infant.	*kuṛ-a*, young.
	[Euphonic changes of the formatives *di*, *du*, and *dei*, after consonants.]	
di	*kâṭ-chi* (*kâṇ-di*), a spectacle.	*kâṇ*, to see.
	têr-chchi (*têr-di*), intelligence.	*têr*, to ascertain.
	uṛal-chchi (*uṛal-di*), a whirling	*uṛal*, to whirl.
	nan-dri (*nal-di*), a benefit.	*nal*, good.
	veṟ-ṟi (*vel-di*), victory.	*vel*, to conquer.
	pugaṛ-chchi (*pugaṛ-di*), praise	*pugaṛ*, to praise.
	ât-chi (*âḷ-di*), possession.	*âḷ*, to possess.
	âṭ-ṭi (*âḷ-di*), a woman.	*âḷ*, a person.
du	*toṇ-du* (*tol-du*), *ton-dru* (*tol-du*), } antiquity.	*tol*, old.
dei	*peṭ-ṭei* (*peṇ-dei*), a hen.	*peṇ*, female.
	paraṭ-tei (*paraṇḍ-dei*), shagginess.	*paraṇḍu*, to scratch.
	toṇ-ḍei (*toḷ-dei*), the throat.	*toḷ*, to perforate.
	ûṭ-tei (*ûn-dei*), uncleanness.	*ûn*, flesh.
n	*kaḍ-an*, debt (= *kaḍ-am*).	*kaḍ-u*, harsh? *kaḍ-a*, to pass over.
	aṟ-an, virtue (= *aṟ-am*).	*aṟ-u*, to cut, to define.

FORMATIVE.	NOUN.	ROOT.
bu	*mara-bu*, usage.	*mara*, ancient?
	paṇ-bu, quality.	*paṇ*, fit for use.
	en-bu, a bone.	= *elum-bu*, the same.
mbu	*nara-mbu*, a vein, fibre.	= *nâr*, fibre.
	iḍu-mbu, haughtiness, oppression.	*iḍ-u*, to press.
ppu	*seva-ppu*, redness.	*se*, *sev*, red.
	kaṟu-ppu, blackness.	*kaṟ-u*, black.
ppei	*kala-ppei*, a plough.	= *kala-m*, a vessel.
am	*paṛ-am*, a ripe fruit.	*paṛ-u*, old, mature.
	nal-am, a benefit.	*nal*, good.
	[Illustrations of nouns ending in *am*, which double and harden the final consonant of the root before *am*.]	
g = *kk* + *am*	*âkk-am*, increase.	*âg-u*, to become.
ṅg = *kk* + *am*	*vîkk-am*, a swelling.	*vîṅg-u*, to swell.
ñj = *chch* + *am*	*achch-am*, fear.	*añj-u*, to fear.
ḍ = *ṭṭ* + *am*	*kûṭṭ-am*, a company.	*kûḍ-u*, to join.
ṇḍ = *ṭṭ* + *am*	*tôṭṭ-am*, a garden (= *toḍ-u*).	*tôṇḍ-u*, to dig.
nd = *tt* + *am*	*nîtt-am*, swimming.	*nînd-u*, to swim.
mb = *pp* + *am*	*virupp-am*, a desire.	*virumb-u*, to desire.
âm	*kuṛ-âm*, a company.	*kuṛ-u*, to gather together.
mei	*muṟei-mei*, order.	*muṟei*, a turn.
	ei-mei, closeness.	*ei*, to be close (the number five).
ây	*kuṛ-ây*, a tube.	comp. *kuṛ-i*, a hole.
	pâ-y, a mat.	*pâ-vu*, to spread.
ar	*śuḍ-ar*, brightness.	*śuḍ-u*, to be hot.
	pud-ar, a thicket.	*pud-u*, new, fresh.
âr	*pug-âr*, fog.	*pug-u*, to enter.
ir	*kuḷ-ir*, cold.	comp. *kuḷ-i*, to bathe.
	ug-ir, a finger-nail.	*ug-u*, to shed.
rei	*kudi-rei*, a horse.	*kud-i*, to leap?
	[I do not include amongst the following nouns ending in *al* verbal nouns properly so called, which retain the force of a verb, and may be preceded by a nominative. The nouns I cite as specimens are secondary forms of still more primitive nouns; or else the verbs from which they are formed are uncertain.]	
al	*pei-(y)-al*, a boy (= *peid-al*).	*pei* = *paśu*, green, fresh.
	uḍ-al, the body.	*uḍ-u*, to put on.
	puś-al, a hurricane (= *puyal*).	*puy*, to seize?

FORMATIVE.	NOUN.	ROOT.
	ur-al, a mortal.	= *ur-am*, strength.
	vay-al, a rice field.	*vei*, to place ?
	vaṇḍ-al, sediment at bottom of tanks.	?
alei	*śuḍ-alei*, a burning ground.	*śuḍ-u*, to burn.
	maṛ-alei, childhood.	*maṛ-a*, young.
	viḍud-alei (= *viḍu-ttal*), release).*	*viḍ-u*, to leave.
il	*mug-il*, a cloud.	comp. *mug-iṛ*, to fold up, as a flower its petals.
	toṭṭ-il, a cradle.	= *toṭṭ-i*, a trough.
	viṭṭil, a grasshopper.	*veṭṭ-u*, to cut, to clip ?
ul	*alg-ul*, the female waist.	*alg-u*, to diminish (ultimate base *al*, not).
vi	*kuru-vi*, a small bird.	*kur-u*, small, tender.
vu	*tura-vu*, a large well.	comp. *tuṟei*, a ford.
vei	*iḍa-vei*, a lane.	comp. *iḍ-am*, place.
	paṟa-vei, a large bird.	*paṟ-a*, to fly.
aṛ	*id-aṛ*, a petal of a flower.	?
	ag-aṛ, a fort ditch.	= *agaṛ*, to dig.
aḷ	*ad-aḷ*, skin.	?
uḷ	*ar-uḷ*, grace.	*ar-u*, to trickle down, to be precious.
	por-uḷ, substance, wealth.	*por-u*, to unite with.
uḷei	*ur-uḷei*, a wheel.	= *ur-uḷ*, a wheel.
ṟ*u*	*kiṇa-*ṟ*u*, a well.	= *kêṇ-i*, a well, a mine ?
	*veḷi-*ṟ*u*, paleness.	*veḷ*, white.

4. *Nouns of Agency.*—The participial nouns of the Dravidian languages are largely used as nouns of agency; but such nouns are also formed in each of the Dravidian dialects in a more direct and primitive manner by suffixing *i* to the verbal root—*e.g.*, *uṇ(ṇ)-i* (Tam. and Can.), an eater, from *uṇ*, to eat; *kol(l)-i* (Tam. and Can.), a killer, from *kol*, to kill. The Dravidian languages in borrowing feminine derivative nouns from Sanskrit, change the final *î* of the Sanskrit feminine into short *i*—*e.g.*, *sunda-rî*, Sans. a fair woman, becomes *sundari*. But this final *i* of feminine derivatives, which is directly borrowed

* *Talei*, head, place, is a good deal used in the classical dialect as a sign of the locative case; but the other words ending in *alei*=*al*, seem to show that *viḍudalei* is formed, not from *viḍu-talei*, but from *viḍudal-ei*. The form *viḍudal* is a verbal noun, properly so called, in common use.

from Sanskrit, is not to be confounded with the more distinctively Dravidian *i*, by suffixing which nouns of agency or operation are formed, without reference to gender, whether masculine, feminine, or neuter. It is also to be distinguished from the *i* which in Sanskrit is sometimes used as a suffix of nouns of agency, generally masculines—*e.g.*, *kâr-i-n*, a doer, *kav-i-s*, a poet, literally, a speaker, in borrowing which from Sanskrit, the Dravidian languages invariably reject the sign of the nominative, and use the crude theme (*e.g.*, *kavi*) instead.

Possibly *i*, the Dravidian suffix of nouns of agency, may have sprung from the same origin as the *i* by which similar nouns are sometimes formed in Sanskrit; but it appears certain that it has not been directly borrowed from Sanskrit, and it does not appear even to have been introduced into the Dravidian languages in imitation of it. Its independence of a direct Sanskrit origin will sufficiently appear from the following statement of the manner in which it is used.

(1.) Dravidian nouns of agency formed by suffixing *i*, are destitute of gender; their gender depends entirely upon the connection—*e.g.*, *panei-(y)-êr-i*, Tam. a Palmyra climber (from *panei*, a Palmyra, and *êr-u*, to climb), may be considered as masculine, because men only are climbers of the palmyra; *man-veṭṭ-i*, Tam. a native spade, a hoe (from *maṇ*, the ground, and *veṭṭ-u*, to dig or cut), is in like manner neuter by the necessity of the case; but both these nouns, and all similar nouns, when regarded from a grammatical point of view, are destitute of gender in themselves, and may be applied at discretion to objects of any gender.

(2.) Nouns of agency may be formed in this manner from primitive, underived nouns, as well as from verbal roots—*e.g.*, *nâr-kâl-i*, Tam. a chair, literally that which has four feet, from *nâḻ-u*, four, and *kâl*, a foot.

(3.) When nouns of agency are formed from verbs, the suffix is often added, not to the crude root, but to the conjugational theme, or that form of the root which appears in the infinitive and in the aorist—*e.g.*, *uṇg-i*, Tam. (as well as *uṇ(ṇ)-i*), an eater.

(4.) My chief reason for regarding this suffix as a true and ancient Dravidian form, and as not directly borrowed from Sanskrit, whatever may have been its ulterior relation to it, consists in the very extensive use which is made of nouns of agency formed by means of this suffix, not only in the Tamil classics, but also in the language of the peasantry. It appears in the names of plants and animals, in the names of many of the objects of nature, in old compounds, in proverbs, in nicknames, in the very highest and in the very lowest connections, and to a much larger extent in all these varieties of use, than in Sanskrit itself. The following Tamil examples cannot be supposed to have been derived from Sanskrit precedents :—*kaḷ(ḷ)-i*, euphorbia, from *kaḷ*, toddy, sweet sap ; *veḷ(ḷ)-i*, silver, from *veḷ*, to be white ; *pul-i*, the cheetah, or leopard, from *pul*, small ; *ili*, a person or thing that has nothing, from *il*, not ; *âṛ-i*, the sea, from *âṛ-u*, to be deep. Compare also the following compounds : *vaṛi-kâṭṭ-i*, a guide, literally, a way-shower ; *vânam-bâḍ-i*, the lark, literally the heaven-singer ; *toṭṭâl-vâḍ-i*, the sensitive plant, literally, if (one) touch, the witherer, or as we should prefer to say, touch-me-and-I-wither.

Adverbs.—It is unnecessary in a work of this kind to enter into the investigation of the Dravidian adverbs, for, properly speaking, the Dravidian languages have no adverbs at all. Every word that is used as an adverb in the Dravidian languages is either a noun, declinable or indeclinable, or a verbal theme, or the infinitive or gerund of a verb ; and illustrations of the manner in which those words acquire an adverbial force and of their use will be found in the ordinary grammars of each of the Dravidian dialects. Much use is made in each of the dialects of a peculiar style of adverb formed by means of reiterative, mimetic syllables, to which is added the verbal participle saying, or the infinitive to say, or so as to say. Thus *maḍa-maḍa(v)endru iḍi viṛundadu*, Tam. it thundered terribly, literally, the thunderbolt fell, saying *maḍa-maḍa*. These mimetic adverbs may be invented at pleasure, though some of them are so commonly used that they have acquired a place in dictionaries.

COMPARATIVE PARADIGM OF A DRAVIDIAN VERB. WHERE LANGUAGES CONTAIN TWO DIALECTS, A HIGHER OR MORE ANCIENT, AND A LOWER OR COLLOQUIAL, THE CONJUGATIONAL FORMS HERE GIVEN ARE THOSE OF THE FORMER.

Root: Tam. *śey*, to do; Mal. *chey*; Tel. *chêy-u*; Can. *gey*; Tuḷu, *maḷpu* (= Can. *mâḍ-u*), to do or make; Coorg *key*.

AFFIRMATIVE MOOD.—*Present Tense.*

	TAMIL.	MALAYÂḶAM.	TELUGU.	CANARESE.	TUḶU.	COORG.
I do.	*śeygindrên, śeygindranen*	*cheyyunnên.*	*chêyuchunnânu.*	*geydapem.*	*maḷpuve.*	*keyuvi, keyuvaḷe.*
Thou doest.	*śeygindrây, śeygindri, śeygindranei.*	(*cheyyunnây*).	*chêyuchunnâvu.*	*geydapay.*	*maḷpuva.*	*keyuvi.*
He does.	*śeygindrân, śeygindranan.*	*cheyyunnân.*	*chêyuchunnâḍu.*	*geydapam.*	*maḷpuve.*	*keyuva, keyuvaḷa.*
She does.	*śeygindrâḷ, śeygindranaḷ.*	*cheyyunnâḷ.*	*chêyuchunnadi.*	*geydapaḷ.*	*maḷpuvaḷ'.*	
It does.	*śeygindradu.*	(*cheyyunnadu*).		*geydapudu.*	*maḷpunḍu.*	
We do.	*śeygindrôm, śeygindrêm, śeygindrâm, śeygindranam.*	*cheyyunnôm, cheyyunnêṅṅaḷ.*	*chêyuchunnâmu.*	*geydapevu, geydapem.*	*maḷpuva.*	*keyuva, keyuvaḷa.*
Ye do.	*śeygindrîr śeygindranir.*	(*cheyyunnîr*).	*chêyuchunnâru.*	*geydapir.*	*maḷpuvar'.*	*keyuvira.*
(Persons) They do.	*śeygindrâr, śeygindranar.*	*cheyyunnâr, cheyyunnôr.*		*geydapar.*	*maḷpuver'.*	*keyuva, keyuvaḷa.*

(Things) They do.	*śeygindra, śeygindrana.*	(*cheyyunnava*).	*chêyuchunnavi.*	*geydapuvu.*	*maḷpuva.*	*keyuva, keyuvaḷa.*
PRESENT VERBAL PARTICIPLES.						
Doing.	*śeya, śeyya* (also future).	...	*chêyuchu, chêyuchunnu.*	*geyutum, geyvutum, geyutte, geyyute,* &c.	*maḷtoṇdu.*	*keyuta, kejj'ṇḍ'.*
PRESENT RELATIVE PARTICIPLES.						
That does.	*śeygindra.* Tamil poets use also a present formed from *ânindru* — *e.g.*, *śeyânindrên,* I do. Every termination taken by *gindru* is taken also by *ânindru.*	*cheyyunna.*	*chêyuchunna.*	*geyva* (also future). Instead of the regularly inflected form of the verb, *geygum* is also used in all genders, numbers, and persons, and for the past and future, as well as the present tense.	*maḷpu.*	*keyuva* (also future).

COMPARATIVE PARADIGM OF A DRAVIDIAN VERB—*Continued.*

Affirmative Mood.—*Past Tense.*

	Tamil.	Malayâḷam.	Telugu.	Canarese.	Tuḷu. Imperfect.	Tuḷu. Perfect.	Coorg.
I did.	*śeydên, śeydanen.*	*cheyden, cheydanên.*	*chêsitini.*	*geydem.*	*maḷte.*	*maḷt'de.*	*kejjam.*
Thou didst.	*śydây, śeydi, śydei, śeydanei.*	*(cheydâyi.)*	*chêsitivi.*	*geyday.*	*maḷta.*	*maḷt'da.*	*kejjiya.*
He did.	*śeydân, śeydanan.*	*cheydân, cheydanan.*	*chêsenu.* (He, She, It)	*geydam.*	*maḷte.*	*maḷt'de.*	*kejja, kejjana, kejjat'.* (He, She)
She did.	*śeydâḷ, śeydanaḷ.*	*cheydâḷ.*		*geydaḷ.*	*maḷtaḷ'.*	*maḷt'daḷ'.*	
It did.	*śeydadu.*	*(cheydadu).*		*geydudu, geyditu, geydattu.*	*maḷt'ṇḍ'.*	*maḷt'd'-ṇḍ'.*	*kejjat'.*
We did.	*śeydôm, śeydêm, śeydâm.*	*cheydôm.*	*chêsitimi.*	*geydevu, geydem.*	*maḷta.*	*maḷt'da.*	*kejjat'.*
	śeydanem, śeydanam.		*chêsitiri.*				
Ye did.	*śeydîr, śeydanir.*	*(cheydîr).*	*chêsiri.* (Ye, Persons)	*geydir.*	*maḷtar'.*	*maḷt'dar'.*	*kejjira.*
(Persons) They did.	*śeydâr, śeydanar.*	*cheydâr, cheydanar.*		*geydar.*	*maḷter'.*	*maḷt'der'.*	*kejjat'.* (Persons, Things)
(Things) They did.	*śeyda, śeydana.*	*(cheydana.)*	*chêsenu.*	*geyduvu.*	*maḷta.*	*maḷt'da.*	

Past Verbal Participles.

	Tamil.	Malayâḷam.	Telugu.	Canarese.	Tuḷu. Imperfect.	Tuḷu. Perfect.	Coorg.
Having done.	*śeydu, śeybu, śeyyâ. śeyyû, śeydena.*	*cheydu.*	*chêsi.*	*geydu.*	*maḷti.*	*maḷt'd', maḷt'di.*	*kejit'.*

Past Relative Participles.

That did.	*śeyda.* *N.B.*—Instead of the more fully developed preterite, the poets use also *śeydu* for I did, *śeydum* for we did.	*cheyda.*	*chêsina.*	*geyda.* *geygum* also used in all genders, numbers, and persons, instead of the regularly inflected verb.	*malti.* *malt'd'*, *malt'di.*	*kejja.*

Affirmative Mood.—*Future Tense.* (*Aorist.*)

I will do.	*śeyvên, śeyven, śeyvanen, śeyvan, śeyval.*	*cheyvên, cheyvan.*	*chêyudunu.*	*geyven.*	*malpe.*	*keyuvam.*
Thou wilt do.	*śeyvây, śeyvi, śevei.*	(*cheyvâyi*).	*chêyuduvu.*	*geyvay.*	*malpa.*	*keyuviya.*
He will do.	*śeyvân, śeyvan, śeyvanan.*	*cheyvan, cheyvôn.*	...	*geyvam.*	*malpe.*	
She will do.	*śeyvâḷ, śeyvaḷ, śeyvanaḷ.*	*cheyvâḷ, cheyvaḷ.*	*chêyunu.*	*geyvaḷ.*	*malpaḷ.*	*keyu.*
It will do.	*śeyyum, śeyvadu.*	*cheyyum.*	...	*geyvudu.*	*malpu.*	
We will do.	*śeyvôm, śeyvêm, śeyvâm, śeyvam, śeyvanam, śeyvanem.*	*cheyvôm.*	*chêyudumu.*	*geyvevu, geyvem.*	*malpa.*	*keyuva.*
Ye will do.	*śeyvîr, śeyvanir.*	...	...	*geyvir.*	*malpar'.*	*keyuvira.*
(Persons.) They will do.	*śeyvâr, śeyba* (*en*, to say, takes also *enmar, enmâr, enmanâr.*)	*cheyvâr, cheyvar, cheyvôr.* (*enmar* as in Tam).	*chêyuduru.*	*geyvar.*	*malper'.*	
(Things.) They will do.	*śeygum, śeyva, śeyna.*	*cheyyum.*	*chêyunu.*	*geyvuru.*	*malpa.*	*keyu.*

COMPARATIVE PARADIGM OF A DRAVIDIAN VERB—*Continued.*

Future Verbal Participles.

	Tamil.	Malayâḷam.	Telugu.	Canarese.	Tuḷu.	Coorg.
About to do.	*śeyvân.*	*cheyvân.*	...	...	*maḷtoṇḍu* (also present).	*keyuta, kejj'ṇḍ'* (also present).

Future Relative Participle.

	Tamil.	Malayâḷam.	Telugu.	Canarese.	Tuḷu.	Coorg.
That will do.	*śeyyum;* also the uninflected root *śey.* (1.) Instead of the more fully inflected form of the future, the poets also use *gu* and *du* in the first person sing. (and *gum* and *dum* in the plur.)—*e.g., śeygu, śeydu,* I will do; *śeygum, śeydum,* We will do. See also the paradigm of the past tense. (2.) The poets also often insert *gu* between *śey* and the sign of tense—*e.g., śeyguven* for *śeyvên,* I will do; *śeyguva* for *śeyva,* they (neut.) will do.	*cheyyum* (*cheyva*).	*chêyu.*	*geyva* (also present).	*maḷpu* (also present).	*keyuva* (also present).

Imperative Mood.

Do thou.	śey, śeyyây, śeymô, śeydi* (śeygu).	chey.	chêyumu, chêyumô, chêyi.	gey, geyya, geyvudu.	maḷpula.	keyi.
Do ye.	śeyyîr, śeymin, śeyminîr, śeydîr* (śeygu).	cheyvin.	chêyuṇḍu, chêyuṇḍi.	geyyim, geyvudu.	maḷpule.	keyiri.

Infinitive Mood.

To do.	śeyya, śeyga, śeyguba, śeyyiya.	cheyya, cheyga.	cheya.	geyya, geyyal, geyye.	maḷpuni, present, to make. maḷtini, perf., to have made. maḷtidini, pluperf., to have had made. second infinitive or supine, *maḷpere*, to make.	keyuvak'.

Negative Mood.—*Aorist.*

(Common to all tenses, but most used with a future signification.)

I do not, did not, or will not do.	śeyyên.	cheyyên.	chêyanu.	geyyem.	...	...
Thou do.	śeyyây.	cheyyâ (impers.)	chêyavu.	geyyay.	...	...
He do.	śeyyân.	cheyyân.	chêyaṇḍu.	geyyam.	...	...
She do.	śeyyâḷ.	cheyyâḷ.	chêyadu.	geyyaḷ.	...	...
It do.	śeyyâdu, śeyyâ.	cheyyâ (impers.)		geyyadu.	...	...

* I regard these two forms rather as preterites than as imperatives.

COMPARATIVE PARADIGM OF A DRAVIDIAN VERB—*Continued.*

Negative Mood.—*Aorist—Continued.*

	Tamil.	Malayâḷam.	Telugu.	Canarese.	Tuḷu.	Coorg.
					Imperfect. Perfect.	
We do not, did not, or will not do.	*śeyyôm, śeyyêm, śeyyâm.*	*cheyyâ* (impers.)	*chêyamu.*	*geyyeva, geyyem.*	...	...
Ye do.	*śeyyîr.*	*cheyyâ* do.	*chêyaru.*	*geyyir.*	...	...
(Pers.) They do.	*śeyyâr.*	*cheyyâr.*		*geyyar.*	...	...
(Things) They do.	*śeyyâ, śeyyâvana.*	*cheyyâ* (impers.)	*chêyavu.*	*geyyavu.*	...	...
Negative Verbal Participle.						
Not doing, not having done, or not being about to do.	*śeyyâ, śeyyâdu, śeyyâdê, śeyyâmal.*	*cheyyâ, cheyyâd', cheyyâde.*	*chêyaka.*	*geyyade.*	*maḷpande.*	*keyate.*
Negative Relative Participle.						
That does not, did not, or will not do.	*śeyyâ, śeyyâda.*	*cheyyâda, cheyyâde, cheyâtta.*	*chêyani.*	*geyyada.*	*maḷpandi.*	*keyata.*
Negative Imperative.						
Do not thou.	*śeyyâdê, śeyyêl, śeyyal, śeyanmô, śeyarka* (*n* and **r** for *l*).	*cheyyâyga* (deprecative, also infinitive).	*chêyakuma, chêyakumô, chêyaka.*	...	...	...

Do not ye.	*śeyyâdêyum, śeyâmin, śeyanmin, śeyarpîr*; also *śeyarka.*	*cheyyâyvin.*	*chêyakuṇḍu, chêyakaṇḍi.*	...	...	...

NEGATIVE MOOD.—*Present Tense.*

I do not.	*śeygindrilên** (= *śeygindr'-ilên*).	*cheyyâyinnu* (impers.)	...	...	*maḷpuji.*	*keya, keyule*; also future.
Thou doest not.	...				*maḷpuja.*	
He does not.	...				*maḷpuje.*	
She does not.	...				*maḷpujaḷ'.*	
It does not.	...				*maḷpuji.*	
We do not.	...	*cheyyâyinnu* (impers.)	...	...	*maḷpuja.*	*keya, keyule*; also future.
Ye do not.	...				*maḷpujar'.*	
(Pers.) They do not.	...				*maḷpujer'.*	
(Things) They do not.	...				*maḷpuja.*	

NEGATIVE MOOD.—*Past Tense.*

I did not.	*śeydilên, ceydên-ilên.*	*cheyyâññu* (impers.)	...	...	*maḷtiji.* *maḷt'diji.*	*kejjile.*
Thou didst not.	do.	*cheyyâññu* (do.)	...	...	*maḷtija.* *maḷt'dija.*	
He did not.	do.	*cheyyâññân.*	...	...	*maḷtije.* *maḷt'dije.*	
She did not.	do.	*cheyâññâḷ.*	...	...	*maḷtijaḷ'.* *maḷt'dijaḷ'.*	
It did not.	do.	*cheyyâññu* (impers.)	...	...	*maḷtiji.* *maḷt'diji.*	

* This form is properly a compound, the negative portion of which is the conjugated noun *ilên* or *ilan*, I am one who is not = I am not. It may be used in each number and person like any other conjugated noun.

COMPARATIVE PARADIGM OF A DRAVIDIAN VERB—*Continued.*

NEGATIVE MOOD.—*Past Tense—Continued.*

	TAMIL.	MALAYÂḶAM.	TELUGU.	CANARESE.	TUḶU.	COORG.
					Imperfect. Perfect.	
We did not.	*śeydilên,ceydên-ilên.*	*cheyâññu* (impers.)	...	...	*maḷtija. maḷt'dija.*	*kejjile.*
Ye did not.	do.	*cheyâññu* (do.)	...	...	*maḷtijar'. maḷt'dijar'.*	
(Pers.) They did not.	do.	*cheyâññâr.*	...	...	*maḷtijer'. maḷt'dijer'.*	
(Things) They did not.	do.	*cheyâññu* (impers.)	...	...	*maḷtija. maḷt'dija.*	

NEGATIVE MOOD.—*Future Tense.*

	TAMIL.	MALAYÂḶAM.	TELUGU.	CANARESE.	TUḶU.	COORG.
I will not do.	*śeyyalên.*	*cheyyâyum, cheyyâyu* (impers.)	...	...	*maḷpaye.*	*keya, keyule;* also present.
Thou wilt not do.	do.				*maḷpaya.*	
He will not do.	do.				*maḷpaye.*	
She will not do.	do.				*maḷpayaḷ'.*	
It will not do.	do.				*maḷpand'.*	
We will not do.	do.	*cheyyâyum, cheyyâyu* (impers.)	...	...	*maḷpaya.*	*keya, keyule;* also present.
Ye will not do.	do.				*maḷpayar'.*	
(Pers.) They will not do.	do.				*maḷpayer'.*	
(Things) They will not do.	do.				*maḷpaya.*	

Negative Verbal Participles.

Pres., Not doing.	See Neg. Aorist.	See Neg. Aorist.	...	...		
Past, Not having done.	do.	*cheyâññu.*	...	...	See Neg. Aorist.	See Neg. Aorist.
Fut., Not being about to do.	do.	*cheyyâyvân.*	...	...		

Negative Relative Participles.

Pres., That does not	...	See Neg. Aorist.	...	...		
Past, That did not do.	...	*cheyyâñña.*	...	...	See Neg. Aorist.	See Neg. Aorist.
Fut., That will not do.	...	See Neg. Aorist.	...	...		

PART VII.

GLOSSARIAL AFFINITIES.

THE comparison of the words of languages used to be conducted in so loose a manner, without definite principles, without regard to dialectic changes, and to the neglect of the comparison of grammatical forms and structure, that this branch of philology long fell into not undeserved disgrace. A comparative vocabulary, however carefully prepared, appears to me to be of much less philological value than a comparative grammar. Isolated nouns and verbs are very apt to get corrupted in the lapse of time, and to adopt one phase of meaning after another, till the original meaning is overlaid or forgotten; whilst declensional and conjugational forms—the bones and sinews of a language—retain for ages both their shape and their signification with greater persistency. Nevertheless, I regard the comparison of words, when carefully and cautiously conducted, as an important help to the determination of lingual affinities; and it will be found, I think, that the following vocabularies bear independent testimony, in their own degree, to the same result at which we arrived by grammatical comparison—viz., that the Dravidian idioms exhibit traces of an ancient, deep-seated connection with Præ-Sanskrit,—the assumed archaic mother-tongue of the Indo-European family,—whilst at the same time the traces they exhibit of relationship to the languages of the Scythian group, especially to the Ugrian tongues, are, on the whole, closer, more distinctive, and more essential.

SECTION I.—INDO-EUROPEAN AFFINITIES.

1. INDEBTEDNESS OF SANSKRIT TO THE DRAVIDIAN LANGUAGES.

Before entering upon the comparison of Dravidian with Sanskrit words, it is desirable to disentangle the subject from extraneous questions by a preliminary examination of words which appear to have been borrowed by Sanskrit from the Dravidian languages. I have long felt persuaded that some words of Dravidian origin have found their way into Sanskrit vocabularies; and I have no doubt that a still larger number of words have been introduced into Sanskrit from various other extraneous sources. I have already discussed the question (in Part I., on "Sounds") whether it was from the Dravidian languages that the Sanskrit derived its "cerebral" or lingual consonants.

There is probably almost as large a proportion of Dravidian words in Sanskrit, as of British words in English: but this probability has generally remained unnoticed; and wherever any word was found to be the common property of the Sanskrit and any of the Dravidian tongues, it was at once assumed to be a Sanskrit derivative. Doubtless, the number of Sanskrit derivatives, properly so called, which have been introduced into the Dravidian languages, is very great; but those words are almost always recognised and admitted to be derivatives by Tamil and Telugu lexicographers, and carefully distinguished from *national* or native Dravidian words. In a few cases, as might be expected, but in a few cases only, some doubt exists whether a particular word was borrowed by the Sanskrit from the Tamil, or by the Tamil from the Sanskrit. Sanskrit lexicographers and grammarians were not always so discriminate as their Dravidian brethren; and if any writer had happened to make use of a local or provincial word, that is, a word belonging to the vernacular of the district in which he resided (and it was natural that such words should occasionally be used, for variety of metre or some other cause, especially after Sanskrit had ceased to be a spoken tongue), every such word, provided only it were found written in Sanskrit characters, was forthwith set down in the vocabularies as Sanskrit. Some words of Greek or Roman origin, such as *denarius*, ὥρα, λεπτὸν (in the sense of a minute of a degree), and even the Greek names of the signs of the Zodiac, have found their way into Sanskrit. If so, it may safely be concluded that a more considerable number of words belonging to the old Dravidian vernaculars must have obtained a footing in the Sanskrit vocabularies.

The grounds or conditions on which I think any word contained in the Sanskrit lexicons may be concluded to be of Dravidian origin, are as follows:—

(i.) When the word is an isolated one in Sanskrit, without a root and without derivatives, but is surrounded in the Dravidian languages with collateral, related, or derivative words; (ii.) when Sanskrit possesses other words expressing the same idea, whilst the Dravidian tongues have the one in question alone; (iii.) when the word is not found in any of the Indo-European tongues allied to Sanskrit, but is found in every Dravidian dialect, however rude; (iv.) when the derivation which the Sanskrit lexicographers have attributed to the word is evidently a fanciful one, whilst Dravidian lexicographers deduce it from some native Dravidian verbal theme of the same or a similar signification, from which a variety of words are found to be derived; (v.) when the signification of the word in the Dravidian languages is evidently radical and physiological, whilst the Sanskrit signification is metaphorical, or only collateral; (vi.) when native Tamil and Telugu scholars, notwithstanding their high estimation of Sanskrit, as the language of the gods and the mother of all literature, classify the word in question as a purely Dravidian one;—when any of these reasons is found to exist, and more especially when several or all of them coincide, I conceive we may safely conclude the word in question to be Dravidian, not a Sanskrit derivative.

Words probably borrowed by Sanskrit from the Dravidian tongues.

akkâ, a mother. For the wide Scythian relationship of this word, and proof of its derivation by the Sanskrit from the Indian vernaculars, see the list of Scythian Affinities. "Apparently a foreign word."—Williams' Sans. Dict. Comp. *Acca Larentia*, Lat. Mother of the Lares.

attâ, *atti*, a mother, an elder sister, a mother's elder sister. See Scythian Affinities. "Probably a word borrowed from the Deccan."—Williams' Sans. Dict.

aṭavi, a jungle, a forest. The root of this word is represented by Sanskrit pandits to be *aṭ*, to roam, because a forest is a place where people and animals roam, which is evidently a fanciful derivation. All the Dravidian languages contain a primary root *aḍ*, the radical signification of which is nearness, closeness; and this monosyllabic root is modified and expanded so as to signify every variety of closeness. Amongst other derived words we have in Tamil *aḍar*, to be crowded, to grow thick together (like the trees of a forest); and there can be little doubt that it was from this verbal root, not from any native Sanskrit one, that *aṭâvi* (in Tamil and Telugu *aḍavi*) was derived. Even the formative *vi* is one which is distinctively Dravidian—*e.g.*, *kêḷvi*, Tam. hearing, from *kêḷ*, to hear.

aṇi, *âṇi*, the pin of the axle of a cart; derived, native pandits say, from *aṇ*, to sound. On comparing this word with the Tamil *âṇi*, a nail, a pin or peg of any kind, it seems evident that they are not different words, but one and the same; and the only question is, which is the original? The Tamil word is connected with a family of roots, each of which has a real affinity in signification to that of a nail, considered as a fastening—*e.g.*, *aṇ-ei*, to embrace, to tie; *aṇ-i*, to put on; *aṇ-avu*, to cleave to; *aṇ-u*, to touch. The derivation of the Sanskrit word from this Dravidian root is, therefore, much more natural than that which Sanskrit pandits have devised. Dr Bühler derives *âṇi* (after the analogy of *pâṇi*, hand = *parni*) from the root *ar*, the original meaning of which was, he supposes, to fit. He compares also *ara*, a spoke. The Dravidian derivation seems to me preferable.

ambâ, *amba*, father, mother; voc. *ambe*, *amba*. This word is found also in some of the Western Indo-European dialects—*e.g.*, Old High German and Oscan *amma;* Icelandic *amma*, grandmother; German *amme*, nurse. Notwithstanding this, it has so many collateral forms in the Dravidian languages, that I am inclined to believe it Dravidian. See illustrations of its Scytho-Indian character in the Scythian Affinities.

âli, a woman's female friend. Compare *âli*, Tel. a wife; *âlu*, a feminine affix; Gônd, *âlî*, a wife.

kaṭuka, *kaṭu*, sharp, pungent, fierce; assumed Sanskrit derivation *kaṭ*, to go. The corresponding Dravidian word is in Tamil *kaḍ-u*, the root meaning of which appears to be 'excessive.' Dr Bühler derives *kaṭu* from *kṛit*, to cut, and thinks *kaṭu* stands for *kartu*. The word *kaṭu* is deeply rooted in Sanskrit, and is *à priori* unlikely to have been borrowed from the Dravidian tongues; and yet it can scarcely be doubted, I think, that its origin is Dravidian. Not only are the direct derivatives of this word more numerous in Tamil than in Sanskrit, but collateral themes and meanings are also very abundant, whereas in Sanskrit no correlative root exists. *kaḍ-u*, Tam., to be sharp, is one of a cluster of roots which are united together by a family resemblance. Some of those are *kaḍ-u-gu*, to make haste; *kaḍ-i*, to cut, to reprove; *kaḍ-i* (with another formative), to bite; *kaṟi*, probably identical with *kaḍi*, curry; *kaḍu-kaḍu* (a mimetic word), to appear angry; *kâḍu*, and also *kaḍam*, *kaḍaṟu*, a forest. Moreover, the Sanskrit *kaṭuka*, pungent, appears to have been derived from the Tamil *kaḍugu*, mustard. Nouns formed from verbal themes in this manner, by suffixing the formative *ku*, pronounced *gu*, are exceedingly abundant in Tamil.

kalâ, any practical art, mechanical or fine; assumed derivation *kal*, to sound, to count. Tamil makes use of the same word (*kalei* for *kalâ*), but includes in the signification every science, as well as every art. We cannot, I think, doubt the derivation of *kalei* or *kalâ* from the primitive Dravidian root *kal*, to learn (another derivative of which is *kalvi*, learning). The other meanings of the Sanskrit word *kalâ* are so entirely unconnected with this, that it is evident that two different words spelled in the same manner (one of them Dravidian) have erroneously been supposed to be one and the same.

kâvêr-i, turmeric, also the river Kâvêrî (Cauvery), (from its muddy colour): assumed root *kav*, to paint. Greek name of the same river, χάβηρος. Possibly this word may be of Sanskrit origin. I may suggest, however, the possibility of the origin of the name of the river Kâvêrî, from the Dravidian *kâvi*, red ochre, or *kâ* (*kâ-vu*), a grove, and *êr-u*, Tel. a river, or *êr-i*, Tam. a sheet of water. A celebrated temple on the banks of the river exhibits this latter word *kâ*—viz., Tiruvânei-(*k*)*kâ*, near Trichinopoly, 'the sacred grove of the elephant.'

kuṭi, a house; related words *kuṭira*, *kuṭîra*, also *kuṭêra*, a cottage, a hut, and *kuṭumba*, a family: assumed derivation *kuṭ*, to be crooked. There can be little doubt of the derivation of *kuṭa-m*, a water-pot, from *kuṭ*, crooked; but the other words are probably of Dravidian origin. In Tamil *kuḍi* means a house, a habitation; root *kuḍ*, to be together, a lengthened form of which is *kûḍ*, to come together: related Tamil words are *kuḍil* and *kuḍiśei*, a hut; a provincial form of the latter of which is *kuchchu*. In Tel. and Can. *guḍi* means a temple, and *guḍise*. In Can. also *guḍasal-u*, a hut. In Hindus. *guṭi* means a house. By native grammarians these words are considered to be of Dravidian origin; and the existence of the same root in all the Finnish tongues favours the supposition that it was not borrowed by the Dravidian languages from the Sanskrit. Compare the Finnish *kota*, Cheremiss *kuda*, Mordvin *kudo*, Ostiak *chot*, —each signifying a house. Was the Teutonic *cot*, *cote*, &c., also derived from this same Scythian or Finnish source?

kuṇi, *kûṇi*, having a crooked or withered arm,—a cripple? Compare this with *kûn*, Drav. crook-back; a derivative from *kun*, to stoop, an undoubtedly Dravidian root, from which it seems probable that the Sanskrit *kuṇi* or *kûni* has been derived.

kûla, a pond or pool, also a bank; assumed derivation *kûl-a*, to cover. Compare the Tam.-Mal. *kuḷ-am*, and the Tel. *kol-anu*, a tank, a pool. The Tamil *kuḷ-am*, a tank, is derived from *kuḷ-i*, to bathe, ultimate root *kuḷ-u*, to be cold, a pure Dravidian root.

kôṭṭa, *kôṭa*, a fort, a stronghold; assumed derivation *kuṭ*, to be crooked. The Dravidian dialects make use of the same or a similar word for a fort, viz., *kôṭa* in Tel., *kôṭe* in Can., and *kôṭṭei* in Tam. Tamil having another and very ancient word for a stronghold, viz., *araṇ*, which is certainly a Dravidian root, it might be conjectured that *kôṭṭei* had been borrowed from the Sanskrit. But where did Sanskrit itself obtain this word? Probably from a Dravidian root after all; for we could not desire a better or more natural derivation than the Tam.-Mal. *kôḍ-u*, a line, a diagram, a line of circumvallation, which is sometimes used, especially in Malayâḷam, to denote also a walled town, a fortification—*e.g.*, *Kôḻi-kôḍu*, Mal., Calicut. *kôḍu* itself is a verbal noun from *koḍ-u*, crooked, as in *koḍun-Damiṛ*, bad Tamil, literally crooked Tamil. *kôḍ-u*, when used adjectivally, becomes *kôṭṭ-u*.

khaṭvâ, *khaṭṭâ*, a couch, a cot; assumed derivation *khaṭṭ*, to screen. Compare the Tam.-Mal. *kaṭṭ-il*, a cot, from *kaṭṭ-u*, to tie or bind. The word *kaṭṭ-u* is thoroughly and essentially Dravidian, and one which abounds with derivatives and related words.

nânâ, several, various, multiform. No good Sanskrit derivative for this word can be assigned. Bopp derives it from certain assumed obsolete demonstratives signifying this and that.

May it not have been derived from the Dravidian *nâl-u* (class. Tam. *nân-gu*), four, this numeral being constantly used in the Dravidian languages to signify several, various, or an indefinite number of moderate extent? By a corresponding usage the numeral ten is taken to represent any large indefinite number. Thus a Tamilian will say, I was told so and so by four persons —*i.e.*, by several persons; or, We must do as ten people do—*i.e.*, as the world does. A numeral adjective *nâlâ* (from *nâl-u*, four), is occasionally used in Tamil to signify various, though literally meaning fourfold. The Tamil Dictionary gives us, as an instance of the use of *nâlâ*, one which is identical with the instance of the use of *nânâ* given in the Sanskrit Dictionaries, viz., *nâlâ vidam*, in various ways, literally in a fourfold way; with which compare the Sanskrit *nânâ vidha*, in various ways. It must be mentioned, however, that Tamilians consider this *nâlâ* a mistake for the Sanskrit *nânâ*. With respect to the Dravidian relationship of this word, the testimony of Tamil usage, such as it is, stands alone; for in the Tamil dictionaries, and also in the Canarese and Telugu dictionaries, *nânâ* is regarded as Sanskrit.

nîra, water; assumed derivation *nî*, to guide. This derivation shows that the word was not familiar to the Sanskrit pandits. Bopp derives it from *nâra*, water, and that from *snâ*, to bathe. *nîra* and *nâra* may have been originally identical, but a reference to the Dravidian languages will show that *nîra* must have been the older form. The Dravidian *nîr* may perhaps be traced to *nira*, Tam.-Mal. to be level, another derivative of which is *nêr*, Tam. straight. *nîra* is rarely used in Sanskrit in comparison with *ap* (connected with *aqua*), and *uda* (connected with *unda* and ὕδωρ). *jala*, another Sanskrit word for water, is supposed to have been borrowed from the Præ-Sanskrit northern vernaculars; whilst I have little doubt that to *nîra* a Dravidian origin should be ascribed. The corresponding Dravidian word is *nîr* or *nîr-u*; and as this is the only word properly signifying water which the Dravidian dialects possess, they cannot be supposed to have borrowed it from Sanskrit. Telugu ordinarily uses *nîḷḷu* for *nîru* —*i.e.*, the plural (*nîrulu*, corrupted to *nîḷḷu*) for the singular; but *nîru*, the singular, is also occasionally used. *nîr* is in Gônd softened to *îr*, and in Brahui it has become *dîr*. Malayâḷam alone commonly uses for water another word, viz., *veḷḷam*, which properly means a flood. This word is used in Tamil to denote the water with which rice-fields are flooded; and it has probably thence come to signify water in Malayâḷam. Even in that dialect, however, *nîr* is also used. In Tamil the adjective *taṉ*, cool, is so frequently prefixed to *nîr*, that in the colloquial dialect the compound *taṉṉîr*, water, literally cold water, has superseded the original and simple noun. The Tamil *nîndu* (base *nî*), to swim, seems to be closely related to *nîr*, water. If so, it may have an ultimate relation with the Greek νέ-ω, Lat. *no*, *nato*, and also to *nau*, Sans. a boat. Probably *nîr* may also have some ulterior connection with the Greek νηρός and ναρος, wet (and through them with the modern Greek νηρό, water), though these words are supposed (and perhaps correctly) to be derived from νάω, to flow.

paṭṭana, *pattana*, *paṭṭa*, a city, town, or village: assumed derivation *paṭ*, to surround. Beames derives it from *patra*, a leaf, thatch. The Dravidian languages have probably borrowed the word *paṭṭanam* as it stands, from Sanskrit; and yet, as in the case of *kôta*, a fort, it will be found, I think, that the Sanskrit word itself was derived originally from an older shape of the word retained in the Dravidian vernaculars. Professors Wilson and Williams conjecture that *paṭṭa* is probably identical with the *pettah* of Southern India; but the word from which I conceive it to have been derived is *paṭṭi*, a fold for cattle, a pound, a small village,—a word which constitutes the final portion or termination of the names of so many towns and villages in the south—*e.g.*, *Kôvil-paṭṭi*, Temple-town. In Canarese the same word is *haṭṭi*—*e.g.*, Dim-hutty. The ultimate root of *paṭṭi* is probably *paḍu*, to settle down, to sink. Sanskrit seems to have adopted this word *paṭṭi*, in addition to its own *pura* (which is a true Indo-European word), and formed from it first *paṭṭa*, and then *paṭṭana*.

The word *pettah*, a suburb (Tam. *pêṭṭei*), which is referred to by Wilson and Williams, belongs probably to the same root as *paṭṭi*, though it is not so likely to have been the origin of the Sanskrit *paṭṭam*. *pêṭṭei* is derived from *pêḍu*, Tam. a suffix to the names of villages; which, again, is identical with *pâḍu* and *pâḍi*, a place, a settlement, from *paḍu*, to settle down, each of which is suffixed to names of villages like *pêḍu*.

panno, Prakrit, gold. This word is supposed by Ellis to be derived from the Sanskrit *suvarṇa*. May it not have been adopted into Prakrit from the Tamil *pon*, or the Telugu *ponn-u*, gold?

palli, a city, a town, a village, especially an agricultural village. This is without doubt identical with the Dravidian word *paḷḷi*, which is added to various names of places in the south—*e.g.*, Trichinopoly, properly Tiriśirâppaḷḷi, "the city of the three-headed Asura." The Dravidian origin of this word is indicated, if not proved, by the circumstance that it is chiefly, if not exclusively, used to denote places which are within the limits of the Dravidian tongues. From this word I derive the word *paḷḷa*, the name of the principal tribe of agricultural labourers or serfs in the Tamil country.

bhaj, to share.

bhâg-a, a portion. I am doubtful whether to regard these words as derived from the Tamil *pag-u*, to divide, to share, or to suppose both the Sanskrit and the Tamil to be derived from a common and earlier source. Probably the former supposition is in this case the more correct. At all events the Tamil-Malayâḷam *pag-u* is a pure, underived Dravidian root. A noun formed from it, signifying a share, is *pańg-u* (*ńg* for *g*, as is often the case); and a collateral root is *pag-ir*, meaning also to share. The Sanskrit word *pańgu* means lame, and is altogether unconnected with the Tamil one. Other derived nouns are *pagal*, a division, daylight; *pâl* (=*pagal*), a portion; and *pâdi* (*paguḍi*), half.

mîna, a fish; assumed derivation *mî* (*mînâti*), to hurt.

The Dravidian word for fish is *mîn*, a word which is found in every dialect of the family, and is the only word signifying fish which these languages possess. *mîn* is found even in the small list of Dravidian words contained in the Râjmahâl dialect. Gônd has *mînd*. It seems much more probable that the Sanskrit-speaking people borrowed this word from the Indian aborigines, and then incorporated it in their vocabulary with other words signifying the same object, than that the Dravidian inhabitants of the Malabar and Coromandel sea-boards were indebted for the word which denoted so important an article of their food and commerce, to a race of inland people coming from the North-West. Moreover, the derivation of *mîn*, which is supplied by the Dravidian languages, is as beautiful as the Sanskrit derivation is uncouth. The root of *mîn*, a fish, is *min*, to glitter, to be phosphorescent. Hence the glow-worm is *min-mini* by reduplication; and *mîn*, a verbal noun which is formed from *min* by the lengthening of the included vowel (like *tîn*, food, from *tin*, to eat), signifies in poetical Támil a star, as well as a fish—*e.g.*, *vân-mîn*, a star (literally a sky-sparkler); and *aru-mîn*, the Pleiades—*i.e.*, the six stars. Who that has seen the phosphorescence flashing from every movement of the fish in tropical seas or lagoons at night, can doubt the appropriateness of denoting the fish that dart and sparkle through the waters, as well as the stars that sparkle in the midnight sky, by one and the same word—viz., a word signifying that which glows or sparkles?

valaksha, white; assumed derivation *vala*, to go. May not this word be derived from the Dravidian *veḷ*, white? Compare also the related Dravidian words *veḷi*, space, the open air; *veḷḷi*, silver; *veḷichcham*, light. The Hungarian *vilâg*, a light, appears to be an allied word. Has the Slavonian *veli*, white, been borrowed from a Scythian source? or is it one of those ultimate analogies which bind both families together?

val-a, to surround.

valaya-m, a circlet, a bracelet. The Dravidian languages seem to have borrowed the Sanskrit noun, with or without modification; but the verb from which the noun has been formed was itself, apparently, borrowed by Sanskrit from the Dravidian languages. The corresponding Dravidian root is *vaḷ-ei*, to bend, to crook, metaphorically to surround. This word has a larger store of secondary meanings and wider ramifications than the

Sanskrit verb. It is also used as a noun, without any formative addition, when it signifies a hole, a sinuosity—*e.g.*, *eli-vaḷei*, Tam. a rat-hole. Whilst the Tamil makes occasional use of the Sanskrit *valayam*, a bracelet, an armlet; it also uses *vaḷeiyal*, a verbal noun formed from *vaḷei*, its own verbal root, to signify the same thing. Taking these various circumstances into consideration, I conclude that the Dravidian verb has certainly not been borrowed from the Sanskrit, and that the Sanskrit verb has probably been derived from the Dravidian.

valgu, handsome.

valguka, sandal-wood. This word seems to resemble the Tamil-Malayâḷam *aṛagu* (pronounced *aḷagu*), beauty.

śava, a corpse.

śâva, adj., relating to a dead body.

These words are said to be derived from *sav*, to go; but this derivation is surely much less probable than the Dravidian verbal root to die, which is *śâ* in Tam.; *châ*, Mal.; *śâ*, Can.; *sei*, Tuḷu; *cha-chu*, Tel.; Tel. infinitive, *châvaḍama*. The vowel of *śâ* is short in Telugu; and in Tamil, Malayâḷam, and Canarese is short in the preterite tense. *śâ* is undoubtedly a pure Dravidian root. Compare the Samoïede *chawe*, dead. Probably also the Sanskrit *shei* (*sâyati*), to waste away, and *shô*, to be destroyed, have some ulterior connection with it.

śukti, a curl. Tam. *śuttru*, Can. *śuttu*, Tel. *chuṭṭu*, anything round, as a ring, a coil, a roundabout way. Root, *śuttru*, to go round.

sâya, the evening; assumed derivation, *sô*, to destroy, to put an end to. The Tamil-Malayâḷam *śây*, to lean, to incline (a pure Dravidian word), seems to be a much more natural derivation, the evening being the period when the sun inclines to the west.

In the foregoing list of Dravidian words which have found a place in the vocabularies of Sanskrit, I have not included the names of various places and tribes in Southern India which are mentioned in the Sanskrit historical poems, and which have, in consequence, found a place in the dictionaries. In general, the vernacular origin of those words is admitted by Sanskrit lexicographers. In one case, however, a Sanskrit origin has erroneously been attributed to a Dravidian word of this class. Malaya, a mountain or mountainous range in Southern India, is represented as being derived from *mal*, Sans. to hold or contain (sandal-wood). The real origin is unquestionably the Dravidian *mal-a*, or *mal-ei*, a hill or mountain, and also a hilly or mountainous country; and the range of mountains referred to under the name of

Malaya is doubtless that of the Southern Ghauts or the Malayâḷam country, which was called Male by the later Greek and early Arabian geographers.

In some remarks on the first edition of this book in the *Journal of the American Oriental Society for* 1862, presumably written by the editor of the Journal, I find a misapprehension of the point of the preceding paragraphs. The writer says—"We should have expected sound philological method, if anywhere, in the comparison of Dravidian and Sanskrit, considering the accessibility of the material, and the position of the author as an Indian philologist; but of the Sanskrit words compared, at least four-fifths would at once be recognised by a Sanskrit scholar as not ancient or genuine constituents of the language." This is precisely the idea I wished to establish, so that here the writer of those remarks and I do not differ, as he supposed we did, but are quite at one. The object I had in view was to show that there is a class of words, usually regarded as Sanskrit, which are not really "ancient or genuine constituents of the language," but have been introduced into it from the Dravidian vernaculars.

The indebtedness of Sanskrit in some particulars to the Dravidian languages seems now to be generally admitted. Professor Benfey says, in his "Complete Sanskrit Grammar," p. 73 (I quote from Dr Muir's translation, "Sanskrit Texts," Part II., p. 461)—"Sanskrit is a language of great antiquity and of wide diffusion. Long after it had ceased to be vernacularly spoken, it continued to be employed as the organ of culture and religion, and in this capacity it prevailed over extensive regions where there existed alongside of it, not merely a variety of dialects which had been developed out of it, but also several popular dialects which were originally quite distinct from it. From these circumstances it has resulted, not only that forms which have been admitted into the Prakrit dialects have been afterwards adopted into Sanskrit, but, further, that words which were originally quite foreign to the Sanskrit have been included in its vocabulary. To separate these foreign words will only become quite possible when an accurate knowledge of the dialects which have no affinity with Sanskrit shall have been attained."

Dr Gundert, the eminent Dravidian scholar, has turned to good account his "accurate knowledge of the dialects" referred to by Professor Benfey. He expresses himself thus (in an article on the "Dravidian elements in Sanskrit," contained in the *Journal of the German Oriental Society for* 1869)—"It might have been expected beforehand that a great many Dravidian words would have found their way into

Sanskrit. How could the Aryans have spread themselves all over India without adopting a great deal from the aboriginal races they found therein, whom in the course of thousands of years they have subdued, partly by peaceful means, partly by force, and yet imperfectly after all up to this day? In like manner no one can study the Dravidian languages without perceiving that Aryan elements are so deeply imbedded in them that their original nature can be discovered only with difficulty. Long labour and careful comparison of the principal dialects are needed to bring those elements to light. In the beginning of the investigation it may appear easy to distinguish what has been borrowed. Soon, however, it appears how wonderfully the Aryan elements have spread themselves in every direction, so that they present themselves now-a-days in the strangest disguises, and often go far to lead the inquirer astray. Something similar to this appears in Sanskrit also. Dravidian words have not only got themselves naturalised therein, but have allied themselves so intimately to similarly sounding words, that through the passion for etymologising and the overvaluing of their sacred tongue by which the Brahmans are distinguished, they either derive those words anyhow from genuine Aryan roots, or cut the knot by representing the Dravidian roots themselves as Sanskrit. We scarcely ever meet in India a native philologist who would be willing to acknowledge the existence of Dravidian elements in Sanskrit; whilst we meet with many, at least in Malabar, who boldly take upon themselves to derive from corruptions of the Sanskrit the whole of the Dravidian vocabulary, and even Arabic and European names. We Europeans, on the other hand, look simply at the nature of the case. Where peoples speaking differing languages are in constant intercommunication with one another—when they trade or fight with one another, and have many joys and sorrows in common, they naturally borrow much from one another, without examination or consideration. And this must have happened to the greatest extent in the earliest times, when those nations still stood face to face in their primitive condition.

"It might be anticipated, therefore, that as the Aryans penetrated further and further to the south, and became acquainted with new objects bearing Dravidian names, they would as a matter of course adopt the names of those things together with the things themselves."

Selections from Dr Gundert's list of words which he thinks have probably been borrowed by Sanskrit from the Dravidian languages.

Uruṇḍa, the name of a demon, round or rolling, from *uruḷ* (pret. *uruṇḍu*), to roll.

êḍa, eḍaka, a sheep or goat; Drav. *âḍu*, a sheep or goat; root *âḍu*, to frisk; Tuḷu *êḍu*.

karabâla, karavâla, a sword; compare Drav. *kai-vâḷ*, a hand-sword; *vâḷ*, a sword, may be from *vaḷ*, to bend.

Karṇâṭaka, Kar-nâṭ-agam, interior of the black country, from *kar*, black, *nâṭ* (*nâḍu*), country, and *agam*, interior—the black cotton soil of the Dekkan. *nâḍu* means properly the cultivated country, from *naḍ-u*, to plant.

kuṇḍa, a hole; Tam. *kuṇḍu*; Tel. *guṇḍa*; Can. *kuni*; Tam. *kuṛi*.

kurkura, a dog; Drav. *kura*, to make a noise; ultimate root *ku*, to cry.

kêyûra, a bracelet worn on the upper arm; Drav. *kei*, hand, arm, *uru*, to be used.

kôkila, the cuckoo; Drav. *kuyil*. The Dravidian word is generally regarded as a corruption from the Sanskrit. Probably neither word is derived from the other, but each is mimetic. Drav. root *ku*, to cry, with the formative *il*, place.

ghôṭa, a horse; Tel. *gurram*. Compare Tam. *kudirai*, a horse, probably from *kudi*, to leap. (See my own list.)

champaka, the Michelia champaka, a tree with a yellow fragrant flower. Also *jambu*, the rose-apple; Drav. *śembu*, red.

nâranga, the orange; Drav. *nâr*, to smell; Mal. (*nârañña*) *nârañ-gây* (*kây*, fruit), an orange. Compare also, however, Sans. *nâgaranga*, an orange.

piṭa, piṭaka, a large basket; Drav. *piḍ*, to catch, to hold.

putra, son; Drav. root *pud*, new?

punnâga, a tree from the flowers of which a yellow dye is prepared; Drav. *pon*, gold.

pêṭa, a basket; Drav. *peṭṭi*, a box or basket; root, Tel. *peṭ*, to place. [*piḍ*, to hold, contain.]

phala, fruit; Drav. *paṛam, paḷam*, ripe fruit; root *paṛ*, to become old. (Tel. *paṇḍu* is from the same root.)

marutta, a medicine-man, a sorcerer; Drav. *marundu* (oblique *maruttu*), medicine.

markaṭa, a monkey; Drav. root *mara*, a tree.

muktâ, a pearl; Prakrit *muttâ*; Tam. *muttu*. Probably both Sanskrit and Tamil words are from *mut*, the equivalent of Tamil *mudal*, first; root *mu* or *mi*, to be first—the *first* of gems.

Bhillas, probably *Billas*, from the Drav. *vil, bil*, a bow, bowmen.

râtri, night; Drav. *irâ, iravu*; Tel. *rê*; root, *ir*, to be dark (*ir-uḷ*, darkness).

virala, loose; Tam.-Mal. *viral*, expansion, from *viri*, to expand.

hêramba, a buffalo; Drav. *eruma, erma*.

śringavêra, ginger. The whole of this word seems to be Dravidian. Ginger is in Tamil and Malayâḷam *inji* or *inchi*, and this word seems to have commenced with *s* originally, as in Canarese the parallel word is *śûnti*. (See *Indian Antiquary*, Nov. 1872, contribution by Dr Burnell.) In earlier times, Dr Burnell says, the Greeks procured this article almost exclusively from Malabar. *inchi*, ginger, would naturally take the addition of *vêr*, the Dravidian word for root (from *vir*, to expand); also Sans. *vêra*, saffron. *vêra* in both words seems to have been intended to mean a bulbous root.

Dr Gundert adduces many other words which I do not insert here, as they appear to me too conjectural. I am doubtful indeed whether much dependence can be placed on several of the words I have quoted.

The following additional illustration, however, which he gives in a different connection, is worthy of consideration. The Sanskrit *rûpa*, form, is in Tamil *uruvam*, *uruvu*, which seem undoubtedly *tadbhavas*. But there is also in Tamil an independent verb, *uru*, to be firm, solid, &c., of which another shape is *uṟu*; and from this *uṟu* comes the Tamil noun *uṟuppu*, a member of the body, the body itself, a form—*e.g.*, the sign of a case is called the *uṟuppu* of the case. Dr Gundert does not doubt that the Sanskrit *rûpa* is derived from this Dravidian *uṟuppu*, even though *uruvu* may be a *tadbhava* of *rûpa*.

The following instances of words probably borrowed by Sanskrit from the Dravidian languages are selected from a list of such words beginning with *a*, *â*, contained in an article by Mr Kittel in the *Indian Antiquary* (No. for August 1872) on "The Dravidian Element in Sanskrit Dictionaries."

aṭṭa, an upper loft; Drav. *aṭṭa*, the same; root *aḍ*, to place one thing upon another.

aṭṭa, boiled rice, food; Drav. *aḍ*, to cook, past participle *aṭṭa*.

aṭṭa (properly *haṭṭa*), a market, a market-place; Drav. *haṭṭa* (*haṭṭi*), a hamlet, properly *patti*. See *paṭṭanam* in my list.

âm, yes; Drav. *âm*, yes, literally it is or will be, the aorist future (neuter singular) of *â-gu*, to become.

âra-kûṭa, brass, a combination of metals; Drav. *kûṭṭa*, union; root *kuḍ*, to join.

âṭa, *âḍa*, as a suffix, playing with, tending after—*e.g.*, *vâchâṭa*, talkative; Drav. *âḍu*, to play, to use.

âla, as a suffix, possessing—*e.g.*, *Malayâla*, mountain possessing, *aśva-vâla*, horse possessing; Drav. *âḷ*, to possess.

âli, a ditch; Drav. *âḷi*, a deep place; root *âḷ*, to be deep.

A few words are appended by Mr Kittel which do not begin with *a*. I quote those that have not been adduced already.

pâlana, the milk of a cow that has recently calved; Drav. *pâl*, milk.
valli, a creeper; Drav. *vaḷḷi*, the same; root *vaḷ*, to bend, to surround.
mukura, *mukula*, a bud; Drav. *muguḷ*; root *mug*, to shut up as a flower.
kuṭa, an earthenware vessel; Drav. root *kuḍ*, to take in, receive.
kuṭhara, an axe; Drav. *kaḍi*, to cut.

The other words adduced by Mr Kittel appear to me to belong, not to the class of words actually borrowed by Sanskrit from the Dravidian languages, but to that of words which are the common property of both families. This is shown by the number of Mr Kittel's illustrations derived from one initial vowel alone to be a very large class; and it is evident that in many instances the Dravidian use of the word, or its relationships, throws light on the use of the word in Sanskrit.

2. Sanskrit Affinities.

I now proceed to point out the existence of another class of Sanskrit affinities in the vocabularies of the Dravidian languages. The words contained in the following list are true, underived Dravidian roots, yet they seem to be so closely allied to certain Sanskrit words, that they may reasonably be concluded to be the common property of both families of tongues. Possibly one or two words may have been borrowed at an early period by the one language from the other; but in most cases, if not in every case, there is a preponderance of evidence in favour of the mutually independent origin of both the Sanskrit word and the Dravidian one, from a source which appears to have been common to both. The various words appear to be too deeply seated in each family of languages, to have too many ramifications, and (whilst they retain a family likeness) to differ too widely, either in sound or in signification, to allow of the supposition of a direct derivation of the one from the other. Moreover, notwithstanding the general resemblance of the Dravidian words contained in the following list to the Sanskrit ones with which they are compared, and notwithstanding the prejudice of native grammarians in favour of everything Sanskrit, these words are invariably regarded by native scholars as independent of Sanskrit, and as underived (*dêśya*) national Dravidian words. Consequently, if a connection can be traced, as I think it can, between these words and the corresponding Sanskrit ones, it must be the connection of a common origin. I place in another and subsequent list those Dravidian words which appear to be more directly allied to Greek or Latin, Persian, or some other extra-Indian member of the Indo-European family, than to Sanskrit. In this list I place those Dravidian words which appear to be allied to the Sanskrit alone, or more directly to Sanskrit than to any other Indo-European language; and it is remarkable how few such words there are, compared with those of the other class. A comparison of the two following lists will, I think, lead to the conclusion that the Indo-European elements contained in the Dravidian languages were introduced into those languages before Sanskrit separated from its sisters, or at least before Sanskrit, as a separate tongue, came in contact with the Dravidian family.

The Dravidian words which follow are quoted from Tamil, if it is not expressly mentioned that it is otherwise. Where it is certain that the final vowel or syllable of a Dravidian word is no part of the root, but is a separable formative accretion, or a particle which has been added merely for euphony, or for the purpose of facilitating enunciation, I have separated such vowel or syllable from the genuine portion of the word by a hyphen.

Words which appear to be the common property of Sanskrit and the Dravidian tongues.

aḍi, to strike, to beat, to kill.

ud-ei, to kick, to stamp; *uḍ-ei*, *oḍ-i*, to break. Comp. *uṭh*, *ûṭh*, Sans. to strike, to knock down.

aḍ-ei, to get in, to attain, to possess. Comp. *aḍ*, Vedic-Sans. to pervade, to attain.

an-u, Tel., *en*, Tam., to speak, to say. Comp. *aṇ*, Sans. to sound.

ar-u, to be scarce, precious, dear. Comp. Sans. *arh.* to deserve; *argha*, value.

ûr-u, to creep; in the higher dialect of the Tamil, to ride (as in a palanquin). Comp. Sans. *ur*, to go.

kaḍ-a, to pass by or over. Comp. *kaṭ*, Sans. to go.

kaḍ-u, to ache, to be hot, pungent, fierce, swift. This is one of a cluster of roots united together by a family resemblance. Some of these are the following:—*kaḍ-i*, to bite; *kaḍ-i*, with another formative, to cut, to reprove; *kaḍ-u-gu*, to make haste; *kar-i* (probably identical with *kaḍ-i*), curry; *kaḍukaḍu*, an intensitive form of *kaḍ-u*. *kaḍ-am*, *kaḍ-aru*, more commonly *kâḍ-u*, a forest; *kaḍ-u-gu*, mustard. Supposing *kaḍ-u* to have meant originally to be excessive, or to have acquired that meaning, another root will then appear to be related to it, viz., *kaḍ-a*, to pass; Sans. *kaṭ*, to go. Comp, Sans. *kaṭu*, *kaṭuka*, sharp, pungent, vehement; assumed root *kaṭ*, to go. Dr Bühler's derivation of *kaṭu* (in his paper on the origin of the linguals of the Sanskrit, see p. 35), from *kṛit*, to cut (*kartu* = *kaṭu*), seems much more probable; and supposing this derivation to be correct, the connection between the Sanskrit and the Dravidian words turns out to be one of primary, and not merely of secondary, meanings. The word *kaṭu* is deeply rooted in Sanskrit, and is unlikely to have been borrowed from another tongue. It is still more unlikely that the Dravidian languages borrowed the word from Sanskrit. Not only are the direct derivatives of this word more numerous in Tamil than in Sanskrit, but collateral themes and meanings also abound, whereas in Sanskrit no collateral root exists. It seems therefore clear that this root, meaning primarily to cut or bite, must have been the common property of both Sanskrit and Tamil. Probably the Sanskrit secondary word *kaṭuka*, pungent, mustard, has been directly derived from the Tamil *kaḍu-gu*, mustard; nouns like this, formed by appending *gu* to the verbal theme, being specially characteristic of Tamil.

kaṛudei, an ass; Tel. *gâḍide*, Can. *katte*. Comp. Sans. *khara*, an ass. The Sanskrit word is borrowed and used by the Tamil poets; but it is never confounded with *kaṛudei*, which is considered to be a purely Dravidian word. Nevertheless, *kaṛudei* appears to be allied to *khara* in origin, and also to the Persian *char*, and the Kurdish *kerr*. Comp. the Laghmani *karatik*, a female ass.

kinna, Can. small, Tuḷu *kini*, Tel. *chinna*, Tam. *śinna*. Comp. *kaṇa*, Sans. a minute particle; also *kanîka*, *kanîya*, small, young. There is no doubt of the Tamil *śinna* having been softened from *kinna*; but I have some doubt whether the *n* has not been corrupted from **r**, for the ultimate root to which *śinna* is referred by Dravidian scholars is *śi***r**-*u*.

key, Coorg, to do; Tuda *kei*, Kota *kê*, Gônd *kî*, Old Can. *gey*, Coll. Can. *gêy*, Tel. *chêy*, Mal. *chey*, Tam. *śey*.

kei, hand; all Dravidian dialects. Telugu has in addition *kêlu* and *chey-i* or *chêy-i*.

The harder form is probably the more ancient; hence the words we have to compare with corresponding words in other languages are *key*, to do, and *kei*, hand. It cannot be doubted that these words were originally identical, like *kar*, to do, and *kar-a*, hand, in Sanskrit. *key* would naturally become *kei*, of which we see an appropriate instance in *gei-du*, having done, in colloquial Canarese, which is the shape the older and more classical *gey-du* has taken. Though it seems certain that these words were originally identical, it does not seem quite so clear which of the two meanings, 'to do' or 'the hand,' was the original one. It would be very natural to call the hand the doer; on the other hand, 'to do' is an abstract word, which cannot well have come into use until a large number of doings and doers had been provided with special names. Some word for hand would be required at a much earlier stage, and it is conceivable that to do meant first of all to use the hand.

Compare these words with *kar* (*kṛi*), Sans. to do, and *kar-a*, hand. The *k* of *kṛi* is changed to *ch* in some of the tenses of the verb (*e.g.*, *chakâra*, I did), just as we have seen above that the Dravidian *k* changes (still more systematically) into *ch*. The *r* of *kar* (or *kṛi*) always retains its place in Sanskrit; and it appears in the corresponding Zend *kar*, to make (*e.g.*, *karôiti*, he made; compare Sans. *karôti*, he does), and also in those western Indo-European languages in which this root appears—*e.g.*, Irish *caraim*, I perform). It is retained in the New Persian *kar* (*kardam*, I did), but seems to have disappeared in the Old Persian *ki*, to do, and also in some inflexional forms in the North Indian vernaculars—*e.g.*, Prakrit *ka-da*, and Maṛathi *kê-lâ*, made, the former supposed to be a weakening of *kar-da* or *kra-da*, the latter for *karilâ*. The included vowel of *kar*, Sans. changes in some inflexions to *kur*. Though there are traces of the existence of *kar*, to do, in most, if not all, of the Indo-European languages, it is not certain that there are any traces of *kar-a*, hand. The Greek χείρ (gen. χερ-ός), and the Old Latin *kir*, hand, are supposed to be connected rather with *har* (*hṛi*), to take, than with *kar* (*kṛi*), to do. The Sanskrit *śaya*, lying down, one of the meanings attributed to which is 'hand,' seems to me to have no connection either with *kar-a* or the Dravidian *kei* (Tel. *chey*). But it seems impossible to avoid the conclusion that between the Sanskrit pair of words, *kar*, to do, and *kar-a*, the hand, and the Dravidian pair, *key*, to do, and *kei*, the hand, a close connection subsists. The existence of *kar*, to do or make, in Zend, shows that the Sanskrit word was not borrowed from the Dravidian; besides which, it occupies too important a place in Sanskrit to allow that supposition to be entertained. It is equally impossible to suppose that the Dravidian languages borrowed *key*, to do, and *kei*, hand, from Sanskrit. *kei*, hand, is found in every Dravidian dialect, however rude; and *key*, to do, or its equivalents, is found in every dialect except the Tuḷu, which shows by its retention of the noun *kei* that it must originally have possessed the verb also. Each of these words *key* and *kei* holds as essential a place in the Dravidian languages as *kar* and *kar-a* in Sanskrit, and each of them has developed a host of derivatives and compounds. The Sans. *kara*, hand, and *karma*, work, are freely borrowed by the Dravidian dialects; but these words are never confounded with their vernacular equivalents, *kei*, hand, and *śeygei*, *śeyal*, *śeydi*, Tam. action, occurrence. There is also an old *tadbhava* of *karma* in use in all the dialects, viz., *kam* (also *kammam* in Tam.), meaning 'work,' especially smith's work, from a comparison of which with *śeygei*, &c., we see how easily the Sanskrit derivative can be distinguished from the Dravidian word. Comp. Sans. *karma-kâra*, a mechanic, a blacksmith, with *kammâra*, the *tadbhava* of the same in Canarese. This proves conclusively that *kam* is not Dravidian, but Sanskrit.

If, then, it may certainly be concluded that the Sanskrit pair of words and the Dravidian are closely connected, and if it may be concluded with equal certainty that neither of these languages borrowed them from the other, we cannot, as it appears to me, escape from the conclusion that they are the common property of both. If this be the case, they bear testimony either to the intimate association of the Dravidian and the Sanskrit speaking peoples in very early times, or to their original oneness. This oneness, however, does not stop here, nor does it prove the Dravidian languages to be exclusively or distinctively Aryan; for it will be shown hereafter, under the head of Scythian affinities, that this same pair of words is found in the Tatar and Finnish languages as well as in the Aryan and Dravidian, and in particular that the Dravidian word for 'hand' reproduces itself in all those languages with an almost perfect exactness.

kur-al, Tam. noise, voice; root *kur*, to make a noise. Comp. Sans. *kar*, to shout; *gar*, to sound. Possibly the Tam. *kôṛi*, the *gallus gallinaceous*, is connected with *kur;* and if so, the word *gallus* itself will appear to be related to *kôṛi*, *gallus* being instead of *garrus;* comp. *garrulus*. The ultimate root of the Tam. *kur* appears to be *ku*, to sound (probably a mimetic word), as in *ku-y-il*, the Indian cuckoo.

kudirei, a horse; Can. *kudure*, probably from *kudi*, to leap. Comp.

Sans. *ghoṭa*, a horse. The Dravidian languages have borrowed *ghôṭa* from Sans. (in Tamil *gôṛam, gôḍagam*), said to be from *ghuṭ*, to retaliate; but *kudirei* is regarded as an underived, indigenous Dravidian word. It is probable, however, that the two words are ultimately related.

kiṛ-i, to tear. Comp. *khur*, Sans. to cut, to scratch.

keḍ-u, to spoil or destroy, or (intransitively) to be spoiled or destroyed; verbal noun *kêḍ-u*, ruin; relative participle *keṭṭa* (*ṭṭ* for *ḍḍ*), bad; Tel. *cheḍ-u*. Comp. Sans. *khid*, to suffer pain or misery, and its verbal noun *khêda*, sorrow, distress. Comp. also *khiṭ*, to terrify, and its derivative *khêṭ*, bad, low; Greek *κῆδος*, sorrow. If these words are allied to the Dravidian one, as they appear to be, it must be in virtue of a common origin, for there is not a more distinctively Dravidian word in existence than *keḍ-u.*

koḍ-u, Tam.-Mal. fierce, extreme, rough, literally crooked—*e.g.*, *koḍ-ukku*, Tam. the claws of the crab; *koḍ-il*, Mal. pincers. Comp. Sans. *kuṭ*, crooked.

śil-ir, to tremble, to have the hair standing on end. Comp. *chêl*, Sans. to shake, to tremble.—See also subsequent list under *kuḷir*, cold.

śe, to be red; Can. *kena, ken; chem, chen.* This root forms the basis of many adjectives and nouns (*e.g.*, *śen*, red), but is not used anywhere in its primitive, unformed shape. Comp. *śoṇa*, Sans. to be red.

śevi, Tam.; *chevi*, Mal.-Tel., the ear; Can. *kivi*, Tuḷu *keppi.* Comp. *śrava*, the ear, Sans., from *śru*, to hear.

taḍ-i, a stick, a club; verbal theme, *taḍi*, to be thick or heavy; *taṭṭ-u.* to hit. Comp. *taḍ*, Sans. to strike, to beat.

tî, fire. Comp. Sans. *dî*, the base of *dîp*, to shine.

tûv-u, to sprinkle gently (as dust).

*tû***r***-u*, to drizzle, to scatter, to spread abroad (as a report).

The transitive of *tû***r***-u* is *tû***rr***-u* (pronounced *tûttru*), to winnow. The ultimate root of all these words evidently is *tû*, which is also a Tamil form of the root. Comp. *dhû* Sans. to shake, to agitate; a derivative from which is *dhûli*, dust. Comp. also *tûsta*, dust (derivative *tuś*, to sprinkle), with which our own word dust is evidently identical. From Sans. *dhûli*, Tamil has borrowed *tûḷi, tûḷ*, dust, and also *tûs-i;* but there cannot be any doubt of the Tamil verbs *tûv-u* and *tû***r***-u* being underived Dravidian themes. *dhû* or *tû* appears, therefore, to be the common property of both families of languages; whilst it is in the Dravidian family that the original meaning of this root appears to have been most faithfully preserved.

naḍ-a, to walk. Comp. the Sanskrit theme *naṭ* (said to be from *nṛit*), to dance, to act; derivatives from which are *naṭa*, dancing, *nâṭaka*, a drama, a play. It seems improbable that the Sanskrit word has been borrowed from the Dravidian tongues; and yet it seems certain that the Dravidian word has not been borrowed from Sanskrit; for Telugu and Canarese make a broad distinction between the Sans. derivative *naṭinchu* or *naṭisu*, to dance, and their own theme *naḍuchu* or *naḍi*, to walk; and whilst Sanskrit has many words signifying walking, the Dravidian languages have *naḍ*, alone. *naḍ-u*, to plant, means also in Malayâḷam to enter, to walk, probably to plant the foot; *naḍêr* (*naḍei*), a way, a derivative from this root, is one of the words adduced by *Kumarila-bhatta* as specimens of the non-Sanskritic words contained in the Dravidian languages. Probably, therefore, the Sanskrit *naṭ*, *nṛit*, and the Dravidian *naḍ*, have been derived from a common source.

ney, to weave. Comp. Sans. *nah*, to spin, originally to join together. Comp. also Greek νήθω; German *nahen*, to sew; Latin *necto*. *nûl*, Tam. thread, to spin, seems to be a verbal noun from a lost root *nu*, which must have meant to join together, like the Sans. *nah*.

pal, many; as a verb, to be multiplied. Comp. Sans. *pulu*, much, more commonly *puru*.

pâḍ-u, Drav. to sing. Comp. Sans. *paṭh*, to read, to recite. The Sans. *paṭh*, is, I have no doubt, the theme from which the corresponding Tel. *paṭh-i*, and the Tamil *paḍ-i*, to read, have been borrowed; and the Tamil *pâḍa-m*, a lesson, is clearly derived from the Sans. *pâṭha*, reading. *pâḍ-u*, to sing, however, and *pâṭṭ-u*, a song (Tel. *pâṭa*, Can. *pâṭ-u*, Gônd *pâṭâ*), do not seem to be derivatives from Sanskrit; but I suspect them to be ultimately related to *paṭh-a* and *pâṭha*, as descended from some ancient source common to both. The ideas expressed are nearly related; for the reading of all Hindûs (and all Orientals) is a sort of *cantilena*; and even the Sanskrit derivative *paḍi*, to read, often receives in colloquial Tamil the meaning to sing.

pâl, Tam. Mal. and Can. a portion, a part, a half. Comp. Sans. *phal*, to divide; also Latin *par-s*, a portion. *pâl* appears to be identical with *pagal*, Tam. a division (also daylight), from *pag-u*, to divide. The medial *g* was softened away, as in *pâdi*, half, originally *pagudi*, from the same root *pag-u*. See Semitic affinities of this word.

pira, other—*e.g.*, *pira-n*, another man. Comp. *para*, Sans. in the sense of other, different, foreign, a sense which it often bears—*e.g.*, *para-dêśa*, a foreign country. It is with this preposition, and not with *pra*, before, forward, that I think the Tamil *pira*, other, should be compared. The use of the Tam. *pira*, and that of the Sans. *para* (in the signification adduced above) are identical; and we might naturally suppose the Tamil word to have been derived from the Sanskrit. Tamil, however, whilst it admits that *para* was borrowed from Sanskrit, regards *pira* as an indigenous theme. The **r** of *pira* is unknown to Sanskrit, and is considered to be a distinctive mark of Dravidian words. Tamil has another word, *pir-a-gu*, after (ultimate base *pir*), which is generally considered to be independent of, and unconnected with, *pira*, other; and yet that this very meaning, after, is one of the many significations which are attributed to *para* in Sanskrit. Possibly both in Tamil and in Sanskrit, after, may have been the first meaning; other, the secondary one. Comp. also *pira*, Tam. to be born = to come after.

It may be concluded, I think, that *para* and *pira* are radically allied; and yet the supposition that the one is derived from the other is inadmissible. Each is too deeply seated in its own family of tongues to allow of this supposition, and we seem, therefore, to be driven to conclude that both have been derived from a common source.

por-u, to bear. Comp. Sans. *bhṛi* (*bhar*), to bear. It is impossible to suppose that either of these words has been borrowed by the one language from the other; yet they appear to be nearly related. See next section.

pâl, milk. The Dravidian languages do not seem to contain the verbal theme from which this word is derived. We may compare it with the Sanskrit *pâyasa*, milk, and also with *pâya*, water, Zend *péo*, Affghan *poï*; all of which words are derived from *pâ*, Sans. to drink—a root which runs through almost all the Indo-European languages. Possibly the Dravidian *pâl*, milk, may be a verbal noun formed from this very theme; for a large number of verbal nouns are formed in Tamil by simply adding *al* or *l* to the root. Notwithstanding this, the purely Dravidian character and connections of this word *pâl*, preclude the supposition of its *direct* derivation from the Sanskrit *pâ*. If *pâl*, milk, could be considered as identical with *pâl*, a portion, its root would be *pag-u*, to divide. It is difficult, however, to see why milk should have been called a portion, a share. A poetical, but very common, name for *ariśi*, unboiled rice, in Tamil is *amudu-paḍi*, the ambrosial portion or allowance. Was it in some such sense that milk was called *pâl*?

peś-u, to speak; Can. *pêḷ-u*. Comp. *bhâsh*, Sans. to speak.

pû, a flower, or to blossom, Tam., Tel., and Can. Comp. *phull-a*, Sans. to blossom, and *pushpa*, a flower. Looking, however, at the Marâṭhi *phûl*, a flower, from *phulla*, the Dravidian *pû* seems likely to have been derived from the Sanskrit after all. Tamil has an ancient word of its own for flowers, *malar*.

val, strong; *val-mei*, strength. Comp. Sans. *bal-a*, strength. See also next section.

3. Extra Sanskritic or West Indo-European Affinities:

Dravidian words which appear to be specially allied to, or specially to resemble, words that are contained in the languages of the Western or Non-Sanskritic branches of the Indo-European family.

Some of the words contained in the following list have Sanskrit as well as West-Aryan analogies; but they have been placed in this, rather than in the preceding list, because the West-Aryan affinities appear to be clearer and more direct than the Sanskrit ones. The greater number, however, of the words that follow, though apparently connected with the Western tongues, and especially with Greek and Latin, exhibit little or no analogy to any words contained in Sanskrit. If the existence of this class of analogies can be established, it may be concluded either that the Dravidians were at an early period near neighbours of the West-Aryan tribes, subsequently to the separation of those tribes from the Sanskrit-speaking people; or, more probably, that both races were descended from a common source. The majority of the Dravidian words which exhibit West-Aryan resemblances, do not belong to that primary, rudimental class to which the words that the Dravidian languages have in common with the Scythian are to be referred. Nevertheless, they are so numerous, many of them are so interesting, and, when all are viewed together, the analogy which they bring to light is so remarkable, that an ultimate relation of *some* kind between the Dravidian and the Indo-European families, may be regarded as probable.

As before, the Dravidian words are to be regarded as Tamil, except it is stated that they are taken from some other dialect.

aś-ei, to shake. Comp. *σεί-ω*, to shake, to move to and fro.

aru-vi, a waterfall; from *ar-u*, to trickle down. Comp. *riv-us*, Lat.

a brook, Eng. river; also the verbal theme of those words, ῥέ-ω or ῥύ-ω (as in ῥύη), to flow; Sans. *sru* or *ru*, to run.

al-ei, to wander, to be unsteady: *alei*, as a noun, means a wave. Comp. ʼαλά-ομαι, to wander, ἄλη; Germ. *welle*, Armen. *alik'*, a wave.

av-â, desire; also *âv-al*, a verbal noun, derived from an obsolete root *âv-u*, to desire. Comp. Sans. *av*, of which one of the rarer meanings is to desire. The affinity between *avâ* and the Latin *ave-o*, to desire, is still more complete, inasmuch as this is the only meaning of the word in Latin, as in Tamil. See also Semitic Affinities.

avv-a, Tel. a grandmother. In Tuda *av* means a mother. In Canarese *avva* or *avve* means either a mother or grandmother, or generally, an old woman. The ordinary Tamil form of this word is *auv-ei*, an honorific term for a matron, an elderly lady, but *avv-ei* is also used. Comp. the Latin *av-us*, a grandfather; *avi-a*, a grandmother; *av-unculus*, a maternal uncle.

âvi, a spirit, literally vapour, breath; then life, and also a spirit: verbal theme *âvi*, to yawn, to breathe. Comp. the Greek ἄω, to blow; also Sans. *vâ*, to blow.

iṛ-u, to draw, to pull. Comp. ἐρύ-ω, to draw. Comp. also *eḷe*, the Canarese equivalent of *iṛu*, with ἕλκ-ω, to drag, a word which is probably related to ἐρύ-ω, through that alliance of *r* to *l* which is apparent in all languages.

iru-mbu, iron; from *iru*, *ir*, the ultimate root, and *mbu*, a formative euphonised from *bu* or *vu*: Tel. *inumu*. Comp. the Lat. *æs*, *æris*, Saxon *iren*, Danish *iern*, Old Ger. *êr*, Armen. *erketh*. The *r* of these words appears to have been hardened from *s*, as may be concluded from comparing them with the German *eisen* and the Sanskrit *ayas*. Though I compare this word with Sanskrit, I do not suppose the one to be derived from the other. The root of the Tamil word (*ir*) appears to mean dark; and *iruḷ*, darkness, appears to be another derivative from it; perhaps also *irâ*, night.

în-u, to bring forth young, Tam. Can., said of cattle especially. Comp. Eng. to *ean* or *yean* (Shakspeare *ean*), Anglo-Sax. *eanian*.

uyar, high; when used as a verb, to raise (ultimate root probably *u*, that). Comp. ἀείρ-ω, to raise up; also ἀερ in ἀέρ-θην' (Aor. pass.), and in the adverb ἀέρ-δην, lifted up. Comp. also ἄηρ, the air; Armenian *wor*, high; Ossete *arw*, heaven.

ur-i, Can. Tuḷu, to burn; Tam. *er-i*. Comp. *ur-o*, Lat. to burn; Armenian *ôr*, fire; Afghan *or*, *wur*. There are also some Semitic analogies—*e.g.*, Hebrew *ûr*, fire, and *ôr*, light.

uḷ-ei, mire. Comp. ἕλ-ος, a marsh.

ûḷ-ei, howling. Lat. *ululo*, to howl; Greek ὀλολύζω; English *howl* (mimetic words).

ey, to shoot (an arrow), to cast (a dart). Comp. ἰός, an arrow, ἵω, to shoot, to cast, ἵημι, to send.

eṛ-u, to rise, to get up. Comp. Lat. *ori-or*, to rise, to get up. *eṛu-ñâyiru*, Tam. the rising sun, may be compared with the Latin *ori-ens sol.*

ell-a, all. The classical Tamil forms *el-âm*, all we, *el-îr*, all ye, show that the root is *el*. Tel.-Can. *ella*, all; colloquial Tam. *ellâ*. The meaning of *el*, from which that of 'all' was derived, appears to have been 'boundary.' The primitive meaning seems to have been 'where?'

Comp. Ossete *al*, *ali*, all; Saxon *eal*; old High German *al*; English *all*. Probably the Greek ὅλ-ος and the Hebrew *kol* are allied rather to our own 'whole,' Lat. *sal-vus*, Sans. *sarva*, than to the Dravidian and Germanic *el*, all.

êr, a plough; also in classical Tam. the work of ploughing; Can.-Tuḷu *êr-u*, a plough. We find also in Canarese *âr-u*, a plough, which appears to be a different form of the same word. Judging by analogy *êr* must be a lengthened form of *er*, a verbal root, of which the meaning must have been to plough. This verbal root no longer exists in a separate shape, but it seems to survive in *erud-u*, the ox, *erumei*, the buffalo, literally, as appears, the ploughing animals. In Tuḷu both animals are called *êr'* (*er'*). In Tam. *er-u*, in Tel. *êr-u*, means also manure, especially cow-dung. There is in Tamil a secondary verb, *er-ukku*, to hew, to cut, which seems to contain a reminiscence of the primitive meaning of *êr*. This meaning appears more distinctly in the classical Canarese *âr-u*, a plough, which seems to be a lengthened secondary form of *ar-u*, to cut, to sever, a root still in common use in each dialect (comp. *ar-u*, *âr-u*, six). The verb meaning 'to plough' in actual use at present is Tam.-Mal. *uṛ-u*; Can. *uḷ-u*; Tuḷu *ur*.

Comp. Lat. *ar-o*; Greek ἀρό-ω, ἀρο-τὸς; Lith. *aru*. I do not feel sure of the existence of any relationship between these and the Dravidian words, but the resemblance is worthy of notice. Dr Schlegel in his "Sinico-Aryaca" (Batavia 1872) connects all the Indo-European words which designate the plough and its uses, and which contain the root *ar*, *er*, *ir*, *or*, with the Sanskrit *ar* (*ri* or *ṛi*), signifying to cut or hurt, and ultimately with the Chinese *li*, sharp, ground to a point, whence are derived various compounds, also pronounced *li*, with the signification of to plough, &c. From this basis he derives the renowned designation of Aryas or Âryas, as meaning 'the ploughing people.' If the Sanskrit *ri* or *ṛi* ordinarily or naturally meant to cut, or even if it could be clearly proved to have ever meant to cut at all, this explanation of the meaning of the words used for plough and ploughing in the Indo-European languages would have carried more weight. I should then also have felt surer of the relationship of the Dravidian words with the Indo-European *ar'*, to cut, being an undoubtedly Dravidian root, and probably the origin of *âr*, Can. a plough. The radical meaning of *ṛi*, however, seems rather to be to run.

ôr-am, border, brim, margin, coast. Comp. Lat. *ora*, border, margin. *ôr-am* has no connection with any Dravidian word signifying mouth; probably therefore its resemblance to the Latin *ora* is accidental. The corresponding word in Gujarâthi, Marâṭhi, and Hindi, is *kôr*.

kaḍ-i, to cut, to rend, to reprove; *katti*, a knife, a sword. Comp. Sans. *kṛit*, to cut, but especially the English cut; Norman-French *cotu*; Welsh *cateia*, to cut; Lat. *caed-o*. The Persian and Ossete *kard*, a knife, and probably also the Dravidian *katti*, a knife. *kattiri*, scissors, is from *kartari*, Sans., a derivative of *kṛit*.

kaṇ, the eye; *kâṇ* (in the preterite *kaṇ-ḍu*), to see; also secondarily, to mark, to consider, to think. In the latter sense it becomes *kaṇṇu* in Tamil, but the base remains unchanged. In (*kanu*, *kannu*) Telugu, the ordinary *n*, the nasal of the dental row, is used instead of *ṇ*, the cerebral nasal. Comp. the Welsh *ceniaw*, to see; English *ken*, view, power or reach of vision, to ken, to know by sight. In Webster's "English Dictionary" *kanna* was said to be 'an eye' in Sanskrit; whereas it is exclusively a Dravidian word. This error may be compared with Klaproth's representing *kuruta*, blind, as a Sanskrit word, instead of referring it to the Dravidian languages, to which alone it belongs. There is a curious word in Sanskrit *kâṇa*, one-eyed, which seems to have some Dravidian relationship. It becomes in Bengali *kâṇâ*, blind, which, in form at least, is identical with the Dravidian negative *kâṇâ*, that sees not. Possibly the Dravidian *kâṇ*, to see, *kaṇṇu*, to consider, may have some ulterior connection with the Gothic *kunn-an*, to know; Greek *γνῶ-ναι*; Sans. *ñâ*; Latin *gna* (*gnarus*); Old High German *chann*. The different shades of meaning which are attributed in Greek to γιῶ-ναι and εἰδέ-ναι, seem to corroborate this supposition; for the latter is represented as meaning to know by reflection, to know absolutely, whereas the former means to perceive, to mark, and may therefore have an ulterior connection with the Dravidian root.

karaḍi, a bear, from *karaḍu*, rough, knotty, uneven, the ultimate base of which must be *kara* or *kar*. The Tuda word for 'a bear' is *karsh* (*kar*). Comp. the Persian *chars*, Kurd *harj*, and even the Latin *urs-us*. Comp. also the Samoïede *korgo*, and the Tungusian *kuti*.

kaṛug-u, an eagle. Comp. Persian *kergish*; Ossete *kartziga*; also Sans. *garuḍa*, the mythical eagle; *gṛidhra*, a vulture.

kaḷ-a, Can. to steal; Tam. *kaḷavu*, Mal. *kaḷḷ-am*, a theft. Comp. Lat. *clep-o*, to steal; Greek κλαπ-εἰς. See also Scythian Affinities.

gav-i, Can. a cave, a cell, *kapp-u*, Can. a pit-fall; *keb-i*, Tam. a cave. The equivalent Sanskrit words are *guhâ*, a cavern, from *guh*, to conceal, and *gaha*, a cave, from *gah*, to be impervious. *guhâ* has become in Tamil *kugei*. It seems doubtful whether the Canarese *gavi* and the Tamil *kabi* are not both *tadbhavas* of *guhâ*. On the supposition that they are independent words, comp. the Lat. *cave-a*, a cavity, a den, from *cav-us*, hollow; theme *cav-o*, to hollow out; and with this the Telugu *kapp-u*, to cover over, probably the origin of the Tamil *kapp-al*, a ship. See also Scythian Affinities.

kây, to be hot, to burn. The Tel. *kâ-gu* (also *kâ-lu*), Can. *kây-u*, to burn, and the Can. *kâge*, heat, compared with the Tamil *kâṅgei*, show that the ultimate root is *kâ*, to which *y* or *gu* is added dialectically as a formative. The only Sans. word which seems to be related to this Drav. one, is *kâm-a*, to desire; and we should not, perhaps, have suspected this to be related, were it not for its connection with the Hebrew *ḥâm-ad*, to desire, and the derivation of that word from *ḥâm-am* (base *ḥâm*), to be warm. Comp. with the Dravidian *kâ* or *kây*, the Greek καί-ω (Attic κά-ω), to burn, to be hot. The words seem identical. Liddell and Scott represent καίω to be connected with the Sanskrit *such*, to dry. How much more nearly it appears to be connected with the Dravidian *kây*! Besides, the Dravidian languages have another word which seems to have a real relation to *sush-a*—viz., *suḍ-u*, to burn.

kiṇḍ-u, to stir, to search, to turn up the ground. Comp. κεντ-έω, to prick, to goad, to spur on.

kiṛa, old (not by use, but with respect to length of life); ultimate root *kiṛ*, beneath, that which has gone down. Comp. Sans. *jar-as*, age, but especially the Greek words signifying age, aged—viz. γῆρα-ς, γήραι-ός, γεραι-ός, γέρ-ων. See also the Scythian affinities of this word.

kiṛa-mei (base *kiṛa*), a week, literally property, possession, each portion of a week being astrologically regarded as the property or inheritance of some planet. Comp. Ossete *kuri, kôre*, a week; Georgian *kuire*. Possibly these words are derived from the Greek κυρι-ακή, Sunday, the Lord's day; but whence is the Greek word derived? from κύρι-ος, a lord, a possessor, the base of which may perhaps be allied to the Tamil *kiṛa*, possession. The ultimate root of *kiṛa* is doubtless *kiṛ*, ordinarily lengthened to *kîṛ*, beneath; hence *kiṛa-mei* means that which is beneath one, under his power, in his possession.

kiḷ-ei, a young branch. Comp. Ossete *kalius;* Servian *galusa;* Greek κλάδος, a young shoot, a branch. The theme of the Greek word is κλά-ω, to lop, to break; and the Tamil *kiḷ-ei*, considered as a verbal theme, means not only to sprout, but also to pluck off. *kiḷḷ-u*, to pinch, to pluck, is a collateral theme.

kupp-ei, sweepings, refuse, dung, a dung-heap. Comp. κόπρος, dung, dirt, a farm-yard.

kuṟ-u, short, brief: derivative verb *kuṟu-gu*, to diminish: collateral root *kuṟ-ei*, a defect, to be or make defective. Comp. Persian *chord*, short; German *kurz;* Latin *curt-us*, short, small, defective. On comparing the Latin word *curt-us*, with such words as *sert-us*, connected, from *ser-o*, it may be concluded that *curt-us* is derived from an obsolete verbal theme *cur-o*, which would be identical with the Tamil *kuṟ-u*. Comp. Greek κυρτός, curved.

kuru-ḍu, blindness, blind: ultimate base *kuru* (like *kiṛa*, the ultimate base of *kiṛaḍu*, old). Comp. Persian *kûr;* Kurd *kor;* Ossete *kurm*, blind.

kuri, Can. a sheep, Tel. *gorre*, Tuda *gurri*. Comp. Irish *kaora*, Georg. *chhuri*.

kuḷ-ir, cold, Tam. and Can.: ultimate base, by analogy, *kuḷ-u;* Telugu and Canarese *chali*, cold: collateral root, *śilir*, Tam. to tremble with cold. *kûdal* and *kûdir*, cold, are doubtless derivative or allied words. Comp. German *kühl;* Saxon *cyl, col, cele;* Russian *cholod;* English *cool, cold;* Latin *gelu;* English *chill*. See also Scythian Affinities.

kêḷ, to hear, Tam. and Can. Comp. Latin *aus-cul-to*, to hear, to listen;

also the Greek *κλύ-ω*, to hear; Welsh *clyw*, hearing; Irish *cluas*, the ear; Lithuanian *klau*, to hear; Latin *clu-o*, to be called. See also the Scythian Affinities.

kol, to kill. Comp. Russian *kolyu*, to stab; and especially the English *kill* and *quell*. See also Scythian Affinities.

śâtt-u, to close a door, to shut; Saxon *scytt-an*, to shut in; Dutch *schutt-en*, to stop; English *to shut*.

śâḍ-i (pronounced *jâḍi*), a jar. Probably from Port. *jarra;* English *jar*.

śâl, a bucket, a furrow. Comp. *σηλ-ία*, any flat board or tray with a raised rim. See also Semitic Affinities.

śivar-u, Can. a splinter. Comp. English *a shiver*.

sîṟ-u (pronounced *sûṟ-u*), to hiss; Can. *sîr-u*, to be angry. Comp. *συρ-ίζω*, to pipe, also to hiss; Latin *su-surr-us*, a whispering, or whistling. Our English word 'hiss' is evidently mimetic; but *sîṟu* and its allied roots bear no trace of an imitative origin.

śuḍ-u, Tam. and Can. to heat, to burn, to fire: secondary theme *śuḍ-ar*, Tam. to shine. Comp. Persian *sus-an;* Kurd *sodj-an;* Ossete *suds-in*, to burn. Comp. also Sans. *sush*, and Latin *sicc-o*, to dry.

śuvei, taste, flavour. Comp. English *sap*, German *saft*.

śurung-u, to shrink. Comp. English *shrink*, German *schrumpfen*.

śepp-u, to speak. Comp. *ἔπ-ω* (for Γέπω), to speak.

śel, to go, to proceed. This is unquestionably a Dravidian root, and abounds in derivatives—*e.g.*, *śel*, the white ant; *śel-avu*, expenditure; *śel-vam*, prosperity. It forms its preterite also in a manner which is peculiar to pure Dravidian verbs. It is obviously allied to the Sanskrit *śal*, to go or move; *śel*, to move, to tremble; *chal* and *char*, to go, to shake, to totter; and also to the Hindustani derivative *chal*, to go. Close as these analogies are, *śel* appears to bear an equally close resemblance to *cel*, the obsolete Latin root, signifying to go, from which are formed *celer*, and also *ex-cell-o* and *præ-cell-o*. The same root is in Greek *κελ*—*e.g.*, *κέλ-ης*, a runner; and *κέλλω*, to urge on.

tag-u, fit, proper, worthy. Comp. German *taug-en*, to be fit for; Gothic *dug-an;* German *tugend*, virtue; *tüchtig*, fit, able; English *doughty*.

tayir, curds. Comp. Greek *τυρ-ός*, cheese; Sans. *dhayî*, drinking, sipping, sucking.

tin, to eat, to eat light food, to eat away; *tindri*, eatables. Comp. *τένδ-ω*, to nibble, to eat daintily; *τένθης*, a gourmand.

tiṟ-a (pronounced nearly like *tuṟa*), to open; *tiṟa-vu*, an opening, a way, a means. Comp. Greek *θύρα*, a door; German *thür;*

Old High German *tor;* Gothic *daur;* Sans. *dvâra;* Vedic-Sans. *dur.* These words are commonly derived from the Sans. theme *dvṛi,* to obstruct, to cover; but as they all mean not the door-leaf, but the door-way, and metaphorically a way, or means, this derivation of them from a root meaning to close seems less natural than that of the Dravidian *tira* or *tora* (Can. *tera*), to open. Comp. *tṛî,* Sans. to pass; *tiras,* through.

tîṇḍ-u, to touch, to kindle. Comp. Gothic *tandya,* I kindle. Possibly there may be a remote connection also with the Sans. *danh,* to burn, the intensitive of which is *dandah.* On the other hand, the *ṇ* of the Tam. *tîṇḍ-u* is probably euphonic, for it disappears in the Can. *tîḍ-u,* and in the Tam. transitive form of the verb *tîṭṭ-u,* to whet.

teḷ, clear. Comp. δῆλ-ος, clear, manifest.

tol-ei (base *tol*), distance, limit, end. As a verb, *tol-ei* signifies to end, or come to an end. Comp. Greek τέλ-ος, an end, and τῆλ-ε, far off, which Buttmann derives from τέλ-ος.

tripp-u, Tel. to turn; from which, by corruption, *tippu,* the ordinary form of the word, has been derived; Can. *tiru-pu;* Tamil *tiru-ppu.* These are causal or active verbs, and the corresponding neuter or intransitive verb signifying to turn, is in Tel. *tiru-gu,* in Tam. *tiru-mbu.* Canarese has *tiru-hu, tiru-vu,* and *tiru-gu.* There are also a few related themes—*e.g., tiru-gu,* Tam. to twist or turn, and *tiri,* the same; from which is derived *tirigei,* a mill. From a comparison of these words, it is manifest that their common base is *tir,* to turn, to which various formative additions have been made, for the purpose of expressing modifications of meaning. Comp. Greek τρέπ-ω, to turn; which bears a remarkable likeness to the Tel. *tripp-u,* and the initial portion of which (with that of our English *turn*), seems closely allied to the Dravidian base. Possibly also the Sans. *tarku,* a spindle, is either a collateral word or one which has been directly borrowed by Sanskrit from the Dravidian tongues.

naś-u, to crush, to squash. Comp. νάσσ-ω, to squeeze close, to stamp down.

nar-a, Can. a tendon, a sinew; sometimes, but improperly, a vein or artery; adjectivally wiry, stringy. Tel. *naramu,* Tam. *narambu,* Râjmahâl *nâru.* A secondary form of the word is *nâr,* fibre, from the base *nar;* with which compare the Latin *nerv-us* and the Greek νεῦρ-ον, a tendon, a ligament.

nin-ei, to think, to remember; Can. *nen-e, nen-a.* This word is undoubtedly a Tamil primitive, and is probably the basis of *neñj-u,* Tam.-Mal. the mind, the heart; also the diaphragm. [With respect to this double signification of the word *neñj-u*, compare the twofold meaning of φρὴν, in Greek, viz., the diaphragm or chest (supposed to be the seat of the mental faculties), and also the mental faculties themselves.] If there is any analogy between the Dravidian *nin* or *nen*, and the Sanskrit *man*, to think, it comes to light only by comparing it with the corresponding Greek word νό-εω, by reduplication νενό-ημαι. μνά-ομαι, to think on, to remember, and μέν-ος, wish, are in perfect accordance with the Sanskrit *mana*, and are probably more ancient than νό-εω; of which the initial ν has been changed either from μ or from γν (γνῶναι). The Dravidian *nen* or *nin* may in like manner, I conceive, have been changed from an older *men* or *min*, allied to *man-a* and μέν-ος.

nînd-u (also *nîñj-u*), to swim; *nîchch-u* and *nîtt-al*, swimming; Tel. *îd-u*, Can. *îs-u*, *îj-u*, Tuḷu *ñându*, to swim: Tel. derivative noun, *îta*, swimming. A comparison of these words shows that the final *ndu* of the Tamil verb has been euphonised from *du*. The base of this verb seems to be simply *nîd* or *nî*; of which *mî*, Can. to bathe, is probably a collateral form. Comp. *nî* with the Latin *no* (*navi*), to swim; Greek νέ-ω, also νή-χω; Sans. *nau*, Greek ναῦ-ς, a boat. Comp. also *nîd-u* (the supposititious original of both *nînd-u* and *îd-u*) with the Latin secondary verb *nat-o*. Bopp derives these Indo-European words from *snâ*, Sans. to bathe, and that from *sna*, to flow; but it is only in the Dravidian tongues and in Latin and Greek that we find the meaning of swim.

ney, to weave. Probably *nûl*, a thread, and also, as a verb, to spin, is a word of collateral origin. As *tûḷ*, dust, from *tû*, to scatter, so *nûl*, a thread, may be supposed to be derived from an obsolete *nu*, to spin; and this root would naturally be concluded to be a correlative of *ney*, to weave. Comp. Greek νέ-ω, to spin, νή-μα, a thread; and more especially the Latin *neo*, which not only means to spin, to entwine, but also, secondarily, to weave —*e.g.*, *tunicam quam molli neverat auro.*—Virg. A collateral root, and one which bears, perhaps, a still closer analogy to the Dravidian *ney*, to weave, is that which we find in the German *nah-en*, to sew: Latin *nec-to*, to knit, to join; and Sans. *nah*, to bind, to tie.

paḍ-u, (1.) to suffer, to receive or feel an impression; a word which is used as an auxiliary in all the Dravidian languages in the formation of passive verbs; derivative noun *pâṭ-u*, Tel. and Can. a suffering. Comp. Sans. *bâdh*, to give trouble; *bâdha*, trouble.

Especially comp. Latin *pat-ior*, and Greek *παθ-εῖν*, each of which has precisely the same meaning as the Dravidian verb. (2.) To fall, to sink, to settle down. This verb is identical with the preceding one; but the meaning, to fall, which it bears more or less distinctly in each dialect, in addition to that of to suffer, suggests a different set of affinities. Comp. Slavonian *pad*, to fall; Sans. *pat* (Prakrit *paḍ*), to fall, to fly; Zend *pat*, to fly; Latin *pet* in *im-pet-o*, to fall upon; Greek *πέτ-ομαι*, to fly, and also *πίπτ-ω*, to fall.

paṇ, Tam.-Mal. to make, to work, to produce: colloquial form *paṇṇu*; Tel. *pannu*. This word is evidently allied to the Sanskrit *paṇ*, to do business, to negotiate; the noun corresponding to which, *paṇa*, means business, hence property. This noun, *paṇa*, has been borrowed by the Dravidian languages; but the signification it bears is money. Whilst *paṇa-m*, money, is always admitted by Dravidian grammarians to be a Sanskrit derivative, they regard *paṇ*(*ṇ*)-*u*, to make, to work, as a primitive Dravidian word; and this view is confirmed by the circumstance that it stands at the head of a large family of derivatives and collaterals, some of which are *paṇṇ-ei*, tillage, a rice-field; *paṇ-i*, service, humility; in Mal. it means also difficulty, toil; *pani*, Tel. work; *paṇikku*, Tam. a clever performance. It is especially worthy of notice that *paṇ-i*, as a verbal root, signifying to be subservient, to obey, to worship, has become in its turn the parent of a host of derivative words. This word is not to be confounded with *paṇi*, Tam. to say, to order, a *tadbhava* of *bhaṇ*, Sans. to speak; from which also the Tuḷu *paṇpu*, to say, is probably derived. Another form of the latter word in Tam. is *pannu*, to say.

I have no doubt that *paṇ*, to make, to work, has an ulterior connection with the Sanskrit *paṇ*, to negotiate; but it appears to have a still closer connection with the Greek *πον-έω*, to toil, to work hard, *πόν-ος*, work, a task, and *πέν-ομαι*, to work, to toil. Comp. also the Babylonian *ban-as*, to do, to make.

pamp-u, Tel. to send; also as a noun, a sending. Comp. Greek *πέμπω*, to send, and *πομπ-ή*, a sending. This resemblance amounts almost to identity, and yet it is very doubtful whether it is not merely accidental. The form this word takes in Tamil and Malayâḷam is *anapp-u*, and in Telugu it takes two forms, one with an initial *p* and one without—*e.g.*, *anuch-u*, *anup-u*, *amp-u*, *ampiñch-u*, *anichipuchch-u*, to send or cause to send, and *panuch-u*, *panup-u*, *pamp-u*, *pampiñch-u*, the same. We have also *ampakam* and *pampu*, dismission. Probably *ampa*, Tel.

an arrow (*ambu*, Tam.), is a related word. It seems clear from a comparison of these words in both languages that the word we must compare with *πέμπ-ω* is not *pamp-u*, but *panup-u;* and that the *p* of *panup-u* does not belong to the root, but is a formative, alternating, according to the custom of the language, with *ch*, as in *panuch-u*. The resemblance to the Greek is considerably lessened hereby; but it would disappear altogether if the initial *p* of *pampu* should have to be given up. It appears to me uncertain whether *anup-u* or *panup-u* were the original form, but the analogy of the Tamil and Malayâḷam leads me to assign the preference to *anup-u*. If so, the change from *anup-u* to *panup-u* must be regarded as a corruption, and no argument can be built upon it. Dr Gundert supposes the root of this word to be *an* (= *en*, Tam.-Mal.), to say, and considers *anuppu*, to send, Tam.-Mal., as meaning to cause to say. To cause to say in Canarese is *enisu*. Another word meaning to say in Tamil is *pann-u*, another again *paṇi*. See previous word *paṇ*. In Tuḷu, *paṇpu* is to say.

paṛ-u, to be old, to become ripe; *paṛa-m*, a ripe fruit; Can. *paḷa* (*ṛ* changed into *ḷ*); Tel. *paṇḍu* (*ṛ* changed dialectically into *ḍ* and then nasalised). Comp. Persian *ber*, fruit; Armenian *perk;* Latin *fru-or*, *fru-x*. Comp. also the Sans. *phala*, fruit, a word which has been borrowed by the Tamil in the sense of effect or profit, but which is never confounded by it with its own *paṛa-m*. I suspect *phala*, however, to be identical in origin with the Drav. *paṛa*, *paḷa*.—See also the Semitic analogies of this word. Another form of this word, with a slightly different meaning, is *paṛa*, Tam., *paḷe*, Can. old, long in use, of ancient date. Comp. Greek *παλαι-ός*, old, ancient; *πάλαι*, in olden times.

pal, many, various; *pal-ar*, many people; *pal-a*, many things. The ordinary adjectival form of this word, which is used in the colloquial dialect without discrimination of number or gender, is *pala*, but *pal* is more classical. There is also a verb formed from the same base, *pal-gu*, to become many, to be multiplied, to increase. There is probably a connection between this word and the Sans. *pulu*, more correctly *puru*, perhaps for *paru*, much [from *pṛî*, to fill (*pi-par-mi*)]; but it still more closely resembles the Greek *πολύς*, *πολύ*, many, much, the Latin *plus*, and the Goth. and Old Germ. *filu*, much. Comp. *palar*, many persons, with *οἱ πολλοί*, the many, the majority.—See Scythian Affinities.

paḷḷ-i, a town, a village, a school, a place of worship for foreigners, especially in Malayâḷam. Trichinopoly = *Tiriśirâ-ppaḷḷi*, the city of the three-headed (*Râkshasa*). Comp. πόλις, a city, from πολέω, to haunt, to frequent.

palli is found in Sanskrit dictionaries, but I consider it to be a purely Dravidian word; root probably *paḷ*, hollow.

piy-kk-u, to rend in pieces, to card, to comb cotton, to pick. Comp. πέκ-ω, to comb; English to pick (?)

pir-i, to divide; also *pôṛ*, to cleave, and *pâl*, a portion. Comp. Sans. *phal-a*, to divide; but especially the Latin *par-s*, a portion; also *portio*, from the supposititious root *por-o* or *par-o*, to apportion, to divide. The Greek πόρ-ω, in the sense of im-*par*-ting, is doubtless an allied word.—See also the Semitic Affinities.

piḷḷ-ei, Tam. a child; Tel. *pilla*, Can. *piḷḷe*, Latin *puell-us*, *puell-a*, a boy, a girl; compare with *pullus*, the young of an animal. If the Latin word is derived from *puer-ulus*, it is probably unconnected with *pill-ei*. Perhaps a more reliable affinity is that of *fil-ius*, *fil-ia*, a son, a daughter, supposed to mean literally a suckling.—See also the Scythian Vocabulary.

pugaṛ, to praise. Comp. Old Prussian *pagir-u*, I praise, and the corresponding noun *pagir-sna*, praise,

puṛudi, also *pûṛi* and *pûṛdi*, dust; Can. *puḷil*, sand. Comp. Latin *pulvis*.

puṟ-am, a side, especially the outside, the exterior, the back—*e.g.*, *appuṟam*, that side; *ippuṟam*, this side: adjectivally *puṟ-attu*, external: adverbially *puṟambâga* (*puṟam-b'-âga*), externally; as a verbal theme *puṟappaḍu* (*puṟa-(p)-paḍu*), to set out; Can. *pora-ge*, outside; *pora-ḍu*, to set forth. There is, doubtless, an ulterior connection between *puṟa-m*, the outside, externally, and *piṟa*, other, after; yet they are not to be regarded as one and the same word; and *puṟam* has affinities of its own, as well as meanings of its own. Comp. Greek παρά, beside, in which one of the meanings of the Dravidian word appears, whilst the meaning of 'side' is not conveyed by the correlative Sanskrit *para*. Comp. especially the Latin *foris*, abroad; *forum*, a public place; *fori*, the decks of a ship, with the Canarese *pora*, outside. This seems a more natural derivation of *foris* than the Greek θύρα, Sans. *dvâra*, a door, a word which I have compared with the Dravidian *tiṟa*, to open. In the Dravidian languages *f* is unknown, and *p* is always used instead.

pûs-ei, a cat, especially in the South-Tamil idiom; Mal. *pûchcha*. In the Cashgar dialect of the Afghan, *pusha* signifies a cat. Comp. Irish *pus*, a cat; English *puss*.

pill-i, Tel. a cat. *pul-i* signifies a tiger, or more correctly a cheetah, or hunting leopard, in all the Dravidian dialects. Comp. Persian *pelang*, a tiger, but especially the Latin *feles* or *felles*, a cat, a word which is also used to denote various animals of a similar character.

peṇ, a female. Comp. Lat. *femina*.

per-u, great; another form of the same adjective in Tamil, and perhaps a more ancient one, is *par-u*. Possibly *pal-a*, many, is a related root, seeing that there appears to be the same relation between *per-u* or *par-u*, great, and *pal-a*, many, that there is between *śir-u*, small, and *śil-a*, few. *per-u*, great, is also used as a verbal theme, and in that connection it signifies to increase, to grow. Comp. Sans. *puru*, *pulu*, much, *barh*, *varh*, to be pre-eminent, but especially the Zend *berez* and *barez*, great, *berezaiti*, to grow.

per-u, to obtain, to get or beget, to bear, to bring forth; verbal noun *pêr-u*, a bringing forth or birth, a thing obtained or a benefit. *pir-a*, to be born, to proceed from, is doubtless a related word; and there is probably a relationship between these words (especially the latter) and *pira*, other, *pir-agu*, after, *pura-m*, the exterior, and even *por-u*, to bear or sustain. Comp. the Lat. *par-io*, *pe-per-i*, to bring forth, to acquire. Possibly the ultimate base of all these words is the Indo-European preposition, *pra*, signifying progressive motion, expansion, excess, &c.; and the Zend form of this preposition, *fra*, indicates the propriety of classing the Latin *fru-x* with the other derivatives. See also the Semitic Vocabulary.

pei-(y)-an, a boy, a servant; also *pei-(y)-al* and *pei-dal*; Mal. *pei-dal*; Can. *hei-da*. The termination *al*, *dal*, is that of the abstract verbal noun; and consequently *peiyal* might be applied to a youth of either sex, a child, though restricted in Tamil to the masculine. Malayâḷam has *âṇ pei-dal*, a boy, *peidal-âḷ*, a girl: root *paś*=*pei*, green, fresh, young. Comp. Greek παῖς, παιδ-ὸς, a boy or girl, a servant; Laconian πόιρ; Latin *puer*; Persian *bach*, a boy, *puser*, a son; Swedish *poike*; English *boy*. The Sanskrit *putra*, a son, has also been supposed to be derived from this theme. See also Scythian Affinities.

por-u, to sustain, to bear, to suffer patiently, *por-u-ppu*, responsibility, *por-u-mei*, patience. Comp. Sans. *bhṛi* (*bhar*), to bear; Gothic *bair-an*, *bâr*, *bêram*, to bear; Old High German *bêran*, *pêran*; English *bear*, *bore*; Old English *bearn*, a child; Greek φέρ-ω; Latin *fer-o*. Tamil distinguishes between this word and *pir-a*, to be born, though both are probably from the same base. Latin in like manner distinguishes between *par-io* and *fer-o*; whilst the Teutonic tongues make no difference between *bear*, to sustain, and *bear*, to bring forth. They constitute one word, from which is formed the past participle to be born or borne, and also the noun birth.

poṛ-u-du, *pôṛ-du*, time; theme *poṛ*, probably to divide. Comp. Sans. *vâr-a*, time; Pers. *bâr*, the theme of *bâri*, once; Lat. *ber*, the suffix of time, which appears in the names of the months from Septem-*ber* to Decem-*ber*.

pô, to go; also *pô-gu* (with the usual formative addition of *gu*). The imperative of *pôgu* is *pô*. Laghmani (an Afghan dialect) *pâk*, to go; Greek *βα-ω*, to go; Lat. *va-do*, to march; Heb. *bô*, to come, occasionally to go.

pôḍ-u, to put. Comp. Dutch *poot-en*, to set or plant; Danish *pod-er*, to graft; English *to put*.

biḷ-u, Can. to fall; Tam. *viṛ-u*. Comp. English *to fall*; German *fall-en*.

mag-an, a son, a male. Comp. Gothic *mag-us*, a boy, a son, from the verbal theme *mag*, originally to grow, then to be able; Gaelic *mak*, a son; Tibetan *maga*, son-in-law. Comp. also Lat. *mas*, a male.

man, to remain, to abide (root of *manĕi*, house). Comp. Lat. *manere*.

may-ir, hair. Probably from *mayi*, Mal. black = Tam. *mei*. Comp. Persian *mui*; Armenian *mas*, hair.

mar-a, to forget. Comp. Lithuanian *mirsz*, to forget.

mâ, a male, particularly the male of the lion, elephant, horse, and swine—*e.g.*, *ari-mâ*, a male lion. Comp. Lat. *mas*, a male.

mâṛg-u, to die, to languish, to mingle, *mâṛ*, to be confused, to be lazy; *mâḷ*, to die, to perish. Comp. Lat. *marc-eo*, to wither, to be faint, to be languid or lazy, and also the Greek *μαραίνω*, which in the passive voice signifies to waste away, or die. Possibly all these words have a remote connection with *mṛi* (*mar*), Sans. to die. It would seem, however, that there is a closer connection between the Latin and Greek secondary themes here adduced and the Tamil than between the Sanskrit and the Tamil. *marka*, Vedic Sans., according to some, means dying away.

mig-u, much, great: as a verbal theme, to be much. *miñj-u*, to abound (from *mij*, nasalised), is a collateral root. Related words, Tel. *migal-u*, remainder, that which is too much; *migula* and *migala*, adverb and adjective, much, exceedingly, also *mikkili*, the same ; Can. *mig-u*, to exceed, also *migil-u*, both as a verb and as a noun ; ancient dialect of Can. *migal*, much, *mogga*, and also *moggara*, *mokkaḷa*, a mass, a heap, an assemblage.

The Sanskrit *mahâ*, great, from *mah* (originally perhaps *magh*), to grow, is frequently used in the Dravidian dialects, but it is always considered to be a Sanskrit derivative, not the original base from which the above-mentioned Dravidian words have been derived. This view is confirmed by the circumstance that the Dravidian languages have no word signifying much, except *mig-u*, and its correlatives. The Dravidian words quoted above, bear a much closer resemblance to the corresponding words in the Classical and Germanic tongues than to the Sanskrit. Thus, the Latin *mag-nus, mag-is ;* the Persian *mih* or *meah ;* the Greek μέγα or μεγάλος ; the Old High German *mihhil, michil ;* Norse *mikil ;* Danish *megen* ; English *migh-t ;* Scotch *mickle*, appear to be more closely connected with the Tam. *mig-u*, the Can. *migal* and *mokkala*, and the Tel. *migala* and *mikkili*, than with the Sans. *mah-at*. The final *al* of the Dravidian words is one of the most common formatives of verbal nouns. See the section on "Roots."

mûṛ-gu, muṛu-gu, to plunge, to sink. *amiṛ* appears to be a softened form of the same word ; and probably the *g* of *mûrgu* is only a formative. Comp. Lat. *merg-o*, to plunge, to immerse: *margo*, however, is supposed to bear the same relation to Sans. *majj* that *frango* does to Sans. *bhanj* (originally perhaps *bhranj*).

mugil, Tam. and ancient Can. a cloud. Comp. Sans. *mêgha*, a cloud, from *mih* (*mêhati*), to sprinkle. The word *mêgha* has been borrowed from Sanskrit by the Dravidian languages, and is now more commonly used than *mugil*. The latter, however, is found in the classics, is much used by the peasantry, and appears to be a pure Dravidian word. Doubtless *mêgha* and *mugil* are ultimately allied ; but there seems to be a special connection between the Dravidian word and the Greek ὀ-μίχλ-ή, a cloud, the Lithuanian *migla*, the Slavonian *mgla*, and the Gothic *milh-ma ;* in each of which the *l* of *mugil* retains its place. Dr Gundert derives *mugil* from Can. *muchch-u* (*mug*), to cover over, to shut in, with the addition of the formative *il*.

muyal, to labour, to endeavour. Comp. Lat. *mol-ior*, to endeavour, to strive ; Greek μῶλ-ος, the toil of war ; Eng. *to moil*, to labour or strive.

muṟumuṟu, to grumble, to murmur. A very similar word *moṟumoṟu*, to murmur, would naturally be regarded as identical with *murumuru;* but a different origin is ascribed to each. *moru-moru* is said to be simply and solely a mimetic word, one of a large class of imitative, reduplicated exclamations—*e.g.*, he said *moru-moru*—*i.e.*, he spoke angrily; his head said *kiru-kiru*—*i.e.*, it went round. *murumuru*, on the other hand, it is said, is not purely imitative, but is supposed to be regularly formed by reduplication from *muru*, the base of *muru-kku*, to twist, to chafe; and the signification of grumbling, and being discontented, has arisen from that of chafing. Whatever be the derivation of the Tamil word, it may be compared with the Latin *murmuro*, to mutter. The Latin word is evidently an imitative one, the reduplication of the syllable *mur* being used to signify the continuance of a low muttering sound. *mur* has doubtless some connection with the base of *musso*, *mussito*, to mutter or grumble. Comp. also the Greek expression to say *μῦ μῦ*, to mutter, to grumble. The Old Prussian *murra*, to murmur, is evidently related. See also the Scythian Affinities. The Tamil word means not only to utter a muttering sound, but also 'to express discontent, to be angry;' and in this it goes beyond the meaning of the corresponding Latin *murmuro*. Muttering is in Tamil expressed by *muṇa-muṇa*, a somewhat similar, yet independent, imitative word.

mûkk-u, the nose: theme *mug-ar*, Tam.-Mal. to smell. Comp. Greek *μυκτήρ*, the nose. The Greek word is said to be derived from *μύζω*, to moan, to mutter, to suck in, or from *μύξα*, the discharge from the nose (Latin *mucus*). It is worth consideration, however, whether the Dravidian derivation is not, after all, a more probable one.

mel, fine, thin, soft, tender; *mell-a*, softly, gently. Comp. Latin *moll-is*, soft, tender, pliant; Greek *μαλακός*, soft, gentle, tender. The derivation of the Latin *mollis*, from *movilis*, seems inconsistent with the connection which subsists between *mollis* and *μαλακός*; and the resemblance of both to the Dravidian *mel* is remarkable. Comp. Sans. *mridu*, soft, which is in Tamil *med-u*. I can scarcely think *mel*, like *med-u*, derived from *mṛidu*.

rây, Tel. a stone. Bearing in mind the mutual interchange of *r* and *l*, we may perhaps compare this word with the Greek *λᾶ-ας* or *λαί-α*, a stone. *rây* seems to correspond to Tam. *arei* (another form of *pârei*), a rock.

val, strong; *val-i-ya*, *van-mei* (*val-mei*), strength. The Dravidian languages have borrowed, and frequently use, the Sans. *bala* (in

Tamil *balan*, *balam*, and even *valam*); and it might at first be supposed that this is the origin of *vali*, &c. I am persuaded, however, that the words cited above have not been derived from Sanskrit, but have been the property of the Dravidian languages from the beginning. The Dravidian *val* has given birth to a large family, not only of adjectives and nouns, but also of derivative verbs, which have no connection whatever with anything Sans.—*e.g.*, *val-am*, the right hand; *val-i*, to drag, to row; *val-u*, to grow strong; *val-iya*, spontaneously, &c.; and if this word is not to be regarded as Dravidian, this family of languages must be supposed to be destitute of a word to express so necessary and rudimental an idea as strong. *val*, also, more closely resembles the Latin *val-eo*, to be strong, and *val-idus*, than the Sanskrit *bala-m*.

vaḷ, fertility, abundance; *vaḷ-ar*, and many related verbs, to rear, to cause to grow. Comp. Latin *al-o*, to nourish. Connection doubtful.

vângu, to receive, to take. Comp. German *(emp)fangen*.

viṇḍ-u, the wind. Comp. Latin *vent-us*; English *wind*. The Tamil word seems to be derived from *viṇ*, the sky: its resemblance to *vent-us* and *wind* is, therefore, probably accidental, the root of those words being *vâ*, to blow (Sans.), and their Sans. equivalent *vâta*.

viṟei, to shiver from cold, to grow stiff from cold. Comp. Greek φρίσσ-ω, to tremble, to shiver; ῥιγ-έω, to shiver or shudder with cold; ῥῖγ-ος, frost, cold, a shivering from cold; also Latin *frig-eo*, to be cold; *frig-us*, cold; *rig-eo*, *rig-or*, to be stiff, as from cold; English *to freeze*.

vîṇ, useless, vain. Comp. Latin *van-us*, empty, unreal, frivolous, vain.

vêṇḍ-u, to wish, to want. Comp. English *want* from Saxon *wanian*, to fail. The corresponding Can. word is *bêḍu*, but this has also the shape of *bêṇḍu*. Another Can. form is *bêku*, from an older *bêḷku*. The root must have been *vêḷ*, which means in High Tam. to desire.

vêṟ-u, different, other. Comp. Latin *var-us*, the secondary meaning of which is different, dissimilar; also *var-ius*, diversified, various, different from something else. Root of *vêṟ-u*: *veṟ-u*, void; the primitive meaning of which seems to have been 'distant.'

SECTION II.—SEMITIC AFFINITIES,

OR DRAVIDIAN WORDS WHICH APPEAR TO BE ALLIED TO HEBREW AND ITS SISTER TONGUES.

The number of such words in the Dravidian languages is not great; and it might be objected that in attempting to establish the existence of this class of affinities, in addition to affinities of the Indo-European and Scythian classes, I prove nothing by attempting to prove too much. I answer, that I do not attempt to establish anything or to prove anything. I content myself with adducing facts. I submit to the reader a list of words which exhibit some interesting points of resemblance between the Dravidian vocabulary and the Hebrew. I am doubtful whether any of those resemblances is of such a nature as to furnish evidence of relationship, but I am not doubtful of the desirableness of giving them a place in this list. They will serve at least to show whether further investigation in this direction is likely to be rewarded with important results or not. In some of the instances which will be adduced, the Semitic words appear to resemble Indo-European words, as well as words belonging to the Dravidian languages; but it will be found that the Dravidian analogies appear in general to be closer than the Indo-European, and it is for that reason that the words are inserted in this list rather than in the preceding one. In some instances, again, the only resemblances to the Semitic words are such as are Dravidian.

If the existence of Semitic affinities in the Dravidian languages could be established, it would not be possible to explain those affinities by supposing them to have been introduced by the Jews who have settled on some parts of the Malabar coast; for the Jews, whether "black" or "white," have carefully preserved their traditional policy of isolation; they are but a small handful of people at most; they have never penetrated far into the interior, even on the Malabar coast, whilst on the Coromandel coast, where Tamil is spoken, they are entirely unknown; and the Dravidian languages were fully formed, and Tamil, it is probable, had been committed to writing, long before the Jews made their appearance in India. Whatever words, therefore, might appear to be the common property of Hebrew and the Dravidian languages, would have to be regarded either as indicating an ancient, pre-historic intermixture or association of the Dravidians with the Semitic race, or rather perhaps as constituting traces of the original oneness of the speech of the Noachidæ.

app-â, father! vocative of *app-an*. This word for father is found unaltered in all the Dravidian dialects, except the Tuḷu, in which, strange to say, *appe* means mother; *amme*, father. This *appe* may possibly be a hardened form of *avve*. Comp. Can. *avve*, a mother, or grandmother. *amme*, Tuḷu father, is allied to the Tam. *ammân*, mother's brother, also father, though rarely used in the latter sense. The Mech, a Bhutân dialect, has *appa* for father; the Bhotiya *aba;* the Singhalese *appâ*. Analogies will also be found in the Scythian vocabulary.

In all the languages of the Indo-European and Semitic families the ultimate base of the words which denote father, is *p* or *b*, and that of the words which denote mother is *m*. The difference between those two families consists in this, that the Indo-European words *commence* with the consonants *p* or *m*—*e.g.*, *pater*, *mater*, from the Sans. roots *pâ*, to protect; *mâ*, to make (a child in the womb); whilst in the Semitic languages, those consonants are preceded by a vowel—*e.g.*, Hebrew *âb*, father; *êm*, mother. Comp. also, however, *ambâ*, Sans. mother. In this particular the Dravidian languages follow the Semitic rule—*e.g.*, Tam. *app-an*, father; *amm-âḷ*, mother. The resemblance between *appan* (vocative *appâ*), and the Chaldee *abbâ*, father (Syriac *âbô*), is remarkable. It is so close, that in the Tamil translation of Gal. iv. 6, *abba*, father, there is no difference whatever, either in spelling or in sound, between the Aramaic word *abbâ* (which by a phonetic law becomes *appâ* in Tamil), and its natural and proper Tamil rendering *appâ;* in consequence of which it has been found necessary to use the Sans. derivative *pidâ-(v)-ê*, instead of the Tamil *appâ*, as the translation of the second word.

amm-â, mother! vocative of *amm-ei* or *amm-âḷ*, mother. Comp. Heb. *êm*, mother; Syr. *âmô*. See also the Scythian and Indo-European affinities of this word, which are still closer than the Semitic.

âr-u, a river; Tel. *êr-u:* correlative root *êri*, Tam. a natural reservoir of water. Comp. Hebrew *y'ôr*, a river; Coptic *jaro*. See also Scythian Analogies.

al, not. In all the Dravidian dialects *al* negatives the attributes of a thing; *il*, its existence; *êl* (and sometimes *al*), is prohibitive. The vowel is transposed in Telugu, and *lê* (the base of *lêdu*), used instead of *il*. Comp. the negative and prohibitive particles of the Hebrew, *al* and *lô;* also the corresponding Arabic and Chaldaic *lâ*. *lô* in Hebrew negatives the properties of a thing, like *al* in Tamil, and another particle, *aïn*, a substantive mean ing nothing, is used to negative the existence of it. This idiom is one which remarkably accords with that of the Dravidian languages. Comp. also the Chaldee *lêth*, it is not, a compound of *lâ*, the negative particle, and *îth*, the substantive verb 'it is' (a compound resembling the Sans. *nâsti*), with the corresponding Tel. *lêdu* (Tam. *iladu*), it is not, which is compounded of *lê*, the negative particle, and *du*, the formative of the third person neuter of the aorist. See also Sanskrit and Scythian Affinities.

av-â, desire: a related word is *âval*, also desire, which is a verbal noun derived from the assumed root *âv-u*, to desire (Marâṭhi *âvaḍ*, love). The Telugu form of this word is *âkali*. *k* between two vowels often becomes *v*. Comp. Heb. *avvah*, desire, a verbal noun derived from *âvâh*, to desire. The ultimate base of the Hebrew *âv* or *av* is identical not only with the Tamil *âv* or *av*, but with the Latin *av-eo*, to desire, and the Sanskrit *av-a*, of which to desire is one of the rarer meanings. Comp. also Heb. *âbâh*, to will.

ir-u, to be; Brahui, *ar*. Comp. Babylonian *ar*, to be; also Coptic *er* or *el*, and the Egyptian auxiliary *ar*. The Dravidian word appears to mean primarily to sit, secondarily to be—*i.e.*, to be *simpliciter*, without doing anything.

iṟ-a, the ultimate base of *iṟa-ngu*, neut., to descend, and its transitive *iṟa-kku*, to cause to descend. Comp. Heb. *yârad* (biliteral base *yar*), to descend.

ur-i, Can. to burn; Tam. *er-i*. Comp. Heb. *ûr*, fire, *ôr*, light.—(See also Indo-European Affinities.)

ûr, a city, a town, a village. Comp. Heb. *âr* or *'îr*, a city; Babylonian *er*, Assyrian *uru*, Accadian *'uri*.

eṟ-i, to cast, to shoot. Comp. Heb. *yârâh* (biliteral base *yar*), to cast, to shoot.

erum-ei, a buffalo, especially a cow buffalo; Tuḷu, *ermma*. Comp. Heb. *rêm*, a buffalo or wild ox. Resemblance probably accidental. Root of the Drav. word *er* (obsol.), to plough; root of the Heb. probably *rûm*, to be high.

kûr, a sharp point. Comp. Heb. *kûr*, to pierce, to bore; Sans. *khur*, to cut.

śây, to lean, to recline. Comp. Heb. *shâ'an* (biliteral base, *sha'* or *sha*), to lean.

śina-m, anger: verb. *śina-kku*, to be angry. Comp. Heb. *sânê*; Chald. *senê*, to hate; Heb. *sinah*, hatred. The corresponding Can. word being *kini*, to be offended, *śina-m* is probably softened from *kina-m*. Analogy doubtful.

śir-u, to hiss. Comp. Heb. *shârak* (biliteral base *shar*), to hiss; Greek *συρίζω*, to pipe, to hiss.

śum-ei, a burden: verb. *suma-kku*, to bear, to carry. Comp. Heb. *sâmak* (biliteral base *sam*), to support, to uphold, to weigh heavily on.

śuv-ar, a wall. Comp. Heb. *shûr*, a wall.

śevv-ei, equal, level, correct: base *śev* or *śe*. A nasalised, adjectival form of the same root is *śen*—*e.g.*, *śen-Damiṛ*, correct Tamil, the classical dialect of the Tamil language. From *śe*, *śev*, or *śen*, is formed *śemm-ei* (*śen-mei*), an abstract of the same meaning as *śevvei*. Comp. Heb. *śhâvâh;* Chald. *shevâ* (biliteral base *shav* or *shev*), to be equal, to be level. If the Sanskrit *sama*, even, is at all connected with the Tamil *śev* or *śen*, the connection is remote; whereas the Tamil and the Hebrew words seem to be almost identical.

nâṭṭ-u, to fix, to set up, to establish: ulterior verbal theme *naḍ-u*, to plant. Comp. Heb. *nâtâ'* (biliteral base *nat*), to plant, to set up, to establish.

nîṭṭ-u, to lengthen, to stretch out; formed by causative reduplication of the final consonant from *nîḍ-u* (also *nîḷ*), long. Comp. Heb. *nâtâh* (biliteral base *nat*), to stretch out.

nôkk-u, to look direct at, to address. Comp. Heb. *nôkah* (base *nok*), straight forward, over against.

paṛ-u, to become ripe, to fruit; *paṛa-m*, a ripe fruit. Comp. Heb. *pârâh*, to be fruitful, to bear fruit; *pâraḥ*, to blossom, to break forth (biliteral base of both, *par*). Especially comp. *perî*, fruit. Comp. also Armenian *perk*, and Persian *ber*, fruit. Doubt, however, is thrown upon the affinity of these words with the Dravidian *paṛ-u*, in consequence of the root-meaning of *paṛ-u* (*paṛ-a*) being, to become old, to be accustomed.

pâl, a part, a portion, a class; Can. *pâl-u*, Tuḷu *per';* collateral Tam. roots *pir-i*, to divide; *piḷ-a*, also *pôṛ*, to cleave. Comp. Heb. *pâlâh*, *pâlâ*, *pâlaḥ*, *pâlag*, *pâlal;* and also (by the interchange of *r* and *l*) *pârash*, *pâras*, and Chald. *perâs*, to separate, to divide, to distinguish, &c. All these words (like the Tam. *pâl* and *pir-i*, and also *pagîr*, to divide), include the idea of separation into parts.—See also the Indo-European analogies of these roots—*e.g.*, Sans. *phal-a*, to divide; Latin *pars*, and *por-tio*, a portion.

peṟ-u, to obtain, to bear or bring forth, to get or beget; verbal noun *pêṟ-u*, a bringing forth or birth, a thing obtained, a benefit: collateral root, *piṟ-a*, to be born; *pir-a*, Tam. other, after;

pur-a, outside. Comp. Heb. *pârâh*, to be fruitful; *perî*, fruit; *pâraḥ*, to blossom, to break forth. The connection between *paṛ-am*, Tam., and *perî*, Heb. fruit, cannot be depended upon; but there seems to be an intimate relation between *per-u*, to bear, *pir-a*, to be born, and the Semitic words which are here adduced, as well as the Latin *par-io*, *pe-per-i*.

bâ, Can. to come; Tam. *vâ*. Comp. Heb. *bô*, to come, to come in; Babylonian, *ba*, to come.

mây, to die, to put to death. Comp. Heb. *mûth*, to die. Comp. also *muwo*, dead, in the Lar, a Sindhian dialect.

mâr-u, to change; Can. to sell; base *mar-u*, other. Comp. Heb. *mûr*, to change or exchange, of which the *niphal* is *nâmar*, as if from a base in *mârar* or *mâr*; *mâhar*, *mâḥar*, to change, to buy. The corresponding Syriac *môr* means to buy.

miśukka-n, a poor, worthless fellow; *miśukk-ei*, a worthless article. Comp. Heb. *miskên*, poor, unfortunate. The Hebrew word is derived from *sâkan*; but Gesenius says a new verb arose from this in several Semitic languages, the initial *m* of which was radical. It is singular that it has also found its way into Tamil; Mal. *miskên*. This word *miskên* has found its way (probably by means of the Saracens) into several European languages—*e.g.*, French *mesquin*. Tamil does not contain the root of this word; it may therefore be concluded to have been borrowed from the Arabic or some Semitic dialect.

mett-a, Tel. (Tam. *mettei*, Can. *motte*), a bed, a cotton bed, a cushion. The Dravidian word appears to be derived from *mel*, soft. Comp., however, the Heb. *mittâh*, a bed, a cushion, a litter, from *nâtâh*, to stretch out; Latin *matta*.

SECTION III.—SCYTHIAN AFFINITIES;

OR,

Dravidian words which appear to exhibit a near relationship, or at least a remarkable resemblance, to words contained in some of the languages of the Scythian group, particularly to the Ugro-Finnish dialects.

The majority of the affinities that follow are clearer and more direct than the Indo-European or Semitic affinities which have been pointed out in the preceding lists. Many of the words which will be adduced as examples are words of a *primary* character—words which carry a certain amount of authority in comparisons of this kind. A considerable number of the Dravidian words in the following list have Sanskrit or Indo-European affinities, as well as Scythian; a very few also have Semitic affinities; but I have preferred placing them in this list, because the Scythian affinities appear to be either the most numerous or the closest. Such words, though they are but few, are of peculiar interest, as tending to prove the primitive oneness of the Scythian and Indo-European groups of tongues. In some instances I have given a place in this list to words which I have already placed in the Indo-European list, and the affinities of which I have stated *in loco* I consider more distinctively Indo-European than Scythian. I have inserted them here also, in order to make the comparison more complete.

I have already said that I consider the comparison of words of less importance towards the determination of affinities than the comparison of grammatical forms and spirit. It may be capable of proof that two languages are as nearly related as Latin and Greek, whilst the bulk of the words in each of those languages, including many of those that are most essential to the expression of the wants of daily life, may be found to be totally different from the corresponding words in the other. If this is the case with the Aryan languages, most of which exhibit traces of having been highly cultivated from, and even before, the first dawn of history, much more is it to be expected in the case of the uncultivated, or but recently cultivated, languages of the so-called Scythian stock. The earliest cultivated language of this family (the Medo-Scythian of the Behistun inscriptions) has passed away altogether from the world, or been absorbed by other languages; and those inscriptions are the only proof of its existence which it has left behind. The Finnish, the Hungarian, and the Turkish languages have been cultivated only within the last few centuries; whilst a far greater number of the Scythian dialects have up to the present day received no literary cultivation whatever. They are spoken by roving hordes leading a rude pastoral life, by agricultural serfs, or by still more barbarous tribes living by fishing or the chase; and the only literary records the languages they speak contain consist of a few songs, with the addition perhaps of a recently executed translation of one of the Gospels. Consequently, whilst those languages exhibit distinct traces of a common origin, or at least of development in the lines and in accordance with the rules of a common formative force, they differ from one another in details in a degree which it is hardly possible for a student of other families of tongues to conceive. It would scarcely, therefore, be in accordance with analogy to expect to discover in the languages of the Scythian stock any very considerable number of words closely resembling words that are contained in the long-isolated and far more highly developed Dravidian tongues; especially if it be supposed, as I have always supposed, that the Dravidian tongues exhibit traces of their existence at a time prior to the final separation of the Indo-European tongues from the Scythian, when words and meanings of words did not belong exclusively to the one rather than to the other, but were the common property of both. It may be objected that the argument derived from Scythian affinities is weakened by the fact that the Scythian words which correspond with certain words in the Dravidian tongues are not found altogether in one dialect, but exist some in one and some in another of the Scythian languages. I admit that such coincidences are not perfectly conclusive; but I must remind the reader that he is obliged to be content with such partial coincidences with regard to the inter-relationship of the Scythian languages themselves.

For the Scythian affinities apparent in the Dravidian pronouns and numerals, see the sections devoted to those parts of speech.

akk-a, Can. and Tel. elder sister; Tam. *akkei, akkâ,* and *akk-âḷ;* Marâṭhi *akâ.* In Sans. *akkâ* signifies a mother; and an improbable Sans. derivation has been attributed to it by native scholars. I believe this word to be one of those which the Sans. has borrowed from the indigenous Dravidian tongues; and this supposition is confirmed by its extensive use in the Scythian group. The Sans. signification of this word, a mother, differs, it is true, from the ordinary Dravidian meaning, an elder sister; but mother is one of its meanings in poetical Tamil, and a comparison of its significations in various languages shows that it was originally used to denote any elderly female relation, and that the meaning of the ultimate base was probably 'old.' The following are Scythian instances of the use of this root with the meaning of elder sister, precisely as in the Dravidian languages:—Tungusian *oki* or *akin;* Mongolian *achan;* Tibetan *achche;* a dialect of the Turkish *ege;* Mordvin *aky;* other Ugrian idioms *iggen.* The Lappish *akke* signifies both wife and grandmother. The Mongol *aka,* Tungusian *aki,* and the Uigur *acha,* signify an elder brother; whilst the signification of old man is conveyed by the Ostiak *iki,* the Finnish *ukko,* and the Hungarian *agg.* Even in the Ku, a Dravidian dialect, *akke* means grandfather. The ultimate base of all these words is probably *ak,* old. On the other hand, *akka,* in Osmanli Turkish, means a younger sister; and the same meaning appears in several related idioms. It may, therefore, be considered possible that *akka* meant originally sister; and then elder sister or younger sister, by secondary or restricted usage. The derivation of *akka*, from a root signifying old, would appear to be the more probable one.

It is proper here to notice the remarkable circumstance that the Dravidian languages, like those of the Scythian group in general, are destitute of any common term for brother, sister, uncle, aunt, &c., and use instead a set of terms which combine the idea of relationship with that of age—*e.g.*, elder brother, younger brother, elder sister, younger sister, and so on.

att-an, father; *att-ei*, mother; also *âtt-an*, a superior (masc.); *âtt-âḷ*, mother. We find in the Sans. lexicons *attâ*, a mother, an elder sister, a mother's elder sister; also *atti*, in theatrical language, an elder sister. I regard this word also, as used in Sanskrit, as probably of Dravidian origin; and it will be found that in one or another of the related meanings of father or mother, it has a wide range of usage throughout the Scythian tongues. The change of *tt* in some Dravidian dialects into *śś* or *chch*, is in perfect accordance with generally prevalent laws of sound. Hence the Malayâḷam *achch-an* and the Canarese *ajj-a*, grandfather, are identical with the Tamil *att-an*; and probably the Hindi and Marâṭhi *âjâ*, a grandfather, is a related word, if not identical. *attei*, mother (Tam.), is *achcha*, also *achchi*, in Mal. *att-ei*, Tam., *att-e*, Can., *att-a*, Tel., have also the meanings of mother-in-law, sister-in-law, paternal aunt; and the corresponding Singhalese *att-â* means a maternal grandmother; meanings which are not found in Sans. In South Malayâḷam *âchchi* means mother, matron.

For the Scythian analogies of these words, compare Finnish *aïti*, mother, together with the following words for father—viz., Turkish *ata*; Hungarian *atya*; Finnish *âtta*; Cheremiss *âtyâ*; Mordvin *atai*; Ostiak *ata*. Comp. also Lappish *aija*, grandfather, and also *attje*. It is remarkable that *atta* is also found in Gothic—*e.g.*, *attan*, father; *aithein*, mother. Comp. also ἄττα, and Latin *atta*, a salutation used to old men, equivalent to father. If we might seek for a Dravidian root for this widely used word, we may perhaps find it in the Tamil *attu*, to join, to lean upon.

ann-ei, mother; honorifically, elder sister. *ann-ei* and *amm-ei* are probably correlative forms of the same base, *m* being sometimes softened into *n*. Comp. however Finnish and Hungarian *anya*, mother; Mordvin *anai;* Ostiak *ane;* and also *anna* and *ana* in two dialects of the Turkish. The Hindi *annî*, a nurse, is possibly the same word.

app-an, father. Comp. the following words for father-in-law—viz., Ostiak *ûp*, *ôp;* Finnish *appi;* Hungarian *ip*, *ipa*, *apos*. See also Semitic Analogies.

amm-âḷ, *amm-ei*, *amm-an*, mother: the word is also used honorifically in addressing matrons. Another form of this word in Malayâḷam is *umma*, mother. The following are correlative words, *amm-âÿ*, maternal grandmother, aunt by the mother's side, and *amm-ân*, mother's brother, also sometimes father's. Comp. Samoïede *amma*, mother; Jeneseï *amma* or *am;* Estrian *emma;* Finnish *emâ*. Comp. also Ostiak *in-a*, woman, wife; Hungarian *eme*. See also Sanskrit and Semitic Analogies. The Sans. *ambâ* or *ammâ*, mother, properly a name or title of Durgâ, seems to be derived from the Dravidian word. The bloody rites of Durgâ, or Kâlî, were probably borrowed from the demonolatrous aborigines by the Brahmans; and *amma*, mother, the name by which she was known and worshipped—her only Dravidian name—would naturally be borrowed at the same time. Comp. also the Scindian *amâ* and the Malay *ama*, mother.

It is remarkable that in Tuḷu the words which denote father and mother seem to have mutually changed places. In Tuḷu *amm-e*, is father, *appe*, mother. See an explanation of this in the Semitic Analogies. Comp. the Mongolian *ama*, father; also Sans. *amba*, father. In Tibetan and its sister dialects, *pa* or *po* denotes a man; *ma* or *mo*, a woman; and these words are post-fixed to nouns as signs of gender—*e.g.*, *Bot-pa*, a Tibetan man, *Bot-mà*, a Tibetan woman.

ar-u, *âr*, precious, dear, scarce. Comp. Hungarian *aru*, *âr*, price; Finnish and Lappish *arwo*. Comp. also Sans. *argha*, value, price, from *argh*, *arh*, to deserve.

al, *êl*, the prohibitive particle, *noli*—*e.g.*, *koḍêl* (from *koḍ-u*, give), give not; Santâl prohibitive *âlâ*. Comp. Lappish *ali* or *ele;* Ostiak *ilâ;* and Finnish *âlâ*. See also Semitic Analogies. The Sans. *alam* cannot properly be called a prohibitive particle; it means enough.

avva, Tel., a grandmother; Tam. *avv-a*, a matron, an elderly woman; Can. *avve*, a mother or grandmother; Tuda *av*. Comp. Mordvin *ava*, mother. See also Indo-European Analogies.

al-ei, a wave; Can. *ale;* as a verbal theme *alei* means to wander, to be unsteady. Comp. Finnish *allok*, a wave; comp. also Armenian *alik*. See especially West Indo-European Affinities.

âr-u, a river; Tel. *êru*. Comp. Lesghian *or;* Avar *uor;* Yakutan (Siberian Turkish) *oryas;* Lappish *wiro;* Ostiak *jeaga*. Comp. also Armenian *aru;* Coptic *jaro;* and Hebrew *ôr*, *yeôr*.

âm, it is, yes; root *â*, to become. Comp. Vogul *âm*, yes; Hung. *âm*, yes, surely.

iru-mbu, iron. Comp. Motor (a Samoïede dialect), *ur*, iron. See also Indo-European Analogies.

îd-u, Tel. to swim; Can. *îj-u;* Tam. *nîñj-u*. Comp. Hung. *usz*, to swim; Ostiak *ûdem;* Finnish *uin*.

ûr, a city. Compare Basque *iri*, a city. See Semitic Analogies.

uḷ, to be in, to be; as a noun, a being, an entity, a thing; as a postposition, in, within; Ancient Can. *ôḷ*. As a verb *uḷ* is very irregular; and the *ḷ*, though radical, is often euphonised into *ṇ*. The primitive form and force of the root are apparent in the Tamil appellative verb *uḷḷadu* (*uḷ(ḷ)-adu*), it is, there is; the Can. *uḷḷavu* (*uḷ(ḷ)-a-vu*), there are; and such nouns as *kaḍavuḷ* (*kaḍa-(v)-uḷ*), Tam. God, literally the surpassing or transcendent Being; and *uḷ(ḷ)-am*, the mind, that which is within. *uḷḷadu* (*uḷ-du*) has in Tamil been euphonised into *uṇḍu* (like *koḷ-du*, having taken, into *koṇḍu*), and this euphonised appellative forms the inflexional base of the Telugu verb *uṇḍu*, to be. Comp. with *uḷ*, to be, the Ugrian substantive verb *ol*, to be—*e.g.*, Cheremiss *olam*, I am; Syrianian *voli*, I was; Finnish *olen*, I am. Comp. also the Turk. *ôl*, Hung. *vol*, to be.

The primitive meaning of the Dravidian *uḷ*, seems to be 'within,' in which sense it is still used as a postposition in Tamil.

eṛud-u, to write, to paint. Comp. Hung. *ir*, to write; Manchu *ara;* Fin. *kir*. Tel. *vrâyu*, to write, corresponds, not to the Tamil *eṛud-u*, but to *varei*, Can. *bare*, to draw lines.

èlu-mbu, bone. Comp. Fin. *lua;* Samoïede *luy*, bone.

okk-a, Mal. all; *oka*, Tel. one. Comp. Mordvin *wok*, all.

kaḍ-i, *kar-i*, to bite. Comp. Lapp. *kask*, to bite; Hung. *harap* (*h* in Hungarian corresponding with *k* in Finnish). See Indo-European Affinities.

kaṭṭ-u, to bind, to tie. Comp. the following words, each of which has the same signification: Hung. *köt;* Ostiak *kattem* (to fasten, to catch); Syrianian *kuta;* Finn. *keitt;* Lapp. *karet;* also Hung. *köttel*, rope.

kan, an eye. Comp. Chinese *ngan*, *yen*.

kaṇṇîr, tears. Comp. Finn. *kônyv;* Hung. *könny*. The Tamil word (*kaṇ-nîr*) literally signifies eye-water, so that this resemblance is probably accidental.

kapp-al, a ship, a vessel, probably a verbal noun from *kapp-u*, Tel. to cover over; derivative Telugu noun *kapp-u*, a covering. The verb is not found in Canarese or Tamil, but the Canarese noun *kapp-u*, a subterraneous room, a pit-fall for catching elephants (covered over with branches of trees and grass), and the Tamil noun *kappal*, a ship, properly a decked vessel, in contradistinction to *paḍugu*, an open vessel, are evidently identical in origin with the Telugu verb and noun. The Malay word for 'ship' is *kapâl;* but this has probably been borrowed direct from Tamil, and forms one of a small class of Malay words which have sprung from a Dravidian origin, and which were introduced into the Eastern Archipelago, either by means of the Klings (Kalingas) who settled there in primitive times, or by means of the Arab traders, whose first settlements in the East were on the Malabar coast, where the Malayâḷam, the oldest daughter of the Tamil, is spoken. The following Scythian words for 'ship' appear to be analogous to the Tamil, and have certainly not been borrowed from it: Vogul *kap* or *kaba;* Samoïede *kebe;* Jenesei *kep;* Yerkesian *kaf;* Ostiak *chap*. See also the analogies adduced under the word *kebi*, a cave.

kar-u, black, an euphonised form of which is *kâr;* Gujarâthi *karo*. Comp. Turkish *quara* or *kara;* Calmuck *chara;* Mongolian *k'ara;* Japanese *kuroi*. One of the eight words belonging to the language of the ancient Turks of the Altæ, recorded by the Chinese, was *koro*, black. See Introduction. These Scythian affinities are too distinct to admit of the smallest doubt. There is evidently a connection between this Scytho-Dravidian root and the Sanskrit *kâla*, black; Tamil *kâḷam;* from which there is a derivative, *kâṛagam*, that throws light on the relation of *kâla* to *kar-u*. Comp. Greek κέλ-αινος. „ Probably also *kṛi* (*kar*), the radical portion of *kṛishna*, Sans. black (adjectival form *kârshṇa*), is related to the same Scythian theme, and ultimately to *kâl-a*.

kara-ḍi, a bear, from *kara-ḍu*, rough. Comp. Samoïede *korgo;* Tungusian *kuti*, *kuuti*. See also Indo-European Affinities.

kaṛu-gu, an eagle. Comp. Ostiak *kuruk*, an eagle. See also Indo-European Affinities.

kaṛutt-u, the throat; also *kur-al*, the wind-pipe. Comp. Vogul *kuryd*, the throat; Finnish *kurkku, kero, kerri;* Kurd *g'eru;* Lappish *karas, kirs.* Comp. also the Slavonian *gorlo;* Sans. *grîva, gala.*

kal, a stone. Comp. Lappish *kalle*, also *kedke* or *kerke;* Lesghian *gul;* Kamtschadale *kual, kualla.* Probably these words have an ulterior connection with the Finnish *kiwi;* Hungarian *kö;* Ostiak *key, kaück.* Comp. also (through the interchange of *l* and *r*) the Tamil *kâṛ*, gravel, a pebble, with the Greek χεϱ-άς, gravel, and χεϱ-μάς, a stone, and the Armenian *k'ar, kuar*, a stone. The Dravidian root cannot be traced further than *kal*, a stone; but the corresponding Lappish *kalle* appears to be derived from, or connected with, *kalw-at*, to become hard. Comp. also *karra*, Lappish, hard, rough.

kaḷḷ-am, kaḷa-vu, a theft. Comp. Lappish *keles*, a lie; Hung. *tsal*, to cheat; also Sans. *chhala*, fraud.

kâṟṟ-u (pronounced *kâttr-u*), wind. Probably from *kâl*, one of the meanings of which is wind, with the formative addition of *du* (*kâl-du* = *kâttru*); Tel. *gâli.* Comp. Kangazian (a Turkish dialect) *kat*, wind; Sojoten (a Samoïede dialect) *kat;* other Samoïede dialects *chat, kada* (also a storm, *charru*); Georg. *kari;* Jurazen *chada.*

kây, to heat, or be hot, to burn to boil. Comp. Finnish *keite, keitta*, to boil, to cook; Hungarian *keszil.* Comp. especially the Indo-European affinities of this word.

kâl, foot; Tuda *kôl;* Tuḷu *kâr.* Comp. Mongol *k'ul;* Ostiak *kur;* Tungusian *chalgan, halgan;* Permian *kok;* Ossete *kach, koch;* Vogul *lal;* Korean *pal;* Canton-Chinese *koh;* Hung. *gyalog*, on foot.

kiṛa, old, aged. Comp. Hung. *kor;* Oriental Turkish *chari;* other Turkish idioms, *kar, kart;* Wotiak *keres;* Lesghian *heran.* See the Indo-European analogies of this word.

kîḷ, Can. below; Tam. *kîṛ;* ultimate base *kiṛ.* Comp. Wolgian *kilgi, kelga*, deep. From the Tamil *kiṛ* is derived *kiṛ-angu*, a bulbous root, with which we may perhaps compare the Slavonian *koren*, Jeneseï *koryl*, a root.

kudir-ei, a horse; Can. *kudur-e.* The Sanskrit *ghôṭa*, a horse, may possibly have an ulterior connection with the Dravidian word; but I cannot suppose the Dravidian word to have been borrowed from the Sanskrit one, for the Tamil occasionally borrows and uses *ghôṭa* (in Tam. *ghôṛam*, also *gôḍagam;* Tel. *gurram-u*), in addition to its own *kudir-ei;* besides which Tamil provides us with a probable derivation of *kudirei*, viz., *kudi*, to leap.

The Scythian analogies are Jeneseï *kut* and Lesghian *kota*. Comp. also Malay *kuda*.

kuḍ-i, a habitation; *kuḍ-il*, *kuḍis-ei*, a hut, a cottage; probably from *kuḍ* (base of *kûḍ*), to come together. In Tel. and Can., *guḍ-i* means a temple. A similar word, *kuṭa* or *kuṭi*, is also contained in Sanskrit.—See Sanskrit Affinities. It has a place in each of the dialects of the Finnish family—*e.g.*, Mordvin *kudo*, a house; Cheremiss *kuda*, Finnish *kota*, Ostiak *chot*, Lappish *kata*. I suspect the Saxon *cot* had a similar origin.

kuḷ-ir, cold, to become cold: ultimate base *kuḷ*; related words *kûd-al* and *kûd-ir*, cold; also Tel. and Can. *chali*, cold. *śil-ir*, Tam. to tremble, seems to be a collateral root. With *kuḷ-ir* comp. Lappish *kal-ot*, to freeze; Finnish *cyl-ma*; and with *chali* (Tel. and Can.) comp. Permian *cheli*, cold.—See also Indo-European Affinities.

kei, hand.

key, to do. In all the Dravidian dialects *kei* is hand. In Telugu *kêlu* is also found. The most common form of this word in Telugu is *chey-i* or *chêy-i*. The word signifying to do is almost identical, viz., *key*, *chey*, &c.—See Sanskrit Affinities. Comp. the following words in Scythian dialects;—Hungarian *kêz* (pronounced *keis*), Finnish *kchêsi* (root *kâ*—*e.g.*, genitive *kâ-an*), Estnian *kâsi*, Ostiak *ket*, Lappish *kât*, Permian *ki*, Lasian *ke*, Mingrelian *che*, Quasi-Qumuq (a Turkish dialect) *kâya*, Turkish *kol*, Mongol *ghar*, Tungusian *gala*. The Hungarian has both *kar* and *kêz*; but the former is used to signify arm, the latter hand—a distinction which seems to prove that those roots, though perhaps ultimately related, have long been independent of one another. The words in the various Scythian languages signifying to do appear to stand in the same relation to the word for hand that they do in the Aryan and Dravidian languages. Comp. the Turkish *kyl*, to do; Mongol *ki*, Manchu *gai*, Mordvin *kâ*. These words resemble the Aryan *kar*, to do, but still more closely the Dravidian *kî*, *ke*, &c. The substantial identity of the Indo-European words for hand and to do, with the Scythian words, and of the Dravidian with both, seems to furnish us, as I have shown under the head of Sanskrit Affinities, with a reliable illustration of the original oneness of all these languages.

kapp-u, Can. a subterraneous room, a pitfall; Tam. *keb-i*, a cave. Comp. Mongol and Manchu *kobi*, a cavity, a cave; Ostiak *kaba*, *kebi*, *kavi*, a chamber. Comp. also *kapp-al*, Tam. a ship, from *kapp-u*, Tel. to cover over.—See Indo-European Affinities.

kivi, Can. the ear; Tam. and Tel. (euphonically softened) *chevi*, Tuḷu *keppi*, Tuda *kevi*, Brahui *khaff*: probably related words *kâd-u*, the ear, and *kêḷ*, to hear. Comp. the following Scythian words signifying the ear:—Samoïede dialects *ko, ku, kus;* Korean *kui*, Ossete *k'us*, Kurd *g'oh*, Turkish dialects *kulak*. With the softened Dravidian form *śevi*, comp. also Sans. *śravas*, the ear.

kêl-u, Tel. the hand. Comp. Kuralian *kell* and Georgian *cheli*, the hand. See also *kei*.

kêḷ, to hear; *kêḷ-vi*, hearing. Comp. Finnish *kuul-en*, to hear; Syryanian *kyla*, Cheremiss *kol-am*, Hung. *halla*, also *ker*, to ask, Lappish *kull-et* (*kullem*, hearing), Ostiak *kûdj-em*. Notice the change of the final *l* of the other Finnish dialects into *dj* in Ostiak, a sort of cerebral consonant, somewhat similar in sound to the final *ḷ* of the corresponding Tamil *kêḷ*.—See also the Indo-European affinities of this word.

kol, to kill. Comp. Finnish *kuol*, to die; Cher. *kol-em*, Syry. *kula*, Hung. *hal*.—See also Indo-European Analogies.

kôn, a king, a ruler; in honorific usage a shepherd, or man of the shepherd caste; *kôn-mei*, royal authority. Another form of the same word is *kô*, a king, a god. *kôyil* in ordinary Tamil means a temple; in the Old Tamil of the Syrian inscriptions it means a palace, literally *kô-il*, the king's house. It is hard to determine whether *kô* or *kôn* is to be regarded as the primitive form of this word. Comp. the Turkish and Mongolian *khân*, also *khagân*, a ruler; Ostiak *khon*.

kôṛ-i, the domestic fowl; Can. *kôḷi*, Tuḷu, *kôri*, Tel. *kôḍi*, Gônd *kôr* (from *ku* or *kû*, to call, to cry as a bird (from which comes *kûyil*, Tam. the cuckoo, and *kural*, the voice). This word is the common term which is used in the Dravidian languages for both the cock and the hen. If it is required to express the gender, *śêval*, Tam. a cock, or *peṭṭei*, a hen, is prefixed adjectivally to the common term *kôṛi*. The Sanskrit *kukkuṭa*, a cock, may possibly be derived by reduplication from *ku*, to cry as a bird, and if so it is identical in origin with the Drav. *kôṛi*, both words being formed from a mimetic verbal theme. The Scythian analogies, on the other hand, seem closer and more direct. Comp. Vogul *kore*, Ostiak *korek*, *kurek*, Permian *korech, kuryg, kuraga*. It looks as if the North-Asian tongues borrowed this word directly from the Dravidian; for the domestic fowl had its origin in India, where the wild variety still exists; and when it was introduced into Upper Asia, the name by which it was known in India would naturally be introduced along with the fowl itself. That name being, not Sanskrit, but Dravidian, it would almost appear as if the domestic fowl had been introduced from India into Central and Northern Asia prior to the irruption into India of the Aryan race, and the consequent cessation of intercourse between the Drâvidians and the Scythians. The Dravidian word seems to have found its way into two languages of the western branch of the Indo-European family, viz., the Persian and the Russian. Comp. Persian *khor-os*, a cock; *kour-ek*, a poulet; and the Russ *kûr*, a cock; *kûr-itsa*, a fowl; diminutive, *kûr-otchka*, a chicken.

śâral, rain driven by the wind: in the usage of the Southern Tamilians, the rain brought by the south-west monsoon. Comp. Samoïede *sarre*, Permian *ser*, Votiak *sor*, rain.

śa, or *śâg-u*, to die; Tel. *chachu* (base *cha*). Comp. Samoïede *chawe* and *chabbi*, dead.—See Sanskrit Affinities.

chêr-u, mud. Comp. *chedo*, *zerta*, *choti*, and *chat'*, Lesghian words for clay.

tal-a, Tel. the head; Can. *tal-e*, Tam. *tal-ei*. Comp. Mongol *tolo-gai*, Calmuck *tol-go*, Buriat *tul-gai*, Samutan (a Tungusian dialect) *döll*; other Tungusian dialects *düll*, *del*, *deli*, Turkish *tor*.

tî, fire. The more commonly used Tamil word for fire is *neruppu*, Tel. *nippu*, *nippuka*; but *tî* is the more classical Tamil word, and it is much used by the mass of the people in the southern districts of the country; classical Can. *tî*, Tuḷu *tû*. The Scythian affinities of this word for fire, are peculiarly distinct—*e.g.*, Samoïede *tu*, *tui*, *ti*, *ty*, Manchu *tua*, Hungarian *tüz*, Ostiak *tût*, Tungus. *togo*, Lesghian *tze*, *zi*, *zie*, Finnish *tuli*, Lappish *tall*, Mongol *dul*. Comp. also Gaelic *teine*, Welsh *tân*, and Persian *tigh*. Sans. *têjas*, brilliancy, is from *tij*, to be sharp. Comp., however, *div*, Sans. to be bright, and especially *dî* and *dîp*, to shine.

têr, chariot. Comp. Mongol *t'ereg*, chariot.

tôl, skin; Can. *togal-u*. Comp. Vogul *toul*, *towl*, skin.

nakk-u, to lick; derivative noun *nâkku*; ultimate form *nâ*, the tongue. Comp. Ostiak *nal*, to lick, and *nâl*, the tongue; Samoïede *nawa*, the tongue; *nâlige*, Can. the tongue. Comp. Hung. *nyelo*.

nag-ei, to laugh, laughter. Comp. Ostiak *nâg-am*, to laugh; *nâch*, laughter; Hung. *nevet*.

nây, a dog; probably from *nâ*, the tongue = the animal that licks. Comp. *nohai*, a dog; Calmuck *nokoi*, *nochoi*. In Telugu, a fox is *nakka*, from *nakku*, to prowl. Another word for dog in classical Tamil is *nayakkan*, from *naya*, to be affectionate.

neṟṟi (pronounced *nettri*), the forehead (from *neṟi*, to stand upright); Tel. *nud-ur*. Comp. Lesghian *nata, nodo, nete-bek*, the forehead.

nôḍ-u, Can. to see, to perceive; *nôkk-u*, Tam.-Mal. Comp. Mongol *nüdu*, the eye.

ñâyiṟ-u, nêyiṟ-u, Tam.-Mal.; *nêsar-u*, class. Can. the sun. Comp. Hung. *nyâr* (= *ñâr*), summer; *nap*, a day; also Mongol *nar-an*, the sun; Ostiak *naï*, Afghan *nmar*.

paśu, green; *pul*, grass. Hung. *pazsit*, grass; Vogul *piza*, Ostiak *pady*.

pei-(y)-an, peî-(y)-al, Tam.-Mal. a boy, a servant; *pei-dal*, Tam. and Mal. but especially the latter, a boy or girl, a child; Can. *heida* (for *peida*), a boy or girl. *peiyan* is a masculine; the words in *al* and *dal* are verbal nouns, and therefore neuters. *dal* is as common a formative of verbal nouns even in Tamil as *al*, and the two forms are mutually convertible. *peiyal* and *peidal* being abstracts, are therefore capable of denoting either sex. The theme or base of these words is evidently *pei*, a softened form of *paś-u* (*paś-u* = *pay-u* = *pei*). Hence *paśan-gaḷ*, Tam. the older form, is often used as the colloquial plural, instead of *peiyan-gaḷ*, which is now reckoned more correct.

Comp. the following Ugrian words for son:—Vogul *py, pu;* Mordvin and Syry. *pi;* Votiak *pyes;* Finnish *poika;* Hungarian *fiu;* Estrian *poeg;* Ostiak *pach, poch, pagul, pagam, pyram;* Lappish *patja*. The Swedish *poike* appears to be derived from the Finnish *poika;* and the Greek παῖ-ς, the Latin *pu-er*, and the English *boy*, are evidently related words. See Indo-European Affinities. The Dravidian languages appear to contain the ultimate theme of all these words—viz., *pei*, Tam. to be green or fresh, a word which has been softened from *paś-u* (*pay-u*, convertible into *pei*), green, by a common Dravidian law.

paṛ-a, old (by reason of use); Can. *paḷa-ya*, old, what is old. Comp. Mordvin *peres;* Syry. *pörys;* Ostiak *pirich*, old. See Indo-European Affinities.

pal, tooth (*pandri* = *pal-di*, Tam. a hog, the animal with a tooth or tusk). Comp. Lappish *pane, padne;* Wolgian *padne, paï, pin;* Ostiak *pank, penk, pek;* Cher. *py*.

pal, pala, many, various. Comp. Finnish *palyo;* Manchu *fulu*.

pâl, a part, a division, a half. Comp. the following Ugrian words signifying a half:—Samoïde *peâleâ;* Cher. *pêle;* Lappish *beâle;* Ostiak *pêlek;* Hungarian *fél.* See also Semitic Affinities.

piḍ-ú, to catch. Comp. Finnish *pidan,* to catch.

pir-agu (base *pir*), behind, after. Comp. Ostiak *pir, pira,* behind, hindermost; Finnish *pera.* See Indo-European and Semitic Affinities.

piḷḷ-ei, a child. Comp. Yarkand Tartar *billa,* a child. What is the origin of the Hindi *pillâ,* a cub, a pup? See also Indo-European Affinities.

pu-gei, smoke (Tel. *pog-a*). Comp. Hung. *fûs,* smoke; also the following words signifying vapour in the Turkish dialects: *bug, buch, bugu.* Comp. also the English *fog.*

peṉ, a female; Can. *heṉn-u.* Comp. Lappish *hene,* a female.

pokkil-i, Tel. the navel (ultimate root probably *poy,* Tam. hollow). Comp. Ostiak *puklam,* the navel.

bayir, Can. the belly; Tam. *vayir-u;* Gônd *pir.* Comp. Kangaẓian (a Turkish dialect) *bar,* the belly; Armenian *port;* Albanian *bark;* Ostiak *perga;* Mordvin *pak.*

bâḷ, Can. to exist; Tam. *vâṛ,* to flourish, to live prosperously. Comp. Oriental Turkish *bôl,* to exist; Hung. *boldog,* happy.

man-a, Can. a house: class. Tam. *man-ei.* Comp. Samoïede *men,* a house; Vogul *unneh.* Theme of the Drav. word *man,* to abide, to exist; *maniki,* Tel. existence, home.

mar-am, a tree, wood; Can. *mar-a;* Tel. *mân-u* (for *mrân-u*). Comp. Lappish *muor, muorra,* a tree, wood; Quasi-Qumuk Turkish *murm, murch;* Mongol *modo;* Tomsk. *madji;* Finnish *metsa;* Lettish *mes.*

mar-i, offspring, the young of certain animals, as the deer, the horse, the ass, &c.; also in Can. a young child; Mongol *mori,* a horse; Manchu *morin;* also German *mähre;* Old German *marah;* Gaelic *marc.* According to Aug. Schlegel (Sinico Aryaca), the root of the Mongol *mori,* &c., is found in the Chinese *ma,* a horse, with the addition of *ri* as a suffix. Probably the Drav. word is from *mar-u,* other.

mal-a, Can., Mal., Tel. a hill, a mountain; Tam. *mal-ei.* This Drav. root has found its way into the Sans. lexicons as the base of *Malaya,* the Sans. name of the Western Ghauts—*Malayâḷam,* or as the later Greek and Arabian geographers called it, "Male." It has probably given their name also to the Mâl-dives or Mal-dives, the *dives* (Sans. *dwîpa*), or islands, pertaining to Male or Malayâḷam. Comp. Albanian *malli,* a hill;

Vogul *molima;* Permian *mylk;* Volgian (by a change of *l* into *r*), *mar;* Samoïede *mari;* Avar *mehr;* Finnish *mâki.*

murumuru, to grumble (not wholly a mimetic word). Comp. Finnish *muraj*, and Hungarian *morog*, to murmur. See also Indo-European Affinities.

mun, before; Hung. *emun, umun*, before. The *e* or *u* of the Hung. word is prosthetic. Chinese for face is *mien* or *min.*

vân, heaven; also *mân.* Comp. Mordvin *mânel*, heaven; Tungus. *ñyan;* dialect of the Kukies in the Chittagong hills, *van.*

vây, the mouth. Comp. Samoïede *aiw-a*, mouth; Lappish *saiwe;* Hung. *ayak*, lip; *szay*, mouth.

viṛ-i, to watch, to keep awake. Comp. Finnish *vir-ot*, to watch; Hung. *vir-ad.*

velich-am, light; *vilakk-u*, a light. Comp. Hung. *vilâg*, a light.

I append a list of Hungarian affinities kindly furnished me by Dr Gundert, in addition to those which have already been adduced. The Drávidian words cited are Tamil, if it is not mentioned that they are otherwise.

	Hung.		Hung.
âḷa, Can. deep.	*ala.*	*tônru*, to appear.	*tûnni.*
kaśappu, bitter.	*keserû.*	*poḍi*, powder, dust.	*por.*
kiru, Can. little.	*kis, kits.*	*pôr*, battle.	*per.*
kiṭṭa, near.	*kôzel.*	*pêś-u*, to speak.	*besze.*
śûppu, to suck.	*szop.*	*beṭṭa*, Can. mountain.	*bertz.*
śêr, to gather.	*szed.*	*mägu*, child.	*magzat.*
śerippu, shoe.	*tzipello.*	*mâḷ*, to perish.	*mul.*
śiragu, wing.	*szarny.*	*muyal* (Tuḷu *nosalu*), a hare.	*nyûl.*
śol, speak.	*szol.*	*mulei*, breast (woman's)	*melly.*
śôr (Can. and Tulu *sôru*), to leak.	*tsorge.*	*ve*, to boil.	*buz-in.*
śuḍu, to heat.	*sûl*, to roast; *sût*, to bake.	*vinei*, action, sin.	*bûn*, sin.
sûl, pregnancy.	*szûl*, to bring forth.	*vir*, to unfold.	*virr*, to dawn.
śurukku, narrow.	*szorit, szûck.*		*virâg*, to blossom.
tarei, to sprout.	*terem.*	*viṛu* (Tuḷu *bur*), to fall.	*bukni.*
tiḷei, to be full.	*tel, tôl*, full, fill.	*vit*, to sow.	*vet.*

The following Chinese, Japanese, and Mongolian affinities are chiefly selected from lists contained in Mr Edkins' "China's Place in Philology." There is a remarkable amount of agreement, especially between the Dravidian languages and the Mongolian, in principles and forms; but I notice few traces of resemblance in the vocabulary.

	CHINESE.
kan, eye.	*ngan.*
śey, chey, to do.	*tsu.*
mei, ink.	*mek.* Comp. Greek μέλας.
akka, elder sister.	*aka*, elder brother.
paḍ-ar, to expand.	*bat*, to extend.
kaṭṭ-u, to tie, a tie.	*kit*, to tie, a tie.
śid-ar, to scatter.	*sat*, to scatter, to sow. Comp. Lat. *ser-o.*
paḍ-u, to suffer, used as a passive auxiliary.	*bad, bit*, to spread, then to be acted upon; used as a sign of the passive.

	JAPANESE.
iru, to be.	*ari, iri, ori, uri*, to be, to dwell.
karu, black.	*kurô* or *kuroi*, black.
para, to spread.	*baru, haru*, to extend.
paṛa, old.	*burui, furui*, old.

	MONGOLIAN.
karu, black.	*kara*, black.
paḍ-ar, to expand.	*badarahu, badaral*, extension.
kei, hand.	*gar.* Comp. Sans. *kara.*

I trust the reader will remember that in comparing Dravidian words with words belonging to other families of speech,—Semitic, Indo-European, and Scythian,—I am quite aware of the danger of mistaking accidental assonances for proofs of relationship. "If," as Max Müller justly remarks (ii. 283), "instead of being satisfied with pointing out the faint coincidences in the lowest and most general elements of speech, scholars imagine they can discover isolated cases of minute coincidence amidst the general disparity in the grammar and dictionary, their attempts become unscientific and reprehensible." I am fully persuaded that many of the resemblances I have tabulated in these lists will turn out to be resemblances and nothing more. It will be found also that the resemblance diminishes or disappears in the course of inquiry, and therefore that it must have been accidental. I am equally persuaded, however, that *all* the resemblances I have pointed out will not be found to be the result of accident; and I consider it an aid to further, more extended, and more searching inquiry, and therefore not unscientific, to draw the attention of scholars to such resemblances as exist—whatever their nature or degree. It is desirable, in the interest of scientific inquiry itself, to indicate the various directions in which such inquiry should be made, and to furnish some means of forming an idea as to whether it is likely to be rewarded with success or not.

APPENDIX.

I.

EVIDENCE THAT THE TUDA, KÔTA, GÔND, KHOND OR KU, RÂJMAHÂL, AND ORÂON LANGUAGES ARE DRAVIDIAN TONGUES, AND THAT THERE IS A DRAVIDIAN ELEMENT IN BRAHUI.

THE Tuda, Kôta, Gônd, Khond or Ku, Râjmahâl, and Orâon languages being rude, uncultivated idioms and little known, it appears to be desirable to furnish the reader with proofs of the assertion that those languages belong to the same Dravidian stock as Tamil and Telugu, Malayâḷam, Tuḷu, and Canarese. It seems also desirable to point out the evidence on which the assertion that there is a Dravidian element in Brahui rests. The substance of this chapter was included in the introduction in the first edition of this work, but I have now thought it best to place it in the Appendix.

1. TUDA.—It used to be supposed that the language of the Tudas was altogether *sui generis*, or at least that it was unconnected with any of the languages of the neighbouring plains. In adopting the conclusion that the Tuda language belonged to the Dravidian stock, and giving it a place, in consequence, in the first edition of this work among the Dravidian dialects whose grammar was about to be compared, the evidence on which I placed most reliance was that of a list of words and short sentences kindly communicated to me by the Rev. F. Metz, of the Basel Missionary Society, missionary on the Nilgherry Hills. Mr Metz's acquaintance with the Tuda language was even then greater than that acquired by any other European ; but in the eighteen years that have elapsed since then it has become still more extensive and perfect. I am indebted to him for many valuable communications respecting the hill tribes and their languages. The Rev. Dr Pope has also applied himself very zealously to the study of the Tuda language ; and the publication, in Colonel Marshall's book on the Tudas, of Dr Pope's "Outlines of the Grammar of the Tuda Language," with copious lists of words, constitutes an era in the history of the language of this rude but interesting tribe. I cannot do better than refer the reader to that grammar for fuller information. I shall content myself here with transcribing the concluding paragraphs.

"§ 44. On the whole, I venture to think that

"(1.) The Tuda is a language which was once highly inflexional; but having lost most of its inflexions, the people, who have evidently degenerated in every way as the result of isolation, have not replaced them by significant particles or auxiliaries to the same extent as the other South Indian tribes, and the language has thus dwindled down to a mere skeleton. It now barely suffices for the purposes of a very barbarous people.

"2. The language seems to have been originally old Canarese, and not a distinct dialect. The Tudas were probably immigrants from the Canarese country, and have dwelt in the Nîlagiris for about 800 years. A few Tamil forms were introduced by the Poligars. Intercourse with the Badagars has probably modernised a few of the forms, and introduced some words. Of Telugu influences I see no trace. Nor can I trace any resemblance in Tuda to Malayalam in any of the points where that dialect differs from its sisters."—"*Outlines of the Tuda Grammar*," included in Colonel Marshall's "*Phrenologist amongst the Todas.*"

2. Kôta.—Whilst the language and customs of the Tudas have always been regarded with peculiar interest, the Kôtas (a tribe of craftsmen, residing from an unknown antiquity on the Nilgherry Hills), being exceedingly filthy in their habits, and addicted beyond all other low-caste tribes to the eating of carrion, have generally been shunned by Europeans; and, in consequence, their language is less known than that of the Tudas. Notwithstanding this, the following paradigm of the Kôta pronouns, and of the present and preterite tense of its verb, furnished me by Mr Metz, will show that the language of this tribe is essentially Dravidian :—

Present—Future. Go, or shall go.	Past. Went.
âne hôgape.	*hôsipe.*
nî hôgapi.	*hôdi.*
avane hôgako.	*hôda* (it went, *hôte*).
nâme hôgapême.	*hôsipême.*
nîve hôgapîri.	*hôsipiri.*
avare hôgako.	*hôsiko.*

In this paradigm the first person plural, both of the pronoun and of the verb, and the second person plural of the verb, accord most with Tamil; the other forms agree most with Ancient Canarese, particularly the formative suffix of the present tense of the verb. In the use of *h* instead of *p* (*hôgu*, to go, instead of *pôgu*), the Kôta accords with the modern Canarese. The third person of the Kôta verb, which is formed both in the singular and the plural, by the suffix *ko*, seems at first sight entirely non-Dravidian, but in reality it is in perfect agreement with several poetic forms in Old Tamil and Old Canarese. The sign of the genitive case in Kôta is *a*, of the dative *ke*, of the locative *olge*,—all which forms correspond with those which are found in the other dialects. The preterite is formed by changing *ga* into *ji*—*e.g.*, *hôgako*, he goes; *hôgiko*, he went. In this also we see a family resemblance to the manner in which the other dialects, especially the Telugu, form their preterites. The Kôta forms its infinitive by the addition of *alik* to the root—*e.g.*, *tin*, eat; *tinalik*, to eat. The infinitives of the corresponding verb in Canarese are *tinna*, *tinnalu*, *tinnalike*. On the whole, though certain analogies with Tamil and also with Tuda may be observed in the Kôta, I regard this language as more nearly allied to the Canarese than to any other Dravidian idiom.

3. Gônd.—A grammar and vocabulary of the Gônd language were published ni 1849 by the Rev. J. E. Dribery, at Bishop's College, Calcutta, and a paper on the language of the Seoni Gônds, by Dr Manger, including "The Song of Sandsumjee," appeared shortly after in the *Journal of the Bengal Asiatic Society.* A translation of the Gospels of St Matthew and St Mark into Gôndi by the Rev. J. Dawson, of the Free Church of Scotland Mission, published in 1872–3 at Allahabad, throws much new light upon the language of this tribe, besides forming an interesting commencement to its literary history; and this has been followed up by an epitome of Gônd Grammar and a list of words by the same author in the *B. A. S. Journal.* These publications contain so many proofs of the close affinity of the Gônd language to Tamil, Telugu, and Canarese, that it seems quite unnecessary to prove in detail that it is a member of the Dravidian family. It is not so easy to determine to which of the cultivated Dravidian dialects it is most nearly allied. In many respects it accords most with Telugu, its neighbour to the south and east; but, on the whole, it seems more closely allied to Tamil, though locally of all Dravidian dialects the farthest removed from it—a proof that the claim of Tamil to be considered as the best representative of the primitive condition of these languages is not destitute of foundation.

The chief particulars in which Gônd agrees with Telugu, rather than with Tamil or with Canarese, are as follows :—

(1.) The pronouns of the first and second persons, especially the second person plural, have most resemblance to Telugu. Compare *mikun,* Gônd, to you, Telugu, *mîku,* with the Tamil *umakku,* and the Canarese *nimage.*

(2.) Another point of resemblance to Telugu consists in the absence of a feminine form of the pronoun of the third person singular and of the third person of the verb, and the use of the neuter singular for the feminine singular.

(3.) The Gônd preterite verbal participle is formed, like the Telugu, by the addition of *si* to the root, instead of the *du,* which is so largely employed by Tamil and Canarese.

(4.) A considerable number of roots of secondary importance have been borrowed by the Gônd from the Hindi; and a small number of Sanskrit *tadbhavas* seem to have been borrowed by it from the Telugu—*e.g., nattur,* blood, from the Telugu *netturu,* a corrupt derivative from the Sanskrit *ractam.*

In some instances again Gônd agrees remarkably with Canarese—*e.g.,* the Gônd infinitive is in *âlê* or *ilê.* In Telugu and Tamil the infinitive is invariably in *a*; the Tamil has a verbal noun ending in *al,* of which the dative is used as a supine; and the High Tamil occasionally, but Canarese ordinarily, uses this very form *al* as an infinitive. Gônd also like Canarese sometimes prefers *k* where the Telugu has *ch* and the Tamil *s*—*e.g.,* the ear, is in Tamil *śevi,* Telugu *chevi,* Canarese *kivi,* in Gônd also *kaui.* To do, is in Tamil *śey,* Telugu *chêy,* Canarese *gêy* (*g* hard), Gônd *ki.* Such agreements of the Gônd with the Canarese are rare; but the particulars in which the Gônd agrees with the Tamil, though the Telugu country lies between it and the country in which the Tamil is spoken, are numerous and important. The following are specimens of this agreement :—

(1.) Telugu has but one form for the plural of nouns substantive, the suffix *lu*; Tamil has two, *ar* and *gaḷ,* the former epicene, the latter neuter : Gônd also has two, *ôr* and *k.*

(2.) Gônd, like colloquial Tamil, makes much use of a double plural for personal pronouns and the personal terminations of verbs, by combining *ôr* and *k,* like the Tamil *ar* and *gaḷ*—*e.g.,* compare the Gônd *ôr* and *ôrk,* they, with the colloquial

Tamil *avar* and *avargaḷ; ândur, ândurk*, they are or were, with the Tamil *ânâr, ânârgaḷ*.

(3.) The instrumental case in Telugu is formed by the addition of *chêta:* Gônd, like the Tamil, uses *âl*.

(4.) Gônd differs from Telugu, and accords with Tamil in retaining unaltered the initial vowel of its pronouns in the oblique cases. Thus, from *adi*, Telugu, it, comes *dêni*, of it; Tamil *adin*, of it; Gônd *adenâ*.

(5.) The Telugu negative particles are *lêdu*, there is not, and *kâdu*, it is not; the corresponding particles in Tamil are *illei* and *alla;* in Gônd *hillê* and *hallê*.

(6.) Telugu systematically uses *ḍ* instead of Tamil vocalic *ṛ;* the Gônd retains the *r* of Tamil; *e.g.*, *êḍu* or *aḍalu*, Telugu, to weep; Tamil *aṛa*, Gônd *ara*. So also compare *êḍu*, Telugu, seven, with Tamil *êṛu* and Gônd *yêr-ung*.

(7.) Gônd, like Ancient Tamil, forms its future by appending *k* to the root. Compare Gônd *kî-kâ*, I will do, with Ancient Tamil *śey-gu;* compare also Ancient Canarese *gey-gum*, used for all tenses and persons.

(8.) A number of Gônd roots denoting objects of primary importance correspond with the Tamil rather than the Telugu—*e.g.*,

	TELUGU.	TAMIL.	GÔND.
three,	*mûḍu*,	*mûndru*,	*mûṇḍ*.
tree,	*mânu*,	*maram*,	*marrâ*.
great,	*pedda*,	*peru, paru*,	*par*.

In a large number of instances Gônd, though retaining the same roots as the other Dravidian dialects, modifies those roots after a fashion peculiar to itself. This will appear on comparing the following Tamil and Gônd words :—

	TAMIL.	GÔND.
boy,	*peidal*,	*pêṇḍgâl*.
to fall,	*viṛa*,	*ara*.
to fill,	*nira*,	*niha*.
light,	*velicham*,	*verchi*.
many, much,	*pala*,	*valle*.
district,	*nâḍu*,	*nâr* (a village).
dew,	*pani*,	*pîni* (cold).
break,	*aḍei*,	*urêha*.

Notwithstanding the affinities between the Gônd and the other Dravidian dialects which have now been mentioned and illustrated, Gônd possesses a large number of roots which are not found elsewhere, and exhibits peculiarities of grammatical structure of such a nature as amply to justify our regarding it as a distinct dialect. The difference existing between Tamil and Telugu sinks into insignificance when compared with the difference between the Gônd and every other dialect of the Dravidian family.

The principal particulars in which the grammatical structure of the Gônd differs from that of the other dialects are as follows :—

(1.) Like the idioms of Northern India, the Gônd evinces a tendency to confound the dative with the accusative, though in possession of both forms.

(2). It has lost the relative participle of the other Dravidian dialects, and uses instead *bô*, the relative pronoun of the Hindi. Here we have an indubitable instance of the grammar of one language being affected by the grammar of another. It is remarkable that the relative participle is retained by the Ku.

(3.) It has a passive voice, formed, as in some of those Northern idioms, by prefixing the past participle of the active voice to the substantive verb.

(4.) The remote and proximate demonstratives (*illi, hi*) which in Tamil are *avar, ivar,* in Telugu *vâru, vîru,* are in Gônd corrupted into *ôr* and *êr.* The neuter plurals, which in Tamil are *avei, ivei,* in Gônd are *âû, tâ;* but a form more in accordance with Tamil is preserved in some of the oblique cases—viz., *ave* and *ive.*

(5.) The base of the interrogative pronouns in Tamil, Telugu, Canarese, Malayâlam is *y,* often softened into *e.* In Gônd it is *b*—*e.g., bôr,* who? (masculine singular), *bâd,* who, which? (neuter-feminine singular); plurals, *bôrk, bâû,* what men? what women and things? *bâ,* why? This Gônd *ba* resembles the Tulu interrogative *vô,* which Dr Gundert derives from *e-v-u.*

(6.) Instead of the regularly formed negative voice of the other dialects, the Gônd forms its negative verbs by simply prefixing the negative particles *hille* or *halle,* to the verb. For example, thou art not, or thou becomest not (in Tamil *âgây,* in Telugu *kâvu*), is in Gônd *halle âyvi.* A similar use of the negative particle is found in the Kota language. The only thing in the other dialects which at all corresponds to this is the occasional formation in poetical Tamil of a negative verb by the insertion of the negative particle *al* between the root of the verb and the pronominal suffix—*e.g., pêś-al-ên,* I speak not, for *pêś-ên.*

(7.) The chief difference, however, in point of grammatical structure between the Gônd and the other Dravidian dialects, consists in its peculiarly elaborate and complete conjugational system. In this particular it is rivalled by the Tulu alone. (See "The Verb: Conjugational System.") Tamil, Malayâlam, and Canarese possess only a present, an indefinite past, and a future—the future more or less aoristic. Telugu, in addition to these tenses, has a regularly formed aorist. The indicative and the imperative are the only moods which these dialects possess, and they are destitute of a passive voice properly so called. All modifications of mood and tense are formed by means either of auxiliary verbs or of suffixed particles. Whilst the more cultivated Dravidian idioms are so simple in structure, the speech of the Gônd boasts in a system of verbal modification and inflexions almost as elaborate as that of Turkish. It has a passive voice: in addition to the indicative and the imperative moods, it possesses a potential: in the indicative mood, where Tamil has only three tenses, it has a present, an imperfect definite, an indefinite past, a perfect, a conditional, and a future, each of which is regularly inflected: like the other idioms, it has a causal verb, but it stands alone in having also an inceptive. In these particulars the Gônd grammar has acquired a development peculiar to itself, perhaps in some degree through the influence of the highly inflected Santâl, its Kôlarian neighbour to the northward.

There is a peculiar refinement in the grammar of the Gônd which is deserving of notice. The possessive forms of the personal pronouns agree in number and gender with the substantives they qualify. Thus, whilst 'my hand' is *nâvâ kei* (Tel. *nâ kei,* Tam. *enadu kei*), 'my son' is *nâvôr marri,* in which *nâvôr,* my, *meus,* is a masculine singular formed from *mâv',* abbreviated from *mâvâ,* with the addition of *ôr,* he (or they, the plural being used for the singular, like Tel. *vâru,* Tam. *avar*). The corresponding Tam. *enadu* (in *enadu magan,* my son) is in itself distinctively a neuter, formed from *du,* the affix of the neuter singular; and yet it is used without distinction of gender (or number in the colloquial dialect) to qualify masculines and feminines. In the Tamil poetical dialect *enadu*, my, is replaced in the plural by *ena*—*e.g.*, *ena keigal*, my hand. The Gônd possessive of the personal pronoun has all four forms complete :—

nâwôr.	*tammur.*	my brother (masc.)
nâwâ.	*selâr.*	my sister (fem.-neut.)
nâwôrk.	*tammurk.*	my brothers (masc. plur.)
nâwông.	*selârk.*	my sisters (fem.-neut. plur.)

4. Ku.*— The Khond, Kandh, or Ku language, undoubtedly a Dravidian idiom, has generally been considered as identical with the Gônd. It was stated long ago by Captain Blunt in the *Asiatic Researches*, vol. vii., on the authority of a native Jaghiredar, that the Gônds and the Khonds are totally distinct races. Notwithstanding this, prior to the publication of the first edition of this work, I had not met with any account of their languages in which they were regarded as different, though in truth their differences are numerous and essential. In many particulars Ku accords more closely than Gônd with Tamil, Telugu, and the other Dravidian tongues ; in some things less so. For example :—

(1.) Gônd forms its infinitive in *âlê* or *îlê ;* Ku, like Telugu, Tamil, and modern Canarese, forms its infinitive by suffixing *a*, sometimes *va* or *pa*. Thus, to become, is in Gônd *âyâlê ;* in Telugu *kâ ;* in Canarese *âgal* or *âga ;* in Tamil *âga ;* in Ku *âva*.

(2.) Ku retains the simplicity of the conjugational system of the other Dravidian dialects, in contradistinction to the elaborateness of the Gônd.

(3.) Gônd forms its negatives by prefixing to the indicative aorist the separate negative particles *hille* or *halle*. In this point Ku differs from Gônd, and agrees with the other dialects. Thus, I do not, is in Gônd *hille kîyôn ;* in Tamil *śeyyên ;* in Telugu *chêyanu ;* in Canarese *gêyenu* ; in Ku *giênu*.

In the following instances Ku accords more closely with Tamil and Canarese, though locally very remote, than with its nearer neighbour, Telugu.

(1.) Telugu forms its plural by the use of *lu* alone, except in some of the oblique forms of the 'rational' demonstratives. Ku, like Tamil, makes a difference between the plurals of nouns which denote rational beings, and those of nouns of the inferior class. The Tamil suffix of the first class of plurals is *ar*, of the second class *kal ;* the corresponding suffixes in Ku are *âru* or *ru*, and *kâ*.

(2.) Telugu forms its masculine singular by means of the suffix *ḍu :* Canarese and Tamil by *anu* and *an*. Ku by means of the suffix *âñu* or *ânyu*. Thus, compare *vâḍu*, Telugu, he, with the Tamil *avan*, Canarese *avanu*, Ku *avâñu*.

(3.) Ku pronouns bear a closer resemblance to the Tamil and Canarese than to the Telugu and Gônd, as will appear from the following comparative view :—

	Telugu.	Gond.	Tamil.	Canarese.	Ku.
I,	*nênu.*	*anâ.*	*yân* (ancient).	*ân* (ancient).	*ânu.*
we,	*mêmu.*	*amât.*	*yâm* (do.)	*âm* (do.)	*âmu.*
thou,	*nîvu.*	*ima.*	*nî.*	*nînu.*	*înu.*

* See a lucidly arranged grammar of this language prepared by Mr Lingam Latchmajî, Deputy Translator to the Ganjam Agency, and published in Oriya characters in the *Calcutta Christian Observer* for May and June 1853. I have not seen any notice in any scientific work or periodical of this valuable contribution to our knowledge of the Indian languages.

	TELUGU.	GOND.	TAMIL.	CANARESE.	KU.
ye,	*mîru.*	*îmat.*	*nîr.*	*nîvu.*	*îru.*
he, remote.	*vâḍu.*	*ôr.*	*avan.*	*avanu.*	*avâñu.*
he, proximate.	*vîḍu.*	*êr.*	*ivan.*	*ivanu.*	*ivâñu.*

(4.) In the Dravidian languages contingency is expressed by the addition of a particle to any verbal tense, person or number. This subjunctive suffix is in Telugu *êni*, or *ê*; in Canarese *re*, *râ*, or *âgyu*. One of the suffixes employed in the Tamil is *kâl*, which in the speech of the vulgar becomes *kâ*; and this very particle *kâ*, added, as in Tamil, to the preterite, is the suffix by which the Ku also forms conditional or contingent verbs—*e.g.*, If I do, is in Telugu *nênu chêyudunêni*; in Canarese *nânu gêyidare*; in colloquial Tamil this is *nân cheydâkkâ*; in Ku also (from the root *gi*, to do), it is *ânu gitekkâ*.

On the other hand, in the following particulars Ku agrees more closely with Telugu than with Tamil or Canarese.

(1.) It uses the neuter singular to denote the feminine singular.

(2.) The oblique cases or "inflexions" of the pronouns of the first and second persons, singular and plural, are identical with those of Telugu.

(3.) The case terminations of Ku are nearly in accordance with those of Telugu.

(4.) The pronominal signs suffixed to the Ku verbs accord on the whole better with Telugu than with any other dialect—*e.g.*, in Tamil the second and third persons plural end differently, the one *îr*, the other *âr*; in Telugu they end alike—both generally in *aru*; in Ku also both these persons end alike in *eru*.

(5.) In Canarese all relative participles, including that of the relative verb, end in *a*; in Tamil all relative participles, with the exception of that of the future, have the same ending. In Telugu the relative participle of the indefinite or aoristic tense ends in *eḍi* or *eṭi*; and in the Ku also the relative past participle exhibits this ending. Thus, *âna*, Tamil, that became; in Canarese *âda*; in Telugu (indefinite tense), *ayyêti*; in Ku the same form is *âti*.

The various particulars now mentioned prove Ku to be distinct from Gônd; and though it is allied to it, it is allied only in the same manner as to the other Dravidian languages. In some points this language differs from all the other dialects of the family; for example, it forms its past verbal participles not by means of the suffixes *du*, *i*, or *si*, the only suffixes known in the other dialects, but by suffixing to the root *â*, sometimes *sâ* or *jâ*, after the manner of some of the languages of Northern India. In the other dialects of this family, with the exception of the Tulu, the negative verb possesses only one tense, an aorist; the Ku, in addition to this negative aorist, has also, like the Tulu, a negative preterite—a decided advantage over the other dialects. The Ku suffixes of the present verbal participles are also different from those which are found in the other Dravidian dialects. The formative suffix of the present verbal participle is in Telugu *chu* or *tu*; in the Canarese *uta* or *ute*; in the Ku it is *i* or *pi*.

5. RÂJMAHÂL.—The lists of words hitherto published do not go a great way towards proving this language distinctively Dravidian. The evidence of the pronouns and lowest numeral is clear; but the other distinctively Dravidian words found in the lists are not numerous. For the present, perhaps, all that can be said with certainty is that the Râjmahâl contains a distinctively Dravidian element. When it has been examined as carefully as the Orâon, it may be possible to speak of its relationship in stronger terms. It is commonly stated that

it is almost the same as the Orâon ; but this opinion, though probably correct, requires confirmation.

The principal and most essentially Dravidian words I have noticed are as follows :—

I,	*en.*
we,	*en* (*nam*, *om*).
thou,	*nina.*
you,	*nina* (*nima* in *nimki*, yours).
he, she, it,	*âth.*
they,	*owar.*
this,	*îh.*
that,	*âh.*
here,	*ino.*
there,	*ano.*
one,	*art*, *ort.*
why,	*endhar.*
dative suffix,	*ku.*

eye,	*kânê.*	Drav.	*kan.*
nose,	*muna.*	do.	*mûkku.*
tooth,	*pâla.*	do.	*pal.*
ear,	*kêdu.*	do.	*kâdu.*
hand,	*kêkha.*	do.	*kei.*
hair,	*tale.*	do.	'head.'
tree,	*man.*	do.	*mân-u.*
flower,	*phûp.*	do.	*pû.*
fish,	*mîn.*	do.	*mîn.*
dove,	*pûrah.*	do.	*purâ.*
scorpion,	*tîlah.*	do.	*têḷ.*
pain,	*nôgi.*	do.	*nôgu.*
above,	*mêkthi.*	do.	*mêl.*
mother,	*aya.*	do.	*âyi.*
daughter,	*moki.*	do.	*mag-aḷ.*
man,	*al*, *alla.*	do.	*âḷ.*
come,	*bar-en.*	do.	*bar-a.*
go,	*ek-en.*	do.	*êg-a.*

Unfortunately the inflexions of the Râjmahâl noun and verb are not given in any of the lists, so that with the exception of a very few incidental particulars the grammatical construction of this language remains unknown. In the particulars that follow the construction is Dravidian. The dative postposition is *ku ; m* is the sign of the plural of the pronouns of the first and second person, replacing *n* of the singular ; *ar* is the sign of the plural of pronouns of the third person.

6. ORÂON. Much light has been thrown on the construction and vocabulary of the Orâon by an article on that language in the *Journal of the Bengal Asiatic Society*, vol. xxxv., by the Rev. F. Batsch, a missionary who has laboured amongst the Orâons in Chûtiâ Nâgpûr.

The personal pronouns, which are very regular and distinctively Dravidian, are as follows :—

	I.	WE.	THOU.	YOU.
nom.	*en.*	*em.*	*nin.*	*nim.*
gen.	*engha.*	*emhai.*	*ninghai.*	*nimhai.*
dat.	*engage.*	*emage.*	*ningâge.*	*nimâge.*
acc.	*engan.*	*eman.*	*ninin.*	*nimin, nimanum.*
abl.	*engusti.*	*emgustin.*	*ningusti.*	*nimgustim.*
instru.	*enganti.*	*emanti.*	*ninante.*	*nimanti.*
loc.	*engmi.*	*emanu, emanum.*	*ninganu.*	*nimganu.*
agent.	*enim.*	*emim.*	*ninim.*	*nimim.*

(1.) *em*, we, is the ordinary plural of the first person, used when we means more than two. *nâm*, which is equally Dravidian, means, it is said, 'we two.' This use of *nâm* as a dual may throw light on the origin of the plural inclusive of the other Dravidian languages.

(2.) The third person is represented only by *ds*, he, *ad*, it or she, *dr*, they. Notice the Dravidian epicene plural in *r*. What? is *end*.

(3.) Postpositions. *ge*, to, for; *nu*, upon; *mund*, before; *mechla*, above; *kuti*, besides; *katha*, beyond; *menya*, up; *kinya*, beneath. These are purely Dravidian words. *gusti*, from, I cannot identify.

(4.) Numerals. One, *onta;* two, *enr;* three, *mund;* four, *ndch*. Adjectival numerals—*ort âlao*, one man, *irib âlar*, two men. The rest of the numerals are borrowed from the northern vernaculars.

(5.) Words certainly Dravidian are *âl*, man, *pal*, tooth, *khan*, eye, *boi*, mouth, *moy*, nose, *bar*, come.

(6.) With the exception of the words cited above, the rest of the Orâon nouns, adjectives, and verbs present scarcely any point of resemblance to Dravidian words. The mass of the words in the Orâon vocabulary may be Kôlarian, but do not seem to be Dravidian. This instance tends to show that languages may be cognate, whilst yet the proof may survive only in the pronouns, the first few numerals, and the structure.

7. Dravidian Element in Brahui.—In many of the particulars in which the Brahui is found to be allied to the Dravidian tongues, it is equally allied to each of the families of tongues included in the Scythian group, so that to that extent it would be safest to content ourselves with saying that the non-Aryan element contained in Brahui—the element which is incapable of being affiliated to the Indo-Persic—appears to be Scythian, using the term Scythian in its widest sense. Thus in Brahui, as in the Dravidian dialects, and in the whole of the Scythian tongues, the cases of nouns are denoted by postpositions. The gender of nouns is expressed, not by their inflexions, but by prefixed separate words. The number of nouns is ordinarily denoted by the use of separate particles of pluralisation, such as many, several, &c. When a noun stands alone without any such sign of plurality, its number is considered to be indefinite, and it is then regarded as singular or plural according to the context, or the number of the verb with which it agrees. This rule is more characteristic of Tamil than of the other Dravidian idioms. Adjectives are destitute of comparatives and superlatives.

On the other hand, there are certain particulars in which the Brahui appears to me to present traces of the existence of a distinctively Dravidian element. The observations I made on the Brahui in the first edition of this work were founded on a brief grammar and vocabulary of the language contained in vol. vii. of the *Journal of the Bengal Asiatic Society*. A fuller grammar and vocabulary has now been supplied by Dr Bellew, in his book entitled "From the Indus to the Tigris" (Trübner, 1873), and it appears to me that the theory I advocated—(not that the Brahui was a Dravidian language, but that "it evidently contained a Dravidian element, an element which was probably derived from the remnant of some ancient Dravidian race incorporated with the Brahuis")—has been confirmed.

(1.) The Brahui pronoun of the second person singular is *nî*, thou, precisely as in all the Dravidian tongues. The plural of this pronoun—viz., *num*, you (*numd*, of you), is also wonderfully in accordance with old Dravidian forms. The Canarese is *nîm*, you; the Orâon *nim;* the old Tamil possessive is *num-a*, you (in which we see traces of an obsolete base *num* or *nûm*, you); and the ordinary base of the oblique cases of this pronoun in Tamil is *um*. It has been objected that there is nothing distinctively Dravidian in these forms, seeing that *ni*, thou, appears in some shape in the Australian dialects, in Chinese, and in many of the languages of High

Asia. This pronoun of the second person has undoubtedly a very wide range, as has been shown *in loco*, but it is remarkable that throughout India and the countries adjacent to India it is found only in the Dravidian languages and the Brahui. The change from *ní* in the singular to *num* in the plural appears to me still more distinctively Dravidian.

(2.) Whilst *nîm* or *nûm* is to be considered as the most classical form of the plural of the Dravidian pronoun of the second person, *nîr* is the form ordinarily used in a separate shape in Tamil, *mîru* in Telugu; and in consequence of this plural termination in *r*, in nearly all the Dravidian idioms the second person plural of the verb in the indicative mood ends, not in *im* or *um*, but in *îr*, *eru*, *âru*, *iri*, &c. The same peculiarity reappears in the Brahui. Whilst the separate pronoun ends in *m*, *r* is the pronominal sign of the second person of the verb—*e.g.*, *areri*, ye are, *arer*, they are; with which compare the Canarese *iru*(*tt*)*îri*, ye are, *iru*(*tt*)*âre*, they are.

(3.) A remarkable analogy between the Brahui and the Dravidian languages is apparent in the reflexive pronoun *ten*, self, *se*. In the Dravidian languages this pronoun is *tan* or *tân*, and is regularly declined, whilst the nominative is also used adverbially in the sense of 'indeed.' In Brahui *ten* is similarly used, not as a particle, nor only as an adverb, but as a pronoun, and is declined as regularly as the other pronouns.

(4.) Nouns form their plurals by adding *k*, as in Gônd—*e.g.*, *hulî*, a horse, *hulîk*, horses.

(5.) The root of the substantive verb in Brahui is *ar*, in Tamil and Canarese *ir*.

(6.) Bopp remarks that the three lowest numerals could never be introduced into any country by foreigners. The truth of this remark is illustrated by several circumstances of which Bopp could scarcely have been aware. From five upwards the numerals of the Orâon are foreign. From four upwards the Brahui numerals are of Indo-European origin (*e.g.*, *char*, four, *panj*, five, *shash*, six); and in the compound numerals twenty-one and twenty-two, the words for one and two are also Indo-European, but the separate numerals one, two, three, are totally unconnected with the Sanskrit family, and two of them are identical with Dravidian numerals. In Brahui, two is *irat*; compare Can. *eraḍu*, two; Tam. *irat*-(*tu*), twofold or double. In Brahui, three is *musit*; compare Can. *mûr-u*; Tel. *mûḍ-u*; Tulu *mûji*. The Dravidian bases of these numerals are *ir*, two, *mu*, three; and if we notice the terminations of the Brahui numerals (one, *asit*, two, *irat*, three, *musit*), it is obvious that the second syllable of each of these words, *it* or *at*, is merely a neuter formative, like that which we find in the Dravidian languages (*e.g.*, compare *ir*, the base and numeral adjective 'two,' with *iraḍu*, the abstract neuter noun): consequently the agreement of the Brahui with the Dravidian numerals, both in the base and in the formative, is complete. If we remember the interchangeable relation of *s* and *r*, and if we regard the Canarese *mûr*, three, and the Brahui *mus*, as an instance of this interchange, as I think we may safely do (illustrated as it is by the Tulu *mûji*), we may also venture to connect the Dravidian numeral base *or*, one, with the Brahui *as*. This connection, however is doubtful, whereas there cannot be any doubt respecting two and three. It is worthy of notice that one is *achat* in Pehlevi.

(7.) In the class of auxiliary words (prepositions, conjunctions, &c.) compare the Brahui *mont*, opposite, with the Tamil *munnê*, before.

The number of nouns and verbs in Brahui which can with certainty be identified with Dravidian roots is not considerable, but it is equal to the number found in the Orâon vocabulary.

	BRAHUI.	DRAVIDIAN.		BRAHUI.	DRAVIDIAN.
eye,	*khan,*	*khan, kan.*	stone,	*khal,*	*kal.*
mouth,	*bâ,*	*bây, vây, boi.*	bow,	*bil,*	*bil, bir, vil.*
ear,	*khaf,*	*kivi, kâd-u, kâû.*	saw,	*ara,*	*ara-m.*
face,	*mon,*	*mun,* before.	scorpion,	*telt,*	*têḷ.*
brain,	*milî,*	*mûḷei.*	to cut,	*hare,*	*aru, ari.*
son,	*mâr,*	*marri* (Gônd).	to beat,	*khal,*	*kol* (to kill).
mother,	*âi,*	*âyi.*	to do,	*ke, kar,*	*ke, ge, chey.*
water,	*dîr,*	*nîr.*	to come,	*bar,*	*bar, var.*
milk,	*pâhlt,*	*pâl.*	to be,	*ar,*	*ir.*

The analogies between the Brahui and the Dravidian languages which have now been pointed out, are much closer than any analogy which subsists between the Dravidian languages and the Bodo, the Dhimal, and the languages of the other tribes on the north-eastern frontier of India which were termed "Tamulian" by Mr Hodgson. Those analogies appear to me to be almost as remote as those of the Tibetan family; and are not only less numerous, but also of a less essential character and less distinctive than the analogies which are discoverable between the Kôlarian tongues and the Dravidian. Compare the following list of Dravidian words of primary importance with analogous words in the Brahui, and with the words in the Bodo and Dhimal which correspond in signification :—

	DRAVIDIAN.	BRAHUI.	BODO.	DHIMAL.
thou,	*nî,*	*nî,*	*nang,*	*nâ.*
you,	*num,*	*num,*	*nangchûr,*	*nyêl.*
we,	*nâm,*	*nân,*	*jong,*	*kyel.*
self,	*tan,*	*ten,*	*goui,*	*tâi.*
one,	*or,*	*as-it,*	*chê,*	*ê.*
two,	*irad-u,*	*irat,*	*gnê,*	*gne.*
three,	*mûr-u,*	*mus-it*	*thâm,*	*sûm.*
eye,	*kan,*	*khan,*	*mogon,*	*mî.*
ear,	*kivi,*	*khaf,*	*khomâ,*	*nâhâthong.*
water,	*nîr,*	*dîr,*	*dôi,*	*chî.*
stone,	*kal,*	*khal,*	*onthâi,*	*ûnthûr.*

It seems unnecessary to give a larger number of instances; for whilst the Brahui does appear to a certain extent to contain Dravidian forms and words, the Bodo and Dhimal, and to them may be added most of the other dialects of the north-eastern forests, present no *special* analogies whatever; and contain only a few of those structural affinities which they have in common, not only with the Dravidian, but with the Tibetan, and with every language and family of languages of the Scythian group.

II.

REMARKS ON THE PHILOLOGICAL PORTION OF MR GOVER'S "FOLK-SONGS OF SOUTHERN INDIA."

Real nature of the theory respecting the relationship of the Dravidian languages to the languages of the Scythian group, advocated in the first edition of this work.

WHAT follows is the principal portion of an article contributed by me to the *Madras Mail* in 1872. In reprinting it here, I leave the third person, as used in the article, unchanged. It was with much regret that I heard a few months afterwards of Mr Gover's sudden, untimely death, which was a great loss in many respects to Southern India.

Mr Gover's "Folk-Songs of Southern India" took the Indian public by surprise. A few slips and inaccuracies—perhaps we might safely say, not a few—are inevitable in a work professing to illustrate the ideas and feelings of five or six different peoples by means of poetical translations of the most popular songs current in the different languages and dialects spoken by them; but the plan of the work is so novel, the execution on the whole so able, the style of the accompanying prose dissertations and explanations so vivid and graphic, and the sympathy of the writer with the better qualities of the mass of the people whose songs he translates so warm, that his book may safely be characterised as one of the most interesting contributions to the knowledge of the people of Southern India that have yet appeared. The writer has struck a new vein in the literary mine, and his remarkable success will, we doubt not, lead other labourers in that mine to turn their efforts in the same, or a similar, direction. The defects of the book are the shadows of its most conspicuous merits. If the writer had been less ardent and—if we may be permitted to say so—less exaggerative, he would probably have been less appreciative. If he had evinced more caution and less confidence, if he had used qualifying expressions more freely, his work would probably have had less attraction for the majority of readers.

The songs translated by Mr Gover do not, as he himself remarks, touch the question of roots and derivatives. His main object is, by means of those songs, to bring more fully into view than has yet been done the better side of the moral nature of the Dravidians. Notwithstanding this, philological questions are occasionally referred to throughout the book, and the greater part of the introduction is devoted to the discussion of the most interesting philological question affecting Southern India—viz., the relationship of the Dravidian languages to other families of tongues. The remarks we are about to make relate exclusively to this question, and in making them we hope it will not be supposed that we wish to detract in any way from the merits of the book before us, viewed as a whole.

Mr Gover informs us that Dr Caldwell, in his "Comparative Grammar of the Dravidian Languages" (that is, the Tamil, Telugu, Canarese, &c.), was mistaken in classifying those languages with the Scythian or Turanian group (which, by the way, he did in the main only, not absolutely), and that the advance of philological science since that book was written has proved those languages to be simply and purely Indo-European, or Aryan. This position was taken by Mr Gover, it appears, in some papers read by him two years ago before the Royal Asiatic Society, and also in an article in the *Cornhill Magazine* for November last year. In a letter to the *Athenæum*, he adduces, in confirmation of his theory, the high authority of Dr Pope's name; but pending the publication by Dr Pope of the materials Mr Gover says he has prepared, we must be forgiven for dealing exclusively at present with what Mr Gover himself has written.

Mr Gover appears to us to be labouring under some misapprehension with regard to the enormous advance he supposes philological science has made since Dr Caldwell's book was published. During the sixteen years that have elapsed since then, he says, "new means of analysis have been furnished by the great German writers on language, new rules of classification have been adopted, the whole science of philology has been recast, Max Müller has won his fame. As it had been shown that Wilkins and Carey were wrong in deriving the Dravidian languages from the Sanskrit, so it is now known that Caldwell and Rask were equally wrong in holding the theory of their Scythian origin. This theory was an error, leading to gigantic mistakes, but it has been dispelled by the progress of philological inquiry." "The science of language, which seems to have sprung into the world like Minerva, fully grown and armed, has during the past few years thrown vast light upon this dark subject." If all this advance has been made since Dr Caldwell's book was written, Mr Gover's statement that it was written sixteen years ago must have been a slip of the pen. He must have meant to say that the book was written sixty years ago, in the præ-scientific age, seeing that the first portion of Grimm's German

Grammar, in which the laws of sounds were for the first time analysed, was given to the world in 1811; that Bopp's Comparative Grammar, by far the most important work of the kind that has ever appeared, was published in 1833; and that Max Müller, who had long already had an European reputation, must surely be considered to have won his fame by 1849, when the first volume of his great edition of the "Rig-Veda" appeared. Dr Caldwell's book, which appeared as late as 1856, is only of yesterday in comparison with the works of those masters of philological science. It may be added—though this does not of itself suffice to prove Dr Caldwell's theory to be right—that Max Müller was, and we believe still is, an upholder of that theory.

It is also to be remembered that the enormous advance in philological science which Mr Gover dilates upon, though a real and great advance as far as it goes, is, after all, confined within very narrow limits. The range within which philology has learnt to deal with its materials, and pursue its objects in a tolerably scientific method is still, we believe, in a considerable degree confined to the intercomparison of the principal languages of the Aryan family. Each of those languages is so thoroughly known, that no scholar, however fond of theorising he may be, can expect to be able to pass off his assumptions about anything connected with it as facts. Beyond the intercomparison of those languages * very little philology worthy of being called scientific has yet appeared, and when people attempt to go further we generally find them amusing themselves with accidental resemblances, and indulging in ingenious guesses pretty much as of old. Within the Aryan range, not more than one grain of assumption to four grains of fact is considered admissible. Beyond that range, we may consider ourselves fortunate if we find ourselves favoured with one grain of fact to four of assumption! It would have been no loss to science if Dr Caldwell had contented himself with comparing the Dravidian languages one with another, and calling attention to the parallelisms and coincidences which he found between them and other languages, without attempting to build any theory thereupon respecting their ultimate relationship. In this particular Mr Gover has improved upon Dr Caldwell. *He* does not theorise! He would not consent to consider his view of the Aryan relationship of the Dravidian languages as a plausible theory,—a theory supported by a certain number of facts,—a theory which may eventually be proved to be true,—all which we are prepared to consider it. He evidently regards it, and

---

* To which must be added Dr Bleek's "Comparative Grammar of the South African Languages."

insists on our regarding it, not as a theory, but as a truth which has already been scientifically demonstrated!

It would have been well if Mr Gover had made himself quite sure of perfectly apprehending Dr Caldwell's Scythic theory, before regarding its refutation and the establishment of his own Aryan theory in its place, as not only of considerable moment from a philological point of view, but as of vast moral and political importance. According to him, Dr Caldwell's theory was that the Dravidians are a Turanian people, an offshoot of the Finnish tribes, and their languages purely and simply Turanian. In reality his theory was not so different from Mr Gover's as Mr Gover appears to suppose. For this misapprehension Dr Caldwell himself was partly to blame. He used expressions at times implying his belief in the affiliation of the Dravidian languages, not to the Aryan family, but to the Turanian group of families, whilst, in those portions of his book in which he discussed the question in greater detail, he attributed almost as much importance to the Aryan affinities as to the Turanian, contenting himself with holding that the Turanian affinities were more numerous and more essentially characteristic. He felt it hard, we presume, to be obliged always to use a round-about mode of expression, and so laid himself open to misapprehension by often using the word "Scythian" alone for short. His lists of Glossarial Affinities would almost satisfy Mr Gover's views. He adduced eighty-four Dravidian roots which he considered Scythian, and of these he stated that twenty-five appeared to be also Aryan. On the other hand, not including words which appeared to him to have been borrowed by the Sanskrit from the Dravidian vernaculars, he gave a list of twenty-one roots common to the Sanskrit and the Dravidian, and a hundred and six roots common to the Dravidian and the western representatives of the Aryan family. He considered also that those hundred and six roots "must have been introduced into the Dravidian languages before the Sanskrit separated from its sisters, or at least before the Sanskrit as a separate tongue came in contact with the Dravidian family." These roots, he said, "are so numerous, many of them are so remarkable, and when all are taken together the analogy which they bring to light is so distinct that an ultimate relation of *some* kind between the Dravidian and Indo-European families may be regarded as conclusively established" (p. 453). In the same page he suggests two alternative suppositions as to the nature of this relationship, one of which is that "it must be concluded that both races were descended from a common source."* He did not, however, consider

* The following might also have been adduced:—"A consideration of the Dravidian demonstrative and interrogative vowels tends to confirm the supposition

the Aryan origin of the Dravidian languages capable of being proved by glossarial affinities alone, such as he had adduced. He considered grammatical structure, methods of dealing with materials, and vital spirit, as of more importance in determining the relationship of long separated tongues than mere verbal resemblances, many of which might turn out on further investigation to be fallacious; and, in consequence of the preponderance of the evidence that appeared to him to be furnished from this quarter, he considered "the propriety of placing these languages in the Scythian group rather than in the Indo-European indicated;" yet, notwithstanding this, he called attention, in connection with almost every point discussed in the book, to the "deep-seated Indo-Europeanisms" which he found imbedded in the grammatical structure of these languages. The fullest statement of his theory is in page 50 of the Introduction. "Whilst, therefore," he says, "I classify the Dravidian family of languages as essentially and in the main Scythian, I consider them as of all Scythian tongues those which present the most numerous, ancient, and interesting analogies to the Indo-European languages. The position which this family occupies, if not mid-way between the two groups, is on that side of the Scythian group on which the Indo-European appears to have been severed from it. If this view be correct (as I think it will be shown to be), the Indo-Europeanisms which are discoverable in the Dravidian languages carry us back to a period beyond all history, beyond all mythology, not only prior to the separation of the western branches of the Indo-European race from the eastern, but prior also to the separation of the yet undivided Indo-Europeans from the Scythian stock."

"On the whole, we appear to have reason to conclude that the various forms of the pronoun of the first person singular which have now been compared, are identical, and that this word was the common property of mankind prior to the separation of the Indo-European tribes from the rest of the Japhetic family" (p. 306). "A similar form of the accusative being extensively prevalent, as we have seen,

---

I have already expressed that the Dravidian family has retained some Præ-Sanskritic elements of immense antiquity, and in particular that its demonstratives, instead of having been borrowed from the Sanskrit, represent those old Japhetic bases from which the primary demonstratives of the Sanskrit itself, as well as of various other members of the Indo-European family, were derived" (p. 345). "Instead of supposing the Dravidian dialects to have borrowed these demonstratives (which are still purer than the Persian) from the Sanskrit (which are irregular and greatly corrupted), it is more reasonable to suppose that the Dravidian demonstrative vowels retain and exhibit the primæval bases from which the demonstratives of the Sanskrit and of all other Indo-European tongues have been derived" (p. 340).

in the Scythian tongues, it would be unreasonable to derive the Dravidian case-sign from the Indo-European. In this instance it is better to conclude that both families have retained a relic of their original oneness" (p. 221). "The hypothesis of the existence of a remote original affinity between the Dravidian languages and the Sanskrit, or rather between those languages and the Indo-European tongues, of such a nature as to allow us to give the Dravidian languages a place in the Indo-European group, is altogether different from the notion of a direct derivation of those languages from the Sanskrit. The hypothesis of a remote original affinity is favoured by some interesting analogies both in the grammar and also in the vocabulary, which will be noticed in their place" (p. 29). "Indo-European analogies are so intimately connected with the individuality and vital essence of the Dravidian languages, that it seems impossible to suppose them to be merely the result of early association, however intimate. It is only on the supposition of the existence of a remote or partial relationship that they appear to be capable of being fully explained" (p. 340).

In another passage the theory of spontaneous development *ab intra* was advanced for the purpose of accounting for certain tendencies in the Indo-European direction observable in the treatment of the gender of nouns:—"(These tendencies) are not the result of Sanskrit influences, of which no trace is perceptible in this department of Dravidian grammar, but have arisen from the progressive mental cultivation of the Dravidians themselves" (p. 171). The pages are those of the first edition; and respecting the real nature of the theory of Dravidian relationship advocated therein, some degree of misapprehension seems to have been entertained by some other persons besides Mr Gover.

If Mr Gover had noticed these and similar passages, he could hardly have supposed the difference between Dr Caldwell's theory and his own to be so great and essential, and pregnant with such momentous consequences to the governors and the governed as he has done. There is no reason why an upholder of Dr Caldwell's theory should not hail with pleasure any well-considered attempt to bring the Indo-Europeanisms of the Dravidian languages more fully to light. The question between Dr Caldwell and Mr Gover is only one of less or more. Dr Caldwell's theory is so wide—it takes us so far back into the mist of ages—that there seems to be room in it for as many new theories as are likely to be invented. Room could be found in it even for Mr Gover's theory, if only its sharp corners were a little smoothed away. One of those sharp corners is the exclusiveness of his theory, as it is held by him at present. He will not consent to give and take, but must have all. We are not sure whether his theory will fare better for this in the end, when it comes to be carefully scrutinised by the great scholars in Europe. Doubtless Mr Gover will hold that so much of Dr Caldwell's book as advocates the existence of Aryan elements in the Dravidian languages is perfectly sound. His only objection doubtless will be that it does not go far enough. Yet it was precisely this part of the book which met with the severest criticism. The editor of the *Journal of the American Oriental Society*, whilst attributing some weight to the evidence adduced by Dr Caldwell from correspondences of form and spirit in favour of the relationship of the Dravidian languages with the Scythian, thought all that part of the work which concerned the comparison of those languages with any other than the Scythian so nearly destitute of scientific value that its omission would have been a gain rather than a loss! Here, as we often see, doctors differ; and here, it is evident, that Mr Gover may expect to find rocks ahead in his exclusion of all Scythian elements from the Dravidian languages, and his affiliation of them, simply and absolutely, to the Aryan family. In comparing the Dravidian languages with the Aryan, he will enjoy many advantages, in consequence of the facilities afforded him, not only by the grammars and dictionaries, but by the extensive, ancient literatures of the languages compared; but freedom from criticism will not be one of the advantages he will enjoy. The evidence he adduces must be capable of enduring a far more searching examination than that adduced by Dr Caldwell in support of his elastic Scythic theory. It is much more easy to discover an error in a comparison when both terms are accurately known, than when one only is accurately known, and the other is known only very imperfectly. When Dr Caldwell wandered off, in search of Dravidian affinities, over the trackless steppes of Central Asia, and amongst the fogs and fens of Siberia, whilst it would be extremely easy for him to go astray and lose his way, it would not be so easy to follow him up and prove, point by point, where, when, and how he had gone astray. But when Mr Gover attempts to prove the Dravidian languages as distinctively Aryan as the Sanskrit, or the Greek, or even as the Celtic, he works at our own door, before our own eyes, in the full light of the most carefully elaborated works of the best masters in philological science; and if he should happen at any time to speculate a little too wildly, or to make too positive an assertion about something not perfectly warranted by the evidence, plenty of scholars will be ready to be down upon him in a trice.

Mr Gover says that it is probably not extravagant or untrue to say that there is not one true Dravidian root common to the three great branches—Tamil, Telugu, and Canarese—that cannot be clearly shown to be Aryan. He takes as a specimen the word *pey*, devil, and tells us that the true meaning is not "devil," but "light," and signified originally "the bright one," that is, the deity. The name being Aryan, the deity denoted by this name was also Aryan, and was identical with the element light. But some of the Dravidians, cut off from the better teaching of the fathers of their race, degenerated in their worship, and thus a god was changed into a devil! This idea is plausible, and it is ingeniously worked out; but its accuracy depends on the nature of the evidence on which the alleged original signification of the word is based. It is an interesting question of roots and derivatives, and Mr Gover's discussion of it is earnest and vigorous. Our only doubt is as to whether his argument is conclusive. This is a point, however, on which Mr Gover feels no doubt at all.

He argues first that the root of the Tamil word *pêy* is identical with the first part of the Sanskrit word for devil, *piśâcha*, which was derived from a root signifying 'light;' and then, that the Tamil relationships of this word combine to show that 'light' was its original meaning. We may remark, at the outset, that, even if these statements were correct, they would not prove that the being now worshipped as a devil was originally a bright being, a god. It would be necessary to know something of the history of the words; to ascertain whether the root meaning had remained unchanged up to the time of its application to the worship of this god or devil; or whether it might not have sustained one of those accidental twists so common in all languages, which are found to act as the starting point of new and unexpected meanings. It would not be safe to assume that, because the oldest shape of the root of the English word 'money' is the Sanskrit *man*, 'to think,' therefore money acquired this name because it is something that people 'think' a great deal about. The ultimate derivation might be correct, yet the assumption founded upon it would be erroneous. It would be found that the word 'money' received an accidental twist in the direction of its modern meaning. We should be taken to the temple of Juno Moneta in Rome, the *Mint* in which money was first coined, and there we should see how the change of meaning took place,—the goddess's name being derived from *moneo*, to warn, and this probably being an offshoot from *man*, to think. Where the modern meaning of a word differs very widely from the root meaning, we must always be on the look-out for some such accidental change. We have, therefore, to ask not only whether it is a fact that the Sanskrit *piśâcha* comes from a root meaning to adorn, to shine, but also whether that was the sense in which the word came to be so applied. It looks extraordinary that the name of the very worst class of spirits known to the Sanskrit-speaking races should have been intended to have a meaning so much better than that of the names of the half divine Asuras, Daityas, Dânavas, Nâgas, Râkshasas, and Yakshas, and equal in beauty, as well as similar in signification, to that of the Devas, the divine beings, themselves. When we seek for an explanation of the reason why the term *Piśâcha* came to be applied to malignant beings, Sanskrit authorities supply us with derivations which differ widely from Mr Gover's. Dr Rost derives *piśâcha* from *api* + *śach*, to attack, and says that when *api* is used as a preposition it generally loses its initial *a*. Native scholars supply us with a derivation which is in accordance with native ideas as to the character and habits of the *piśâcha*. *Piśâcha*, according to them, means an 'eater of flesh,' and is substantially identical with the regular compound, *piśit-asi*, a word which has the same meaning. This view is corroborated by the fact that *peśi*, a noun regularly formed from the root *piś*, means both a lump of flesh, and the name of a female fiend. Compare the Tamil *pêychchi*, a female devil. How a noun signifying 'flesh' comes from a root signifying 'to adorn,' is the only question that remains, and that ceases to present any difficulty when it is remembered that that root signifies also to 'form,' to 'figure,' to 'organize,' and even to 'put on,' to 'cover.'

We now come to the consideration of the Tamil word *pêy*, and here our course is comparatively clear. Whatever may be said for or against the idea that the Sanskrit *piśâcha* was originally a 'bright being,' Mr Gover does not consider *pêy* derived from *piśâcha* by corruption or abbreviation, but holds merely that the roots are identical. The Dravidian tongues, he says, do not need these foreign analogies to show that *pey*, a devil, comes from a root meaning light. He might, we think, have made out a plausible case for the direct derivation of *pêy* from *piśâcha*. [Dr Gundert is in favour of this derivation.] Some Sanskrit words have in this way got abbreviated, and both the abbreviated form and the unabbreviated are in use. Probably, however, Mr Gover was right in not committing himself to the direct derivation of *pêy* from *piśâcha*. Though the words are, to a certain extent, interchangeable, yet people who are skilled in diabolical refinements draw a distinction between them. *Pêy*, they say, means the ghost of a human being that has become powerful and malignant. It has a name and a place of residence, and is systematically worshipped. The *piśâcha*, on the other hand, they say, has no home, or name, or worship. The *bhûta*, they add, is a demon of a somewhat higher order, an attendant on the Brahmanical demon-gods. It is still more worthy of notice that *pêy* has meanings which *piśâcha* has not. In combination with names of plants, *pêy* means 'wild, uncultivated, useless for human food;' in combination with names of animals it means 'mad.' We often find that the use of a word in combination throws light on its original meaning. This may be so in this case—or it may not—as it is possible that this application to plants and animals may be only a metaphorical transfer of the older meaning of 'devil.' Still, in either case, the direct derivation of *pêy* from *piśâcha*, a word which is never used in this way, may be regarded as uncertain, though possible.

We have now to deal with the Dravidian evidence adduced by Mr Gover to show that *pêy* comes from a root meaning light. He begins his argument by stating that another form of the word in Tamil is *pênam*, a devil, and this he says appears in Khond as *pennu*, the name of the deity, the meaning of which name is the 'sun' or 'light.' Its ultimate connection is with the Sanskrit *pins* and the Greek φαίνω. From this he argues, that whether amongst the Khonds or the Tamilians, the worship of the devil was originally the worship of the light of the sun. Unfortunately for Mr Gover's theory, there is no such word for devil in the Tamil language as *pênam*, though it is true that in Malayâḷam there is a word meaning devil, *pêna*, which would in Tamil be *pênei*. In Tamil, however, we have a corresponding word *pê*, a word meaning foam, froth, which is represented as identical with *pênam*, a fuller form of the same word; and this *pênam* in turn is identical with the Sanskrit *phena*, froth. It looks as if the two words *pêy*, devil, and *pe*, froth, with the more correct form of the latter, *pênam*, were somehow connected. From *pê*, foam, would come *pêyi*, one who foams, one from whose mouth *pê* comes, and *pêyi* would naturally be abbreviated into *pêy*. What more natural origin than this could be desired for *pêy*, devil? Mr Gover may possibly object that, however plausible it may be, it leaves the Tamil word for devil as far as ever from the sweetness and light it ought to denote.*

After discussing the inferences that may be drawn from *pênam* being a Tamil word for devil, he proceeds to adduce examples of Dravidian words beginning with *p*, *b*, or *v*, and meaning light, for the purpose of proving that *pey* also must (could, would, or should) mean light. One of the words he adduces is *veyyil*, the heat of the sun. The root of this word, however, means not light, but heat. It is from *ve*, to be

* Mr Beames suggested to me the possibility of the derivation of *pêy*—if derived from Sanskrit at all—from *prêta*, a corpse, also a ghost, one of the Prakrit forms of which would, according to the usual rule, be *pêya*. *preta* (in Tamil *pirêdam*) occasionally has in Tamil the meaning of ghost; but *pêy* never means corpse. *pêyam* is unknown in Tamil.

hot, one of the commonest roots in the language, and very prolific of derivatives. The two Tamil roots that really mean light, *oḷ*, a shining light, and *veḷ*, a diffused light, cannot be brought into any harmony with *pêy*. Another word which he adduces is *piei*, which he says "in ancient Tamil was the moon." It looks as if he had been following Dr Hunter's authority here, as we find that in his "Comparative Dictionary of the Non-Aryan Languages," Hunter puts *pirei*, for moon, under the head of Ancient Tamil. The word, however, is equally modern and ancient, and it means, not the moon itself, except by poetic licence, but the waxing and waning moon, the crescent moon. And to this the derivation of the word points. The most natural derivation is *pir*, the root of *pira*, other, and *piraṛ*, to change. The meaning of *pirei* is doubtless 'that which changes,' 'the changing phases of the moon.'

The word on which Mr Gover appears to place his chief dependence is *pagal*, day, 'the light time,' which he divides quite correctly into *pag*, the root, and *al*, a formative termination. He might have quoted the same word in all the Dravidian dialects, but he contents himself with the Tuluva, and three Dravidian dialects of Central India—the Madi, the Rutluk, and the Madia—evidently following Hunter herein. If *pag*, the verbal root of this word *pagal*, day, really meant light, it would be an interesting, if not a perfectly conclusive, argument in favour of Mr Gover's view. And why should not this be its meaning? It is certainly very natural that the word for the day, as distinguished from the night, should mean light; and it is natural also that a person, finding light placed first in the list of meanings in most dictionaries, should conclude that this was regarded by the authors of those dictionaries as the root meaning of the word. But however natural these assumptions may be, they are mere assumptions after all; and the second of the two, the assumption that Tamil dictionaries are accustomed to place the root meaning first, and to follow this up by derivative meanings in the order of their development, is notoriously erroneous. We are persuaded that the author of the "Chaturakarâdi," the most classical Tamil dictionary, saw quite clearly that it was a pure old form of verbal noun. He gives the form of the same verbal noun in common use as an equivalent, and two other verbal nouns nearly equivalent; and yet he places these words in the middle of the list of meanings, instead of at the beginning. We shall adhere to his meanings, but shall take the liberty of arranging them in the order in which he himself, if he had studied the matter, must have supposed them to have been developed. The succession of meanings will be found to afford some interesting examples of the association of ideas. *Pagal*, verbal noun, from the root *pag-u*, to divide: meanings—1, *paguttal*, 'division;' 2, 'a division;' 3, *piridal*, 'partition;' 4, *piḷattal*, 'splitting,' 'cleaving a thing into two equal portions;' 5, 'middle,' the middle of anything being the point where the division or cleavage takes place; 6, 'the middle pin of a yoke' (a particular application of the new meaning 'middle'); 7, 'the middle of the day,' 'midday,' 'noon' (another and more important example of the same); 8, 'the sun,' the cause of noonday brightness; 9, 'light;' 10, 'the whole period of daylight,' the day, as distinguished from the night; 11, 'the day,' inclusive of the night; 12, 'time.' That *pagal* meant, and still means, especially midday, is well illustrated by the fact that the phrase *Pagaleikku mêl* (and the corresponding Telugu phrase) means, not 'after the day is over,' but simply 'afternoon.'

We see now that the root meaning of *pagal* is not light, as Mr Gover supposed it to be, but division, and with this disappears every trace of evidence from Dravidian sources in favour of the supposition that the Tamil *pêy* was not so black as he has been painted, but was originally a bright being, a deity. Mr Gover informs us that a hundred other examples might be adduced in favour of this meaning of the word *pêy;* but it is impossible, of course, for us to deal with them until we know what they are. It is evident that Mr Gover was diligently looking out all over India for words for light beginning with the letter *p*, and in this inquiry he appears to have found only a very little help in Dr Hunter's lists. Of the seventeen South Indian words for light given by Dr Hunter, none begin with a *p*, so none could be made use of; but amongst the twenty-one words for light contained in the list of words belonging to the dialects of Central India, fortunately one word beginning with a *p* was found, and here it is. "In another dialect," says Mr Gover, "*peymoro* is the light." The Keikadi of Dr Hunter's lists is that other dialect. There are two letters different in Dr Hunter. He gives the word as *paymaro*, not as *peymoro*. This makes the resemblance of the first syllable to the Tamil *pêy* a little more doubtful; but apart from this, one would like to know the signification of the second portion of the word, and the literal meaning of the entire word. It looks like a compound, and therefore requires explanation. One of our reasons for thinking so is that it resembles so much a word for day (not light) in another Central Indian dialect, the Yerukala of Dr Hunter's lists. The word is given in two shapes, *pammaru* and *pangamaru*. This word must surely be a compound; and if so, it is only when we come to know the real meaning of each part of the compound that we shall be able to determine its ulterior relationship. In this particular Dr Hunter's lists of words cannot always be trusted. When the questioner does not know the language of the person questioned, and the person questioned is equally ignorant of the language of the questioner, the result will sometimes be of an amusing rather than a satisfactory nature.

"It has always been easy," Mr Gover says, "to change a god into a devil. The last word used is an illustration, for devil is a clear derivative from *deva*, and is closely related to deity. That gods have ere now been changed into devils is certain, of which perhaps the best proof is the fact that the word *deva*, a god amongst the Sanskrit-speaking race, denotes a demon amongst the monotheistical Zoroastrians." Mr Gover's illustration of this change is a remarkable, if not a satisfactory one. He evidently considers the derivation of our English *devil*—like that of the French *diable*, the Italian *diavolo*, and the German *teufel*, from the διαβολος of the Greek New Testament—as an old-world theory which the advance of science has annihilated. As the final *l* in devil keeps its place in all the European languages, we should be tempted to advise Mr Gover to retain it, and then he would be able to give the word an interesting extension. *Deval* is the Hindustani for a temple, and the name must denote, not the house of God, but a place where devils are worshipped!

Mr Gover's philology is used throughout to support his ethnology. He considers it of great moral and political importance to prove that the Dravidians are an Aryan, not a Scythian race. The Scythian theory, he says, "shuts up the doors of sympathy and fellow-feeling between the Dravidian peoples and their English conquerors, and relegates the former to that particular human race which is lowest in the scale of humanity, and therefore farthest from their Aryan fellow-subjects." Whether the Scythic theory be ever refuted on philological grounds or not, we think Mr Gover need not distress himself by attributing to it such deplorable consequences. He quotes Dr Farrar's estimate of the Scythian or Turanian peoples, as if it corroborated his own; but the exceptions mentioned by Dr Farrar deprive his estimate of the value it might otherwise have possessed. The exceptions, he says, are the Chinese, Finns, Magyars, and Turks. He ought to have added the Japanese. This is an extraordinary mode of stating an exception, though whether it is correctly attributed to Dr Farrar we know not. It is as if he had said, the Turanians belong to the lowest strata of humanity, with the exception of nineteen-twentieths of their number who occupy a very respectable position among the upper strata. It may have been meant that whatever be said of the intellectual advancement of certain Turanian peoples, yet in so far as their moral nature is concerned, it is undeniable that all Turanians are inferior to all Aryans. Even when thus limited, this statement is still far too sweeping. Few people consider the Turks morally inferior to the modern Greeks, and no one would dream of placing the (Hungarian) Magyars either morally or intellectually below the Roumanians or the Croats. Progress in civilisation depends not only on race, but also, and perhaps in a still greater degree, on climate and external circumstances. Moral development is profoundly affected by religion and political history. If the Gônds, the Khonds, and the other Dravidian tribes of Central India are Aryans, as the civilised Dravidians are now asserted to be, it is plain that Aryan blood alone is not all-sufficient, and that isolation amongst forests and mountains makes Aryans sometimes look marvellously like Scythians. Those 'Veddahs of Ceylon' (in Tamil *Vêḍar*, huntsmen), who are introduced as examples of Turanian "imperfectibility," are probably the Dravidian aborigines of the island. According to Mr Gover, therefore, they must be Aryans. On the other hand, this discussion ceases to have any special importance or significance, when Dr Caldwell's Scythic theory is correctly apprehended. If the Dravidian race separated from the great primitive Asian hordes before the final separation from the same hordes of the Aryan tribes,—if we suppose it to have taken its origin at so high a point as this in the stream of time,—it is evident that every attempt to differentiate between Aryans and Turanians, in so far as the Dravidians are concerned, may almost as well be abandoned. In physiological characteristics and capacity for intellectual and moral development, the Dravidians are probably fit to be classified with the most favoured race; and, being a primitive race themselves, it is of little importance to what other primitive races we affiliate them.

III.

SUNDARA PÂṆḌYA.

THE following are the extracts from the Muhammedan historians referred to in the Introduction, with Colonel Yule's remarks, and a few additional particulars.

Passages from Polo's contemporary, Rashiduddin, quoted in Sir H. Elliot's "History of India" (new edition, p. 69).

"M'abar, from Kûlam to Silâwar (should be Nilâwar = Nellore), extends 300 parasangs along the shore. . . . . The king is called Dewar, which means in the M'abar language 'the Lord of wealth.' . . . . Within the last few years (written towards 1300) Sundar Bandi was Dewar, who, with his three brothers, obtained power in different directions, and Malik al-Taki-uddin, brother of Shaikh Jumaluddin, was his minister and adviser, to whom he assigned the government of Fatan, Malefatan, and Bâwal (read Kâil as it is in some MSS.)" Here, says Colonel Yule, we have Polo's Senderbandi Dewar and his brothers. Moreover, in Ramusio's edition of Polo, the brother princes are not five, but four, as in Rashid. . . . . "In the year 692 A.H. (A.D. 1293) the Dewar died, and his wealth and possessions fell into the hands of his adversaries and opponents, and Shaik Jumaluddin, who succeeded him, obtained, it is said, an accession of 700 bullock-loads of jewels," &c.

The Persian history of Wassaf has some particulars the same and some differing. The third volume of the new edition of Elliot contains some of those passages from Wassaf, which Von Hammer embodies in his "History of the Ilkhans of Persia." It is plain from these that Rashid-uddin copied from Wassaf, or *vice versâ*. "M'abar is the coast which stretches from the Persian Sea, through a length of 300 farsangs, to Nilâwar. Its princes are called Diwar or Lord." He then gives exactly the same account of Sundar Bandi being Dewar of M'abar and dying in A.H. 692 (A.D. 1293) as that given by Rashiduddin. There is a difference only as to his successor. Instead of making the Muhammedan Jumaluddin succeed, Elliot's translation from Wassaf ran, "It is related by Malik âl Islâm Jumaluddin that out of that treasure (left by Sundar Bandi) 7000 oxen, laden with precious stones and pure gold and silver *fell to the share of the brother who succeeded him.*"

At a later date we have the following :—

"Kales Dewar, the ruler of M'abar, enjoyed a highly prosperous life, extending to forty and odd years, during which time neither any foreign enemy entered his country, nor any severe malady confined him to bed. His coffers were replete with wealth, insomuch that in the treasury of the city of Mardi [this is what Von Hammer has as Shahrmandi = Shahrpandi = the city of the Pâṇḍi, Madura] there were 1200 crowns of gold, &c., &c. This fortunate and happy sovereign had two sons, the elder named Sundar Pandi, who was legitimate, his mother being joined to the Dewar by lawful marriage, and the younger named Tira Pandi [Pirebendi of Von Hammer = Vîra Pâṇḍi?], was illegitimate. . . . As Tira Pandi was remarkable for his shrewdness and intrepidity, the ruler nominated him as his successor. His brother, Sundar Pandi, being enraged at this supercession, killed his father in a moment of rashness and undutifulness, towards the close of the year A.H. 709 (1310 A.D.), and placed the crown on his head in the city of Mardi [Madurei is often mispronounced by the vulgar Marudei], and induced the troops who were there to support his interests, and conveyed some of the royal treasures which were deposited there to the city of Mankûl (Menkpu in Von Hammer). . . . . Upon this his brother Tira Pandi, being resolved on avenging his father's blood, followed to give him battle, and on the margin of a lake which in their language they call Talâchi (Ham., Telaji), the opponents came to action. . . . . Tira Pandi, wounded, fell into the hands of the enemy. . . . . Manâr Barmûl (Ham., Permel), the son of the daughter of Kales Dewar, who espoused the cause of Tira Pandi, being at that time at Karâmhatti, near Kâlûl [Von Hammer, Kiramjetti, in the country of Kail], sent him assistance both in men and money, which was attended with a most fortunate result. Sundar Pandi . . . at last met with the chastisement due to his ingratitude; for in the middle of the year A.H. 710 (A.D. 1310) Tira Pandi, having collected an army, advanced to oppose him; and Sundar Pandi, trembling and alarmed, fled from his native country, and took refuge under the protection of Alauddin of Delhi, and Tira Pandi became firmly established in his hereditary kingdom." Colonel Yule remarks—"This Sundar Pandi is quite different from the man of four brethren; first, because the latter had been dead eighteen years before this escape to Delhi; second,—but no more reasons seem wanted after that! The notion that floats in my mind is that the real kings of Madura were Kales and his sons Sundar and Tira Pandi, and that Marco Polo's Sender Bandi, Asciar, and brethren, were a separate family, probably of adventurers, who had got possession of the coast country, and perhaps paid some nominal homage to Madura. But then Kales's name ought to be in the Madura lists as predecessor of Sundara Pandi."

With reference to the Kales Dewar of Wassaf, circa 1309–10, it is deserving of notice that according to the Singhalese records the Pâṇḍyan king at that time was called Kulaśêkhara; and that this was a different Kulaśêkhara from the one already mentioned in the Introduction appears from the fact that he is represented, not as being conquered by the Singhalese, but as carrying the war into the Singhalese territory. Bhuvaneka Bâhu the first, as I am informed by Mr Rhys Davids, began to reign in A.D. 1303, and died in 1314; and at the end of his reign Âryachakravarti, in command of an army sent by the Pâṇḍyan king Kulasêkhara, took the capital of Ceylon and carried off the celebrated tooth-relic. The names of Sundara and Vîra are not mentioned by the Singhalese narratives in connection with this Kulaśêkhara. I have many inscriptions in my possession relating to the reign of Kulaśêkhara, but as none of them contains any date, except the year of the king's reign, I am unable to determine when he lived, or whether there were one or two of the name. From the tenor of the inscriptions it is my impression that they all refer to one and the same person, and probably the second king of the name, rather than the first. I have two inscriptions of one Vîra Pâṇḍya; but this Vîra could not have been the Vîra represented by the Muhammedan historians as Sundara's brother and rival, or by the Singhalese annalists as his rival, for these inscriptions, unlike his, are dated, and according to them the date of this Vîra Pâṇḍya's accession was A.D. 1437. The discrepancy between Rashiduddin's statement that the Sundar Pandi, who died in A.D. 1293, was succeeded by his Muhammedan minister, and Wassaf's statement that he was succeeded by his brother, is not a very serious one. Both statements may have been in a measure true. There is a discrepancy, however, in Wassaf's own account of his two Sundars which seems to me at present irreconcilable. According to him, as to Rashiduddin, Sundar Pandi, the Dewar of M'abar, died in A.D. 1293, the year after Marco Polo's visit; yet Kales, the father of the other Sundar Pandi and Tira Pandi, who was murdered by Sundar in A.D. 1310, had been Dewar of M'abar for forty and odd years, and during the whole of that time had enjoyed unexampled peace and prosperity! Wassaf here seems somehow to have misapprehended his authorities, for he provides no room for his first Sundar during Kales's long reign.

After the above was written, an interesting extract from the Singhalese historical records, regarding the invasion of Kulaśêkhara's territory by the Singhalese, was published in the *Journal of the Asiatic Society of Bengal*, No. 2, 1872, by Mr T. W. Rhys Davids, then district judge, Anurâdhâpûra, Ceylon, an eminent Singhalese scholar. This extract is too long to give here *in extenso*, but the substance of it is as follows :—

The Pâṇḍu king Parâkrama, of the city of Madura, became terrified by the army with which *King Kulaśêkhara* was preparing to attack him, and sent ambassadors to the great king of Ceylon, Parâkrama Bâhu, to supplicate his help. Before anything could be done, Kulaśêkhara, the king, had surrounded Madura with a large army, and taken prisoner the Pâṇḍu king and his army. On hearing this, Parâkrama Bâhu, the great king, sent his general, Lankârapura, with a great army, filling several hundred ships, with orders to slay Kulaśêkhara, and establish in that kingdom some one who came of the stock of the kings of Pâṇḍu. This general with his army landed at a place called Laśśilla, and there defeated the army of a Tamil named Arak. The rulers of five districts then came up with an army, and after a fierce fight were defeated. Other six rulers with their forces joined the five, but they also were overthrown. Then, at the order of Parâkrama Bâhu, the general set up a pillar of victory at a place near Râmêśwara, and formed a town called Parâkrama, where he lived. Whilst he was there Kulaśêkhara sent *Sundara, the Pâṇḍu king*, with many councillors, to attack him, but the Singhalese general beat them in three pitched battles. He then fought several battles with Âlawanâ Perumâl and other chiefs, and took various countries, villages, and towns. Kulasêkhara then entered on a campaign in the Kandaya district, but was defeated, and was obliged to take refuge, with his warriors, in a city which they barricaded. The Singhalese, however, broke in, and Kulaśêkhara escaped through a gate in disguise. Thereupon the Singhalese celebrated a festival of victory, and made *Vîra Pâṇḍu* king with great ceremony. The narrative then goes on to relate how Kulaśêkhara, after his flight in disguise, fortified himself in the stronghold of Toṇḍamâna, and afterwards sallying thence retook Kandayaru, defeating two of Lankârapura's lieutenants, and how Lankârapura again defeated him, re-established peace, and confirmed Vîra Pâṇḍu on the throne, restoring the banished Tamil nobles to their lands, and anointing Vîra Pâṇḍu in the city of Madura.

We find here again the very same three names that appear in the Muhammedan histories—Kales (doubtless Kulaśêkhara), Sundara, and Vîra: and both narratives, though differing in other particulars, agree in leaving Vîra on the throne. The dates differ very considerably. Parâkrama Bâhu the Great, king of Ceylon, ascended the throne in 1153 A.D., and died in 1186. His expedition against the Pâṇḍyan country appears to have commenced in 1173; whilst Wassaf represents Vîra Pâṇḍi as finally triumphing over his brother Sundara, the murderer of their father Kales, in 1310 A.D. It is difficult to suppose that there were two trios of contemporary Madura princes, named severally Kulaśêkhara, Sundara, and Vîra, the latter two of whom were on opposite sides; and if there were only one such trio, it follows that either the Singhalese or the Muhammedan narrators—(surely not the Singhalese, who are remarkably trustworthy)—must have fallen into a chronological error of more than a hundred years. The Sundara of the Singhalese narrative presents few or no points of resemblance to the Sundara of the inscriptions and the Saiva revival, the last sovereign of the old Pâṇḍya line; but so far as appears at present, there is no insuperable difficulty in the way of identifying this more eminent Sundara with the first Sundara of the Muhammedan historians, who died in 1293, and the Sender of Marco Polo, who was alive 1292.

According to the Muhammedan historians the flight to Delhi of Sundara, the murderer of Kulaśêkhara, led to the invasion of the

Madura country by Malik Kafûr. I avail myself again of Colonel Yule's kindness. Additional statement by Wassaf, not given in the printed extracts. "In the last year but one of Alauddin's reign (A.D. 1315), he sent his general Hazârdinâri (*alias* Malik Kafûr), with four lakhs of men, to conquer M'abar. The Raja of M'abar hid himself in the jungles. The booty was tremendous; 700 elephants, and gold to such extent that every soldier had 25 lbs.! The farmer-general, Surajuddin, desired to place his treasure in security (and was plundered, whereupon he took poison). . . . The son, Malik Nizamuddin, betook himself to the court of Alauddin to complain of this robbery, and obtained, with the restoration of a part of his property, the administration of the finances, which had been entrusted to his grandfather Jumaluddin Et Thaibi, and his father Surajuddin." According to Ferishta, Malik Kafûr conquered M'abar as far south as Rameshwar, or Adam's Bridge, opposite Ceylon, where he built a mosque. M'abar was regarded by Ferishta as a portion of the Belâla kingdom of Dwârasamudra. Ibn Batuta, who appears to have visited Madura in A.D. 1348–9, found the country still under Muhammedan rule. The Pâṇḍya kings after a time got the better of the Muhammedan intruders and resumed their ancient sway, but I am unable to fix the date. The earliest dated inscription of this second line of Pâṇḍyas in my possession is that of Vîra Pâṇḍya in A.D. 1437.

IV.

ARE THE PARIARS (PAREIYAS) OF SOUTHERN INDIA DRAVIDIANS?

It has been commonly supposed by Anglo-Indians, that certain tribes and castes inhabiting Southern India, especially the Pareiyas, Paḷḷas, Puleiyas, and similar tribes, belong to a different race from the mass of the inhabitants. The higher castes are styled Hindûs, or else Tamilians, Malayâḷis, &c., according to their language and nation; but those names are withheld from some of the ruder and more primitive tribes, and from the Pareiyas and other agricultural slaves. As this supposition, and the use of words to which it has given rise, are frequently met with both in conversation and in books, it seems desirable to inquire whether, and to what extent, this opinion may be regarded as correct.

It is necessary here to premise some remarks on the meaning of the term Hindû. This term is used in India in a variety of ways, but its most common, as well as its best authorised meaning, is that of an adherent of the system of religion called Hindûism. It is true that this use of the term is liable to serious objection, inasmuch as the term Hindû originally meant, and ought still to mean, an Indian—an inhabitant of India—irrespective of the religion to which he belonged. It seems hardly fair to use a term which in itself has not a theological, but a geographical meaning, to denote the adherents of one out of several religions which prevail in the region to which the term applies. There is no such inconsistency pertaining to the use of the terms Buddhist, Jaina, Muhammedan, or Christian. Notwithstanding this, in consequence of the difficulty of finding any other convenient term to denote the followers of the Brahmanical religion, or the religion of the Vedas and Purâṇas, and also in consequence of the followers of this religion forming the great majority of the inhabitants of India, people have been led to adopt the national name as a term of religious nomenclature. This meaning has been made authoritative by its use in official documents, and by a decision of one of the courts, to the effect that the term Hindûs, as used in the 'Indian Succession Act,' is meant to denote the adherents of the religion called Hindûism, in consequence of which Indian Christians are declared not to be Hindûs in the meaning of the Act. This being the case, it seems to have become desirable that the term Hindû should now cease to be used in any other sense. Consistency in the use of terms is of more importance than accuracy of etymology. It may, therefore, be admitted—using the word in this sense—that the Tudas, the Khonds, and many of the Gônds are not Hindûs, and also that some of the predatory wandering tribes are probably not Hindûs; though, geographically, they have all as much right to the name of Hindû as the Brahmans themselves. In some of these cases, however, it would be safer to say merely that such and such classes are not regarded as orthodox Hindûs. As for the Pareiyas and the lower castes generally in the more civilised districts of the country, they are Hindûs by religion, like the rest of the community. The Brahmans and the Pareiyas equally worship S'iva and Vishnu, and therefore are equally Hindûs. The differences between them pertain to caste, not to religion.

Many persons, especially in Northern India, have been accustomed to use the term Hindû as synonymous with Aryan. They call the Brahmans and the higher castes of Northern India Hindûs, but withhold the name from the aboriginal races. This seems an improper use of words, inasmuch as it denationalises not only the low-caste inhabitants of the northern provinces and the rude forest tribes of Central India, but also the whole of the Dravidian inhabitants of the Peninsula; notwithstanding the proofs that exist that they crossed the Sind, Hind, or Ind-us, and occupied the Sapta Sindhu, or 'country of the seven rivers'—the Vaidik name of India, as far as India was at that time known—before the arrival of the Aryans, and that they have therefore a better claim to be called Hind-ûs than the Aryans themselves. To deprive the Dravidians and other primitive races of the name of Hindû, seems as unjust as it would be to deprive all persons of Anglo-Saxon descent of the name of Englishman, and to restrict that name to the descendants of Norman families.

Some again mix the two meanings—the religious and the ethnological—together, and thus, as it appears to me, produce inextricable confusion. Thus Mr Beames, in a note to the Introduction to his "Comparative Grammar of the Aryan Vernaculars of Northern India," p. 39, says, "For the information of readers in Europe it may be necessary to explain that the word Hindû is always used in India as a religious term, denoting those Aryans who still adhere to the Brahmanical faith, and who in most parts of India constitute the majority of the population." I should have considered this definition perfectly correct if the word Aryans had been omitted; but as it stands, it either includes Dravidians amongst Aryans, contrary, I believe, to Mr Beames's own opinion, or it refuses the name of Hindû to those Dravidians in Madras and elsewhere, who consider themselves, and are generally considered by others, amongst the most orthodox and zealous Hindûs in India. In Southern India, Dravidians are invariably called Hindûs in public documents; and the University of Madras divides candidates for its honours amongst the Hindû community into two classes only, Brahmans and 'other Hindûs;' by the term, other Hindûs, denoting all persons 'not Brahmans' who are adherents of the Hindû religion. Notwithstanding this, in Southern India itself the term Hindû has sometimes been restricted to the higher castes, and denied to the Pareiyas and other castes supposed to hold an inferior place in the social system. In this classification the term high-caste, without distinction of Aryan or Dravidian, occupies the place of the word Aryan in Mr Beames's definition. This restriction of the name of Hindû to those of the higher castes who adhere to the Brahmanical religion prevails chiefly, as might be expected, amongst persons who belong to the higher castes themselves, but Europeans have sometimes fallen into the same style of expression. For instance, in regard to the Shânârs, a tribe in Tinnevelly, a considerable proportion of the members of which have become Christians, it has sometimes been said by Europeans that they are 'not Hindûs.' This style of expression is owing, I believe, to a misapprehension, inasmuch as the Shânârs, in their original condition, before their reception of Christianity, were adherents of the ordinary Hindû religion, though generally it was a low type of that religion which they followed. They were certainly not Aryans, except on the supposition that all Dravidians are Aryans, but in this respect they were only in the same predicament as the rest of the Tamil castes, whether higher or lower. The practice of demonolatry does not make a man cease to be a Hindû by religion, the demonolatry of the aborigines having been incorporated with the worship of Rudra from very early, if not even from Vaidik times. The greater number of the Buddhists in Ceylon are demonolaters—the origin of demonolatry in Ceylon and India being no doubt the same; yet, though demonolatry is further removed from Buddhism than from Hindûism, we do not think of saying that the Singhalese are not Buddhists. There is an element of recognised demonism in the Saivism of every part of India, in some places more, in others less. It is a question only of less or more; and the adherents of the more, as well as of the less are Hindûs. The notion that the Shânârs are not Hindûs is a notion unknown to the Hindûs themselves. By the Hindûs they are regarded as simply one caste out of many. We must now, however, bring this digression to an end, and resume our inquiry respecting the relationship of the Pareiyas.

The Pareiyas (called in Telugu Mâlavâṇḍlu = Mâlas) are not the only caste or class of people in the Dravidian parts of India, who are commonly regarded as outcasts, nor are they the lowest or most degraded of those classes; but partly because they are the most numerous servile tribe (their numbers amounting in some places to so much as a fifth of the population), and partly because they are more frequently brought into contact with Europeans than any similar class, in consequence of the majority of the domestic servants of Europeans throughout the Madras Presidency being Pareiyas, they have come to be regarded by some persons as *the* low-caste race of Southern India. Hence, besides the above-mentioned discrepancies in the application of the name Hindû, there are various errors afloat respecting the origin of the Pareiyas and their position in the caste scale, which require to be noticed before entering on the question now to be discussed, 'Are the Pareiyas Dravidians?'

Europeans were generally led to suppose, on their arrival in India several generations ago, that the Pareiyas were either the illegitimate offspring of adulterous intercourse, or were persons who had been excluded from caste for their crimes. This notion appears to have been invented and propagated by the Brahmans and the higher castes, and must have originated, in part, in their wish to justify their exclusive, unsocial behaviour towards the Pareiyas, on principles which they supposed that Europeans would approve. In part, also, it may have originated in an error arising from the uncritical habit of the Hindû mind—viz., the error of transferring to Southern India and to the Dravidian tribes, the fictions which were devised in Northern India to account for the origin of the new castes, or so called mixed classes, of the North. Those northern castes or classes seem to have come into being through the operation of two causes; first, through the subdivision of the original castes of Vaiśyas and servile or S'ûdra Aryans, in accordance with the progressive subdivision of labour; and secondly, through the introduction of one aboriginal tribe after another within the pale of Aryan civilisation, as the religion and civil polity of the Sanskrit-speaking race spread throughout the country, and as the primitive inhabitants were transformed from Dasyus, Nishâdas, and Mlechchas, into S'ûdras. In Manu and similar S'âstras, no mention is made of either of these causes; but the new or mixed castes are attributed exclusively to fictitious mixtures of the older castes. The more respectable of the new castes are attributed to the legal intermarriage of persons belonging to different castes of recognised respectability; another and inferior set of castes are attributed to the adulterous intercourse of persons of equal respectability, but of different caste, or of high-caste men with low-caste women; whilst the lowest castes of all are represented to have sprung from the adulterous intercourse of high-caste women with low-caste men, and are said also to constitute the receptacle of persons who had been socially excommunicated for offences against their caste.

Whatever amount of truth may be contained in this representation of the origin of the castes of Northern India (and I think it most probably a fiction throughout), it may confidently be affirmed that the Dravidian castes had no such origin. The only 'mixed caste' known in Southern India, is that which consists of the children of the dancing girls attached to the temples. Of this class the female children are brought up in the profession of their mothers, the males as temple florists and musicians. In all ordinary cases, when children are born out of wedlock, if there is no great disparity in rank or caste between the parents, the rule is that the caste of the child is that of the less honourable of the two castes to which its parents belong. Where considerable disparity exists, and where the dereliction of rank is on the woman's side—as, for example, where a high-caste woman, or even a woman belonging to the middling castes, has formed an intimacy with a Pareiya man, neither the caste of the father nor any other caste has much chance of being recruited or polluted by the addition of the woman's illegitimate offspring. The child rarely sees the light; the mother either procures an abortion or commits suicide. To suppose, therefore, as Europeans have sometimes been led to suppose, that the entire caste of Pareiyas (including its subdivisions, and the 'left hand' castes corresponding to it) has come into existence in the surreptitious manner described above, or that it is composed of persons who have been excluded from other castes for their crimes, is a baseless dream, which seems too preposterous for serious refutation. Though it is probable that it was from the statements of natives that the Anglo-Indian community originally derived this notion, yet I never met with any natives, learned or unlearned, by whom the notion appeared to be entertained; and the Pareiyas themselves, who regard their lowly caste with feelings of pride and affection, which are very different from what might be expected of them, would resent this representation of their origin, if they had ever heard of it, with indignation.

Anglo-Indians who are not acquainted with the vernacular languages, often designate Pareiyas as outcasts, as persons who are without caste, or as persons who have no caste to lose. It is true that the Pareiya servants of Europeans will sometimes vaunt that they belong to 'master's caste;' and some masters are said to have found to their cost that their Pareiya servants practise no scrupulous, superstitious distinctions respecting meats and drinks. Notwithstanding this, to suppose that the Pareiyas have literally no caste, is undoubtedly an error. The Pareiyas constitute a well-defined, distinct, ancient caste, independent of every other; and the Pareiya caste has subdivisions of its own, its own peculiar usages, its own traditions, and its own jealousy of the encroachments of the castes which are above it and below it. They constitute, perhaps, the most numerous caste in the Tamil country. In the city of Madras they number twenty-one per cent. of the Hindû population; the Veḷḷâḷas, who come next to them, numbering fourteen per cent. Though the Pareiyas themselves will admit that they belong—or, as they would prefer to say, that they belong *at present*—to the lowest division of castes, and are not fabled to have sprung from even the least noble part of Brahmâ; nevertheless, they are not the lowest of the castes comprised in this lowest division. I am acquainted with several castes in various parts of the Tamil country, which are considered lower than the Pareiyas in the social scale; and in this enumeration I do not include the Paḷḷas, a caste between whom and the Pareiyas there is an unsettled dispute respecting precedence. The treatment which the Pareiyas receive from the castes above them, is doubtless unjust and indefensible; but it is not generally known by those Europeans who sympathise in the wrongs of the Pareiyas, that, whenever they have an opportunity, the Pareiyas deal out the very same treatment to the members of castes which are inferior to their own—*e.g.*, the caste of shoemakers, and the lowest caste of washermen; that they are, equally with the higher castes, filled with that compound of pride of birth, exclusiveness, and jealousy, called 'caste feeling;' and that there is no contest for precedence amongst the higher castes of longer standing, or of a more bitter character, than that which is carried on between the Pareiyas and the Paḷḷas. In the insane dispute about pre-eminence, which is always being carried on in Southern India between the 'right hand' and the 'left hand' castes, the Pareiyas range themselves on the right hand, the Paḷḷas on the left; and it is chiefly by these two castes that the fighting part of the controversy is carried on. Now that Europeans are better acquainted with Indian affairs, the theory of the illegitimate origin of the Pareiyas is more rarely found to be entertained; and, as the study of the native languages extends, the supposition that they are outcasts, or that they have no caste, will soon disappear likewise.

The question before us having been cleared of popular errors and extraneous matter, we now come to the consideration of that question itself. Are the Pareiyas Dravidians? Are the forest tribes, the lower castes, and the so-called 'outcasts,' that speak the Dravidian languages, especially the Tamil Pariahs (properly *Pareiyas*), the Telugu Mâlas, and the Malayâḷam Puleiyas (who may be taken as the representatives of the class), of the same origin and of the same race as the Dravidians of the higher castes? Whilst both classes have a right to be called Hindûs, are the higher castes alone Dravidians, Tamilians, Malayâḷis, &c.? and are the Pareiyas and people of similar castes to be regarded as belonging to a different race?

On the whole, I think it more probable that the Pareiyas are Dravidians; nevertheless, the supposition that they belong to a different race, that they are descended from the true aborigines of the country —a race older than the Dravidians themselves—and that they were reduced by the first Dravidians to servitude, is not destitute of probability. It may be conceived that as the Aryans were preceded by the Dravidians, so the Dravidians may have been preceded by an older, ruder, and perhaps blacker race, of whom the Dôms and other Chandâlas of Northern India, and the Pareiyas, and other low tribes of the Peninsula, are the surviving representatives. If this primitive race existed prior to the arrival of the Dravidians, it would naturally happen that some of them would take refuge from the intruders in mountain fastnesses and pestilential jungles—like the Râjîs or Dôms of the Himâlayas, the Weddas of Ceylon, and the Mala-(y)-araśas of the Southern Ghauts; whilst others, probably the majority of the race, would be reduced to perpetual servitude, like the Pareiyas, Puleiyas, and Pallas. The history of the subjection of the Præ-Aryan S'ûdras of Northern India, would thus form the counterpart and supplement of the history of the subjection of a still older race. Though, however, all this may be conceived to be possible, and though there may not be any *à priori* improbability in it, it is more to the purpose to state such circumstances and considerations as appear to be adducible in its support.

(1.) The Pareiyas, the Pallas, the Puleiyas, and several other low-caste tribes, are generally slaves to the higher castes, and most of them appear always to have been in an enslaved condition; and it is more natural to suppose that they were reduced to a servile condition by conquest, than to suppose that entire tribes were enslaved by the operation of ordinary social causes. If, then, the castes referred to were a subjugated people, they must have settled in the country at an earlier period than their conquerors, and probably belonged to a different race.

(2.) The low-caste inhabitants of Southern India are distinguished from the entire circle of the higher castes by clear, unmistakable marks of social helotry. The title of 'S'ûdra,' which has generally been assumed by the higher castes, or which was conferred upon them by the Brahmans, is withheld from the low-caste tribes; they are not allowed to enter within the precincts of the temples of the *Dii majorum gentium;* and wherever old Hindû usages survive unchecked, as in the native protected states of Travancore and Cochin, the women belonging to those castes are prohibited (or were, till lately) from wearing their 'cloth' over their shoulders, and obliged to leave the entire bust uncovered, in token of social inferiority. It may be argued, that broadly marked class distinctions like the above-mentioned, which separate the people of ten or twenty different castes or tribes from the rest of the population, are incompatible with the supposition of an original identity of race.

(3.) There are various traditions current amongst the Pareiyas to the effect that the position which their caste occupied in native society at some former period was very different from what it is now, and much more honourable. Wilks observes that there is a tradition that the Canareśe Pareiyas were once an independent people, with kings of their own. The Tamil Pareiyas sometimes boast that at an ancient period theirs was the most distinguished caste in the country. They say that they were reduced to their present position, as a punishment for the haughty behaviour of their ancestors to some ancient king; on which occasion the Veḷḷâḷas, or caste of cultivators, who are now called Tamiṛar, or Tamilians, *par excellence*, were raised to the place which had previously been occupied by themselves. There is a similar tradition that the Kuravas, or gipsy basket-makers, were once kings of the hill country in the south.

(4.) In various parts of the country Pareiyas and members of similar castes enjoy peculiar privileges, especially at religious festivals. Thus, at the annual festival of *Égâttâḷ*, the only mother—a form of Kâlî, and the tutelary goddess of the 'Black town' of Madras—when a *tâli*, or bridal necklace (answering to our wedding-ring), was tied round the neck of the idol in the name of the entire community, a Pareiya used to be chosen to represent the people as the goddess's bridegroom. Similar privileges are claimed by Pareiyas in other parts of the country, especially at the worship of divinities of the inferior class, such as the village *ammâs*, or mothers, and the guardians of boundaries; and these peculiar rights, which are conceded to them by the higher castes, may be supposed to amount to an acknowledgment of their ancient importance; like the privileges claimed at the coronation of Rajput princes by the Bhills, a northern race of aborigines. It has always been the policy of Hindû rulers to confer a few empty privileges upon injured races as a cheap compensation for injuries; and it has generally been found, where an inquiry has been made, that such privileges possess an historical signification. Mr Walhouse, in an article entitled "Archæological Notes," in the *Bombay Antiquary* for July 1874, adds a few instances of the privileges enjoyed by the lower castes. "At Melkotta, the chief seat of the followers of Râmânuja Âchárya, and at the Brahman temple at Bailur, the Holeyars or Pareyars have the right of entering the temple on three days in the year, specially set apart for them. In the great festival of Siva at Trivalûr, in Tanjor, the head man of the Pareyars is mounted on the elephant with the god, and carries his *chauri*. In Madras, too" [in addition to the custom mentioned above by myself], "the mercantile caste, and in Vizagapatam the Brahmans, had to go through the form of asking the consent of the lowest castes to their marriages, though the custom has now died out." The principle underlying these customs is thus explained:—"It is well known," he says, "that the servile castes in Southern India once held far higher positions, and were indeed masters of the land on the arrival of the Brahmanical races. Many curious vestiges of their ancient power still survive in the shape of certain privileges, which are jealously cherished, and, their origin being forgotten, are much misunderstood. These privileges are remarkable instances of survivals from an extinct order of society—shadows of a long-departed supremacy, bearing witness to a period when the present haughty high-caste races were suppliants before the ancestors of degraded classes whose touch is now regarded as pollution."

(5.) The strongest argument which can be adduced in support of the Præ-Dravidian origin of the Pareiyas and similar castes, consists in the circumstance that the national name of Tamilians, Malayâḷis, Kannaḍis, &c., is withheld from them by the *usus loquendi* of the Dravidian languages, and conferred exclusively upon the higher castes. When a person is called a Tamiṛan, or Tamilian, it is meant that he is neither a Brâhman nor a member of any of the inferior castes, but a Dravidian S'ûdra. The name is understood to denote, not the language which is spoken by the person referred to, but the nation to which he belongs; and as the lower castes are never denoted by this national name, it would seem to be implied that they do not belong to the nation, though they speak its language, but belong, like the Tamil-speaking Brahmans and Muhammedans, to a different race.

I may here mention an argument occasionally urged in support of the same view of the case, which is founded, I believe, upon an error. It has been said that the name Pareiya, or Paṛiah, is synonymous with that of the Pahârias (from *pahâr*, a hill), a race of mountaineers, properly called Mâlers, inhabiting the Râjmahâl Hills, in Bengal; and hence it is argued that the Pareiyas may be considered, like the Pahârias, as a race of non-Aryan, non-Dravidian aborigines. It is an error, however, to suppose that there is any connection between those two names. The word Pariah, properly Pareiya, denotes not a mountaineer, but a drummer, a word regularly derived from *parei*, a drum, especially the great drum used at funerals. The name Pareiya is, in fact, the name of a hereditary occupation, the Pareiyas being the class of people who are generally employed at festivals, and especially at funerals, as drummers. It is true that their numbers are now so great that many of them are never so employed, and that the only employment of the great majority is that of agricultural labourers; but whenever and wherever the din of the *parei* happens to be heard we may be assured that a Pareiya is the person who is engaged in beating it. As the whole caste, though perhaps the most numerous in the circle of the low-castes, is denominated by this name, it appears probable that originally drumming was their principal employment.

The origin of the term *Mâla*, applied to the Telugu Pareiyas, is uncertain. *Mâl* means black in Tamil, but the corresponding word in Telugu is not *mâl*, but *nalla*. The Purâṇas speak of a tribe of barbarians called Mâlas, but their location has been considered doubtful. I should be inclined to identify the Puranic name with that of the Mâlers, the primitive hill people of the Râjmahâl hills; it seems hazardous, however, to attribute the same origin to the name of the Telugu Pareiyas. Mr C. P. Brown suggests, but does not adopt, the derivation of the name from the Telugu verb *mâl*-uṭa, to be without, the meaning deducible from which, 'the destitute,' would seem to suit the circumstances of the case. The name of the Malayâḷam *Pulayas* (Tam. *Puleiyas*), is derived from *pula*, flesh, pollution; but the ultimate root seems to be *pul*, little. The caste which is considered the lowest in the Malayâḷam country, perhaps the lowest in any of the Dravidian provinces, is that of the Nâyâḍis, or Nâyaḍis, a race of dwellers in the jungles. Nâyâḍi means one who hunts with dogs; Nâyaḍi, an eater of dogs. The members of this caste are required to retire seventy-two steps from high-caste people, Pulayas thirty-six, Kaṇiyârs twenty-four. It seems difficult to suppose that tribes which are now regarded as so degraded belonged originally to the same race as the higher castes themselves; but the difficulty, though one that requires careful consideration, may not be found to be insuperable. The circumstances and arguments that have now been alleged in favour of the non-Dravidian origin of the lower castes, possess undoubtedly a considerable degree of strength; but I proceed to show that they are not perfectly conclusive, and that they are to some extent counterbalanced by considerations adducible on the other side.

(1.) The argument which is drawn from the servile condition of the Pareiyas fails to establish the conclusion: because it is certain that there are many slaves in various parts of the world who do not differ from their masters in race, though they do in status. The Russian serfs were Slavonians, and the Magyar serfs Magyars, equally with their masters. Illustrations of the inconclusiveness of the argument may be drawn also from Dravidian life. The more wealthy of the Shâṇârs—a caste inhabiting the extreme south—have slaves in their employment, some of whom belong to a subdivision of the Shâṇâr caste. These servile Shâṇârs appear to have been slaves from a very early period; and yet they are admitted even by their masters to belong to the same race as themselves. There are also servile subdivisions of some other castes. Thus, a portion of the Maravas of the southern provinces are slaves to the Poligars, or Marava chieftains; and even of the Veḷḷâḷas, or Tamilian cultivators, there are not a few families who are slaves to the temples. Various circumstances might contribute to the reduction of the Pareiyas, &c., to servitude, irrespective of difference or inferiority of race. In the wars of barbarous nations, it often happens that both conquerors and conquered belong to the same race, and even to the same tribe. In a civilised age, the conquerors may be content with governing and taxing the conquered; but in a ruder age, and especially in a tropical climate, where labour is distasteful, the vanquished are ordinarily reduced to the condition of slaves. In such cases we shall meet with a phenomenon exactly parallel to that of the Pareiyas—viz., a servile tribe speaking the language and exhibiting the physiological peculiarities of their masters, and yet separated from them by an impassable barrier. Other causes, however, in addition to that of war, may have been in operation, such as poverty, or a state of society resembling the feudal system, or even a trade in slaves, like that which in Africa sets not only nation against nation, but village against village. At all events, taking into account the probability that these and similar social evils may have existed at an early period, it does not seem more difficult to account for the enslaved condition of the Pareiyas, without supposing them to have been of a different race from their masters, than it is to account for the serfdom, till lately, of the Russian peasantry, or for the existence of slavery amongst nearly all the primitive Indo-European races, without the help of any such supposition. It is worthy of notice also, that whilst the Pareiyas, Paḷḷas, and Puleiyas are generally slaves, some of the castes that are included in the lower division—including some of the very lowest—consist wholly of freemen.

(2.) The traditions that have been mentioned respecting the honourable position formerly occupied by the Pareiyas, do not establish the point in hand. Supposing them to rest (which they do not appear to do) on an historical foundation, they prove, not an original difference of race, but only the ancient freedom of the Pareiyas, and the respectability of their social rank, before their reduction to slavery.

(3.) The circumstance that the entire circle of the lower castes, including the Pareiyas, are separated from the higher by badges of social distinction, and denied the national names of Tamilian, Malayâḷi, &c., is one which must be admitted to possess great weight. Though the argument which may be deduced from this circumstance is a very strong one, it does not appear to be absolutely conclusive, for it is in accordance with the genius of Hindû legislation to punish poverty by civil and social disabilities; and high-caste pride might naturally take the shape of an exclusive appropriation even of the national name. We find a parallel use of words in the Sanskrit S'âstras, in which nations that are admitted in those S'âstras to be of Kshatriya origin (*e.g.*, the Yavanas and Chînas), are termed Mlêchchas, not in consequence of difference of race, but solely in consequence of their disuse of Brahmanical rites. There is a still closer parallel in the law of

Manu, that Brahmans who took up their abode in the Dravidian country —probably in Manu's time an uncleared forest—should be regarded as Mlêchchas.

(4.) There does not seem to be anything in the physiology of the Pareiyas, in their features, or in the colour of their skin, which warrants us to suppose that they belong to a different race from their high-caste neighbours. The comparative blackness of their complexion has led some persons to suppose them to be descended from a race of Negrito aborigines; but this hypothesis seems to be unnecessary. The swarthiness of the complexion not only of the Pareiyas, but also of the Puleiyas of the Malayâḷam country (a still blacker caste), may be accounted for by their continual employment for many ages in the open air, exposed to the full force of the vertical sun. If the Fellahs, or labourers, and Bedouins, or wandering shepherds, of Egypt, are admitted to be Arabs of pure blood, notwithstanding the deep brown of their complexion, it would seem to be unnecessary to suppose the Pareiyas, who labour in a hotter sun than that of Egypt, to be of a different race from the rest of the Dravidians, in order to account for their complexions being a shade darker. In no country in the world are features and complexion so variable as in India; but caste, as it exists in India, and especially as it affects the condition of the lower classes, is unknown in every other country in the world. Separate for ever from the society of their fellow-countrymen a class of agricultural labourers or slaves: prohibit all intermarriage with families in more easy circumstances: require them to live by themselves in wretched wigwams, removed to a considerable distance from the village inhabited by the respectable householders: compel them to work hard the whole year round in the open air in an inter-tropical climate—in a country where the sun comes twice in the year right over head: let all possibility of their rising to a higher condition of life, or obtaining a more sedentary, shady employment be for ever precluded: prohibit education: pay them no wages: feed them scantily and clothe them still more scantily: encourage drunkenness and the eating of carrion: prohibit the women from dressing themselves with ordinary regard for decency:—treat them, in short, for twenty centuries as the Brahmans and high-caste Dravidians have treated the Pareiyas and other low-castes, and it will be unnecessary to have recourse to the theory of their intermixture with a primitive race of Africans or Negritoes in order to account for the coarseness of their features, their dwarfishness, or the blackness of their skin. Notwithstanding all this, though the Pareiyas and Puleiyas, as a class, are darker than any other class in the South, we find amongst them almost as great a variety of colour as amongst other classes of Hindûs; and occasionally we may notice complexions that are as clear as those of the higher castes, together with considerable regularity of feature. When Pareiyas have risen to a position of competence and comfort, and S'ûdras have become impoverished, and been obliged to work hard in the sun all day, their complexion is affected as well as their social position; and in a few generations the S'ûdra is said to become dark, the Pareiya fair.

I admit that the features of the Pareiyas differ somewhat from those of the high-caste Veḷḷâḷas, or cultivators, as the features of every caste in India differ somewhat from those of every other caste; yet there is no difference between the cultivator and the Pareiya in the shape of their heads. Not only from their peculiarities of feature and dress, but even from the shape of their heads, we are generally able to distinguish Tamilians or Telugus from the Afghan or Turco-Tatar Muhammedans of India. But looking at the shape of their heads alone, and leaving complexion and features out of account, it is impossible to distinguish a Tamilian, or high-caste Dravidian, from a Pareiya or any other member of the lower castes. Difference in feature is of little or no account in this inquiry, for it is notorious that castes which proceed from the same origin differ from one another both in features and in mental characteristics, as widely as if they inhabited different and distant countries. The soldier or robber castes of Kaḷḷas and Maravas, differ as much from the higher castes in their features as the Pareiyas, and in habit of mind still more. Nevertheless, they claim to be considered as pure Tamilians. The caste title of the Maravas, 'Dêva,' is the same as that of the old kings of the Pâṇḍya and Chôla dynasties. Chieftains of their race still possess the principalities of Shevagunga and Râmnâd, which are called 'the two Maravas;' and the latter, the prince of Ramnad, has claimed from an ancient period to be considered as Sêtupati, or hereditary guardian of Rama's bridge. The other tribe, the Kaḷḷas, have a king of their own, the Toṇḍamân Râjâ, or Râjâ of Puducottah; they claim a relationship to the ancient kings of the Chôla country; and they are regarded by the Tamilian Veḷḷâḷas, or cultivators, as next in rank to themselves. It is possible—though not, I think, probable—that these castes settled in the Tamil country subsequently to the settlement of the mass of the population; but it does not follow that they belonged to a non-Dravidian race; for the course which I have supposed the Kaḷḷas and Maravas to have followed, is precisely that which was followed on the decline of the power of the Pâṇḍyas, by various Telugu and Canarese castes that are unquestionably Dravidians.

(5.) The essential unity of all the Dravidian dialects argues the unity of the race, inclusive of the lower castes. The mixed origin of the Hindûs of the Gaura provinces may be conjectured, not only from historical notices, but from an examination of the component elements of the northern vernaculars. In those vernaculars we can trace the existence of two lingual currents, the Aryan and the non-Aryan, the one running counter to the other; but in no dialect of the Dravidian languages are such traces discoverable of any extraneous idiom which appears to have differed in character from that of the mass of the language. All the grammatical forms of primary importance in all the Dravidian dialects cohere together and form one harmonious system. If the Pareiyas and the other servile castes were supposed to be a different race from the Dravidians, and the only surviving descendants of the true aborigines, it would be necessary to regard the isolated mountain tribes, the Tudas, Gôṇḍs, &c., as remnants of the same aboriginal race; and if this theory were correct, the languages of those long isolated tribes should be found to differ essentially from Telugu and the Tamil. On the contrary, no essential difference in grammatical structure, or in the more important names of things, has been discovered in them; but the Gôṇḍ and Ku, Tuda and Kôta dialects, belong demonstrably to the same family as the more cultivated Dravidian tongues. It is also worthy of notice that though the Pareiyas and the other servile classes in the plains live in hamlets by themselves, removed to a considerable distance from the villages in which their high-caste masters reside, there is no trace amongst them of any difference in idiom, of peculiar words, or of peculiar forms of speech. The only difference apparent, consists in their mispronunciation of Sanskrit derivatives, arising from their general want of education; and in many instances, even this difference is not found to exist.

On the whole, therefore, the supposition that the lower castes in the Dravidian provinces belong to a different race from the higher, appears to me to be untenable. It seems safer to hold, that all the indigenous tribes who were found by the Aryans in Southern India, belonged substantially to one and the same race. It is probable enough that the Dravidians were broken up into tribes before the Aryan immigration, and that the distinctions, not only of richer and poorer, but also of master and slave, had already come into existence amongst them. Those distinctions may have formed the foundation of the caste system, which their Brahmanical civilisers built up, and which was moulded by degrees into an exact counterpart of the caste system of Northern India.

V.

ARE THE NEILGHERRY (NÎLAGIRI) TUDAS DRAVIDIANS?

THE following observations on the relationship of the Tudas to the rest of the Dravidians need not perhaps have been republished. They appeared necessary in the first edition, the theory advocated being then, so far as I am aware, new. Since then the researches of various scholars, and in particular the lifelong researches of the Rev. F. Metz, have removed a great deal of the mystery that hung around this subject, and it seems now to be universally admitted that the Tudas are a Dravidian tribe. Mr Metz called my attention to the circumstance that there was a statement in Assemann to the effect that there was formerly a Christian church in Todamale. I have found the statement in question; but as this Todamale is merely one of the names contained in a list of places on the Malabar coast in which there were churches, which was compiled by or for Menezes, Archbishop of Goa, in 1599, I question whether the place referred to were identical with the Neilgherries. A book on the Tudas has recently been published by Colonel Marshall, of the Bengal Staff Corps, entitled "A Phrenologist amongst the Tudas; or, the Study of a Primitive Tribe in South India; History, Character, Customs, Religion, Infanticide, Polyandry, Language." The twenty-ninth chapter contains a summary of Tuda grammar by the Rev. Dr Pope, including a collection of Tuda words and sentences supplied by Mr Metz. Colonel Marshall's book is so elaborate and exhaustive that it seems to render every other book or tractate on the Tudas unnecessary. In reprinting the following observations, I do so only on account of the interest that attaches, or may be supposed to attach, to them as the first statement in print of that view of the question which is now regarded as established.

The Tudas, or aboriginal inhabitants of the Neilgherry (Nîlagiri) Hills, have been commonly supposed to belong to a different race from the Dravidians of the plains. The reasons that have been adduced in support of this supposition appear to me inconclusive. Unfortunately, so much exaggeration and error are included in those reasons, arising from the sentimental interest with which everything connected with the Tudas has been invested by tourists, that there is not much satisfaction in dealing with the question.

(1.) The difference of the religion of the Tudas from what is called Hindûism, or the Brahmanical religion, is alleged to prove that they belong to a different race to their low country neighbours.

It is quite true that the Tuda religion differs greatly from the Brahmanical; but it will be shown in another portion of this Appendix that the original religion of the majority of the Dravidians of the plains differed from Brahmanism almost as widely, and that the religion of the Gônds and Khonds, who are as certainly Dravidians as the Tamil people themselves, is very different from the religion of the Brahmans, and in some particulars not unlike that of the Tudas.

(2.) The manners and customs of the Tudas are said to be altogether *sui generis*, and such as to indicate an origin different from that of the people of the plains.

Many of the customs of this tribe are certainly remarkable, but it is an error to regard them as peculiar to the Tudas, and *sui generis*. Polyandria is practised by the Tudas, but it is practised also by the Coorgs and Khonds, whose Dravidianism cannot be questioned; and female infanticide is not confined to the Tudas, but is unfortunately too well known in various parts of India. The Tudas are not the only Indian people who live a wandering, pastoral life, who subsist entirely upon milk and grain, who dwell in huts formed of twisted bamboos, who wear no covering upon their heads, who let their hair grow to almost its full length, or who never wash their clothes and seldom their bodies from their birth to their death. Each of those customs is practised by various other Indian tribes, though not all of them, perhaps, by any tribe but the Tudas; and though the Tudas may observe some customs of minor importance which are quite peculiar to themselves—(*e.g.*, the Tuda men do not, like other long-haired Dravidians, tie their long hair in a knot like women, but allow it to cluster round their head in natural curls. The bamboo huts, also, in which they dwell, are built on the plan of a perfect equilateral arch)—yet the observance of a few peculiar customs by a caste which is so isolated as the Tudas, cannot be regarded as a proof of difference of race; for every caste in India, whether Aryan or Dravidian, whether high or low, has some custom or another which is entirely peculiar to itself—generally some peculiarity in dress, in the ornaments worn by the women, or in the manner in which their houses are built.

(3.) The Tudas are said to be a fine manly, athletic race, with European features, Roman noses, hazel eyes, and great physical strength; and hence it is concluded that they differ from the Tamilians and other Dravidians in origin, as well as in appearance.

It is admitted that the Tudas are a hardy, fine-looking race, as might be expected from their simple mode of life and the bracing mountain air they breathe; but it is also certain that many of the statements that are commonly made, both in conversation and in books, respecting their physical characteristics are mere romance. As regards size and strength of body they will not bear a comparison with the natives of the north-western provinces, or even with the Telugu farmers and palanquin bearers. The supporters of the Celtic or Indo-European origin of the Tudas are wont to rest the chief weight of their theory in the Roman noses of their protégés; but aquiline noses are not unfrequently met with amongst the people of the plains, though they have not had the good fortune to attract so much of the notice of tourists: and after all, the nose which is most commonly seen on the Tuda face is not an aquiline nose, but simply a large nose. Even if it were universally aquiline, it would reveal nothing respecting the origin of the Tudas; for physiology makes little account of noses, but much of heads, and the shape of the heads of the Tudas does not differ in any material point from that of the low country Dravidians. Even their features do not differ from those of the people of the plains to a greater degree than their isolated situation for many ages would lead us to expect. It is true that the Tudas have brown or hazel eyes and curly or wavy hair; and this alone would give them a different appearance from the black-eyed, straight-haired people of the plains. The colour of their eyes may be the result of their long residence in the temperate climate of the hills; but this circumstance, when considered as an argument for difference of race, is neutralised by the dark colour of their hair, approaching to black, and especially by the darkness of the colour of their skin. It has not hitherto been noticed by writers on the Nilgherries, but it is nevertheless a fact, that, notwithstanding the long residence of the Tudas on a cold, cloudy mountain region, the colour of their skin is considerably darker than that of the more modern hill race, the Badagas, a race of people who immigrated from the Canarese country not many centuries ago, and is many shades darker than that of the majority of the natives of the Malabar coast. The darkness of the complexion of the Tudas appears to prove that they came originally from the eastern or sun-burnt side of the range of Ghauts; and that long before they took up their abode on the hills they had formed a constituent portion of the low country population. [It should be observed also, that this inference exactly accords with the results that have been deduced from the examination of the Tuda language contained in Appendix I. It has there been shown that the language of the Tudas is essentially Dravidian, and that it appears, on the whole, more nearly allied to Tamil, the language which is spoken in the plains on the eastern side, than to any other dialect.]

After weighing the various considerations that have now been adduced, we may, I think, safely adopt the conclusion that the Tudas belong to the same race and stock as the mass of the Dravidians, though long separated from the rest of the race, and isolated from its civilisation. It may, at least, be confidently asserted that the evidence of the Dravidian origin of the Tudas greatly preponderates over that of every other supposition.

VI.

DRAVIDIAN PHYSICAL TYPE.

LINGUAL comparison appears to me to be the best available guide to a knowledge of the præ-historic relationship of the Dravidian family, but as physiology has in some instances contributed to the discovery of the affiliation of races, it seems desirable to inquire whether in this instance also it can render us any help. The general conclusion to which we are led seems to be that whilst the physical type of the Dravidians of Southern India, including that of the uncivilised Tudas, seems to be substantially identical with that of the Aryans, the type of the Dravidians of Central India, as represented by the uncivilised, or but partially civilised, Gônds, seems to be generally Mongolian. If this conclusion be admitted, and if it be admitted also that the Gônds belong to the same race as the Dravidians of the South, one of the questions that will come up for consideration will be, have the Gônds degenerated? or, have the South Indian Dravidians risen?

I must here premise that my remarks relate exclusively to the Dravidian race properly so called, whether civilised or uncivilised, not to the aboriginal races of India generally. Many of the physical characteristics which Mr Hodgson attributes to the Tamilians, may undoubtedly be observed in the sub-Himâlayan tribes of Nepâl and Assam, and in a smaller degree in the Santâls and other Kôls; but the inexpediency of using as a general appellation so definite a term as Tamilian, appears from the error into which some writers have fallen of attributing the same or similar physical characteristics to the Dravidians or Tamilians of Southern India, who differ almost as much from the Himâlayan tribes as do the Brahmans themselves.

Mr Hodgson thus distinguishes the "Aryans" from the "Tamilians:" "A practised eye will distinguish at a glance between the Arian and

Tamilian style of features and form—a practised pen will readily make the distinction felt—but to perceive and to make others perceive, by pen or pencil, the physical traits that separate each group or people of Aryan or of Tamilian extraction from each other group would be a task indeed! In the Aryan form there is height, symmetry, lightness, and flexibility: in the Aryan face an oval contour with ample forehead and moderate jaws and mouth; a round chin, perpendicular with the forehead, a regular set of distinct and fine features; a well raised and unexpanded nose, with elliptic nares; a well-sized and freely opened eye, running directly across the face; no want of eye-brows, eye-lash, or beard; and lastly, a clear brunet complexion, often not darker than that of the most southern Europeans. In the Tamilian form, on the contrary, there is less height, less symmetry, more dumpiness and flesh: in the Tamilian face, a somewhat lozenge contour caused by the large cheek bones, less perpendicularity in the features to the front, occasioned not so much by defect of forehead or chin, as by excess of jaws and mouth; a larger proportion of face to head, and less roundness in the latter; a broader, flatter face, with features less symmetrical, but perhaps more expression, at least of individuality; a shorter, wider nose, often clubbed at the end and furnished with round nostrils; eyes less, and less fully opened, and less evenly crossing the face by their line of aperture; ears larger, lips thicker, beard deficient; colour brunet, as in the last, but darker on the whole, and, as in it, various. Such is the general description of Indian Aryans and Turanians." Mr Hodgson states also in several places that a Mongolian stamp is impressed on all the aborigines of India. "Look steadfastly," he says, "on any man of an aboriginal race, and say if a Mongol origin is not palpably inscribed on his face.

Probably there was little if any reference to the Tamilians, properly so called, in this striking comparative description of the Brahmans of Northern India and of the forest tribes of the Himâlayas and the Vindhyas; but through the vague use of the appellation "Tamilian," it seems probable that Professor Max Müller was led to suppose the same description applicable to the Dravidians proper, or original inhabitants of the south. Founding his remarks on this description, which he quotes and eulogises (in his "Turanian Researches," included in Bunsen's "Outlines of Universal History"), he says: "From the most ancient times to the period of the Puranas, we meet everywhere with indications, more or less distinct, of two races brought into contact in the Indian peninsula:" and again, "The traveller in India to the present day, though he would look in vain for the distinctive features of a Brahman, a Kshattriya, or a Vaisya, feels the conviction irresistibly growing upon him, as he passes along the streets of cities, or the roads of villages, *whether north or south of the Vindhyas*, that everywhere he is brought in contact with at least two races of man, distinct in mind as well as in body." It is evident also from a quotation from a paper of Dr Stevenson's, which he subjoins, that by those "two races of man" he understood "the higher and lower orders of natives"—"the Brahmans and other castes allied to them, and the lower or non-Aryan castes of the Hindû population." We thus arrive at the conclusion that Mr Hodgson's description of the physical peculiarities which he calls "Tamilian,"—that is, as he understands the term, Turanian or Mongolian,—has come to be accepted as a faithful portraiture of the non-Aryan Hindûs generally, including the non-Aryans south of the Vindhyas—*i.e.*, the entire mass of the Dravidian people. The Professor quotes also those notices from the Puranas in which the type of the Nishâda features is given.—He is "a being," they say, "of the complexion of a charred stake, with flattened features, and of dwarfish stature." "The inhabitants of the Vindhya mountains are called his descendants. According to the Matsya-purâṇa, they were as black as collyrium. According to the Bhâgavata-purâṇa, they had short arms and legs, were black as a crow, with projecting chin, broad and flat nose, red eyes, and tawny hair. The Padma-purâṇa adds a wide mouth, large ears, and a protuberant belly, and particularises their descendants as Kirâṭas, Bhillas, Bahanakas, Bhramaras, and Pulindas." In the next chapter the Professor states that he "accepts for his starting point this general distinction between Aryas and Nishâdas, which, whether suggested by physical features or proved by the evidence of grammar, may be considered as an undisputed fact;" and he then proceeds to inquire "whether they can be subdivided into distinct groups." Finally he distinguishes, yet on lingual evidence alone, between "two classes of Nishâdas, the Tamilic, in the narrower sense of the word, and the Bhotîya or Sub-Himalayan."

Leaving out of consideration at present the Kôls, Santâls, and other Nishâda tribes now called Kolarians, we have to turn our attention to the question of the physical type of the Dravidians, properly so called. The Gôṇḍs may probably have been considered Nishâdas, equally with the Kôls, but there is no proof that the Dravidians of the south were ever designated by this name. They seem always to have been called by local names, as Kalingas, Chôlas, Pâṇḍyas, &c.; and on the whole there seems to me to be a decided preponderance of evidence in favour of their physical type being Caucasian, or identical with that of the Aryans. A writer in the *Journal of the Eastern Archipelago* (Dr Logan), treating of the Dravidians exclusively, thinks that there is a strong Melanesian or Indo-African element in the Tamil physiology; and accounts for it by the supposition that a negro race overspread India and Ultra India, not only before the arrival of the Aryans, but even before the arrival of the Scythians. He sees an evidence of this in the colour of the Dravidians, and in the exceeding variety of physical type and features which he observes amongst them. Yet even in his opinion, and in this point at least I think he is quite correct, the Tamilians are "intellectually more Europeanised than any other Tartaro-Iranian race." The theory of M. de Quatrefages, in the *Journal des Savants* for December 1873, agrees in the main with Dr Logan's. He supposes India, long before the historical period, to have been inhabited by a black race resembling the Australians; that subsequently, but still before the commencement of the historical period, a yellow race entered India from the north-east; and that it was from the mixture of these two races that the Dravidians arose. He accounts in this way for the facts, as he supposes them to be, that the Dravidians are yellow in the north and black in the south. I am doubtful, however, whether the colour of any portion of the Gônds and Orâons inclines to yellow. Colonel Dalton's photographs, and the verbal descriptions of various observers, represent them as nearly black.

Omitting for the present the question of colour, it does not appear to me that there is any essential difference between the heads or features of the Dravidians and those of the Brahmans. There is, it is true, a great variety of feature, as well as of colour, apparent amongst the Dravidians; but though the varieties of feature, or rather of physiognomy, which one observes are numerous, the differences are generally so minute and unimportant that in the absence of any class-difference in the shape of the head, they are consistent with the supposition of oneness of blood, and may safely be referred to local, social, and individual causes of difference. The long continued operation of the caste-law of the Hindûs appears to me to be quite sufficient to account for the differences of feature and expression that are observed to exist. Like oil and water in the same vessel, or ingredients which may be mixed mechanically, but will not combine chemically, the various castes into which the Dravidians were arranged by their Brahman preceptors have lived side by side for ages, probably in some instances for twenty centuries, without commingling. For ages there has been no intermarriage, no social intercourse, no common bond of sympathy. Rank has become hereditary, as well as occupation; and not only rank, but even intellect, temperament, character, and physical characteristics. It would be surprising indeed if under such circumstances "varieties of man" did not make their appearance, and if ethnologists, looking at the question from a distance, did not sometimes doubt whether they could all be referred to a single race of pure blood. "Some," says Dr Logan, speaking of the Tamilians in particular, "are exceedingly Iranian, more are Semitico-Iranian, some are Semitic, others Australian, some remind us of Egyptians, while others again have Malayo-Polynesian, and even Simang and Papuan features."

In comparing the physical type of the Dravidians with that of Mongolians and Aryans, it would be improper to restrict the comparison to the lower classes; for the high-caste Dravidians claim to be regarded as the purest representatives of their race. Their institutions and manners have been Aryanised; but it is pure Dravidian blood which flows in their veins. There *may* possibly be some doubt whether the lower castes were not intermixed with an anterior race: but the higher castes call themselves Tamilians, Malayâḷis, &c., *par excellence*; and their special right to those national appellations is always admitted, in terms at least, by the lower castes themselves. When we compare the physical type of cultivated, high-caste Dravidians with that of the Brahmans, no essential difference whatever, and very little difference of any kind, can be observed. In many instances the features of the high-caste Dravidian women are as delicately formed and regular as those of Brahman women themselves, whilst their complexions are equally fair; and if any difference appears, it consists not in Mongolian breadth of face, but in greater elongation and narrowness. The Dravidian type of head will even bear to be directly compared with the European. Compare, for instance, the heads of the Tamil or Telugu pleaders and translators in any Zillah court with that of the presiding English judge; and it is evident that the Dravidian heads differ from the English only in being smaller and narrower,—with a preponderance in the former of the signs of timidity and subtilty, in the latter of physical and moral courage.

It is especially deserving of consideration that the Neilgherry Tudas, who of all Dravidian tribes have been most thoroughly guarded by their secluded position from Brahmanical influences, instead of being more Mongol-like or Negro-like than the Aryanised Dravidians, are so distinctively Caucasian in the opinion of many persons, that they have been regarded as Celts, Romans, Jews, &c.; and the chief difficulty that exists is that of inducing people to be content with the statement that the Tudas are proved by their language and colour to be identical in origin with the Dravidians of the plains.

Amongst the lower class of the Dravidians, I have occasionally observed a type of head which is somewhat inclined to be what is called Mongolian, that is, it exhibits unusual breadth across the cheek-bones, a pyramidal forehead, a somewhat oblique position of the eyes, and a pyramidal nose with a broad base. On the other hand, Mongolian smoothness of skin, scantiness of hair, flatness of face, and the peculiar monotonous olive hue of the Mongolian complexion, are never met with; and it should be observed with respect to the other elements of the Mongolian type, that it is chiefly, if not solely, amongst the lower classes that they are seen, and that they do not constitute the class-type of any caste whatever. They are exceptional instances, which scarcely at all affect the general rule; and I have no doubt that similar exceptional instances could easily be pointed out amongst the lower classes of our own race.

The physical type of a race may best be determined by the shape of the head and the more permanent peculiarities of feature, irrespective of the complexion, or colour of the skin; for every one who has lived in India must have learned to regard colour as a deceptive evidence of relationship and race. It is a disputed question, it is true, whether the blackness of the colour of the skin of certain races is owing to climate or not. On the one hand, if we follow any of the intertropical lines of latitude round the world, we shall find it passing through different zones of colour—olive, copper-coloured, black, and even white; on the other hand, if we confine our attention to India alone, climate and colour seem to be associated as cause and effect. Looking at the facts that have come under my own observation in India, it is not clear to me that blackness of complexion must be regarded as an inexplicable phenomenon—a fact irrespective of climate. It is true that the Brahmans as a class are much fairer than the Pareiyas as a class: but the conviction is forced upon the mind of every observer, by the hundreds of instances he meets with in daily life, that the colour of the features of the Hindûs is mainly a result of the external circumstances in which they are placed with respect to climate, occupation, and mode of life. As a rule, they seem to be dark-complexioned in proportion as they are exposed to the sun in out-door labour, and fair in proportion as they live a sedentary life; and consequently colour, if an evidence of anything specific, seems to be an evidence mainly of the social status of the individual and his family. We cannot, therefore, expect from considerations of colour and complexion much real help towards determining the race to which the Dravidians belong.

The influence of climate alone, in darkening or blanching the colour of the skin, seems to be greater than is commonly supposed; and India furnishes many instances of this influence. Perhaps the best Indian instance of the influence of climate in modifying colour with which I am acquainted is furnished by the fairness of the complexion of the greater proportion of the natives of the Malabar coast, compared with the very dark hue of a like proportion of the natives of the coast of Coromandel, who belong to the same or similar castes, and who follow similar occupations. The natives of the Coromandel coast are exposed for ten months in the year to a very high degree of dry heat, in a level country, bare of wood.* The natives of the Malabar coast are exposed to a similar degree of heat for not more than two months out of the twelve, and a similar degree of drought is on that coast unknown. Their sky is almost always laden with moisture; the quantity of rain that falls is generally treble the quantity that falls on the eastern coast in the same latitude. The country is everywhere well wooded, and the houses of the people are generally nestled in deep, cool groves; and, in consequence, in the same degree of latitude, and with a difference in longitude of only a degree or half a degree, the skin of the people on the western side of the Ghauts (or central mountain range of Southern India) is almost as much fairer than that of the people on the eastern side, as the complexion of the Brahmans of any of the eastern provinces is fairer than that of the labouring classes in the same province. Notwithstanding this difference in complexion there is no difference in race, for it seems certain that the Malayâḷis are descended from an early colony of Tamilians; and an equally remarkable difference in complexion is apparent amongst the members of those more recent Tamil colonies which have settled in Malayâḷam.

Towards the southern extremity of the peninsula, the breadth of the central mountain range is greatly diminished, and there is easy access from the Tamil country into Travancore by the Aramboly Pass. By this pass, and by similar breaks and gaps still farther south, the Tamilians of the old Pâṇḍya kingdom forced their way into Malayâḷam, and possessed themselves of the southern portion of Travancore. The government of this province has again reverted to the Travancorians, in whose hands it has been for several centuries; but the bulk of the population continue to be Tamilians, as far as the vicinity of Trivandrum, the Travancore capital. Up to that limit the majority of the people on the Travancore side of the mountain barrier belong to the same castes as in the British district of Tinnevelly, on the eastern side: they speak the same language, and follow the same occupations; they occasionally intermarry, and their features are perfectly similar; yet,

---

* In my own neighbourhood in Tinnevelly, I never knew the thermometer lower at any period of the year, day or night, than 70°. The average fall of rain in the same neighbourhood, during the twenty-eight years I registered it, was only a little above 22 inches!

notwithstanding this, they differ so materially with respect to colour, that a stranger would naturally suppose them to belong to different races. A remarkable instance of difference of colour under these circumstances is furnished by the Shânârs—a caste chiefly engaged in the cultivation of the palmyra—who are found in considerable numbers on each side of the Ghauts, up to the very foot of the mountains. The Shânârs on the western side of the mountain range are separated from their fellow caste-men on the eastern side by a space of only about fifteen or twenty miles as the crow flies; and the only difference in their circumstances is the difference in the climate, which is caused by the precipitation of the moisture of the south-western monsoon on the western side of the Ghauts, and its interception from the eastern side. In consequence of this difference in the climate alone, the Shânârs who reside on the eastern side of the Ghauts are amongst the blackest of the Tamilians, while on the Travancore side the same class of people, engaged in the same occupations, are almost as fair as the Brahmans of the Carnatic. This fact, which is patent to the observation of every one in the neighbourhood, is perhaps one of the most remarkable illustrations in existence of the influence of climate in modifying the colour of the skin.

Another and better known evidence is furnished by the circumstance that many of the descendants of the Portuguese who settled in India several centuries ago, are now blacker than the Hindûs themselves. The class of people referred to are a mixed race, descended from European fathers and native mothers, yet instead of being the fairer for their admixture with European blood, many of them are of a darker colour than the natives from whom, on the maternal side, they are descended, and who belonged chiefly to the fair portion of the population of the Malabar coast. Even amongst the Brahmans, though supposed to be a pure, unmixed race, differences of colour are frequently observed. It is supposed to be unlucky to meet a black Brahman or a fair Pareiya, the first thing in the morning. The Brahmans of Northern India are generally fairer than those of the south, with the exception of the Nambûris, or high-caste Brahmans of the Malabar coast, who appear to be amongst the fairest of their race.

Professor Max Müller (in his paper on the Bengali in one of the Reports of the British Association) thought he found in the Gônds and other non-Aryanised Dravidians evidences of the existence of a race "closely resembling the Negro;" and said that "the existence of the same dark race in the south of India is authenticated by Strabo." In the main, Strabo's statement will, I believe, be found to corroborate the view I have taken. He says, "The Southern Indians resemble the Æthiopians *in colour*, but *in features* and *in hair* they resemble the rest of the Indians (for on account of the moisture of the climate the hair does not become woolly); but the Northern Indians resemble the Egyptians." This statement of Strabo throws light on a passage in Herodotus, in which a black race, apparently Hindûs, are said to have been brigaded with the fairer Indians in the army of Xerxes. He says, "Æthiopians from the eastward—from the sun-rising—from Asia—marched with Indians, but differed not from other Æthiopians except in their language and their hair; for the Libyan Æthiopians have the woolliest hair of all men, but those people are straight-haired." Herodotus supplies us with a fact, Strabo with the right explanation of that fact. Herodotus is silent with respect to the *features* of the Eastern Æthiopians; Strabo asserts that their features resembled those of the rest of the Indians.

On the other hand, it must be admitted that on the Malabar coast itself, where a moist climate and an abundance of shade seem to favour the blanching of the colour of the skin, the Puleiyas, a caste of agricultural slaves, are noted for their exceeding blackness. On the Coromandel coast, where the people are blacker on the whole by several degrees than on the Malabar coast, I have met with individuals belonging to various castes, even amongst the higher castes, as black as the Puleiyas; but I cannot say that I am acquainted with any caste or class on either coast which can vie with the Puleiyas in being so universally black. In conjunction with this blackness, however, I have not noticed anything in the shape of the head or in the features of the Puleiyas tending to connect them with a Negrito race, or with any other race than their Dravidian masters. The difference seems to me one of colour alone; and I must be content, I fear, for the present to leave this difference in colour unaccounted for. The Puleiyas are also a very diminutive race, but that is of very little consequence ethnologically, as it is easily accounted for by the half-starved condition in which they have been kept from generation to generation. Sir George Campbell ("Ethnology of India") makes some observations on the blackness of this tribe. He says, "The blackest of the aboriginal tribes live in the densest forest country, in a most malarious climate. Even on this very western coast I find the aboriginal helots of Malabar described as being of the deepest black." He looks to immigration by sea (and if so, probably from Africa) as the modifying cause; but though it is true that Arabs, Jews, and Persians came to the western coast of India by sea in considerable numbers, it does not appear probable that the Puleiyas, a helot tribe, who if they were not of the same race with their masters must have been in the country before their arrival, could have crossed the sea at so early a period.

Most modern observers consider the physical type of the Gônds Mongolian; but Colonel Dalton, in his "Descriptive Ethnology of Bengal," appears to think their prevailing type that of the Negro. He says of the Gônds (p. 283), "They are singularly ill-favoured, and though some of the wealthier families have formed alliances with other races which have improved their looks, I can point to many who have tried this in vain, and who show to this day features more closely resembling the lower Negro type than any I have met with amongst the tribes of Bengal. They often have short, crisp, curly hair, and though it is said, and no doubt truly, that this is far removed from the regular woolly covering of a Negro's head, I have generally found such hair in conjunction with features very noticeably Negro in type, and accompanying a very dark skin. They are larger and heavier in build than the Orâons or Kôls, and with none of the graceful physique to be found in both those tribes."

I have not had an opportunity of seeing any members of this race for myself, and the descriptions I have met with do not quite agree; but, on the whole, it appears to be the prevailing opinion that the most characteristic type of the features of the Gônds is not Negrito, but Mongolian. The Rev. Mr Hislop, a careful observer, describes the Gônd of the Nâgpûr country thus ("Papers relating to the Aboriginal Tribes of the Central Provinces," 1866, p. 71)—"A little below the average height of Europeans, and in complexion darker than the generality of Hindûs, bodies well-proportioned, but features rather ugly: a roundish head, distended nostrils, wide mouth, thickish lips, straight black hair, and scanty beard and mustaches. . . . . Both hair and features are decidedly Mongolian." In another passage he describes the Gônds as darker than the generality of Hindûs, but without any resemblance to the African race. It may be asked, however, if they are decidedly Mongolian, whence their blackness of complexion? Blackness is not a Mongolian characteristic. In his introduction to the "Central Provinces Gazetteer," 1870, p. 110, Mr Charles Grant speaks of the Gônds as "intermixed with the Hindû population, and sometimes so closely as to have almost lost *the flat head, the squat nose, and the thick lips*, which are the facial characteristics of their race. . . . . Their possessions, though still pretty considerable in extent, mostly lie in jungle tracts of little value. The proprietary lists show, it is true, Gônd owners even in the richest districts, but these are not of the true non-Aryan blood, but half-bred chiefs, generally claiming Rajput ancestry. Such was the origin of the royal line of Gârha-Mandla, and probably of most of the families which call themselves Râj-Gônd or Royal Gônd. If so, however, the lower blood is dominant, for in appearance most of them obstinately retain the Turanian type." Mr Beames, speaking of such classes of people, says, "Mixed races call themselves Rajputs, and claim to come from Chitor or Ajmer, unconscious that their high cheek-bones, flat noses, and narrow pig-like eyes, give the lie as they speak to their absurd pretensions."—"Comparative Grammar," p. 258. Mr Hislop says, "This tendency to claim connection with Rajputs is not peculiar to ambitious Gônds. It prevails among the Bhils of Malwa, and is not unknown to the wandering Keikâdis of the Dekkan, both of whom boast of being Yâdavas or Powârs, or some other equally high-born section of the Kshattriyas." The difference between the Gônds in their original condition and the Aryans, in respect of intellectual calibre, seems to have been as marked as the difference in their features. Mr Grant says, "They were as little fitted to cope with men of Aryan descent in peace as in war; and though slow centuries of enervation under an Indian sky had relaxed the northern vigour of the races to whom they had once before succumbed, yet in every quality and attainment which can give to one people superiority over another, there was probably as much difference between Hindûs and Gônds as between Anglo-Americans and Red Indians, or between Englishmen and New Zealanders."—"Introduction to Central Provinces Gazetteer," p. 14.

Notwithstanding the low mental development of the Gônds, according to the estimate of them given above, a distinction is drawn in their favour in the same paper, between them and their more Mongolian neighbours the Kôls. "The Gônds," it is said, "are capable of approaching far more nearly to the Aryan level of organisation than any other of the aboriginal tribes of Central India" ("Introduction," p. 77); and in confirmation of this general statement we find that the Gônds established themselves as an independent power in the sixteenth and seventeenth centuries, and that "under their easy, eventless sway the rich country over which they ruled prospered, their flocks and herds increased, and their treasures filled," p. 83. "The leaders of the Kolarians never rose above the status of predatory chiefs, while the Gônd princes founded kingdoms, received high titles of nobility from the Mogol emperors, and even in their decadence were treated by their Marâṭha conquerors with all the form due to established royalty," p. 110.

If the Gônds are Dravidians, as the fact that their language is Dravidian seems to show, it is remarkable that the physical type of the

Dravidians of Southern India, including even the Tudas of the Nilgherry Hills, should differ so widely from that of the Gônds, and that in intellectual power and capacity for civilisation, the Southern Dravidians —not including the Tudas—should be so greatly their superiors. The South Indian is an Aryan in looks, and rivals the Aryans in culture : it is only in his speech that he shows himself a member of the same race as the Gônds and a non-Aryan. How is this to be accounted for? There does not seem any ground for supposing that the Gônds became intermixed to any considerable extent with the more distinctively Mongolian Kôls; nor does there appear to be any case on record in which people possessed of a Caucasian type of feature are known to have exchanged it for a Mongolian type. An ascent from the Mongolian type to the Caucasian is not unknown; but, conversely, it is not known, I believe, that there has been any descent from the Caucasian to the Mongolian. It would seem, therefore, that it only remains that we should suppose the original type of the whole Dravidian race to have been Mongolian, as that of the Gônds generally is up to the present time, and attribute the Caucasian type now universally apparent amongst the Dravidians of South India to the influence of culture, aided perhaps in some small degree by intermixture with Aryans. If the type of all the Dravidians could be proved to have been originally identical with that of the Gônds, the result would be one of great value, not only for the history of Indian civilisation, but for the natural history of the human race. It would tend to show that mental improvement and the acquisition of a higher style of physical beauty go hand in hand.

The possibility, at least, of such a change taking place under circumstances favourable to mental development is proved by the fact that similar changes from the Mongolian type to the Caucasian have already taken place in India itself and in other parts of the world. The danger of taking fixity of type for granted is illustrated by the change that has passed over the Muhammedans of India. When I speak of the Muhammedans of India I do not refer to a class of Muhammedans found in considerable numbers in Southern India, on both coasts and also in Ceylon, who are called by the Europeans Lubbies or Moormen, and by natives S'ônagas—that is, Yavanas—and who are descended from Arab merchants and their native wives, with a large addition of native converts. I refer to the higher and much more numerous class of Indian Muhammedans commonly called Paṭâns. These are partly descended from the Afghân or Paṭân invaders of India, and partly from the Mogol invaders; but the great majority are descendants of the Tatar-Turkish soldiers and camp-followers, who accompanied both the Afghâns and the Mogols. Probably many of the so called Afghân invaders of India were Seljukian Turks; the Mogols were, as their name seems to import, Mongolians; and the hordes that followed the fortunes of both classes of invaders, were a mixed race—a *colluvies gentium*—comprising various tribes and races of Mongolian and Tatar-Turkish origin, called by the Hindûs Turushkas, in Tamil Turukkas, or more commonly Tulukkas—*i.e.*, Turks. The proportion of Persians and other races of Indo-European origin who accompanied the Afghâns and Mongols in their expeditions, was exceedingly small. Hence, the Muhammedans of India may be regarded as a Tatar-Mongolian people; and we might naturally expect to observe in them those physiological peculiarities of the High Asian races which must have characterised the majority of their ancestors on their first arrival in India, and which are still apparent in all their distinctiveness, not only in the Mongolians, but in the Siberian Turks. Notwithstanding this, we generally search in vain amongst the Indian Muhammedans for signs of a Tatar origin. With the exception of a somewhat greater breadth of face and head, and a more olive complexion, they do not now differ from the Hindûs, properly so called, in any essential point. They exhibit, it is true, special peculiarities of physiognomy and expression; but every Hindû tribe or caste has, in like manner, a peculiar physiognomy of its own, by which it differs from every other tribe. A change appears to have passed over the physiology of the Muhammedans of India similar to that which the Osmanli Turks and the Magyars have experienced since they settled in Europe, and which has transformed them from Tatars into Europeans.

I cannot forbear bringing out more fully the argument founded on the change which has passed over the Turks and Magyars by citing the words of Dr W. B. Carpenter ("Cyclopædia of Anatomy and Physiology"), as condensed by Archdeacon Pratt ("Scripture and Science not at Variance," sixth edition, p. 115):—"The Turks of Europe and Western Asia so clearly accord in physical character with the great bulk of European nations, and depart so widely from the Turks of Central Asia, that many writers have referred the former to the (so-called) Caucasian rather than to the Mongolian stock. Yet historical and philological evidence sufficiently proves that the Western Turks originally belonged to the Central Asia group of nations, with which the eastern portion of their nation still remains associated, not only in its geographical position, but in its language, physical character, and habits of life; and that it is in the western, and not the eastern, that the change has taken place. Any result arising from intermixture of the Turkish race with the inhabitants of the countries they conquered, Dr Carpenter shows to be altogether inadequate to explain the phenomena. Another instance of the same modification is to be found in the Magyar race, which forms a large part of the population of Hungary, including the entire nobility of that country. This race, which is not inferior in mental or physical character to any in Europe, is proved by historical and philological evidence to have been a branch of the great northern Asiatic stock, which was expelled about ten centuries ago from the country it then inhabited, bordering on the Uralian mountains; and in its turn expelled the Sclavonian nations from the fertile parts of Hungary, which it has occupied ever since. Having thus exchanged their abode from the most rigorous climate of the old continent—a wilderness in which Ostiaks and Samoiedes pursue the chase during only the milder season—for one in the south of Europe, in fertile plains abounding in rich harvests, the Magyars gradually laid aside the rude and savage habits which they are recorded to have brought with them, and adopted a more settled mode of life. In the course of a thousand years their type of cranial formation has been changed from the pyramidal to the elliptical; and they are become a handsome people, with fine stature and regular European features, with just enough of the Tatar cast of countenance, in some instances, to call their origin to mind. Here again, it may be said that the intermixture of the conquering with the conquered race had a great share in bringing about this change; but a similar reply must be returned, for the existing Magyars pride themselves greatly on the purity of their descent; and the small influence of Sclavonic blood which may have taken place from time to time, is by no means sufficient to account for the complete change of type which now manifests itself. The women of pure Magyar race are said by good judges to be singularly beautiful, far surpassing either German or Sclavonian females. A similar modification, but in less degree, appears to have taken place in the Finnish tribes of Scandinavia. These may almost certainly be affirmed to have the same origin with the Lapps; but whilst the latter retain, though inhabiting Europe, the nomadic habits of their Mongolian ancestors, the former have adopted a much more settled mode of life, and have made considerable advances in civilisation, especially in Esthonia, where they assimilate with their Russian neighbours. And thus we have in the Finns, Lapps, and Magyars, three nations or tribes, of whose descent from a common stock no reasonable doubt can be entertained, and which exhibit the most marked differences in cranial characters, and also in general conformation, the Magyars being as tall and well-made as the Lapps are short and uncouth." Mr Edkins also remarks (in "China's Place in Philology") that the Turks of the east, even those of Chinese Turkestan, have more of the European physiognomy than the Mongols. So also, he says, the Muhammedans of North China have the western type of face.

These well authenticated changes from a Mongolian or lower type of feature to a Caucasian or higher type, prove the possibility, if not the probability, of a similar change having taken place amongst the Dravidians. If the mass of the Dravidians, when they parted company from the Gônds, were as distinctively Turanians in physical type as the Gônds are now said to be, and if it is certain that their type is now incapable of being distinguished from that of the Aryans, except in point of complexion,—and that not in general in a considerable degree,—the improvement that has taken place in their physical type does not seem to be too great to be accounted for in the main by the influence of external circumstances. It seems to have arisen in the first instance from the fortunate exchange they made of a region of hills and forests for a region of extensive, well-watered plains, admirably adapted for agriculture, and favourably situated for the development of a progressive civilisation.

On the other hand, perhaps, we cannot safely conclude that an exaggerated Mongolian type of features was from the beginning the inheritance of the whole of the Turanian tribes. It may be that that type was developed in the course of time in the steppes of High Asia; and it is certain that the tribes amongst whom it has acquired a peculiar degree of permanence are the Tibetans and the Mongolian nomads, who still inhabit the original seats of their race.

The Indian tribes which are now most distinctly characterised by Mongolian peculiarities, are those which entered India by the North-East, and are probably of Tibetan origin. The Garos and other forest tribes on the Bhûtân frontier, as described by Mr Hodgson, seem to be decidedly Mongolian; and the Kôls and Santâls are probably descended from a similar stock. The existence at an early period in the vicinity of Orissa, of barbarous tribes differing in appearance from the rest of the Hindûs, and exhibiting a Mongolian or foreign type, is attested by the following passage in the "Periplus Maris Erythraei." After referring to the region watered by the Godavery and Kistna, the author says: "After this, keeping the sea on the right hand and sailing northwards, we come upon certain barbarous tribes, as the Κιῤῥίδαι (Sans. *Kirâṭas*?) a race of people with flattened noses (evidently Mongolians), also the horse-faces and the long-faces, all of whom are said to be cannibals. Then sailing eastwards, and having a certain sea on the right, we come to the Ganges." The statement of Strabo which has already been quoted, joined to the negative evidence of this passage, seems to show that at the Christian era, the civilised, cultivated Dravidians (the Pâṇḍyas, Chôlas, Kalingas, &c.) did not materially differ in physiognomy or personal appearance from the northern Hindûs; and that certain barbarous inhabitants of the jungles, who are barbarians still, were the only tribes that appeared to be distinctively Mongolian. The Gondali of Ptolemy, who are classed among 'the Bitti,' and distinguished from 'the Phyllitæ' (probably the Bhills), were probably the Gônds, but it is not said whether or not they differed in appearance from the more cultivated Dravidians. Some writers, I think erroneously, speak of the 'jet blackness' of the Gônds; and the Râjmahâl people are said to be black. Notwithstanding this, according to the account of that accurate observer, Dr Buchanan Hamilton, the features of the Mâlers or Râjmahâl hill people, do not essentially differ from the Aryan type. "Their lips are full, but not at all like those of the Negro. Their faces are oval, not shaped like a lozenge as those of the Chinese are. Their eyes, instead of being hid in fat and placed obliquely like those of the Chinese, are exactly like those of Europeans." We have seen that some of the Vindhya Nishâdas are described in the Purâṇas to be 'as black as crows;' but without debating the accuracy of the portrait of those primitive tribes, which the Purâṇas have drawn, and which seems to be confirmed on the whole by the photographs in Colonel Dalton's "Ethnology of Bengal," it will suffice for the present to remind the reader that those very Purâṇa writers entertained so different an impression respecting the mass of the Dravidians of the south, that they fell into the opposite error of Aryanising them, and supposed the Kalingas, Pâṇḍyas, Chôlas, Kêralas, and other Dravidians, to be descended from Aryan princes of the Lunar line.

It was not until after the above was written that I became acquainted with Sir George Campbell's "Ethnology of India." His impression of the similarity in the physical type of the higher castes amongst the Southern Dravidians to that of the Aryans of northern India is as strong as mine, whilst the reason for the similarity he assigns is different. He says (p. 15), "I draw no wide ethnological line between the northern and southern countries of India, not recognising the separate Dravidian classification of the latter as properly ethnological. It seems to me that among all the Hindû tribes the Aryan element now prevails, and that the presence, more or less, of the aboriginal element is only a question of degree. As a question of degree I do not think that there is at any geographical parallel any decided line. A change of language takes place where passing southward we exchange the Maraṭṭa for Telugu and Canarese. But looking at the people, we see no radical change of feature or characteristics. It may well be that although the people speaking a Dravidian language in the South may always by force of numbers have linguistically prevailed over each separate batch of immigrants, and so far annexed them; still by successive immigration, notwithstanding a Dravidian form of speech, the Aryan blood has come in reality greatly to prevail. The mere fact that they are recognised as orthodox Hindûs seems to imply the northern origin of all the better castes in the South, and that is their own account of their origin. I have no doubt the southern Hindûs may generally be classed as Aryans, and that the southern society is in its structure, its manners, and its laws and institutions, an Aryan society. After all, in their main characteristics the southern people are very like those of the North. Among some of the inferior tribes of the South the remains of the thick lips, the very black skin, and other features may still be traced; but, colour perhaps excepted, the aboriginal features are probably gradually wearing away." He regards the race that preceded the Aryans in the occupation of India as having been a race of Negritoes. "I take as a great division of tribes and castes the black aboriginal tribes of the interior hills and jungles. There can, I suppose, be no doubt that they are the remnants of the race which occupied India before the Hindûs. They are evidently the remains of an element the greater portion of which has been absorbed by, or amalgamated with, the modern Indian race, and which, mixed in various degrees with the high-featured immigrants, has contributed to form the Hindû of to-day. In the South their speech still forms the basis of the modern languages." As regards features, he thinks with Colonel Dalton, that lower races would gradually assimilate themselves to a higher race living amongst them, though inferior to themselves in number. Professor Huxley's views of Dravidian ethnology, together with those of Professor de Quatrefages, seem to be substantially identical with Sir George Campbell's. So also are those of Dr Logan already referred to.

This theory of the origin of the people of Southern India, considered from an ethnological point of view alone, seems nearly perfect. The only ethnological facts it does not appear to account for are the difference between the small, black Puleiyas of the Malabar coast and the large, brown, and comparatively handsome Tudas of the Nilgherries, the fairness of some entire tribes of low-caste Dravidians—*e.g.*, the Mâdigas or 'Chucklers' of the Telugu country, and the combination of Mongolian features with a black complexion in the Gônds and Orâons of the Central Provinces. It cannot be expected, however, that any theory should perfectly meet and explain all the peculiarities observable amongst mixed races, especially where their mixture dates from præ-historic times. Notwithstanding the *prima facie* attractiveness of this theory, I am doubtful whether ethnology is entitled to settle the question, without any reference to the evidence furnished by history and philology. The historic and linguistic difficulties in the way of the acceptance of this theory seem to me to be very considerable.

The better castes of Southern India—that is, those that have the *entrée* of the temples and the members of which are regarded as "orthodox Hindûs"—are too numerous to suit the hypothesis in question. Judging by the results of the census of the city of Madras, the higher Dravidian castes (not including Brahmans) form at least four-fifths of the entire population of Southern India. Small bodies of men belonging to the Aryan or North Indian race might have migrated to the South, and amalgamated with Dravidian tribes, in the manner supposed by the theory under consideration, without any record of their migration surviving, except perhaps in the lighter complexion of their descendants. But it seems difficult to suppose that such an immense migration as the theory requires—whether all at once or in successive waves—can have taken place, subsequently to the composition of the Vedas, during the period covered by the epic poems and the Purâṇas, without leaving behind it some trace of itself, either in Sanskrit or in Dravidian literature, in coins or inscriptions, or at least in the northern names and relationships of the principal castes. The account in the Mâhâ-bhârata of the marriage of Arjuna to a daughter of the king of the Pâṇḍyas may be regarded as a specimen of the notices we should have expected everywhere to find. In this very manner traces of the northern relationship of certain princely families in the South still survive. Those families not only call themselves Kshatriyas, but keep up their connection with the great Râjput families of the north, by occasional intermarriages. A certain number of floating popular traditions, such as that such and such castes are descended from such and such Solar or Lunar kings, are, I admit, in favour of the theory; but such traditions have no place in the literature, and seem to me to be pretty much on a par with the tradition of the artificers of the South, to the effect that they are the descendants of Viśva-karma, the architect of the universe. Castes that have really a northern origin, as the Brahmans and a few offshoots of the Râjputs, are always recognised as such by the caste names they retain.

The theory in question seems irreconcilable also with the great preponderance of Dravidian over Sanskrit names of places in Ptolemy and the other Greek geographers. The only names of Sanskrit origin they give us are those of the river Kâvêrî, Cape Comorin, the promontory Kory, the city of Madura, and the town Brachme, together with the names of two of the Southern princes, Pandion and Kerobotras. All the rest of the names, whether belonging to the coast or to the interior, are purely Dravidian, from which it may fairly be concluded that the great bulk of the population was even then Dravidian, not Aryan. The distinction drawn between the district of Ariace and that of Damirice (Lymirice) (see "Introduction,") would seem also to show that the settlements of the two races were even then clearly defined. Brahmans had doubtless established themselves in various places in the Grecian period, and apparently their influence was extending, but there is no evidence that the bulk of the people in the South then consisted of Aryans, or that they had already been Brahmanised. It is an important fact, conveying an inference in the same direction, that as late as the seventh century Kumârila-bhaṭṭa, himself said to be a South Indian Brahman, and the first Indian scholar who clearly discerned a difference between Sanskrit and the Dravidian vernaculars, styled the Dravidas and Andhras (the Tamil and Telugu people) "Mlechchas," meaning thereby rude, aboriginal, non-Brahmanised tribes (see "Introduction"). If the great bulk of the South Indians, including the whole of the better castes, had been Aryans in origin, equally with himself, and as orthodox Hindûs as himself—as probably they would have been if they had been Aryans—it is difficult to suppose that he would have made use of this contemptuous expression.

The theory in question seems to me inconsistent with the insignificant position occupied in the speech of the cultivated Dravidians by Sanskrit, the language of literature amongst the Indo-Aryans, or the Prâkrits, the old Indo-Aryan vernaculars. The Aryans were so masterful a people, with so high a conception of the divine origin and excellence of everything belonging to themselves, that wherever they established themselves they Aryanised everything they found. There is no instance on record of an aboriginal language holding its ground in the face of an Aryan occupation. In Northern and Western India, and in Bengal and Orissa, where the course of events was in accordance with this theory—that is, where Aryan colonies gradually spread themselves over the country, conquering and partly absorbing the aboriginal population—the ancient vernaculars have so completely disappeared that it has now become a debated point whether any traces of them survive in the structure or vocabulary of the speech of the Aryan colonists. It is held by many that it is highly probable, if not certain, that every word and form in the modern vernaculars of Northern India is Aryan. The Aryan immigrants could not be expected to be so numerous at any time in the South as they were in those parts of India which were nearest the first settlements of their race in the Panjâb. It might therefore be argued that the languages of the Southern aborigines might be expected to hold their ground better than those of the aborigines of the North. This may freely be granted; and yet some kind of proportion between race and language ought to be observable. If four-fifths of the population in the South are Aryans, four-fifths, at least, of the grammatical principles and words of the Southern languages ought to be Sanskritic. I say this result *at least* should follow; because all experience seems to show that a much smaller proportion of the Aryan race would suffice to exert a much larger degree of influence. It is not as if the people in the South conquered by the Aryans had been a highly civilised people, with a cultivated language and a literature of their own. The theory under consideration supposes them to have been in a condition similar to that in which the aboriginal tribes and the lower castes remain still. It supposes, indeed, the Gônds, the Tudas, the Puḷeiyas, and similar tribes to be the truest, least changed representatives of the ancient Dravidians. Though, therefore, the Afghâns lost their language on their arrival in India, and adopted the languages of the highly cultivated races they conquered—(*Græcia capta ferum victorem cepit*)—it seems improbable that the Aryans, especially when supposed to arrive in such large numbers, would exchange their own language, as the hypothesis supposes them to have done, for the languages of people who were greatly inferior to themselves in civilisation, and on whom they found it so easy to impose their own religion and civil polity.

If we should suppose that the Aryan immigration to Southern India consisted, not of large masses of people, but of small isolated parties of adventurers, like that which is said to have colonised Ceylon; if we should suppose that the immigrants consisted chiefly of a few younger sons of Aryan princes, attended by small bodies of armed followers and a few Brahman priests—the result would probably be that a certain number of words connected with government, with religion, and with the higher learning, would be introduced into the Dravidian languages, and that the literary life of these languages would then commence, or at least would then receive a new development, whilst the entire structure of their grammar and the bulk of their vocabulary would remain unchanged. The result which I have supposed would take place is in fact the very condition of things we actually see, and it may, therefore, I think, be concluded that it fairly represents the reality. The only influence Sanskrit has exerted is seen in the enrichment of the Dravidian stock of words; and the only influence exerted by Prâkrits is seen in the mode in which a certain number of those words are pronounced. The position the speech of the Aryans would naturally have acquired in Southern India, if the whole, or even if a considerable portion, of the higher castes had been Aryan in origin, may be illustrated by what has actually taken place in the neighbouring island of Ceylon. Whether we accept the story of Vijaya as historically true or not, it cannot be doubted that several centuries before the Christian era Ceylon was conquered by a small party of Aryan adventurers, probably from Magadha. The previous inhabitants of the island were a rude race, represented now only by the "Weddahs," and probably allied to, if not identical with, the primitive Dravidians. And what was the result? The result was that the Aryan speech—the Pâli-Prâkrit—became supreme, and that the speech of the aborigines disappeared, leaving only a very few traces behind. Even the language spoken by the Veddahs has been found to be substantially Aryan. The fact that the name the Aryans gave to Ceylon (Tâmraparṇî) was identical with the name of the principal river south of the Kâvêrî on the opposite coast of the mainland, would seem to show that the party led by Vijaya was an offshoot from a similar party that had established itself at an earlier period on the banks of the Tamraparṇi, probably at Kolkei, the first seat, according to tradition, of the rule of the Pâṇḍya princes. If so, however, looking at the insignificance of the position occupied on the mainland by the speech of the Aryans, compared with the importance of the position occupied by it in Ceylon, the proportion of Aryans to Dravidians on the mainland must have been very much smaller than in the island, and is therefore very difficult to reconcile with the hypothesis that the great bulk of the inhabitants of Southern India are Aryans by origin, not Dravidians.

On the whole, therefore, I am unable as yet to commit myself to the acceptance of the hypothesis in question, though I confess myself unable to set up in its room a hypothesis that will cover the whole ethnological field with such apparent ease. Further research seems to be required; and a careful comparison of the physical type of the lower castes in Southern India with that of the rude, aboriginal tribes of the Central Provinces, seems to be specially desirable. The second volume of Dr Muir's "Sanskrit texts" (new edition) contains much information, from North Indian sources, respecting the Aryan immigration to the South. The conclusions at which he has arrived have thus been summarised. "The evidence he has adduced all tends to show that the Aryans gradually made their way downwards from the North, but that the force of their incursive wave was weakened as it passed the Vindhya mountains, and failed to make any serious impression beyond the limits of Mahârâshtra; leaving the Dravidian tongues of the peninsula as monuments to record what manner of people had dwelt in that land in previous ages."

VII.

ANCIENT RELIGION OF THE DRAVIDIANS.

Religious usages are sometimes found to throw light on the origin or relationship of races. Similarity in the religious ideas and practices of any two primitive tribes strengthens any evidence of their relationship that may be furnished by similarity of language. Let us see whether any light can be thrown on the question of the relationship of the Dravidians by an inquiry into their religious usages. *A priori*, this inquiry seems likely to lead to some result, inasmuch as the religions of the ancient Indo-European nations and the old Scythian religions of Upper Asia present many essential points of difference. In the earliest times we find amongst the nations of the Indo-European family the universal prevalence of certain tenets and usages, which each of those nations appears to have inherited from the common progenitors of the race. Their objects of worship were either the sun, the sky, water, fire, and other elements of nature personified, or a Pantheon of heroes and heroines; and one of the most characteristic of their religious usages was the maintenance of a distinct order of priests, generally hereditary, who were venerated as the depositaries of ancient traditions and spiritual power. In whatever race these religious peculiarities appear to have prevailed, we shall probably find on inquiry that there are reasons for attributing to that race an Indo-European origin or relationship: and in like manner a family likeness (exceedingly dissimilar from the particulars now mentioned) will be found to characterise the religious practices of the nations and peoples of the Scythian group.

In endeavouring to ascertain the characteristics of the primitive Dravidian religion, we are met by a serious but not insurmountable difficulty. The Brahmans, by whom the Aryan civilisation was grafted on the old Dravidian stock, laboured assiduously, if not to extirpate the old Dravidian religion, yet at least to establish their own in its room as a religion of paramount obligation; and they are generally supposed to have succeeded in accomplishing this object. Notwithstanding their success, however, it is still possible in some degree to discriminate between the practices introduced by the Brahmans and the older religion of the Dravidian people. If, for instance, any usages are found to prevail extensively in Southern India, and especially amongst the ruder and less Aryanised tribes, which are derived neither from the Vêdas nor from the Purâṇas, neither from Buddhism nor from Jainism, such usages may be concluded to be relics of the religious system of the Dravidian aborigines. Many such usages do actually exist. Several religious systems widely differing from the Brahmanical are discoverable amongst the Dravidian nations, and are especially prevalent amongst the rude inhabitants of the jungles. Hence, we are not quite destitute of the means of comparing the characteristics of the ancient Dravidian religion prior to the introduction of Brahmanism (or what is commonly called Hindûism), with the religious usages that prevailed amongst the High Asian races.

The system which prevails in the forests and mountain fastnesses throughout the Dravidian territories, and also in the south of the peninsula amongst the lower classes and a portion of the middle classes, and which appears to have been still more widely prevalent at an early period, is a system of demonolatry, or the worship of evil spirits by means of bloody sacrifices and frantic dances. This system seems to have been introduced from the Tamil country into Ceylon, where it is now mixed up with Buddhism. On comparing this Dravidian system of demonolatry and sorcery with Shamanism*—the superstition which prevails amongst the Ugrian races of Siberia and the hill-tribes on the south-western frontier of China, which is still mixed up with the Buddhism of the Mongols, and which seems to have been the old religion of the whole Tatar race before Buddhism and Muhammedanism were disseminated amongst them—we cannot avoid the conclusion that those two superstitions, though practised by races so widely separated, are not only similar but identical.

I shall here point out the principal features of resemblance between the Shamanism of High Asia and the demonolatry of the Dravidians,† as still practised in many districts in Southern India.

* This word Shamanism is formed from Shaman, the name of the magician-priest of the North Asian demonolaters. *Shaman,* though a name appropriated by demonolaters, is of Buddhistic origin, and was adopted from the Mongolians. It is identical with *Śamaṇa,* the Tamil name for a Buddhist, and is derived from the Sanskrit word *Śramaṇa,* a Buddhist ascetic. The use of this word *Shaman,* in Siberia, must be of comparatively modern origin; but the system of religion into which it has been adopted and incorporated is one of the oldest superstitions in the world.

† A full account of the peculiarities of the Dravidian demonolatry was contained in a small work of mine (now out of print), called "The Shânârs of Tinnevelly,"

1. The Shamanites are destitute of a regular priesthood. Ordinarily the father of the family is the priest and magician; but the office may be undertaken by any one who pleases, and at any time laid aside. Precisely similar is the practice existing amongst the rude tribes of Southern India. Ordinarily it is the head of the family, or the headman of the hamlet or community, who performs the priestly office; but any worshipper, male or female, who feels so disposed, may volunteer to officiate, and becomes for the time being the representative and interpreter of the demon.

2. The Shamanites acknowledge the existence of a supreme God, but they do not offer him any worship, believing that he is too good to do them any harm. The same acknowledgment of God's existence and the same neglect of his worship characterise the religion of the Dravidian demonolaters.

3. Neither amongst the Shamanites, nor amongst the primitive, un-Brahmanised demonolaters of India is there any trace of belief in the metempsychosis.

4. The objects of Shamanite worship are not gods or heroes, but demons, which are supposed to be cruel, revengeful, and capricious, and are worshipped by bloody sacrifices and wild dances. The officiating magician or priest excites himself to frenzy, and then pretends, or supposes himself, to be possessed by the demon to which worship is being offered; and whilst in this state he communicates, to those who consult him, the information he has received. The demonolatry

---

published by the Society for the Propagation of the Gospel. I think I proved in that work that the demonolatry of the Shânârs, and other primitive tribes of Southern India, did not originate with the Brahmans, or in any local development of the religion of the Brahmans; but that, on the contrary, the element of demonology which is contained in the Puranic system was borrowed from this old Dravidian superstition. The Buddhists of Ceylon seem to have borrowed their demonolatry from the Dravidians of the old Pâṇḍya kingdom: if so, it cannot be unreasonable to suppose that it was from the same or a similar source that the Brahmans borrowed the demoniacal element contained in their religion. It appears to me that an element of demonism, ready to receive further development, may be traced even in the Aitareya Brâhmaṇa of the Rig-veda, in connection with the character attributed, and the worship offered, to Rudra, afterwards identified with Śiva. I apprehend that we have a mythical record of the adoption of the aboriginal demonolatry into the Brahmanical system, and of the object in view in this alliance, in the Puranic story of the sacrifice of Daksha. According to that story, Śiva (*i.e.*, Śaiva Brahmanism) found himself unable to subdue the old elementary divinities, and to secure to himself the exclusive homage at which he aimed, till he called in the aid of the demons (the demonolatry of the aborigines), and put himself at their head in the person of his (*pro-re-natus*) son, Vîra-bhadra; a demigod whose wife, emanation, or representative, Bhadra-kâlî, is regarded by the Shânârs as their patroness and mother.

practised in India by the more primitive Dravidian tribes is not only similar to this, but the same. Every word used in the foregoing description of the Shamanite worship would apply equally well to the Dravidian demonolatry; and in depicting the ceremonies of the one race we depict those of the other also.

Compare the following accounts of the demonolatrous rites of the Shamanites of Siberia and those of the demonolaters of India. The description of the Shamanite worship is formed from a series of arranged quotations from the descriptions which various Russian travellers and ecclesiastics have given of the superstitions of the Ostiaks, the Samoïedes, the Siberian Turks, and other pagan inhabitants of Northern Asia, to which are added some extracts from Marco Polo, and Colonel Yule's notes thereon. The account of the Dravidian superstitions is mainly taken from my paper on "the Tinnevelly Shânârs," a paper which was written before I was aware of the identity of the demonolatry of Siberia with that of Southern India.

Shamanite Demonolatrous Rites.—"When the Shaman, or magician, performs his superstitious rites, he puts on a garment trimmed with bits of iron, rattles, and bells: he cries horribly, beats a sort of drum, agitates himself, and shakes the metallic appendages of his robe; and at the same time the bystanders increase the din by striking with their fists upon iron kettles. When the Shaman, by his horrible contortions and yells, by cutting himself with knives, whirling and swooning, has succeeded in assuming the appearance of something preternatural and portentous, the assembled multitude are impressed with the belief that the demon they are worshipping has taken possession of the priest, and regard him accordingly with wonder and dread. When he is quite exhausted with his exertions, and can no longer hold out, he makes a sign that the spirit has left him, and then imparts to the people the intimations he has received."

Marco Polo, speaking of some rude tribes of Central Asia, southward of the Burman frontier, not then converted to Buddhism (Colonel Yule's edition, vol. ii. pp. 53–61), says—

"And let me tell you that in all those three provinces that I have been speaking of, to wit, Carajan, Vochan, and Yachi, there is never a leech. But when any one is ill they send for the devil-conjurers, who are the keepers of their idols. When these are come the sick man tells what ails him, and then the conjurers incontinently begin playing on their instruments, and singing, and dancing; and the conjurers dance to such a pitch that at last one of them will fall to the ground lifeless, like a dead man. And then the devil entereth into his body.

And when his comrades see him in this plight they begin to put questions to him about the sick man's ailment. And he will reply, 'Such or such a spirit hath been meddling with the man, for that he hath angered the spirit and done it some despite.' Then they say, 'We pray thee to pardon him, and to take of his blood or of his goods what thou wilt, in consideration of thus restoring him to health.' And when they have so prayed, the malignant spirit that is in the body of the prostrate man will (mayhap) answer, 'The sick man hath also done great despite unto such another spirit, and that one is so ill-disposed that it will not pardon him on any account;'—this at least is the answer they get if the patient be like to die. But if he is to get better, the answer will be that they are to bring two sheep, or may be three, and to brew ten or twelve jars of drink, very costly, and abundantly spiced. Moreover, it will be announced that the sheep must be all black-faced, or of some other particular colour as it may happen; and then all those things are to be offered in sacrifice to such and such a spirit whose name is given. And they are to bring so many conjurers, and so many ladies, and the business is to be done with a great singing of lauds, and with many lights and store of good perfumes. That is the sort of answer they get if the patient is to get well. And then the kinsfolk of the sick man go and procure all that has been commanded, and do as has been bidden, and the conjurer who had uttered all that gets on his legs again.

"So they fetch the sheep of the colour prescribed, and slaughter them, and sprinkle the blood over such places as have been enjoined, in honour and propitiation of the spirit. And the conjurers come, and the ladies, in the number that was ordered, and when all are assembled and everything is ready, they begin to dance and play and sing in honour of the spirit. And they take flesh-broth, and drink, and lign-aloes, and a great number of lights, and go about hither and thither, scattering the broth and the drink and the meat also. And when they have done this for a while, again shall one of the conjurers fall flat and wallow there, foaming at the mouth, and then the others will ask if he have yet pardoned the sick man? And sometimes he shall answer yes! and sometimes he shall answer no! And if the answer be no, they shall be told that something or other has to be done all over again, and then he shall be pardoned; so this they do. And when all that the spirit has commanded has been done with great ceremony, then it will be announced that the man is pardoned and shall be speedily cured. So when they at length receive such a reply, they announce that it is all made up with the spirit, and that he is propitiated, and they fall to eating and drinking with great joy and mirth, and he who had been lying lifeless on the ground gets up and takes his share. So when they have all eaten and drunken, every man departs home. And presently the sick man gets sound and well."

The following are Colonel Yule's notes on the above :—

Note 7.—Compare Mr Hodgson's account of the sub-Himalayan Bodos and Dhimals : "All diseases are ascribed to supernatural agency. The sick man is supposed to be possessed by one of the deities, who racks him with pain as a punishment for impiety or neglect of the god in question. Hence not the mediciner, but the exorcist, is summoned to the sick man's aid."—(*J. A. S. B.*, xviii. 728.)

Note 8.—Mr Hodgson again—"Libations of fermented liquor always accompany sacrifice—because, to confess the whole truth, sacrifice and feast are commutable words, and feasts need to be crowned with copious potations."—(*Ibid.*)

Note 9.—And again—"The god in question is asked what sacrifice he requires? a buffalo, a hog, a fowl, or a duck, to spare the sufferer? . . . . anxious as I am fully to illustrate the topic, I will not try the patience of my readers by describing all that vast variety of black victims and white, of red victims and blue, which each particular deity is alleged to prefer."—(*Ibid*, and p. 732.)

Note 10.—The same system of devil-dancing is prevalent among the tribes on the Lu-Kiang, as described by the Roman Catholic missionaries. The conjurers are there called Mumos.

"Marco's account of the exorcism of evil spirits in cases of obstinate illness exactly resembles what is done in similar cases by the Burmese, except that I never saw animals sacrificed on such occasions."—(Sir A. Phayre.)

Mouhot says of the wild people of Cambodia called Stiens : "When any one is ill they say that the evil spirit torments him ; and to deliver him they set about the patient a dreadful din which does not cease night or day, until some one among the bystanders falls down as if in a syncope, crying out, "I have him—he is in me—he is strangling me !" Then they question the person who has thus become possessed. They ask him what remedies will save the patient ; what remedies does the evil spirit require that he may give up his prey? Sometimes it is an ox or a pig ; but too often it is a human victim."—(*Journal of the Royal Geographical Society*, xxxii. 147.)

In fact, these strange rites of Shamanism, devil-dancing, or what not, are found with wonderful identity of character among the non-Aryan races over parts of the earth most remote from one another, not only among the vast variety of Indo-Chinese tribes, but among the Tamilian tribes of India, the Veddahs of Ceylon, the races of Siberia, and the red nations of North and South America. Hinduism has assimilated these "prior superstitions of the sons of Tur," as Mr Hodgson calls them, in the form of Tantrika mysteries, whilst in the wild performance of the dancing dervishes at Constantinople we see perhaps again the infection of Turanian blood breaking out from the very heart of Mussulman orthodoxy.

"Dr Caldwell has given a striking account of the practice of devil-dancing among the Shanars of Tinnevelly, which forms a perfect parallel in modern language to our traveller's description of a scene of which he also had manifestly been an eye-witness."

Thus far Colonel Yule. I now adduce the passage from my own paper, of which Colonel Yule quoted the principal portion.

Shânâr Demonolatrous Rites.—"When it is determined to offer a sacrifice to a devil, a person is specially appointed to act the part of priest; for devil-worship is not, like the worship of the deities, appropriated to a particular order of men, but may be performed by any one who chooses. The officiating priest is styled a devil-dancer. Usually the head man, or one of the principal men of the village officiates; but sometimes the duty is voluntarily undertaken by some devotee, male or female, who wishes to gain notoriety, or in whom the sight of the preparations has awakened a sudden zeal. The officiating priest is dressed up for the occasion in the vestments and ornaments appropriated to the particular devil that is worshipped. The object in view in donning the demon's insignia is doubtless to strike terror into the imagination of the beholders; but the party-coloured dress and grotesque ornaments, the cap and trident and jingling bells, of the performer, bear so close a resemblance to the usual adjuncts of a pantomime that an European would find it difficult to look grave. The musical instruments, or rather the instruments of noise, which are chiefly used in the devil-dance are the drum and the horn; with occasionally the addition of a clarionet when the parties can afford it. But the favourite instrument, because the noisiest, is that which is called the bow. A series of bells of various sizes is fastened to the frame of a gigantic bow, the strings are tightened so as to emit a musical note when struck, and the bow rests on a large empty brazen pot. The instrument is played on by a plectrum, and several musicians join in the performance. One strikes the strings of the bow with the plectrum, another produces the bass by striking the brazen pot with his hand, and a third beats time and improves the harmony by a pair of cymbals. When the preparations are completed, and the devil-dance is about to commence, the music is at first comparatively slow, and the dancer seems impassive and sullen, and either he stands still or moves about in gloomy silence. Gradually, as the music becomes quicker and louder, his excitement begins to rise. Sometimes to help him to work himself up into a frenzy he uses medicated draughts, cuts and lacerates his flesh till the blood flows, lashes himself with a huge whip, presses a burning torch to his breast, drinks the blood which flows from his own wounds, or drinks the blood of the sacrifice, putting the throat of the decapitated goat to his mouth. Then, as if he had acquired new life, he begins to brandish his staff of bells, and dance with a quick, but wild, unsteady step. Suddenly the *afflatus* descends. There is no mistaking that glare, or those frantic leaps. He snorts, he stares, he gyrates. The demon has now taken bodily possession of him, and though he retains the power of utterance and of motion, both are under the demon's control, and his separate consciousness is in abeyance. The bystanders signalise the event by raising a long shout attended with a peculiar vibratory noise. The devil-dancer is now worshipped as a present deity; and every bystander consults him respecting his disease, his wants, the welfare of his absent relations, and the offerings which are to be made for the accomplishment of his wishes. As the devil-dancer acts to admiration the part of a maniac, it requires some experience to enable a person to interpret his dubious or unmeaning replies, his muttered voice, and uncouth gestures; but the wishes of the parties who consult him help them greatly to interpret his meaning."

A similar system prevails in the hilly districts of Mysore, as appears from an article on the demon-worship practised in the Malnâd district in that province, in the *Indian Antiquary* for September 1872, by Mr Narasimmiyengar of Bangalore. There also the priest "works himself to a state bordering on frenzy, and whatever he may utter in that condition is considered to be a supernatural revelation."

A still more extraordinary outburst of demoniacal frenzy takes place amongst the Kûrs, Kûrkus, or Muâsîs, a people of Chûtiâ Nâgpûr, in connection with the worship of one of their divinities. These people belong to the Kôlarian, not to the Dravidian stock, but their religion, like that of the old Dravidians, seems to be mainly a worship of evil spirits. "The divinity may be invoked at any time, and in all sickness and misfortunes his votaries confidently appeal to him. The Baiga is always the medium of communication, but he assembles the people to aid him in the invocation. Musical instruments are produced, dancing commences, and the invocation to the spirit is chanted until one or more of the performers manifest possession by wild rolling of the eyes and involuntary spasmodic action of the muscles. The affection appears contagious, and old women and others who have not been dancing become influenced by it in a manner that is horrible to contemplate. Captain Samuells, who frequently witnessed the incantation, is confident that no deception whatever is practised. The affection, says Captain Samuells, comes on like a fit of ague, lasting sometimes for a quarter of an hour, the patient or possessed person writhing and trembling with intense violence, especially at the commencement of the paroxysm. Then he is seen to spring from the ground into the air, and a succession of leaps follows, all executed as if he were shot at by some unseen agency. During this stage of the seizure he is supposed to be quite unconscious, and rolls into the fire, if there be one, or under the feet of the dancers, without sustaining injury from the heat or pressure. This lasts for a few minutes only, and is followed by the spasmodic stage. With hands and knees on the ground, and hair loosened, the body is convulsed, and the head shakes violently, whilst from the mouth issues a hissing or gurgling noise. The patient next evincing an inclination to stand on his legs, the bystanders assist him, and place a stick in his hand, with the aid of which he hops about, the spasmodic action of the body still continuing, and the head performing by jerks a violently fatiguing circular movement. This may go on for hours, though Captain Samuells says that no one in his senses could continue such exertion for many minutes. When the Baiga is appealed to, to cast out the spirit, he must first ascertain whether it is Gansâm himself, or one of his familiars, that has possessed the victim. If it be the great Gansâm, the Baiga implores him to desist, meanwhile gently anointing the victim with butter; and if the treatment is successful, the patient gradually and naturally subsides into a state of repose from which he rises into consciousness, and restored to his normal state, feels no fatigue or other ill-effects from the attack. This is certainly the most thorough form of demon-worship with which we have met, and one that must appear to its votaries to testify to its own reality each time it is resorted to."—(Colonel Dalton's "Ethnology of Bengal," p. 232.)

It seems to me unnecessary to say anything more in proof of the substantial identity of the demonolatry of Central and Southern India with the Shamanism of Central and Northern Asia. It may be alleged that similarity in mental characteristics and social circumstances alone might give rise to this similarity in religious ideas and practices, and I admit this to be possible, nay probable, but it seems to me more probable still that both the superstitions which have now been described have sprung from a common origin: and I may add that the conformity which has been traced between the old religion of the Dravidians and that which was once the religion of almost all the Scythian nations and tribes corroborates the suspicion of the Scythian relationship, on the whole, of the Dravidian race.

Whilst the demonolatrous rites which I have now described appear to have constituted the prevailing superstition of the ancient Dravidians, we meet also with traces of the existence of systems that correspond in part to those which prevailed amongst the Indo-European races.

The religion of the Khonds, Kandhs, or Kus, though it contains a demonolatrous element, may be described as in the main a worship of gods of rivers and mountains, of gods of the earth and the sky, and of the gods of elements and *genii loci*. It is in part an elementary worship, which may be allied in principle to that of the Aryans, but which differs widely from it in spirit and form, and appears to be quite independent of it in origin. This remark especially applies to that section of the Khonds which used to practise human sacrifices, and delighted in cruelty and gloom. A worship of gods of rivers and mountains similar to that of the Khonds is found amongst some of the Kôls, and also amongst the Sub-Himâlayan and Bhûtân tribes described by Mr Hodgson,—in most instances modified by an element of terror, and intermixed with demon worship pure and simple.

Amongst the Dravidians of the plains scarcely any reliable trace of the worship of the elements has ever been discovered, except in so far as it can be shown to have had a Brahmanical origin. Indeed there is reason to believe that the old Vedic or Elementary worship of the Brahmans had already merged into the mythological and mystical system of the Purâṇas, before the Brahmans effected a settlement in the South. So far as appears, every usage of the plains which is not of Brahmanical origin is either identical with Shamanism or allied to it.

The religion of the Tudas of the Neilgherry (Nîlagiri) hills exhibits some peculiarities which have been regarded as 'Scytho-Druidical.' The peculiar veneration with which the Tudas regard the manes of ancestors; their sacrifices to secure the peace of the dead; the prominence given in their worship to offerings of milk and clarified butter; their freedom from the worship of idols; the religious veneration with which they regard a sacred bell which is hung up in their temples or sacred dairies; their abstinence from flesh, and living entirely on grain and milk; their exclusion of women from all share in the rites of worship, and even from the precincts of their temples; their practice of polyandria;—these and analogous peculiarities of the religious system and social life of the Tudas accord to a certain extent with usages which prevailed in the earliest ages amongst most of the tribes of the Indo-

European race. Our ignorance of the history of the Tudas, and of the circumstances which compelled them to take refuge in the Neilgherry hills, renders it difficult, if not impossible, to determine whether their religion sprang from the same origin as the Dravidian demonolatry, whether it is to be placed to the account of their early association with some Indo-European race, or whether it was a spontaneous development of the Tuda mind.

The religion of the Tudas has sometimes been called Druidical, Celto-Druidical, or identical with the religion of the ancient Celts; but, with the exception of the performance of some of their rites in the deep gloom of sacred groves,—a practice which was not peculiar to the Celts alone, but which prevailed amongst various ancient nations,—it does not appear that there is anything distinctively or certainly Druidical in the existing system of the Tudas.

Since the appearance of the above remarks in the first edition of this work, much progress has been made in the study of the religion and usages of the Tudas, through the researches of Colonel Marshall, and especially those of the Rev. F. Metz. Most of the information respecting the Tudas acquired by Mr Metz during a long life of missionary labour amongst the hill tribes of the Neilgherries, will be found in Colonel Marshall's book. It is now known that the Tudas have a priestly family or clan; that the bell-god they venerate so highly is a memorial of the bell worn by a succession of sacred cows; that the men of the tribe eat flesh once a year in a dense forest; and, in particular, that the cows that are slaughtered at and after a funeral, are not 'sacrifices to secure the peace of the dead,' but are a provision made to supply the spirit of the deceased with milk (the chief food of this pastoral race) in the other world. Colonel Marshall, after describing the rites of the Tudas in detail, thus comments on the items of information he has furnished in chap. xxii. pp. 186—189: "What we have seen in Tuda rites and ceremonies is little else than the arrangements which a pastoral and communistic people have made for the provision and care of an article of food, doubtless at one time essential, not merely for due sustenance, but to their very existence in the land. These customs having through the course of ages so mellowed as to have acquired all the effect and influence of sanctity, we find ourselves now in the interesting position of actual witnesses to the growth of the earliest germs of religious belief and observance, as they develop in the mind of primitive man from the material nucleus whence they originated.

"We note that the stage when the cow, the milk-giver and support on which the people have depended almost from all time, has grown, from an object of the greatest solicitude, to become one of deep reverence and (so far as they have yet learnt to express themselves) of worship. The flesh is not eaten. Its milk is almost sacred. The chattels of early herds (the cow-bell in particular) have matured into gods, and dairies bear the conception of temples. We find that common milkmen have, by virtue of the sacred nature of such office, advanced in popular estimation until they are viewed in the aspect of priests. The high priest, from being a servant of certain gods, has become confused with godhead itself. A family, styling itself 'sons of the gods,' has developed (though without arrogation to caste pretensions) into a Levitical clan, inheritors of the highest priestly office; its males being prepared and chastened thereto in sacred groves, by the use of a plant set apart for the purpose, and by abstinence from sensual pleasures; the females of the entire tribe being not only excluded from participation in such duties, but debarred approach to all holy precincts. They acknowledge the existence of gods, *perhaps* even of a Supreme God (Ûsuru Swâmi), but their ideas on the subject are quite undeveloped. I think I trace in them a partiality to the regard of *light*—apart from fire—as, *par excellence*, the manifestation of deity. . . . . I submit this suggestion as one having a possible value in determining the ethnic affinities of the Tuda race, and as pointing to an interesting stage in Turanian progress,—that whence various creeds have sprung and ramified. The Tuda religion has not the slightest sympathy with idolatry, nor does it pay attention to natural objects, as trees or rivers; to birds, beasts, or reptiles; nor to the elements. No offerings to a god, whether of flesh (human or animal) or fruit of the soil, are made; no human victims, and no self-torture. It is not that they have risen above such prejudices; they seem to me rather not to have attained the stage when religious observances commence. Circumcision is not performed. The memory of forefathers is piously regarded, but the feeling has not expanded through veneration into any form of hero-worship. They believe in transmigration, but whether of soul or body, probably few have formed any distinct ideas. [They dispose of their dead by cremation.] The funeral service seems to favour the idea that the transition of the soul is the dogma which, though unexpressed, lies like an instinct in their minds; coupled with the idea that the soul is a living solid—a real duplicate Tuda requiring food. [They generally abstain from the eating of flesh, but] the practice certainly forms at present no part of their religious observance. I would place the state of their belief in witchcraft and the work of demons and other unseen agencies somewhat on a parallel with that of their knowledge of divine work. Neither one nor the other troubles them much. Though they do, to a certain extent, practise demonolatry, they do not do so with the enthusiasm of other primitive races of South India. Indeed I had not one opportunity of witnessing feats of exorcism.

"I incline to the belief that in any matters of religion beyond what I have described, they have been influenced through the proximity of cognate races, who themselves, again, have at different periods been variously Hinduised or inoculated with the strange customs of other tribes in India, cognate or otherwise. Thus, through the Âryans, the Tuda sense of adoration has been educated; more gods have been introduced than he knows what to do with; and his natural love of relics has been intensified and improved. From being at first memorials of cattle herds, the relics have grown to be venerated as souvenirs of ancestors. On the other hand, the mildness and contentedness of the tribe have (so I think) led them to drop or to avoid much of the demonolatrous habit of other members of that Dravidian race to which they belong. Certainly any superior ideas; any notions of the soul, or of sin, and all forms of invocation in prayer, small as even collectively they may appear to be, bear the appearance of their having come to them through the instrumentality of the Âryans; partly, no doubt, from Brahmanical sources: in part, perhaps, in course of some very early contiguity, antecedent to the migration of either race, from a common cradle-land, into India."

The supposition of the Druidical character of the Tuda religion arose in part from the error of attributing to the Tudas various remains which were peculiar to an earlier and apparently extinct race. Those remains consist of cairns or barrows, cromlechs, kist-vaens, and circles of upright, loose stones, which are nearly identical in form with those that are found in Europe in the ancient seats of the Celts: and whatever mystery may hang over the origin of those remains, and over the race of which they are the only surviving relics, there seems no reason for hesitating to style them Druidical. It must be understood, however, that the term 'Druidical' is used not scientifically, but only in a vague general sense, like that in which the word 'Scythian' is used. In the cairns or barrows referred to, vases, cinerary urns, and other vessels of glazed pottery are often found, which sometimes contain human bones, more or less charred, and mixed with ashes, sometimes a little animal charcoal alone. Most of these vessels have a peculiar glaze * of a rich red colour, with a zig-zag ornamentation: some have

* Dr Hunter, of the Madras School of Art, an eminent authority on these matters, explains that this is not what is technically called a glaze, but a peculiar, skilfully executed polish. See *Indian Antiquary*, 1873, in a paper by the Rev. Mr Phillips.

a black glaze. Brass and iron implements of agriculture and of war have often been discovered in them: in several instances a bell has been found, as in some of the Celtic barrows in England; and occasionally gold ornaments have come to light. Though these remains seem to be undoubtedly Druidical in character, it does not follow that they belong to a period of very high antiquity. On the contrary, they can set up no claim to an antiquity equal to that of many Druidical remains found in Europe.

The rich glaze of the pottery; the elegance of the shape of some of the vessels (compared with the rude cinerary urns discovered in the British barrows); the presence of implements of iron; the representations of processions with musical instruments and led horses, which are rudely sculptured on the sides of some of the cromlechs; the presence of gold ornaments;—all these circumstances denote a superior civilisation to that of the primitive Celts, and therefore probably a much later origin of the relics. If it be true, as it is confidently asserted (though I have been unable to ascertain the truth of the statement), that a Roman aureus was discovered in one of the barrows, the race by which those Druidical rites were practised must have survived for several centuries after the Christian era, if not down to a comparatively late time.

At first it was supposed that cairns and other so-called Druidical remains were discoverable only on the Neilgherry hills; and hence it was natural that these remains should at first be attributed to the Tudas, the supposed aborigines of the Neilgherries, who are as peculiar in their customs as in their language. On further research it was found that the people to whom those remains belonged had practised agriculture; whereas the Tudas were ignorant of agriculture, and appeared to have always lived a pastoral, wandering life. It was subsequently discovered that the Tudas neither claimed the cairns and cromlechs as belonging to themselves or their ancestors, nor regarded them with reverence; that their rites of sepulture were altogether different from those of the ancient people who used those cairns; and that they ascribed them to a people still more ancient than themselves, by whom they asserted that the plateau of the Neilgherries was inhabited prior to their arrival. Sometimes they designated the cairns as burial places of the Kurubas or Kurumbas, a race of nomad shepherds who once overspread a considerable part of the Tamil country (possibly the 'nomadic Sôræ' of Ptolemy), and of whom a few scattered relics still inhabit the slopes of the Neilgherries. It appeared, however, that similar cairns or barrows, containing a great variety of similar remains, but of a more advanced order and in a better condition, existed in immense numbers on the Âna-mala hills,—a range of hills on the south side of the great Coimbatoor gap, which forms the commencement and the northern face of the Southern Ghauts; and further investigation proved their existence, not only in mountain ranges, but in almost every part of the Dekhan and Peninsular India, from Nagpore to Tinnivelly, and also in various districts in the presidency of Bombay. Similar remains are found also in Circassia and Russia; and circles of stones surrounding ancient graves are found both on the Southern Arabian coast and in the Somali country in Africa.

This discovery has had the effect of disconnecting the cairns and other so-called Druidical remains of the Neilgherries from the Tudas, almost as completely as from any other Dravidian race or tribe that now exists; and the question of the origin of the relics which have been discovered in such numbers not only in the Neilgherries, but in many other parts of India, and in the plains as well as on the mountains, and also the ulterior question of the relationship and history of the people of whom these relics are the only monuments that remain, have now become problems of a more general and of a deeply interesting character. Captain Meadows Taylor has discovered and examined a large number of these remains at Rajan Koloor, in Sorapoor, and also at Siwarji, near Ferozabad, on the Bhima; and has devoted much attention to the comparison of them with similar remains found in England. He calls them 'Scytho-Celtic,' or 'Scytho-Druidical.'

More is now known about the cairns of the Neilgherries than was known when the above remarks first appeared. The late Mr Breeks, of the Madras Civil Service, devoted much time and labour to the examination of those remains, in which he was much assisted by Mr Metz. Mr Breeks was understood to have a book on the subject nearly ready for publication at the time of his death. That book has not yet appeared, but I am indebted to private communications from Mr Metz for the following items of information. There are no less than six different kinds of cairns and cromlechs on the Neilgherries, of which only one kind, that called *azârams*, small stone circles, can be attributed to the ancient Tudas. The Tudas make use of those circles up to the present day as places for the burning of their dead. Of the structures generally called cromlechs, one kind is called *Bîra-kallu* (Can. 'hero-stones'). These appear to be sculptured memorials of great men, and some of them are evidently modern. Memorials of a similar nature are still erected by the Kurumbas, one of the Neilgherry tribes. Another kind was erected, he says, by the Baḍagas, the most numerous of the Neilgherry tribes, after their arrival from the Canarese country several centuries ago. The kist-vaens, Mr Metz says, are called *Môriara mane*, the house of the Môrias or Maurias, whom he identifies with Usbeck Tatars, or the Maurya race.

It is in these kist-vaens that the pottery with the rich red glaze is found, and many of the clay figures found in them are represented with a high Tatar head-dress. These remains are not claimed by any of the races now existing on the hills, and seem to be of considerable antiquity. One of the cairns of this description opened by Mr Breeks had an immense tree growing out of it and over it, which was supposed to be at least eight hundred years old.

The Neilgherry cairns and the cairns of a similar nature found elsewhere in India have often been styled Druidical remains. Whether they are properly called Druidical or not, they are not on this account necessarily Celtic, for the practice of rites of what is called a Druidical character and the use of cairns and barrows were not confined to the Celts, but appear to have prevailed also amongst the Finns, the Euraskians, and the other Scythians by whom Europe was inhabited prior (?) to the arrival of the Celtic race; and traces of the same system of religion and sepulture have been discovered in various parts of Northern and Central Asia. The other term, 'Scytho-Druidical,' seems an unobjectionable one.

It is a remarkable illustration of the uninquiring habit of the Indian mind, that though cairns of various kinds are found in so many districts in India, no class of Hindûs know anything of the race to which they belonged, and that neither in Sanskrit literature nor in that of the Dravidian languages is any tradition on the subject contained. The Tamil people are said sometimes to call the cairns by the name of *pâṇḍu-kuṛis*. I have not heard this word used myself, nor do I find it in Winslow's "Tamil Dictionary," but it sounds like a word really used by some class of the people. *kuṛi* means a pit or grave, and *pâṇḍu* denotes anything connected with the Pâṇḍus, or Pâṇḍava brothers, to whom, all over India, ancient mysterious structures are generally attributed. To call anything 'a work of the Pâṇḍavas' is equivalent to terming it 'Cyclopean' in Greece, 'a work of the Picts' in Scotland, or 'a work of Nimrod' in Asiatic Turkey; and it means only that the structure to which the name is applied was erected in some remote age, by a people of whom nothing is now known. In Malayâḷam the term appears not as Pâṇḍu(k)kuṛi, but as Pâṇḍi(k)kuṛi, which seems to mean a sepulchre of the Tamilians [called Pâṇḍis in Malabar, from their connection with the Pâṇḍyan kingdom], but is defined in Gundert's Dictionary to mean an ancient sepulchre. This form of the word and explanation would seem to disconnect the term altogether from the Pâṇḍava brothers. In the extreme south of the peninsula where I have myself lived—on both sides of the Ghauts—the principal peculiarity of the cairns I have met with is that they contain a very large urn or jar, filled with human bones, sometimes partially charred, with a number of beautiful little vessels of various shapes made of glazed pottery, and with relics of iron weapons. These urns are sometimes found in large numbers crowded together, without being enclosed in stone chambers or surrounded with circles of stones, but simply embedded in the earth. The name given to this sepulchral urn in Tinnevelly is *mudu muttar tâṛi.* If this were a correct word, it would mean the *tâṛi*, or jar, in which were placed those 'persons who were emancipated by reason of age' or 'in the ancient period.' This explanation would be quite suitable to the ideas that now prevail in the Tamil country with regard to the people who were interred in those jars. They are supposed to be people who had shrunk through age to so small a size that they were generally put in little lamp-niches in the walls of the houses to keep them out of the way of harm; but when at last their friends were thoroughly tired of them, they were put in these sepulchral jars and left to die. I need scarcely say that the human remains found in these jars are of the ordinary size, and it is evident that they had generally been burnt before being collected and placed in the jar. I mention this tradition only for the purpose of showing that the people of these times know nothing whatever about the people so interred. They do not know even whether they belonged to the same race as themselves or not.

It has often been suggested that these remains may have belonged to the Buddhists, and the proficiency in the arts the relics exhibit would render this supposition a very natural one. I have never noticed anything, however, which would distinctively connect these urns with the Buddhists, though traditions about the Jainas still survive; and the people are never found to entertain the idea that the inhabitants of the urns were Buddhists or Jainas. In the northern part of the Tamil country these urns, as appears from Winslow's Dictionary, are called *mada madakka* (*t*)*tâṛi*, the jar which boils up violently, or boils over. It is evident that this name was originally the same as that already mentioned, but it is not quite clear which was the original and which the corruption. The meaning given by Winslow is identical—"a large earthen jar wherein very old persons in ancient times were placed and interred." In Dr Gundert's "Malayâḷam Dictionary" (Appendix), the word *nannu : nannaṅṅâḍi* is thus explained: "A kind of cairn; of two kinds; 1, a deep and narrow clay urn (*kuṛi-tâḷi*), buried perpendicularly, with a stone lid, containing bones, the tools of the deceased, &c.; 2, a monument of stone slabs having three sides and a roof, but open towards the east, containing underground as above. (Pâlghât, South Malabar.) The popular belief is that in Trêtâyuga men became very old and shrank to the size of a cat, when they were put into these pots or monuments in order not to trouble the living."

It is evident that further investigation is required before the mystery that hangs over the class of people that disposed of their dead in these cairns and urns is dispelled. Nothing that can be regarded as distinctively connecting them with, or disconnecting them from, any race or the followers of any religion, has, so far as I am aware, been yet discovered, and tradition is utterly at fault. The supposition that the builders of the cairns had settled in India earlier than the Dravidians, and were expelled by the Dravidians from the plains, and forced to take refuge in the hills and jungles, where they gradually died out, would accord with some of the circumstances now mentioned; but it is inconsistent with the proofs of the civilisation of the race we meet with, and in particular with the beauty of their pottery. If it should be held, on the other hand, that they were a race of nomadic Scytho-Druidical shepherds, who wandered into India *after* it was peopled and settled, and then wandered out again, the circumstance that these remains are found most plentifully in remote mountainous regions renders this supposition an improbable one. The improbability of the supposition would, however, be diminished if we were to suppose that this shepherd people, instead of retracing their steps and wandering out of India, formed alliances with the Dravidians, and gradually merged in the mass of the Dravidian race.

Whether the people to whom these remains belonged were or were not Dravidians, identical with the Dravidians of the present time in everything but the mode in which they disposed of their dead, is a point which cannot be settled till we know something more of them; but it cannot be regarded as probable that their peculiar rites of sepulture had their origin in India.* The resemblance of the barrows, cromlechs, &c., and their contents to the Druidical remains which are discovered in the ancient seats of the Celtic and Scythian races in Europe, seems to be too remarkable to be accounted for on any other supposition than that of their derivation from a common origin. Hence the people by whom Druidical rites were introduced into India must have brought them with them from Central Asia; and this would favour the conclusion that they must have entered India at a very early

* See a paper on this subject, by the Rev. Maurice Phillips, in the *Indian Antiquary* for 1873.

period—a period perhaps as early as the introduction of Druidical rites into Europe. On this supposition it seems to be necessary to suppose that they kept themselves separated from the various races that entered India subsequently, and that they imitated the civilisation of the newer immigrants without abandoning their own peculiarities. It is an argument against this supposition, however, that it has to be held that those people have everywhere disappeared, and that not even the faintest tradition of their existence survives.

On a review of the various particulars which have been mentioned above respecting the religious usages of the Non-Aryanised Dravidians, including the Khonds and the Tudas, and also the unknown race that practised *quasi* Druidical rites, it may be concluded that a large number, perhaps the majority, of the ancient Dravidian inhabitants of India were demonolaters or Shamanites, like the majority of the ancient Scythian tribes of Upper Asia, whilst it also seems probable that there existed amongst them a strong under-current of Indo-European tendencies. This result exactly accords with the supposition which has already been deduced from lingual comparison respecting the relationship or affiliation of the Dravidian race, viz., that in basis and origin it is rather Scythian than Indo-European, but with a deep-seated and very ancient admixture of the Indo-European element.

INDEX.